Mike Holt's Illustrated Guide to

ELECTRICAL EXAM PREPARATION

Theory • Calculations • Motor Controls • Code

Includes the NEC® Exam Practice Questions Book

Based on the 2011 NEC®

This Workbook Suitable for all electrical exams based on the NEC®, such as:
AMP, ICC, Local Exam Boards, Pearson Vue, Professional Testing, Prov, PSI, Prometric

MIKE HOLT ENTERPRISES, INC.
TM
Since 1974
www.MikeHolt.com

Mike Holt Enterprises, Inc.
888.NEC.CODE (632.2633) • www.MikeHolt.com • Info@MikeHolt.com

NOTICE TO THE READER

Mike Holt's Illustrated Guide to Electrical Exam Preparation 2011 Edition

First Printing: April 2011

Technical Illustrator: Mike Culbreath
Cover Design: Madalina Iordache-Levay
Layout Design and Typesetting: Cathleen Kwas

ISBN 978-1-932685-63-3

For more information, call 888.NEC.CODE (632.2633), or E-mail Info@MikeHolt.com.

I dedicate this book to the
Lord Jesus Christ,
my mentor and teacher.
Proverbs 16:3

One Team

To Our Instructors and Students:

We're committed to providing you the finest product with the fewest errors, but we're realistic and know that there'll be errors found and reported after the printing of this book. The last thing we want is for you to have problems finding, communicating, or accessing this information. It's unacceptable to us for there to be even one error in our textbooks or answer keys. For this reason, we're asking you to work together with us as One Team.

Students: Please report any errors you may find to your instructor.

Instructors: Please communicate these errors to us by sending an email to corrections@mikeholt.com.

Our Commitment:

We'll continue to list all of the corrections that come through for all of our textbooks and answer keys on our Website. The most up-to-date answer keys will always be available to instructors to download from our instructor Website. We don't want you to have problems finding this updated information, so we're outlining where to go for all of this below:

To view textbook and answer key corrections: Students and instructors go to our Website, www.MikeHolt.com, click on "Books" in the sidebar of links, and then click on "Corrections."

To download the most up-to-date answer keys: Instructors go to our Website, www.MikeHolt.com, click on "Instructors" in the sidebar of links and then click on "Answer Keys." On this page you'll find instructions for accessing and downloading these answer keys.

If you're not registered as an instructor you'll need to register. Your registration will be sent to our educational director who in turn will review and approve your registration. In your approval E-mail will be the login and password so you can have access to all of the answer keys. If you have a situation that needs immediate attention, please contact the office directly at 888.NEC.CODE (632.2633).

Call 888.NEC.CODE (632.2633) or visit us online at www.MikeHolt.com

Table of Contents

Introduction

Mike Holt's Illustrated Guide to *NEC* Exam Preparation

This edition of *Mike Holt's Illustrated Guide to NEC Exam Preparation* is intended to provide you with the knowledge to pass your exam the first time. The writing style of this textbook, as with all of Mike Holt's products, is meant to be informative, practical, informal, easy to read, and applicable for today's electrical professional. Also, just like all of Mike Holt's textbooks, it contains hundreds of detailed color-coded illustrations that apply to today's electrical installations.

Passing an important electrical exam is the dream of all those who care about improving themselves and their families. Unfortunately, many don't pass the exam at all, and few pass it the first time. The primary reason people fail their exam is because they're not prepared on the technical material and/or they don't know how to take the exam.

Most electrical exams contain questions on electrical theory, basic electrical calculations, the *Code*, and important and difficult *National Electrical Code* calculations. This textbook contains hundreds of illustrations, examples, and almost 3,200 practice questions covering all of these subjects and ten Practice Quizzes, seven Challenge Quizzes, and two NEC final exams. *Mike Holt's Illustrated Guide to NEC Exam Preparation* is intended to be used with the *2011 National Electrical Code.*

The Scope of this Textbook

This textbook covers the general installation requirements contained in the *NEC* Articles 90 through 830 that Mike considers to be of critical importance. This textbook contains the following stipulations:

- **Power Systems and Voltage.** All power-supply systems are assumed to be solidly grounded and any of the following voltages: 120V single-phase, 120/240V single-phase, 120/208V three-phase, 120/240V three-phase, or 277/480V three-phase, unless identified otherwise.
- **Electrical Calculations.** Unless the question or example specifies three-phase, the questions and examples are based on a single-phase power supply.
- **Rounding.** All calculations are rounded to the nearest ampere in accordance with 220.5(B).
- **Conductor Material.** Conductors are considered copper, unless aluminum is identified or specified.
- **Conductor Sizing.** Conductors are sized based on a THHN copper conductor terminating on a 75°C terminal in accordance with 110.14(C), unless the question or example identifies otherwise.
- **Overcurrent Device.** The term "overcurrent device" in this textbook refers to a molded case circuit breaker, unless identified otherwise. Where a fuse is identified, it's to be of the single-element type, also known as a "one-time fuse," unless identified otherwise.

  Author's Comment: Because the neutral conductor of a solidly grounded system is always grounded to the earth, it's both a "grounded conductor" and a "neutral" conductor. To make it easier for the reader of this textbook, we will refer to the "grounded" conductor of a solidly grounded system as the "neutral" conductor.

Journeyman or Master/Contractor Units

If you're using this textbook to pass a Journeyman Exam, complete Units 1 through 9 in Chapters 1 and 2 of the textbook (including the unit calculation practice and challenge questions), as well as the *NEC* quizzes in Chapter 5.

If you're using this textbook to pass a Master/Contractor's Exam, complete Chapters 1–4 in their entirety (including the unit calculation practice and challenge questions) as well as the *NEC* quizzes in Chapter 5.

Chapter 4 includes a bonus unit on Basic Motor Controls. Some states include motor control questions on both Journeyman and Master's level exams, while many do not. If your state includes motor control principles in the exam, be sure to study this chapter.

For additional help in preparing for an exam, you can expand your study program with DVDs that accompany this textbook.

About This Textbook

This textbook is divided into five chapters, which are further divided into units. Chapters 1 through 3 are the calculations section of the textbook.

- Chapter 1. Electrical Theory
- Chapter 2. *NEC* Calculations
- Chapter 3. Advanced *NEC* Calculations

Chapter 4 is a bonus chapter that provides basic motor control theory to help prepare for the exams in some states that include this requirement. Chapter 5 includes the complete Mike Holt's *NEC Exam Practice Questions* book to help you become really proficient in answering questions on the Code.

Each unit of this part of the textbook contains objectives, explanations with graphics, examples, steps for calculations, formulas, and practice calculations. As you read through the textbook, be sure to take the time to review the author's comments, graphics, and examples with your 2011 *Code* book.

The writing style of this textbook is intended to be informal and relaxed. The color graphics are included to help make the learning easy and fun.

After you've read each unit, you need to take time to complete the unit questions. Each of the 13 units in chapters 1 through 4 include the following:

- Unit Practice Questions
- Unit Challenge Questions

The calculations study of the first three chapters will help you learn to use the *NEC* tables and perform calculations based on the *Code*. The material in Chapter 5 will help you in answering *NEC* questions.

Important Features for the 2011 Edition of This Textbook

In order to better meet the needs of our customers, we have improved the layout of this textbook with some new feaures, in addition to the features from the 2008 edition which were so successful. These features include:

- Special Sections which contain additional information to better help you understand a concept are identified with a light gray background and colored frame.
- Important electrical formulas are represented by green text throughout the book.
- Examples or practical application questions with their answer and solution have a light yellow background.
- Graphics that contain a 2011 *Code* change will have a green border with a green 2011 CC icon next to the heading.
- Any *NEC* changes will be in green underlined text in all graphics. If you see a green bordered graphic with no green underlined text, it most likely indicates that the *Code* change is the removal of some text. Graphics without a color border support the concept being discussed, but nothing in the graphic was affected by a change for 2011.

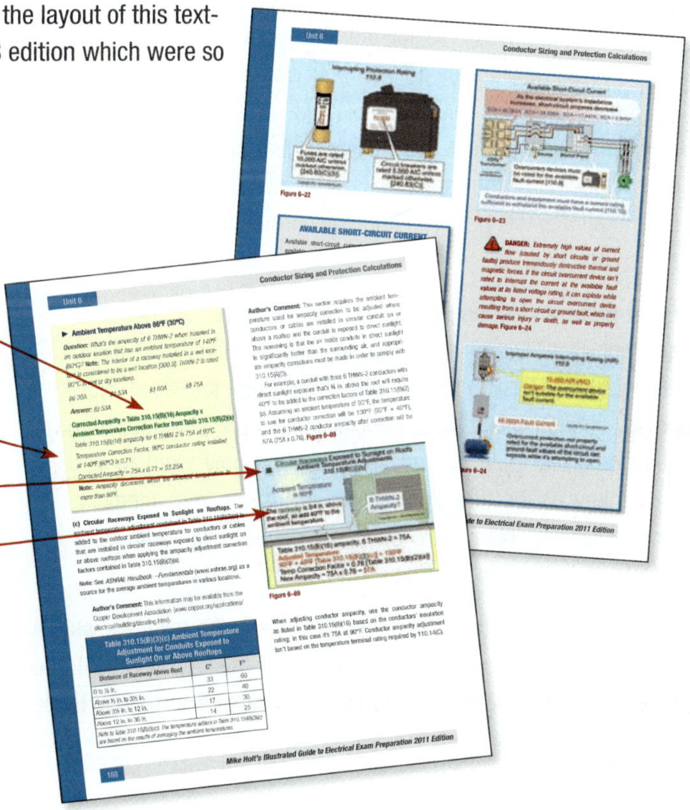

Chapter 5 includes three types of *Code* quizzes. You may want to intersperse the *NEC* review questions with your study of the first three chapters of the textbook, or you may want to complete the first three chapters first, and then work on the *NEC* review questions. Be sure to use your 2011 *Code* book to answer the review questions (quizzes). These quizzes are:

- **Practice Quizzes in Straight Order**. Each of the ten Units of Chapter 5 include a 100 question set of practice questions given in the same order as found in the *Code* book. You should complete these Practice Quizzes to begin with. If you are short on time before your exam, complete all of the straight order questions of all 10 units first, then return to the random order questions as time allows.
- **Practice Quizzes in Random Order.** Also provided in each of the 10 Units of Chapter 5 are 50 questions in random order to give you more practice in finding answers in the *Code* book.
- **NEC Challenge Quizzes.** The seven challenge quizzes will help you hone your skills in finding *Code* requirements. Complete these after you have done the practice questions to provide a good *Code* review. The questions in the challenge quizzes don't follow the chapters of the *Code* book; they're organized in a random manner, and you might find them harder to answer. Scores for the first few challenge quizzes might be somewhat lower than you would like to see. But, as you go through this textbook and take the review and practice quizzes, you'll learn a great deal and gain a better understanding of the material. This improved knowledge and understanding will help you improve on the challenge quizzes as you proceed.
- **Final Exams.** To complete your review, there are two 100 question Final Exams that will help you evaluate your exam taking skills. Answer these questions from the 2011 NEC book. Practice using your *Code* book for the straight-order questions, and then as you progress, you may want to see how many of the questions you can answer from memory. Most licensing exams are open book, but check with your testing authority in your region.

If you have difficulty with a question or section in the textbook, skip it for the moment and get back to it later. Don't frustrate yourself! The answer key is intended to be very clear, so be sure to review those questions that you miss.

If there are *NEC* questions that you don't understand after reading the answer key, don't hesitate to ask your co-workers or fellow students about them. Additional study of the *Code* questions on a chapter-by-chapter basis is available using our Understanding the *National Electrical Code* book which includes many illustrations and clear explanations.

Cross-References and Author's Comments

Cross References. This textbook contains several *NEC* cross-references to other related *Code* requirements to help you develop a better understanding of how the *NEC* rules relate to one another. These cross-references are indicated by *Code* section numbers in brackets, an example of which is "[90.4]."

> **Author's Comments:** "Author's Comments," written by Mike, are intended to help you understand the *NEC* material, and to bring to your attention things of which you should be aware.

Difficult Concepts

As you progress through this textbook, you might find that you don't understand every explanation, example, calculation, or comment. Don't become frustrated, and don't get down on yourself. There are DVDs that can help you learn this material. Remember, this is the *National Electrical Code* and sometimes the best attempt to explain a concept isn't enough to make it perfectly clear. If you're still confused, visit www.MikeHolt.com, and post your question on the *Code* Forum for help.

Different Interpretations

Some electricians, contractors, instructors, inspectors, engineers, and others enjoy the challenge of discussing the *NEC* requirements, hopefully in a positive and productive manner. This give-and-take is important to the process of better understanding the *Code* requirements and application. However, if you're going to get into an *NEC* discussion, please don't spout out what you think without having the actual *Code* book in your hand. The professional way of discussing an *NEC* requirement is by referring to a specific section, rather than talking in vague generalities.

QR Codes

QR Code

What is this? It is a QR Code and gives you the ability to use your smartphone to take a photo (using a barcode reader app) and be directed to a website. For example, the QR Code to the left when captured will direct your smartphone to the Mike Holt Enterprises website. We have included these in various places in our book to make it easier for you to go directly to the website page referenced. In order to use a QR code, you will need an app for your phone that allows your phone to read this barcode. Your phone may already have the ability to scan this barcode, but if not visit the website www.mobile-barcodes.com/qr-code-software for more information.

Textbook Errors and Corrections

Humans develop the text, graphics, and layout of this textbook, and since currently none of us are perfect, there may be a few errors. This can occur because the *NEC* is dramatically changed each *Code* cycle; new articles are added, some are deleted, some are relocated, and many are renumbered. We take great care in researching the *NEC* requirements to ensure this textbook is correct. If you believe there's an error of any kind in this textbook (typographical, grammatical, technical, or anything else), no matter how insignificant, please let us know.

Any errors found after printing are listed on our Website, so if you find an error, first check to see if it's already been corrected. Go to www.MikeHolt.com, click on the "Books" link, and then the "Corrections" link (www.MikeHolt.com/bookcorrections.htm).

If you don't find the error listed on the Website, contact us by sending an E-mail to Corrections@MikeHolt.com. Be sure to include the book title, page number, and any other pertinent information.

You Tube

Visit the Mike Holt channel on YouTube to see video clips that accompany this and our other 2011 books (www.youtube.com/user/MikeHoltNEC).

Journeyman and Master/Contractor Intermediate Library

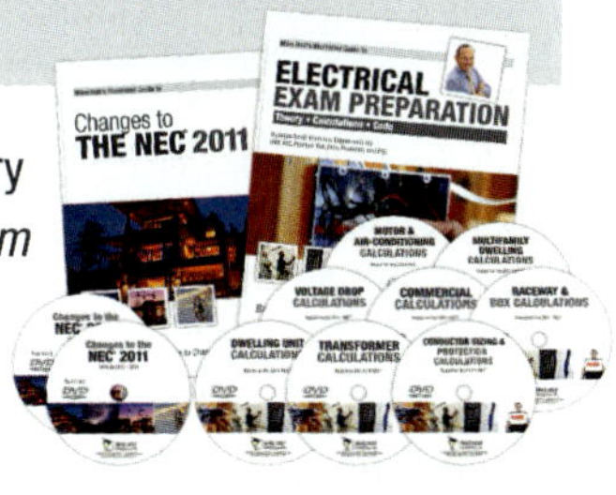

The Journeyman Intermediate Library includes the full-color *Electrical Exam Preparation* textbook and seven DVDs, as well as Mike's 2011 *Changes to the NEC* textbook and two DVDs. The Master/Contractor Intermediate Library includes everything in the Journeyman Library, plus three additional Calculation DVDs. For more information, visit www.MikeHolt.com/ExamPrep.

Journeyman and Master/Contractor Comprehensive Library

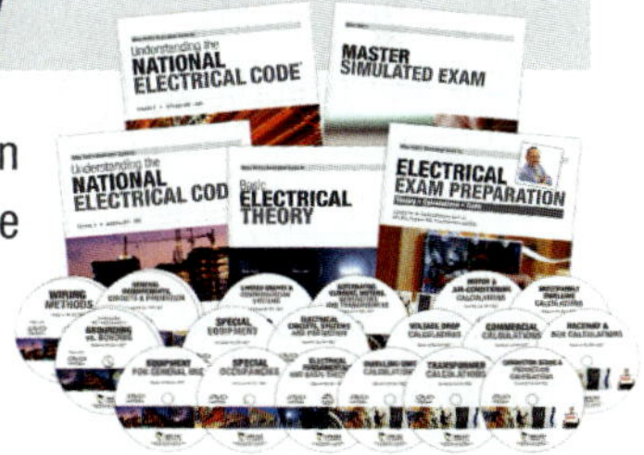

The Comprehensive Exam Preparation Library is based on a full term of live classes. You'll learn everything you need to know to pass your exam the first time. Mike's dynamic style and detailed graphics easily explain the most difficult subjects.

The Comprehensive Library includes the following:

- *Understanding the NEC*, Volume 1 textbook, plus 7 DVDs
- *Understanding the NEC,* Volume 2 textbook, plus 3 DVDs
- *Basic Electrical Theory* textbook/workbook, plus 3 DVDs
- *Electrical Exam Preparation* textbook/workbook, plus 5 DVDs for Journeyman, 8 DVDs for Master
- Simulated Exam

For more information, visit www.MikeHolt.com/ExamPrep.

Passing Your Exam

This textbook was designed to help you prepare for your *National Electrical Code* exam.

Understanding the Emotional Aspects of Learning

To learn effectively, you must develop an attitude that learning is a process that will help you grow both personally and professionally. The learning process has an emotional as well as an intellectual component that we must recognize. To understand what affects our learning, consider the following:

Positive Image. Many feel disturbed by the expectations of being treated like children and we often feel threatened with the learning experience.

Uniqueness. Each of us will understand the subject matter from different perspectives and we all have some unique learning challenges and needs.

Resistance to Change. People tend to resist change and resist information that appears to threaten their comfort level of knowledge. However, we often support new ideas that support our existing beliefs.

Dependence and Independence. The dependent person is afraid of disapproval and often will not participate in class discussion and will tend to wrestle alone. The independent person spends too much time asserting differences and too little time trying to understand others' views.

Fearful. Most of us feel insecure and afraid of learning, until we understand the process. We fear that our performance will not match the standard set by us or by others.

Egocentric. Our ego tendency is to prove someone is wrong, with a victorious surge of pride. Learning together without a win-lose attitude can be an exhilarating learning experience.

Emotional. It's difficult to discard our cherished ideas in the face of contrary facts when overpowered by the logic of others.

Getting the Best Grade

Studies have concluded that for students to get their best grades, they must learn to get the most from their natural abilities. It's not how long you study or how high your IQ is, it's what you do and how you study that counts the most. To get your best grade, you must make a decision to do your best and follow as many of the following techniques and suggestions as possible.

Reality. These instructions are a basic guide to help you get the maximum grade. It's unreasonable to think that all of the instructions can be followed to the letter all of the time. Day-to-day events and unexpected situations must be taken into consideration.

Support. You need encouragement in your studies and you need support from your loved ones and employer. To properly prepare for your exam, you need to study 10 to 15 hours per week for about 3 to 6 months.

Communication with Your Family. Good communication with your family is very important because studying every night and on weekends can cause much tension and stress. Try to get their support, cooperation, and encouragement during this difficult time. Let them know the benefits to the family and what passing the exam means. Be sure to plan some special time with them during this preparation period; don't go overboard and neglect them.

Stress. Stress can really take the wind out of you. It takes practice, but get into the habit of relaxing before you begin your studies. Stretch, do a few sit-ups and push-ups, take a 20-minute walk, or a few slow, deep breaths. Close your eyes for a couple of minutes, and deliberately relax the muscle groups that are associated with tension, such as the shoulders, back, neck, and jaw.

Attitude. Maintaining a positive attitude is important. It helps keep you going and helps keep you from becoming discouraged.

Training. Preparing for the exam is the same as training for any other event. Get plenty of rest and avoid intoxicating drugs, including alcohol. Stretching or exercising each day for at least 10 minutes helps you get in a better mood. Eat light meals such as pasta, chicken, fish, vegetables, fruit, and so forth. Try to avoid red meat, butter, sugar, salt, and high-fat content foods. They slow you down and make you tired and sleepy.

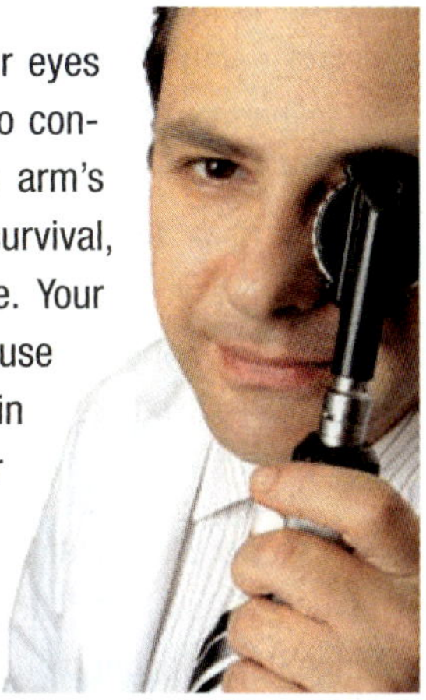

Eye Care. It's very important to have your eyes checked! Human eyes weren't designed to constantly focus on something less than an arm's length away. Our eyes were designed for survival, spotting food and enemies at a distance. Your eyes will be under tremendous stress because of prolonged reading, which can result in headaches, fatigue, nausea, squinting, or eyes that burn, ache, water, or tire easily. Be sure to tell your eye doctor that you are studying to pass an exam (bring this textbook and the *Code* book with you) and that you expect to do a tremendous amount of reading and writing. Reading glasses can reduce eye discomfort.

Reducing Eye Strain. Be sure to look up occasionally, away from near tasks to distant objects. Your work area should be three times brighter than the rest of the room. Don't read under a single lamp in a dark room. Try to eliminate glare. Mixing of fluorescent and incandescent lighting can be helpful.

Posture. Sit up straight, with your chest up and your shoulders back, so both eyes are an equal distance from what you're viewing.

Getting Organized. Our lives are so busy that simply making time for homework and exam preparation is almost impossible. You can't waste time looking for a pencil or missing paper. Keep everything you need together. Maintain folders, one for notes, one for exams and answer keys, and one for miscellaneous items.

Study Location. It's very important that you have a private study area available at all times. Keep your materials there. The dining room table is not a good spot.

Time Management. Time management and planning are very important. There simply are not enough hours in the day to get everything done. Make a schedule that allows time for work, rest, study, meals, family, and recreation. Establish a schedule that's consistent from day to day. Have a calendar and immediately plan your exam preparation schedule. Try to follow the same routine each week and try not to become overtired. Learn to pace yourself to accomplish as much as you can without the need for cramming.

Speak Up in Class. If you're in a classroom setting, the most important part of the learning process is participation. If you don't understand the instructor's point, ask for clarification. Don't try to get attention by asking questions you already know the answers to.

Study With a Friend. Studying with a friend can make learning more enjoyable. You can push and encourage each other. You're more likely to study if someone else is depending on you. Students who study together perform above average because they try different approaches and explain their solutions to each other. This kind of interaction is a significant aid to learning retention. Those who study alone may spend much of their time reading and rereading the text and trying the same approach time after time with less success.

Study Anywhere/Anytime. To make the most of your limited time, always keep a copy of the book(s) with you. Any time you get a free minute, study! Continue to study any chance you get. You can study at the supply house when waiting for your material; you can study during your coffee break, or even while you're at the doctor's office. Become creative!

You need to find your best study time. For some, it's late at night when the house is quiet. For others, it's the first thing in the morning before things get going.

Set Priorities. Once you begin your study, stop all phone calls, TV shows, radio, snacks, and other interruptions. You can always take care of it later.

Preparing to Take the Exam

Get Advance Information. Check with the testing authorities in advance to be certain you know what reference books and what kind of calculator you're allowed to take with you to the exam site. Find out if you're allowed to make notes in your *Code* book, or if the testing site will provide you with a *Code* book. If your state is using computerized testing, find the Website of the testing company and review any information that they make available. Take any sample online test(s) on the testing company's Website so you're familiar with the testing process.

Have the Proper Supplies. First of all, make sure you have everything needed several days before the exam. The night before the exam is not the time to be out buying pencils, calculators, and batteries. You should have a checklist (prepared in advance) of everything you can possibly need the night before the exam. The following is a sample checklist to get you started:

- Six sharpened #2H pencils or two mechanical pencils with extra #2H leads. The type with the larger lead is better for filling in the answer key.
- Two calculators. Most examining boards require quiet, paperless calculators. Solar calculators are great, but there may not be enough light to operate them. Find out what type of calculators will be allowed for the exam. Some exams don't allow scientific calculators, so be sure that you don't find yourself with a calculator you can't use!
- Spare batteries. Two sets of extra batteries should be taken. It's very unlikely you'll need them, but…
- Extra glasses if you use them.
- A wristwatch to ensure you'll stay on track.
- All your reference materials, even the ones not on the list. Let the proctors tell you which ones aren't permitted.
- Bring something to drink. Coffee is excellent.
- Some fruit, nuts, aspirin, etc.
- Know where the exam is going to take place and how long it takes to get there. Arrive at least 30 minutes early.
- Bring a jacket.

Meals. It's also a good idea to pack a lunch rather than going out if a lunch break is allowed. It can give you a little extra time to review the material for the afternoon portion of the exam, and it reduces the chance of coming back late.

Taking the Exam

Being prepared for an exam means more than just knowing electrical concepts, the *Code*, and the calculations. Have you felt prepared for an exam, and then choked when actually taking it? Many good and knowledgeable people didn't pass their exam because they didn't know "how to take an exam."

Taking exams is a learned process that takes practice and involves strategies. The following suggestions are designed to help you develop your strategies:

Relax. This is easier said than done, but it's one of the most important factors in passing your exam. Stress and tension cause us to choke or forget. Everyone has had experiences where they became tense and couldn't think straight. The first step is becoming aware of the tension, and the second step is to make a deliberate effort to relax. Make sure you're comfortable; remove clothes if you're hot, or put on a jacket if you're cold.

There are many ways to relax and you have to find a method that works for you. Two of the easiest methods that work very well for many people follow:

- Breathing Technique: Take a few slow deep breaths every few minutes. Don't confuse this with hyperventilation, which is abnormally fast breathing.

- Single-Muscle Relaxation: When we're tense or stressful, many of us do things like clench our jaw, squint our eyes, or tense our shoulders without even being aware of it. If you find a muscle group that does this, deliberately relax that one group. The rest of the muscles will automatically relax also. Try to repeat this every few minutes, and it will help you stay more relaxed during the exam.

Understand the Question. To answer a question correctly, you must first understand the question. One word in a question can totally change the meaning of it. Carefully read every word of every question. Underlining key words in the question will help you focus.

Skip the Difficult Questions. Contrary to popular belief, you don't have to answer one question before going on to the next one. The irony is that the question you get stuck on is one that you'll probably get wrong anyway. This will result in not having enough time to answer the easy questions. You'll get all stressed-out worrying that you won't complete the exam on time, and a chain reaction is started. More people fail their exams this way than for any other reason.

Many states are using computerized testing, but even in the computerized format you're usually able to mark a question for later review and return to that question after you've answered the easier ones.

The following strategy should be used to avoid getting into this situation:

- First Pass: Answer the questions you know. Give yourself about 30 seconds for each question. If you can't find the answer in your reference book within the 30 seconds, go on to the next question. Chances are that you'll come across the answers while looking up another question. The total time for the first pass should be 25 percent of the exam time.

- Second Pass: This pass is done the same as the first pass except that you allow a little more time for each question, about 60 seconds. If you still can't find the answer, go on to the next one. Don't get stuck. The total time for the second pass should be about 30 percent of the exam time.

- Third Pass: See how much time is left and subtract 30 minutes. Spend the remaining time equally on each question. If you still haven't answered the question, it's time to make an educated guess. Never leave a question unanswered.
- Fourth Pass: Use the last 30 minutes of the exam to transfer your answers from the exam booklet to the answer key. Read each question and verify that you selected the correct answer on the test book. Transfer the answers carefully to the answer key. With the remaining time, see if you can find the answer to those questions you guessed at.

Guessing. When time is running out and you still have unanswered questions, GUESS! Never leave a question unanswered.

You can improve your chances of getting a question correct by the process of elimination. Many times, there are a couple of choices that can be easily eliminated as illogical or outside the range of expected answers.

How do you pick one of the remaining answers? Some people toss a coin, others count up how many of the answers were As, Bs, Cs, and Ds and use the one with the most as the basis for their guess.

Checking Your Work. The first thing to check (and you should be watching out for this during the whole exam) is to make sure you mark the answer in the correct spot. People have failed the exam by one-half of a point. When they reviewed their exam, they found they correctly answered several questions on the test booklet, but marked the wrong spot on the exam answer sheet. They knew the answer was "(b) False" but marked in "(d)" in error. Another thing to be very careful of, is marking the answer for, let's say question 7, in the spot reserved for question 8.

Changing Answers. When re-reading the question and checking the answers during the fourth pass, resist the urge to change an answer. In most cases, your first choice is best and if you aren't sure, stick with the first choice. Only change answers if you are positive that you made a mistake. Multiple choice exams are graded electronically so be sure to thoroughly erase any answer that you changed. Also erase any stray pencil marks from the answer sheet.

Rounding Off. You should always round your answers to the same number of places as the exam's answers.

Example: If an exam has multiple choice of:

(a) 2.10 (b) 2.20 (c) 2.30 (d) none of these

And your calculation comes out to 2.16, don't choose the answer (d) none of these. The correct answer is (b) 2.20, because the answers in this case are rounded off to the nearest tenth.

Example: It could be rounded to tens, such as:

(a) 50 (b) 60 (c) 70 (d) none of these.

For this group, an answer such as 67 will be (c) 70, while an answer of 63 will be (b) 60. The general rule is to check the question's choice of answers and then round off your answer to match it.

Things To Be Careful Of

- Don't get stuck on any one question.
- Read each question carefully.
- Be sure you mark the answer in the correct spot on the answer sheet.
- Don't get flustered or extremely tense.

Summary

- Make sure everything is ready and packed the night before the exam.
- Don't try to cram the night before the exam—if you don't know it by then, it's too late!
- Have a good breakfast. Get the thermos and energy snacks ready.
- Take all your reference books. Let the proctors tell you what you can't use.
- Know where the exam is to be held and arrive early.
- Bring identification and your confirmation papers from the license board if this is required.
- Review your *NEC* while you wait for your exam to begin.
- Try to stay relaxed.
- Determine the time per question for each pass and don't forget to save 30 minutes for transferring your answers to the answer key.
- Remember—in the first pass answer only the easy questions. In the second pass, spend a little more time with each question, but don't get stuck. In the third pass, use the remainder of the time minus 30 minutes to answer the remaining questions. In the fourth pass, check your work and transfer the answers to the answer key.

Watch Mike's How to Prepare for an Exam on YouTube. Use this QR code to go to directly to the video, or visit the Mike Holt channel to see this and other video clips at www.youtube.com/MikeHoltNEC.

How to Use the *National Electrical Code*

The *National Electrical Code* is written for persons who understand electrical terms, theory, safety procedures, and electrical trade practices. These individuals include electricians, electrical contractors, electrical inspectors, electrical engineers, designers, and other qualified persons. The *Code* isn't written to serve as an instructive or teaching manual for untrained individuals [90.1(C)].

Learning to use the *NEC* is like learning to play the game of chess; it's a great game if you enjoy mental warfare. When learning to play chess, you must first learn the names of the game pieces, how the pieces are placed on the board, and how each piece moves.

Once you understand the fundamentals, you're ready to start playing the game. Unfortunately, at this point all you can do is make crude moves, because you really don't understand how all the information works together. To play chess well, you'll need to learn how to use your knowledge by working on sub-tle strategies before you can work your way up to the more intriguing and complicated moves.

Not a Game

Electrical work isn't a game, and it must be taken very seriously. Learning the basics of electricity, important terms and concepts, as well as the basic layout of the *NEC* gives you just enough knowledge to be dangerous. There are thousands of specific and unique applications of electrical installations, and the *Code* doesn't cover every one of them. To safely apply the *NEC*, you must understand the purpose of a rule and how it affects the safety aspects of the installation.

NEC Terms and Concepts

The *NEC* contains many technical terms, so it's crucial for *Code* users to understand their meanings and their applications. If you don't understand a term used in a *Code* rule, it will be impossible to properly apply the *NEC* requirement. Be sure you understand that Article 100 defines the terms that apply to two or more *Code* articles. For example, the term "Dwelling Unit" is found in many articles; if you don't know what a dwelling unit is, how can you apply the requirements for it?

In addition, many articles have terms unique for that specific article and definitions of those terms are only applicable for that given article. For example, Section 250.2 contains the definitions of terms that only apply to Article 250—Grounding and Bonding.

Small Words, Grammar, and Punctuation

It's not only the technical words that require close attention, because even the simplest of words can make a big difference to the application of a rule. The word "or" can imply alternate choices for equipment wiring methods, while "and" can mean an additional requirement. Let's not forget about grammar and punctuation. The location of a comma can dramatically change the requirement of a rule.

Slang Terms or Technical Jargon

Electricians, engineers, and other trade-related professionals use slang terms or technical jargon that isn't shared by all. This makes it very difficult to communicate because not everybody understands the intent or application of those slang terms. So where possible, be sure you use the proper word, and don't use a word if you don't understand its definition and application. For example, lots of electricians use the term "pigtail" when describing the short conductor for the connection of a receptacle, switch, luminaire, or equipment. Although they may understand it, not everyone does.

NEC Style and Layout

Before we get into the details of the *NEC*, we need to take a few moments to understand its style and layout. Understanding the structure and writing style of the *Code* is very important before it can be used and applied effectively. The *National Electrical Code* is organized into ten major components.

1. Table of Contents
2. Article 90 (Introduction to the *Code*)
3. Chapters 1 through 9 (major categories)
4. Articles 90 through 840 (individual subjects)
5. Parts (divisions of an article)
6. Sections and Tables (*Code* requirements)

7. Exceptions (*Code* permissions)
8. Informational Notes (explanatory material)
9. Annexes (information)
10. Index

1. Table of Contents. The Table of Contents displays the layout of the chapters, articles, and parts as well as the page numbers. It's an excellent resource and should be referred to periodically to observe the interrelationship of the various *NEC* components. When attempting to locate the rules for a particular situation, knowledgeable *Code* users often go first to the Table of Contents to quickly find the specific *NEC* Part that applies.

2. Introduction. The *NEC* begins with Article 90, the introduction to the *Code*. It contains the purpose of the *NEC*, what's covered and what isn't covered along with how the *Code* is arranged. It also gives information on enforcement and how mandatory and permissive rules are written as well as how explanatory material is included. Article 90 also includes information on formal interpretations, examination of equipment for safety, wiring planning, and information about formatting units of measurement.

3. Chapters. There are nine chapters, each of which is divided into articles. The articles fall into one of four groupings: General Requirements (Chapters 1 through 4), Specific Requirements (Chapters 5 through 7), Communications Systems (Chapter 8), and Tables (Chapter 9).

Chapter 1 General
Chapter 2 Wiring and Protection
Chapter 3 Wiring Methods and Materials
Chapter 4 Equipment for General Use
Chapter 5 Special Occupancies
Chapter 6 Special Equipment
Chapter 7 Special Conditions
Chapter 8 Communications Systems (Telephone, Data, Satellite, Cable TV and Broadband)
Chapter 9 Tables–Conductor and Raceway Specifications

4. Articles. The *NEC* contains approximately 140 articles, each of which covers a specific subject. For example:

Article 110 General Requirements
Article 250 Grounding and Bonding
Article 300 Wiring Methods
Article 430 Motors and Motor Controllers
Article 500 Hazardous (Classified) Locations
Article 680 Swimming Pools, Fountains, and Similar Installations
Article 725 Remote-Control, Signaling, and Power-Limited Circuits
Article 800 Communications Circuits

5. Parts. Larger articles are subdivided into parts.

Because the parts of a *Code* article aren't included in the section numbers, we have a tendency to forget what "part" the *NEC* rule is relating to. For example, Table 110.34(A) contains working space clearances for electrical equipment. If we aren't careful, we might think this table applies to all electrical installations, but Table 110.34(A) is located in Part III, which only contains requirements for "Over 600 Volts, Nominal installations." The rules for working clearances for electrical equipment for systems 600V, nominal, or less are contained in Table 110.26(A)(1), which is located in Part II—600 Volts, Nominal, or Less.

6. Sections and Tables.

Sections. Each *NEC* rule is called a "*Code* Section." A *Code* section may be broken down into subsections by letters in parentheses (A), (B), and so on. Numbers in parentheses (1), (2), and so forth, may further break down a subsection, and lowercase letters (a), (b), and so on, further break the rule down to the third level. For example, the rule requiring all receptacles in a dwelling unit bathroom to be GFCI protected is contained in Section 210.8(A)(1). Section 210.8(A)(1) is located in Chapter 2, Article 210, Section 8, Subsection (A), Sub-subsection (1).

Many in the industry incorrectly use the term "Article" when referring to a *Code* section. For example, they say "Article 210.8," when they should say "Section 210.8." Section numbers in this book are shown without the word "Section," unless they begin a sentence. For example, Section 210.8(A) is shown as simply 210.8(A).

Tables. Many *Code* requirements are contained within tables, which are lists of *NEC* requirements placed in a systematic arrangement. The titles of the tables are extremely important; you must read them carefully in order to understand the contents, applications, limitations, and so forth, of each table in the *Code*. Many times notes are provided in or below a table; be sure to read them as well since they're also part of the requirement. For example, Note 1 for Table 300.5 explains how to measure the cover when burying cables and raceways, and Note 5 explains what to do if solid rock is encountered.

7. Exceptions. Exceptions are *Code* requirements or permissions that provide an alternative method to a specific requirement. There are two types of exceptions—mandatory and permissive. When a rule has several exceptions, those exceptions with mandatory requirements are listed before the permissive exceptions.

Mandatory Exceptions. A mandatory exception uses the words "shall" or "shall not." The word "shall" in an exception means that if you're using the exception, you're required to do it in a particular way. The phrase "shall not" means it isn't permitted.

Permissive Exceptions. A permissive exception uses words such as "shall be permitted," which means it's acceptable (but not mandatory) to do it in this way.

8. Informational Notes. An Informational Note contains explanatory material intended to clarify a rule or give assistance, but it isn't a *Code* requirement.

9. Annexes. Annexes aren't a part of the *NEC* requirements, and are included in the *Code* for informational purposes only.

Annex A. Product Safety Standards
Annex B. Application Information for Ampacity Calculation
Annex C. Raceway Fill Tables for Conductors and Fixture Wires of the Same Size
Annex D. Examples
Annex E. Types of Construction
Annex F. Critical Operations Power Systems (COPS)
Annex G. Supervisory Control and Data Acquisition (SCADA)
Annex H. Administration and Enforcement
Annex I. Recommended Tightening Torques

10. Index. The Index at the back of the *NEC* is helpful in locating a specific rule.

Changes to the *NEC* since the previous edition(s), are identified by shading, but rules that have been relocated aren't identified as a change. A bullet symbol "•" is located on the margin to indicate the location of a rule that was deleted from a previous edition. New articles contain a vertical line in the margin of the page.

How to Locate a Specific Requirement

How to go about finding what you're looking for in the *Code* depends, to some degree, on your experience with the *NEC. Code* experts typically know the requirements so well they just go to the correct rule without any outside assistance. The Table of Contents might be the only thing very experienced *NEC* users need to locate the requirement they're looking for. On the other hand, average *Code* users should use all of the tools at their disposal, including the Table of Contents and the Index.

Table of Contents. Let's work out a simple example: What *NEC* rule specifies the maximum number of disconnects permitted for a service? If you're an experienced *Code* user, you'll know Article 230 applies to "Services," and because this article is so large, it's divided up into multiple parts (actually eight parts). With this knowledge, you can quickly go to the Table of Contents and see it lists the Service Equipment Disconnecting Means requirements in Part VI.

> **Author's Comment:** The number 70 precedes all page numbers because the *NEC* is NFPA Standard Number 70.

Index. If you use the Index, which lists subjects in alphabetical order, to look up the term "service disconnect," you'll see there's no listing. If you try "disconnecting means," then "services," you'll find that the Index specifies that the rule is located in Article 230, Part VI. Because the *NEC* doesn't give a page number in the Index, you'll need to use the Table of Contents to find the page number, or flip through the *Code* to Article 230, then continue to flip through pages until you find Part VI.

Many people complain that the *NEC* only confuses them by taking them in circles. As you gain experience in using the *Code* and deepen your understanding of words, terms, principles, and practices, you'll find the *NEC* much easier to understand and use than you originally thought.

Customizing Your *Code* Book

One way to increase your comfort level with the *Code* is to customize it to meet your needs. You can do this by highlighting and underlining important *NEC* requirements, and by attaching tabs to important pages. Be aware that if you're using your *Code* book to take an exam, some exam centers don't allow markings of any type.

Highlighting. As you read through this textbook, be sure you highlight those requirements in the *Code* that are the most important or relevant to you. Use yellow for general interest and orange for important requirements you want to find quickly. Be sure to highlight terms in the Index and the Table of Contents as you use them.

Underlining. Underline or circle key words and phrases in the *NEC* with a red pen (not a lead pencil) and use a 6-inch ruler to keep lines straight and neat. This is a very handy way to make important requirements stand out. A small 6-inch ruler also comes in handy for locating specific information in the many *Code* tables.

Tabbing the *NEC*. By placing tabs on *Code* articles, sections, and tables, it will make it easier for you to use the *NEC*. However, too many tabs will defeat the purpose. You can order a set of *Code* tabs designed by Mike Holt online at www.MikeHolt.com, or by calling 1.888.NEC.CODE (632.2633).

About the Author

Mike Holt

Mike Holt worked his way up through the electrical trade from an apprentice electrician to become one of the most recognized experts in the world as it relates to electrical power installations. He has worked as a journeyman electrician, master electrician, and electrical contractor. Mike's experience in the real world gives him a unique understanding of how the *NEC* relates to electrical installations from a practical standpoint. You'll find his writing style to be direct, nontechnical, and practical.

Did you know that he didn't finish high school? So if you struggled in high school or if you didn't finish it at all, don't let this get you down, you're in good company. As a matter of fact, Mike Culbreath, Master Electrician, who produces the finest electrical graphics in the history of the electrical industry, didn't finish high school either. So two high school dropouts produced the text and graphics in these textbooks! However, realizing success depends on one's continuing pursuit of education. Mike immediately attained his GED (as did Mike Culbreath) and ultimately attended the University of Miami's Graduate School for a Master's degree in Business Administration (MBA).

Mike Holt resides in Central Florida, is the father of seven children, and has many outside interests and activities. He's a six-time National Barefoot Water-Ski Champion (1988, 1999, 2005, 2006, 2007, and 2008), has set many national records, has competed in three World Championships (2006, 2008, and 2010) and continues to train and work out year-round so that he can qualify to ski in the 2012 World Barefoot Championships at the age of 61!

What sets him apart from some, is his commitment to living a balanced lifestyle; placing God first, family, career, then self.

Mike Holt—Special Acknowledgments

First, I want to thank God for my godly wife who's always by my side and my children, Belynda, Melissa, Autumn, Steven, Michael, Meghan, and Brittney.

A special thank you must be sent to the staff at the National Fire Protection Association (NFPA), publishers of the *NEC*—in particular Jeff Sargent for his assistance in answering my many *Code* questions over the years. Jeff, you're a "first class" guy, and I admire your dedication and commitment to helping others understand the *NEC*. Other former NFPA staff members I would like to thank include John Caloggero, Joe Ross, and Dick Murray for their help in the past.

A personal thank you goes to Sarina, my long-time friend and office manager. It's been wonderful working side-by-side with you for over 25 years nurturing this company's growth from its small beginnings.

About the Graphic Illustrator

Mike Culbreath

Mike Culbreath devoted his career to the electrical industry and worked his way up from an apprentice electrician to master electrician. While working as a journeyman electrician, he suffered a serious on-the-job knee injury. With a keen interest in continuing education for electricians, he completed courses at Mike Holt Enterprises, Inc. and then passed the exam to receive his Master Electrician's license. In 1986, after attending classes at Mike Holt Enterprises, Inc., he joined the staff to update material and later studied computer graphics and began illustrating Mike Holt's textbooks and magazine articles. He's worked with the company for almost 25 years and, as Mike Holt has proudly acknowledged, has helped to transform his words and visions into lifelike graphics.

Special Acknowledgments

I want to thank my wonderful children, Dawn and Mac, who have had to put up with me during the *Code* revision seasons.

I would like to thank Steve Arne, our amazing technical editorial director, Eric Stromberg, an electrical engineer and super geek (and I mean that in the most complimentary manner, this guy is brilliant), and Ryan Jackson, an outstanding and very knowledgeable code guy, for helping me keep our graphics as technically correct as possible.

I also want to give a special thank you to Cathleen Kwas for making me look good with her outstanding layout design and typesetting skills. I would also like to acknowledge Belynda Holt Pinto, our Chief Operations Officer and the rest of the outstanding staff at Mike Holt Enterprises, for all the hard work they do to help produce and distribute these outstanding products.

And last but not least, I need to give a special thank you to Mike Holt for not firing me about 25 years ago when I "borrowed" one of his computers and took it home to begin the process of learning how to do computer illustrations. He gave me the opportunity and time needed to develop my computer graphic skills. He's been an amazing friend and mentor since I met him as a student many years ago. Thanks for believing in me and allowing me to be part of the Mike Holt Enterprises family.

Mike Holt Enterprises Team

Editorial Team

I want to thank **Toni Culbreath** and **Barbara Parks** who worked tirelessly to proofread and edit the final stages of this publication. Their attention to detail and dedication to this project is greatly appreciated.

Production Team

I want to thank **Cathleen Kwas** who did the layout and production of this book. Her desire to create the best possible product for our customers is greatly appreciated.

Video Team Members

The following special persons provided assistance in the development of this textbook; particularly in ensuring that the technical content is accurate. In addition, they all provided outstanding technical advice as they served on the video team along with author Mike Holt and a guest appearance by graphic illustrator Mike Culbreath.

Steve Arne
Technical Training Consultant
Arne Electro Tech
Rapid City, S.Dak.
ElectricalMaster.com

Steve Arne has worked in various positions in the electrical industry since 1974 including electrician, electrical contractor, full-time instructor, and department chair in technical postsecondary education. Steve has developed and taught curriculum for many electrical training courses as well as university business and leadership courses. He's completed a Bachelor's degree in Technical Education and a Master's degree in Administrative Studies. Currently, he provides electrician exam prep and continuing education *Code* classes in South Dakota, Wyoming, and surrounding states using Mike Holt's textbooks and material. He enjoys seeing a student's "lights come on" as they come to a point of understanding and have the "ah-ha" experience of learning something new.

Steve has worked for Mike Holt as a technical editor and video team participant since 2002, and used Mike Holt's books in his classes for a number of years before that. Steve is very thankful to have been associated with an industry leader like Mike who provides excellent training products to help students progress in the electrical industry. Steve has been active in the South Dakota Electrical Council, serving on the Board of the Black Hills Chapter in various capacities and is the current Chapter President and a state board member.

Steve and his wife Deb live in Rapid City, S.Dak. where they're both active in their church and community, and love to spend time with their children and grandchildren. Most of all, Steve and Deb both endeavor to put God first in their lives and in their home.

Dennis Carlson
Master Electrician/Electrical Instructor
The Industrial Company (T.I.C.)
Steamboat Springs, Colorado
Ticus.com

Dennis Carlson started in the electrical trade in 1980 with Simmons Electric based in Greeley, Colorado and did residential and commercial work with them until 1985. He then went to work for Atkinson Electric based out of Ft. Collins, Colorado until 1987, also doing residential and commercial work.

Dennis has since worked on various industrial projects for TIC (The Industrial Company) as a journeyman, electrical foreman, and project coordinator. He is presently the Manager of the Electrical Craft Training Program for TIC.

Dennis instructs levels first, second, third, and fourth year trainees. With the use of Mike Holt's *NEC* Exam Preparation book, he has had a success rate of 90 percent with his fourth year trainees on the Colorado State electrical exam.

Dennis lives in Steamboat Springs, with his wife Cindy. Their son Josh will be attending college in the Fall, studying for an engineering degree, and specializing in robotics. Their daughter is enrolled at CSU in Ft. Collins studying for a degree in Art.

John Mills
Master Electrician/Electrical Instructor
Premier Electrical Company/Dade County School Board
Miami Springs, Florida

John Mills is an instructor for Mike Holt Enterprises, Inc. and is a Certified Electrical Contractor, Certified Inspector, Plan Reviewer, and CBO. John started in the electrical trade in 1980 as a helper and attended an ABC Apprenticeship Program, then worked his way up to Master Electrician. John has been an instructor for 20 years, teaching master and journeyman exam preparation courses and Florida State certification courses.

John resides in Miami, Florida with his wife Corina and their four sons. John's hobbies are working with wood and metal. He makes wooden bowls and furniture from trees that have been cut down. He enjoys making things for his children as well as fishing, family picnics, and vacations with his family.

Michael P. Pillarella
Owner, Pillarella School of Electrical Code & Theory
Assonet, MA
www.pillarellaschool.com

Michael Pillarella holds a Master's degree in Education. In addition, he holds a Bachelor of Science degree in Industrial Arts and an Associates degree in Electric and Electronics Engineering Technology.

Mike established his own proprietary school opening the Pillarella School of Electrical Code & Theory in 2007. His proudest moment as an instructor was when his son, Tim, earned his Master's license. Tim was the first to receive his license as an attendee of the school.

In 1988, Mike established and became the President of E.M.I. Electrical Contractors, Inc. providing over 20 years of service to the South Coast area. He put this education to good use by becoming a Certified Electrical Related/Shop Instructor, and the Outside Electrical Projects Manager within the Massachusetts Public School System.

Mike is also a licensed Master Electrician in Massachusetts, New Hampshire, Vermont, Rhode Island, and Maine and an approved continuing education provider in those states. He's also approved to teach OSHA Outreach Construction Courses. He is President of the Massachusetts Electrical Contractors Association Bristol Chapter and First Vice President and Education Chairman of the International Association of Electrical Inspectors Roger Williams Chapter

Brian Spaziani
Director of Program Development
Mike Holt Enterprises
Allentown, PA
www.MikeHolt.com

Brian Spaziani worked his way up through the ranks of the electrical field from apprentice to journeyman while employed by his father's company, Spaziani Electric (then Mark A. Spaziani Jr., Electrical Contractor).

Brian served in the U.S. Navy as an electronics technician working on shipboard communications equipment. After the Navy, he obtained his master's license. He worked for several large contractors on projects up to a billion dollars. Brian began developing training programs for his workers, where he discoverd he enjoyed teaching more than anything.

In 2004, Brian started an electrician's program at a post-secondary school in Philadelphia. His program trains 300 students a year with awards for retention of 99 percent. After almost six years, Brian opened his own school, Advance Electrical Training in Allentown, mainly providing license test preparation services.

As a consultant, Brian revised Mike Holt's apprenticeship curriculum into a fully customizable program that can meet any electrical training need. Brian is now the Director of Program Development at Mike Holt Enterprises where he assists schools and instructors with development, implementation, and operation of new and revised programs.

Brian and his wife Shannon live in Allentown, PA. They have been married for 12 years and have four children; Brian II, Andrew, Anthony, and Emily. They are very involved with their children's school and sports activities, which keeps their days action packed year round.

Eric Stromberg
Electrical Engineer/Instructor
Stromberg Engineering, Inc.
Lake Jackson, TX
www.strombergengineering.com

Eric Stromberg started in the Electrical field by working as a journeyman electrician for a small contractor in the Houston area while going to college pursuing a degree in Electrical Engineering. After graduation, in 1982, Eric worked as an electronic technician where he installed and maintained life safety control systems in high rise buildings. In 1989, Eric went to work for Dow Chemical where he designed power distribution systems for major industrial complexes in the U.S., Spain, Brazil, and Germany. Eric was very involved in both creating Electrical standards and procedures as well as checking existing standards and procedures for alignment with national standards.

He also worked as a Construction Manager where he ensured *Code* compliancy of installations as well as provided field engineering support. Eric currently has his own business and spends a good deal of time teaching classes in both the *National Electrical Code* and electrical circuits. He is also a member of the Electrical Safety and Licensing Advisory Board for the State of Texas.

Eric lives in Lake Jackson, Texas, with his wife Jane. They have three children: Ainsley, Austin, and Brieanna. Ainsley is a teacher in Boston who will be getting married in the summer of 2011. Austin will be enlisting in the Air Force, and Brieanna started college in the Fall of 2010.

James Thomas
Master Electrician/Electrical Instructor
James Sprunt Community College
Kenansville, North Carolina
www.jamessprunt.edu

James Thomas has been working in the electrical field since 1985, and is licensed in the State of North Carolina. He has worked in residential, commercial, and industrial electrical jobs. James has been an instructor teaching electrical and electronic courses (including the *National Electrical Code*) full time at James Sprunt Community College in Kenansville, NC for over 16 years and has taught thousands of individuals. He has taught at Pitt Community College in Greenville, NC; Cape Fear Community College in Wilmington, NC; and Sampson Community College in Clinton, NC.

James earned a diploma in Electrical Installation and Maintenance; a Bachelor's degree in Business Management from Mount Olive College in Mount Olive, NC; and a Master's degree in Industrial Technology from East Carolina University in Greenville NC. James also served in the Air Force Reserve in Goldsboro NC for over 22 years.

Notes

CHAPTER 1

ELECTRICAL THEORY

Essential for Journeyman and Master's Licensing Exams

Notes

UNIT 1

Electrician's Math and Basic Electrical Formulas

INTRODUCTION TO UNIT 1—ELECTRICIAN'S MATH AND BASIC ELECTRICAL FORMULAS

In order to construct a building that will last into the future, a strong foundation is a prerequisite. The foundation is a part of the building that isn't visible in the finished structure, but is essential in erecting a building that will have the necessary strength to endure.

The math and basic electrical concepts of this unit are very similar to the foundation of a building. The concepts in this unit are the essential basics that you must understand, because you'll build upon them as you study electrical circuits and systems. As your studies continue, you'll find that a good foundation in electrical theory and math will help you understand why the *NEC* contains certain provisions.

This unit includes math and electrical fundamentals. You'll be amazed at how often your electrical studies return to the basics of this unit. Ohm's law and the electrical formulas related to it are the foundation of all electrical circuits.

Every student begins at a different level of understanding, and you may find this unit an easy review, or you may find it requires a high level of concentration. In any case, be certain that you fully understand the concepts of this unit and are able to successfully complete the questions at the end of the unit before going on. A solid foundation will help in your successful study of the rest of this textbook.

PART A—ELECTRICIAN'S MATH

Introduction

Numbers can take different forms:

Whole numbers: 1, 20, 300, 4,000, 5,000
Decimals: 0.80, 1.25, 0.75, 1.15
Fractions: ½, ¼, ⅝, ⁴⁄₃
Percentages: 80%, 125%, 250%, 500%

You'll need to be able to convert these numbers from one form to another and back again, because all of these number forms are part of electrical work and electrical calculations.

You'll also need to be able to do some basic algebra. Many people have a fear of algebra, but as you work through the material here you'll see there's nothing to fear.

1.1 Whole Numbers

Whole numbers are exactly what the term implies. These numbers don't contain any fractions, decimals, or percentages. Another name for whole numbers is "integers."

1.2 Decimals

The decimal method is used to display numbers other than whole numbers, fractions, or percentages such as, 0.80, 1.25, 1.732, and so on.

1.3 Fractions

A fraction represents part of a whole number. If you use a calculator for adding, subtracting, multiplying, or dividing, you need to convert the fraction to a decimal or whole number. To change a fraction to a decimal or whole number, divide the numerator (the top number) by the denominator (the bottom number).

► **Examples**

⅙ = one divided by six = 0.166
⅖ = two divided by five = 0.40
³⁄₆ = three divided by six = 0.50
⁵⁄₄ = five divided by four = 1.25
⁷⁄₂ = seven divided by two = 3.50

1.4 Percentages

A percentage is another method used to display a value. One hundred percent (100%) means all of a value; fifty percent (50%) means one-half of a value, and twenty-five percent (25%) means one-fourth of a value.

For convenience in multiplying or dividing by a percentage, convert the percentage value to a whole number or decimal, and then use the result for the calculation. When changing a percent value to a decimal or whole number, drop the percentage symbol and move the decimal point two places to the left. Figure 1–1

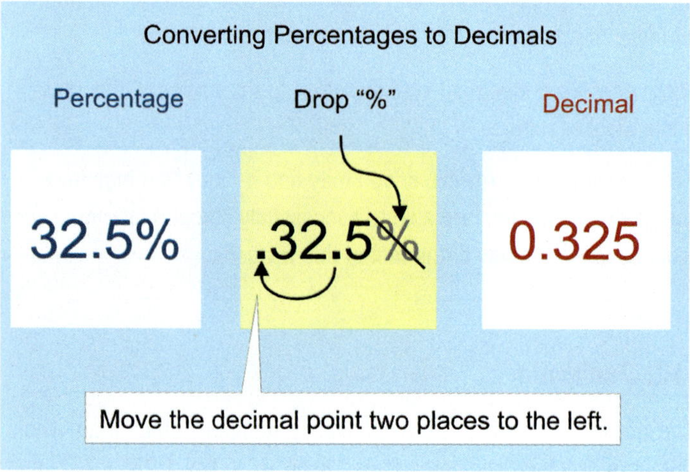

Figure 1–1

► Examples

Percentage	*Number*
32.50%	*0.325*
80%	*0.80*
125%	*1.25*
250%	*2.50*

1.5 Multiplier

When a number needs to be changed by multiplying it by a percentage, the percentage is called a multiplier. The first step is to convert the percentage to a decimal, then multiply the original number by the decimal value.

► Example 1

Question: *An overcurrent device (circuit breaker or fuse) must be sized no less than 125 percent of the continuous load. If the load is 80A, the overcurrent device will have to be sized no smaller than _____.* **Figure 1–2**

(a) 75A *(b) 80A* *(c) 100A* *(d) 125A*

Answer: *(c) 100A*

Step 1: Convert 125 percent to a decimal: 1.25

Step 2: Multiply the value of the 80A load by 1.25 = 100A

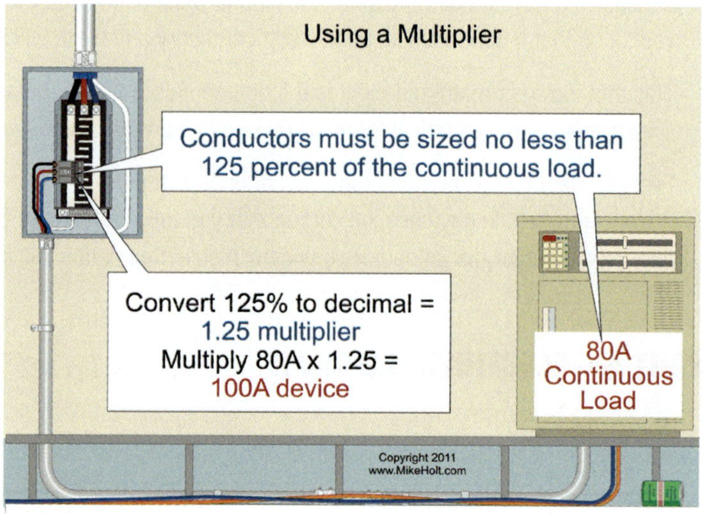

Figure 1–2

► Example 2

Question: *The maximum continuous load on an overcurrent device is limited to 80 percent of the device rating. If the overcurrent device is rated 50A, what's the maximum continuous load permitted on the overcurrent device?* **Figure 1–3**

(a) 40A *(b) 50A* *(c) 75A* *(d) 100A*

Answer: *(a) 40A*

Step 1: Convert 80 percent to a decimal: 0.80

Step 2: Multiply the value of the 50A device rating by 0.80 = 40A

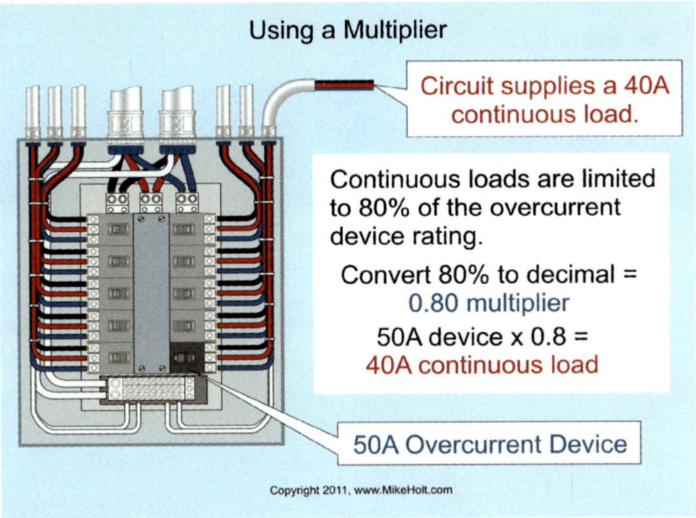

Figure 1–3

1.6 Percent Increase

Use the following steps to increase a number by a specific percentage:

Step 1: Convert the percent to a decimal value.

Step 2: Add one to the decimal value to create the multiplier.

Step 3: Multiply the original number by the multiplier found in Step 2.

▶ Example 1

Question: *How do you increase the whole number 45 by 35 percent?*

Step 1: Convert 35 percent to decimal form: 0.35

Step 2: Add one to the decimal value: 1 + 0.35 = 1.35

Step 3: Multiply 45 by the multiplier 1.35: 45 x 1.35 = 60.75

▶ Example 2

Question: *If the feeder demand load for a range is 8 kW and it's required to be increased by 15 percent, the total calculated load will be ______.* **Figure 1–4**

(a) 6.80 kW (b) 8 kW (c) 9.20 kW (d) 15 kW

Answer: *(c) 9.20 kW*

Step 1: Convert the percentage increase required to decimal form: 15 percent = 0.15

Step 2: Add one to the decimal: 1 + 0.15 = 1.15

Step 3: Multiply 8 by the multiplier 1.15: 8 kW x 1.15 = 9.20 kW

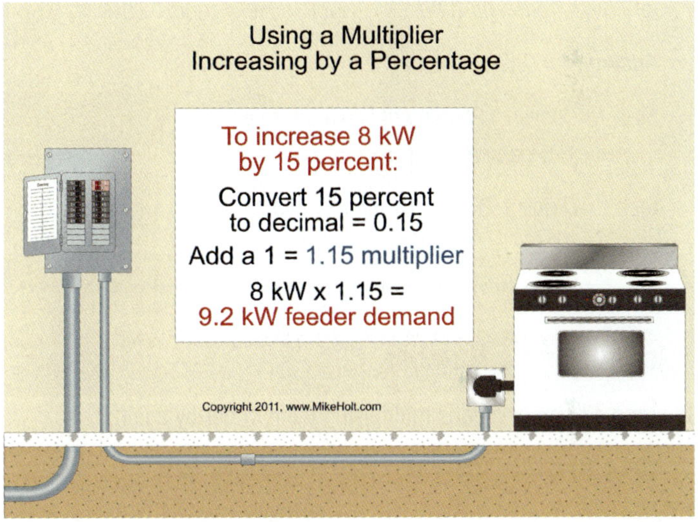

Figure 1–4

1.7 Reciprocals

To obtain the reciprocal of a number, convert the number into a fraction with the number one as the numerator (the top number). It's also possible to calculate the reciprocal of a decimal number. Determine the reciprocal of a decimal number by following these steps:

Step 1: Convert the number to a decimal value.

Step 2: Divide the value into the number one.

► **Example 1**

Question: *What's the reciprocal of 80 percent?*

(a) 0.80 (b) 100% (c) 125% (d) 150%

Answer: *(c) 125%*

Step 1: Convert 80 percent into a decimal (move the decimal two places to the left): 80 percent = 0.80

Step 2: Divide 0.80 into the number one: 1/0.80 = 1.25 or 125 percent

► **Example 2**

Question: *What's the reciprocal of 125 percent?*

(a) 75% (b) 0.80 (c) 100% (d) 125%

Answer: *(b) 0.80*

Step 1: Convert 125 percent into a decimal: 125 percent = 1.25

Step 2: Divide 1.25 into the number one: 1/1.25 = 0.80 or 80 percent

1.8 Squaring a Number

Squaring a number means multiplying the number by itself.

$10^2 = 10 \times 10 = 100$ or $23^2 = 23 \times 23 = 529$

► **Example 1**

Question: *What's the power consumed in watts by a 12 AWG conductor that's 200 ft long, and has a total resistance of 0.40 ohms, if the current (I) in the circuit conductors is 16A? (Answers are rounded to the nearest 50).*

Formula: Power = I^2 x R

(a) 50W (b) 100W (c) 150W (d) 200W

Answer: *(b) 100W*

$P = I^2 \times R$
I = 16A
R = 0.40 ohms

$P = 16A^2 \times 0.40$ ohms
P = 16A x 16A x 0.40 ohms
P = 102.40W

► **Example 2**

Question: *What's the area in square inches (sq in.) of a trade size 1 raceway with an inside diameter of 1.049 in.?*

Formula: Area = $\pi \times r^2$
$\pi = 3.14$
r = radius (equal to 0.50 of the diameter)

(a) 0.34 sq in. (b) 0.50 sq in. (c) 0.86 sq in. (d) 1 sq in.

Answer: *(c) 0.86 sq in.*

Area = $\pi \times r^2$
Area = $3.14 \times (0.50 \times 1.049)^2$
Area = 3.14×0.5245^2
Area = 3.14 x (0.5245 x 0.5245)
Area = 3.14 x 0.2751
Area = 0.86 sq in.

► **Example 3**

Question: *What's the sq in. area of an 8 in. pizza?* **Figure 1–5A**

(a) 25 sq in. (b) 50 sq in. (c) 64 sq in. (d) 75 sq in.

Answer: *(b) 50 sq in.*

Area = $\pi \times r^2$
Area = $3.14 \times (0.50 \times 8)^2$
Area = 3.14×4^2
Area = 3.14 x (4 x 4)
Area = 3.14 x 16
Area = 50 sq in.

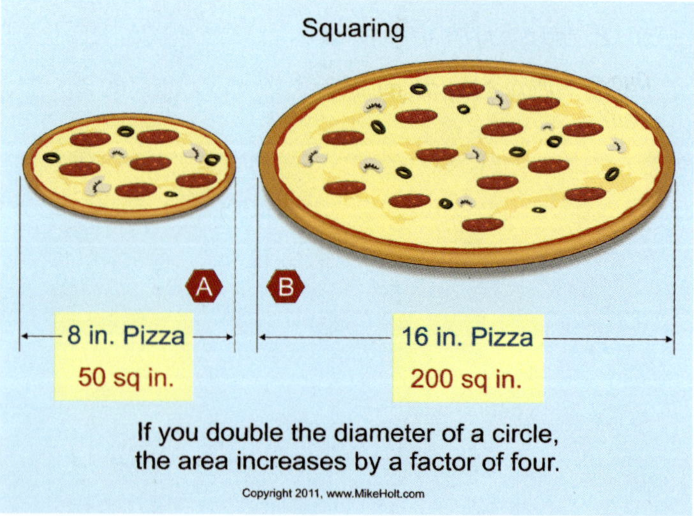

Figure 1–5

▶ **Example 4**

Question: *What's the sq in. area of a 16 in. pizza?* **Figure 1–5B**

(a) 100 sq in. (b) 150 sq in. (c) 200 sq in. (d) 256 sq in.

Answer: *(c) 200 sq in.*

Area = π x r²
Area = 3.14 x (0.50 x 16)²
Area = 3.14 x 8²
Area = 3.14 x (8 x 8)
Area = 3.14 x 64
Area = 200 sq in.

Author's Comment: As you see in Examples 3 and 4, if you double the diameter of the circle, the area contained in the circle is increased by a factor of four! By the way, a large pizza is always cheaper per sq in. than a small pizza.

1.9 Parentheses

Whenever numbers are in parentheses, complete the mathematical function within the parentheses before proceeding with the rest of the problem.

Parentheses are used to group steps of a process in the correct order. For instance, adding the sum of 3 and 15 to the product of 4 and 2 equals 26.

(3 + 15) + (4 x 2) = 18 + 8 = 26

▶ **Example**

Question: *What's the current of a 36,000W, 208V, three-phase load?* **Figure 1–6**

Ampere (I) = Watts/(E x 1.732)

(a) 50A (b) 100A (c) 150A (d) 360A

Answer: *(b) 100A*

Step 1: Perform the operation inside the parentheses first—determine the product of: 208V x 1.732 = 360V

Step 2: Divide 36,000W by 360V = 100A

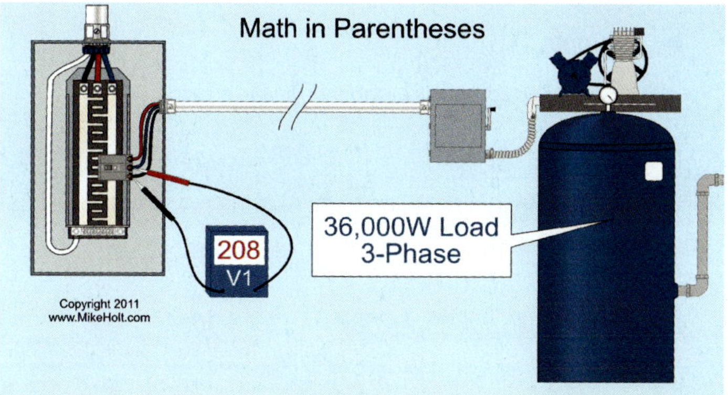

$$I = \frac{P}{(E \times \sqrt{3})} \quad I = \frac{36{,}000W}{(208V \times 1.732)} \quad I = \frac{36{,}000W}{360} = 100A$$

Whenever numbers are in parentheses, we must complete the mathematical function within the parentheses before proceeding with the rest of the problem.

Figure 1–6

1.10 Square Root

Deriving the square root of a number ($\sqrt{n}$) is the opposite of squaring a number. The square root of 36 is a number that, when multiplied by itself, gives the product 36. The $\sqrt{36}$ equals six, because six, multiplied by itself (which can be written as 6^2) equals the number 36.

Because it's difficult to do this manually, just use the square root key of your calculator.

$\sqrt{3}$: Following your calculator's instructions, enter the number 3, then press the square root key = 1.732.

$\sqrt{1{,}000}$: enter the number 1,000, then press the square root key = 31.62.

If your calculator doesn't have a square root key, don't worry about it. For all practical purposes in using this textbook, the only number you need to know the square root of is 3. The square root of 3 equals approximately 1.732.

To add, subtract, multiply, or divide a number by a square root value, determine the decimal value and then perform the math function.

► **Example 1**

Question: *What's 36,000W/(208V x* $\sqrt{3}$*) equal to?*

(a) 100A (b) 120A (c) 208A (d) 360A

Answer: *(a) 100A*

Step 1: Determine the decimal value for the $\sqrt{3} = 1.732$

Step 2: Divide 36,000W by (208V x 1.732) = 100A

► **Example 2**

Question: *The phase voltage of a 120/208V system is equal to 208V/*$\sqrt{3}$*, which is _____.*

(a) 120V (b) 208V (c) 360V (d)480V

Answer: *(a) 120V*

Step 1: Determine the decimal value for the $\sqrt{3} = 1.732$

Step 2: Divide 208V by 1.732 = 120V

1.11 Volume

The volume of an enclosure is expressed in cubic inches (cu in.). It's determined by multiplying the length, by the width, by the depth of the enclosure.

► **Example**

Question: *What's the volume of a box that has the dimensions of 4 x 4 x 1½ in.?* **Figure 1–7**

(a) 12 cu in. (b) 20 cu in. (c) 24 cu in. (d) 30 cu in.

Answer: *(c) 24 cu in.*

1½ = 1.50
4 x 4 x 1.50 = 24 cu in.

Author's Comment: The actual volume of a 4 in. square electrical box is less than 24 cu in. because the interior dimensions may be less than the nominal size and often corners are rounded, so the allowable volume is given in the *NEC* Table 314.16(A).

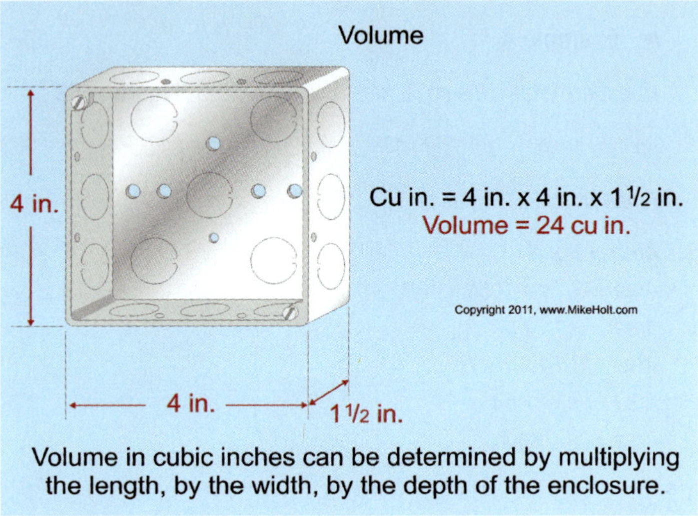

Figure 1–7

1.12 Kilo

The letter "k" is used in the electrical trade to abbreviate the metric prefix "kilo," which represents a value of 1,000.

To convert a number which includes the "k" prefix to units, multiply the number preceding the "k" by 1,000.

► **Example 1**

Question: *What's the wattage value for an 8 kW rated range?*

(a) 8W (b) 800W (c) 4,000W (d) 8,000W

Answer: *(d) 8,000W*

To convert a unit value to a "k" value, divide the number by 1,000 and add the "k" suffix.

► **Example 2**

Question: *What's the kW rating of a 300W load?* **Figure 1–8**

(a) 0.30 kW (b) 30 kW (c) 300 kW (d) 3,000 kW

Answer: *(a) 0.30 kW*

kW = Watts/1,000
kW = 300W/1,000 = 0.30 kW

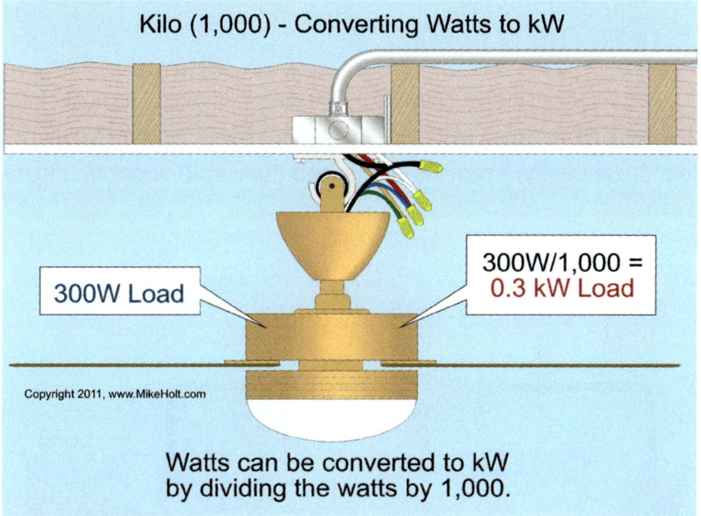

Figure 1–8

Author's Comment: The use of the letter "k" isn't limited to "kW." It's also used for kVA (1,000 volt-amperes), kcmil (1,000 circular mils) and other units such as kft (1,000 feet).

1.13 Rounding Off

There's no specific rule for rounding off, but rounding to two or three "significant digits" should be sufficient for most electrical calculations. Numbers below five are rounded down, while numbers five and above are rounded up.

0.1245—fourth number is five or above =
0.125 rounded up

1.674—fourth number is below five =
1.67 rounded down

21.99—fourth number is five or above =
22 rounded up

367.20—fourth number is below five =
367 rounded down

Rounding Answers for Multiple Choice Questions

You should round your answers in the same manner as the multiple choice selections given in the question.

► **Example**

Question: *The sum* of 12, 17, 28, and 40 is equal to _____.*

(a) 70　　(b) 80　　(c) 90　　(d) 100

Answer: *(d) 100*

**A sum is the result of adding numbers.*

The sum of these values equals 97, but that answer isn't listed as one of the choices. The multiple choice selections in this case are rounded off to the closest "tens."

1.14 Testing Your Answer for Reasonableness

When working with any mathematical calculation, don't just blindly do the calculation and assume it's correct. When you perform a mathematical calculation, you need to know if the answer is greater than or less than the values given in the problem. Always do a "reality check" to be certain that your answer isn't nonsense. Even the best of us make mistakes at times, so always examine your answer to make sure it makes sense!

► **Example**

Question: *The input of a transformer is 300W; the transformer efficiency is 90 percent. What's the transformer output?* **Figure 1–9**

(a) 270W　　(b) 300W　　(c) 333W　　(d) 500W

Answer: *(a) 270W*

Since the output has to be less than the input (300W), you won't have to perform any mathematical calculation; the only multiple choice selection that's less than 300W is (a) 270W.

The math to work out the answer is:
300W x 0.90 = 270W

To check your multiplication, use division:
270W/0.90 = 300W

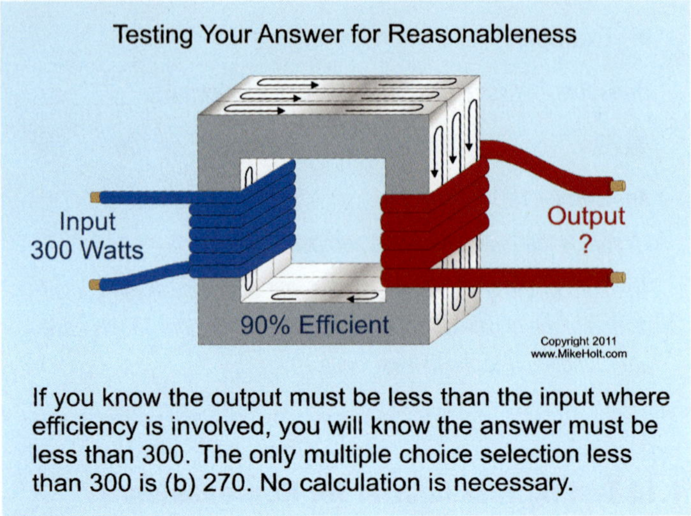

Figure 1–9

Author's Comment: One of the nice things about mathematical equations is that you can usually test to see if your answer is correct. To do this test, substitute the answer you arrived at back into the equation you're working with, and verify that it indeed equals out correctly. This method of checking your math will become easier once you know more of the formulas and how they relate to each other.

PART B—BASIC ELECTRICAL FORMULAS

Introduction

Now that you've mastered the math and understand some basics about electrical circuits, you're ready to take your knowledge of electrical formulas to the next level. One of the things we're going to do here is strengthen your proficiency with Ohm's Law.

Many false notions about the application of Article 250—Grounding and Bonding and Chapter 3—Wiring Methods (both in the *NEC*) arise when people use Ohm's Law only to solve practice problems on paper but lack a real understanding of how that law works and how to apply it. After completing this unit, you'll have that understanding, and won't be subject to those false notions—or the unsafe conditions they lead to.

But we won't stop with Ohm's Law. You're also going to have a high level of proficiency with the power equation. One of the tools for handling the power equation with ease—and Ohm's Law—is the power wheel. You'll be able to use it to solve all kinds of problems.

1.15 Electrical Circuit

A basic electrical circuit consists of the power source, the conductors, and the load. A switch can be placed in series with the circuit conductors to control the operation of the load (turning it on or off). **Figure 1–10**

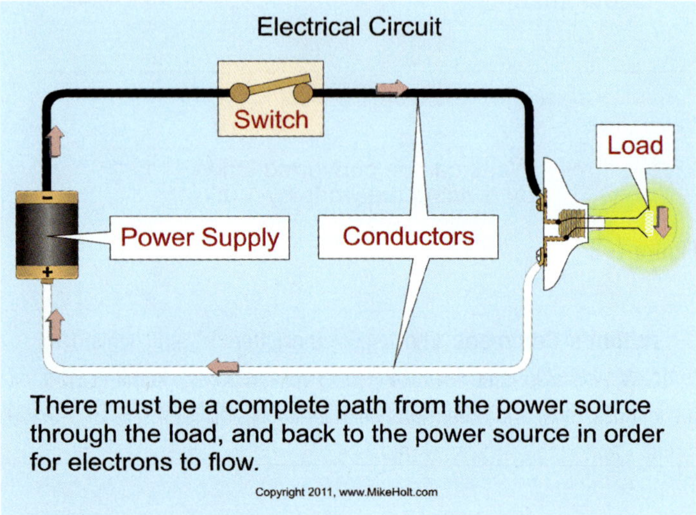

Figure 1–10

Author's Comment: According to the "electron current flow theory," current always flows from the negative terminal of the source, through the circuit and load, to the positive terminal of the source.

1.16 Power Source

The power necessary to move electrons out of their orbit around the nucleus of an atom can be produced by chemical, magnetic, photovoltaic, and other means. The two categories of power sources are direct current (dc) and alternating current (ac).

Direct Current

The polarity and the output voltage from a direct-current power source never change direction. One terminal is negative and the other is positive, relative to each other. Direct-current power is often produced by batteries, direct-current generators, and electronic power supplies. **Figure 1–11**

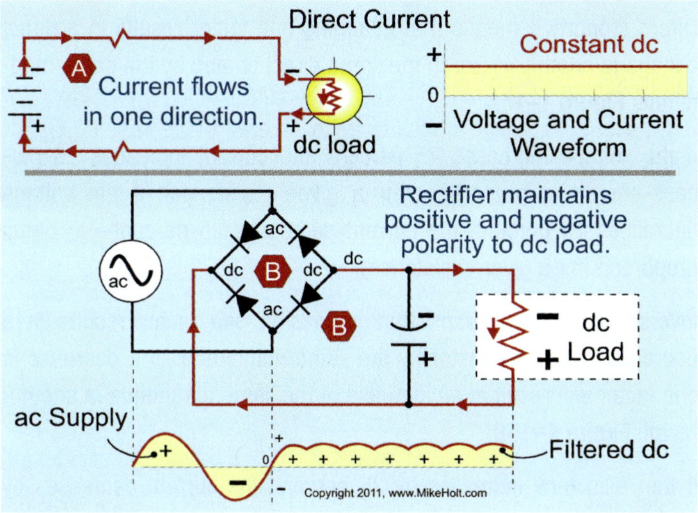

Figure 1–11

Direct current is used for electroplating, street trolley and railway systems, or where a smooth and wide range of speed control is required for a motor-driven application. Direct current is also used for control circuits and electronic instruments.

Alternating Current

Alternating-current power sources produce a voltage that changes polarity and magnitude. Alternating current is produced by an alternating-current power source such as an alternating-current generator. The major advantage of alternating current over direct current is that voltage can be changed through the use of a transformer. Figure 1–12

> **Author's Comment:** Alternating current accounts for more than 90 percent of all electric power used throughout the world.

1.17 Conductance

Conductance, or conductivity, is the property of a metal that permits current to flow. The best conductors in order of their conductivity are silver, copper, gold, and aluminum. Copper is most often used for electrical applications. Figure 1–13

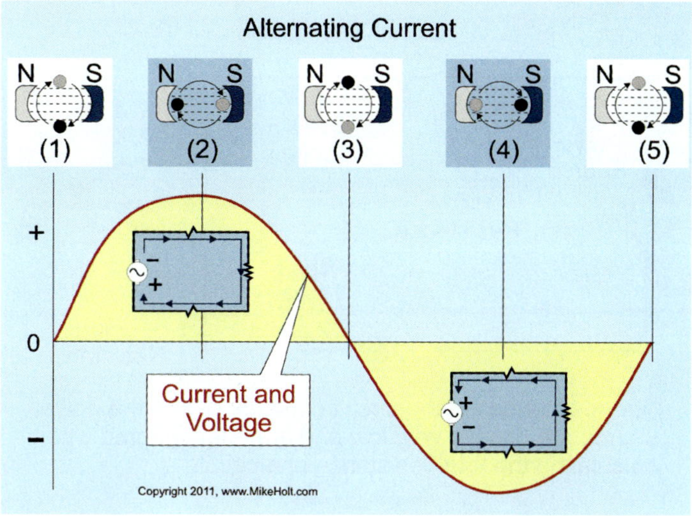

Figure 1–12

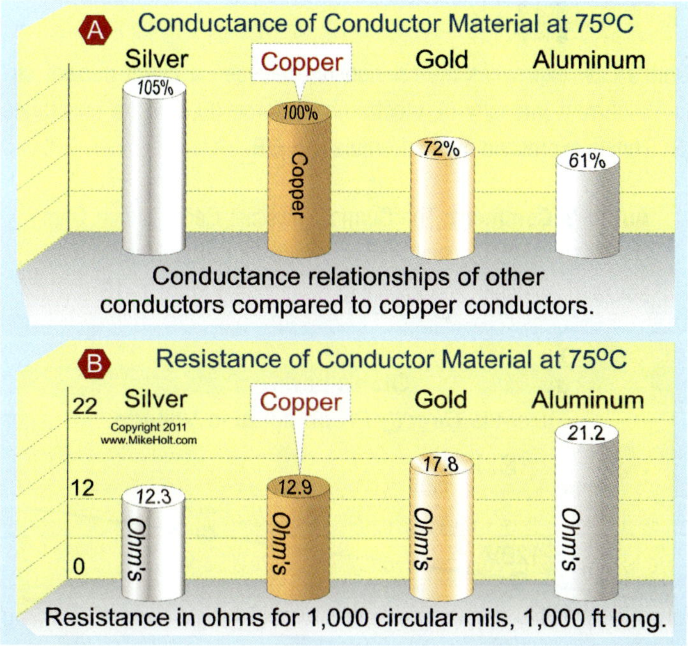

Figure 1–13

1.18 Circuit Resistance

The total resistance of a circuit includes the resistance of the power supply, the circuit wiring, and the load. Appliances such as heaters and toasters use high-resistance conductors to produce the heat needed for the application. Because the resistances of the power source and conductor are so much smaller than that of the load, they're generally ignored in circuit calculations. Figure 1–14

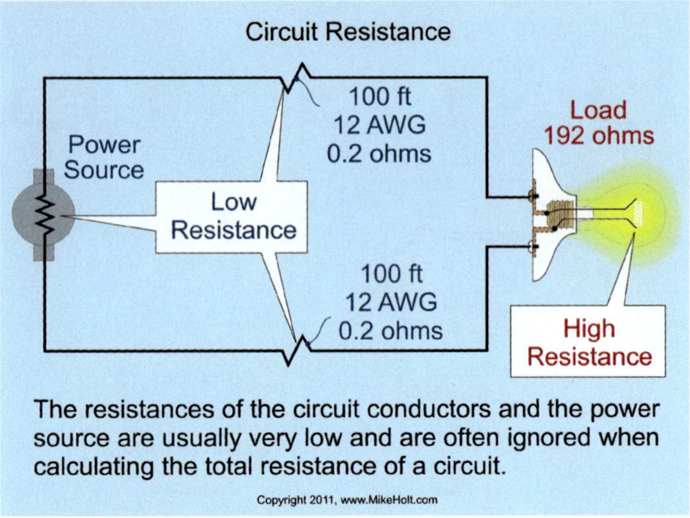

Figure 1–14

1.19 Ohm's Law

Ohm's Law expresses the relationship between a direct-current circuit's current intensity (I), electromotive force (E), and its resistance (R). This is expressed by the formula: **I = E/R**.

> **Author's Comment:** The German physicist Georg Simon Ohm (1787-1854) stated that current is directly proportional to voltage, and inversely proportional to resistance. **Figure 1–15**

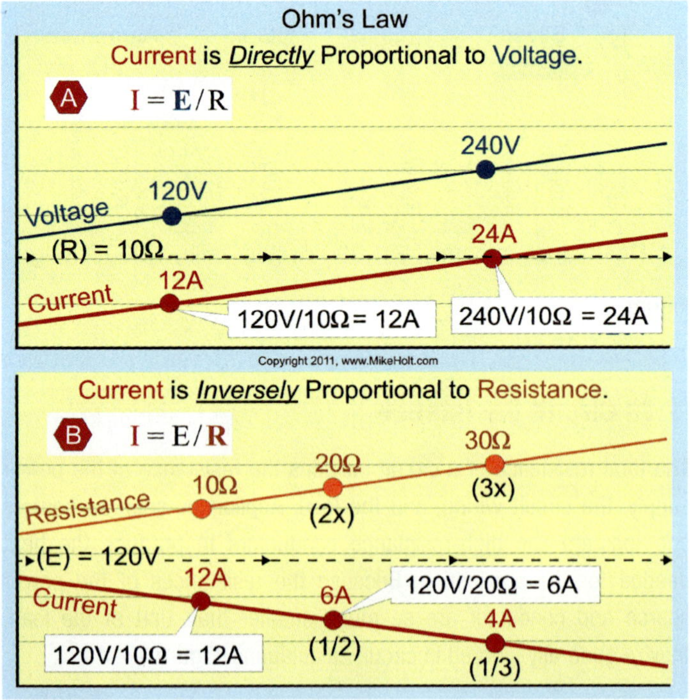

Figure 1–15

Direct proportion means that changing one factor results in a direct change to another factor in the same direction and by the same magnitude. **Figure 1–15A**

If the voltage increases 25 percent, the current increases 25 percent—in direct proportion (for a given resistance). If the voltage decreases 25 percent, the current decreases 25 percent—in direct proportion (for a given resistance).

Inverse proportion means that increasing one factor results in a decrease in another factor by the same magnitude, or a decrease in one factor will result in an increase of the same magnitude in another factor. **Figure 1–15B**

If the resistance increases by 25 percent, the current decreases by 25 percent—in inverse proportion (for a given voltage), or if the resistance decreases by 25 percent, the current increases by 25 percent—in inverse proportion (for a given voltage).

1.20 Ohm's Law and Alternating Current

Direct Current

In a direct-current circuit, the only opposition to current flow is the physical resistance of the material through which the current flows. This opposition is called resistance and is measured in ohms.

Alternating Current

In an alternating-current circuit, there are three factors that oppose current flow: the resistance of the material; the inductive reactance of the circuit; and the capacitive reactance of the circuit.

> **Author's Comment:** For now, we'll assume that the effects of inductance and capacitance on the circuit are insignificant and they'll be ignored.

1.21 Ohm's Law Formula Circle

Ohm's Law, the relationship between current, voltage, and resistance expressed in the formula, **E = I x R**, can be transposed to **I = E/R** or **R = E/I**. In order to use these formulas, two of the values must be known.

> **Author's Comment:** Place your thumb on the unknown value in **Figure 1–16**, and the two remaining variables will "show" you the correct formula.

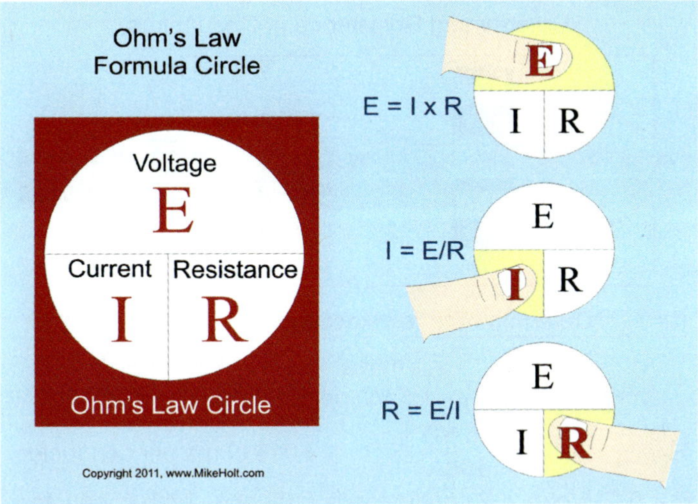

Figure 1–16

▶ Current Example

Question: *120V supplies a lamp that has a resistance of 192 ohms. What's the current flow in the circuit?* **Figure 1–17**

(a) 0.50A *(b) 0.60A* *(c) 1.30A* *(d) 2.50A*

Answer: *(b) 0.60A*

Step 1: What's the question? What's "I?"

Step 2: What do you know? E = 120V, R = 192 ohms

Step 3: The formula is ***I = E/R***

Step 4: The answer is I = 120V/192 ohms

Step 5: The answer is I = 0.625A

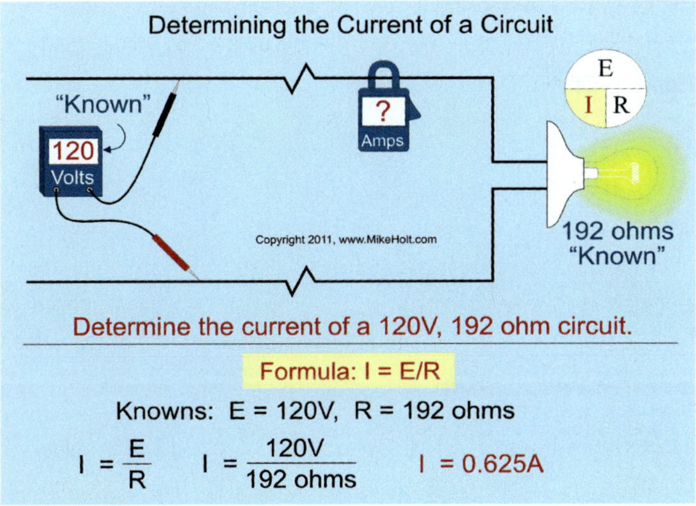

Figure 1–17

▶ Voltage-Drop Example

Question: *What's the voltage drop over two 12 AWG conductors (resistance of 0.20 ohms per 100 ft) supplying a 16A load located 50 ft from the power supply?* **Figure 1–18**

(a) 1.60V *(b) 3.20V* *(c) 16V* *(d) 32V*

Answer: *(b) 3.20V*

Step 1: What's the question? What's "E?"

Step 2: What do you know about the conductors?

I = 16A, R = 0.20 ohms. The NEC lists the alternating-current resistance of 1,000 ft of 12 AWG as 2 ohms [Chapter 9, Table 8]. The resistance of 100 ft is equal to 0.20 ohms. **Figure 1–19**

Step 3: The formula is ***E = I x R.***

Step 4: The answer is E = 16A x 0.20 ohms

Step 5: The answer is E = 3.20V

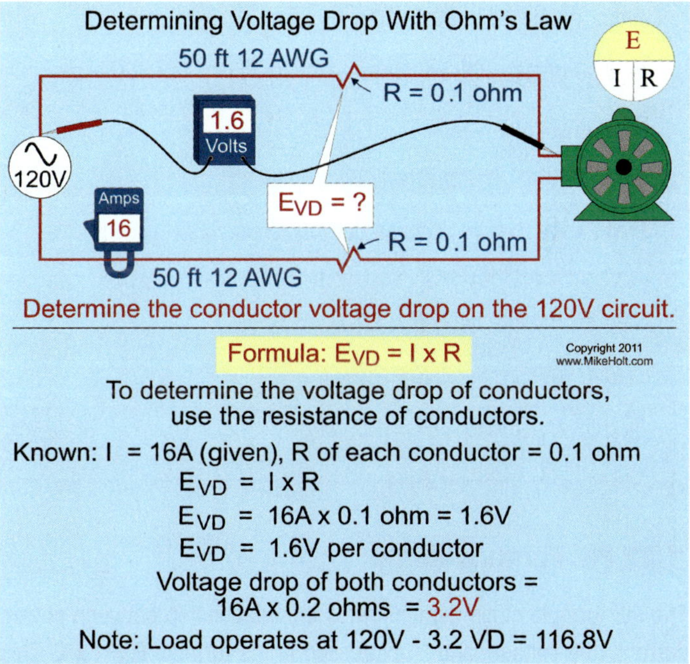

Figure 1–18

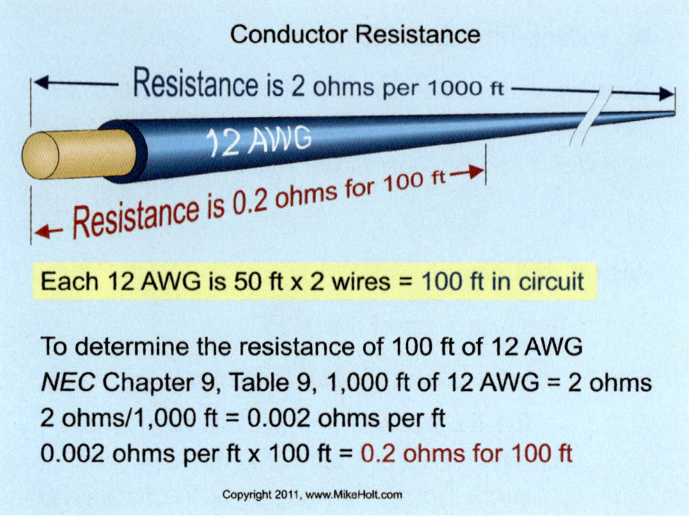

Figure 1–19

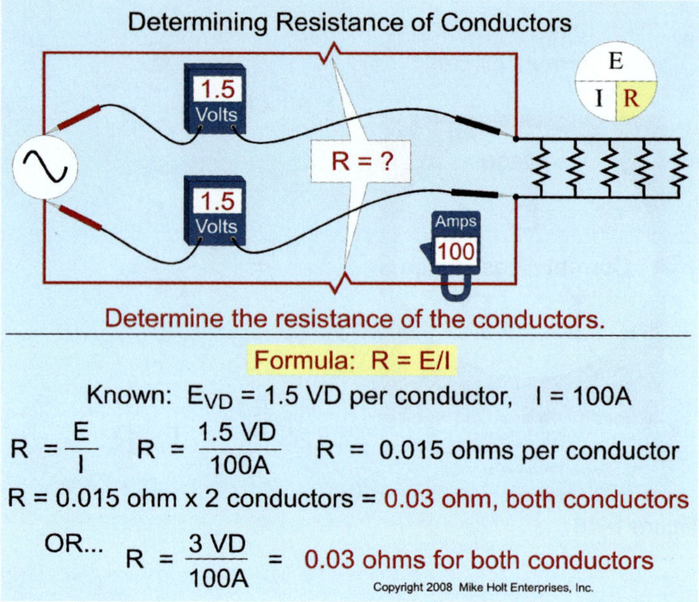

Figure 1–20

▶ Resistance Example

Question: *What's the resistance of the circuit conductors when the conductor voltage drop is 3V and the current flowing in the circuit is 100A?* **Figure 1–20**

(a) 0.03 ohms (b) 2 ohms (c) 30 ohms (d) 300 ohms

Answer: *(a) 0.03 ohms*

Step 1: What's the question? What's "R?"

Step 2: What do you know about the conductors?
E = 3V dropped, I = 100A

Step 3: The formula is ***R = E/I***

Step 4: The answer is R = 3V/100A

Step 5: The answer is R = 0.03 ohms

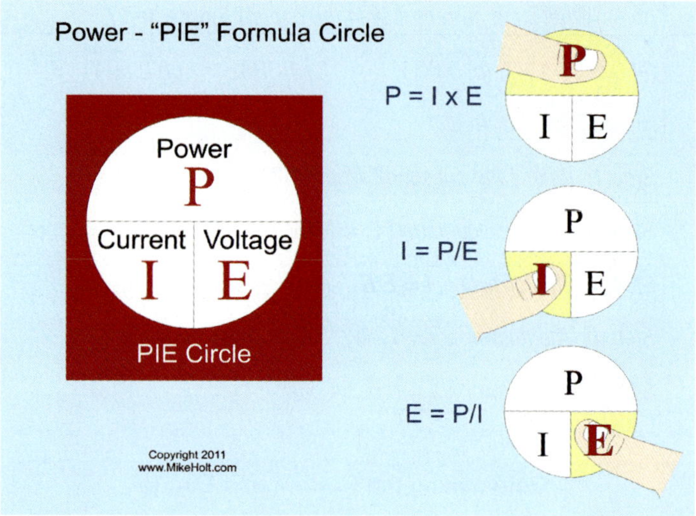

Figure 1–21

1.22 PIE Formula Circle

The PIE formula circle demonstrates the relationship between power, current, and voltage, and is expressed in the formula **P = I x E**. This formula can be transposed to **I = P/E** or **E = P/I**. In order to use these formulas, two of the values must be known.

> **Author's Comment:** Place your thumb on the unknown value in **Figure 1–21** and the two remaining variables will "show" you the correct formula.

► Power Loss Example

Question: *What's the power loss in watts for two conductors that carry 12A and have a voltage drop of 3.60V?* **Figure 1–22**

(a) 4.30W *(b) 24W* *(c) 43.20W* *(d) 432W*

Answer: *(c) 43.20W*

Step 1: What's the question? What's "P?"

Step 2: What do you know? I = 12A, E = 3.60V.

Step 3: The formula is ***P = I x E****.*

Step 4: The answer is P = 12A x 3.60V.

Step 5: The answer is 43.20W.

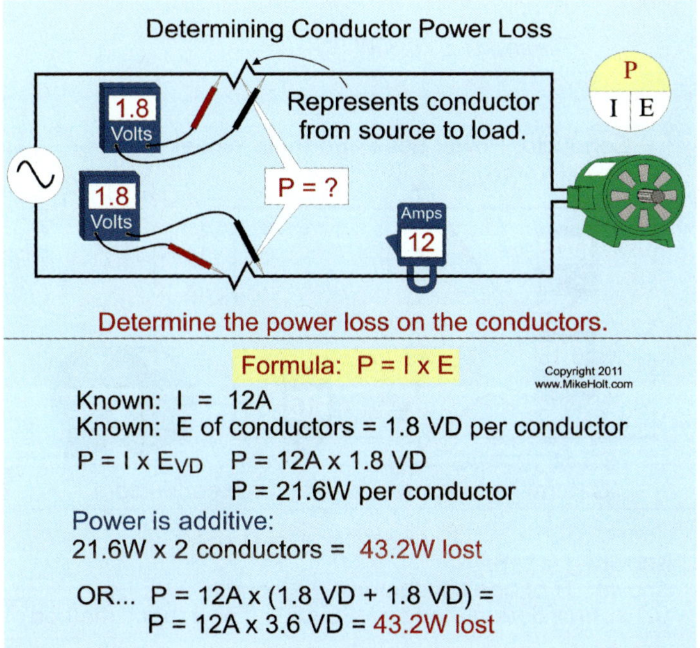

Figure 1–22

► Current Example

Question: *What's the current flow in amperes through a 7.50 kW heat strip rated 230V when connected to a 230V power supply?* **Figure 1–23**

(a) 25A *(b) 33A* *(c) 39A* *(d) 230A*

Answer: *(b) 33A*

Step 1: What's the question? What's "I?"

Step 2: What do you know? P = 7,500W, E = 230V.

Step 3: The formula is ***I = P/E****.*

Step 4: The answer is I = 7,500W/230V.

Step 5: The answer is 32.60A.

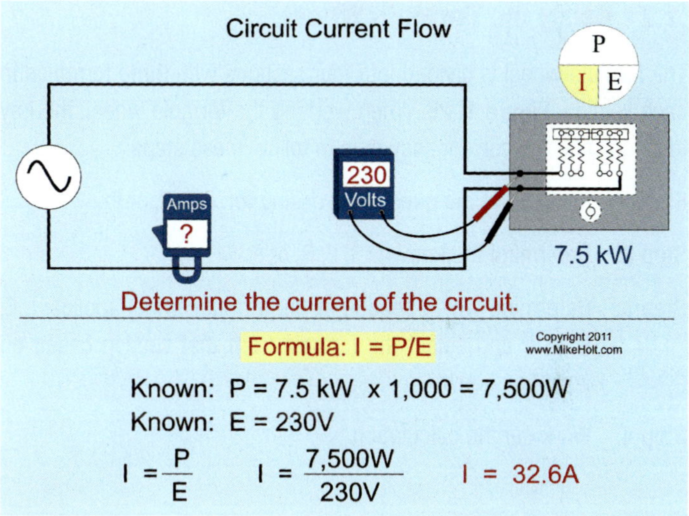

Figure 1–23

1.23 Formula Wheel

The formula wheel is a combination of the Ohm's Law and the PIE formula wheels. The formulas in the formula wheel can be used for direct-current circuits or alternating-current circuits with unity power factor. **Figure 1–24**

> **Author's Comment:** Unity power factor is explained in Unit 3. For the purpose of this unit, we'll assume a power factor of 1.0 for all alternating-current circuits.

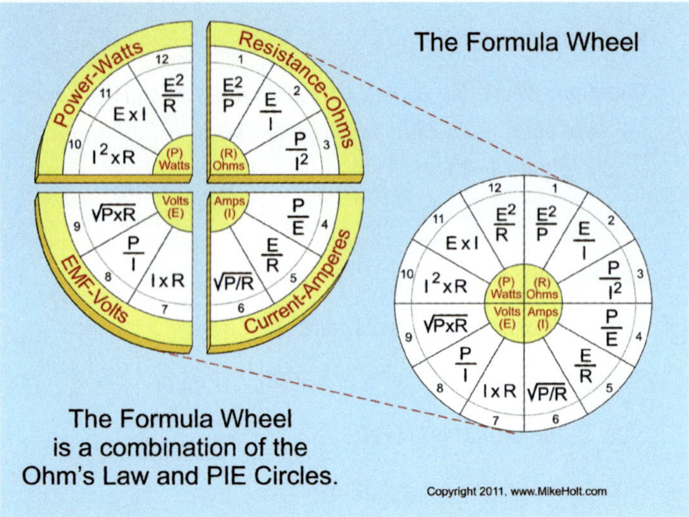

Figure 1–24

1.24 Using the Formula Wheel

The formula wheel is divided into four sections with three formulas in each section. Figure 1–25. When working the formula wheel, the key to calculating the correct answer is to follow these steps:

Step 1: Know what the question is asking for: I, E, R, or P.

Step 2: Determine the knowns: I, E, R, or P.

Step 3: Determine which section of the formula wheel applies: I, E, R, or P and select the formula from that section based on what you know.

Step 4: Work out the calculation.

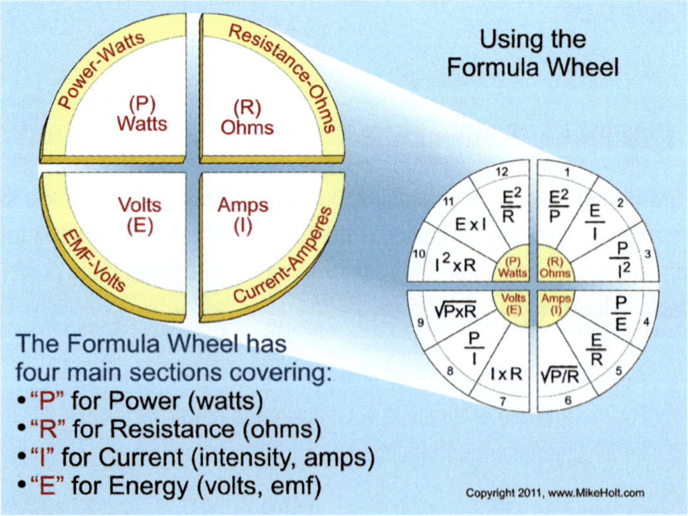

Figure 1–25

► Example

Question: *The total resistance of two 12 AWG conductors, 75 ft long is 0.30 ohms, and the current through the circuit is 16A. What's the power loss of the conductors?* **Figure 1–26**

(a) 20W *(b) 75W* *(c) 150W* *(d) 300W*

Answer: *(b) 75W*

Step 1: What's the question? What's the power loss of the conductors "P?"

Step 2: What do you know about the conductors?
I = 16A, R = 0.30 ohms

Step 3: What's the formula? ***P = I² x R***

Step 4: Calculate the answer: P = 16A² x 0.30 ohms = 76.80W.
The answer is 76.80W.

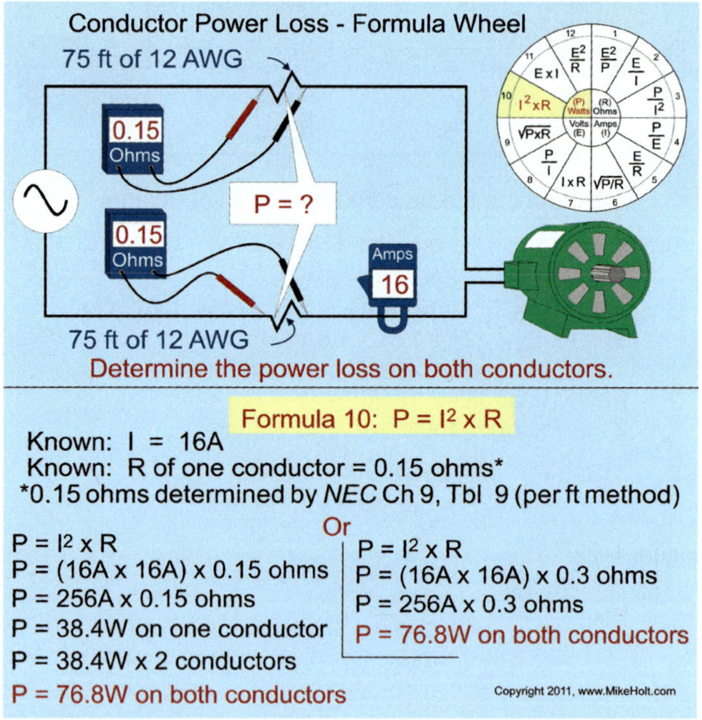

Figure 1–26

1.25 Power Losses of Conductors

Power in a circuit can be either "useful" or "wasted." Most of the power used by loads such as fluorescent lighting, motors, or stove elements is consumed in useful work. However, the heating of conductors, transformers, and motor windings is wasted work. Wasted work is still energy used; therefore it must be paid for, so we call wasted work "power loss."

► **Example**

Question: *What's the conductor power loss in watts for a 10 AWG conductor that has a voltage drop of 3 percent in a 240V circuit, and carries a current flow of 24A?* **Figure 1–27**

(a) 17W *(b) 173W* *(c) 350W* *(d) 450W*

Answer: *(b) 173W*

Step 1: What's the problem asking you to find? What's wasted "P?"

Step 2: What do you know about the conductors?

I = 24A
E = 240V x 3%
E = 240V x 0.03
E = 7.20V

Step 3: The formula is ***P = I x E****.*

Step 4: Calculate the answer: P = 24A x 7.20V = 172.80W. The answer is 172.80W.

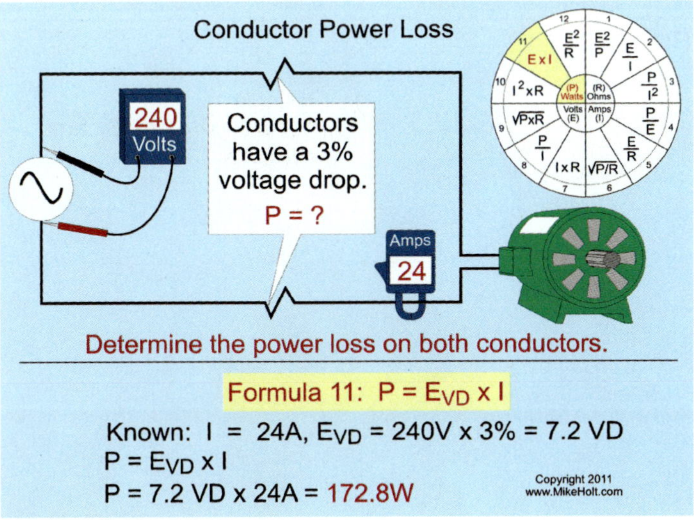

Figure 1–27

1.26 Cost of Power

Since electric bills are based on power consumed in watts, we should understand how to determine the cost of power.

► **Example**

Question: *What does it cost per year (at 8.60 cents per kWh) for the power loss of two 10 AWG circuit conductors that have a total resistance of 0.30 ohms with a current flow of 24A?* **Figure 1–28**

(a) $1.30 *(b) $13* *(c) $130* *(d) $1,300*

Answer: *(c) $130*

Step 1: Determine the amount of power consumed:

P = I2 x R
P = $24A^2$ x 0.30 ohms
P = 172.80W

Step 2: Convert the answer in Step 1 to kW:

P = 172.80W/1,000W
P = 0.1728 kW

Step 3: Determine the cost per hour:

(0.086 dollars per kWh) x 0.17280 kW = 0.01486 dollars per hr

Step 4: Determine the dollars per day:

0.01486 dollars per hr x (24 hrs per day) = 0.3567 dollars per day

Step 5: Determine the dollars per year:

0.3567 dollars per day x (365 days per year) = $130.20 per year

Author's Comment: That's a lot of money just to heat up two 10 AWG conductors for one circuit. Imagine how much it costs to heat up the conductors for an entire building!

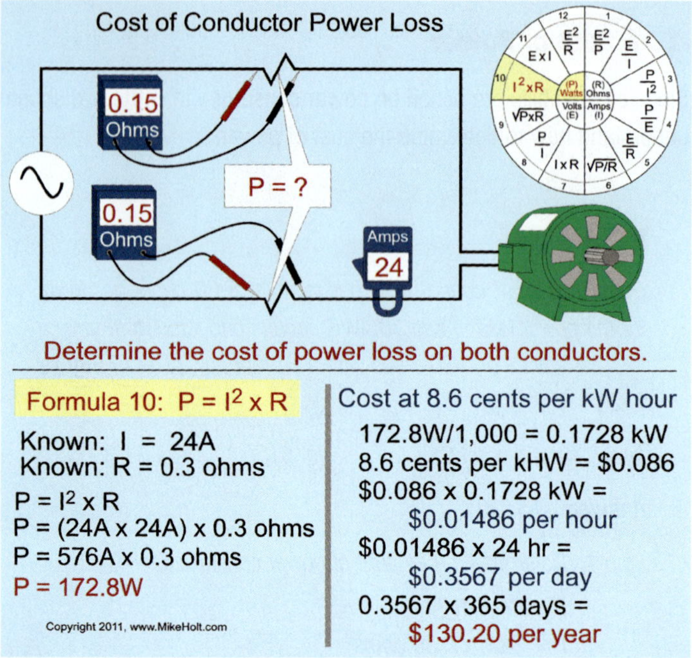

Figure 1–28

1.27 Power Changes with the Square of the Voltage

The voltage applied to a resistor dramatically affects the power consumed by that resistor. Power is determined by the square of the voltage. This means that if the voltage is doubled, the power will increase four times. If the voltage is decreased 50 percent, the power will decrease to 25 percent of its original value. **Figure 1–29**

▶ Power Example at 230V

Question: *What's the power consumed by a 9.60 kW heat strip rated 230V connected to a 230V circuit?* **Figure 1–30**

(a) 7.85 kW (b) 9.60 kW (c) 11.57 kW (d) 25 kW

Answer: *(b) 9.60 kW*

Step 1: What's the problem asking you to find?
Power consumed by the resistance.

Step 2: What do you know about the heat strip?
You were given "P = 9.60 kW" in the statement of the problem.

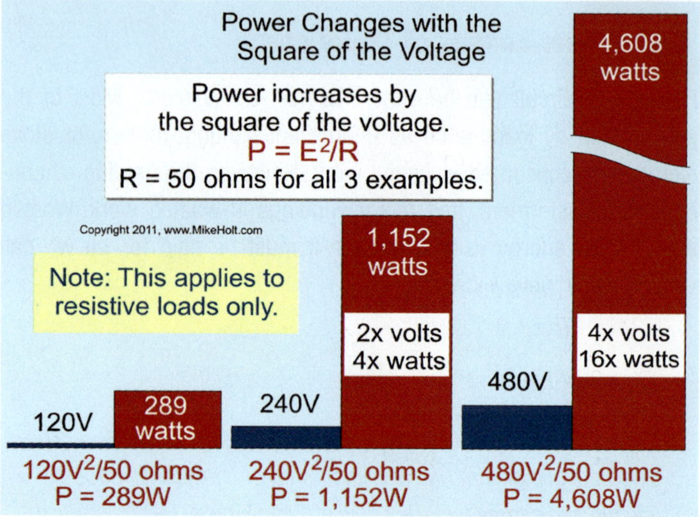

Figure 1–29

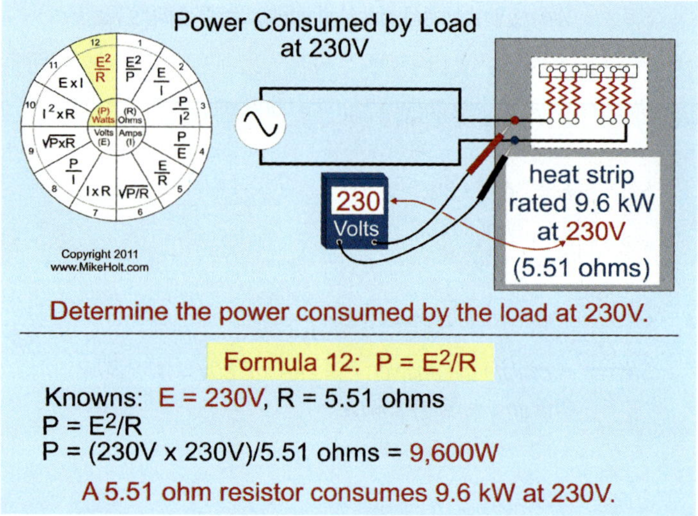

Figure 1–30

► Power Example at 208V

Question: *What's the power consumed by a 9.60 kW heat strip rated 230V connected to a 208V circuit?* **Figure 1–31**

(a) 7.85 k *(b) 9.60 kW* *(c) 11.57 kW* *(d) 208 kW*

Answer: *(a) 7.85 kW*

Step 1: What's the problem asking you to find?
The power consumed by the resistance.

Step 2: What do you know about the heat strip?
$E = 208V$, $R = E^2/P$
$R = 230V \times 230V/9{,}600W$
$R = 5.51$ ohms

Step 3: The formula to determine power is: ***P = E2/R***.

Step 4: The answer is:
$P = 208V^2/5.51$ ohms
$P = 7{,}851W$ or 7.85 kW

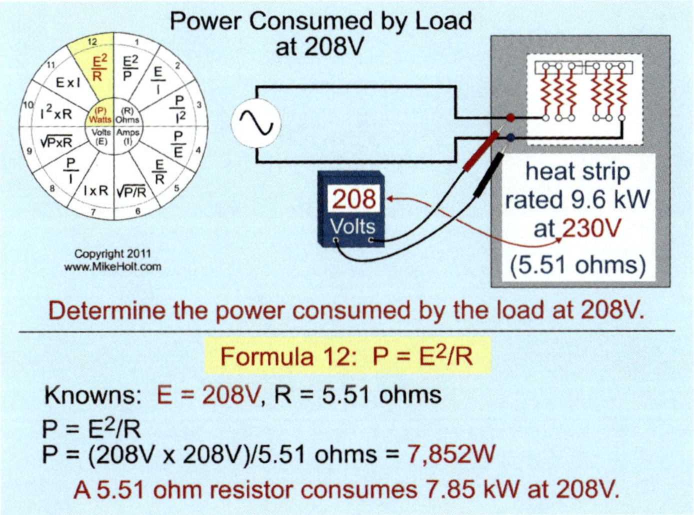

Figure 1–31

Author's Comment: It's important to realize that the resistance of the heater unit doesn't change—it's a property of the material through which the current flows and isn't dependent on the voltage applied.

Thus, for a small change in voltage, there's a considerable change in the power consumption by this heater.

Author's Comment: The current flow for this heat strip is **I = P/E**.

$P = 7{,}851W$
$E = 208V$
$I = 7{,}851W/208V$
$I = 38A$

► Power Example at 240V

Question: *What's the power consumed by a 9.60 kW heat strip rated 230V connected to a 240V circuit?* **Figure 1–32**

(a) 7.85 kW *(b) 9.60 kW* *(c) 10.45 kW* *(d) 11.57 kW*

Answer: *(c) 10.45 kW*

Step 1: What's the problem asking you to find?
The power consumed by the resistance.

Step 2: What do you know about the resistance?
*$R = 5.51$ ohms**

The resistance of the heat strip is determined by the formula* **$R = E^2/P$.

E = Nameplate voltage rating of the resistance, 230V

P = Nameplate power rating of the resistance, 9,600W

$R = E^2/P$
$R = 230V^2/9{,}600W$
$R = 5.51$ ohms

Step 3: The formula to determine power is: **$P = E^2/R$**

Step 4: The answer is:
$P = 240V \times 240V/5.51$ ohms
$P = 10{,}454W$
$P = 10.45$ kW

Author's Comment: The current flow for this heat strip is **I = P/E**.

$P = 10{,}454W$
$E = 240V$
$I = 10{,}454W/240V$
$I = 44A$

As you can see, when the voltage changes, the power changes by the square of the change in the voltage, but the current changes in direct proportion to the change in the voltage.

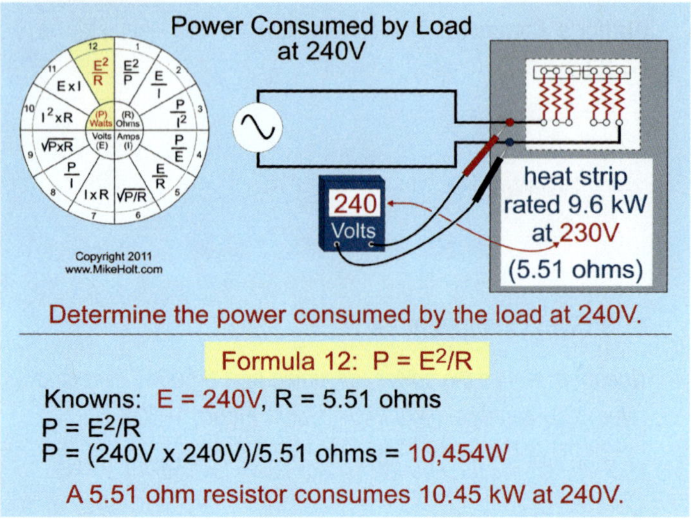

Figure 1–32

CONCLUSION TO UNIT 1—ELECTRICIAN'S MATH AND BASIC ELECTRICAL FORMULAS

You've gained skill in working with Ohm's Law and the power equation, and can use the power wheel to solve a wide variety of electrical problems. You also know how to calculate voltage drop and power loss, and can relate the costs in real dollars.

As you work through the practice questions, you'll see how well you've mastered the mathematical concepts and how ready you are to put them to use in electrical formulas. Always remember to check your answer when you're done—then you'll know you have a correct answer every time. As useful as these skills are, there's still more to learn. But, your mastery of the basic electrical formulas means you're well prepared. Work through the questions that follow, and go back over the instructional material if you have any difficulty. When you believe you know the material in Unit 1, you're ready to tackle the electrical circuits of Unit 2.

UNIT 1 Practice Questions

PRACTICE QUESTIONS FOR UNIT 1—ELECTRICIAN'S MATH AND BASIC ELECTRICAL FORMULAS

PART A—ELECTRICIAN'S MATH

1.3 Fractions

1. The decimal equivalent for the fraction "½" is ______.

   (a) 0.50
   (b) 0.70
   (c) 2
   (d) 5

2. The approximate decimal equivalent for the fraction "4⁄18" is ______.

   (a) 0.20
   (b) 2.50
   (c) 3.50
   (d) 4.50

1.4 Percentages

3. To change a percent value to a decimal or whole number, drop the percentage sign and move the decimal point two places to the ______.

   (a) right
   (b) left
   (c) depends
   (d) none of these

4. The decimal equivalent for "75 percent" is ______.

   (a) 0.075
   (b) 0.75
   (c) 7.50
   (d) 75

5. The decimal equivalent for "225 percent" is ______.

   (a) 0.225
   (b) 2.25
   (c) 22.50
   (d) 225

6. The decimal equivalent for "300 percent" is ______.

   (a) 0.03
   (b) 0.30
   (c) 3
   (d) 30.00

1.5 Multiplier

7. The method of increasing a number by another number is done by using a ______.

   (a) percentage
   (b) decimal
   (c) fraction
   (d) multiplier

8. An overcurrent device (circuit breaker or fuse) must be sized no less than 125 percent of the continuous load. If the load is 16A, the overcurrent device will have to be sized at no less than ______.

   (a) 17A
   (b) 20A
   (c) 23A
   (d) 30A

9. The maximum continuous load on an overcurrent device is limited to 80 percent of the device rating. If the overcurrent device is rated 100A, the maximum continuous load is ______.

   (a) 72A
   (b) 80A
   (c) 90A
   (d) 125A

1.6 Percent Increase

10. The feeder calculated load for an 8 kW load, increased by 20 percent is ______.

(a) 8 kW
(b) 9.60 kW
(c) 10 kW
(d) 12 kW

1.7 Reciprocals

11. What's the reciprocal of 1.25?

(a) 0.80
(b) 1.10
(c) 1.25
(d) 1.50

12. A continuous load requires an overcurrent device sized no smaller than 125 percent of the load. What's the maximum continuous load permitted on a 100A overcurrent device?

(a) 75A
(b) 80A
(c) 100A
(d) 125A

1.8 Squaring a Number

13. Squaring a number means multiplying the number by itself.

(a) True
(b) False

14. What's the power consumed in watts by a 12 AWG conductor that's 100 ft long and has a resistance (R) of 0.20 ohms, when the current (I) in the circuit is 16A?

Formula: Power = I^2 x R

(a) 50W
(b) 75W
(c) 100W
(d) 200W

15. What's the approximate area in square inches of a trade size 2 raceway?

Formula: Area = π x r^2, π = 3.14, r = radius (½ of diameter)

(a) 1 sq in.
(b) 2 sq in.
(c) 3 sq in.
(d) 4 sq in.

16. The numeric equivalent of 4^2 is ______.

(a) 2
(b) 8
(c) 16
(d) 32

17. The numeric equivalent of 12^2 is ______.

(a) 3.46
(b) 24
(c) 144
(d) 1,728

1.9 Parentheses

18. What's the maximum distance that two 14 AWG conductors can be run if they carry 16A and the maximum allowable voltage drop is 10V?

D = (Cmil x E_{vd})/(2 x K x I)

The cmil area of 14 AWG = 4,110 cmil [Chapter 9, Table 8]
D = (4,110 Cmil x 10V)/(2 x 12.90 ohms x 16A)

(a) 50 ft
(b) 75 ft
(c) 100 ft
(d) 150 ft

19. What's the current in amperes of an 18 kW, 208V, three-phase load?

Current: I = VA/(E x $\sqrt{3}$)

Current: I = 18,000W/(208V x 1.732)

(a) 25A
(b) 50A
(c) 100A
(d) 150A

1.10 Square Root

20. Deriving the square root of a number is almost the same as squaring a number.

(a) True
(b) False

21. What's the approximate square root of 1,000?

(a) 3
(b) 32
(c) 100
(d) 500

22. The square root of 3 is ______.

(a) 1.50
(b) 1.732
(c) 9
(d) 729

1.11 Volume

23. The volume of an enclosure is expressed in ______, and is calculated by multiplying the length, by the width, by the depth of the enclosure.

(a) cubic inches
(b) weight
(c) inch-pounds
(d) none of these

24. What's the volume (in cubic inches) of a 4 x 4 x 1.50 in. box?

(a) 20 cu in.
(b) 24 cu in.
(c) 30 cu in.
(d) 33 cu in.

1.12 Kilo

25. What's the kW of a 75W load?

(a) 0.075 kW
(b) 0.75 kW
(c) 7.50 kW
(d) 75 kW

1.13 Rounding Off

26. The approximate sum of 2, 7, 8, and 9 is equal to ______.

(a) 20
(b) 25
(c) 30
(d) 35

1.14 Testing Your Answer for Reasonableness

27. The output power of a transformer is 100W and the transformer efficiency is 90 percent. What's the transformer input if the output is lower than the input?

Formula: Input = Output/Efficiency

(a) 90W
(b) 100W
(c) 110W
(d) 125W

PART B—BASIC ELECTRICAL FORMULAS

1.15 Electrical Circuit

28. An electrical circuit consists of the ______.

(a) power source
(b) conductors
(c) load
(d) all of these

29. According to the electron flow theory, electrons leave the ______ terminal of the source, flow through the conductors and load(s), and return to the ______ terminal of the source.

(a) positive, negative
(b) negative, positive
(c) negative, negative
(d) positive, positive

1.16 Power Source

30. The polarity and the output voltage from a direct-current power source changes direction. One terminal will be negative and the other will be positive at one moment, then the terminals switch polarity.

(a) True
(b) False

31. Direct current is used for electroplating, street trolley and railway systems, or where a smooth and wide range of speed control is required for a motor-driven application.

(a) True
(b) False

32. The polarity and the output voltage from an alternating-current power source never change direction.

(a) True
(b) False

33. The major advantage of alternating-current over direct-current is the ease of voltage regulation by the use of a transformer.

(a) True
(b) False

1.17 Conductance

34. Conductance is the property that permits current to flow.

(a) True
(b) False

35. The best conductors, in order of their conductivity, are gold, silver, copper, and aluminum.

(a) True
(b) False

36. Conductance, or conductivity, is the property of metal that permits current to flow. The best conductors in order of their conductivity are ______.

(a) gold, silver, copper, aluminum
(b) gold, copper, silver, aluminum
(c) silver, gold, copper, aluminum
(d) silver, copper, gold, aluminum

1.18 Circuit Resistance

37. The circuit resistance includes the resistance of the ______.

(a) power source
(b) conductors
(c) load
(d) all of these

38. Often the resistances of the power source and conductor are ignored in circuit calculations.

(a) True
(b) False

1.19 Ohm's Law

39. The Ohm's Law formula, **I = E/R**, states that current is ______ proportional to the voltage, and ______ proportional to the resistance.

(a) indirectly, inversely
(b) inversely, directly
(c) inversely, indirectly
(d) directly, inversely

40. Ohm's Law demonstrates the relationship between circuit ______.

(a) intensity
(b) EMF
(c) resistance
(d) all of these

1.20 Ohm's Law and Alternating Current

41. In a direct-current circuit, the only opposition to current flow is the physical resistance of the material. This opposition is called reactance and is measured in ohms.

(a) True
(b) False

42. In an alternating-current circuit, the factor(s) that oppose current flow is(are) ______.

(a) resistance
(b) inductive reactance
(c) capacitive reactance
(d) all of these

1.21 Ohm's Law Formula Circle

43. What's the voltage drop of two 12 AWG conductors (0.40 ohms) supplying a 16A load, located 100 ft from the power supply?

Formula: E_{vd} = I x R

(a) 1.60V
(b) 3.20V
(c) 6.40V
(d) 12.80V

44. What's the resistance of the circuit conductors when the conductor voltage drop is 7.20V and the current flow is 50A?

Formula: R = E/I

(a) 0.14 ohms
(b) 0.30 ohms
(c) 3 ohms
(d) 14 ohms

1.22 PIE Formula Circle

45. What's the power loss in watts of a conductor that carries 24A and has a voltage drop of 7.20V?

Formula: P = I x E

(a) 175W
(b) 350W
(c) 700W
(d) 2,400W

46. What's the approximate power consumed by a 10 kW heat strip rated 230V, when connected to a 208V circuit?

Formula: P = $E^{2/R}$

(a) 8.20 kW
(b) 9.30 kW
(c) 10.90 kW
(d) 11.20 kW

1.23 Formula Wheel

47. The formulas in the power wheel apply to ______.

(a) direct-current circuits
(b) alternating-current circuits with unity power factor
(c) direct-current circuits or alternating-current circuits
(d) a and b

1.24 Using the Formula Wheel

48. When working any formula, the key to calculating the correct answer is following these four steps:

    Step 1: Know what the question is asking you to find.
    Step 2: Determine the knowns of the circuit.
    Step 3: Select the formula.
    Step 4: Work out the formula calculation.

    (a) True
    (b) False

1.25 Power Losses of Conductors

49. Power in a circuit can be either "useful" or "wasted." Wasted work is still energy used; therefore it must be paid for, so we call wasted work "______."

    (a) resistance
    (b) inductive reactance
    (c) capacitive reactance
    (d) power loss

50. The total circuit resistance of two 12 AWG conductors (each 100 ft long) is 0.40 ohms. If the current of the circuit is 16A, what's the power loss of both conductors?

    Formula: $P = I^2 \times R$

    (a) 75W
    (b) 100W
    (c) 300W
    (d) 600W

51. What's the conductor power loss for a 120V circuit that has a 3 percent voltage drop and carries a current flow of 12A?

    Formula: $P = I \times E$

    (a) 43W
    (b) 86W
    (c) 172W
    (d) 1,440W

1.26 Cost of Power

52. What does it cost per year (at 8 cents per kWh) for the power loss of a 12 AWG conductor (100 ft long) that has a total resistance of 0.40 ohms and a current flow of 16A?

    Formula: Cost per Year = Power for the Year in kWh x $0.08

    (a) $33
    (b) $54
    (c) $72
    (d) $89

1.27 Power Changes with the Square of the Voltage

53. The voltage applied to a resistor dramatically affects the power consumed by that resistor because power is affected in direct proportion to the voltage.

    (a) True
    (b) False

54. What's the power consumed by a 10 kW heat strip that's rated 230V, if it's connected to a 115V circuit?

    Formula: $P = E^2/R$

    (a) 2.50 kW
    (b) 5 kW
    (c) 7.50 kW
    (d) 15 kW

UNIT

1

Challenge Questions

CHALLENGE QUESTIONS FOR UNIT 1—ELECTRICIAN'S MATH AND BASIC ELECTRICAL FORMULAS

PART A—ELECTRICIAN'S MATH

1.12 Kilo

1. One kVA is equal to ______.

   (a) 100 VA
   (b) 1,000V
   (c) 1,000W
   (d) 1,000 VA

PART B—BASIC ELECTRICAL FORMULAS

1.17 Conductance

2. Which of the following is the most conductive?

   (a) Bakelite
   (b) Oil
   (c) Air
   (d) Salt water

1.19 Ohm's Law

3. If the contact resistance of a connection increases and the current of the circuit (load) remains the same, then the voltage dropped across the connection will ______.

   (a) increase
   (b) decrease
   (c) remain the same
   (d) can't be determined

4. To double the current of a circuit when the voltage remains constant, the R (resistance) must be ______.

   (a) doubled
   (b) reduced by half
   (c) increased
   (d) none of these

5. An ohmmeter is being used to test a relay coil. The equipment instructions indicate that the resistance of the coil should be between 30 and 33 ohms. The ohmmeter indicates that the actual resistance is less than 22 ohms. This reading most likely indicates ______.

   (a) the coil is okay
   (b) an open coil
   (c) a shorted coil
   (d) a meter problem

1.23 Formula Wheel

6. To calculate the energy consumed in watts by a resistive appliance, you need to know ______ of the circuit.

   (a) the voltage and current
   (b) the current and resistance
   (c) the voltage and resistance
   (d) any of these pairs of variables

7. The power consumed by a resistor can be expressed by the formula **I^2 x R**. If 120V is applied to a 10 ohm resistor, the power consumed will be ______.

   (a) 510W
   (b) 1,050W
   (c) 1,230W
   (d) 1,440W

8. Power loss in a circuit because of heat can be determined by the formula ______.

(a) P = R x I
(b) P = I x R
(c) P = I^2 x R
(d) none of these

9. The energy consumed by a 5 ohm resistor is ______ than the energy consumed by a 10 ohm resistor, assuming the current in both cases remains the same.

(a) more
(b) less

10. When a load rated 500W at 115V is connected to a 120V power supply, the current of the circuit will be ______. Tip: At 120V, the load consumes more than 500 watts, but the resistance of the load remains constant.

(a) 2.70A
(b) 3.80A
(c) 4.50A
(d) 5.50A

1.27 Power Changes with the Square of the Voltage

11. A 120V rated toaster will produce ______ heat when supplied by 115V.

(a) more
(b) less
(c) the same
(d) none of these

12. When a 100W, 115V lamp operates at 230V, the lamp will consume approximately ______.

(a) 150W
(b) 300W
(c) 400W
(d) 450W

13. A 1,500W resistive heater is rated 230V and is connected to a 208V supply. The power consumed by this load at 208V will be approximately ______.

(a) 1,225W
(b) 1,625W
(c) 1,750W
(d) 1,850W

14. The total resistance of a circuit is 10.20 ohms. The load has a resistance of 10 ohms and the wire has a resistance of 0.20 ohms. If the current of the circuit is 12A, then the power consumed by the circuit conductors (0.20 ohms) is approximately ______.

(a) 8W
(b) 29W
(c) 39W
(d) 45W

UNIT
2 Electrical Circuits

INTRODUCTION TO UNIT 2—ELECTRICAL CIRCUITS

Unit 1 laid a foundation for your continuing study of electricity. The math, basic electrical concepts, and electrical formulas you learned are essential to understanding the topics covered in Unit 2.

The basic requirements of a practical electrical circuit are the presence of an electrical source, an electrical load, and a complete path of current flow from the source to the load and returning again to the source. The path of current flow can be configured in many ways. The way this path is designed is one factor that determines the amount of current flow at any specific point of the circuit, and how many volts are measured across any particular component. The configuration of the current-flow path can be expressed as a series path, a parallel path, or a combination series-parallel path.

In this unit, you'll learn about series circuits, parallel circuits, combinations of series and parallel circuits, and a special application called a multiwire branch circuit. Multiwire branch circuits have unique safety requirements, and the *NEC* makes special provisions for using them. Be sure to understand the roles of current and voltage in each of these different types of circuits and how to find the total resistance of a given circuit. The questions at the end of the unit will help you solidify your understanding of these circuits.

This unit makes use of some direct-current (dc) circuits and some alternating-current (ac) circuits, and their similarities in series and parallel resistive circuits will be explained. In Unit 3, more about the differences between direct-current and alternating-current circuits will be explained as you continue to learn about how electricity works.

PART A—SERIES CIRCUITS

Introduction

A series circuit is a circuit in which a specific amount of current leaves the voltage source and flows through every electrical device in a single path before it returns to the voltage source.

It's important to understand that in a series circuit, current is identical through ALL circuit elements of the circuit. **Figure 2–1**

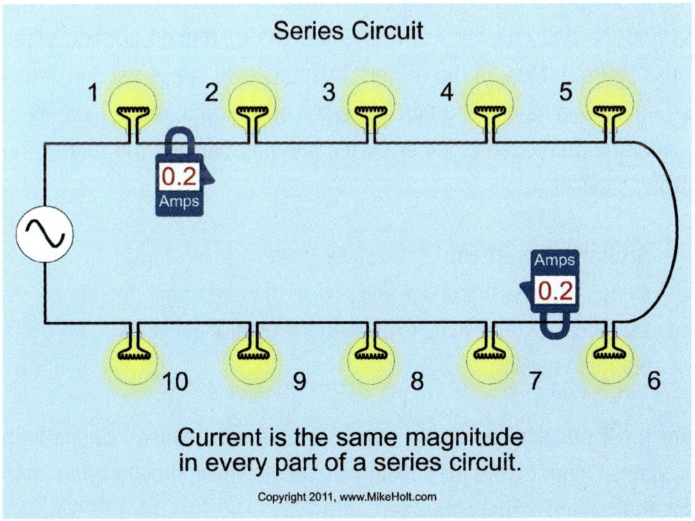

Figure 2–1

2.1 Practical Uses of the Series Circuit

In a series circuit, if any part of the circuit is open, the current in the circuit will stop.

Lighting

A series circuit isn't generally useful for lighting because if one lamp burns out, all the other lamps on the circuit will go out. Figure 2–2

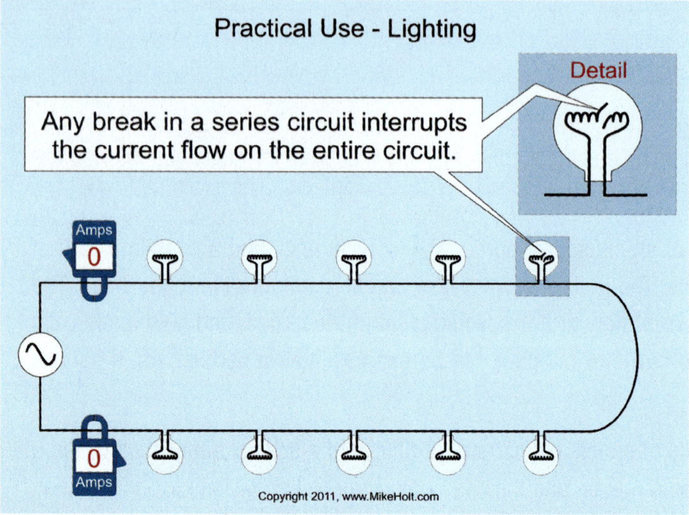

Figure 2–2

> **Author's Comment:** There are some special applications such as airport runway lighting that make use of series circuits.

Older strings of Christmas lights were made using series circuits—if one lamp burned out, it required examining EVERY lamp in order to find the bad one because the entire string stopped burning when this occurred! Most of the newer Christmas light lamps used in series string lighting have a shorting bar. When one lamp burns out, the lamp leads are connected together by the shorting bar and the rest of the string stays lit.

> **Author's Comment:** If, however, there are ten lamps in the string, and one burns out, the rest of the lamps will operate at 10 percent higher voltage, causing the other nine lamps to burn out more quickly.

For most practical purposes, series circuits, also called "closed-loop systems," aren't used for building wiring; however, they're often used for control and signal circuits.

Control Circuit

Closed-loop (series) circuits are often used for the purpose of controlling (starting and stopping) electrical equipment. Figure 2–3

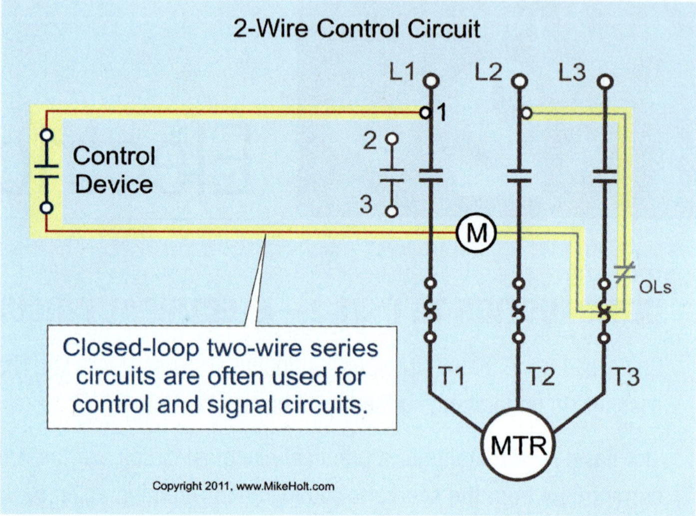

Figure 2–3

Signaling Circuit

Two-wire closed-loop (series) circuits are often used to give a signal that something has occurred. They can indicate that a door is open, a process is operating, or that there's fire or smoke. For example, the discontinuation of current flow when part of the circuit opens is important for the operation of burglar alarm circuits. Figure 2–4

Internal Equipment Wiring

The internal wiring of many types of equipment is connected in series. For example, a 115/230V dual-rated motor connected to a 230V circuit must have the internal windings connected in series so that each winding will receive at least 115V. Figure 2–5

2.2 Understanding Series Calculations

It's important to understand the relationship between current, voltage, resistance, and power in series circuits. Figure 2–6

Resistance

Resistance opposes the flow of electrons. In a series circuit, the total circuit resistance is equal to the sum of all the series resistances. Resistance is additive: $R_T = R_1 + R_2 + R_3 + R_4$. Figure 2–7

R_1 Power Supply	0.05 ohms
R_2 Conductor No. 1	0.15 ohms
R_3 Appliance	7.15 ohms
R_4 Conductor No. 2	+ 0.15 ohms
R_T Total Resistance	7.50 ohms

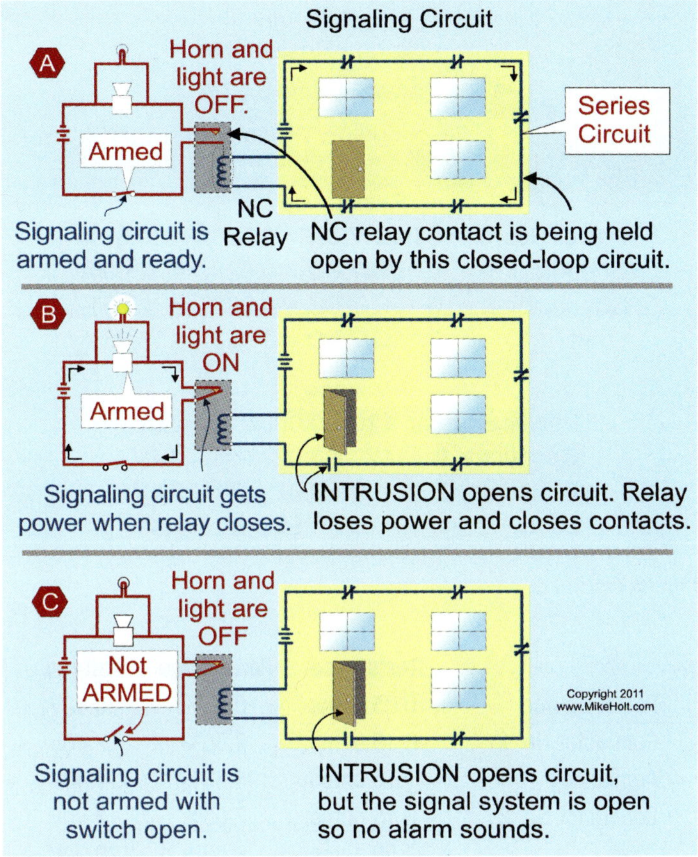

Figure 2–4

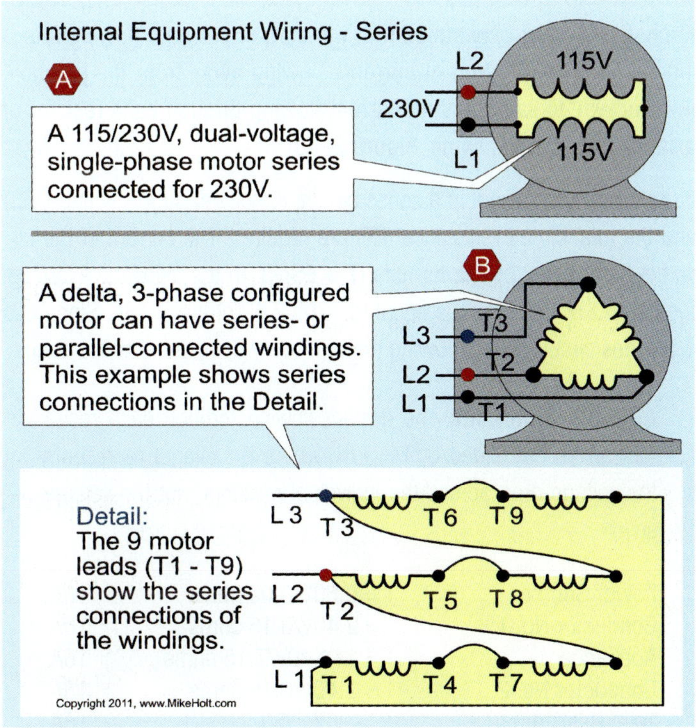

Figure 2–5

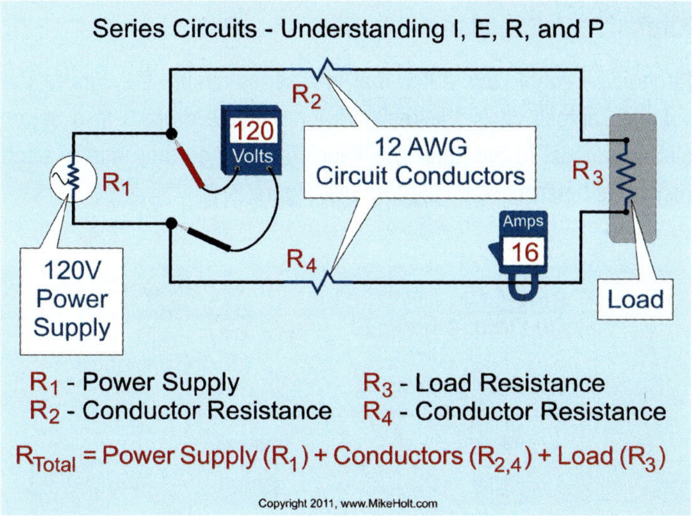

Figure 2–6

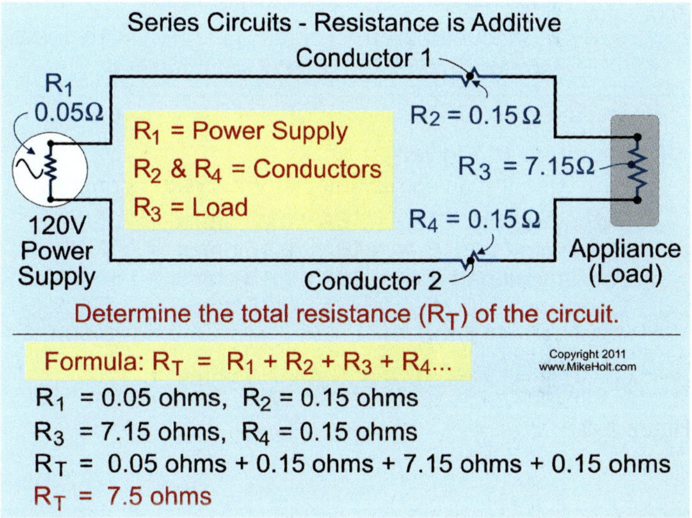

Figure 2–7

Voltage

The voltage, also called electromotive force (EMF), provides the pressure necessary to move electrons through the circuit. However, the power supply, the conductors, and the appliance all have resistance that opposes the current flow (although the power supply's resistance is usually ignored). The opposition (resistance) to current flow (amperes) results in a drop of the circuit voltage (voltage drop), and is calculated by the formula $\mathbf{E_{vd} = I \times R}$.

Kirchoff's Voltage Law

Kirchoff's Voltage Law states that in a series circuit, the sum of the voltages across all of the resistors (or "voltage drops") in a series circuit is equal to the applied voltage. The voltage drop across each resistor is determined by the formula: **Figure 2–8**

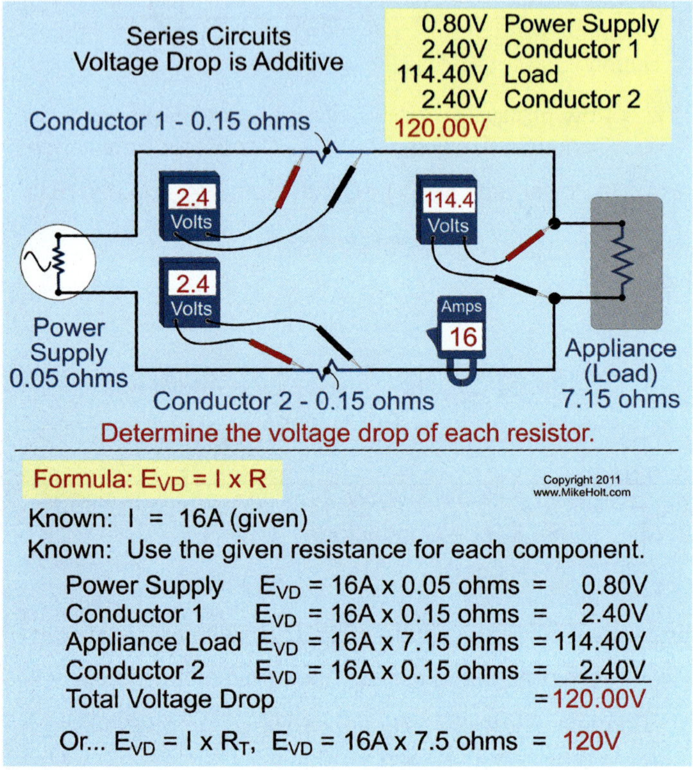

Figure 2–8

E_{vd} = I x R

I = Current of circuit

R = Resistance of resistor

Power Supply	16A x 0.05 ohms	0.80V
Conductor 1	16A x 0.15 ohms	2.40V
Appliance	16A x 7.15 ohms	114.40V
Conductor 2	16A x 0.15 ohms	+ 2.40V
Total	16A x 7.50 ohms	120.00V

In addition, the voltage of the power supply is distributed or divided among the circuit resistors according to the Resistance Law of Proportion. The Resistance Law of Proportion means that the supply voltage is distributed among all the resistors, according to the proportion of resistance each resistor has relative to the total resistance. **Figure 2–9**

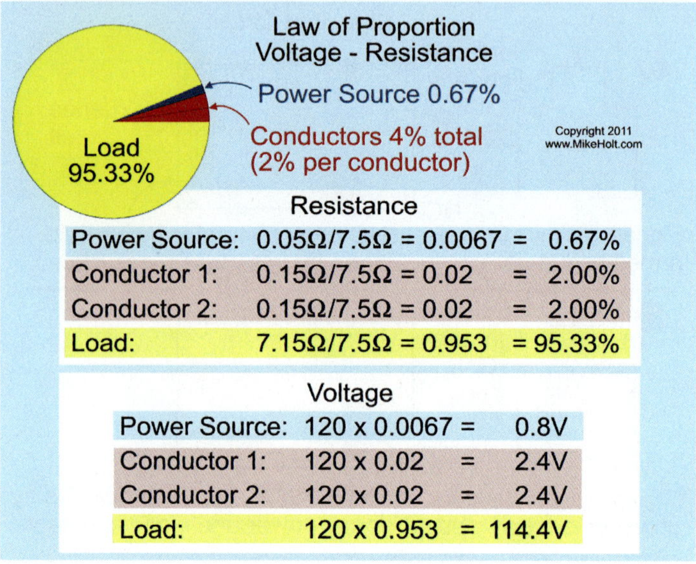

Figure 2–9

	Resistance	Percentage	Voltage
Power Source	0.05 ohms	0.67%	0.80V
Conductor No. 1	0.15 ohms	2.00%	2.40V
Appliance	7.15 ohms	95.33%	114.40V
Conductor No. 2	+ 0.15 ohms	2.00%	2.40V
Total	7.50 ohms	100%	120.00V

Kirchoff's Current Law

Kirchoff's Current Law states that the sum of currents flowing into a junction equals the sum of currents flowing away from the junction. Another way to say it is that, current flowing through each resistor of a series circuit is the same. **Figure 2–10**

To calculate the current in a series circuit, the power-supply voltage (ES) and the total circuit resistance (RT) are required. The current of the circuit is determined by the formula **IT = ES/RT**. In the following example, the current of the circuit is equal to 120V/7.50 ohms = 16A. Since this is a series circuit, 16A is flowing through every component of the circuit.

> **Author's Comment:** The current flowing through each resistor can be calculated by I = E/R, where E (voltage) represents the voltage drop across the individual resistors, not the voltage source.

Power Source	I = 0.80V/0.05 ohms	16A
Conductor No. 1	I = 2.40V/0.15 ohms	16A
Appliance	I = 114.40V/7.15 ohms	16A
Conductor No. 2	I = 2.40V/0.15 ohms	16A
Total Resistance	I= 120V/7.50	16A

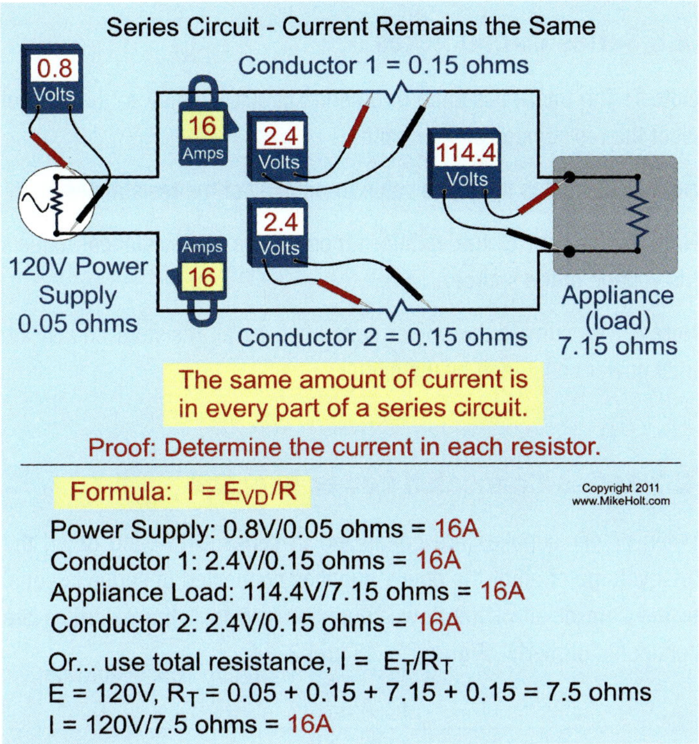

Figure 2–10

Power

The power consumed in a series circuit equals the sum of the power consumed by all of the resistors in the series circuit. The Law of Conservation of Energy states that the power supply (a battery, and so forth) will only produce as much power as that consumed by the circuit elements. Power is a result of current flowing through a resistance and is calculated by the formula $P = I^2 \times R$.

► Example

Power Source	*$P = 16A^2 \times 0.05$ ohms*	*12.80W*
Conductor No. 1	*$P = 16A^2 \times 0.15$ ohms*	*38.40W*
Appliance	*$P = 16A^2 \times 7.15$ ohms*	*1,830.40W*
Conductor No. 2	*$P = 16A^2 \times 0.15$ ohms*	*38.40W*

Power can also be calculated according to the Resistance Law of Proportion.

	Resistance	Percentage	Power
Power Source	0.05 ohms	0.67%	12.80W
Conductor No. 1	0.15 ohms	2.00%	38.40W
Appliance	7.15 ohms	95.33%	1,830.00W
Conductor No. 2	+ 0.15 ohms	2.00%	38.40W
Total Resistance	7.50 ohms	100%	1,920.00W

2.3 Series Circuit Calculations

When performing series circuit calculations, follow these steps: **Figure 2–11**

Step 1: Determine the resistance of each resistive element in the circuit. Often, the resistance of each element is given in the problem. If you know the nameplate voltage and power (wattage) rating of the appliance or equipment, determine its resistance by the formula $R = E^2/P$.

E = Nameplate voltage rating

P = Nameplate power rating

Step 2: Calculate the total resistance (R_T) of the circuit,
$R_{T} = R_1 + R_2 + R_3 + R_4$.

Step 3: The current of the circuit is determined by the formula:
$I = E_S/R_T$.

E_S = Voltage Source

R_T = Total circuit resistance (Step 2)

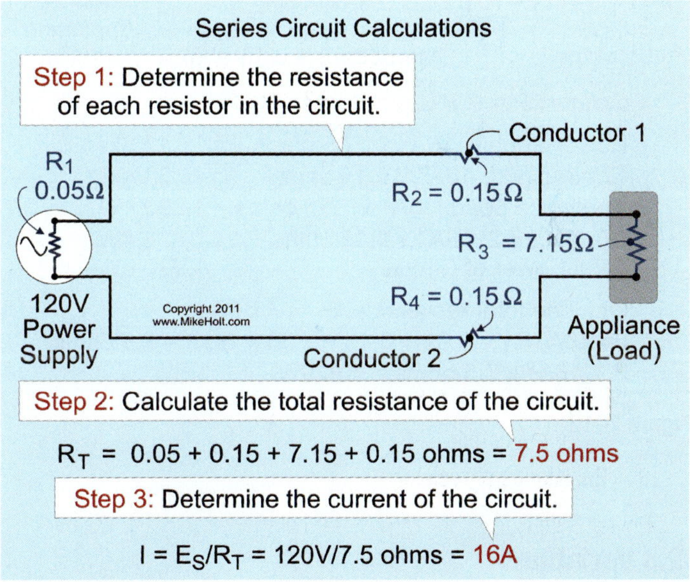

Figure 2–11

2.4 Power Calculations

If you know the current of the circuit and the resistance of each resistor, the power of each resistor is determined by the formula **$P = I^2 \times R$**. **Figure 2–12**

I^2 = Current of circuit (squared) (Step 3)
R = Resistance of the resistor (Step 1)

The power of the circuit is determined by adding up the power of all of the resistors, or by the formula **$P = I^2 \times R_T$**.

I^2 = Current of the circuit (squared)
R_T = Resistance total of the circuit

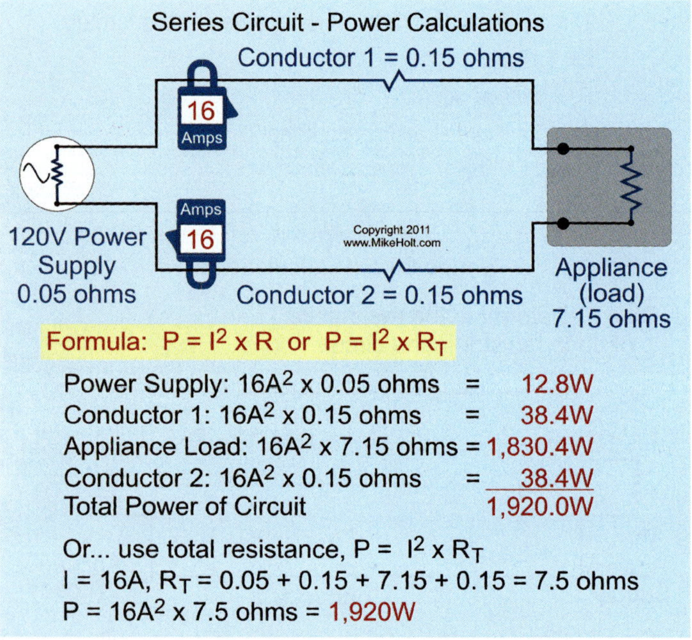

Figure 2–12

2.5 Variations

There are often many different ways to solve an electrical circuit problem involving voltage, current, resistance, and power. It's also often possible to verify or check one's calculations by solving the problem different ways.

2.6 Series Circuit Notes

Note 1: The total resistance of a series circuit is equal to the sum of all of the resistances of the circuit.

Note 2: Current is the same value through all of the resistances.

Note 3: The sum of the voltage drops across all resistances equals the voltage of the source.

Note 4: The sum of the power consumed by all resistors equals the total power consumed by the circuit.

2.7 Series-Connected Power Supplies

When power supplies are connected in series with each other, the total voltage of all of the power supplies connected in series is equal to the sum of all of the power supplies (provided the polarities are connected properly). **Figures 2–13 and 2–14**

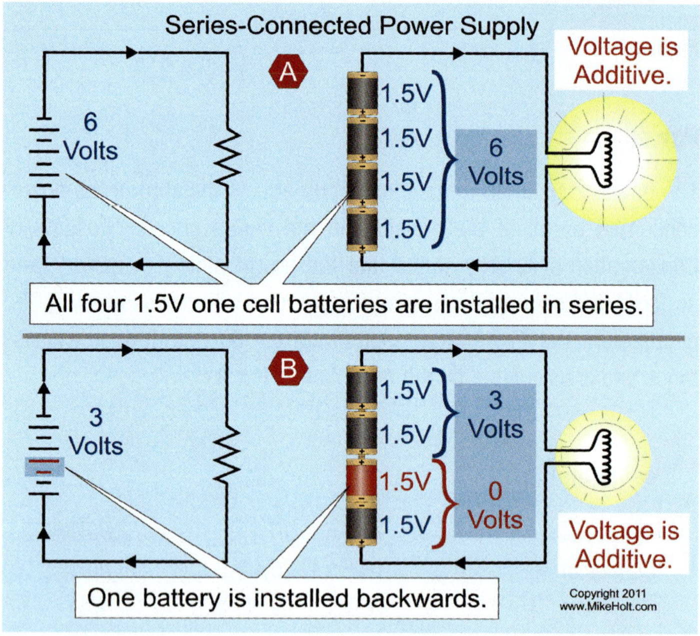

Figure 2–13

PART B—PARALLEL CIRCUITS

Introduction

"Parallel" is a term used to describe a method of connecting electrical components so there are two or more paths through which current may flow.

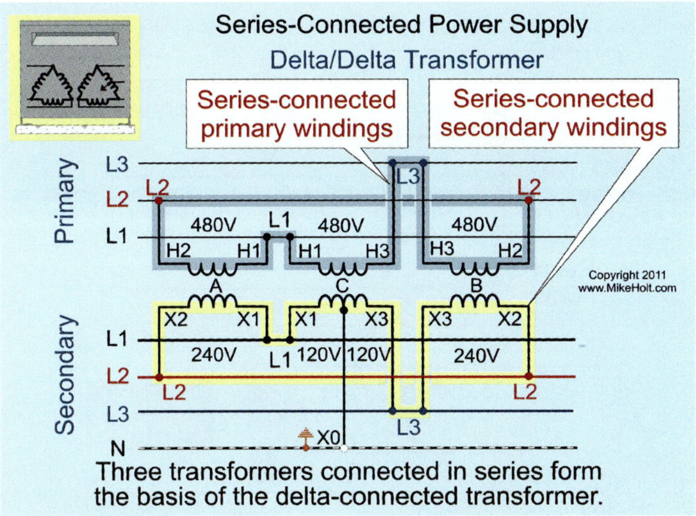

Figure 2–14

A parallel circuit is one with several different paths over which the electricity can travel. It's like a river that's been divided up into smaller streams and all the streams come back to form the river once again. Figure 2–15

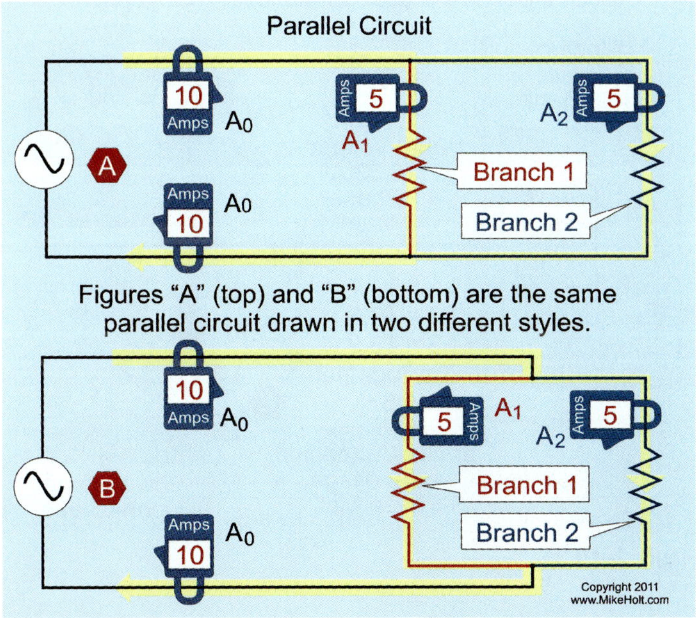

Figure 2–15

A parallel circuit has different characteristics than a series circuit. For one, the total resistance of a parallel circuit isn't equal to the sum of the resistors. The total resistance in a parallel circuit is always less than any of the branch resistances. Adding more parallel resistances to the paths causes the total resistance in the circuit to decrease.

2.8 Practical Uses of the Parallel Circuit

Parallel circuits are used for most building wiring.

Receptacles

When wiring receptacles on a circuit, they're connected in parallel to each other. Figure 2–16

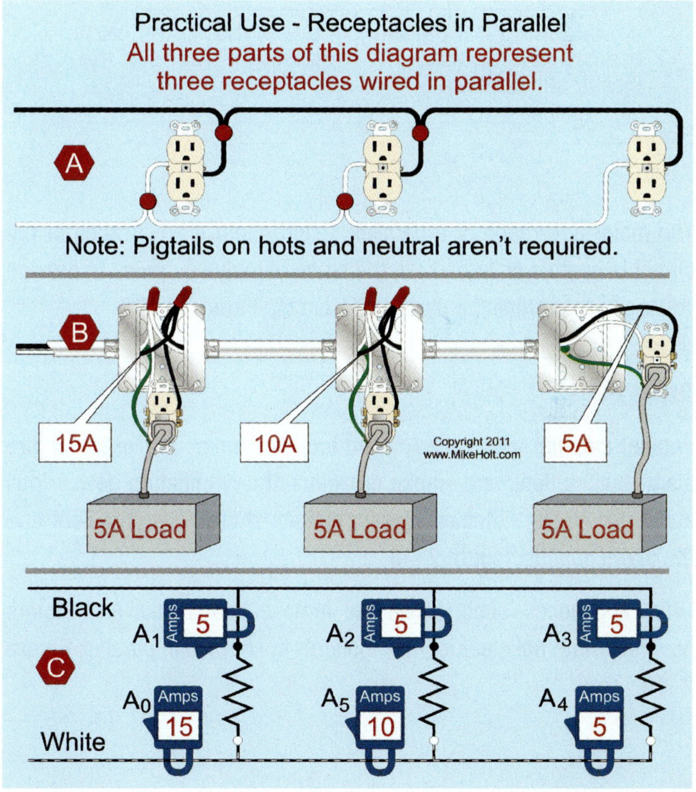

Figure 2–16

Lighting

Another example is lights connected in parallel to each other. **Figure 2–17A**

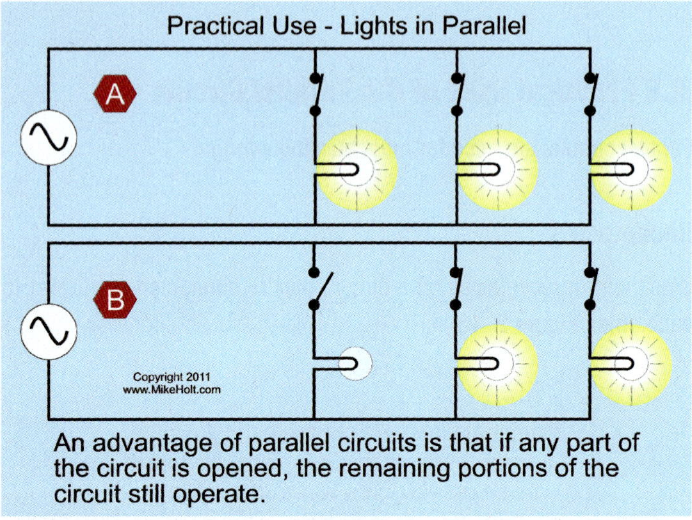

Figure 2–17

The major advantage of a parallel circuit is that if any branch of the circuit is opened or turned off, the power supply continues to provide voltage to the remaining parts of the circuit. **Figure 2–17B**

Other Uses

Parallel circuits, also called "open-loop systems," are used for fire alarm pull stations and smoke detectors. If any initiating device (pull station or smoke detector) closes, the signal circuit is complete and the alarm sounds. **Figure 2–18**

Often appliances, such as electric furnace heat banks and motors have their internal electrical components connected in parallel. **Figure 2–19**

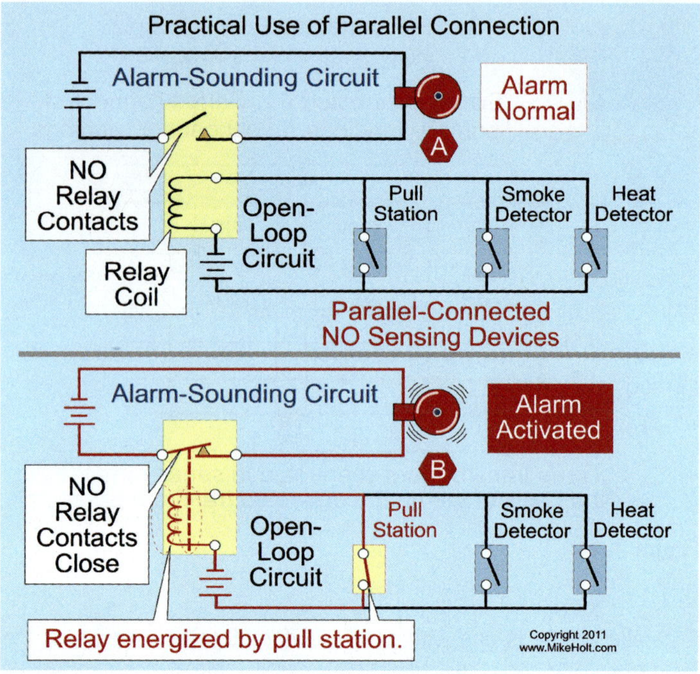

Figure 2–18

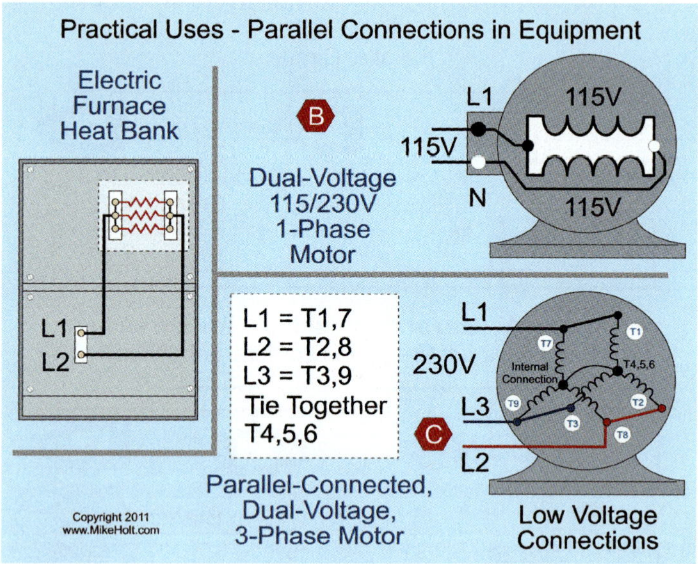

Figure 2–19

2.9 Understanding Parallel Calculations

It's important to understand the relationship between voltage, current, power, and resistance in parallel circuits.

Voltage

In a pure parallel circuit (one with no resistors in series with the parallel resistors), the voltage drop across each resistance is equal to the voltage supplied by the power source (ignoring any voltage drop in the source and conductors). **Figure 2–20**

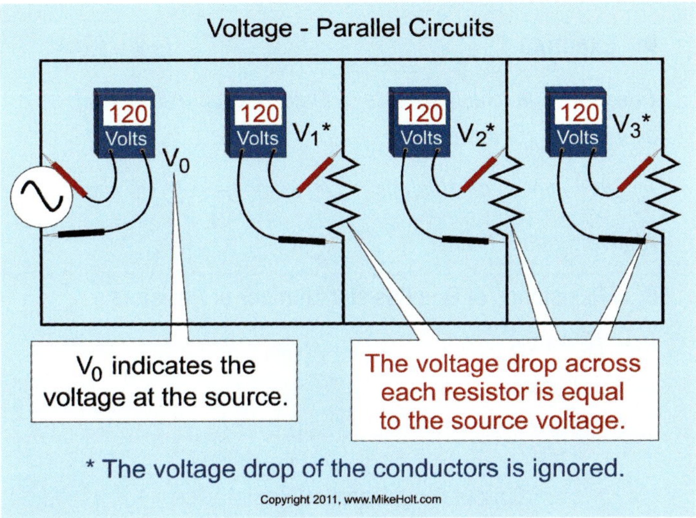

Figure 2–20

For the moment, we'll ignore the voltage drop and power loss effects of the conductor and power supply as it's usually much, much smaller than the voltage drop across the resistive elements.

Kirchoff's Current Law

In a parallel circuit, current from the power source will branch in different directions and magnitudes. The current in each branch is dependent on the resistance of each branch. Kirchoff's Current Law states that the total current provided by the source to a parallel circuit is equal to the sum of the currents of all of the branches.

The current in each branch is calculated by the formula **I = E/R**. **Figure 2–21**

E = Voltage of each branch.
R = Resistance of each branch (appliance).

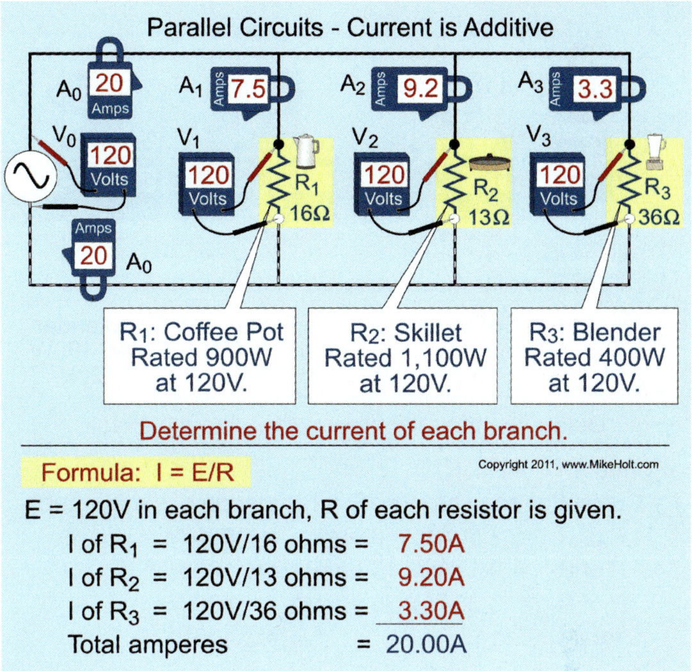

Figure 2–21

The current of each branch is as follows: **I = E/R**

Coffee Pot (R_1)	P = 120V/16 ohms	7.50A
Skillet (R_2)	P = 120V/13 ohms	9.20A
Blender (R_3)	P = 120V/36 ohms	+ 3.30A
Total Current (R_T)		20.00A

Author's Comment: The resistances and currents have been rounded off.

Power

When current flows through a resistor, power is consumed. The power consumed by each branch of the parallel circuit is determined by the formulas:

$P = I^2 \times R$ or $P = E \times I$ or $P = E^2/R$

The total power consumed in a parallel circuit equals the sum of the power in each branch. **Figure 2–22**

Using the formula $P = I^2 \times R$, determine the power of each resistor:

Coffee Pot	$P = 7.50A^2 \times 16$ ohms	900W
Skillet	$P = 9.20A^2 \times 13$ ohms	1,100W
Blender	$P = 3.30A^2 \times 36$ ohms	+ 400W
Total Circuit Power		2,400W

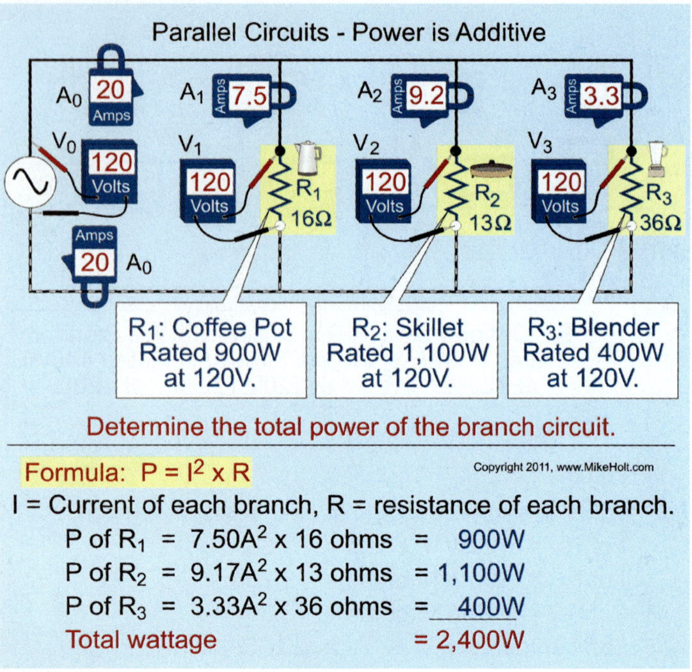

Figure 2–22

2.10 Circuit Resistance

Calculating total circuit resistance is different in series and parallel circuits. In a series circuit, the total circuit resistance is equal to the sum of the resistances. Figure 2–23A.

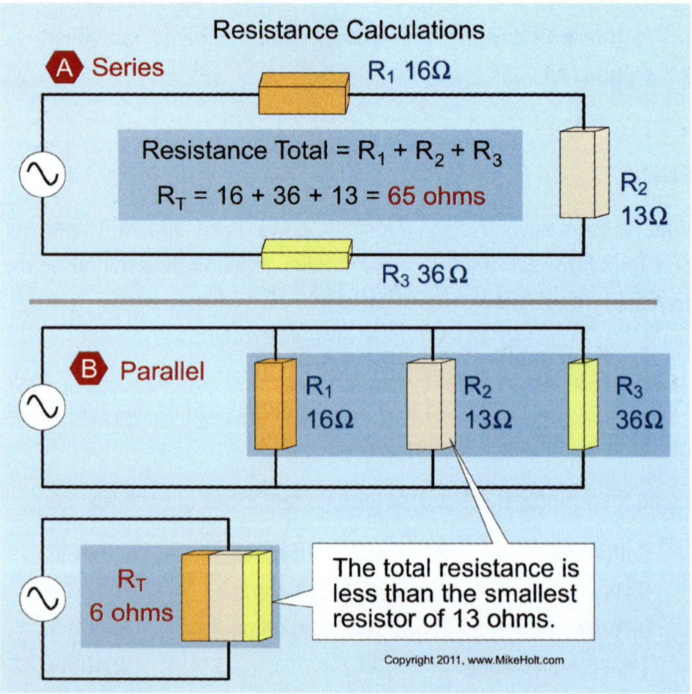

Figure 2–23

In a parallel circuit, the total circuit resistance is always less than the smallest individual resistance. Figure 2–23B

There are three basic methods of calculating the total resistance of a parallel circuit: the Equal Resistance method, the Product-Over-Sum method, and the Reciprocal method.

Equal Resistance Method

When all of the resistors of the parallel circuit have the same resistance, the total circuit resistance is found by dividing the resistance of one resistive element by the total number of resistors in parallel.

> ► **Example 1**
>
> ***Question:*** *The total resistance of three 10 ohm resistors in parallel is _____.* **Figure 2–24**
>
> *(a) 3.33 ohms (b) 10 ohms (c) 20 ohms (d) 30 ohms*
>
> ***Answer:*** *(a) 3.33 ohms*
>
> **R_T = Resistance of One Resistor/Number of Resistors**
>
> *R_T = 10 ohms/3*
>
> *R_T = 3.33 ohms*

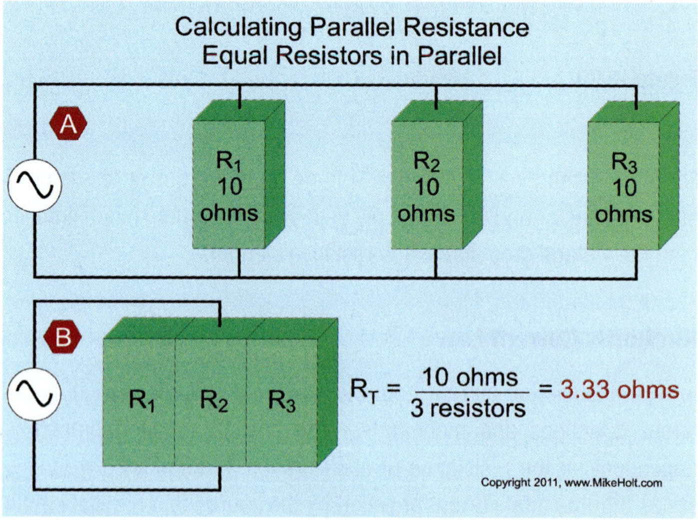

Figure 2–24

► Example 2

Question: *The total resistance of ten 10 ohm resistors in parallel is ______.*

(a) 1 ohm (b) 10 ohms (c) 50 ohms (d) 100 ohms

Answer: *(a) 1 ohm*

R_T = Resistance of One Resistor/Number of Resistors

R_T = 10 ohms/10

R_T = 1 ohm

Product-Over-Sum Method

This method is used to calculate the resistance of two resistors at a time:

$R_T = (R_1 \times R_2)/(R_1 + R_2)$

Author's Comment: The term "product" means the answer obtained when numbers are multiplied. The term "sum" means the answer obtained by adding a group of numbers.

► Example 1

Question: *The resistance of a 900W coffee pot is 16 ohms and the resistance of a 1,100W skillet is approximately 13 ohms. The appliances are connected in parallel. What's the total resistance of the two appliances?* **Figures 2–25A and 2–25B**

(a) 7.20 ohms (b) 13 ohms (c) 16 ohms (d) 29 ohms

Answer: *(a) 7.20 ohms*

RT = (R1 x R2)/(R1 + R2)

R_T = (16 x 13)/(16 + 13)

R_T = 7.20 ohms

The total resistance of a parallel circuit is always less than the smallest resistance.

The Product-Over-Sum method can be used to determine the resistance total for more than two resistors in a parallel circuit, but only two resistors can be dealt with at a time. If more than two resistors are in parallel, the Product-Over-Sum method must be applied several times, each time considering the equivalent resistance of the last two resistors looked at as a "new" resistance for the equation.

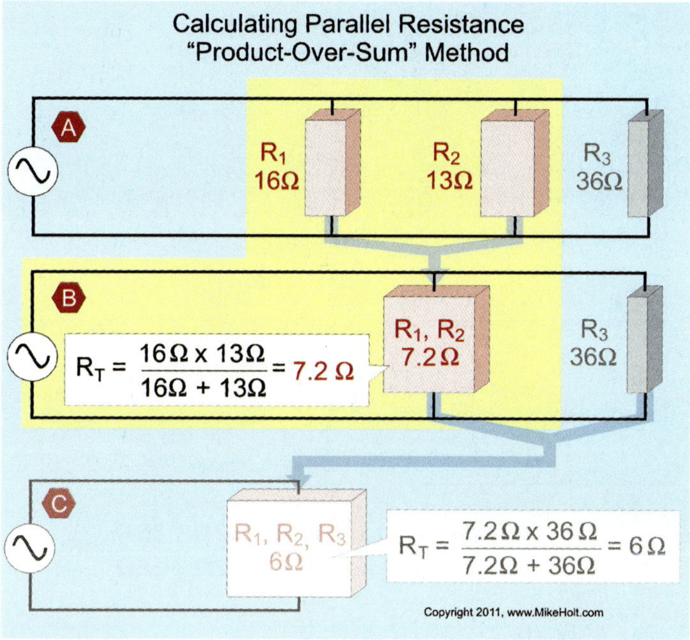

Figure 2–25

► Example 2

Question: *What's the total resistance of a 16 ohm resistor, a 13 ohm resistor, and a 36 ohm resistor connected in parallel?* **Figure 2–26**

(a) 6 ohms (b) 26 ohms (c) 43 ohms (d) 65 ohms

Answer: *(a) 6 ohms*

The 16 ohm and 13 ohm resistors are treated as an "equivalent" single resistor of 7.20 ohms (previous example). The resistance of the circuit will be calculated as follows: **Figures 2–26B and 2–26C**

RT = (R1,2 x R3)/(R1,2 + R3)

R_T = (7.20 x 36)/(7.20 + 36)

R_T = 6 ohms

Author's Comment: The answer must be less than the smallest resistor of the circuit (13 ohms).

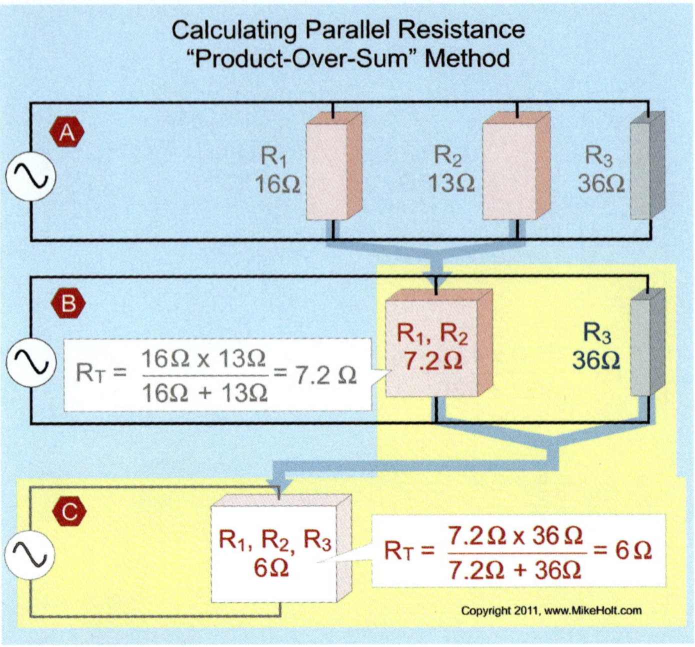

Figure 2–26

Reciprocal Method

The advantage of the Reciprocal method in determining the total resistance of a parallel circuit is that this formula can be used for as many resistors as the parallel circuit contains.

$R_T = 1/((1/R_1) + (1/R_2) + (1/R_3) ...)$

► **Example**

Question: *What's the resistance total of 16 ohm, 13 ohm, and 36 ohm resistors connected in parallel?*

(a) 6 ohms (b) 13 ohms (c) 16 ohms (d) 36 ohms

Answer: *(a) 6 ohms*

$R_T = 1/((1/16 \text{ ohms}) + (1/13 \text{ ohms}) + (1/36 \text{ ohms}))$

$R_T = 1/(0.0625 \text{ ohms} + 0.0769 \text{ ohms} + 0.0278 \text{ ohms})$

$R_T = 1/(0.1672 \text{ ohms})$

$R_T = 6 \text{ ohms}$

2.11 Parallel Circuit Notes

A parallel circuit has the following characteristics:

Note 1: A parallel circuit has two or more paths through which current flows.

Note 2: Total resistance is less than the smallest individual resistor. Total resistance in a parallel circuit is calculated with the following formula:

$R_T = 1/((1/R_1) + (1/R_2) + (1/R_3) ...)$

Note 3: The sum of the currents through each path is equal to the total current that flows from the source.

Note 4: Total power is equal to the sum of the branches' powers.

Note 5: Voltage the is same across each component of the parallel circuit.

2.12 Parallel-Connected Power Supplies

When power supplies are connected in parallel, the voltage remains the same, but the current (or in the case of batteries the amp-hour capacity) increases. To place batteries in parallel to each other, connect them with the proper polarity, which is positive (+) to positive (+) and negative (–) to negative (–). Figure 2–27A

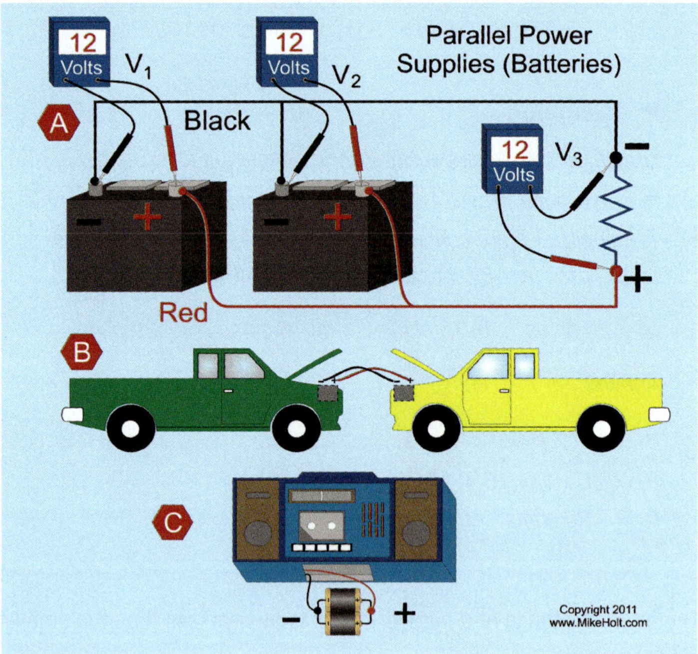

Figure 2–27

Author's Comment: When jumping a car battery, place the red cables on the positive (+) terminals and the black cables on the negative (–) terminals. Figure 2–27B

Batteries are often connected in parallel in radios, toys, and other appliances that operate on direct-current power. Figure 2–27C

PART C—SERIES-PARALLEL CIRCUITS

Introduction

A series-parallel circuit is a circuit that contains some resistors in series and some in parallel to each other. That portion of the series-parallel circuit that contains resistors in series must comply with the rules for series circuits. That portion of the series-parallel circuit that contains resistors in parallel complies with the rules for parallel circuits. However, it's good to remember that Ohm's Law always prevails. Figure 2–28

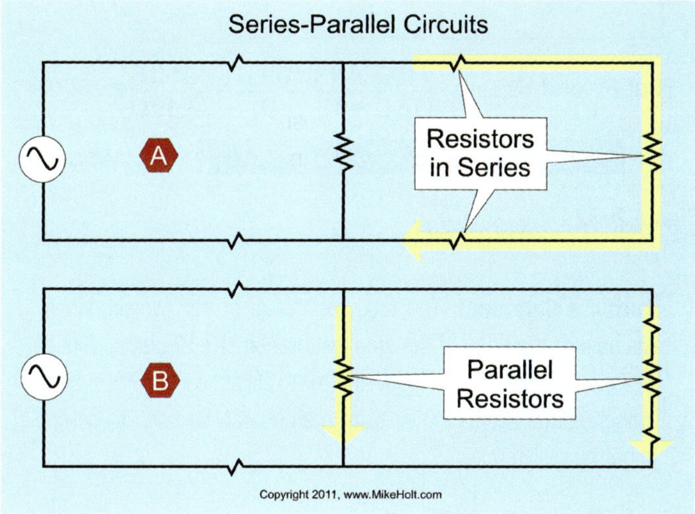

Figure 2–28

2.13 Review of Series and Parallel Circuits

To understand series-parallel circuits, we must review the rules for series and parallel circuits.

Series Circuit Review, Figure 2–29

Note 1: The total resistance of a series circuit is equal to the sum of all of the resistances of the circuit.

Note 2: Current is constant.

Note 3: The sum of the voltage drop of all resistors must equal the voltage of the source.

Note 4: The sum of the power consumed by all resistors equals the total power of the circuit.

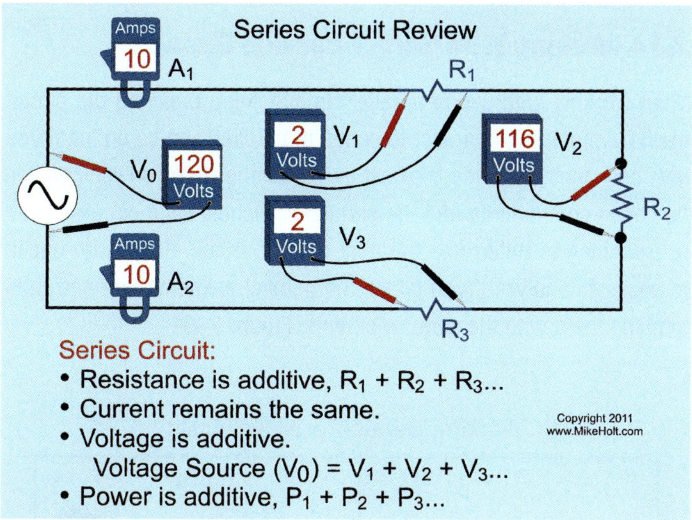

Figure 2–29

Parallel Circuit Review, Figure 2–30

Note 1: A parallel circuit has two or more paths through which current flows.

Note 2: Total resistance is less than the smallest individual resistor. Total resistance in a parallel circuit is calculated with the following formula:

$$R_T = 1/((1/R_1) + (1/R_2) + (1/R_3) ...)$$

Note 3: The sum of the currents through each path is equal to the total current that flows from the source.

Note 4: Total power is equal to the sum of the branches' powers.

Note 5: Voltage is the same across each component of the parallel circuit.

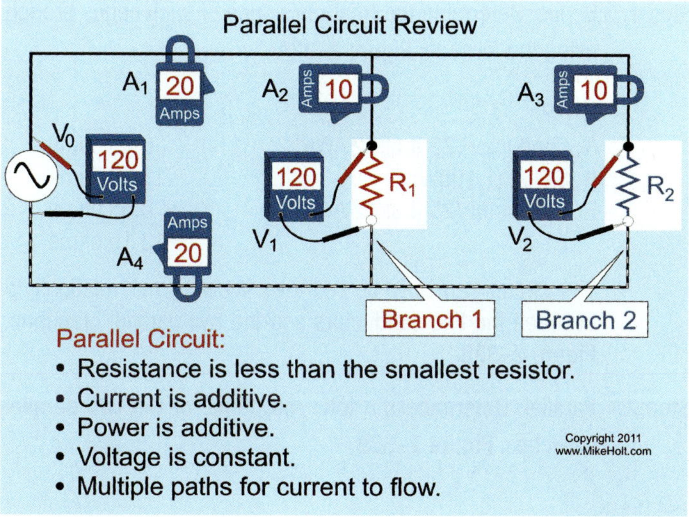

Figure 2–30

2.14 Working With Series-Parallel Circuits

When working with series-parallel circuits, keep breaking the circuit down from series to parallel to series to parallel, and so on, until you have only one resistance. It's best to redraw the circuit so you can see the series components and the parallel branches. Each circuit should be examined to determine the best plan of attack. Some turn out to be easier to analyze if you tackle the parallel elements first and then combine them with the series elements. **Figure 2–31**

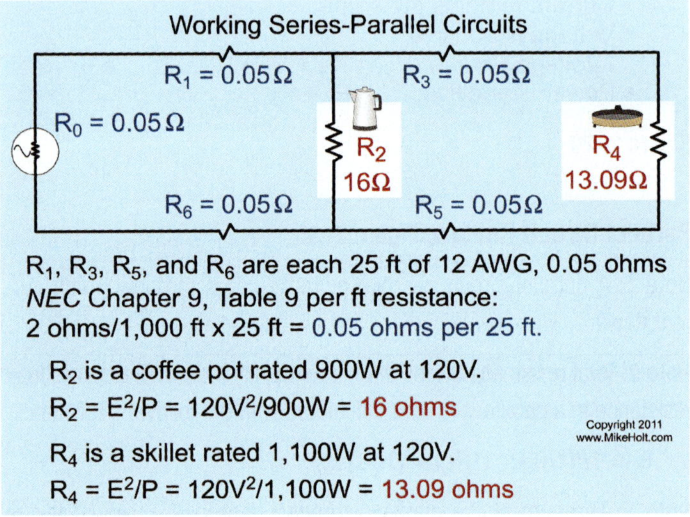

Figure 2–31

Other circuits are best worked by combining series elements first and then combining the result with the parallel resistances. In **Figure 2–31**, the series combination of R_3, R_4, and R_5 is the first step.

Step 1: Series: Determine the total resistance of each series branch using the formula: **Figure 2–32A**

$$R_{T = R3} + R_4 + R_5$$

R_3 Conductor (25 ft of 12 AWG)	0.05 ohms
R_4 Skillet (1,100W)	13.09 ohms
R_5 Conductor (25 ft of 12 AWG)	+ 0.05 ohms
	13.19 ohms

The circuit can now be redrawn showing the relationship between the two conductors and the two parallel branches. **Figure 2–32B**

Step 2: Parallel: Determine the total resistance of the two parallel branches. **Figure 2–32B**

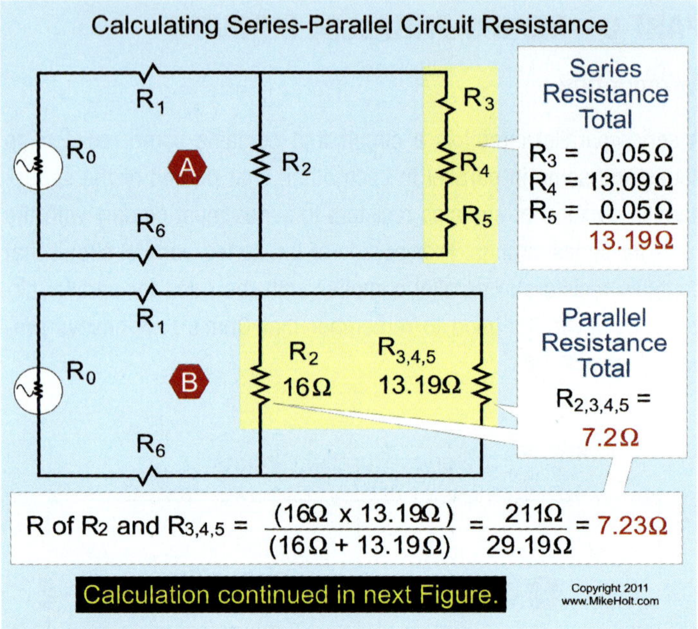

Figure 2–32

Author's Comment: The total resistance of the two branches will be less than that of the smallest branch (13.19 ohms). Since we're only trying to determine the total resistance of two parallel branches, the Product-Over-Sum method can be used to determine the resistance.

$$R_{T = (R2} \times R_{3,4,5})/(R_2 + R_{3,4,5})$$

$$R_T = (16 \text{ ohms} \times 13.19 \text{ ohms})/(16 \text{ ohms} + 13.19 \text{ ohms})$$

$$R_T = 7.23 \text{ ohms}$$

Author's Comment: When working with series-parallel circuits, keep breaking the circuit down from series to parallel to series to parallel, and so forth, until you have only one resistor. **Figure 2–33**

2.15 Voltage

Even though the current is different in the different resistors, remember that Ohm's Law always works. Every complicated problem is really just a series of easy problems waiting to be worked out. To calculate the voltage of each resistor, consider each one on a case-by-case basis and multiply its value by the current flowing through it.

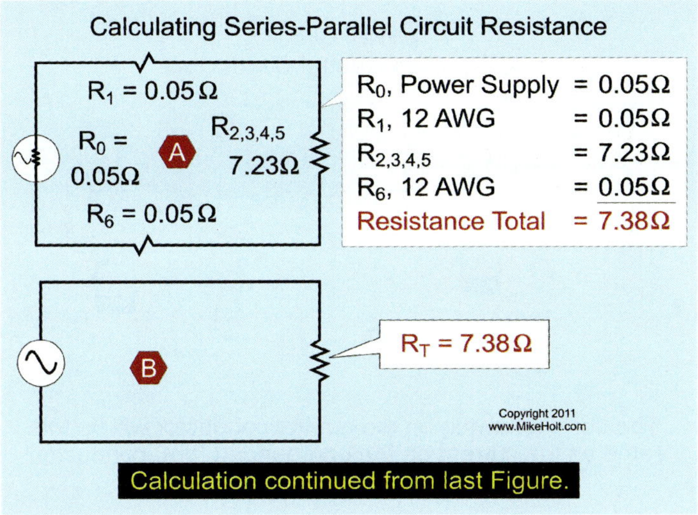

Figure 2–33

PART D—MULTIWIRE BRANCH CIRCUITS

Introduction

Understanding series, parallel, and series-parallel circuits is the foundation for understanding multiwire branch circuits. A multiwire branch circuit is a circuit consisting of two or more ungrounded conductors (hot wires) that have a voltage difference between them, and an equal voltage between each ungrounded conductor and the neutral conductor [Article 100]. A typical 3-wire, 120/240V, single-phase circuit is an example. **Figure 2–34**

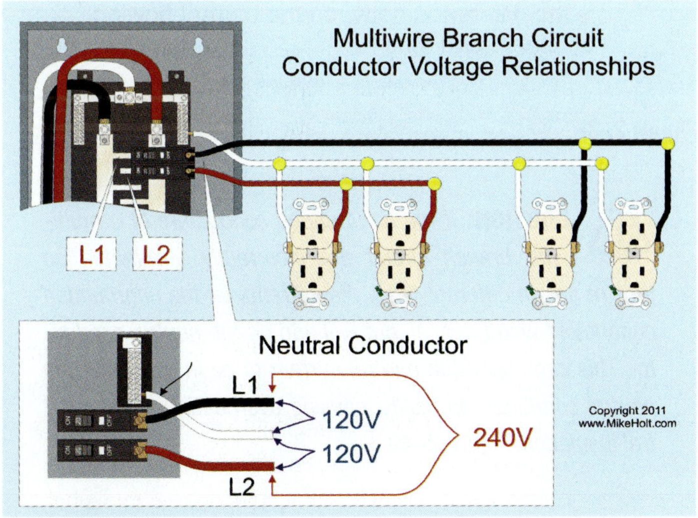

Figure 2–34

2.16 Neutral Conductor

The *NEC* defines a neutral conductor as the conductor connected to the neutral point of a system that's intended to carry current under normal conditions [Article 100]. **Figure 2–35**

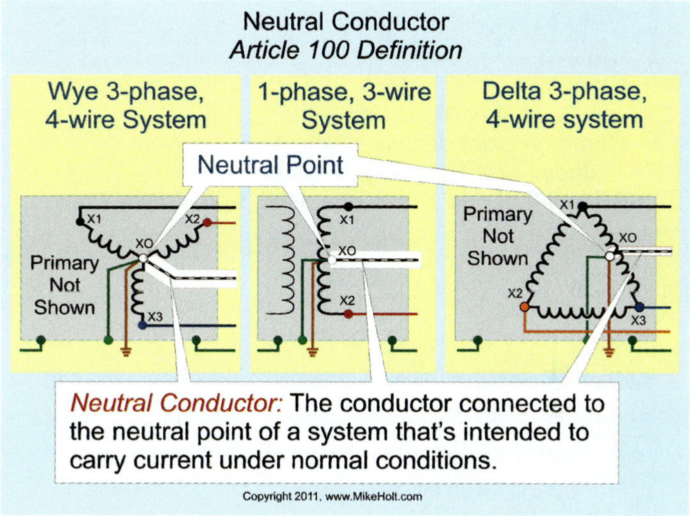

Figure 2–35

Author's Comment: The neutral conductor of a solidly grounded system is required to be grounded to the earth, therefore this conductor is also called a "grounded conductor."

The term "Neutral Point" in the *Code* is defined as the common point on a 4-wire, three-phase, 120/208V or 277/480V wye-connected system, the midpoint of a 3-wire, 120/240V single-phase system, or the midpoint of the single-phase portion of a 120/240V, three-phase delta-connected system [Article 100]. **Figure 2–36**

The definition of "Neutral Point" describes the point to which the neutral conductor is connected.

2.17 Grounded Conductor

The "grounded conductor," according to the *NEC*, is a circuit or system conductor that's intentionally grounded [Article 100]. In the case of home wiring (3-wire, 120/240V, single-phase), the grounded conductor is often called the "neutral conductor," and it will be either white or gray in color in accordance with the *National Electrical Code* [200.6].

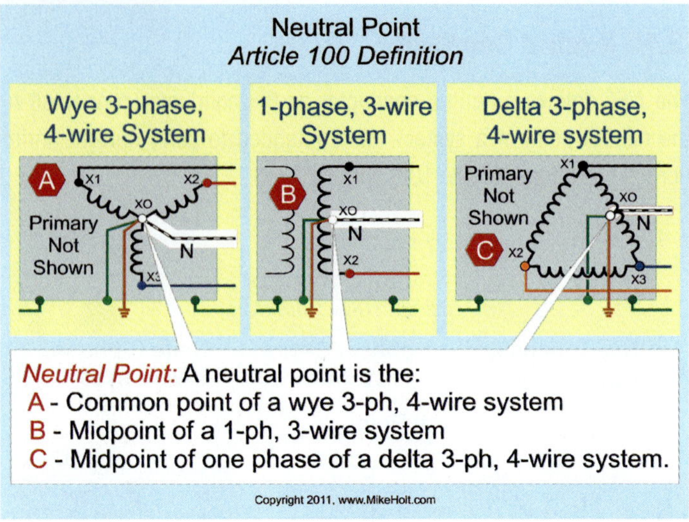

Figure 2–36

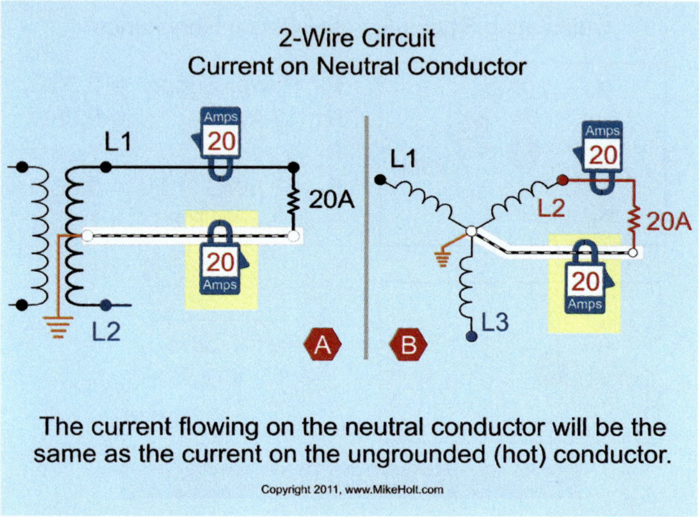

Figure 2–37

Author's Comment: When a grounded conductor is also used as a neutral conductor, this textbook will refer to it as a "neutral conductor" except in the *Code* questions at the end of each unit, which will follow the *NEC* wording.

2.18 Current Flow on the Neutral Conductor

To understand the current flow on the neutral conductor, review the following circuits.

2-Wire Circuit

The current flowing in the neutral conductor of a 2-wire circuit is the same as the current flowing in the ungrounded (hot) conductor. **Figure 2–37**

3-Wire, 120/240V, Single-Phase Circuit

The current flowing in the neutral conductor of a 3-wire, 120/240V, single-phase circuit equals the difference in current flowing in the ungrounded conductors (I_N = L1–L2), **Figure 2–38**. The reason is that at any instant the currents on the two ungrounded conductors oppose each other. **Figure 2–39**

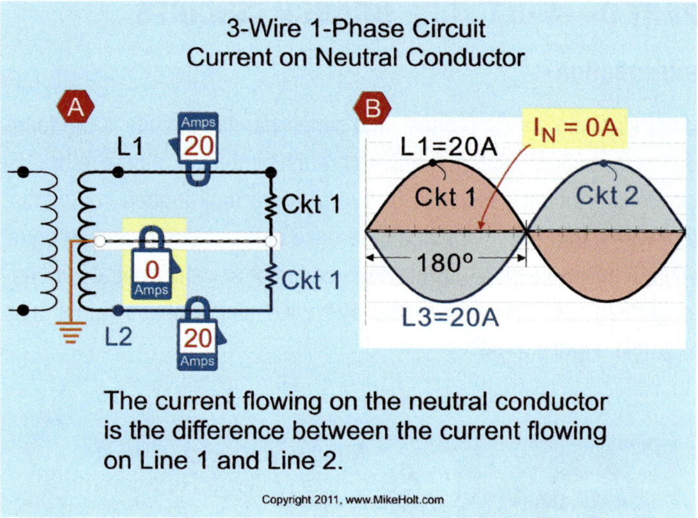

Figure 2–38

CAUTION: *If the ungrounded conductors of a multiwire branch circuit are incorrectly terminated so they're not on different lines, the currents on the ungrounded conductors won't cancel, but will add on the neutral conductor. This can cause the neutral current to be in excess of the neutral conductor ampacity, causing overheating of the neutral insulation.* **Figure 2–40**

Author's Comment: This is one reason white neutral conductors sometimes turn brown or black.

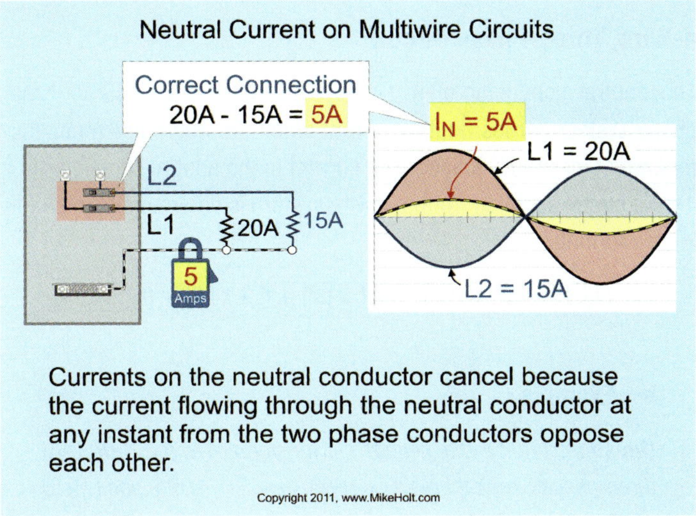

Figure 2–39

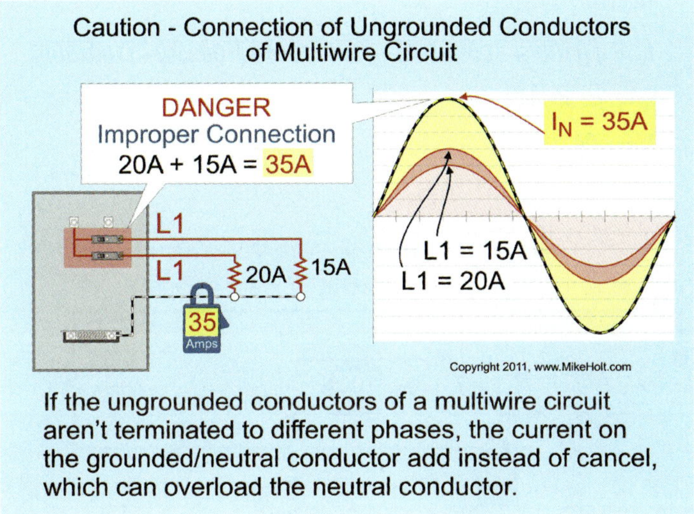

Figure 2–40

2.19 Balanced Systems

If the current in each ungrounded conductor of a multiwire branch circuit is the same, the neutral conductor carries 0A. This applies to 3-wire, 120/240V, single-phase and all three-phase circuits, regardless of configuration or voltage. Figure 2–41

2.20 Unbalanced Current

The current flowing in the neutral conductor of a multiwire branch circuit is called "unbalanced current."

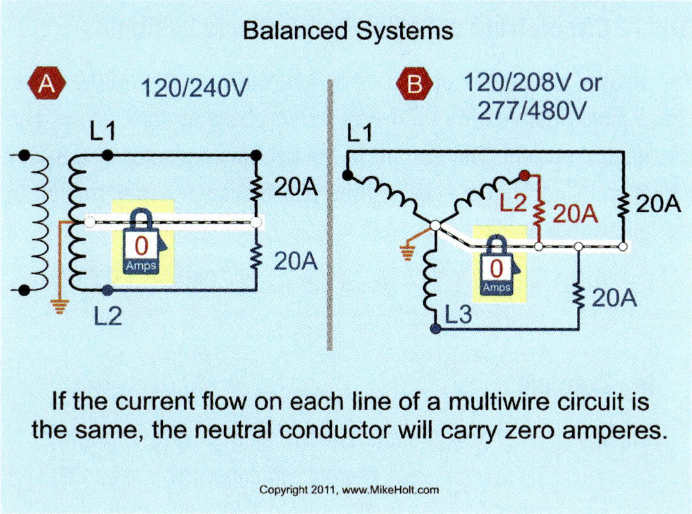

Figure 2–41

3-Wire, 120/240V, Single-Phase Circuit

The neutral conductor of a 3-wire, 120/240V, single-phase circuit only carries current when the current in the ungrounded conductors isn't identical. The unbalanced current is determined by the following formula: Figure 2–42

$I_N = L1 - L2$

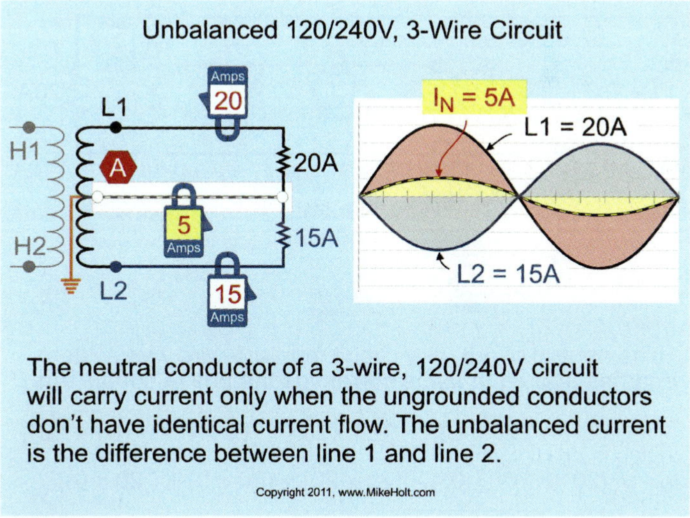

Figure 2–42

3-Wire Circuit from a 4-Wire, Three-Phase System

The neutral conductor of a 3-wire, 120/208V or 277/480V, three-phase circuit derived from a 4-wire, three-phase system always carries neutral current. The current in the neutral conductor of a 3-wire circuit supplied from a 4-wire, three-phase system is determined by the following formula:

$$I_N = \sqrt{[(L1^2 + L2^2 + L3^2) - [(L1 \times L2) + (L2 \times L3) + (L1 \times L3)]]}$$

► Example

Question: *What's the neutral current for a 3-wire, 120/208V, single-phase circuit, if each ungrounded conductor carries 20A, and the circuit is supplied from a 4-wire, 120/208V, three-phase system?* **Figure 2–43**

(a) 0A *(b) 20A* *(c) 80A* *(d) 100A*

Answer: *(b) 20A*

$I_N = \sqrt{[(20^2 + 20^2 + 0) - (20^2 + 0 + 0)]}$

$I_N = \sqrt{400}$

$I_N = 20A$

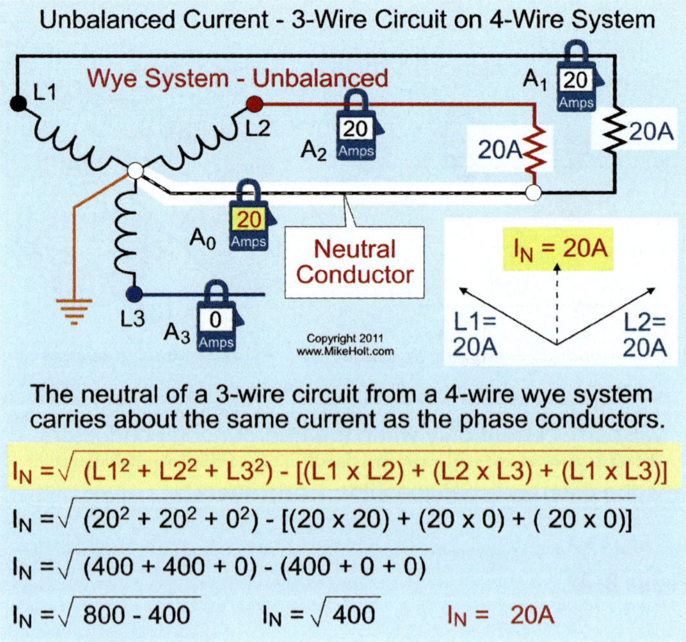

Figure 2–43

4-Wire, Three-Phase Circuit

The neutral conductor of a 4-wire, 120/208V or 277/480V, three-phase system carries neutral current when the ungrounded conductors aren't identically loaded. The current in the neutral conductor of a 4-wire circuit supplied from a 4-wire system is determined by the following formula:

$$I_N = \sqrt{[(L1^2 + L2^2 + L3^2) - [(L1 \times L2) + (L2 \times L3) + (L1 \times L3)]]}$$

► Example

Question: *What's the neutral current for a 4-wire, 120/208V, three-phase circuit if Line 1 = 100A, Line 2 = 100A, and Line 3 = 50A?* **Figure 2–44**

(a) 0A *(b) 50A* *(c) 100A* *(d) 125A*

Answer: *(b) 50A*

$I_N = \sqrt{[(100^2 + 100^2 + 50^2) - [(100 \times 100) + (100 \times 50) + (100 \times 50)]]}$

$I_N = \sqrt{2{,}500A}$

$I_N = 50A$

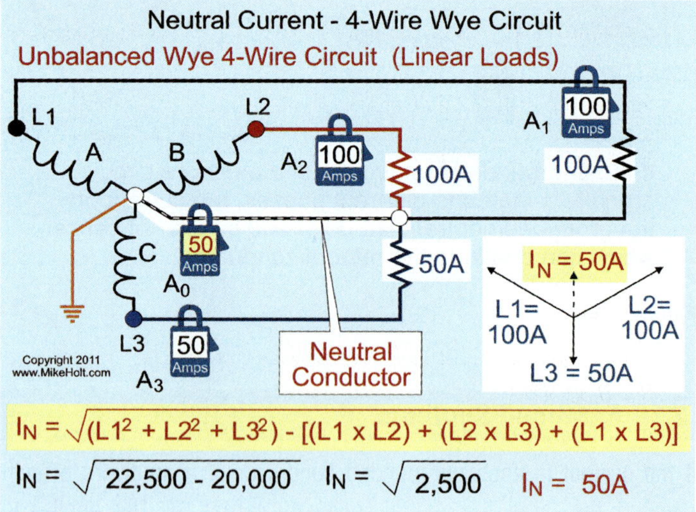

Figure 2–44

2.21 Multiwire Branch Circuits

Multiwire branch circuits are more cost-effective than 2-wire circuits in that they have fewer conductors for a given number of circuits, which enables the use of a smaller raceway. In addition, multiwire branch circuits result in lower circuit voltage drop.

Reduced Number of Conductors. Normally it requires four wires to install two 120V single-phase circuits. By using a multiwire branch circuit, which allows sharing the neutral between the two circuits, this installation can be made using three wires. Likewise, the six conductors required for three 120V circuits on a three-phase system can be replaced by a multiwire branch circuit of four conductors; three ungrounded conductors sharing a neutral conductor between them.

Reduced Raceway Size. If the number of circuit conductors is reduced, the size of the raceway can often be reduced. Reducing the number of conductors and installing a smaller raceway is very cost-effective in terms of savings in both material and labor.

Reduced Circuit Voltage Drop. The voltage drop of the circuit conductors is dependent upon the magnitude of current and conductor resistance: $E_{vd} = I \times R$.

2-Wire Circuit Voltage Drop

A typical 2-wire circuit has current flow in both the ungrounded and neutral conductors. Therefore, the circuit voltage drop includes the voltage drop of both conductors.

> ### ► Example
>
> ***Question:*** *What's the voltage drop of two 12 AWG conductors, each 75 ft long, supplying a 2-wire, 20A load? The resistance for 1,000 ft of 12 AWG copper is 2 ohms.* **Figure 2–45**
>
> *(a) 2V (b) 3V (c) 4V (d) 6V*
>
> ***Answer:*** *(d) 6V*
>
> ***Evd = I x R***
>
> *I = 20A*
>
> *R = (2 ohms per 1,000 ft/1,000) x 75 ft x 2 wires*
>
> *R = 0.30 ohms*
>
> E_{vd} *= 20A x 0.30 ohms*
>
> E_{vd} *= 6V*

Multiwire Branch-Circuit Voltage Drop

A balanced 3-wire, single-phase or 4-wire, three-phase multiwire branch circuit has current flowing only in the ungrounded circuit conductors. Therefore, the circuit voltage drop for the line-to-neutral only includes the voltage drop of one conductor. The line-to-line voltage drop is found by multiplying the line-to-neutral voltage drop by 1.732.

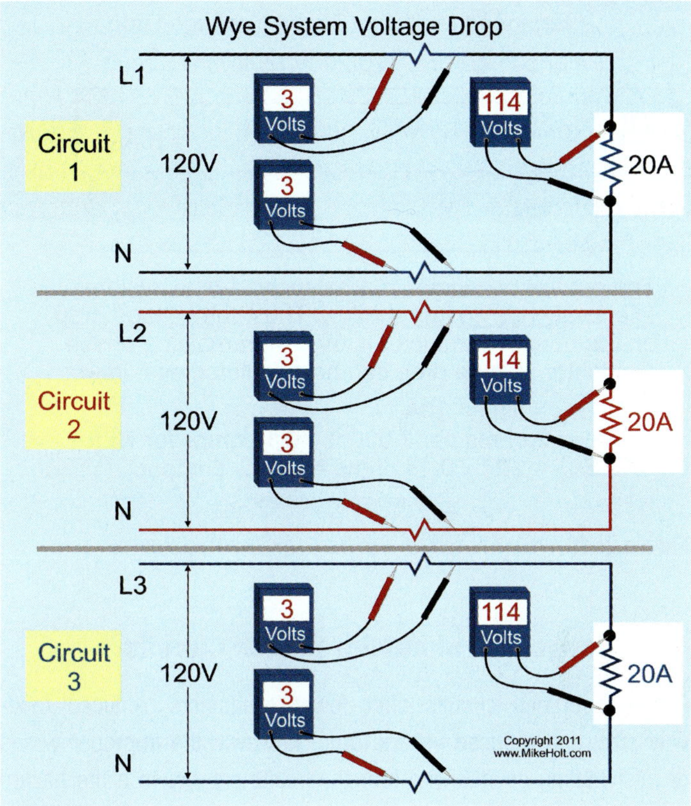

Figure 2–45

> ### ► Example
>
> ***Question:*** *What's the line-to-neutral voltage drop over each line conductor of a balanced 4-wire multiwire branch circuit? Each conductor is 12 AWG, 75 ft long, supplying a 20A load.* **Figure 2–46**
>
> *(a) 2V (b) 3V (c) 4V (d) 6V*
>
> ***Answer:*** *(b) 3V*
>
> *The neutral conductor in a balanced 4-wire system effectively has 0A of current flow (the three return currents cancel each other out because of their phase relationship). Thus, by Ohm's Law, the voltage drop over this conductor is 0V. The remaining phase conductor voltage drop can be calculated as follows:*
>
> ***Evd = I x R***
>
> *I = 20A*
>
> *R = (2 ohms per 1,000 ft/1,000) x 75 ft x 1 wire*
>
> *R = 0.15 ohms*
>
> E_{vd} *= 20A x 0.15 ohms*
>
> E_{vd} *= 3V*

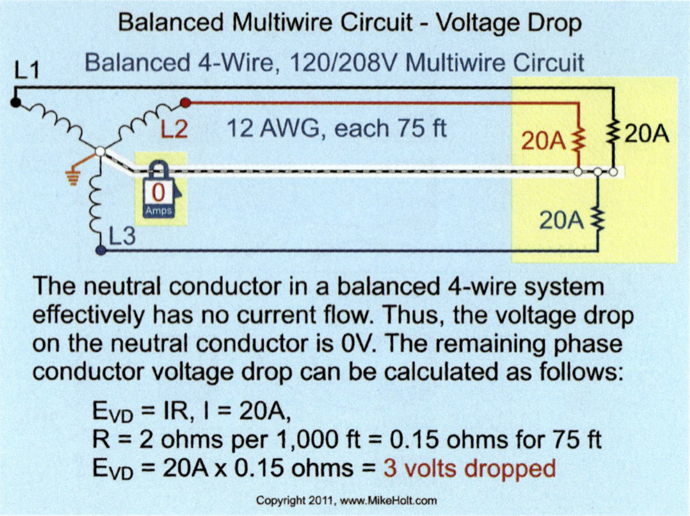

Figure 2–46

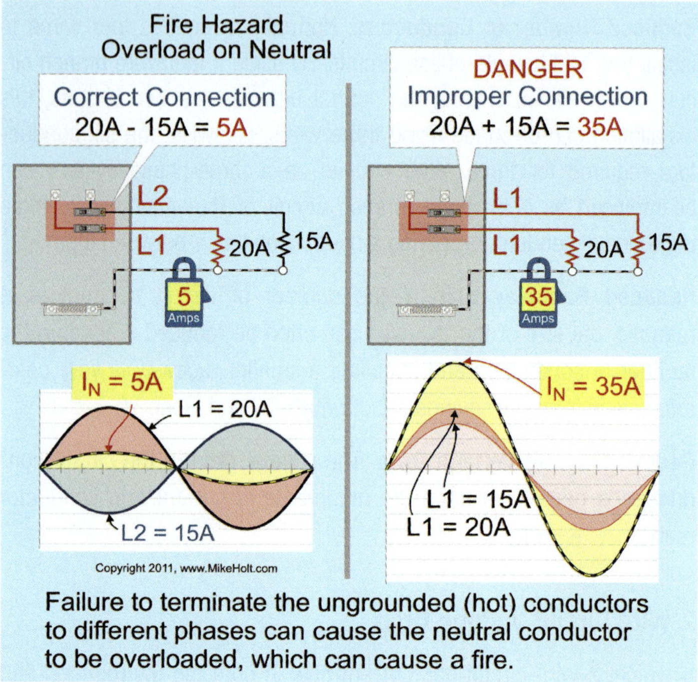

Figure 2–47

2.22 Dangers of Multiwire Branch Circuits

Multiwire branch circuits offer fewer conductors, reduced raceway size, and reduced voltage drop. However, the improper wiring or mishandling of multiwire branch circuits can cause a fire hazard because of conductor overloading and/or the destruction of connected equipment.

Fire Hazard

Failure to terminate the ungrounded conductors to separate phases or lines may cause the neutral conductor to become overloaded from excessive neutral current, and the insulation may be damaged or destroyed. Conductor overheating is known to decrease insulating material service life, potentially resulting in a fire from arcing faults in hidden locations. It's difficult to predict just how long conductor insulation will last under normal operating conditions, but heat does decrease its life span. Figure 2–47

Destruction of Equipment as Well as Fire Hazard

The opening of the ungrounded or neutral conductor of a 2-wire circuit during the replacement of a device doesn't cause a safety hazard, so the pigtailing of these conductors isn't required.

If the continuity of the neutral conductor of a multiwire branch circuit is interrupted (opened), there can be a fire and/or destruction of electrical equipment resulting from overvoltage or undervoltage.

► **Example**

A 3-wire, 120/240V circuit supplies a 1,200W, 120V hair dryer and a 600W, 120V television. If the neutral conductor is interrupted, it will cause the 120V television to operate at 160V and consume 1,067W of power (instead of 600W) for only a few seconds before it burns up. Figure 2–48

Step 1: Determine the resistance of each appliance.

R = E2/P

Hair Dryer

$R = 120V^2/1{,}200W$

R = 12 ohms

Television

$R = 120V^2/600W$

R = 24 ohms

Step 2: Determine the current of the circuit.

I = E/R

I = 240V/(12 ohms + 24 ohms)

I = 6.70A

Step 3: Determine the operating voltage for each appliance.

$$E = I \times R$$

Hair dryer operates at = 6.70A x 12 ohms
Hair dryer operates at = 80V

Television operates at = 6.70A x 24 ohms
Television operates at = 160V

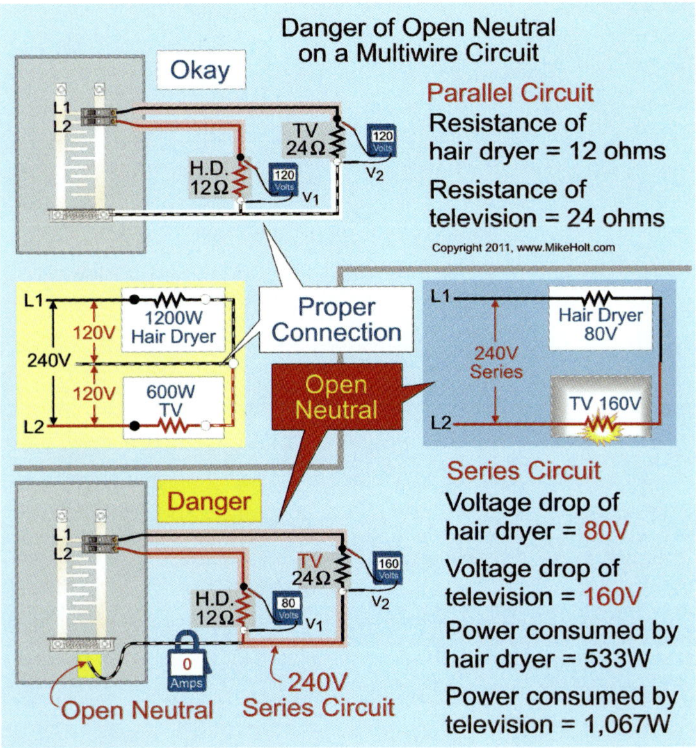

Figure 2–48

2.23 *NEC* Requirements

Because of the dangers associated with an open neutral conductor, the *NEC* specifies that the continuity of the neutral conductor of a multiwire branch circuit can't be dependent upon any wiring device [300.13(B)]. In other words, the neutral conductors of a multiwire branch circuit must be spliced together, and a wire (pigtail) brought out to the device. This way, if the receptacle is removed, it doesn't result in an open neutral conductor. **Figure 2–49**

Each multiwire branch circuit must have a means to simultaneously disconnect all ungrounded conductors at the point where the branch circuit originates [210.4(B)].

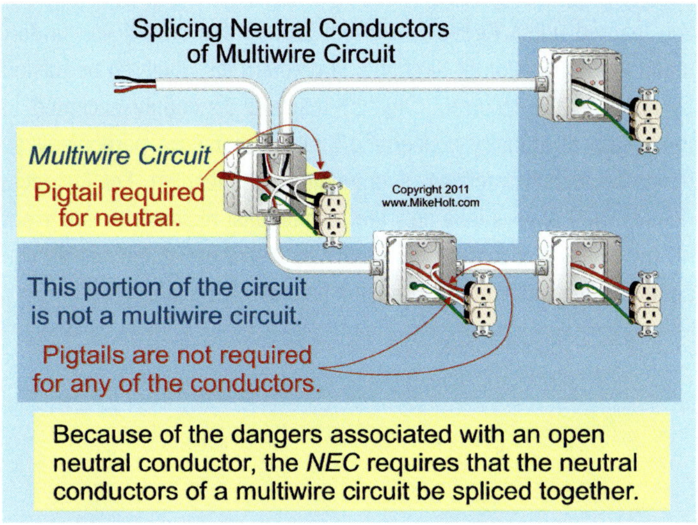

Figure 2–49

Author's Comment: Individual single-pole breakers with handle ties identified for the purpose, or a breaker with a common internal trip, can be used for this application [240.15(B)(1)]

CAUTION: *This rule is intended to prevent people from working on energized circuits they thought were disconnected.*

CONCLUSION TO UNIT 2—ELECTRICAL CIRCUITS

In completing this unit, you've laid another block in the foundation of your understanding of electricity. You've learned about series circuits, parallel circuits, and combinations of series and parallel circuits. It's important to be able to look at a circuit and visualize the relationship between the components and be able to understand why there are different levels of voltage or current in various locations of the circuit. This ability will greatly enhance your troubleshooting success on real branch circuits.

In this unit, you learned about a special circuit called a "multiwire branch circuit." There are special *Code* considerations for multiwire branch circuits. You now know how important it is to correctly install multiwire branch circuits with neutral connections that are very securely made. A neutral must never be opened on an energized multiwire branch circuit, as this can result in placing both undervoltages and overvoltages on circuit components, which can result in damage.

You learned about Kirchoff's Current Law in this unit. If you understand the application of Kirchoff's law, you're less likely to be misled by some of the incorrect "myths" that are commonly accepted in the electrical industry concerning fault current flow, particularly as it relates to the practices of grounding and bonding. For instance, does current always take only the path of least resistance? Is current always seeking a path to the earth? Ponder these questions as you continue your study of the intriguing field of electricity.

UNIT 2 Practice Questions

PRACTICE QUESTIONS FOR UNIT 2—ELECTRICAL CIRCUITS

PART A—SERIES CIRCUITS

Introduction

1. A series circuit is a circuit in which a specific amount of current leaves the voltage source and flows through every electrical device in a single path before it returns to the voltage source.

   (a) True
   (b) False

2.1 Practical Uses of the Series Circuit

2. Series circuits are often used for ______ applications.

   (a) signal
   (b) control
   (c) a and b
   (d) none of these

3. A 115/230V rated motor connected to a 230V circuit must have the windings connected in series so that each winding will receive at least 230V.

   (a) True
   (b) False

2.2 Understanding Series Calculations

4. Resistance opposes the flow of electrons. In a series circuit, the total circuit resistance is equal to the sum of all of the resistances in series.

   (a) True
   (b) False

5. The opposition to current flow results in a voltage drop of the circuit voltage.

   (a) True
   (b) False

6. Kirchoff's Voltage Law states that in a series circuit, the sum of the voltage drops across all of the resistors equals the applied voltage.

   (a) True
   (b) False

7. No matter how many resistances there are in a series circuit, the sum of the voltages across all of the resistances equals the voltage of the source according to the Resistance Law of Proportion.

   (a) True
   (b) False

8. Kirchoff's Current Law states that in a series circuit, the current is ______ through the transformer, the conductors, and the appliance.

   (a) proportional
   (b) distributed
   (c) additive
   (d) the same

9. The power consumed in a series circuit is equal to the power consumed by the largest resistance in the series circuit.

   (a) True
   (b) False

2.3 Series Circuit Calculations

10. To determine the resistance of each resistive element in the circuit, use the formula $R = E^2/VA$. E is the rated voltage of the resistance, and VA is the rated power of the resistor.

    (a) True
    (b) False

11. To calculate the total resistance of the circuit, use the formula:

    $R_{T = R1} + R_2 + R_3 + ...$

    (a) True
    (b) False

12. The current of the circuit can be determined by the formula $I = E_S/R_T$.

    (a) True
    (b) False

2.4 Power Calculations

13. If you know the current of the circuit and the resistance of each resistor, the power of each resistor can be determined by the formula $P = I^2 \times R$.

    (a) True
    (b) False

2.5 Variations

14. There can never be variations in the formulas used or the order in which they're used for series circuits.

    (a) True
    (b) False

2.7 Series-Connected Power Supplies

15. When power supplies are connected in series, the circuit voltage remains the same as when only one power supply is connected to it, provided that all the polarities are connected properly.

    (a) True
    (b) False

PART B—PARALLEL CIRCUITS

Introduction

16. A parallel circuit has two or more paths in which current can flow.

    (a) True
    (b) False

2.9 Understanding Parallel Calculations

17. In a parallel circuit, the voltage drop across each resistance is equal to the sum of the voltage drops of each of the resistors in parallel.

    (a) True
    (b) False

18. According to Kirchoff's Current Law, the total current provided by the source to a parallel circuit equals the sum of the currents of all of the branches.

    (a) True
    (b) False

19. The total power consumed in a parallel circuit equals the sum of the power of all branches.

    (a) True
    (b) False

2.10 Circuit Resistance

20. In a parallel circuit, the total circuit resistance is always greater than the smallest resistance.

    (a) True
    (b) False

21. The total resistance of a parallel circuit can be calculated by the ______ method.

(a) equal resistance
(b) product-over-sum
(c) reciprocal
(d) any of these

22. According to the equal resistance method, when all the resistances of the parallel circuit have the same resistance, divide the resistance of one element by the largest resistor in parallel.

(a) True
(b) False

23. The product-over-sum method is used to calculate the resistance of ______ resistance(s) at a time.

(a) one
(b) two
(c) three
(d) four

24. The advantage of the reciprocal method is that the formula can be used for as many resistances as the parallel circuit contains.

(a) True
(b) False

2.12 Parallel-Connected Power Supplies

25. When power supplies are connected in parallel, the voltage remains the same, but the current or ampere-hour capacity is increased.

(a) True
(b) False

PART C—SERIES-PARALLEL CIRCUITS

Introduction

26. A ______ is a circuit that contains some resistances in series and some resistances in parallel with each other.

(a) parallel circuit
(b) series circuit
(c) series-parallel circuit
(d) none of these

27. That portion of the series-parallel circuit that contains resistances in series must comply with the rules for series circuits.

(a) True
(b) False

28. That portion of the series-parallel circuit that contains resistances in parallel must comply with the rules for parallel circuits.

(a) True
(b) False

2.14 Working With Series-Parallel Circuits

29. When working with series-parallel circuits, it's best to redraw the circuit so you can see the series components and the parallel branches.

(a) True
(b) False

PART D—MULTIWIRE BRANCH CIRCUITS

Introduction

30. A multiwire branch circuit has two or more ungrounded conductors having a potential difference between them, and having an equal difference of potential between each ungrounded conductor and the grounded conductor.

(a) True
(b) False

31. A neutral conductor is the conductor connected to the ______ of a system that's intended to carry neutral current under normal conditions.

(a) grounding electrode
(b) neutral point
(c) intersystem bonding termination
(d) earth

2.16 Neutral Conductor

32. An ungrounded delta system contains a neutral point.

(a) True
(b) False

33. The common point on a 4-wire, three-phase, 120/208V wye-connected system is defined by the *Code* as the ______.

(a) wye point
(b) neutral point
(c) bridge point
(d) ungrounded point

2.17 Grounded Conductor

34. The grounded conductor is a conductor that's intentionally grounded to the earth.

(a) True
(b) False

2.18 Current Flow on the Neutral Conductor

35. The current in the neutral conductor of a 2-wire circuit is ______ of the current in the ungrounded conductor.

(a) 0 percent
(b) 70 percent
(c) 80 percent
(d) 100 percent

36. A balanced 3-wire, 120/240V, single-phase circuit is connected so that the ungrounded conductors are from different transformer lines (Line 1 and Line 2). The current in the neutral conductor is ______ of the ungrounded conductor current.

(a) 0 percent
(b) 70 percent
(c) 80 percent
(d) 100 percent

37. The neutral conductor of a 3-wire, 120/240V, single-phase circuit only carries the unbalanced current when the circuit isn't balanced.

(a) True
(b) False

38. If the ungrounded conductors of a multiwire branch circuit aren't terminated to different phases, this can cause the neutral current to exceed the neutral conductor's ampacity.

(a) True
(b) False

2.19 Balanced Systems

39. If the current in each ungrounded conductor of a multiwire branch circuit is the same, the neutral conductor carries 0A.

(a) True
(b) False

40. What's the neutral current for a 4-wire, 120/208V circuit, where L1 = 20A, L2 = 20A, and L3 = 20A?

(a) 0A
(b) 10A
(c) 20A
(d) 60A

2.20 Unbalanced Current

41. The current flowing in the neutral conductor of a multiwire branch circuit is called unbalanced current.

(a) True
(b) False

42. The neutral conductor of a 3-wire, 120/240V, single-phase circuit only carries current when the current in the ungrounded conductors isn't identical.

(a) True
(b) False

43. The neutral conductor of a 3-wire, 120/208V or 277/480V circuit supplied from a 4-wire, three-phase system never carries neutral current.

(a) True
(b) False

44. The neutral conductor of a 4-wire, 120/208V or 277/480V, three-phase system has neutral current flow when the ungrounded conductors are equally loaded.

(a) True
(b) False

2.21 Multiwire Branch Circuits

45. Multiwire branch circuits have more conductors for a given number of circuits, which requires the use of a larger raceway.

(a) True
(b) False

46. A balanced multiwire branch circuit has current flow only on the ungrounded conductors.

(a) True
(b) False

47. What's the voltage drop of two 12 AWG conductors, each 100 ft in length, supplying a 2-wire, 16A load? The resistance of 12 AWG conductors is 2 ohms per 1,000 ft.

(a) 3.20V
(b) 6.40V
(c) 7.20V
(d) 9.60V

48. What's the voltage drop of each ungrounded conductor of a 4-wire multiwire branch circuit? Each conductor is 12 AWG, 100 ft in length, supplying a 16A load. The resistance of 12 AWG conductors is 2 ohms per 1,000 ft.

(a) 3.20V
(b) 6.40V
(c) 7.20V
(d) 9.60V

2.22 Dangers of Multiwire Branch Circuits

49. The improper wiring or mishandling of multiwire branch circuits can cause _____ connected to the circuit.

(a) overloading of the ungrounded conductors
(b) overloading of the grounded conductors
(c) destruction of equipment
(d) b and c

50. The opening of the ungrounded or neutral conductor of a _____ circuit during the replacement of a device doesn't cause a safety hazard, so the pigtailing of these conductors isn't required.

(a) 2-wire
(b) 3-wire
(c) 4-wire
(d) all of these

2.23 *NEC* Requirements

51. Because of the dangers associated with an open neutral conductor, the continuity of the ______ conductor in a multiwire branch circuit can't depend upon the receptacle.

    (a) ungrounded
    (b) grounded
    (c) a and b
    (d) none of these

UNIT 2 Challenge Questions

CHALLENGE QUESTIONS FOR UNIT 2—ELECTRICAL CIRCUITS

PART A—SERIES CIRCUITS

2.2 Understanding Series Calculations

1. A series circuit contains two resistors, one rated 4 ohms and the other rated 8 ohms. If the total voltage drop across both resistors equals 12V, then the current that passes through either resistor will be ______.

   (a) 1A
   (b) 2A
   (c) 4A
   (d) 8A

2. A series circuit has four 40 ohm resistors and the power supply is 120V. The voltage drop of each resistor will be ______.

   (a) one-quarter of the source voltage
   (b) 30V
   (c) the same across each resistor
   (d) all of these

3. The power consumed in a series circuit is ______.

   (a) the sum of the power consumed by each load
   (b) determined by the formula $PT = I^2 \times RT$
   (c) determined by the formula $PT = E \times I$
   (d) all of these

4. The reading on Voltmeter 2 (V2) is ______. See Figure 2–50.

   (a) 5V
   (b) 6V
   (c) 7V
   (d) 10V

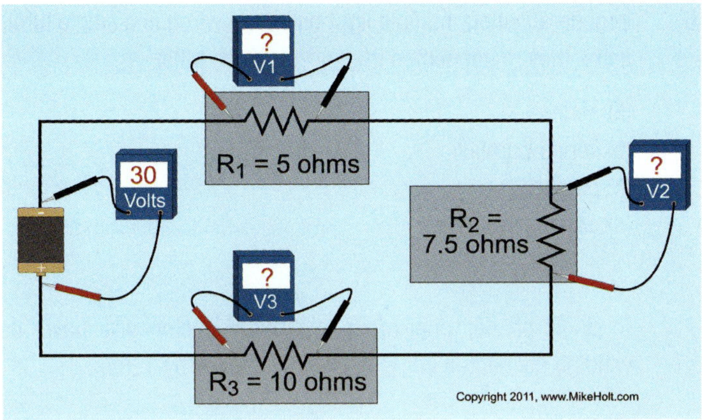

Figure 2–50

5. The voltmeter connected across the switch reads ______. See Figure 2–51.

   (a) 3V
   (b) 6V
   (c) 12V
   (d) 18V

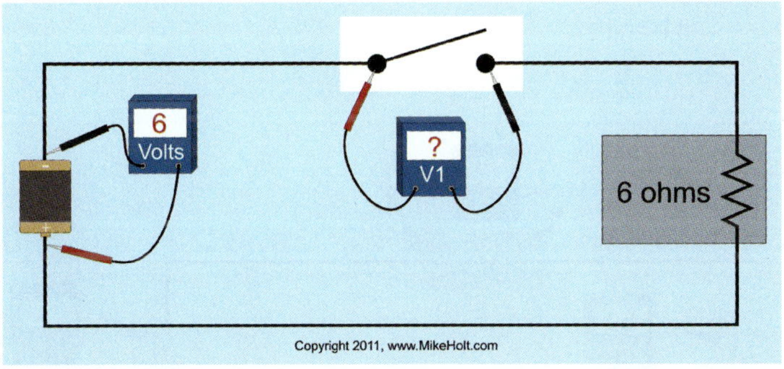

Figure 2–51

PART B—PARALLEL CIRCUITS

2.9 Understanding Parallel Calculations

6. In general, when multiple light bulbs are wired in a single luminaire, they're connected in _____ to each other.

(a) series
(b) series-parallel
(c) parallel
(d) order of wattage

7. A single-phase, dual-rated, 120/240V motor will have its winding connected in _____ when supplied by 120V.

(a) series
(b) parallel
(c) series-parallel
(d) parallel-series

8. The voltmeters shown in **Figure 2–52** are connected _____ each of the loads.

(a) in series to
(b) across
(c) in parallel to
(d) b and c

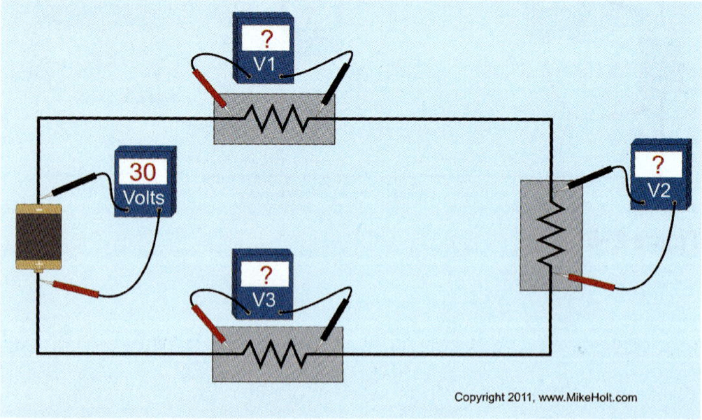

Figure 2–52

9. If the supply voltage is 120V, the total energy consumed for four 10 ohm resistors will be more if all of the resistors are connected _____.

(a) in series
(b) in series-parallel
(c) in parallel
(d) any of these

2.10 Circuit Resistance

10. A parallel circuit has three resistors. One resistor is rated 2 ohms, one is rated 3 ohms, and the other is rated 5 ohms. The total resistance of the parallel circuit is _____. Remember, the total resistance of any parallel circuit is always less than the smallest resistor.

(a) 0.50 ohms
(b) 1 ohm
(c) 2 ohms
(d) 3 ohms

Figure 2–53 applies to the next three questions:

11. In **Figure 2–53**, the total current of the circuit can be measured by ammeter _____.

(a) A1
(b) A2
(c) A3
(d) none of these

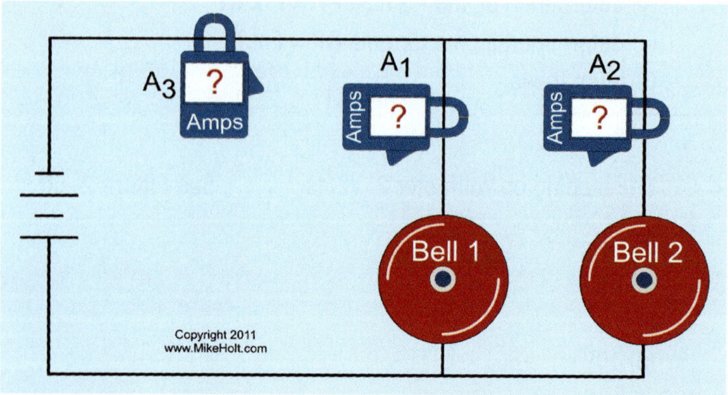

Figure 2–53

12. If Bell 2 consumes 12W of power when supplied by two 12V batteries (connected in series), the resistance of this bell is ______. See **Figure 2–53**.

(a) 12 ohms
(b) 24 ohms
(c) 36 ohms
(d) 48 ohms

13. Determine the total circuit resistance of the parallel circuit shown in **Figure 2–53** based on the following facts:

1. The current on ammeter 1 reads 0.75A.
2. The voltage of the circuit is 30V.
3. Bell 2 has a resistance of 48 ohms.

Tip: The total resistance of a parallel circuit is always less than the smallest resistor.

(a) 22 ohms
(b) 32 ohms
(c) 42 ohms
(d) 60 ohms

PART C—SERIES-PARALLEL CIRCUITS

2.14 Working With Series-Parallel Circuits

Figure 2–54 applies to the next three questions:

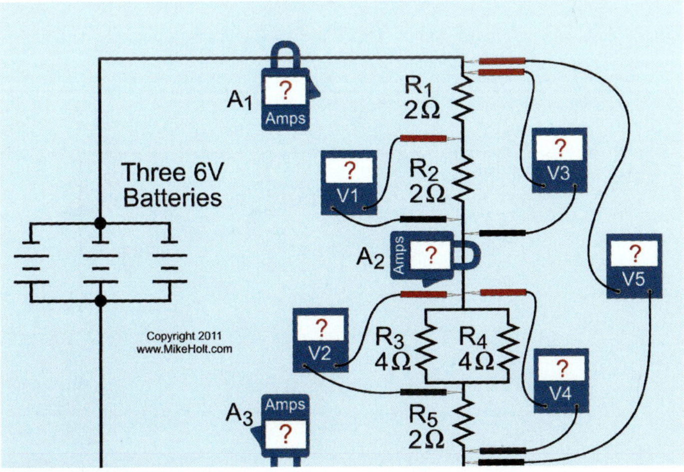

Figure 2–54

14. The total current of the circuit shown in **Figure 2–54** can be read on ______.

(a) Ammeter 1
(b) Ammeter 2
(c) Ammeter 3
(d) all of these

15. The reading of Voltmeter 2 (V2) is ______. See **Figure 2–54**.

(a) 1.50V
(b) 4V
(c) 5V
(d) 8V

16. The reading of V4 is ______. See **Figure 2–54**.

(a) 1.50V
(b) 3V
(c) 5V
(d) 8V

Figure 2–55 applies to the next two questions:

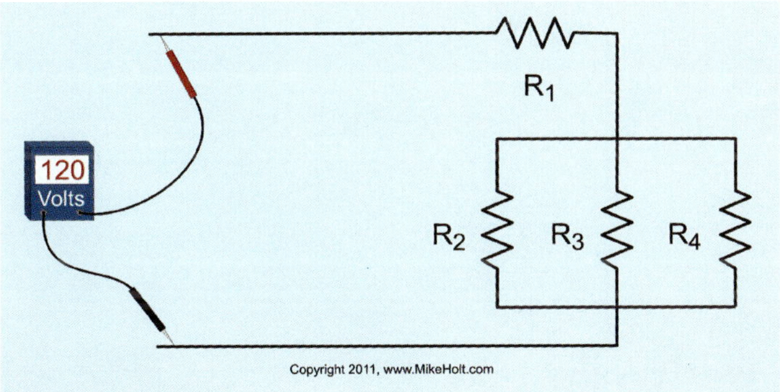

Figure 2–55

17. Resistor R_1 has a resistance of 5 ohms and resistors R_2, R_3, and R_4 have a resistance of 15 ohms each. The total resistance of this series-parallel circuit is ______. See **Figure 2–55**.

(a) 10 ohms
(b) 25 ohms
(c) 35 ohms
(d) 50 ohms

18. What's the voltage drop across R_1, if R_1 is equal to 5 ohms and the total resistance of R_2, R_3, and R_4 is 5 ohms? See **Figure 2–55**.

(a) 33V
(b) 40V
(c) 60V
(d) 120V

PART D—MULTIWIRE BRANCH CIRCUITS

2.22 Dangers of Multiwire Branch Circuits

19. If the neutral of the circuit in the diagram is opened, the circuit becomes one series circuit of 240V. Under this condition, the current of the circuit is ______. Tip: Determine the total resistance. See **Figure 2–56**.

(a) 0.25A
(b) 0.58A
(c) 0.67A
(d) 2.25A

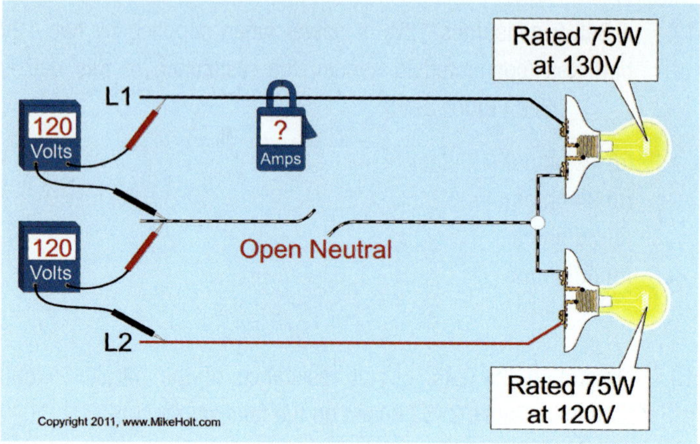

Figure 2–56

UNIT 3

Understanding Alternating Current

INTRODUCTION TO UNIT 3—UNDERSTANDING ALTERNATING CURRENT

Direct-current (dc) circuits and alternating-current (ac) circuits have similarities as well as differences. In resistive circuits, direct-current and alternating-current circuits have many similarities. The calculations of resistors used in series, parallel, or series-parallel combination circuits discussed in the preceding unit applies to both direct-current and alternating-current circuits. In contrast, this unit focuses on the special characteristics of alternating current and how it's generated, distributed, and utilized.

The practical use of electric power depends on the efficient generation and distribution of power to the point of utilization. The principles of magnetism and induction are important in the generation and transformation of alternating-current power. The flow of direct current in a circuit is opposed by resistance, but because of the changing current flow of an alternating-current circuit, alternating-current is opposed by a property called impedance. Impedance is a combination of resistance, inductive reactance, and capacitive reactance.

Be sure to study this unit carefully so you'll understand the differences between alternating-current and direct-current circuits. There are some types of equipment that rely on the characteristics of the changing magnetic field developed by alternating-current power to function, such as the alternating-current motors and transformers that will be covered in Unit 4.

PART A—UNDERSTANDING ALTERNATING CURRENT

Introduction

Because alternating current is inexpensive to transmit compared to direct current, alternating current has become the dominant form of electricity in our modern infrastructure. In the early days of commercially available electric power, direct current was more common. But, economics won out. Applying alternating current safely or effectively, however, requires an understanding of certain concepts that border on the complex. All of those concepts build on what you've already learned.

3.1 Current Flow

In order for current to flow in a circuit, the power supply must apply sufficient electromotive force (voltage) to cause the electrons to move. The movement of the electrons themselves doesn't produce any useful work. It's the effects that the moving electrons have on the loads they flow through that are important. The effects of electron movement are the same regardless of the direction of the current flow. Figure 3–1

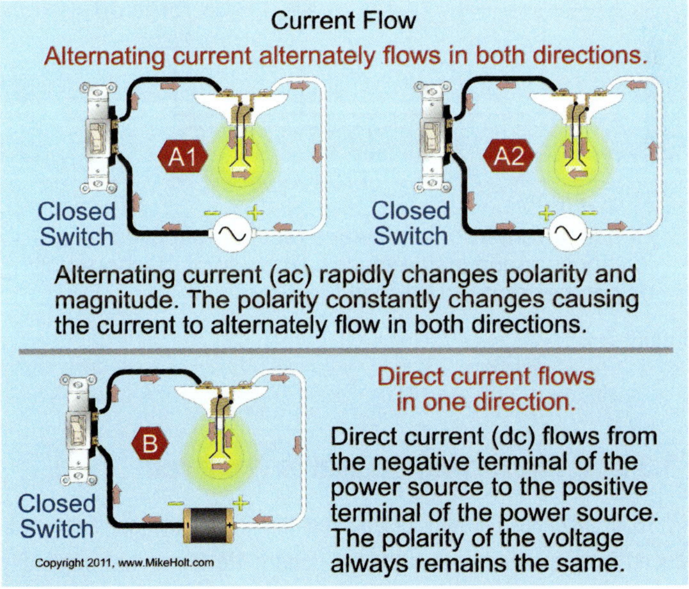

Figure 3–1

3.2 Why Alternating Current Is Used

Alternating current is primarily used because it can be transmitted inexpensively by transforming it to high-transmission level voltages and then converting this voltage back to lower distribution voltage levels. High-voltage transmission lines allow for the transmission of alternating-current at high voltage, and relatively low current. High-voltage transmission with the outcome of lower current results in reduced voltage drop in the transmission lines. Conductors and electrical equipment are sized based on the current in the lines, so the lower current levels also allow the use of smaller wire and smaller electrical equipment.

Direct-Current Use. There are other applications however, particularly in electronic equipment, where only direct current can perform the desired function. This is accomplished by rectifying alternating-current to direct-current to power these electronic loads. Figure 3–2

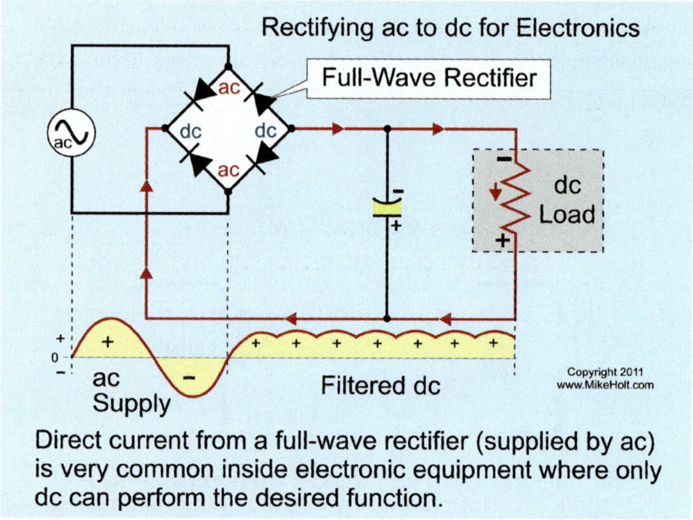

Figure 3–2

3.3 How Alternating Current Is Produced

In 1831, Michael Faraday discovered that electricity could be produced from a source other than a battery. He knew that electricity produced magnetism, and wondered why magnetism couldn't produce electricity. Faraday discovered that when he moved a magnet inside a coil of wire, he got a pulse of electricity. When he pulled the magnet out, he got another pulse. He also got the same reaction when he moved the coil toward and away from the magnet.

Faraday's experiments revealed that when a magnetic field moves through a coil of wire, the lines of force of the magnetic field cause the electrons in the wire to flow in a specific direction. When the magnetic field moves in the opposite direction, electrons in the wire flow in the opposite direction. Electrons flow only when there's motion of the conductors relative to the magnetic field. Figure 3–3

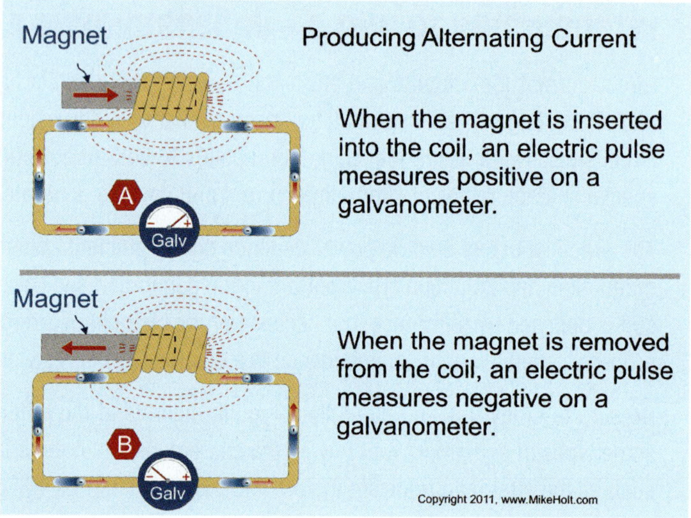

Figure 3–3

3.4 Alternating-Current Generator

A simple alternating-current generator consists of a loop of wire rotating between the lines of force between the opposite poles of a magnet. The halves of each conductor loop travel through the magnetic lines of force in opposite directions, causing the electrons within the conductor to move in a given direction. The magnitude of the voltage produced depends upon the number of turns of wire, the strength of the magnetic field, and the speed at which the coil rotates. Figure 3–4

The rotating conductor loop is called a "rotor" or "armature." "Slip" or "collector" rings and carbon brushes are used to connect the output voltage from the generator to an external circuit.

In generators that produce large quantities of electricity, the conductor coils are stationary and the magnetic field revolves within the coils. The magnetic field is produced by an electromagnet, instead of a permanent magnet. Using electromagnets permits the strength of the magnetic field (and thus the lines of force) to be modified, thereby controlling the output voltage. Figure 3–5

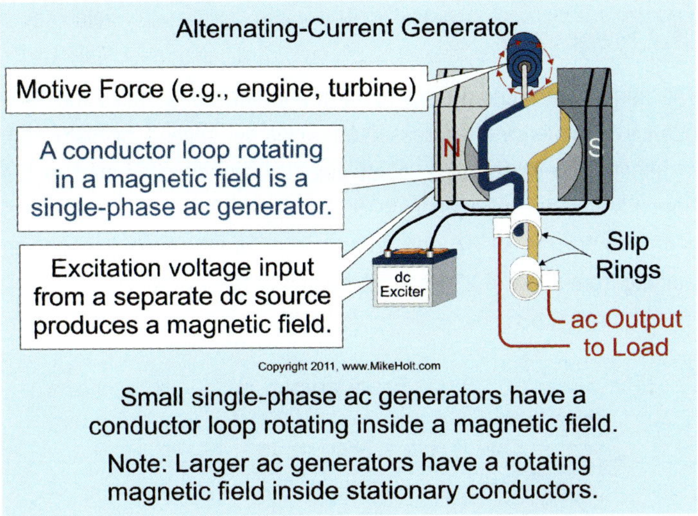

Figure 3–4

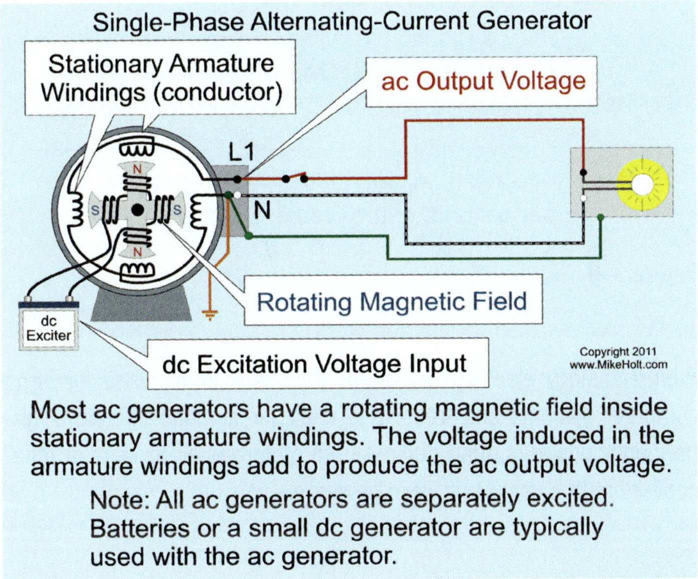

Figure 3–5

3.5 Waveform

A waveform image is used to display the level and direction of current and voltage.

Direct-Current Waveform

A direct-current waveform displays the direction (polarity) and magnitude of the current or voltage. Figure 3–6

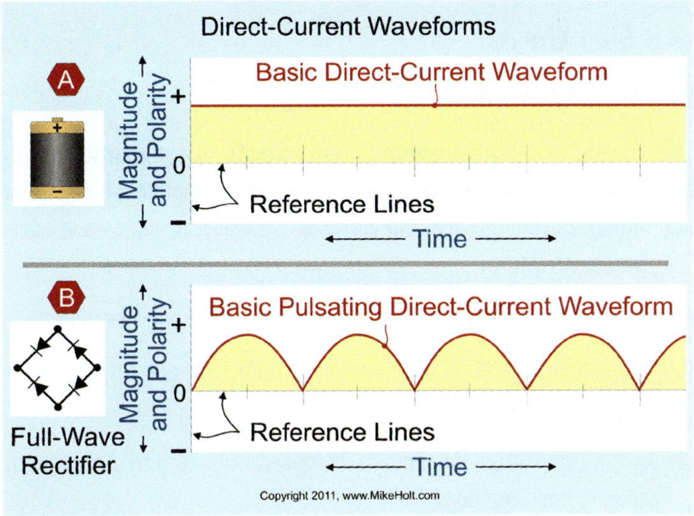

Figure 3–6

Alternating-Current Waveform

An alternating-current waveform displays the level and direction of the current and voltage for every instant of time for one full revolution of the rotor. Figure 3–7

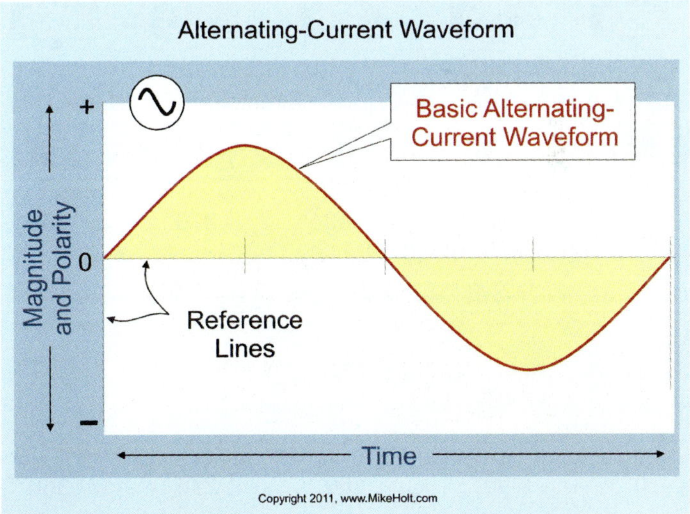

Figure 3–7

3.6 Sine Wave

Sinusoidal Waveform

The waveform for alternating-current circuits is symmetrical, with positive above and negative below the zero reference level. For most alternating-current circuits, the waveform is called a "sine wave" or a "sinusoidal waveform."

Figure 3–8 shows the relationship of the waveform and the rotor.

(1) The voltage starts at zero, when the rotor isn't cutting any magnetic lines of force.

(2) As the rotor turns, the voltage increases from zero to a maximum value in one direction.

(3) It then decreases until it reaches zero.

(4) At zero, the voltage reverses polarity and increases until it reaches a maximum value at this opposite polarity.

(5) It decreases until it reaches zero again.

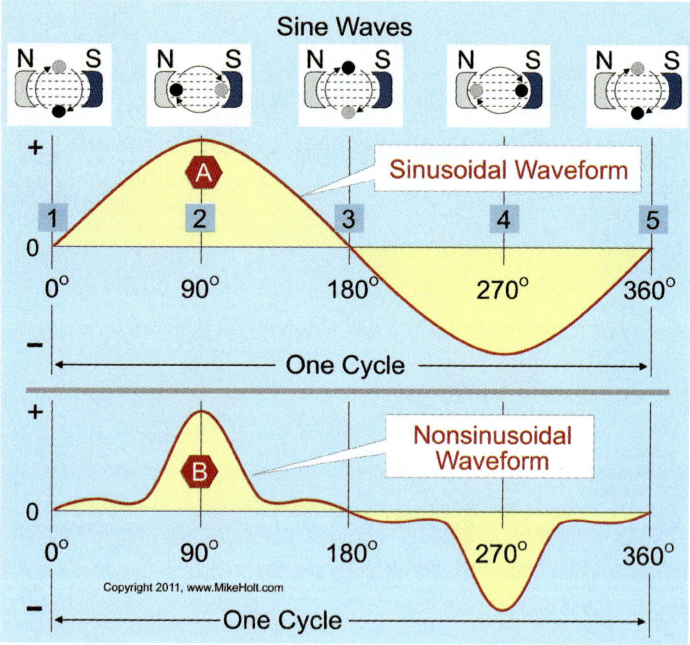

Figure 3–8

3.7 Frequency

The number of times a rotor turns in one second is called the "frequency." Frequency is expressed as cycles per second, or Hertz (Hz), in honor of Heinrich Hertz. Most electrical power generated in the United States has a frequency of 60 Hz, **Figure 3–9**. Many other parts of the world use 50 Hz, and some use different power frequencies ranging from a low of 25 Hz to a high of 125 Hz.

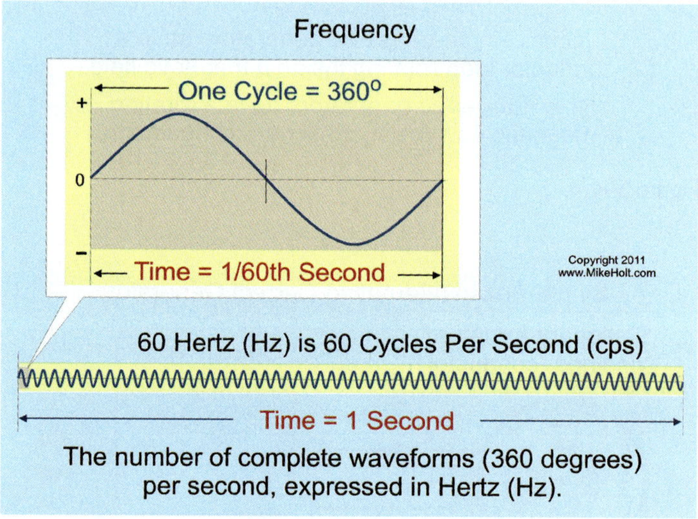

Figure 3–9

High-frequency electrical power of 415 Hz is often used for large computer systems and 400 Hz is used for airplane lighting. High-frequency power is often derived from motor-generator sets or other converters that use 60 Hz input power.

3.8 Phase

"Phase" is a term that indicates the time or degree relationship between two waveforms, such as voltage-to-current or voltage-to-voltage. When two waveforms are in step with each other, they're said to be "in-phase." In a purely resistive alternating-current circuit, the current and voltage are in-phase. This means that, at every instant, the current is exactly in step with the applied voltage. They both reach their zero and peak values at the same time. **Figure 3–10**

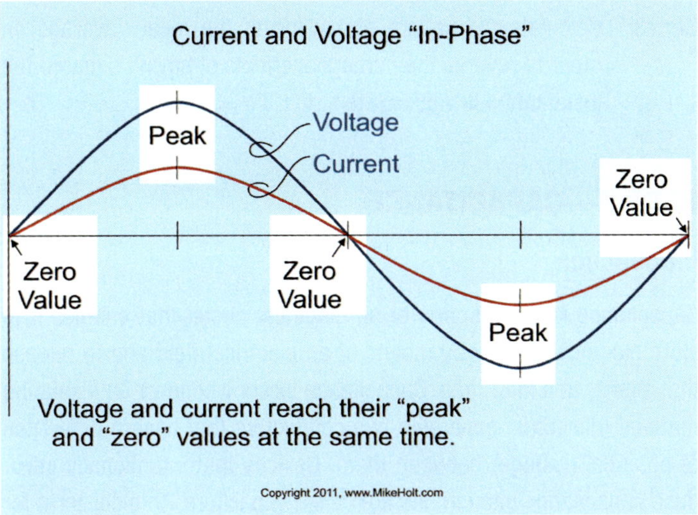

Figure 3–10

3.9 Degrees

Phase differences are often expressed in degrees; one full waveform equals 360 degrees. For example, a three-phase generator has each of its windings out-of-phase with each other by 120 degrees. Figure 3–11

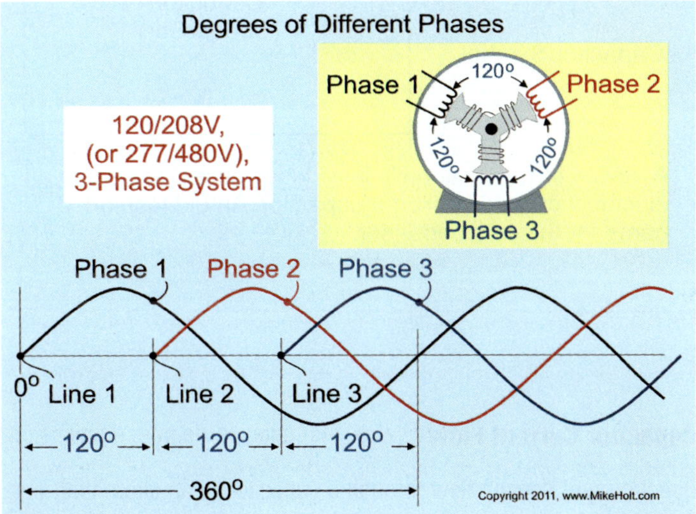

Figure 3–11

3.10 Lead or Lag

When describing the relationship between two different waveforms that aren't in phase, meaning that they don't simultaneously reach their peaks and zero-crossings, they're often described as having leading or lagging relationships..

Leading

It's easy to become confused about which waveform leads and which one lags behind. The best way to remember this is to look at which waveform finishes its cycle first. In Part A of Figure 3–12, the voltage waveform (designated by E2) finishes its waveform cycle before the current waveform, so the voltage waveform "leads" the current waveform. It can also be said that the current lags the voltage.

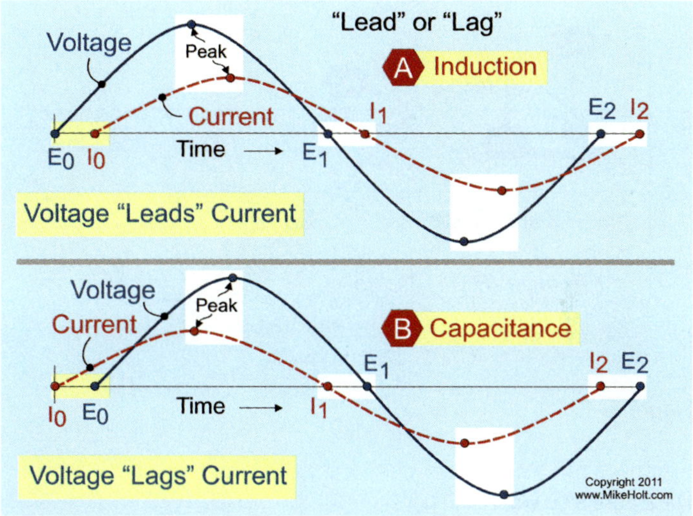

Figure 3–12

Lagging

In Figure 3–12B, the voltage waveform in Part B finishes its waveform cycle after the current waveform (designated by I2 in Figure 3–12). In this case the voltage "lags" the current, or the current can be said to lead the voltage.

3.11 Values of Alternating Current

There are many important values in alternating-current waveforms. Some of the most important include instantaneous, peak, and effective. Figure 3–13

Instantaneous Value

The value at a moment of time. Depending upon the instant selected, it can range anywhere from zero, to peak, to negative peak value. Figure 3–13A1

Peak Value

The maximum value the current or voltage waveform reaches. **Figure 3–13A2**

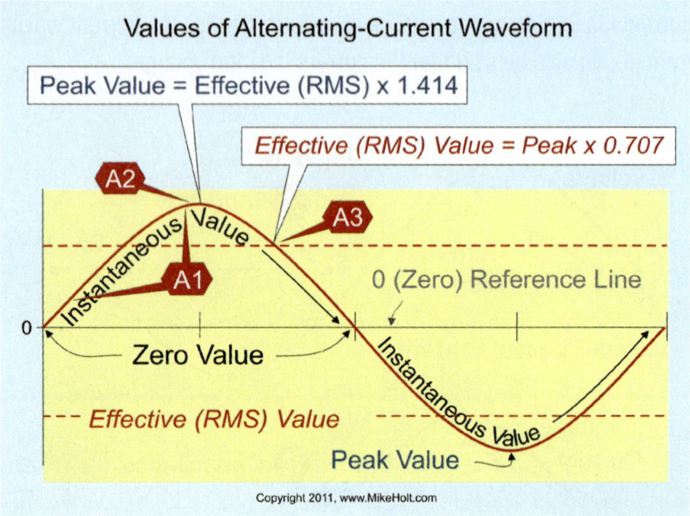

Figure 3–13

For a pure sine wave:

Peak Value = Effective Value/0.707
Peak Value = Effective Value x 1.414
Effective Value = Peak Value x 0.707

Effective Value

Effective alternating-current voltage or effective ac current is the equivalent value of direct-current voltage or dc current that will produce the same amount of heat in a resistor, **Figure 3–13A3**. For a pure sine wave:

Effective Value = RMS Value

RMS Value

Root-Mean-Square (RMS) describes the steps (in reverse) necessary to determine the effective voltage or current value. **Figure 3–13A3**

Step 1: Square the instantaneous waveform values; this turns all of the negative portions into positive portions.

Step 2: Determine the mean (average) of the instantaneous values of the waveform.

Step 3: Calculate the square root value of the mean (average) in order to reverse the numerical effects of having squared the instantaneous values (Step 1).

PART B—CAPACITANCE

Introduction

Capacitance is the property of an electrical circuit that enables it to store electrical energy by means of an electrical field and to release that energy at a later time. Capacitance exists whenever an insulating material (dielectric) separates two conductors that have a difference of potential (voltage) between them. Devices that intentionally introduce capacitance into circuits are called capacitors. An older term for these components is "condensers." **Figure 3–14**

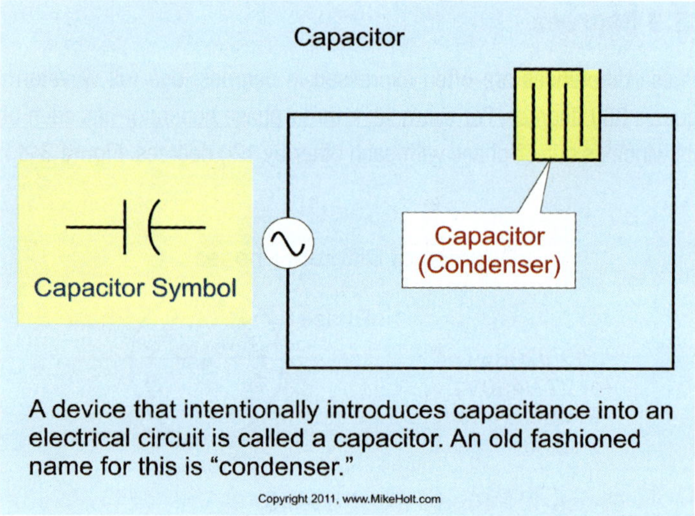

Figure 3–14

Capacitor Current Flow

Direct current doesn't flow through a capacitor. In an alternating-current circuit, the electrons in the circuit move back and forth to alternately charge the capacitor, first in one direction, and then in the other. A capacitor permits current to flow because of its ability to store energy and then discharge the energy as the alternating current flows in the opposite direction.

Capacitors as Filters

Figure 3–15 shows a diagram of a full-wave rectifier, which makes use of four rectifiers. A rectifier is a device that allows current to flow in only one direction, thus converting alternating current to direct current. Each rectifier only provides current flow for one-half of the alternating-current sine wave, which isn't a very practical dc current. Connecting four rectifiers into the full-wave rectifier circuit shown provides a bridge circuit which allows different rectifiers to alternately provide current to the load during each half of the sine wave alternation, while always keeping the same direct-current polarity on the load. This provides a partial solution, however the current produced is still not a pure dc current, but what's called "pulsating dc current." A capacitor can be used to level out the pulsating dc current into a filtered dc current.

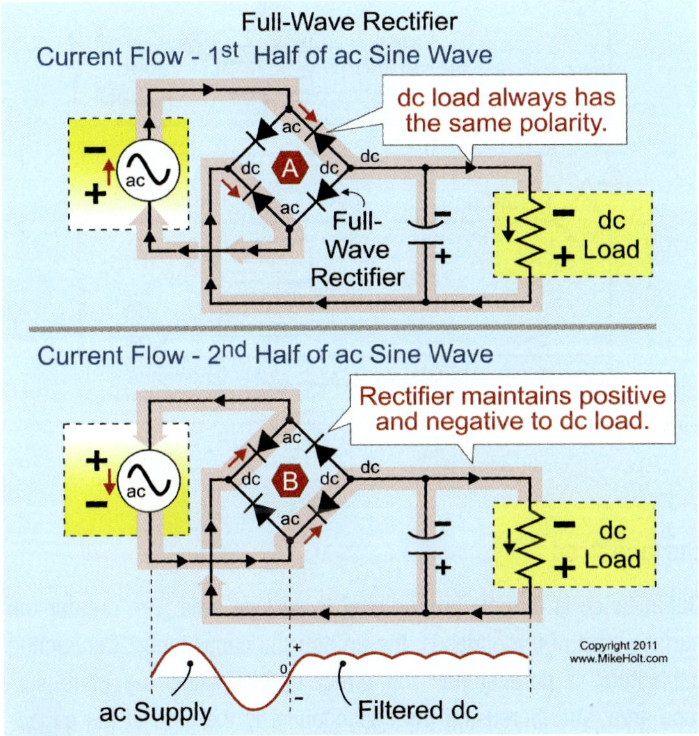

Figure 3–15

Author's Comment: As a full-wave rectifier converts the alternating-current voltage to filtered direct-current voltage, the capacitor will be continuously charged. Figure 3–15

3.12 Charged Capacitor

When a capacitor has a potential difference between the conductors (plates), the capacitor is charged. One plate has an excess of free electrons and the other plate has a lack of them. The plate with the excess electrons has an overall negative charge (–), while the plate from which electrons were removed has an overall positive charge (+). A difference of potential (voltage) exists between the plates. Figure 3–16

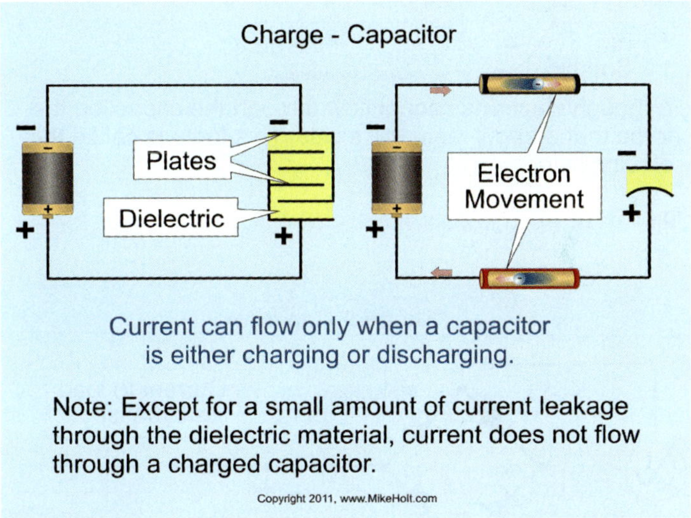

Figure 3–16

3.13 Electrical Field

Although the electrons can't flow, the force that attracts them still exists; this force is called the electrical field. The electrical field can be thought of as lines of electrical force that exist between the capacitor plates. Figure 3–17

The more the capacitor is charged, the stronger the electrical field. If the capacitor is overcharged, the electrons from the negative plate could be pulled through the insulation to the positive plate. If this happens, the capacitor is said to have broken down (shorted). Figure 3–18

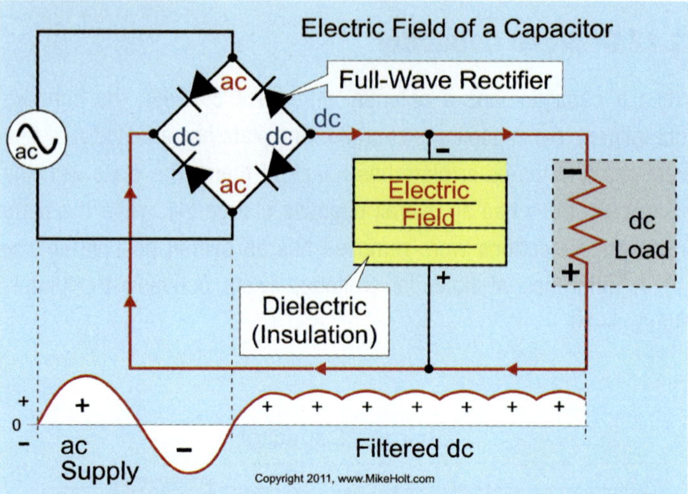

Although electrons cannot flow through the capacitor, the force that attracts them still exists. This force is called the electric field.

Figure 3–17

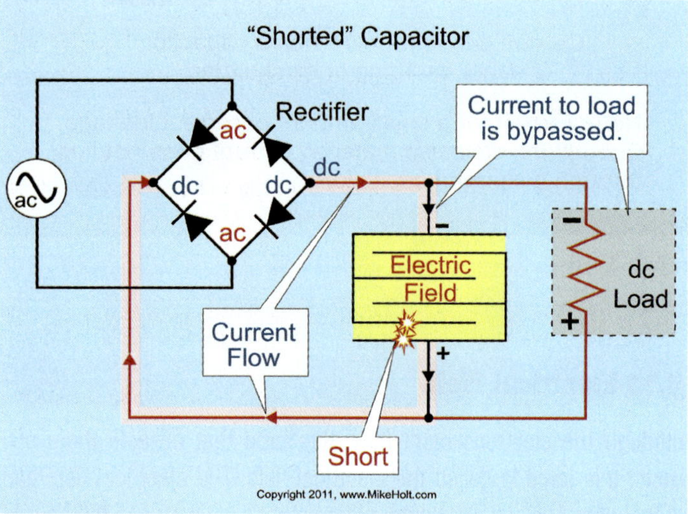

Figure 3–18

3.14 Discharging a Capacitor

To discharge a capacitor, all that's required is a conducting path connected across the terminals of the capacitor. The free electrons on the negative plate will then flow through the external circuit to the positive plate.

CAUTION: *Be careful when working on a circuit that contains capacitors (such as those found in variable speed drives). Capacitors can store large amounts of energy for a long period of time. They can present a shock hazard even after the power has been removed.*

3.15 Determining Capacitance

Factors that determine the capacitance of a capacitor are the surface area of the plates, the distance between the plates, and the insulating material or dielectric between the plates.

Plate Distance

Capacitance is inversely proportional to the distance between the capacitor plates. The closer the plates of the capacitor are to each other, the greater the capacitance and, conversely, the greater the distance is between the plates, the lower the capacitance. **Figure 3–19**

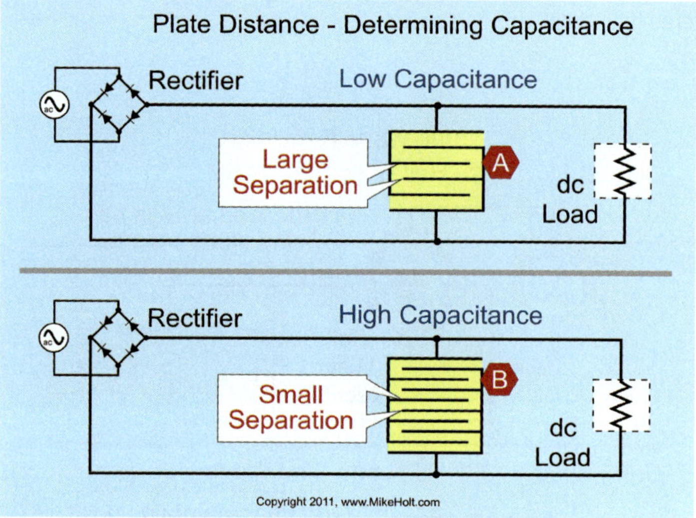

Figure 3–19

Surface Area

Capacitance is directly proportional to surface area. The greater the surface area of the plates is, the greater the capacitance. Connecting capacitors in parallel has the effect of increasing the plate surface area, and increasing the capacitance by the sum of the capacitors. Connecting capacitors in series has the effect of increasing the dielectric, and decreasing the capacitance. **Figure 3–20**

Dielectric Strength

Dielectric strength indicates the maximum voltage that can be applied across the dielectric safely. **Figure 3–21**

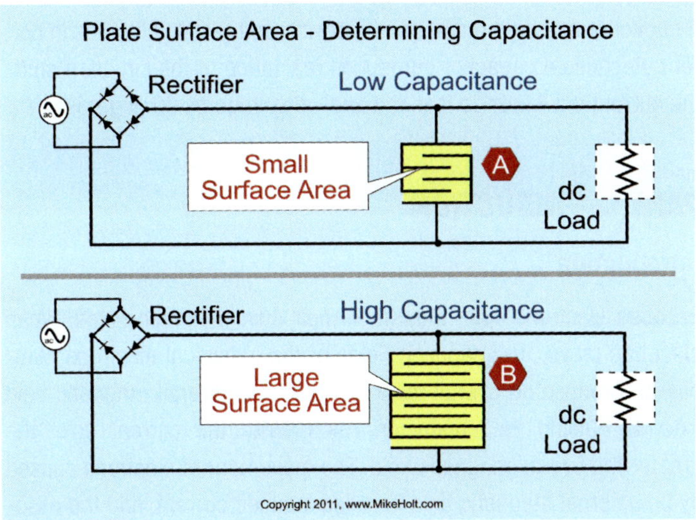

Figure 3–20

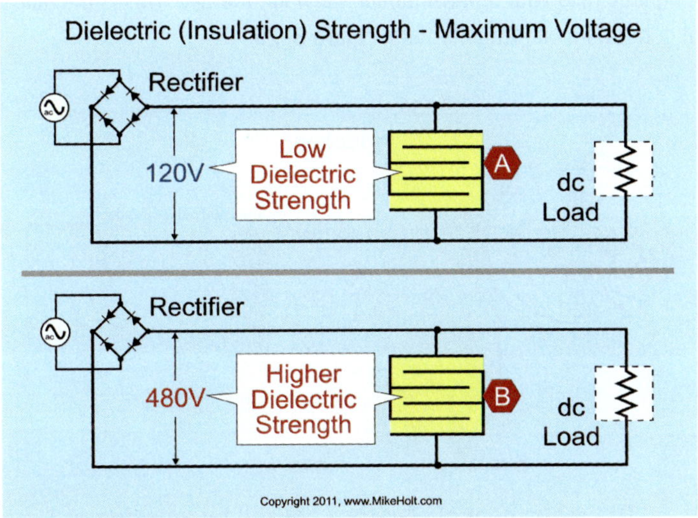

Figure 3–21

3.16 Uses of Capacitors

Capacitors have many uses in electronic circuits, as well as applications that are more familiar to electricians. Capacitors aid in starting single-phase alternating-current motors by creating a phase displacement in the motor windings. Later in this unit, we'll discuss power factor and the role that capacitors play in correcting low power factor. Capacitors can be used to prevent arcing across the contacts of electric switches. A capacitor connected across the switch contacts provides a path for current flow until the switch is fully open and the danger of arcing has passed. **Figure 3–22**

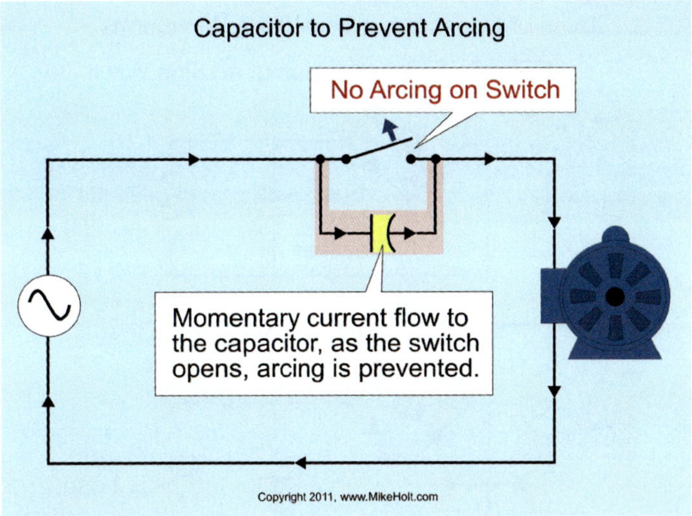

Figure 3–22

Electronic Power Supplies

One use of capacitors is to smooth out pulsating direct-current waveforms, such as those which would be present through a direct-current load if the capacitor wasn't present. A full-wave bridge rectifier transforms the alternating-current waveform from the source into a pulsating direct-current waveform—the capacitor then smoothes out the waveform and makes a near-steady direct-current voltage across the direct-current load. **Figure 3–23**

3.17 Phase Relationship

A capacitor is a device that resists changes in voltage. As the alternating-current sine wave reaches a positive peak, the capacitor fully charges to the same polarity. Then, as the ac current passes peak and decreases, the capacitor begins to discharge which has the effect of resisting the change of the alternating-current circuit voltage value. This results in what's called "capacitive reactance" and a shifting of the current waveform out-of-phase to the voltage waveform. **Figure 3–24**

One way to think of this is that the capacitor responds to changes in current by increasing or decreasing its own amount of charge. Therefore, the voltage waveform change lags the current waveform change. The opposition offered to the flow of ac current by a capacitor is called "capacitive reactance." This is expressed in ohms and abbreviated X_C.

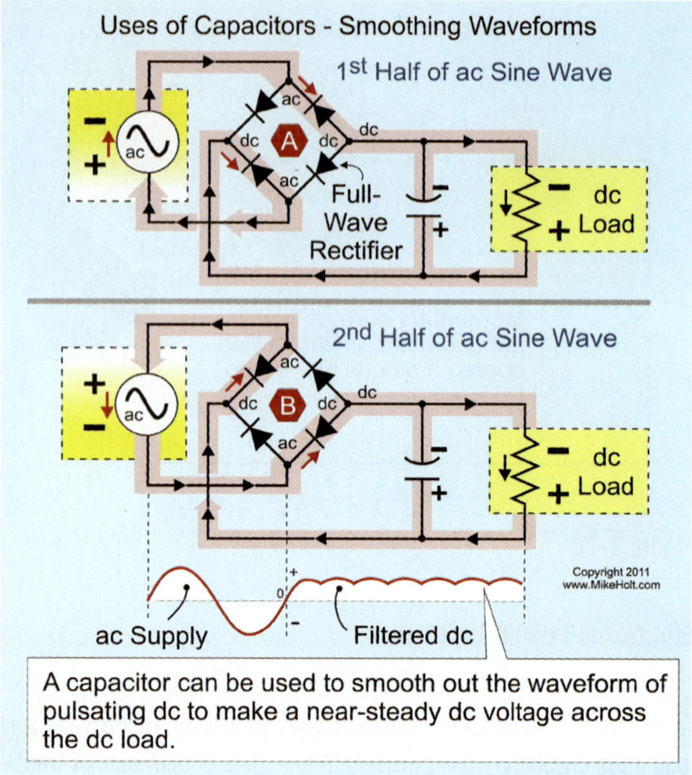

Figure 3–23

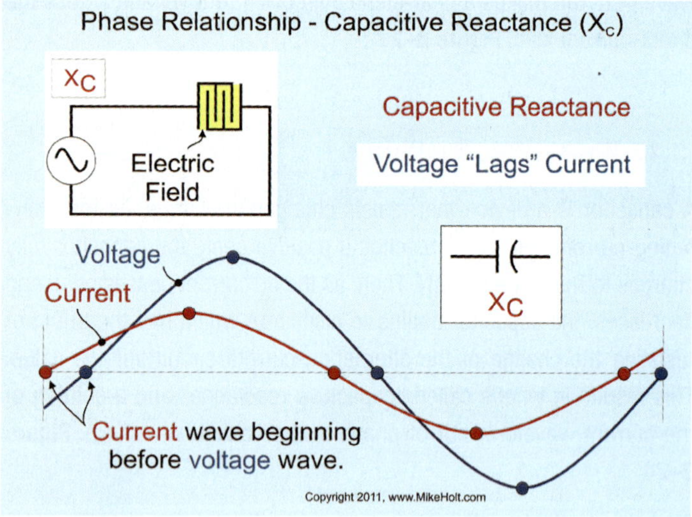

Figure 3–24

Capacitive reactance is calculated using the following equation:

$X_C = 1/(2 \times \pi \times f \times C)$

where π equals 3.14, "f" is the frequency in hertz, "C" is the capacitance in farads, and "X_C" is expressed in ohms.

A capacitor can be thought of as a device that resists changes in current. Because a capacitor introduces reactance to the circuit, it shifts the current waveform to lead the applied voltage by 90 degrees.

PART C—INDUCTION

Introduction

Because electrons spin, they have their own magnetic fields. When electrons move, the magnetic fields of the individual electrons combine to produce an overall magnetic field. The overall magnetic field extends outside the conductor. The greater the current flow, the greater the overall magnetic field. The movement of electrons caused by an external magnetic field is called induced current, and the associated potential that's established is called induced voltage. In order to induce voltage, all that's required is a conductor and an external magnetic field with relative motion between the two. This is the basis of generators and transformers. Figure 3–25

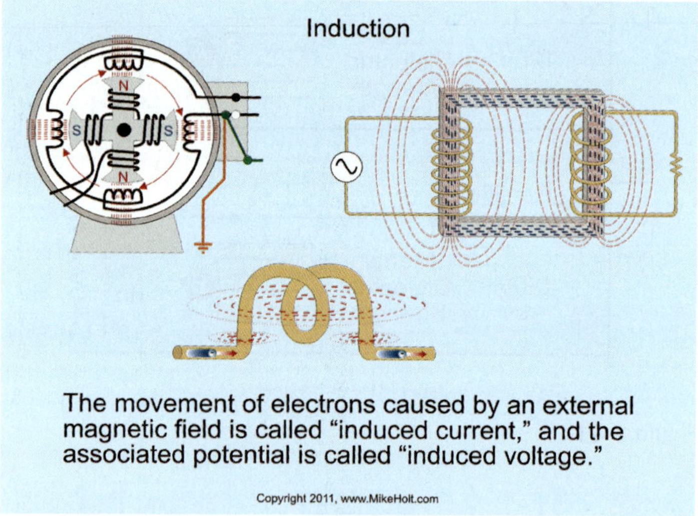

Figure 3–25

Inductance is the property of an electrical circuit that enables it to store electrical energy by means of an electromagnetic field and to release this energy at a later time.

3.18 Self-Induction

As the ac current through a conductor increases, an expanding electromagnetic field is created through the conductor. The expanding magnetic flux lines cut through the conductor itself (which, in effect, is in motion relative to the field), thus inducing voltage within the conductor.

When the current within the conductor decreases, the electromagnetic field collapses, and again the magnetic flux lines through the conductor cut through the conductor itself. The voltage induced within the conductor caused by its own expanding and collapsing magnetic field is known as "self-induced voltage." **Figure 3–26**

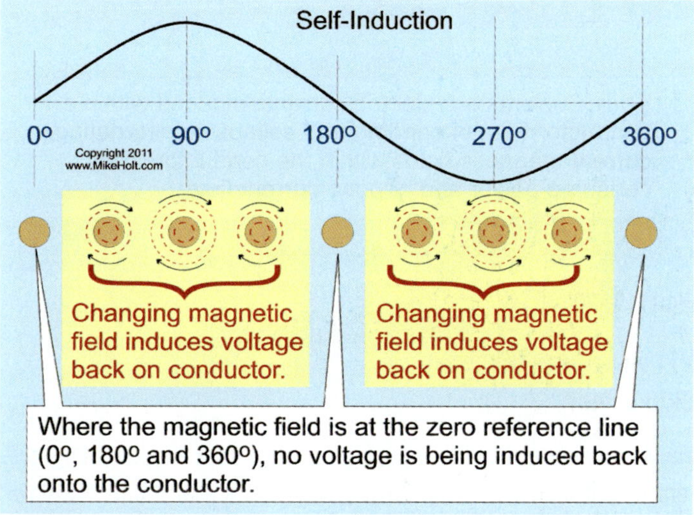

Figure 3–26

3.19 Induced Voltage and Applied Current

The induced voltage in a conductor carrying alternating current always opposes the change in current flowing through the conductor. The induced voltage that opposes the current flow is called "counter-electromotive force" (CEMF), or "back-EMF."

The waveform of the induced voltage in the conductor (CEMF) is 90 degrees out-of-phase with the circuit current and 180 degrees out-of-phase with the applied voltage waveform. CEMF either opposes or aids the conductor current flow. **Figure 3–27**

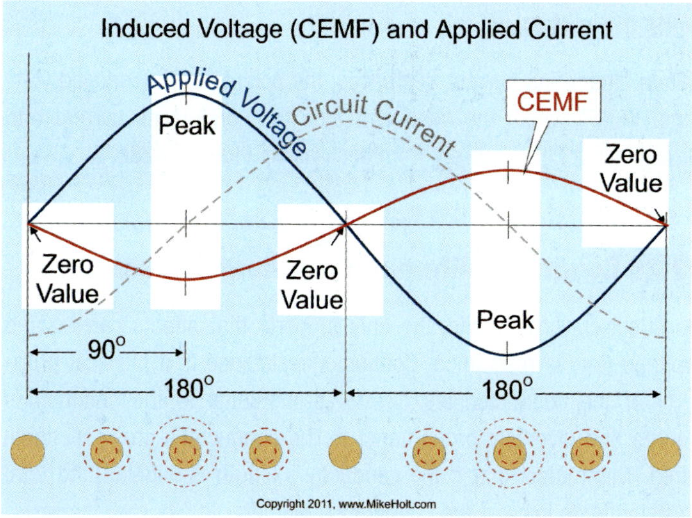

Figure 3–27

Opposes Current Flow

When alternating current increases, the polarity of the induced voltage (CEMF) within the conductor opposes the conductor's current and tries to prevent the current from increasing. **Figure 3–28A**

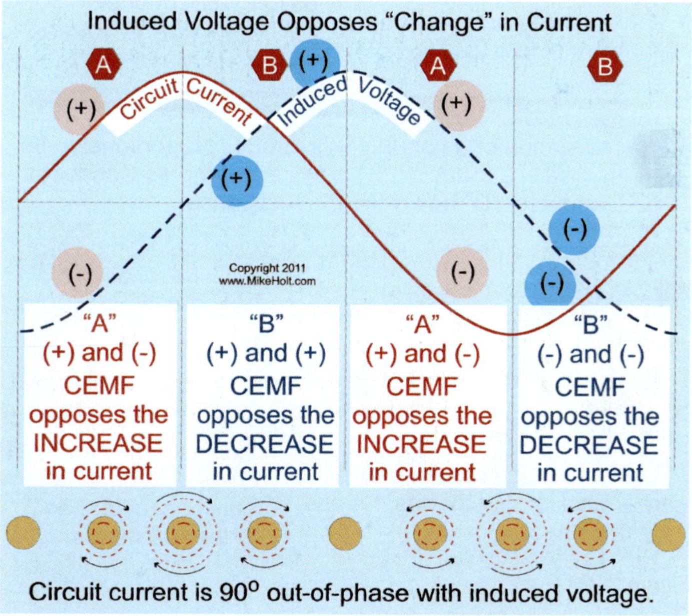

Figure 3–28

Aids Current Flow

When alternating current decreases, the polarity of the induced voltage (CEMF) within the conductor aids the conductor's current and tries to prevent the current from decreasing. Figure 3–28B

3.20 Conductor Alternating-Current Resistance

In direct-current circuits, the only property that affects current and voltage flow is resistance. Conductor resistance is a physical property of the conductor. It's directly proportional to the conductor's length and inversely proportional to the conductor's cross-sectional area. This means that if the conductor's length is doubled, the total resistance doubles; if the conductor's diameter is reduced, the resistance increases. Increases in temperature also result in an increase in resistance. Figure 3–29

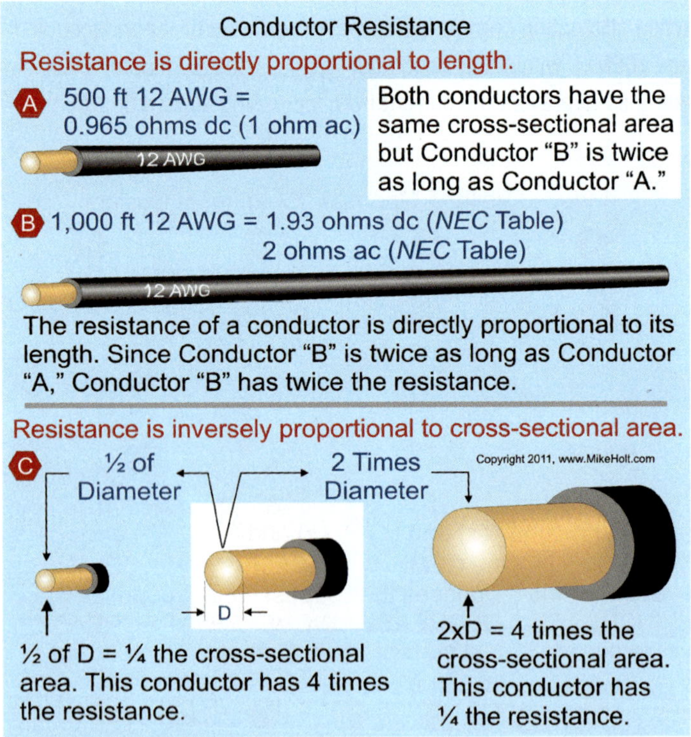

Figure 3–29

For alternating-current circuits, one must factor in the effects of eddy currents and skin effect, in addition to the resistance of the conductor.

Eddy Currents

Eddy currents are small independent currents that are produced as a result of the expanding and collapsing magnetic field from an alternating-current circuit. Eddy currents flow erratically through a conductor, consume power, and increase the opposition to current flow. Figure 3–30

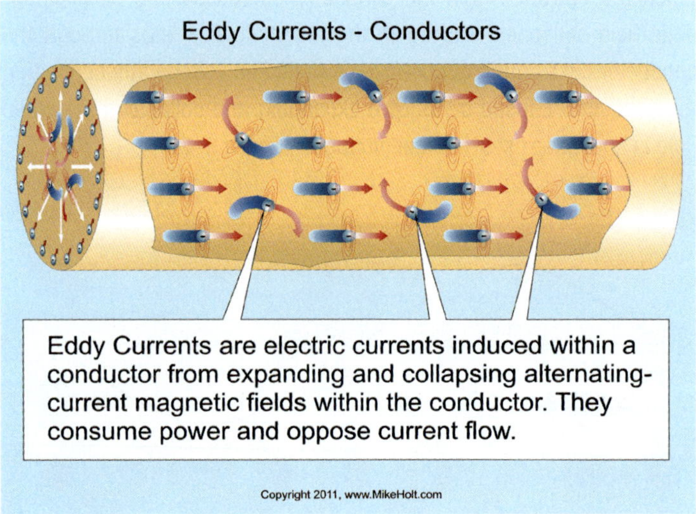

Figure 3–30

Skin Effect

The expanding and collapsing magnetic field from an alternating-current circuit induces voltage in the conductors that repels the flowing electrons toward the surface of the conductor. This results in a decrease of the effective conductor cross-sectional area because more current (electrons) flows near the conductor surface than at the center. The decreased usable conductor cross-sectional area causes an increased opposition to current flow. Figure 3–31

3.21 Conductor Shape

The physical shape of a conductor affects the amount of self-induced voltage within the conductor itself. When a conductor is coiled into adjacent loops (helically wound), it's called a "winding." The expanding and collapsing magnetic flux lines of alternating current flowing through the conductor loops interact and add together to create a strong overall magnetic field. As the combined flux lines expand and collapse they cut additional conductor loops, creating greater self-inductance in each loop. Figure 3–32

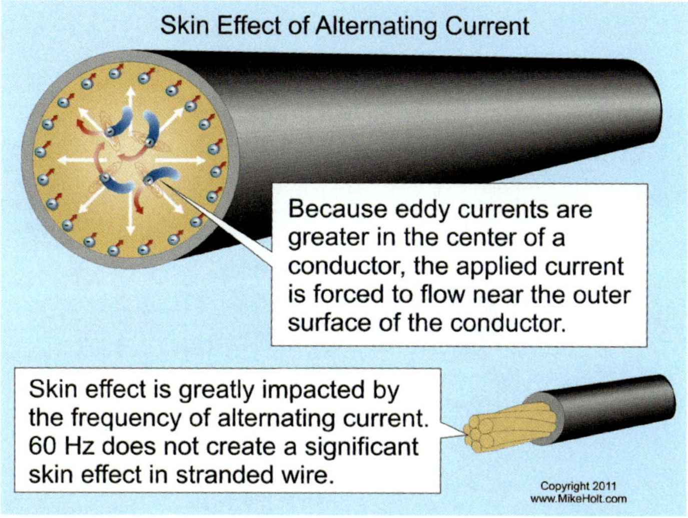

Figure 3–31

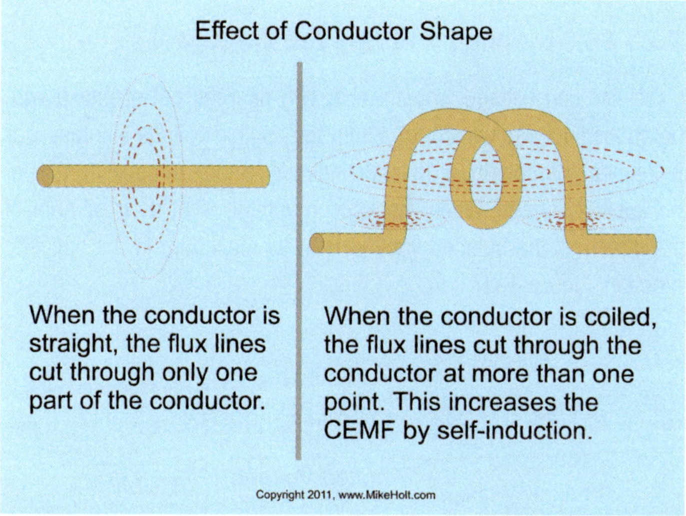

Figure 3–32

The amount of the self-induced voltage created within the winding is directly proportional to the current flow, the winding (conductor length and number of turns), and the frequency at which the expanding and collapsing magnetic fields cut through the conductors of the winding.

Current

The greater the winding current is, and the greater the alternating magnetic field, the greater the CEMF will be within the winding.

Winding

The greater the number of winding conductor loops (turns) and the closer the windings, the greater the CEMF produced within the winding will be. Figure 3–33

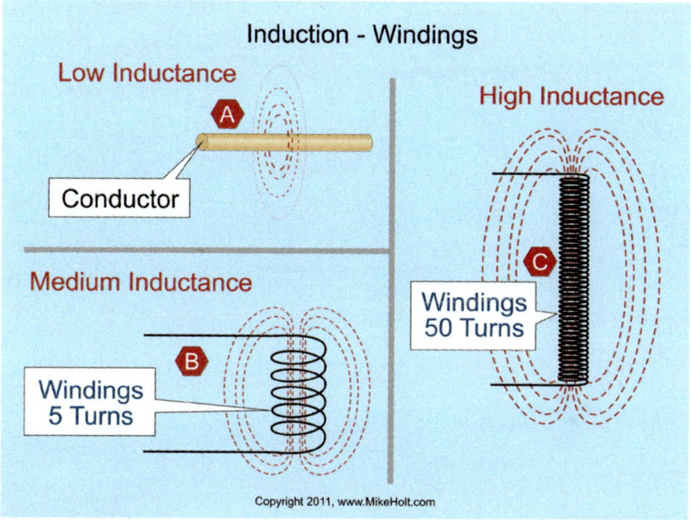

Figure 3–33

Frequency

Self-induced voltage depends upon the frequency at which the magnetic field expands or collapses. Therefore, the greater the frequency is, the greater the CEMF induced within the winding will be.

3.22 Magnetic Cores

The core material also has an effect on self-inductance in a winding (coil).

Core Material

Because an iron core provides an easy path for magnetic flux, windings with soft iron cores produce greater self-inductance than windings with an air core. Figure 3–34

Core Length

Longer cores result in fewer flux lines; this results in reduced self-inductance. If the core length is doubled, the CEMF decreases by 50 percent. Figure 3–35

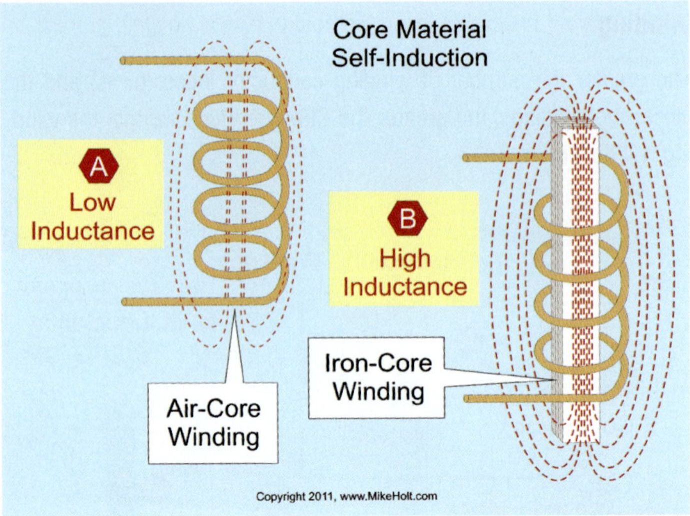

Figure 3–34

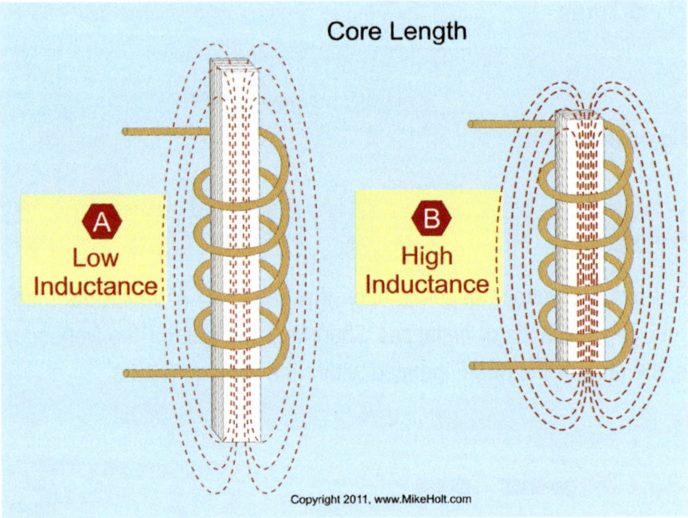

Figure 3–35

Core Area

Self-inductance (CEMF) is directly proportional to the cross-sectional area of the core, and inversely proportional to its length. This means that if the core area is doubled, the CEMF increases 200 percent. **Figure 3–36**

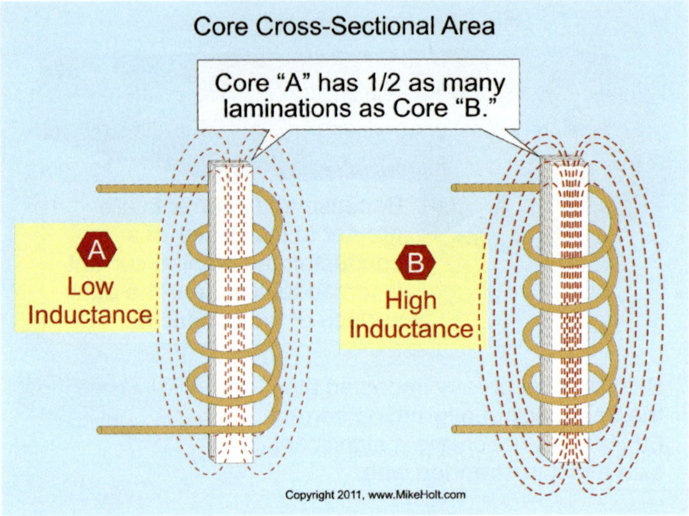

Figure 3–36

3.23 Self-Induced and Applied Voltage

A self-induced voltage waveform is 180 degrees out-of-phase with the applied voltage waveform. When the applied voltage increases, or decreases, the polarity of the self-induced voltage is opposite that of the applied voltage. When the applied voltage is at its maximum in one direction, the induced voltage is at its maximum in the opposite direction. **Figure 3–37**

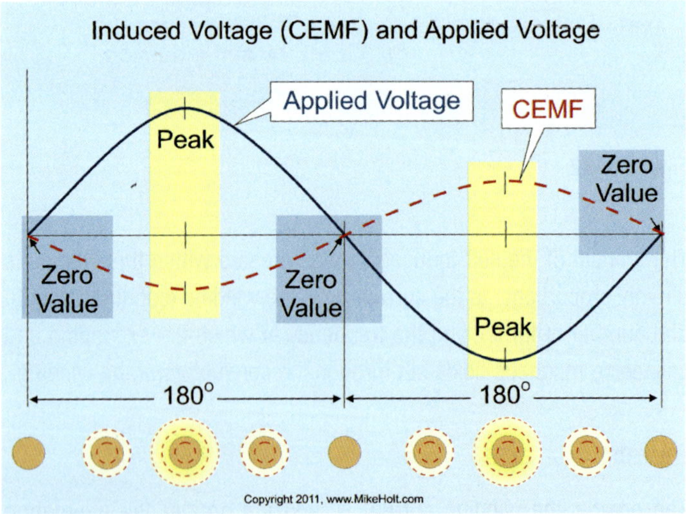

Figure 3–37

3.24 Inductive Reactance

Alternating-current flow in a conductor is limited by the conductor's resistance and self-induced voltage (CEMF). Self-induced voltage (CEMF) acts to oppose the change in current flowing in the conductor. This property is called "inductive reactance" and it's measured in ohms.

Inductive Reactance

Inductive reactance is abbreviated X_L and can be calculated by the following equation, where "f" is frequency with units of hertz, "L" is inductance with units of Henrys, and $\pi = 3.14$.

$$X_L = 2 \times \pi \times f \times L$$

Author's Comment: Just remember that alternating-current flow contains an additional element (reactance) that opposes the flow of electrons, besides conductor resistance.

3.25 Phase Relationship

In a purely inductive circuit, the CEMF waveform is 90 degrees out-of-phase with the circuit current waveform and 180 degrees out-of-phase with the applied voltage waveform. As a result, the applied voltage waveform leads the current waveform by 90 degrees. **Figure 3–38**

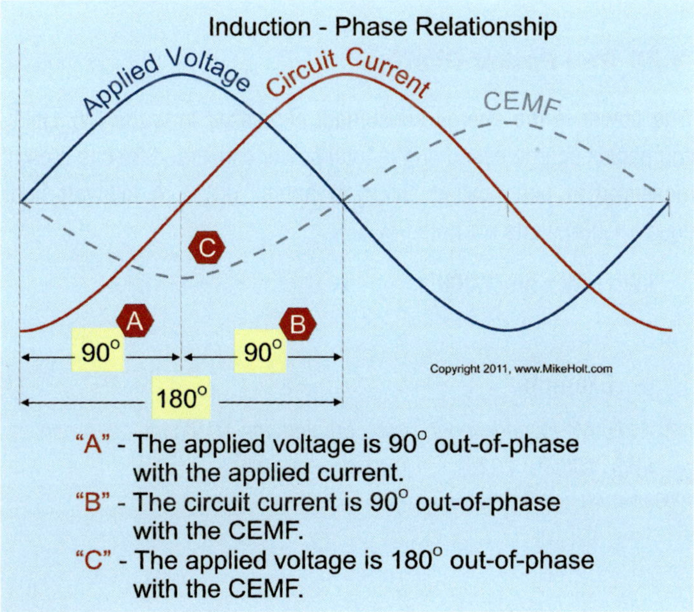

Figure 3–38

Author's Comment: Just remember that an alternating-current circuit contains inductive reactance because the voltage and current aren't in-phase with each other.

3.26 Uses of Induction

The major use of induction is in transformers, motors, and generators. **Figure 3–39**

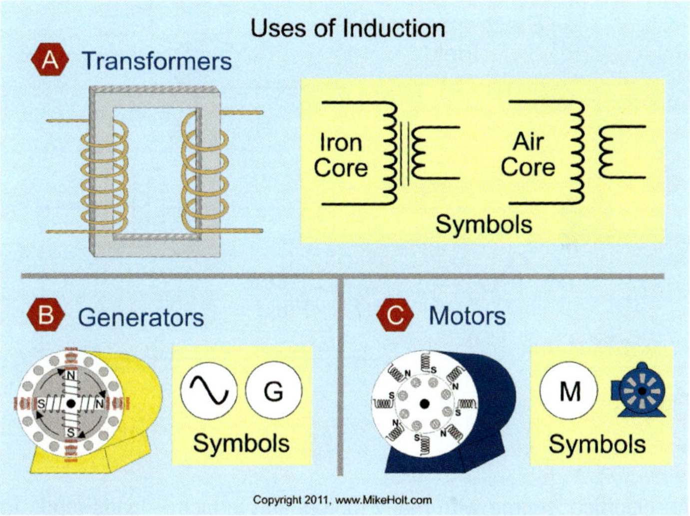

Figure 3–39

PART D—POWER FACTOR

Introduction

The out-of-phase relationship between voltage and current in alternating-current circuits that serve reactive loads such as motors often leads to a situation where more power is being delivered to the load than is actually used. This situation is very common in industrial plants where a large number of high horsepower motors are installed, resulting in a highly inductive load and a low power factor.

Electric utilities typically impose penalties in their rate structure for customers with low power factor, so electricians should understand power factor and how to correct it in order to procure utility bill savings for their customers or their employer.

Inductors and Capacitors

Inductors and capacitors are energy storage devices in alternating-current and direct-current circuits. Energy is stored in the electromagnetic field of an inductor and the electric field of a capacitor. Figure 3–40

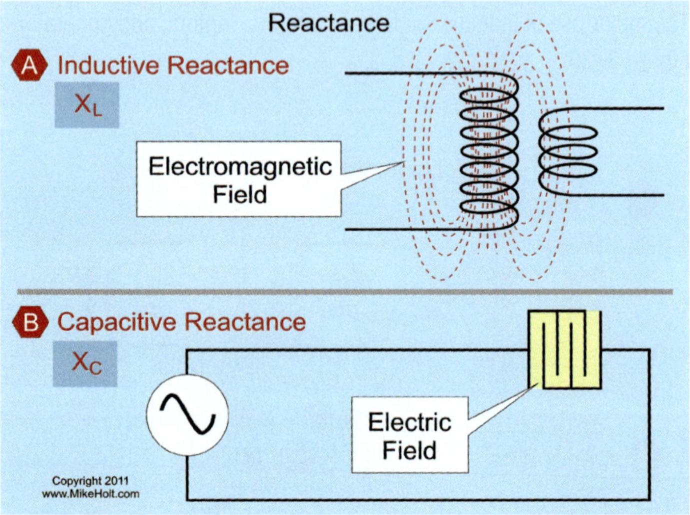

Figure 3–40

An electrical source with many motors and inductive loads tends to have a high amount of inductive reactance and a low power factor. Adding capacitors will help counteract high inductance and increase the power factor.

3.27 Apparent Power (Volt-Amperes)

If you measure voltage and current in an inductive or capacitive circuit, and multiply them together, the product is the apparent power supplied to the circuit by the source. Apparent power is expressed in volt-amperes (VA). Circuits and equipment must be sized to the circuit VA load.

Apparent Power = Volts x Amperes

► **Example**

Question: *What's the apparent power in VA of a 1 hp, 115V motor that has a full-load current rating of 16A?* **Figure 3–41**

(a) 1,320 VA *(b) 1,840 VA* *(c) 1,920 VA* *(d) 2,400 VA*

Answer: *(b) 1,840 VA*

VA = E x I

VA = 115V x 16A

VA = 1,840 VA

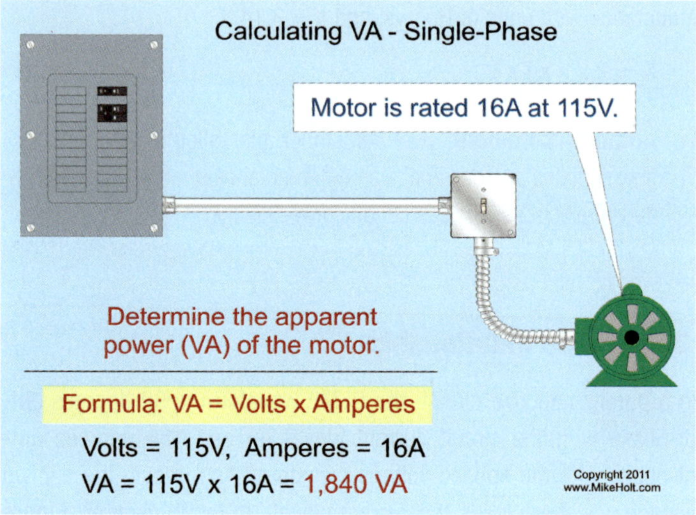

Figure 3–41

3.28 True Power (Watts)

True power is the energy consumed, expressed in watts (W). Utility companies charge based on the total power consumed for one month, measured in units called "kilowatt hours" (kWh). A kilowatt hour equals 1,000 watts x 1 hour.

kWh = W x hrs/1,000

► **Example**

A 100W incandescent lamp, burning for 10 hours uses one kWh: 100W x 10 hrs = 1,000 Wh = 1 kWh

Direct Current

To determine the true power (W) consumed by a direct-current circuit, multiply the volts (E) by the amperes (I):

W = E x I

Alternating Current

In an alternating-current circuit, true power (W) is determined by multiplying the circuit volts (E), by the amperes (I), times the power factor (PF):

W = E x I x PF

3.29 Power Factor

Alternating-current inductive or capacitive reactive loads cause the voltage and current sine waves to be out-of-phase with each other. Power factor measures how far the current waveform is out-of-phase with the voltage waveform. Figure 3–42

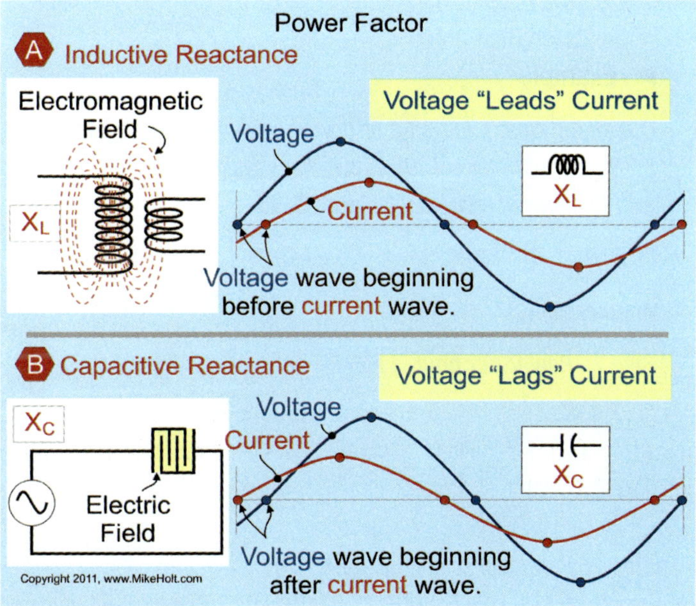

Figure 3–42

Power factor is defined as a ratio of true power (W) to apparent power, which is expressed in volt-amperes (VA):

Power Factor (PF) = True Power (W)/Apparent Power (VA)

3.30 Unity Power Factor

When an alternating-current circuit supplies power to a purely resistive load, such as incandescent lighting or heating elements, the circuit voltage and current are in-phase with each other.

Because the voltage and current reach their zero and peak values at the same time, there's no leading or lagging of the voltage to the current. Therefore, the power factor of the load is 100 percent (or 1.00), and this condition is called "unity power factor." Figure 3–43

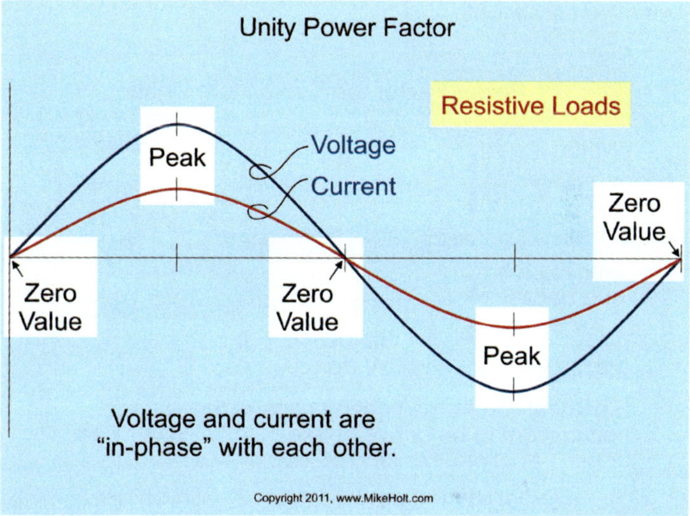

Figure 3–43

3.31 Power Factor Formulas

The relationship between true power (Watts), apparent power (VA), and power factor can be shown as:

Power Factor (PF) = True Power (Watts)/Apparent Power (VA)
Apparent Power (VA) = True Power (W)/Power Factor (PF)
True Power (Watts) = Apparent Power (VA) x Power Factor (PF)

► Power Factor (PF) Example

Question: *Assuming 100 percent efficiency, what's the power factor for each ballast rated 0.75A at 120V for a 2 x 4 fixture containing four 40W lamps (two lamps per ballast)?* **Figure 3–44**

(a) 69% (b) 75% (c) 89% (d) 95%

Answer: *(c) 89%*

PF = W/VA

PF = 80W/(0.75A x 120V)

PF = 80W/(90VA)

PF = 0.888 or 89%

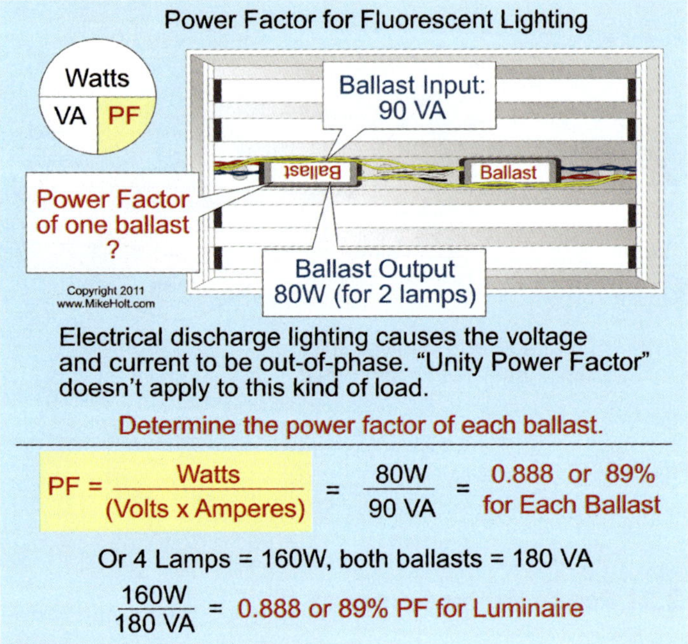

Figure 3–44

► Apparent Power (VA) Example

Question: *What's the apparent power in VA of a fluorescent ballast that has a power factor of 89 percent when it's connected to two 40W lamps?*

(a) 70W (b) 80 VA (c) 90 VA (d) 100W

Answer: *(c) 90 VA*

VA = W/PF

VA = 80W/0.89 PF

VA = 89.90 VA

Note: *Apparent power is expressed in VA; therefore, neither (a) nor (d) can be the correct answer.*

► True Power (Watts) Example

Question: *What's the true power of a 16A load rated 120V, with a power factor of 85 percent?*

(a) 1,632W (b) 1,800W (c) 1,920W (d) 2,400W

Answer: (a) 1,632W

Watts = VA x PF

Watts = (120V x 16A) x 0.85 PF

Watts = 1,632W

True power (watts) is equal to volts times amperes times power factor.

True power is always equal to or less than apparent power and is expressed in watts or kilowatts.

3.32 Cost of True Power

The cost of electrical power is based on the true power consumed during a month, multiplied by the cost per kWh (1,000W for a period of one hour).

► Example

Question: *What's the cost of power consumed per month (at $0.09 per kWh) for a 120V circuit that's faulted to a ground rod with 25 ohms of resistance?* **Figure 3–45**

(a) $10 (b) $25 (c) $37 (d) $55

Answer: *(c) $37*

Step 1: ***Power per hour = E2/R***

E = 120V

R = 25 ohms

P = (120V x 120V)/25 ohms

P = 576W

Step 2: Power consumed per day:

576W x 24 hours = 13,824Wh or 13.824 kWh

Step 3: Power consumed in 30 days:

13.824 kWh x 30 days = 415 kWh

Step 4: Cost of power at $0.09 per kWh:

415 kWh x $0.09 = $37.33

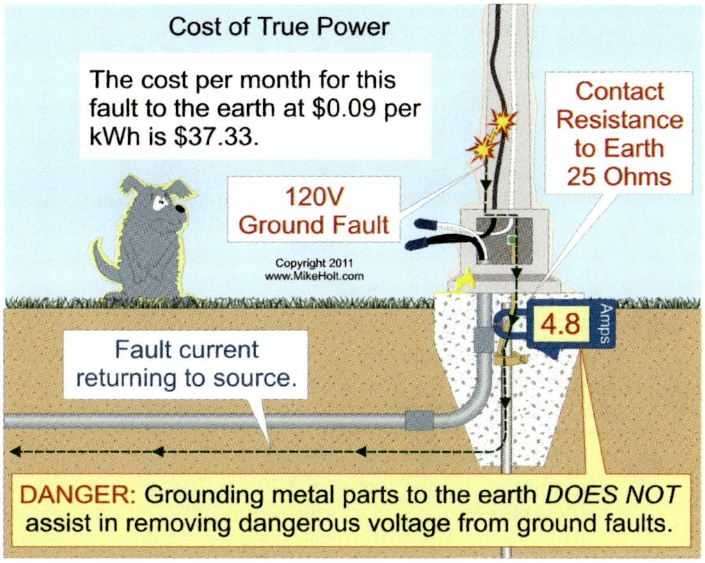

Figure 3–45

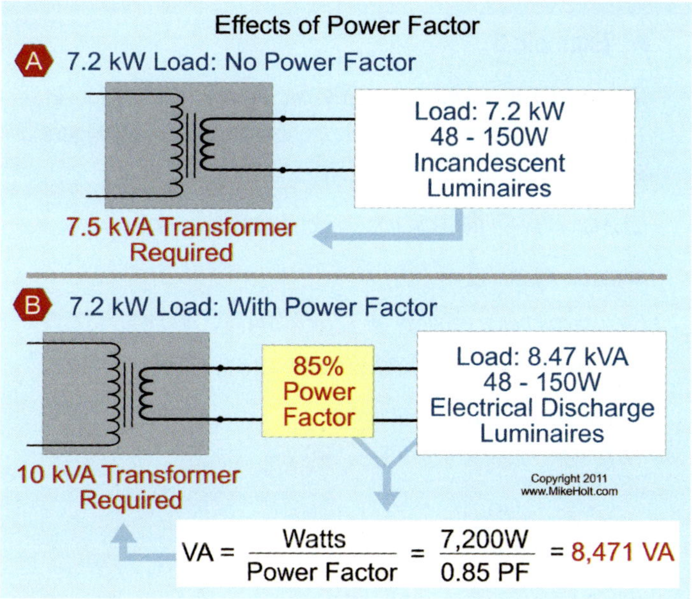

Figure 3–46

3.33 Effects of Power Factor

Apparent power (VA) is used for sizing circuits and equipment. Because the VA of the load is greater than the watts of the load, fewer loads can be supplied by each branch circuit. More circuits and panels, and larger transformers may be required.

▶ Example 1

Question: *What size transformer is required for 48, 150W incandescent luminaires (noncontinuous load)?* **Figure 3–46A**

(a) 3 kVA *(b) 5 kVA* *(c) 7.50 kVA* *(d) 10 kVA*

Answer: *(c) 7.50 kVA*

kVA = (48 Fixtures x 150W)/1,000
kVA = 7,200W/1,000
kVA = 7.20 kVA

Author's Comment: Transformers are always sized based on kVA, not kW because transformers are an inductive load which results in apparent power. Apparent power is measured in kVA, while kW is used only for true power such as resistive loads.

▶ Example 2

Question: *What size transformer is required for 48, 150W electric discharge luminaires that have a power factor of 85 percent (noncontinuous load)?* **Figure 3–46B**

(a) 3 kVA *(b) 5 kVA* *(c) 7.50 kVA* *(d) 10 kVA*

Answer: *(d) 10 kVA*

kW = (48 fixtures x 150W)/1,000
kW = 7,200W/1,000
kW = 7.20 kW

Apparent Power = kW/PF
Apparent Power = 7.20 kW/0.85 PF
Apparent Power = 8.47 kVA

Transformers are sized for apparent power (kVA), not true power.

► Example 3

Question: *How many 20A, 120V circuits are required for 48, 150W incandescent luminaires (noncontinuous load)?* **Figure 3–47A**

(a) 2 circuits (b) 3 circuits (c) 4 circuits (d) 5 circuits

Answer: *(b) 3 circuits*

Each circuit has a capacity of: 120V x 20A = 2,400 VA

Each circuit can have: 2,400W/150W = 16 luminaires

The number of circuits required is:
48 luminaires/16 luminaires = 3 circuits

► Example 4

Question: *How many 20A, 120V circuits are required for 48, 150W electric discharge luminaires (noncontinuous load) that have a power factor of 85 percent?* **Figure 3–47B**

(a) 4 circuits (b) 6 circuits (c) 8 circuits (d) 12 circuits

Answer: *(a) 4 circuits*

Circuits are loaded according to VA, not watts!

VA of each luminaire equals:

VA = Watts/PF
VA = 150W/0.85 PF
VA = 176 VA

Each circuit has a capacity of: 120V x 20A = 2,400 VA
Each circuit can have: 2,400 VA/176 VA = 13 luminaires

The number of circuits required is:
48 luminaires/13 luminaires per circuit = 4 circuits

If the building has 480 luminaires, 40 circuits will be needed instead of 30 and the transformer will have to be rated at least 100 kVA, instead of 75 kVA.

Author's Comment: The VA and/or amperage rating is commonly marked on the nameplate or ballast of inductive luminaires for use in branch circuit sizing. The circuit isn't based on the lamp wattage rating alone. [220.14(D)]

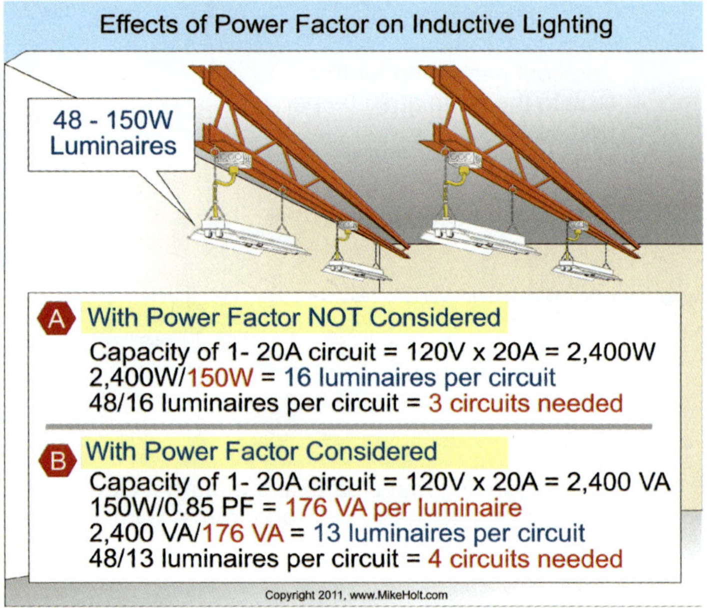

Figure 3–47

PART E—EFFICIENCY

Introduction

Electricity is used because of its convenience in transferring energy to operate lighting, heating, controls, motors, and so on. In this transfer of energy, there are power losses (waste) in the conductors, the power supply, and the load itself. The total amount of power loss in watts is indicated by the term "efficiency."

Efficiency describes how much input energy is used for its intended useful purpose, and is expressed as a ratio of output true power to input true power. Naturally, the output power can never be greater than the input power. **Figure 3–48**

If equipment is rated at 100 percent efficiency (there is none), that means that 100 percent of the input energy is consumed for its intended useful purpose.

When equipment is rated at 90 percent efficiency, only 90 percent of the input power is used for its intended useful purpose. Another way of saying this is that 10 percent of the input power is wasted.

Power Loss

When energy isn't used for its intended purpose, this condition is called "power loss." Conductor resistance, mechanical friction, and other factors can contribute to increased power losses, or a reduced efficiency rating.

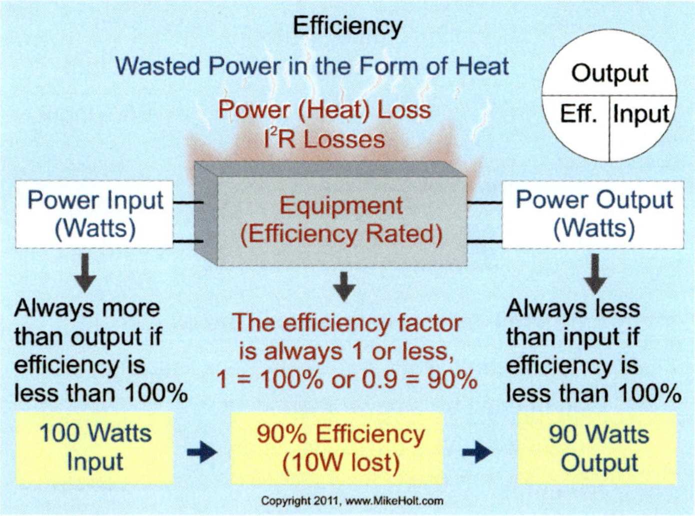

Figure 3–48

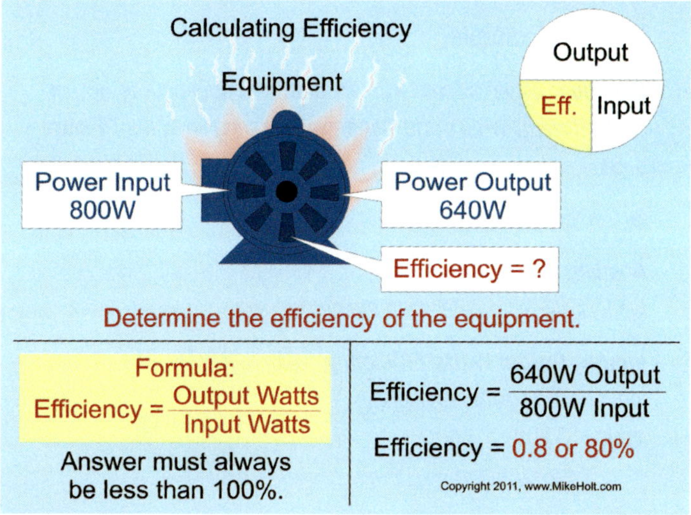

Figure 3–49

3.34 Efficiency Formulas

The formulas that are often used for efficiency calculations include:

Efficiency = Output Watts/Input Watts
Input Watts = Output Watts/Efficiency
Output Watts = Input Watts x Efficiency

▶ Efficiency Example 1

Question: *If the output of a load is 640W and the input is 800W, what's the efficiency of the equipment?* **Figure 3–49**

(a) 60% *(b) 70%* *(c) 80%* *(d) 100%*

Answer: *(c) 80%*
Efficiency is always less than 100%.

Efficiency = Output Watts/Input Watts
Efficiency = 640W/800W
Efficiency = 0.80 or 80%

▶ Efficiency Example 2

Question: *If the output of a 5 hp direct-current motor is 3,730W (746W x 5) and the input is 4,800W (40A x 120V), what's the efficiency of the motor?* **Figure 3–50**

(a) 60% *(b) 78%* *(c) 80%* *(d) 100%*

Answer: *(b) 78%*

Efficiency = Output Watts/Input Watts
Efficiency = 3,730W/4,800W
Efficiency = 0.777 or 77.70%

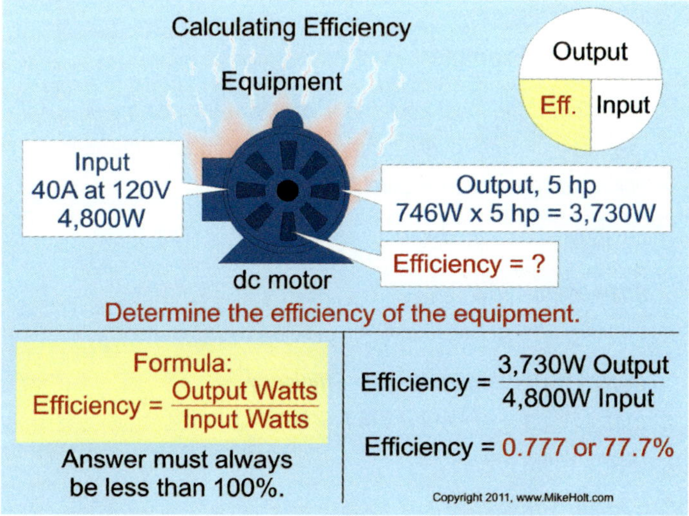

Figure 3–50

▶ Input Example

Question: *If the output is 250W and the equipment is 88 percent efficient, what's the input power rating in watts?* **Figure 3–51**

(a) 200W *(b) 250W* *(c) 285W* *(d) 325W*

Answer: *(c) 285W*

Input is always greater than the output.

Input = Output Watts/Efficiency

Input = 250W/0.88 Efficiency

Input = 284W

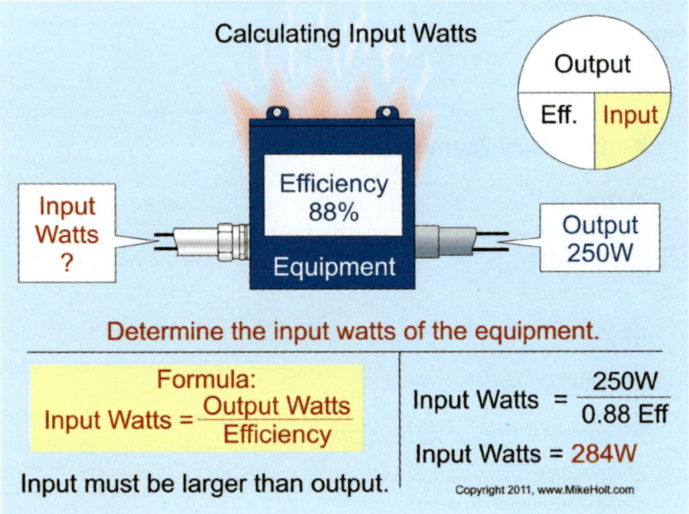

Figure 3–51

▶ Output Example

Question: *If the input power to a load is 479W and the equipment is rated at 87.60 percent efficiency, what's the output power rating in watts?* **Figure 3–52**

(a) 350W *(b) 420W* *(c) 500W* *(d) 550W*

Answer: *(b) 420W*

Output is always less than input.

Output Watts = Input Watts x Efficiency

Output Watts = 479W x 0.876 Efficiency

Output Watts = 419.60W

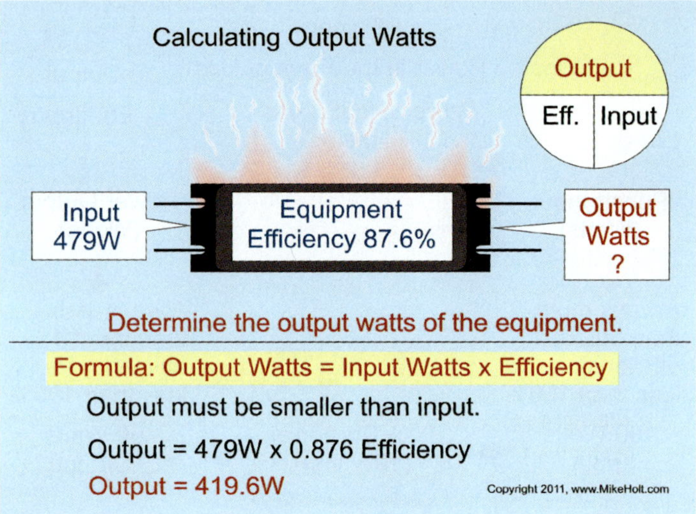

Figure 3–52

CONCLUSION TO UNIT 3—UNDERSTANDING ALTERNATING CURRENT

You now have a solid understanding of the basic concepts of alternating current. You know where it comes from and why it's used, and you understand the various properties that characterize the current in a given circuit or system.

Your knowledge of what lead and lag mean will help you understand power factor. Remember that three-phase alternating current has three waveforms that, when conditions are perfect, have sinusoidal shapes and are 120 degrees out-of-phase with each other.

You now understand what a capacitor is, some of its uses, and why it works the way it does. You've also learned the equation for capacitive reactance. Capacitors have many uses, not all of which have been discussed here. For example, capacitors are often combined in circuits with inductors to form "tank circuits" in devices called "power conditioners."

Induction, like capacitance and impedance, is one of the fundamental properties of alternating-current circuits. Now that you understand inductance, you're ready to learn the basic theory behind three important types of inductive devices—motors, generators, and transformers.

You understand apparent power, true power, power factor, and unity power factor, and you know that it's possible to use capacitors to correct power factor.

You know that no circuit is 100 percent efficient—all circuits and equipment have some power loss. The ability to calculate efficiency and power loss is now part of your skill set. While you don't normally have to use this skill, you may find it useful when troubleshooting or when deciding whether to replace old equipment.

UNIT
3 Practice Questions

PRACTICE QUESTIONS FOR UNIT 3—UNDERSTANDING ALTERNATING CURRENT

PART A—UNDERSTANDING ALTERNATING CURRENT

3.1 Current Flow

1. The movement of electrons themselves doesn't produce any useful work. It's the effects that the moving electrons have on the loads through which they flow that are important.

(a) True
(b) False

3.2 Why Alternating Current is Used

2. Alternating current is primarily used because it can be transmitted inexpensively due to the ability to easily transform alternating-current for high-voltage transmission.

(a) True
(b) False

3.3 How Alternating Current is Produced

3. When a magnetic field moves through a coil of wire, the lines of force of the magnetic field cause the electrons in the wire to flow in a specific direction. When the magnetic field moves in the opposite direction, electrons in the wire flow in the opposite direction.

(a) True
(b) False

3.4 Alternating-Current Generator

4. A simple alternating-current generator consists of a loop of wire rotating across the lines of force between the opposite poles of a magnet.

(a) True
(b) False

5. In alternating-current generators that produce large quantities of electricity, the conductor coils are stationary and the magnetic field revolves within the coils.

(a) True
(b) False

6. The output voltage of a generator depends upon the ______.

(a) number of turns of wire
(b) strength of the magnetic field
(c) speed at which the coil rotates
(d) all of these

3.5 Waveform

7. A waveform image is used to display the level and direction of current, but not voltage.

(a) True
(b) False

8. The waveform for alternating-current circuits displays the level and direction of the current and voltage for every instant of time for one full revolution of the rotor.

(a) True
(b) False

3.6 Sine Wave

9. A ______ wave is a waveform that's symmetrical with positive above and negative below the zero reference level.

(a) nonsinusoidal
(b) nonsymmetrical
(c) sine
(d) any of these

3.7 Frequency

10. The number of complete waveforms in one second is called the "frequency." Frequency is expressed as _____ or cycles per second.

(a) degrees
(b) a sine wave
(c) phase
(d) Hertz

3.8 Phase

11. The term "Phase" is used to indicate the time or degree relationship between two waveforms, such as voltage-to-current or voltage-to-voltage.

(a) True
(b) False

12. In a purely resistive alternating-current circuit, the current and voltage are _____. This means that they both reach their zero and peak values at the same time.

(a) in-phase
(b) out-of-phase
(c) a or b
(d) none of these

3.9 Degrees

13. Phase differences are expressed in degrees; one full waveform is equal to _____.

(a) 90°
(b) 120°
(c) 180°
(d) 360°

14. A three-phase generator has each of its windings out-of-phase with each other by _____.

(a) 90°
(b) 120°
(c) 180°
(d) 360°

15. Phase differences are expressed in _____.

(a) sine waves
(b) phases
(c) Hertz
(d) degrees

3.10 Lead or Lag

16. When describing the relationship between voltage and current waveforms, if the _____ waveform finishes first, then it can be said that the current is lagging.

(a) current
(b) resistance
(c) voltage
(d) none of these

17. If the voltage waveform finishes before the current waveform, the voltage is said to _____ the current waveform.

(a) lead
(b) lag
(c) be in-phase with
(d) none of these

18. When the current waveform finishes before the voltage waveform, the voltage _____ the current waveform.

(a) leads
(b) lags
(c) is in-phase with
(d) none of these

3.11 Values of Alternating Current

19. _____ is the value of the voltage or current at a moment of time.

(a) "Peak"
(b) "Root-mean-square"
(c) "Effective"
(d) "Instantaneous"

20. The peak value is equal to the effective value ______.

(a) times 0.707
(b) times 1.41
(c) divided by 1.41
(d) times 0.58

21. ______ is the maximum value that ac current or voltage reaches, both for positive and negative polarity.

(a) "Peak"
(b) "Root-mean-square"
(c) "Instantaneous"
(d) none of these

22. The effective value is equal to the peak value ______.

(a) times 0.707
(b) times 1.41
(c) divided by 2
(d) times 0.58

23. Effective alternating-current voltage or effective alternating current is the equivalent value of direct-current voltage or direct current that will produce the same amount of heat in a resistor.

(a) True
(b) False

24. ______ describes the steps necessary to determine the effective voltage or current value.

(a) "Peak"
(b) "Root-mean-square"
(c) "Instantaneous"
(d) none of these

PART B—CAPACITANCE

Introduction

25. ______ is a property of an electrical circuit that enables it to store electrical energy by means of an electric field and to release this energy at a later time.

(a) "Capacitance"
(b) "Induction"
(c) "Self-induction"
(d) none of these

26. A half-wave rectifier can be used to convert alternating-current voltage into direct-current voltage allowing it to continuously charge a capacitor during both alternations of the alternating-current sine wave.

(a) True
(b) False

3.12 Charged Capacitor

27. When a capacitor has a potential difference between the plates, it's said to be ______. One plate has an excess of free electrons, and the other plate has a lack of them.

(a) induced
(b) charged
(c) discharged
(d) shorted

3.13 Electrical Field

28. If a capacitor is overcharged, the electrons from the negative plate could be pulled through the insulation to the positive plate. The capacitor is said to have ______.

(a) charged
(b) discharged
(c) been induced
(d) shorted

3.14 Discharging a Capacitor

29. To discharge a capacitor, all that's required is a(n) ______ path between the terminals of the capacitor. The free electrons on the negative plate then flow through the external circuit to the positive plate.

    (a) conductive
    (b) insulating
    (c) open
    (d) all of these

30. Even when power is removed from the circuit, capacitors can store large amounts of energy for a long period of time, and can discharge and arc if inadvertently shorted or grounded out.

    (a) True
    (b) False

3.15 Determining Capacitance

31. Factors that determine the capacitance of a capacitor are the ______.

    (a) surface area of the plates
    (b) distance between the plates
    (c) dielectric between the plates
    (d) all of these

3.16 Uses of Capacitors

32. Capacitors are used to start single-phase alternating-current motors and to prevent arcing across the contacts of electric switches.

    (a) True
    (b) False

3.17 Phase Relationship

33. A capacitor is a device that resists changes in current. Because a capacitor introduces reactance to the circuit, it shifts the current waveform to ______.

    (a) lead the applied voltage by 90°
    (b) lag the applied voltage by 90°
    (c) lead the applied voltage by 180°
    (d) lag the applied voltage by 180°

34. The opposition offered to the flow of alternating-current by a capacitor is called capacitive reactance, which is expressed in ohms and abbreviated ______.

    (a) X_C
    (b) X_L
    (c) Z
    (d) none of these

PART C—INDUCTION

Introduction

35. When electrons move, the magnetic fields of the individual electrons combine to produce an overall magnetic field. The greater the current flow, the greater the overall magnetic field around the conductor.

    (a) True
    (b) False

36. The movement of electrons caused by an external magnetic field is called ______ current, and the associated potential that's established is called ______ voltage.

    (a) circuit
    (b) applied
    (c) induced
    (d) none of these

37. In order to induce voltage, relative motion is required between a conductor and a ______ field. This is the basis of the generator and transformer.

    (a) voltage
    (b) current
    (c) magnetic
    (d) none of these

3.18 Self-Induction

38. As the alternating-current through a conductor increases, an expanding and collapsing electromagnetic field through the conductor induces a voltage within the conductor. This is known as ______ voltage.

    (a) applied
    (b) circuit
    (c) self-induced
    (d) none of these

3.19 Induced Voltage and Applied Current

39. The induced voltage in a conductor carrying alternating current opposes the change in current flowing through the conductor. The induced voltage that opposes the current flow is called "______."

    (a) CEMF
    (b) counter-electromotive force
    (c) back-EMF
    (d) all of these

40. The waveform of the CEMF is ______ out-of-phase with the applied voltage.

    (a) 90°
    (b) 120°
    (c) 180°
    (d) 360°

41. When alternating current increases, the polarity of the CEMF within the conductor tries to prevent the current from increasing.

    (a) True
    (b) False

42. When alternating current decreases, the polarity of the induced voltage within the conductor tries to prevent the current from decreasing.

    (a) True
    (b) False

3.20 Conductor Alternating-Current Resistance

43. In direct-current circuits, the only property that opposes current flow is ______.

    (a) impedance
    (b) reactance
    (c) resistance
    (d) none of these

44. Conductor resistance is directly proportional to the conductor's length and cross-sectional area.

    (a) True
    (b) False

45. For alternating-current circuits, the ______ of a conductor oppose(s) the current flow in the circuit.

    (a) eddy currents
    (b) skin effect
    (c) resistance
    (d) all of these

46. Eddy currents are small independent currents induced within the conductor because of direct current.

    (a) True
    (b) False

47. The expanding and collapsing magnetic field within the conductor induces a voltage in the conductors (CEMF) that repels the flowing electrons toward the surface of the conductor. This is called "______."

    (a) eddy currents
    (b) induced voltage
    (c) impedance
    (d) skin effect

3.21 Conductor Shape

48. The magnitude of self-induced voltage within a winding is directly proportional to the current flow, the winding, and the frequency at which magnetic fields cut through the winding.

(a) True
(b) False

3.22 Magnetic Cores

49. Because an iron core provides an easy path for magnetic flux, windings with soft iron cores produce a greater self-inductance than windings with air cores.

(a) True
(b) False

3.23 Self-Induced and Applied Voltage

50. Self-induced voltage is 180° out-of-phase with the ______. When the applied voltage is at its maximum in one direction, the induced voltage is at its maximum in the opposite direction.

(a) applied current
(b) applied voltage
(c) induced voltage
(d) induced current

3.24 Inductive Reactance

51. Self-induced voltage opposes the change in current flowing in the conductor. This is called "inductive reactance" and is abbreviated ______.

(a) X_L
(b) X_C
(c) Z
(d) none of these

3.25 Phase Relationship

52. In a purely inductive circuit, the CEMF waveform is ______ out-of-phase with the applied voltage waveform.

(a) 90°
(b) 120°
(c) 180°
(d) 360°

53. In an inductive circuit, the CEMF waveform is 90° out-of-phase with the current waveform and 180° out-of-phase with the applied voltage waveform, making the voltage waveform lead the current waveform by ______.

(a) 90°
(b) 120°
(c) 180°
(d) 360°

3.26 Uses of Induction

54. A common practical use of induction is for ______.

(a) motors
(b) transformers
(c) generators
(d) all of these

PART D—POWER FACTOR

Introduction

55. Energy is stored in the electromagnetic field of an inductor and the electric field of a capacitor.

(a) True
(b) False

3.27 Apparent Power (Volt-Amperes)

56. If you measure voltage and current in an inductive or capacitive circuit and then multiply them together, you obtain the circuit's ______.

(a) true power
(b) power factor
(c) apparent power
(d) none of these

3.28 True Power (Watts)

57. To determine the true power consumed by a direct-current circuit, multiply the volts by the amperes.

(a) True
(b) False

58. The true power of an alternating-current circuit equals volts times amperes.

(a) True
(b) False

3.29 Power Factor

59. Alternating-current inductive or capacitive reactive loads cause the voltage and current to be in-phase with each other.

(a) True
(b) False

60. Power factor is a measurement of how far the current is out-of-phase with the voltage.

(a) True
(b) False

3.30 Unity Power Factor

61. When an alternating-current circuit supplies power to a purely ______ load, the circuit voltage and current are in-phase with each other. This condition is called "Unity Power Factor."

(a) capacitive
(b) inductive
(c) resistive
(d) any of these

3.32 Cost of True Power

62. What does it cost per year (at $0.09 per kWh) for ten 150W recessed luminaires to operate if they're turned on for six hours a day?

(a) $150
(b) $300
(c) $500
(d) $800

3.33 Effects of Power Factor

63. Because apparent power (VA) is greater than true power (W), more loads can be placed on a circuit, so fewer circuits and panels, and smaller transformers might be required.

(a) True
(b) False

64. When sizing circuits or equipment, always size the circuit components and transformers according to the apparent power (VA), not the true power (W).

(a) True
(b) False

65. What's the true power of a 10A circuit operating at 120V with unity power factor?

(a) 1,200 VA
(b) 2,400 VA
(c) 1,200W
(d) 2,400W

66. What size transformer is required for a 100A, 240V, single-phase noncontinuous load with unity power factor?

(a) 15 kVA
(b) 25 kVA
(c) 37.50 kVA
(d) 50 kVA

67. What size transformer is required for a 100A, 240V, single-phase noncontinuous load that has a power factor of 85 percent?

(a) 15 kVA
(b) 25 kVA
(c) 37.50 kVA
(d) 50 kVA

68. How many 20A, 120V circuits are required for forty-two, 300W incandescent luminaires (noncontinuous load)?

(a) 3 circuits
(b) 4 circuits
(c) 5 circuits
(d) 6 circuits

69. How many 20A, 120V circuits are required for forty-two, 300W HID luminaires (assume this is a noncontinuous inductive load) that have a power factor of 85 percent?

(a) 5 circuits
(b) 6 circuits
(c) 7 circuits
(d) 8 circuits

PART E—EFFICIENCY

Introduction

70. In the transfer of electrical energy, there are power losses in the conductors, the power supply, and the load itself.

(a) True
(b) False

71. Efficiency describes how much input energy is used for its intended purpose.

(a) True
(b) False

3.34 Efficiency Formulas

72. If the output power is 1,320W and the input power is 1,800W, what's the efficiency of the equipment?

(a) 62%
(b) 73%
(c) 80%
(d) 100%

73. If the input power of a 1 hp direct-current motor is 1,128W and the output power is 746W, what's the efficiency of the motor?

(a) 66%
(b) 74%
(c) 87%
(d) 100%

74. If the output power is 1,600W and the equipment is 88 percent efficient, what are the input amperes at 120V?

(a) 10A
(b) 15A
(c) 20A
(d) 25A

75. If a transformer is 97 percent efficient, for every 1 kW input, there will be ______ output.

(a) 970W
(b) 1,000W
(c) 1,030W
(d) 1,200W

UNIT
3 Challenge Questions

CHALLENGE QUESTIONS FOR UNIT 3—UNDERSTANDING ALTERNATING CURRENT

PART A—UNDERSTANDING ALTERNATING CURRENT

3.2 Why Alternating Current is Used

1. Alternating current is primarily used because it can be transmitted inexpensively due to the ease of transforming to high-transmission voltage and then transforming this voltage back to low-distribution voltage.

   (a) True
   (b) False

2. One of the advantages of a higher-voltage system as compared to a lower-voltage system (for the same wattage loads) is ______.

   (a) reduced voltage drop
   (b) reduced power use
   (c) large currents
   (d) lower electrical pressure

3. The advantage of alternating-current over direct-current is that alternating-current provides for ______.

   (a) better speed control
   (b) ease of voltage variation
   (c) lower resistance at high currents
   (d) none of these

3.5 Waveform

4. A waveform represents ______.

   (a) the magnitude and direction of current or voltage
   (b) how current or voltage can vary with time
   (c) how output voltage can vary with the generator armature
   (d) all of these

3.7 Frequency

5. The frequency of an alternating-current waveform is the number of times the current or voltage goes through 360 degrees in ______.

   (a) 1⁄10 second
   (b) 1 second
   (c) 5 seconds
   (d) 60 seconds

6. How much time does it take for 60 Hz alternating-current to travel through 180 degrees?

   (a) 1⁄120 second
   (b) 1⁄90 second
   (c) 1⁄80 second
   (d) 1⁄40 second

3.11 Values of Alternating Current

7. The heating effects of 10A of alternating current as compared to 10A of direct current are ______.

   (a) the same
   (b) less
   (c) greater
   (d) none of these

8. If the peak value of an alternating-current system is 50A, the RMS value will be approximately ______.

   (a) 25A
   (b) 30A
   (c) 35A
   (d) 40A

9. The maximum value of 120V direct current is equal to the peak value of an equivalent 120V of alternating current.

   (a) True
   (b) False

10. 120V is the reading shown on a voltmeter. This is an indication of the _____ value of the voltage source.

(a) average
(b) peak
(c) effective
(d) instantaneous

PART B—CAPACITANCE

3.15 Determining Capacitance

11. The insulating material between the surface plates of a capacitor is called the "_____."

(a) inhibitor
(b) electrolyte
(c) dielectric
(d) regulator

12. If three capacitors are to be connected together, which connection will provide the highest capacitance?

(a) Connect all three in series.
(b) Connect all three in parallel.
(c) Connect the capacitors in a combination of series and parallel.
(d) none of these

3.16 Uses of Capacitors

13. In a circuit that has only capacitive reactance (X_C), the voltage and current are said to be out-of-phase to each other because the voltage _____.

(a) leads the current by 90°
(b) lags the current by 90°
(c) leads the current
(d) none of these

3.17 Phase Relationship

14. Capacitive reactance is measured in _____.

(a) ohms
(b) volts
(c) watts
(d) Henrys

PART C—INDUCTION

15. Inductive reactance is abbreviated as _____.

(a) I^2R
(b) LX
(c) XL
(d) Z

16. Inductive reactance is measured in _____.

(a) farads
(b) watts
(c) ohms
(d) coulombs

3.21 Conductor Shape

17. The total opposition to current flow in an alternating-current circuit is expressed in ohms and is called "_____."

(a) impedance
(b) conductance
(c) reluctance
(d) none of these

18. Impedance is present in _____ type circuit(s).

(a) resistance
(b) direct-current
(c) alternating-current
(d) none of these

19. Conductor resistance to alternating-current flow is ______ the resistance to direct current.

(a) higher than
(b) lower than
(c) the same as
(d) none of these

PART D—POWER FACTOR

3.28 True Power (Watts)

20. If you multiply the voltage by the current in an inductive or capacitive circuit, the answer will be the ______ of the circuit.

(a) watts
(b) true power
(c) apparent power
(d) all of these

21. The apparent power of a 19.20A, 120V load is ______.

(a) 0.233 kVA
(b) 1.23 kVA
(c) 2.30 kVA
(d) 230 kVA

3.29 Power Factor

22. A wattmeter is connected in ______ in the circuit.

(a) series
(b) parallel
(c) series-parallel
(d) none of these

23. True power is always voltage times current for ______.

(a) all alternating-current circuits
(b) direct-current circuits
(c) alternating-current circuits at unity power factor
(d) b and c

24. Power consumed (watts) in either a single-phase alternating-current or direct-current system is always equal to ______.

(a) $I \times R^2$
(b) E x R
(c) $I^2 \times R$
(d) E/(I x R)

25. The power consumed by a 208V, 76A, three-phase circuit that has a power factor of 89 percent is ______.

(a) 24,367W
(b) 27,379W
(c) 35,808W
(d) 212,456W

26. The true power of a 2.10 kVA, single-phase load with a power factor of 91 percent is ______.

(a) 0.191 kW
(b) 1.75 kW
(c) 1.91 kW
(d) 2.10 kW

3.30 Unity Power Factor

27. Power factor in an alternating-current circuit is unity (100 percent), if the circuit contains only ______.

(a) induction motors
(b) transformers
(c) reactance coils
(d) resistive loads

28. Three 8 kW electric-discharge lighting bank circuits, which have a 92 percent power factor, are connected to a 230V, three-phase source. The current flow of these lights is ______.

(a) 37A
(b) 50A
(c) 65A
(d) 75A

3.31 Power Factor Formulas

29. Assuming 100 percent efficiency, what's the power factor for each ballast rated 0.65A at 120V for a fixture containing two 34W lamps?

(a) 67%
(b) 77%
(c) 87%
(d) 97%

30. What's the apparent power in VA of a fluorescent ballast that has a power factor of 90 percent when connected to two 34W lamps?

(a) 76 VA
(b) 86 VA
(c) 96 VA
(d) 106 VA

31. What's the true power of a 12A load rated 120V, with a power factor of 80 percent?

(a) 1,050W
(b) 1,150W
(c) 1,250W
(d) 1,350W

3.32 Cost of True Power

32. The cost of electrical power is based on the true power consumed during a month, multiplied by the cost per kWh (1,000W for a period of one hour).

(a) True
(b) False

33. What's the cost of power consumed per month (at $0.10 per kWh) for a 10 ohm ground rod having a ground-fault voltage of 120V?

(a) $75
(b) $85
(c) $95
(d) $105

3.33 Effects of Power Factor

34. Apparent power (VA) is used for sizing circuits and equipment. Because the VA of the load is greater than the watts of the load, fewer loads can be supplied by each branch circuit.

(a) True
(b) False

35. What size transformer is required for fifty, 100W luminaires that have a power factor of 90 percent (noncontinuous load)?

(a) 2 kVA
(b) 4 kVA
(c) 6 kVA
(d) 8 kVA

36. How many 20A, 120V circuits are required for fifty, 100W luminaires that have a power factor of 90 percent (noncontinuous load)?

(a) 3 circuits
(b) 5 circuits
(c) 7 circuits
(d) 9 circuits

PART E—EFFICIENCY

3.34 Efficiency Formulas

37. Motor efficiency can be determined by which of the following formulas?

(a) hp x 746W
(b) hp x 746W/VA Input
(c) hp x 746W/W Input
(d) Input W/(hp x 746W)

38. The efficiency ratio of a 4,000 VA transformer winding with a secondary VA of 3,600 VA is _____ percent.

(a) 70
(b) 80
(c) 90
(d) 110

UNIT

4

Motors and Transformers

INTRODUCTION TO UNIT 4—MOTORS AND TRANSFORMERS

Electric motors are used to convert electrical energy into mechanical energy that can be used to do work and accomplish a productive goal. Motors are an essential component of our industrialized society, so it's important for electricians to understand the basic operational characteristics of motors and how to properly install and connect them.

There are many different types of specialized motors. This unit discusses the most commonly used direct-current (dc) motors and alternating-current (ac) motors. Some of the important things covered in this unit include the differences between full-load current rating, full-load ampere rating, and locked-rotor current.

Generators are used to convert mechanical energy into electrical energy. Direct-current generators, single-phase alternating-current generators, and three-phase alternating-current generators are introduced in this unit. Generators can be found everywhere from very large units at utility generating plants, to emergency generators at hospitals and manufacturing plants, to small residential standby units.

The ability to distribute alternating-current (ac) at high voltages with low line losses and then transform that alternating current to lower voltages for local distribution systems and utilization equipment is one of the most attractive features of using alternating current as opposed to direct current for distribution systems. Transformers are also used within premises wiring systems to provide the necessary voltages for utilization equipment and applications such as control circuits.

Transformers operate using the principle of mutual induction, which accomplishes the transfer of energy from one system to a second system with no physical connection between the two. In this unit we'll explain some basic transformer principles and you'll be introduced to three-phase transformer configurations.

PART A—MOTOR BASICS

Introduction

Electric motors are among the most common loads on electrical systems of commercial and industrial occupancies. Think of the sheer number of things that must move in some way. Every pump, fan, compressor, conveyor, or other device that moves material or objects, requires either a motor or an engine powered by steam, air pressure, internal combustion, or some other force.

A motor is a device that converts electrical energy into motion. Computers contain many small motors (in the fans, DVDs, CD drives, hard drives, and other devices), as do automobiles (in which electrically operated motors have steadily been replacing vacuum operated and fluid operated motors). Where there's motion, there's probably an electric motor.

Electricians typically work with various configurations of motors that are powered by 120V, 208V, 240V, or 480V supplies. A solid understanding of the fundamentals of motor operation, motor calculations, motor circuits, and motor controls is essential for success as an electrician. The goal of this unit is to provide you with that basic understanding and prepare you for learning more about this important subject. Motor calculations are covered in Unit 7 of this textbook.

4.1 Motor Principles

A motor must have two opposing magnetic fields in order to rotate.

Stator. The stationary field winding of a motor is mounted on the stator, which is the part of the motor that doesn't turn. For some small permanent magnet motors, there's no field winding because the field is produced by permanent magnets.

Rotor. The rotating part of the motor is referred to as either the "rotor" or the "armature."

4.2 Dual-Voltage Alternating-Current Motors

Dual-voltage alternating-current motors are made with two field windings, each rated for the lower of two possible operating voltages. The field windings are connected in parallel for low-voltage operation and in series for high-voltage operation.

For example, a 230/460V dual-rated motor has its windings connected in series if supplied by a 460V source, or the windings are connected in parallel if supplied by a 230V source. Figure 4–1

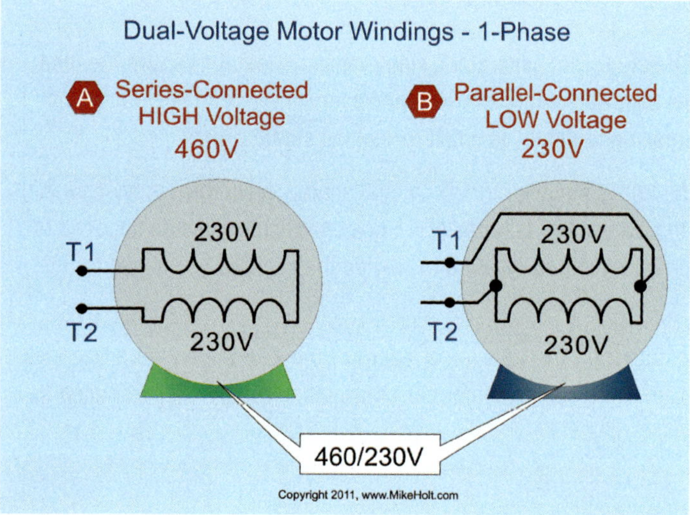

Figure 4–1

Author's Comment: The *NEC* describes voltages as either nominal or rated. "Nominal" voltage refers to the approximate expected utility voltage; for example, a 120/240V system. However, because of circuit voltage drop, the actual voltage at the load is less than 120V or 240V. Therefore, equipment is often rated at a value lower than the nominal system voltage, such as 115V or 230V.

4.3 Motor Horsepower Ratings

The output mechanical work of a motor is measured or rated in horsepower (hp).

Author's Comment: The conversion of mechanical work to electrical energy is measured in watts, where one horsepower = 746W.

CAUTION: *746W is the electrical output value for each horsepower. But this value isn't the input electrical rating required to calculate the motor nameplate current rating.*

► Horsepower Example

Question: *What size motor, in horsepower, produces an output of 15 kW?* **Figure 4–2**

(a) 5 hp (b) 10 hp (c) 20 hp (d) 30 hp

Answer: *(c) 20 hp*

Horsepower = Output Watts/746
Horsepower = 15,000W/746W
Horsepower = 20 hp

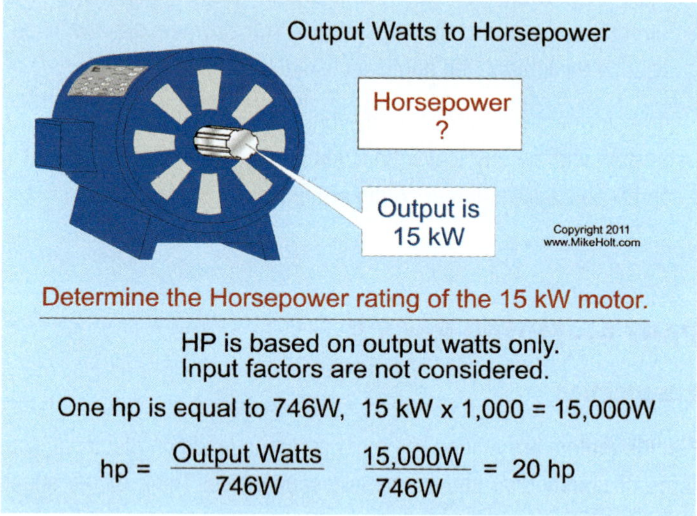

Figure 4–2

▶ Output Watts Example

Question: *What's the output watts rating of a 10 hp, alternating current, 480V, three-phase motor with an efficiency rating of 75 percent and a power factor of 70 percent?* **Figure 4–3**

(a) 5 kW *(b) 6 kW* *(c) 7.50 kW* *(d) 8 kW*

Answer: *(c) 7.50 kW*

Output Watts = hp x 746W

Output Watts = 10 hp x 746W

Output Watts = 7,460W

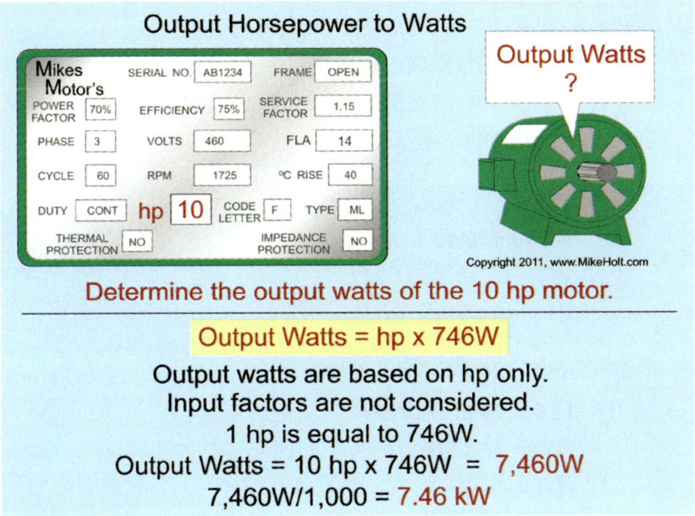

Figure 4–3

Efficiency, power factor, phases, and voltage have nothing to do with determining the output watts of a motor! But calculating motor output watts helps you understand how motor nameplate current numbers are developed.

4.4 Motor Current Ratings

Motor Full-Load Ampere (FLA) Rating

The motor nameplate full-load ampere (FLA) rating is the current in amperes that the motor draws while carrying its rated horsepower load at its rated voltage. **Figure 4–4**

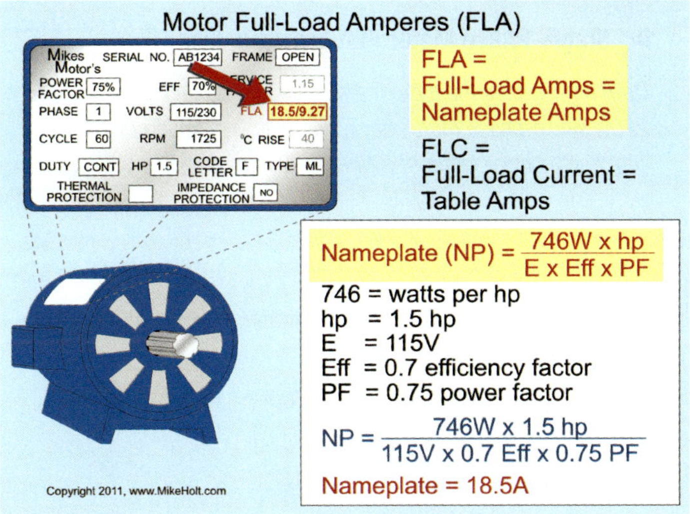

Figure 4–4

Actual Motor Current

The actual current drawn by a motor depends upon the load on the motor and the voltage at the motor terminals. If the load increases, the current also increases or if the motor operates at a voltage below its nameplate rating, the operating current increases.

⚠ **CAUTION:** *To prevent damage to motor windings from excessive heat (because of excessive current), never load a motor above its horsepower rating and be sure the supply voltage matches the motor's voltage rating.*

4.5 Calculating Motor FLA

The motor nameplate full-load ampere (FLA) rating can be determined by:

Single-Phase

FLA = (Motor hp x 746W)/(E x Eff x PF)

Three-Phase

FLA = (Motor hp x 746W)/(E x 1.732 x Eff x PF)

► Single-Phase Motor FLA Example

Question: *What's the motor nameplate FLA rating for a 7.50 hp, 230V, single-phase motor, having an efficiency rating of 93 percent and a power factor of 87 percent?* **Figure 4–5**

(a) 16A *(b) 19A* *(c) 24A* *(d) 30A*

Answer: *(d) 30A*

Step 1: Determine the motor output watts:

Output Watts = hp x 746W
Output Watts = 7.50 hp x 746W
Output Watts = 5,595W

Step 2: Determine the motor input watts:

Input = Output/Eff
Input = 5,595W/0.93 Eff
Input = 6,016W

Step 3: Determine the motor input VA:

VA = Watts/PF
VA = 6,016W/0.87 PF
VA = 6,915 VA

Step 4: Determine the motor amperes:

FLA = VA/E
FLA = 6,915W/230V
FLA = 30A

OR

FLA = (hp x 746W)/(E x Eff x PF)
FLA = (7.50 hp x 746W)/(230V x 0.93 Eff x 0.87 PF)
FLA = 30A

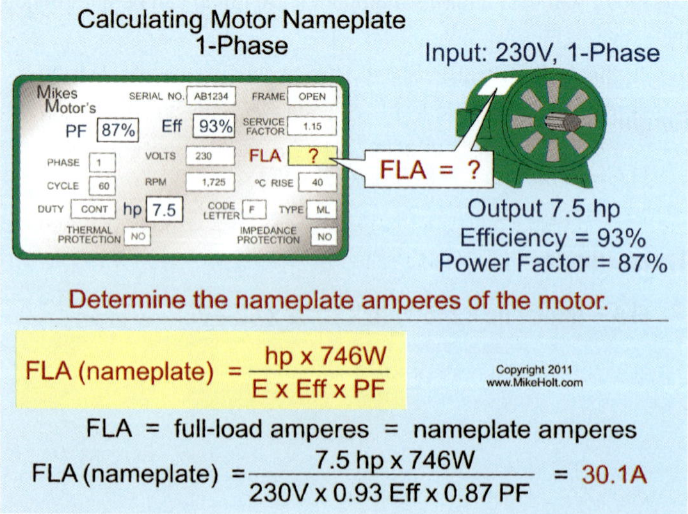

Figure 4–5

► Three-Phase Motor FLA Example

Question: *What's the motor FLA rating for a 40 hp, 208V, three-phase motor having an efficiency rating of 80 percent and a power factor of 90 percent?*

(a) 76A *(b) 84A* *(c) 99A* *(d) 115A*

Answer: *(d) 115A*

Step 1: Determine the motor output watts:

Output Watts = hp x 746W
Output Watts = 40 hp x 746W
Output Watts = 29,840W

Step 2: Determine the motor input watts:

Input Watts = Output/Eff
Input Watts = 29,840W/0.80 Eff
Input Watts = 37,300W

Step 3: Determine the motor input VA:

VA = Watts/PF
VA = 37,300W/0.90 PF
VA = 41,444 VA

Step 4: Determine the motor amperes:

FLA = VA/(E x 1.732)
FLA = 41,444VA/(208V x 1.732)
FLA = 115A

OR

FLA = (hp x 746W)/(E x 1.732 x Eff x PF)
FLA = (40 hp x 746W)/
(208V x 1.732 x 0.80 Eff x 0.90 PF)
FLA = 115A

4.6 Motor-Starting Current

When voltage is first applied to the field winding of an induction motor, only the conductor resistance opposes the flow of current through the motor winding. Because the conductor resistance is so low, the motor has a very large inrush current (a minimum of six times the full-load ampere rating). **Figure 4–6A**

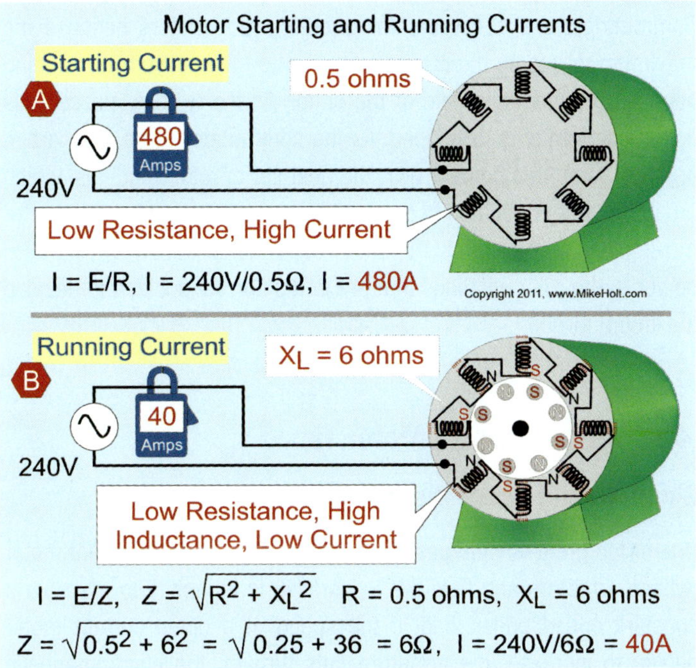

Figure 4–6

4.7 Motor-Running Current

However, once the rotor begins turning, the rotor-bars (winding) are increasingly cut by the stationary magnetic field, resulting in an increasing counter-electromotive force. Figure 4–6B

We learned previously that CEMF opposes the applied voltage, resulting in an increased opposition to current flow within the conductor. This is called inductive reactance. The increase in inductive reactance, because of self-induction, causes the impedance of the conductor winding to increase which results in reduced current flow.

4.8 Motor Locked-Rotor Current (LRC)

If the rotating part of the motor winding (armature) becomes jammed so that it can't rotate, no more CEMF is produced in the motor winding. This results in decreased conductor impedance to the point that it's effectively a short circuit. Result—the motor operates at locked-rotor current (LRC), which is about six times the running current value, and causes the motor winding to overheat to the point that it will be destroyed if the current isn't quickly stopped.

Author's Comment: The *National Electrical Code* requires that most motors be provided with overcurrent protection to prevent damage to the motor winding because of locked-rotor current.

4.9 Motor Overload Protection

Motors must be protected against excessive winding heat. Motors must not be overloaded; they must operate near their nameplate voltage, and measures must be taken to prevent the motor from jamming (LRC). If a motor is overloaded or if it operates at a voltage below its rating, the operating current can increase to a value above the motor full-load ampere (FLA) rating. The excessive operating current may damage the motor winding from excessive heat.

Figure 4–7 shows a type of overload device called a "melting-alloy overload." Other types of overload devices that provide motor overload protection include the dashpot type and bimetallic type, as well as solid-state overload relays.

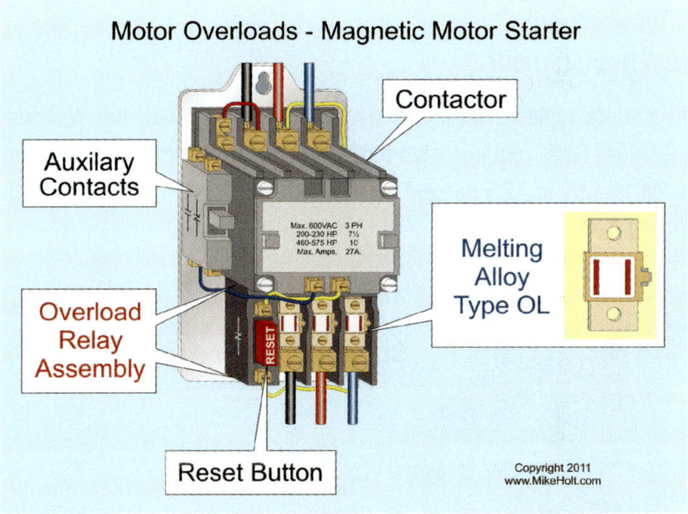

Figure 4–7

Author's Comment: Motors are designed to operate with an inrush current of six to eight times the motor-rated FLA for short periods of time without damage to the motor windings. Figure 4–8

However, if a motor operates at LRC for a prolonged period of time, the motor insulation and lubrication can be destroyed by excessive heat. Most motors can operate at 600 percent of the motor's FLA satisfactorily for a period of less than one minute or 300 percent of the motor's FLA for not more than three minutes.

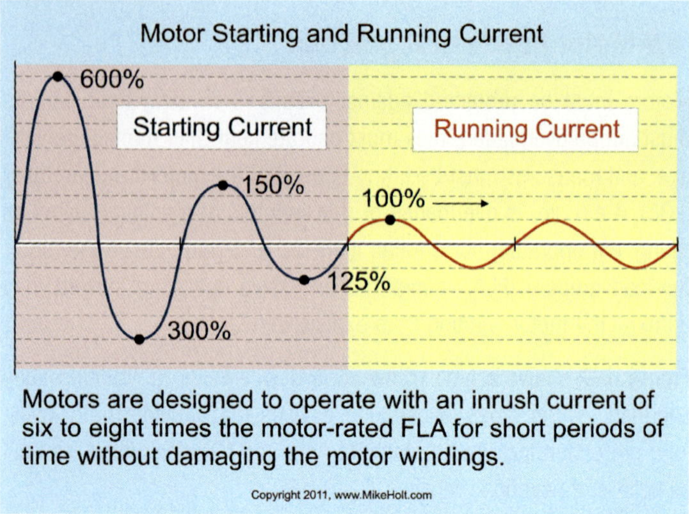

Figure 4–8

NEC Requirement

To protect against excessive heat from an overload, the *National Electrical Code* requires standard overload protection devices to be sized at 115 to 125 percent of the motor FLA rating [430.32(A)(1)]. **Figure 4–9**

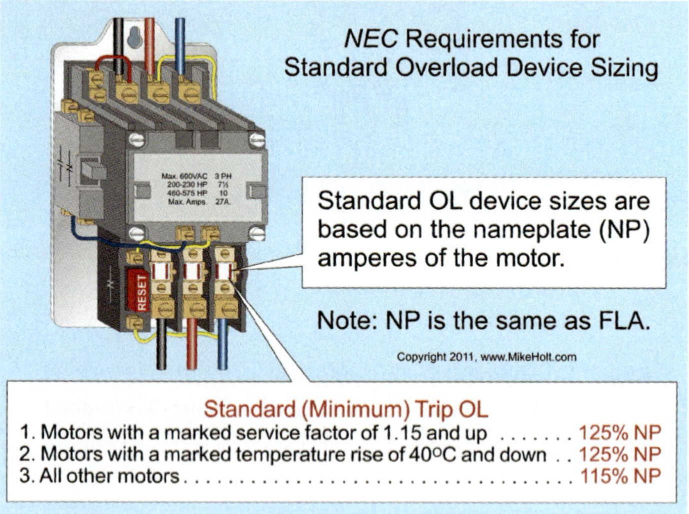

Figure 4–9

4.10 Direct-Current Motor Principles

Direct-current motors use brushes (pieces of conductive carbon) with springs to hold them in contact with a commutator. A commutator is a ring around the rotor shaft that has segments with insulation between them.

Commutators are necessary for direct-current motors because the maximum torque on the rotor develops when the active rotor winding opposes the magnetic field of the stator. As the winding passes this point, less torque is developed. As the commutator turns, the carbon brushes come into contact with the next set of rotor windings, which are in the proper position to oppose the stator field and keep the rotor moving. As the rotor turns, the brush-commutator set always supplies power to the rotor windings that are in the correct position to develop maximum torque.

4.11 Direct-Current Motor Types

Shunt-Wound Direct-Current Motor

One of the great advantages of the shunt-wound direct-current motor (whose armature and field are in parallel) is its ability to maintain a constant speed under load. If the speed of a direct-current motor begins to increase, the armature cuts through the electromagnetic field at an increasing rate. This results in a greater armature CEMF, which acts to cut down on the increased armature current, resulting in the motor slowing back down.

Placing a load on a direct-current motor causes the motor to slow down, which reduces the rate at which the armature is cut by the field flux lines. As a result, the armature CEMF decreases, resulting in an increase in the applied armature voltage and current. The increased current results in an increase in motor speed. This gives shunt-wound direct-current motors a built-in system for regulating their own speed. For these reasons, computer disk drives and recording equipment use direct-current motors exclusively.

Series-Wound Direct-Current Motor

Series-wound direct-current motors (those in which the field winding and the armature winding are connected in series) have poor speed regulation, and slow down considerably when a load is applied. When unloaded, they often run at a very high rpm and in some cases they tend to "run away" and increase speed to the point of damaging the motor. However, series direct-current motors have very good torque characteristics. One of the best examples of a series-wound direct-current motor is the starter motor on your automobile, which has very high torque to start the engine and is connected to a load so that it doesn't overspeed.

4.12 Reversing the Rotation of a Direct-Current Motor

To reverse the rotation of a direct-current motor, you must reverse either the stator field or the armature magnetic field. This is accomplished by reversing either the field or armature current. Because most direct-current motors have the field and armature windings fed from the same direct-current power supply, reversing the polarity of the power supply simultaneously changes the field and armature. This results in the motor continuing to run in the same direction.

The polarity of either the field or armature must be changed by disconnecting and interchanging the polarity of the leads of the field winding (while leaving the armature polarity unchanged), or interchanging the polarity of the armature (while leaving the field polarity unchanged). Figure 4–10

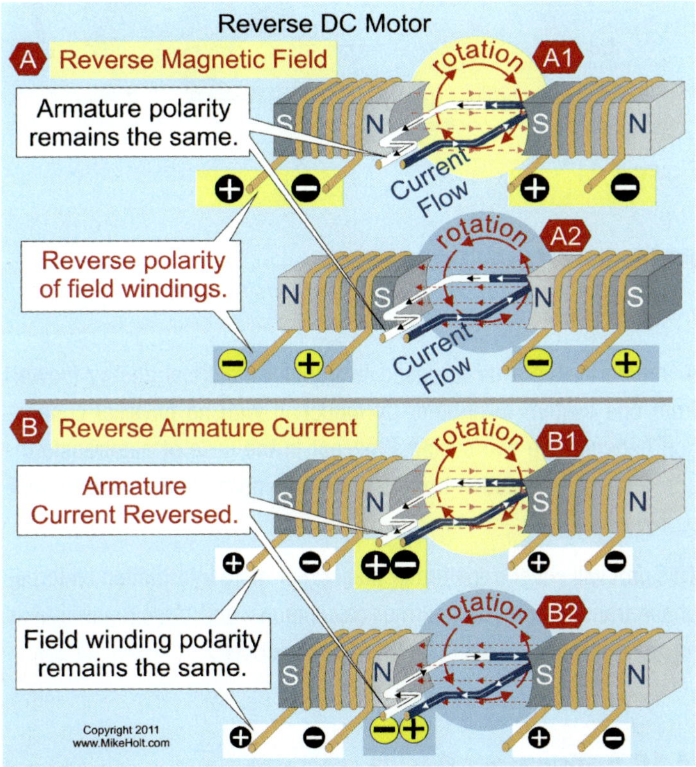

Figure 4–10

4.13 Alternating-Current Induction Motor

In an alternating-current induction motor, the stator produces a rotating magnetic field.

The rotor is a series of coils (windings) that are connected in a closed loop. The rotating magnetic field of the stator induces currents flowing in the rotor windings (thus, induction motor). These rotor currents generate a magnetic field that opposes the magnetic field of the stator, thereby causing the rotor to turn. This is why the rotor of an induction motor always turns with an rpm slightly less than the rpm of the stator's magnetic field.

4.14 Alternating-Current Motor Types

Squirrel-Cage Induction Motor

The most common type of alternating-current motor is the induction motor, which has no physical connection between its rotating member (the rotor), and the stationary member surrounding it (the stator).

Three-phase alternating-current squirrel-cage induction motors are used in almost all major industrial applications. They're called squirrel-cage motors because the rotor consists of bars that are either parallel to the shaft or at a slight angle and are connected together at the ends by shorting rings. These bars would resemble a hamster or squirrel cage if you were to remove the core material around them.

As the magnetic field from the stator of an induction motor rotates, the field induces voltage in the rotor bars as it cuts across them. Conditions for generator action exist—a conductor (rotor bars), a magnetic field (from the field winding), and relative motion between them. The generated voltage causes current to flow from bar to bar through the shorting rings. The conditions for motor action are now present—a conductor (each rotor bar) has current flowing through it in a magnetic field (from the stator field). This produces torque in the rotor causing it to turn.

Synchronous Motor

In a synchronous motor, the rotor is actually locked in step with the rotating stator field and is dragged along at the synchronous speed of the rotating magnetic field. Synchronous motors maintain their speed with a high degree of accuracy. Small synchronous motors are used for clock motors.

Large synchronous motors are often found in large industrial facilities driving loads such as compressors, crushers, and large pumps. Sometimes they're operated unloaded, meaning that nothing is attached to their shafts. In this application, the synchronous motor is being "overexcited," meaning that a large amount of direct current is being fed into the rotor through the slip rings. The synchronous motor acts as though it were a large capacitor when it's in this condition and can be used for power factor correction.

Wound-Rotor Motor

Wound-rotor induction motors are used only in special applications because of their complexity. Wound-rotor induction motors only operate on three-phase alternating-current power. They're similar to an induction motor; however, the rotor windings are connected in a wye configuration and the points of the wye are brought out through slip rings to an external controller.

Resistors are usually inserted into the rotor winding circuit during start-up in order to reduce the inrush current. As the motor increases speed, the value of the resistance is changed to lower values. Ultimately, the rotor windings are shorted, thereby allowing the motor to achieve full speed.

The wound-rotor motor can also be used in applications that require some speed control. Today, however, it's more common to use a Variable Speed Drive coupled to an induction motor.

Universal Motor

Universal motors are fractional horsepower motors that operate equally well on alternating current and direct current. They're used for vacuum cleaners, electric drills, mixers, and light household appliances. These motors have the inherent disadvantage associated with direct-current motors, which is the need for commutation. The problem with commutators is that as the motor operates, motor parts rub against each other and wear out.

4.15 Reversing the Rotation of an Alternating-Current Motor

Some alternating-current single-phase motors are constructed so that they can be reversed easily and some aren't. In order to reverse a single-phase alternating-current induction motor, it's necessary to change the relative polarity of the start winding in relation to the run winding. The motor nameplate will contain the wiring connection information for forward and reverse operation.

A three-phase motor can be reversed by swapping any two of the three power line conductors. Industry practice is to reverse Line 1 and Line 3. This can be done by reconnecting the motor, or a special reversing starter can be used to switch these connections for a motor that will be run in both directions during normal operation. **Figure 4–11**

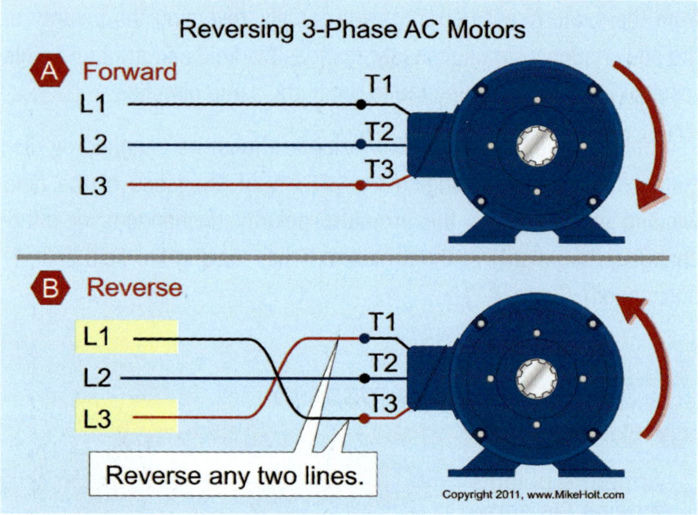

Figure 4–11

PART B—TRANSFORMERS

Introduction

A transformer is a device used to transfer electrical energy (power) from one system to another by induction with no physical connection between the two systems, except in the case of autotransformers. Other than isolation transformers, transformers are used to raise or lower voltages.

This part will cover transformer basics. For more information on three-phase transformers, transformer calculations, and *Code* requirements for transformers, refer to Unit 12 in this textbook.

4.16 Transformer Basics

Primary versus Secondary

The transformer winding connected to the voltage source is called the primary. The transformer winding connected to the load is called the secondary. Transformers can be used to either raise or lower voltage.

Mutual Induction

The energy transfer of a transformer is accomplished because the electromagnetic lines of force from the primary winding induce a voltage in the secondary winding. This process is called mutual induction. Figure 4–12

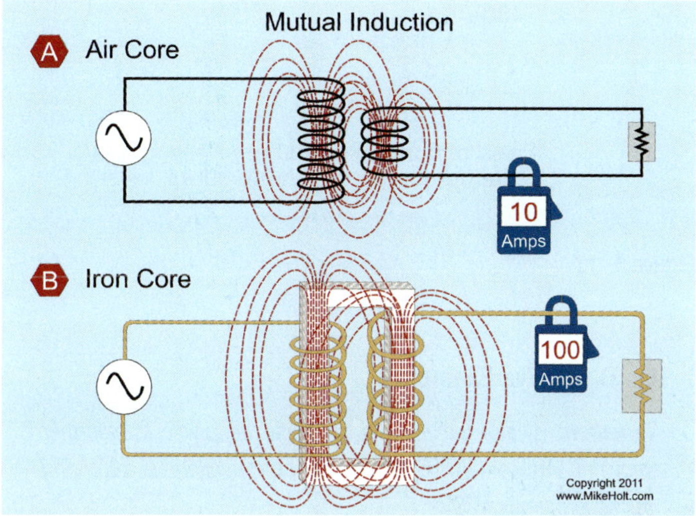

Figure 4–12

The voltage level that can be induced in the secondary winding, from the primary magnetic field, is a function of the number of secondary conductor loops (turns) that are cut by the primary electromagnetic field.

4.17 Secondary Induced Voltage

Voltage induced in the secondary winding of a transformer is equal to the sum of the voltages induced in each loop of the secondary winding. For example, if a transformer has three windings on the secondary and each secondary winding has 80V induced, the secondary voltage is 240V. Figure 4–13

The induced voltage in each loop of the secondary winding depends on the number of secondary conductor loops (turns), as compared to the number of primary turns. Figure 4–14

If both windings have the same number of turns, and if all of the magnetism set up by the primary passes through the secondary, the secondary will deliver the same voltage and power as the primary. This is how an isolation transformer works. Figure 4–15

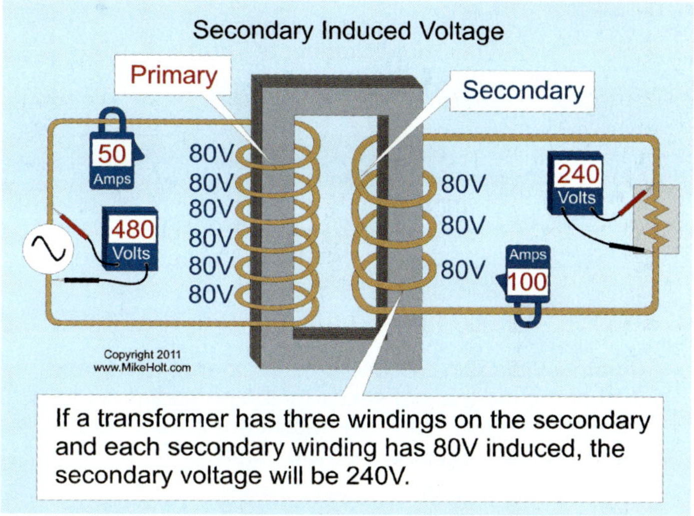

Figure 4–13

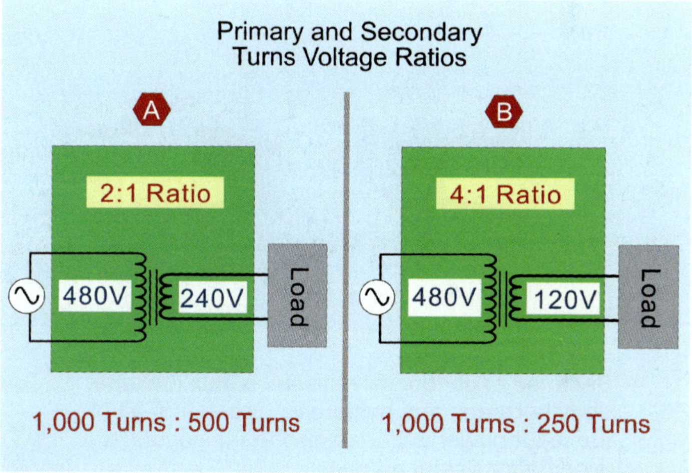

Figure 4–14

4.18 Efficiency

Because of conductor resistance, flux leakage, eddy currents, and hysteresis losses, not all of the input power is transferred to the secondary winding of a transformer for useful purposes. Transformer losses are typically quite small with efficiency approaching 95 to 97 percent. Thus, for most practical purposes, transformer efficiency can be ignored. Figure 4–16

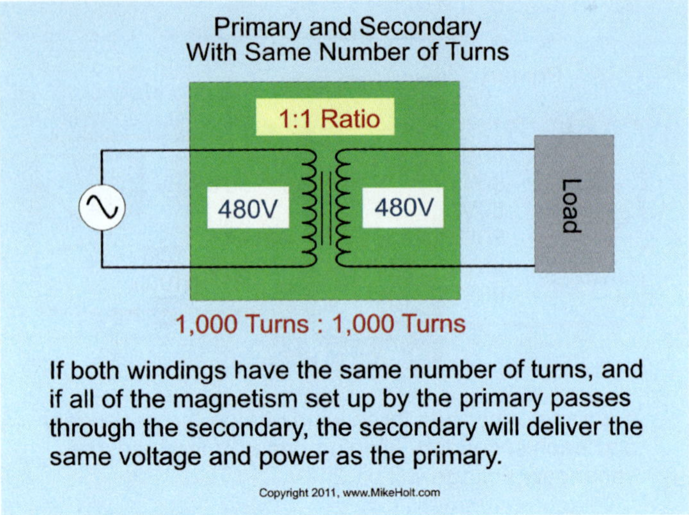

Figure 4–15

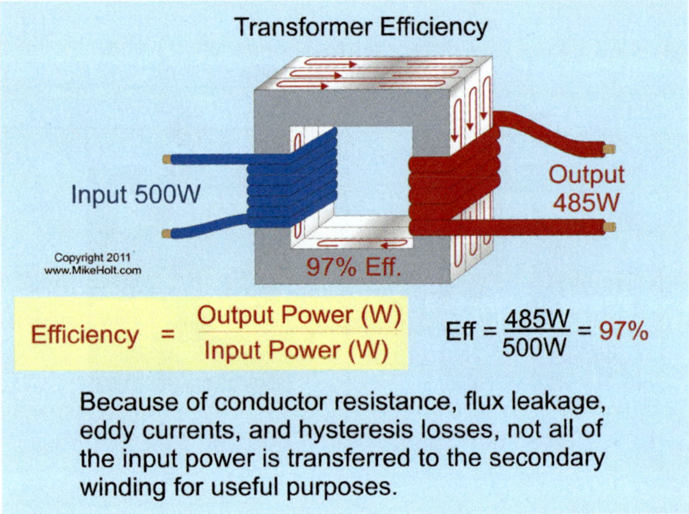

Figure 4–16

4.19 Transformer Turns Ratio

The relationship of the primary winding voltage to the secondary winding voltage is the same as the relationship between the number of turns of wire on the primary and the number of turns on the secondary. This relationship is called "turns ratio." Figure 4–17

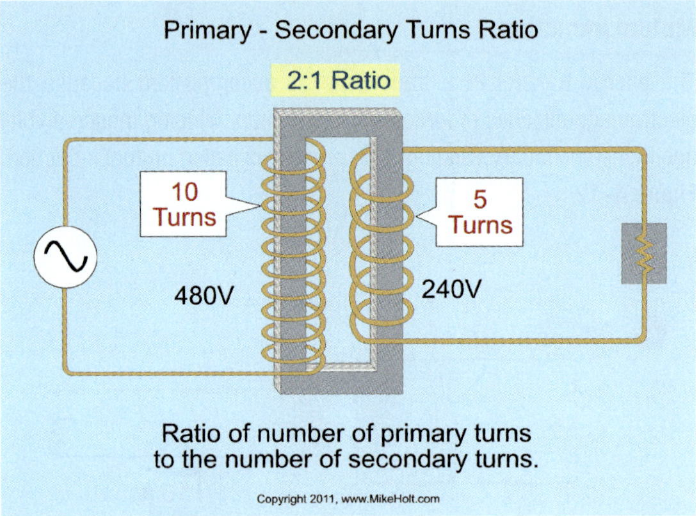

Figure 4–17

▶ Delta/Wye Example

Question: *What's the turns ratio of the delta/wye transformer shown in* **Figure 4–18** *if the primary phase voltage is 480V and the secondary is 120V?*

(a) 1:4 *(b) 1:2* *(c) 2:1* *(d) 4:1*

Answer: *(d) 4:1*

▶ Delta/Delta Example

Question: *What's the turns ratio of the delta/delta transformer shown in* **Figure 4–19** *if the primary phase voltage is 480V and the secondary is 240V?*

(a) 1:4 *(b) 1:2* *(c) 2:1* *(d) 4:1*

Answer: *(c) 2:1*

▶ Secondary Voltage Example 1

Question: *What's the secondary voltage of the transformer shown in* **Figure 4–20** *if the turns ratio is 10:1 and the primary voltage is 120V?*

(a) 6V *(b) 12V* *(c) 24V* *(d) 48V*

Answer: *(b) 12V*

The turns ratio is 10:1. This means the voltage ratio is also 10:1. Since the primary voltage is 120V, the secondary voltage is 10 times smaller, 120V/10 = 12V.

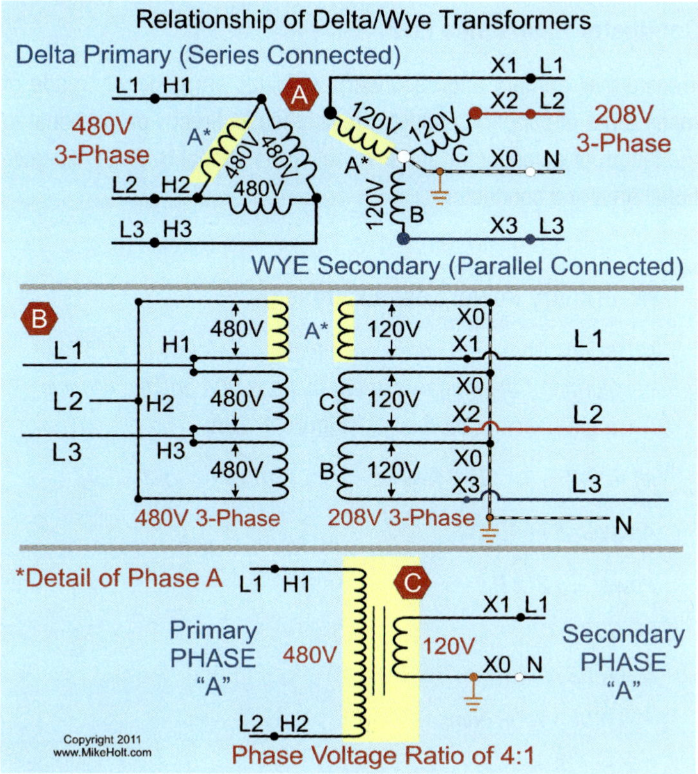

Figure 4–18

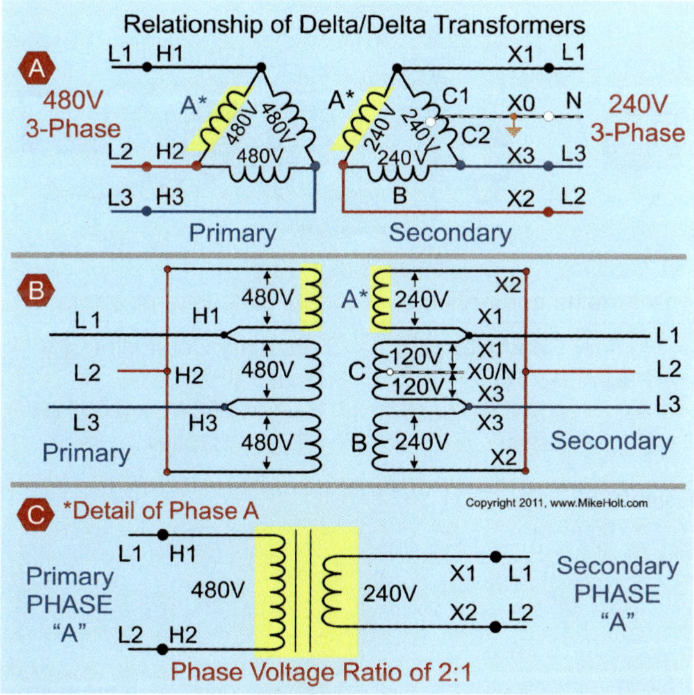

Figure 4–19

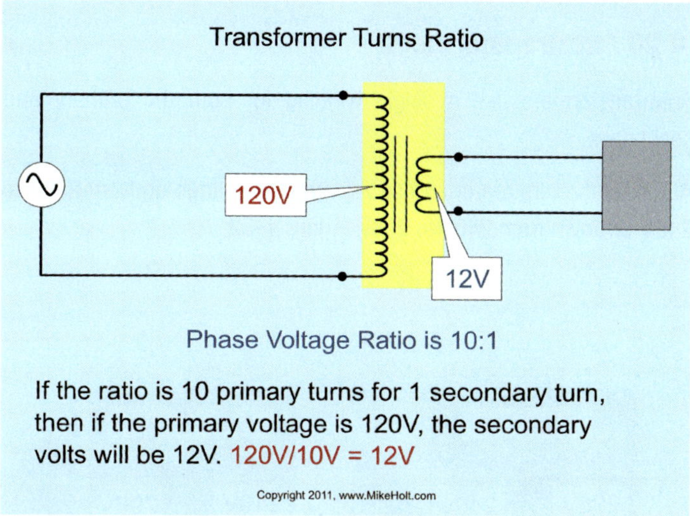

Figure 4–20

▶ Secondary Voltage Example 2

Question: *What's the secondary voltage of the transformer shown in* **Figure 4–21** *if the turns ratio is 10:1 and the primary voltage is 240V?*

(a) 6V *(b) 24V* *(c) 48V* *(d) 120V*

Answer: *(b) 24V*

Since the primary voltage is 240V, the secondary voltage is 10 times smaller, 240V/10 = 24V.

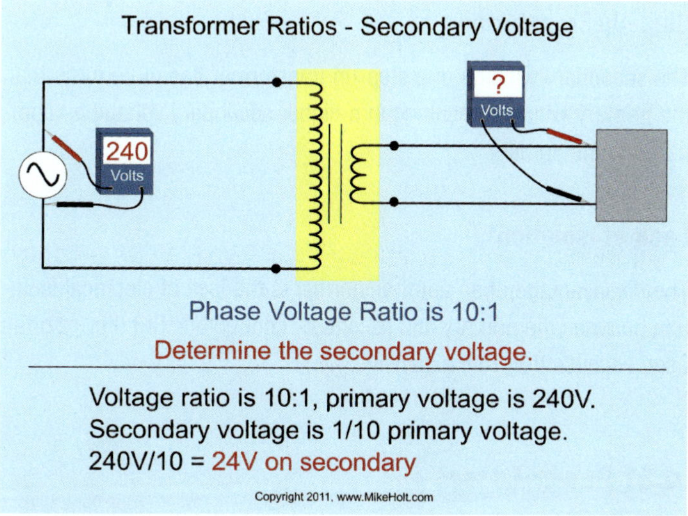

Figure 4–21

4.20 Autotransformers

Autotransformers use a single winding for both the primary and secondary.

Autotransformers are often used to step the voltage up from 208V to 240V, or down from 240V to 208V. Figure 4–22

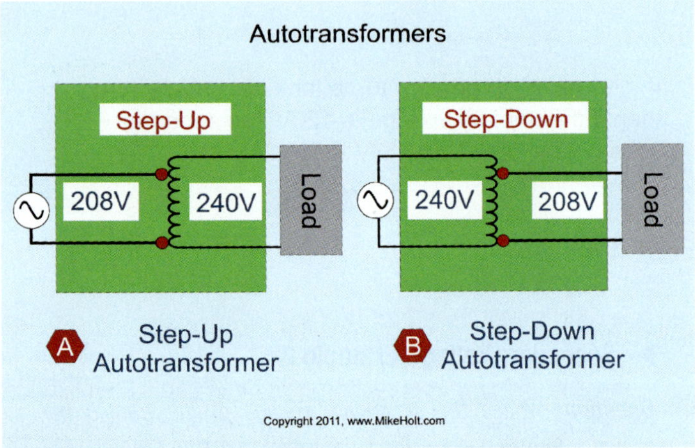

Figure 4–22

Step-Down Transformer

The secondary winding of a step-down transformer has fewer turns than the primary winding, resulting in a lower secondary voltage as compared to the primary.

Step-Up Transformer

The secondary winding of a step-up transformer has more turns than the primary winding, resulting in a higher secondary voltage as compared to the primary.

Lack of Isolation

The disadvantage of an autotransformer is the lack of electrical isolation between the primary and secondary conductors. But they're often used because they're inexpensive.

4.21 Power Losses

In an ideal transformer, all the primary power is transferred from the primary winding to the secondary winding. But real-world transformers have power losses because of conductor resistance, flux leakage, eddy currents, and hysteresis losses.

Conductor Resistance Loss

Transformer primary and secondary windings are generally made of many turns of copper. Conductor resistance is directly proportional to the length of a conductor and inversely proportional to the cross-sectional area of a conductor.

► Primary Power Loss Example

Question: *What's the primary conductor power loss of a 75 kVA transformer if the primary current rating is 90A and the winding has a resistance of 0.08 ohms?* **Figure 4–23A**

(a) 400W *(b) 648W* *(c) 1,100W* *(d) 1,300W*

Answer: *(b) 648W*

Power = I2 x R

I = 90A

R = 0.08 ohms

P = 90A² x 0.08 ohms

P = 648W

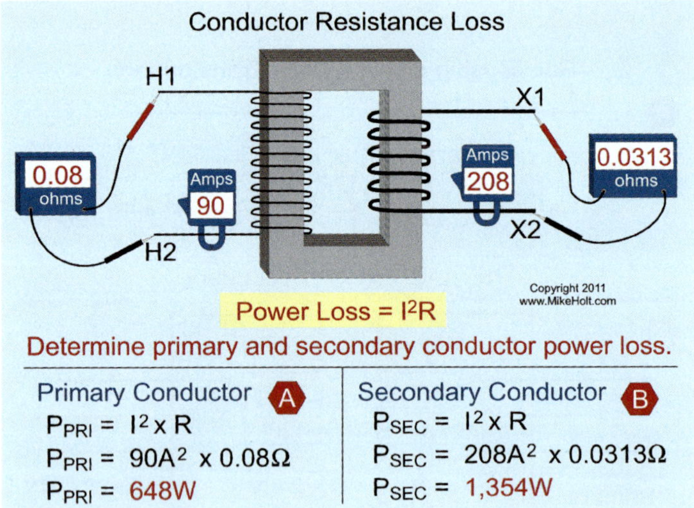

Figure 4–23

► Secondary Power Loss Example

Question: *What's the secondary conductor power loss of a 75 kVA transformer if the secondary current rating is 208A and the winding has a resistance of 0.0313 ohms?* **Figure 4–23B**

(a) 1,354W (b) 1,800W (c) 2,100W (d) 2,700W

Answer: *(a) 1,354W*

Power = I2 x R

I = 208A

R = 0.0313 ohms

P = $208A^2$ x 0.0313 ohms

P = 1,354W

Flux Leakage Loss

The leakage of the electromagnetic flux lines between the primary and secondary windings of transformers also represents wasted energy. **Figure 4–24**

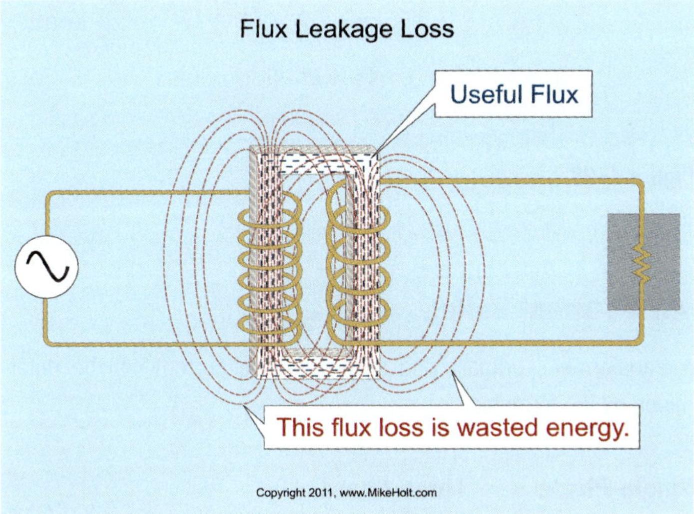

Figure 4–24

Eddy Currents

Iron is the only metal used for transformer cores because it's easy to magnetize. However, the expanding and collapsing electromagnetic field from alternating current induces a voltage in the iron core. These circulating eddy currents cause the core to heat up without any useful purpose. To reduce losses because of eddy currents, long laminated iron cores, separated by insulation (usually lacquer) are used. **Figure 4–25**

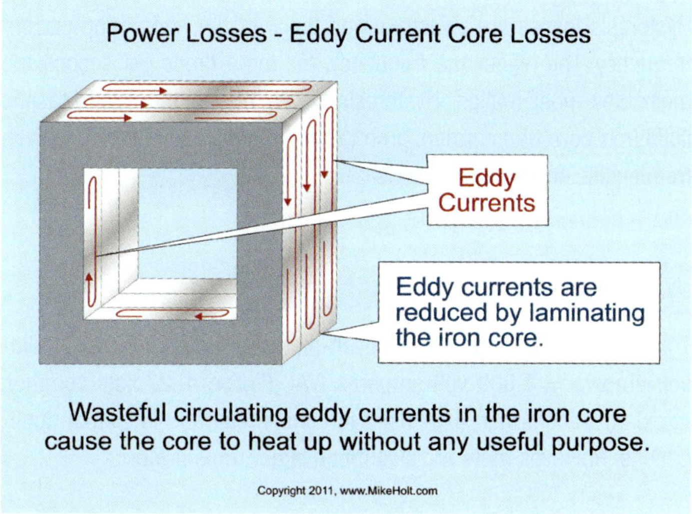

Figure 4–25

Hysteresis Losses

As current flows through a transformer, the iron core is temporarily magnetized by the electromagnetic field created by the alternating current. Each time the primary magnetic field expands and collapses, the core molecules realign themselves to the changing polarity of the electromagnetic field. The energy required to realign the core molecules to the changing electromagnetic field is called the "hysteresis loss of the core." **Figure 4–26**

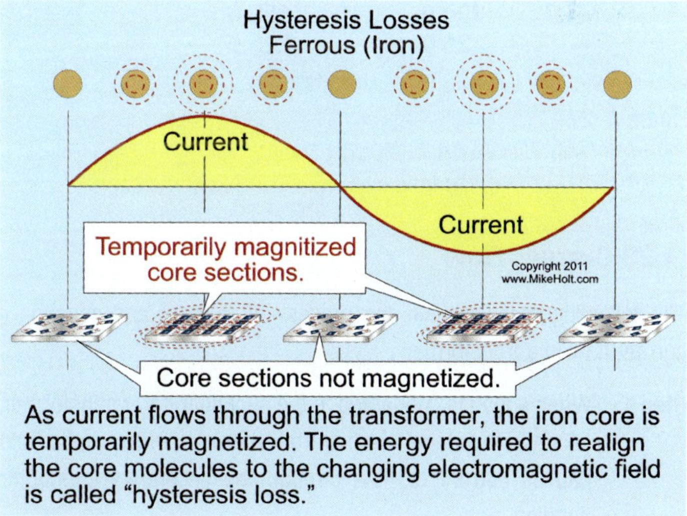

Figure 4–26

Hysteresis losses are directly proportional to the alternating-current frequency. The higher the frequency, the more times per second the molecules must realign. Hysteresis loss is one of the main reasons solid iron-core transformers aren't used in applications involving high frequencies and nonlinear loads.

4.22 Transformer kVA Rating

Transformers are rated in kilovolt-amperes (kVA), where 1 kilovolt-ampere = 1,000 volt-amperes (VA). **Figure 4–27** lists common standard transformer sizes used in commercial and industrial applications. However, there are also much larger transformers.

Standard Transformer Ratings - In kVA

Single-Phase	Three-Phase
1.0	3.0
1.5	6.0
2.0	9.0
3.0	15.0
5.0	22.5
7.5	25.0
10.0	30.0
15.0	37.5
25.0	45.0
37.5	50.0
50.0	75.0
75.0	112.5
100.0	150.0
125.0	225.0

Figure 4–27

4.23 Current Flow

The following steps explain the process of primary and secondary current flow in a transformer.

Step 1: When a load is connected to the secondary of a transformer, secondary voltage induced from the primary magnetic field causes current to flow through the secondary conductor winding.

Step 2: The secondary current flow in the secondary winding creates an electromagnetic field that opposes the primary electromagnetic field.

Step 3: The flux lines from the secondary magnetic field effectively reduce the strength of the primary flux lines, and as a result, less CEMF is generated in the primary winding conductors. With less CEMF to oppose the primary applied voltage, the primary current increases in direct proportion to the secondary current. **Figure 4–28**

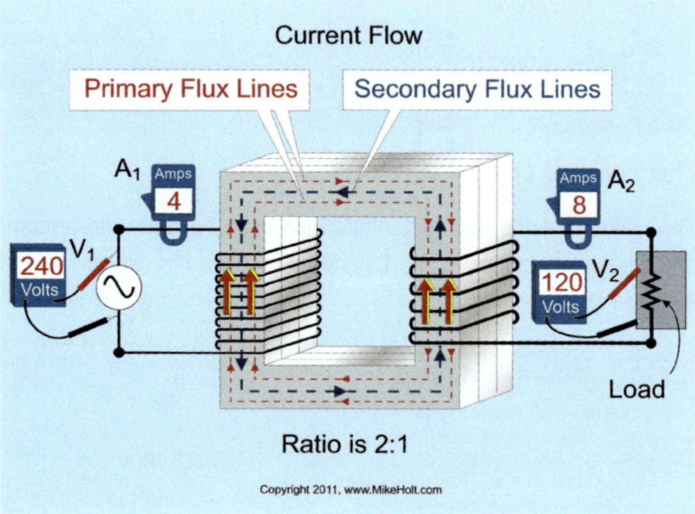

Figure 4–28

4.24 Current Rating

A transformer's primary and secondary line current can be determined by the formulas:

Single-Phase
I = VA/E

Three-Phase
I = VA/(E x 1.732)

▶ Single-Phase Example

Question: *What's the maximum primary and secondary line current at full load for a 480/240V, 25 kVA, single-phase transformer?* **Figure 4–29**

(a) 52/104A (b) 104/52A (c) 104/208A (d) 208/104A

Answer: *(a) 52/104A*

$I_{primary}$ = VA/E

$I_{primary}$ = 25,000 VA/480V

$I_{primary}$ = 52A

$I_{secondary}$ = VA/E

$I_{secondary}$ = 25,000 VA/240V

$I_{secondary}$ = 104A

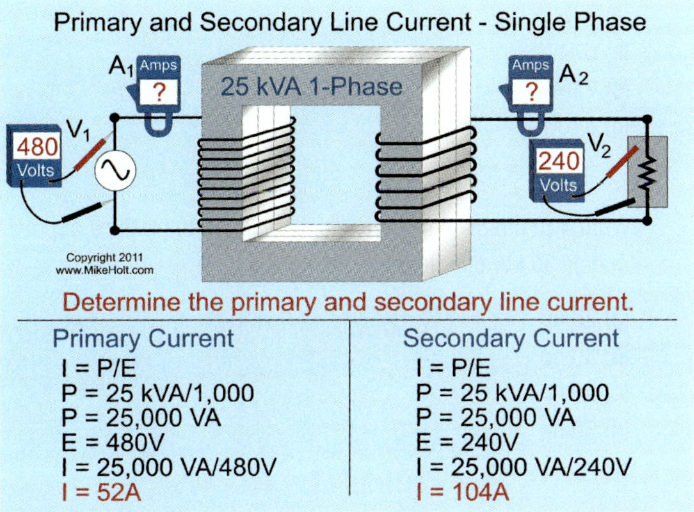

Figure 4–29

▶ Three-Phase Example

Question: *What's the maximum primary and secondary line current at full load for a 480/208V, 37.50 kVA, three-phase transformer?* **Figure 4–30**

(a) 45/104A (b) 104/40A (c) 140/120A (d) 208/140A

Answer: *(a) 45/104A*

$I_{primary}$ = VA/(E x 1.732)

$I_{primary}$ = 37,500 VA/(480V x 1.732)

$I_{primary}$ = 45A

I secondary = VA/(E x 1.732)

$I_{secondary}$ = 37,500 VA/(208V x 1.732)

$I_{secondary}$ = 104A

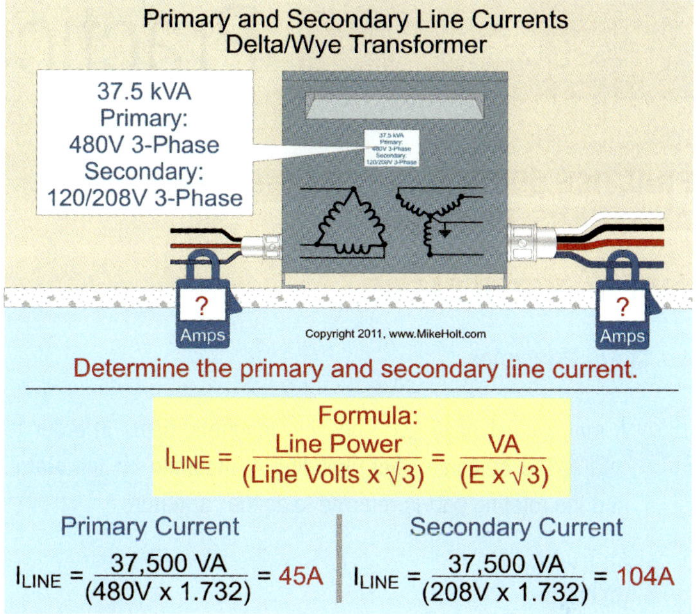

Figure 4–30

CONCLUSION TO UNIT 4—MOTORS AND TRANSFORMERS

Article 430 of the *National Electrical Code* addresses motors, motor circuits, and motor controllers. It's one of the largest of all the *NEC* articles. Now that you've studied basic motor theory, motor calculations, motor circuits, and motor controls, you can see why this is so. Although you've learned much here, you'll benefit from learning even more, especially if you're going to do commercial or industrial work.

Unit 7 of this textbook provides a study of motor calculations. Unit 12 provides more information about transformer calculations and the *Code* requirements for transformer installations and grounding. Be sure to continue your studies with these important topics.

UNIT 4 Practice Questions

PRACTICE QUESTIONS FOR UNIT 4—MOTORS AND TRANSFORMERS

PART A—MOTOR BASICS

4.1 Motor Principles

1. A motor must have two opposing magnetic fields in order to rotate. The stationary field winding is mounted on the stator, and the rotating part is referred to as the "armature."

   (a) True
   (b) False

4.2 Dual-Voltage Alternating-Current Motors

2. Dual-voltage alternating-current motors are made with two field windings. The field windings are connected in ______ for low-voltage operation and in ______ for high-voltage operation.

   (a) series, parallel
   (b) parallel, series
   (c) series, series
   (d) parallel, parallel

3. For a dual-voltage 230/460V motor, the field windings are connected in parallel for ______ operation and in series for _____ operation.

   (a) 230V, 460V
   (b) 460V, 230V
   (c) 230V, 230V
   (d) 460V, 460V

4.3 Motor Horsepower Ratings

4. Motors are used to convert electrical energy into mechanical work and the output mechanical work of a motor is rated in horsepower. 1 hp = ______.

   (a) 476W
   (b) 674W
   (c) 746W
   (d) 840W

5. What size motor, in horsepower, is required to produce approximately 30 kW of output?

   (a) 20 hp
   (b) 30 hp
   (c) 40 hp
   (d) 50 hp

6. What's the approximate output of a 15 hp motor?

   (a) 11 kW
   (b) 15 kW
   (c) 22 kW
   (d) 31 kW

7. What's the approximate output of a 5 hp, 480V, three-phase motor?

   (a) 3.75 kW
   (b) 4.75 kW
   (c) 6.75 kW
   (d) 7.75 kW

4.4 Motor Current Ratings

8. The nameplate motor FLA rating describes the motor current rating when it carries its rated horsepower load at its rated ______.

(a) power
(b) resistance
(c) CEMF
(d) voltage

9. The actual motor current depends upon the load on the motor and the operating voltage at the motor terminals.

(a) True
(b) False

10. The motor FLA rating is used when sizing motor conductors or circuit protection.

(a) True
(b) False

4.5 Calculating Motor FLA

11. What's the nameplate FLA for a 5 hp, 230V, single-phase motor with a 93 percent power factor and an 87 percent efficiency rating?

(a) 10A
(b) 20A
(c) 28A
(d) 35A

12. What's the nameplate FLA for a 20 hp, 208V, three-phase motor with a 90 percent power factor and an 80 percent efficiency rating?

(a) 51A
(b) 58A
(c) 65A
(d) 80A

4.6 Motor-Starting Current

13. When a motor starts, the current drawn is at least ______ times the motor FLA; this is known as "motor locked-rotor amperes" (LRA).

(a) 0.80
(b) 1.25
(c) 3
(d) 6

4.7 Motor-Running Current

14. Once a motor begins turning, the rotor windings are increasingly cut by the stationary magnetic field, resulting in an increasing counter-electromotive force.

(a) True
(b) False

4.8 Motor Locked-Rotor Current (LRC)

15. If the rotating part of the motor winding is jammed so that it can't rotate, no CEMF is produced in the motor winding. As a result, the motor operates at ______ and the windings will be destroyed by excessive heat.

(a) FLA
(b) FLC
(c) LRC
(d) any of these

4.9 Motor Overload Protection

16. Motors must be protected against excessive winding heat by a properly sized overload protection device, based on the motor ______ current rating.

(a) FLA
(b) FLC
(c) LRC
(d) any of these

4.10 Direct-Current Motor Principles

17. Direct-current motors use brushes with springs to hold them in contact with a(n) ______.

(a) rotor
(b) stator
(c) armature
(d) commutator

4.11 Direct-Current Motor Types

18. If the speed of a shunt-wound direct-current motor begins to increase, the armature cuts through the electromagnetic field at an increasing rate. This results in a greater armature CEMF, which acts to cut down on the increased armature current, resulting in the motor speeding up.

(a) True
(b) False

19. Placing a load on a shunt-wound direct-current motor causes the motor to slow down, which increases the rate at which the field flux lines are cut by the armature. As a result, the armature CEMF increases resulting in an increase in the applied armature voltage and current. The increased current results in increased motor speed.

(a) True
(b) False

4.12 Reversing the Rotation of a Direct-Current Motor

20. To reverse the rotation of a direct-current motor, you must reverse the ______.

(a) stator field
(b) rotor field
(c) a and b
(d) a or b

4.13 Alternating-Current Induction Motor

21. In an alternating-current induction motor, the stator produces a rotating magnetic field that induces current in the rotor windings. The rotor current generates a magnetic field in opposition to the magnetic field of the stator, thereby causing the rotor to turn.

(a) True
(b) False

4.14 Alternating-Current Motor Types

22. In a(n) ______ motor, the rotor is actually locked in step with the rotating stator field and is dragged along at the speed of the rotating magnetic field.

(a) wound-rotor
(b) induction
(c) synchronous
(d) squirrel-cage

23. ______ motors are fractional horsepower motors that operate equally well on alternating current and direct current and are used for vacuum cleaners, electric drills, mixers, and light household appliances.

(a) Alternating-current
(b) Universal
(c) Wound-rotor
(d) Synchronous

4.15 Reversing the Rotation of an Alternating-Current Motor

24. Swapping ______ of the line conductors can reverse a three-phase alternating-current motor's rotation.

(a) one
(b) two
(c) three
(d) four

PART B—TRANSFORMERS

4.16 Transformer Basics

25. A ______ is used to raise or lower voltage and it has the ability to transfer electrical energy from one system to another with no physical connection between the two systems.

 (a) capacitor
 (b) motor
 (c) relay
 (d) transformer

26. The transformer winding that's connected to the source is called the "______" winding and the transformer winding that's connected to the load is called the "______."

 (a) secondary, primary
 (b) primary, secondary
 (c) depends on the wiring
 (d) none of these

27. The energy transfer ability of a transformer is accomplished because the primary electromagnetic lines of force induce a voltage in the secondary winding.

 (a) True
 (b) False

4.17 Secondary Induced Voltage

28. Voltage induced in the secondary winding of a transformer is dependent on the number of secondary turns as compared to the number of primary turns.

 (a) True
 (b) False

4.18 Efficiency

29. Because of conductor resistance, flux leakage, eddy currents, and hysteresis losses, not all of the input power is transferred to the secondary winding for useful purposes.

 (a) True
 (b) False

30. For most practical purposes, transformer efficiency can be ignored.

 (a) True
 (b) False

4.19 Transformer Turns Ratio

31. The relationship of the number of turns of wire on the ______ as compared to the number of turns on the ______ is called "turns ratio."

 (a) primary, secondary
 (b) secondary, primary
 (c) primary, primary
 (d) secondary, secondary

32. If the primary phase voltage is 480V and the secondary phase voltage is 240V, the turns ratio is ______.

 (a) 1:4
 (b) 1:2
 (c) 2:1
 (d) 4:1

4.20 Autotransformers

33. Autotransformers use separate windings for the primary and secondary.

 (a) True
 (b) False

4.21 Power Losses

34. Wasteful circulating ______ in the iron core cause(s) the core to heat up without any useful purpose.

 (a) conductor resistance
 (b) flux leakage
 (c) eddy currents
 (d) hysteresis losses

35. _____ can be reduced by dividing the core into many flat sections or laminations.

(a) Conductor resistance
(b) Flux leakage
(c) Eddy currents
(d) Hysteresis losses

36. As current flows through the transformer, the iron core is temporarily magnetized. The energy required to realign the core molecules to the changing electromagnetic field is called "_____."

(a) conductor resistance
(b) flux leakage
(c) eddy currents
(d) hysteresis loss

37. The leakage of electromagnetic flux lines between the primary and secondary windings of a transformer represents wasted energy.

(a) True
(b) False

4.22 Transformer kVA Rating

38. Transformers are rated in _____.

(a) Henrys
(b) kW
(c) W
(d) kVA

4.23 Current Flow

39. The primary electromagnetic field induces a voltage in the secondary. As the secondary current flows, it produces an electromagnetic field that reduces the strength of the primary flux lines. This results in an increase in primary current.

(a) True
(b) False

40. Current flow in a secondary transformer winding creates an electromagnetic field that opposes the primary electromagnetic field resulting in less primary CEMF. The primary current automatically increases in direct proportion to the secondary current.

(a) True
(b) False

UNIT

4

Challenge Questions

CHALLENGE QUESTIONS FOR UNIT 4—MOTORS AND TRANSFORMERS

PART A—MOTOR BASICS

4.3 Motor Horsepower Ratings

1. The input VA of a 5 hp (15.20A), 230V, three-phase motor is closest to ______.

   (a) 4,600 VA
   (b) 5,300 VA
   (c) 6,100 VA
   (d) 7,500 VA

2. The input VA of a 1 hp (16A), 115V, single-phase motor is ______.

   (a) 1,650 VA
   (b) 1,840 VA
   (c) 2,960 VA
   (d) 3,190 VA

4.11 Direct-Current Motor Types

3. A(n) ______ type of electric motor tends to "run away" if it isn't always connected to its load.

   (a) direct-current series
   (b) direct-current shunt
   (c) alternating-current induction
   (d) alternating-current synchronous

4. A(n) ______ motor has a wide speed range.

   (a) alternating-current
   (b) direct-current
   (c) synchronous
   (d) induction

4.12 Reversing the Rotation of a Direct-Current Motor

5. If the two line (supply) leads of a direct-current series motor are reversed, the motor will ______.

   (a) not run
   (b) run backwards
   (c) run the same as before
   (d) become a generator

6. To reverse a direct-current series motor, we may simply reverse the supply (power) leads.

   (a) True
   (b) False

4.14 Alternating-Current Motor Types

7. The ______ induction motor is used only in special applications and is always operated on three-phase alternating-current power.

   (a) compound
   (b) synchronous
   (c) split-phase
   (d) wound-rotor

8. The rotating part of a direct-current motor or generator is called the ______.

   (a) shaft
   (b) rotor
   (c) armature
   (d) b or c

PART B—TRANSFORMERS

4.19 Transformer Turns Ratio

9. A transformer winding has a voltage turns ratio of 2:1. The current flowing through the secondary winding will be ______ the current flowing through the primary winding.

(a) higher than
(b) lower than
(c) the same as
(d) none of these

10. The primary winding of a transformer has 100 turns and the secondary winding has 10 turns. What's the current flowing through the primary winding if the current flowing through the secondary winding is 5A?

(a) 0.50A
(b) 5A
(c) 10A
(d) 25A

11. Which winding of a current transformer (CT) carries more current?

Tip: An induction clamp-on ammeter operates on the principle of the meter acting as the secondary winding.

(a) The primary winding.
(b) The secondary winding.
(c) The interwinding.
(d) The tertiary winding.

12. If a transformer primary winding has 900 turns and the secondary winding has 90 turns, which winding of the transformer has a larger conductor in cross-sectional area?

(a) The primary winding.
(b) The secondary winding.
(c) The interwinding.
(d) The autowinding.

13. If the primary transformer winding operates at 480V and the secondary at 240V, which winding has a larger conductor in cross-sectional area?

(a) The tertiary winding.
(b) The secondary winding.
(c) The primary winding.
(d) The windings are equal.

14. If the transformer winding voltage turns ratio is 5:1 and the current flowing through the secondary winding is 10A, the current flowing through the primary winding will be ______.

(a) 1A
(b) 2A
(c) 10A
(d) 25A

15. A transformer primary winding operates at 240V, the secondary winding operates at 12V, and the secondary load is two 100W lamps. What's the secondary current flow if the transformer winding is rated 80 percent efficient?

(a) 1A
(b) 17A
(c) 28A
(d) 200A

16. A transformer primary winding operates at 240V, the secondary at 120V, and the load is 1,500W. If the transformer is rated 92 percent efficient, what's the current flowing through the primary winding of this transformer?

(a) 6.80A
(b) 7.80A
(c) 8.60A
(d) 9.90A

17. The approximate primary kVA of a transformer that supplies a 208V, 100A, three-phase load is ______. See Figure 4–31.

(a) 21 kVA
(b) 30 kVA
(c) 42 kVA
(d) 72.50 kVA

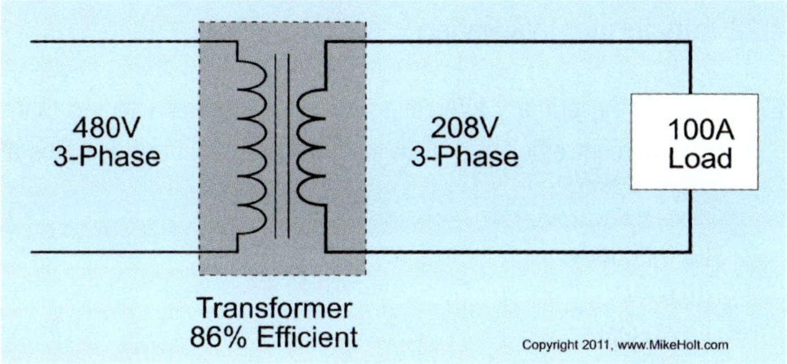

Figure 4–31

18. The primary current of the 480/208V transformer shown in Figure 4–31 is ____.

(a) 12A
(b) 25A
(c) 50A
(d) 90A

19. The secondary voltage of the transformer shown in Figure 4–32 is ____.

(a) 6V
(b) 12V
(c) 24V
(d) 30V

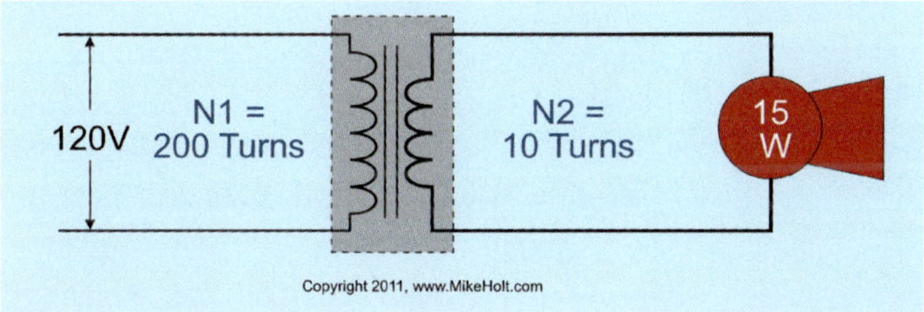

Figure 4–32

20. The primary load in watts for a transformer (rated 95 percent efficient) that supplies a 500W load is ____. See Figure 4–33.

(a) 400W
(b) 475W
(c) 526W
(d) 550W

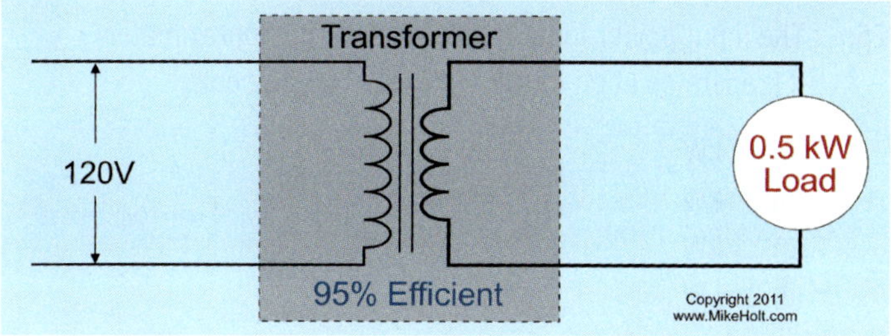

Figure 4–33

21. The primary current of the transformer is ____. See Figure 4–33.

(a) 0.416A
(b) 3.56A
(c) 4.38A
(d) 41.60A

22. The primary winding of a transformer operates at 240V, the secondary at 12V, and the load consists of two 100W lamps. What's the load on the secondary winding if the transformer winding is rated 92 percent efficient?

(a) 200 VA
(b) The same as the primary VA.
(c) Can't be calculated.
(d) none of these

23. The secondary winding of a transformer operates at 24V and it supplies a load that has a rating of 5A. If the transformer is rated 90 percent efficient, what's the secondary VA load rating?

(a) 120 VA
(b) The same as the primary VA.
(c) Can't be calculated.
(d) a and b

24. A primary transformer winding operates at 240V, the secondary at 12V, and the load is two 100W lamps. What's the primary VA load if the transformer is rated 92 percent efficient?

(a) 0.217 VA
(b) 185 VA
(c) 217 VA
(d) 275 VA

25. The input power for a 20 kW load will be approximately ______ if it operates at an efficiency level of 65 percent.

(a) 11 kW
(b) 20 kW
(c) 31 kW
(d) 33 kW

4.21 Power Losses

26. When the current in the steel core of a transformer has risen to a point where high flux density has been reached and additional increases in current produce few additional flux lines, the metal core is said to be ______.

(a) maximized
(b) saturated
(c) full
(d) none of these

4.22 Transformer kVA Rating

27. What's the primary kVA rating for a transformer winding that's 100 percent efficient if a 5A load on the secondary operates at 12V?

(a) 0.06 kVA
(b) 6 kVA
(c) 30 kVA
(d) 600 kVA

CHAPTER

2

NEC CALCULATIONS

Essential for Journeyman and Master's Licensing Exams

Notes

UNIT 5

Raceway and Box Calculations

INTRODUCTION TO UNIT 5—RACEWAY AND BOX CALCULATIONS

Anyone who's ever pulled wire into a conduit understands the reason for maximum limits on the wire fill for raceways. Trying to pull too many conductors into a raceway can damage the conductor insulation due to the friction and mechanical abuse. We've all heard a joke about tying a wire-pulling rope onto the hitch of the service truck and "locking in the hubs." At least, we hope this is a joke and not an accurate recounting of an installation.

Chapter 9, Table 1 provides the maximum limits the *Code* recognizes for wire fill in terms of a percentage of the raceway's interior cross-sectional area. This unit explains those limits and provides instruction regarding the use of the associated tables in Chapter 9 to calculate conductor fill. How to use the tables in Annex C when all of the conductors in the raceway are the same size (total cross-sectional area including insulation) is also covered.

Wireway abuse results from disregarding the limits on the radius of bends required for making transitions into and out of the wireway, and the number of conductors and splices allowed. There are specific rules in the *NEC* to help plan wireway installations that are in compliance and much easier to work with.

The *Code* provides a limit to the number of conductors allowed in outlet boxes, based on Table 314.16(A). This limit is often joked about as being the "maximum number of conductors that can be installed in the outlet box while using the persuasion of your hammer handle." This method doesn't follow the *NEC's* guidance set forth in 314.16(B). In this unit, you'll learn how to properly calculate the maximum number of conductors and "conductor equivalents" to be installed in an outlet box. Be sure to read this material carefully so you'll understand what the *Code* means by "conductor equivalents."

An explanation of the sizing requirements of 314.28(A)(1) and (2) for larger pull boxes, junction boxes, and conduit bodies which enclose conductors 4 AWG and larger, rounds out the information provided here in Unit 5.

PART A—RACEWAY FILL

Introduction

Raceways must be large enough to avoid damaging the insulation when conductors are pulled into the raceway. Chapter 9 and Annex C of the *NEC* are the primary references for determining allowable conductor fill in raceways. For the most common condition, where multiple conductors of the same size are installed together in a raceway, the maximum number of conductors permitted can be determined from the tables in Annex C. For situations where conductors of different sizes are mixed together in a raceway, Chapter 9 contains the information necessary to calculate the required raceway size. Because different conductor types (THW, TW, THHN, and so forth) have different thicknesses of insulation, the number and size of conductors permitted in a given raceway often depend on the conductor type used.

Author's Comment: This unit is based on the use of solidly grounded ac systems, 600V or less, using 90°C insulated copper conductors sized to 75°C terminals unless otherwise specified.

5.1 Understanding the *NEC*, Chapter 9 Tables

Table 1—Conductor Percent Fill

The maximum percentage of allowable conductor fill is listed in Chapter 9, Table 1. It's based on common conditions where the length of the conductor and number of raceway bends are within reasonable limits [Chapter 9, Table 1, Note 1]. **Figure 5–1**

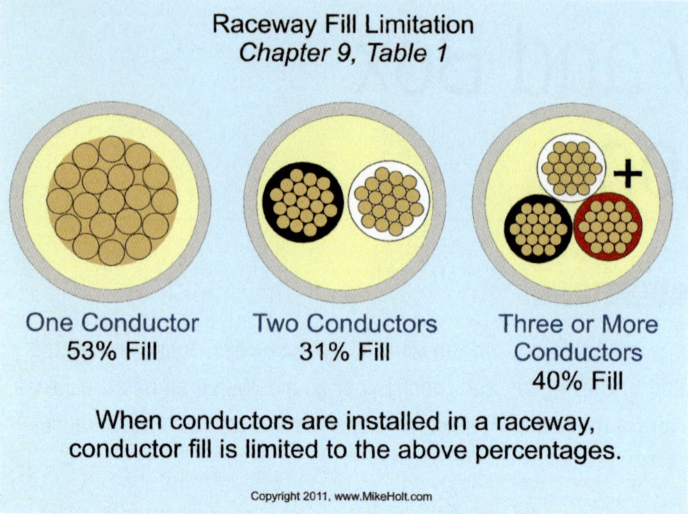

Figure 5–1

Notes to Tables, Note 1—Conductors all the Same Size

When all conductors in a conduit or tubing are the same size (total cross-sectional area including insulation), the number of conductors permitted in a raceway can be determined by simply looking at the tables located in Annex C—Raceway Fill Tables for Conductors and Fixture Wires of the Same Size.

Table 1 of Chapter 9, Maximum Percent Conductor Fill

Number of Conductors	Percent Fill Permitted
1 conductor	53% fill
2 conductors	31% fill
3 or more conductors	40% fill
Raceway 24 inches or less	60% fill, Note 4

- Tables C.1 through C.12(a) are based on maximum percent fill as listed in Chapter 9, Table 1.
- Table C.1—Conductors and fixture wires in electrical metallic tubing (EMT)
- Table C.1(A)—Compact conductors in electrical metallic tubing (EMT)
- Table C.2—Conductors and fixture wires in electrical nonmetallic tubing (ENT)
- Table C.2(A)—Compact conductors in electrical nonmetallic tubing (ENT)
- Table C.3—Conductors and fixture wires in flexible metal conduit (FMC)
- Table C.3(A)—Compact conductors in flexible metal conduit (FMC)
- Table C.4—Conductors and fixture wires in intermediate metal conduit (IMC)
- Table C.4(A)—Compact conductors in intermediate metal conduit (IMC)
- Table C.5—Conductors and fixture wires in liquidtight flexible nonmetallic conduit (gray type) (LFNC-B)
- Table C.5(A)—Compact conductors in liquidtight flexible nonmetallic conduit (gray type) (LFNC-B)
- Table C.6—Conductors and fixture wires in liquidtight flexible nonmetallic conduit (orange type) (LFNC-A)
- Table C.6(A)—Compact conductors in liquidtight flexible nonmetallic conduit (orange type) (LFNC-A)

Author's Comment: The annex doesn't have a table for LFNC of the black type (LFNC-C).

- Table C.7—Conductors and fixture wires in liquidtight flexible metal conduit (LFMC)
- Table C.7(A)—Compact conductors in liquidtight flexible metal conduit (LFMC)
- Table C.8—Conductors and fixture wires in rigid metal conduit (RMC)
- Table C.8(A)—Compact conductors in rigid metal conduit (RMC)
- Table C.9—Conductors and fixture wires in rigid PVC conduit, Schedule 80
- Table C.9(A)—Compact conductors in rigid PVC conduit, Schedule 80
- Table C.10—Conductors and fixture wires in rigid PVC conduit, Schedule 40
- Table C.10(A)—Compact conductors in rigid PVC conduit, Schedule 40
- Table C.11—Conductors and fixture wires in Type A, rigid PVC conduit
- Table C.11(A)—Compact conductors in Type A, rigid PVC conduit
- Table C.12—Conductors and fixture wires in Type EB, PVC conduit
- Table C.12(A)—Compact conductors in Type EB, PVC conduit

▶ Annex C—Table C.1—EMT

Question: *How many 14 RHH conductors (without cover) can be installed in trade size 1 EMT?* **Figure 5–2**

(a) 13 (b) 16 (c) 19 (d) 25

Answer: *(b) 16 conductors [Annex C, Table C.1]*

Note 2 at the end of Annex C, Table C.1 indicates that an asterisk (*) with conductor insulation types RHH, RHW*, and RHW-2* means that these types don't have an outer covering. Insulation types RHH, RHW, and RHW-2 (without the asterisk) do have an outer cover. This is a cover (which may be a fibrous material) that increases the dimensions of the conductor more than the thin nylon cover encountered with conductors such as THHN.*

Question: *How many 8 THHN conductors can be installed in a trade size 3/4 EMT?* **Figure 5–3**

(a) 3 (b) 5 (c) 6 (d) 8

Answer: *(c) 6 conductors [Annex C, Table C.1]*

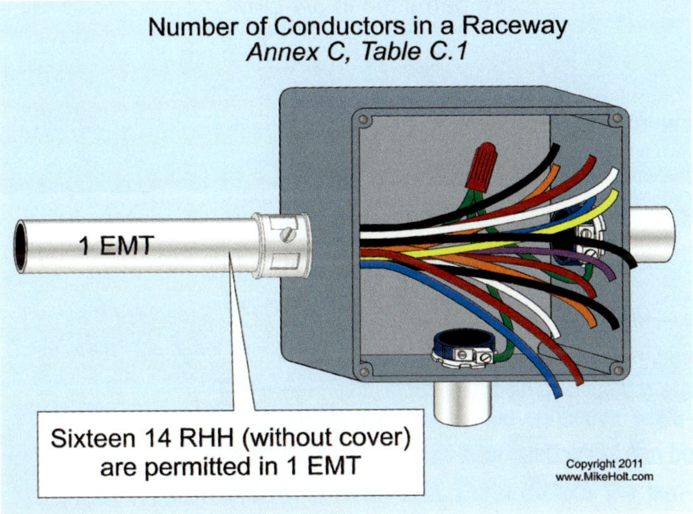

Figure 5–2

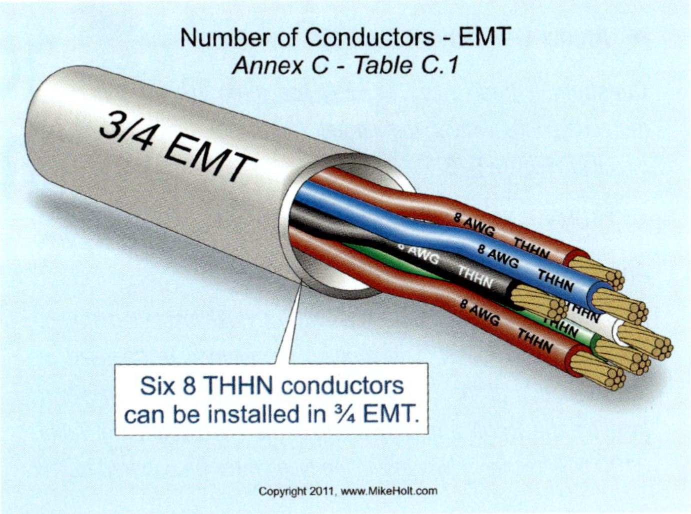

Figure 5–3

▶ Annex C—Table C.2A—Compact Conductors in ENT

Question: *How many 6 XHHW compact conductors can be installed in trade size 1¼ ENT?* **Figure 5–4**

(a) 6 (b) 10 (c) 13 (d) 16

Answer: *(b) 10 conductors [Annex C, Table C.2A]*

Compact stranding is the result of a manufacturing process where the standard conductor is compressed to the extent that the voids between the strands of wires are virtually eliminated [Annex C, Table C.1(a) footnote]. Unless the question specifically states compact conductors, assume that the conductors aren't the compact type.

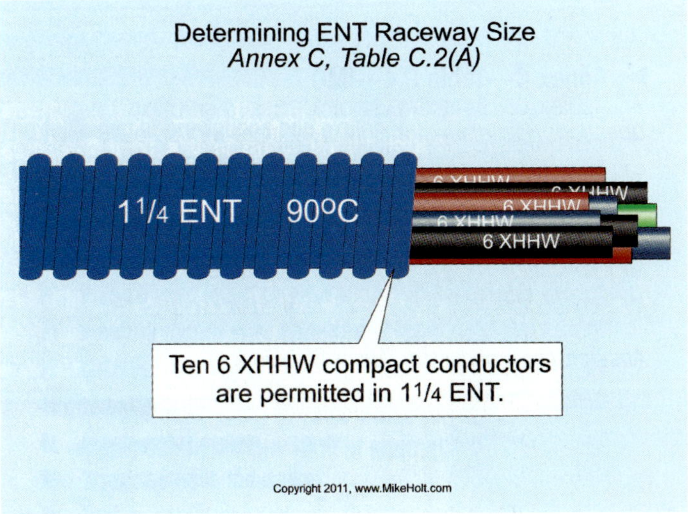

Figure 5–4

► Annex C—Table C.3—FMC

Question: *If trade size 1¼ FMC has three THHN conductors (not compact), what's the largest conductor permitted to be installed?* **Figure 5–5**

(a) 1 THHN (b) 1/0 THHN (c) 2/0 THHN (d) 3/0 THHN

Answer: *(a) 1 THHN [Annex C, Table C.3]*

It's common to see conductors with a dual insulation rating, such as THHN/THWN. This type of conductor can be used in a dry location at the THHN 90°C ampacity, or if used in a wet location, the THWN ampacity rating of the 75°C column of Table 310.15(B)(16) for THWN insulation types must be adhered to.

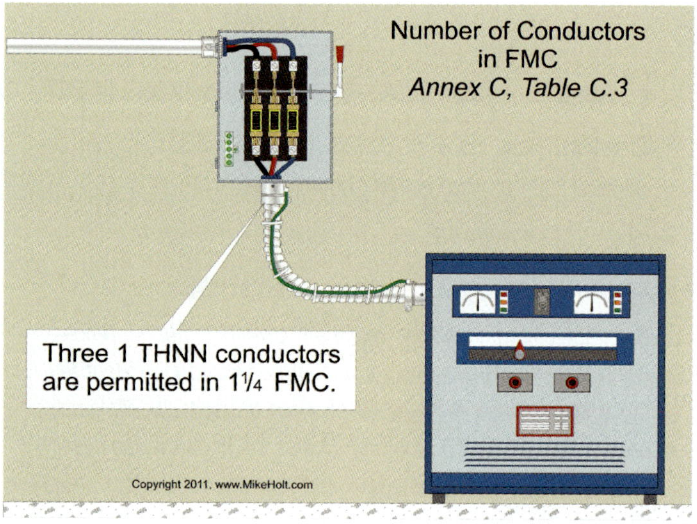

Figure 5–5

► Annex C—Table C.4—IMC

Question: *How many 4/0 RHH conductors with an outer cover can be installed in trade size 2 IMC?*

Note: *RHH insulation with an outer cover has no asterisk (*).*

(a) 1 conductor (b) 2 conductors
(c) 3 conductors (d) 4 conductors

Answer: *(c) 3 conductors [Annex C, Table C.4]*

► Annex C—Table C.7—Fixture Wire in LFMC

Question: *How many 18 TFFN conductors can be installed in trade size ¾ LFMC?* **Figure 5–6**

(a) 14 conductors (b) 26 conductors
(c) 30 conductors (d) 39 conductors

Answer: *(d) 39 conductors [Annex C, Table C.7]*

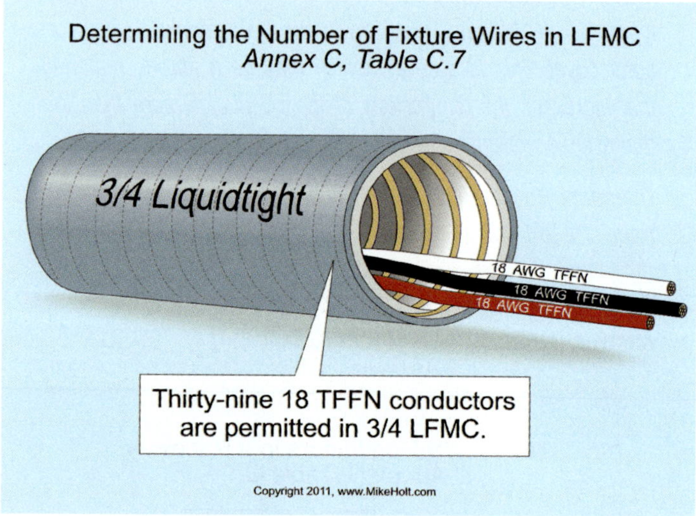

Figure 5–6

► Annex C—Table C.9—PVC Schedule 80

Question: *What's the smallest trade size PVC Schedule 80 raceway that can be used for the installation of a single 3/0 THHN as a grounding electrode conductor?* **Figure 5–7**

(a) Trade size ½ (b) Trade size ¾
(c) Trade size 1 (d) Trade size 1¼

Answer: (b) Trade size 3/4 [Annex C, Table C.9]

Question: *If trade size 2 PVC Schedule 80 has three THHN compact conductors, what's the largest conductor permitted to be installed?*

(a) 1/0 THHN (b) 4/0 THHN
(c) 250 kcmil THHN (d) 300 kcmil THHN

Answer: (d) 300 kcmil THHN [Annex C, Table C.9(A)]

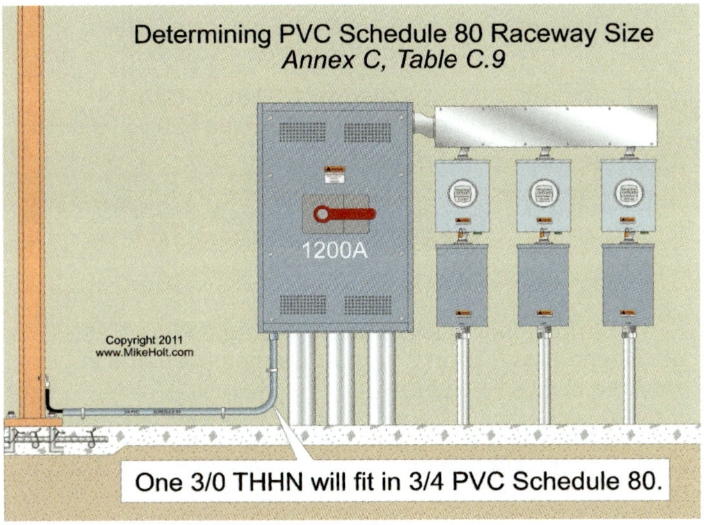

Figure 5–7

▶ Annex C—Table C.10—PVC Schedule 40

Question: *What's the smallest trade size PVC Schedule 40 raceway that can be used for the installation of four 1/0 THHN conductors?* **Figure 5–8**

(a) Trade size3/4	*(b) Trade size 1*
(c) Trade size 1 1/2	*(d) Trade size 2*

Answer: *(c) Trade size 1½ [Annex C, Table C.10]*

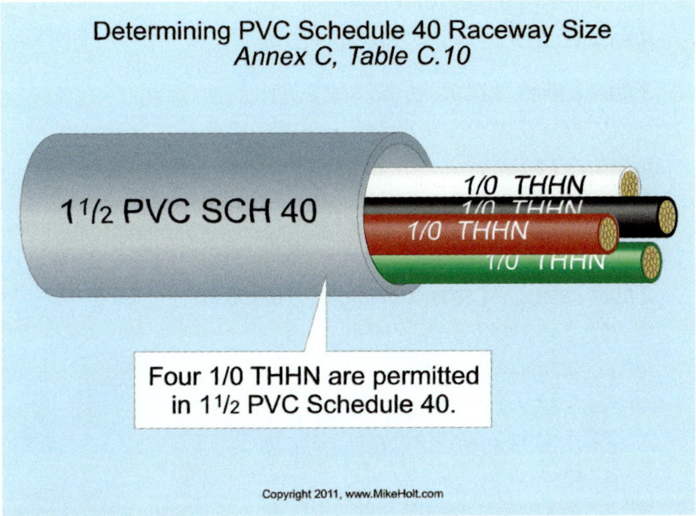

Figure 5–8

▶ Annex C—Table C.10(a)—Compact Conductors in PVC Schedule 40

Question: *If a trade size 2 PVC Schedule 40 raceway has three THHN compact conductors, what's the largest conductor permitted to be installed?*

(a) 1/0 THHN	*(b) 4/0 THHN*
(c) 350 kcmil THHN	*(d) 750 kcmil THHN*

Answer: *(c) 350 kcmil THHN [Annex C, Table C.10(A)]*

Notes to Tables, Note 2—Used for Physical Protection

The percentages listed in Table 1 apply only to complete raceway systems and aren't intended to apply to sections of raceways used to protect wiring from physical damage. **Figure 5–9**

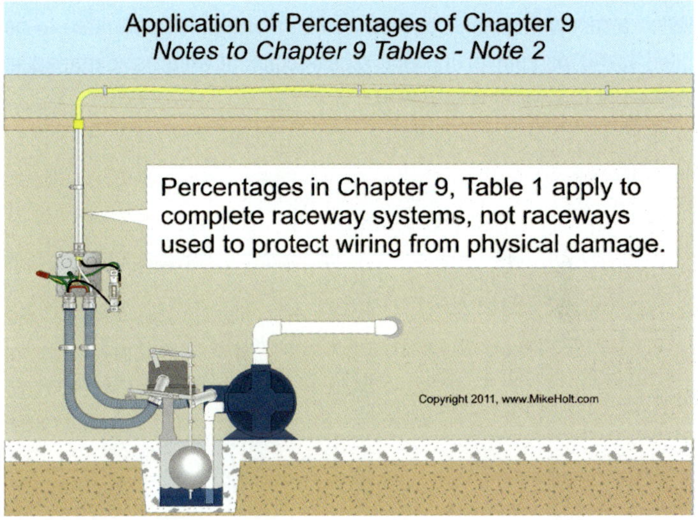

Figure 5–9

Notes to Tables, Note 3—Equipment Grounding Conductors

When equipment grounding and bonding conductors are installed in a raceway, the actual area of the conductor must be used to calculate raceway fill, **Figure 5–10** . Chapter 9, Table 5 can be used to determine the cross-sectional area of insulated conductors and Chapter 9, Table 8 can be used to determine the cross-sectional area of bare conductors (see Chapter 9, Notes to Tables, Note 8).

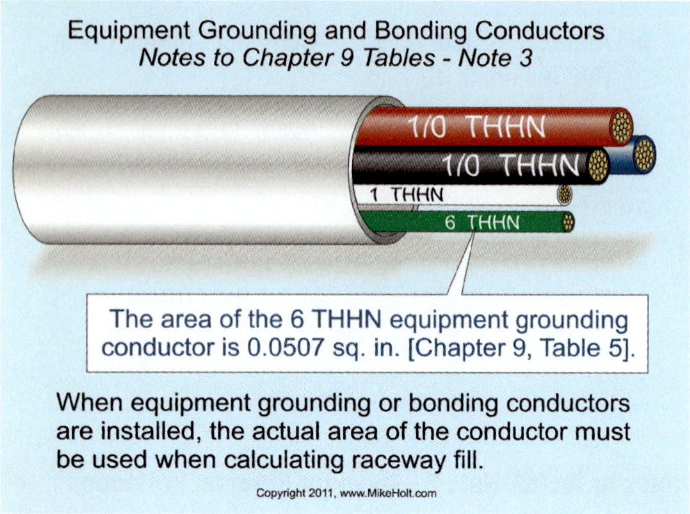

Figure 5–10

Notes to Tables, Note 4—Raceways not Exceeding 24 Inches

When a raceway doesn't exceed 24 in. in length, it's permitted to be filled to 60 percent of its total cross-sectional area as identified in Table 4 of Chapter 9. **Figure 5–11**

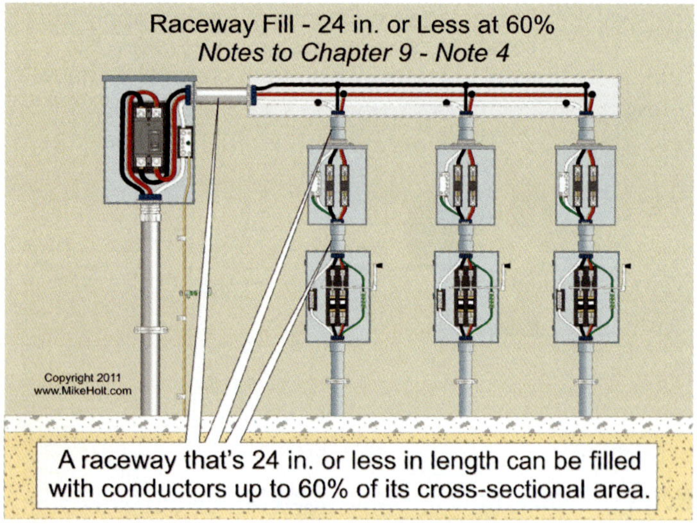

Figure 5–11

Notes to Tables, Note 5—Multiconductor Cables

For multiconductor cables, the actual cross-sectional area of the cable is to be used for raceway sizing. The cross sectional area of a circle is calculated by taking 3.14 x the square of the radius of the circle. **Figure 5–12**

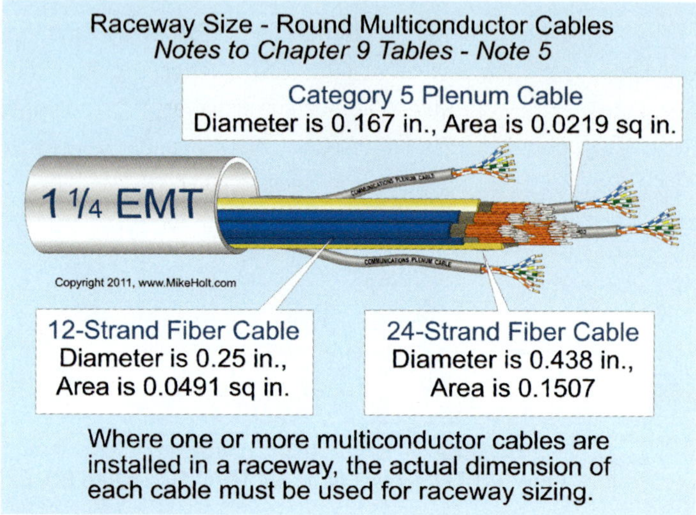

Figure 5–12

Question: *What Is the total are occupied in a raceway for the following cables?*

4 Category 5 plenum cables, dia = 0.167 in.
2 fiber cables, 24 strand, dia = 0.438 in.
3 fiber cables, 12 strand, dia = 0.25 in.

(a) 0.0254 (b) 0.1203 (c) 0.5363 (d) 0.9578

Answer: *(c) 0.5363 sq in.*

4 Cat 5 plenum cables, diameter = 0.167 in.
r = d/2 r = 0.167/2 = 0.0835 in.
Area = 3.14 x r^2
Area = 3.14 x 0.0835 in. x 0.0835 in.
Area = 0.0219 sq in. x 4 = 0.0876 sq in.

3 fiber cables, 12 strand, dia = 0.25 in.
r = d/2 r = 0.25/2 = 0.125 in.
Area = 3.14 x r^2
Area = 3.14 x 0.125 in. x 0.125 in.
Area = 0.0491 sq in. x 3 = 0.1473 sq in.

2 fiber cables, 24 strand, diameter = 0.438 in.
r = d/2 r = 0.438/2 = 0.219 in.
Area = 3.14 x r^2
Area = 3.14 x 0.219 in. x 0.219 in.
Area = 0.1507 sq in. x 2 = 0.3014 sq in.

Cat 5	*0.0876 sq in.*
12- strand	*0.1473 sq in.*
24-strand	*0.3014 sq in.*
	0.5363 sq in.

Notes to Tables, Note 6—Different Size Conductors

Use Table 4 and Table 5 when sizing raceways for conductors of different sizes. Table 4 provides the cross-sectional area of raceways, while Tables 5 and 5A give the cross-sectional areas of conductors. This is also the method to use when doing calculations for raceways of 24 in. and shorter, as Annex C doesn't account for the 60 percent fill allowance provided by Table 4. **Figure 5–13**

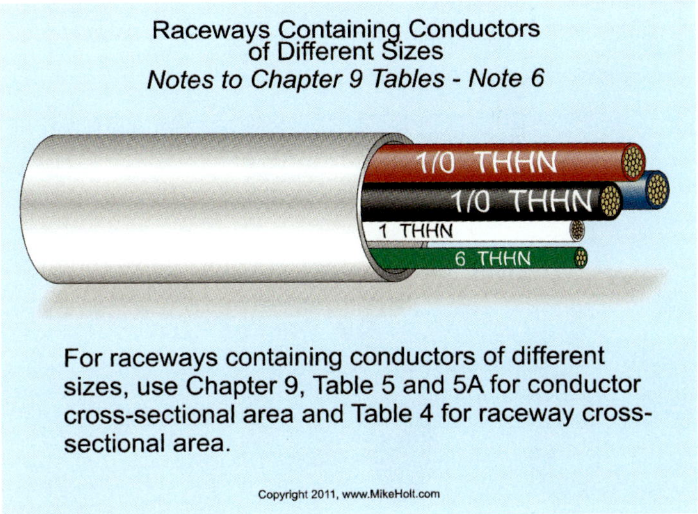

Figure 5–13

Notes to Tables, Note 7—Rounding

When the calculated number of conductors (all of the same size including insulation) results in 0.80 or more, the next higher whole number of conductors can be used.

> ***Question:*** *How many 8 THHN conductors can be installed in a trade size 3/4 EMT?* **Figure 5–14**
>
> *(a) 3* *(b) 5* *(c) 6* *(d) 8*
>
> ***Answer:*** *(c) 6 conductors*
>
> *8 THHN = 0.0366 sq in [Chapter 9 Table 5]*
>
> *3/4 EMT 40% fill = 0.213 sq in. [Chapter 9 Table 4]*
>
> *0.213 sq in./0.0366 sq in. = 5.82 conductors we are allowed to use 6 conductors per Chapter 9 Notes to Tables, Note 7*
>
> *When the calculated number of conductors, all of the same size including insulation results in 0.80 or more, the next higher number of conductors can be used [Chapter 9, Notes to Tables, Note 7]*

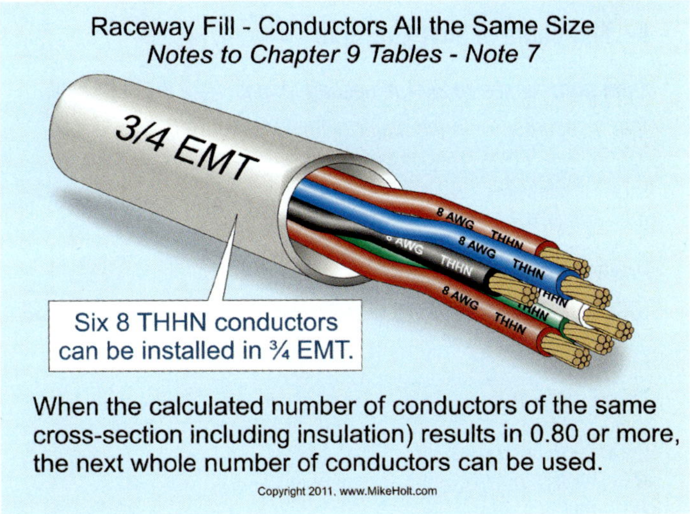

Figure 5–14

Notes to Tables, Note 8—Bare Conductors

The dimensions for bare conductors are listed in Chapter 9, Table 8. **Figure 5–15**

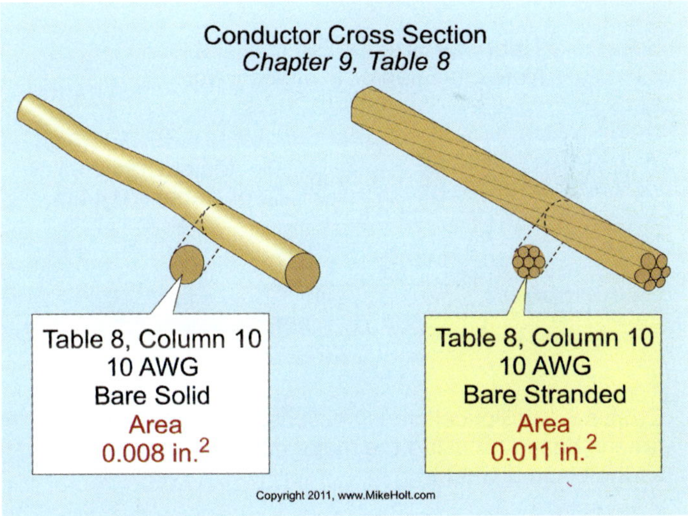

Figure 5–15

Notes to Tables, Note 9

A multiconductor cable or flexible cord is treated as a single conductor for calculating percentage conduit fill area. For cables with elliptical cross sections, the cross-sectional area is based on using the major diameter of the ellipse as the circle diameter.

► NM cable in EMT Example

Question: *What size EMT is needed for one 12-2 w/G NM cable that measures 7⁄16 on the major diameter?* **Figure 5–16**

(a) Trade size ½ *(b) Trade size ¾*
(c) Trade size 1 *(d) Trade size 1¼*

Answer: *(a) Trade size ½*

Area = 3.14 x r²

D = 7⁄16 in.
D = 0.4375 in.

R = D/2
R = 0.4375 in./2
R = 0.22 in.

Area = 3.14 x 0.22 in. x 0.22 in.
Area = 0.1520 sq in.

Use the one wire column (53%) of Chapter 9, Table 4 for EMT:

Trade size ½ EMT provides 0.161 sq in., which is larger than 0.1520 sq in. and will meet the minimum requirement.

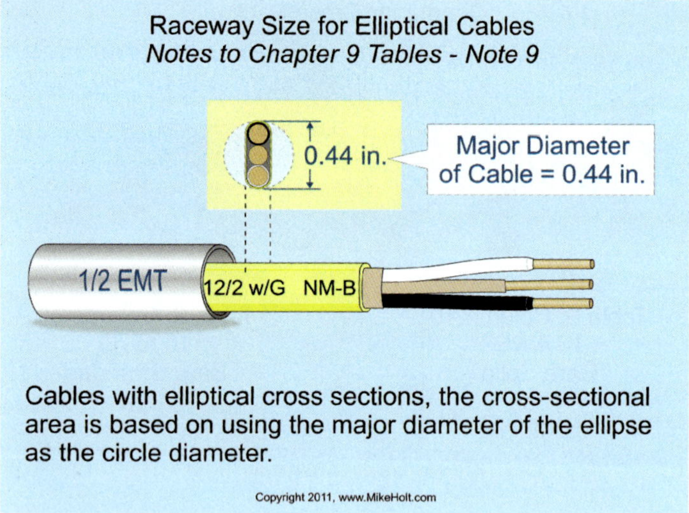

Figure 5–16

Notes to Tables—Raceway Cross-Sectional Area

The sixth column of this table (Total Area 100%) gives the total cross-sectional area in square inches of the raceway. There are also 31% (2 wires), 40% (3 or more wires), 53% (1 wire), and 60% (nipple) cross-sectional area columns based on the number of conductors in accordance with Chapter 9, Table 1.

► Raceway Cross-Sectional Area Example 1

Question: *What's the cross-sectional area of permitted conductor fill for a trade size 1 EMT raceway 30 inches long that contains four conductors?* **Figure 5–17**

(a) 0.346 sq in. *(b) 1.013 sq in.*
(c) 2.067 sq in. *(d) 3.356 sq in.*

Answer: *(a) 0.346 sq in.*
[Chapter 9, Notes to Tables, Note 4 and Table 4, 40% column]

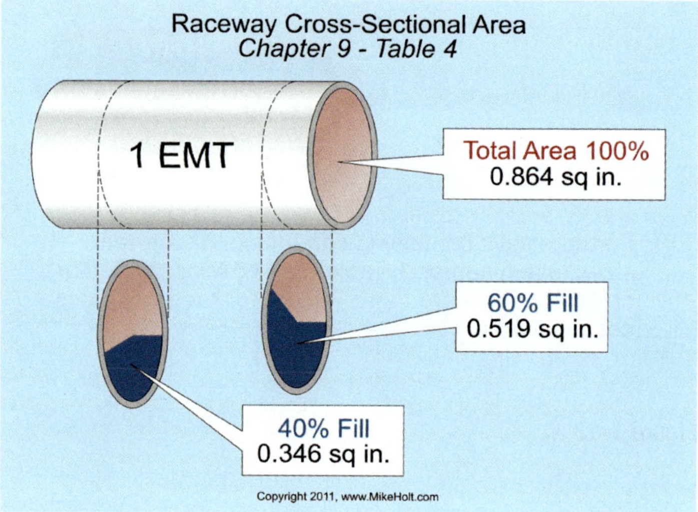

Figure 5–17

► Raceway Cross-Sectional Area Example 2

Question: *What's the cross-sectional area of permitted conductor fill for a trade size 2 EMT raceway that's 20 inches long?* **Figure 5–18**

(a) 1.342 sq in. *(b) 2.013 sq in.*
(c) 2.067 sq in. *(d) 3.356 sq in.*

Answer: *(b) 2.013 sq in.*
Reminder: For a raceway 24 in. and shorter, use the 60% column [Chapter 9, Notes to Tables, Note 4 and Table 4, 60% column]

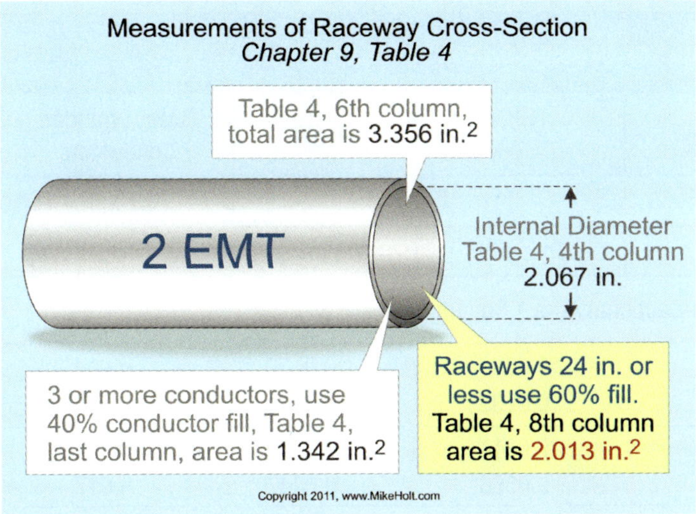

Figure 5–18

▶ Raceway Cross-Sectional Area Example 3

Question: *What's the cross-sectional area of permitted conductor fill for a trade size 2 EMT raceway 30 inches long that contains four conductors? See* **Figure 5–18**.

(a) 1.342 sq in. *(b) 2.013 sq in.*
(c) 2.067 sq in. *(d) 3.356 sq in.*

Answer: *(a) 1.342 sq in.*
[Chapter 9, Table 1 and Table 4, 40% column]

▶ Raceway Cross-Sectional Area Example 4

Question: *What's the minimum size EMT raceway required for three conductors with a wire fill of 0.25 sq in.?*

(a) Trade size ½ *(b) Trade size 1*
(c) Trade size 1¼ *(d) Trade size 1½*

Answer: *(b) Trade size 1*

▶ Raceway Cross-Sectional Area Example 5

Question: *What's the minimum size Schedule 80 PVC raceway required for three conductors with a wire fill of 0.35 sq in.?*

(a) Trade size ½ *(b) Trade size 1*
(c) Trade size 1¼ *(d) Trade size 1½*

Answer: *(c) Trade size 1¼*

Table 5—Dimensions of Insulated Conductors and Fixture Wires

Chapter 9, Table 5 lists the cross-sectional area of insulated conductors and fixture wires (see **Table 5–1**).

▶ Table 5—THHN

Question: *What's the cross-sectional area for one 10 THHN conductor?* **Figure 5–19**

(a) 0.0097 sq in. *(b) 0.0172 sq in.*
(c) 0.0211 sq in. *(d) 0.0278 sq in.*

Answer: *(c) 0.0211 sq in.*

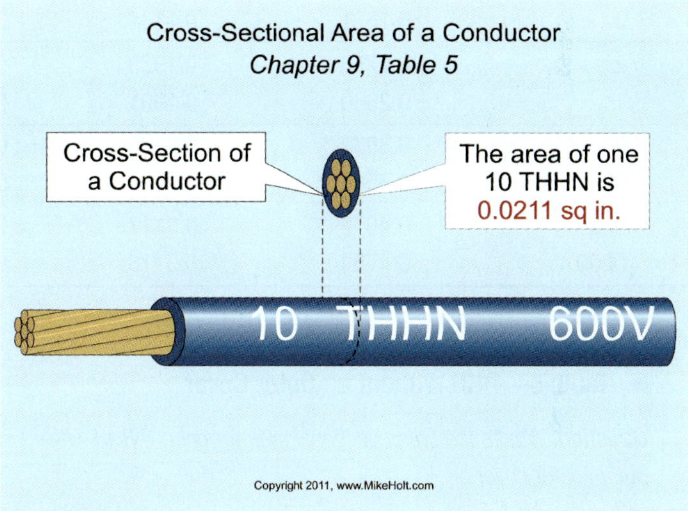

Figure 5–19

▶ Table 5—RHW With an Outer Cover

Question: *What's the cross-sectional area for one 10 RHW conductor with an outer cover?*

(a) 0.0172 sq in. *(b) 0.0206 sq in.*
(c) 0.0278 sq in. *(d) 0.0437 sq in.*

Answer: *(d) 0.0437 sq in.*

Table 5–1: Commonly Used Conductor Cross-Sectional Area

Column 1	RHH/RHW With Cover	RHH/RHW Without Cover	TW or THW	THHN THWN	XHHW	BARE Stranded Conductors
	Chapter 9, Table 5					Chapter 9 Table 8
	Column 2	Column 3	Column 4	Column 5	Column 6	
Size AWG/kcmil	Approximate Cross-Sectional Area – Square Inches					
14	0.0293	0.0209	0.0139	0.0097	0.0139	0.004
12	0.0353	0.0260	0.0181	0.0133	0.0181	0.006
10	0.0437	0.0333	0.0243	0.0211	0.0243	0.011
8	0.0835	0.0556	0.0437	0.0366	0.0437	0.017
6	0.1041	0.0726	0.0726	0.0507	0.0590	0.027
4	0.1333	0.0973	0.0973	0.0824	0.0814	0.042
3	0.1521	0.1134	0.1134	0.0973	0.0962	0.053
2	0.1750	0.1333	0.1333	0.1158	0.1146	0.067
1	0.2660	0.1901	0.1901	0.1562	0.1534	0.087
0	0.3039	0.2223	0.2223	0.1855	0.1825	0.109
00	0.3505	0.2624	0.2624	0.2233	0.2190	0.137
000	0.4072	0.3117	0.3117	0.2679	0.2642	0.173
0000	0.4754	0.3718	0.3718	0.3237	0.3197	0.219

► **Table 5—RHH Without an Outer Cover**

Question: *What's the cross-sectional area for one 10 RHH without an outer cover?*

(a) 0.0117 sq in. *(b) 0.0252 sq in.*
(c) 0.0278 sq in. *(d) 0.0333 sq in.*

Answer: *(d) 0.0333 sq in.*

The note at the end of Table 5 states that conductor Types RHH, RHW, and RHW-2 without outer coverings are identified on the table with an asterisk (*).

Author's Comment: The difference in the insulation thickness between RHH and THHN can be determined from Table 310.104(A) Conductor Applications and Insulations. You will find that 10 RHH has an insulation thickness of 45 mils while 10 THHN has an insulation thickness of 20 mils.

Table 5A—Dimensions of Compact Insulated Conductors

Chapter 9, Table 5A, lists the cross-sectional areas for compact copper and aluminum building wires. These conductors use specially shaped strands so that the overall size of the conductor is more compact. The outer covering is marked as a compact conductor.

► **Table 5—THHN Compact Conductors**

Question: *What's the cross-sectional area for one 1 THHN compact conductor?*

(a) 0.0117 sq in. *(b) 0.1352 sq in.*
(c) 0.2733 sq in. *(d) 0.5216 sq in.*

Answer: *(b) 0.1352 sq in.*

► Table 5—Compact Conductors

Question: *What's the cross-sectional area for one 4/0 XHHW compact conductor?*

(a) 0.0117 sq in. *(b) 0.1352 sq in.*
(c) 0.2733 sq in. *(d) 0.5216 sq in.*

Answer: *(c) 0.2733 sq in.*

Table 8—Conductor Properties

Chapter 9, Table 8 contains conductor properties such as the cross-sectional area in circular mils, the number of strands per conductor, the cross-sectional area in square inches for bare conductors, and the direct-current resistance at 75°C for both copper and aluminum conductors.

► Bare Conductor—Cross-Sectional Area

Question: *What's the cross-sectional area for one 10 AWG bare stranded conductor?* **Figure 5–20**

(a) 0.008 sq in. *(b) 0.011 sq in.*
(c) 0.038 sq in. *(d) a or b*

Answer: *(b) 0.011 sq in. [Chapter 9, Table 8]*

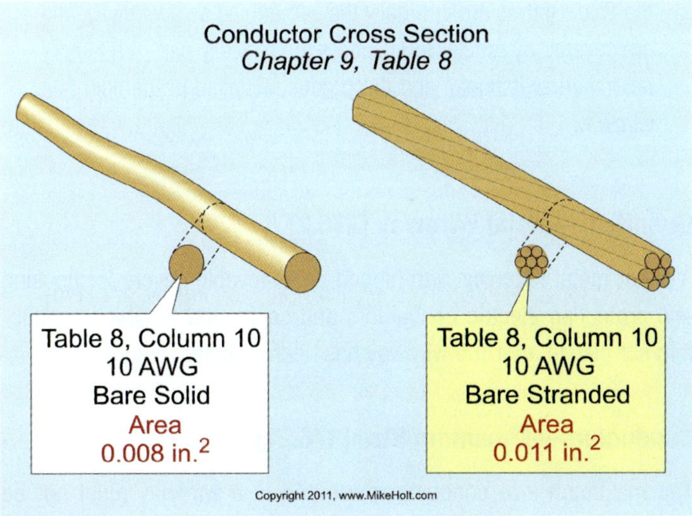

Figure 5–20

5.2 Raceway Calculations

Annex C—Tables 1 through 12 can't be used to determine raceway sizing when conductors of different sizes are installed in the same raceway. When this situation is encountered, use the following steps to determine the raceway size and nipple size:

Step 1: Determine the cross-sectional area (in square inches) for each conductor from Chapter 9, Table 5 for insulated conductors and from Chapter 9, Table 8 for bare conductors.

Step 2: Determine the total cross-sectional area for all conductors.

Step 3: Size the raceway according to the percent fill as listed in Chapter 9, Table 1. Chapter 9, Table 4 includes the various types of raceways with columns representing the allowable percentage fills; such as 40 percent for three or more conductors, and 60 percent for raceways 24 in. or less in length. Be careful when selecting the raceway from Chapter 9, Table 4 as this table is divided up into numerous tables for each raceway type, and you must choose the correct section of the table for the type of raceway for which you're performing the calculations.

► Raceway Size

Question: *What's the minimum size Schedule 40 PVC raceway required for three 500 kcmil THHN conductors, one 250 kcmil THHN conductor, and one 3 THHN conductor.* **Figure 5–21**

(a) Trade size 2 *(b) Trade size 2½*
(c) Trade size 3 *(d) Trade size 3½*

Answer: *(c) Trade size 3*

Step 1: Determine the cross-sectional area of the conductors [Chapter 9, Table 5].

500 THHN 0.7073 sq in. x 3 wires = 2.1219 sq in.
250 THHN 0.3970 sq in. x 1 wire = 0.3970 sq in.
3 THHN 0.0973 sq in. x 1 wire = 0.0973 sq in.

Step 2: Total cross-sectional area of all conductors = 2.6162 sq in.

Step 3: Size the conduit at 40 percent fill [Chapter 9, Table 1] using Chapter 9, Table 4 (be sure to select the table for PVC Schedule 40). Trade size 3 Schedule 40 PVC has an allowable cross-sectional area of 2.907 sq in. for over two conductors in the 40 percent column.

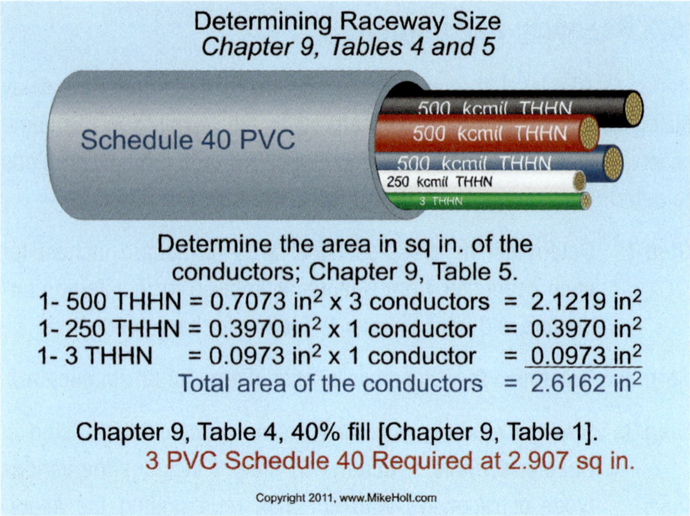

Figure 5–21

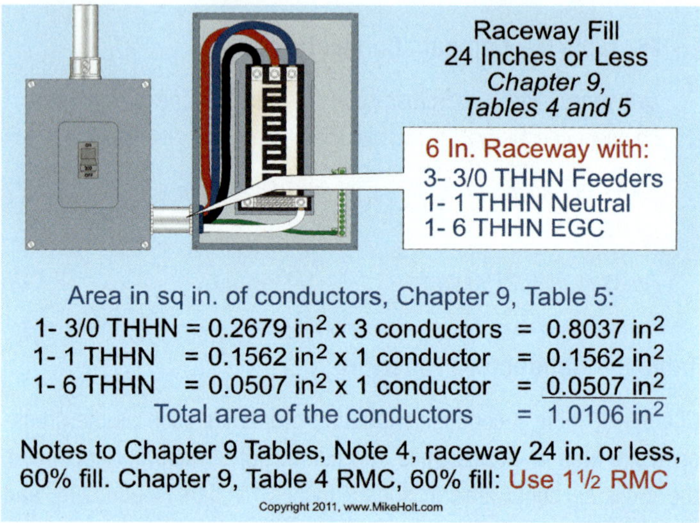

Figure 5–22

▶ Raceway 24 in. or Less in Length

Question: *What size RMC 24 in. or less in length is required for three 3/0 THHN conductors, one 1 THHN conductor, and one 6 THHN conductor?* **Figure 5–22**

(a) Trade size ½ *(b) Trade size 1*
(c) Trade size 1½ *(d) Trade size 2*

Answer: *(c) Trade size 1½*

Step 1: Determine the cross-sectional area of the conductors [Chapter 9, Table 5].

3/0 THHN 0.2679 sq in. x 3 wires = 0.8037 sq in.
1 THHN 0.1562 sq in. x 1 wire = 0.1562 sq in.
6 THHN 0.0507 sq in. x 1 wire = 0.0507 sq in.

Step 2: Total cross-sectional area of the conductors = 1.0106 sq in.

Step 3: Size the conduit at 60 percent fill [Chapter 9, Table 1, Note 4] using Chapter 9, Table 4.

Trade size 1¼ nipple = 0.0916 sq in., too small
Trade size 1½ nipple = 1.243 sq in., just right
Trade size 2 nipple = 2.045 sq in., larger than required

5.3 Wireways

Wireways are commonly used where access to the conductors within the raceway is required to make terminations, splices, or taps to several devices at a single location. Their high cost precludes their use for other than short distances, except in some commercial or industrial occupancies where the wiring is frequently revised.

Author's Comment: Both metal wireways [376] and nonmetallic wireways [378] are often called "troughs" or "gutters" in the field. Gutters are not really the same thing as a wireway, and are covered by Article 366. Gutters are typically part of a factory fabricated switchgear, and the product installed in the field is a wireway.

Definition—Metal Wireway [376.2]

A sheet metal raceway with hinged or removable covers for housing and protecting electric conductors and cable, and in which conductors are placed after the wireway has been installed. **Figure 5–23**

Conductors—Maximum Size [376.21]

The maximum size conductor permitted in a wireway must not be larger than that for which the wireway is designed.

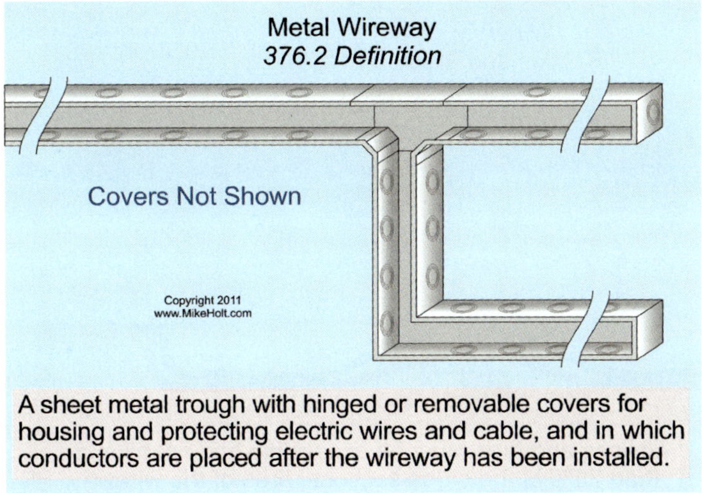

Figure 5–23

Number of Conductors and Ampacity [376.22]

(a) Number of Conductors. The maximum number of conductors permitted in a wireway is limited to 20 percent of the cross-sectional area of the wireway. Figure 5–24

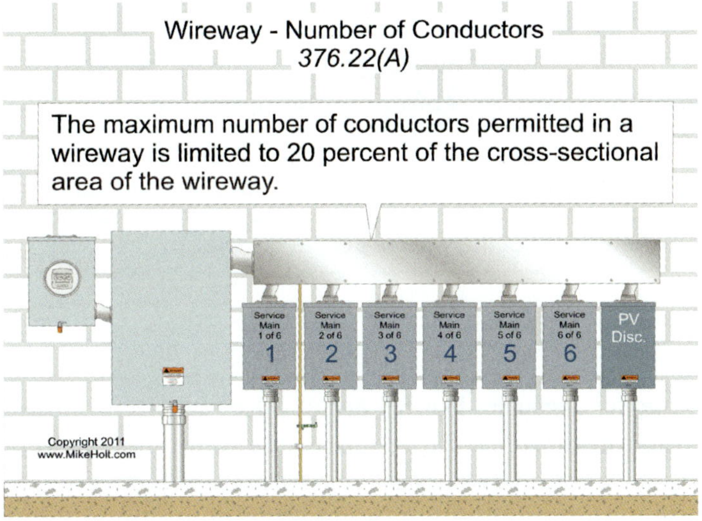

Figure 5–24

► Wireway Cross-Sectional Area

Question: *What's the cross-sectional area of a 6 in. x 6 in. wireway?*

(a) 6 sq in. (b) 16 sq in. (c) 36 sq in. (d) 66 sq in.

Answer: *(c) 36 sq in.*

The cross-sectional area is found by multiplying height by depth: 6 in. x 6 in. = 36 sq in.

► Wireway Allowable Conductor Fill Area

Question: *What's the maximum allowable conductor fill in square inches for a 6 in. x 6 in. wireway?*

(a) 5 sq in. (b) 6.50 sq in. (c) 7.20 sq in. (d) 8.90 sq in.

Answer: *(c) 7.20 sq in.*

36 sq in. x 0.20 = 7.20 sq in. [376.22(A)]

► Wireway Conductor Fill

Question: *What's the maximum number of 500 kcmil THHN conductors that can be installed in a 6 in. x 6 in. wireway?* Figure 5–25

(a) 4 (b) 6 (c) 10 (d) 20

Answer: *(c) 10*

36 sq in. x 0.20 = 7.20 sq in. [376.22(A)]

500 kcmil THHN = 0.7073 sq in. [Chapter 9, Table 5]

Maximum Allowable Area/Area per Conductor = Number of Conductors

7.20 sq in./0.7073 sq in. = 10.17 conductors

10 conductors can be installed.

Note: *Conductor ampacity adjustment for bundling isn't required because there are fewer than 30 current-carrying conductors [376.22(B)].*

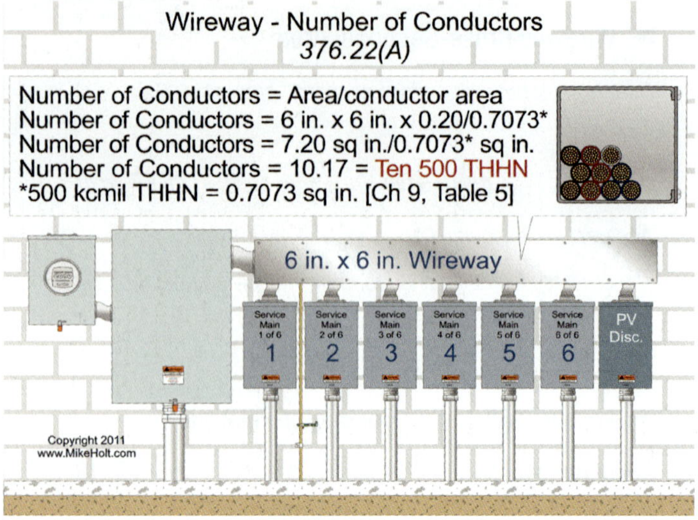

Figure 5–25

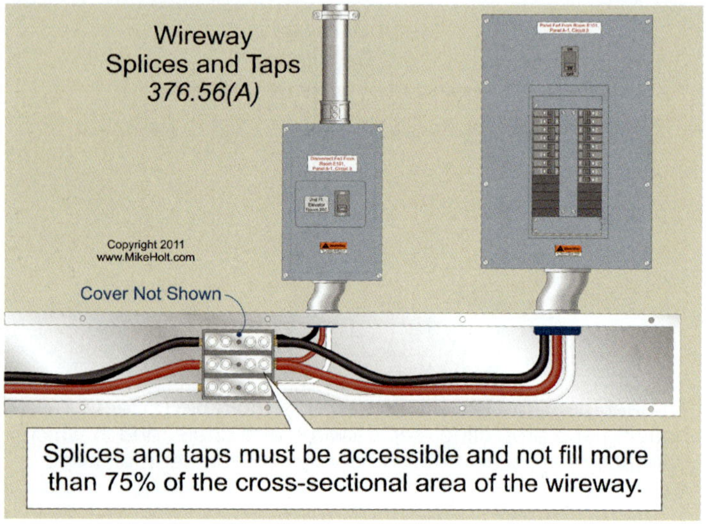

Figure 5–26

▶ Wireway Conductor Fill

Question: *What size wireway is required for three 500 kcmil THHN, one 250 kcmil THHN, and four 4/0 THHN conductors?*

(a) 4 in. x 4 in. *(b) 6 in. x 6 in.*
(c) 8 in. x 8 in. *(d) 10 in. x 10 in.*

Answer: *(b) 6 in. x 6 in.*

Find the conductor area [Chapter 9, Table 5]

500 kcmil THHN = 0.7073 sq in. x 3 = 2.1219 sq in.
250 kcmil THHN = 0.3970 sq in.
4/0 THHN = 0.3237 sq in. x 4 =1.2948 sq in.
Total Conductor Area = 3.8137 sq in.

The wireway must not be filled to over 20 percent of its cross-sectional area [376.22(A)]. Twenty percent is equal to one-fifth, so we can multiply the required conductor area by five to find the minimum square inch area required.

Conductor Area x 5 = Required Wireway Minimum Area
3.8137 sq in. x 5 = 19.07 sq in.

A 6 in. x 6 in. wireway has a cross-sectional area of 36 sq in. and will be large enough.

Wireway Splices and Taps. Splices and taps must not fill more than 75 percent of the wiring space at any cross section [376.56]. **Figure 5–26 and 5–27**

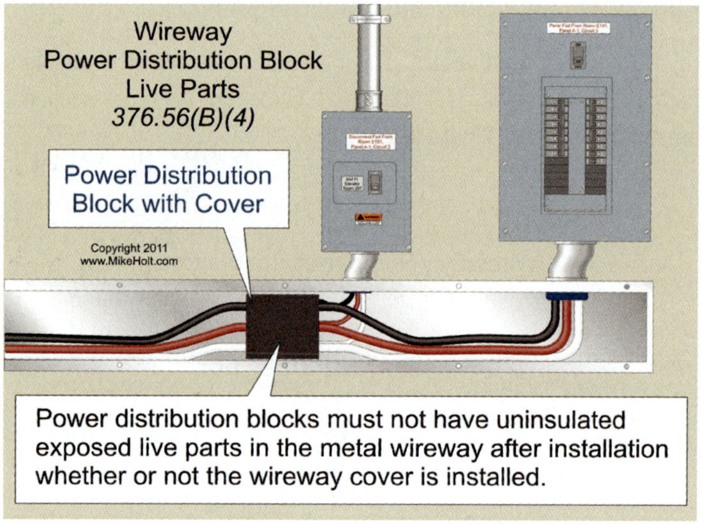

Figure 5–27

Sizing for Conductor Bending Radius. Where conductors are bent within a metal wireway, the wireway must be sized to meet the bending radius requirements contained in Table 312.6(A), based on one wire per terminal [367.23(A)]. **Figure 5–28**

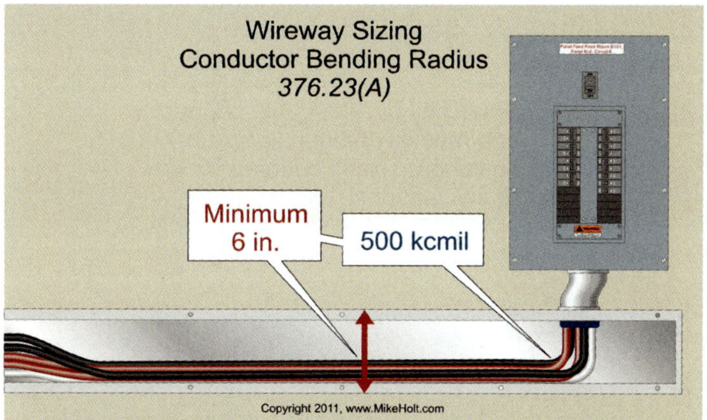

Where conductors are bent, the wireway must be sized to meet the bending radius of Table 312.6(A), based on one wire per terminal.

Figure 5–28

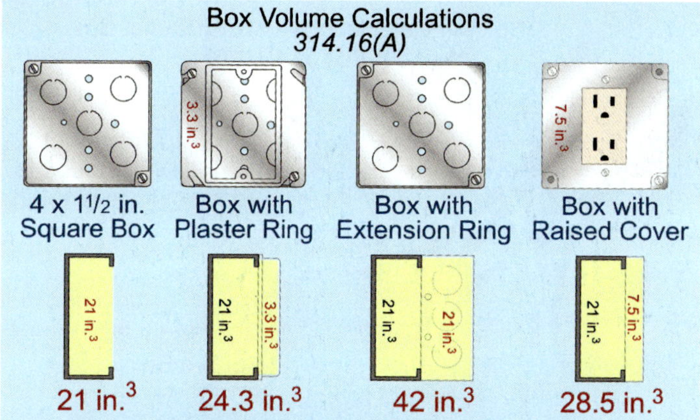

The volume of a box includes the volume of its assembled parts that are marked with their cu in. or are made from boxes listed in Table 314.16(A).

Figure 5–29

5.4 Tips for Raceway Calculations

Tip 1: Take your time.

Tip 2: Use a ruler or a straightedge when using tables, and highlight key words and important sections.

Tip 3: Watch out for different types of raceways and conductor insulations, particularly RHH/RHW with or without an outer cover.

Tip 4: Watch for the difference between conductors and compact conductors.

PART B—OUTLET BOX FILL CALCULATIONS [314.16]

Introduction

Boxes must be of sufficient size to provide free space for all conductors. An outlet box is generally used for the attachment of devices and luminaires and has a specific amount of space (volume) for conductors, devices, and fittings. The volume taken up by conductors, devices, and fittings in a box must not exceed the box fill capacity. The volume of a box is the total volume of its assembled parts, including plaster rings, industrial raised covers, and extension rings. The total volume includes only those parts that are marked with their volumes in cubic inches [314.16(A)] or included in Table 314.16(A) of the *NEC*. **Figure 5–29**

5.5 Sizing Box—Conductors All the Same Size [Table 314.16(A)]

When all of the conductors in an outlet box are the same size (insulation doesn't matter), Table 314.16(A) can be used to:

(1) Determine the number of conductors permitted in the outlet box, or

(2) Determine the size outlet box required for the given number of conductors.

Author's Comment: If the outlet box contains switches, receptacles, luminaire studs, luminaire hickeys, manufactured cable clamps, or equipment grounding conductors, then we must make an allowance for these items, which is not reflected in Table 314.16(A) .

► Outlet Box Size

Question: *What's the minimum depth for a 4 in. square outlet box which contains six 12 THHN conductors and three 12 THW conductors?* **Figure 5–30**

(a) 4 x 1¼ in. square *(b) 4 x 1½ in. square*
(c) 4 x 2⅛ in. square *(d) 4 x 2⅛ in. with extension*

Answer: *(b) 4 x 1½ in. square*

Table 314.16(a) permits nine 12 AWG conductors; the insulation type isn't a factor when calculating box fill.

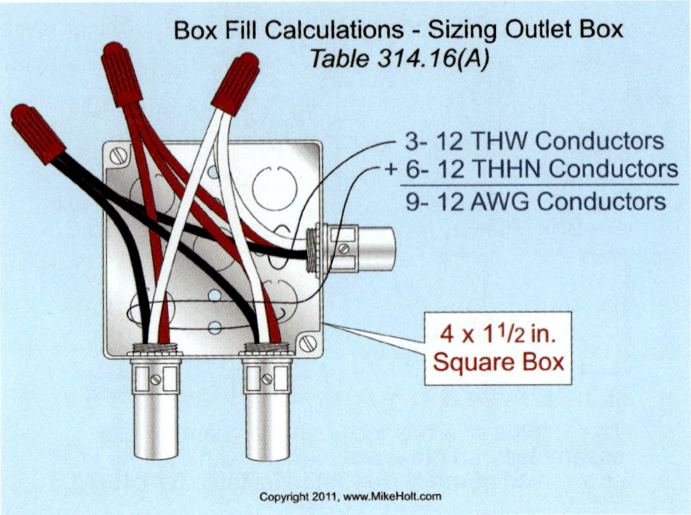

Figure 5–30

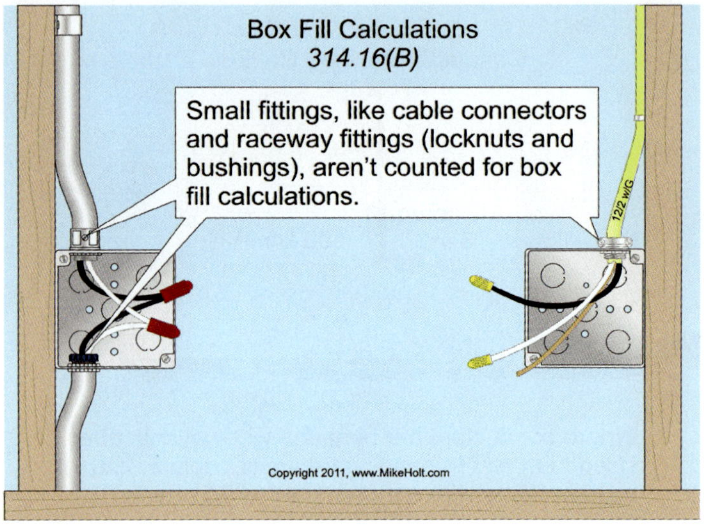

Figure 5–31

▶ Number of Conductors in an Outlet Box

Question: *Using Table 314.16(A), how many 14 THHN conductors are permitted in a 4 x 1½ in. round box?*

(a) 7 conductors *(b) 9 conductors*
(c) 10 conductors *(d) 11 conductors*

Answer: *(a) 7 conductors*

5.6 Conductor Equivalents

Box Fill Calculations [314.16(B)].

The calculated conductor volume determined by (1) through (5) and Table 314.16(B) are added together to determine the total volume of the conductors, devices, and fittings. Raceway and cable fittings, including locknuts and bushings, aren't counted for box fill calculations. Figure 5–31

Table 314.16(B) Volume Allowance Required per Conductor	
Conductor AWG	Volume cu in.
18	1.50
16	1.75
14	2.00
12	2.25
10	2.50
8	3.00
6	5.00

(1) Conductor Volume. Each unbroken conductor that runs through a box and each conductor that terminates in a box is counted as a single conductor volume in accordance with Table 314.16(B). Each loop or coil of unbroken conductor having a length of at least twice the minimum length required for free conductors in 300.14 must be counted as two conductor volumes. Conductors that originate and terminate within the box, such as pigtails, aren't counted at all. Figures 5–32 and 5–33

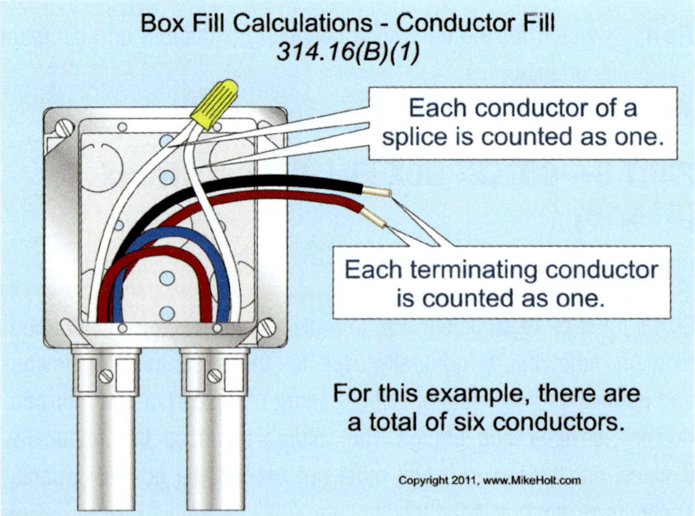

Figure 5–32

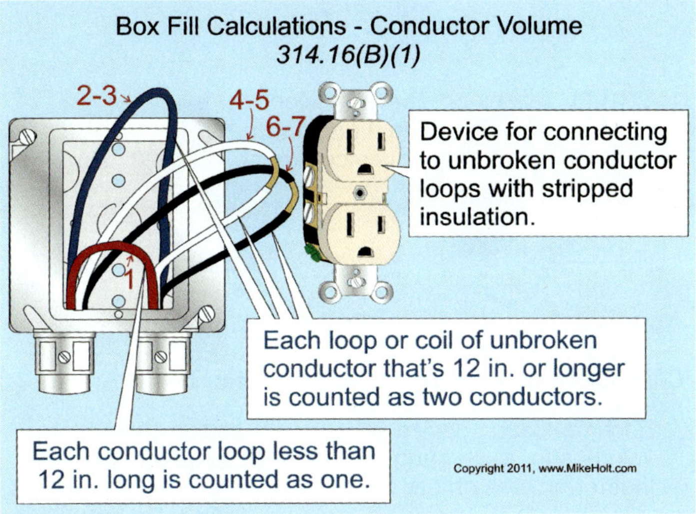

Figure 5–33

Author's Comment: According to 300.14, at least 6 in. of free conductor, measured from the point in the box where the conductors enter the enclosure, must be left at each outlet, junction, and switch point for splices or terminations of luminaires or devices.

Exception: Equipment grounding conductors, and up to four 16 AWG and smaller fixture wires, can be omitted from box fill calculations if they enter the box from a domed luminaire or similar canopy, such as a ceiling paddle fan canopy. Figure 5–34

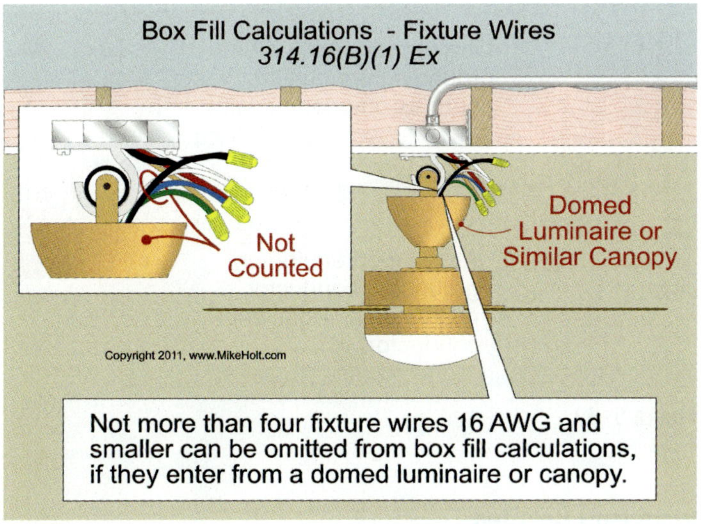

Figure 5–34

(2) Cable Clamp Volume. One or more internal cable clamps count as a single conductor volume in accordance with Table 314.16(B), based on the largest conductor that enters the box. Cable connectors that have their clamping mechanism outside the box aren't counted. Figure 5–35

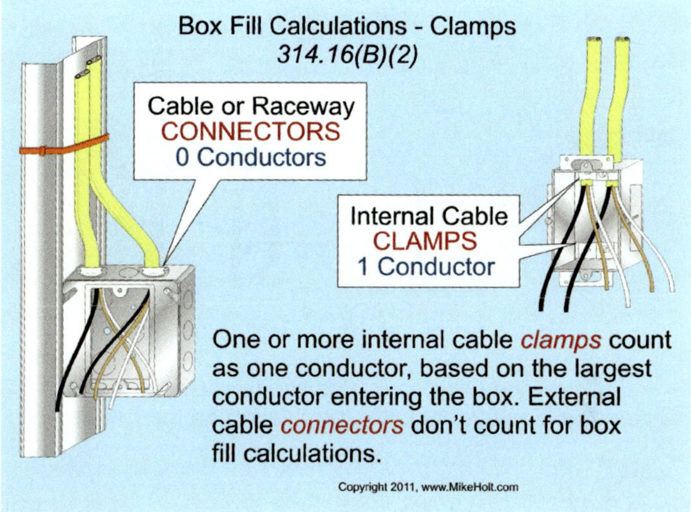

Figure 5–35

(3) Support Fitting Volume. Each luminaire stud or luminaire hickey counts as a single conductor volume in accordance with Table 314.16(B), based on the largest conductor that enters the box. Figure 5–36

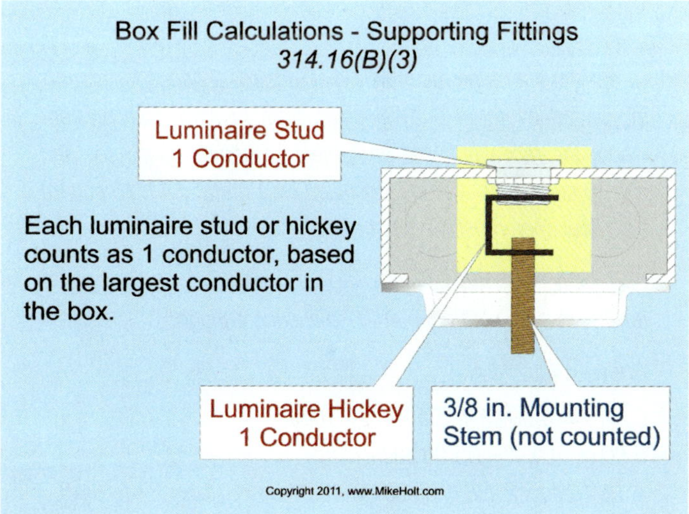

Figure 5–36

(4) Device Yoke Volume. Each single gang device yoke (regardless of the ampere rating of the device) counts as two conductor volumes based on the largest conductor that terminates on the device in accordance with Table 314.16(B). **Figure 5–37**

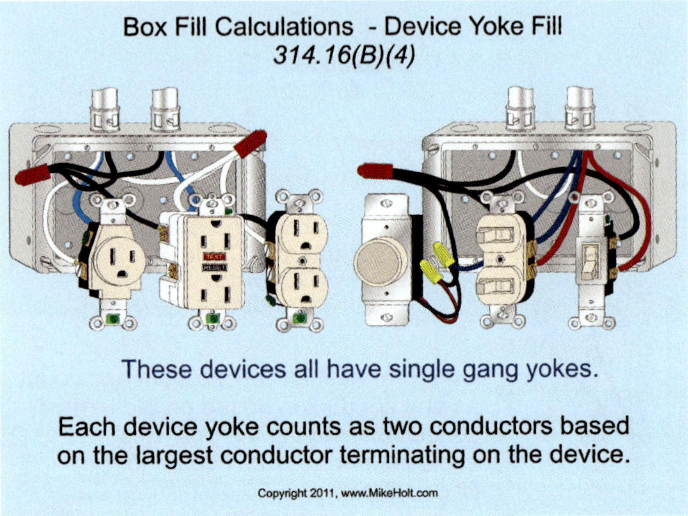

Figure 5–37

Each multigang device yoke counts as two conductor volumes for each gang based on the largest conductor that terminates on the device in accordance with Table 314.16(B). **Figure 5–38**

> **Author's Comment:** A device that's too wide for mounting in a single gang box is counted based on the number of gangs required for the device.

Question: *If a range receptacle that requires 2 gangs for mounting is fed by three 6 AWG conductors In a raceway system where the raceway is the equipment grounding conductor, and a 1.30 cu in. plaster ring is installed on a metal 4 11/16 square box, how deep must the box be?*

(a) 1 ¼ in. *(b) 1 ½ in.*
(c) 2 ⅛ in. *(d) none of these is deep enough*

Answer: *(c) 2 ⅛ in.*

6 AWG = 5.00 cu in. [Table 314.16(B)]
5.00 cu in. x 7 = 35.00 cu in.
4 11/16 sq x 2 1/8 deep box = 42.00 cu in. [Table 314.16(A)]
42.00 + 1.30 cu in. = 43.30 cu in.

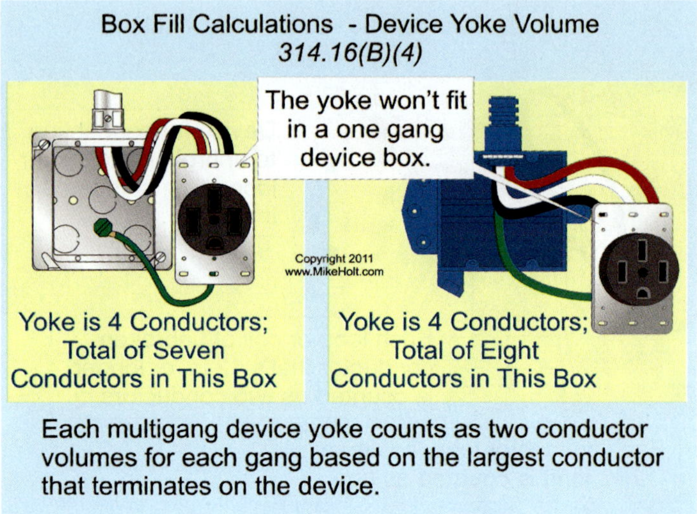

Figure 5–38

(5) Equipment Grounding Conductor Volume. All equipment grounding conductors in a box count as a single conductor volume in accordance with Table 314.16(B), based on the largest equipment grounding conductor that enters the box. Insulated equipment grounding conductors for receptacles having insulated grounding terminals (isolated ground receptacles) [250.146(D)] count as a single conductor volume in accordance with Table 314.16(B). **Figure 5–39**

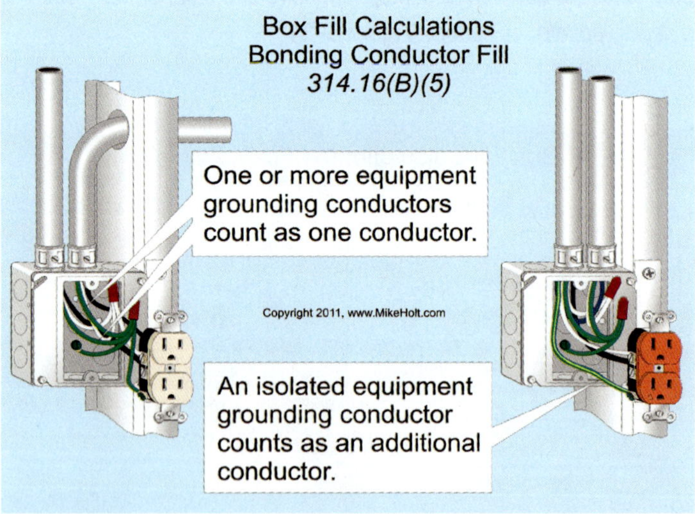

Figure 5–39

What Isn't Counted

Wire connectors, cable connectors, raceway fittings, and conductors that originate and terminate within the outlet box (such as equipment bonding jumpers and pigtails) aren't counted for box fill calculations [314.16(A)].

▶ Number of Conductors

Question: *What's the total number of conductors used for the box fill calculations in* **Figure 5–40**?

(a) 5 conductors *(b) 7 conductors*
(c) 9 conductors *(d) 11 conductors*

Answer: *(d) 11 conductors*

Switch and conductors	*5 – 14 AWG †*
Receptacles and conductors	*4 – 14 AWG ††*
Equipment grounding conductor	*1 – 14 AWG*
Cable clamps	*+ 1 – 14 AWG*
Total	*11 – 14 AWG*

†two conductors for the device and three conductors terminating

††two conductors for the device and two conductors terminating

Each 14 AWG counts as 2 cu in. [Table 314.16(B)].

11 conductors x 2 cu in. = 22 cu in.

If the cubic inch volume of the mud ring isn't stamped on it, or given in the problem, we can't include it in the box volume. Without knowing the mud ring volume, a 4 in. square by 2⅛ in. deep box is the minimum required for this example.

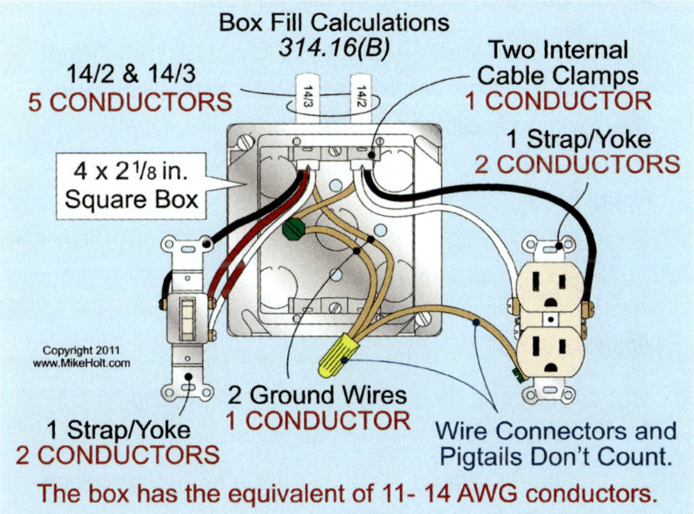

Figure 5–40

5.7 Outlet Box Sizing [314.16(B)]

To determine the size of the outlet box when the conductors are of different sizes (insulation isn't a factor), follow these steps:

Step 1: Determine the number and size of conductor equivalents in the box.

Step 2: Determine the volume of the conductor equivalents from Table 314.16(B).

Step 3: Size the box by using Table 314.16(A).

▶ Example: Calculating Different Size Conductors

Question: *What's the minimum depth 4 in. square outlet box required for one 14/3 w/G Type NM cable that terminates on a 3-way switch, and one 12/2 w/G Type NM cable that terminates on a receptacle? The box has internally installed cable clamps.* **Figure 5–41**

(a) 4 x 1¼ in. square *(b) 4 x 1½ in. square*
(c) 4 x 2⅛ in. square *(d) any of these*

Answer: *(c) 4 x 2⅛ in. square*

Step 1: Determine the number of each size conductor.

14 AWG	
14/3 NM =	*3 – 14 AWG*
Switch	*+ 2 – 14 AWG*
Total	*5 – 14 AWG*
12 AWG	
12/2 NM	*2 – 12 AWG*
Cable clamp	*1 – 12 AWG*
Receptacle	*2 – 12 AWG*
Equipment grounding conductor	*+ 1 – 12 AWG*
Total	*6 – 12 AWG*

All equipment grounding conductors count as one conductor, based on the largest equipment grounding conductor entering the box [314.16(B)(5)].

Step 2: Determine the volume of the conductors [Table 314.16(B)].

14 AWG	*2 cu in. each*
2 cu in. x 5 conductors	*10 cu in.*
12 AWG	*2.25 cu in. each*
2.25 cu in. x 6 conductors	*13.50 cu in.*
Total Volume	*10 cu in. + 13.50 cu in.*
Total Volume	*23.50 cu in.*

Step 3: Select the outlet box from Table 314.16(A).

4 x 2⅛ in. square, 30.30 cu in. meets the minimum cu in. requirements

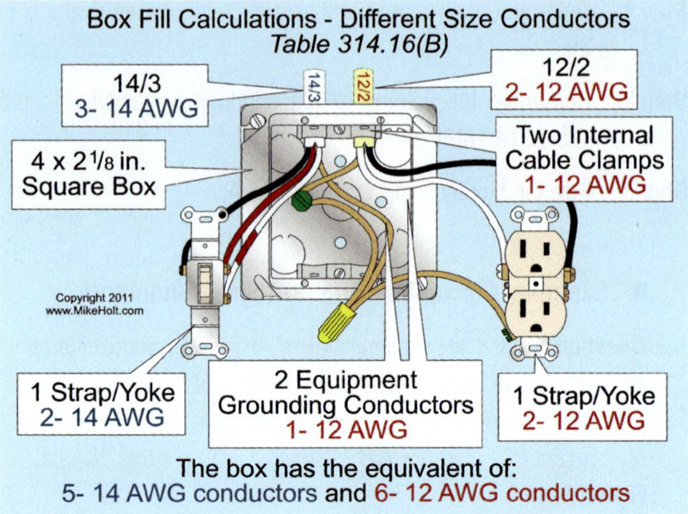

Figure 5–41

► Domed Fixture Canopy [314.16(B)(1) Ex]

Question: *A round 4 x ½ in. box has a total volume of 7 cu in. and has factory-installed internal cable clamps. Can this pancake box be used with a lighting luminaire that has a domed canopy? The branch-circuit wiring is 14/2 w/G NM cable, and the luminaire has two 16 AWG fixture wires and one 16 AWG ground wire.* **Figure 5–42**

(a) Yes *(b) No*

Answer: *(b) No*

The box is limited to 7 cu in., and the conductor equivalents total 8 cu in. [314.16(B)(1) Ex].

Step 1: Determine the number and size of conductors within the box.

Fixture wires, including the fixture equipment grounding conductor aren't counted when the fixture has a domed canopy.

14/2 NM	*2 – 14 AWG*
Cable clamps	*1 – 14 AWG*
Ground wire	*+ 1 – 14 AWG*
Total	*4 – 14 AWG conductors*

Step 2: Determine the volume of the conductors [Table 314.16(B)].

14 AWG = 2 cu in.

Four 14 AWG conductors = 4 wires x 2 cu in. = 8 cu in.

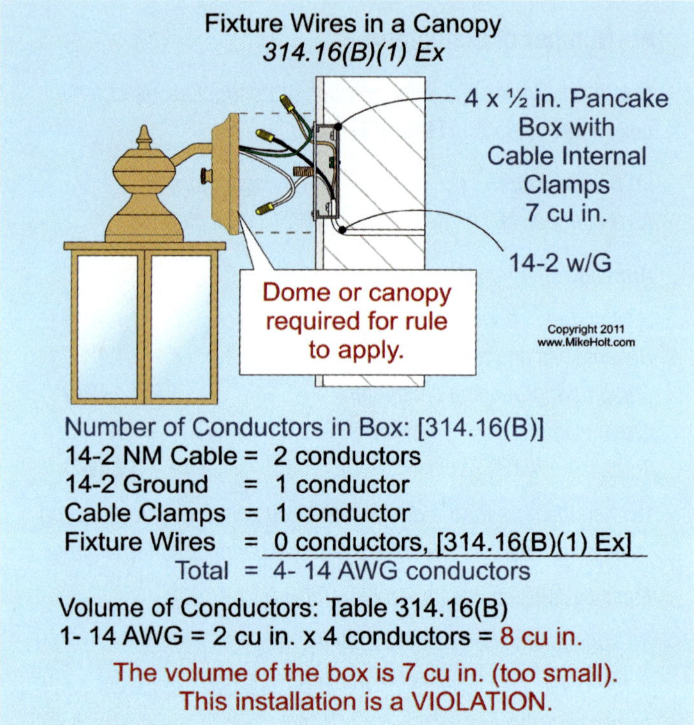

Figure 5–42

► Conductors Added to an Existing Box

Question: *How many 14 AWG conductors can be pulled through a 4 x 2 ⅛ in. square box that has a plaster ring of 3.60 cu in.? The box already contains two receptacles, five 12 AWG conductors, and one 12 AWG equipment grounding conductor.* **Figure 5–43**

(a) 4 conductors *(b) 5 conductors*
(c) 6 conductors *(d) 7 conductors*

Answer: *(b) 5 conductors*

Step 1: Determine the number and size of the existing conductors.

Two Receptacles (2 yokes x 2 conductors)	*4 – 12 AWG conductors*
Five 12 AWG	*5 – 12 AWG conductors*
One equipment grounding conductor	*+ 1 – 12 AWG conductors*
Total	*10 – 12 AWG conductors*

Step 2: Determine the volume of the existing conductors [Table 314.16(B)].

12 AWG conductor = 2.25 cu in.
10 wires x 2.25 cu in. = 22.50 cu in.

Step 3: Determine the space remaining for the additional 14 AWG conductors.

Remaining space = Total space less the area required for existing conductors

Total space = 30.30 cu in. (box) [Table 314.16(A)] + 3.60 cu in. (ring) = 33.90 cu in.

Remaining space = 33.90 cu in. – 22.50 cu in. (ten 12 AWG conductors)

Remaining space = 11.40 cu in.

Step 4: Determine the number of 14 AWG conductors permitted in the spare space.

Conductors added = Remaining space/added conductors' volume

Conductors added = 11.40 cu in./2 cu in. = 5.70 [Table 314.16(B)]

Conductors added = 5
(Rounding up doesn't apply to box fill.)

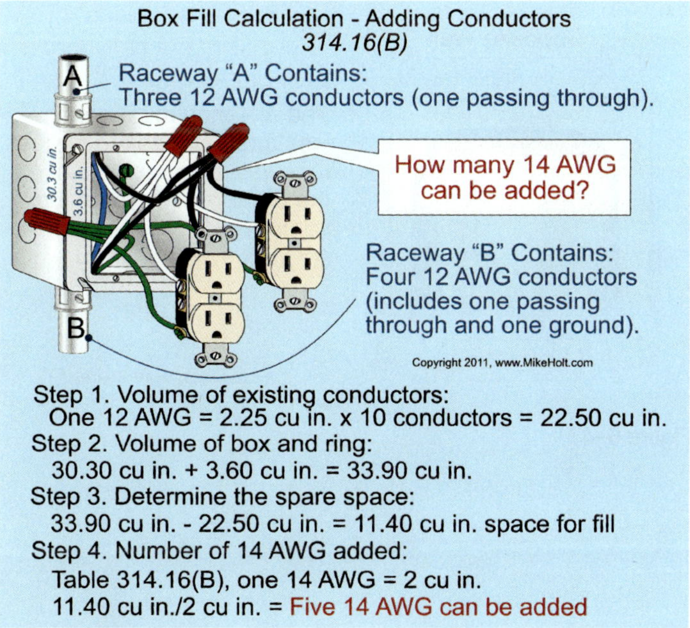

Figure 5–43

Tips for Outlet Box Sizing

Tip 1: If conductors are the same size, add them together and size the box using the AWG size columns of Table 314.16(A).

Tip 2: If the box contains different sizes of conductors, use Table 314.16(B) to find the area of each conductor, add them up, and size the box from Table 314.16(A) using the cu in. column.

Tip 3: Practice sizing boxes on the jobsite or in your own home, or by drawing out a picture problem to solve.

PART C—PULL BOXES, JUNCTION BOXES, AND CONDUIT BODIES

Introduction

Pull boxes, junction boxes, and conduit bodies must be sized to permit conductors to be installed so that the conductor insulation isn't damaged. For conductors 4 AWG and larger, pull boxes, junction boxes, and conduit bodies must be sized in accordance with 314.28 of the *NEC*. **Figure 5–44**

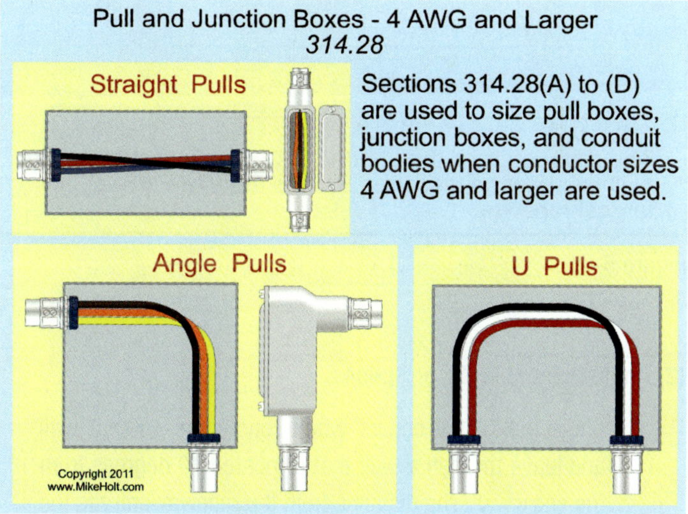

Figure 5–44

5.8 Pull/Junction Box Sizing Requirements

Boxes and Conduit Bodies for Conductors 4 AWG and Larger [314.28]

Boxes and conduit bodies containing conductors 4 AWG and larger that are required to be insulated must be sized so the conductor insulation won't be damaged.

(A) Minimum Size. For raceways containing conductors 4 AWG or larger, the minimum dimensions of boxes and conduit bodies must comply with the following:

(1) Straight Pulls. The minimum distance from where the conductors enter to the opposite wall must not be less than eight times the trade size of the largest raceway. **Figure 5–45**

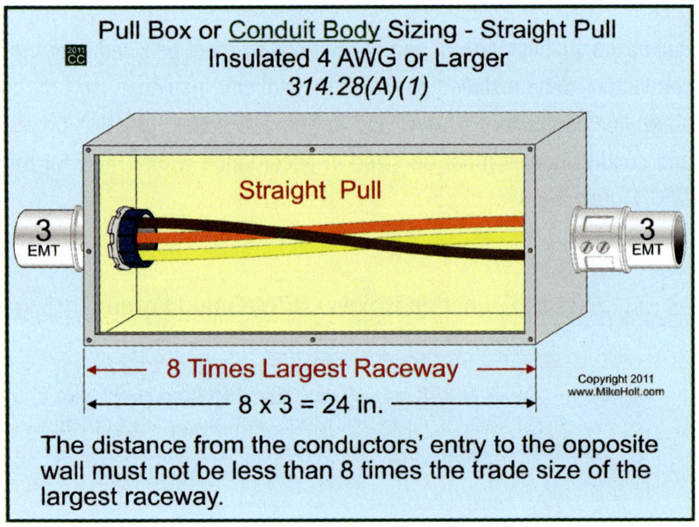

Figure 5–45

(2) Angle Pulls, U Pulls, or Splices.

- Angle Pulls. This occurs when conductors enter a wall and leave through a wall that is located 90 degrees from the entry wall. The distance from the raceway entry to the opposite wall must not be less than six times the trade size of the largest raceway, plus the sum of the trade sizes of the remaining raceways on the same wall and row. **Figure 5–46**

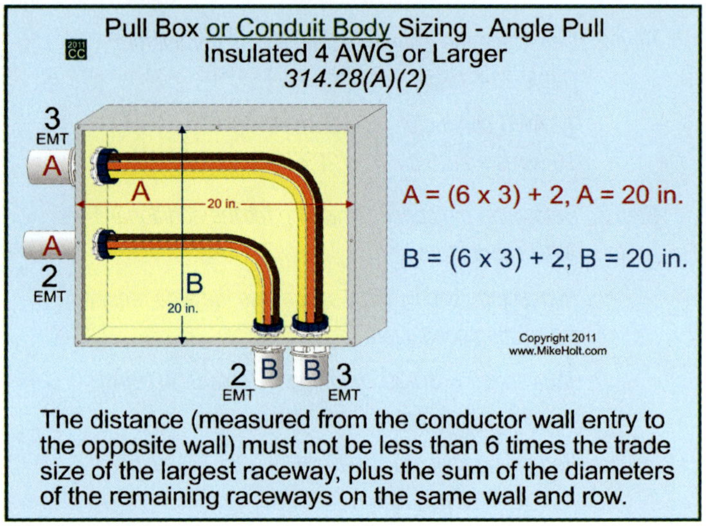

Figure 5–46

- U Pulls. When a conductor enters and leaves from the same wall, the distance from where the raceways enter to the opposite wall must not be less than six times the trade size of the largest raceway, plus the sum of the trade sizes of the remaining raceways on the same wall and row. **Figure 5–47**

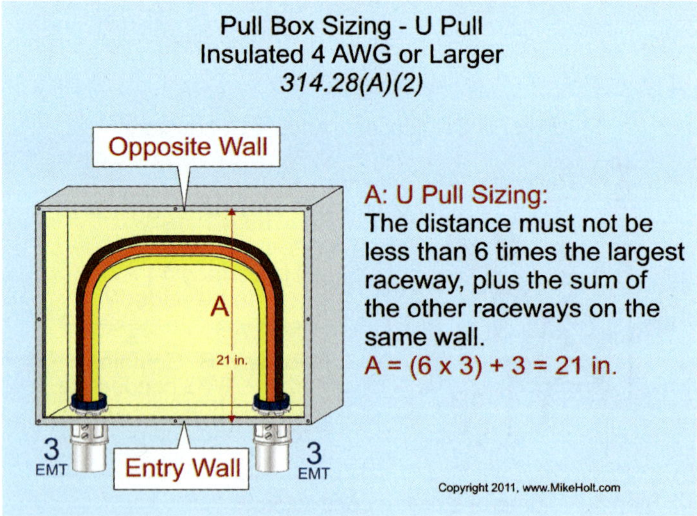

Figure 5–47

- Splices. When conductors are spliced, the distance from where the raceways enter to the opposite wall must not be less than six times the trade size of the largest raceway, plus the sum of the trade sizes of the remaining raceways on the same wall and row. **Figure 5–48**

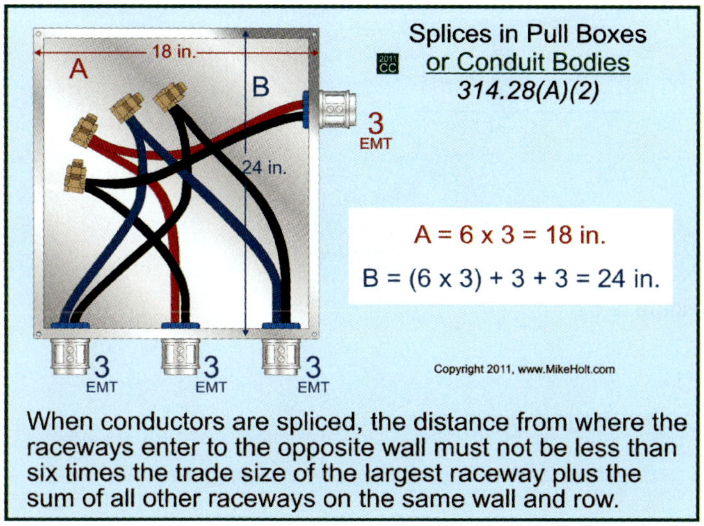

Figure 5–48

- Rows. Where there are multiple rows of raceway entries, each row is calculated individually and the row with the largest distance must be used. **Figure 5–49**

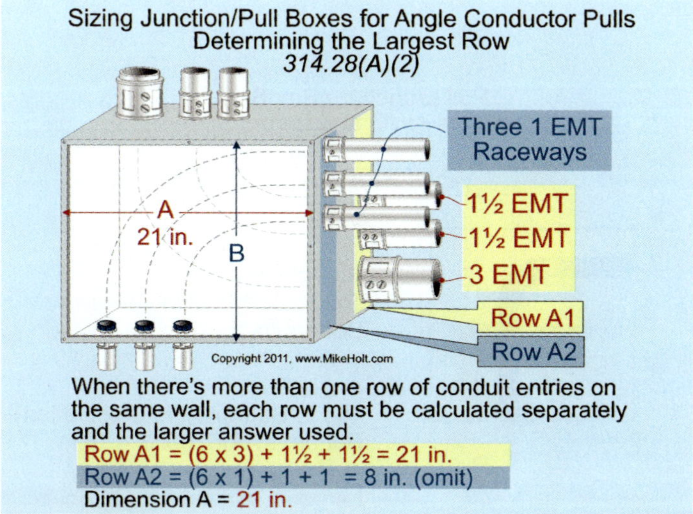

Figure 5–49

- Distance Between Raceways. The distance between raceways enclosing the same conductor must not be less than six times the trade size of the largest raceway, measured from the raceways' nearest edge-to-nearest edge. **Figure 5–50**

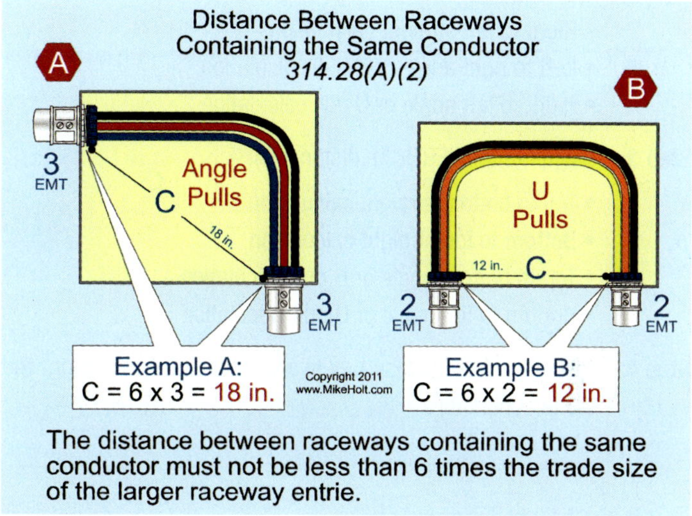

Figure 5–50

Exception: When conductors enter an enclosure with a removable cover, such as a conduit body or wireway, the distance from where the conductors enter to the removable cover must not be less than the bending distance as listed in Table 312.6(A) for one conductor per terminal. **Figure 5–51**

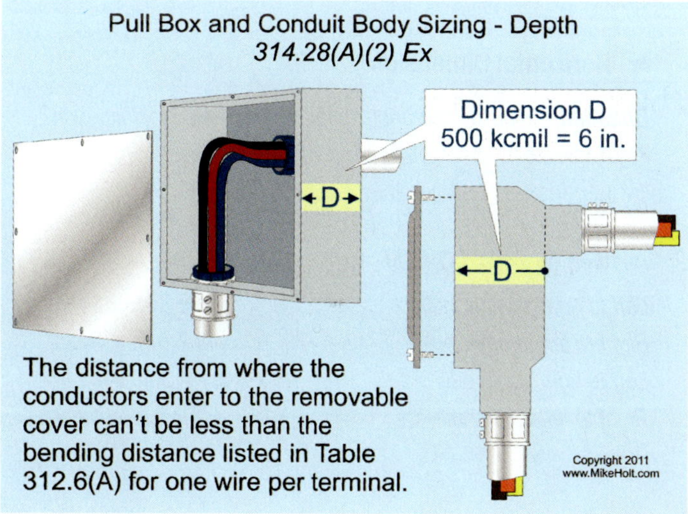

Figure 5–51

5.9 Pull/Junction Box Sizing Tips

When sizing pull and junction boxes, follow these suggestions:

Step 1: Always draw out the problem.

Step 2: Calculate the HORIZONTAL distance(s):

- Left to right straight calculation
- Right to left straight calculation
- Left to right angle or U pull calculation
- Right to left angle or U pull calculation

Step 3: Calculate the VERTICAL distance(s):

- Top to bottom straight calculation
- Bottom to top straight calculation
- Top to bottom angle or U pull calculation
- Bottom to top angle or U pull calculation

Step 4: Calculate the distance between raceways enclosing the same conductors.

5.10 Pull Box Examples

Pull Box Sizing

A junction box contains two trade size 3 raceways on the left side and one trade size 3 raceway on the right side. The conductors from one of the trade size 3 raceways on the left wall are pulled through the trade size 3 raceway on the right wall. The conductors from the other trade size 3 raceways on the left wall are pulled through a trade size 3 raceway at the bottom of the pull box.

► Horizontal Dimension

Question: *What's the horizontal dimension of this box?* **Figure 5–52**

(a) 18 in. *(b) 21 in.* *(c) 24 in.* *(d) 30 in.*

Answer: *(c) 24 in. [314.28]*

Left to right straight pull	*8 x 3 in. = 24 in.*
Right to left straight pull	*8 x 3 in. = 24 in.*
Left to right angle pull	*(6 x 3 in.) + 3 in. = 21 in.*
Right to left angle pull	*No calculation*

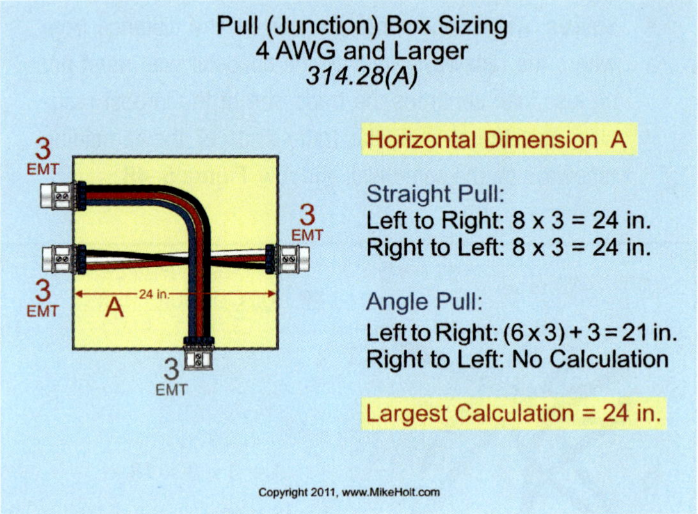

Figure 5–52

► Vertical Dimension

Question: *What's the vertical dimension of this box?* **Figure 5–53**

(a) 18 in. *(b) 21 in.* *(c) 24 in.* *(d) 30 in.*

Answer: *(a) 18 in. [314.28]*

Top to bottom straight	*No calculation*
Bottom to top straight	*No calculation*
Top to bottom angle	*No calculation*
Bottom to top angle	*6 x 3 in. = 18 in.*

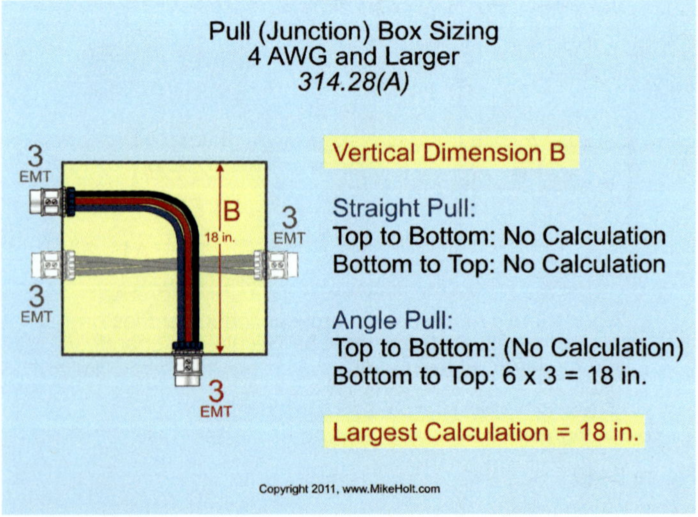

Figure 5–53

▶ Distance Between Raceways

Question: *What's the minimum distance between the two trade size 3 raceways that contain the same conductors?* **Figure 5–54**

(a) 18 in. *(b) 21 in.* *(c) 24 in.* *(d) 30 in.*

Answer: *(a) 18 in. [314.28]*

6 x 3 in. = 18 in.

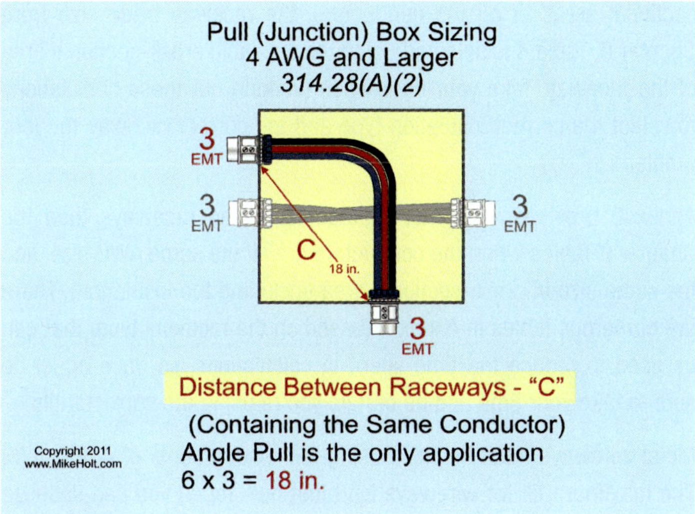

Figure 5–54

Pull Box Sizing

A pull box contains a trade size 2 and trade size 3 raceway on the left side, a trade size 3 raceway on the top, and a trade size 2 raceway on the right side. The trade size 2 raceways are a straight pull and the trade size 3 raceways are an angle pull.

▶ Horizontal Dimension

Question: *What's the horizontal dimension of the box?* **Figure 5–55**

(a) 20 in. *(b) 24 in.* *(c) 28 in.* *(d) 30 in.*

Answer: *(a) 20 in. [314.28(A)(2)]*

Left to right straight pull	*8 x 2 in. = 16 in.*
Right to left straight pull	*8 x 2 in. = 16 in.*
Left to right angle pull	*(6 x 3 in.) + 2 in. = 20 in.*
Right to left angle pull	*No calculation*

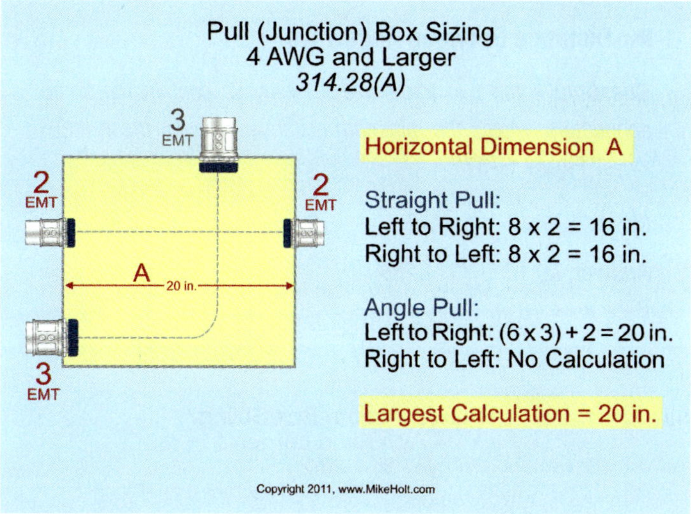

Figure 5–55

▶ Vertical Dimension

Question: *What's the vertical dimension of the box?* **Figure 5–56**

(a) 14 in. *(b) 18 in.* *(c) 21 in.* *(d) 26 in.*

Answer: *(b) 18 in. [314.28(A)(2)]*

Top to bottom straight	*No calculation*
Bottom to top straight	*No calculation*
Top to bottom angle	*6 x 3 in. = 18 in.*
Bottom to top angle	*No calculation*

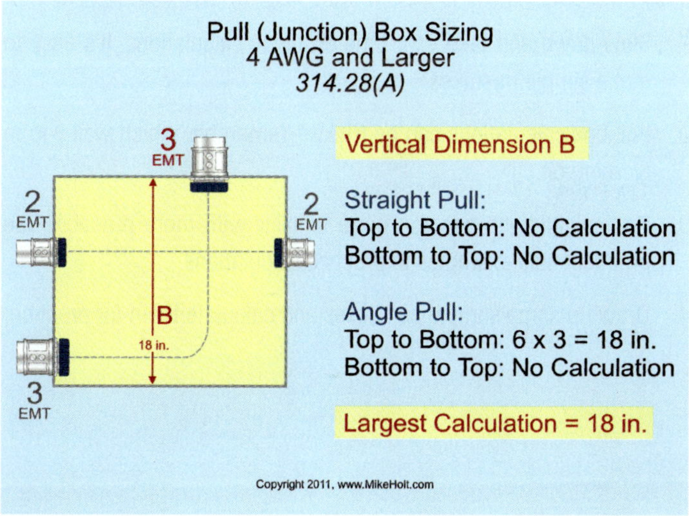

Figure 5–56

► Distance Between Raceways

Question: *If the two trade size 3 raceways contain the same conductors, what's the minimum distance between these raceways?* **Figure 5–57**

(a) 18 in. *(b) 21 in.* *(c) 24 in.* *(d) 30 in.*

Answer: *(a) 18 in. [314.28(A)(2)]*
6 x 3 in. = 18 in.

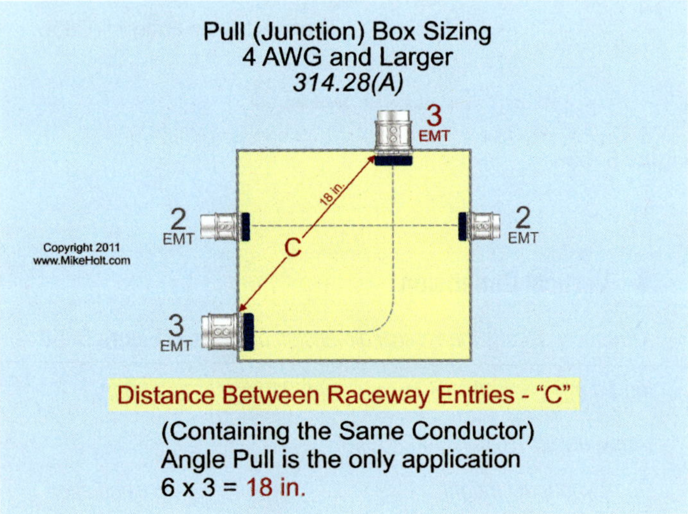

Figure 5–57

Summary

1. Slow down and take your time on these calculations. It's easy to make simple mistakes.
2. Pull box calculations can be tricky—remember which wall you're working on.
3. Box calculations become more familiar with more practice. Use practical field examples to practice calculations.
4. Draw up some sample pull boxes and calculate them for practice.

CONCLUSION TO UNIT 5—RACEWAY AND BOX CALCULATIONS

The importance of protecting conductor insulation during installation is understood by every electrician. The principles covered in this unit have gone far toward helping you achieve that goal.

In this unit, you learned how to use the tables in Chapter 9 of the *NEC* when completing raceway fill calculions. First, the area of the conductor is found, using Chapter 9, Table 5 for insulated conductors or Chapter 9, Table 8 for bare conductors. Then after totaling the cross-sectional areas of all the conductors, the raceway trade size from Chapter 9, Table 4 is selected using the available cross-sectional area of the raceway. Take your time when working out these calculations to select the correct insulation type and the correct raceway for your problem.

Annex C provides a quicker method for sizing raceways than the Chapter 9 Tables when the conductors are all the same AWG size, and the same size in cross-sectional area (including the insulation). There are numerous tables in Annex C (based on the raceway type) that can be used to reduce the time spent in calculations, so once again be sure to take your time and be certain you're using the correct table.

Metal wireways must be sized using the requirements of Article 376. The maximum fill for wireways isn't just how much you can squeeze into them. There are specific limits on conductor cross-sectional area, number of conductors, and wire-bending radius. Following the rules of Article 376 will provide a much safer installation and takes the mystery out of sizing wireways.

Maintaining proper outlet box fill is important as you rough-in the installation. There are a number of details that were covered in determining the correct box size to be used that will be important on an exam. Be sure to remember what items are counted in box fill calculations, and review the information if necessary.

Junction box and pull box calculations only come into play when the conductors are 4 AWG and larger. Straight pulls, angle pulls, and U pulls were all covered in this unit, as well as an often forgotten requirement that applies to two raceways that contain the same conductors. Always draw out a problem involving junction or pull boxes so that you'll be able to visualize it and properly apply the calculations you've learned.

UNIT

5

Practice Questions

Please use the 2011 *Code* book to answer the following questions, which are based on the 2011 *NEC*.

PRACTICE QUESTIONS FOR UNIT 5—RACEWAY AND BOX CALCULATIONS

PART A—RACEWAY FILL

5.1 Understanding the *NEC*, Chapter 9 Tables

1. When all the conductors are the same size (total cross-sectional area including insulation), the number of conductors permitted in a raceway can be determined by simply looking at the Tables in ______ of the *NEC*.

(a) Chapter 9
(b) Annex B
(c) Annex C
(d) Annex D

2. When equipment grounding conductors are installed in a raceway, the actual area of the conductor must be used when calculating raceway fill.

(a) True
(b) False

3. When a raceway doesn't exceed 24 in. in length, the raceway is permitted to be filled to ______ percent of its cross-sectional area.

(a) 31
(b) 40
(c) 53
(d) 60

4. How many 16 TFFN conductors can be installed in trade size ¾ electrical metallic tubing?

(a) 26
(b) 29
(c) 30
(d) 40

5. How many 6 RHH conductors (without outer cover) can be installed in trade size 1¼ electrical nonmetallic tubing?

(a) 7
(b) 13
(c) 16
(d) 25

6. How many 1/0 XHHW conductors can be installed in trade size 2 flexible metal conduit?

(a) 6
(b) 7
(c) 13
(d) 16

7. How many 12 RHH conductors (with outer cover) can be installed in a trade size 1 IMC raceway?

(a) 4
(b) 5
(c) 7
(d) 11

8. Three THHN compact conductors are needed in a trade size 2 rigid metal conduit. What's the largest compact conductor that can be installed?

(a) 4/0 AWG
(b) 250 kcmil
(c) 350 kcmil
(d) 500 kcmil

9. The actual area of conductor fill is dependent on the raceway size and the number of conductors installed. If there are three or more conductors installed in a raceway, the total area of conductor fill is limited to ______ percent.

(a) 31
(b) 40
(c) 53
(d) 60

10. What's the cross-sectional area in square inches for a 10 THW conductor?

(a) 0.0172 sq in.
(b) 0.0243 sq in.
(c) 0.0252 sq in.
(d) 0.0278 sq in.

11. What's the cross-sectional area in square inches for a 14 RHW conductor (without an outer cover)?

(a) 0.0172 sq in.
(b) 0.0209 sq in.
(c) 0.0252 sq in.
(d) 0.0278 sq in.

12. What's the cross-sectional area in square inches for a 10 THHN conductor?

(a) 0.0117 sq in.
(b) 0.0172 sq in.
(c) 0.0211 sq in.
(d) 0.0252 sq in.

13. What's the cross-sectional area in square inches for a 12 RHH conductor (with an outer cover)?

(a) 0.0117 sq in.
(b) 0.0252 sq in.
(c) 0.0327 sq in.
(d) 0.0353 sq in.

14. What's the cross-sectional area in square inches for an 8 AWG bare solid conductor?

(a) 0.013 sq in.
(b) 0.027 sq in.
(c) 0.038 sq in.
(d) 0.045 sq in.

5.2 Raceway Calculations

15. The number of conductors permitted in a raceway is dependent on the ______.

(a) area of the raceway
(b) percent area fill as listed in Chapter 9, Table 1
(c) area of the conductors as listed in Chapter 9, Tables 5 and 8
(d) all of these

16. A 200A feeder installed in Schedule 80 PVC has three 3/0 THHN conductors, one 2 THHN conductor, and one 6 THHN conductor. What size raceway is required?

(a) A trade size 2 raceway.
(b) A trade size 2½ raceway.
(c) A trade size 3 raceway.
(d) A trade size 3½ raceway.

17. What size rigid metal conduit is required for three 4/0 THHN conductors, one 1/0 THHN conductor, and one 4 THHN conductor when the raceway is 24 in. or less in length?

(a) A trade size 1½ rigid metal conduit.
(b) A trade size 2 rigid metal conduit.
(c) A trade size 2½ rigid metal conduit.
(d) A trade size 3 rigid metal conduit.

18. An existing trade size ¾ rigid metal conduit that does not exceed 24 in. in length contains four 10 THHN conductors and one 10 AWG (bare stranded) ground wire. How many additional 10 THHN conductors can be installed?

(a) 5
(b) 7
(c) 9
(d) 11

5.3 Wireways

19. What's the cross-sectional area of a 4 in. x 4 in. wireway?

(a) 6 sq in.
(b) 16 sq in.
(c) 36 sq in.
(d) 66 sq in.

20. What's the maximum allowable sq in. of conductor fill for a 4 in. x 4 in. wireway?

(a) 2.40 sq in.
(b) 3.20 sq in.
(c) 5.30 sq in.
(d) 12 sq in.

21. What's the maximum number of 400 kcmil THHN conductors that can be installed in a 6 in. x 6 in. wireway?

(a) 4
(b) 6
(c) 10
(d) 12

PART B—OUTLET BOX FILL CALCULATIONS [314.16]

5.5 Sizing Box—Conductors All the Same Size [Table 314.16(A)]

22. What size box is the minimum required for six 14 THHN conductors and three 14 THW conductors?

(a) A 4 x 1¼ square box.
(b) A 4 x 1½ round box.
(c) A 4 x 1¼ round box.
(d) A 4 x 2⅛ square box.

23. How many 10 AWG conductors are permitted in a 4 x 1½ square box?

(a) 8 conductors
(b) 9 conductors
(c) 10 conductors
(d) 11 conductors

5.6 Conductor Equivalents

24. Table 314.16(A) doesn't take into consideration the volume of ______.

(a) switches and receptacles
(b) luminaire studs and hickeys
(c) internal cable clamps
(d) all of these

25. When determining the number of conductors for box fill calculations, which of the following statements is(are) true?

(a) A luminaire stud or hickey is considered as one conductor for each type, based on the largest conductor that enters the outlet box.
(b) Internal factory cable clamps are considered as one conductor for one or more cable clamps, based on the largest conductor that enters the outlet box.
(c) The single gang device yoke is considered as two conductors, based on the largest conductor that terminates on the strap (device mounting fitting).
(d) all of these

26. When determining the number of conductors for box fill calculations, which of the following statements is(are) true?

(a) Each conductor that runs through the box without a splice or leaving a loop long enough to splice is considered as one conductor.
(b) Each conductor that originates outside the box and terminates in the box is considered as one conductor.
(c) Wirenuts, cable connectors, raceway fittings, and conductors that originate and terminate within the outlet box (equipment bonding jumpers and pigtails) aren't counted for box fill calculations.
(d) all of these

27. It's permitted to omit one equipment grounding conductor and not more than ______ that enter a box from a luminaire canopy.

(a) five fixture wires
(b) four 16 AWG fixture wires
(c) four 18 AWG fixture wires
(d) b and c

28. Can a round 4 x ½ in. box marked as 8 cu in. with manufactured cable clamps supplied with 14/2 W/G NM be used with a luminaire that has two 18 TFN conductors and a canopy cover?

(a) Yes
(b) No

5.7 Outlet Box Sizing [314.16(B)]

29. What size outlet box is required for one 12/2 W/G NM cable that terminates on a switch, one 12/3 W/G NM cable that terminates on a receptacle, and the box has manufactured cable clamps?

(a) A 4 x 1¼ square box.
(b) A 4 x 1½ square box.
(c) A 4 x 2⅛ square box.
(d) A 3 x 2 x 3½ device box

30. How many 14 AWG conductors can be pulled through a 4 x 1½ square box with a plaster ring marked 3.60 cu in.? The box already contains two duplex receptacles, five 14 AWG conductors, and two grounding conductors.

(a) one conductor
(b) two conductors
(c) three conductors
(d) four conductors

PART C—PULL BOXES, JUNCTION BOXES, AND CONDUIT BODIES

5.8 Pull/Junction Box Sizing Requirements

31. When conductors 4 AWG and larger are installed in boxes and conduit bodies, the enclosure must be sized according to which of the following requirements?

(a) The minimum distance for straight pull calculations from where the conductors enter to the opposite wall must not be less than eight times the trade size of the largest raceway.
(b) The distance for angle pull calculations from the raceway entry to the opposite wall must not be less than six times the trade size diameter of the largest raceway, plus the sum of the diameters of the remaining raceways on the same wall and row.
(c) The distance between raceways enclosing the same conductor(s) must not be less than six times the trade size diameter of the largest raceway.
(d) all of these

32. When conductors enter an enclosure opposite a removable cover, the distance from where the conductors enter to the removable cover must not be less than ______.

(a) six times the largest raceway
(b) eight times the largest raceway
(c) a or b
(d) none of these

The following information applies to the next three questions.

A junction box contains two trade size 2½ raceways on the left side and one trade size 2½ raceway on the right side. The conductors from one trade size 2½ raceway (on the left wall) are pulled through the raceway on the right wall. The other trade size 2½ raceway conductors (on the left wall) are pulled through a trade size 2½ raceway at the bottom of the pull box.

33. What's the minimum distance from the left wall to the right wall?

(a) 18 in.
(b) 20 in.
(c) 21 in.
(d) 24 in.

34. What's the minimum distance from the bottom wall to the top wall?

(a) 15 in.
(b) 18 in.
(c) 21 in.
(d) 24 in.

35. What's the minimum distance between the raceways that contain the same conductors?

(a) 15 in.
(b) 18 in.
(c) 21 in.
(d) 24 in.

The following information applies to the next three questions.

A junction box contains two trade size 2 raceways on the left side, and two trade size 2 raceways on the top.

36. What's the minimum distance from the left wall to the right wall?

    (a) 14 in.
    (b) 21 in.
    (c) 24 in.
    (d) 28 in.

37. What's the minimum distance from the bottom wall to the top wall?

    (a) 14 in.
    (b) 18 in.
    (c) 21 in.
    (d) 24 in.

38. What's the minimum distance between the trade size 2 raceways that contain the same conductors?

    (a) 12 in.
    (b) 18 in.
    (c) 21 in.
    (d) 24 in.

UNIT

5

Challenge Questions

Please use the 2011 *Code* book to answer the following questions, which are based on the 2011 *NEC*.

CHALLENGE QUESTIONS FOR UNIT 5—RACEWAY AND BOX CALCULATIONS

PART A—RACEWAY FILL

5.2 Raceway Calculations

1. A trade size 3 Schedule 40 PVC raceway contains seven 1 RHW conductors without outer cover. How many 2 THW conductors may be installed in this raceway with the existing conductors?

   (a) 11
   (b) 15
   (c) 20
   (d) 25

5.3 Wireways

2. What size wireway is required for three 400 kcmil THHN, one 250 kcmil THHN, four 4/0 THHN conductors, and three 8 THHN conductors?

   (a) A 4 in. x 4 in. wireway.
   (b) A 6 in. x 6 in. wireway.
   (c) An 8 in. x 8 in. wireway.
   (d) A 10 in. x 10 in. wireway.

PART B—OUTLET BOX FILL CALCULATIONS [314.16]

5.7 Outlet Box Sizing [314.16(B)]

3. Determine the minimum number of cubic inches required for two 10 AWG conductors passing through a box, four 14 AWG conductors spliced in the box, two 12 AWG conductors terminating to a receptacle, and one 12 AWG equipment bonding jumper from the receptacle to the box.

   (a) 18.50 cu in.
   (b) 20 cu in.
   (c) 21.75 cu in.
   (d) 22 cu in.

4. When determining the number of conductors in a box that has one 14/3 W/G NM cable, one switch, and two internal cable clamps, the count will equal _____.

   (a) 6 conductors
   (b) 7 conductors
   (c) 8 conductors
   (d) 10 conductors

PART C—PULL BOXES, JUNCTION BOXES, AND CONDUIT BODIES

5.8 Pull/Junction Box Sizing Requirements

Figure 5–58 applies to the next four questions.

5. The minimum horizontal dimension for the junction box shown in the diagram in **Figure 5–58** is _____.

   (a) 18 in.
   (b) 20 in.
   (c) 21 in.
   (d) 24 in.

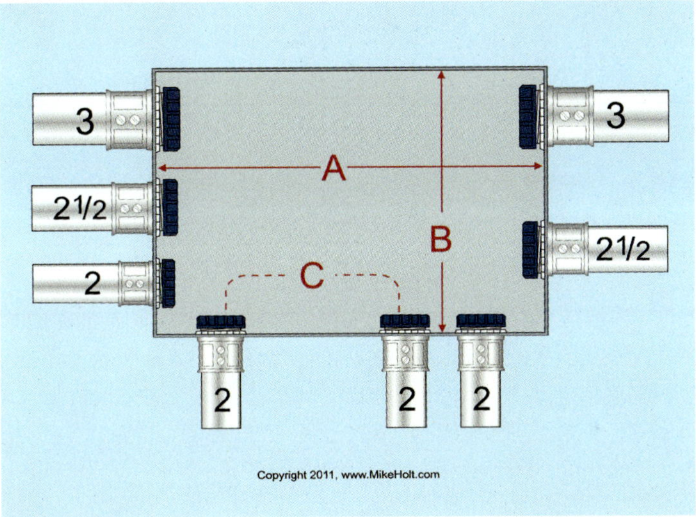

Figure 5–58

6. The minimum vertical dimension for the junction box shown in Figure 5–58 is ______.

(a) 16 in.
(b) 18 in.
(c) 20 in.
(d) 24 in.

7. The minimum distance between the two trade size 2 raceways that contain the same Conductor C, as illustrated in Figure 5–58 is ______.

(a) 12 in.
(b) 18 in.
(c) 24 in.
(d) 30 in.

8. If a trade size 3 raceway entry (250 kcmil) is in the wall opposite a removable cover, the distance from that wall to the cover must not be less than ______. Figure 5–58

(a) 4 in.
(b) 4½ in.
(c) 5 in.
(d) 6 in.

Notes

UNIT 6

Conductor Sizing and Protection Calculations

INTRODUCTION TO UNIT 6—CONDUCTOR SIZING AND PROTECTION CALCULATIONS

Every conductor has a certain amount of resistance. Any time current flows through a conductor there's resistance, and heat is generated. The amount of heat produced is directly proportional to the resistance of the wire and the square of the current flow. In order to determine what size conductor is needed to carry a certain amount of current, the heat that will be generated must be taken into consideration. The number of conductors in the same raceway that are carrying current can affect this decision, as can the ambient or surrounding temperature.

This unit explains how to evaluate these factors and make the proper choice in sizing electrical conductors, and how to select the proper conductor based on the temperature rating of the equipment terminals. This can become a complicated choice, and you should study this unit carefully to learn how to make the right conductor sizing decisions.

The amount of current that a conductor is allowed to carry must be limited to a level that won't cause destructive overheating of the conductor or of the equipment or structure in which it may be in contact. In order to make sure that the amount of current in a conductor is kept within safe limits, overcurrent protection is used to open the circuit. Generally this protection is provided by installing a fuse or circuit breaker, of a size based on the conductor's ampacity, at the point where the conductor receives its supply. The general rules for overcurrent protection are covered in this unit, along with exceptions to the general rules; for example, those for tap conductors and special cases such as motor circuits. Motor circuits will be covered in more depth in Unit 7. Some specific overcurrent applications and tap rules will be covered to help you become familiar with the rules for sizing overcurrent devices in this unit.

PART A—GENERAL CONDUCTOR REQUIREMENTS

Introduction

All conductors used for general applications covered by the NEC are made from copper and aluminum. But beyond the conductor material, there are other characteristics that affect how conductors can be used and how their ampacity is calculated. These include the temperature rating of the insulation, the conditions under which the conductors are installed (for example, whether they're in free air, in a raceway, or direct buried), the ambient temperature, and the temperature rating of the terminal, device, or equipment to which the conductors are connected.

Author's Comment: This unit is based on the use of solidly grounded ac systems, 600V or less, using 90ºC insulated copper conductors sized to 75ºC terminals unless otherwise specified.

6.1 Conductor Insulation [Table 310.104(A)]

Table 310.104(A) of the *NEC* provides information on conductor properties such as permitted use, maximum operating temperature, and other insulation details. The *NEC* includes wiring methods that are considered suitable for use [110.8]. **Figure 6–1**

The following abbreviations and explanations will be helpful in understanding Tables 310.15(B)(16) and 310.104(A).

- -2 Conductor is permitted to be used at a continuous 90ºC operating temperature
- F Fixture wire (solid or 7-strand) [Table 402.3]
- FF Flexible fixture wire (stranded) [Table 402.3]
- H Usually indicates a 75ºC insulation rating
- HH Usually indiates a 90ºC insulation rating
- N Nylon outer cover
- T Thermoplastic insulation
- W Wet or damp location

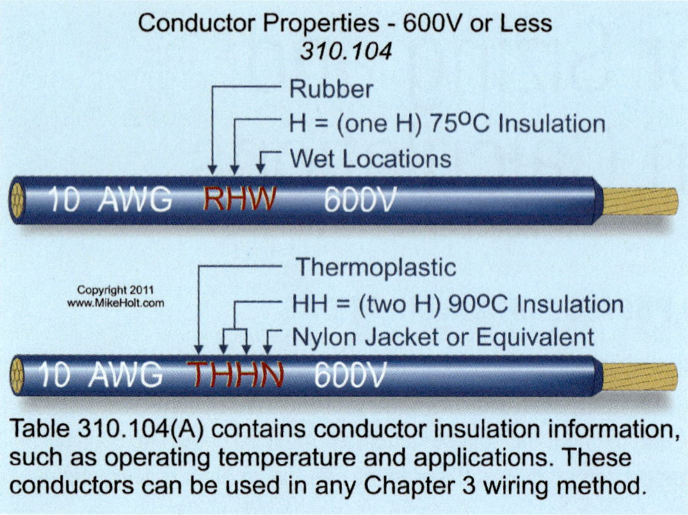

Figure 6–1

For more information about fixture wires, see Article 402, Table 402.3, and Table 402.5. For more information on flexible cords and flexible cables, see Article 400, Table 400.4, Table 400.5(A), and Table 400.5(B).

It's common to see conductors with a dual insulation rating, such as THHN/THWN. This type of conductor can be used in a dry location at the THHN 90°C ampacity, or if used in a wet location, the THWN ampacity rating of the 75°C column of Table 310.15(B)(16) for THWN insulation types must be adhered to. When a -2 is added at the end of an insulation type, such as THWN-2, that means that the conductor can be used in a wet or dry location at the 90°C ampacity rating.

Table 310.104(A) Conductor Applications and Insulations

Type Letter	Column 2	Column 3	Column 4	Column 5	Column 6
	Insulation	Maximum Operating Temperature	Application	Sizes Available AWG or kcmil	Outer Covering
RHH	Flame-retardant	90°C	Dry and damp locations	14 – 2,000	Moisture-resistant, flame-retardant, nonmetallic
RHW	Flame-retardant, moisture-resistant thermoset	75°C	Dry and wet locations	14 – 2,000	Moisture-resistant, flame-retardant, nonmetallic
RHW-2	Flame-retardant, moisture-resistant thermoset	90°C	Dry and wet locations	14 – 2,000	Moisture-resistant, flame-retardant, nonmetallic
THHN	Flame-retardant, heat-resistant thermoplastic	90°C	Dry and damp locations	14 – 1,000	Nylon jacket or equivalent
THHW	Flame-retardant, moisture- and heat-resistant thermoplastic	75°C 90°C	Wet locations Dry and damp locations	14 – 1,000	None
THW	Flame-retardant, moisture- and heat-resistant thermoplastic	75°C	Dry and wet locations	14 – 2,000	None
THW-2	Flame-retardant, moisture- and heat-resistant thermoplastic	90°C	Dry and wet locations	14 – 1,000	None
THWN	Flame-retardant, moisture- and heat-resistant thermoplastic	75°C	Dry and wet locations	14 – 1,000	Nylon jacket or equivalent
THWN-2	Flame-retardant, moisture- and heat-resistant thermoplastic	90°C	Dry and wet locations	14 – 1,000	Nylon jacket or equivalent
TW	Flame-retardant, moisture-resistant thermoplastic	60°C	Dry and wet locations	14 – 2,000	None
USE	Heat- and moisture-resistant	75°C	See Article 338	14 – 2,000	Moisture-resistant nonmetallic
USE-2	Heat- and moisture-resistant	90°C	See Article 338	14 – 2,000	Moisture-resistant nonmetallic

Table 310.15(B)(16) Allowable Ampacities of Insulated Conductors Based on Not More Than Three Current-Carrying Conductors and Ambient Temperature of 30°C (86°F)*

Size	Temperature Rating of Conductor, See Table 310.13						Size
	60°C (140°F)	75°C (167°F)	90°C (194°F)	60°C (140°F)	75°C (167°F)	90°C (194°F)	
AWG kcmil	TW UF	RHW THHW THW THWN USE XHHW	RHH RHW-2 THHN THW-2 THWN-2 THHW USE-2 XHHW XHHW-2	TW UF	RHW THHN THW THWN USE XHHW	RHH RHW-2 THHN THW-2 THWN-2 THHW USE-2 XHHW XHHW-2	AWG kcmil
	Copper			Aluminum/Copper-Clad Aluminum			
14*	15	20	25				14*
12*	20	25	30	15	20	25	12*
10*	30	35	40	25	30	35	10*
8	40	50	55	35	40	45	8
6	55	65	75	40	50	55	6
4	70	85	95	55	65	75	4
3	85	100	115	65	75	85	3
2	95	115	130	75	90	100	2
1	110	130	145	85	100	115	1
1/0	125	150	170	100	120	135	1/0
2/0	145	175	195	115	135	150	2/0
3/0	165	200	225	130	155	175	3/0
4/0	195	230	260	150	180	205	4/0
250	215	255	290	170	205	230	250
300	240	285	320	195	230	260	300
350	260	310	350	210	250	280	350
400	280	335	380	225	270	305	400
500	320	380	430	260	310	350	500

*See 240.4(D)

► **Table 310.104(A)**

Question: Which of the following describe Type TW insulation? **Figure 6–2**

(a) Thermoplastic insulation.
(b) Suitable for dry or wet locations.
(c) A maximum operating temperature of 60°C.
(d) all of these

Answer: *(d) all of these*

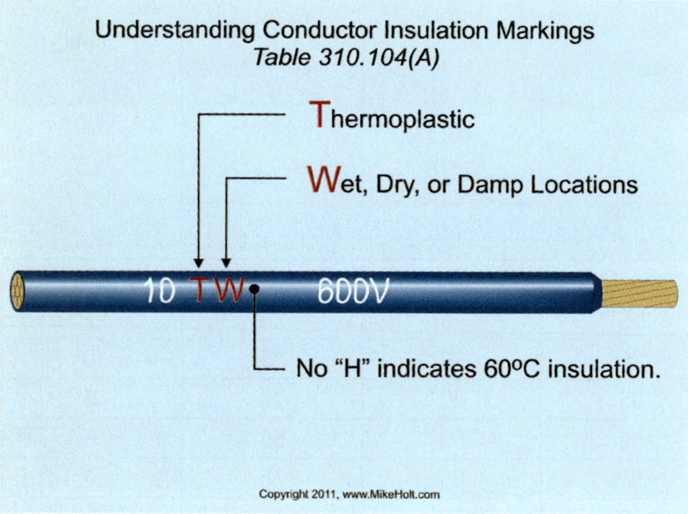

Figure 6–2

Not all conductor types are Included in Article 310. Article 400 covers flexible cords and cables and Article 402 covers fixture wires.

► **Table 400.4 Flexible Cord Example**

Question: *SJO can be described as ______.*

(a) oil-resistant thermoset outer covering
(b) usable In damp locations
(c) 300V insulation
(d) all of these

Answer: *(d) all of these*

► **Table 402.3**

Question: *Which of the following describes Type TFFN insulation?*

(a) Stranded fixture wire.
(b) Thermoplastic insulation with a nylon outer cover.
(c) Suitable for dry and wet locations.
(d) both a and b

Answer: *(d) both a and b*

Author's Comment: Be sure to use the tables in Article 400 for flexible cords and cables and Article 402 for fixture wires.

6.2 Conductor Sizing [110.6]

Conductors are sized according to the American Wire Gage (AWG) from 40 AWG through 4/0 AWG. The smaller conductors are represented by the larger numbers, with the AWG size numbers decreasing as the conductor size increases. Wire sizes above 1 AWG are sizes 1/0, 2/0, 3/0, and 4/0. Conductors larger than 4/0 AWG are identified according to their cross-sectional area in circular mils, such as 250,000 cmil, 300,000 cmil, 500,000 cmil, and so on The circular mil size is usually expressed in kcmil (1,000 circular mils), such as 250 kcmil, 300 kcmil, and 500 kcmil. **Figure 6–3**

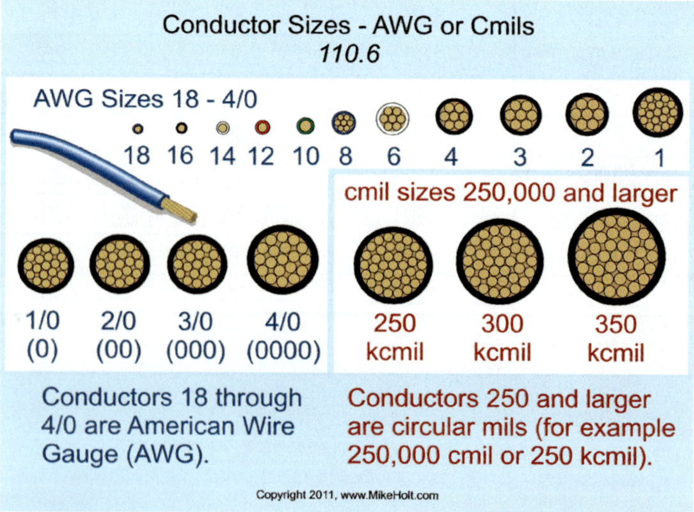

Figure 6–3

6.3 Smallest Conductor Size [310.106(A)]

The smallest size conductors permitted by the NEC for branch circuits, feeders, or services are 14 AWG copper [Table 310.106(A)]. However, some local codes require a minimum 12 AWG for commercial and industrial installations. Conductors smaller than 14 AWG are permitted for:

- Class 1 remote-control circuits [725.43]
- Fixture wire [402.6]
- Motor control circuits [Table 430.72(B)]

6.4 Conductor Size—Terminal Temperature Rating [110.14(C)]

Conductors are to be sized to the lowest temperature rating of any terminal, device, or conductor of the circuit in accordance with the equipment terminal temperature rating as follows:

Circuits Rated 100A and Less [110.14(C)(1)(a)]

Equipment terminals rated 100A or less and pressure connector terminals for 14 AWG through 1 AWG conductors, must have the conductor sized to the 60ºC temperature rating listed in Table 310.15(B)(16), unless the terminals are marked for 75°C conductors. **Figure 6–4**

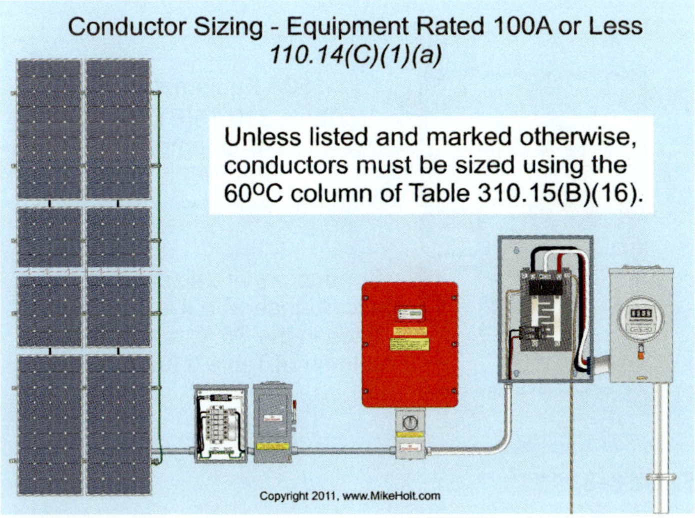

Figure 6–4

Author's Comment: Conductors are sized to prevent the overheating of terminals, in accordance with listing standards. For example, a 50A circuit with 60°C terminals requires the circuit conductors to be sized not smaller than 6 AWG, in accordance with the 60°C ampacity listed in Table 310.15(B)(16). An 8 THHN insulated conductor has a 90°C ampacity of 55A in a dry location, but 8 AWG can't be used for this circuit because the conductor's operating temperature at full-load ampacity (55A) will be near 90°C, which is well in excess of the 60°C terminal rating.

► Terminal Rated 60ºC [110.14(C)(1)(a)(2)

Question: *What size THHN conductor is required for a 50A circuit where the terminals aren't marked with a temperature rating?* **Figure 6–5**

(a) 10 AWG *(b) 8 AWG* *(c) 6 AWG* *(d) 4 AWG*

Answer: *(c) 6 AWG*

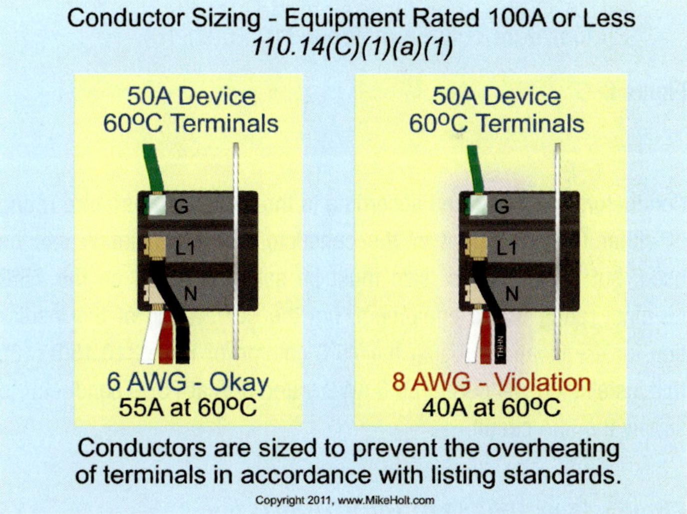

Figure 6–5

Conductors must be sized to the lowest temperature rating of either the equipment or the conductor. Equipment terminals for 100A and less that aren't marked are to be sized using the 60ºC column. THHN insulation can be used, but the conductor size must be selected based on the 60ºC terminal rating of the equipment, not the 90ºC rating of the insulation. Using the 60ºC column of Table 310.15(B)(16), this 50A circuit requires a 6 AWG conductor (rated 55A at 60ºC).

► Terminal Rated 75°C [110.14(C)(1)(a)(3)

Question: *What size THHN conductor is required for a 50A circuit where the terminals are all listed for use at 75°C?* **Figure 6–6**

(a) 10 AWG (b) 8 AWG (c) 6 AWG (d) 4 AWG

Answer: *(b) 8 AWG*

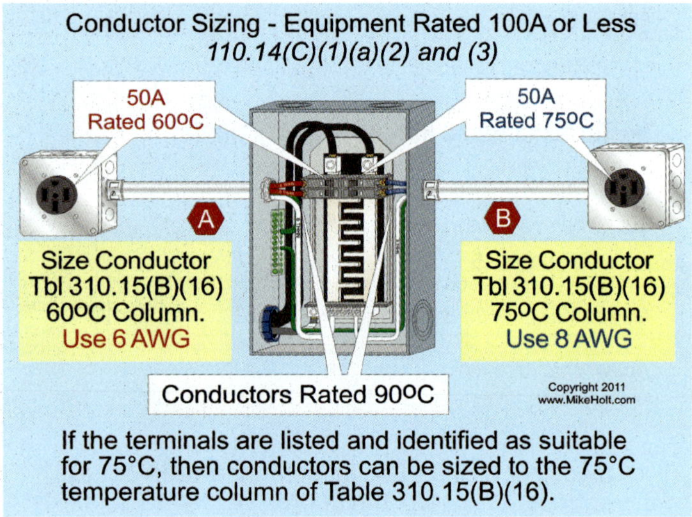

Figure 6–6

Conductors must be sized according to the lowest temperature rating of either the equipment or the conductor. THHN insulation can be used, but the conductor size must be selected based on the 75°C terminal rating of the equipment, not the 90°C rating of the insulation for dry locations. Using the 75°C column of Table 310.15(B)(16), this installation will permit an 8 AWG (rated 50A at 75°C) conductor to supply the 50A circuit.

Circuits Over 100A [110.14(C)(1)(b)(1) and (2)]

Terminals for equipment rated over 100A and pressure connector terminals for conductors larger than 1 AWG must have the conductor sized according to the 75°C temperature rating listed in Table 310.15(B)(16). **Figure 6–7**

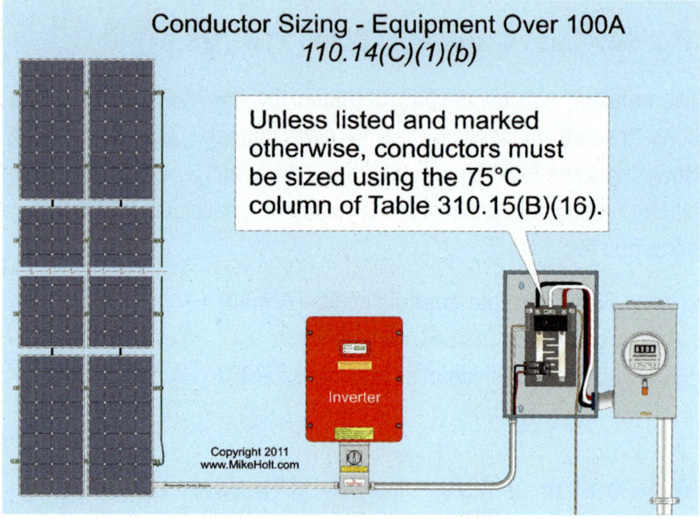

Figure 6–7

► Over 100A [110.14(C)(1)(b)(2)

Question: *What size THHN conductor is required to supply a 150A feeder?* **Figure 6–8**

(a) 1/0 AWG (b) 2/0 AWG (c) 3/0 AWG (d) 4/0 AWG

Answer: *(a) 1/0 AWG*

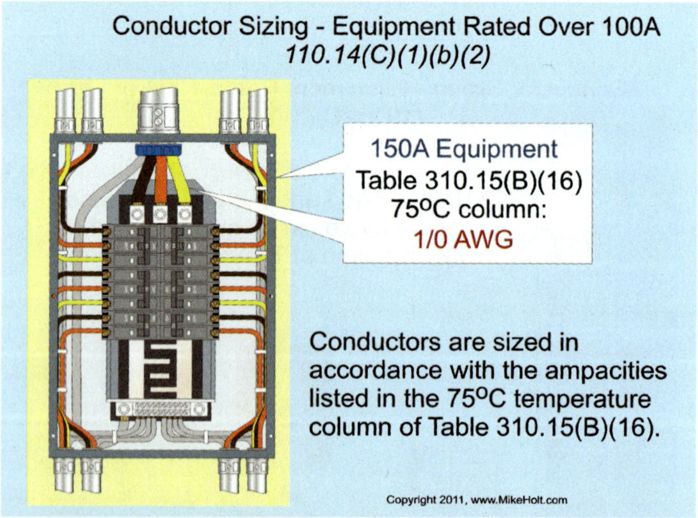

Figure 6–8

The conductors in this example must be sized to the lowest temperature rating of either the equipment or the conductor. THHN conductors can be used, but the conductor size must be selected according to the 75ºC terminal rating of the equipment when sizing for over 100A. Using the 75ºC column of Table 310.15(B)(16), this will require a 1/0 AWG conductor (rated 150A at 75ºC) to supply the 150A circuit.

The 90ºC ampacity column could only be used if the conductors and connectors are rated at least 90ºC. Most equipment terminals are now rated 75ºC, bus bar connections made with 90ºC rated connectors are one of the few components that may be rated 90ºC. **Figure 6–9**

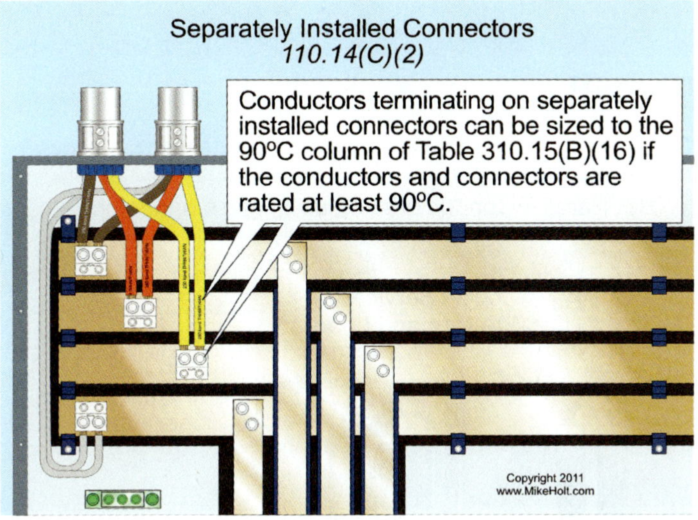

Figure 6–9

Minimum Conductor Size Table

When sizing conductors, the following table must be used to determine the minimum size conductor to meet the requirements of 110.14(C).

Circuit Rating	60°C	75°
50A	6 AWG	8 AWG
60A	4 AWG	6 AWG
70A	4 AWG	4 AWG
100A	1 AWG	3 AWG
125A	—	1 AWG
150A	—	1/0 AWG
200A	—	3/0 AWG
225A	—	4/0 AWG

What's the purpose of THHN if we can't use its higher ampacity at 90°C for conductor sizing?

The advantage of THHN insulated conductors is that the 90°C insulation rating allows for a higher conductor ampacity for conductor ampacity "adjustment" and/or "correction" in accordance with 310.15(B)(2)(a) and 310.15(B)(3)(a). The higher ampacity of THHN, as compared to the terminal temperature rating, will often permit the use of a conductor without having to increase its size because of conductor ampacity adjustment or correction. The advantage of THHN isn't that it permits a smaller circuit conductor, but that you might not have to install a larger conductor because of ampacity adjustments or corrections.

CAUTION: *Conductor voltage drop, ambient temperature correction, and conductor bundle adjustment factors are additional elements that must be considered in sizing conductors. These subjects are covered later in this textbook.*

Author's Comment: This is explained in detail in Part B of this unit.

6.5 Conductors in Parallel

Parallel conductors permit a smaller cross-sectional area per ampere, resulting in significant cost savings. **Figure 6–10**

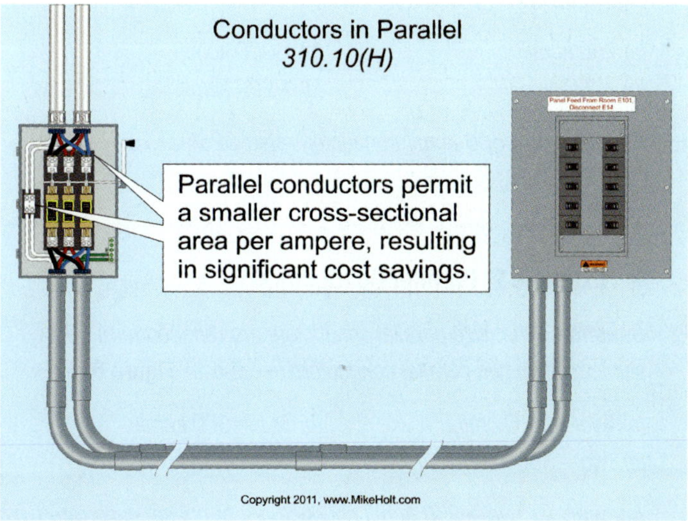

Figure 6–10

The following table demonstrates the circular mil area required per ampere for copper conductors.

Conductor Size	Circular Mils Chapter 9, Table 8	Ampacity 75°C	Circular Mils Per Ampere
1/0 AWG	105,600 cmil	150A	704 cmil
3/0 AWG	167,800 cmil	200A	839 cmil
250 kcmil	250,000 cmil	255A	980 cmil
500 kcmil	500,000 cmil	380A	1,316 cmil
750 kcmil	750,000 cmil	475A	1,579 cmil

As can be seen in the above table, 750 kcmil requires more than twice as much copper (1,579 cmil) to carry one ampere of current as compared to 1/0 AWG (704 cmil). With the high cost of copper, one must determine when it's cost effective to parallel an installation. However, the NEC only permits the paralleling of conductors when the following requirements of Section 310.10(H) are met.

Sizing Parallel Conductors

The next two examples show the difference between single conductors and parallel conductors for a 600A service with a 550A calculated load.

► Example 1: Single Conductors

Question: *What size conductor is required for a 600A service?* **Figure 6–11**

(a) 750 kcmil *(b) 1,000 kcmil*
(c) 1,250 kcmil *(d) 1,500 kcmil*

Answer: *(d) 1,500 kcmil conductor, rated 625A at 75°C [Table 310.15(B)(16)].*

► Example 2: Parallel Conductors

Question: *What size parallel conductors are required for a 600A service, using two parallel conductors per phase?* **Figure 6–12**

(a) Two—250 kcmil *(b) Two—300 kcmil*
(c) Two—350 kcmil *(d) Two—750 kcmil*

Answer: *(c) Two—350 kcmil conductors per phase, each rated 310A are suitable [Table 310.15(B)(16)].*

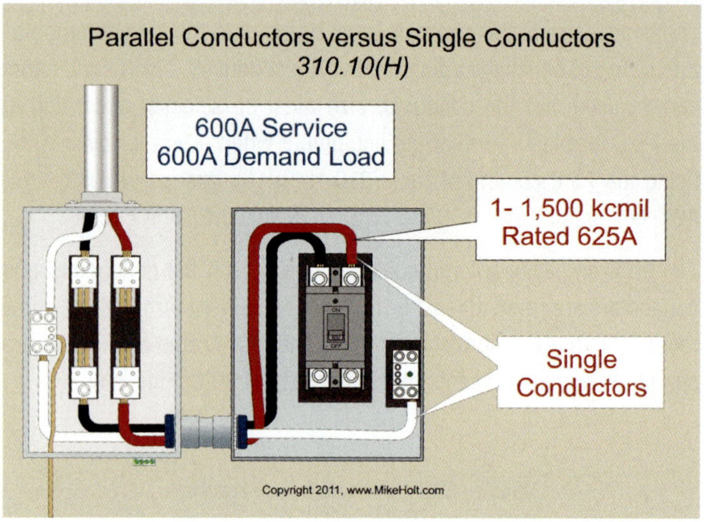

Figure 6–11

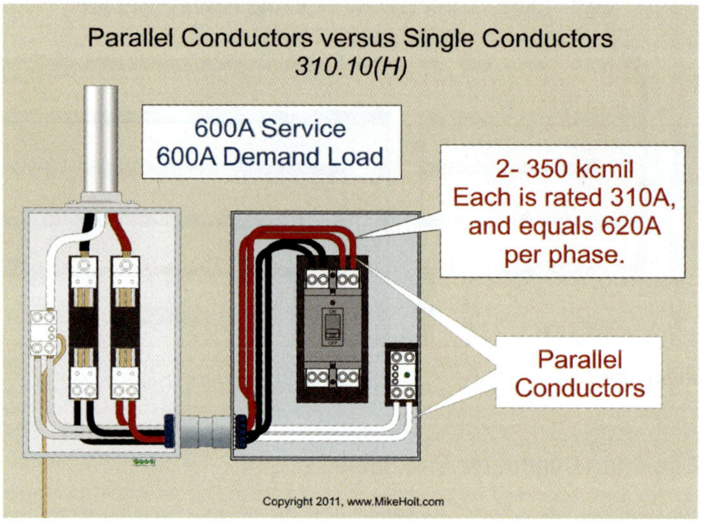

Figure 6–12

If we parallel the conductors, we can use two 350 kcmil conductors (total 700 kcmil) instead of one 1,500 kcmil conductor per phase.

► Example 3: Parallel Conductors

Question: *What size parallel conductors are required for a 600A service, using three parallels per phase?* **Figure 6–13**

(a) Three—3/0 AWG *(b) Three—4/0 AWG*
(c) Three—250 kcmil *(d) Three—300 kcmil*

Answer: *(a) Three—3/0 AWG conductors per phase, each rated 200A are suitable [Table 310.15(B)(16)].*

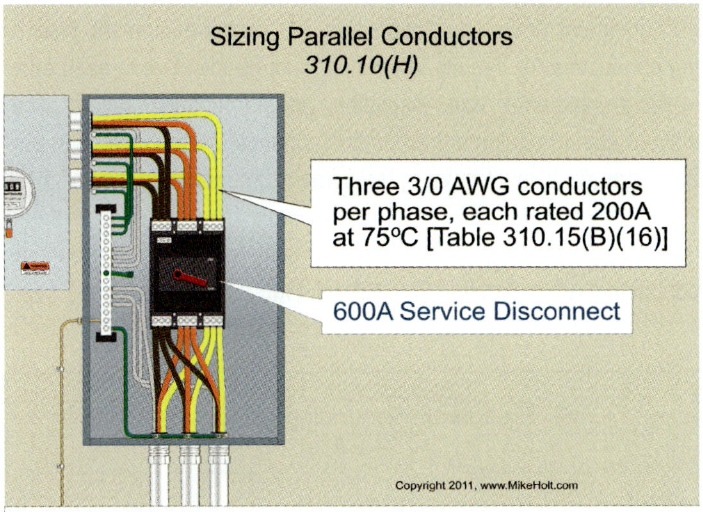

Figure 6–13

If we parallel the conductors three per-phase, we can use three 3/0 AWG conductors per phase.

6.6 *NEC* Requirements for Conductors in Parallel [310.10(H)]

(1) General. Ungrounded and neutral conductors sized 1/0 AWG and larger can be connected in parallel (electrically joined at both ends). When circuit conductors are run in parallel, the current must be evenly distributed between the individual parallel conductors. Figure 6–14

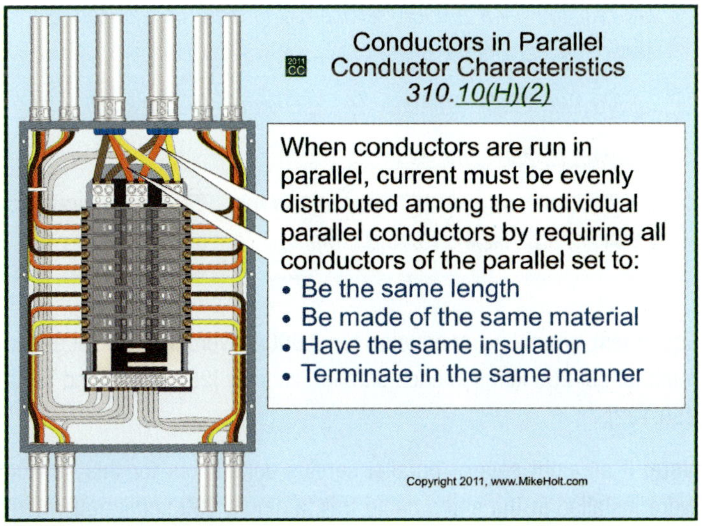

Figure 6–14

(2) Conductor Characteristics. All circuit conductors within a parallel set must:

(1) Be the same length.

(2) Consist of the same conductor material (copper, aluminum, or copper-clad aluminum).

(3) Be the same size in circular mil area (minimum 1/0 AWG).

(4) Have the same insulation type (like THHN).

(5) Terminate in the same manner (set screw versus compression).

(3) Separate Raceways or Cables. Raceways or cables containing parallel conductors must have the same electrical characteristics and the same number of conductors. Figure 6–15

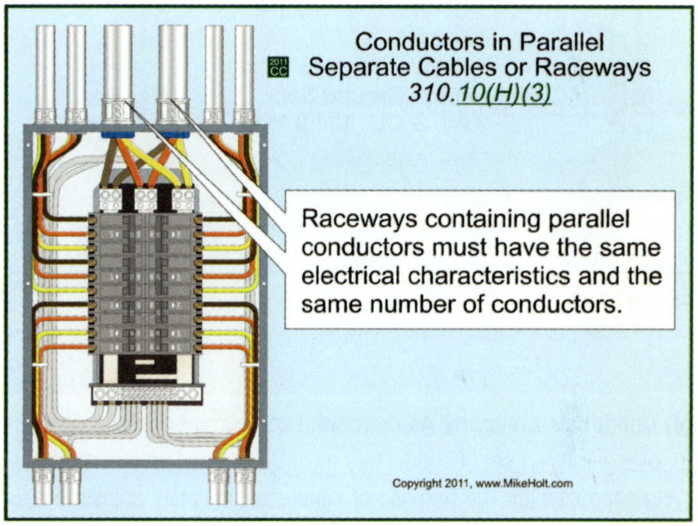

Figure 6–15

Author's Comment: If one set of parallel conductors is run in a metallic raceway and the other conductors are run in PVC conduit, the conductors in the metallic raceway will have an increased opposition to current flow (impedance) as compared to the conductors in the nonmetallic raceway. This results in an unbalanced distribution of current between the parallel conductors. Without getting into the details, this isn't good.

Paralleling is done in sets. Parallel sets of conductors aren't required to have the same physical characteristics as those of another set to achieve balance.

Author's Comment: For example, a 400A feeder with a neutral load of 240A can be paralleled as follows: **Figure 6–16**

- Phase A, Two—250 kcmil THHN aluminum, 100 ft
- Phase B, Two—3/0 THHN copper, 104 ft
- Phase C, Two—3/0 THHN copper, 102 ft
- Neutral, Two—1/0 THHN aluminum, 103 ft
- Equipment Grounding Conductor, Two—3 AWG copper, 101 ft

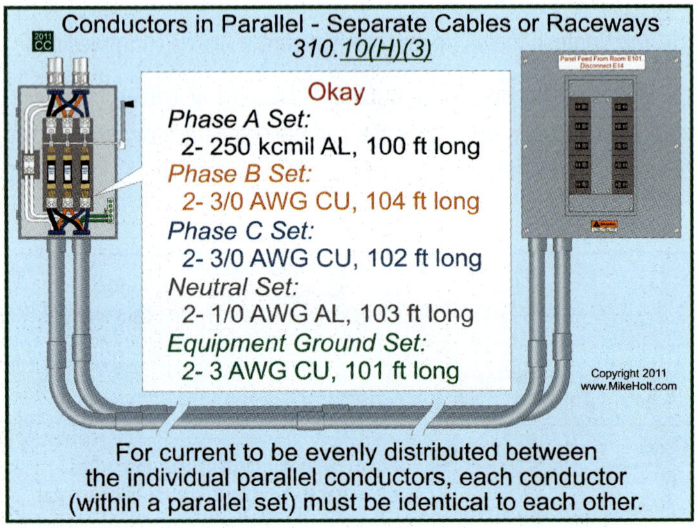

Figure 6–16

(4) Conductor Ampacity Adjustment. Each current-carrying conductor of a paralleled set of conductors must be counted as a current-carrying conductor for the purpose of conductor ampacity adjustment, in accordance with Table 310.15(B)(3)(a). **Figure 6–17**

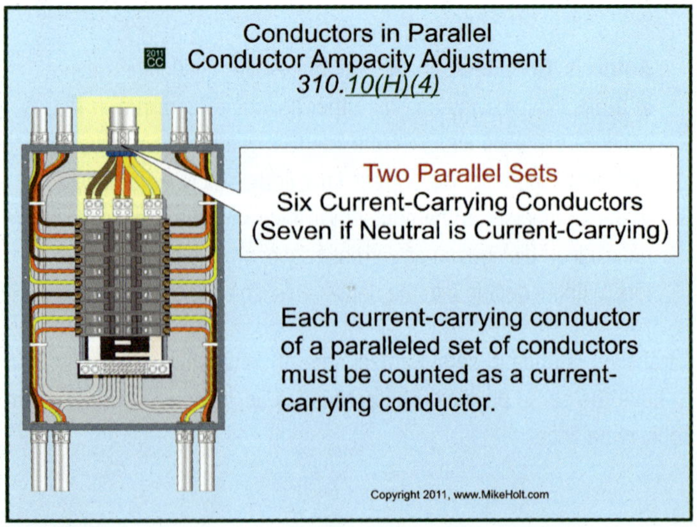

Figure 6–17

(5) Equipment Grounding Conductors. The circuit equipment grounding conductors for circuits in parallel must be identical to each other in length, material, size, insulation, and termination. Where raceways requiring equipment grounding conductors are installed in parallel, they each must have an equipment grounding conductor sized in accordance with 250.122. The minimum 1/0 AWG rule for parallel conductors of 310.10(H)(1) doesn't apply to equipment grounding conductors run in parallel [250.122(F)]. **Figure 6–18**

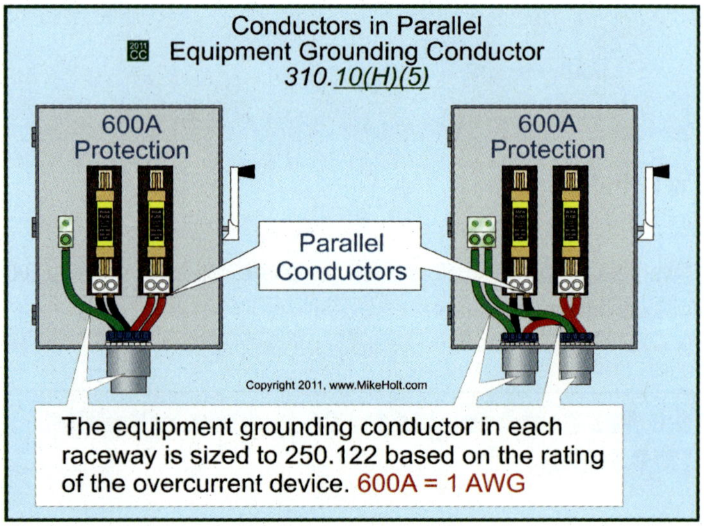

Figure 6–18

Question: *What size parallel equipment grounding conductors are required for a 2,000A service, using eight parallel sets of service conductors per phase?*

(a) 3/0 AWG (b) 4/0 AWG (c) 250 kcmil (d) 300 kcmil

Answer: *(c) 250 kcmil*

2,000A/8 raceways = 250A per parallel run. 250 kcmil is rated 255A at 75°C [Table 310.15(B)(16)].

Equipment grounding conductor for 2,000A overcurrent device is a minimum of 250 kcmil in each parallel raceway [250.122(F) and Table 250.122]

Note: If all eight sets of parallel service conductors for this service were installed in the same cable tray, a single 250 kcmil equipment grounding conductor would be required in the cable tray [250.122(F)].

6.7 Overcurrent Protection [Article 240]

An overcurrent is defined as current in excess of the equipment rating caused by an overload, short circuit, or ground fault [Article 100 Definition]. Figure 6–19

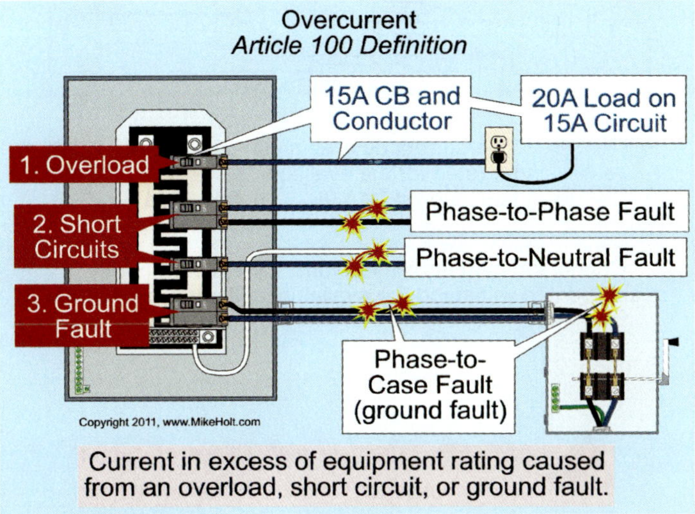

Figure Figure 6–19

An overcurrent device protects the circuit by opening the device when the current reaches a value that will cause an excessive or dangerous temperature rise (overheating) in conductors. This is the actual ampere rating of the overcurrent device, such as 15A, 20A, or 30A [240.6(A)]. The NEC lists standard sized overcurrent devices of: 15, 20, 25, 30, 35, 40, 45, 50, 60, 70, 80, 90, 100, 110, 125, 150, 175, 200, 225, 250, 300, 350, 400, 450, 500, 600, 700, 800, 1,000, 1,200, and 1,600A [240.6(A)]. Figure 6–20

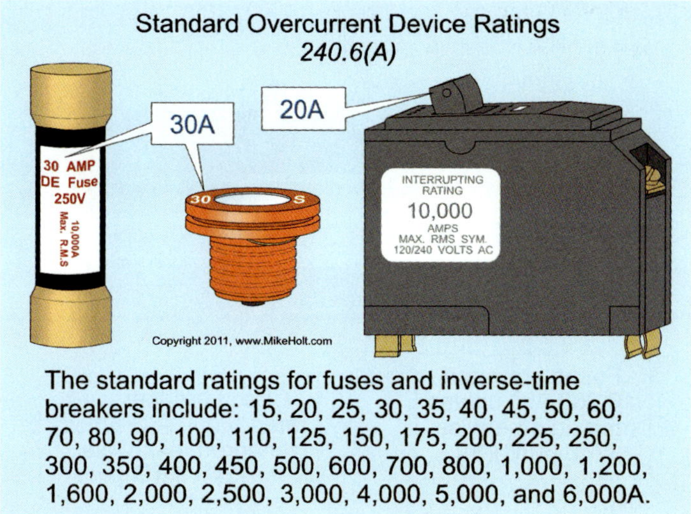

Figure 6–20

Interrupting Protection Rating [110.9]

Overcurrent devices such as circuit breakers and fuses are intended to interrupt the circuit, and they must have an interrupting rating sufficient for the short-circuit current available at the line terminals of the equipment [110.9]. Figure 6–21

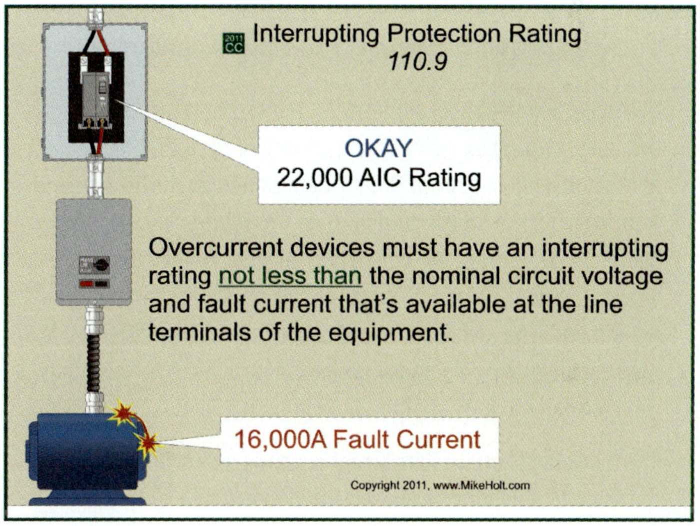

Figure 6–21

Author's Comments:

- See the definition of "Interrupting Rating" in Article 100.
- Unless marked otherwise, the ampere interrupting rating for circuit breakers is 5,000A [240.83(C)], and for fuses it's 10,000A [240.60(C)(3)]. Figure 6–22

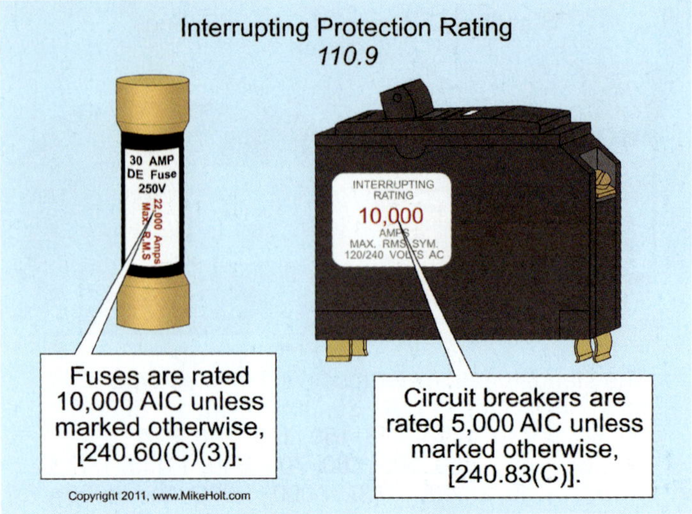

Figure 6–22

AVAILABLE SHORT-CIRCUIT CURRENT

Available short-circuit current is the current, in amperes, available at a given point in the electrical system. This available short-circuit current is first determined at the secondary terminals of the utility transformer. Thereafter, the available short-circuit current is calculated at the terminals of service equipment, then at branch-circuit panelboards and other equipment. The available short-circuit current is different at each point of the electrical system. It's highest at the utility transformer and lowest at the branch-circuit load.

The available short-circuit current depends on the impedance of the circuit, which increases moving downstream from the utility transformer. The greater the circuit impedance (utility transformer and the additive impedances of the circuit conductors), the lower the available short-circuit current. Figure 6–23

Factors that impact the available short-circuit current at the utility transformer include the system voltage, the transformer kVA rating, and its impedance (expressed in a percentage on the equipment nameplate). Properties that affect the impedance of the circuit include the conductor material (copper versus aluminum), conductor size, conductor length, and motor-operated equipment supplied by the circuit.

> **Author's Comment:** Many people in the industry describe Amperes Interrupting Rating (AIR) as "Amperes Interrupting Capacity" (AIC).

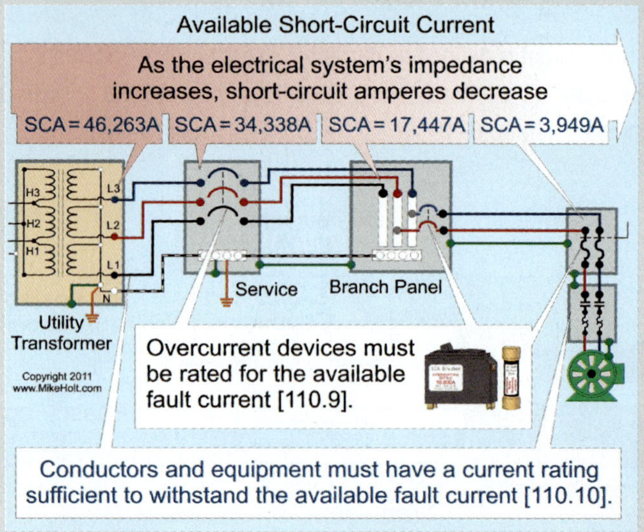

Figure 6–23

DANGER: *Extremely high values of current flow (caused by short circuits or ground faults) produce tremendously destructive thermal and magnetic forces. If the circuit overcurrent device isn't rated to interrupt the current at the available fault values at its listed voltage rating, it can explode while attempting to open the circuit overcurrent device resulting from a short circuit or ground fault, which can cause serious injury or death, as well as property damage.* Figure 6–24

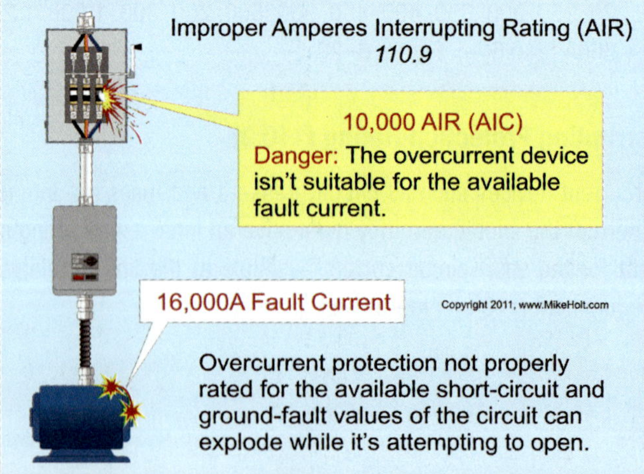

Figure 6–24

SHORT-CIRCUIT CALCULATION

The available short-circuit current at the transformer is found with the formula:

Isca = VA/(E x 1.732 x Z%) for three-phase

Isca = Short-Circuit Current Available
VA = Transformer VA Rating
E = Voltage
Z% = Transformer Percent Impedance
A 1.732 multiplier is included for three-phase transformers.

Author's Comment: This calculation is made assuming a condition called "infinite buss" which means that the impedance on the primary side of the transformer, including the impedance of the utility lines to that point, is ignored. This results in a higher short-circuit current than will be experienced in an actual situation, but many other factors may also affect the actual fault current, and in a very sophisticated system, an engineering study may be warranted.

► Example 1: Short-Circuit Calculation

Question: *What's the available short-circuit current for a 112.50 kVA, 208V, three-phase transformer with 3.20 percent impedance?*

(a) 220A (b) 400A (c) 5,450A (d) 9,759A

Answer: *(d) 9,759A*

Isca = VA/(E x 1.732 x Z%)
Isca = 112,500VA/(208V x 1.732 x 0.032)
Isca = 9,759A

► Example 2: Short-Circuit Calculation

Question: *What's the available short-circuit current for a 30 kVA, 208V, three-phase transformer with 6.30 percent impedance?*

(a) 275A (b) 950A (c) 1,321A (d) 5,450A

Answer: *(c) 1,321A*

Isca = VA/(E x 1.732 x Z%)
Isca = 30,000VA/(208V x 1.732 x 0.063)
Isca = 1,321A

6.8 Overcurrent Protection of Conductors—General Requirements [240.4]

There are many different rules for protecting conductors and equipment. It's not simply 12 AWG wire and a 20A breaker. The general rule is that conductors must be protected at the point where they receive their supply in accordance with their ampacities, as listed in Table 310.15(B)(16), **Figure 6–25**. Other methods of protection are permitted or required as listed in Subsections (A) through (G) of Section 240.4.

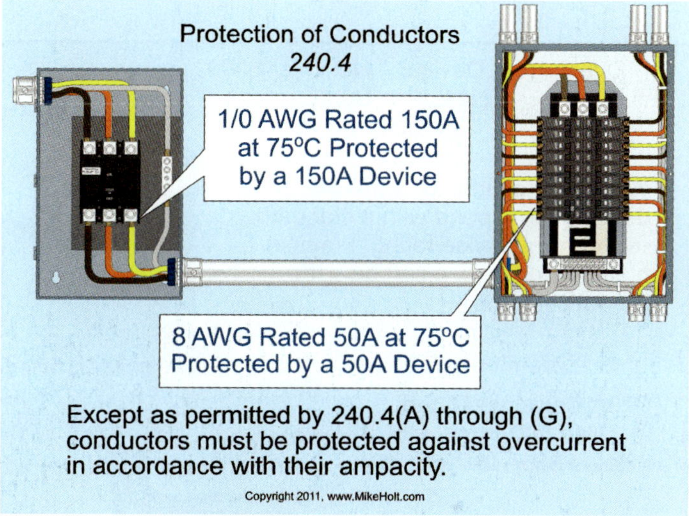

Figure 6–25

(A) Power Loss Hazard. Conductor overload protection isn't required, but short-circuit protection is required where the interruption of the circuit will create a hazard, such as in a material-handling electromagnet circuit or a fire pump circuit.

(B) Overcurrent Devices Rated 800A or Less. The next higher standard rating of overcurrent device (above the ampacity of the ungrounded conductors being protected) is permitted, provided all of the following conditions are met:

(1) The conductors don't supply branch circuits for more than one receptacle.

(2) The ampacity of a conductor, after ampacity adjustment and/or correction, doesn't correspond with the standard rating of a fuse or circuit breaker in 240.6(A).

(3) The overcurrent device rating doesn't exceed 800A.

► Overcurrent Protection 800A and Less Example

Question: *What's the maximum size overcurrent device that can be used to protect 500 kcmil conductors, where each conductor has an ampacity of 380A at 75°C, in accordance with Table 310.15(B)(16) and the calculated load is 370A?* **Figure 6–26**

(a) 300A (b) 350A (c) 400A (d) 500A

Answer: *(c) 400A*

This "next size up" rule doesn't apply to feeder tap conductors [240.21(B)], or transformer secondary conductors [240.21(C)].

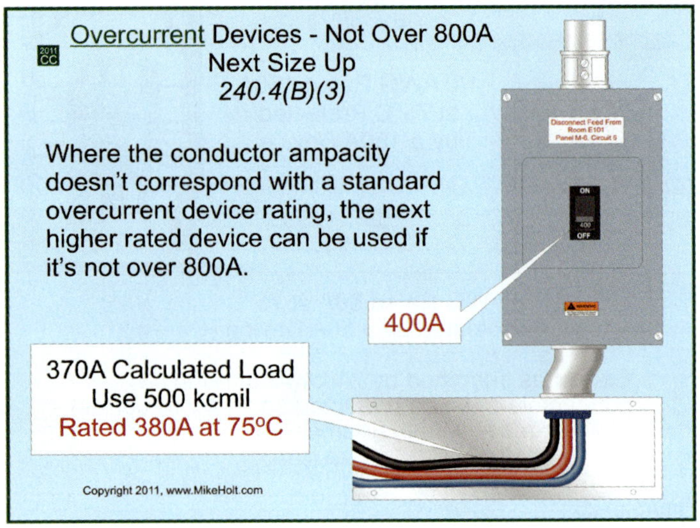

Figure 6–26

(C) Overcurrent Devices Rated Over 800A. If the circuit's overcurrent device exceeds 800A, the conductor ampacity, after ampacity adjustment and/or correction, must not be less than the rating of the overcurrent device.

► Overcurrent Protection Over 800A Example

Question: *What's the minimum size of conductors allowed to be protected by a 1,200A overcurrent device using three sets of conductors per phase with terminals rated at 75°C?* **Figure 6–27**

(a) 400 kcmil (b) 500 kcmil (c) 600 kcmil (d) 750 kcmil

Answer: *(c) 600 kcmil*

Three sets of 600 kcmil conductors per phase, where each conductor has an ampacity of 420A at 75°C, in accordance with Table 310.15(B)(16).

420A x 3 = 1,260A

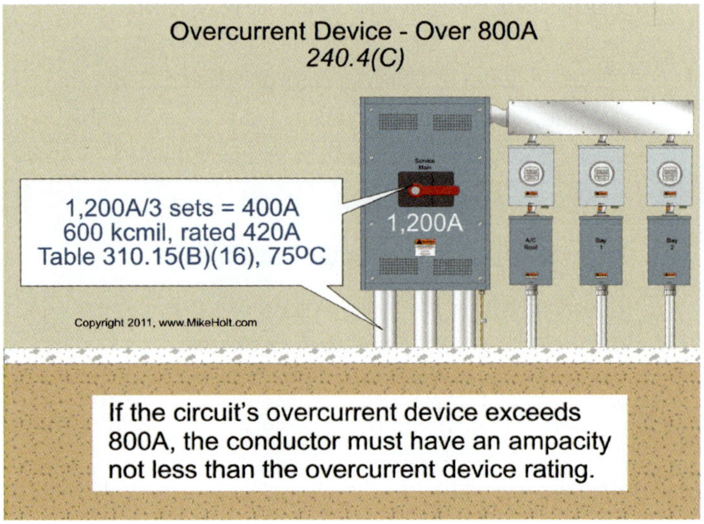

Figure 6–27

(D) Small Conductors. Unless specifically permitted in 240.4(E) or (G), overcurrent protection must not exceed the following after ampacity adjustment and/or correction according to 310.15: **Figure 6–28**

(1) 18 AWG Copper—7A

(2) 16 AWG Copper—10A

(3) 14 AWG Copper—15A

(4) 12 AWG Aluminum/Copper-Clad Aluminum—15A

(5) 12 AWG Copper—20A

(6) 10 AWG Aluminum/Copper-Clad Aluminum—25A

(7) 10 AWG Copper—30A

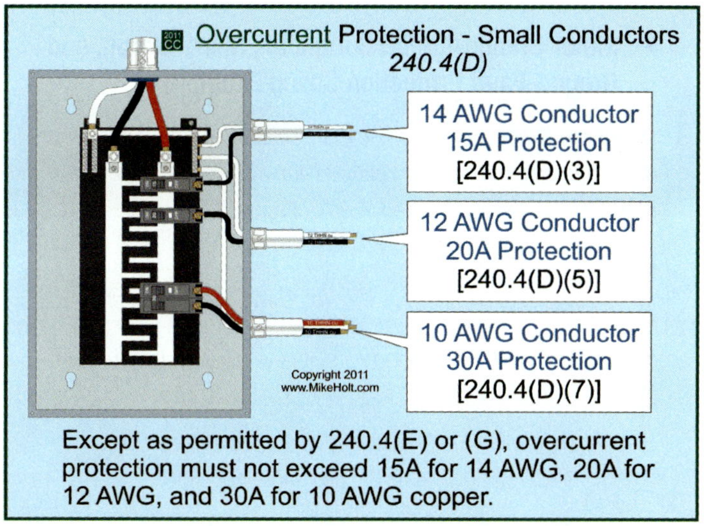

Figure 6–28

(E) Tap Conductors. Tap conductors must be protected against overcurrent as follows:

(1) Household Ranges and Cooking Appliances and Other Loads, 210.19(A)(3) and (4)

(2) Fixture Wire, 240.5(B)(2)

(3) Location in Circuit, 240.21

(4) Reduction in Ampacity Size of Busway, 368.17(B)

(5) Feeder or Branch Circuits (busway taps), 368.17(C)

(6) Single Motor Taps, 430.53(D)

(F) Transformer Secondary Conductors. The primary overcurrent device sized in accordance with 450.3(B) is considered suitable to protect the secondary conductors of a 2-wire (single voltage) system, provided the primary overcurrent device doesn't exceed the value determined by multiplying the secondary conductor ampacity by the secondary-to-primary transformer voltage ratio.

▶ Transformer Secondary Conductor Sizing Example

Question: *What's the minimum secondary conductor size required for a 2-wire, 480V to 120V transformer rated 1.50 kVA (terminals rated 75°C)?* Figure 6–29

(a) 16 AWG (b) 14 AWG (c) 12 AWG (d) 10 AWG

Answer: *(b) 14 AWG*

Primary Current = VA/E

VA = 1,500 VA

E = 480V

Primary Current = 1,500 VA/480V

Primary Current = 3.13A

Primary Protection [450.3(B)] = 3.13A x 1.67

Primary Protection = 5.22A or 5A Fuse

Secondary Current = 1,500 VA/120V

Secondary Current = 12.50A

Secondary Conductor = 14 AWG, rated 20A at 75°C, Table 310.15(B)(16)

The 5A primary overcurrent device can be used to protect 14 AWG secondary conductors because it doesn't exceed the value determined by multiplying the secondary conductor ampacity by the secondary-to-primary transformer voltage ratio (5A = 20A x 120V/480V).

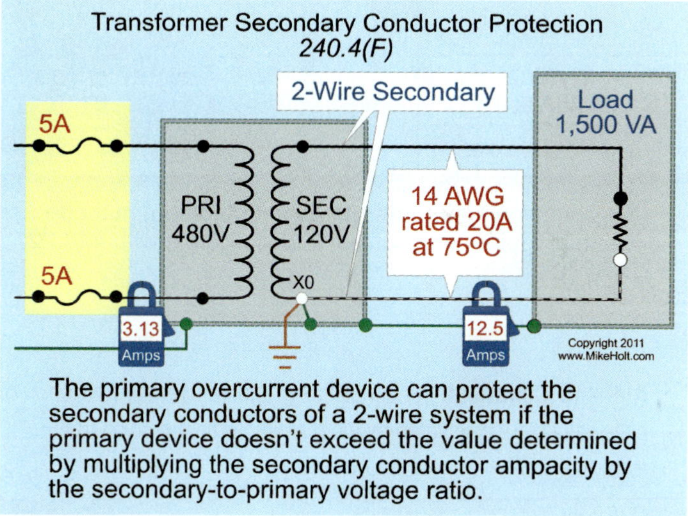

Figure 6–29

(G) Overcurrent Protection for Specific Applications. Overcurrent protection for specific equipment and conductors must comply with that referenced in Table 240.4(G).

Air-Conditioning and Refrigeration [Article 440]. Air-conditioning and refrigeration equipment, and their circuit conductors, must be protected against overcurrent in accordance with 440.22.

> **Author's Comment:** Typically, the branch-circuit ampacity and protection size is marked on the equipment nameplate [440.4(A)].

► Air Conditioner Overcurrent Protection Sizing Example

Question: *What size branch-circuit overcurrent device is required for an air conditioner (18A) when the nameplate indicates the minimum circuit ampacity is 23A, with maximum overcurrent protection of 40A (terminals rated 75°C) ?* **Figure 6–30**

(a) 12 AWG, 40A protection *(b) 12 AWG, 50A protection*
(c) 12 AWG, 60A protection *(d) 12 AWG, 70A protection*

Answer: *(a) 12 AWG, 40A protection*

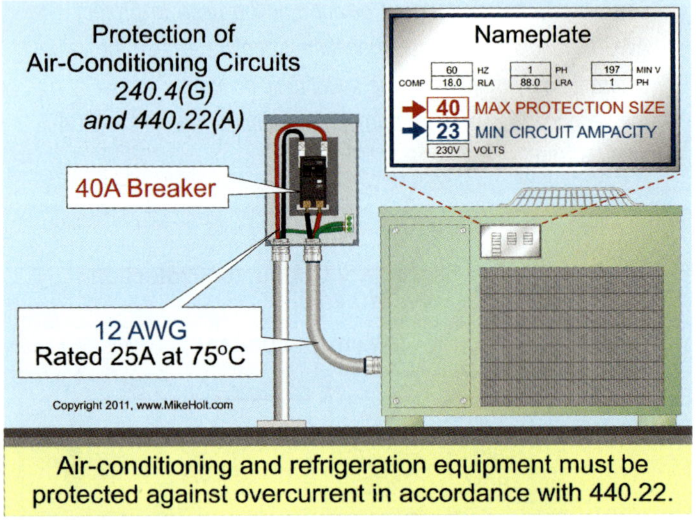

Figure 6–30

Author's Comment: Air-conditioning and refrigeration nameplate values are calculated by the manufacturer according to the following:

- Branch-Circuit Conductor Size [440.32]
  18A x 1.25 = 22.50A, 12 AWG rated 25A at 75°C
- Branch-Circuit Protection Size [440.22(A)]
  18A x 2.25 = 40.50A, 40A maximum overcurrent protection device size [240.6(A)]
- Motors [Article 430]. Motor circuit conductors must be protected against short circuits and ground faults in accordance with 430.52 and 430.62 [430.51].

► Motor Branch-Circuit Conductor, Short-Circuit, and Ground-Fault Protection Sizing Example

Question: *What size branch-circuit conductor and overcurrent device (circuit breaker) is required for a 7½ hp, 230V, three-phase motor (terminals rated 75°C) ?* **Figure 6–31**

(a) 10 AWG, 30A breaker *(b) 10 AWG, 60A breaker*
(c) 10 AWG, 70A breaker *(d) 8 AWG, 90A breaker*

Answer: *(b) 10 AWG, 60A breaker (or use 50A if it will handle motor starting current)*

Step 1: Determine the branch-circuit conductor size [Table 310.15(B)(16), 430.22, and Table 430.250]:

22A x 1.25 = 28A, 10 AWG, rated 35A at 75°C

Step 2: Determine the branch-circuit protection size [240.6(A), 430.52(C)(1) Ex 1, Table 430.250].

Inverse Time Breaker: 22A x 2.50 = 55A
Next size up = 60A

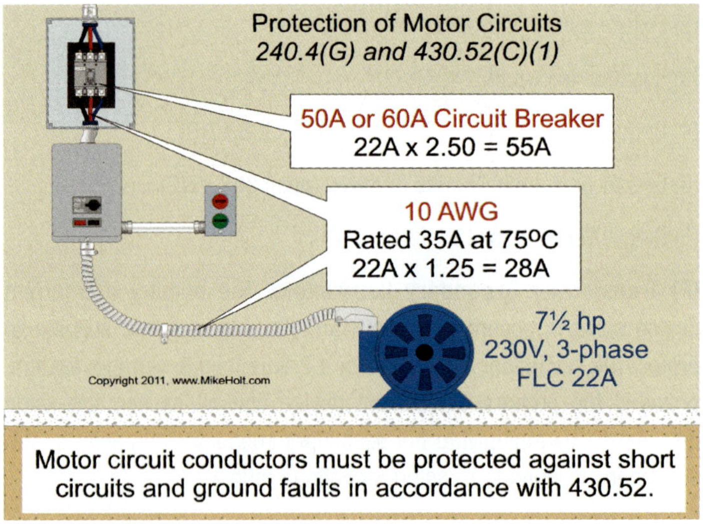

Figure 6–31

Motor Control [430]

Motor control circuit conductors must be sized and protected in accordance with 430.72.

Remote-Control, Signaling, and Power-Limited Circuits [725]

Remote-control, signaling, and power-limited circuit conductors must be protected against overcurrent in accordance with 725.43.

6.9 Overcurrent Protection of Conductors—Specific Requirements

When sizing and protecting conductors for equipment, be sure to apply the specific NEC requirement(s).

- Air-Conditioning [440.22 and 440.32]
- Appliances [422.10 and 422.11]
- Branch Circuits [210.20]
- Electric Heating Equipment [424.3]
- Motors [Article 430]
  - Branch Circuits [430.22 and 430.52]
  - Feeders [430.24 and 430.62]
  - Remote Control [430.72]
- Panelboards [408.36(A)]
- Transformers [240.21 and 450.3]
- Feeder Conductors [215.2 and 215.3]
- Service Conductors [230.42 and 230.90(A)]
- Tap Conductors [240.21(B)]
- Transformer Secondary Conductors [240.21(B)]

Branch-Circuit Overcurrent Protection

Conductors must be sized no less than 125 percent of the continuous loads, plus 100 percent of the noncontinuous loads, based on the terminal temperature rating ampacities as listed in Table 310.15(B)(16), before any ampacity adjustment [110.14(C) and 210.19(A)(1)].

► Branch-Circuit Overcurrent Protection Example

Question: *What size branch-circuit conductor and overcurrent protection is required for a 44A continuous load if the equipment terminals are rated 75°C as permitted by 110.14(C)(1)(a)(3)?* **Figure 6–32**

(a) A 10 AWG and 30A circuit breaker
(b) An 8 AWG and 50A circuit breaker
(c) A 6 AWG and 60A circuit breaker
(d) A 4 AWG and 80A circuit breaker

Answer: *(c) A 6 AWG and 60A circuit breaker*

Since the load is 44A continuous, the conductor must be sized to have an ampacity of not less than 55A (44A x 1.25) [210.19(A)(1)]. According to Table 310.15(B)(16), 75°C column, a 6 AWG conductor is suitable, because it has an ampere rating of 65A at 75°C before any conductor ampacity adjustment and/or correction is applied. The overcurrent device must be sized at 60A (44 x 1.25) which protects the 6 AWG conductor within its ampacity rating [210.20(A)]. **Figure 6–33**

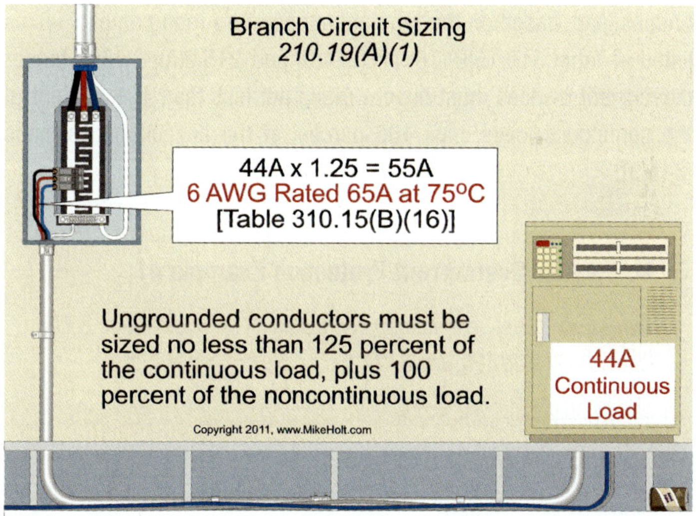

Figure 6–32

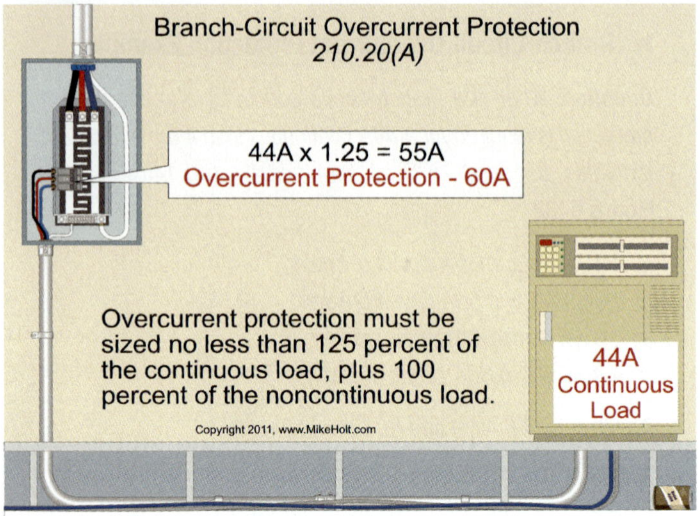

Figure 6–33

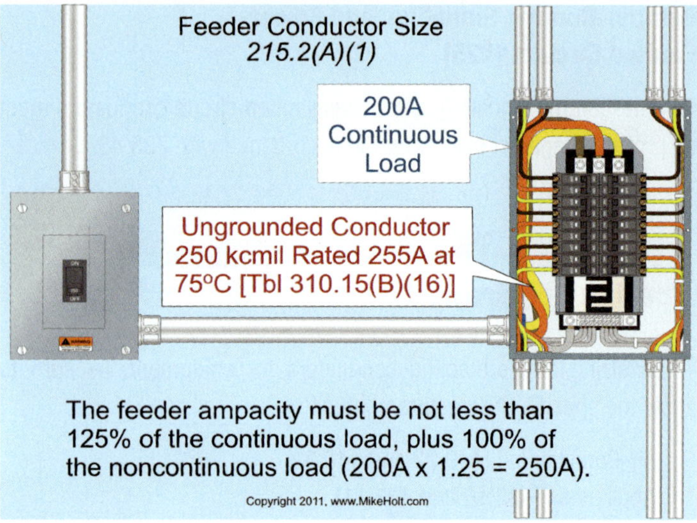

Figure 6–34

Feeder Overcurrent Protection

The minimum feeder-circuit conductor ampacity, before the application of any adjustment and/or correction factors, must be no less than 125 percent of the continuous load, plus 100 percent of the noncontinuous load, based on the terminal temperature rating ampacities as listed in Table 310.15(B)(16) [110.14(C) and 215.2(A)(1)]. The feeder overcurrent devices must have a rating not less than 125 percent of the continuous loads, plus 100 percent of the noncontinuous loads [215.3].

► Feeder Overcurrent Protection Example #1

Question: *What size feeder conductor is required for a 200A continuous load?* **Figure 6–34**

(a) 4/0 AWG (b) 250 kcmil (c) 400 kcmil (d) 500 kcmil

Answer: *(b) 250 kcmil*

200 x 1.25 = 250A
250 kcmil has an ampacity of 255A at 75°C

► Feeder Overcurrent Protection Example #2

Question: *What size neutral conductor is required in the feeder for a 200A continuous load?*

(a) 3/0 AWG (b) 250 kcmil (c) 400 kcmil (d) 500 kcmil

Answer: *(a) 3/0 AWG*

The neutral of a feeder circuit is allowed to be sized at 100% of the continuous load [215.2(A)(1) Ex 2]. In no case can the neutral for a feeder be sized smaller than required by 250.122 [215.2(A)(2)]. **Figure 6–35**

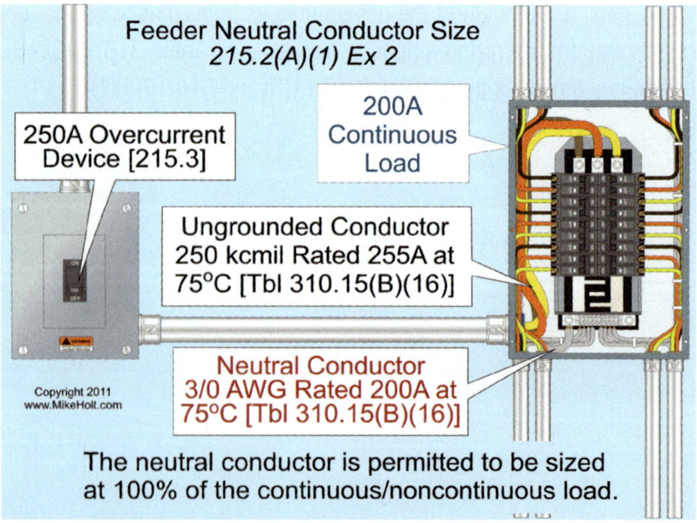

Figure 6–35

► Feeder Overcurrent Protection Example #3

Question: *What size feeder overcurrent device is required for a 200A continuous load?* **Figure 6–36**

(a) 200A *(b) 225A* *(c) 250A* *(d) 300A*

Answer: *(c) 250A*

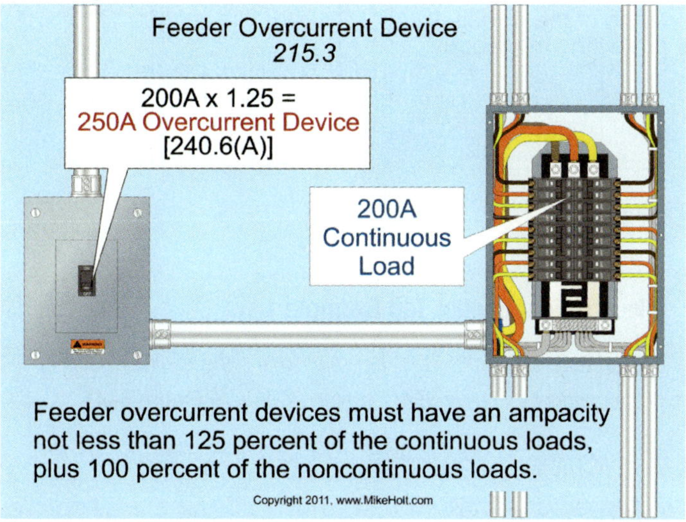

Figure 6–36

Overcurrent Protection Location in Circuit [240.21]

Except as permitted by (A) through (H), overcurrent devices must be placed at the point where the branch or feeder conductors receive their power. Tap and secondary conductors aren't permitted to supply another conductor (tapping a tap isn't permitted). **Figure 6–37**

(A) Branch-Circuit Taps. Branch-circuit taps are permitted in accordance with 210.19.

(B) Feeder Tap Conductors. Conductors can be tapped from a feeder as specified in 240.21(B)(1) through (B)(5).

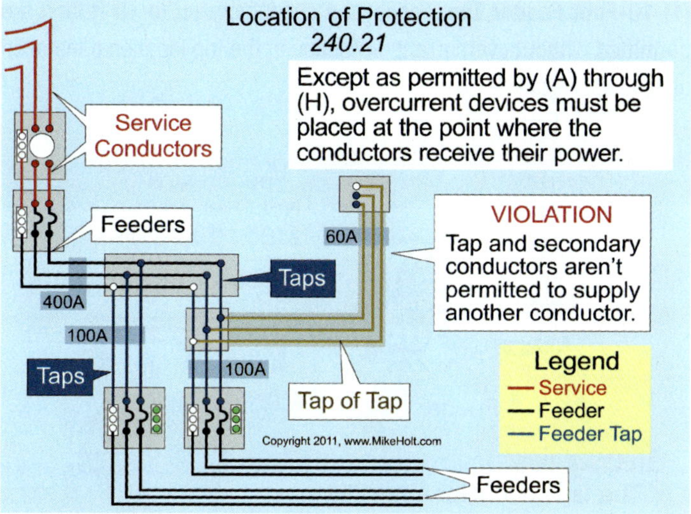

Figure 6–37

► Feeder Tap Conductors Example

Question: *What size tap conductors will be required for a 150A circuit breaker if the calculated continuous load is 100A?* **Figure 6–38**

(a) 3 AWG, rated 100A *(b) 2 AWG, rated 115A*
(c) 1 AWG, rated 130A *(d) 1/0 AWG, rated 150A*

Answer: *(d) 1/0 AWG, rated 150A*

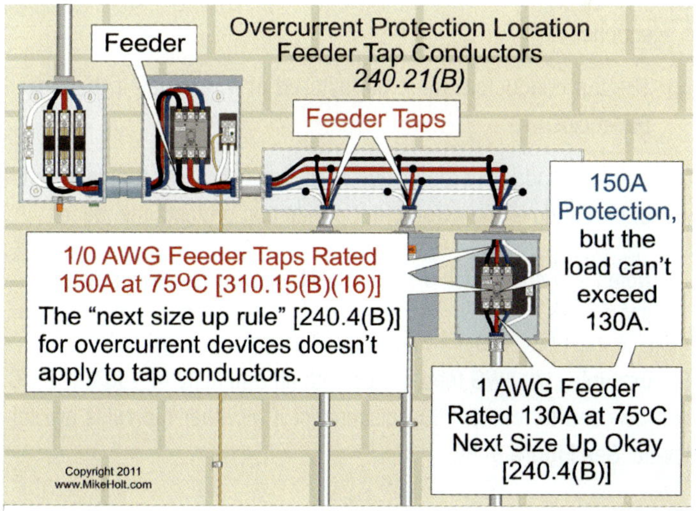

Figure 6–38

(1) 10-Foot Feeder Tap. Feeder tap conductors up to 10 ft long are permitted without overcurrent protection at the tap location if installed as follows: Figure 6–39

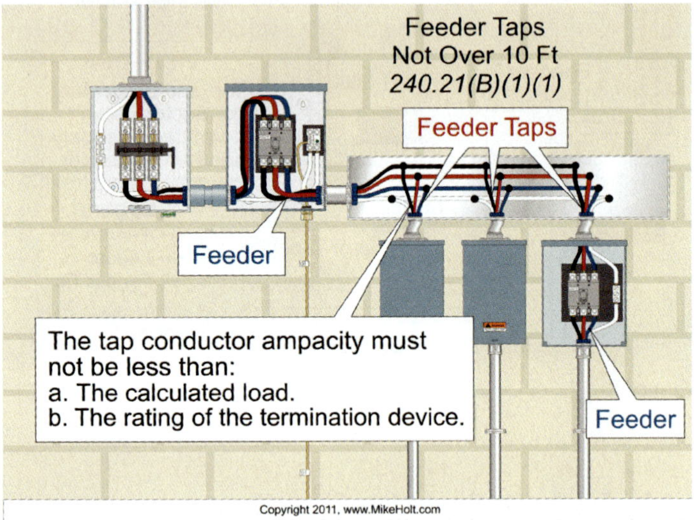

Figure 6–39

(1) The ampacity of the tap conductor must not be less than:

a. The calculated load in accordance with Article 220, and

b. The rating of the device or overcurrent device supplied by the tap conductors.

(2) The tap conductors must not extend beyond the equipment they supply.

(3) The tap conductors must be installed in a raceway if they leave the enclosure.

(4) The tap conductors must have an ampacity not less than one-tenth of the rating of the overcurrent device that protects the feeder.

Note: See 408.36 for the overcurrent protection requirements for panelboards.

For example, 1/0 AWG feeder taps with an ampacity of 150A at 75°C, can be used to feed a 150A disconnect if all other tap rules are followed. See Figure 6–39.

10-Foot Feeder Tap

A 400A breaker protects a set of 500 kcmil feeder conductors. There are three taps fed from the 500 kcmil feeders that supply disconnects with 200A, 150A, and 100A overcurrent devices. Figure 6–40

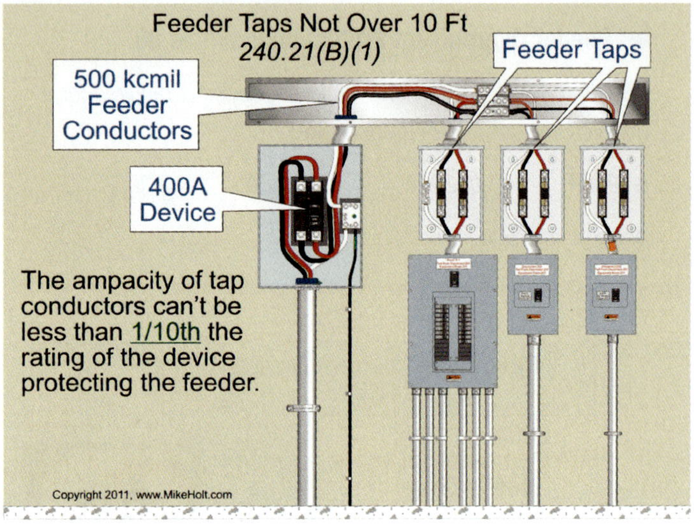

Figure 6–40

► 10-Foot Feeder Tap Example 1

Question: *Using the 10-ft tap rule, what's the minimum size of the conductors required to feed the 200A tap?* Figure 6–41

(a) 3 AWG *(b) 1/0 AWG* *(c) 3/0 AWG* *(d) 250 kcmil*

Answer: *(c) 3/0 AWG*

3/0 AWG has an ampacity of 200A at 75°C, and is greater than one-tenth of the rating of the 400A overcurrent device [Table 310.15(B)(16)].

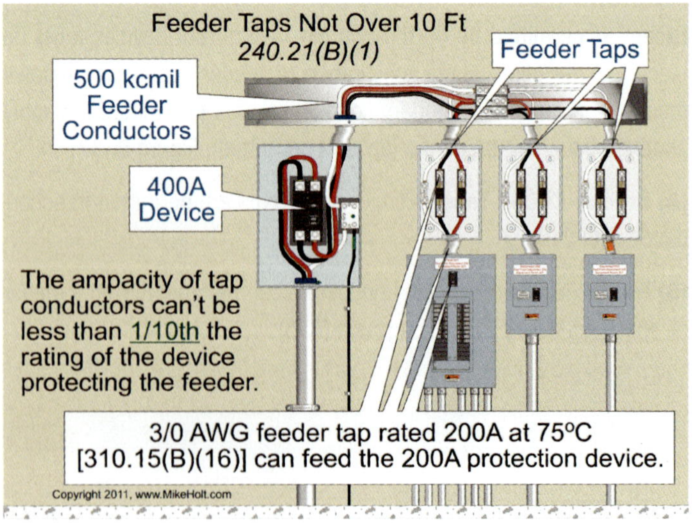

Figure 6–41

► 10-Foot Feeder Tap Example 2

Question: *Using the 10-ft tap rule, what's the minimum size of the conductors required to feed the 150A tap?* **Figure 6–42**

(a) 3 AWG *(b) 1/0 AWG* *(c) 3/0 AWG* *(d) 250 kcmil*

Answer: *(b) 1/0 AWG*

1/0 AWG has an ampacity of 150A at 75°C, and is greater than one-tenth of the rating of the 400A overcurrent device [Table 310.15(B)(16)].

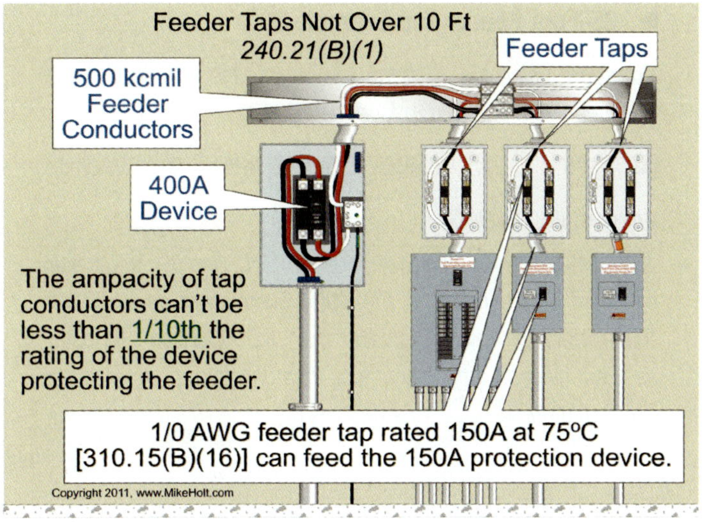

Figure 6–42

► 10-Foot Feeder Tap Example 3

Question: *Using the 10-ft tap rule, what's the minimum size of the conductors required to feed the 100A tap?* **Figure 6–43**

(a) 3 AWG *(b) 1/0 AWG* *(c) 3/0 AWG* *(d) 250 kcmil*

Answer: *(a) 3 AWG*

3 AWG has an ampacity of 100A at 75°C, and is greater than one-tenth of the rating of the 400A overcurrent device [Table 310.15(B)(16)].

A 400A breaker protects a set of 500 kcmil feeder conductors. There are three taps fed from the 500 kcmil feeders that supply disconnects with 200A, 150A, and 30A overcurrent devices.

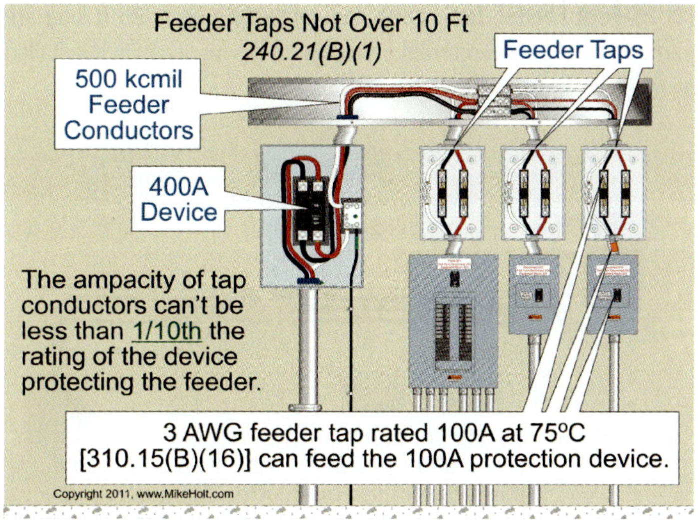

Figure 6–43

► 10-Foot Feeder Tap Example 4

Question: *Using the 10-ft tap rule, what's the minimum size of the conductors required to feed the 30A tap?* **Figure 6–44**

(a) 12 AWG *(b) 8 AWG* *(c) 1/0 AWG* *(d) 3/0 AWG*

Answer: *(b) 8 AWG*

8 AWG has an ampacity of 50A at 75°C, and is greater than one-tenth of the rating of the 400A overcurrent device [Table 310.15(B)(16)]. Anything smaller than 8 AWG can't be used, as it will have an ampacity of less than one-tenth of 400A (40A) in the 75°C column.

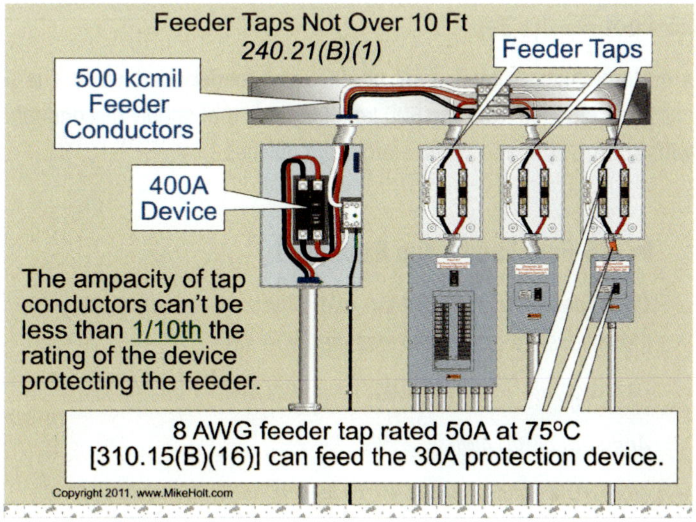

Figure 6–44

(2) 25-Foot Feeder Tap. Feeder tap conductors up to 25 ft long are permitted without overcurrent protection at the tap location if installed as follows: **Figure 6–45**

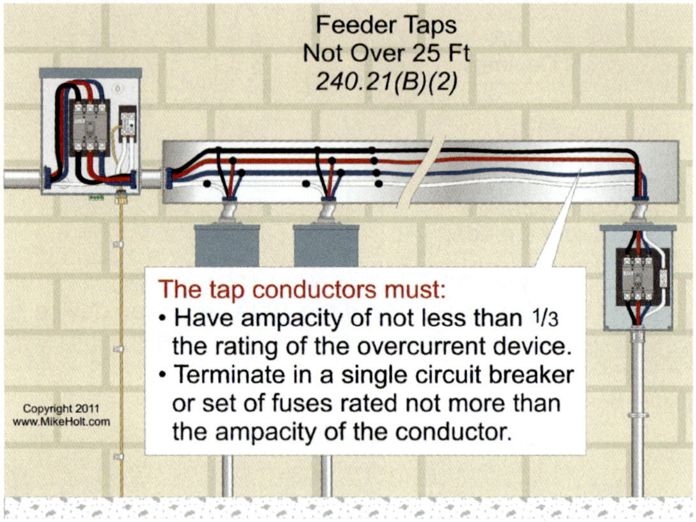

Figure 6–45

(1) The ampacity of the tap conductors must not be less than one-third the rating of the overcurrent device that protects the feeder.

(2) The tap conductors terminate in a single circuit breaker, or set of fuses rated no more than the tap conductor ampacity in accordance with 310.15 [Table 310.15(B)(16)].

(3) The tap conductors must be protected from physical damage by being enclosed in a manner approved by the authority having jurisdiction, such as within a raceway.

25-Foot Feeder Tap

A 400A breaker protects a set of 500 kcmil feeder conductors. There are three taps fed from the 500 kcmil feeders that supply disconnects with 200A, 150A, and 100A overcurrent devices.

► 25-Foot Feeder Tap Example 1

Question: *Using the 25-ft tap rule, what's the minimum size of the conductors required to feed the 200A tap?*

(a) 3 AWG (b) 1/0 AWG (c) 3/0 AWG (d) 250 kcmil

Answer: *(c) 3/0 AWG*

3/0 AWG is rated 200A at 75°C, and is greater than one-third of the rating of the 400A overcurrent device [Table 310.15(B)(16)].

► 25-Foot Feeder Tap Example 2

Question: *Using the 25-ft tap rule, what's the minimum size of the conductors required to feed the 150A tap?*

(a) 3 AWG (b) 1/0 AWG (c) 3/0 AWG (d) 250 kcmil

Answer: *(b) 1/0 AWG*

1/0 AWG has an ampacity of 150A at 75°C, and is greater than one-third of the rating of the 400A overcurrent device [Table 310.15(B)(16)].

► 25-Foot Feeder Tap Example 3

Question: *Using the 25-ft tap rule, what's the minimum size of the conductors required to feed the 100A tap?*

(a) 3 AWG (b) 1/0 AWG (c) 3/0 AWG (d) 250 kcmil

Answer: *(b) 1/0 AWG*

1/0 AWG has an ampacity of 150A at 75°C, and is greater than one-third of the rating of the 400A overcurrent device [Table 310.15(B)(16)]. Anything smaller than 1/0 AWG can't be used, as it will have an ampacity of less than one-third of 400A in the 75°C column.

Author's Comment: Taps may originate at the overcurrent device using multiple terminals per line. For instance, a 400A breaker can feed two 3/0 AWG feeder conductors using double-barrel terminal lugs, and each feeder may then feed two individual 200A panelboards as long as the appropriate tap rules for a 10-foot or 25-foot tap rule are followed.

(3) Taps Supplying a Transformer. Feeder tap conductors that supply a transformer must be installed as follows:

(1) The primary tap conductors must have an ampacity not less than one-third the rating of the overcurrent device.

(2) The secondary conductors must have an ampacity that, when multiplied by the ratio of the primary-to-secondary voltage, is at least one-third the rating of the overcurrent device that protects the feeder conductors.

(3) The total length of the primary and secondary conductors must not exceed 25 ft.

(4) Primary and secondary conductors must be protected from physical damage by being enclosed in a manner approved by the authority having jurisdiction, such as within a raceway.

(5) Secondary conductors terminate in a single circuit breaker, or set of fuses rated no more than the tap conductor ampacity in accordance with 310.15 [Table 310.15(B)(16)].

(4) Taps over 25 ft Long. Where the feeder is in a high bay manufacturing building over 35 ft high at the walls and meets 9 conditions.

(5) Outside Feeder Tap of Unlimited Length Rule. Outside feeder tap conductors can be of unlimited length without overcurrent protection at the point they receive their supply if installed as follows: Figure 6–46

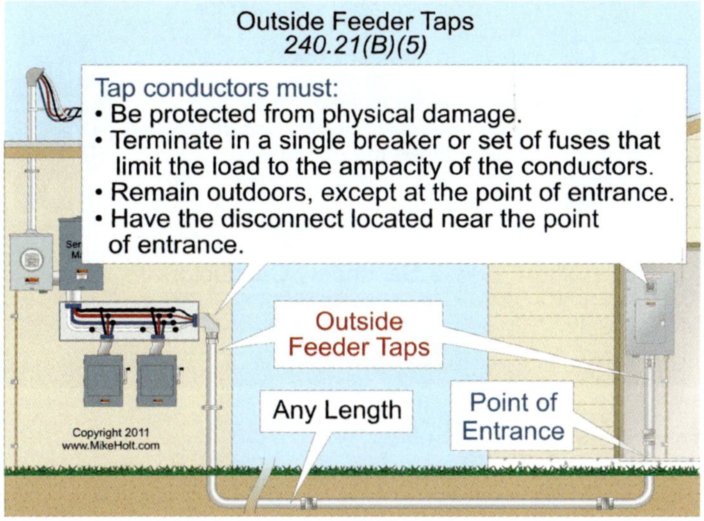

Figure 6–46

(1) The tap conductors must be suitably protected from physical damage in a raceway or manner approved by the authority having jurisdiction.

(2) The tap conductors terminate at a single circuit breaker or a single set of fuses that limits the load to the ampacity of the conductors.

(3) The overcurrent device for the tap conductors must be an integral part of the disconnecting means or it must be located immediately adjacent to it.

(4) The disconnecting means must be located at a readily accessible location either outside the building or structure, or nearest the point of entry of the conductors.

(C) Transformer Secondary Conductors. A set of conductors supplying single or separate loads is permitted to be connected to a transformer secondary without overcurrent protection at the secondary, in accordance with (1) through (6):

> **Author's Comment:** The "next size up rule" [240.4(B)] for overcurrent devices does not aply to transformer secondary conductors. Figure 6–47

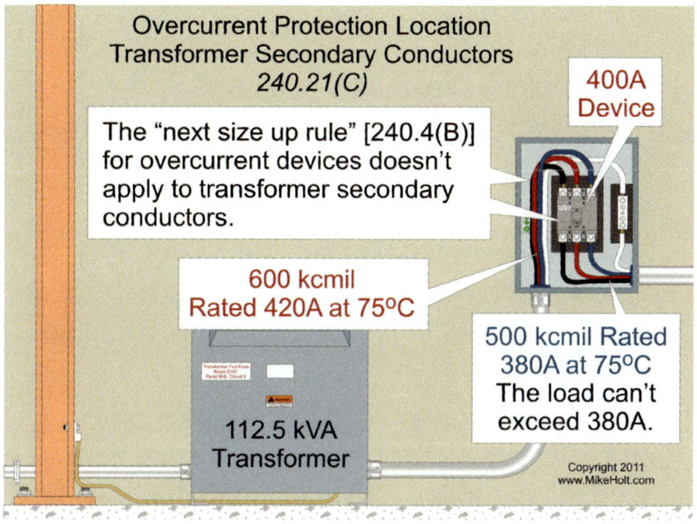

Figure 6–47

(1) Protection by Primary Overcurrent Device. The primary overcurrent device sized in accordance with 450.3(B) is considered suitable to protect the secondary conductors of a 2-wire system, provided the primary protection device doesn't exceed the value determined by multiplying the secondary conductor ampacity by the secondary-to-primary transformer voltage ratio.

► Transformer Secondary Conductor Sizing Example

Question: *What's the minimum size secondary conductor required for a 2-wire, 480V to 120V transformer rated 1.50 kVA (terminals rated 75°C)?* **Figure 6–48**

(a) 16 AWG (b) 14 AWG (c) 12 AWG (d) 10 AWG

Answer: *(b) 14 AWG*

Primary Current = VA/E

VA = 1,500 VA
E = 480V

Primary Current = 1,500 VA/480V
Primary Current = 3.13A

Primary Protection [450.3(B)] = 3.13A x 1.67
Primary Protection [450.3(B)] = 5.22A or 5A Fuse

Secondary Current = 1,500 VA/120V
Secondary Current = 12.50A

Secondary Conductor = 14 AWG, rated 20A at 75°C, Table 310.15(B)(16)

The 5A primary protection device can be used to protect 14 AWG secondary conductors because it doesn't exceed the value determined by multiplying the secondary conductor ampacity by the secondary-to-primary transformer voltage ratio (5A = 20A x 120V/480V).

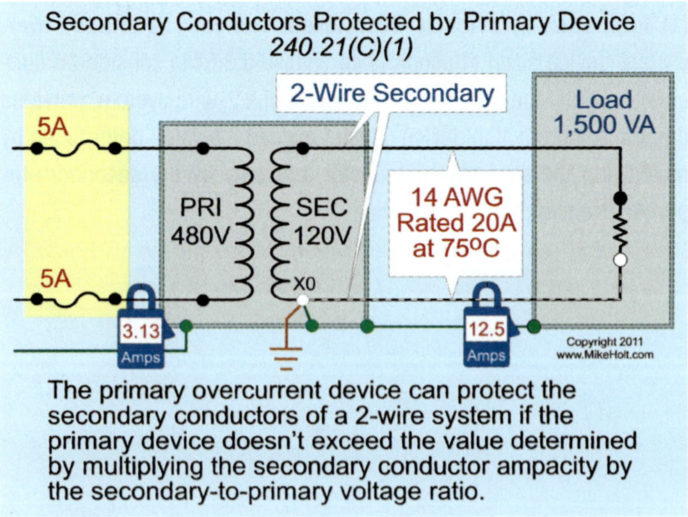

Figure 6–48

(2) 10-Foot Secondary Conductors. Secondary conductors can be run up to 10 ft without overcurrent protection if installed as follows:

(1) The ampacity of the secondary conductor must not be less than: **Figure 6–49**

a. The calculated load in accordance with Article 220,

b. The rating of the device supplied by the secondary conductors or the overcurrent device at the termination of the secondary conductors, and

c. Not less than one-tenth the rating of the overcurrent device protecting the primary of the transformer, multiplied by the primary-to-secondary transformer voltage ratio.

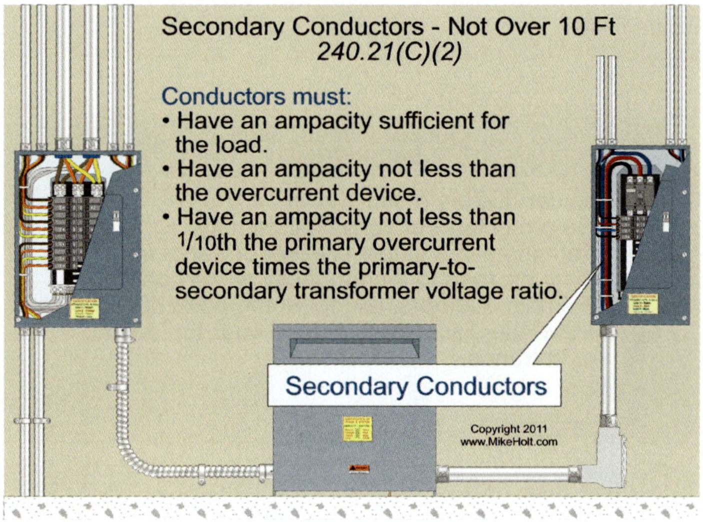

Figure 6–49

Note: See 408.36 for the overcurrent protection requirements for panelboards.

(2) The secondary conductors must not extend beyond the switchboard, panelboard, disconnecting means, or control devices they supply.

(3) The secondary conductors must be enclosed in a raceway.

(4) Outside Secondary Conductors of Unlimited Length. Outside secondary conductors can be of unlimited length, without overcurrent protection at the point they receive their supply, if they're installed as follows: **Figure 6–50**

(1) The conductors must be suitably protected from physical damage in a raceway or manner approved by the authority having jurisdiction.

(2) The conductors must terminate at a single circuit breaker or a single set of fuses that limit the load to the ampacity of the conductors.

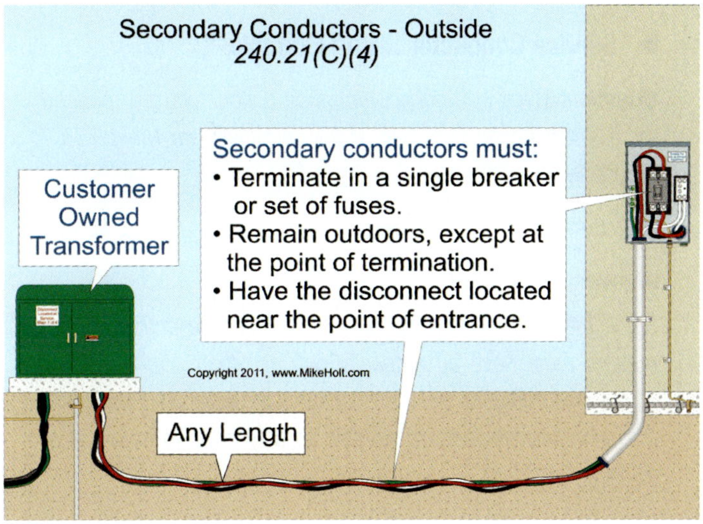

Figure 6–50

(3) The overcurrent device for the ungrounded conductors must be an integral part of a disconnecting means or it must be located immediately adjacent thereto.

(4) The disconnecting means must be located at a readily accessible location that complies with one of the following:

a. Outside of a building or structure.

b. Inside, nearest the point of entrance of the conductors.

c. Where installed in accordance with 230.6, nearest the point of entrance of the conductors.

▶ Transformer Outdoor Secondary Conductor Sizing Example

Question: *When outdoor secondary conductors are used to feed a 100A circuit breaker which is backfeeding a 225A main-lug-only panelboard, what's the minimum size required for the secondary conductors?*

(a) 3 AWG (b) 1 AWG (c) 4/0 AWG (d) 250 kcmil

Answer: *(a) 3 AWG*

(5) Secondary Conductors from a Feeder Tapped Transformer. Transformer secondary conductors must be installed in accordance with 240.21(B)(3).

(6) Secondary Conductors Not Over 25 ft Long. Where the length of secondary conductors doesn't exceed 25 ft and complies with the following: Figure 6–51

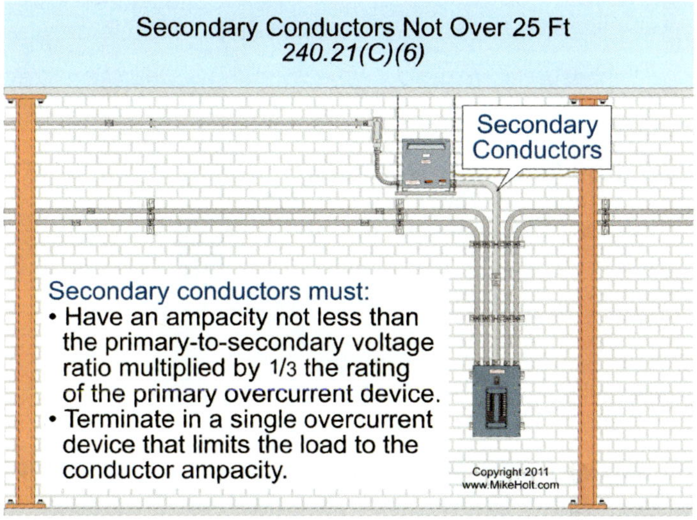

Figure 6–51

(1) The secondary conductors must have an ampacity not less than the value of the primary-to-secondary voltage ratio multiplied by one-third of the rating of the overcurrent device protecting the primary of the transformer.

(2) The conductors must terminate at a single circuit breaker or a single set of fuses that limit the load to the ampacity of the conductors.

(3) The conductors must be suitably protected from physical damage in a raceway or manner approved by the authority having jurisdiction.

▶ Transformer Secondary Conductor Sizing Example

Question: *What size secondary conductors are the minimum required from a 45 kVA, 120/208V, three-phase transformer to feed a 175A main breaker panelboard less than 25 ft away, serving 125A of continuous load?* Figure 6–52

(a) 1/0 AWG (b) 2/0 AWG (c) 4/0 AWG (d) 250 kcmil

Answer: *(b) 2/0 AWG*

125A x 1.25 = 156A which is the minimum ampacity required for a continuous load [215.2(A)(1)]. At least a 175A conductor is required to feed the 175A circuit breaker in the panel [240.21(C)(6)]. 2/0 AWG is rated 175A at 75°C [Table 310.15(B)(16)].

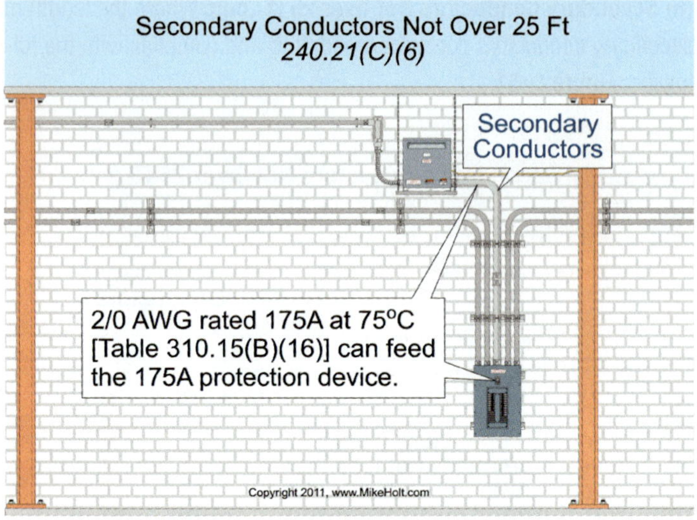

Figure 6–52

(D) Service Conductors. Service conductors must be protected against overload by the service disconnect overcurrent device in accordance with 230.91.

Size and Rating [230.42]

(A) Load Calculations. Service-entrance conductors must have sufficient ampacity for the loads to be served in accordance with Parts III, IV, or V of Article 220.

(1) Continuous and Noncontinuous Loads. The ampacity of the service-entrance conductors, before the application of any adjustment or correction factors, must be sized no smaller than 125 percent of the continuous loads, plus 100 percent of the noncontinuous loads, based on the terminal temperature rating ampacities as listed in Table 310.15(B)(16), before any ampacity adjustment [110.14(C)].

> **Author's Comment:** See 215.3 for the sizing requirements of feeder overcurrent devices for continuous and noncontinuous loads.

▶ Service Conductor Sizing Example

Question: *What size service-entrance conductors are required for a 200A continuous load, if the terminals are rated 75°C?* Figure 6–53

(a) 2/0 AWG (b) 3/0 AWG (c) 4/0 AWG (d) 250 kcmil

Answer: *(d) 250 kcmil*

Since the load is 200A continuous, the service-entrance conductors must have an ampacity not less than 250A (200A x 1.25). According to the 75°C column of Table 310.15(B)(16), 250 kcmil conductors are suitable as they have an ampacity of 255A at 75°C.

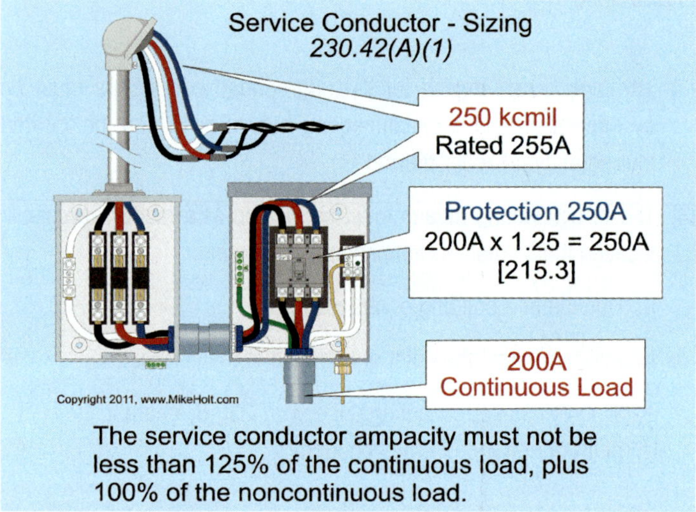

Figure 6–53

Overload Protection Required [230.90]

Each ungrounded service conductor must have overload protection at the point where the service conductors terminate [240.21(D)]. Figure 6–54

230.90(A) Overcurrent Device Rating. The rating of the overcurrent device must not be more than the ampacity of the conductors.

Ex 2: Where the ampacity of the ungrounded conductors doesn't correspond with the standard rating of overcurrent devices as listed in 240.6(A), the next higher overcurrent device can be used, if it doesn't exceed 800A [240.4(B)].

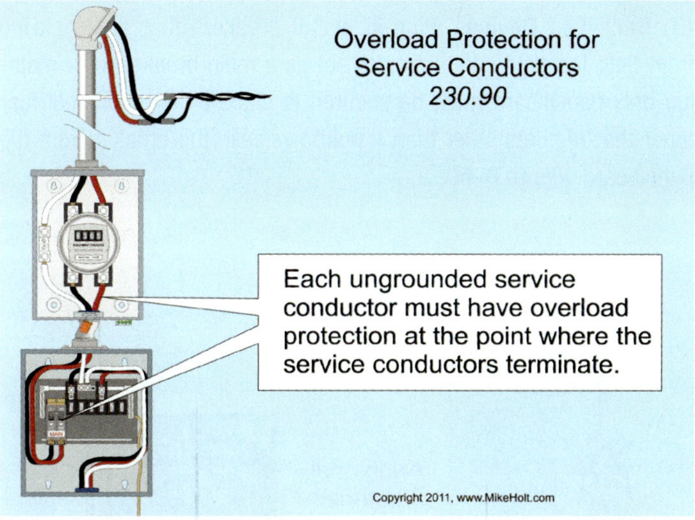

Figure 6–54

Author's Comment: Two sets of parallel 500 kcmil THHN conductors (each rated 380A at 75°C) can be protected by an 800A overcurrent device. Figure 6–55

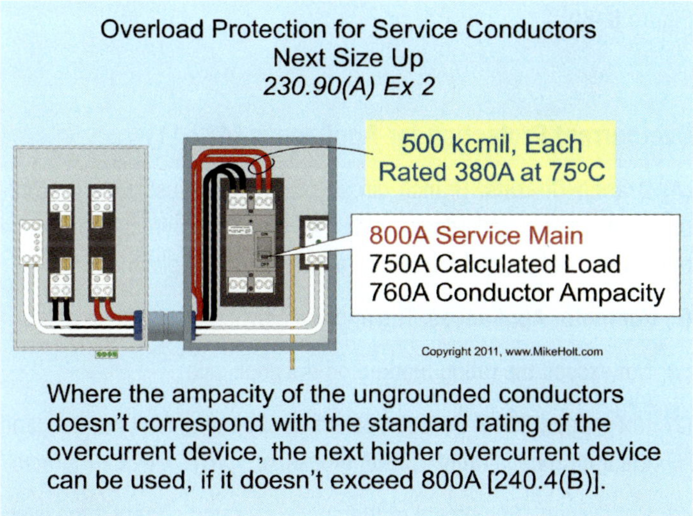

Figure 6–55

Ex 3: The combined ratings of two to six service disconnecting means can exceed the ampacity of the service conductors provided the calculated load, in accordance with Article 220, doesn't exceed the ampacity of the service conductors. Figure 6–56

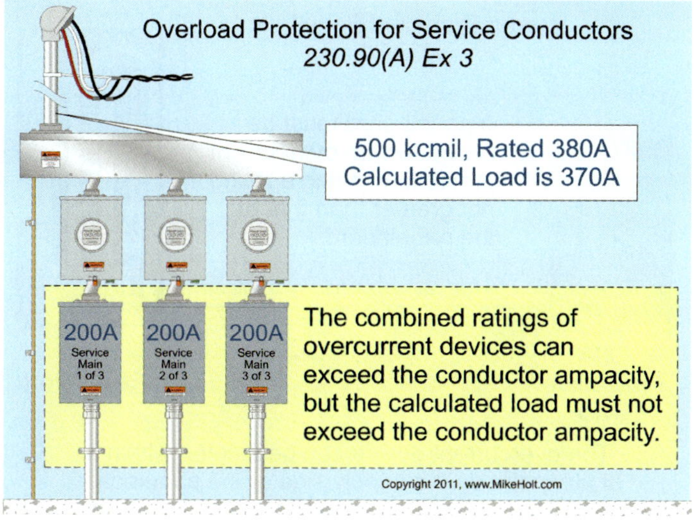

Figure 6–56

Ex 5: Overload protection for 3-wire, single-phase, 120/240V dwelling unit service conductors can be in accordance with 310.15(B)(7). Figure 6–57

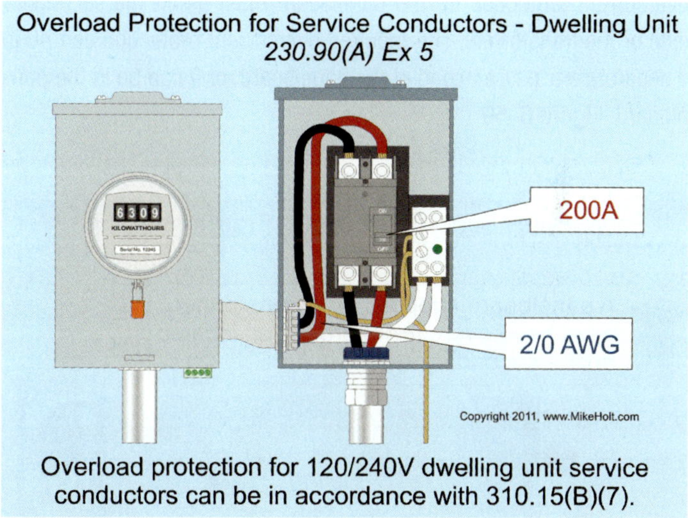

Figure 6–57

Overcurrent Protection of Panelboards [408.36]

Each panelboard must be provided with overcurrent protection located within, or at any point on the supply side of, the panelboard. The overcurrent device must have a rating not greater than that of the panelboard, and it can be located within or on the supply side of the panelboard. Figure 6–58

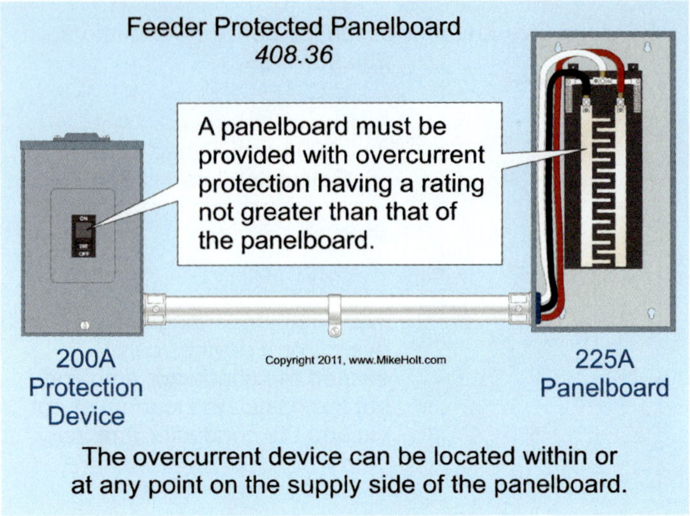

Figure 6–58

Ex 1: Individual overcurrent protection isn't required for panelboards used as service equipment in accordance with 230.71.

(B) Panelboards Supplied Through a Transformer. When a panelboard is supplied from a transformer, as permitted in 240.21(C), the overcurrent protection for the panelboard must be on the secondary side of the transformer. The required overcurrent protection can be in a separate enclosure ahead of the panelboard, or it can be in the panelboard. Figure 6–59

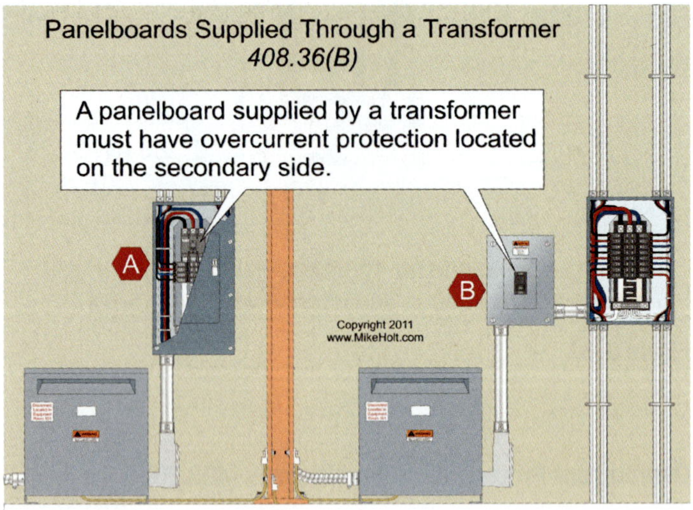

Figure 6–59

(D) Back-Fed Devices. Plug-in circuit breakers that are back-fed from field-installed conductors to act as a main breaker for a main-lug-only panelboard must be secured in place by an additional fastener that requires other than a pull to release the breaker from the panelboard. Figure 6–60

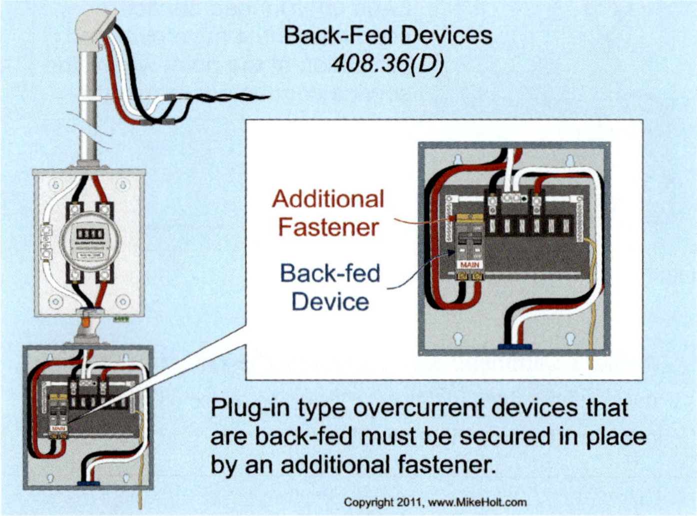

Figure 6–60

Overcurrent Protection for Appliances [422.11]

(A) Branch-Circuits. Branch-circuit conductors must have overcurrent protection in accordance with 240.4, and the overcurrent device rating must not exceed the rating marked on the appliance.

(E) Nonmotor Appliances. The appliance overcurrent device must:

(1) Not exceed the rating marked on the appliance,

(2) Not exceed 20A if the overcurrent device rating isn't marked, and the appliance is rated 13.30A or less, or

(3) Not exceed 150 percent of the appliance rated current if the overcurrent device rating isn't marked, and the appliance is rated over 13.30A. Where 150 percent of the appliance rating doesn't correspond to a standard overcurrent device ampere rating listed in 240.6(A), the next higher standard rating is permitted.

► Appliance Overcurrent Protection Example

Question: *What's the maximum size overcurrent protection for a 4,500W, 240V water heater?* **Figure 6–61**

(a) 20A (b) 30A (c) 40A (d) 50A

Answer: *(b) 30A*

Appliance Rated Current = 4,500W/240V

Appliance Rated Current = 18.75A
Conductor/Protection Size = 18.75A x 1.50 [422.11]
Conductor/Protection Size = 28A, next size up, 30A [240.6(A)]

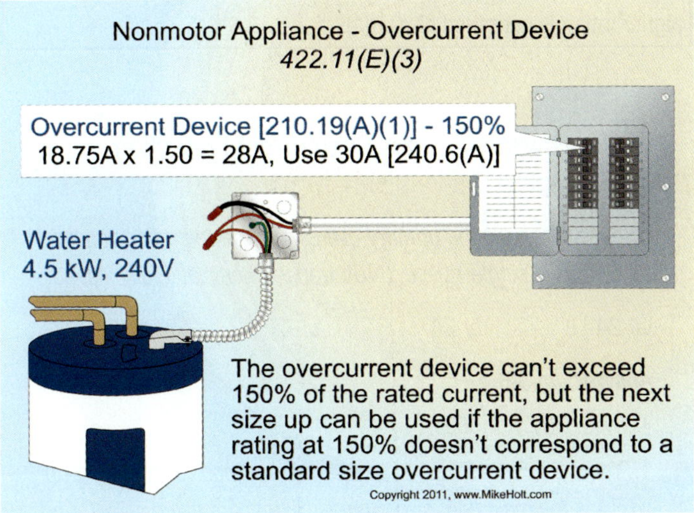

Figure 6–61

Storage Water Heaters [422.13]

An electric water heater having a capacity of 120 gallons or less is considered a continuous load for the purpose of sizing branch circuits.

Author's Comment: Branch-circuit conductors and overcurrent devices must have a rating of at least 125 percent of the ampere rating of a continuous load [210.19(A)(1) and 210.20(A)].

► Appliance Conductor Sizing Example

Question: *What's the calculated continuous load for conductor sizing for a 4,500W, 240V water heater? The terminal temperature rating isn't marked.*

(a) 15A (b) 24A (c) 30A (d) 35A

Answer: *(b) 24A*

I = P/E
P = 4,500W
E = 240V

I = 4,500W/240V
I = 18.75A

Calculated Continuous Load for Conductor Sizing = 18.75A x 1.25

Calculated Continuous Load for Conductor Sizing = 23.43A

Author's Comment: In the previous example, the overcurrent device was sized at 30A, so 10 AWG conductors are the minimum size required [240.4(D)]. When the equipment terminal temperature rating isn't marked, the 60°C Column of Table 310.15(B)(16) must be used for conductor sizing [110.14(C)(1)(a)].

Article 424 contains the installation requirements for fixed electrical equipment used for space heating, such as heating cables, unit heaters, boilers, or central systems [424.1].

Author's Comment: Wiring for fossil-fuel heating equipment, such as gas, oil, or coal central furnaces, must be installed in accordance with Article 422, specifically 422.12. Also, local building codes and mechanical codes may include requirements for the heating plant, such as the location of disconnect switches.

Branch Circuits for Electric Space-Heating [424.3]

(B) Branch-Circuit Sizing. For the purpose of sizing branch-circuit conductors, fixed electric space-heating equipment is considered a continuous load.

Author's Comment: The branch-circuit conductors and overcurrent devices for fixed electric space-heating equipment must have a rating not less than 125 percent of the total heating load [210.19(A)(1) and 210.20(A)].

► Electric Space-Heating Branch-Circuit Sizing Example

Question: *What size conductor and overcurrent device are required for a 9,600W, 240V fixed electric space heater (with 75°C terminals) that has a 3A blower motor?* **Figure 6–62**

(a) 10 AWG, 30A *(b) 8 AWG, 40A*
(c) 6 AWG, 60A *(d) 4 AWG, 80A*

Answer: *(c) 6 AWG, 60A*

Step 1: Determine the total load:

I = VA/E
I = 9,600 VA/240V
I = 40A + 3A = 43A

Step 2: Size the conductors at 125 percent of the total current load [110.14(C), 210.19(A)(1), and Table 310.15(B)(16)]:

Conductor = 43A x 1.25
Conductor = 53.75A, round to 54A [220.5(B)]
6 AWG, rated 65A at 75°C

Step 3: Size the overcurrent device at 125 percent of the total current load [210.20(A), 240.4(b) and 240.6(A)]:

Overcurrent Protection = 43A x 1.25
Overcurrent Protection = 53.75A, next size up is 60A

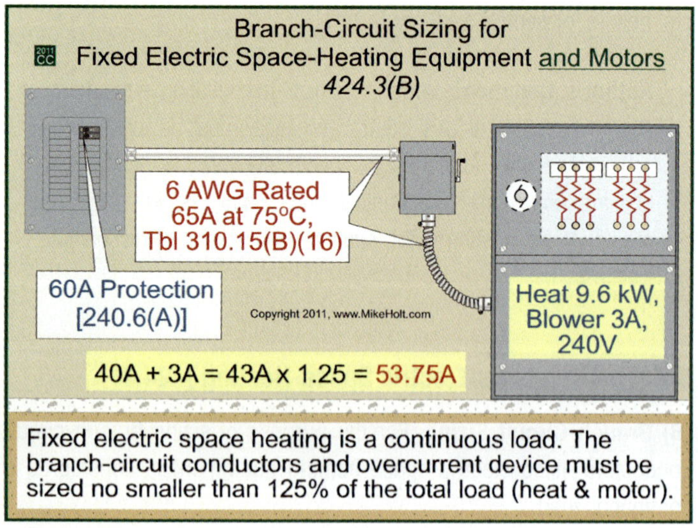

Figure 6–62

Overcurrent Protection for Transformers Not Over 600V. The primary winding of a transformer must be protected against overcurrent in accordance with the percentages listed in Table 450.3(B) and all applicable notes.

Table 450.3(B) Overcurrent Protection for Transformer

Primary Current Rating	Maximum Protection
9A or More	125%, see Note 1
Less Than 9A	167%
Less Than 2A	300%

Note 1. Where 125 percent of the primary current doesn't correspond to a standard rating of a fuse or nonadjustable circuit breaker, the next higher rating is permitted [240.6(A)].

► Transformer Primary Overcurrent Protection Example 1

Question: *What's the primary overcurrent device rating required for a 400VA, single-phase, 240V transformer that's fully loaded?*

(a) 2A *(b) 3A* *(c) 7A* *(d) 10A*

Answer: *(b) 3A*

400VA/240V = 1.666A

1.70A x 300% = 5.10A There is no provision for rounding up, so 3A is the maximum size. Standard sizes are listed in 240.6(A) but non-standard sizes are available from some manufacturers.

► Transformer Primary Overcurrent Protection Example 2

Question: *What's the primary overcurrent device rating required for a 2 kVA, single-phase, 240V transformer that's fully loaded?*

(a) 2A *(b) 5A* *(c) 7A* *(d) 10A*

Answer: *(d) 10A*

2,000VA/240V = 8.33A

8.33A x 167% = 13.90A There is no provision for rounding up, so 10A is the maximum standard size.

► Transformer Primary Overcurrent Protection Example 3

Question: *What's the primary overcurrent device rating and conductor size required for a 45 kVA, three-phase, 480V transformer that's fully loaded? The terminals are rated 75°C.* **Figure 6–63**

(a) 8 AWG, 40A *(b) 6 AWG, 50A*
(c) 6 AWG, 60A *(d) 4 AWG, 70A*

Answer: *(d) 4 AWG, 70A*

Step 1: Determine the primary current:

I = VA/(E x 1.732)
I = 45,000 VA/(480V x 1.732)
I = 54A

Step 2: Determine the primary overcurrent device rating [240.6(A)]:

54A x 1.25 = 68A, next size up 70A, Table 450.3(B), Note 1

Step 3: The primary conductor must be sized to carry 54A continuously (54A x 1.25 = 68A) [215.2(A)(1)] and be protected by a 70A overcurrent device [240.4(B)]. A 4 AWG conductor rated 85A at 75°C meets all of the requirements [110.14(C)(1) and 310.15(B)(16)].

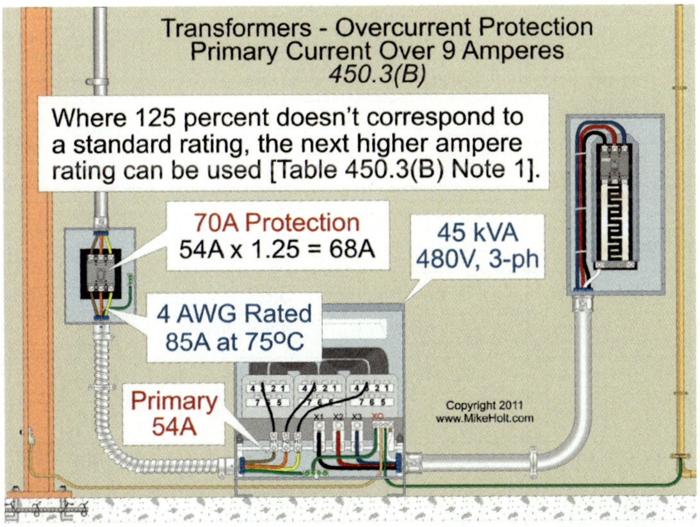

Figure 6–63

Secondary protection isn't required for transformers with more than 9A of secondary current if the primary is protected at 125 percent [Table 450.3(B)].

PART B—CONDUCTOR AMPACITY

Introduction

The insulation temperature rating of a conductor is limited to an operating temperature that prevents serious heat damage to the conductor's insulation. If the conductor carries excessive current, the I^2R heating within the conductor can destroy the conductor insulation. To limit elevated conductor operating temperatures, the current flow (amperes) in the conductors must be limited.

The temperature rating of a conductor is the maximum temperature at any location along its length that the conductor can withstand over a prolonged time period without experiencing serious degradation. The main factors to consider for conductor operating temperature are ambient temperature, heat generated internally from current flow through the conductor, the rate at which heat can dissipate, and adjacent load-carrying conductors [310.15(A)(3) Note No. 1].

6.10 Conductor Ampacity

The ampacity of a conductor is the current the conductors can carry continuously under specific conditions of use [Article 100 definition]. **Figure 6–64** Conductor ampacities are listed in Table 310.15(B)(16) under the condition of no more than three current-carrying conductors bundled together in an ambient temperature of 86°F. **Figure 6–65**

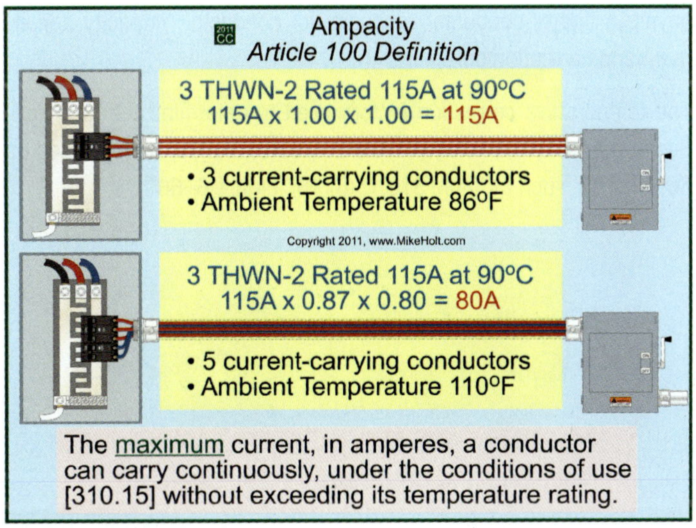

Figure 6–64

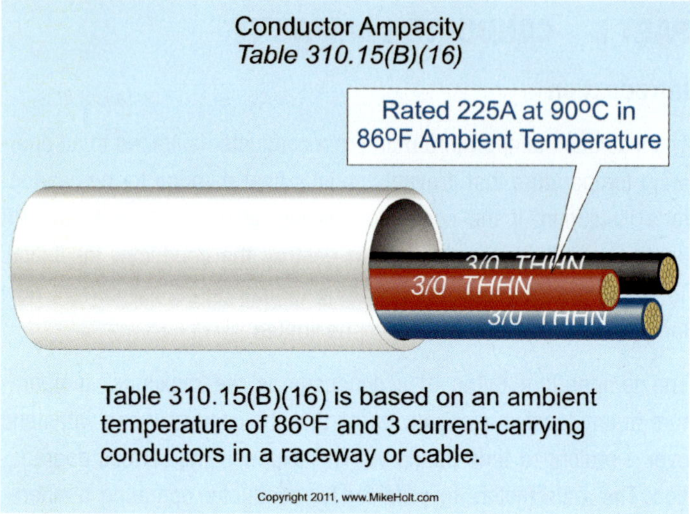

Figure 6–65

6.11 Ambient Temperature Correction Factors [Table 310.15(B)(2)(a)]

The ampacity of a conductor as listed in Table 310.15(B)(16) is based on the conductor operating at an ambient temperature of 86°F (30°C). When the ambient temperature is other than between 78°F and 86°F (30°C) for a prolonged period of time, the conductor ampacity listed in Table 310.15(B)(16) must be corrected [310.15(B)(2)].

Even though 90°C rated conductor ampacities can't be used for sizing circuit conductors because of the temperature limitations on the equipment terminals [110.14(C)(1)], they offer the opportunity of having a higher conductor ampacity for conductor ampacity adjustment and correction purposes.

The temperature correction factors used to determine the new conductor ampacity are listed in Table 310.15(B)(2)(a) for tables based on 86°F (30°C), such as Table 310.15(B)(16). Figure 6–66

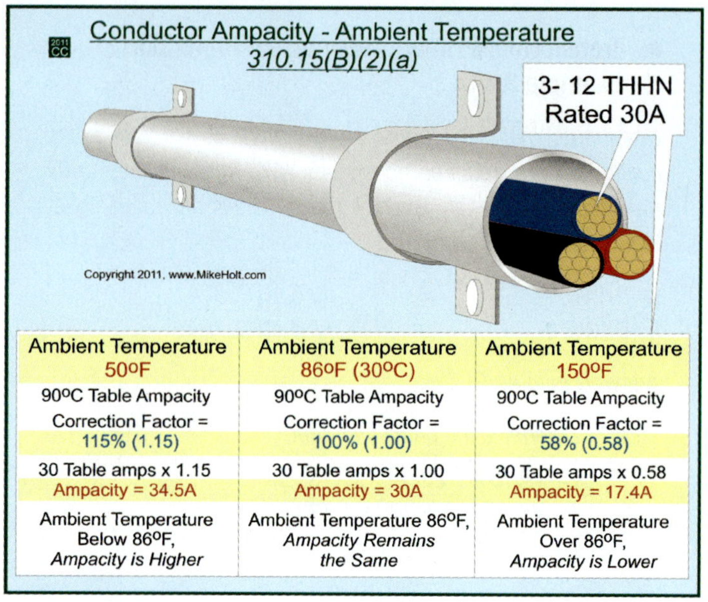

Figure 6–66

Table 310.15(B)(2)(a) Ambient Temperature Correction Factors Based on 86°F

Ambient Temperature °F	Ambient Temperature °C	Correction Factor 75°C Conductors	Correction Factor 90°C Conductors
50°F or less	10°C or less	1.20	1.15
51-59°F	11-15°C	1.15	1.12
60-68°F	16-20°C	1.11	1.08
69–77°F	21–25°C	1.05	1.04
78–86°F	26–30°C	1.00	1.00
87–95°F	31–35°C	0.94	0.96
96–104°F	36–40°C	0.88	0.91
105–113°F	41–45°C	0.82	0.87
114–122°F	46–-50°C	0.75	0.82
123–131°F	51–-55°C	0.67	0.76
132–140°F	56–60°C	0.58	0.71
141–149°F	61–65°C	0.47	0.65
150-158°F	66-70°C		
159–167°F	71–75°C		0.50
168-176°F	76-80°C		0.41
177-185°F	81-85°C		0.29

Author's Comment: When correcting conductor ampacity for elevated ambient temperature, the correction factor used for THHN conductors is based on the 90°C rating of the conductor in a dry location. If the conductor is dual rated, such as having both a THWN and THHN rating, then the 75°C rating of the conductor must be used in a wet location, since THWN is a 75°C rated conductor and the wet location will require the use of the THWN characteristics. THWN-2 is an insulation type that's acceptable in a wet location and is rated for 90°C in either a wet or dry location. When raceways are installed in wet locations, the conductors installed inside them are considered to be in wet locations and must be of a type allowed in wet locations [300.9 and 310.10(C)].

The following formula can be used to determine the conductor's new ampacity when the ambient temperature isn't 86ºF (30ºC). **Figure 6–67**

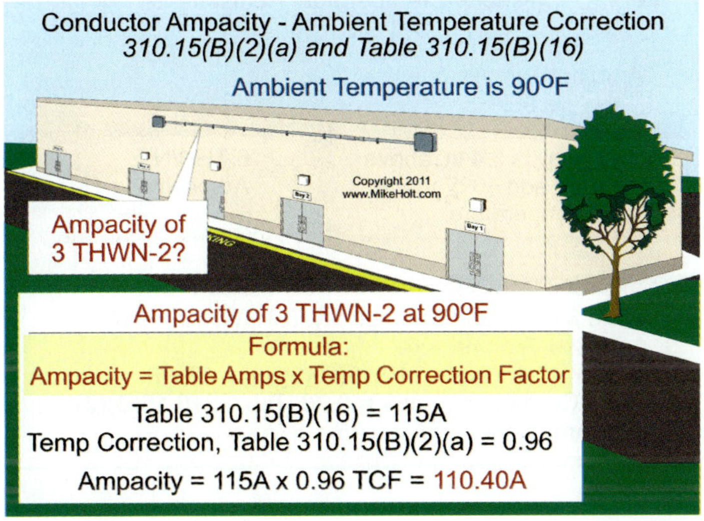

Figure 6–67

◆ **Corrected Conductor Ampacity—Ambient Temperature Correction Formula**

Corrected Ampacity = Table 310.15(B)(16) Ampacity x Ambient Temperature Correction Factor

Author's Comment: When different ampacities apply to a conductor length, the higher ampacity can be used for the entire circuit if the reduced ampacity length isn't in excess of 10 ft and its length doesn't exceed 10 percent of the length of the part of the circuit with the higher ampacity [310.15(A)(2) Ex].

► Ambient Temperature Below 86ºF

Question: *What's the ampacity of 12 THHN when installed in a location that has an ambient temperature of 50ºF?* **Figure 6–68**

(a) 20A *(b) 25A* *(c) 31A* *(d) 34.50A*

Answer: *(d) 34.50A*

Corrected Ampacity = Table 310.15(B)(16) Ampacity x Ambient Temperature Correction Factor from Table 310.15(B)(2)(a)

Table 310.15(B)(16) ampacity for 12 THHN installed in a dry location is 30A at 90ºC.

The temperature Correction Factor for a 90ºC conductor installed in an ambient temperature of 50ºF is 1.15.

Corrected Ampacity = 30A x 1.15 = 34.50A

Note: Ampacity increases when the ambient temperature is less than 86ºF (30ºC).

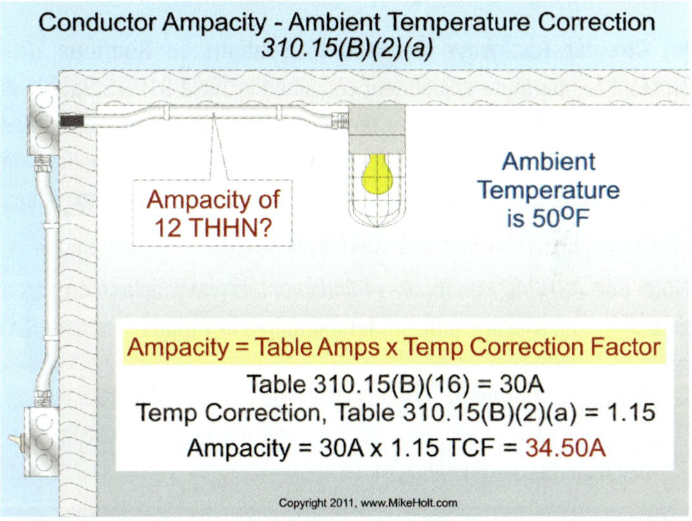

Figure 6–68

► Ambient Temperature Above 86°F (30°C)

Question: *What's the ampacity of 6 THWN-2 when installed in an outdoor location that has an ambient temperature of 140°F (60°C)?* **Note:** *The interior of a raceway installed in a wet location is considered to be a wet location [300.9]. THWN-2 is rated 90°C in wet or dry locations.*

(a) 35A *(b) 53A* *(c) 60A* *(d) 75A*

Answer: *(b) 53A*

Corrected Ampacity = Table 310.15(B)(16) Ampacity x Ambient Temperature Correction Factor from Table 310.15(B)(2)(a)

Table 310.15(B)(16) ampacity for 6 THWN-2 is 75A at 90°C.

Temperature Correction Factor, 90°C conductor rating installed at 140°F (60°C) is 0.71.

Corrected Ampacity = 75A x 0.71 = 53.25A

Note: *Ampacity decreases when the ambient temperature is more than 86°F.*

(c) Circular Raceways Exposed to Sunlight on Rooftops. The ambient temperature adjustment contained in Table 310.15(B)(3)(c) is added to the outdoor ambient temperature for conductors or cables that are installed in circular raceways exposed to direct sunlight on or above rooftops when applying the ampacity adjustment correction factors contained in Table 310.15(B)(2)(a).

Note: See *ASHRAE Handbook—Fundamentals* (www.ashrae.org) as a source for the average ambient temperatures in various locations.

> **Author's Comment:** This information may be available from the Copper Development Association (www.copper.org/applications/electrical/building/derating.html).

Table 310.15(B)(3)(c) Ambient Temperature Adjustment for Conduits Exposed to Sunlight On or Above Rooftops

Distance of Raceway Above Roof	C°	F°
0 to ½ in.	33	60
Above ½ in. to 3½ in.	22	40
Above 3½ in. to 12 in.	17	30
Above 12 in. to 36 in.	14	25

Note to Table 310.15(B)(3)(c): The temperature adders in Table 310.15(B)(3)(c) are based on the results of averaging the ambient temperatures.

> **Author's Comment:** This section requires the ambient temperature used for ampacity correction to be adjusted where conductors or cables are installed in circular conduit on or above a rooftop and the conduit is exposed to direct sunlight. The reasoning is that the air inside conduits in direct sunlight is significantly hotter than the surrounding air, and appropriate ampacity corrections must be made in order to comply with 310.15(A)(3).
>
> For example, a conduit with three 6 THWN-2 conductors with direct sunlight exposure that's ¾ in. above the roof will require 40°F to be added to the correction factors of Table 310.15(B)(2)(a). Assuming an ambient temperature of 90°F, the temperature to use for conductor correction will be 130°F (90°F + 40°F), and the 6 THWN-2 conductor ampacity after correction will be 57A (75A x 0.76). **Figure 6–69**

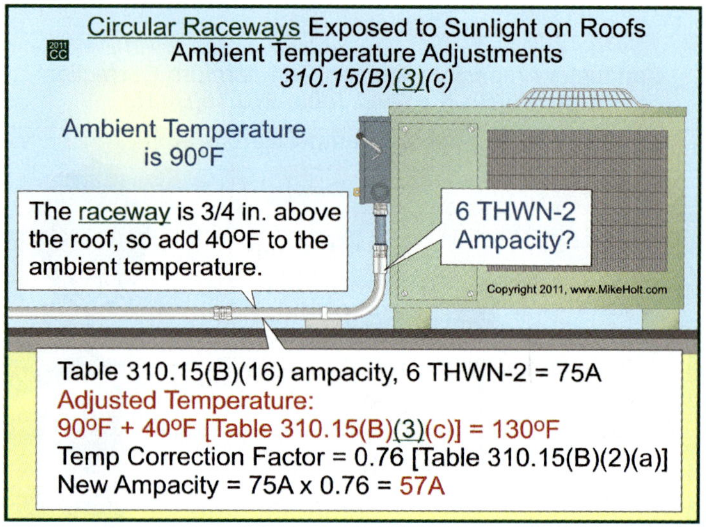

Figure 6–69

When adjusting conductor ampacity, use the conductor ampacity as listed in Table 310.15(B)(16) based on the conductors' insulation rating; in this case it's 75A at 90°F. Conductor ampacity adjustment isn't based on the temperature terminal rating required by 110.14(C).

► Conductor Size

Question: *What is the maximum corrected ampacity of an 8 THWN-2 conductor installed in a circular raceway exposed to sunlight on a roof, 3/4 in. above the roof where the ambient temperature is 90°F?* **Figure 6–70**

(a) 20A (b) 41.80A (c) 56.20A (d) 65.40A

Answer: *(b) 41.80A*

Corrected Ampacity = Table 310.15(B)(16) Amperes x Ambient Temperature Correction Factor from Table 310.15(B)(2)(a)

90°F + 40°F = 130°F [Table 310.15(B)(3)(c)]

Ambient Temperature Correction Factor for 130°F = 0.76 [Table 310.15(B)(2)(a)]

8 THWN-2 has an ampacity of 55A [Table 310.15(B)(16)]

New Ampacity = 55A x 0.76 = 41.80A

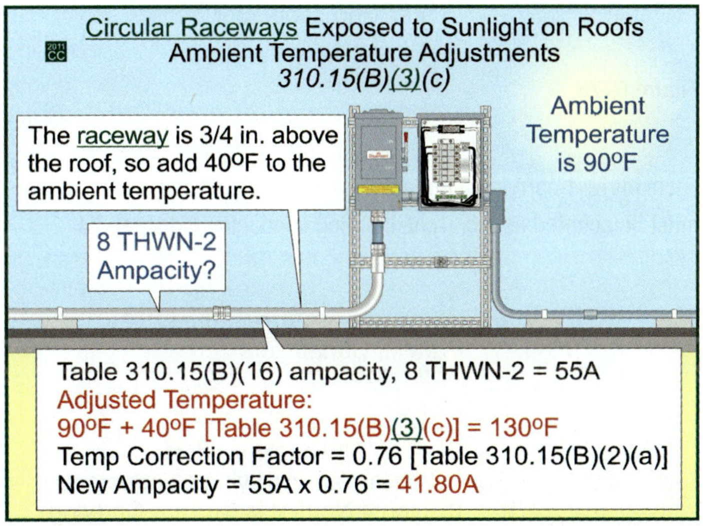

Figure 6–70

► Conductor Size

Question: *What size THHN/THWN conductor is required to supply a 40A noncontinuous load in a dry location if the conductors pass through an ambient temperature of 100°F?* **Figure 6–71**

(a) 10 AWG (b) 8 AWG (c) 6 AWG (d) 4 AWG

Answer: *(b) 8 AWG*

Corrected Ampacity = Table 310.15(B)(16) Amperes x Ambient Temperature Correction Factor from Table 310.15(B)(2)(a)

For a dry location, use the 90°C column for THHN. For a wet location, use the 75°C column for THWN

Ambient Temperature Correction Factor for 100°F = 0.91 for THHN

The Table 310.15(B)(16) ampacity for 10 THHN is 40A at 90°C in a dry location

10 THHN = 40A x 0.91 = 36.40A

Table 310.15(B)(16) ampacity for 8 THHN/THWN is 55A at 90°C in a dry location: use the THHN column

8 THHN = 55A x 0.91 = 50A

If this were in a wet location, would 8 THHN/THWN still be adequate?

Table 310.15(B)(16) ampacity for 8 THHN/THWN is 50A at 75°C in a wet location: use the THWN column

Ambient Temperature Correction Factor for 100°F = 0.88 for THWN

8 THWN = 50A x 0.88 = 44A

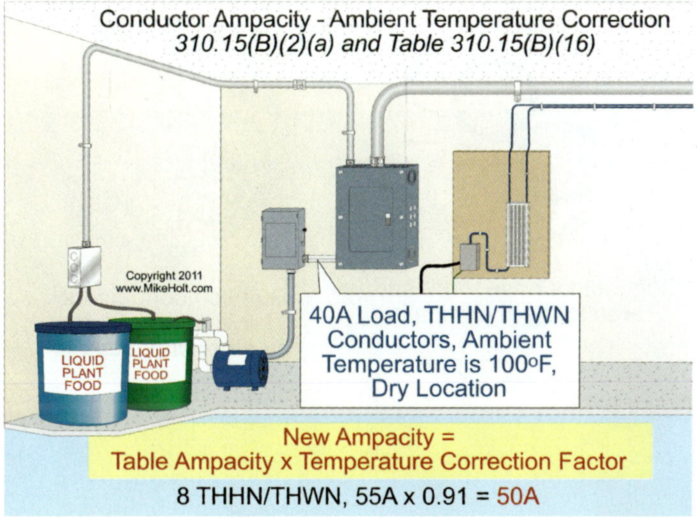

Figure 6–71

Author's Comment: The conductor to the load must have an ampacity of 40A after applying the ambient temperature correction factor. In this example, the 8 THHN/THWN has sufficient ampacity after correction in either a wet or dry location. That's not always the case, so when using dual-rated insulation types, watch the wet or dry location situation carefully and use the column that corresponds to the location. Also remember to double check your wire size by referring to 110.14(C) for the terminal temperature rating requirements. In this case, the ampacity for 8 AWG at 60º C is 40A, so 8 AWG will be satisfactory even if the equipment terminals had a 60 degree temperature rating.

6.12 Conductor Bundling Ampacity Adjustment Factors [Table 310.15(B)(3)(a)]

When conductors are bundled together, the ability of the conductors to dissipate heat is reduced. The NEC requires that the ampacity of a conductor be reduced whenever four or more current-carrying conductors are bundled together. **Figure 6–72**. The higher insulation temperature rating of 90ºC rated conductors provides a greater conductor ampacity for use in ampacity adjustment, even though conductors must be sized based on the column that corresponds to the temperature listing of the terminals [110.14 (C)(1)].

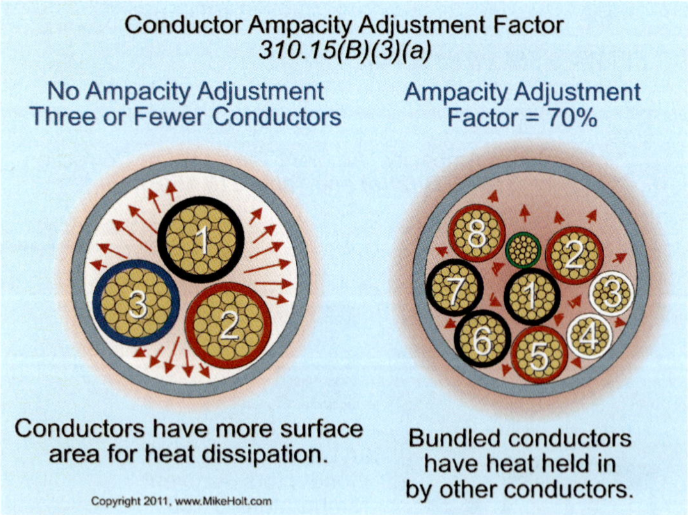

Figure 6–72

Conductor Bundle. Where the number of current-carrying conductors in a raceway or cable exceeds three, or where single conductors or multiconductor cables are installed without maintaining spacing for a continuous length longer than 24 in., the allowable ampacity of each conductor, as listed in Table 310.15(B)(16), must be adjusted in accordance with the adjustment factors contained in Table 310.15(B)(3)(a). **Figure 6–73**

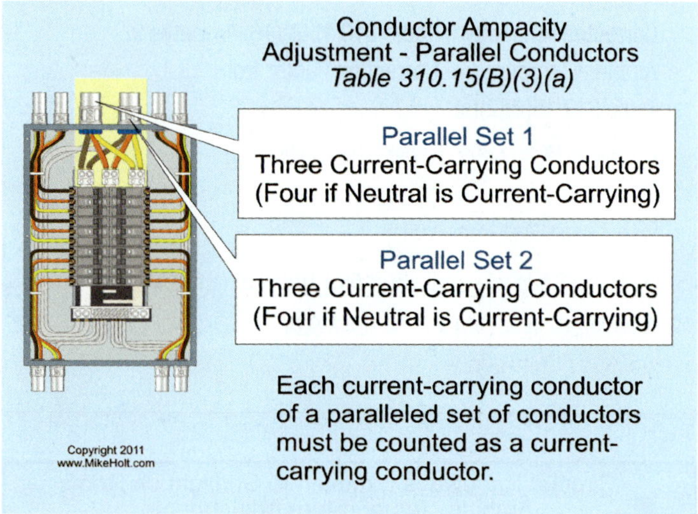

Figure 6–73

Each current-carrying conductor of a paralleled set of conductors must be counted as a current-carrying conductor. **Figure 6–74**

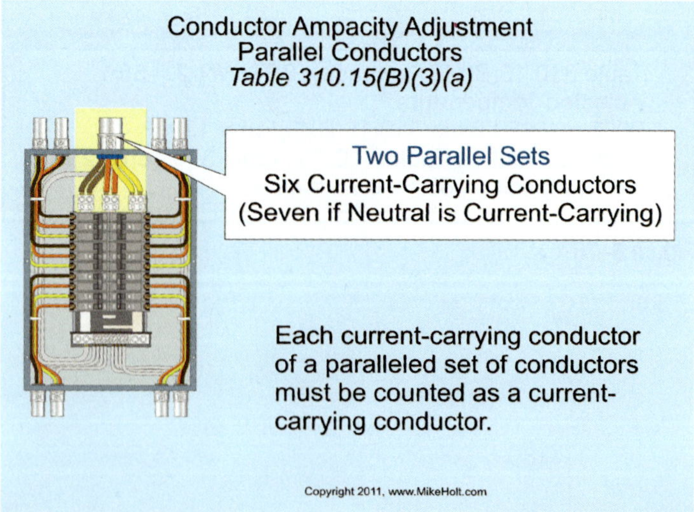

Figure 6–74

The ampacity adjustment factor used to determine the new ampacity is listed in Table 310.15(B)(3)(a). The following formula can be used to determine the new conductor ampacity when more than three current-carrying conductors are bundled together:

◆ **Conductor Bundling Ampacity Adjustment Formula**

Adjusted Ampacity = Table 310.15(B)(16) Ampacity x Bundled Ampacity Adjustment Factor from Table 310.15(B)(3)(a)

Table 310.15(B)(3)(a)

Number of Current–Carrying	Adjustment Factor
1–3 Conductors	1.00
4–6 Conductors	0.80
7–9 Conductors	0.70
10–20 Conductors	0.50

Author's Comments:

- The neutral conductor might be a current-carrying conductor, but only under the conditions specified in 310.15(B)(5). Equipment grounding conductors are never considered current carrying [310.15(B)(6)].
- When correcting or adjusting conductor ampacity, the ampacity is based on the temperature insulation rating of the conductor as listed in Table 310.15(B)(16), not the temperature rating of the terminal [110.14(C)].
- Where more than three current-carrying conductors are present and the ambient temperature isn't between 78°F and 86°F, the ampacity listed in Table 310.15(B)(16) must be corrected and adjusted for both conditions.

► Conductor Ampacity

Question: *What's the ampacity of each 10 THHN conductor when four current-carrying conductors are installed in a raceway or cable in a dry location?* **Figure 6–75**

(a) 20A *(b) 24A* *(c) 29A* *(d) 32A*

Answer: *(d) 32A*

Adjusted Ampacity = Table 310.15(B)(16) Ampacity x Bundled Ampacity Adjustment Factor from Table 310.15(B)(3)(a)

The Table 310.15(B)(16) ampacity for 10 THHN is 40A at 90°C.

The bundled adjustment factor for four current-carrying conductors is 0.80.

Adjusted Ampacity = 40A x 0.80 = 32A

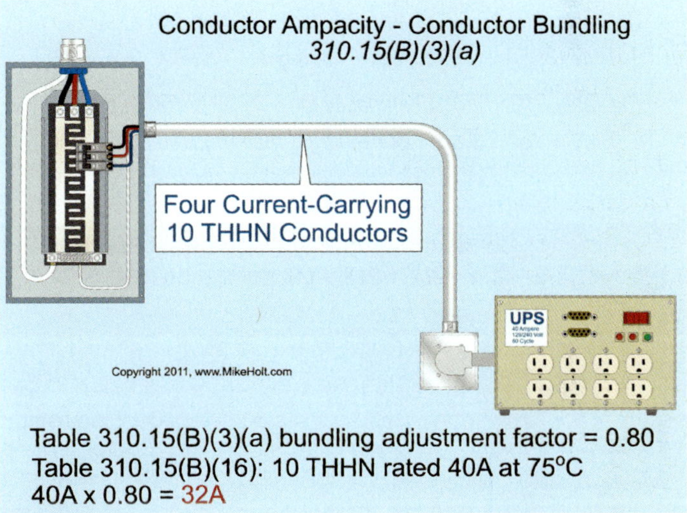

Figure 6–75

► Conductor Size

Question: *A raceway contains four current-carrying conductors. What size conductor is required to supply a 40A noncontinuous load in a dry location?* **Figure 6–76**

(a) 12 THHN (b) 10 THHN (c) 8 THHN (d) 6 THHN

Answer: *(c) 8 THHN*

The conductor must have an ampacity of 40A after applying the bundled adjustment factor.

Adjusted Ampacity = Table 310.15(B)(16) Ampacity x Bundled Ampacity Adjustment Factor from Table 310.15(B)(3)(a)

The Table 310.15(B)(16) ampacity for 10 THHN is 40A at 90°C

Bundled Adjustment Factor for 4 conductors = 0.80 [Table 310.15(B)(3)(a)]
10 THHN = 40A x 0.80 = 32A—too small

The Table 310.15(B)(16) ampacity for 8 THHN is 55A at 90°C
8 THHN = 55A x 0.80 = 44A—just right

The Table 310.15(B)(16) ampacity for 6 THHN is 75A at 90°C
6 THHN = 75A x 0.80 = 60A—larger than required by the NEC

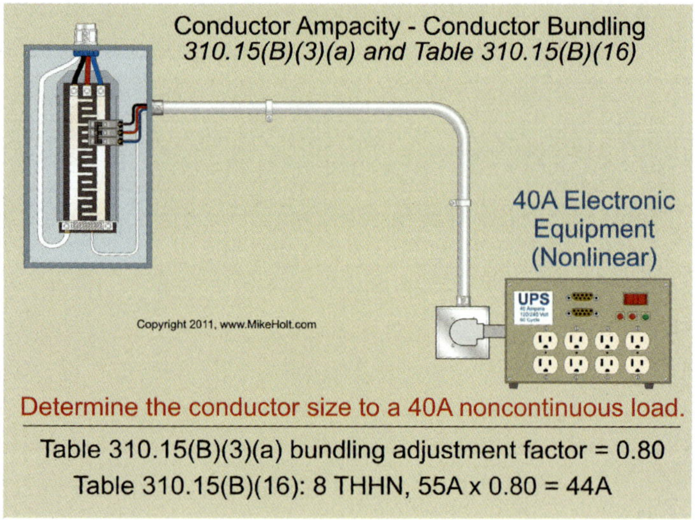

Figure 6–76

Author's Comment: Not all conductors are considered current-carrying. For example, an equipment grounding conductor doesn't normally carry current and isn't counted as a current-carrying conductor [310.15(B)(6)]. Some neutral conductors are considered current-carrying and others aren't, depending on the conditions described in 310.15(B)(5). Of course, all ungrounded conductors are considered current-carrying. See Section 6.14 of this unit for specific information on how to determine the number of current-carrying conductors. Conductor bundling ampacity adjustment factors don't apply to conductors in a raceway not exceeding 24 in. in length. [310.15(B)(3)(a)(2)]. **Figure 6–77**

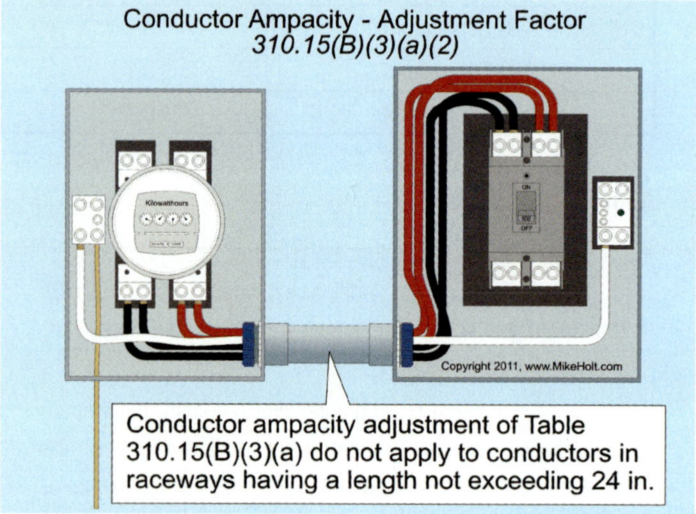

Figure 6–77

The conductor ampacity adjustment factors of Table 310.15(B)(3)(a) don't apply to Type AC or Type MC cable when [310.15(B)(3)(a)(4)]: **Figure 6–78**

(a) The cables do not have an overall outer jacket.

(b) Each cable has not more than three current-carrying conductors,

(c) The conductors are 12 AWG copper, and

(d) No more than 20 current-carrying conductors (ten 2-wire cables or six 3-wire cables) are bundled without maintaining spacing, are stacked, or are supported on "bridle rings."

Author's Comment: When 11 or more 2-wire cables or 7 or more 3-wire cables (more than 20 current-carrying conductors) are bundled or stacked for more than 24 in., an ampacity adjustment factor of 60 percent must be applied.

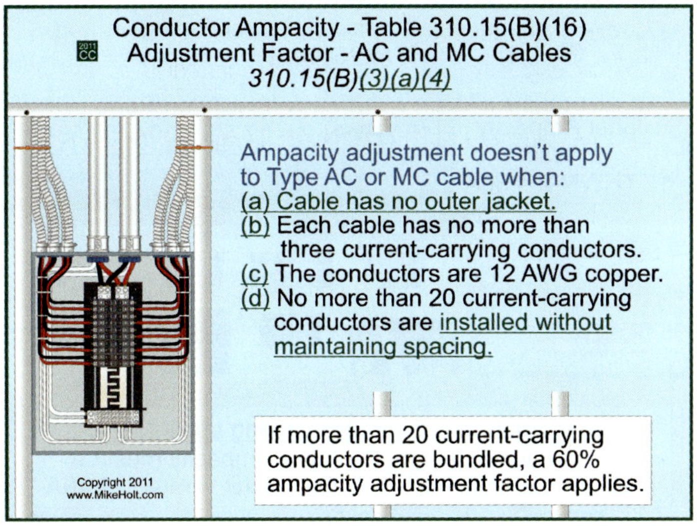

Figure 6–78

6.13 Ambient and Conductor Bundling Adjustment

If the ambient temperature is other than 86ºF and there are more than three current-carrying conductors bundled together, then the ampacity listed in Table 310.15(B)(16) must be adjusted and corrected for both conditions. Figure 6–79

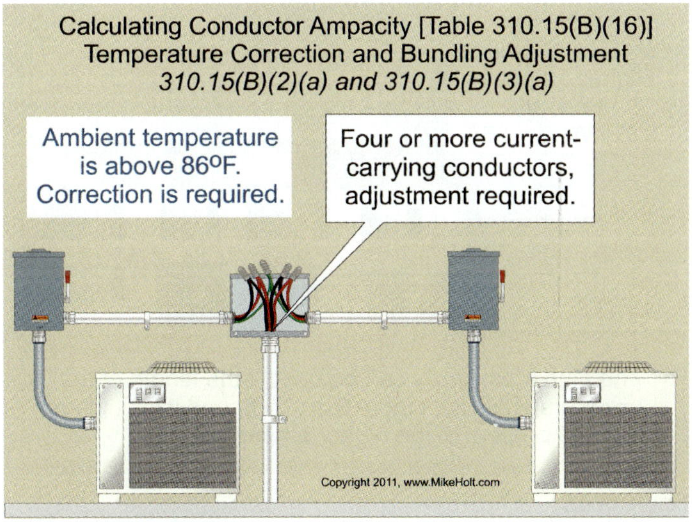

Figure 6–79

The following formula can be used to determine the new conductor ampacity when both ambient temperature correction and bundled adjustment factors apply:

Adjusted/Corrected Ampacity = Table 310.15(B)(16) Ampacity x Temperature Correction Factor x Bundled Adjustment Factor

► Conductor Ampacity Example 1

Question: *What's the ampacity of four current-carrying 8 THHN conductors installed in an ambient temperature of 90ºF in a dry location?* **Figure 6–80**

(a) 25A *(b) 40A* *(c) 55A* *(d) 60A*

Answer: *(b) 40A*

Adjusted/Corrected Ampacity = Table 310.15(B)(16) Ampacity x Temperature Factor x Bundled Adjustment Factor

The Table 310.15(B)(16) ampacity of 8 THHN is 55A at 90ºC.

The temperature correction factor for 90ºC conductor insulation at 90ºF is 0.96 [Table 310.15(B)(2)(a)].

The bundled adjustment factor for four conductors is 0.80 [Table 310.15(B)(3)(a)].

Adjusted/Corrected Ampacity = 55A x 0.96 x 0.80 = 42.24A

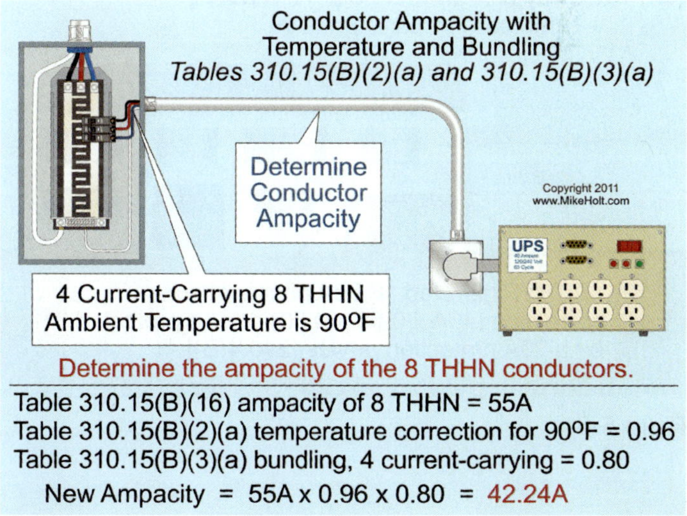

Figure 6–80

▶ Conductor Ampacity Example 2

Question: *What's the ampacity of four current-carrying 10 THWN-2 conductors installed in a circular raceway less than 1/2 in. above a rooftop with an ambient temperature of 90ºF?* **Figure 6–81**

(a) 15.30A (b) 18.56A (c) 25.34A (d) 31.25A

Answer: *(b) 18.56A*

Adjusted/Corrected Ampacity = Table 310.15(B)(16) Ampacity x Temperature Factor x Bundled Adjustment Factor

The Table 310.15(B)(16) ampacity of 10 THWN-2 is 40A at 90ºC.

Ambient Temperature + Adjustment for Raceways above Rooftop = 90ºF + 60ºF = 150ºF

Temperature correction factor for 90ºC conductor insulation at 150ºF is 0.58 [Table 310.15(B)(2)(a)].

The bundled adjustment factor for four conductors is 0.80 [Table 310.15(B)(3)(a)].

Adjusted/Corrected Ampacity = 40A x 0.58 x 0.80 = 18.56A

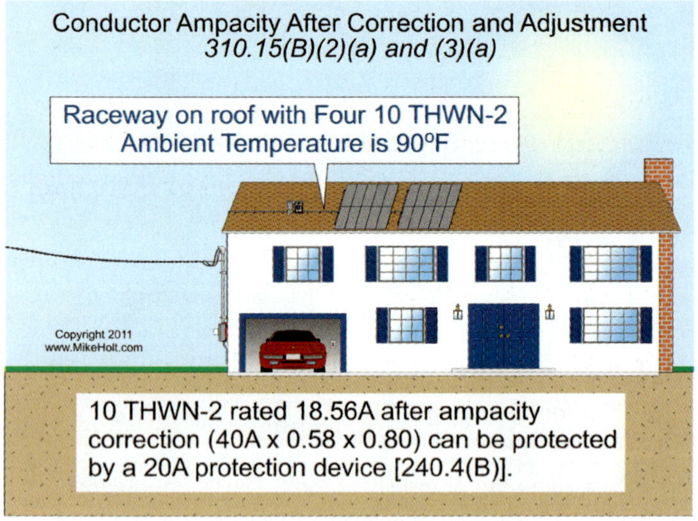

Figure 6–81

If a single length of conductor has two ampacities, the lower ampacity must be used for the entire circuit [310.15(A)(2)]. **Figure 6–82**

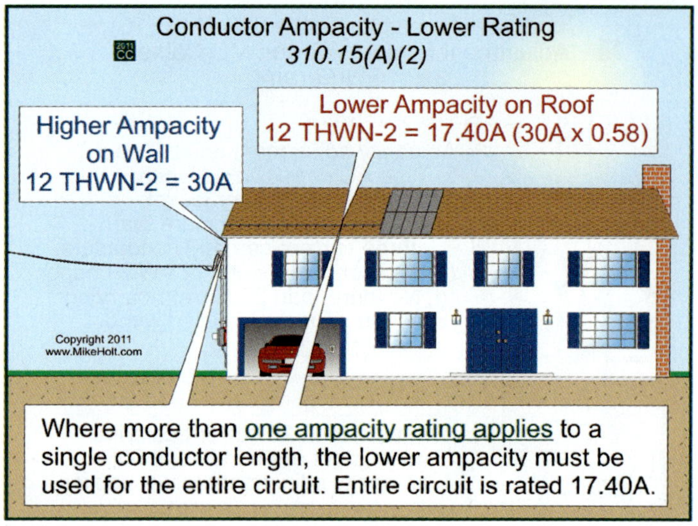

Figure 6–82

When different ampacities apply to a conductor length, the higher ampacity can be used for the entire circuit if the reduced ampacity length isn't in excess of 10 ft and its length doesn't exceed 10 percent of the length of the part of the circuit with the higher ampacity [310.15(A)(2) Ex]. **Figures 6–83 and 6–84**

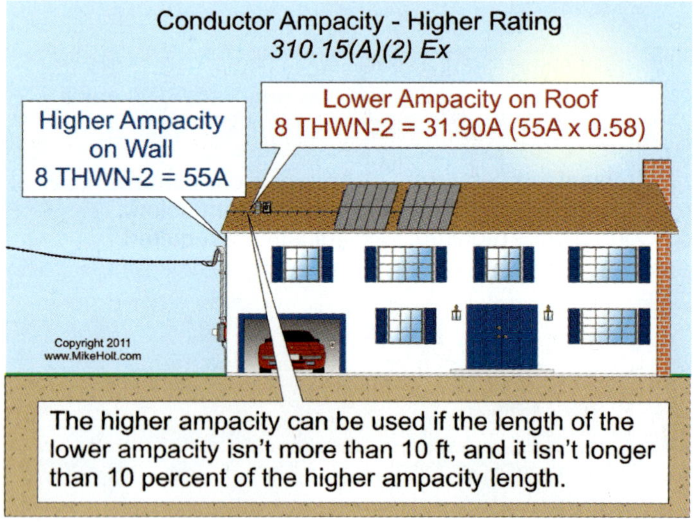

Figure 6–83

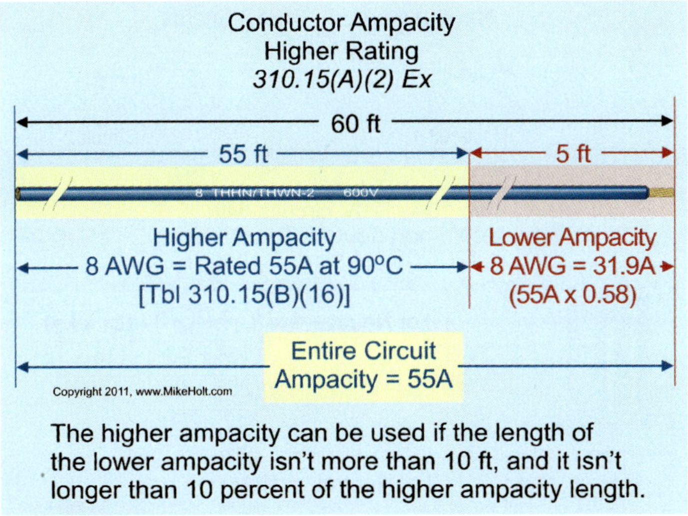

Figure 6–84

6.14 Current-Carrying Conductors

The Table 310.15(B)(3)(a) adjustment factors only apply when there are more than three current-carrying conductors bundled together. Naturally, all phase conductors are considered current carrying, and the following factors help determine which other conductors are also considered current carrying:

Two-Wire Circuits

Both the neutral and ungrounded conductors of a 2-wire circuit carry current and both are considered current carrying. Figure 6–85

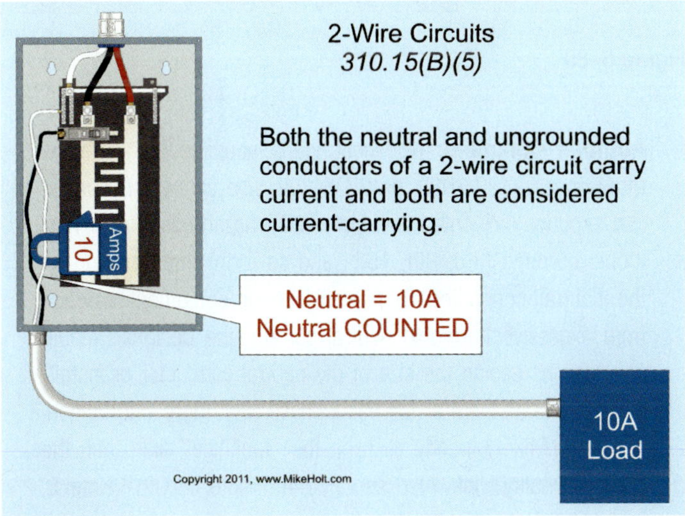

Figure 6–85

Neutral Conductor—Balanced Circuits [310.15(B)(5)(a)]

A neutral conductor that carries only the unbalanced current from other conductors of the same circuit isn't considered a current-carrying conductor. Figure 6–86

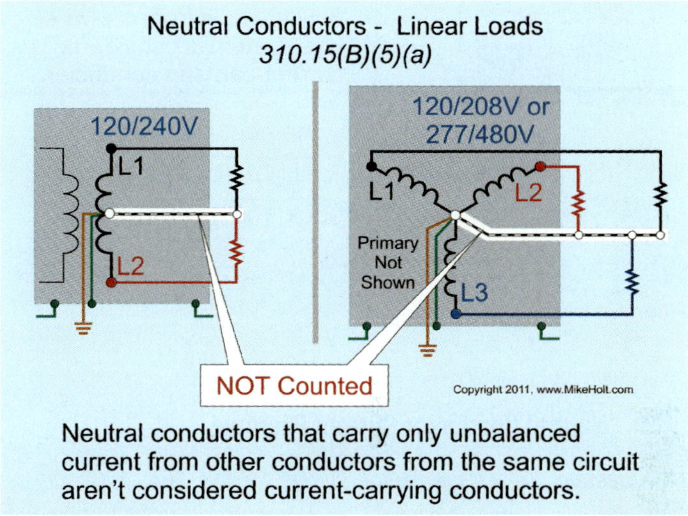

Figure 6–86

Neutral Conductor—Unbalanced 3-Wire Wye Circuit [310.15(B)(5)(b)]

The neutral conductor of a 3-wire circuit of a 4-wire, three-phase, wye-connected system carries approximately the same current as the line-to-neutral load currents of the other conductors and is considered a current-carrying conductor, Figure 6–87. In such a situation, one of the line-to-neutral currents isn't present and can be zeroed out of the neutral current formula, resulting in the following formula:

- **3-Phase Wye Secondary Neutral Current Formula**

$$I_{Neutral} = \sqrt{(I_{Line1}^2 + I_{Line2}^2 + I_{Line3}^2) - [(I_{Line1} \times I_{Line2}) + (I_{Line2} \times I_{Line3}) + (I_{Line1} \times I_{Line3})]}$$

- **Unbalanced 3-Wire Wye Secondary Neutral Current Formula**

$$I_{Neutral} = \sqrt{(I_{Line1}^2 + I_{Line2}^2) - (I_{Line1} \times I_{Line2})}$$

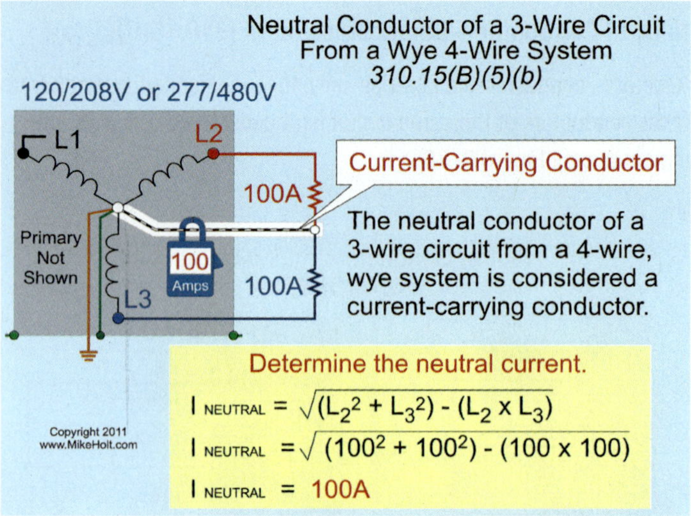

Figure 6–87

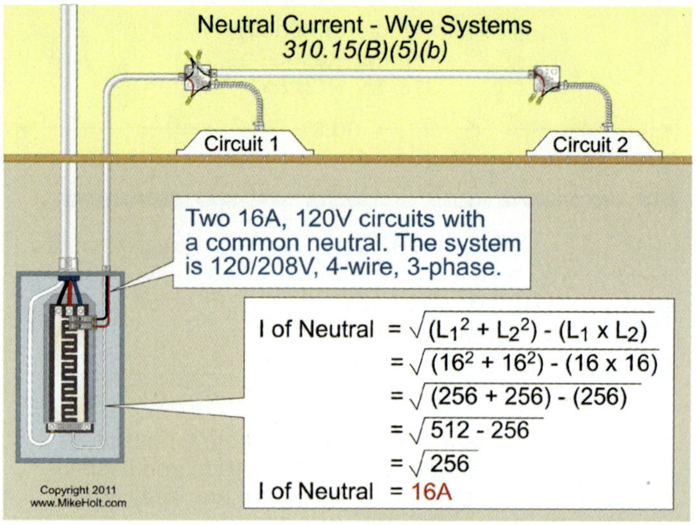

Figure 6–88

► Neutral Conductor Current Example

Question: *What's the neutral current for two 16A, 120V circuits with a common neutral? The system is a 120/208V, three-phase, 4-wire, wye-connected system that supplies fluorescent lighting.* **Figure 6–88**

(a) 8A *(b) 16A* *(c) 32A* *(d) 40A*

Answer: *(b) 16A*

$$I_{Neutral} = \sqrt{(I_{Line1}^2 + I_{Line2}^2) - (I_{Line1} \times I_{Line2})}$$

$$I_{Neutral} = \sqrt{(16^2 + 16^2) - (16 \times 16)}$$

$$I_{Neutral} = \sqrt{(512 - 256)}$$

$$I_{Neutral} = \sqrt{256}$$

$$I_{Neutral} = 16A$$

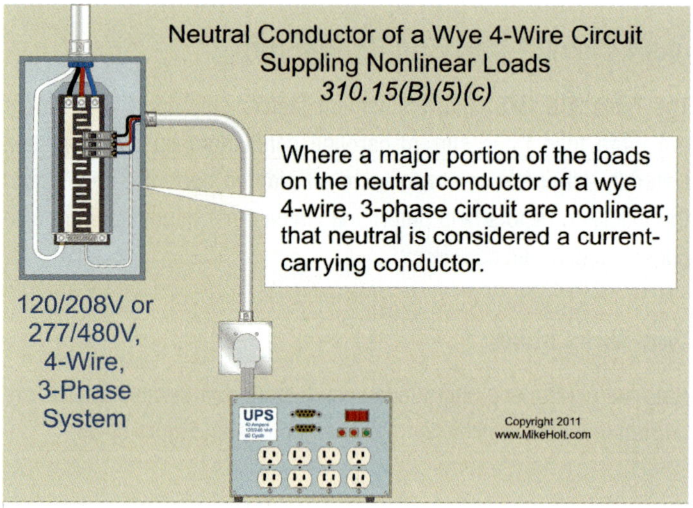

Figure 6–89

Neutral Conductor—Nonlinear Loads [310.15(B)(5)(c)]

The neutral conductor for a 4-wire, 3-phase wye circuit is considered a current-carrying conductor where the major portion of the load consists of nonlinear loads. **Figure 6–89**

CAUTION: *Nonlinear loads produce harmonic currents that add on the neutral conductor, and the current on the neutral can be as much as twice the current on the ungrounded conductors.* **Figure 6–90**

Author's Comment: Nonlinear loads supplied by a 4-wire, three-phase, 120/208V or 277/480V wye-connected system can produce unwanted and potentially hazardous triplen harmonic currents (3rd, 9th, 15th, and so forth) that can add on the neutral conductor. To prevent fire or equipment damage from excessive harmonic neutral current, the designer should consider increasing the size of the neutral conductor or installing a separate neutral for each phase. For more information, visit www.MikeHolt.com, click on the "Technical" link, then the "Power Quality" link. Also see 210.4(a) Note, 220.61 Note 2, and 450.3 Note 2.

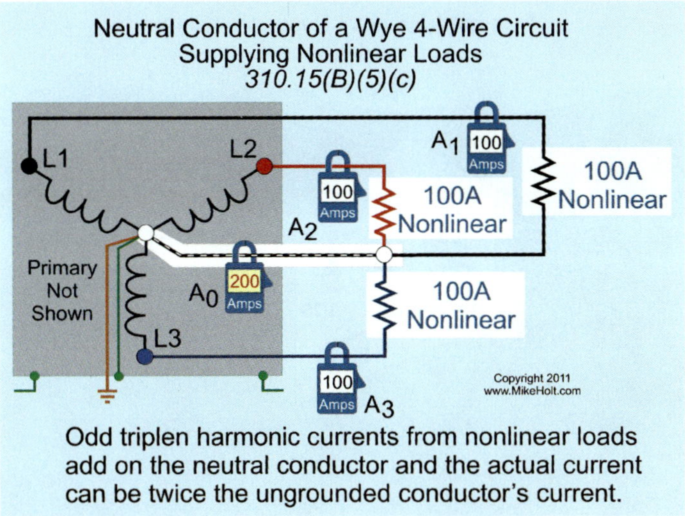

Figure 6–90

Grounding and Bonding Conductors [310.15(B)(6)]

Grounding and bonding conductors don't normally carry current and aren't considered current carrying. Figure 6–91

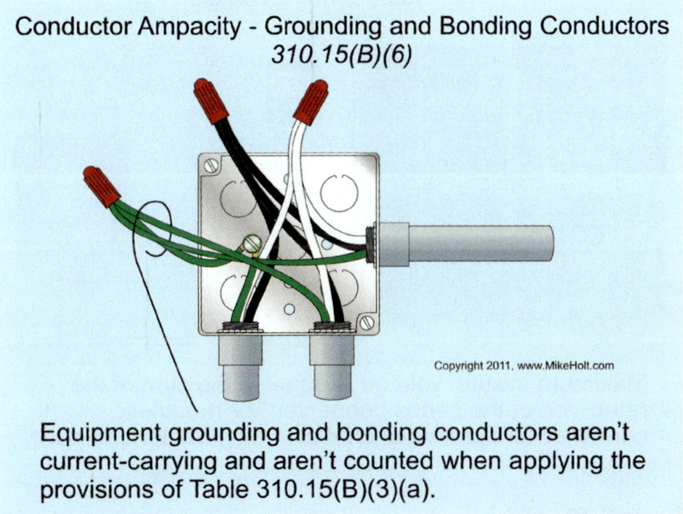

Figure 6–91

Author's Comment: Grounding and bonding conductors aren't counted when adjusting conductor ampacity for the effects of conductor bundling. [310.15(B)(6)] They do occupy space in the raceway and are included in raceway fill calculations. See Chapter 9, Table 1, Note 3.

6.15 Wireway Conductor Ampacity [376.22(B)]

Wireways are commonly used where access to the conductors within the raceway is required to make terminations, splices, or taps to several devices at a single location.

Conductor Ampacity Adjustment Factors. When more than 30 current-carrying conductors are installed in any cross-sectional area of the wireway, the conductor ampacity, as listed in Table 310.15(B)(16), must be adjusted in accordance with Table 310.15(B)(3)(a). Figure 6–92

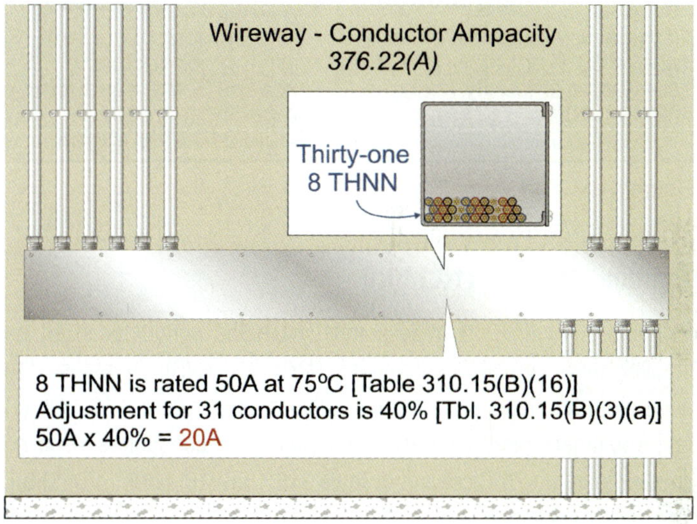

Figure 6–92

Signaling and motor control conductors between a motor and its starter used only for starting duty aren't considered current carrying for conductor ampacity adjustment.

Adjustment for 31 conductors is 40% [Table 310.15(B)(3)(a)]
50A x 40% = 20A

6.16 Conductor Sizing Summary

The ampacity of a conductor changes with changing conditions. The factors that affect conductor ampacity include: Figure 6–93

- The allowable ampacity as listed in Table 310.15(B)(16).
- The ambient temperature correction factors, if the ambient temperature isn't 86ºF, from Table 310.15(B)(2)(a).
- Conductor ampacity adjustment factors apply if four or more current-carrying conductors are bundled together from Table 310.15(B)(3)(a).

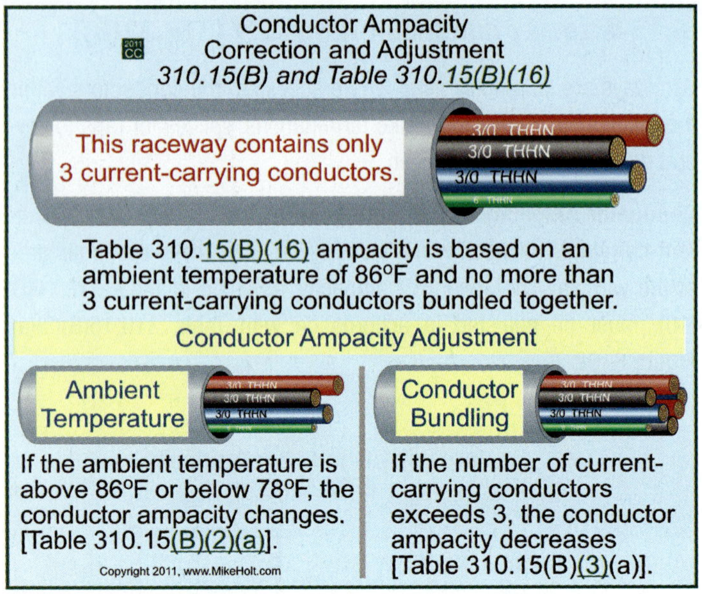

Figure 6–93

Terminal Ratings [110.14(C)]

Equipment rated 100A or less must have the conductor sized no smaller than the 60°C column of Table 310.15(B)(16) unless the equipment terminals are rated for a higher temperature [110.14(C)(1)(a)]. Equipment rated over 100A must have the conductors sized no smaller than the 75°C column of Table 310.15(B)(16) [110.14(C)(1)(b)]. The higher insulation temperature rating of conductors such as THHN allow the use of the 90°C column for ampacity correction and adjustment calculations.

PART C—ARTICLE 690 SOLAR PV SYSTEMS

Introduction

Article 690 applies to photovoltaic (PV) electrical energy systems, array circuit(s), inverter(s), and charge controller(s) for PV systems, which may be interactive with other electrical power sources (electric utility) or stand-alone with or without energy storage (batteries). Figure 6–94

6.17 Maximum Voltage [690.7]

(A) Maximum PV System Voltage. Maximum PV system voltage is equal to the sum of the rated open-circuit voltage (Voc) of the series-connected PV modules as corrected for the lowest-expected ambient temperature in accordance with Table 690.7.

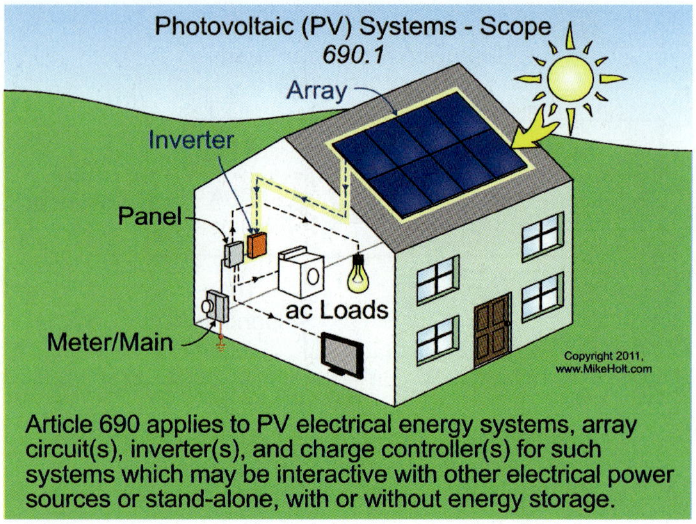

Figure 6–94

Open-circuit voltage temperature coefficients supplied in the instructions for PV modules **must** be used to calculate the maximum PV system voltage instead of Table 690.7. Figure 6–95

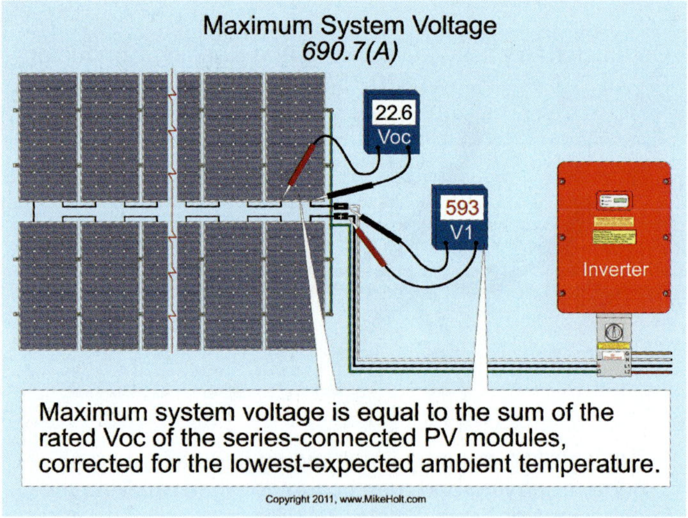

Figure 6–95

Note: One source for lowest-expected ambient temperature is the Extreme Annual Mean Minimum Design Dry Bulb Temperature found in the *ASHRAE Handbook—Fundamentals*. See http://www.solarabcs.org/permitting/map/.

> **Author's Comment:** PV module voltage has an inverse relationship with temperature, which means that at lower temperatures, PV modules' voltage raises and at higher temperatures, PV modules' voltage falls from its nameplate rating.

Table 690.7 Voltage Correction Factors		
Lowest-Expected Ambient Temperature °C	°F	Temperature Correction Factor
0 to 4	32 to 40	1.10
-1 to -5	23 to 31	1.12
-6 to -10	14 to 22	1.14
-11 to -15	5 to 13	1.16
-16 to -20	4 to -4	1.18
-21 to -25	-5 to -13	1.20
-26 to -30	-14 to -22	1.21
-31 to -35	-23 to -31	1.23
-36 to -40	-32 to -40	1.25

► PV System Voltage Based on Table 690.7

Question: *Using Table 690.7, what's the maximum PV source circuit voltage for twenty-three modules each rated Voc 22.60, at an ambient temperature of -7°C?* **Figure 6–96**

PV Voc Table 690.7 = Module Voc × Table 690.7 Correction Factor × # Modules per Series String

PV Voc = 22.60 Voc × 1.14 × 23 modules

PV Voc = 593V

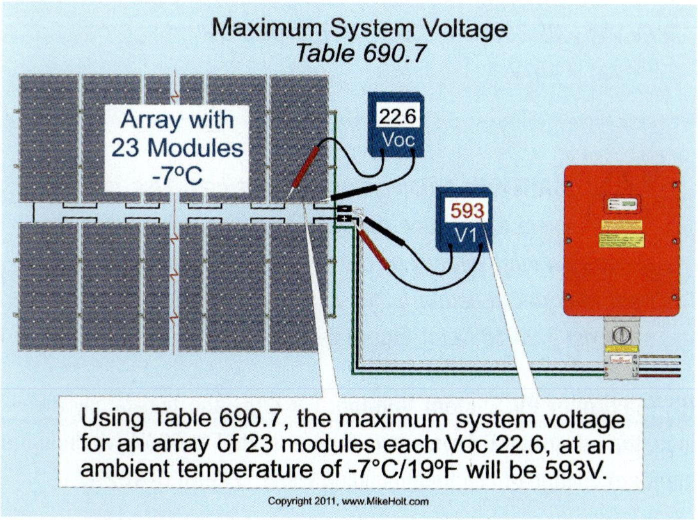

Figure 6–96

► PV System Voltage Based on Manufacturer Temperature Coefficient %/°C

Question: *Using the manufacturer's temperature coefficient -0.31%/°C, what's the maximum PV source circuit voltage for twenty-three modules each rated Voc 22.60, at a cell temperature of -7°C?* **Figure 6–97**

PV VOc = Rated Voc × {1 + [(Min. Temp. °C - 25°C) × Module Coefficient %/°C]} × # Modules per Series String

PV Voc = 22.60 Voc × {1+ [(-7°C - 25°C) × -0.31%/°C]} × 23 modules

PV Voc = 22.60 Voc × {1 + [-32°C × -0.31%/°C]}) × 23 modules

PV Voc = 22.60 Voc × {1 + 9.92%} × 23 modules

PV Voc = 22.60 Voc × 1.0992 × 23 modules

PV Voc = 571V

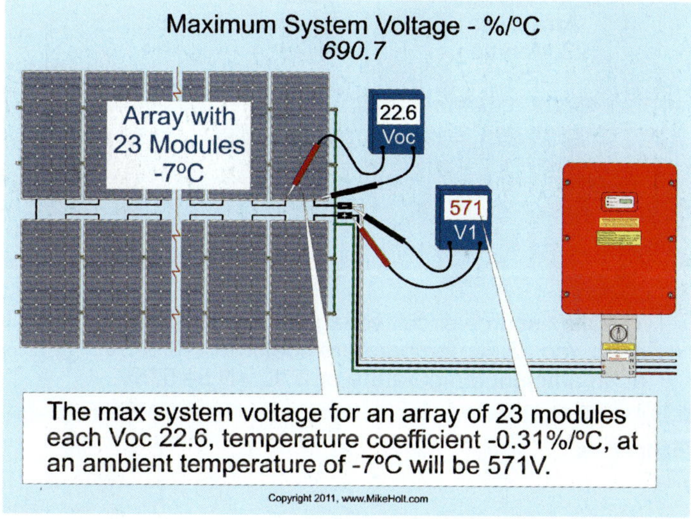

Figure 6–97

► PV System Voltage Based on Manufacturer Temperature Coefficient V/°C

Question: *Using the manufacturer's temperature coefficient -0.075V/°C, what's the maximum PV source circuit voltage for twenty-three modules each rated Voc 22.60, at an ambient temperature of -7°C?* **Figure 6–98**

PV Voc (V/°C) = {Rated Voc + [(Min. Temp. °C - 25°C) × Module Coefficient V/°C]} × # Modules per Series String

PV Voc = {22.60V + [(-7°C - 25°C) × -0.075V/°C]} × 23

PV Voc = {22.60V + [-32°C × -0.075V/°C)) × 23

PV Voc = (22.60V + 2.40V) × 23

PV Voc = 25V × 23

PV Voc = 575V

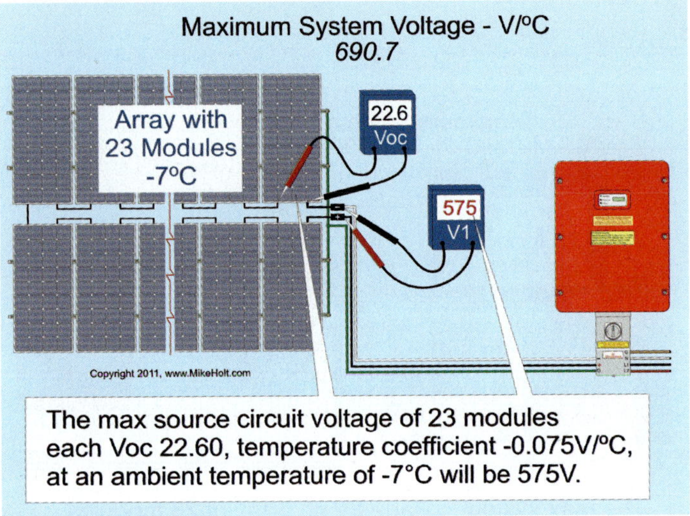

Figure 6–98

Author's Comment: Inverters require a minimum dc voltage to start; therefore PV voltage calculations should be performed to ensure the modules can produce sufficient voltage during the heat of the day to start the system [110.3(B)]. **Figure 6–99**

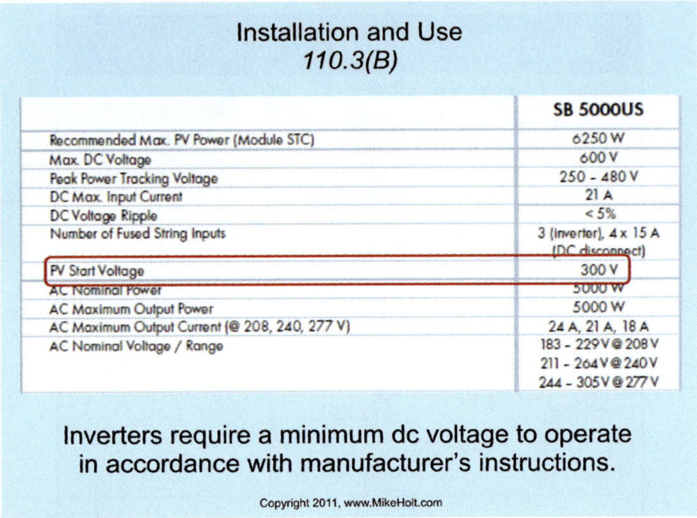

	SB 5000US
Recommended Max. PV Power (Module STC)	6250 W
Max. DC Voltage	600 V
Peak Power Tracking Voltage	250 - 480 V
DC Max. Input Current	21 A
DC Voltage Ripple	< 5%
Number of Fused String Inputs	3 (inverter), 4 x 15 A (DC disconnect)
PV Start Voltage	300 V
AC Nominal Power	5000 W
AC Maximum Output Power	5000 W
AC Maximum Output Current (@ 208, 240, 277 V)	24 A, 21 A, 18 A
AC Nominal Voltage / Range	183 - 229V @ 208 V 211 - 264V @ 240 V 244 - 305V @ 277 V

Figure 6–99

► PV System Voltage Based on Manufacturer Temperature Coefficient %/°C

Question: *Using the manufacturer's temperature coefficient -0.31%/°C, what's the maximum PV source circuit voltage for twenty-three modules each rated Voc 22.60, at a cell temperature of 67.8°C?* **Figure 6–100**

PV Voc = Rated Voc × {1 + [(Min. Temp. °C - 25°C) × Module Coefficient %/°C]} × # Modules per Series String

PV Voc = 22.60 Voc × {1+ [(67.8°C - 25°C) × -0.31%/°C]} × 23 modules

PV Voc = 22.60 Voc × {1 + [42.8°C × -0.31%/°C]}) × 23 modules

PV Voc = 22.60 Voc × {1 + (-13.27%)} × 23 modules

PV Voc = 22.60 Voc × 0.8673 × 23 modules

PV Voc = 451V

CAUTION: *Illumination at dawn and dusk is sufficient to produce dangerous voltage, even when the sun isn't shining directly on the PV modules. Although moonlight may not generate lethal voltages, a shock hazard may still exist [690.18 Note].* **Figure 6–101**

(C) Maximum PV System Voltage. For one- and two-family dwellings, the maximum PV system voltage is limited to 600V, which is the standard voltage of electrical building wiring. **Figure 6–102**

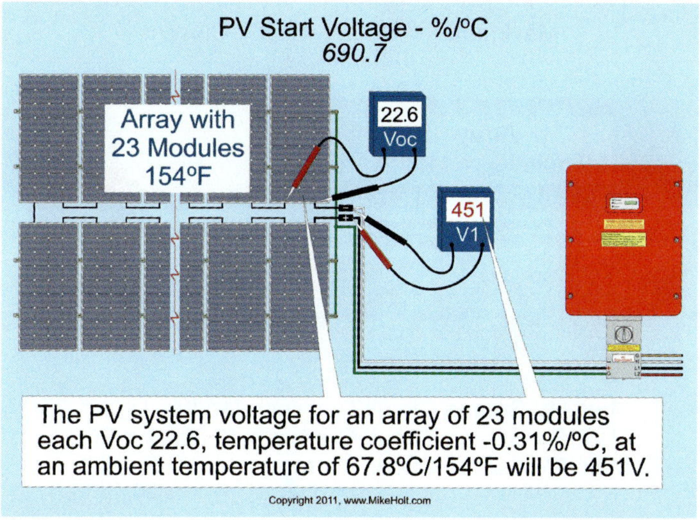

Figure 6–100

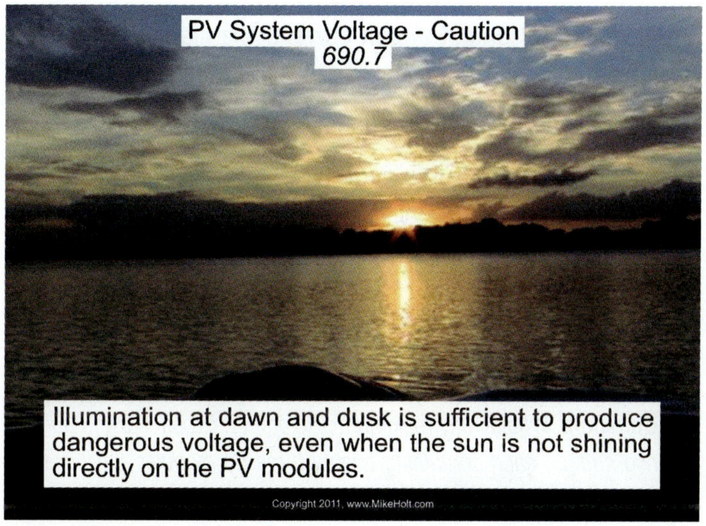

Figure 6–101

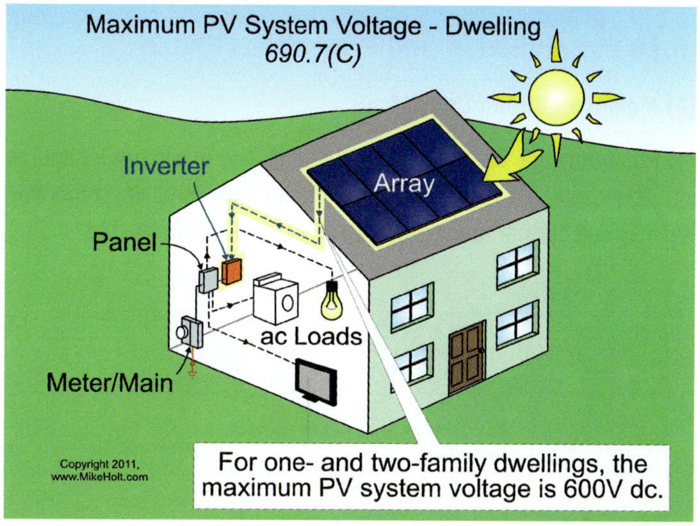

Figure 6–102

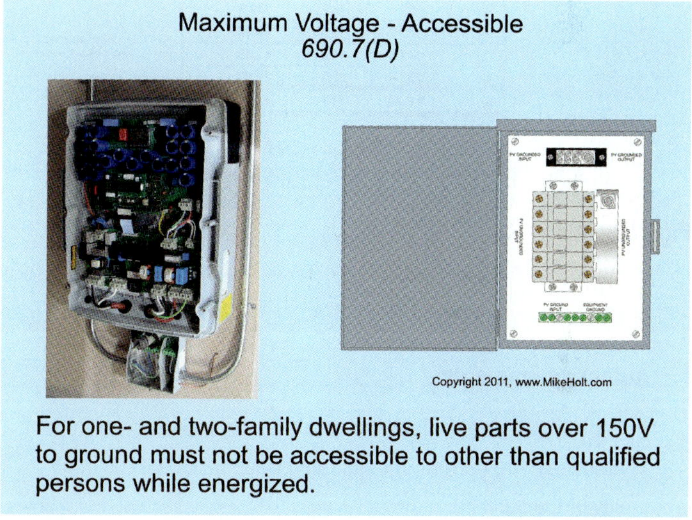

Figure 6–103

Accessible. In one- and two-family dwellings, live parts over 150V to ground must only be accessible to qualified persons [690.7(D)]. **Figure 6–103**

Bipolar Source and Output Circuits. For 2-wire circuits connected to bipolar systems, the maximum system voltage is the highest voltage between the conductors of the 2-wire circuit if all of the following conditions apply [690.7(E)]:

(1) One conductor of each circuit of a bipolar subarray is solidly grounded.

Exception: The operation of ground-fault or arc-fault devices (abnormal operation) shall be permitted to interrupt this connection to ground when the entire bipolar array becomes two distinct arrays isolated from each other and the utilization equipment.

(2) Each circuit is connected to a separate subarray.

(3) The equipment is clearly marked with a label as follows:

WARNING — BIPOLAR PHOTOVOLTAIC ARRAY DISCONNECTION OF NEUTRAL OR GROUNDED CONDUCTORS MAY RESULT IN OVERVOLTAGE ON ARRAY OR INVERTER.

6.18 Circuit Sizing and Protection [690.8]

(A) Maximum Circuit Current.

(1) Maximum PV Source Circuit Current. The maximum PV source circuit current is calculated by multiplying the module nameplate short-circuit current rating (Isc) by 125 percent. **Figure 6–104**

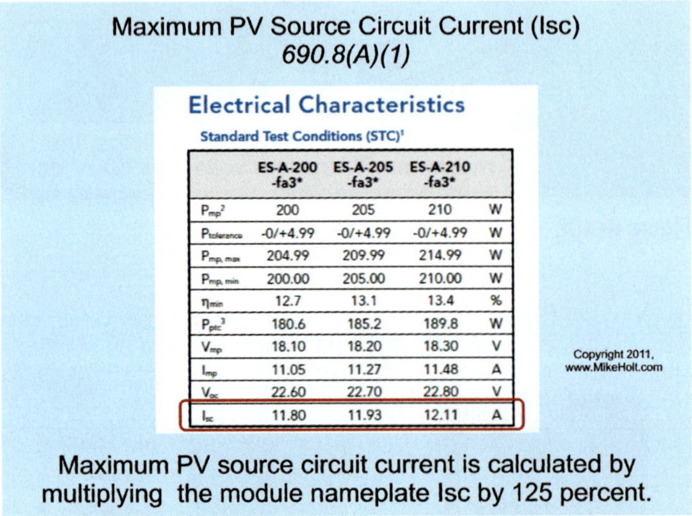

	ES-A-200 -fa3*	ES-A-205 -fa3*	ES-A-210 -fa3*	
P_{mp}[2]	200	205	210	W
$P_{tolerance}$	-0/+4.99	-0/+4.99	-0/+4.99	W
$P_{mp, max}$	204.99	209.99	214.99	W
$P_{mp, min}$	200.00	205.00	210.00	W
η_{min}	12.7	13.1	13.4	%
P_{ptc}[3]	180.6	185.2	189.8	W
V_{mp}	18.10	18.20	18.30	V
I_{mp}	11.05	11.27	11.48	A
V_{oc}	22.60	22.70	22.80	V
I_{sc}	11.80	11.93	12.11	A

Figure 6–104

Author's Comments:

- The 125% current multiplier is due to the module's ability to produce more current than its rated value based on the intensity of the sunlight.
- The PV source circuit consists of the circuit conductors between the PV modules and the terminals of the combiner or inverter dc input terminals if no combiner is used. [690.2].

▶ Maximum PV Source Circuit Current

Question: *What's the maximum PV source circuit current for twenty-three series connected dc modules having a nameplate Isc of 11.80A?* **Figure 6–105**

Maximum PV Source Circuit Current = Module Isc × 1.25

Maximum PV Source Circuit Current = 11.80A × 1.25

Maximum PV Source Circuit Current = 14.75A

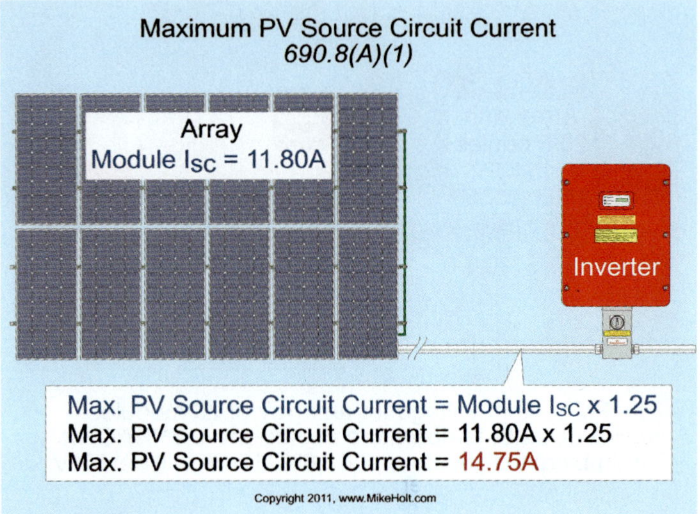

Figure 6–105

(2) Maximum PV Output Circuit Current. The maximum PV output circuit current is equal to the sum of parallel PV source circuit currents as calculated in 690.8(A)(1).

Author's Comment: The PV output circuit consists of circuit conductors between the PV source circuit (combiner) and the dc input terminals of the inverter or dc disconnect.

▶ Maximum PV Source Circuit Current

Question: *What's the maximum PV output circuit current for two strings, each containing twenty-three dc modules having a nameplate Isc of 11.80A?* **Figure 6–106**

Maximum PV Output Circuit Current = (Module Isc × 1.25)* × Number of Strings

Maximum PV Output Circuit Current = (11.80A × 1.25) × 2*

Maximum PV Output Circuit Current = (14.75A) × 2*

Maximum PV Output Circuit Current = 29.50A

**690.8(A)(1)*

(3) Maximum Inverter Output Circuit Current. The maximum inverter output current is equal to the continuous output current marked on the inverter nameplate or installation manual. **Figure 6–107**

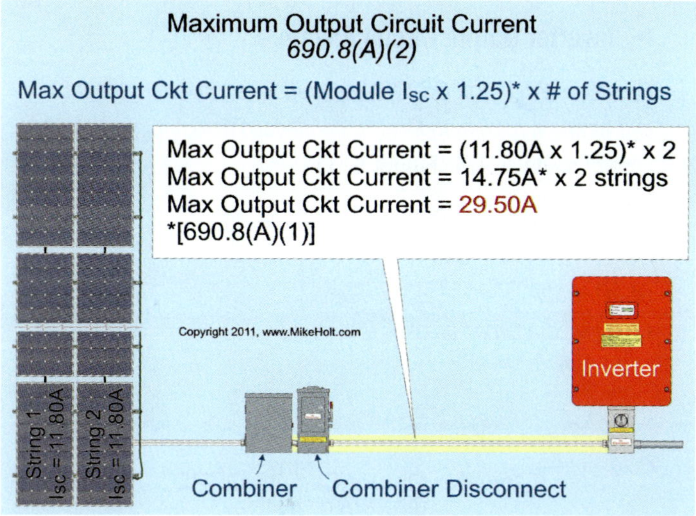

Figure 6–106

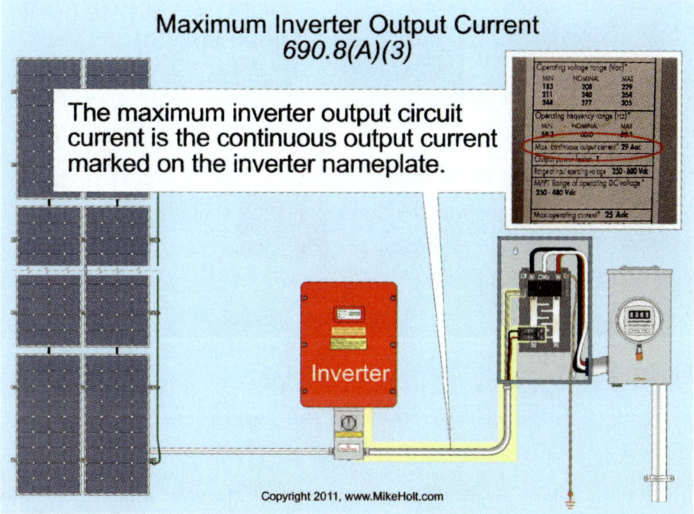

Figure 6–107

Author's Comment: The inverter output circuit consists of the circuit conductors from the inverter output terminals or ac modules [690.6(B)] to ac premises wiring.

(B) Ampacity and Overcurrent Protection Device (OCPD) Ratings.

(1) Overcurrent Devices. Where conductor overcurrent protection is required [690.9], it must be.

(a) Overcurrent devices must be sized not less than 125 percent of 690.8(A) circuit current.

Author's Comment: The 125% current multiplier is because the modules are expected to provide continuous current for more than three hours.

► PV Source Circuit

Question: *Where required, size the OCPD for a single PV source circuit having a nameplate Isc of 11.80A?* **Figure 6–108**

OCPD = (Module Isc × 1.25)* × 1.25

OCPD = (11.80A × 1.25) × 1.25*

OCPD = (14.75A) × 1.25*

OCPD = 18.44A

OCPD = 20A [240.6(A)]

**690.8(A)(1)*

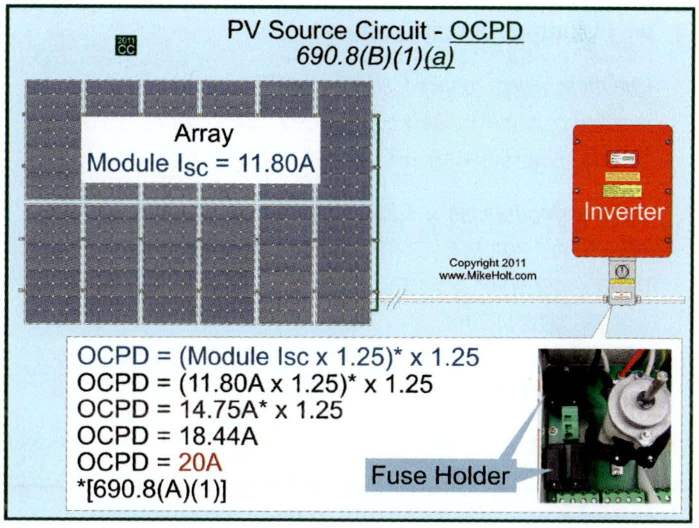

Figure 6–108

Author's Comment: The PV source circuit OCPD isn't permitted to exceed the maximum overcurrent rating marked on the PV module nameplate [110.3(B)]. **Figure 6–109**

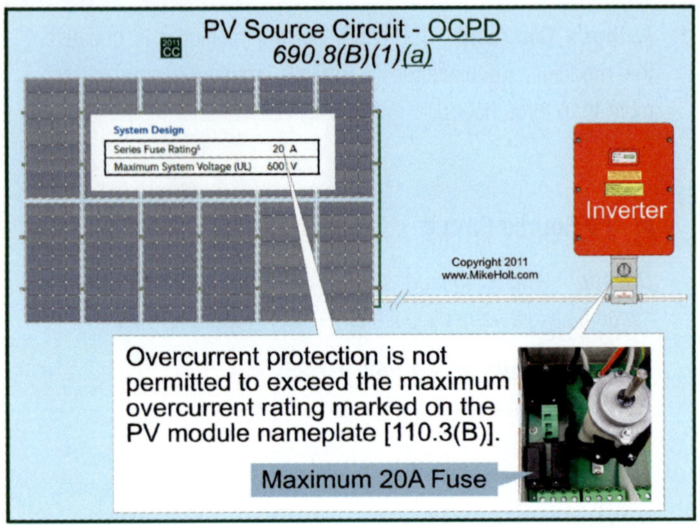

Figure 6–109

► PV Output Circuit Example

Question: *Where required, size the OCPD for a PV output circuit supplied by two PV source circuits, each having nameplate Isc of 11.80A?* **Figure 6–110**

OCPD = (Module Isc × 1.25 × Number of Strings)* × 1.25

OCPD = (11.80A × 1.25 × 2 strings) × 1.25*

OCPD = (29.50A) × 1.25*

OCPD = 36.88A

OCPD = 40A [240.6(A)]

**690.8(A)(2)*

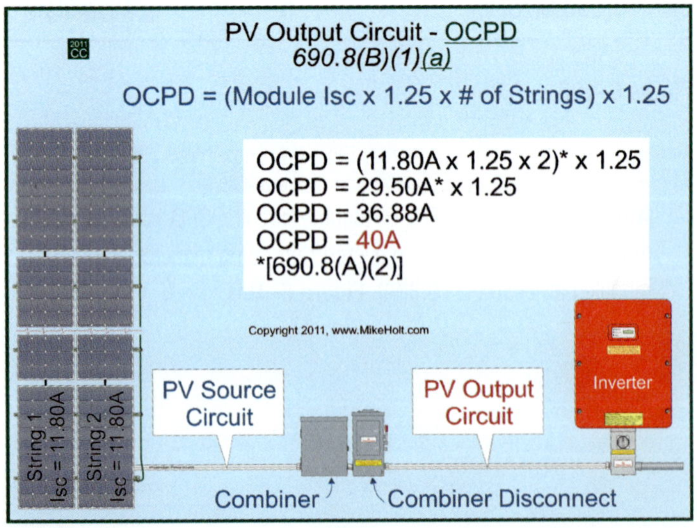

Figure 6–110

► Inverter Output Circuit Example

Question: *What size OCPD is required for an inverter output circuit having a maximum inverter continuous ac output nameplate current rating of 24A?* **Figure 6–111**

OCPD = Inverter ac Output Current Rating* × 1.25

OCPD = 24A × 1.25*

OCPD = 30A

OCPD = 30A circuit breaker [240.6(A)]

**690.8(A)(3)*

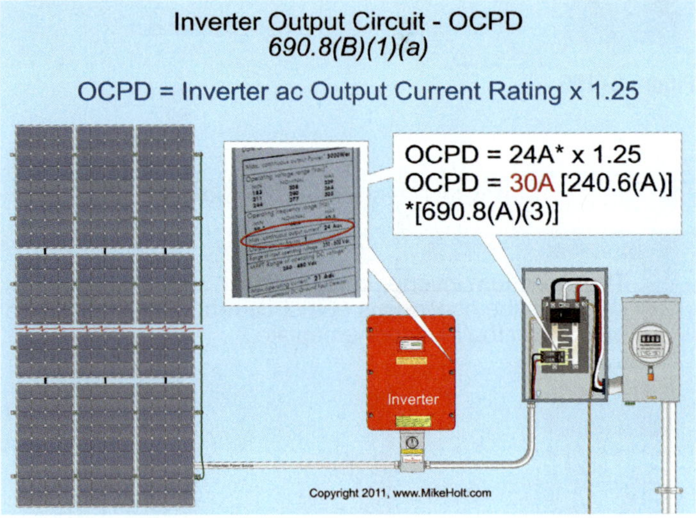

Figure 6–111

(c) Where overcurrent devices operate at greater than 40°C, the ampacity rating of the OCPD must be adjusted in accordance with manufacturer's temperature correction factors. **Figure 6–112**

Author's Comment: Single element fuses are insignificantly impacted by elevated ambient temperature.

(2) Conductor Ampacity. PV circuit conductors must be sized to the larger of 690.8(B)(2)(a) or 690.8(B)(2)(b).

(a) PV circuit conductors must be sized to carry not less than 125 percent of 690.8(A) current before the application of conductor ampacity correction [310.15(B)(2)(a) and 310.15(B)(3)(c)] and adjustment [310.15(B)(3)(a)]. **Figure 6–113**

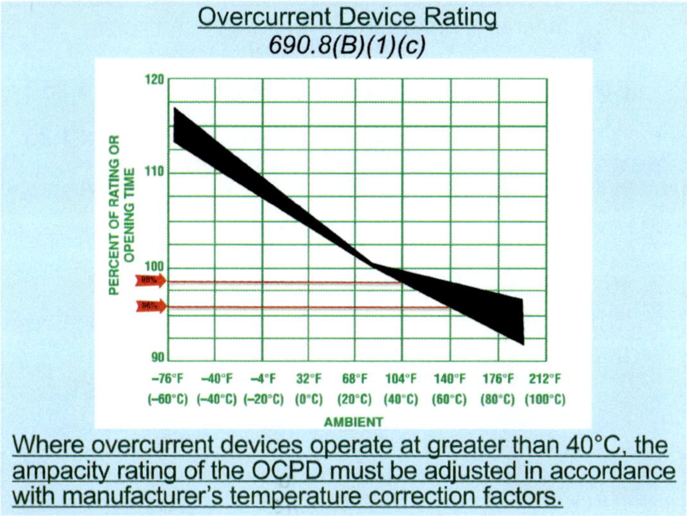

Figure 6–112

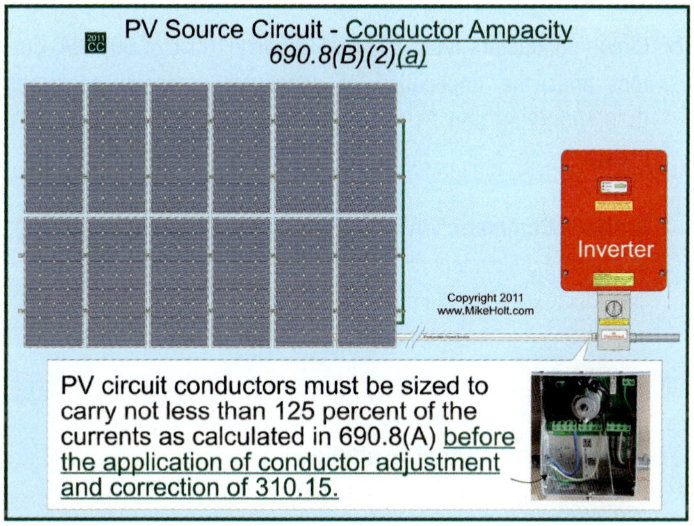

Figure 6–113

► PV Source Circuit Example

Question: *What's the minimum PV source circuit conductor ampacity before the application of conductor correction or adjustment for a string having a short-circuit current rating of 11.80A; assuming all terminals are rated 75°C?* **Figure 6–114**

Conductor Ampacity = (Module Isc × 1.25)* × 1.25

Conductor Ampacity = (11.80A × 1.25) × 1.25*

Conductor Ampacity = (14.75A) × 1.25*

Conductor Ampacity = 18.44A

Conductor Ampacity = 14 AWG rated 20A at 75°C [Table 310.15(B)(16)]

**690.8(A)(1)*

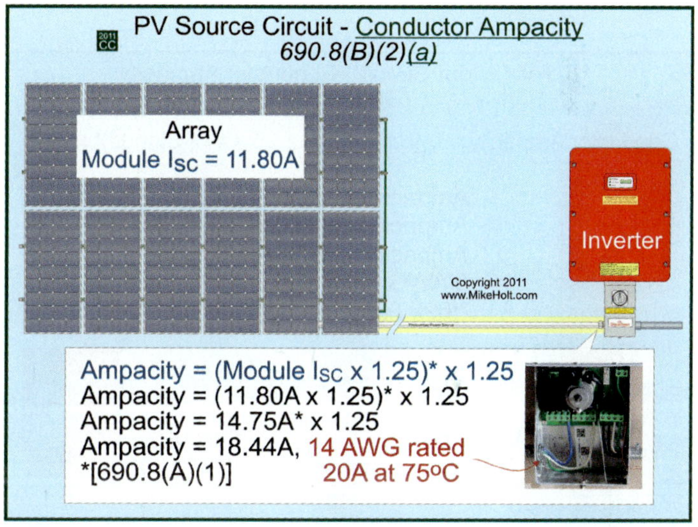

Figure 6–114

Author's Comment: Conductors terminating on terminals rated 75°C are sized in accordance with the ampacities listed in the 75°C temperature column of Table 310.15(B)(16) [110.14(C)(1)(a)(3)].

▶ PV Output Circuit Example

Question: *What's the minimum PV output circuit conductor ampacity, before the application of conductor correction or adjustment, supplied by two PV source circuits, each having a short-circuit current rating of 11.80A; assuming all terminals are rated 75°C?* **Figure 6–115**

Conductor Ampacity = (Module Isc × 1.25 × Number of Source Circuits)* × 1.25

Conductor Ampacity = (11.80A × 1.25 × 2 strings) × 1.25*

Conductor Ampacity = 29.5A × 1.25*

Conductor Ampacity = 36.88A

Conductor Ampacity = 8 AWG rated 50A at 75°C [Table 310.15(B)(16)]

**690.8(A)(2)*

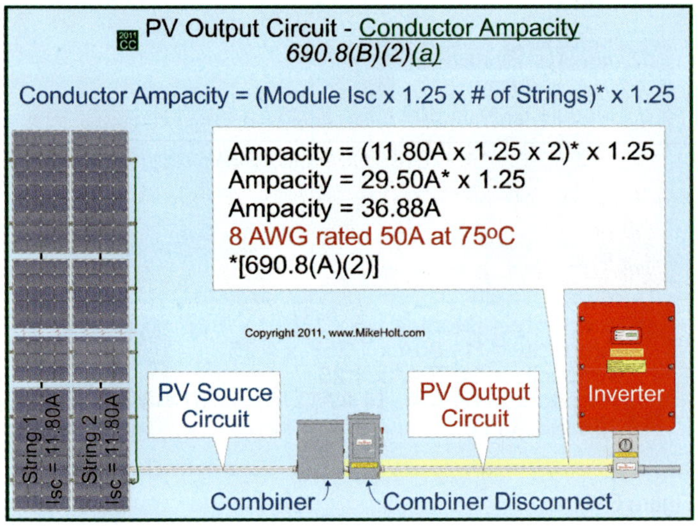

Figure 6–115

▶ Example—Inverter Output Circuit Example

Question: *What's the minimum inverter ac output circuit conductor ampacity, before the application of conductor correction or adjustment, if the maximum continuous nameplate ac rating of the inverter is 24A; assuming all terminals are rated 75°C?* **Figure 6–116**

Conductor Ampacity = Inverter Nameplate Rating* × 1.25

Conductor Ampacity = 24A × 1.25*

Conductor Ampacity = 30A

Conductor Ampacity = 10 AWG rated 35A at 75°C [310.15(B)(16)]

**690.8(A)(3)*

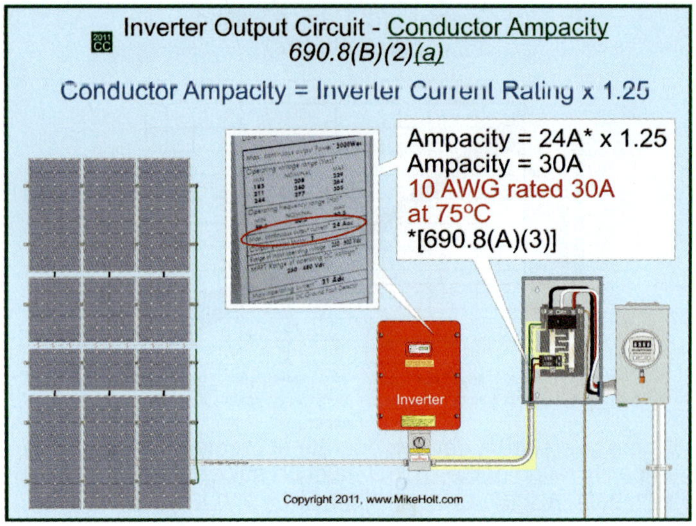

Figure 6–116

(b) Circuit conductors must be sized to carry 100% of 690.8(A) current after the application of conductor ampacity correction [310.15(B)(2)(a) and 310.15(B)(3)(c)] and adjustment [310.15(B)(3)(a)].

Author's Comment: When performing conductor ampacity correction and adjustment calculations, use the conductor ampacity listed in the 90°C column of Table 310.15(B)(16) for THWN-2 insulated conductors [310.15(B)].

▶ PV Source Circuit Example

Question: *What's the PV source circuit conductor ampacity after temperature correction for two current-carrying size 12 THWN-2 conductors in a circular raceway on the roof, ambient temperature is 90°F with 60°F temperature added in accordance with Table 310.15(B)(3)(c), supplying modules having a nameplate Isc rating of 11.80A?* **Figure 6–117**

Conductor Ampacity = Table 310.15(B)(16) Ampacity at 90°C Column x Temperature Correction

Temperature Correction = 0.58, Table 310.15(B)(2)(a) based on 150°F (ambient plus 60°F roof temperature adder)

Conductor Ampacity = 30A x 0.58

Conductor Ampacity = 17.40A, which has sufficient ampacity after correction and adjustment to supply 690.8(A)(1) calculated current of 14.75A (11.80A x 1.25).

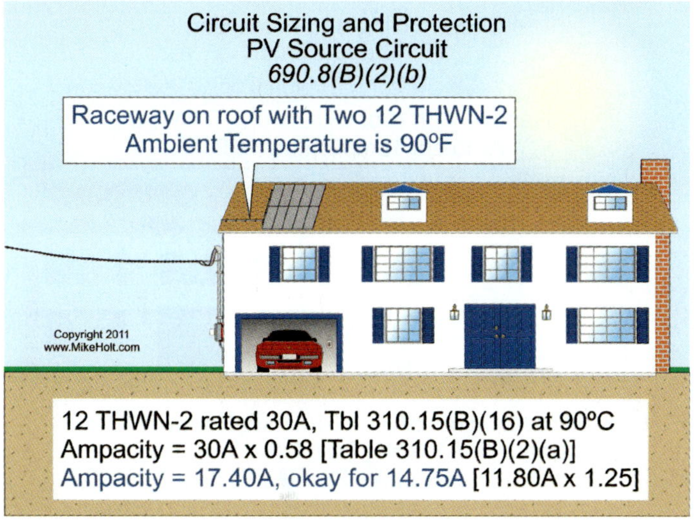

Figure 6–117

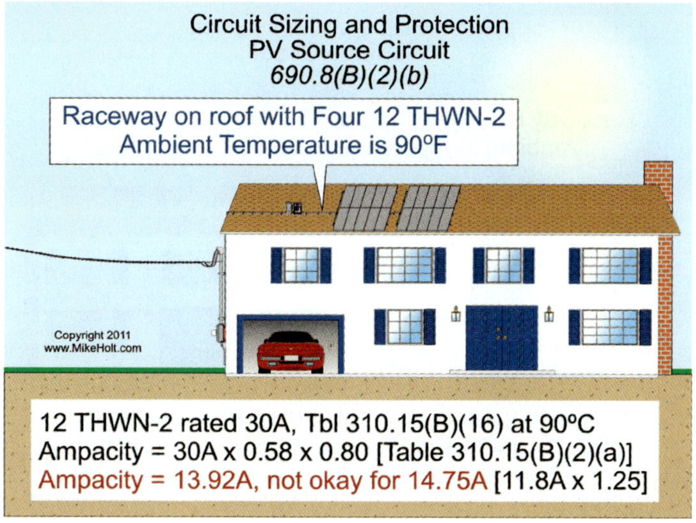

Figure 6–118

► PV Source Circuit Example

Question: *What's the PV source circuit conductor ampacity after temperature correction and adjustment for four current-carrying size 12 THWN-2 conductors in a circular raceway on the roof, ambient temperature is 90°F with 60°F temperature added in accordance with Table 310.15(B)(3)(c), supplying modules having a nameplate Isc rating of 11.80A for each circuit?* **Figure 6–118**

Conductor Ampacity = Table 310.15(B)(16) Ampacity at 90°C Column x Temperature Correction x Adjustment

Temperature Correction = 0.58, Table 310.15(B)(2)(a) based on 150°F (ambient plus 60°F roof temperature adder)

Adjustment = 0.80, Table 310.15(B)(3)(a), based on four current-carrying conductors in a raceway

Conductor Ampacity = 30A x 0.58 x 0.80

Conductor Ampacity = 13.92A, which does not have sufficient ampacity to supply carry 690.8(A)(2) calculated current of 14.75A [11.80A x 1.25], therefore a 10 AWG THWN-2 conductor would be required.

► PV Source Circuit Example

Question: *What's the PV source circuit conductor ampacity after temperature correction and adjustment for four current-carrying size 10 THWN-2 conductors in a circular raceway on the roof where the ambient temperature is 90°F with 60°F temperature added in accordance with Table 310.15(B)(3)(c), supplying modules having a nameplate Isc rating of 11.80A for each circuit?* **Figure 6–119**

Conductor Ampacity = Table 310.15(B)(16) Ampacity at 90°C Column x Temperature Correction x Adjustment

Temperature Correction = 0.58, Table 310.15(B)(2)(a) based on 150°F (ambient plus 60°F roof temperature adder)

Adjustment = 0.80, Table 310.15(B)(3)(a), based on four current-carrying conductors in a raceway

Conductor Ampacity = 40A x 0.58 x 0.80 [Tables 310.15(B)(2)(a), 310.15(B)(3)(c), and 310.15(B)(3)(a)]

Conductor Ampacity = 18.56A, which has sufficient ampacity after correction and adjustment to supply 690.8(A)(1) calculated current of 14.75A (11.80A x 1.25)

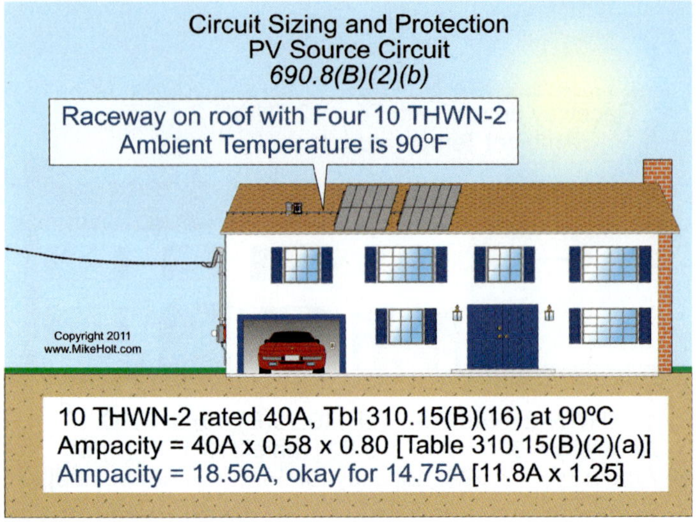

Figure 6–119

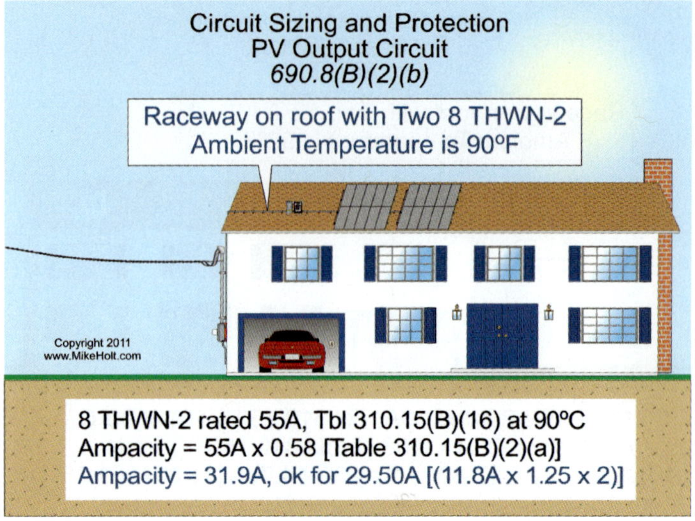

Figure 6–120

▶ PV Output Circuit Example

Question: *What's the PV output current ampacity after temperature correction for two current-carrying 8 size THWN-2 conductors in a circular raceway on the roof where the ambient temperature is 90°F supplied by two parallel PV source circuits, each having a Isc rating 11.80A?* **Figure 6–120**

Conductor Ampacity = Table 310.15(B)(16) Ampacity at 90°C Column x Temperature Correction

Temperature Correction = 0.58, Table 310.15(B)(2)(a) based on 150°F (ambient plus 60°F roof temperature adder)

Conductor Ampacity = 55A x 0.58 [Tables 310.15(B)(2)(a) and 310.15(B)(3)(c)]

Conductor Ampacity = 31.90A, which has sufficient ampacity after correction and adjustment to supply 690.8(A)(2) calculated current of 29.5A (11.80A x 1.25 x 2)

▶ Inverter Output Circuit Example

Question: *What's the ampacity of two current-carrying size 12 THWN-2 conductors installed at a location where the ambient temperature is 90°F?*

Conductor Ampacity = Table 310.15(B)(16) Ampacity at 90°C Column x Temperature Correction

Temperature Correction = 0.96, Table 310.15(B)(2)(a) based on 90°F ambient temperature

Conductor Ampacity = 30A x 0.96 [Table 310.15(B)(2)(a)]
Conductor Ampacity = 28.80A

(c) The overcurrent protection device is sized to protect the conductor after the application of conductor ampacity correction and adjustment of 310.15 in accordance with 240.4. **Figure 6–121**

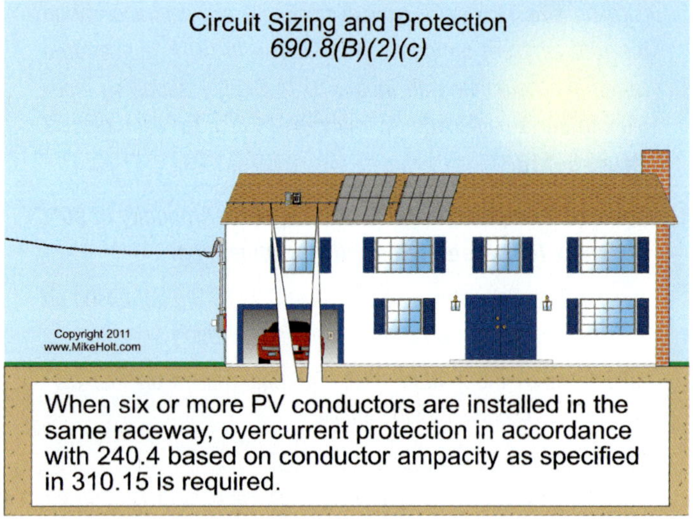

Figure 6–121

Author's Comments:

- Overcurrent protection is only required when six or more PV conductors are installed in the same raceway [690.9(A) Ex].
- When the ampacity of a conductor doesn't correspond with the standard size OCPD of 250.6(A), the next higher standard rating of overcurrent device is permitted, as long as the next size doesn't exceed 800A [240.4(B)].

▶ PV Source Circuit Example

Question: *PV source circuit supplies six current-carrying size 10 THWN-2 conductors in a circular raceway placed on the roof, ambient temperature 90°F with 60°F temperature added in accordance with Table 310.15(B)(3)(c), and modules nameplate Isc rating of 11.80A?*

Conductor Ampacity = Table 310.15(B)(16) Ampacity at 90°C Column x Temperature Correction x Adjustment

Temperature Correction = 0.58, Table 310.15(B)(2)(a) based on 150°F (ambient plus 60°F roof temperature adder)

Adjustment = 0.80, Table 310.15(B)(3)(a), based on six current-carrying conductors in a raceway

Conductor Ampacity = 40A x 0.58 x 0.80

Conductor Ampacity = 18.56A, has sufficient ampacity to carry 690.8(A)(1) calculated current of 14.75A [11.80A x 1.25], and is permitted to be protected by a 20A OCPD as calculated in 690.8(B)(1)(a) [240.4(B) and 690.8(C)].

▶ PV Output Circuit Example

Question: *What's the PV output current ampacity after temperature correction for two current-carrying size 6 THWN-2 conductors in a circular raceway placed on the roof, ambient temperature 90°F with temperature added in accordance with Table 310.15(B)(3), supplied by two parallel PV source circuits, each having a Isc rating 11.80A?*

Conductor Ampacity = Table 310.15(B)(16) Ampacity at 90°C Column x Temperature Correction

Temperature Correction = 0.58, Table 310.15(B)(2)(a) based on 150°F (ambient plus 60°F roof temperature adder)

Conductor Ampacity = 75A x 0.58 [Tables 310.15(B)(2)(a) and 310.15(B)(3)(c)]

Conductor Ampacity = 43.50A, has sufficient ampacity to carry 690.8(A)(2) calculated current of 29.5A [11.80A x 1.25 x 2], and is permitted to be protected by a 40A OCPD as calculated in 690.8(B)(1)(a) [240.4 and 690.8(C)].

▶ Inverter Output Circuit Example

Question: *What's the ampacity of two current-carrying size 12 THWN-2 conductors installed at a location where the ambient temperature is 90°F?*

Conductor Ampacity = Table 310.15(B)(16) Ampacity at 90°C Column x Temperature Correction

Temperature Correction = 0.96, Table 310.15(B)(2)(a) based on 90°F ambient temperature

Conductor Ampacity = 30A x 0.96 [Table 310.15(B)(2)(a)]

Conductor Ampacity = 28.80A, has sufficient ampacity to carry 690.8(A)(3) calculated current of 24A and is permitted to be protected by a 30A OCPD as calculated in 690.8(B(1)(a) [240.4(B) and 690.8(B)].

6.19 Overcurrent Protection [690.9]

(A) Circuits and Equipment. PV source circuits, PV output circuits, inverter output circuits, and equipment must have overcurrent protection in accordance with Article 240. **Figure 6–122**

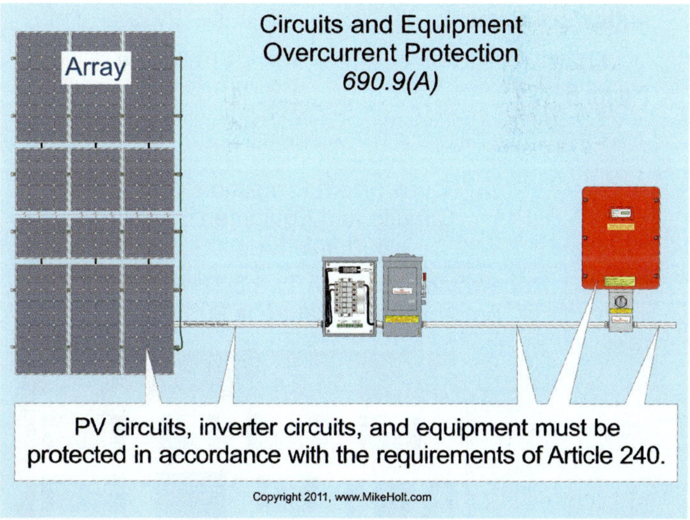

Figure 6–122

Author's Comment: For an ungrounded system [690.35], both positive and negative conductors require overcurrent protection; for grounded systems, only one conductor requires overcurrent protection, typically the positive conductor [240.15].

Ex: Overcurrent protection isn't required for PV dc circuits where the short-circuit currents (Isc) from all sources can't exceed the ampacity of the PV circuit conductors or the maximum overcurrent device size specified on the PV module nameplate. **Figure 6–123**

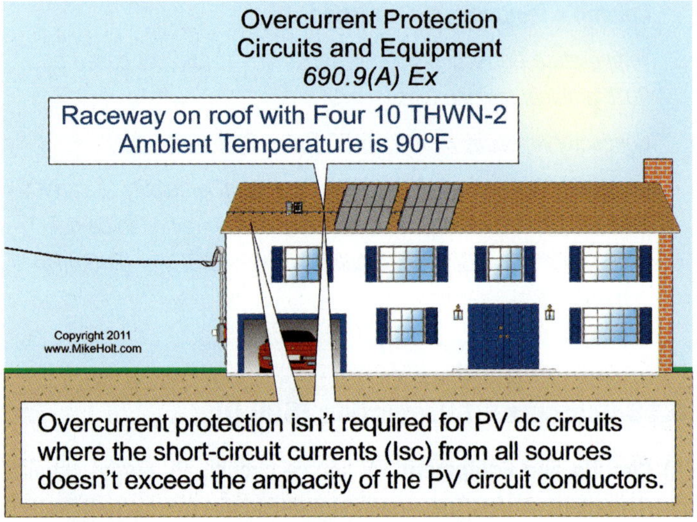

Figure 6–123

Author's Comment: This occurs when the PV source or PV output circuits consist of no more than four conductors. **Figure 6–124**

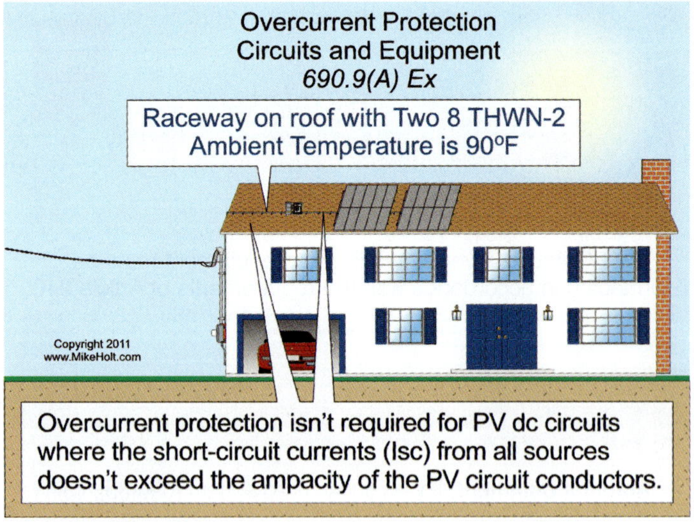

Figure 6–124

(C) PV Source Circuits. Overcurrent devices for PV source circuits are not required to be readily accessible [690.9(C)]. **Figure 6–125**

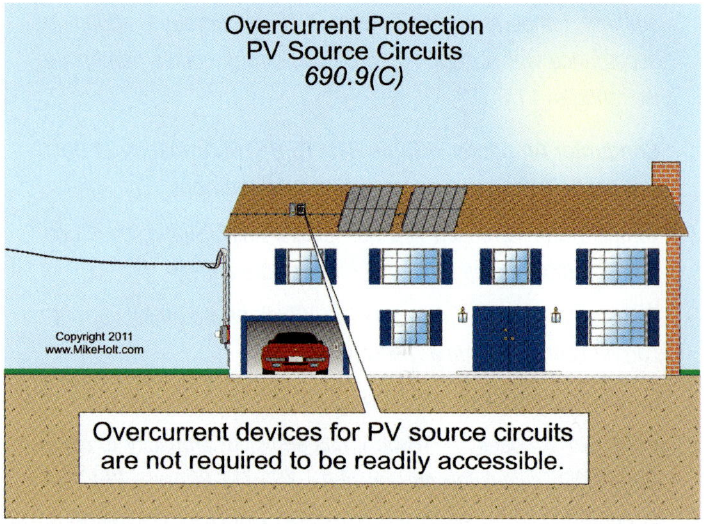

Figure 6–125

Standard sizes of supplementary overcurrent devices come in 1A increments up to and including 15A, higher standard values are in accordance with 240.6(A) [690.9(C)]. **Figure 6–126**

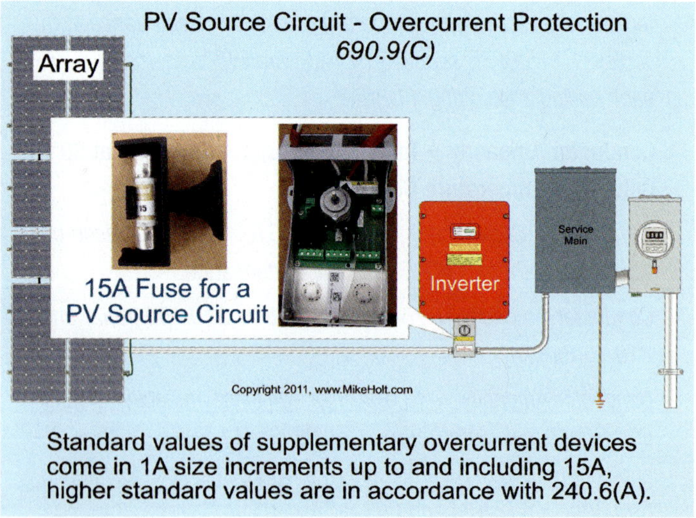

Figure 6–126

(D) Direct-Current Rating. Fuses or circuit breakers for PV dc circuits must be listed for use in dc circuits and must have the appropriate voltage, current and interrupt ratings. Figure 6–127

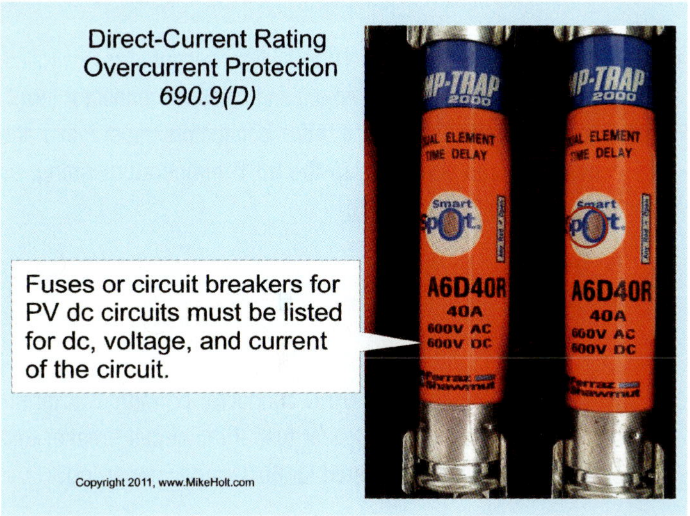

Figure 6–127

CONCLUSION TO UNIT 6—CONDUCTOR SIZING AND PROTECTION CALCULATIONS

The sizing of conductors and overcurrent protection is much more complicated than it appears at first. This unit has provided an insight into the numerous factors that must be taken into account in properly sizing conductors and providing for their protection.

Temperature is a key factor in the resistance of a conductor, and consequently temperature affects a conductor's current-carrying capacity. High temperature on conductors can lead to the breakdown of conductor insulation *and* damage to equipment terminals. Therefore, when sizing conductors, the ampacity values given in the NEC *tab*les must be corrected for ambient temperatures that differ from the ambient of 86° F, on which the Code tables *ar*e based. A bundle of current-carrying conductors will have increased operating temperatures, so the NEC also requires that an adjustment be made when bundling more than three current-carrying conductors together.

This unit also taught you that conductors must not be sized to a higher temperature column of the ampacity table than the rating that the equipment terminals allow. This means that even though you install a 90°C rated conductor such as THHN, a lower ampacity column must be used to match the terminal rating. This confusing requirement results in mistakes on exam pr*oble*ms, so review this part of the unit again if you're not sure how to apply Section 110.14(C) of the Code.

Overcurrent protection must be sized correctly to protect the circuit wiring and equipment from damage that can result from overheating. This unit covered common overcurrent sizing requirements as well as some of the exceptions to the general rules of Article 240. A number of specific examples of overcurrent protection were explained along with examples of how to size the overcurrent devices in order to help you understand that there are specific rules for many types of equipment or situations that don't follow the general overcurrent protection requirements.

UNIT 6

Practice Questions

Please use the 2011 *Code* book to answer the following questions, which are based on the 2011 *NEC*.

PRACTICE QUESTIONS FOR UNIT 6—CONDUCTOR SIZING AND PROTECTION CALCULATIONS

PART A—GENERAL CONDUCTOR REQUIREMENTS

6.1 Conductor Insulation [Table 310.104(A)]

1. THHN can be described as ______.

(a) thermoplastic insulation with a nylon outer cover
(b) suitable for dry and wet locations
(c) having a maximum operating temperature of 90°C
(d) a and c

6.2 Conductor Sizing [110.6]

2. Conductor sizes are expressed in American Wire Gage (AWG) from 40 AWG through 4/0 AWG. Conductors larger than ______ are expressed in circular mils.

(a) 1 AWG
(b) 1/0 AWG
(c) 3/0 AWG
(d) 4/0 AWG

3. The smallest size conductor permitted for branch circuits, feeders, and services for residential, commercial, and industrial locations is ______.

(a) 14 AWG copper
(b) 12 AWG aluminum
(c) 12 AWG copper
(d) a and b

6.4 Conductor Size—Terminal Temperature Rating [110.14(C)]

4. Equipment terminals rated 100A or less (receptacles, switches, circuit breakers, fuses, and so on) and pressure connector terminals for 14 AWG through 1 AWG conductors must have the conductor sized according to the 60°C temperature rating, as listed in Table 310.15(B)(16).

(a) True
(b) False

5. What's the minimum size THHN conductor permitted to terminate on a 70A circuit breaker or fuse if the circuit breaker and equipment terminals are listed for 60°C conductor sizing?

(a) 8 AWG
(b) 6 AWG
(c) 4 AWG
(d) 2 AWG

6. What's the minimum size THHN conductor that's permitted to terminate on a 50A circuit breaker or fuse if the circuit breaker and equipment terminals are listed for 75°C conductor sizing?

(a) 10 AWG
(b) 8 AWG
(c) 6 AWG
(d) 4 AWG

7. Terminals for equipment rated over 100A and pressure connector terminals for conductors larger than 1 AWG must have the conductor sized according to the 75°C temperature rating, as listed in Table 310.15(B)(16).

(a) True
(b) False

8. What size THHN/THWN conductor is required for an air-conditioning unit if the nameplate requires a conductor ampacity of 34A? The terminals of all the equipment and circuit breakers are rated 75°C and the raceway is installed outdoors in a wet location.

(a) 14 AWG
(b) 12 AWG
(c) 10 AWG
(d) 8 AWG

9. What's the minimum size THHN conductor required for a 150A circuit breaker or fuse for a nonmotor circuit? Be sure to comply with the requirements of 110.14(C)(1)(b).

(a) 1/0 AWG
(b) 2/0 AWG
(c) 3/0 AWG
(d) 4/0 AWG

10. In general, THHN (90°C) conductor ampacities can't be used when sizing conductors. When more than three current-carrying conductors are bundled together, or if the ambient temperature is greater than 86°F, the allowable conductor ampacity must be decreased. THHN provides a greater ampacity for conductor adjustment purposes.

(a) True
(b) False

11. What size conductor is required to supply a 190A noncontinuous load in a dry location? The terminals are rated 75°C.

(a) 2/0 AWG
(b) 3/0 AWG
(c) 4/0 AWG
(d) 300 kcmil

6.5 Conductors in Parallel

12. Phase and grounded conductors sized ______ AWG and larger are permitted to be connected in parallel.

(a) 1
(b) 1/0
(c) 2/0
(d) 3/0

13. To ensure that currents are evenly distributed between parallel conductors, each conductor within a parallel set must be installed in the same type of raceway (metallic or nonmetallic) and must be the same length, material, circular mils, insulation type, and must terminate in the same method.

(a) True
(b) False

14. When equipment grounding conductors are installed in parallel, each raceway must have a full-size equipment grounding conductor sized according to the overcurrent device rating of that circuit.

(a) True
(b) False

15. All parallel equipment grounding conductors are required to be a minimum 1/0 AWG.

(a) True
(b) False

16. What size equipment grounding conductor is required in each raceway for an 800A, 500 kcmil feeder paralleled in two raceways?

(a) 1 AWG
(b) 2 AWG
(c) 3 AWG
(d) 1/0 AWG

17. If an 800A service has a calculated load of 750A, what size 75°C conductors are required for the service ungrounded conductors if the conductors are paralleled in two raceways?

(a) 4/0 AWG
(b) 250 kcmil
(c) 500 kcmil
(d) 750 kcmil

18. What size ungrounded conductors are required for a 250A feeder paralleled in two raceways?

(a) 3 AWG
(b) 2 AWG
(c) 1/0 AWG
(d) 2/0 AWG

6.7 Overcurrent Protection [Article 240]

19. One of the purposes of conductor overcurrent protection is to protect the conductors against excessive or dangerous heat.

(a) True
(b) False

20. Overcurrent devices must be designed and rated to clear fault current and must have a short-circuit interrupting rating sufficient for the available fau*lt* levels. If the minimum interruption rating isn't marked on the overcurrent device, according to the NEC the minimum for circuit breakers is ______ and ______ for fuses.

(a) 5,000A, 5,000A
(b)5,000A, 10,000A
(c) 10,000A, 5,000A
(d) 10,000A, 10,000A

21. Which of the following is a standard size for circuit breakers and fuses?

(a)25A
(b) 90A
(c) 350A
(d) any of these

22. Where a circuit supplies continuous loads or any combination of continuous and noncontinuous loads, the rating of the overcurrent device must not be less than the noncontinuous load plus ______ of the continuous load.

(a) 80 percent
(b) 100 percent
(c) 125 percent
(d) 150 percent

6.8 Overcurrent Protection of Conductors—General Requirements [240.4]

23. The maximum overcurrent device size for 14 AWG is 15A, 12 AWG is 20A, and 10 AWG is 30A. This is a general rule, but it doesn't apply to motors or air conditioners according to 240.4(G).

(a) True
(b) False

24. If the ampacity of a conductor doesn't correspond with the standard ampere rating of a fuse or circuit breaker, the next size up overcurrent device is permitted. This applies only if the conductors supply multioutlet receptacles for portable cord-and-plug-connected loads.

(a) True
(b) False

25. What size conductor is required for a 70A breaker that supplies a 70A noncontinuous load where the terminals are rated 75°C?

(a) 8 AWG
(b) 6 AWG
(c) 4 AWG
(d) any of these

6.9 Overcurrent Protection of Conductors—Specific Requirements

26. What size feeder overcurrent device is required for a 100A continuous load?

(a) 100A
(b) 125A
(c) 150A
(d) 200A

27. Feeder tap conductors not over 25 ft are permitted, providing the ______.

(a) ampacity of the tap conductors isn't less than one-third the rating of the overcurrent device protecting the feeder conductors being tapped
(b) tap conductors terminate in a single circuit breaker or set of fuses that limit the load to the ampacity of the tap conductors
(c) tap conductors are suitably protected from physical damage
(d) all of these

28. Outside transformer secondary conductors can be of unlimited length without overcurrent protection at the point they receive their supply if ______.

(a) the conductors are suitably protected from physical damage
(b) the conductors terminate at a single circuit breaker or a single set of fuses that limits the load to the ampacity of the conductors
(c) a and b
(d) none of these

PART B—CONDUCTOR AMPACITY

6.10 Conductor Ampacity

29. The temperature rating of a conductor is the maximum operating temperature the conductor insulation can withstand (without serious damage) over a prolonged period of time. The ______ provide guidance for adjusting conductor ampacities for different conditions.

(a) conductor allowable ampacities
(b) ambient temperature correction factors
(c) over three current-carrying conductors adjustment factors
(d) all of these

6.11 Ambient Temperature Correction Factors [Table 310.15(B)(2)(a)]

30. The ampacities listed in Table 310.15(B)(16) apply only when the ambient temperature is 40°C and there are no more than two current-carrying conductors bundled together. If the ambient temperature isn't 40°C, or there are more than two current-carrying conductors in a raceway, the allowable ampacities must be adjusted to reflect the ampacity under the conditions of use.

(a) True
(b) False

31. What's the ampacity of an 8 THHN conductor when installed in a walk-in cooler (dry location) if the ambient temperature is 50°F?

(a) 40A
(b) 50A
(c) 55A
(d) 57A

32. What size THHN conductor is required to feed a 16A noncontinuous load when the conductors are in an ambient temperature of 100°F in a dry location? The circuit is protected with a 20A overcurrent device.

(a) 14 AWG
(b) 12 AWG
(c) 10 AWG
(d) 8 AWG

6.12 Conductor Bundling Ampacity Adjustment Factors [Table 310.15(B)(3)(a)]

33. When four or more current-carrying conductors are bundled together for more than ______, the conductor allowable ampacity must be reduced according to the factors listed in Table 310.15(B)(3)(a).

(a) 12 in.
(b) 24 in.
(c) 36 in.
(d) 48 in.

34. What's the ampacity of each 1/0 THHN conductor when there are four current-carrying conductors installed in a raceway in a dry location?

(a) 111A
(b) 136A
(c) 153A
(d) 171A

35. A raceway contains eight current-carrying conductors. What size conductor is required to feed a 21A noncontinuous lighting load in a dry location? The overcurrent device is rated 30A.

(a) 14 THHN
(b) 12 THHN
(c) 10 THHN
(d) any of these

6.13 Ambient and Conductor Bundling Adjustment

36. What's the ampacity of each 10 THHN conductor when there are eight current-carrying conductors installed in the same raceway and the ambient temperature is 100°F in a dry location?

(a) 21A
(b) 25A
(c) 32A
(d) 40A

6.14 Current-Carrying Conductors

37. The neutral conductor that carries only the unbalanced current from a 3-wire delta circuit, or 4-wire, three-phase wye circuit, is considered a current-carrying conductor for the purpose of applying the adjustment factors of Table 310.15(B)(3)(a).

(a) True
(b) False

38. The neutral conductor of a balanced 4-wire, three-phase wye circuit, that's at least 50 percent loaded with nonlinear loads (electric-discharge lighting, electronic ballasts, dimmers, controls, computers, laboratory test equipment, medical test equipment, recording studio equipment, and so forth) isn't considered a current-carrying conductor for the purpose of applying bundle adjustment factors.

(a) True
(b) False

39. The neutral conductor of a 3-wire wye circuit from a 4-wire, three-phase, wye system isn't considered a current-carrying conductor for the purpose of applying bundle adjustment factors.

(a) True
(b) False

6.15 Conductor Sizing Summary

40. The ampacity of a conductor can be different along the length of the conductor. The higher calculated ampacity can be used if the length of the lower ampacity is no more than 10 ft, or no more than 10 percent of the length of the higher ampacity circuit conductors, whichever is less.

(a) True
(b) False

41. Terminals are presumed to be rated 60°C for equipment 100A or less and 75°C for equipment terminals rated over 100A unless the terminal temperature rating is specified. Regardless of the conductor ampacity, conductors must be sized no smaller than required by the terminal temperature rating.

(a) True
(b) False

PART C—ARTICLE 690 SOLAR PV SYSTEMS

42. The ______ of a dc photovoltaic source circuit or output circuit, must be calculated as the sum of the rated open-circuit voltage of the series-connected photovoltaic modules multiplied by the correction factor provided in Table 690.7.

(a) minimum allowable ampacity of conductors
(b) maximum allowable ampacity of conductors
(c) minimum photovoltaic system voltage
(d) maximum photovoltaic system voltage

43. For PV systems, one source for lowest-expected ambient temperature is the "Extreme Annual Mean Minimum Design Dry Bulb Temperature" found in the ASHRAE Handbook — Fundamentals.

(a) True
(b) False

44. For one- and two-family dwellings, the maximum PV system voltage is ______V.

(a) 240
(b) 208
(c) 480
(d) 600

45. For PV systems, in one- and two-family dwellings, live parts over 150V to ground must not be ______ while energized.

(a) accessible to an inspector
(b) accessible to an electrician
(c) accessible to an unqualified person
(d) all of the above

46. The PV source circuit current is calculated by multiplying the sum of the parallel module nameplate short-circuit current ratings (Isc) by 125 percent.

(a) True
(b) False

47 The PV output circuit current is equal to the sum of parallel PV source circuit maximum currents as calculated in ______.

(a) 690.8(A)(1)
(b) 690.8(A)(2)
(c) 690.8(A)(3)
(d) none of the above

48. The maximum PV inverter output circuit current is equal to the ______ output current rating.

(a) average
(b) peak
(c) continuous
(d) intermittent

49. Currents of photovoltaic systems are to be considered ______.

(a) safe
(b) continuous
(c) noncontinuous
(d) inverted

50. Overcurrent devices for PV systems shall be rated to carry not less than ______ percent of the maximum currents calculated in 690.8(A).

(a) 80
(b) 100
(c) 125
(d) 250

51. The overcurrent device ratings in photovoltaic systems operated at temperatures greater than ______, shall comply with the manufacturer's temperature correction factors.

(a) 32 degrees C
(b) 40 degrees C
(c) 32 degrees F
(d) 40 degrees F

52. Overcurrent devices for PV source circuits must be readily accessible.

(a) True
(b) False

53. Fuses or circuit breakers for PV dc circuits must be ______ for use in dc circuits and shall have the appropriate voltage, current, and interrupt ratings.

(a) identified
(b) approved
(c) recognized
(d) listed

UNIT 6

Challenge Questions

Please use the 2011 *Code* book to answer the following questions, which are based on the 2011 *NEC.*

CHALLENGE QUESTIONS FOR UNIT 6—CONDUCTOR SIZING AND PROTECTION CALCULATIONS

PART A—GENERAL CONDUCTOR REQUIREMENTS

6.7 Overcurrent Protection [Article 240]

1. A continuous load of 27A requires the circuit overcurrent device to be sized at ______.

(a) 20A
(b) 30A
(c) 35A
(d) 40A

2. What size overcurrent device is required for a 45A continuous load? The circuit is in a raceway with 14 current-carrying conductors.

(a) 45A
(b) 50A
(c) 60A
(d) 70A

3. A 65A continuous load requires a ______ overcurrent device.

(a) 60A
(b) 70A
(c) 75A
(d) 90A

4. A department store feeder (continuous load) supplies a lighting load of 103A. The minimum size overcurrent device permitted for this feeder is ______.

(a) 110A
(b) 125A
(c) 150A
(d) 175A

PART B—CONDUCTOR AMPACITY

6.11 Ambient Temperature Correction Factors [Table 310.15(B)(2)(a)]

5. A 2 TW conductor is installed in a location where the ambient temperature is expected to be 102°F. The temperature correction factor for conductor ampacity in this location is ______.

(a) 0.71
(b) 0.82
(c) 0.88
(d) 0.96

6. If the ambient temperature is 71°C, the minimum insulation temperature rating that a conductor must have and still have the capacity to carry current is ______.

(a) 60°C
(b) 90°C
(c) 105°C
(d) 120°C

6.12 Conductor Bundling Ampacity Adjustment Factors [Table 310.15(B)(3)(a)]

7. The ampacity of six current-carrying 4/0 XHHW aluminum conductors installed in a ground floor slab (wet location) is ______.

(a) 135A
(b) 144A
(c) 185A
(d) 210A

6.13 Ambient and Conductor Bundling Adjustment

8. The ampacity of 15 current-carrying 10 RHW aluminum conductors in a raceway in an ambient temperature of 75°F is ______.

   (a) 12A
   (b) 15A
   (c) 22A
   (d) 30A

9. A(n) ______ THHN conductor is required for a 19.70A noncontinuous load if the ambient temperature is 75°F and there are nine current-carrying conductors in the raceway in a dry location.

   (a) 14
   (b) 12
   (c) 10
   (d) 8

10. The ampacity for each of nine current-carrying 10 THW conductors installed in a 20 in. long raceway is ______.

   (a) 25A
   (b) 30A
   (c) 35A
   (d) 40A

11. The ampacity for each of 10 current-carrying 6 THHW conductors installed in an 18 in. long conduit in a dry location having an ambient temperature of 39°C is ______.

   (a) 40A
   (b) 68A
   (c) 75A
   (d) 90A

6.14 Current-Carrying Conductors

12. A raceway contains the following: one 4-wire, multiwire branch circuit that supplies a balanced incandescent 120V lighting load; one 4-wire, multiwire branch circuit that supplies a balanced 120V fluorescent lighting load; two conductors that supply a receptacle; and one equipment grounding conductor. The system is 120/208V, three-phase. Taking these factors into consideration, how many of these conductors are considered current carrying?

   (a) 7 conductors
   (b) 8 conductors
   (c) 9 conductors
   (d) 11 conductors

13. There's a total of nine 10 THW conductors in a raceway. The system voltage is 120/208V, three-phase. One conductor is an equipment grounding conductor, four conductors supply a 4-wire, multiwire branch circuit for balanced electric-discharge luminaires, and the remaining conductors supply a 4-wire, multiwire branch circuit for balanced incandescent luminaires. Taking all of these factors into consideration, how many of these conductors are considered current carrying?

   (a) 6 conductors
   (b) 7 conductors
   (c) 9 conductors
   (d) 10 conductors

Part C—Article 690 Solar PV systems

Solar PV Calculations - 690.7

14. Using Table 690.7, what's the maximum PV source circuit voltage for twenty-five modules each rated Voc 20.60, at an ambient temperature of -7°C?

   (a) 447V
   (b) 566V
   (c) 575V
   (d) 587V

15. Using the manufacturer's temperature coefficient -0.31%/ºC, what's the maximum PV source circuit voltage for twenty-five modules each rated Voc 20.60, at a cell temperature of -7°C?

(a) 447V
(b) 566V
(c) 575V
(d) 587V

16. Using the manufacturer's temperature coefficient -0.075V/ºC, what's the maximum PV source circuit voltage for twenty-five modules each rated Voc 20.60, at an ambient temperature of -7°C?

(a) 447V
(b) 566V
(c) 575V
(d) 587V

17. Using the manufacturer's temperature coefficient -0.31%/ºC, what's the maximum PV source circuit voltage for twenty-five modules each rated Voc 20.60, at a cell temperature of 67.8°C?

(a) 447V
(b) 566V
(c) 575V
(d) 587V

Solar PV Calculations - 690.8(A)(1)

18. What's the maximum PV source circuit current for twenty-three series connected dc modules having a nameplate Isc of 10.80A?

(a) 10.8A
(b) 13.5A
(c) 17A
(d) None of these

19. What's the maximum PV output circuit current for two strings, each containing twenty-three dc modules having a nameplate Isc of 10.80A?

(a) 10.8A
(b) 13.5A
(c) 17A
(d) None of these

Solar PV Calculations - 690.8(B)(1)(a)

20. Where required, size the OCPD for a single PV source circuit having a nameplate Isc of 10.80A?

(a) 15A
(b) 20A
(c) 25A
(d) 35A

21. Where required, size the OCPD for a PV output circuit supplied by two PV source circuits, each having nameplate Isc of 10.80A?

(a) 15A
(b) 20A
(c) 25A
(d) 35A

22. What size OCPD is required for an inverter output circuit having a maximum inverter continuous ac output nameplate current rating of 24A?

(a) 15A
(b) 20A
(c) 25A
(d) 30A

Solar PV Calculations - 690.8(B)(2)(a)

23. What's the minimum PV source circuit conductor ampacity before the application of conductor correction or adjustment for a string having a short-circuit current rating of 10.80A; assuming all terminals are rated 75°C?

(a) 14 AWG
(b) 12 AWG
(c) 10 AWG
(d) 8 AWG

24. What's the minimum PV output circuit conductor ampacity, before the application of conductor correction or adjustment, supplied by two PV source circuits, each having a short-circuit current rating of 10.50A; assuming all terminals are rated 75°C?

(a) 14 AWG
(b) 12 AWG
(c) 10 AWG
(d) 8 AWG

25. What's the minimum inverter ac output circuit conductor ampacity, before the application of conductor correction or adjustment, if the maximum continuous nameplate ac rating of the inverter is 24A; assuming all terminals are rated 75°C?

(a) 14 AWG
(b) 12 AWG
(c) 10 AWG
(d) 8 AWG

Solar PV Calculations - 690.8(B)(2)(b)

26. What's the PV source circuit conductor ampacity after temperature correction for two current-carrying size 12 THWN-2 conductors in a circular raceway on the roof, ambient temperature is 90°F with 60°F temperature added in accordance with Table 310.15(B)(3)(c), supplying modules having a nameplate Isc rating of 10.50A?

(a) 11A
(b) 14A
(c) 17A
(d) None of these

27. What's the PV source circuit conductor ampacity after temperature correction and adjustment for four current-carrying size 12 THWN-2 conductors in a circular raceway on the roof, ambient temperature is 90°F with 60°F temperature added in accordance with Table 310.15(B)(3)(c), supplying modules having a nameplate Isc rating of 10.50A for each circuit?

(a) 11A
(b) 14A
(c) 17A
(d) None of these

28. What's the PV output circuit conductor ampacity after temperature correction for two current-carrying 8 THWN-2 conductors in a circular raceway on the roof where the ambient temperature is 90°F supplied by two parallel PV source circuits, each having a Isc rating 10.50A?

(a) 29A
(b) 32A
(c) 55A
(d) none of these

29. What's the ampacity of two current-carrying size 10 THWN-2 conductors installed at a location where the ambient temperature is 90°F?

(a) 29A
(b) 32A
(c) 55A
(d) none of these

Solar PV Calculations - 690.8(B)(2)(c)

30. PV source circuit supplies six current-carrying size 10 THWN-2 conductors in a circular raceway placed on the roof, ambient temperature 90°F with 60°F temperature added in accordance with Table 310.15(B)(3)(c), and modules nameplate Isc rating of 10.50A?

(a) 19A
(b) 32A
(c) 40A
(d) none of these

31. What's the PV output current ampacity after temperature correction for two current-carrying 8 THWN-2 conductors in a circular raceway placed on the roof, ambient temperature 90°F with temperature added in accordance with Table 310.15(B)(3), supplied by two parallel PV source circuits, each having a Isc rating 10.50A?

(a) 19A
(b) 32A
(c) 40A
(d) none of these

32. What's the ampacity of two current-carrying size 10 THWN-2 conductors installed at a location where the ambient temperature is 90°F?

(a) 19A
(b) 29A
(c) 30A
(d) none of these

UNIT 7

Motor and Air-Conditioning Calculations

INTRODUCTION TO UNIT 7—MOTOR AND AIR-CONDITIONING CALCULATIONS

Motor circuits have special requirements that effect how the overcurrent protection is sized and installed. Motors typically draw about six times as much current at start-up as they draw during normal operation. Article 430 provides guidance on how to properly protect the motor from overcurrent and still avoid nuisance tripping of the fuse or circuit breaker protecting the motor. Similar rules are included in Article 440 for air conditioners.

The *Code* definition of "Overcurrent" is made up of three factors: short circuits, ground faults, and overloads. For motors, the function of overcurrent protection is divided into two parts. The short-circuit and ground-fault protection of a motor is usually provided by a fuse or circuit breaker which is sized large enough to let the motor start, but too large to provide overload protection. Overload protection is provided to protect the motor and wiring at a value close to the actual running current of the motor, but with sufficient time delay to allow the motor to start. This protection is often provided by the "heaters" which are overload sensing devices in a magnetic starter.

Article 430 spells out the minimum sizing of conductors for motor branch circuits and feeders as well. When conductors and short-circuit ground-fault protection are sized based on Article 430, the fuse or circuit breaker may appear to be much larger than it should be for the conductors selected. Make sure everything is sized correctly based on Article 430, then don't be concerned. The overcurrent protection rules of Article 240 don't apply to motors or air conditioners, so often an installation may not "look right," even though it complies with the requirements of Article 430 for motors and Article 440 for hermetic air conditioners.

Careful study of this unit will help you understand the sometimes confusing requirements of Articles 430 and 440.

PART A—MOTOR CALCULATIONS

7.1 Scope of Article 430

Scope [430.1]. Article 430 covers motors, motor branch-circuit and feeder conductors and their protection, motor overload protection, motor control circuits, motor controllers, and motor control centers. This article is divided into many parts, the most important being: Figure 7–1

- General—Part I
- Circuit Conductors—Part II
- Overload Protection—Part III
- Branch-Circuit Short-Circuit and Ground-Fault Protection—Part IV
- Feeder-Circuit Short-Circuit and Ground-Fault Protection—Part V
- Control Circuits—Part VI
- Controllers—Part VII
- Motor Control Centers—Part VIII
- Disconnecting Means—Part IX

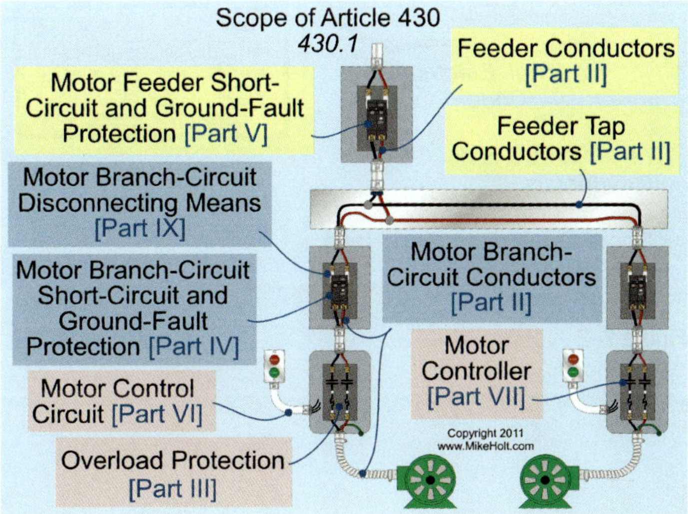

Figure 7–1

Note No. 1: Article 440 contains the installation requirements for electrically driven air-conditioning and refrigeration equipment [440.1]. Also see 110.26(F) for dedicated space requirements for motor control centers.

Author's Comment: This unit is based on the use of solidly grounded ac systems, 600V or less, using 90°C insulated copper conductors sized to 75°C terminals unless otherwise specified.

7.2 FLC versus Motor Nameplate

Motors and their associated equipment must be protected against overcurrent (overload, short circuit, or ground fault) [Article 100]. Due to the special characteristics of induction motors, overcurrent protection is generally accomplished by having the overload protection separated from the short-circuit and ground-fault device.

Part III of Article 430 contains the requirements for motor overload protection, and Part IV of Article 430 contains the requirements for motor short-circuit and ground-fault protection.

Table FLC versus Motor Nameplate Current Rating [430.6]

(A) General Requirements. Figure 7–2

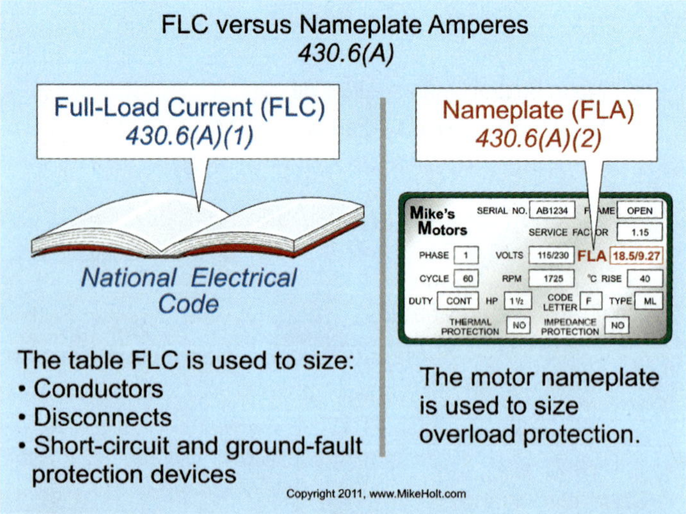

Figure 7–2

(1) Table Full-Load Current (FLC). The motor full-load current ratings listed in Tables 430.247, 430.248, and 430.250 are used to determine the conductor ampacity [430.22], the circuit short-circuit and ground-fault overcurrent device size [430.52 and 430.62], and the ampere rating of disconnecting switches [430.110].

Author's Comment: The actual current rating on the motor nameplate (full-load amperes, or FLA) [430.6(A)(2)] isn't permitted to be used to determine the conductor ampacity (except as covered in 430.22(E) for other than continuous duty), the branch-circuit short-circuit and ground-fault overcurrent device size, nor the ampere rating of disconnecting switches.

Motors built to operate at less than 1,200 RPM or that have high torques may have higher full-load currents, and multispeed motors have full-load current varying with speed, in which case the nameplate current ratings must be used.

Exception No. 3: For a listed motor-operated appliance, the motor full-load current marked on the nameplate of the appliance must be used instead of the horsepower rating on the appliance nameplate to determine the ampacity or rating of the disconnecting means, the branch-circuit conductors, the controller, and the branch-circuit short-circuit and ground-fault protection.

► Table FLC Direct Current Example

Question: *What is the FLC from the NEC Tables for a 5 hp 120V dc motor?*

(a) 28A *(b) 32.20A* *(c) 40A* *(d) 56A*

Answer: *(c) 40A*
5 hp, 120, dc motor = 40A [Table 430.247]

► Table FLC Single-Phase ac Example 1

Question: *What is the FLC from the NEC Tables for a 5 hp 115V ac single-phase motor?*

(a) 28A *(b) 32.20A* *(c) 40A* *(d) 56A*

Answer: *(d) 56A*
5 hp, 125V, ac motor = 56A [Table 430.248]

▶ Table FLC Single-Phase ac Example 2

Question: *What is the FLC from the NEC Tables for a 5 hp 200V ac single-phase motor?*

(a) 28A (b) 32.20A (c) 40A (d) 56A

Answer: *(b) 32.20A*
5 hp, 200V, ac motor = 32.20A [Table 430.248]

▶ Table FLC Single-Phase ac Example 3

Question: *What is the FLC from the NEC Tables for a 5 hp 208V ac single-phase motor?*

(a) 30.80A (b) 32.20A (c) 40A (d) 56A

Answer: *(a) 30.80A*
5 hp, 208V, ac motor = 30.80A [Table 430.248]

▶ Table FLC Single-Phase ac Example 4

Question: *What is the FLC from the NEC Tables for a 5 hp 230V ac single-phase motor?*

(a) 28A (b) 31A (c) 39A (d) 52A

Answer: *(a) 28A*
5 hp, 230V, ac motor = 28A [Table 430.248]

▶ Table FLC Three-Phase ac Example 1

Question: *What is the FLC from the NEC Tables for a 5 hp 230V ac three-phase motor?*

(a) 11A (b) 15.20A (c) 40A (d) 56A

Answer: *(b) 15.20A*
5 hp, 230V, three-phase ac motor = 15.20A [Table 430.250]

▶ Table FLC Three-Phase ac Example 2

Question: *What is the FLC from the NEC Tables for a 25 hp 230V ac three-phase motor?*

(a) 28A (b) 35.20A (c) 40A (d) 68A

Answer: *(d) 68A*
5 hp, 230V, three-phase ac induction motor = 68A [Table 430.250]

▶ Table FLC Three-Phase ac Example 3

Question: *What is the FLC from the NEC Tables for a 25 hp 230V ac three-phase motor with a 90 percent power factor?*

(a) 48A (b) 55.20A (c) 66.50A (d) 74.80A

Answer: *(d) 74.80A*
5 hp, 230V, three-phase ac induction motor = 68A [Table 430.250]
[For a 90 percent power factor multiply the table values by 1.10 per footnote to Table 430.250]
68A x 1.10 = 74.80A

(2) Motor Nameplate Current Rating (FLA). Overload devices must be sized based on the motor nameplate current rating in accordance with 430.31.

> **Author's Comment:** The motor nameplate full-load ampere rating is identified as "full-load amperes" (FLA). The FLA rating is the current in amperes the motor draws while producing its rated horsepower load at its rated voltage, based on its rated efficiency and power factor. **Figures 7–3 and 7–4**

The actual current drawn by the motor depends upon the load on the motor and on the actual operating voltage at the motor terminals. That is, if the load increases, the current also increases, or if the motor operates at a voltage below its nameplate rating, the operating current will increase.

> **Author's Comment:** Other factors that may affect a motor's performance and output include varying duty and environmental factors such as installation at higher elevations. Check with motor manufacturers for more information on these topics.

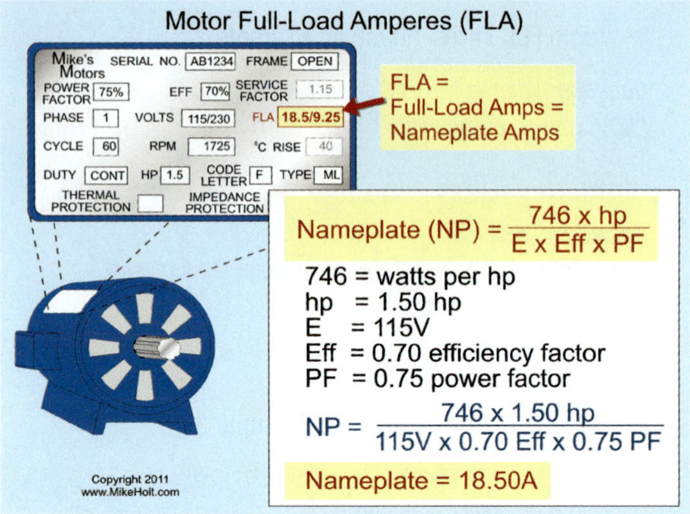

Figure 7–3

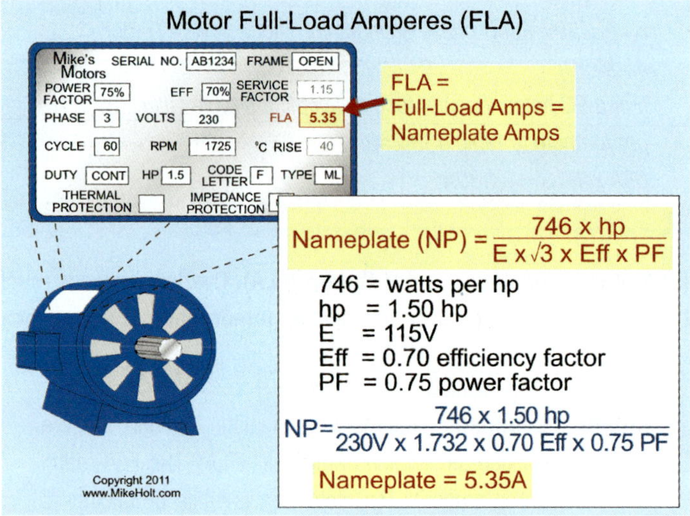

Figure 7–4

CAUTION: *To prevent damage to motor windings from excessive heat (caused by excessive current), never load a motor above its horsepower rating, and be sure the voltage source matches the motor's voltage rating.*

7.3 Highest Rated Motor [430.17]

When selecting the feeder conductors or the feeder short-circuit ground-fault protection device, the highest rated motor must be the highest rated motor FLC (not the highest rated horsepower) [430.17].

► Highest Rated Motor

Question: *Which of the following is the highest rated motor?* **Figure 7–5**

(a) 10 hp, 208V, three-phase *(b) 3 hp, 208V, single-phase*
(c) 3 hp, 120V, single-phase *(d) any of these*

Answer: *(c) 3 hp, 120V, single-phase*

10 hp, 208V, three-phase = 30.80A [Table 430.250]

3 hp, 208V, single-phase = 18.70A [Table 430.248]

3 hp, 120V, single-phase = 34A [Table 430.248]

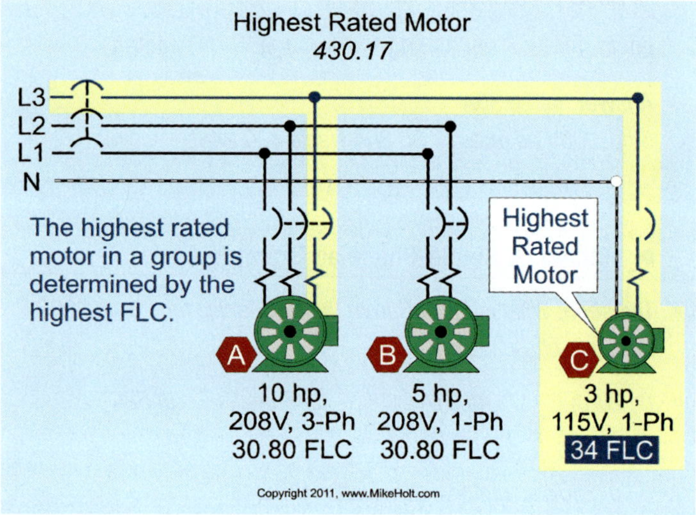

Figure 7–5

7.4 Branch-Circuit Conductor Size

Branch-circuit conductors to a single motor used for continuous duty must have an ampacity of not less than 125 percent of the motor's full-load current (FLC) as listed in Tables 430.247 through 430.250 [430.6(A)(1) and 430.22], **Figure 7–6**. When selecting motor current from one of these tables, note that the last sentence above each table allows us to use the ampacity columns for a range of system voltages without any adjustment. The actual conductor size must be selected from Table 310.15(B)(16) according to the terminal temperature rating (60°C or 75°C) of the equipment [110.14(C)].

Author's Comment: The *Code* book tables list the motor rated current based on motor rated voltages. Common system voltage ranges of 110 to 120, 220 to 240, 440 to 480V are allowed to be used with the motor rated current.

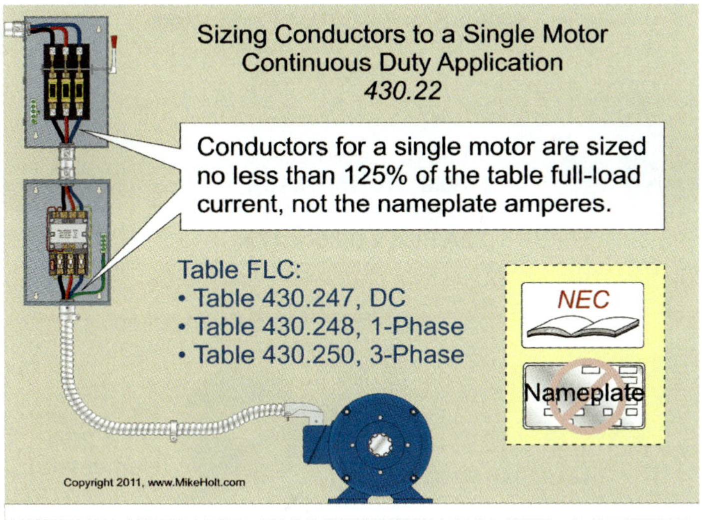

Figure 7–6

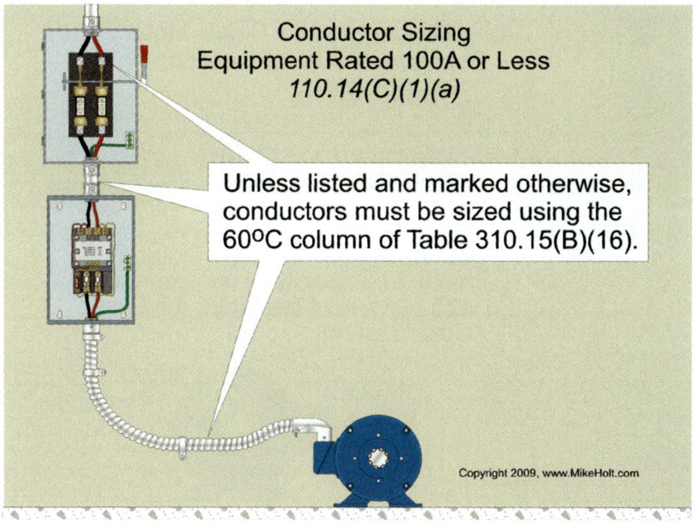

Figure 7–7

THHN/THWN is a common conductor insulation type which can be used in a dry location at the THHN 90°C ampacity, or in a wet location using the 75°C ampacity for the THWN insulation type. Regardless of the conductor insulation type, the conductor must be sized based on the rules of 110.14(C).

Motor applications are considered to be continuous duty unless the nature of the control or apparatus that the motor drives is designed in a way so that the motor won't operate continuously with load [Table 430.22(E) Note]. When a motor isn't continuous duty because of this type of application, the conductors are sized using the percentages of Table 430.22(E). If a motor must stop during the course of performing its function, such as a garage door operator, that is a good sign that it is intermittent duty.

Author's Comment: 110.14(C)(1)(a) tells us that terminals are rated 60°C for equipment rated 100A or less unless marked 75°C. **Figure 7–7** In real life, most terminals are now rated 75°C, so in this unit we'll assume all motors are rated 75°C unless specified 60°C . For equipment with terminals rated over 100A, conductors are sized using the 75°C column of Table 310.15(B)(16). For exam purposes, read the problem carefully to be certain you know what terminal temperature rating the exam question specifies. If unspecified, use the rules of 110.14(C).

► Motor Branch-Circuit Conductors

Question: *What size branch-circuit conductors are required for a 7½ hp, three-phase, 230V motor?* **Figure 7–8**

(a) 14 AWG (b) 12 AWG (c) 10 AWG (d) 8 AWG

Answer: *(c) 10 AWG*

Motor FLC [Table 430.250]:
7 ½ hp, 230V, three-phase FLC = 22A

The conductor is sized no less than 125 percent of motor FLC: 22A x 1.25 = 27.50A, Table 310.15(B)(16), 10 AWG has an ampacity of 35A at 75°C

Note: Any motor application must be considered as continuous duty unless the nature of the apparatus it drives is such that the motor will not operate continuously under any condition of use [Note to Table 430.22(E)]

Author's Comment: The motor full-load current (FLC) is from the *Code* Tables [430.6(A)(1)] which isn't the same thing as the motor full-load amperes (FLA), which is the motor's nameplate rating [430.6(A)(2)].

When a motor is used for other than continuous duty, the nameplate current rating percentages of Table 430.22(E) are used for conductor sizing [430.22(E)].

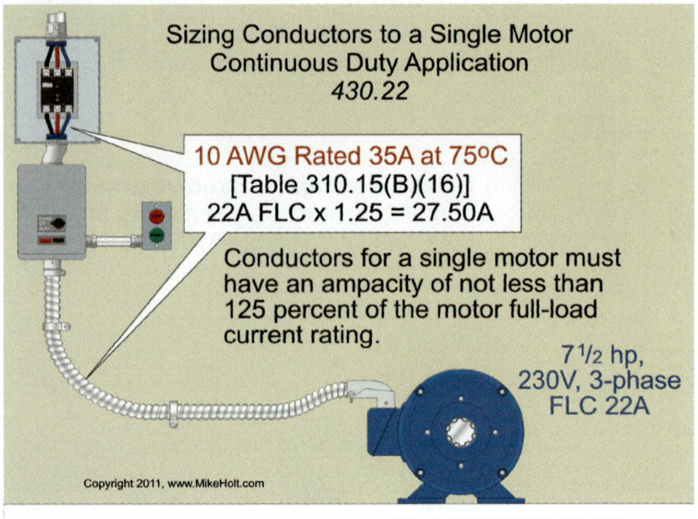

Figure 7–8

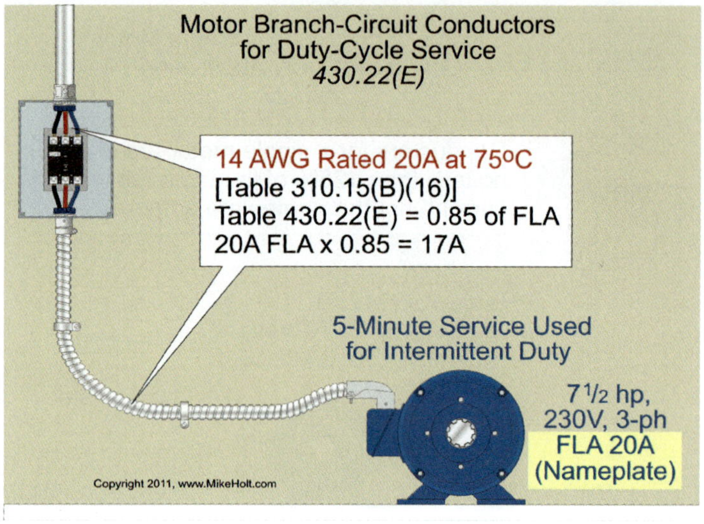

Figure 7–9

► Motor Branch-Circuit Conductors for Duty-Cycle Service [Table 430.22(E)]

Question: *What size branch-circuit conductors are required for a 7½ hp, three-phase, 230V motor with nameplate FLA of 20A, rated for 5-minute service, used for intermittent duty?* **Figure 7–9**

(a) 14 AWG (b) 12 AWG (c) 10 AWG (d) 8 AWG

Answer: *(a) 14 AWG*

Motor FLA from nameplate is used with Table 430.22(E) for Duty-Cycle service FLA = 20A

The conductor is sized no less than 85 percent of motor FLA [Table 430.22(E)]: 20A x 0.85 = 17A, Table 310.15(B)(16), 14 AWG has an ampacity of 20A at 75ºC

Note: The minimum size conductor permitted for building wiring is 14 AWG [Table 310.106(A)]; however, some local codes and many industrial facilities have requirements that 12 AWG be used as the smallest branch-circuit conductor.

Author's Comment: The motor full-load amps from the motor nameplate is used with Table 430.22(E) instead of the full-load current (FLC) from the Code Tables [430.6(A)(1)].

► Motor Branch-Circuit Conductors for Duty-Cycle Service [Table 430.22(E)]

Question: *What size branch-circuit conductors are required for a 7½ hp, three-phase, 230V motor with nameplate FLA of 20A, rated for 30-minute service, used for short-time duty?* **Figure 7–10**

(a) 14 AWG (b) 12 AWG (c) 10 AWG (d) 8 AWG

Answer: *(c) 10 AWG*

Motor FLA from nameplate is used with Table 430.22(E) for Duty-Cycle service FLA = 20A

The conductor is sized no less than 150 percent of motor FLA [Table 430.22(E)]: 20A x 1.50 = 30A, Table 310.15(B)(16), 10 AWG has an ampacity of 35A at 75ºC

Adjustable Speed Drive Conductor Sizing Example

Circuit conductors supplying power conversion equipment included as part of an adjustable-speed drive system must have an ampacity not less than 125 percent of the rated input current to the power conversion equipment [430.122(A)].

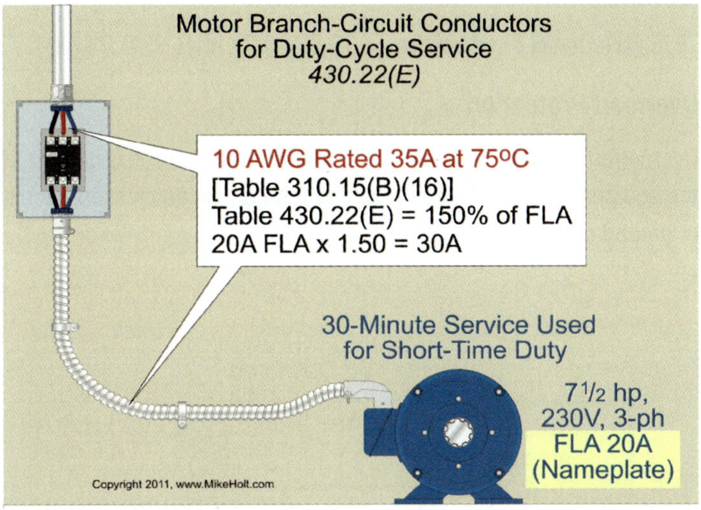

Figure 7–10

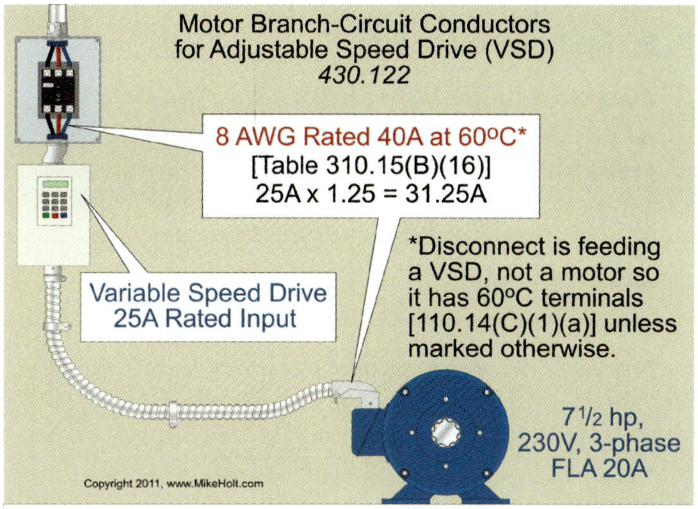

Figure 7–11

► Motor Branch-Circuit Conductors for Adjustable Speed Drive Systems [430.122]

Question: *What size branch-circuit conductors are required for a 7½ hp, three-phase, 230V motor on an adjustable-speed drive system with rated input of 25A when the terminals of the adjustable speed drive are rated 60ºC?* **Figure 7–11**

(a) 14 AWG (b) 12 AWG (c) 10 AWG (d) 8 AWG

Answer: *(d) 8 AWG*

Rated input from variable frequency drive = 25A

25A x 1.25=31.25A Table 310.15(B)(16), 8 AWG has an ampacity of 40A at 60ºC

Note: for adjustable speed drives, see Article 430, Part X. Short-circuit and ground fault protection sizing is still calculated using 430.51 and all other parts of Article 430 Part I through Part IX are applicable unless modified by Part X [430.120].

7.5 Feeder Conductor Size [430.24]

Conductors that supply several motors must have an ampacity of not less than:

(1) 125 percent of the highest rated motor FLC [430.17], plus

(2) The sum of the FLCs of the other motors (on the same line). The motor FLC is found using the *NEC* Tables [430.6(A)(1)], plus

(3) 100 percent of any non-continuous non-motor load, plus

(4) 125 percent of the continuous non-motor load.

Author's Comment: The highest rated motor is based on the motor with the highest full-load current [430.17]. The "other motors in the group" value (on the same line) is determined by balancing the motors' FLCs on the feeder being sized, then selecting the line that has the highest rated motor on it (refer to Section 7.3 and **Figure 7–12**).

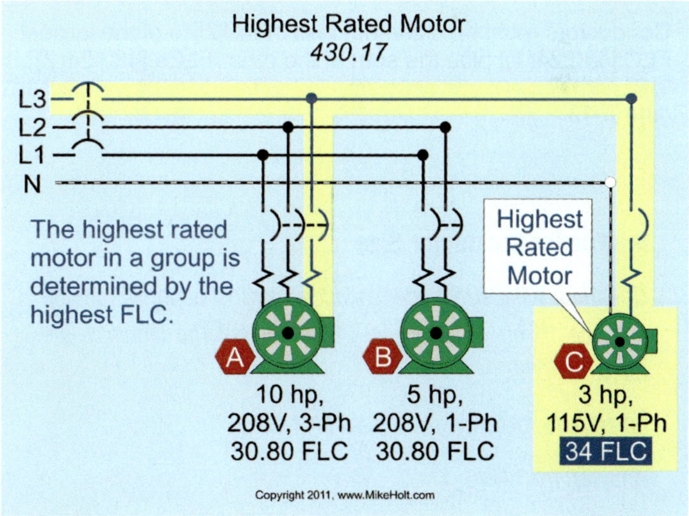

Figure 7–12

► Feeder Conductor Size

Question: *What size feeder conductor is required for two 7½ hp, three-phase, 230V motors? The terminals are rated for 75°C.* **Figure 7–13**

(a) 10 AWG (b) 8 AWG (c) 6 AWG (d) 4 AWG

Answer: *(b) 8 AWG*

(22A x 1.25) + 22A = 49.50A

Note: An 8 AWG conductor is rated 50A at 75°C [Table 310.15(B)(16)].

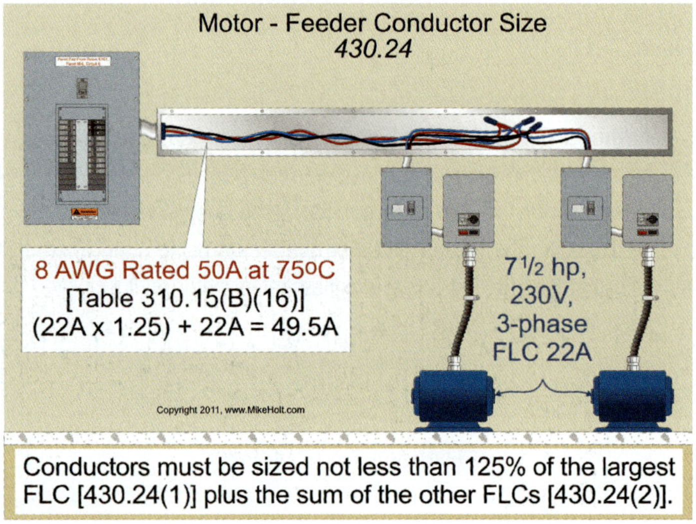

Figure 7–13

► Feeder Conductor Size

Question: *What size feeder conductor is required for two 7½ hp and one 15 hp, three-phase, 230V motors? The terminals are rated for 75°C.*

(a) 10 AWG (b) 8 AWG (c) 3 AWG (d) 4 AWG

Answer: *(c) 3 AWG*

7 ½ hp, three phase, 230V motor = 22A FLC [Table 430.250]
15 hp, three phase, 230V motor = 42A FLC [Table 430.250]
(42A x 1.25) + 22A + 22A = 96.50 A
3 AWG has an ampacity of 100A at 75°C.

7.6 Overload Protection [430.6(A)(2) and 430.32(A)]

Overload Protection

Overcurrent is current, in amperes, greater than the rated current of the equipment or conductors resulting from an overload, short circuit, or ground fault. **Figure 7–14**

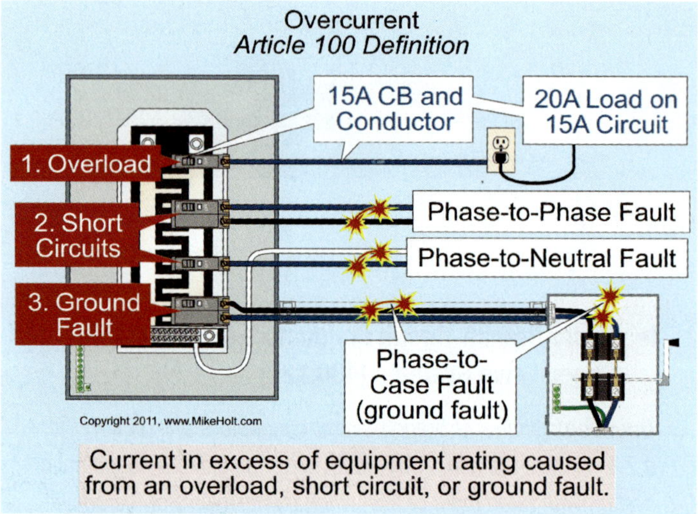

Figure 7–14

In motor circuits, the overcurrent protection function is commonly divided into two separate componenets, one component of providing short-circuit and ground-fault protection and a separate provision for overload protection. Short circuits and ground faults result from faults in the wiring which can carry large amounts of current. Overloads aren't fault conditions, but just the result of excessive current flowing in the circuit. **Figure 7–15**

Overload is the condition where current exceeds the equipment ampere rating, which can result in equipment damage due to dangerous overheating [Article 100]. Overload protection devices, sometimes called "heaters" are intended to protect the motor, the motor control equipment, and the branch-circuit conductors from excessive heating due to motor overload [430.31]. **Figure 7–16**

Overload protection isn't intended to protect against short circuits or ground-fault currents.

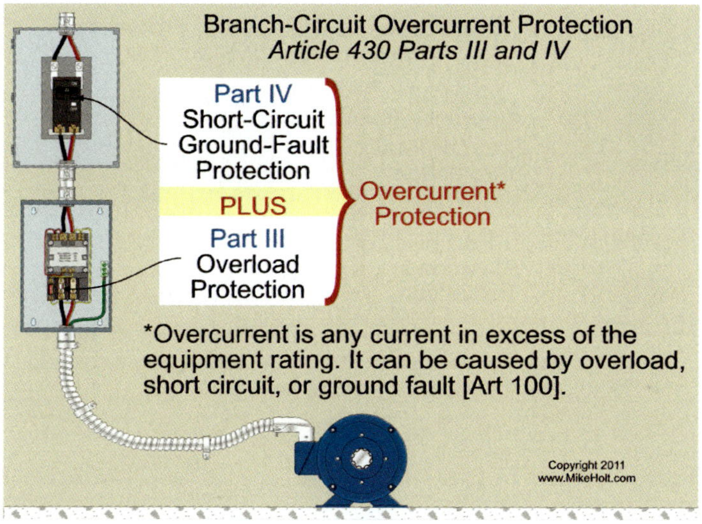

Figure 7–15

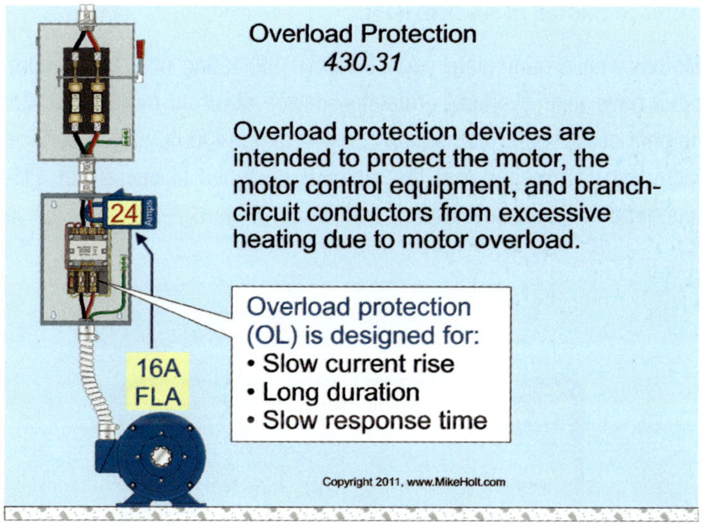

Figure 7–16

Overload protection devices (OLs) are intended to protect motors, motor control apparatus, and motor branch-circuit conductors against excessive heating due to motor overloads and failure to start. It's possible for a motor to become so hot it will burn out or start a fire. Some of the causes of overload are:

Low voltage to the motor.

A locked rotor.

The motor is too small for the application.

Bad bearings.

Single-phasing, meaning one conductor of a three-phase circuit fails, causing it to run on two phases.

Overload devices must have enough time delay built in to stay closed during the high starting current of the motor,

Modern overload devices can take many forms, from simple heaters installed in an overload relay of a magnetic motor starter to more sophisticated means such as entering the nameplate FLA via a computer or other man-to-machine interface. Often the math of 430.32 is not necessary, only the FLA from the nameplate. For testing purposes, we will discuss the math behind overload protection. If overload protection is accomplished using fuses, a fuse must be installed for each ungrounded conductor [430.36 and 430.55]. **Figure 7–17**

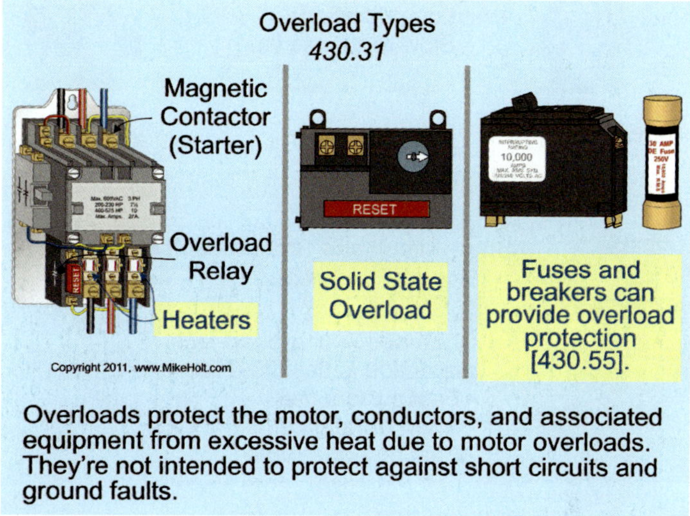

Figure 7–17

Short-Circuit and Ground-Fault Protection

Branch-circuit short-circuit and ground-fault protection devices are intended to protect the motor, the motor control apparatus, and the conductors against short circuits or ground faults, but they're not intended to protect against an overload [430.51]. **Figure 7–18**

Short-circuit or ground-fault protection is designed for fast current rise, short duration, and fast response time. **Figure 7–19**

> **Author's Comment:** The short-circuit and ground-fault protection device required for motor circuits isn't the same thing as the ground-fault circuit-interrupter (GFCI) protection required for personnel [210.8], temporary wiring for receptacles [590.6], or ground-fault protection installed on feeders [215.9 and 240.13] or services [230.95].

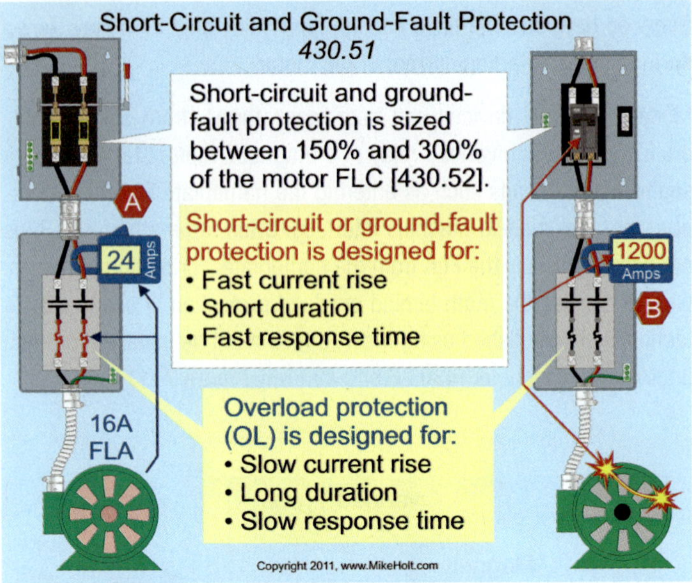

Figure 7–18

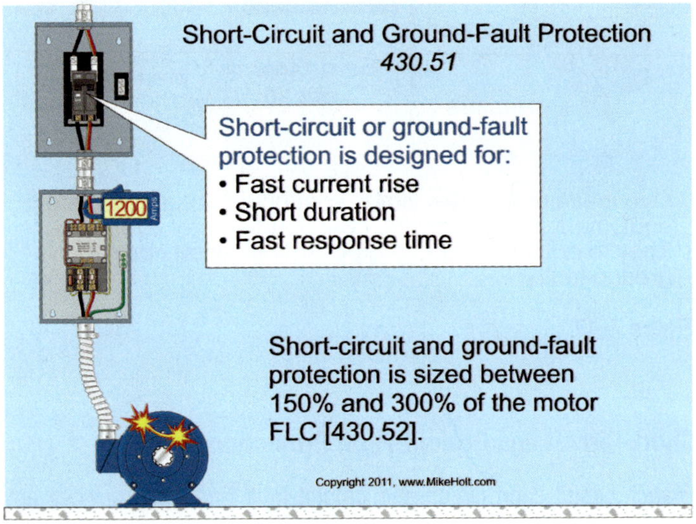

Figure 7–19

In addition to short-circuit and ground-fault protection, motors must be protected against overload. **Figure 7–20** Generally, the motor overload device is part of the motor starter or variable frequency drive (VFD); however, a separate overload device like a dual-element fuse can be used [430.55]. Motors rated more than 1 hp without integral thermal protection, and motors 1 hp or less (automatically started) [430.32(B)], must have an overload device sized in response to the motor nameplate current rating [430.6(A)(2)]. The overload device must be sized no larger than required by 430.32.

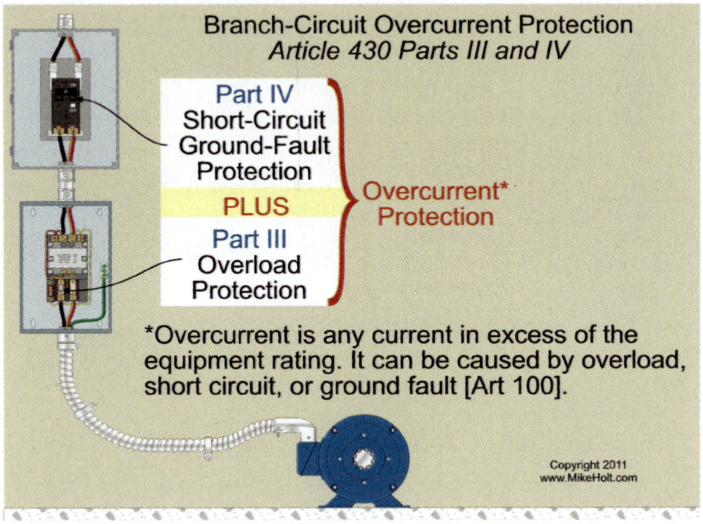

Figure 7–20

Service Factor [430.32(A)(1)]

Motors with a nameplate service factor (SF) rating of 1.15 or more must have their overload protection device sized no more than 125 percent of the motor nameplate current rating [430.6(A)(2)]. A service factor of 1.15 means that the motor is designed to operate at 115 percent of its rated horsepower periodically. **Figure 7–21**

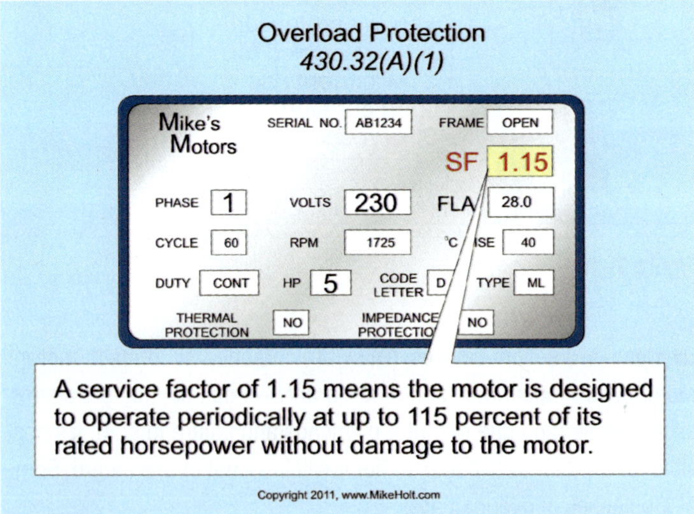

Figure 7–21

Author's Comment: Operation at a higher elevation may require a derating of the motor's service factor. For instance, a motor with a 1.15 service factor at an elevation of 3,300 ft or below is derated to a service factor of 1.00 at 9,000 ft unless the nameplate states that it was designed for a specific elevation. A good resource for motor applications is the website: http://www.electricmotors.com/right-size-motor.html

Motor service factors can be thougth of as safety factors. The service factor indicates how much the motor capacity can be exceeded for short periods without overheating. This is important where loads vary and may peak slightly above the rated torque. A standard design B motor with a service factor of 1.15 can operate at 15% greater than its rated output without overheating. Service factors should be used sparingly as safety margins because if a motor operates continuously above its rated output it will have a short life.

► Service Factor Example 1

Question: *If a dual-element fuse is used for overload protection, what size fuse is required for a 5 hp, 230V, single-phase motor, with a service factor of 1.16, if the motor nameplate current rating is 28A?* **Figure 7–22**

(a) 25A *(b) 30A* *(c) 35A* *(d) 40A*

Answer: *(c) 35A*

Overload protection is sized to the motor nameplate current rating [430.6(A), 430.32(A)(1), and 430.55].

28A x 1.25 = 35A [240.6(A)]

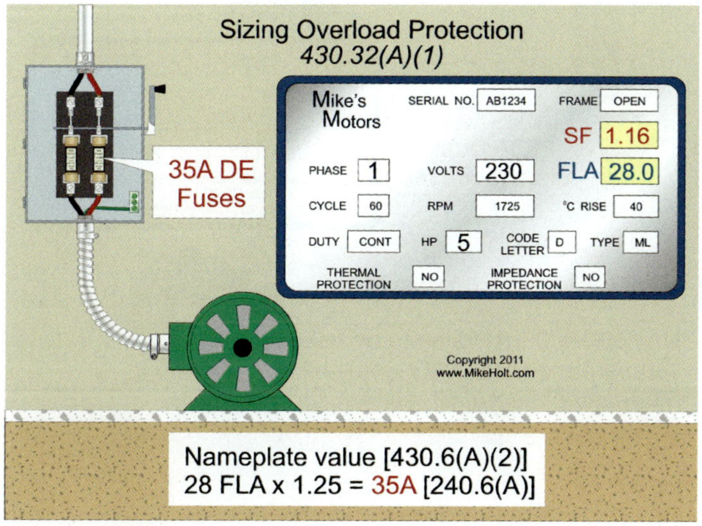

Figure 7–22

In a case where the sensing element or setting or sizing of the motor overload device isn't sufficient to allow the motor to start, or to carry the load, the overload element setting or sizing can be increased, but not to exceed 140 percent for motors with a marked service factor of 1.15 or greater [430.32(C)].

► Service Factor Example 2

Question: *A 35A dual-element fuse is used for overload protection of a 5 hp, 230V, single-phase motor, with a service factor of 1.15, and the motor nameplate current rating is 28A. If the motor is unable to start, what's the maximum size overload allowed?* **Figure 7–23**

(a) 25A *(b) 30A* *(c) 35A* *(d) 40A*

Answer: *(c) 35A*

28A x 1.40 = 39.20A, use a 35A fuse maximum [240.6(A) and 430.32(C)].

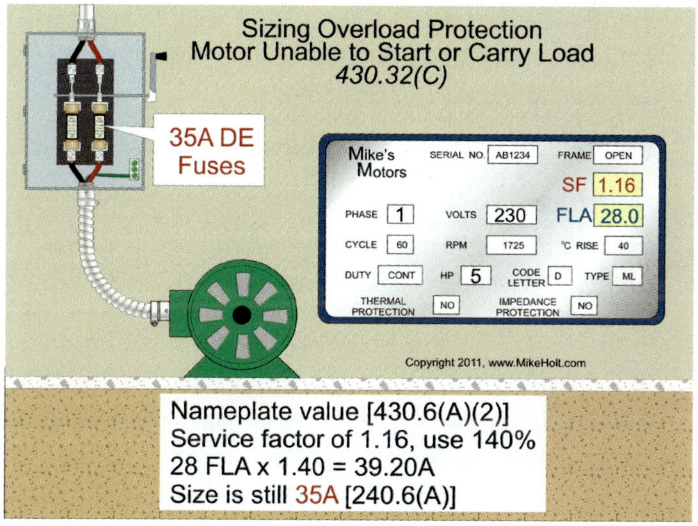

Figure 7–23

Temperature Rise

Motors with a nameplate temperature rise rating not over 40°C must have the overload protection device sized no more than 125 percent of the motor nameplate current rating. A motor with a nameplate temperature rise of 40°C means the motor is designed to operate so that it won't heat up more than 40°C above its rated ambient temperature when operated at its rated load and voltage. Studies have shown that when the operating temperature of a motor is increased 10°C, the motor winding insulating material's anticipated life is reduced by 50 percent. **Figure 7–24**

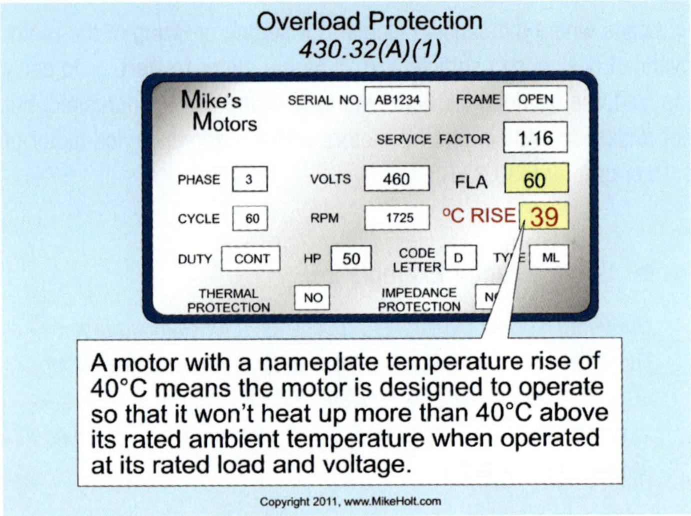

Figure 7–24

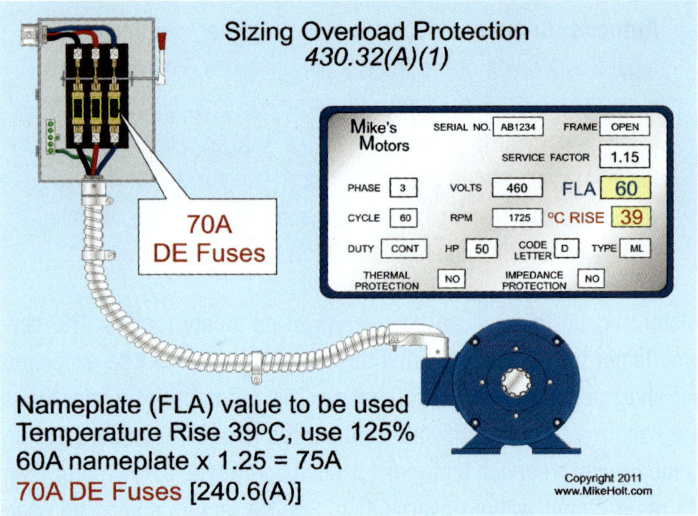

Figure 7–25

▶ Temperature Rise Example 1

Question: *If a dual-element fuse is used for the overload protection, what size fuse is required for a 50 hp, 460V, three-phase motor, with a temperature rise of 39ºC, and a motor nameplate current rating of 60A (FLA)?* **Figure 7–25**

(a) 40A *(b) 50A* *(c) 60A* *(d) 70A*

Answer: *(d) 70A*

Overloads are sized according to the motor nameplate current rating, not the motor FLC rating from the Code book tables.

60A x 1.25 = 75A, use a 70A fuse [240.6(a) and 430.32(A)(1)]

When using a fuse for overload protection, the values of 430.32(A)(1) aren't to be exceeded, so we must round down to the next smaller fuse. Standard fuse sizes are listed in 240.6(A).

In a case where the motor overload isn't of sufficient size to allow the motor to start, the overload size can be increased, but not to exceed 140 percent for motors with a marked temperature rise of 40°C or less [430.32(C)].

▶ Temperature Rise Example 2

Question: *A 70A dual-element fuse is used for overload protection for a 50 hp, 460V, three-phase motor, with a temperature rise of 39ºC, and a motor nameplate current rating of 60A (FLA). If the motor is unable to start, what's the maximum size overload allowed?* **Figure 7–26**

(a) 50A *(b) 60A* *(c) 70A* *(d) 80A*

Answer: *(d) 80A*

60A x 1.40 = 84A, use an 80A fuse maximum [240.6(A)].

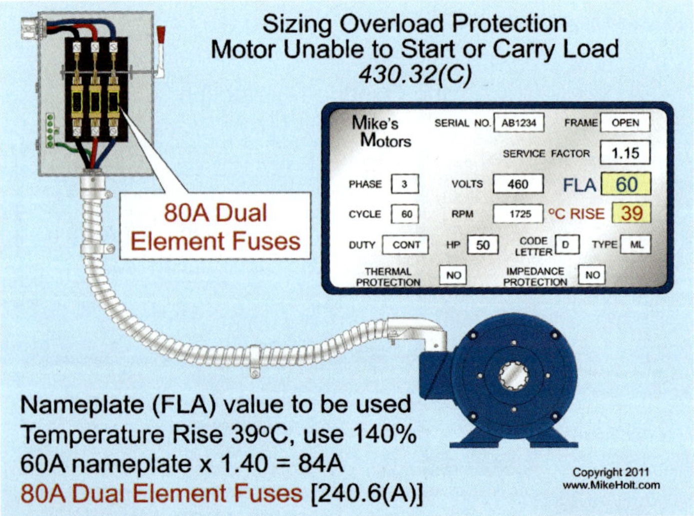

Figure 7–26

All Other Motors

Motors that don't have a service factor rating of 1.15 and up, or a temperature rise rating of 40ºC and less, must have the overload protection device sized at not more than 115 percent of the motor nameplate ampere rating [430.32(A)(1)].

► Other Motors Example 1

Question: *A motor has a nameplate that specifies the following: The service factor is 1.12, with a temperature rise of 41ºC, and a nameplate current rating of 25A. What size dual-element fuse is required when used for overload protection of this motor?* **Figure 7–27**

(a) 20A *(b) 25A* *(c) 30A* *(d) 40A*

Answer: *(b) 25A*

Since 1.12 is less than 1.15 for the service factor, and 41ºC is over 40ºC, the overload protection is sized based on 115 percent of the motor nameplate ampere rating.

25A x 1.15 = 28.75A, round down to 25A [240.6(A)]

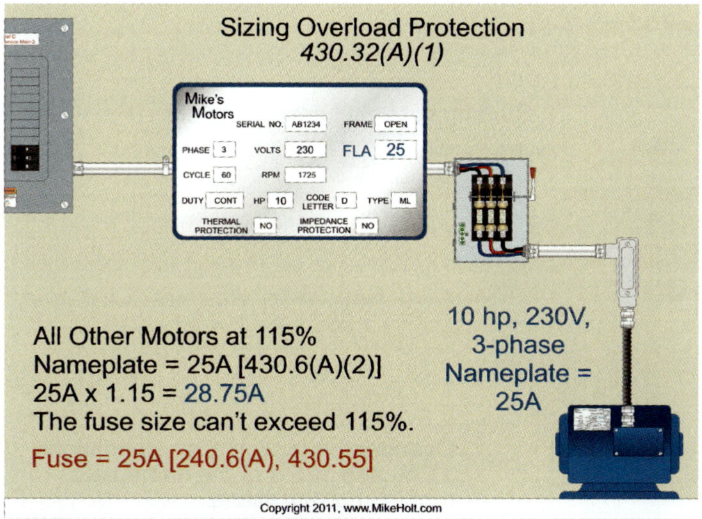

Figure 7–27

In a case where the motor overload isn't of sufficient size to allow the motor to start, the overload size can be increased, but not to exceed 130 percent for motors with a service factor of less than 1.15 and a marked temperature rise of over 40°C [430.32(C)].

► Other Motors Example 2

Question: *A 25A dual-element fuse is used for overload protection for a 10 hp, 230V, three-phase motor, with a temperature rise of 41ºC, a service factor of 1.12, and a motor nameplate current rating of 25A (FLA). If the motor is unable to start, what's the maximum size overload protection allowed?* **Figure 7–28**

(a) 20A *(b) 25A* *(c) 30A* *(d) 40A*

Answer: *(c) 30A*

25A x 1.30 =32.50A, use a 30A maximum fuse size [240.6(A)]

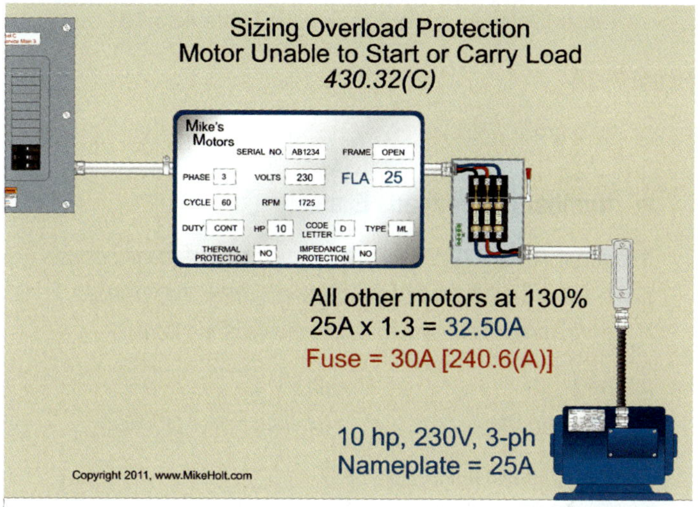

Figure 7–28

Number of Overloads [430.37]

An overload protection device must be installed in ungrounded conductors according to the requirements of Table 430.37. If fuses are used for overload protection, a fuse must be installed in each ungrounded conductor [430.36]. **Figure 7–29**

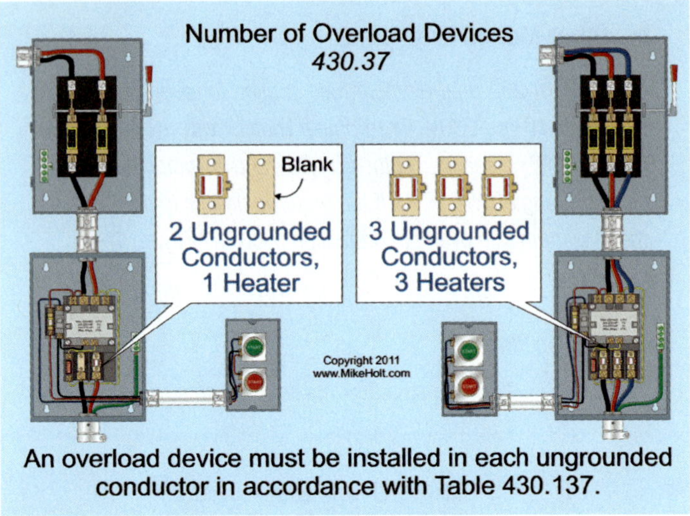

Figure 7–29

▶ Number of Overloads Example

Question: *For a 230V, single-phase motor which does not use fuses for overload protection, overloads must be installed in ______ to meet the minimum requirements of the Code.*

(a) line 1 *(b) line 2*
(c) line 1 and line 2 *(d) either line 1 or line 2*

Answer: *(d)) either line 1 or line 2*
[Table 430.37]

7.7 Branch-Circuit Short-Circuit and Ground-Fault Protection [430.51]

General [430.51]

A branch-circuit short-circuit and ground-fault protective device protects the motor, the motor control apparatus, and the conductors against short circuits or ground faults, but not against overload. Figure 7–30

Author's Comment: Overload protection must comply with the requirements contained in 430.32.

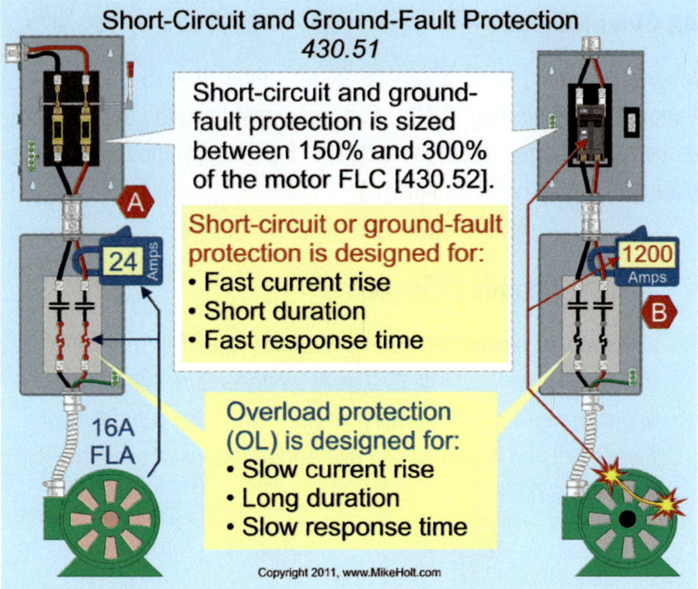

Figure 7–30

Motor-Starting Current. When voltage is first applied to the field winding of an induction motor, only the conductor resistance opposes the flow of current through the motor winding. Because the conductor resistance is so low, the motor will have a very large inrush current. Figure 7–31

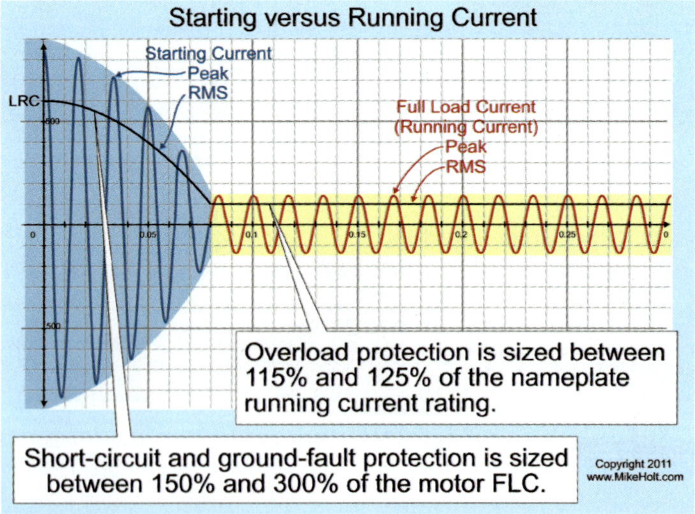

Figure 7–31

Motor-Running Current. Once the rotor comes up to speed, the motor current settles to it's running value.

Motor Locked-Rotor Current (LRC). If the rotating part of the motor winding (armature) becomes jammed so it can't rotate, no counter-electromotive force (CEMF) will be produced in the motor winding. This results in a decrease in conductor impedance to the point that it's effectively a short circuit. As a result the motor will operate at locked-rotor current (LRC), often six times the full-load ampere rating, depending on the motor's code letter rating [430.7(B)]. This will cause the motor winding to overheat and be destroyed if the current isn't quickly reduced or removed.

Author's Comment: The *National Electrical Code* requires that most motors be provided with overcurrent protection to prevent damage to the motor winding because of locked-rotor current.

Branch-Circuit Short-Circuit and Ground-Fault Protection [430.52]

(A) General. The motor branch-circuit short-circuit and ground-fault protective device must comply with 430.52(B) and 430.52(C).

(B) All Motors. A motor branch-circuit short-circuit and ground-fault protective device must be capable of carrying the motor's starting current.

(C) Rating or Setting.

(1) Table 430.52. Each motor branch circuit must be protected against short circuit and ground faults by an overcurrent device sized no greater than the following percentages listed in Table 430.52.

Author's Comment: Instantaneous Trip Breakers are not shown on this chart, as Inverse Time Breakers are much more commonly used.

Branch-Circuit Protection Table 430.52

Circuit Motor Type	Nontime Delay	Dual-Element Fuse	Inverse Time Breaker
Direct Current	150%	150%	150%
Wound Rotor	150%	150%	150%
All Other Motors	300%	175%	250%

► Branch-Circuit Short-Circuit and Ground-Fault Protection Example 1

Question: *What size conductor and inverse time circuit breaker are required for a 2 hp, 230V, single-phase motor?* **Figure 7–32**

(a) 14 AWG, 30A breaker *(b) 14 AWG, 35A breaker*
(c) 14 AWG, 40A breaker *(d) 14 AWG, 45A breaker*

Answer: (a) 14 AWG, 30A breaker

Step 1: Determine the branch-circuit conductor [Table 310.15(B)(16), 430.22(A), and Table 430.248]:

12A x 1.25 = 15A, 14 AWG, rated 20A at 75°C [Table 310.15(B)(16)]

Step 2: Determine the branch-circuit protection [240.6(A), 430.52(C)(1), and Table 430.248]:

12A x 2.50 = 30A

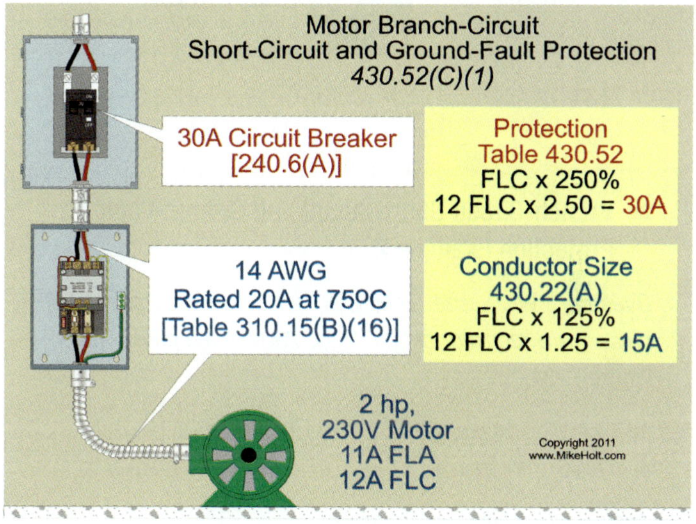

Figure 7–32

Author's Comment: I know it bothers many in the electrical industry to see a 14 AWG conductor protected by a 30A circuit breaker, but branch-circuit conductors are protected against overloads by the overload device, which is sized between 115 and 125 percent of the motor nameplate current rating [430.32]. See 240.4(G) for details.

Exception No. 1: Where the motor short-circuit and ground-fault protective device values derived from Table 430.52 don't correspond with the standard overcurrent device ratings listed in 240.6(A), the next higher overcurrent device rating can be used. **Figure 7–33**

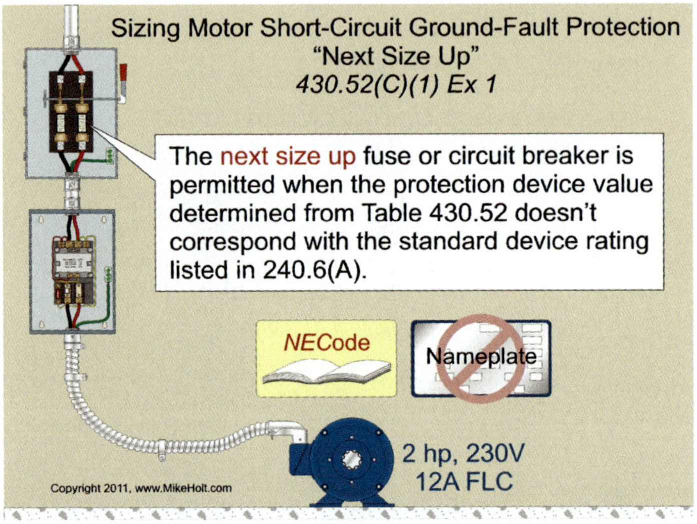

Figure 7–33

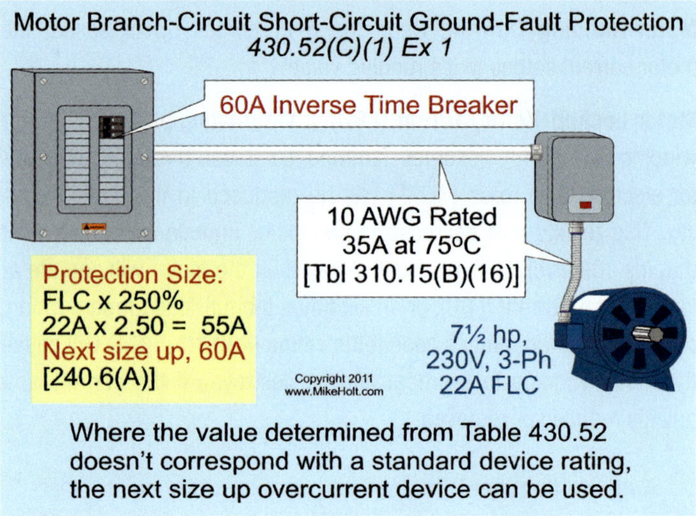

Figure 7–34

► Branch-Circuit Short-Circuit and Ground-Fault Protection Example 2

Question: *What size conductor and inverse time circuit breaker are required for a 7½ hp, 230V, three-phase motor?* **Figure 7–34**

(a) 10 AWG, 50A breaker *(b) 10 AWG, 60A breaker*
(c) 8 AWG, 70A breaker *(d) 8 AWG, 80A breaker*

Answer: *(b) 10 AWG, 60A breaker*

Step 1: Determine the branch-circuit conductor [Table 310.15(B)(16), 430.22(A), and Table 430.250]:

22A x 1.25 = 27.50A, 10 AWG, rated 35A at 75°C [Table 310.15(B)(16)]

Step 2: Determine the branch-circuit protection [240.6(A), 430.52(C)(1) Ex 1, and Table 430.250]:

22A x 2.50 = 55A, next size up = 60A

► Branch-Circuit Short-Circuit and Ground-Fault Protection Example 3

Question: *What size nontime-delay fuses are required for a 2 hp, 230V, single-phase motor?* **Figure 7–35**

(a) 30A fuse *(b) 35A fuse* *(c) 40A fuse* *(d) 45A fuse*

Answer: *(c) 40A fuse*

Determine the branch-circuit protection [240.6(A), 430.52(C)(1), and Table 430.248]:

12A x 3 = 36A, use a 40A nontime-delay fuse

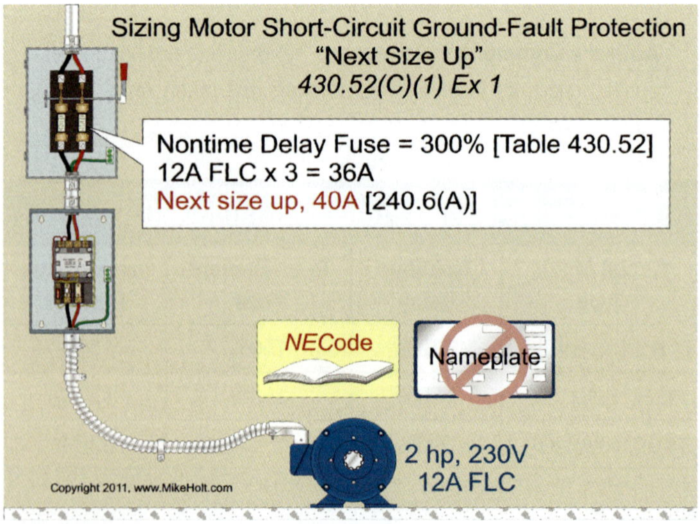

Figure 7–35

► Branch-Circuit Short-Circuit and Ground-Fault Protection Example 4

Question: *What size time-delay fuses are required for a 2 hp, 230V, single-phase motor?*

(a) 25A fuse (b) 30A fuse (c) 35A fuse (d) 40A fuse

Answer: *(a) 25A fuse*

Determine the branch-circuit protection [240.6(A), 430.52(C)(1), and Table 430.248]:

12A x1.75 = 21A, use a 25A time-delay fuse

7.8 Branch-Circuit Summary

Branch-Circuit Conductors [430.22(A)]

Branch-circuit conductors to a single motor must have an ampacity of not less than 125 percent of the motor FLC as listed in Tables 430.247 through 430.250 [430.6(A)]. **Figure 7–36**

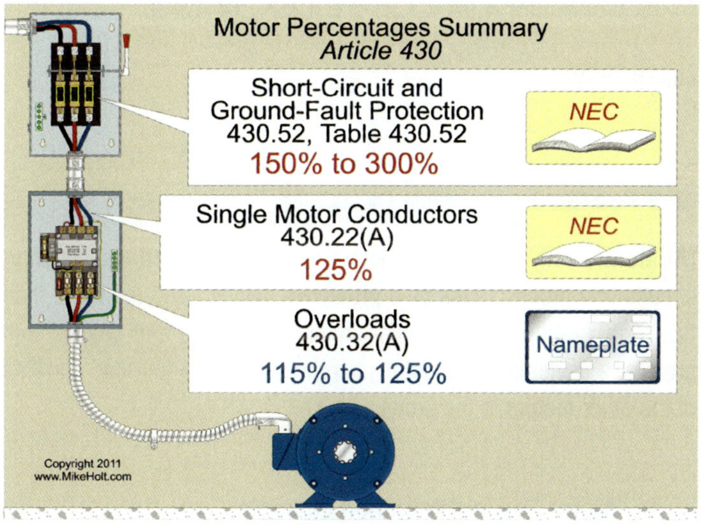

Figure 7–36

Branch-Circuit Short-Circuit Protection [430.52(C)(1)]

The branch-circuit short-circuit and ground-fault protection device protects the motor, the motor control apparatus, and the conductors against overcurrent due to short circuits or ground faults, but not against overloads [430.51]. The branch-circuit short-circuit and ground-fault protection devices are sized by considering the type of motor and the type of protection device and applying the percent of motor FLC listed in Table 430.52. When the protection device values determined from Table 430.52 don't correspond with the standard rating of overcurrent devices as listed in 240.6(A), the next higher overcurrent device can be installed [430.52(C)(1) Ex 1].

Overload Protection [430.32(A)]

Overload protection is sized based on the motor nameplate rating.

► Branch Circuit Summary Example 1

Question: *If an inverse time circuit breaker is used for short-circuit and ground-fault protection, what size circuit breaker and conductor is required for a 5 hp, 230V, single-phase motor having a nameplate current rating of 26A?* **Figure 7–37**

(a) 10 AWG, 50A breaker (b) 10 AWG, 60A breaker
(c) 10 AWG, 70A breaker (d) 8 AWG, 80A breaker

Answer: *(c) 10 AWG, 70A breaker*

Motor FLC = 28A [Table 430.248].

Conductors: 28A x 1.25 = 35A. 10AWG is rated 35A at 75°C [Table 310.15(B)(16)]

Circuit breaker: 28A x 2.50 = 70A [Table 430.52]

Overload Protection: 26A x 1.15 = 29.90 [430.32]

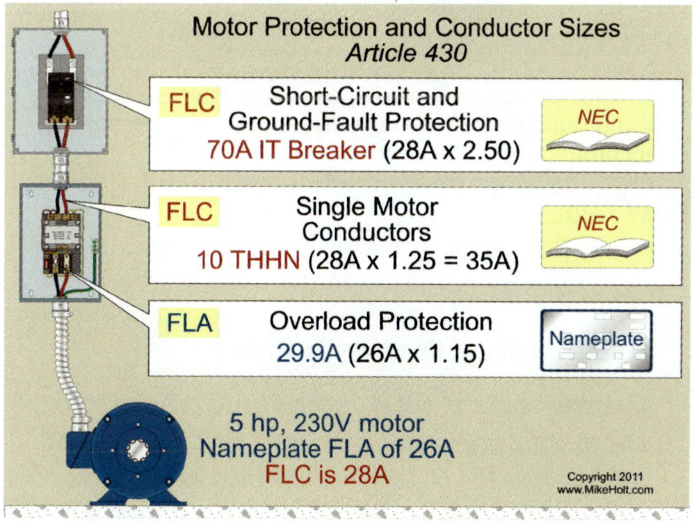

Figure 7–37

Single Overcurrent Device [430.55]

A motor can be protected against overload, short circuit, and ground faults by a single overcurrent device sized to the overload requirements contained in 430.32.

► Branch Circuit Summary Example 2

Question: *What size dual-element fuse is permitted to protect a 5 hp, 230V, single-phase motor with a service factor of 1.15 and a nameplate current rating of 28A from overloads as well as short-circuits and ground-faults?* **Figure 7–38**

(a) 20A (b) 25A (c) 30A (d) 35A

Answer: *(d) 35A*

Overload Protection [430.32(A)(1) and 430.55]

28A x 1.25 = 35A

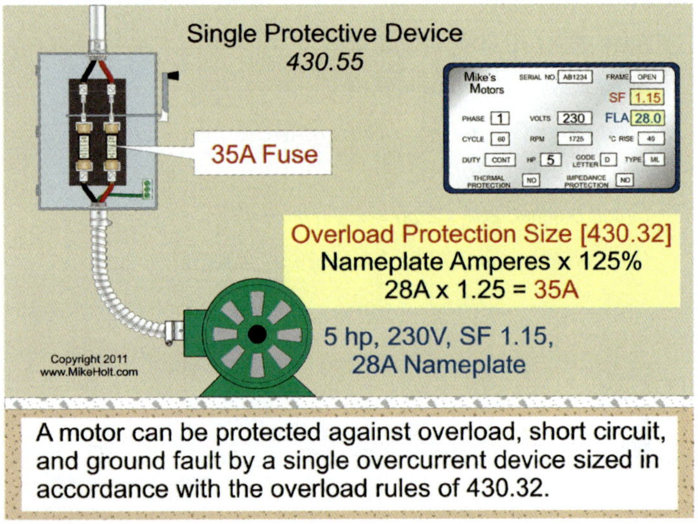

Figure 7–38

► Branch Circuit Summary Example 3

Question: *What size dual-element fuse is permitted to protect a ½ hp, 230V, single-phase motor with a service factor of 1.20 and nameplate FLA of 4.90A from overloads as well as short-circuits and ground-faults?* **Figure 7–39**

(a) 3A (b) 6A (c) 10A (d) 15A

Answer: *(b) 6A*

Overload Protection [430.32(A)(1) and 430.55] (when the nameplate FLA isn't given, we can use the FLC from the Tables)

FLC = 4.90A [Table 430.248]

4.90A x 1.25 = 6.125A. Use a 6A fuse [240.6(A)]

The conductor will be sized at: 4.90A x 1.25 = 6.125A, 14AWG is rated 20A at 75°C [Table 310.15(B)(16)].

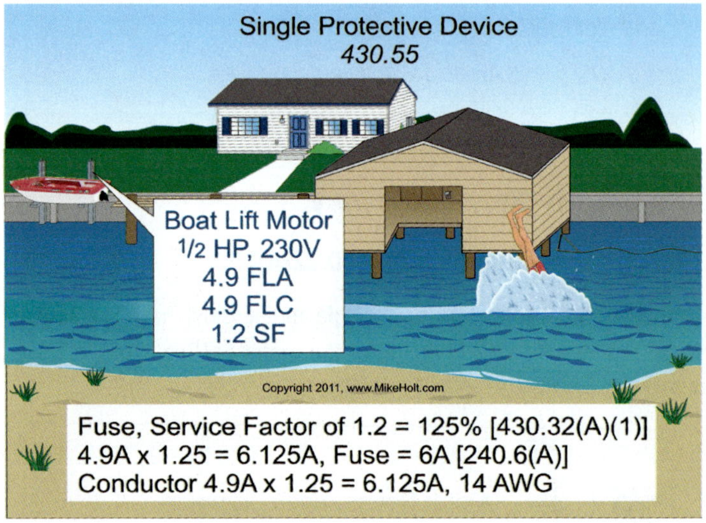

Figure 7–39

7.9 Feeder Protection [430.62]

(A) Motors Only. Feeder conductors must be protected against short circuits and ground faults by a protective device sized not more than the largest rating of the branch-circuit short-circuit and ground-fault protective device for any motor, plus the sum of the full-load currents of the other motors in the group.

► Motor Feeder Protection Example

Question: *What size feeder protection (inverse time breakers with 75°C terminals) and conductors are required for the following two motors?* **Figure 7–40**

Motor 1—10 hp, 460V, three-phase: FLC = 14A [Table 430.250]

Motor 2—20 hp, 460V, three-phase: FLC = 27A [Table 430.250]

(a) 8 AWG, 70A breaker *(b) 8 AWG, 80A breaker*
(c) 8 AWG, 90A breaker *(d) 10 AWG, 90A breaker*

Answer: *(b) 8 AWG, 80A breaker*

Step 1: Determine the feeder conductor size [430.24]:

(27A x 1.25) + 14A = 48A
8 AWG rated 50A at 75°C [110.14(C) and Table 310.15(B)(16)]

Step 2: Feeder protection [430.62(A)] is to be sized no greater than the largest branch-circuit ground-fault and short-circuit overcurrent device plus the other motor FLC.

Step 3: Determine the largest branch-circuit ground-fault and short-circuit overcurrent device [430.52(C)(1) Ex]:

10 hp Motor = 14A x 2.50 = 35A
20 hp Motor = 27A x 2.50 = 68, next size up = 70A

Step 4: Determine the size feeder protection:

Not more than 70A + 14A, = 84A, next size down = 80A [240.6(A)]

The "next size up protection" rule for branch circuits [430.52(C)(1) Ex 1] doesn't apply to the motor feeder overcurrent device rating.

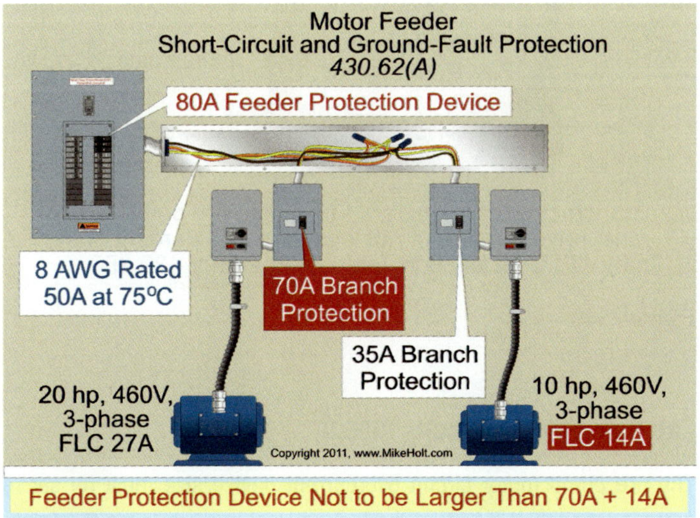

Figure 7–40

7.10 Motor VA Calculations

The measure of mechanical output of a motor is horsepower. Horsepower can be converted to watts by multiplying the horsepower rating by 746 watts per horsepower. Since this is a measure of a motor's output, don't confuse it with the input power required by a motor.

► Single-Phase Motor VA Output Example

Question: *What's the output VA for a dual voltage, 1 hp motor rated 115/230V?*

(a) 746W *(b) 1,000W* *(c) 1,400W* *(d) 1,840W*

Answer: *(a) 746W*
746W x 1 hp = 746W Output power

The input VA of a motor is determined by multiplying the motor volts by the motor amperes. To determine the motor VA rating, the following formulas can be used:

- **Motor Single-Phase VA Formula**

  Motor Single-Phase VA =
  Motor Volt Rating x Motor Ampere Rating

- **Motor Three-Phase VA Formula**

  Motor Three-Phase VA =
  Motor Volt Rating x Motor Ampere Rating x 1.732

► Motor VA—Single-Phase Example

Question: *What's the input VA for a dual voltage, 1 hp motor rated 115/230V?* **Figure 7–41**

(a) 920 VA at 230V *(b) 1,840 VA at 115V*
(c) 1,840 VA at 230V *(d) b and c*

Answer: *(d) b and c*

Motor VA = Volts x FLC
Table 430.248, 115V FLC = 16A, 230V FLC = 8A

VA at 230V = 230V x 8A
VA at 230V = 1,840 VA

VA at 115V = 115V x 16A
VA at 115V = 1,840 VA

Note: Many people believe that a 230V motor consumes less power than a 115V motor, but both motors consume the same amount of power.

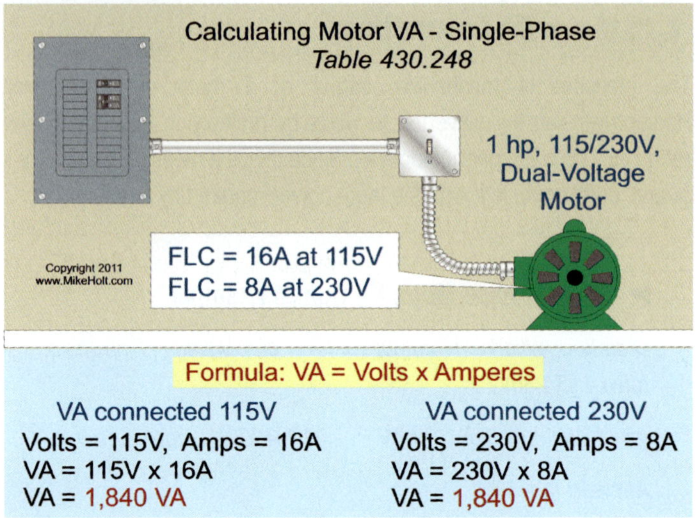

Figure 7–41

► **Motor VA—Three-Phase Example**

Question: *What's the input VA for a 5 hp, 230V, three-phase motor?* **Figure 7–42**

(a) 3,730 VA *(b) 6,055 VA* *(c) 6,440 VA* *(d) 8,050 VA*

Answer: *(b) 6,055 VA [Table 430.250]*

Motor Three-Phase VA = Volts x FLC x 1.732

Table 430.250, FLC = 15.20A

Motor VA = 230V x 15.20A x 1.732

Motor VA = 6,055 VA

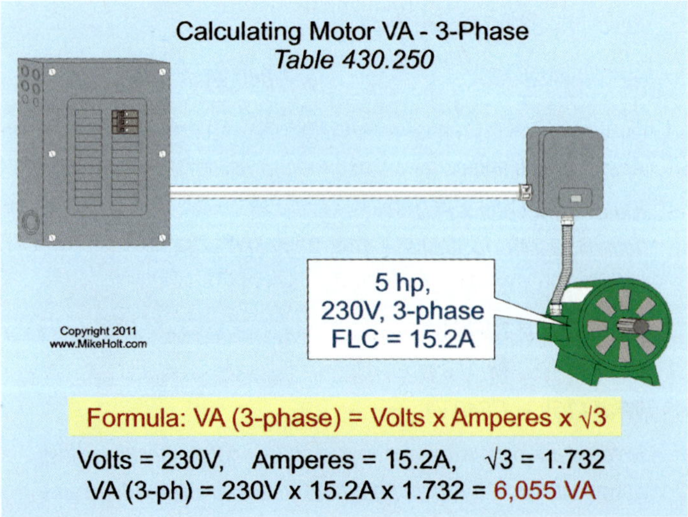

Figure 7–42

7.11 Fire Pump Motor Circuits

Fire Pump Conductor Size

Conductors must be sized no less than 125 percent of the sum of the motor full-load current as listed in Tables 430.248 or 430.250 [695.6(B)(2)].

► **Fire Pump Conductor Size Example**

Question: *What size conductor is required for a 25 hp, 208V, three-phase fire pump motor?* **Figure 7–43**

(a) 6 AWG *(b) 4 AWG* *(c) 3 AWG* *(d) 1 AWG*

Answer: *(c) 3 AWG*

25 hp, 208V, three-phase motor FLC = 74.80A [Table 430.250]

74.80A x 1.25 = 93.50A

3 AWG is rated 100A at 75°C

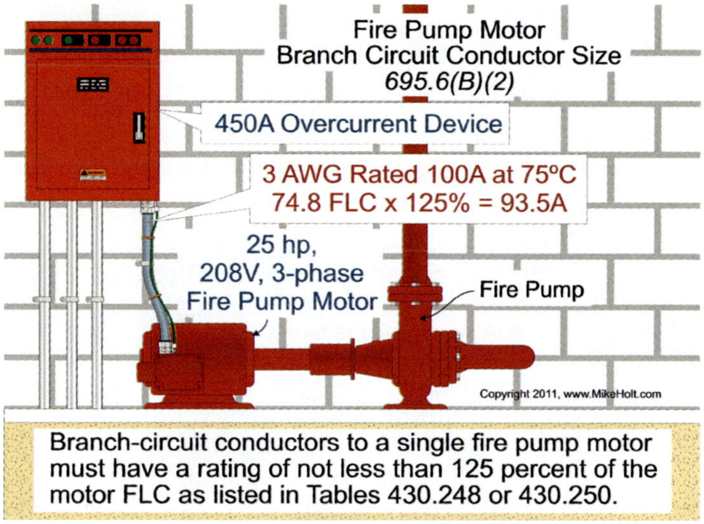

Figure 7–43

Fire Pump Motor Circuits [695.6]

The fire pump motor circuit overcurrent device size must be set to carry indefinitely the sum of the locked-rotor current of the fire pump motor [695.4(B)(2)(a)]. **Figure 7–44**

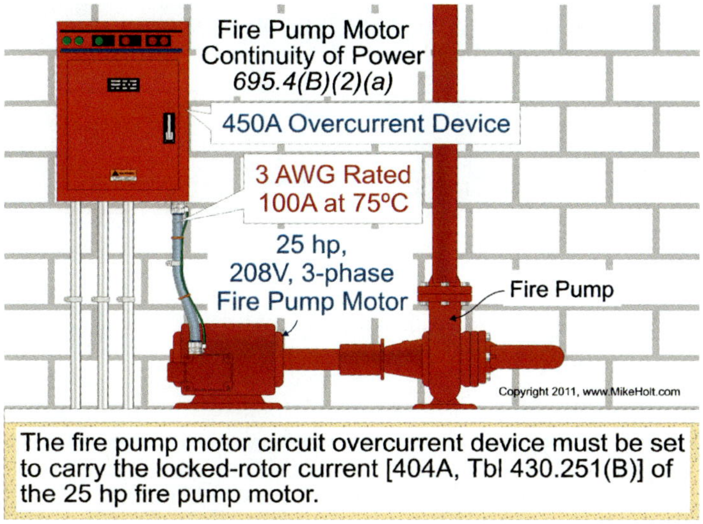

Figure 7–44

► Fire Pump Overcurrent Size Example

Question: *What size overcurrent device is required for a 25 hp, 208V, three-phase fire pump motor? See* **Figure 7–44**.

(a) 100A *(b) 200A* *(c) 400A* *(d) 450A*

Answer: *(d) 450A*

25 hp, 208V, three-phase motor LRC = 404A [Table 430.251(B)]

Next standard size overcurrent device = 450A [240.6(A)]

PART B—AIR-CONDITIONING CALCULATIONS

7.12 Scope of Article 440

Scope [440.1]

Article 440 applies to electrical motor-driven air-conditioning and refrigeration equipment. This article provides for the special considerations necessary for circuits supplying hermetic refrigerant motor-compressors.

Definitions [440.2]

Hermetic Refrigerant Motor-Compressor. A compressor and motor enclosed in the same housing, operating in the refrigerant.

Rated-Load Current. The current resulting when the motor-compressor operates at rated load and rated voltage.

7.13 Other Articles

Other Articles [440.3]

(B) Equipment with No Hermetic Motor-Compressors. Air-conditioning and refrigeration equipment that don't have hermetic refrigerant motor-compressors, such as furnaces with evaporator coils, must comply with Article 422 for appliances, Article 424 for electric space-heating equipment, and Article 430 for motors.

(C) Household Refrigerant Motor-Compressor Appliances. Household refrigerators and freezers, drinking water coolers, and beverage dispensing machines are listed as appliances, and their installation must also comply with Article 422 for appliances. **Figure 7–45**

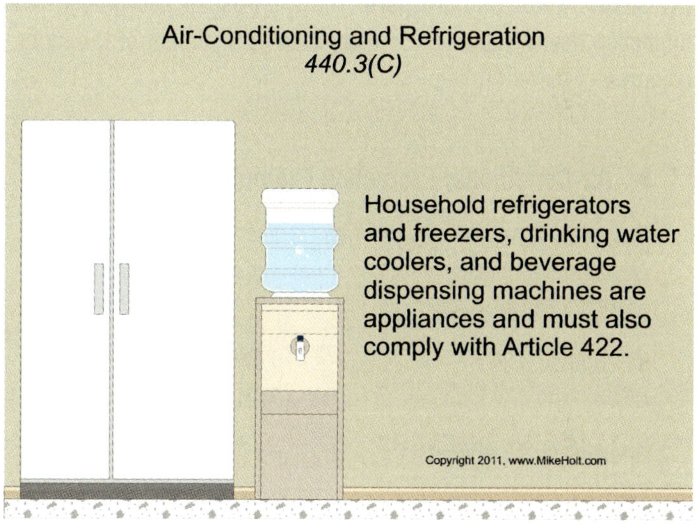

Figure 7–45

Ampacity and Rating [440.6]

(A) Hermetic Refrigerant Motor-Compressor. For a hermetic refrigerant motor-compressor, the rated-load current marked on the nameplate of the equipment is to be used in determining the rating of the disconnecting means, the branch-circuit conductors, the controller, and the branch-circuit short-circuit and ground-fault protection.

Exception No. 1: The branch-circuit selection current must be used instead of the rated-load current if provided on the equipment nameplate.

7.14 Short-Circuit and Ground-Fault Protection

General [440.21]

The branch-circuit conductors, control apparatus, and circuits supplying hermetic refrigerant motor-compressors must be protected against short circuits and ground faults in accordance with 440.22.

> **Author's Comment:** If the equipment nameplate specifies "Maximum Fuse Size," then a one-time or dual-element fuse must be used.

Short-Circuit and Ground-Fault Protection Device Size [440.22]

(A) Single Motor-Compressors. The short-circuit and ground-fault protection device must not be more than 175 percent of the motor-compressor current rating.

▶ Air-Conditioner Protection Example 1

Question: *What size conductor and protection is required for an a/c motor-compressor that has a running current rating of 24A at 230V?* **Figure 7–46**

(a) 10 AWG, 40A *(b) 10 AWG, 60A*
(c) a or b *(d) 10 AWG, 90A*

Answer: *(a) 10 AWG, 40A*

Step 1: Determine the branch-circuit conductor [Table 310.15(B)(16) and 440.32]:

24A x 1.25 = 30A, 10 AWG is rated 35A at 75°C [Table 310.15(B)(16)]

Step 2: Determine the branch-circuit protection [240.6(A) and 440.22(A)]:

24A x 1.75 = 42A, next size down = 40A

If the overcurrent device sized at 175 percent isn't capable of carrying the starting current of the motor-compressor, the next size larger overcurrent device can be used, but in no case can it exceed 225 percent of the motor-compressor current rating [440.22(A)].

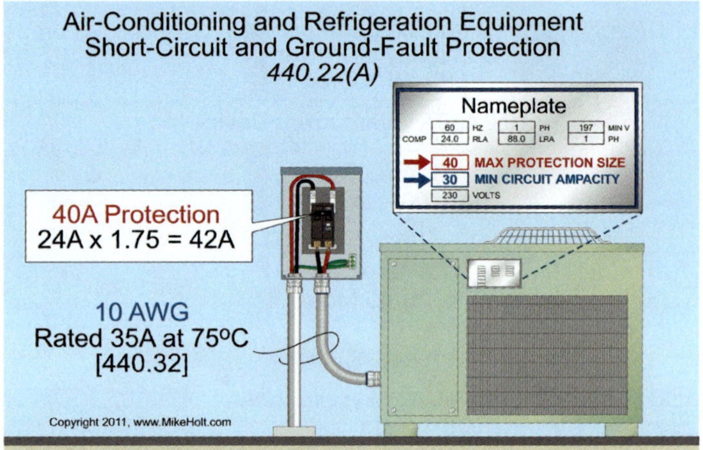

A short-circuit and ground-fault protection device must not be greater than 175% of the equipment load current rating.

Figure 7–46

▶ Air-Conditioner Protection Example 2

Question: *What size protection is required for an a/c hermetic motor-compressor that has a running current of 24A at 230V if the short circuit and ground fault protection device sized at 175 percent isn't sufficient to allow the air-conditioner compressor to start?* **Figure 7–47**

(a) 30A *(b) 40A* *(c) 50A* *(d) 90A*

Answer: *(c) 50A*

Determine the branch-circuit protection [240.6(A) and 440.22(A)]:

24A x 2.25 = 54A, next size down 50A

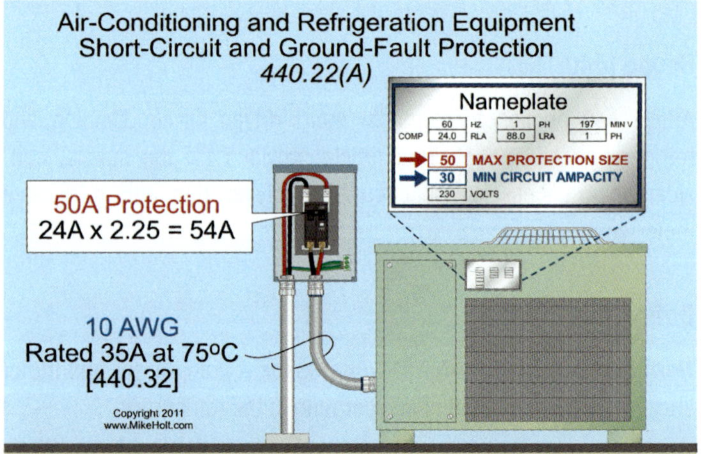

If 175% can't carry the starting current, the overcurrent device can be sized at a maximum of 225%.

Figure 7–47

(B) Several Motor-Compressors. Where the equipment incorporates more than one hermetic refrigerant motor-compressor, or a hermetic refrigerant motor-compressor and other motors or other loads, the equipment short-circuit and ground-fault protection must be sized as follows:

(1) Motor-Compressor Largest Load. The rating of the branch-circuit short-circuit and ground-fault protective device must not be more than the largest motor-compressor short-circuit ground-fault overcurrent device, plus the sum of the rated-load currents of the other compressors.

Author's Comment: The branch-circuit conductors are sized at 125 percent of the largest motor-compressor current, plus the sum of the rated-load currents of the other compressors [440.33].

7.15 Conductor Sizing for a Single Motor-Compressor

Conductor Size for Single Motor-Compressors [440.32]

Branch-circuit conductors to a single motor-compressor must have an ampacity not less than 125 percent of the motor-compressor rated-load current or the branch-circuit selection current, whichever is greater.

Author's Comment: Branch-circuit conductors for a single motor-compressor must have short-circuit and ground-fault protection sized between 175 percent and 225 percent of the rated-load current [440.22(A)].

► Air-Conditioner Conductor Sizing Example

Question: *What size conductor and overcurrent device is required for an 18A, 230V a/c hermetic motor-compressor?* **Figure 7–48**

(a) 12 AWG, 30A	*(b) 10 AWG, 50A*
c) a or b	*(d) 10 AWG, 60A*

Answer: *(a) 12 AWG, 30A*

Step 1: Determine the branch-circuit conductor [Table 310.15(B)(16) and 440.32]:

18A x 1.25 = 22.50A, 12 AWG, rated 25A at 75°C [Table 310.15(B)(16)]

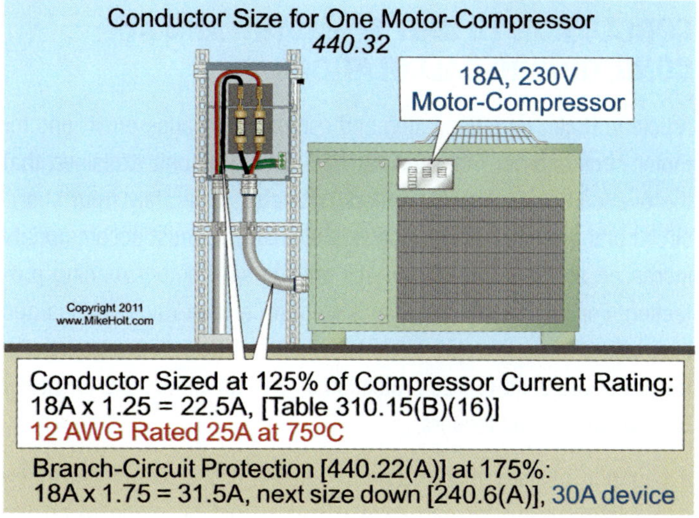

Figure 7–48

Step 2: Determine the branch-circuit protection [240.6(A) and 440.22(A)]:

18A x 1.75 = 31.50A, next size down = 30A

If the 30A overcurrent device isn't capable of carrying the starting current, then the overcurrent device can be sized up to 225 percent of the equipment load current rating. 18A x 2.25 = 40.50A, next size down 40A

Author's Comment: A 30A or 40A overcurrent device is permitted to protect a 12 AWG conductor for an air-conditioning circuit. See 240.4(G) for details.

Conductor Size for Several Motor-Compressors [440.33]

Conductors that supply several motor-compressors must have an ampacity not less than 125 percent of the highest motor-compressor current of the group, plus the sum of the rated load or branch-circuit selection current ratings of the other compressors.

Author's Comment: These conductors must be protected against short circuits and ground faults in accordance with 440.22(B)(1).

CONCLUSION TO UNIT 7—MOTOR AND AIR-CONDITIONING CALCULATIONS

Article 430 can be intimidating and confusing because provisions for motor circuits differ from general *NEC* rules. This unit explained that the overload protection for motors is treated separately from short-circuit and ground-fault protection. Motor circuits must accommodate increased starting current and still provide satisfactory running protection. For this reason, the overcurrent protection rules you learned in Article 240 don't apply to motor circuits. Article 430 contains the rules that are used to size protection as well as conductors for motor branch circuits and feeders.

A common mistake made in motor circuits is the use of the motor nameplate current for calculations that should be made using the full-load current from the Article 430 tables. The nameplate full-load amperes is only used for overload protection; Tables 430.248, 430.249, and 430.250 are used for sizing conductors, short-circuit and ground-fault protection, and disconnect switches. Review the material in this unit regarding 430.6(A) if this isn't clear to you.

Be sure you understand the differences between motor branch circuits and feeders, and how to apply the requirements of Article 430 to size the conductors and short-circuit and ground-fault protection for each.

The rules for sizing conductors and protection for air conditioners are similar to those for motor circuits. Apply the rules from Article 440 when sizing air-conditioner circuits, and be sure to comply with the instructions on the nameplate. Sizing the wiring and protection for an air conditioner is usually as simple as reading the information from the nameplate and trusting that the manufacturer followed the requirements of Article 440 in calculating that information for you.

UNIT 7

Practice Questions

Please use the 2011 *Code* book to answer the following questions, which are based on the 2011 *NEC*.

PRACTICE QUESTIONS FOR UNIT 7—MOTOR AND AIR-CONDITIONING CALCULATIONS

PART A—MOTOR CALCULATIONS

7.2 FLC versus Motor Nameplate

1. Motors and their associated equipment must be protected against overcurrent (overload, short circuit, or ground fault), but because of the special characteristics of induction motors, overcurrent protection is generally accomplished by having the overload protection separate from the short-circuit and ground-fault protection.

   (a) True
   (b) False

2. Which part of Article 430 contains the requirements for motor short-circuit and overload protection?

   (a) Motor and Branch-Circuit Overload Protection—Part III
   (b) Motor Branch-Circuit Short-Circuit and Ground-Fault Protection—Part IV
   (c) a and b
   (d) none of these

7.3 Highest Rated Motor [430.17]

3. When selecting the feeder conductors and short-circuit ground-fault protection device, the highest rated motor must be the highest rated _____.

   (a) horsepower
   (b) full-load current
   (c) nameplate current
   (d) any of these

4. Which is the highest rated FLC of the following?

   (a) 25 hp, 460V, synchronous, three-phase
   (b) 20 hp, 460V, three-phase
   (c) 15 hp, 460V, three-phase
   (d) 3 hp, 120V, single-phase

7.4 Branch-Circuit Conductor Size

5. What AWG size conductor is required for a 5 hp, 230V, single-phase motor? The terminals are rated 75°C.

   (a) 14 AWG
   (b) 12 AWG
   (c) 10 AWG
   (d) 8 AWG

7.5 Feeder Conductor Size [430.24]

6. Feeder conductors that supply several motors must have an ampacity of not less than _____.

   (a) 125 percent of the highest rated motor's FLC
   (b) the sum of the full-load currents of the other motors on the same phase
   (c) a or b
   (d) a and b

7.6 Overload Protection [430.6(A)(2) and 430.32(A)]

7. Overload is the condition where the current is greater than the equipment rating, resulting in equipment damage due to dangerous overheating [Article 100]. Overload protection devices, sometimes called "heaters," are intended to protect the _____ from dangerous overheating.

   (a) motor
   (b) motor control equipment
   (c) branch-circuit conductors
   (d) all of these

8. The *NEC* requires motor overload protection devices to be sized according to the motor full-load current ratings listed in Tables 430.247, 430.248, or 430.250.

(a) True
(b) False

9. If the motor overload protection relay sized according to 430.32(A)(1) isn't capable of carrying the motor starting and running current, a larger overload can be used if sized according to the requirements of 430.32(C).

(a) True
(b) False

10. Motors with a nameplate service factor (SF) rating of 1.15 or more must have the overload protection device sized at no more than _____ percent of the motor nameplate current rating.

(a) 100
(b) 115
(c) 125
(d) 135

11. Motors with a nameplate temperature rise rating not over 40°C must have the overload protection device sized at no more than _____ percent of the motor nameplate current rating.

(a) 100
(b) 115
(c) 125
(d) 135

12. Motors that have a service factor rating of 1.10 must have the overload protection device sized at not more than _____ percent of the motor nameplate ampere rating.

(a) 100
(b) 115
(c) 125
(d) 135

13. If a dual-element fuse is used for overload protection, what size fuse is required for a 5 hp, 208V, three-phase motor with a service factor of 1.15 and a motor nameplate current rating of 16A (FLA)?

(a) 20A
(b) 25A
(c) 30A
(d) 35A

14. If a dual-element fuse is used for overload protection, what size fuse is required for a 30 hp, 460V, three-phase synchronous motor, with a temperature rise of 39°C?

(a) 20A
(c) 25A
(b) 30A
(d) 40A

7.7 Branch-Circuit Short-Circuit and Ground-Fault Protection [430.51]

15. The branch-circuit short-circuit and ground-fault protection device is intended to protect the motor, the motor control apparatus, and the conductors against overcurrent due to _____.

(a) short circuits
(b) ground faults
(c) overloads
(d) a and b

16. In addition to overload protection, each motor and its accessories require short-circuit and ground-fault protection according to 430.52. When sizing the branch-circuit protection device, which of the following factors must be considered?

(a) The motor type, such as induction, synchronous, wound-rotor, single-phase alternating current, three-phase alternating current, and so on
(b) The motor full-load current from the *Code* tables must be used.
(c) The type of protection device to be used such as a nontime-delay fuse, dual-element fuse, or inverse time breaker.
(d) all of these

17. The *NEC* requires motor branch-circuit short-circuit and ground-fault protection to be sized not greater than the percentages listed in Table 430.52. When the short-circuit ground-fault protection device value determined from Table 430.52 doesn't correspond with the standard rating of overcurrent devices as listed in 240.6(A), the next _____ device size is permitted to be used.

(a) smaller
(b) larger
(c) a or b
(d) none of these

18. To determine the percentage of the motor FLC from Table 430.52 that's to be used to size the motor branch-circuit short-circuit and ground-fault protection device, which of the following steps should be used?

(a) Locate the motor type in Table 430.52 such as direct current, wound-rotor, single-phase, or polyphase alternating-current motors.
(b) Select the percentage from Table 430.52 according to the type of protection device such as a nontime-delay fuse, dual-element fuse or inverse time circuit breaker.
(c) After making the necessary calculations, round up to the next standard size overcurrent device.
(d) all of these

19. Where the next size up time-delay (dual-element) fuse isn't sufficient for the starting current of the motor, the rating of the fuse is permitted to be increased, but must in no case exceed _____ percent of the motor full-load current.

(a) 125
(b) 150
(c) 175
(d) 225

20. Conductors are sized at _____ percent of the motor full-load current [430.22(A)], overloads from _____ percent, and the motor short-circuit, ground-fault protection device (inverse time circuit breaker) is sized up to _____ percent of the motor full-load current.

(a) 100, 100, 100
(b) 100, 125, 150
(c) 125, 125, 125
(d) 125, 115, 250

21. Which of the following statements is(are) true for a 10 hp, 208V, three-phase motor with a nameplate current of 29A, terminals are rated 60ºC ?

(a) The branch-circuit conductors can be 8 THHN.
(b) Overload protection is 33A.
(c) Short-circuit and ground-fault protection can be an 80A circuit breaker.
(d) all of these

7.9 Feeder Protection [430.62]

22. Motor feeder conductors for more than one motor (sized according to 430.24) must have a feeder protection device to protect against short circuits and ground faults (not overloads), sized not greater than the _____.

(a) largest branch-circuit short-circuit ground-fault protection device [430.52] of any motor of the group
(b) sum of the full-load currents of the other motors on the same phase
(c) a or b
(d) a and b

7.10 Motor VA Calculations

23. What's the VA input of a dual voltage, 5 hp, three-phase motor rated 460/230V?

(a) 3,027 VA at 460V
(b) 6,055 VA at 230V
(c) 6,055 VA at 460V
(d) b and c

24. What's the input VA of a 3 hp, 208V, single-phase motor?

(a) 3,890 VA
(b) 6,440 VA
(c) 6,720 VA
(d) 9,422 VA

PART B—AIR-CONDITIONING CALCULATIONS

7.14 Short-Circuit and Ground-Fault Protection

25. What size branch circuit short-circuit and ground-fault protection is required for a 24A motor-compressor connected to a 240V circuit?

(a) 40A
(b) 60A
(c) 70A
(d) 90A

26. What size branch circuit short-circuit and ground-fault protection is required for an 18A motor-compressor connected to a 240V circuit?

(a) 30A
(b) 40A
(c) 50A
(d) 60A

7.15 Conductor Sizing for a Single Motor-Compressor

27. What size conductor is required for a 24A motor-compressor connected to a 240V circuit? (75°C rated terminals)

(a) 14 AWG
(b) 12 AWG
(c) 10 AWG
(d)8 AWG

28. What size conductor is required for an 18A motor-compressor connected to a 240V circuit? (75°C rated terminals)

(a) 14 AWG
(b) 12AWG
(c) 10 AWG
(d) 8 AWG

UNIT

7

Challenge Questions

Please use the 2011 *Code* book to answer the following questions, which are based on the 2011 *NEC*.

CHALLENGE QUESTIONS FOR UNIT 7—MOTOR AND AIR-CONDITIONING CALCULATIONS

PART A—MOTOR CALCULATIONS

7.4 Branch-Circuit Conductor Size

1. The branch-circuit conductors of a 5 hp, 230V, single-phase motor with a nameplate rating of 25A must have an ampacity of not less than ______.

   Note: This five-minute-rated motor is used for intermittent duty and, due to the nature of the apparatus it drives, it can't run for more than five minutes at any one time.

   (a) 21A
   (b) 23A
   (c) 33A
   (d) 37A

7.5 Feeder Conductor Size [430.24]

2. The motor feeder conductor size for three 15 hp, 208V, three-phase motors; three 3 hp, 208V, single-phase motors; and three 1 hp, 120V, single-phase motors will be ______. (75°C rated terminals)

   (a) 2/0 AWG
   (b) 3/0 AWG
   (c) 4/0 AWG
   (d) 250 kcmil

7.6 Overload Protection [430.6(A)(2) and 430.32(A)]

3. The standard overload protection device for a 2 hp, 115V motor that has a full-load current rating of 24A and a nameplate rating of 21.50A must not exceed ______.

   (a) 20.60A
   (b) 24.70A
   (c) 29.90A
   (d) 33.80A

7.7 Branch-Circuit Short-Circuit and Ground-Fault Protection [430.51]

4. A 2 hp, 120V motor requires a ______ branch-circuit short-circuit protection device.

   Note: Use an inverse time breaker.

   (a) 20A
   (b) 30A
   (c) 40A
   (d) 60A

5. The branch-circuit short-circuit and ground-fault protection device for a 10 hp, 230V, single-phase motor must not exceed ______.

   Note: Use an inverse time breaker.

   (a) 50A
   (b) 75A
   (c) 80A
   (d) 125A

6. The branch-circuit short-circuit and ground-fault protection (circuit breaker) for a 125 hp, 240V, direct-current motor is ______.

   (a) 400A
   (b) 600A
   (c) 700A
   (d) 800A

7.9 Feeder Protection [430.62]

7. There are three motors; one 5 hp, 230V, single-phase motor with a service factor of 1.20, and two 1½ hp, 120V, single-phase motors. Using an inverse time breaker, the 3-wire feeder conductor protection device after balancing all three motors will be ______.

(a) 60A
(b) 70A
(c) 80A
(d) 90A

8. If an inverse time breaker is used for the feeder short-circuit protection, what size protection is required for the following 460V, three-phase motors?

(1) Motor 1 = 40 hp, 52 FLC
(2) Motor 2 = 20 hp, 27 FLC
(3) Motor 3 = 10 hp, 14 FLC
(4) Motor 4 = 5 hp, 7.60 FLC

(a) 125A
(b) 175A
(c) 200A
(d) 225A

9. The feeder protection for one 25 hp, 208V, three-phase motor, and three 3 hp, 120V, single-phase motors will be ______ after balancing.

Note: Use inverse time breakers.

(a) 200A
(b) 225A
(c) 250A
(d) 300A

10. Which of the following statements about a 30 hp, 460V, three-phase synchronous motor and a 10 hp, 460V, three-phase motor is(are) true? (75°C rated terminals)

(a) The 30 hp motor is supplied by 8 AWG conductors with an 80A breaker.
(b) The 10 hp motor is supplied by 14 AWG conductors with a 35A breaker.
(c) The feeder conductors must be 6 AWG conductors with a 90A breaker.
(d) all of these

UNIT

8

Voltage-Drop Calculations

INTRODUCTION TO UNIT 8—VOLTAGE-DROP CALCULATIONS

When electrical current flows through a conductor, there's a certain amount of voltage drop in the conductor due to its inherent resistance. This is another example of Ohm's Law at work. The results of voltage drop, however, aren't useful work. One of the effects of exorbitant voltage drop is a large amount of heat given off by the conductors. This is wasted power that must be paid for on the utility bill. This wasted power heats up any other conductors in the same raceway or in close proximity. This results in inefficiency at the least, and overheated circuit conductors that can result in damage as a worst-case scenario.

Excessive voltage drop can also result in delivering a voltage to the circuit load that's less than the rated voltage of the equipment. In some cases this may not be a serious problem, but for circuits such as sensitive electronic equipment, it may be critical. The manufacturer's nameplate and installation information should be consulted to determine the acceptable voltage limitations of any particular piece of equipment.

The amount of voltage drop encountered in a particular circuit is directly proportional to the amount of current flow in the circuit and directly proportional to the resistance of the circuit, as predicted by Ohm's Law. The resistance of the circuit is determined by the material of the conductor (copper or aluminum), the cross-sectional area of the conductor, and the length of the conductor.

In this unit, we'll show you how to find all the information necessary to make accurate voltage-drop calculations for either single-phase or three-phase circuits. This will be helpful in designing practical circuits as well as in preparing for an exam.

PART A—CONDUCTOR RESISTANCE CALCULATIONS

Introduction

Ohm's Law expresses the relationship between current, voltage, and resistance in an electric circuit. Most *NEC* applications deal primarily with current (conductor ampacity and equipment ratings) and voltage (nominal system voltage, equipment ratings, and transformer primary and secondary voltages). For most everyday purposes, resistance is ignored in the *Code*. However, all conductor materials have opposition to current flow, and understanding voltage-drop calculations requires knowledge of this phenomenon and how to deal with it. The total opposition to current flow is called "resistance" in direct-current circuits. In alternating-current circuits, the total opposition to current flow includes resistance as well as other components that we'll discuss in this unit. This combined total opposition, in alternating-current circuits, is called "impedance." Both direct-current and alternating-current circuits will be covered in this unit.

Author's Comment: This unit is based on the use of solidly grounded ac systems, 600V or less, using 90ºC insulated copper conductors sized to 75ºC terminals unless otherwise specified.

8.1 Conductor Resistance

Voltage drop is the loss of potential that results when current must overcome the resistance/impedance of a conductor of a circuit. To calculate voltage drop, it is essential that we know the current load of the circuit and the resistance of the conductors. Metals intended to carry electric current are called conductors or wires, and by their nature, they oppose the flow of electrons. Electrical conductors for applications covered by the *NEC* can be solid or stranded, and are most often made from copper or aluminum. All materials oppose the flow of electrons. This opposition to electron movement is known as "resistance." All conductors offer some resistance to electron movement

The conductor's opposition to the flow of current depends on the conductor material (copper or aluminum), its cross-sectional area (wire size), its length, and its operating temperature.

Material

Aluminum is often used when weight or cost are important considerations, but copper is the most common type of metal used for electrical conductors. Gold doesn't tarnish so it's used mostly to plate terminals (electroplating) for some electronic equipment.

Cross-Sectional Area

Conductors are sized according to American Wire Gage (AWG), which ranges from 40 AWG to 4/0 AWG. Conductors larger than 4/0 are identified in thousand circular mils (kcmil), such as 250 kcmil, 350 kcmil, and 500 kcmil. **Figure 8–1**

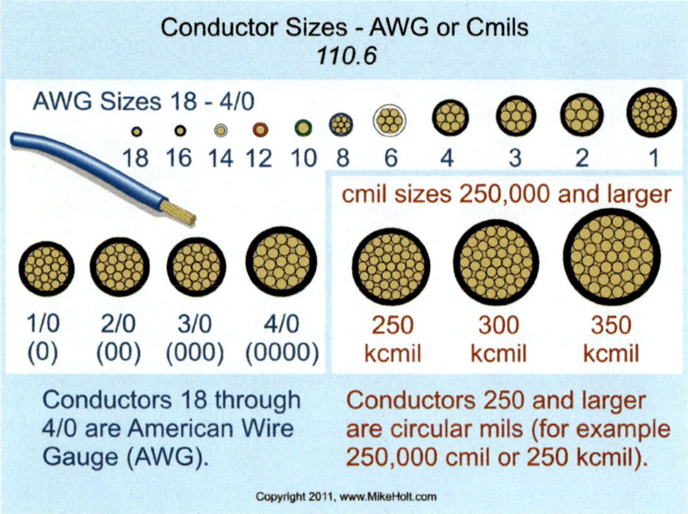

Figure 8–1

The cross-sectional area of a conductor is commonly expressed in circular mils (cmils). This value is found in Chapter 9, Table 8. Notice that the circular mil area is the same for a specific size conductor that is solid or stranded. **Figure 8–2**

The greater the conductor cross-sectional area (the larger the conductor), the greater the number of available electron paths and the lower the conductor resistance. **Figure 8–3**

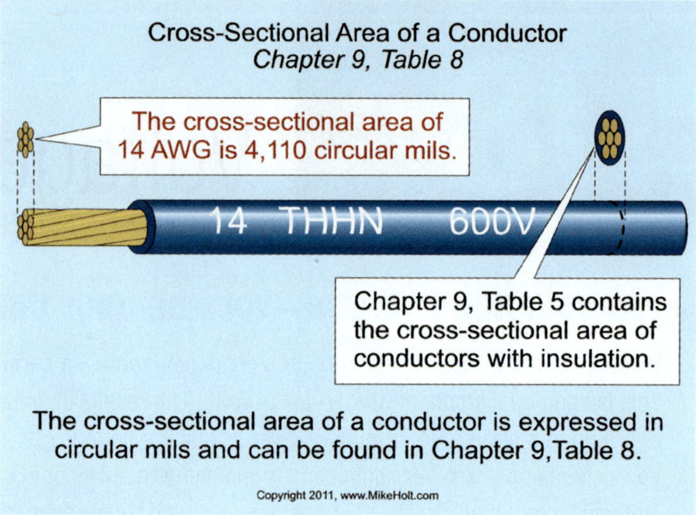

Figure 8–2

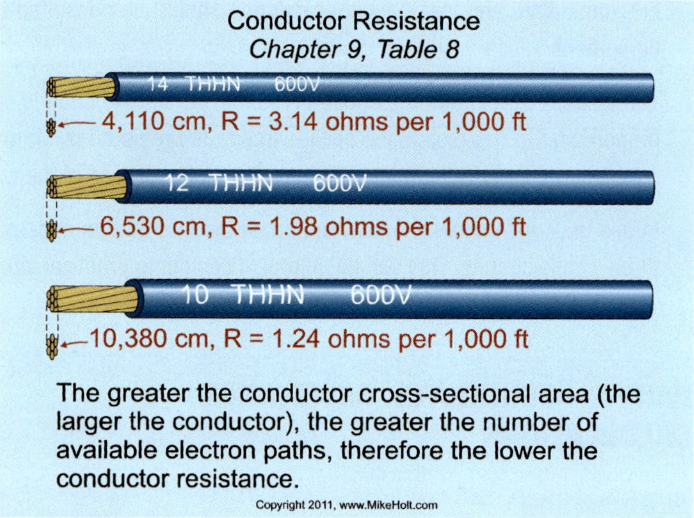

Figure 8–3

Conductor resistance varies inversely with the conductor's size; the smaller the wire size, the greater the resistance, and the larger the wire size, the lower the resistance. **Figure 8–4**

Conductor Length

The resistance of a conductor is directly proportional to its length. **Figure 8–5**

Table 8–1 provides examples of conductor resistance and circular mils area for conductors 1,000 ft long. Longer or shorter lengths will naturally have different conductor resistances.

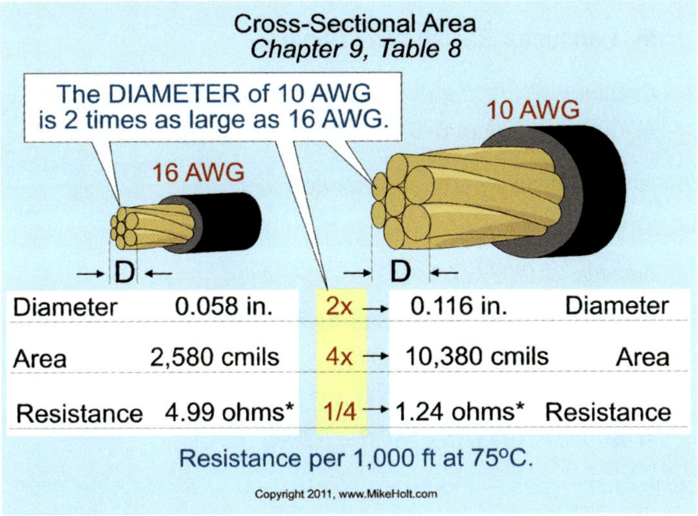

Figure 8–4

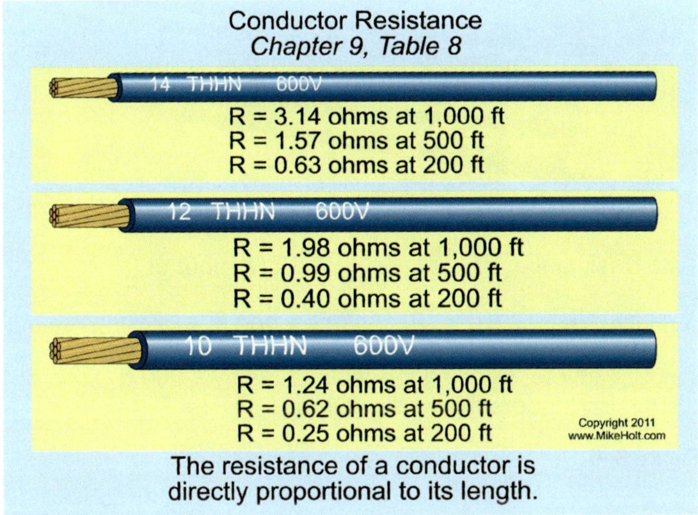

Figure 8–5

Table 8–1. Conductor Properties, *NEC* Chapter 9, Table 8

Conductor Size American Wire Gage	Conductor Resistance Per 1,000 Feet at 75°C	Conductor Diameter Inches	Conductor Area Circular Mils
14 AWG	3.140 ohms (stranded)	0.073	4,110
12 AWG	1.980 ohms (stranded)	0.092	6,530
10 AWG	1.240 ohms (stranded)	0.116	10,380
8 AWG	0.778 ohms (stranded)	0.146	16,510
6 AWG	0.491 ohms (stranded)	0.184	26,240

Temperature

The resistance of a conductor changes with temperature. The amount of change per degree is called the "temperature coefficient." Positive temperature coefficient indicates that as the temperature rises, the conductor resistance also rises; this reduces conductor ampacity. Copper and aluminum conductors have a positive temperature coefficient.

The conductor resistances listed in the *NEC* Chapter 9, Tables 8 and 9, are based on an operating temperature of 75°C. A three-degree rise in temperature results in a one percent increase in conductor resistance for both copper and aluminum conductors. The formula to determine the change in conductor resistance with changing temperature is listed at the bottom of Chapter 9, Table 8 in Note 2. For example, the resistance of copper at 90°C is about five percent more than at 75°C.

Question: *What is the dc resistance of 14 AWG at 75°C?*

(a) 2.25 ohms (b) 3.14 ohms (c) 4.10 ohms (d) 5.45 ohms

Answer: *(b) 3.14 ohms*

At 75°C the resistance of 14 AWG = 3.14 ohms, Chapter 9, Table 8

Temperature Adjustment, Table 8, Note 2:

R for CU = Table R x [1 + (0.00323 x (Temp°C - 75°))]
R for AL = Table R x [1 + (0.00333 x (Temp°C - 75°))]

Question: *What is the dc resistance of 14 AWG at 30°C?*

(a) 1.22 ohms (b) 2.15 ohms (c) 2.67 ohms (d) 3.91 ohms

Answer: *(c) 2.67 ohms*
30°C = 3.14 x [1+ (0.00323) x (30-75))]
30°C = 3.14 ohms x [1 - 0.14535]
30°C = 3.14 ohms x [0.85465]
At 30°C the resistance of 14 AWG = 2.67 ohms

8.2 Conductor Resistance—Direct-Current Circuits [Chapter 9, Table 8]

The *NEC* lists the resistance and area in circular mils for both direct-current and alternating-current circuit conductors. Direct-current circuit conductor resistances are listed in Chapter 9, Table 8, and alternating-current circuit conductor resistances (and reactances) are listed in Chapter 9, Table 9. The tables include both solid and stranded conductors. Stranded conductors will be used in this textbook unless specified otherwise. Table 8 lists both coated copper and uncoated copper. Uncoated copper is our most commonly used conductor; unless specifically stated that the conductor is a coated conductor, use uncoated (for most resistance calculations, there is very little difference between the two).

The direct-current conductor resistances listed in Chapter 9, Table 8 apply to conductors 1,000 ft long and are expressed as kFT on the table. The following formula can be used to determine the conductor resistance for conductor lengths other than 1,000 ft:

◆ Direct-Current Conductor Resistance Formula

Direct-Current Conductor Resistance = (Conductor Resistance Ohms/1,000 ft) x Conductor Length

► Conductor Resistance Copper

Question: *What's the direct-current resistance of 200 ft of 12 AWG copper?*

(a) 0.21 ohms (b) 0.29 ohms 0.396 ohms (d) 0.72 ohms

Answer: *(c) 0.396 ohms*

The direct-current resistance of 12 AWG copper 1,000 ft long is 1.98 ohms [Chapter 9, Table 8].

The direct-current resistance of 200 ft is:
(1.98 ohms/1,000 ft) x 200 ft = 0.396 ohms

► Conductor Resistance Copper

Question: *What's the direct-current resistance of 200 ft of 6 AWG copper?* **Figure 8–6**

(a) 0.021 ohms (b) 0.029 ohms
(c) 0.049 ohms (d) 0.098 ohms

Answer: *(d) 0.098 ohms*

The direct-current resistance of 6 AWG copper 1,000 ft long is 0.491 ohms [Chapter 9, Table 8].

The direct-current resistance of 420 ft is:
(0.491 ohms/1,000 ft) x 200 ft = 0.0982 ohms

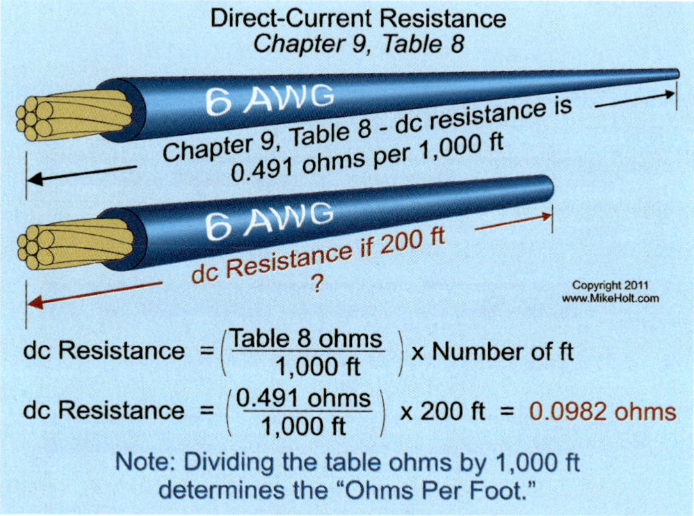

Figure 8–6

► Conductor Resistance Aluminum

Question: *What's the resistance of 200 ft of 1/0 AWG aluminum?* **Figure 8–7**

(a) 0.04 ohms (b) 0.29 ohms (c) 0.60 ohms (d) 0.72 ohms

Answer: *(a) 0.04 ohms*

The resistance of 1/0 AWG aluminum 1,000 ft long is 0.201 ohms [Chapter 9, Table 8].

The resistance of 200 ft is:
(0.201 ohms/1,000 ft) x 200 ft = 0.04 ohms

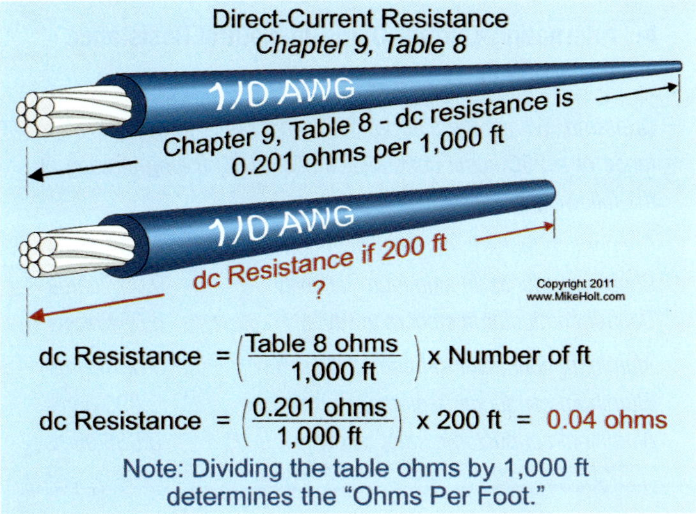

Figure 8–7

8.3 Conductor Resistance—Alternating-Current Circuits

In direct-current circuits, the only property that opposes the flow of electrons is resistance. In alternating-current circuits, the expanding and collapsing magnetic field within the conductor induces an electromotive force that opposes the flow of the alternating current. This opposition to the flow of alternating current is called "inductive reactance."

In addition, alternating current flowing through a conductor generates small, erratic, independent currents called "eddy currents," Figure Figure 8–8.

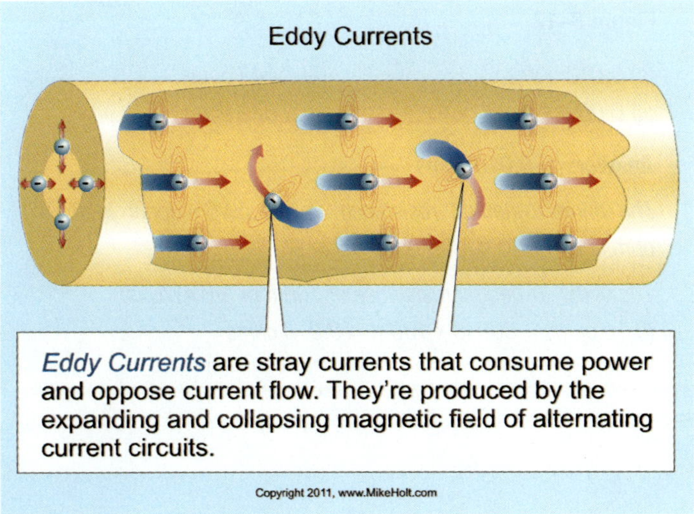

Figure 8–8

Eddy currents are strongest in the center of the conductors and repel the flowing electrons toward the conductor surface. This is known as "skin effect." Skin effect is greatly impacted by the frequency of alternating current. Sixty Hertz creates a less significant skin effect in stranded wire than a higher frequency would. Figure 8–9

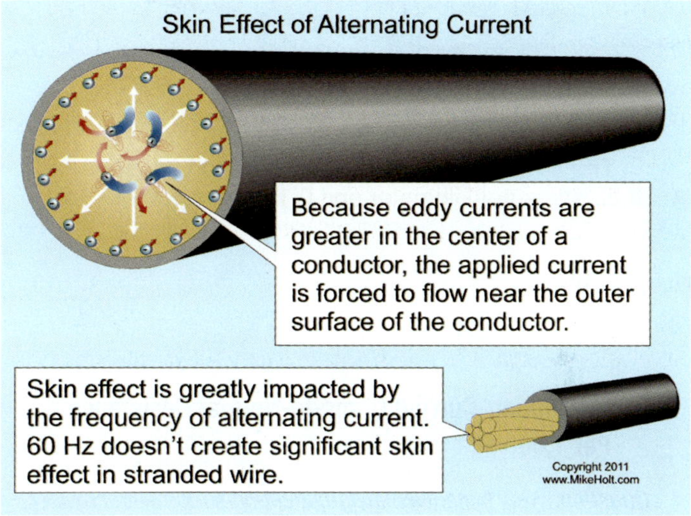

Figure 8–9

Because of skin effect, the effective cross-sectional area of an ac conductor is reduced, which results in an increased opposition to current flow. The total opposition to the movement of electrons in an alternating-current circuit (resistance plus inductive reactance plus skin effect) is called "impedance."

8.4 Alternating-Current Resistance

An alternating-current conductor's opposition to current flow (resistance and reactance) is listed in Chapter 9, Table 9 of the *NEC*. The total opposition to current flow in an alternating-current circuit is called "impedance" and depends on the conductor material (copper or aluminum) and on the magnetic property of the raceway or cable in which the conductors are installed.

The header row of Chapter 9, Table 9 shows, "Ohms to Neutral per Kilometer" and directly under that it reads, "Ohms to Neutral per 1,000 Feet." Each entry on Table 9 follows this format. For example, the alternating-current resistance (impedance) for 2 AWG uncoated copper in a PVC raceway is 0.62 ohms per kilometer and 0.19 ohms per 1,000 ft. In this textbook, we'll use the "Ohms to Neutral per 1,000 Feet" for all calculations. Figure 8–10

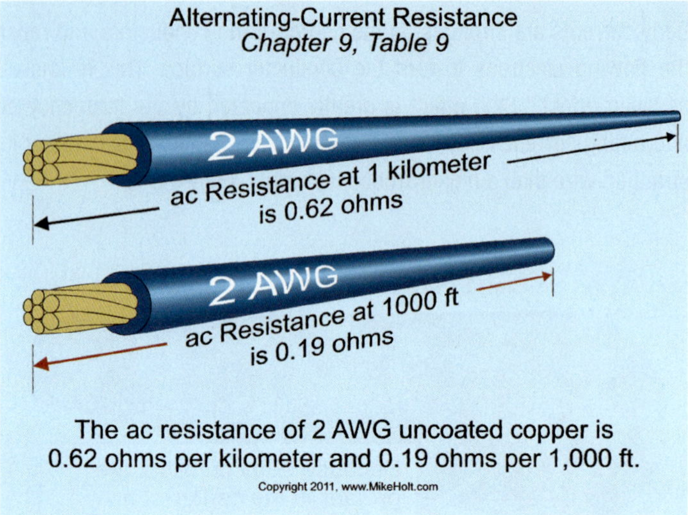

Figure 8–10

▶ Alternating-Current Ohms-to-Neutral Resistance Per 1,000 Ft

Question: *What's the alternating-current ohms-to-neutral resistance of a 500 kcmil uncoated copper conductor that's 1,000 ft long in each of the following raceways?* **Figure 8–11**

Copper conductor in nonmetallic raceway [Chapter 9, Table 9]	*0.027 ohms*
Copper conductor in aluminum raceway	*0.032 ohms*
Copper conductor in steel raceway	*0.029 ohms*

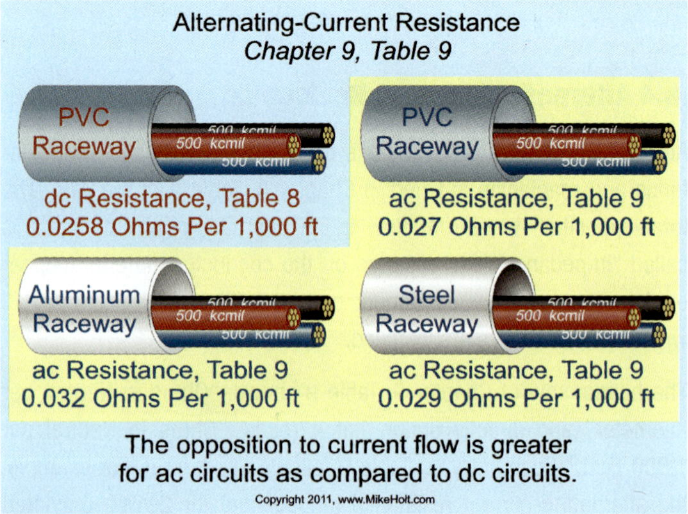

Figure 8–11

▶ Alternating-Current Ohms-to-Neutral Resistance Per 1,000 Ft

Question: *What's the alternating-current ohms-to-neutral resistance of a 250 kcmil conductor that's 1,000 ft long in each of the following raceways?*

Copper conductor in nonmetallic raceway	*0.052 ohms*
Copper conductor in aluminum raceway	*0.057 ohms*
Copper conductor in steel raceway	*0.054 ohms*
Aluminum conductor in nonmetallic raceway	*0.085 ohms*
Aluminum conductor in aluminum raceway	*0.090 ohms*
Aluminum conductor in steel raceway	*0.086 ohms*

Alternating-Current Conductor Resistance Formula

The following formula can be used to determine conductor resistance:

◆ **Alternating-Current Resistance Formula**

Alternating-Current Resistance = (Conductor Ohms-to-Neutral Resistance/ 1,000 ft) x Conductor Length

Author's Comment: Uncoated copper is our most common conductor for general use; unless specifically stated that the conductor is a coated copper wire, use uncoated copper.

▶ Ohms-to-Neutral Resistance Example 1

Question: *What's the alternating-current ohms-to-neutral resistance of 100 ft of 2/0 AWG copper installed in a steel raceway?* **Figure 8–12**

(a) 0.010 ohms *(b) 0.042 ohms*
(c) 0.069 ohms *(d) 0.072 ohms*

Answer: *(a) 0.010 ohms*

The ohms-to-neutral resistance of 2/0 AWG copper is 0.10 ohms per 1,000 ft [Chapter 9, Table 9].

The ohms-to-neutral resistance of 100 ft of 2/0 AWG is:
(0.10 ohms/1,000 ft) x 100 ft = 0.010 ohms

► Ohms-to-Neutral Resistance Example 2

Question: *What's the alternating-current ohms-to-neutral resistance of 100 ft of 500 kcmil aluminum conductors installed in an aluminum raceway?* **Figure 8–13**

(a) 0.0021 ohms *(b) 0.0029 ohms*
(c) 0.0048 ohms *(d) 0.0081 ohms*

Answer: *(c) 0.0048 ohms*

The ohms-to-neutral resistance of 500 kcmil installed in an aluminum raceway is 0.048 ohms per 1,000 ft.

The ohms-to-neutral resistance of 100 ft of 500 kcmil in an aluminum raceway is: (0.048 ohms/1,000 ft) x 100 ft = 0.0048 ohms

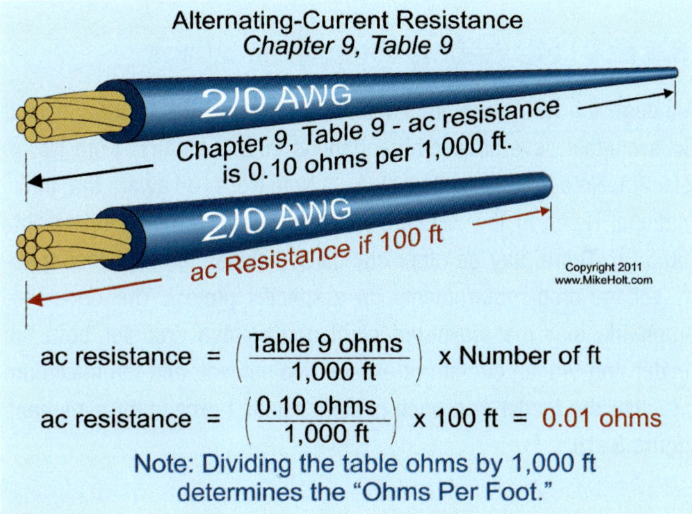

Figure 8–12

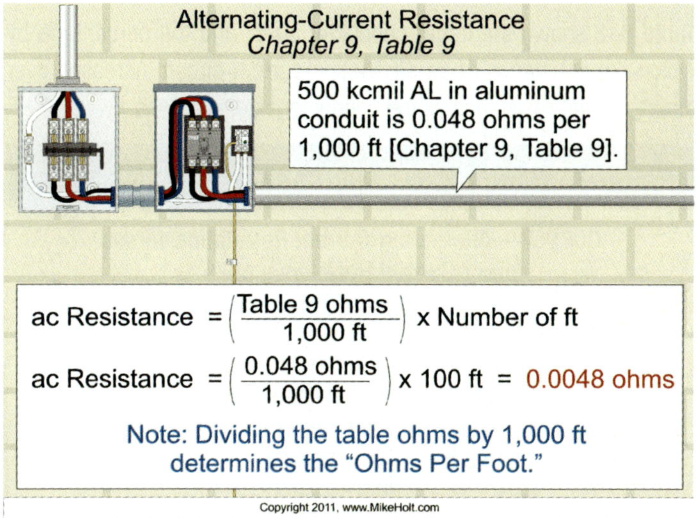

Figure 8–13

8.5 Alternating-Current Resistance as Compared to Direct-Current Resistance

The opposition to current flow (impedance) is greater for alternating-current circuits compared to the resistance of direct-current circuits because of inductive reactance, eddy currents, and skin effect in addition to the resistance of the conductor. **Table 8–2** provides some comparisons between alternating-current resistance and direct-current resistance. Chapter 9, Table 8 provides direct-current resistance values for conductors, and Chapter 9, Table 9 provides alternating-current resistance and reactance values for conductors. These values are presented in a graphical comparison in **Figure 8–14**. Note that for conductors smaller than 1/0 AWG, the two values are essentially equal.

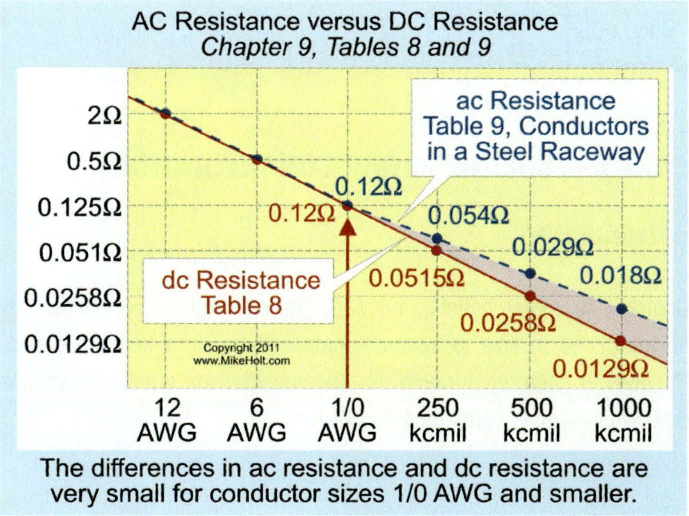

Figure 8–14

Table 8–2 shows the larger conductor sizes, and the percentage by which the resistance of an alternating-current circuit increases over direct-current resistance as the conductor size increases.

Table 8–2

Conductor Size	Alternating-Current Resistance Chapter 9, Table 9	Direct-Current Resistance Chapter 9, Table 8	Alternating-Current resistance greater than direct-current resistance by %
COPPER—Alternating-Current Resistance versus Direct-Current Resistance at 75°C			
250,000	0.054 ohms per 1,000 ft	0.0515 ohms per 1,000 ft	4.85%
500,000	0.029 ohms per 1,000 ft	0.0258 ohms per 1,000 ft	12.40%
1,000,000	0.018 ohms per 1,000 ft	0.0129 ohms per 1,000 ft	39.50%
ALUMINUM—Alternating-Current Resistance versus Direct-Current Resistance at 75°C			
Conductor Size	**Alternating-Current Resistance Chapter 9, Table 9**	**Direct-Current Resistance Chapter 9, Table 8**	**Alternating-Current resistance greater than direct-current resistance by %**
250,000	0.086 ohms per 1,000 ft	0.0847 ohms per 1,000 ft	1.50%
500,000	0.045 ohms per 1,000 ft	0.0424 ohms per 1,000 ft	6.13%
1,000,000	0.025 ohms per 1,000 ft	0.0212 ohms per 1,000 ft	17.92%

PART B—VOLTAGE-DROP CONSIDERATIONS

Introduction

Contrary to many beliefs, the *NEC* doesn't require conductors to be increased in size to accommodate voltage drop in most cases. However, it does recommend that we consider the effects of voltage drop when sizing conductors. **Figure 8–15**

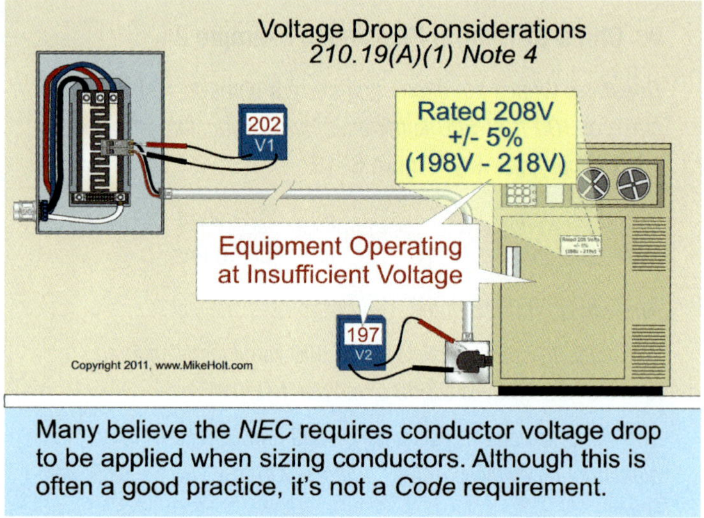

Figure 8–15

8.6 *NEC* Voltage-Drop Recommendations

Although the *NEC* generally doesn't include rules for voltage drop, it does contain several recommendations in 210.19(A)(1) Note No. 4, 215.2(A) Note No. 2, and 310.15(A)(1) Note No. 1. Be aware that informational Notes in the *NEC* are recommendations, not requirements [90.5(C)]. There may be other standards besides the *NEC* that specify voltage-drop requirements on a specific project. The *Code* recommends that the maximum combined voltage drop for both the feeder and branch circuit not exceed five percent, and the maximum on either the feeder or branch circuit shouldn't exceed three percent. **Figure 8–16**

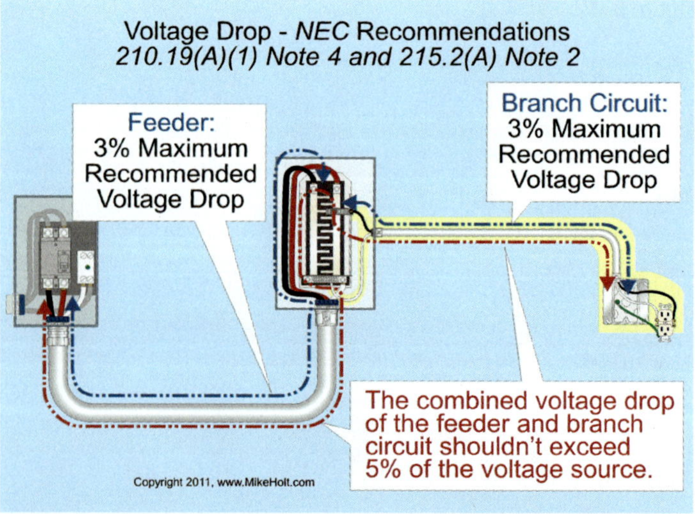

Figure 8–16

The Article 100 definitions for a branch circuit and a feeder are:

Branch Circuit [Article 210]. The conductors between the final overcurrent device and the receptacle outlets, lighting outlets, or other outlets as defined in this article. **Figure 8–17**

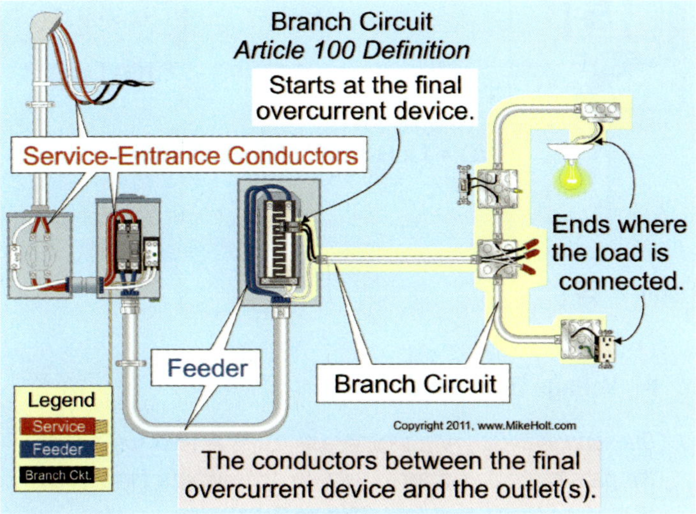

Figure 8–17

Feeder [Article 215]. The conductors between the service equipment, a separately derived system, or other power supply and the final branch-circuit overcurrent device. **Figure 8–18**

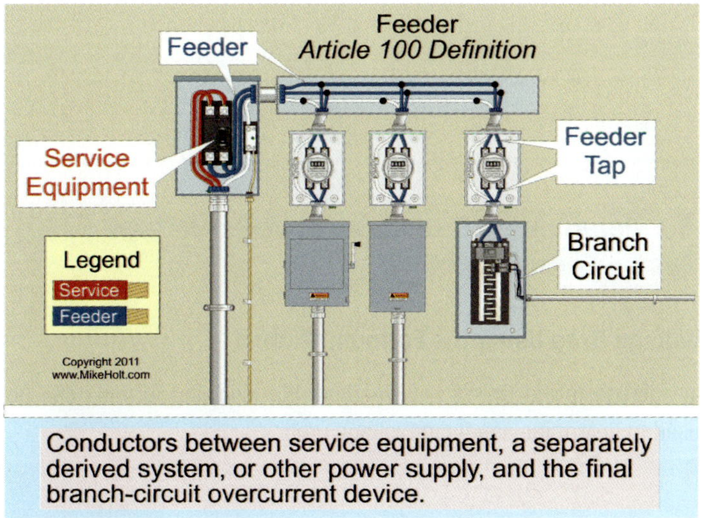

Figure 8–18

► *NEC* Voltage-Drop Recommendation

Question: *What are the minimum NEC recommended operating volts for a 115V rated load that's connected to a 120V source?* **Figure 8–19**

(a) 114V (b) 115V (c) 116V (d) 120V

Answer: *(a) 114V*

The maximum conductor voltage drop recommended for both the feeder and branch circuit is five percent of the voltage source (120V). The total conductor voltage drop (feeder and branch circuit) shouldn't exceed 120V x 0.05 = 6V. The operating voltage at the load is calculated by subtracting the conductor's voltage drop from the voltage source: 120V – 6V = 114V.

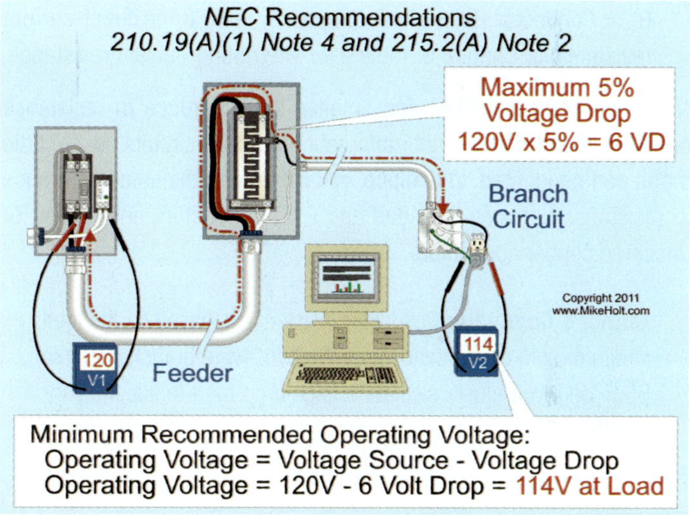

Figure 8–19

Undervoltage harms the performance of electrical equipment. For inductive loads such as motors and heaters it can cause inefficiency, overheating, and shortened life spans. Solid-state equipment such as TVs and computers are also effected by voltage drop. When conductor resistance causes circuit voltage to drop below an acceptable value, the conductor size should be increased.

8.7 Determining Circuit Conductors' Voltage Drop—Ohm's Law Method

The voltage drop of a circuit is in direct proportion to the conductor's resistance and the magnitude (size) of the current. A longer conductor results in greater conductor resistance, and greater conductor voltage drop. Increased current flow will result in greater conductor voltage drop. The voltage drop of the circuit conductors can be determined by the Ohm's Law method or by the formula method:

- **Ohm's Law Method—Single-Phase**

  $E_{vd} = I \times R$

  E_{vd} = Conductor voltage drop expressed in volts.

  I = The load in amperes at 100 percent, not at 125 percent, for motors or continuous loads.

  R* = Conductor Resistance, Chapter 9, Table 8 for direct-current resistance or Chapter 9, Table 9 for alternating-current resistance.

*For conductors 1/0 AWG and smaller, the difference in resistance between direct-current and alternating-current circuits is so little that it can be ignored. In addition, you can ignore the small difference in resistance between stranded and solid conductors and coated or uncoated copper conductors.

> **Author's Comment:** Conductor resistance is based on the total length of both circuit conductors. So if a 2-wire branch circuit is 80 ft long, you must calculate voltage drop for a total conductor length of 160 ft.

► Voltage Drop 120V

Question: *What's the voltage drop of two 12 AWG conductors that supply a 16A, 120V, single-phase load located 100 ft from the power supply?* **Figure 8–20**

(a) 3.20V (b) 6.40V (c) 9.60V (d) 12.80V

Answer: *(b) 6.40V*

$E_{vd} = I \times R$

I = 16A

R = 2 ohms per 1,000 ft [Chapter 9, Table 9]

R = (2 ohms per 1,000 ft/1,000 ft) x 200 ft

R = 0.40 ohms

$E_{vd} = I \times R$

E_{vd} = 16A x 0.40 ohms

E_{vd} = 6.40V

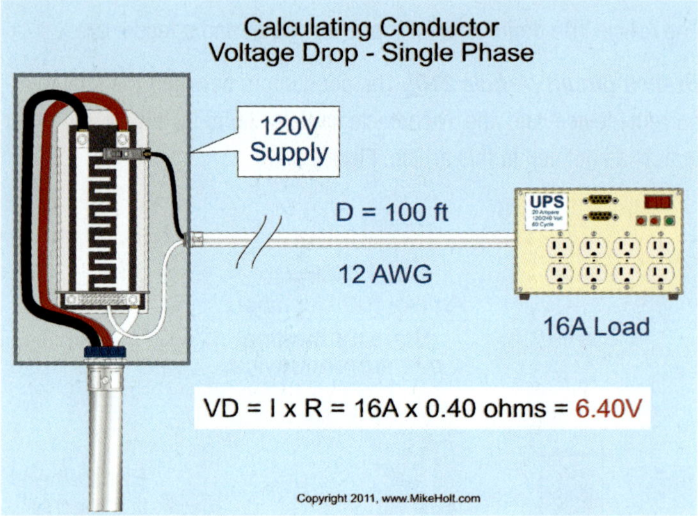

Figure 8–20

► Voltage Drop 240V

Question: *A 240V, 24A, single-phase load is located 100 ft from the panelboard and is wired with 10 AWG. What's the voltage drop of the circuit conductors?* **Figure 8–21**

(a) 3.64V (b) 4.53V (c) 5.76V (d) 9.22V

Answer: *(c) 5.76V*

$E_{vd} = I \times R$

I = 24A

R = 1.20 ohms per 1,000 ft [Chapter 9, Table 9]

R = (1.20 ohms per 1,000 ft/1,000 ft) x 200 ft

R = 0.24 ohms

$E_{vd} = I \times R$

E_{vd} = 24A x 0.24 ohms

E_{vd} = 5.76V

8.8 Determining Circuit Conductors' Voltage Drop—Formula Method

Voltage Drop Using the Formula Method

In addition to the Ohm's Law method, the following formula can be used to determine conductor voltage drop:

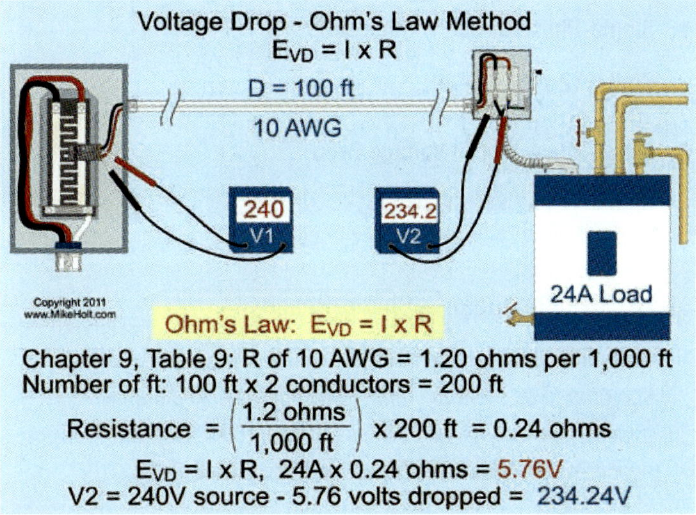

Figure 8–21

◆ **Single-Phase Circuit Voltage Drop**

E_{vd} = (2 x K x I x D)/Cmil

◆ **Three-Phase Circuit Voltage Drop**

E_{vd} = (1.732 x K x I x D)/Cmil

E_{vd} = Volts Dropped: The voltage drop of the circuit expressed in volts.

K = Direct-Current Constant. This constant K represents the direct-current resistance for a 1,000 circular mils conductor that's 1,000 ft long, at an operating temperature of 75°C. The constant K value is 12.90 for copper and 21.20 for aluminum.

> **Author's Comment:** This K value is an approximation that provides a reasonable working voltage drop result. We'll use this approximation in this unit. To find the actual or "True K" value of a conductor, multiply the circular mil area of the conductor by its resistance per ft.

I = Amperes: The load in amperes at 100 percent (not at 125 percent for motors or continuous loads).

D = Distance: The distance the load is from the power supply. Don't use length of wire for this formula.

Cmil = Circular Mils: The circular mils of the circuit conductor as listed in the *NEC* Chapter 9, Table 8.

► Voltage Drop—Single-Phase

Question: *A 24A, 240V single-phase load is located 100 ft from a panelboard and is wired with two 10 AWG conductors. What's the approximate voltage drop of the branch-circuit conductors?* **Figure 8–22**

(a) 4.25V *(b) 5.97V* *(c) 3%* *(d) 5%*

Answer: *(b) 5.97V*

E_{vd} = (2 x K x I x D)/Cmil

K = 12.90, copper

I = 24A

D = 100 ft

Cmil = 10,380 cmil, (10 AWG) [Chapter 9, Table 8]

E_{vd} = (2 x K x I x D)/Cmil

E_{vd} = (2 x 12.90 x 24A x 100 ft)/10,380 cmil

E_{vd} = 5.97V

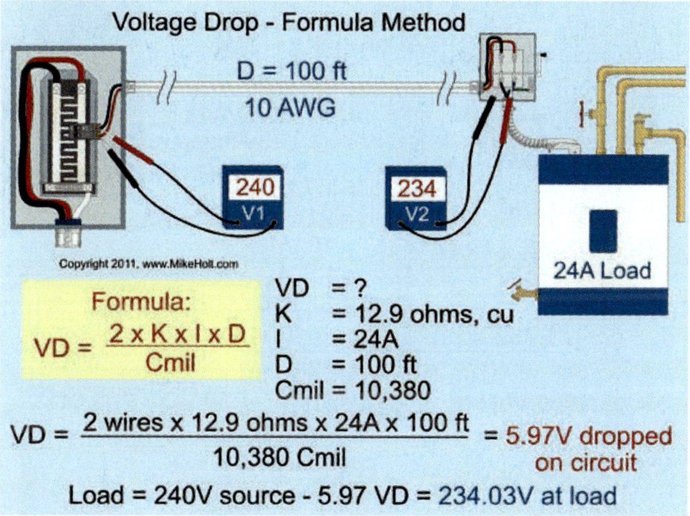

Figure 8–22

► Voltage Drop—Three-Phase

Question: *What is the voltage drop of 1 AWG aluminum conductors that supply a 100A, 208V, three-phase load located 100 ft from the power supply?* **Figure 8–23**

(a) 4.39V (b) 7.00V (c) 3% (d) 5%

Answer: *(a) 4.39V*

$E_{vd} = (1.732 \times K \times I \times D)/Cmil$

K = 21.20, aluminum
I = 100A
D = 100 ft
Cmil = 83,690, (1 AWG) [Chapter 9, Table 8]

$E_{vd} = (1.732 \times 21.20 \times 100A \times 100\ ft)/83{,}690\ cmil$
$E_{vd} = 4.39V$

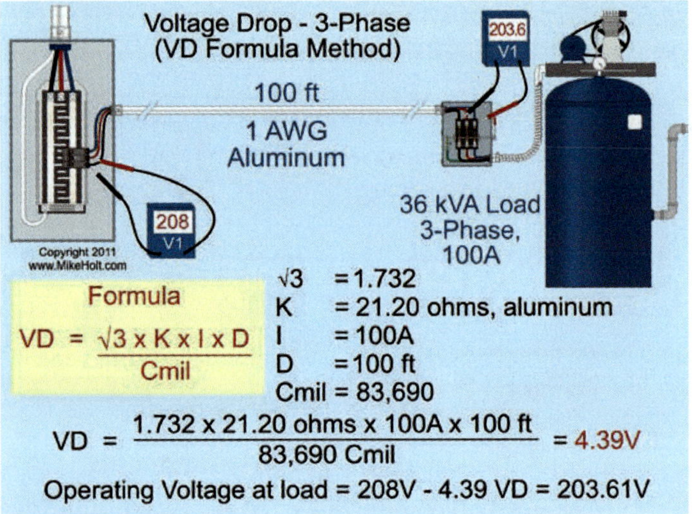

Figure 8–23

8.9 Sizing Conductors to Prevent Excessive Voltage Drop

The size of a conductor (actually its resistance) effects voltage drop. If we want to decrease the voltage drop of a circuit, we can increase the cross-sectional area of the conductor (reduce its resistance). When sizing conductors to prevent excessive voltage drop, use the following formulas:

◆ **Single-Phase Circuit Voltage Drop**

$Cmil = (2 \times K \times I \times D)/E_{vd}$

◆ **Three-Phase Circuit Voltage Drop**

$Cmil = (1.732 \times K \times I \times D)/E_{vd}$

► Size Conductor—Single-Phase

Question: *What size conductor should be used to limit the voltage drop to no more than three percent if the single-phase continuous load of 26A at 230V is located 100 ft from the power supply? The terminals are rated for 75°C.* **Figure 8–24**

(a) 10 AWG (b) 8 AWG (c) 6 AWG (d) 4 AWG

Answer: *(b) 8 AWG*

$Cmil = (2 \times K \times I \times D)/E_{vd}$

K = 12.90, copper
I = 26A at 230V
D = 100 ft

$E_{vd} = 240V \times 0.03$
$E_{vd} = 7.20V$

Cmil = (2 x 12.90 x 26A x 100 ft)/7.20V
Cmil = 9,317 cmil, (10 AWG) [Chapter 9, Table 8]

Note: Section 210.19(A)(1) requires that the conductors for a continuous load be sized not less than 125 percent of the continuous load and 210.20(A) requires that the overcurrent protection device must be not less than 125 percent of the continuous load. The continuous load is 28A so the conductor and overcurrent device must be sized at: 28A x 1.25 = 35A.

The 10 AWG conductor required for voltage drop is rated for 35A at 75°C according to 110.14(C) and Table 310.15(B)(16). However, 240.4(D) requires that 10 AWG can't be protected by an overcurrent device rated more than 30A, so this will not work. We need to size up to 8 AWG conductors protected at 35A.

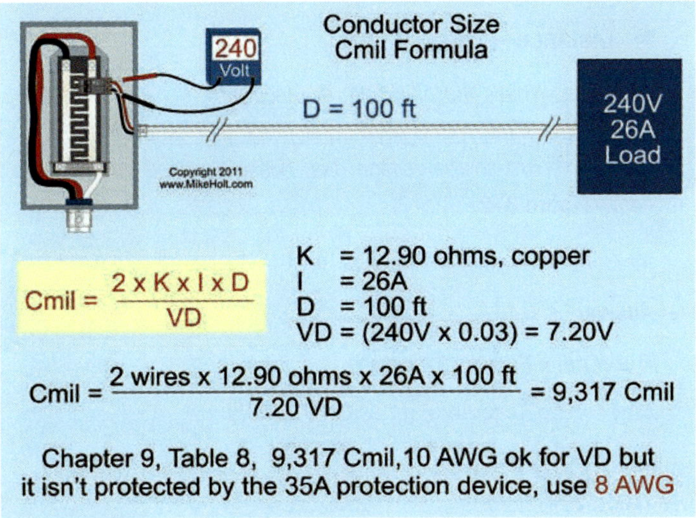

Figure 8–24

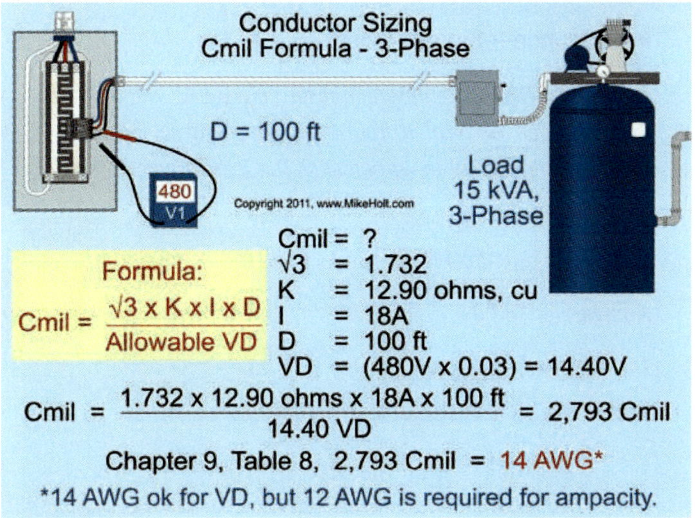

Figure 8–25

▶ Size Conductor—Three-Phase

Question: *What size conductor should be used to limit voltage drop from exceeding three percent if the appliance nameplate indicates 18A at 460V, three-phase and it's located 100 ft from the power supply? The terminals are rated for 75°C.* **Figure 8–25**

(a) 12 AWG (b) 10 AWG (c) 8 AWG (d) 6 AWG

Answer: *(a) 12 AWG*

Cmil = (1.732 x K x I x D)/ E_{vd}

K = 12.90, copper

I = 18A

D = 100 ft

E_{vd} *= 480V x 0.03 = 14.40V*

Cmil = (1.732 x 12.90 x 18A x 100 ft)/14.40V

Cmil = 2,793 cmil, (14 AWG) [Chapter 9, Table 8]

Note: If the problem does not state that this is a continuous load, assume that it is noncontinuous. Section 210.19(A)(1) requires that the conductors for a noncontinuous load be sized not less than 100 percent of the load and 210.20(A) requires that the overcurrent protection device must be not less than 100 percent of the noncontinuous load. The noncontinuous load is 18A so the conductor and overcurrent device must be sized at 18A.

The 14 AWG conductor required for voltage drop is rated for 20A at 75°C according to 110.14(C) and Table 310.15(B)(16). However, 240.4(D) requires that 14 AWG can't be protected by an overcurrent device rated more than 15A, so this will not work. We need to size up to 12 AWG conductors protected at 20A.

8.10 Limiting Conductor Length to Minimize Voltage Drop

Limiting the length of conductors can also reduce voltage drop. The following formulas can be used to help determine maximum conductor length to limit the voltage drop to *NEC* recommendations:

- **Single-Phase Circuit Voltage Drop**

  D = (Cmil x E_{vd})/(2 x K x I)

- **Three-Phase Circuit Voltage Drop**

  D = (Cmil x E_{vd})/(1.732 x K x I)

► Distance—Single-Phase

Question: *What's the maximum distance a 240V, single-phase, 10A load can be located from the panelboard so the voltage drop doesn't exceed three percent? The load is wired with 12 AWG.* **Figure 8–26**

(a) 55 ft (b) 110 ft (c) 182 ft (d) 220 ft

Answer: *(c) 182 ft*

D = (Cmil x E_{vd})/(2 x K x I)

Cmil = 6,530 (12 AWG) [Chapter 9, Table 8]

E_{vd} = 240V x 0.03
E_{vd} = 7.20V

K = 12.90, copper

I = 10A

D = (6,530 cmil x 7.20V)/(2 x 12.90 x 10A)
D = 182.20 ft

► Distance—Three-Phase

Question: *What's the maximum distance a 100A, 208V, three-phase load, wired with 3 AWG conductors, can be located from the panelboard so the voltage drop doesn't exceed three percent?* **Figure 8–27**

(a) 75 ft (b) 125 ft (c) 147 ft (d) 325 ft

Answer: *(c) 147 ft*

D = (Cmil x E_{vd})/(1.732 x K x I)

Cmil = 52,620, (3 AWG) [Chapter 9, Table 8]

E_{vd} = 208V x 0.03
E_{vd} = 6.24V

K = 12.90, copper

I = 100A

D = (52,620 cmil x 6.24V)/(1.732 x 12.90 x 100A)
D = 147 ft

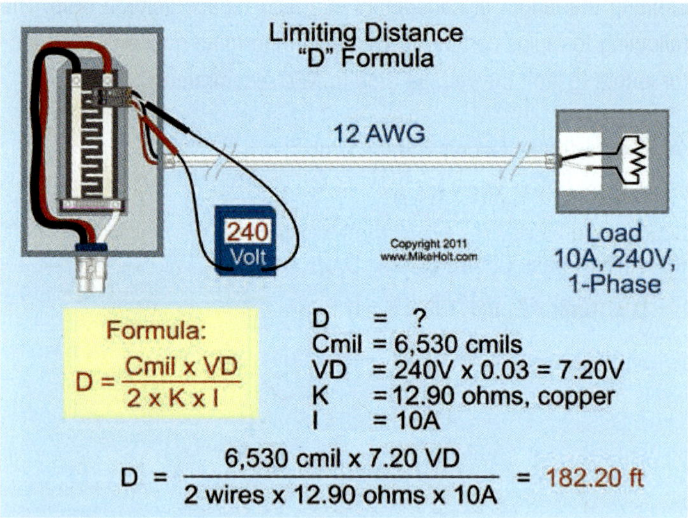

Figure 8–26

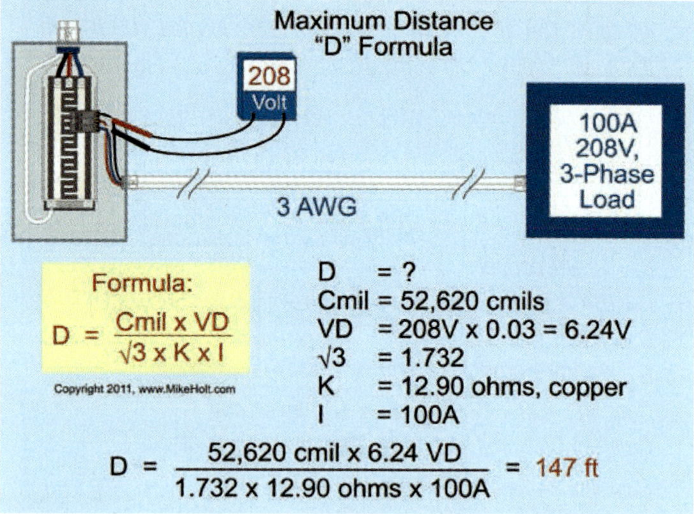

Figure 8–27

8.11 Limiting Current to Limit Voltage Drop

Sometimes the only method of limiting the circuit voltage drop is to limit the load on the conductors. The following formulas can be used to determine the maximum load:

- **Single-Phase Circuit Voltage Drop**

  $I = (Cmil \times E_{vd})/(2 \times K \times D)$

- **Three-Phase Circuit Voltage Drop**

  $I = (Cmil \times E_{vd})/(1.732 \times K \times D)$

▶ Maximum Load—Single-Phase

Question: *What's the maximum recommended load that should be placed on 1/0 AWG aluminum conductors in a nonmetallic raceway to a panelboard located 200 ft from a 240V single-phase power source so the NEC recommendation for voltage drop isn't exceeded?* **Figure 8–28**

(a) 51A (b) 89A (c) 94A (d) 115A

Answer: *(b) 89A*

$I = (Cmil \times E_{vd})/(2 \times K \times D)$

Cmil = 105,600 (1/0 AWG) [Chapter 9, Table 8]

E_{vd} = 240V x 0.03
E_{vd} = 7.20V

K = 21.20, aluminum

D = 200 ft

I = (105,600 cmil x 7.20V)/(2 x 21.20 x 200 ft)
I = 89.66A

Note: The maximum load permitted on 1/0 AWG aluminum at 75°C terminals is 120A [Table 310.15(B)(16)]. This circuit will safely carry the 89.66A without excessive voltage drop, but can't be loaded to the rated value of 120A.

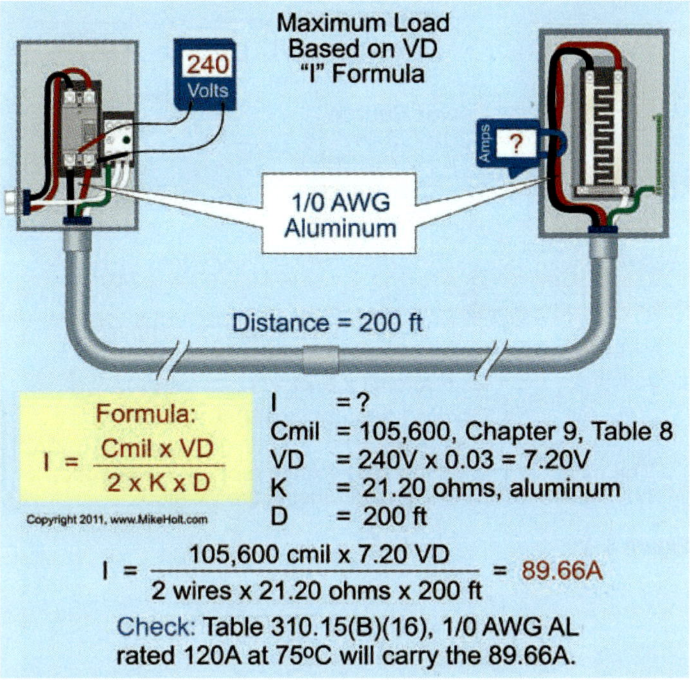

Figure 8–28

▶ Maximum Load—Three-Phase

Question: *What's the maximum recommended load that should be placed on 1 AWG copper conductors in an aluminum raceway to a panelboard located 150 ft from a 208V, three-phase power source so the NEC recommendation for voltage drop isn't exceeded?* **Figure 8–29**

(a) 155A (b) 190A (c) 210A (d) 240A

Answer: *(a) 155A*

$I = (Cmil \times E_{vd})/(1.732 \times K \times D)$

Cmil = 83,690 (1 AWG) [Chapter 9, Table 8]

E_{vd} = 208V x 0.03
E_{vd} = 6.24V

K = 12.90, copper

D = 150 ft

I = (83,690 cmil x 6.24V)/(1.732 x 12.90 x 150 ft)
I = 155.80A

Note: The maximum load of 155.80A limits the voltage drop to no more than three percent. When working this type of problem, don't lose sight of other Code requirements. Table 310.15(B)(16) must also be consulted for the maximum ampacity permitted on 1 AWG at 75°C, which is 130A, so 130A is the working limit for this circuit [110.14(C) and Table 310.15(B)(16)].

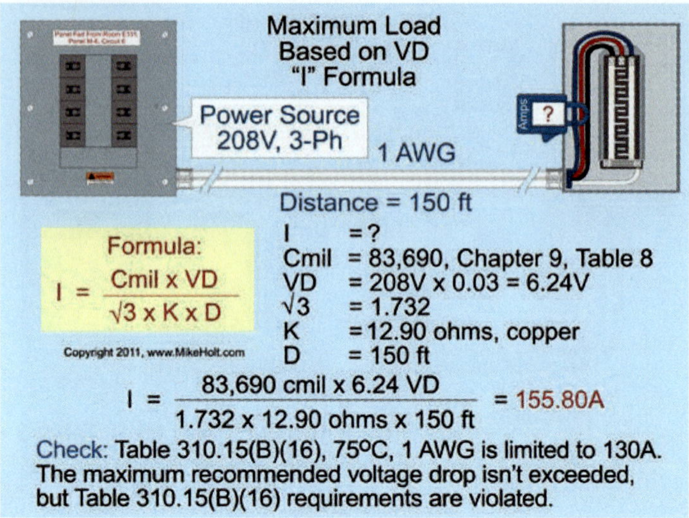

Figure 8–29

CONCLUSION TO UNIT 8—VOLTAGE-DROP CALCULATIONS

This unit explained that voltage drop results anytime there's current flowing through a resistor. Every conductor has resistance (opposition to the flow of electrons), which is determined by factors such as the conductor material, cross-sectional area, length, and operating temperature. Excessive voltage drop results in power losses and possibly under-operating voltage for electrical equipment.

The *Code* provides specific voltage-drop requirements in some special cases, such as for fire pumps, but doesn't generally require conductors to be sized to limit conductor voltage drop. Manufacturers' instructions may require a minimum operating voltage, which means that voltage drop must be considered. In this unit, you learned how to correctly size conductors in order to stay within the *NEC* recommendations for voltage drop.

Transpositions of voltage-drop formulas were reviewed in this unit so that you'll be able to select the proper formula to solve for various unknowns. You now have the tools needed to properly install circuits for proper equipment operation.

If you're not yet fully comfortable with voltage-drop calculations, go back and review this unit carefully and see how each voltage-drop formula relates to Ohm's Law. It all can be traced back to the basics.

UNIT 8

Practice Questions

Please use the 2011 *Code* book to answer the following questions, which are based on the 2011 *NEC.*

PRACTICE QUESTIONS FOR UNIT 8—VOLTAGE-DROP CALCULATIONS

PART A—CONDUCTOR RESISTANCE CALCULATIONS

8.1 Conductor Resistance

1. The larger the cross-sectional area of a conductor, the ______ the number of paths for electrons, which lowers the resistance of the conductor.

(a) greater
(b) fewer

2. Conductor resistance is determined by the ______.

(a) material type
(b) cross-sectional area
(c) conductor length
(d) all of these

3. ______ is the best conductor, better than gold, but the high cost limits its use to special applications, such as fuse elements and some switch contacts.

(a) Silver
(b) Copper
(c) Aluminum
(d) none of these

4. ______ conductors are often used when weight or cost are important considerations.

(a) Silver
(b) Copper
(c) Aluminum
(d) none of these

5. A conductor's cross-sectional area is expressed in AWG or ______.

(a) square inches
(b) mils
(c) circular mils
(d) none of these

6. The resistance of a conductor is directly proportional to its length.

(a) True
(b) False

7. The resistance of a conductor changes with temperature. Temperature coefficient describes the effect that temperature has on the resistance of a conductor. Conductors with a ______ temperature coefficient have an increase in resistance with an increase in temperature.

(a) positive
(b) negative
(c) neutral
(d) none of these

8.2 Conductor Resistance—Direct-Current Circuits [Chapter 9, Table 8]

8. The *National Electrical Code* lists the resistance and area in circular mils for both direct-current and alternating-current conductors. Direct-current conductor resistances are listed in Chapter 9, Table ______ and alternating-current conductor resistances are listed in Chapter 9, Table ______.

(a) 1, 5
(b) 3, 4
(c) 8, 9
(d) 9, 8

9. What's the direct-current resistance of a 6 AWG copper conductor that's 400 ft long?

(a) 0.20 ohms
(b) 0.30 ohms
(c) 0.40 ohms
(d) 0.50 ohms

10. What's the direct-current resistance of a 1 AWG copper conductor that's 200 ft long?

(a) 0.0308 ohms
(b) 0.0311 ohms
(c) 0.0423 ohms
(d) 0.0564 ohms

11. What's the direct-current resistance of a 3 AWG aluminum conductor that's 1,000 ft long?

(a) 0.231 ohms
(b) 0.313 ohms
(c) 0.403 ohms
(d) 0.422 ohms

12. What's the direct-current resistance of a 1/0 AWG aluminum conductor that's 800 ft long?

(a) 0.08 ohms
(b) 0.16 ohms
(c) 0.23 ohms
(d) 0.56 ohms

13. What's the direct-current resistance of a 1 AWG copper conductor that's 100 ft long?

(a) 0.0154 ohms
(b) 0.1620 ohms
(c) 0.2330 ohms
(d) 0.5610 ohms

14. What's the direct-current resistance of a 3 AWG aluminum conductor that's 500 ft long?

(a) 0.0231 ohms
(b) 0.1614 ohms
(c) 0.2015 ohms
(d) 0.2330 ohms

15. What's the direct-current resistance in ohms for three 300 kcmil conductors in a parallel run that's 1,000 ft long?

(a) 0.014 ohms
(b) 0.026 ohms
(c) 0.047 ohms
(d) 0.052 ohms

8.3 Conductor Resistance—Alternating-Current Circuits

16. The intensity of a magnetic field depends on the intensity of alternating current. The greater the current flow, the greater the overall magnetic field.

(a) True
(b) False

17. In alternating-current circuits, the expanding and collapsing magnetic field within the conductor induces an electromotive force that opposes the flow of alternating current. This opposition to the flow of alternating current is called "inductive reactance."

(a) True
(b) False

18. ______ currents are small independent currents that are produced as a result of the expanding and collapsing magnetic field. They flow erratically within the conductor opposing current flow and consuming power.

(a) Lenz
(b) Ohm's
(c) Eddy
(d) Kirchoff's

19. The expanding and collapsing magnetic field induces a counter voltage within the conductors, which repels the flowing electrons toward the conductor surface. This is known as "______ effect."

(a) inductive
(b) skin
(c) surface
(d) watt

8.4 Alternating-Current Resistance

20. The opposition to current flow is greater for alternating-current circuits than for direct-current circuits because of ______.

(a) eddy currents
(b) skin effect
(c) inductive reactance
(d) all of these

21. The alternating-current conductor resistances listed in Chapter 9, Table 9 of the *NEC* are different for copper and aluminum and for nonmagnetic and magnetic raceways.

(a) True
(b) False

22. What's the alternating-current ohms-to-neutral resistance for a 2/0 AWG copper conductor that's 300 ft long?

(a) 0.03 ohms
(b) 0.04 ohms
(c) 0.05 ohms
(d) 0.06 ohms

23. What's the alternating-current ohms-to-neutral resistance for a 500 kcmil copper conductor installed in an aluminum raceway that's 1,000 ft long?

(a) 0.027 ohms
(b) 0.029 ohms
(c) 0.030 ohms
(d) 0.032 ohms

24. What's the alternating-current ohms-to-neutral resistance for a 3 AWG copper conductor that's 100 ft long?

(a) 0.012 ohms
(b) 0.025 ohms
(c) 0.330 ohms
(d) 0.430 ohms

25. What's the alternating-current ohms-to-neutral resistance of a 500 kcmil copper conductor installed in PVC conduit that's 400 ft long?

(a) 0.0108 ohms
(b) 0.0204 ohms
(c) 0.0333 ohms
(d) 0.0431 ohms

26. A 2-wire circuit supplies a 36A load that's located 100 ft from the panelboard. The load is wired with 1 AWG aluminum conductors in PVC conduit. What's the total alternating-current ohms-to-neutral resistance of the circuit conductors?

(a) 0.05 ohms
(b) 0.25 ohms
(c) 0.50 ohms
(d) 0.62 ohms

27. What size copper conductors in a steel raceway can be used to replace 1/0 AWG aluminum that supplies a 110A load? Hint: find a copper conductor with the same resistance per foot as the existing aluminum conductor.

Note: We don't want to increase the circuit voltage drop.

(a) 3 AWG
(b) 2 AWG
(c) 1 AWG
(d) 1/0 AWG

28. What's the circuit voltage if the conductor voltage drop is 3.30V?

Note: Assume three percent voltage drop.

(a) 110V
(b) 115V
(c) 120V
(d) 240V

29. What's the alternating-current ohms-to-neutral resistance for three 1/0 AWG aluminum conductors run in parallel for 1,000 ft?

(a) 0.067 ohms
(b) 0.114 ohms
(c) 0.231 ohms
(d) 0.413 ohms

PART B—VOLTAGE-DROP CONSIDERATIONS

8.6 *NEC* Voltage-Drop Recommendations

30. Because of high demand for electricity, utilities are sometimes forced to reduce their output voltage. In addition, transformers, services, feeders, and branch-circuit conductors oppose the flow of current. The opposition to current flow results in voltage drop. All circuits have voltage drop, simply because all conductors have resistance.

(a) True
(b) False

31. When sizing conductors for feeders and branch circuits, the *NEC* ______ that we take voltage drop into consideration.

(a) assumes
(b) suggests
(c) requires
(d) demands

32. ______ equipment such as motors and electromagnetic ballasts can overheat at reduced voltage. This results in reduced equipment operating life and inconvenience to the customer.

(a) Inductive
(b) Electronic
(c) Resistive
(d) all of these

33. ______ equipment such as computers, laser printers, copy machines, and so forth, can suddenly power down because of reduced voltage, resulting in data losses.

(a) Inductive
(b) Electronic
(c) Resistive
(d) all of these

34. When a conductor resistance causes the voltage to be dropped below an acceptable point, the conductor size should be increased.

(a) True
(b) False

35. How can conductor voltage drop be reduced?

(a) Reduce the conductor resistance.
(b) Increase the conductor size.
(c) Decrease the conductor length.
(d) all of these

36. If the branch-circuit supply voltage is 208V, the maximum recommended voltage drop of the circuit shouldn't be more than ______.

(a) 3.60V
(b) 6.24V
(c) 6.90V
(d) 7.20V

37. If the feeder supply voltage is 240V, the maximum recommended voltage drop of the feeder shouldn't be more than ______.

(a) 3.60V
(b) 6.24V
(c) 6.90V
(d) 7.20V

8.7 Determining Circuit Conductors' Voltage Drop—Ohm's Law Method

38. What's the voltage drop of two 12 AWG conductors supplying a 12A continuous load?

Note: The continuous load is located 100 ft from the power supply.

(a) 3.20V
(b) 4V
(c) 4.76V
(d) 12.80V

8.8 Determining Circuit Conductors' Voltage Drop—Formula Method

39. A 240V, 24A, single-phase load is located 160 ft from the panelboard. The load is wired with 10 AWG. What's the approximate voltage drop of the branch-circuit conductors?

(a) 3.20V
(b) 4.25V
(c) 5.90V
(d) 9.50V

40. A 100A, three-phase load is located 100 ft from the panelboard and is wired with 1 AWG aluminum conductors. What's the approximate voltage drop of the circuit conductors?

(a) 3V
(b) 3.50V
(c) 4.40V
(d) 5V

8.9 Sizing Conductors to Prevent Excessive Voltage Drop

41. A single-phase, 5 hp motor is located 110 ft from a panelboard in a dry location. The nameplate indicates that the voltage is 115V and the FLA is 52A. What size conductor is required?

Note: Apply the NEC recommended voltage-drop limit for this branch circuit.

(a) 10 AWG
(b) 8 AWG
(c) 6 AWG
(d) 3 AWG

42. A single-phase, 5 hp motor is located 110 ft from a panelboard. The nameplate indicates that the voltage is 230V and the FLA is 26A. What size conductor is required?

Note: Apply the NEC recommended voltage-drop limits.

(a) 10 AWG
(b) 8 AWG
(c) 6 AWG
(d) 4 AWG

43. A 480V, 18A, three-phase load is located 300 ft from the panelboard. What size copper conductors are required to prevent the voltage drop from exceeding three percent?

(a) 10 AWG
(b) 8 AWG
(c) 6 AWG
(d) 4 AWG

8.10 Limiting Conductor Length to Minimize Voltage Drop

44. What's the approximate distance that a 240V, 31A, single-phase load can be located from the panelboard so the voltage drop doesn't exceed three percent? The load is wired with 8 AWG copper.

(a) 55 ft
(b) 110 ft
(c) 145 ft
(d) 220 ft

45. What's the approximate distance a 480V, 45A, three-phase transformer, wired with 6 AWG copper can be located from the panelboard so the voltage drop doesn't exceed three percent?

(a) 250 ft
(b) 300 ft
(c) 375 ft
(d) 400 ft

8.11 Limiting Current to Limit Voltage Drop

46. An existing installation consists of 1/0 AWG copper conductors in a nonmetallic raceway to a panelboard located 200 ft from a 240V, single-phase power source. What's the maximum load that can be placed on the panelboard so that the *NEC* recommendations for voltage drop aren't exceeded?

(a) 71A
(b) 94A
(c) 109A
(d) 147A

47. An existing installation contains 2 AWG aluminum conductors in an aluminum raceway to a panelboard located 350 ft from a 480V, three-phase power source. What's the maximum load the conductors can carry without exceeding the *NEC* recommendation for voltage drop?

(a) 49A
(b) 64A
(c) 74A
(d) 85A

UNIT 8 Challenge Questions

Please use the 2011 *Code* book to answer the following questions, which are based on the 2011 *NEC.*

CHALLENGE QUESTIONS FOR UNIT 8—VOLTAGE-DROP CALCULATIONS

PART A—CONDUCTOR RESISTANCE CALCULATIONS

8.1 Conductor Resistance

1. The resistance of a conductor is affected by temperature change. This is called the "______."

(a) temperature correction factor
(b) temperature coefficient
(c) ambient temperature factor
(d) none of these

8.3 Conductor Resistance—Alternating-Current Circuits

2. The total opposition to current flow in an alternating-current circuit is expressed in ohms and is called "______."

(a) impedance
(b) conductance
(c) reluctance
(d) resistance

8.4 Alternating-Current Resistance

3. A 240V, 40A, single-phase load is located 150 ft from an existing junction box. The junction box is located 50 ft from the panelboard and is wired with 4 AWG aluminum wire. The total resistance of the two 4 AWG conductors from the panelboard to the junction box is approximately ______.

(a) 0.03 ohms
(b) 0.04 ohms
(c) 0.05 ohms
(d) 0.08 ohms

4. A load is located 100 ft from a 230V power supply and is wired with 4 AWG aluminum conductors. What size copper conductor can be used to replace the aluminum conductors and not increase the conductor voltage drop?

(a) 8 AWG
(b) 6 AWG
(c) 2 AWG
(d) 1/0 AWG

PART B—VOLTAGE-DROP CALCULATIONS

8.7 Determining Circuit Conductors' Voltage Drop—Ohm's Law Method

5. A 40A, 240V rated single-phase load is 150 ft from a junction box and the junction box is located 50 ft from a panelboard (for a total of 200 ft). If the voltage at the panelboard is 240V, what's the minimum voltage recommended by the *NEC* at the 40A load?

(a) 117.70V
(b) 228.20V
(c) 232.80V
(d) 236.20V

8.8 Determining Circuit Conductors' Voltage Drop—Formula Method

6. What's the voltage drop of two 4 AWG aluminum conductors that supply a 5 hp, 115V, single-phase motor that has a name-plate rating of 55A? The motor is located 95 ft from the power supply.

(a) 3.25V
(b) 5.31V
(c) 6.24V
(d) 7.26V

8.9 Sizing Conductors to Prevent Excessive Voltage Drop

7. A 240V, 40A, single-phase load is located 150 ft from an existing junction box. The junction box is located 50 ft from the panelboard. When the 40A load is on, the voltage at the junction box is calculated to be 236V. The *NEC* recommends that the voltage drop for this branch circuit not exceed three percent of the 240V source (7.20V). What size copper conductor can be installed from the junction box to the load and still meet the *NEC* recommendations for branch circuits?

    (a) 6 AWG
    (b) 3 AWG
    (c) 1 AWG
    (d) 1/0 AWG

8. An existing junction box is located 65 ft from the panelboard and contains 4 AWG aluminum conductors. What size copper conductor can be used to extend this circuit 85 ft and supply a 50A, 208V load?

    Note: Apply the NEC recommended voltage-drop limits.

    (a) 10 AWG
    (b) 8 AWG
    (c) 6 AWG
    (d) 4 AWG

8.10 Limiting Conductor Length to Minimize Voltage Drop

9. How far can a 230V, 50A, three-phase load be located from a panelboard if it's fed with 3 AWG conductors and still meet the *NEC* recommendations for voltage drop for branch circuits?

    (a) 275 ft
    (b) 300 ft
    (c) 325 ft
    (d) 350 ft

8.11 Limiting Current to Limit Voltage Drop

10. Two 8 AWG copper conductors supply a 120V load that's located 225 ft from the panelboard. What's the maximum load in amperes that can be applied to these conductors without exceeding the *NEC* recommendation on conductor voltage drop?

    (a) 0A
    (b) 5A
    (c) 10A
    (d) 15A

UNIT 9

Dwelling Unit Calculations

INTRODUCTION TO UNIT 9—DWELLING UNIT CALCULATIONS

Unit 9 focuses on sizing the service for a one-family dwelling unit. The *NEC* defines a dwelling unit as a single unit, providing complete and independent living facilities for one or more persons, including permanent provisions for living, sleeping, cooking, and sanitation. Figure 9–1

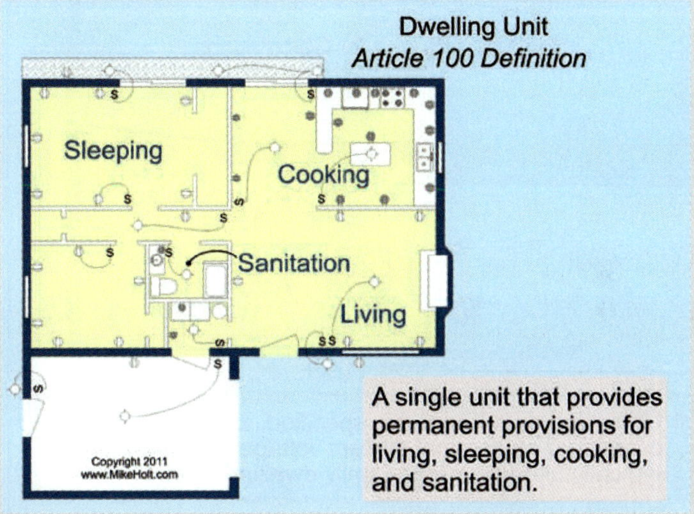

Figure 9–1

The *Code* provides two different calculation methods for this: standard and optional. Both methods are explained in this unit and you should be familiar with both for exam purposes. A good grasp of the material in this unit is important as a basis for the following units which will address multifamily dwellings and commercial calculations, so be sure to study the examples and complete the questions at the end to solidify your understanding.

Sizing a service isn't simply a matter of adding up all of the loads or all of the circuit breaker sizes. The *NEC* recognizes that not all loads will be used simultaneously under normal living conditions, so there are a number of "demand factors" that come into play in sizing an electrical service. It's important to be familiar with all of the requirements of Article 220 so the proper demand factors will be applied to a given installation. There are numerous tables and requirements to follow, but take them one at a time and you'll be able to complete these calculations.

PART A—GENERAL REQUIREMENTS

Introduction

The *NEC* contains detailed requirements for calculating service and feeder loads in many types of occupancies (buildings). Although most of these requirements are located in Article 220, other rules effecting service and feeder loads are scattered throughout the *Code*. When performing load calculations, dwelling units are a special class of occupancy. In the first place, the *Code* permits two different general approaches for load calculations: standard and optional. When using either of these general methods, the rules for dwelling unit calculations also contain a number of demand factors that can't be used in other types of buildings.

Author's Comment: This unit is based on the use of solidly grounded ac systems, 600V or less, using 90°C insulated copper conductors sized to 75°C terminals unless otherwise specified.

9.1 General Requirements

Article 220 provides the requirements for residential branch circuits, feeders, and service calculations [220.1]. Other important articles include: Branch Circuits—210, Feeders—215, Services—230, Overcurrent Protection—240, Wiring Methods—300, Conductors—310, Appliances—422, Electric Space-Heating Equipment—424, Motors—430, and Air-Conditioning Equipment—440.

9.2 Voltages [220.5(A)]

Unless other voltages are specified, branch-circuit, feeder, and service loads must be calculated using the nominal system voltage such as 120, 120/240, 120/208, 240, 347, 277/480, 480, 347/600, or 600. For single-family dwelling unit calculations, the nominal voltage is typically 120/240V. Figure 9–2

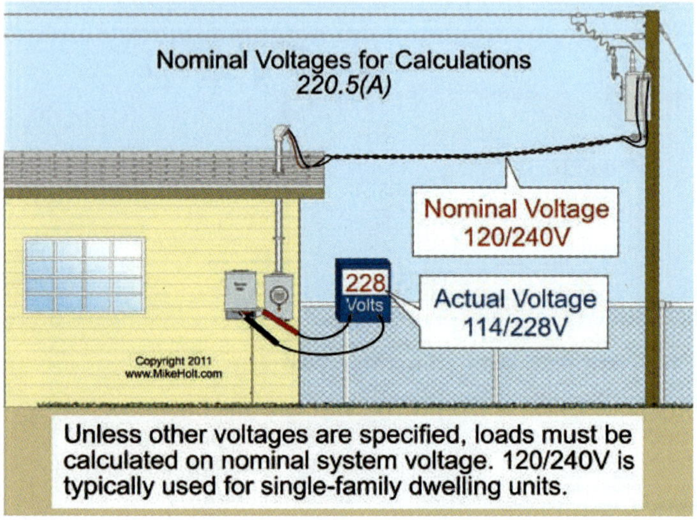

Figure 9–2

Author's Comment: A nominal value is assigned to a circuit for the purpose of conveniently designating its voltage class. The actual voltage at which a circuit operates can vary from the nominal within a range that permits satisfactory operation of equipment [100].

9.3 Fraction of an Ampere [220.5(B)]

Rounding

Where calculations result in a fraction of an ampere, the *Code* permits rounding to the closest ampere, and if the fraction is less than 0.50A, the decimal fractions can be dropped.

Author's Comment: When do you round—after each calculation, or at the final calculation? The *NEC* isn't specific on this issue, so I guess it all depends on the answer you want to see!

According to 424.3(B), fixed electric heating is considered to be a continuous load, and therefore the branch-circuit conductors and overcurrent device for electric space-heating equipment must be sized no less than 125 percent of the total load.

► Electric Space Heating Conductor Sizing Example

Question: *What size conductor is required to supply a 9.60 kVA (40A), 240V, single-phase fixed space heater with a 3A blower motor if equipment terminals are rated 75°C?* **Figure 9–3**

(a) 10 AWG (b) 8 AWG (c) 6 AWG (d) 4 AWG

Answer: *(c) 6 AWG*

Step 1: Determine the total load.

I = VA/E

I = 9,600 VA/240V

I = 40A

Step 2: The conductor is sized at 125 percent of the load [210.19(A)(1)].

Conductor Size = (40A + 3A) x 1.25

Conductor Size = 53.75A, round up to 54A

If we were allowed to round down, then 8 AWG rated 50A at 75°C could be used, but since we must round up, 6 AWG rated 65A at 75°C is required.

Author's Comment: If wiring with Type NM Cable, be aware that the 90°C rating can be used for amapacity adjustment and correction purposes, but the allowable ampacity must not exceed that of a 60°C rated conductor [334.80].

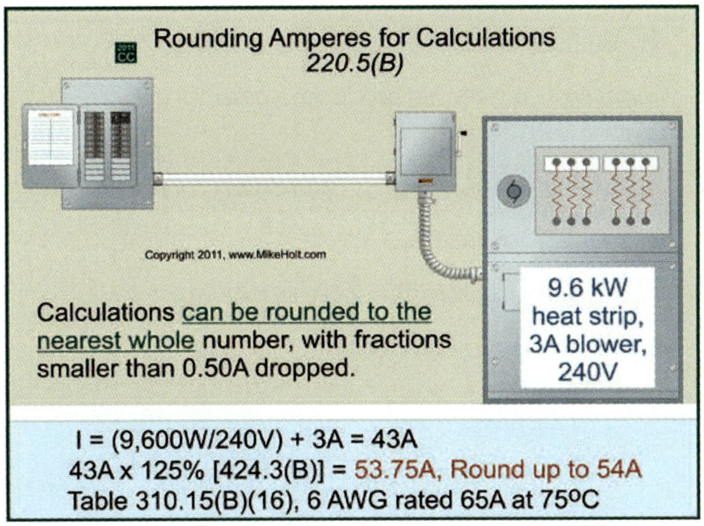

Figure 9–3

9.4 Lighting and Receptacles

General Lighting Calculated Load [220.12]

The *NEC* requires a minimum 3 VA per sq ft for the general lighting and general-use receptacles for the purpose of determining branch circuits and feeder/service calculations. The dimensions for determining the area must be computed from the outside dimensions of the building and must not include open porches, garages, or spaces not adaptable for future use. Figure 9–4

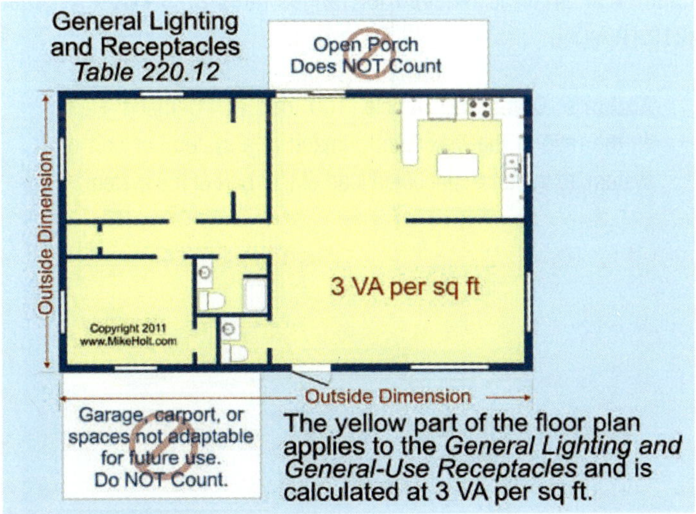

Figure 9–4

Author's Comment: The 3 VA per sq ft rule for general lighting includes all 15A and 20A general-use receptacles, but it doesn't include the small-appliance or laundry circuit receptacles. See 220.14(J) for details.

► General Lighting Load Example [Table 220.12]

Question: *What's the general lighting and receptacle load for a 2,000 sq ft dwelling unit that has 34 convenience receptacles and 12 luminaires rated 100W each?* Figure 9–5

(a) 2,100 VA (b) 4,200 VA (c) 6,000 VA (d) 8,400 VA

Answer: *(c) 6,000 VA*

2,000 sq ft x 3 VA = 6,000 VA

Note: No additional load is required for general-use receptacles and lighting outlets. See 220.14(J).

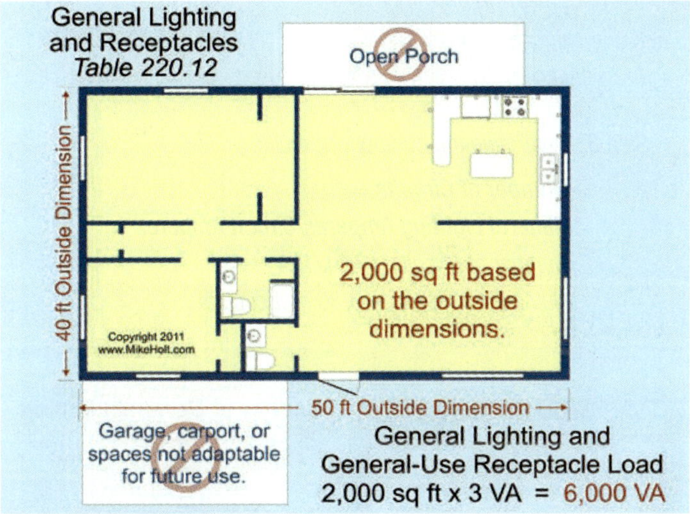

Figure 9–5

Number of Circuits Required [Annex D, Example D1(a)]

The number of branch circuits required for general lighting and receptacles must be determined from the general lighting load and the rating of the circuits [210.11(A)]. To determine the number of branch circuits for general lighting and receptacles, follow these steps:

Step 1: Determine the general lighting VA load:

Living Area Square Footage x 3 VA

Step 2: Determine the general lighting ampere load:

I = VA/E

Step 3: Determine the number of branch circuits:

General Lighting Amperes (Step 2)/Circuit Amperes

► Number of 15 Ampere Circuits Example

Question: *How many 15A circuits are required for a 2,000 sq ft dwelling unit?* **Figure 9–6**

(a) 2 circuits (b) 3 circuits (c) 4 circuits (d) 5 circuits

Answer: *(c) 4 circuits*

Step 1: General Lighting VA = 2,000 sq ft x 3 VA
General Lighting VA = 6,000 VA

Step 2: General Lighting Amperes:

I = VA/E
*I = 6,000 VA/120V**
I = 50A

**Use 120V, single-phase unless specified otherwise.*

Step 3: Determine the number of circuits:

Number of Circuits =
General Lighting Amperes/Circuit Amperes
Number of Circuits = 50A/15A
Number of Circuits = 3.30 or 4 circuits.

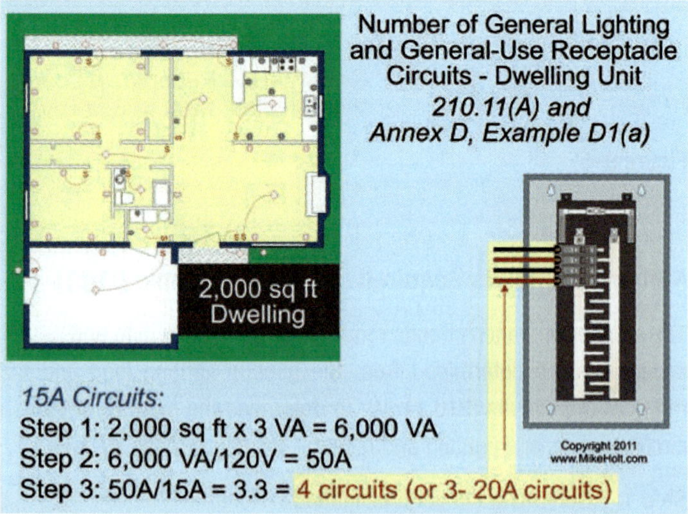

Figure 9–6

► Number of 20 Ampere Circuits Example

Question: *How many 20A circuits are required for a 2,000 sq ft dwelling unit?*

(a) 2 circuits (b) 3 circuits (c) 4 circuits (d) 5 circuits

Answer: *(b) 3 circuits*

Step 1: General Lighting VA = 2,000 sq ft x 3 VA = 6,000 VA

Step 2: General Lighting Amperes:

I = VA/E
I = 6,000 VA/120V
I = 50A

Step 3: Determine the number of circuits:

Number of Circuits =
General Lighting Amperes/Circuit Amperes
Number of Circuits = 50A/20A
Number of Circuits = 2.50 or 3 circuits.

9.5 Cooking Equipment—Branch Circuit [Table 220.55, Note 4]

The branch-circuit calculated load for household ranges and cooking equipment can be determined using Table 220.55, Note 4. The branch-circuit calculated load for one range may be calculated according to the demand factors listed in Table 220.55, but a minimum 40A circuit is required for ranges rated 8.75 kVA and larger [210.19(A)(3)].

Author's Comment: Article 100 defines "Demand Factor" as the ratio of the maximum demand of a system, or part of a system, to the total connected load of that part of the system.

► Less Than 12 kVA, Table 220.55, Column C Example

Question: *What's the minimum branch-circuit conductor ampacity for one 9 kVA range?* **Figure 9–7**

(a) 21A (b) 27A (c) 33A (d) 38A

Answer: *(c) 33A*

The calculated load for one range in Table 220.55, Column C is 8 kVA.

This can be converted to amperes by dividing the power by the voltage:

I = VA/E

*I = (8 kVA x 1,000)/240V**

I = 33A

**Assume 120/240V, single-phase for all calculations unless the question gives a specific voltage and system [220.5(A)].*

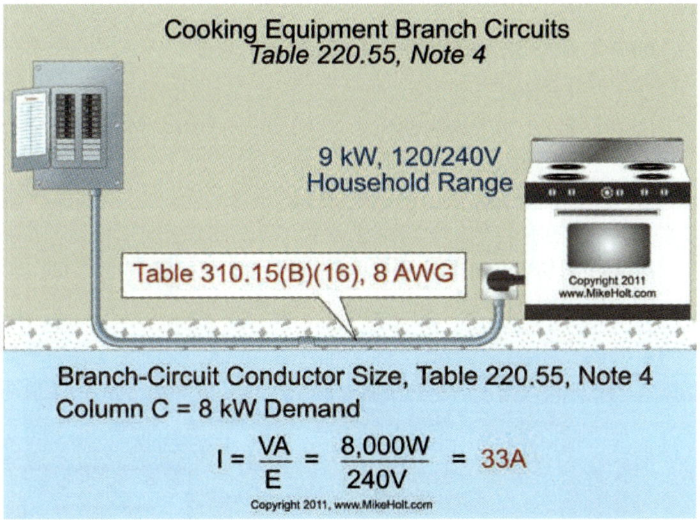

Figure 9–7

Author's Comment: A minimum 40A circuit is required for ranges rated 8.75 kVA and larger [210.19(A)(3)]. Also, notice the footnote to Table 310.15(B)(16) that refers to 240.4(D). The rule in 240.4(D) puts a limit of 30A protection on a 10 AWG conductor, except in specific situations listed in 240.4(E) and 240.4(G).

► More than 12 kVA, Table 220.55, Note 1 Example

Question: *What's the minimum branch-circuit conductor ampacity for one 14 kVA range?* **Figure 9–8**

(a) 33A (b) 37A (c) 50A (d) 58A

Answer: *(b) 37A*

Step 1: Since the range exceeds 12 kVA, follow Note 1 of Table 220.55. The first step is to determine the calculated load as listed in Column C of Table 220.55 for one unit = 8 kVA.

Step 2: We must increase the Column C value (8 kVA) by 5% for each kVA that the range exceeds 12 kVA. In this case, 14 kVA exceeds 12 kVA by 2 kVA.

2 x 5% = 10% increase of the Column C value, resulting in 110%, or a 1.10 multiplier.

Calculated Load = Column C Value x Multiplier

Calculated Load = 8 kVA x 1.10

Calculated Load = 8,800 VA

Step 3: Convert the calculated load to amperes.

I = VA/E

I = 8,800 VA/240V

I = 36.70A

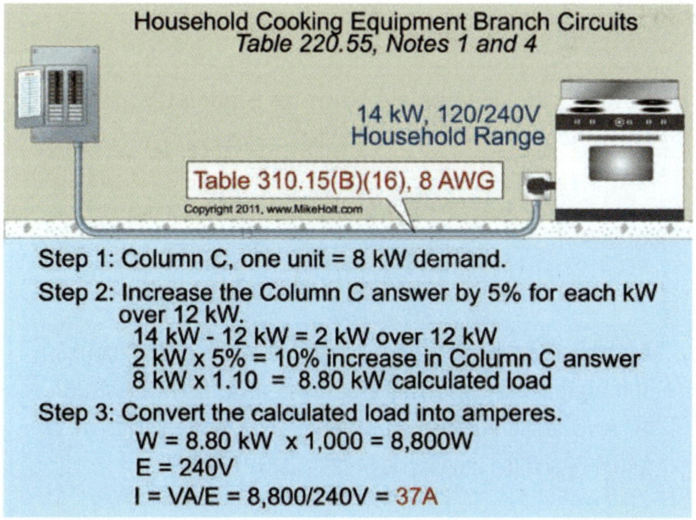

Figure 9–8

Author's Comment: A minimum 40A circuit is required for ranges rated 8.75 kVA and larger [210.19(A)(3)].

► One Counter-Mounted Cooking Unit or One Wall-Mounted Oven Example

Question: *What's the minimum branch-circuit conductor ampacity for one 6 kVA wall-mounted oven?* **Figure 9–9**

(a) 15A (b) 20A (c) 25A (d) 30A

Answer: *(c) 25A*

P = 6 kVA nameplate value

E = 240V (assumed)

I = VA/E

I = 6,000 VA/240V

I = 25A

The branch-circuit load of one wall-mounted oven or one counter-mounted cooking unit must be the nameplate rating of the oven or cooking unit [Table 220.55, Note 4].

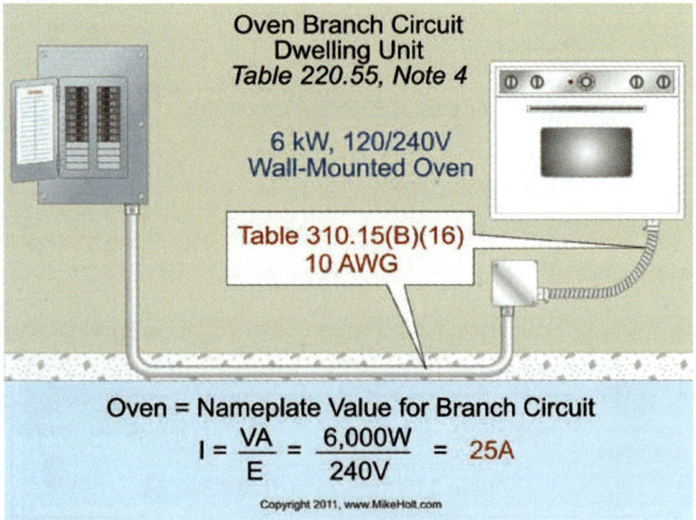

Figure 9–9

Author's Comment: 10 AWG is rated 30A in the 60°C column. The overcurrent device must be sized at a minimum of 25A. 10 AWG is the minimum size allowed due to the limitations of 240.4(D) and the ampacities of Table 310.15(B)(16).

One Counter-Mounted Cooking Unit and Up to Two Wall-Mounted Ovens [Table 220.55, Note 4]

To calculate the load for one counter-mounted cooking unit (cooktop) and up to two wall-mounted ovens, complete the following steps:

Step 1: Add the nameplate ratings of the cooking appliances and treat this total as one range.

Step 2: Determine the kVA load for one unit from Table 220.55, Column C.

Step 3: If the total nameplate rating exceeds 12 kVA, increase Column C (8 kVA) 5% for each kVA, or major fraction (0.50 kVA), that the combined rating exceeds 12 kVA.

► Cooktop and One Wall-Mounted Oven Example

Question: *What's the minimum branch-circuit conductor ampacity for one 6 kVA counter-mounted cooking unit and one 3 kVA wall-mounted oven?* **Figure 9–10**

(a) 25A (b) 33A (c) 38A (d) 42A

Answer: *(b) 33A*

Step 1: Total connected load: 6 kVA + 3 kVA = 9 kVA

Step 2: kVA load for one range, Column C of Table 220.55: 8 kVA

Step 3: Convert the calculated load to amperes:

I = VA/E

I = 8,000 VA/240V

I = 33.30A

Author's Comment: A minimum 40A circuit is required for ranges rated 8.75 kVA and larger [210.19(A)(3)].

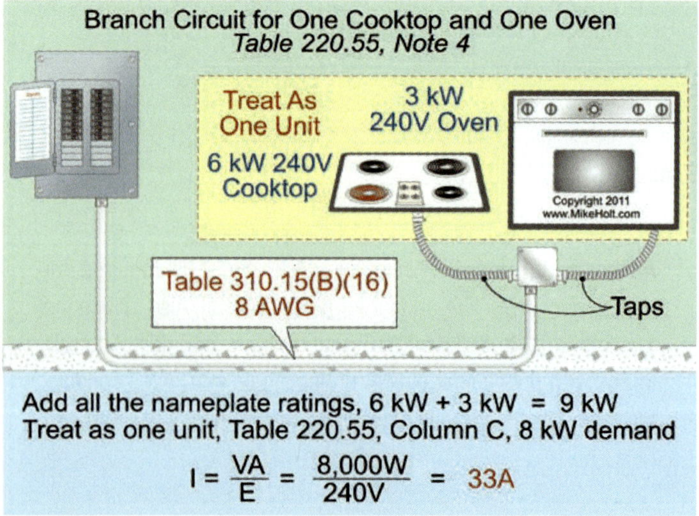

Figure 9–10

► Cooktop and Two Wall-Mounted Ovens Example

Question: *What's the minimum branch-circuit conductor ampacity for one 6 kVA counter-mounted cooking unit (cooktop) and two 4 kVA wall-mounted ovens?* **Figure 9–11**

(a) 22A *(b) 27A* *(c) 33A* *(d) 37A*

Answer: *(d) 37A*

Step 1: Total connected load: 6 kVA + 4 kVA + 4 kVA = 14 kVA

Step 2: Demand load for one range, 8 kVA from Column C of Table 220.55

Step 3: Since the total (14 kVA) exceeds 12 kVA, we must increase Column C (8 kVA) 5% for each kVA that the total exceeds 12 kVA.

14 kVA exceeds 12 kVA by 2 kVA

2 x 5% = 10% increase of the Column C value, resulting in 110%, or a 1.10 multiplier.

Calculated Load = Column C Value x Multiplier

Calculated Load = 8 kVA x 1.10

Calculated Load = 8,800 VA

Step 4: Convert the calculated load to amperes:

I = VA/E

I = 8,800 VA/240V

I = 36.70A

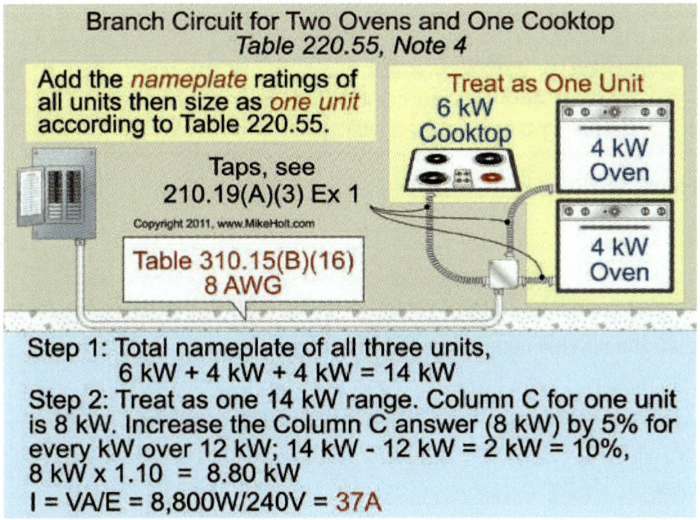

Figure 9–11

Author's Comment: A minimum 40A circuit is required for ranges rated 8.75 kVA and larger [210.19(A)(3)].

PART B—STANDARD METHOD—FEEDER/SERVICE LOAD CALCULATIONS

Introduction

Article 220 of the *NEC* permits two distinctly different methods of calculating residential loads: the standard method in Part III and the optional method in Part IV. The two methods are different and typically give different results. You must use one method or the other; rules from both can't be mixed together. On an exam, you'll usually be told which method to use for a particular question, but if the question doesn't specify a method, use the standard calculation.

9.6 Dwelling Unit Feeder/Service Load Calculations (Article 220, Part III)

Follow these steps to determine the feeder or service size for a dwelling unit using the standard method contained in Article 220, Part III:

Step 1: General Lighting and Receptacles, Small-Appliance, and Laundry Circuits [Table 220.42]

The *NEC* recognizes that the general lighting and receptacle, small-appliance, and laundry circuits won't all be on, or loaded, at the same time and permits a demand factor to be applied to the total connected load [220.52]. To determine the feeder calculated load for these circuits, use the following steps:

Step a: Total Connected Load. Determine the total connected load for:

(1) general lighting and receptacles at3 VA per sq ft [220.12]

(2) two small-appliance circuits each at 1,500 VA [220.52(A)], and

(3) one laundry circuit at 1,500 VA [220.52(B)].

Step b: Demand Factor. Apply the Table 220.42 demand factors to the total connected load.

Step c: First 3,000 VA at 100 percent demand; remaining VA at 35 percent demand.

Step 2: Appliances [220.53]

A 75 percent demand factor is permitted to be applied when four or more appliances are fastened in place, such as a waste disposal, dishwasher, trash compactor, water heater, and so on, and are on the same feeder. This doesn't apply to space-heating equipment [220.51], clothes dryers [220.54], cooking appliances [220.55], or air-conditioning equipment.

Author's Comment: This demand factor is applied to the nameplate rating of the appliances.

Step 3: Clothes Dryer [220.54]

The feeder or service load for electric clothes dryers located in a dwelling unit must not be less than 5,000W or the nameplate rating if greater than 5,000W. The demand factors from Table 220.54 can be applied if there are more than 4 dryers in the dwelling unit. A feeder or service dryer load isn't required if the dwelling unit doesn't contain an electric dryer!

Step 4: Cooking Equipment [220.55]

Household cooking appliances rated over 1¾ kVA can have the feeder and service calculated according to the demand factors of Table 220.55, including Notes 1, 2, and 3.

Step 5: Air-Conditioning versus Heat

Because the air-conditioning and heating loads aren't on at the same time, the smaller of the two loads can be omitted [220.60]. The air-conditioning load is calculated at 100 percent [220.50] and the fixed electric heating load is calculated at 100 percent [220.51].

Step 6: Feeder and Service Conductor Size

Step a: For individual dwelling units of one-family, two-family, and multifamily dwellings, Table 310.15(B)(7) can be used to size 3-wire, single-phase, 120/240V service or feeder conductors, including the feeder neutral conductor, that supply all loads that are part of, or associated with, the dwelling unit. Figure 9–12

Step b: Over 400 Amperes. Size the ungrounded and neutral conductors according to Table 310.15(B)(16).

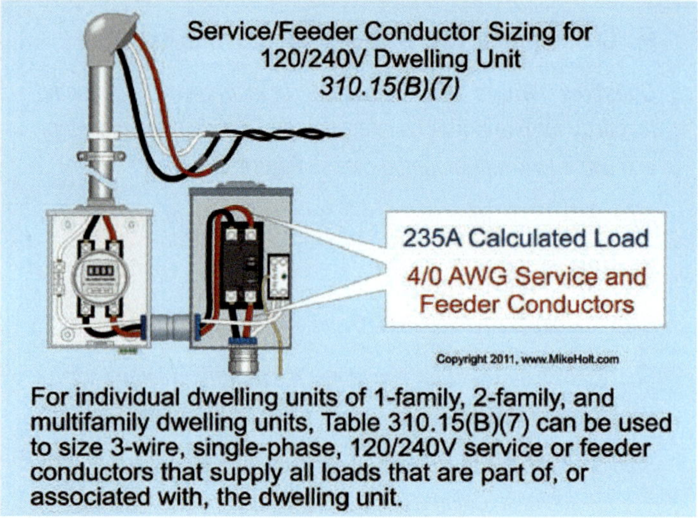

Figure 9–12

Author's Comment: Table 310.15(B)(7) can't be used for service conductors for two-family or multifamily buildings. Figure 9–13

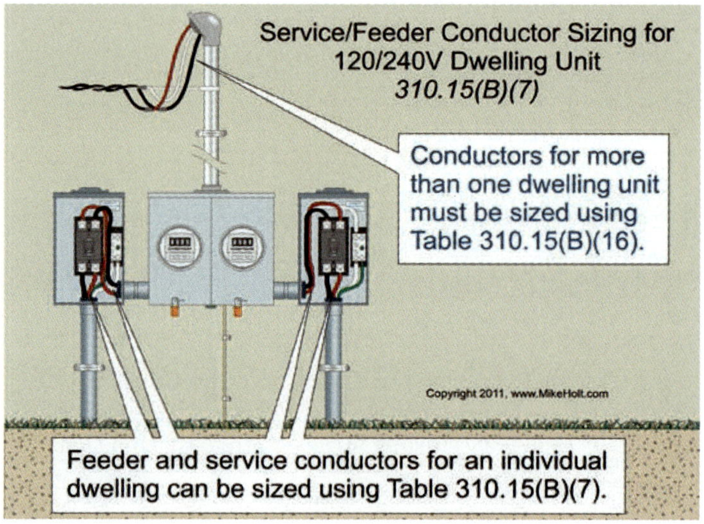

Figure 9–13

Feeder conductors aren't required to have an ampacity rating more than the service conductors [215.2(A)(3)].

Table 310.15(B)(7) Conductor Sizes for 120/240V, 3-Wire, Single-Phase Dwelling Services and Feeders		
Amperes	Copper	Aluminum
100	4 AWG	2 AWG
110	3 AWG	1 AWG
125	2 AWG	1/0 AWG
150	1 AWG	2/0 AWG
175	1/0 AWG	3/0 AWG
200	2/0 AWG	4/0 AWG
225	3/0 AWG	250 kcmil
250	4/0 AWG	300 kcmil
300	250 kcmil	350 kcmil
350	350 kcmil	500 kcmil
400	400 kcmil	600 kcmil

WARNING: *Table 310.15(B)(7) doesn't apply to 3-wire feeder/service conductors connected to three-phase, 120/208V systems because the neutral conductor in these systems always carries neutral current, even when the load on the phases is balanced [310.15(B)(5)(b)]. For more information on this topic, see 220.61(C)(1).* **Figure 9–14**

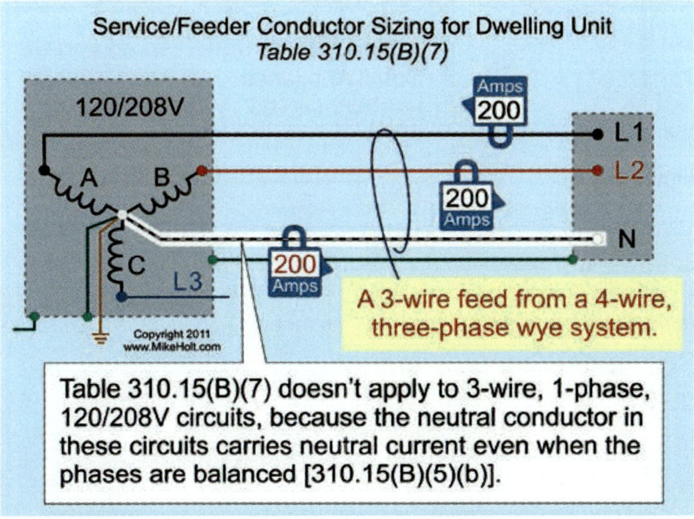

Figure 9–14

Neutral Conductor Sizing. Table 310.15(B)(7) can be used to size the neutral conductor of a 3-wire, single-phase, 120/240V service or feeder that carries all loads associated with the dwelling unit, based on the calculated load in accordance with 220.61.

CAUTION: *Because the service neutral conductor is required to serve as the effective ground-fault current path, it must be sized so it can safely carry the maximum fault current likely to be imposed on it [110.10 and 250.4(A)(5)]. This is accomplished by sizing the neutral conductor in accordance with Table 250.66, based on the area of the largest ungrounded service conductor [250.24(C)(1)].*

► Dwelling Service Conductor Sizing Example

Question: *What size service conductors are required if the calculated load for a dwelling unit equals 195A, and the maximum unbalanced neutral load is 100A?* **Figure 9–15**

(a) 1/0 AWG and 6 AWG *(b) 2/0 AWG and 4 AWG*
(c) 3/0 AWG and 2 AWG *(d) 4/0 AWG and 1 AWG*

Answer: *(b) 2/0 AWG and 4 AWG*

Service Conductor: 2/0 AWG rated 200A [Table 310.15(B)(7)]

Neutral Conductor: 4 AWG is rated 100A in accordance with Table 310.15(B)(7). In addition, 250.24(C) requires the neutral conductor to be sized no smaller than 4 AWG, based on 2/0 AWG service conductors in accordance with Table 250.66.

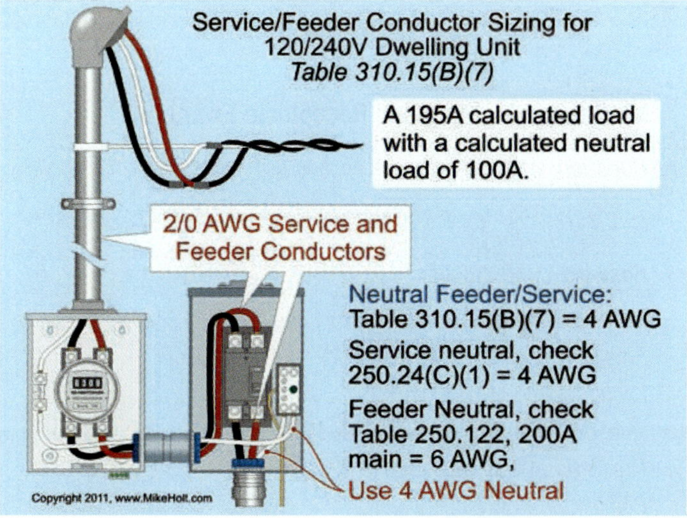

Figure 9–15

9.7 Dwelling Unit Example

Step 1: General Lighting and Receptacle, Small Appliance, and Laundry Demand [Table 220.42]

The demand factors in Table 220.42 apply to the 3 VA per sq ft for general lighting and general-use receptacles [Table 220.12], small-appliance circuits [220.52(A)], and the laundry circuit [220.52(B)].

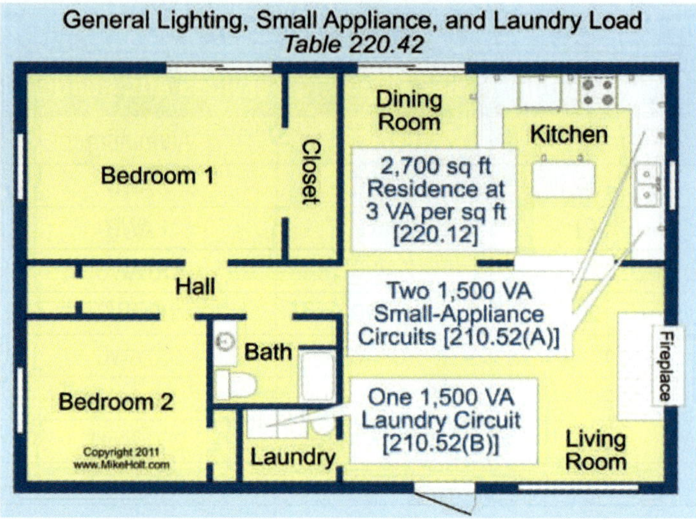

Figure 9–16

► General Lighting and Receptacle Example 1

Question: *What's the general lighting and receptacle, small appliance, and laundry feeder/service calculated load for a 2,700 sq ft dwelling unit?* **Figure 9–16**

(a) 2,700 VA (b) 6,360 VA (c) 8,100 VA (d) 12,600 VA

Answer: *(b) 6,360 VA*

General Lighting/Receptacles (2,700 sq ft x 3 VA) [220.12]	*8,100 VA*		
Small-Appliance Circuits (1,500 VA x 2) [220.52(A)]	*3,000 VA*		
Laundry Circuit (1,500 VA x 1) [220.52(B)]	*+ 1,500 VA*		
Total Connected Load	*12,600 VA*		
First 3,000 VA at 100% [Table 220.42]	*–3,000 VA*	*x 1.00 =*	*3,000 VA*
Remainder at 35%	*9,600 VA*	*x 0.35 =*	*+ 3,360 VA*
Calculated Load			*6,360 VA*

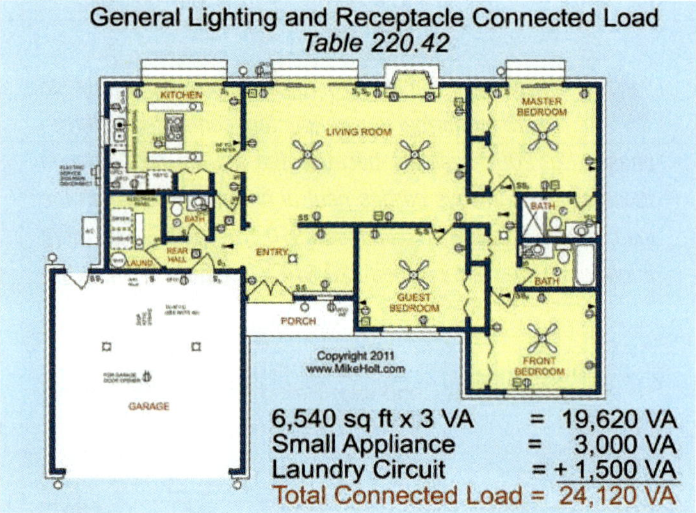

Figure 9–17

► General Lighting and Receptacle Example 2

Question: *What's the general lighting and receptacle, small appliance, and laundry feeder/service calculated load for a 6,540 sq ft dwelling unit?*

(a) 2,700 VA (b) 8,100 VA (c) 10,392 VA (d) 12,600 VA

Answer: *(c) 10,392 VA*

General Lighting/Receptacles (6,540 sq ft x 3 VA) [220.12]	*19,620 VA*		
Small-Appliance Circuits (1,500 VA x 2) [220.52(A)]	*3,000 VA*		
Laundry Circuit (1,500 VA x 1) [220.52(B)]	*+ 1,500 VA*		
Total Connected Load **Figure 9–17**	*24,120 VA*		
First 3,000 VA at 100% [Table 220.42]	*– 3,000 VA*	*x 1.00 =*	*3,000 VA*
Remainder at 35%	*21,120 VA*	*x 0.35 =*	*+ 7,392 VA*
Calculated Load			*10,392 VA*

Step 2: Appliance Calculated Load [220.53]

Add the nameplate ratings of all appliances fastened in place. If there are four or more appliances, apply a 75 percent demand factor to determine the calculated load.

Author's Comment: This demand factor doesn't apply to space-heating equipment [220.51], clothes dryers [220.54], electric ranges [220.55], or air-conditioning equipment.

► Appliance Example 1

Question: *What's the feeder/service calculated load for a dishwasher (1,250 VA), waste disposal (940 VA), and a water heater (4,500 VA)?*

(a) 5,018 VA (b) 6,272 VA (c) 6,690 VA (d) 8,363 VA

Answer: *(c) 6,690 VA*

Dishwasher	*1,250 VA*
Waste Disposal	*940 VA*
Water Heater	*+ 4,500 VA*
Calculated Load	*6,690 VA*

► Appliance Example 2

Question: *What's the feeder/service calculated load for a dishwasher (1,250 VA), trash compactor (1,100 VA), waste disposal (940 VA), and water heater (4,500 VA)?* **Figure 9–18**

(a) 5,843 VA (b) 7,303 VA (c) 7,790 VA (d) 9,738 VA

Answer: *(a) 5,843 VA*

Dishwasher	*1,250 VA*
Trash Compactor	*1,100 VA*
Waste Disposal	*940 VA*
Water Heater	*+ 4,500 VA*
Connected Load	*7,790 VA*

Calculated Load = Connected Load x Demand Factor [220.53]

Calculated Load = 7,790 VA x 0.75

Calculated Load = 5,843 VA

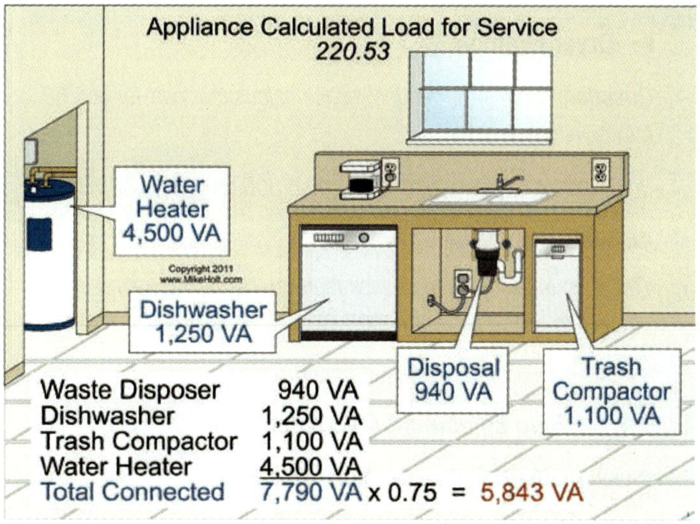

Figure 9–18

Step 3: Dryer Calculated Load [220.54]

The minimum calculated load for a household electric dryer is 5,000 VA or use the nameplate rating if it's higher.

► Dryer Example 1

Question: *What's the feeder/service calculated load for a 4 kVA dryer?* **Figure 9–19**

(a) 3,000 VA (b) 4,000 VA (c) 5,000 VA (d) 5,500 VA

Answer: *(c) 5,000 VA*

The dryer load must not be less than 5,000 VA.

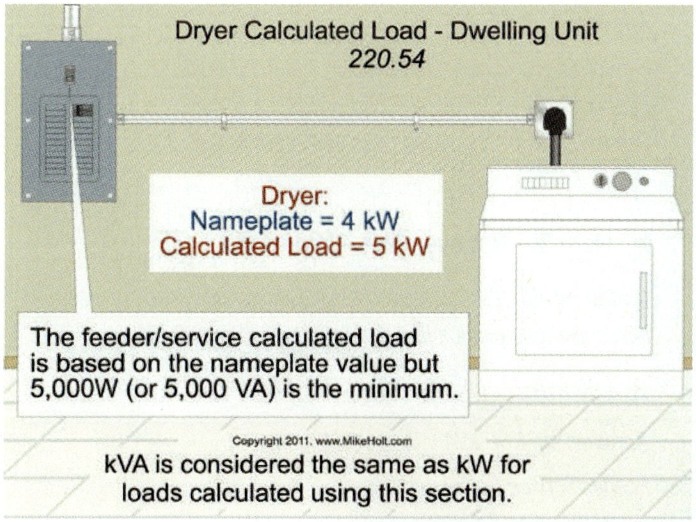

Figure 9–19

▶ Dryer Example 2

Question: *What's the feeder/service calculated load for a 5.50 kVA dryer?*

(a) 3,000 VA (b) 4,000 VA (c) 5,000 VA (d) 5,500 VA

Answer: *(d) 5,500 VA*

The dryer load must not be less than the nameplate rating if the nameplate is greater than 5,000 VA.

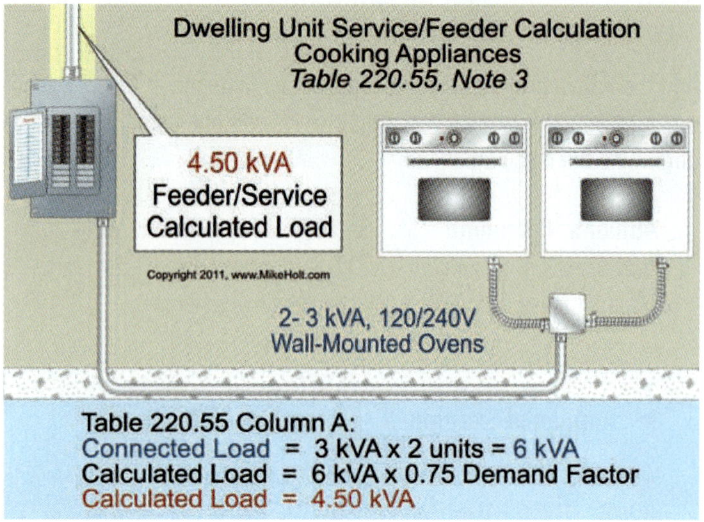

Figure 9–20

Step 4: Cooking Equipment Calculated Load [220.55]

When using Table 220.55, note the following:

- Column A applies to cooking equipment rated over 1¾ kVA but less than 3½ kVA.
- Column B applies to cooking equipment rated 3½ to 8¾ kVA.
- Column C applies to cooking equipment rated 8¾ kVA to 12 kVA.

These columns are used with Notes 1, 2, and 3 for determining feeder/service calculated loads.

▶ Note 3—Over 1¾ and Less Than 3½ kVA—Table 220.55, Column A Figure 9–20

Question: *What's the feeder/service calculated load for two 3 kVA cooking appliances in a dwelling unit?*

(a) 3 kVA (b) 3.90 kVA (c) 4.50 kVA (d) 4.80 kVA

Answer: *(c) 4.50 kVA*

Feeder/Service Connected Load = 3 kVA x 2 units
Feeder/Service Calculated Load = 6 kVA x 0.75
Feeder/Service Calculated Load = 4.50 kVA

▶ Note 3—Not over 8¾—Column B

Question: *What's the feeder/service calculated load for one 6 kVA cooking appliance in a dwelling unit?* Figure 9–21

(a) 3.90 kVA (b) 4.50 kVA (c) 4.80 kVA (d) 6 kVA

Answer: *(c) 4.80 kVA*

Feeder/Service Calculated Load = 6 kVA x 0.80
Feeder/Service Calculated Load = 4.80 kVA

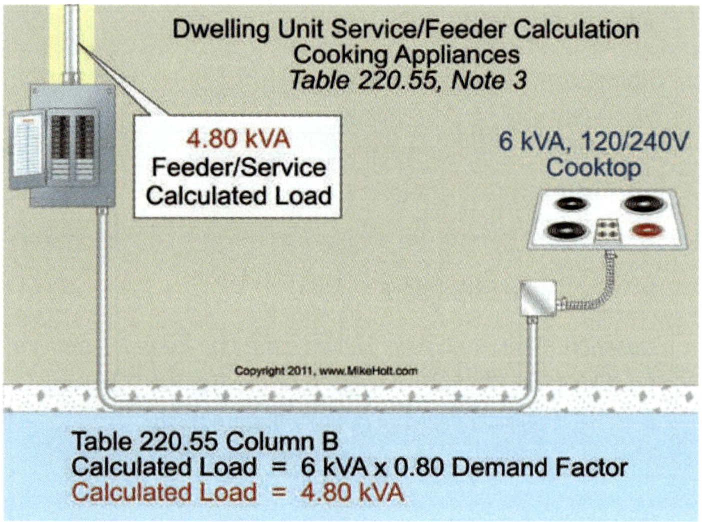

Figure 9–21

▶ Note 3—Columns A and B

Question: *What's the feeder/service calculated load for two 3 kVA ovens and one 6 kVA cooktop in a dwelling unit?* Figure 9–22

(a) 4.50 kVA (b) 4.80 kVA (c) 6 kVA (d) 9.30 kVA

Answer: *(d) 9.30 kVA*

Column A Calculated:	*(3 kVA x 2) x 0.75*	*4.50 kVA*
Column B Calculated:	*6 kVA x 0.80*	*+ 4.80 kVA*
Total Calculated		*9.30 kVA*

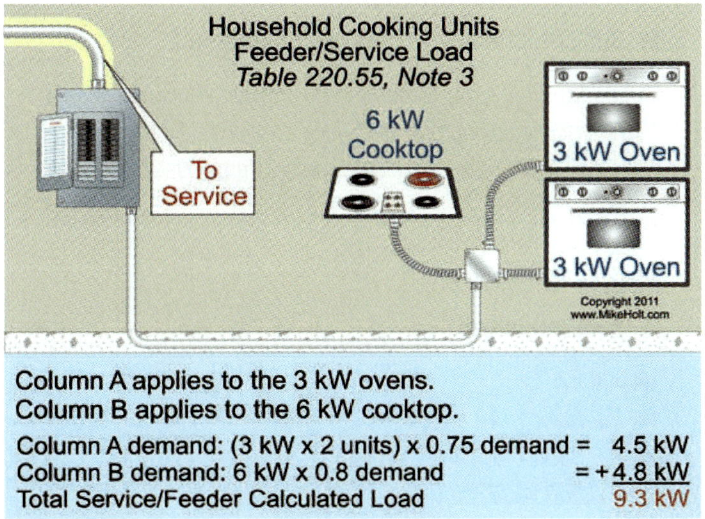

Figure 9–22

► Table 220.55, Column C—Not over 12 kVA

Question: *What's the feeder/service calculated load for an 11.50 kVA range in a dwelling unit?*

(a) 6 kVA *(b) 8 kVA* *(c) 9.20 kVA* *(d) 11.50 kVA*

Answer: *(b) 8 kVA*

Table 220.55, Column C: 8 kVA

► Over 12 kVA—Note 1

Question: *What's the feeder/service calculated load for a 13.60 kVA range in a dwelling unit?*

(a) 6 kVA *(b) 8 kVA* *(c) 8.80 kVA* *(d) 9.20 kVA*

Answer: *(c) 8.80 kVA*

Step a: 13.60 kVA exceeds 12 kVA by 1 kVA and one major fraction of a kVA. The Column C value (8 kVA) must be increased 5% for each kVA or major fraction of a kVA (0.50 kVA or larger) over 12 kVA [Table 220.55, Note 1].

2 x 5% = 10% increase of the Column C value, resulting in 110%, or a 1.10 multiplier.

Step b: ***Calculated Load = Column C Value x Multiplier***

Calculated Load = 8 kVA x 1.10

Calculated Load = 8,800 VA

Step 5: Air-Conditioning versus Heat [220.60]

Compare the air-conditioning load at 100 percent [220.50] against the heating load at 100 percent [220.51] and use the larger of the two loads [220.60].

► Air-Conditioning Calculated Load Example

Question: *What's the calculated VA load for a 230V single-phase air conditioner that contains a 16A compressor and a 1A fan?* **Figure 9–23**

(a) 4 kVA *(b) 5 kVA* *(c) 6 kVA* *(d) 7 kVA*

Answer: *(a) 4 kVA*

A/C VA Load = Volts x Amperes

A/C VA Load = 240V x (16A + 1.00A)

A/C VA Load = 240V x 17A

A/C VA Load = 4,080 VA

4,080 VA/1,000 = 4.08 kVA

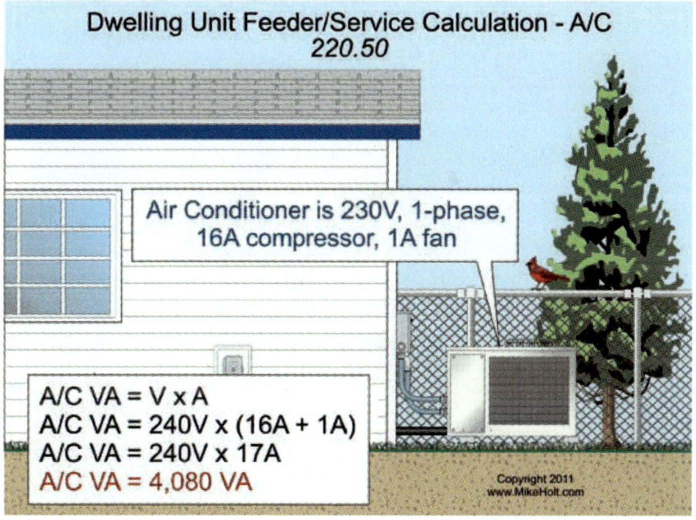

Figure 9–23

Author's Comment: Motors have nameplate ratings of 115V and 230V for use on 120V and 240V nominal voltage systems [Annex D Example D1(b)].

► Air-Conditioning versus Heat Example 1

Question: *What's the feeder/service calculated load for a 5 hp, 230V air-conditioning unit, versus three 3 kVA, 240V baseboard heaters?* **Figure 9–24**

(a) 3,000 VA (b) 6,400W (c) 8,050 VA (d) 9,000W

Answer: *(d) 9,000W*

5 hp, 230V motor draws 28A [Table 430.248]

VA = V x A

VA = 240V x 28A

VA = 6,720 VA

VA = 6,720 VA [220.60]

Heat [220.51]: 3,000 VA x 3 units = 9,000 VA

Use the heat, which is the larger of the two loads

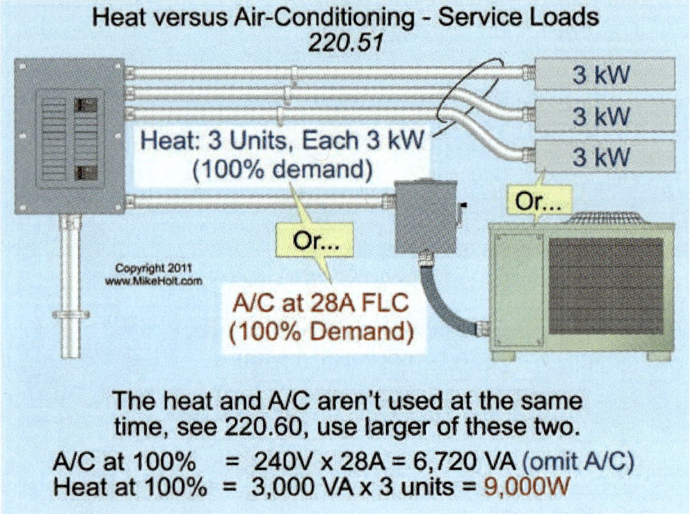

Figure 9–24

► Air-Conditioning versus Heat Example 2

Question: *What's the feeder/service calculated load for a 14A, 240V air-conditioning unit containing an electric heater rated at 9.60 kVA, 240V plus a 3A blower motor?* **Figure 9–25**

(a) 3,910 VA (b) 5,000 VA (c) 10,320 VA (d) 12,500 VA

Answer: *(c) 10,320 VA*

Air-conditioning Unit:

VA = V x A

VA = 240V x 14A

VA = 3,360 VA

VA = 3,360 VA [220.60]

Heat [220.51]:

9,600 VA + (3A x 240V) = 10,320 VA

Use the heat, which is the larger of the two loads

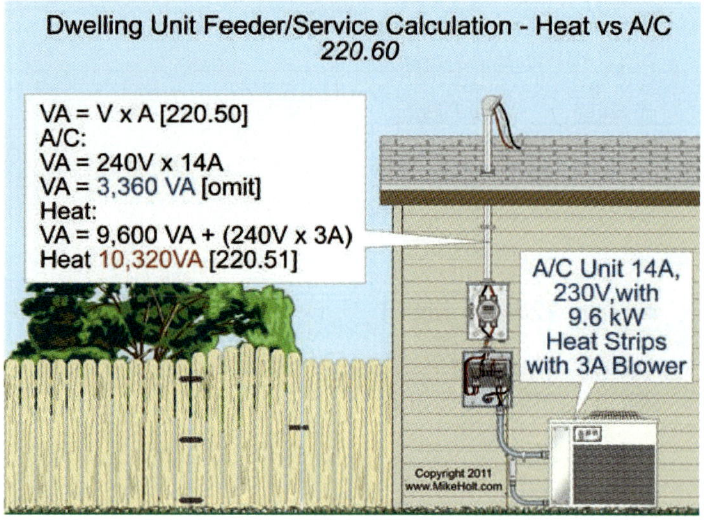

Figure 9–25

Step 6: Service Conductor Size [Table 310.15(B)(7)]

Dwelling Unit Feeder/Service Conductors. For individual dwelling units of one-family, two-family, and multifamily dwellings, Table 310.15(B)(7) can be used to size 3-wire, single-phase, 120/240V service or feeder conductors (including neutral conductors) that serve as the main power feeder. Feeder conductors aren't required to have an ampacity rating greater than the service conductors [215.2(A)(3)].

Author's Comment: Table 310.15(B)(7) permits a smaller feeder/service conductor size than listed in Table 310.15(B)(16) for the same calculated load, but this reduced size conductor is only permitted to be used for conductors that supply all loads to a single dwelling when the service is a 120/240V, 3-wire single-phase service up to 400A.

Neutral Conductor Sizing. Table 310.15(B)(7) can be used to size the neutral conductor of a 3-wire, single-phase, 120/240V service or feeder that serves as the main power feeder, based on the feeder calculated load in accordance with 220.61.

Author's Comment: Because the neutral service conductor is required to serve as the effective ground-fault current path, it must be sized so that it can safely carry the maximum fault current likely to be imposed on it [110.10 and 250.4(A)(5)]. This is accomplished by sizing the neutral conductor in accordance with Table 250.66, based on the total area of the largest ungrounded conductor [250.24(C)(1)].

► Service Conductor Example 1

Question: *What size service conductors (120/240V, single-phase) are required when the calculated load for a dwelling unit equals 195A and the neutral load is 100A?* **Figure 9–26**

(a) 1/0 AWG and 6 AWG *(b) 2/0 AWG and 4 AWG*
(c) 3/0 AWG and 2 AWG *(d) 4/0 AWG and 1 AWG*

Answer: *(b) 2/0 AWG and 4 AWG*

Service Conductor: 2/0 AWG rated 200A [Table 310.15(B)(7)]

Neutral Conductor: 4 AWG is rated 100A in accordance with Table 310.15(B)(7). In addition, 250.24(C) requires the neutral conductor to be sized no smaller than 4 AWG, based on 2/0 AWG service conductors in accordance with Table 250.66.

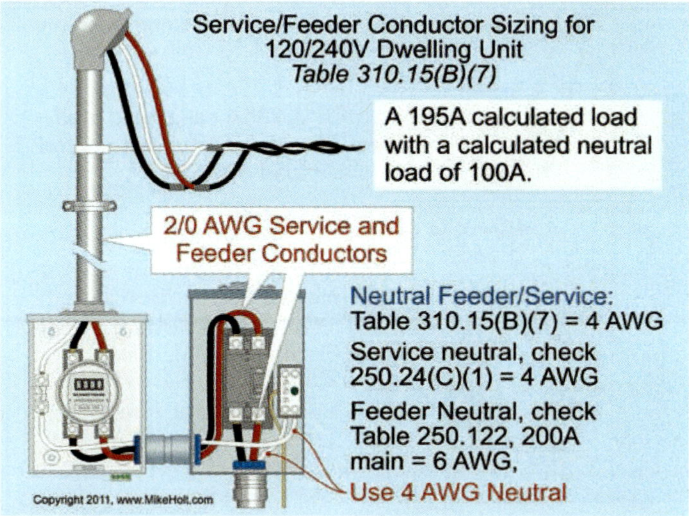

Figure 9–26

► Service Conductor Example 2

Question: *What size service conductors (120/240V, single-phase) are required when the calculated load for a dwelling unit equals 235A and the neutral load is 100A?* **Figure 9–27**

(a) 1/0 AWG and 6 AWG *(b) 2/0 AWG and 4 AWG*
(c) 4/0 AWG and 2 AWG *(d) 4/0 AWG and 1 AWG*

Answer: *(c) 4/0 AWG and 2 AWG*

Service Conductor: 4/0 AWG rated 250A [Table 310.15(B)(7)]

Neutral Conductor: 4 AWG is rated 100A in accordance with Table 310.15(B)(7). In addition, 250.24(C) requires the neutral conductor to be sized no smaller than 2 AWG, based on 4/0 AWG service conductors in accordance with Table 250.66.

Table 310.15(B)(7) doesn't apply to 3-wire, single-phase, 120/208V systems, because the neutral conductor in these systems carries neutral current even when the load on the phases is balanced [310.15(B)(5)(b)]. For more information on this topic, see the NEC 220.61(C)(1). **Figure 9–28**

Author's Comment: 120/208V, single-phase feeders from a 120/208V, three-phase service are sometimes used to supply single-family dwelling units in a multifamily building.

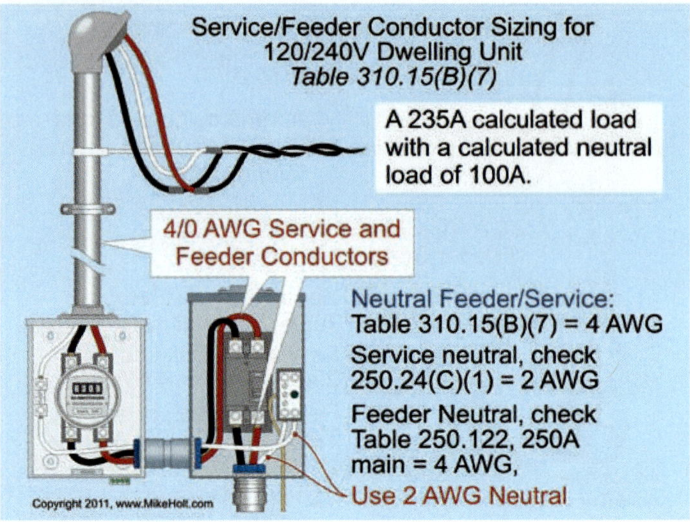

Figure 9–27

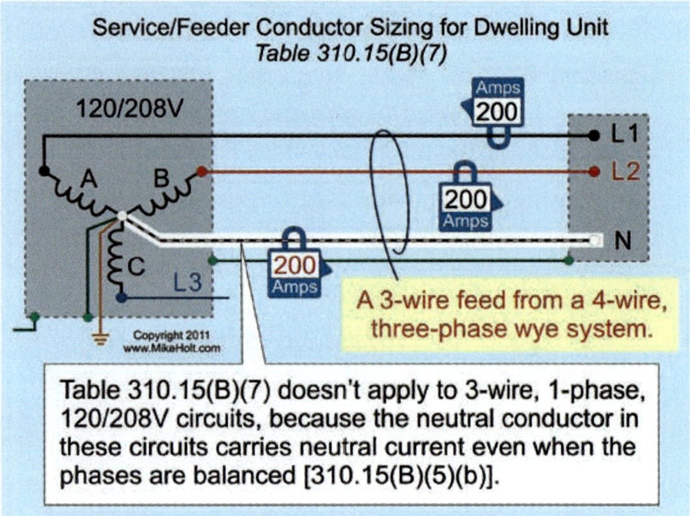

Figure 9–28

► Service Conductor Example 3

Question: *What size service conductors are required when the calculated load for a dwelling unit equals 195A and the maximum unbalanced neutral load is 65A, if supplied from a 120/208V system?*

(a) 1/0 AWG and 6 AWG *(b) 2/0 AWG and 4 AWG*
(c) 3/0 AWG and 4 AWG *(d) 4/0 AWG and 1 AWG*

Answer: *(c) 3/0 AWG and 4 AWG*

Service Conductor: 3/0 AWG rated 200A at 75°C [110.14(C) and Table 310.15(B)(16)]

Neutral Conductor: 6 AWG is rated 65A at 75°C in accordance with Table 310.15(B)(16), but 250.24(C) requires the neutral conductor to be sized no smaller than 4 AWG, based on 3/0 AWG service conductors in accordance with Table 250.66.

PART C—OPTIONAL METHOD—FEEDER/SERVICE LOAD CALCULATIONS

Introduction

Instead of sizing the dwelling unit feeder and/or service phase conductors according to the standard method described in Article 220, Part III, an optional method in Article 220, Part IV can often be used. This method can only be used for dwelling units served by a single 120/240V or 120/208V 3-wire set of service or feeder conductors with an ampacity of 100A or larger [220.82].

9.8 Dwelling Unit Optional Calculations [220.82]

The following steps can be used to determine the feeder or service size for a dwelling unit using the optional method contained in Article 220, Part IV:

Step 1: General Loads [220.82(B)]

The calculated load must not be less than 100 percent for the first 10 kVA, plus 40 percent of the remainder of the following loads:

(1) General Lighting and Receptacles: 3 VA per sq ft

(2) Small-Appliance and Laundry Branch Circuits: 1,500 VA for each 20A small-appliance and laundry branch circuit specified in 220.52.

(3) Appliances: The nameplate VA rating of all appliances and motors that are fastened in place (permanently connected) or located on a specific circuit, except heating and air conditioning.

Note: Be sure to calculate the range and dryer at their nameplate ratings!

Step 2: Heating and Air-Conditioning Load [220.82(C)]

Include the larger of (1) through (6):

(1) Air-Conditioning Equipment: 100 percent

(2) Heat-Pump Compressor without Supplemental Heating: 100 percent

(3) Heat-Pump Compressor and Supplemental Heating: 100 percent of the nameplate rating of the heat-pump compressor and 65 percent of the supplemental electric heating for central electric space-heating systems.

If the heat-pump compressor is prevented from operating at the same time as the supplementary heat, it can be omitted in the calculation.

(4) Space-Heating Units (three or fewer units): 65 percent

(5) Space-Heating Units (four or more units): 40 percent

(6) Thermal Storage Heating: 100 percent

> **Author's Comment:** One form of thermal storage heating involves heating bricks or water at night when the electric rates are lower. Then during the day, the building uses the thermally stored heat.

Step 3: Feeder/Service Conductors [310.15(B)(7)]

400 Amperes and Less. For individual dwelling units of one-family, two-family, and multifamily dwellings, Table 310.15(B)(7) can be used to size 3-wire, single-phase, 120/240V service or feeder conductors (including neutral conductors) that serve as the main power feeder. Feeder conductors aren't required to have an ampacity rating greater than the service conductors [215.2(A)(4)]. The neutral conductor must be sized to carry the unbalanced load according to Table 310.15(B)(7).

Over 400 Amperes. Size ungrounded conductors and the neutral conductor according to Table 310.15(B)(16).

9.9 Optional Calculation Example

► Optional Load Calculation Example 1

Question: *What size service conductor is required for a 1,500 sq ft dwelling unit containing the following loads?* **Figure 9–29**

Cooktop	*6,000 VA*
Disposal	*900 VA*
Dishwasher	*1,200 VA*
Dryer	*4,000 VA*
Ovens (two each)	*3,000 VA*
Water Heater	*4,500 VA*
Air-Conditioning	*17A, 230V*
Electric Heating (one control unit)	*9.60 kVA*

(a) 6 AWG *(b) 4 AWG* *(c) 3 AWG* *(d) 2 AWG*

Answer: *(c) 3 AWG*

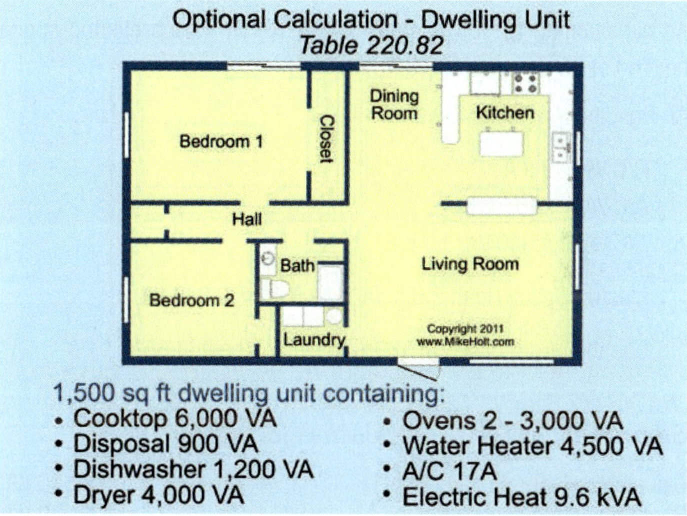

Figure 9–29

Step 1. General Loads [220.82(B)]

General Lighting			
(1,500 sq ft x 3 VA)	4,500 VA		
Small-Appliance Circuits			
(1,500 VA x 2 circuits)	3,000 VA		
Laundry Circuit	1,500 VA		
Appliances (nameplate)			
Cooktop	6,000 VA		
Disposal	900 VA		
Dishwasher	1,200 VA		
Dryer	4,000 VA		
Ovens (each 3 kW)	6,000 VA		
Water Heater	4,500 VA		
Connected Load	31,600 VA		
First 10 kW at 100%	– 10,000 VA	x 1.00 =	10,000 VA
Remainder at 40%	21,600 VA	x 0.40 =	+ 8,640 VA
Calculated General Load			18,640 VA

Step 2: Air-Conditioning versus Heat [220.82(C)]

Air-conditioning at 100 percent [220.82(C)(1)] versus electric space heating at 65 percent [220.82(C)(4)]

Air Conditioner [Table 430.248]:

A/C VA = V x A
A/C VA = 240V x 17A
A/C VA = 4,080 VA,

Electric Space Heat: 9,600VA VA x 0.65 = 6,240 VA

Use the larger of A/C at 100% or electric heat at 65%

Step 3: Feeder/Service Conductors [310.15(B)(7)]

Calculated General Load (Step 1)	18,640 VA
Heat Calculated Load (Step 2)	+ 6,240 VA
Total Calculated Load	24,880 VA

I = VA/E
I = 24,880 VA/240V
I = 103.67A

The feeder/service ungrounded conductor is sized to 110A, 3 AWG [310.15(B)(7)].

Existing Loads [220.87]

For existing installations, the calculation of a feeder or service load is permitted to use actual maximum demand to determine the existing load. The maximum demand for one year* at 125 percent plus the new load must not exceed the ampacity of the feeder [220.87]. If the maximum demand data for one year isn't available, the maximum power demand over a 15-minute period over a 30-day period, is permitted. The recording must be taken when the building or space is occupied based on the larger of the heating or cooling equipment load [220.87 Ex].

When a generator is to be installed in an existing dwelling, it must be sized to comply with Article 220 calculations [702.6].

► Existing Load Calculation Example 1

Question: *If the maximum demand in accordance with 220.87 is 12,480 VA, what size generator would be required for this installation?*

(a) 7 kVA (b) 10 kVA (c) 16 kVA (d) 25 kVA

Answer: *(c) 16 kVA*

Generator Size = 12,480 VA x 1.25
Generator Size = 15,600 VA

PART D—OTHER TOPICS OF INTEREST

9.10 Neutral Calculations [220.61]

The feeder/service neutral load is the maximum unbalanced calculated load between the neutral conductor and any ungrounded conductor as determined by Article 220, Part III.

Because phase-to-phase loads aren't connected to the neutral conductor, they're not considered when sizing the neutral conductor.

► Neutral Not Over 200A

Question: *What size 120/240V, single-phase ungrounded and neutral conductors are required for a one-family dwelling unit with a calculated load of 375A, of which 175A consist of 240V loads?* **Figure 9–30**

(a) Two—350 kcmil and one—350 kcmil
(b) Two—400 kcmil and one—2/0 AWG
(c) Two—400 kcmil and one—350 kcmil
(d) Two—500 kcmil and one—500 kcmil

Answer: *(b) Two—400 kcmil and one—2/0 AWG*

The ungrounded conductor is sized at 375A (400 kcmil) according to Table 310.15(B)(7).

Neutral Load = Total Load Less Phase-to-Phase Loads
Neutral Load = 375A - 175A
Neutral Load = 200A

The neutral conductor must be sized to carry the 200A of neutral current.

Neutral Conductor: A 2/0 AWG conductor is rated 200A [Table 310.15(B)(7)], 250.24(C) requires the neutral conductor to be sized no smaller than 1/0 AWG, based on the 400 kcmil service conductors in accordance with Table 250.66.

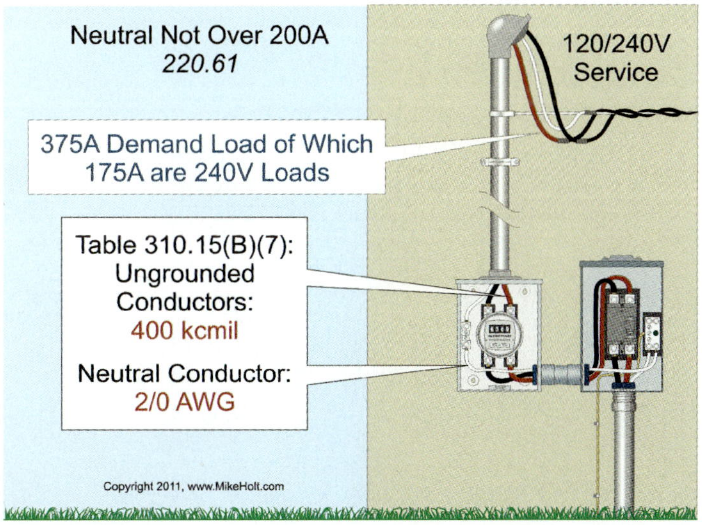

Figure 9–30

Cooking Appliance Feeder/Service Neutral Load [220.61(B)(1)]

The feeder/service cooking appliance neutral load for household cooking appliances, such as electric ranges, wall-mounted ovens, or counter-mounted cooking units is calculated at 70 percent of the calculated load as determined by 220.55.

► Range Neutral

Question: *What's the neutral load (in amperes) for one 14 kVA range?*

(a) 16A *(b) 22.90A* *(c) 25.70A* *(d) 36.70A*

Answer: *(c) 25.70A*

Step 1: Since the range exceeds 12 kVA, we must comply with Note 1 of Table 220.55. The first step is to determine the demand load as listed in Column C of Table 220.55 for one unit = 8 kVA.

Step 2: We must increase the Column C value (8 kVA) by 5% for each kVA that the range exceeds 12 kVA [Table 220.55, Note 1], 14 kVA – 12 kVA = 2 kVA.

2 x 5% = 10% increase of the Column C value, resulting in 110%, or a 1.10 multiplier.

Calculated Load = Column C Value x Multiplier
Calculated Load = 8 kVA x 1.10
Calculated Load = 8.80 kVA

I = VA/E
I = 8,800VA/240V
I = 36.70A

Neutral load at 70%:

Feeder/Service Neutral Calculated Load = 36.70A x 0.70 [220.61(B)(1)]
Feeder/Service Neutral Calculated Load = 25.70A

Dryer Feeder/Service Neutral Load [220.61(B)(1)]

The feeder and service dryer neutral load for electric clothes dryers is calculated at 70 percent of the calculated load as determined by 220.54.

▶ Dryer Over 5 kVA

Question: *What's the feeder/service neutral load for one 5.50 kVA dryer?*

(a) 3.85 kVA *(b) 4.60 kVA*
(c) 5 kVA *(d) 5.50 kVA*

Answer: *(a) 3.85 kVA*

Feeder/Service Neutral Calculated Load = 5.50 kVA x 0.70 [220.61(B)(1)]

Feeder/Service Neutral Calculated Load = 3.85 kVA

See the NEC Annex D Examples D1(a) and D1(b) for more neutral calculations.

▶ Neutral Calculation Example

Question: *What's the minimum size feeder/service neutral required for a 2,700 sq ft single dwelling with:*

- *17A, 230V Air-Conditioning unit, 9 kVA 230V electric heater*
- *Dishwasher (1,250 VA), Waste disposal (940VA), Water Heater (4,500 VA)*
- *Clothes Dryer, (5,000VA) Electric Range (9,500 VA)*
- *The ungrounded conductors are 2/0 AWG copper.*

For the neutral calculation, disregard the 240V loads such as electric heating and air-conditioning and the 240V water heater.

Find the general lighting/receptacle load using the Table 220.42 demand factors:

General Lighting/Receptacles (2,700 sq ft x 3 VA) [220.12]	*8,100 VA*		
Small-Appliance Circuits (1,500 VA x 2) [220.52(A)]	*3,000 VA*		
Laundry Circuit (1,500 VA x 1) [220.52(B)]	*+ 1,500 VA*		
Total Connected Load	*12,600 VA*		
First 3,000 VA at 100% [Table 220.42]	*–3,000 VA*	*x 1.00*	*3,000 VA*
Remainder at 35%	*9,600 VA*	*x 0.35*	*+ 3,360 VA*
Calculated Load			*6,360 VA*
Dishwasher			*1,250 VA*
Waste disposal			*940 VA*
Dryer calculated load from 220.54 times 70% [220.61(B)(1)]:	*5,000 VA*	*x 0.70*	*3,500 VA*
Range calculated load from Table 220.55 times 70% [220.61(B)(1)]:	*8,000 VA*	*x 0.70*	*5,600 VA*
			17,650 VA

Neutral Calculated Load: 17,650VA/240V = 73.54A
4 AWG is rated 85A at 75°C, which is also the minimum required neutral from Table 250.66, based on 2/0 AWG ungrounded conductors [250.24(C)(1)].

9.11 Grounding and Bonding of Service Equipment

Service Equipment Grounding and Bonding [250.24]

(A) Grounded System. Service equipment supplied from a grounded system must have the neutral conductor terminate in accordance with (1) through (5).

(1) Grounding Location. A grounding electrode conductor must connect the service neutral conductor to the grounding electrode at any accessible location, from the load end of the service drop or service lateral, up to and including the service disconnecting means. Figure 9–31

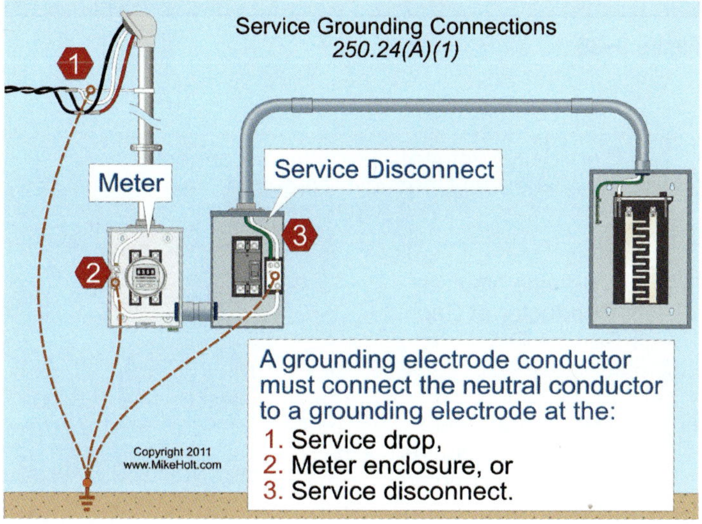

Figure 9–31

Author's Comment: Some inspectors require the service neutral conductor to be grounded (connected to the earth) from the meter socket enclosure, while other inspectors insist that the service neutral conductor be grounded (connected to the earth) only from the service disconnect.

(4) Grounding Termination. When the service neutral conductor is connected to the service disconnecting means [250.24(B)] by a wire or busbar [250.28], the grounding electrode conductor is permitted to terminate to either the neutral terminal or the equipment grounding terminal within the service disconnect.

(5) Neutral-to-Case Connection. A neutral-to-case connection isn't permitted on the load side of service equipment, except as permitted by 250.142(B). Figure 9–32

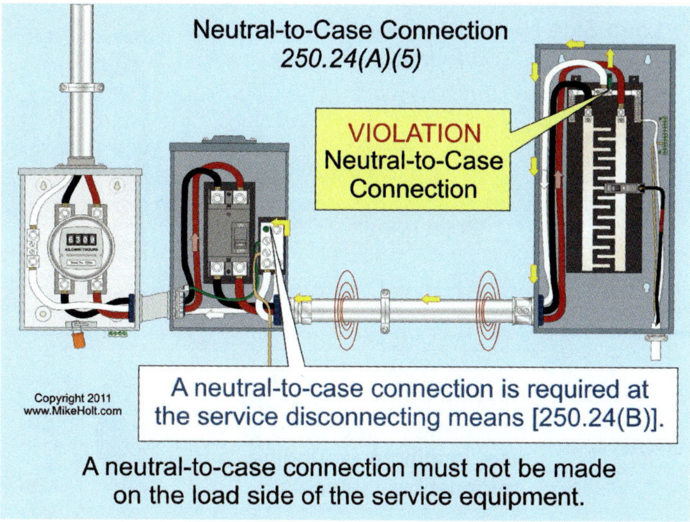

Figure 9–32

Author's Comment: If a neutral-to-case connection is made on the load side of service equipment, dangerous objectionable neutral current will flow on conductive metal parts of electrical equipment [250.6(A)]. Objectionable neutral current on metal parts of electrical equipment can cause electric shock and even death from ventricular fibrillation, as well as a fire. Figures 9–33 and 9–34

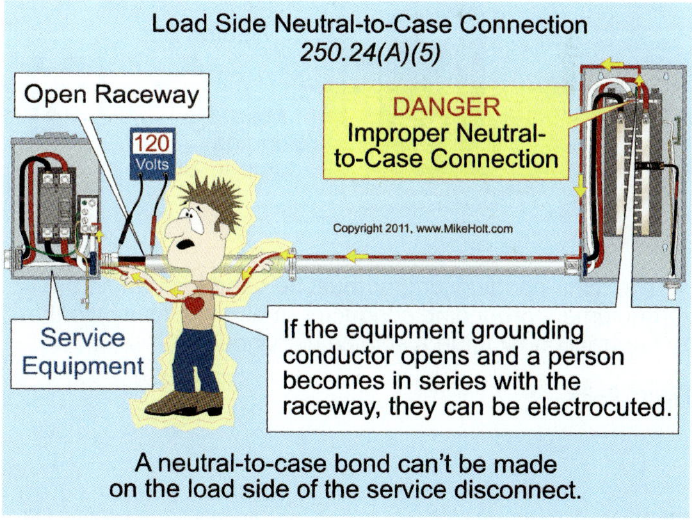

Figure 9–33

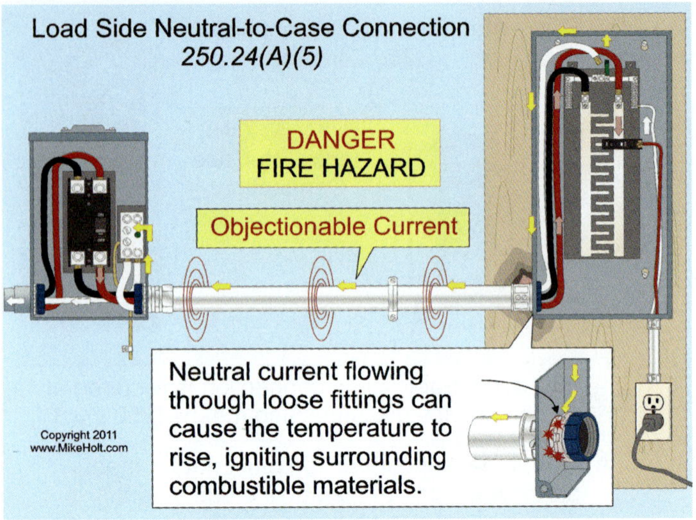

Figure 9–34

(B) Bonding. A main bonding jumper [250.28] must be installed for the purpose of connecting the neutral conductor to the metal parts of the service disconnecting means. Figure 9–35

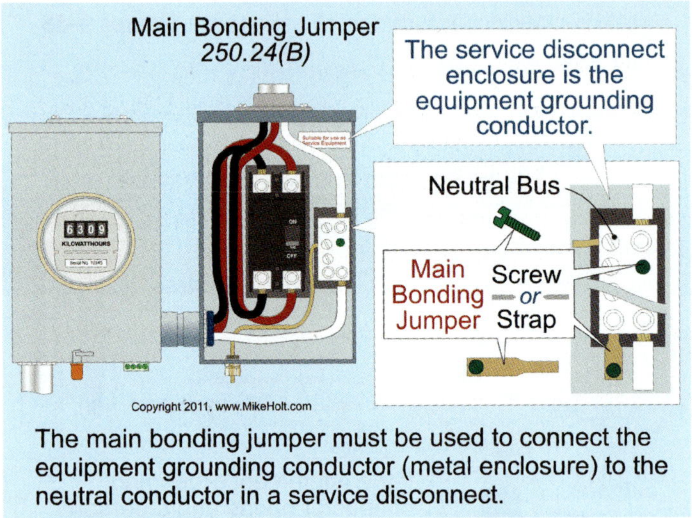

Figure 9–35

(C) Neutral Conductor. A service neutral conductor from the electric utility must terminate to each service disconnecting means via a main bonding jumper [250.24(B)] that's installed between the service neutral conductor and each service disconnecting means enclosure. Figures 9–36 and 9–37

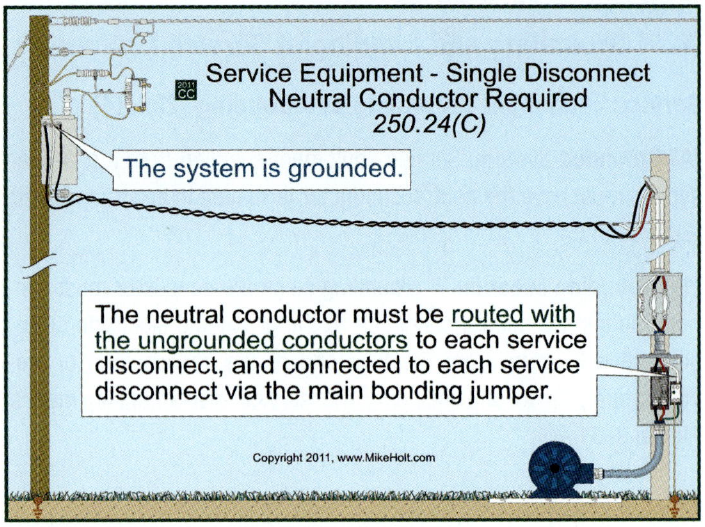

Figure 9–36

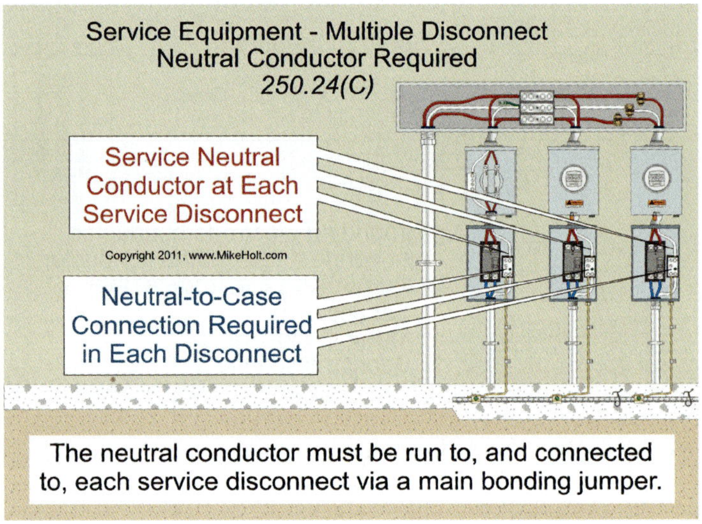

Figure 9–37

Author's Comment: The service neutral conductor provides the effective ground-fault current path to the power supply to ensure that dangerous voltage from a ground fault will be quickly removed by opening the overcurrent device [250.4(A)(3) and 250.4(A)(5)], Figure 9–38. An effective ground-fault current path is an intentionally constructed low-impedance conductive path designed to carry fault current from the point of a ground fault on a wiring system to the electrical supply source [Article 100]. Figure 9–39

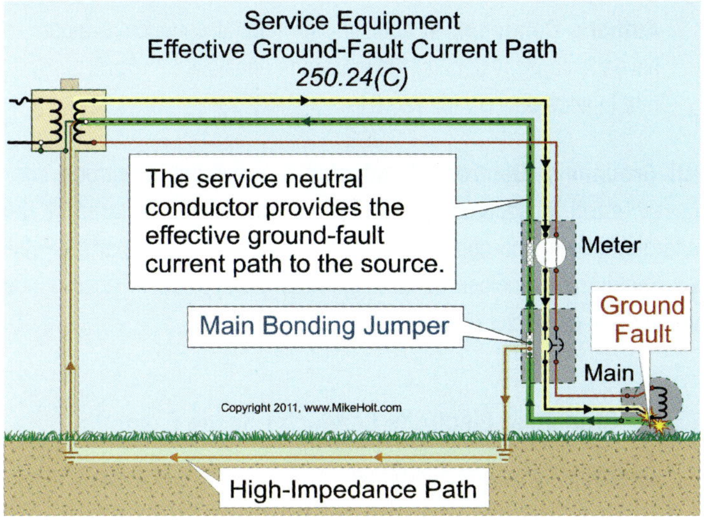

Figure 9–38

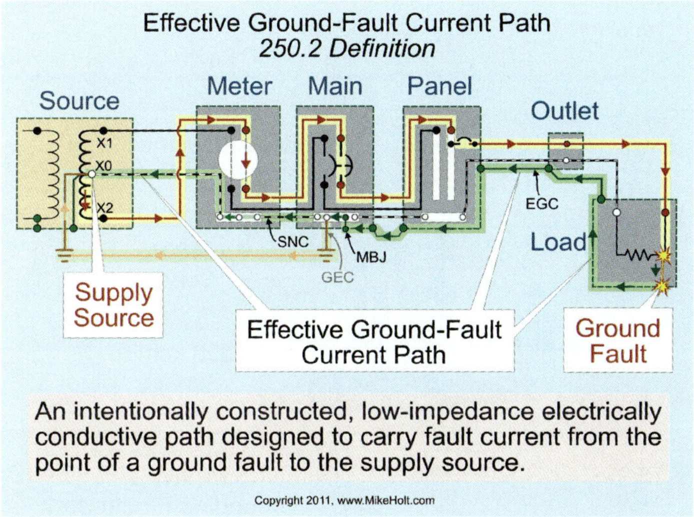

Figure 9–39

DANGER: *Dangerous voltage from a ground fault won't be removed from metal parts, metal piping, and structural steel if the service disconnecting means enclosure isn't connected to the service neutral conductor. This is because the contact resistance of a grounding electrode to the earth is so great that insufficient fault current returns to the power supply if the earth is the only fault current return path to open the circuit overcurrent device.* **Figure 9–40**

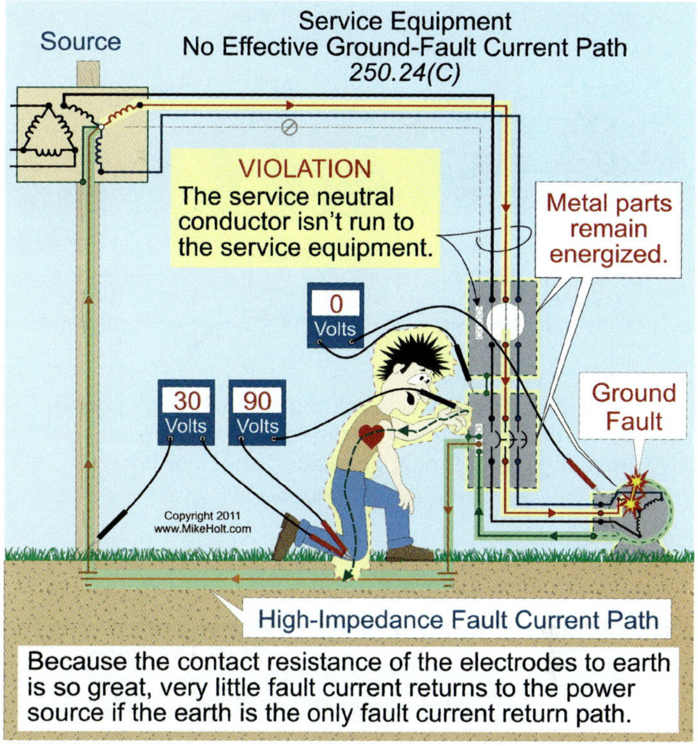

Figure 9–40

Author's Comment: For example, if the neutral conductor is opened, dangerous voltage will be present on metal parts under normal conditions, providing the potential for electric shock. If the earth's ground resistance is 25 ohms and the load's resistance is 25 ohms, the voltage drop across each of these resistors will be half of the voltage source. Since the neutral is connected to the service disconnect, all metal parts will be elevated to 60V above the earth's potential for a 120/240V system. **Figure 9–41**

To determine the actual voltage on the metal parts from an open service neutral conductor, you need to do some complex math calculations. Visit www.MikeHolt.com and go to the "Free Stuff" link to download a spreadsheet for this purpose.

(1) Neutral Conductor Minimum Size. Because the service neutral conductor serves as the effective ground-fault current path to the source for ground faults, it must be sized so it can safely carry the maximum fault current likely to be imposed on it [110.10 and 250.4(A)(5)]. This is accomplished by sizing the neutral conductor in accordance with Table 250.66, based on the cross-sectional area of the ungrounded service conductor. **Figure 9–42**

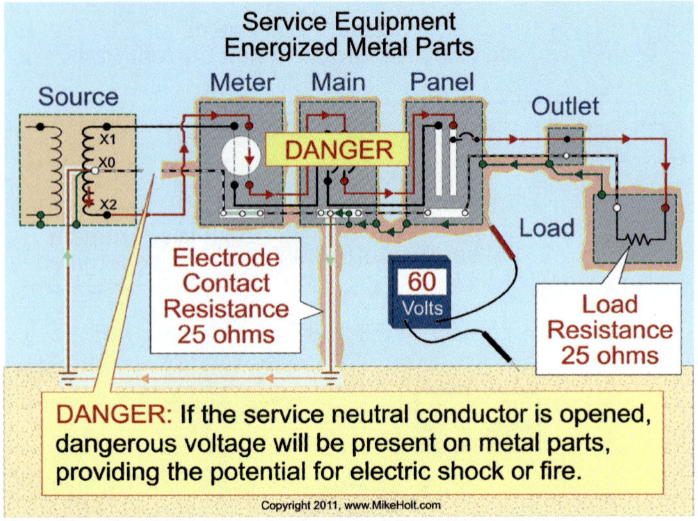

Figure 9–41

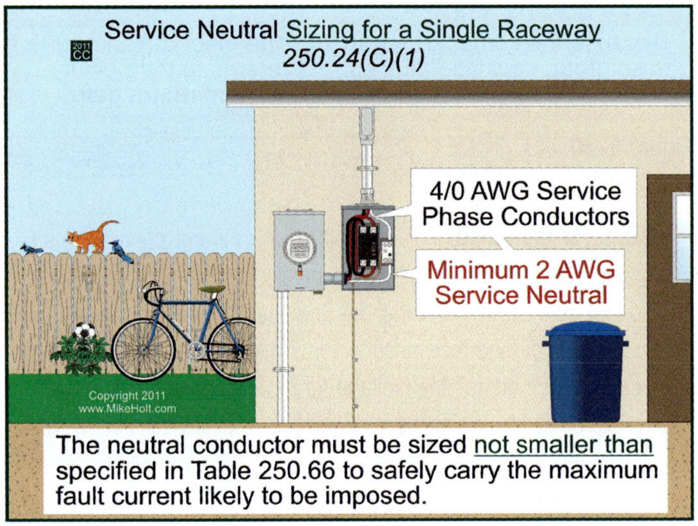

Figure 9–42

Author's Comment: In addition, the neutral conductors must have the capacity to carry the maximum unbalanced neutral current in accordance with 220.61.

(2) Parallel Neutral Conductor. Where service conductors are paralleled, a neutral conductor must be installed in each of the parallel raceways and it must be sized in accordance with Table 250.66, based on the area of the largest service conductor in the raceway. In no case can the neutral conductor in each parallel set be sized smaller than 1/0 AWG [310.10(H)].

Author's Comment: In addition, the neutral conductors must have the capacity to carry the maximum unbalanced neutral current in accordance with 220.61.

(D) Grounding Electrode Conductor. A grounding electrode conductor, sized in accordance with 250.66 based on the area of the ungrounded service conductor, must connect the metal parts of service equipment enclosures to a grounding electrode in accordance with Part III of Article 250.

▶ Grounding Electrode Conductor Sizing Example

Question: *What's the minimum size grounding electrode conductor for a 400A service where the ungrounded service conductors are sized at 500 kcmil?* **Figure 9–43**

(a) 3 AWG *(b) 2 AWG* *(c) 1 AWG* *(d) 1/0 AWG*

Answer: *(d) 1/0 AWG [Table 250.66]*

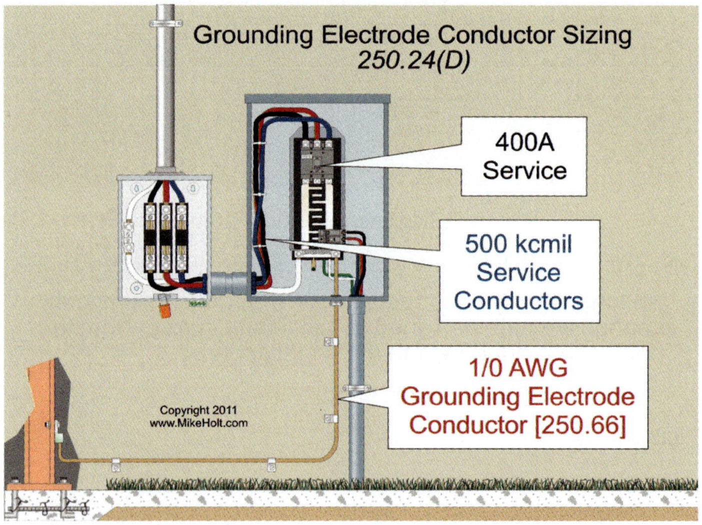

Figure 9–43

Author's Comment: Where the grounding electrode conductor is connected to a ground rod that portion of the conductor that's the sole connection to the ground rod isn't required to be larger than 6 AWG copper [250.66(A)], **Figure 9–44** Where the grounding electrode conductor is connected to a concrete-encased electrode that portion of the conductor that's the sole connection to the concrete-encased electrode isn't required to be larger than 4 AWG copper [250.66(B)]. **Figure 9–45**

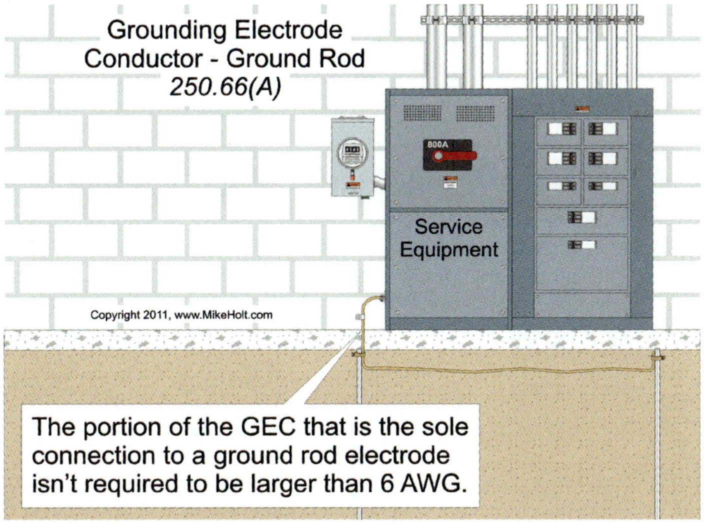

Figure 9–44

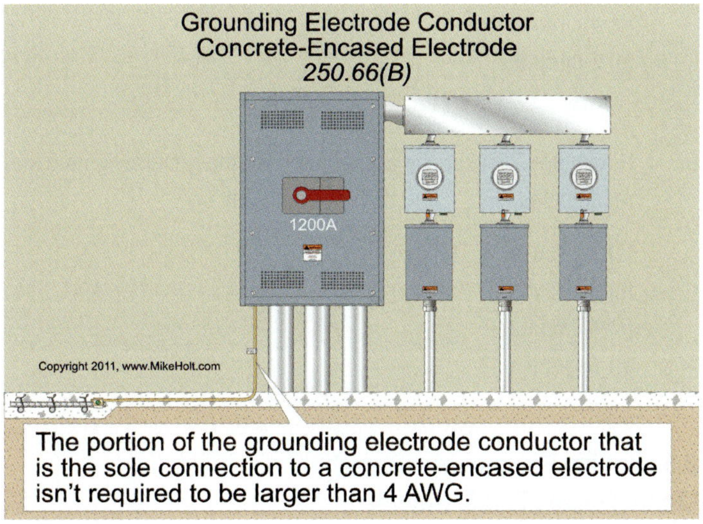

Figure 9–45

CONCLUSION TO UNIT 9—DWELLING UNIT CALCULATIONS

The residential branch circuit, feeder, and service calculations in Unit 9 required you to understand and apply many different demand factors. Since not all loads are used simultaneously in a home, the service to a home is allowed to be sized not on the total possible load, but on a percentage of that, based on what we call "demand factors."

The *Code* doesn't explain how demand factors were derived, and it's not essential that you understand this in order to apply them correctly. Be sure to work on some practice calculations so you understand how to apply the various demand factors to a dwelling unit calculation. It's important to have a good working knowledge of this before going on to the following unit about multifamily dwellings, which will build on the concepts developed in this unit.

The standard calculation and the optional calculation methods were both discussed in this unit. These are two distinctly different calculation methods, so be careful not to mix them together. Which method is better to use? On an exam, you'll likely be told which method to use on a specific question, but if the question doesn't specify a method, use the standard calculation. The optional method is usually faster and easier to apply, so it has a natural advantage for daily use on the job.

UNIT 9

Practice Questions

Please use the 2011 *Code* book to answer the following questions, which are based on the 2011 *NEC*.

PRACTICE QUESTIONS FOR UNIT 9—DWELLING UNIT CALCULATIONS

PART A—GENERAL REQUIREMENTS

9.2 Voltages [220.5(A)]

1. Unless other voltages are specified, feeder and service loads must be computed at a nominal system voltage of ______.

(a) 120V
(b) 120/240V
(c) 120/208V
(d) any of these

9.3 Fraction of an Ampere [220.5(B)]

2. Where a calculation results in a fraction of an ampere that's less than ______, that fraction is permitted to be dropped.

(a) 0.40
(b) 0.45
(c) 0.50
(d) 0.55

9.4 Lighting and Receptacles

Number of Circuits Required [Annex D, Example D1(a)]

3. The number of branch circuits required for general lighting and receptacles must be determined from the general lighting load and the rating of the circuits.

(a) True
(b) False

4. How many 15A general lighting circuits are required for a 2,340 sq ft home?

(a) 2 circuits
(b) 3 circuits
(c) 4 circuits
(d) 5 circuits

5. How many 20A general lighting circuits are required for a 2,100 sq ft home?

(a) 2 circuits
(b) 3 circuits
(c) 4 circuits
(d) 5 circuits

6. How many 20A circuits are required for the general lighting and receptacles for a 1,500 sq ft dwelling unit?

(a) 2 circuits
(b) 3 circuits
(c) 4 circuits
(d) 5 circuits

9.5 Cooking Equipment—Branch Circuit [Table 220.55, Note 4]

7. What's the branch-circuit calculated load (in amperes) for one 11 kW range?

(a) 21A
(b) 27A
(c) 33A
(d) 38A

8. What's the branch-circuit calculated load (in amperes) for one 13.50 kW range?

(a) 33A
(b) 37A
(c) 50A
(d) 58A

One Counter-Mounted Cooking Unit(s) and Up to Two Wall-Mounted Ovens [Table 220.55, Note 4]

9. What's the branch-circuit load (in amperes) for one 6 kW wall-mounted oven rated 240V, single-phase?

(a) 15A
(b) 25A
(c) 30A
(d)40A

10. What's the branch-circuit load (in amperes) for one 4.80 kW counter-mounted cooking unit rated 240V, single-phase?

(a) 15A
(b) 20A
(c) 25A
(d) 30A

11. What's the minimum branch-circuit conductor ampacity for one 6 kW counter-mounted cooking unit and one 3 kW wall-mounted oven rated 240V, single-phase?

(a) 27A
(b) 30A
(c) 35A
(d) 40A

12. What's the minimum branch-circuit conductor ampacity for one 6 kW counter-mounted cooking unit and two 4 kW wall-mounted ovens rated 240V, single-phase?

(a) 21A
(b) 27A
(c) 31A
(d) 40A

PART B—STANDARD METHOD—FEEDER/ SERVICE LOAD CALCULATIONS

9.6 Dwelling Unit Feeder/Service Load Calculations [Article 220, Part III]

13. A minimum of ______ 20A small-appliance branch circuit(s) is(are) required for receptacle outlets in the kitchen, dining room, breakfast room, pantry, and similar areas.

(a) one
(b) two
(c) three
(d) four

14. When sizing the feeder or service, each dwelling unit must have a minimum feeder load of ______ for the two small-appliance branch circuits.

(a) 1,000 VA
(b) 2,000 VA
(c) 3,000 VA
(d) 4,000 VA

15. The *NEC* doesn't require a separate circuit for the washing machine, but does require a separate circuit for the laundry room receptacle or receptacles, of which one can be for the washing machine.

(a) True
(b) False

16. Each dwelling unit must have a feeder load consisting of ______ for the 20A laundry circuit.

(a) 1,500 VA
(b) 2,000 VA
(c) 3,000 VA
(d) 4,500 VA

17. The *NEC* requires a minimum of 3 VA for each square foot of living space for the required general lighting and general-use receptacles for dwelling units. The dimensions for determining the area are computed from the outside of the building and don't include _____.

(a) open porches
(b) garages
(c) spaces not adaptable for future use
(d) all of these

18. The 3 VA for each square foot of living space for general lighting includes receptacles rated 20A, but not the small-appliance or laundry circuit receptacles.

(a) True
(b) False

19. What's the general lighting load and general-use receptacle load for a 2,100 sq ft home that has 74 receptacle outlets and nine recessed luminaires rated at 100W each?

(a) 2,100 VA
(b) 4,200 VA
(c) 6,300 VA
(d) 8,400 VA

20. The *NEC* recognizes that the general lighting and receptacles, and small-appliance and laundry circuits won't all be on or loaded at the same time and permits a(n) _____ to be applied to the total of these loads.

(a) demand factor
(b) adjustment factor
(c) correction factor
(d) correction

21. Because the air-conditioning and heating loads aren't on at the same time they're called "noncoincidental," and it's permissible to omit the smaller of the two loads.

(a) True
(b) False

22. A load demand factor of 75 percent is permitted for _____ or more appliances fastened in place such as waste disposals, dishwashers, trash compactors, water heaters, and so forth.

(a) one
(b) two
(c) three
(d) four

23. The feeder or service calculated load for electric clothes dryers located in dwelling units must not be less than _____.

(a) 5,000W
(b) the nameplate rating
(c) a or b
(d) the greater of a or b

24. A feeder or service dryer load is required even if the dwelling unit doesn't contain an electric dryer.

(a) True
(b) False

25. Household cooking appliances rated 1kW can have the feeder and service loads calculated according to the demand factors of Table 220.55.

(a) True
(b) False

26. Dwelling unit feeder and service ungrounded (hot) conductors are sized according to Table 310.15(B)(7) for _____.

(a) 3-wire, single-phase, 120/240V systems up to 400A
(b) 3-wire, single-phase, 120/208V systems up to 400A
(c) 4-wire, single-phase, 120/240V systems up to 400A
(d) none of these

27. What's the general lighting load for a 2,700 sq ft dwelling unit?

(a) 2,700 VA
(b) 6,840 VA
(c) 8,100 VA
(d) 12,600 VA

28. What's the total connected load for general lighting and receptacles, small-appliance, and laundry circuits for a 6,540 sq ft dwelling unit?

(a) 2,700 VA
(b) 8,100 VA
(c) 12,600 VA
(d) 24,120 VA

29. What's the feeder or service calculated load for one air conditioner (28A, 230V) and three baseboard heaters (3 kW each)?

(a) 3,000 VA
(b) 6,400 VA
(c) 8,050 VA
(d) 9,000 VA

30. What's the feeder or service calculated load for an air conditioner (28A, 230V) and electric space heater (9.6 kW with a 3A, 240V blower motor)?

(a) 3,910 VA
(b) 6,440 VA
(c) 10,320 VA
(d) 10,900 VA

31. What's the feeder or service calculated load for a waste disposal (940 VA), dishwasher (1,250 VA), and a water heater (4,500 VA)?

(a) 5,018 VA
(b) 6,272 VA
(c) 6,690 VA
(d) 8,363 VA

32. What's the feeder or service calculated load for a waste disposal (940 VA), dishwasher (1,250 VA), a trash compactor (1,100 VA), and a water heater (4,500 VA)?

(a) 5,843 VA
(b) 7,303 VA
(c) 7,490 VA
(d) 9,738 VA

33. What's the feeder or service calculated load for a 4 kW dryer?

(a) 3 kW
(b) 4 kW
(c) 5 kW
(d) 6 kW

34. What's the feeder or service calculated load for a 5.50 kW dryer?

(a) 3 kW
(b) 4 kW
(c) 5 kW
(d) 5.50 kW

35. What's the feeder or service calculated load for two 3 kW cooking appliances?

(a) 3.90 kW
(b) 4.20 kW
(c) 4.50 kW
(d) 5.00 kW

36. What's the feeder or service calculated load for one 6 kW cooking appliance?

(a) 3.90 kW
(b) 4.50 kW
(c) 4.80 kW
(d) 6 kW

37. What's the feeder or service calculated load for one 6 kW and two 3 kW cooking appliances?

(a) 4.50 kW
(b) 4.80 kW
(c) 6 kW
(d) 9.30 kW

38. What's the feeder or service calculated load for an 11.50 kW range?

(a) 7 kW
(b) 8 kW
(c) 9 kW
(d) 10 kW

39. What's the feeder or service calculated load for a 13.60 kW range?

(a) 6 kW
(b) 8 kW
(c) 8.80 kW
(d) 9.20 kW

40. What AWG size 120/240V, single-phase feeder/service copper conductors are required for a dwelling unit that has a 190A service calculated load?

(a) 1/0 AWG
(b) 2/0 AWG
(c) 3/0 AWG
(d) 4/0 AWG

41. What's the net calculated load for the general lighting, small-appliance, and laundry circuits for a 1,500 sq ft dwelling unit?

(a) 3,500 VA
(b) 4,200 VA
(c) 5,100 VA
(d) 5,700 VA

42. What's the feeder/service calculated load for an air conditioner (18A, 230V) and electric space heating (4 kW)?

(a) 2,000 VA
(b) 3,910 VA
(c) 4,000 VA
(d) 4,140 VA

43. What's the feeder/service calculated load for a dwelling unit that has one dishwasher (1.50 kW) and one water heater (4 kW)?

(a) 4 kVA
(b) 4.13 kVA
(c) 5.50 kVA
(d) 1,500 kVA

44. What's the calculated load for a 4.50 kW dryer?

(a) 4.50 kW
(b) 5 kW
(c) 5.50 kW
(d) 8 kW

45. What's the calculated load for a 14 kW range?

(a) 8 kW
(b) 8.40 kW
(c) 8.80 kW
(d) 14 kW

46. If the total calculated load is 30 kVA for a 120/240V dwelling unit, what's the feeder/service copper conductor size?

(a) 4 AWG
(b) 2 AWG
(c) 1/0 AWG
(d) 3/0 AWG

47. If a service raceway contains 2 AWG service conductors, what size copper bonding jumper is required for the service raceway?

(a) 8 AWG
(b) 6 AWG
(c) 4 AWG
(d) 3 AWG

48. If a service contains 2 AWG conductors, what's the minimum size grounding electrode conductor required?

(a) 8 AWG
(b) 6 AWG
(c) 4 AWG
(d) 3 AWG

PART C—OPTIONAL METHOD—FEEDER/ SERVICE LOAD CALCULATIONS

9.10 Dwelling Unit Optional Calculations [220.82]

49. When sizing the feeder or service conductor according to the optional method we must:

(a) Determine the total connected load of the general lighting and receptacles, small-appliance and laundry branch circuits, and the nameplate VA rating of all appliances and motors.
(b) Determine the calculated load by applying the following demand factors to the total connected load: The first 10 kVA at 100 percent, and the remainder at 40 percent.
(c) Determine the air-conditioning versus heat calculated load.
(d) all of these.

50. A 1,500 sq ft dwelling unit contains the following loads:

Waste Disposal (1 kVA)
Dishwasher (1.50 kVA)
Water Heater (5 kW)
Dryer (5.50 kW)
Cooktop (6 kW)
Two Ovens (each 3 kW)
Air-Conditioning (3 hp, 230V)
Two separately controlled 5 kW space-heating units

Use the optional method of calculation to determine what size aluminum conductors are required for the 120/240V, single-phase service.

(a) 1 AWG AL
(b) 1/0 AWG AL
(c) 2/0 AWG AL
(d) 3/0 AWG AL

51. A dwelling unit has 2,330 sq ft of living space. In addition, there's a 900 sq ft porch, and a 400 sq ft carport (not a garage) with the following loads:

Waste Disposal (1 kVA)
Dishwasher (1.50 kW)
Trash Compactor (1.50 kVA)
Water Heater (6 kW)
Range (14 kW)
Dryer (4.50 kW)
Air-Conditioning Unit (5 hp 230V)
Baseboard Heat (Four at 2.50 kW each)

Use the optional method to determine what size aluminum conductors are required for the 120/240V, single-phase service.

(a) 1 AWG AL
(b) 1/0 AWG AL
(c) 2/0 AWG AL
(d) 3/0 AWG AL

PART D—OTHER TOPICS OF INTEREST

9.12 Neutral Calculations [220.61]

52. The feeder and service neutral load is the maximum unbalanced calculated load between the neutral conductor and any one ungrounded (hot) conductor as determined by Article 220. Since 240V loads can't be connected to the neutral conductor, 240V loads aren't considered for sizing the feeder grounded conductor.

(a) True
(b) False

53. What size single-phase, 3-wire feeder is required for a 475A calculated load of which 275A consists of 240V loads? Size the conductors based on 75°C terminals in accordance with 110.14(C)(1)(b).

(a) Two 500 kcmil and one 350 kcmil
(b) Two 750 kcmil and one 3/0 AWG
(c) Two 750 kcmil and one 350 kcmil
(d) Two 750 kcmil and one 500 kcmil

54. The feeder or service neutral load for household cooking appliances, such as electric ranges, wall-mounted ovens, or counter-mounted cooking units, is permitted to be calculated at ______ percent of the load as determined by 220.55.

(a) 50
(b) 60
(c) 70
(d) 80

55. What's the dwelling unit service neutral load for one 9 kW range?

(a) 3.50 kW
(b) 5.60 kW
(c) 6.50 kW
(d) 12 kW

56. The service neutral load for household electric clothes dryers is permitted to be calculated at ______ percent of the load as determined by 220.54.

(a) 50
(b) 60
(c) 70
(d) 80

57. What's the feeder neutral load for one 6 kW household dryer?

(a) 4.20 kW
(b) 4.70 kW
(c) 5.40 kW
(d) 6.60 kW

UNIT

9

Challenge Questions

Please use the 2011 *Code* book to answer the following questions, which are based on the 2011 *NEC*.

CHALLENGE QUESTIONS FOR UNIT 9—DWELLING UNIT CALCULATIONS

PART A—GENERAL REQUIREMENTS

9.5 Cooking Equipment—Branch Circuit [Table 220.55, Note 4]

1. The branch-circuit calculated load for one 18 kW range is ______.

(a) 8 kW
(b) 10.40 kW
(c) 12 kW
(d) 18 kW

2. A dwelling unit kitchen has the following appliances: one 9 kW cooktop and one wall-mounted oven rated 5.30 kW. The branch-circuit calculated load for these appliances is ______.

(a) 8 kW
(b) 8.80 kW
(c) 12 kW
(d) 14.30 kW

PART B—STANDARD METHOD—FEEDER/SERVICE LOAD CALCULATIONS

9.6 Dwelling Unit Feeder/Service Load Calculations [Article 220, Part III]

3. An apartment building contains 20 units, each is 840 sq ft. What's the general lighting and general-use receptacle feeder calculated load for each dwelling unit?

Note: Laundry facilities are provided on the premises for all tenants so a laundry circuit isn't required in each unit [210.52(F) Ex 1].

(a) 3,520 VA
(b) 3,882 VA
(c) 4,220 VA
(d) 6,300 VA

4. What's the calculated load for the general lighting, receptacles, small-appliance circuits, and laundry circuits for a 1,800 sq ft dwelling unit?

(a) 4,300 VA
(b) 4,900 VA
(c) 5,415 VA
(d) 5,700 VA

5. How many 15A, 120V branch circuits are required for general-use receptacles and lighting in a 1,800 sq ft dwelling unit?

(a) 1 circuit
(b) 2 circuits
(c) 3 circuits
(d) 4 circuits

6. How many 20A, 120V branch circuits are required for general-use receptacles and lighting in a 2,800 sq ft dwelling unit?

(a) 2 circuits
(b) 4 circuits
(c) 6 circuits
(d) 7 circuits

Appliances [220.53]

7. A dwelling unit contains one of each of the following: dishwasher (1.20 kVA), trash compactor (1.50 kVA), and water heater (4 kVA). The appliance calculated load added to the service is ______.

(a) 5.90 kVA
(b) 6.70 kVA
(c) 7.70 kVA
(d) 8.80 kVA

8. A dwelling unit contains one of each of the following: dishwasher (½ hp) and water heater (4 kVA). What's the appliance calculated load for the dwelling unit?

(a) 4 kVA
(b) 5.10 kVA
(c) 9 kVA
(d) 11 kVA

Clothes Dryer [220.54]

9. A dwelling unit contains a 5.50 kW electric clothes dryer. What's the feeder calculated load for the dryer?

(a) 3.38 kW
(b) 4.50 kW
(c) 5 kW
(d) 5.50 kW

Cooking Equipment [220.55]

10. The feeder load for twelve 1.75 kW cooktops is ______.

(a) 10.50 kW
(b) 12.50 kW
(c) 13.50 kW
(d) 21 kW

11. The minimum neutral for a branch circuit to a 9 kW household range is ______. (See 210.19(A)(3) Ex 2.)

(a) 10 AWG
(b) 12 AWG
(c) 8 AWG
(d) 6 AWG

12. What's the maximum dwelling unit feeder or service calculated load for fifteen 8 kW cooking units?

(a) 38.40 kW
(b) 42 kW
(c) 48 kW
(d) 52 kW

13. What's the feeder calculated load for five 10 kW, five 14 kW, and five 16 kW household ranges?

(a) 21 kW
(b) 25 kW
(c) 28 kW
(d) 33 kW

14. A dwelling unit has one 6 kW cooktop and one 6 kW oven. What's the minimum feeder calculated load for the cooking appliances?

(a) 6.50 kW
(b) 7.10 kW
(c) 7.80 kW
(d) 8.20 kW

15. The maximum feeder calculated load for an 8 kW range is ______.

(a) 6.30 kW
(b) 8 kW
(c) 8.50 kW
(d) 12 kW

16. The minimum feeder calculated load for five 5 kW ranges, two 4 kW ovens, and four 7 kW cooking units is ______.

(a) 16.50 kW
(b) 17.10 kW
(c) 19.50 kW
(d) 28.20 kW

17. The minimum feeder calculated load for two 3 kW wall-mounted ovens and one 6 kW cooktop is ______.

(a) 8.40 kW
(b) 9.30 kW
(c) 9.60 kW
(d) 11 kW

18. If each unit of a duplex apartment requires a 100A main, the resulting 200A service will require ______ conductors.

(a) 1 AWG
(b) 1/0 AWG
(c) 3/0 AWG
(d) 250 kcmil

19. After all demand factors have been taken into consideration, the calculated load for a single dwelling service is a 24,221 VA, 120/240V, single-phase system. The minimum service size is ______.

(a) 70A
(b) 80A
(c) 110A
(d) 125A

PART C—OPTIONAL METHOD—FEEDER/ SERVICE LOAD CALCULATIONS

9.8 Dwelling Unit Optional Calculations [220.82]

20. After all demand factors have been taken into consideration the calculated load for a dwelling unit is 21,560 VA. The minimum service size for this residence will be ______ if the optional method of service calculations is used for a 120/240V, single-phase system. Be sure to read 220.82 carefully!

(a) 80A
(b) 100A
(c) 125A
(d) 150A

21. Using the optional calculations method, determine the calculated load for a 6 kW electric space-heating unit and a 4 kVA air-conditioning unit.

(a) 3,900 VA
(b) 4,000 VA
(c) 5,000 VA
(d) 9,000 VA

22. The total connected load of a dwelling unit is 25 kVA, not including heat or air-conditioning. If the 10 kW of baseboard electric heat is separately controlled in five rooms and the air-conditioning is 6 kVA, then the total service calculated load is ______ if the optional method is used.

(a) 5 kVA
(b) 22 kVA
(c) 23 kVA
(d) 24 kVA

23. Using the optional method, determine the service for the following loads: 1,200 sq ft on the first floor, plus 600 sq ft on the second floor, a 200 sq ft open porch, dishwasher (½ hp), water heater (4 kW), clothes dryer (4 kW), oven (6 kW), cooktop (6 kW), air-conditioning (5 hp, 230V), a single electric space heating unit (6 kW), and pool pump (¾ hp, 115V). The service source voltage is 120/240V, single-phase.

(a) 70A
(b) 80A
(c) 110A
(d) 125A

24. An 1,800 sq ft residence contains the following: a 4 kW water heater, five separately controlled electric space-heating units totaling 10 kW, one 1.50 kW dishwasher, one 6 kW range, one 4.50 kW dryer, two 3 kW ovens, and one 6 kW air conditioner. The 120/240V, single-phase service for the loads will be ______. The optional method of service calculation is to be used.

(a) 100A
(b) 110A
(c) 125A
(d) 150A

25. A dwelling unit has 1,200 sq ft on the first floor, 600 sq ft upstairs (unfinished but adaptable for future use), a 200 sq ft open porch, and the following loads: pool pump (¾ hp), range (13.90 kW), dishwasher (1.20 kW), water heater (4 kW), dryer (4 kW), air-conditioning (5 hp), and electric space heating (6 kW). Using the optional calculation method, what size feeder/service conductor is required for this 120/240V, single-phase service?

(a) 100A service with 4 AWG
(b) 110A service with 3 AWG
(c) 125A service with 2 AWG
(d) 150A service with 1 AWG

CHAPTER 3

ADVANCED *NEC* CALCULATIONS

Essential for Master's Exams

Notes

UNIT 10 Multifamily Dwelling Calculations

INTRODUCTION TO UNIT 10—MULTIFAMILY DWELLING CALCULATIONS

The *NEC* defines "Multifamily Dwellings" as buildings that contain three or more dwelling units. There are many similarities in the electrical requirements for multifamily and single-family dwellings, but there are differences also. The wiring method used for a single-family dwelling unit is often Type NM cable (unless local codes don't allow Type NM). Depending on several factors, such as the number of units, number of stories, the building construction type, and local building codes, a multifamily dwelling may use metal raceways or metallic-sheathed cable. The branch-circuit requirements of Article 210 are almost the same for each of these types of buildings so much of the branch-circuit design is similar.

When sizing the service or feeder conductors for a single-family dwelling in Unit 9, the use of Table 310.15(B)(7) is allowed. Table 310.15(B)(16) must be used instead when sizing conductors for the service or feeder for a multifamily dwelling. However, Table 310.15(B)(7) may still be used for the feeders to an individual dwelling unit within the building.

To size the electrical feeders to individual dwelling units, the requirements of Article 220 that were discussed in Unit 9 may be followed, but the main service that feeds a multifamily dwelling is based on the sum of all of the individual dwelling unit loads with the appropriate demand factors applied.

Demand factors are allowed for multifamily dwellings because diversity in usage is expected, so the maximum connected load isn't likely to be in use simultaneously. Many of the principles explained in Unit 9 will still be used for multifamily dwellings here in Unit 10.

The *NEC* defines a dwelling unit as a single unit, providing complete and independent living facilities for one or more persons, including permanent provisions for living, sleeping, cooking, and sanitation. A free-standing microwave is generally not accepted as the cooking provisions required to meet this definition. Figure 10–1

A multifamily dwelling is a building that contains three or more dwelling units, such as many apartment buildings, condominiums, and some hotels and motels. Figure 10–2 A two-family dwelling isn't considered a multifamily dwelling [Article 100 Definitions]. An example of a two-family dwelling calculation is provided in this unit in Section 10.7.

Author's Comment: Hotels and motels without cooking areas aren't considered dwelling units. Figure 10–3

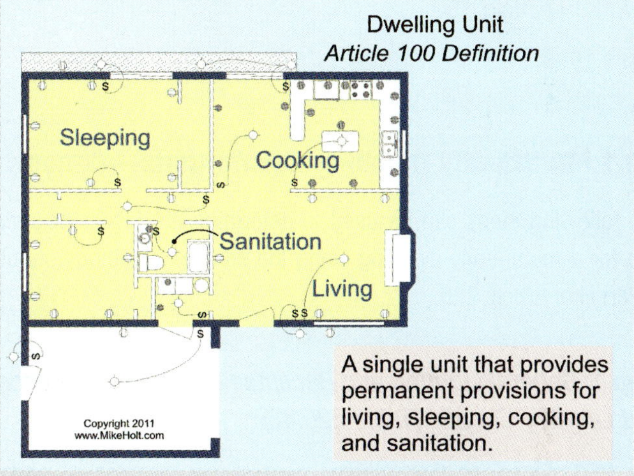

Figure 10–1

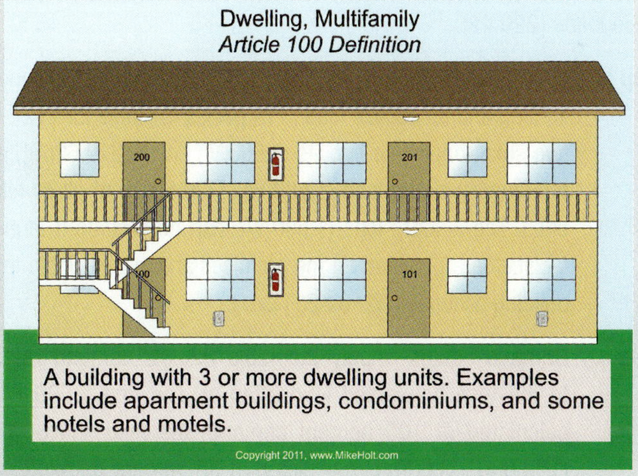

Figure 10–2

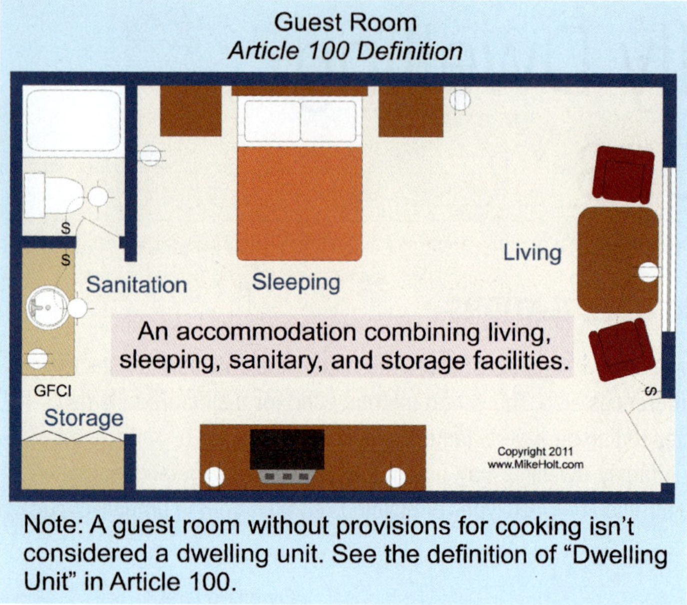

Figure 10–3

10.1 Multifamily Dwelling Calculations—General

The following steps can be used to determine the feeder or service size for a multifamily dwelling using the standard method contained in Part III of Article 220:

Step 1: General Lighting and Receptacles, Small-Appliance and Laundry Circuits [Table 220.42]

The *NEC* recognizes that lighting, general-use receptacles, and the small-appliance and laundry circuits won't all be on, or loaded, at the same time. It permits the following demand factors to be applied to these loads [220.42]:

Step a: Total Connected Load—Determine the total connected general lighting and receptacle load (3 VA per sq ft) [Table 220.12], the two small-appliance circuits (1,500 VA each) [220.52(A)], and the laundry circuit load (1,500 VA) [220.52(B)] of all dwelling units. The laundry load (1,500 VA) can be omitted if laundry facilities are provided on the premises and are available to all building occupants [210.52(F) Ex 1].

Step b: Demand Factor—Apply the Table 220.42 demand factors to the total connected load (Step a). The first 3,000 VA is calculated at 100 percent demand, the next 117,000 VA (120,000 - 3,000) is calculated at 35 percent demand, and the remainder at 25 percent according to Table 220.42.

Step 2: Appliances [220.53]

A demand factor of 75 percent is permitted for four or more appliances fastened in place, such as a dishwasher, kitchen waste disposal, trash compactor, water heater, and so on. This doesn't apply to air-conditioning equipment [220.50], space-heating equipment [220.51], clothes dryers [220.54], or cooking appliances [220.55].

Step 3: Clothes Dryers [220.54]

The feeder or service calculated load for household electric clothes dryers located in dwelling units must not be less than 5,000W (or 5,000 VA), or the nameplate rating (whichever is greater) and may be adjusted according to the demand factors listed in Table 220.54.

> **Author's Comment:** A dryer load isn't required if the dwelling unit doesn't contain an electric dryer. Dryers in common laundry rooms must not have their loads calculated according to this method.

Step 4: Cooking Equipment [220.55]

Household cooking appliances rated over 1¾ kVA can have their feeder and service loads calculated according to the demand factors of Table 220.55 and Notes.

Step 5: Air-Conditioning versus Heat [220.51 and 220.60]

When the air-conditioning and heating loads aren't on at the same time (simultaneously), only the larger of the two loads must be used [220.60].

- *Air-Conditioning.* The air-conditioning load must be calculated at 100 percent [220.50].
- *Heat.* Electric space-heating loads must be calculated at 100 percent [220.51].

Step 6: Feeder and Service Conductor Size

The feeder/service conductors are sized according to Table 310.15(B)(16). Conductors are presumed to be copper unless otherwise stated, and systems are presumed to be single-phase unless otherwise stated.

Author's Comments:

- Table 310.15(B)(7) can be used to size the 120/240V feeder conductors to the individual dwelling units of a multifamily dwelling, but Table 310.15(B)(16) must be used to size service conductors that supply two or more dwelling units.
- Section 110.14(C)(1)(a) states that terminals are rated 60°C for equipment rated 100A or less unless marked 75°C. In real life, most terminals are now rated 75°C, so in this unit, we assume all terminals are rated 75°C unless 60°C is specified. Insulated conductors will be presumed to be 90°C rated. For exam purposes, read the problem carefully to be certain you know what terminal rating the exam question specifies. If unspecified, use the rules of 110.14(C).

PART A—STANDARD METHOD—FEEDER/ SERVICE LOAD CALCULATIONS

Introduction

In Unit 9 you learned how to calculate feeder and/or service loads for single dwelling units, using two different methods: the standard and the optional. In a multifamily building, as with single dwelling units, the *NEC* permits demand factors to be applied to account for the fact that not all connected loads in a multifamily dwelling will operate simultaneously. This part of the unit will provide the standard method of calculation for a multifamily dwelling.

10.2 Multifamily Dwelling Calculation Examples—Standard Method

The following steps can be used to determine feeder and service sizes for a multifamily dwelling using the standard method contained in Article 220, Part III:

Step 1: General Lighting, Small-Appliance, and Laundry Demand [Table 220.42]

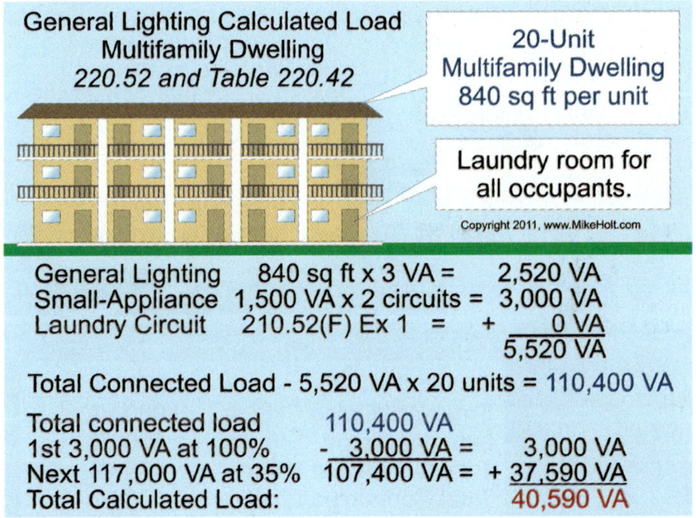

Figure 10–4

► **General Lighting Load Example 1**

Question: *What's the general lighting and receptacle (including small-appliance circuits) calculated load for an apartment building that contains 20 units? Each apartment is 840 sq ft.*

Note: Laundry facilities are provided on the premises for all tenants [210.52(F) Ex 1]. **Figure 10–4**

(a) 5,200 VA (b) 25,500 VA (c) 40,590 VA (d) 110,400 VA

Answer: *(c) 40,590 VA*

General Lighting (840 sq ft x 3 VA)	*2,520 VA*		
Small-Appliance Circuits 2 x 1,500 VA	*3,000 VA*		
Laundry Circuit	*+ 0 VA*		
Connected Load for one unit	*5,520 VA*		
Connected Load [Table 220.42] (5,520 VA x 20 units)	*110,400 VA*		
First 3,000 VA at 100 percent	*– 3,000 VA*	*x 1.00 =*	*3,000 VA*
Next 117,000 VA at 35 percent	*107,400 VA*	*x 0.35 =*	*+ 37,590 VA*
Total Calculated Load			*40,590 VA*

► General Lighting Load Example 2

Question: *What's the general lighting and receptacle calculated load for a 20-unit apartment building? Each unit is 990 sq ft.* **Figure 10–5 and 10–6**

(a) 51,300 VA (b) 74,700 VA (c) 105,600 VA (d) 149,400 VA

Answer: *(a) 51,300 VA*

General Lighting (990 sq ft x 3 VA)	*2,970 VA*		
Small-Appliance Circuits	*3,000 VA*		
Laundry Circuit	*+ 1,500 VA*		
Connected Load for one unit	*7,470 VA*		
Connected Load (7,470 VA x 20 units)	*149,400 VA*		
First 3,000 VA at 100% [Table 220.42]	*– 3,000 VA*	*x 1.00 =*	*3,000 VA*
	146,400 VA		
Next 117,000 VA at 35%	*–117,000 VA*	*x 0.35 =*	*40,950 VA*
Remainder VA at 25%	*29,400 VA*	*x 0.25 =*	*+ 7,350 VA*
Total Calculated Load			*51,300 VA*

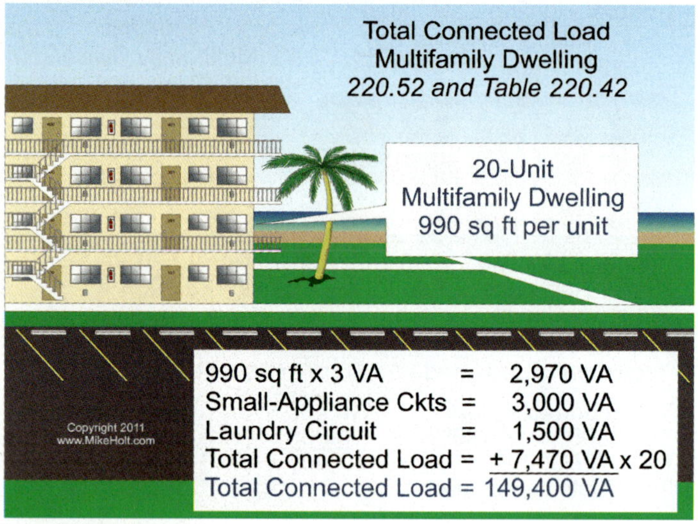

Figure 10–5

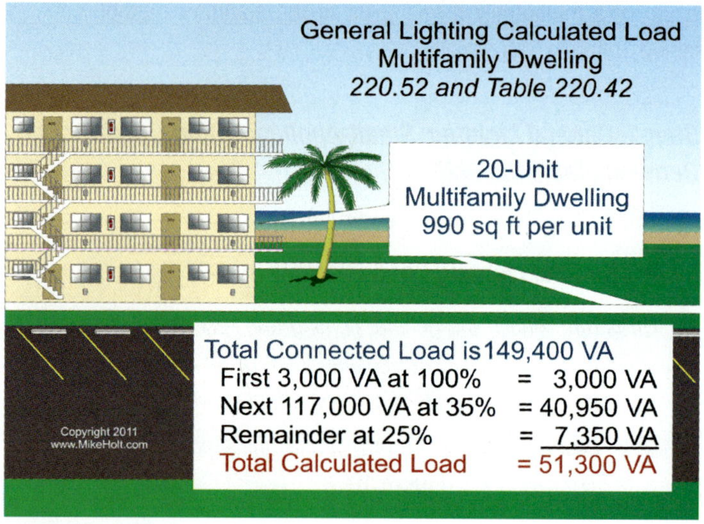

Figure 10–6

Step 2. Appliance Calculated Load [220.53]

► Appliance Load Example 1

Question: *What's the appliance calculated load for the feeder/service to a 20-unit multifamily building that contains a 940 VA waste disposal, a 1,250 VA dishwasher, and a 4,500 VA water heater in each unit?* **Figure 10–7**

(a) 5 kVA (b) 7 kVA (c) 100 kVA (d) 134 kVA

Answer: *(c) 100 kVA*

Disposal	*940 VA*
Dishwasher	*1,250 VA*
Water Heater	*+ 4,500 VA*
Connected Load per Unit	*6,690 VA*
Total Connected Load	*6.690 VAx 20 units =133,800 VA*
Total Calculated Load	*133,800 VA x 0.75* = 100,350 VA*

**Use the total number of appliances to determine if the 75 percent demand factor applies. In this case, there are 60 appliances on the feeder/service conductors [220.53].*

The contribution to the neutral of the feeder/service for the appliance connected load is calculated by first removing the 240V loads, such as the water heater:

Disposal	*940 VA*
Dishwasher	*1,250 VA*
	2,190 VAx 20 units = 43,800 VA
Total Appliance Neutral Calculated Load	*43,800 VA x 0.75 = 32,850 VA*

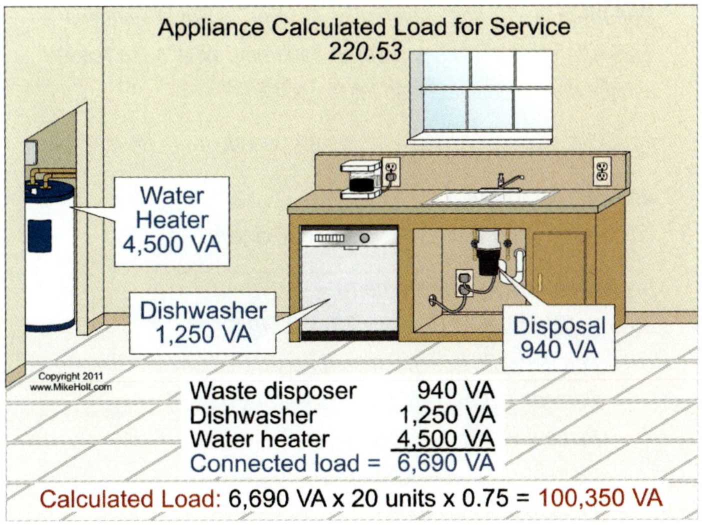

Figure 10–7

► Appliance Load Example 2

Question: *What's the appliance calculated load for the feeder/service to a 35-unit multifamily building that contains a 900 VA waste disposal, a 1,200 VA dishwasher, and a 5,000 VA water heater in each unit?* **Figure 10–8**

(a) 71 kVA (b) 107 kVA (c) 142 kVA (d) 187 kVA

Answer: *(d) 187 kVA*

Disposal	*900 VA*
Dishwasher	*1,200 VA*
Water Heater	*+ 5,000 VA*
Connected Load per Unit	*7,100 VA*
Total Connected Load	*7,100 VA x 35 units = 248,500 VA*
Calculated Load	*248,500 VA x 0.75* = 186,375 VA*

**Use the total number of appliances to determine if the 75 percent demand factor applies. In this case, there are 105 appliances on the feeder/service conductors [220.53].*

The contribution to the neutral of the feeder/service for the appliance connected load is calculated by first removing the 240V loads, such as the water heater:

Disposal	*900 VA*
Dishwasher	*1,200 VA*
	2,100 VAx 35 units = 73,500 VA
Total Appliance Neutral Calculated Load	*73,500 VA x 0.75 = 55,125 VA*

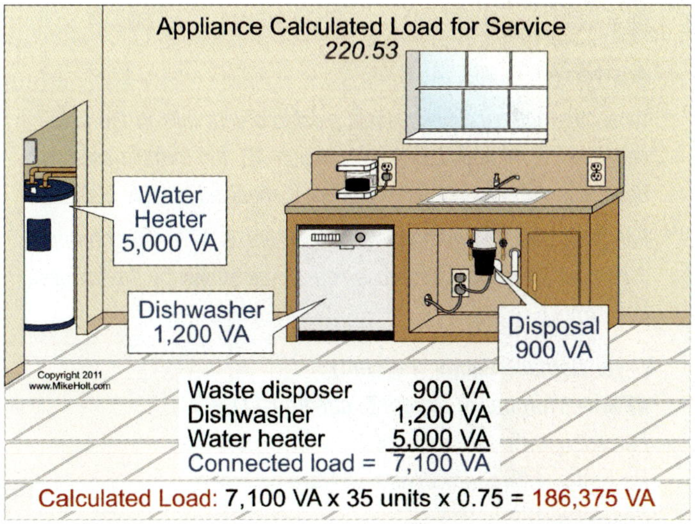

Figure 10–8

Step 3: Household Dryer Calculated Load [220.54]

► Dryer Load Example 1

Question: *A 10-unit multifamily dwelling building contains a 4.50 kVA electric clothes dryer in each unit. What's the feeder/service dryer calculated load for the building?*

(a) 5 kVA (b) 25 kVA (c) 45 kVA (d) 60 kVA

Answer: *(b) 25 kVA*

5 kVA is the minimum load for calculation [220.54]

Connected Load = 5 kVA x 10 Units
Connected Load = 50 kVA

Calculated Load = Connected Load x Demand Factor [Table 220.54]
Calculated Load = 50 kVA x 0.50
Calculated Load = 25 kVA

The contribution to the neutral of the feeder/service for the clothes dryer load is calculated by first multiplying the dryer calculated load times 70 percent [220.61(B)(1)]:

25 kVA x 0.70 = 17.50 kVA

► Dryer Load Example 2

Question: *A 20-unit multifamily dwelling building contains a 5.25 kVA electric clothes dryer in each unit. What's the feeder/service dryer calculated load for the building?* **Figure 10–9**

(a) 5 kVA (b) 27 kVA (c) 39.90 kVA (d) 60 kVA

Answer: *(c) 39.90 kVA*

When the number of household electric dryers falls in the categories of 12 through 23, or 24 through 42, the formula used to determine the demand factor percent is specified in Table 220.54.

For 20 dryers, the demand factor percent is 47 percent minus 1 percent for each dryer exceeding 11, as shown by the following formula:

Dryer Demand Factor (Percent) =
47% – (Number of Dryers Exceeding 11)%
Percent = 47% - (Number of Dryers - 11)%
Percent = 47% - (20 Dryers - 11)%
Percent = 47% - 9%
Percent = 38%

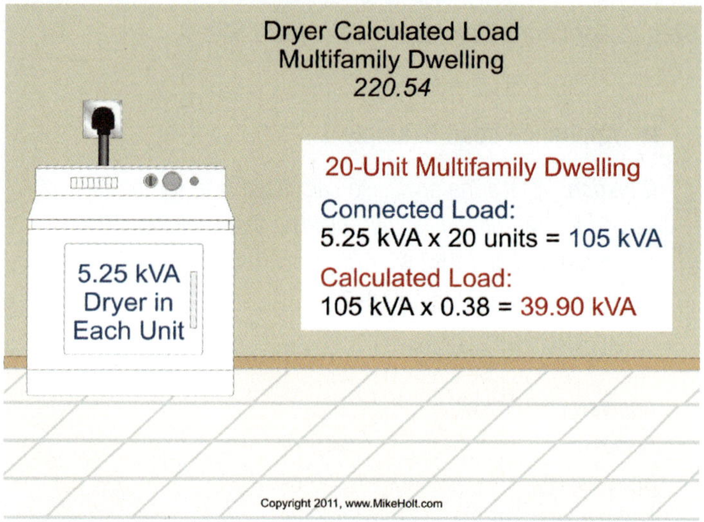

Figure 10–9

Calculated Load = Connected Load x Demand Factor Percent
Connected Load = 5.25 kVA x 20 Units

Calculated Load = 5.25 kVA x 20 Units x 0.38
Calculated Load = 39.90 kVA
Author's Comment: a percentage can be converted to a decimal number as shown in this example to simplify the multiplication.

The contribution to the neutral of the feeder/service for the clothes dryer load is calculated by multiplying the dryer calculated load times 70 percent [220.61(B)(1)]:

39.90 kVA x 0.70 = 27.93 kVA

► Dryer Load Example 3

Question: *A 30-unit multifamily dwelling building contains a 5.25 kVA electric clothes dryer in each unit. What's the feeder/service dryer calculated load for the building?*

(a) 5 kVA (b) 27 kVA (c) 39.90 kVA (d) 50 kVA

Answer: *(d) 50 kVA*
What is the Dryer Demand Factor for 30 dryers?

Dryer Demand Factor (Percent) =
35% – [(Number of Dryers - 23) x 0.50]%
Percent = 35% – [(number of dryers – 23) x 0.50]%
Percent = 35% – [(30 dryers – 23) x 0.50]%
Percent = 35% – (7 x 0.50)%
Percent = 35% – 3.50%
Percent = 31.50%

Calculated Load = Connected Load x Demand Factor Percent

Connected Load = 5.25 kVA x 30 Units

Calculated Load = 5.25 kVA x 30 Units x 0.315

Calculated Load = 49.61 kVA

Step 4: Household Cooking Equipment Calculated Load [220.55]

▶ Table 220.55 Column C—Not Over 12 kVA Example Figure 10–10

Question: *What's the feeder/service calculated load for twenty 9 kVA ranges?*

(a) 9 kVA (b) 20 kVA (c) 35 kVA (d) 45 kVA

Answer: *(b) 35 kVA*

Over 8¾, and less than 12 kVA, look up the kW Demand Load in Table 220.55, Column C.

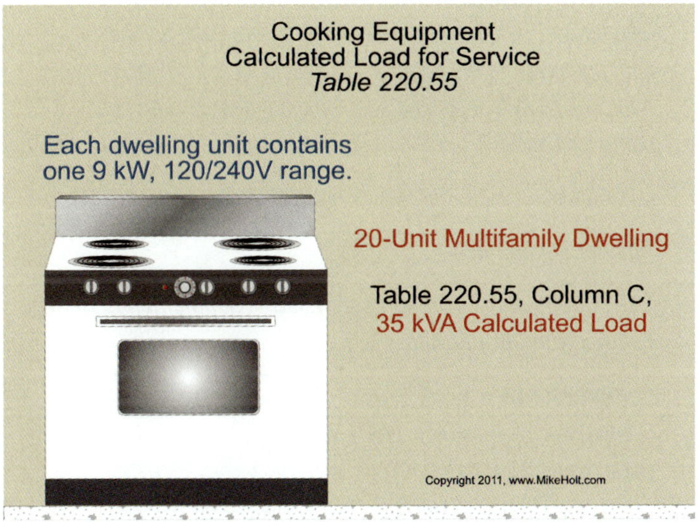

Figure 10–10

▶ Table 220.55, Note 1—Over 12 kVA with Equal Ratings Example

Question: *What's the feeder/service calculated load for twenty 15.60 kVA ranges?*

(a) 28 kVA (b) 30 kVA (c) 38 kVA (d) 42 kVA

Answer: *(d) 42 kVA*

Step a: Column C Demand Load for 20 units: 35 kVA.

Step b: The 15.60 kVA range exceeds 12 kVA by 3.60 kVA.

Increase the Column C Demand Load by 5% for each kVA or major fraction of kVA in excess of 12 kVA.

Step c: 3.60 kVA is equal to 3 kVA plus a major fraction of a kVA, so increase the Column C kVA value by 4 x 5% = 20% increase, resulting in 120%, or a 1.20 multiplier.

Calculated Load = Column C Value x Multiplier

Calculated Load = 35 kVA x 1.20

Calculated Load = 42 kVA

The contribution to the neutral of the feeder/service for the range load is calculated by multiplying the range calculated load times 70 percent [220.61(B)(1)]:

42 kVA x 0.70 = 29.40 kVA

▶ Table 220.55, Note 2—Unequal Ratings Over 12 kVA Example

Question: *What's the feeder/service calculated load for ten ranges rated 9 kVA and ten ranges rated 14 kVA?*

(a) 22 kVA (b) 36 kVA (c) 42 kVA (d) 78 kVA

Answer: *(b) 36 kVA*

Step a: Determine the total connected load:

9 kVA (min. 12 kVA)	*10 ranges x 12 kVA =*	*120 kVA*
14 kVA	*10 ranges x 14 kVA=*	*140 kVA*
Total Connected Load		*260 kVA*

Step b: Determine the average of range ratings:

260 kVA/20 units = 13 kVA average rating.

Step c: Demand load from Table 220.55 Column C:

20 ranges = 35 kVA

Step d: The average of the ranges (13 kVA) exceeds 12 kVA by 1 kVA. Increase the Column C Demand load (35 kVA) by 5%, resulting in 105%, or a 1.05 multiplier

Calculated Load = Column C Value x Multiplier

Calculated Load = 35 kVA x 1.05

Calculated Load = 36.75 kVA

The contribution to the neutral of the feeder/service for the range load is calculated by multiplying the range calculated load times 70 percent [220.61(B)(1)]:

36.75 kVA x 0.70 = 25.725 kVA

► Table 220.55, Note 3 Example

Question: *What's the feeder/service calculated load for ten 3 kVA ovens?*

(a) 10 kVA (b) 15 kVA (c) 20 kVA (d) 30 kVA

Answer: *(b) 15 kVA (closest answer)*

Connected Load = 3 kVA x 10 units = 30 kVA
Calculated Load = 30 kVA x 0.49 [Table 220.55, Column A]
Calculated Load = 14.70 kVA

Step 5: Air-Conditioning versus Heat [220.51]

► Air-Conditioning versus Heat Example 1

Question: *What's the calculated load for air-conditioning versus heat for a 40-unit multifamily building that has an air-conditioning unit (14A, 230V) and two 3 kW heaters in each unit?*

(a) 50 kVA (b) 60 kVA (c) 160 kVA (d) 250 kVA

Answer: *(d) 250 kVA*

Heat = VA x Number of Units [220.51]
Heat = 3 kVA x 2 Units
Heat = 6 kVA x 40 Units
Heat = 240,000 VA

Air-Conditioning VA = V x A
Air-Conditioning VA = 240V x 14A
Air-Conditioning VA = 3,360 VA x 40
Air-Conditioning VA = 134,400 VA, [220.60]
Use the larger of the heating or air-conditioning

Author's Comment: Motors have nameplate ratings of 115V and 230V for use on 120V and 240V nominal voltage systems [Annex D Example D1(b)].

► Air-Conditioning versus Heat Example 2

Question: *What's the air-conditioning versus heat calculated load for a 25-unit multifamily building where each unit has a 17A, 230V air-conditioning unit and 5 kVA of electric heat?*

(a) 5 kVA (b) 6 kVA (c) 125 kVA (d) 160 kVA

Answer: *(c) 125 kVA*

Heat = VA x Number of Units [220.51]
Heat = 5 kVA x 25 Units
Heat = 125 kVA

Air-Conditioning VA = V x A
Air-Conditioning VA = 240V x 17A
Air-Conditioning VA = 4,080 VA x 25
Air-Conditioning VA = 102,000 VA, [220.60]
Use the larger of the heating or air-conditioning loads.

► Air-Conditioning versus Heat Example 3

Question: What's the air-conditioning versus heat calculated load for a 25-unit multifamily building where each unit has a heat pump where the compressor load is 17A, 230V and there's a total of 18 kVA of electric supplemental heat in each heat pump air-handler?

(a) 255 kVA (b) 388 kVA (c) 552 kVA (d) 727 kVA

Answer: *(c) 552 kVA*

Calculated Load = (Compressor Load + Supplemental Heat Load) x Number of Units

Compressor VA = V x A
Compressor VA = 240V x 17A
Compressor VA = 4,080 VA

Calculated Load = (4,080 VA + 18,000 VA) x 25 Units
Calculated Load = 552,000 VA

Step 6: Service Conductor Size [Table 310.15(B)(16)]

► Service Conductor Size Example 1

Question: *What size service copper conductors are required for a 120/240V, single-phase multifamily building that has a calculated load of 93 kVA?* **Figure 10–11**

(a) 300 kcmil (b) 350 kcmil (c) 500 kcmil (d) 600 kcmil

Answer: *(d) 600 kcmil*

I = VA/E
I = 93,000 VA/240V
I = 388A

600 kcmil copper, rated 420A at 75°C [Table 310.15(B)(16)]

According to Annex C, Table C.10, a trade size 3 Schedule 40 PVC raceway will accommodate three 600 kcmil THWN conductors.

If the service conductors are paralleled in two sets:

- *388A/2 raceways = 194A*
- *3/0 AWG is rated 200A at 75°C [Table 310.15(B)(16)], so two 3/0 AWG can be paralleled for this service. A trade size 1½ Schedule 40 PVC raceway will accommodate three 3/0 THWN conductors [Annex C, Table C.10].*

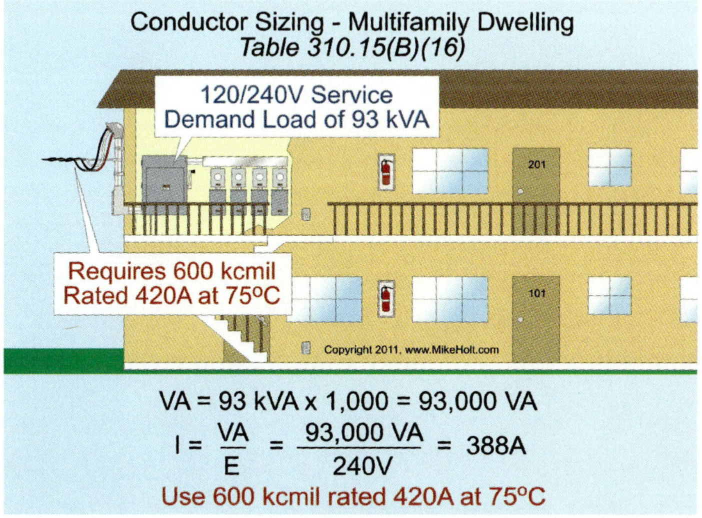

Figure 10–11

Author's Comment: The neutral is allowed to serve as the equipment grounding conductor ahead of the service disconnect, so only three conductors are required in each raceway [250.142(A)].

► Service Conductor Size Example 2

Question: *What size aluminum service conductors are required for a 120/240V, single-phase multifamily building that has a calculated load of 93 kVA?*

(a) 300 kcmil (b) 350 kcmil (c) 600 kcmil (d) 800 kcmil

Answer: *(d) 800 kcmil*

I = VA/E
I = 93,000 VA/240V
I = 388A

800 kcmil aluminum, rated 395A at 75°C [Table 310.15(B)(16)]

According to Annex C, Table C.10, a trade size 3½ Schedule 40 PVC raceway will accommodate three 800 kcmil THWN conductors.

If the service conductors are paralleled in two sets:

- *388A/2 raceways = 194A*
- *250 kcmil aluminum is rated 205A at 75°C [Table 310.15(B)(16)], so two 250 kcmil aluminum conductors can be paralleled for this service. A trade size 2 Schedule 40 PVC raceway will accommodate three 250 kcmil THWN conductors [Annex C, Table C.10].*

If the service conductors are paralleled in three sets:

- *388A/3 raceways = 129.33A*
- *2/0 AWG aluminum is rated 135A at 75°C [Table 310.15(B)(16)], so three 2/0 AWG aluminum conductors can be paralleled for this service. A trade size 1½ Schedule 40 PVC raceway will accommodate three 2/0 THWN conductors [Annex C, Table C.10].*

Author's Comment: Table 310.15(B)(7) only applies to feeder/service conductors for individual 120/240V dwelling units of 400A or less for single-family, two-family, or multifamily buildings. In this building, Table 310.15(B)(7) can be used for the feeder to each apartment, but Table 310.15(B)(16) must be used for sizing the feeder/service conductors that supply the entire building.

► Service Conductor Size Example 3

Question: *What size copper service conductors are required for a multifamily building that has a calculated load of 270 kVA for a 120/208V, three-phase system? Service conductors are run in parallel in two raceways.* **Figure 10–12**

(a) Two–300 kcmil per phase *(b) Two–350 kcmil per phase*
(c) Two–500 kcmil per phase *(d) Two–600 kcmil per phase*

Answer: *(c) Two–500 kcmil per phase*

I = VA/(1.732 x 208V)
I = 270,000 VA/(1.732 x 208V)
I = 270,000 VA/360V
I = 750A

Amperes per Parallel Set = Amperes/Number of Parallel Sets
750A/2 conductors in parallel = 375A per conductor.

A 500 kcmil conductor has an ampacity of 380A at 75°C [Table 310.15(B)(16)]. Table 310.15(B)(7) doesn't apply to services or feeders for multifamily buildings.

Two sets of 500 kcmil conductors (380A x 2) can be protected by an 800A overcurrent device. Their combined ampacity is 760A, but we're allowed to round up to the next standard size overcurrent device [240.4(B) and 240.6(A)].

If the service conductors are paralleled in three sets:

- *750A/3 raceways = 250A*
- *250 kcmil copper is rated 255A at 75°C [Table 310.15(B)(16)], so three 250 kcmil conductors can be paralleled for this service. A trade size 2 Schedule 40 PVC raceway will accommodate three 250 kcmil THWN conductors [Annex C, Table C.10].*

Author's Comment: Throughout this book, we use copper conductors unless otherwise specified [110.5].

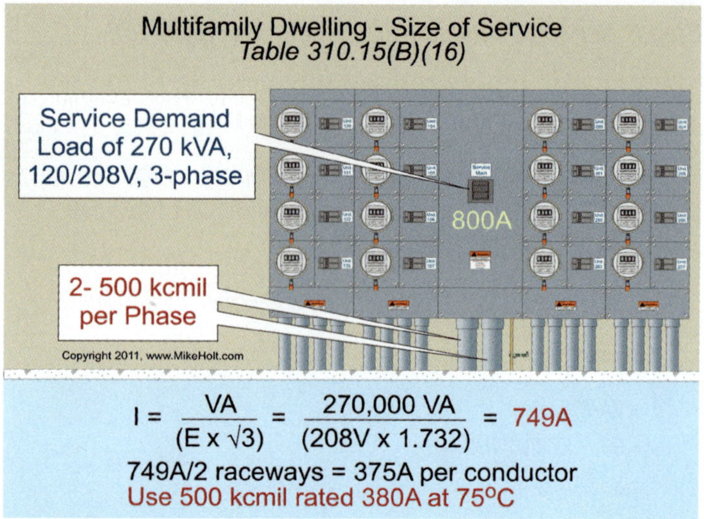

Figure 10–12

10.3 Multifamily Dwelling Calculations—Standard Method Example

The following example demonstrates the steps used to determine feeder and service sizes for a multifamily dwelling using the standard method contained in Article 220, Part III:

► Standard Method Calculated Load Example

Question: *What's the calculated load for a 25-unit apartment building? The system voltage is 120/240V, single-phase. Each apartment is 1,000 sq ft, and contains the following:*

Waste Disposal	*1.50 kVA*
Dishwasher	*1.20 kVA*
Water Heater	*4.50 kVA*
Dryer	*4.50 kVA*
Range	*15.50 kVA*
Air-Conditioning (230V)	*28A*
Electric Space Heating	*7.50 kVA*

(a) 200 kVA (b) 325 kVA (c) 475 kVA (D) 600 kVA

Answer: *(c) 475 kVA*

Step 1: General Lighting, Small-Appliance, and Laundry Demand [Table 220.42]

General Lighting (1,000 sq ft x 3 VA) [220.12]	*3,000 VA*		
Small-Appliance Circuits [220.52(A)]	*3,000 VA*		
Laundry Circuit [220.52(B)]	*+ 1,500 VA*		
	7,500 VA		
Total Connected Load (7,500 VA x 25 units)	*187,500 VA*		
First 3,000 VA at 100 percent [Table 220.42]	*– 3,000 VA*	*x 1.00 =*	*3,000 VA*
	184,500 VA		
Next 117,000 VA at 35 percent	*– 117,000 VA*	*x 0.35 =*	*40,950 VA*
Remainder at 25 percent	*67,500 VA*	*x 0.25 =*	*+ 16,875 VA*
Total Calculated Load			*60,825 VA*

Step 2: Appliance Calculated Load [220.53]

Waste Disposal	*1,500 VA*		
Dishwasher	*1,200 VA*		
Water Heater	*+ 4,500 VA*		
Connected Load	*7,200 VA*	*x 25 units =*	*180,000 VA*
Calculated Load	*180,000 VA*	*x 0.75* =*	*135,000 VA*

**Use the total number of appliances to determine if the 75 percent demand factor applies. In this case, there are 75 appliances on the feeder/service conductors [220.53].*

Step 3: Dryer Calculated Load [220.54]

Dryers must be calculated at a minimum of 5,000 VA or the nameplate, whichever is larger [220.54].

Total Connected Load = 5 kVA x 25 units
Total Connected Load = 125,000 VA

Dryer Demand Factor for 25 dryers (Percent) =
35 percent minus 0.50 percent for each dryer exceeding 23 [Table 220.54].

Percent = 35 - [0.50 x (Number of Dryers Exceeding 23)]
Percent = 35 - [0.50 x (25 Dryers - 23)]
Percent = 35 - (0.50 x 2)
Percent = 35 - 1
Percent = 34%

Calculated Load = Connected Load x Demand Factor Percent
Calculated Load = 125,000 VA x 0.34
Dryer Calculated Load = 42,500 VA

Step 4: Cooking Equipment Calculated Load [220.55]

Step a: Column C Demand Load for 25 units = 40 kVA. [Table 220.55]

Step b: 15.50 kVA – 12 kVA = 3.50 kVA.
3.50 kVA is equal to 3 kVA plus a major fraction of a kVA, so increase to 4

Step c: Increase the Column C Demand Load (40 kVA) by 4 x 5% = 20%: resulting in 120%, or a 1.20 multiplier.

Step d: Range calculated load = Column C Value x Multiplier
Range calculated load = 40 kVA x 1.20
Range calculated load = 48 kVA

Step 5: Air-conditioning versus Heat [220.51]

Air-conditioning VA Load = 28A x 240V x 25 Units
Air-conditioning VA Load = 168,000 VA, (omit) [220.60]

Heat Connected Load = VA x Number of Units [220.51]
Heat Connected Load = 7,500 VA x 25 Units
Heat Connected Load = 187,500 VA

Step 6: Service Conductor Size

Step 1: Total general lighting, small-appliance, and laundry calculated load	*60,825 VA*
Step 2: Total appliance calculated load	*135,000 VA*
Step 3: Total dryer calculated load	*42,500 VA*
Step 4: Range calculated load	*48,000 VA*
Step 5: Total heat calculated load [220.51] (7,500 VA x 25 units)	*+ 187,500 VA*
Total Calculated Load	*473,825 VA*

Service Conductor Amperes = VA/E
Service Conductor Amperes = 473,825 VA/240V
Service Conductor Amperes = 1,974A

PART B—OPTIONAL METHOD—FEEDER/SERVICE LOAD CALCULATIONS

Introduction

In a multifamily building consisting of three or more dwelling units, either the standard method or the optional method can be used to calculate the size of the main service. Part IV of Article 220 provides the optional method which permits demand factors to be applied in recognition of the diversity of usage of all the loads in all the separate units of a multifamily dwelling. In order to apply the optional method for multifamily dwellings, each dwelling unit must be equipped with electric cooking equipment, electric heating and/or air-conditioning, and supplied by no more than one feeder.

10.4 Multifamily Dwelling Unit Calculations [220.84]—Optional Method

The feeder/service calculated load for a building that has three or more dwelling units equipped with electric cooking equipment and either electric space heating or air-conditioning can be calculated in accordance with the demand factors of Table 220.84, based on the number of dwelling units [220.84(A)(1), (2), and (3)]. The feeder/service neutral calculated load must be determined in accordance with 220.61.

House loads for common areas are calculated in accordance with Article 220, Part III and then added to the Table 220.84 calculated load.

> **Author's Comment:** House loads are those not directly associated with the individual dwelling units of a multifamily dwelling. Some examples of house loads are landscape and parking lot lighting, hall and stairway lighting, common laundry facilities, common pool and recreation areas, and so forth.

The following steps can be used to determine feeder and service sizes for a multifamily dwelling using the optional method contained in Article 220, Part IV:

Step 1: Total Connected Load [220.84(C)]

The following connected loads from all the dwelling units are added together, and then the Table 220.84 demand factor is applied to determine the calculated load:

- 3 VA per sq ft for general lighting and general-use receptacles.
- 1,500 VA for each small-appliance circuit (minimum of 2 circuits).
- 1,500 VA for each laundry circuit.
- The nameplate rating of all appliances.
- The nameplate rating of all motors.
- The larger of the air-conditioning load or the space-heating load.

> **Author's Comment:** A laundry circuit isn't required for an individual dwelling unit if common laundry facilities are provided.

Step 2: Calculated Load

The calculated load is determined by applying the demand factor from Table 220.84 to the total connected load (Step 1). The calculated load (kVA) can be converted to amperes by:

◆ **Single-Phase Formula:** $I = VA/E$ **Three-Phase Formula:** $I = VA/(1.732 \times E)$

Step 3: Feeder and Service Conductor Size

The ungrounded conductors are sized according to Table 310.15(B)(16), based on the calculated load.

10.5 Multifamily—Optional Method Example 1 [220.84]

A 120/240V, single-phase system supplies a 12-unit multifamily building. Each 1,500 sq ft unit contains: **Figure 10–13**

Dishwasher	1.50 kVA
Water Heater	4 kVA
Washing Machine	1.20 kVA
Dryer	4.50 kVA
Range	14.40 kVA
Air-Conditioning (230V)	17A, 230V
Electric Space Heating	5 kVA

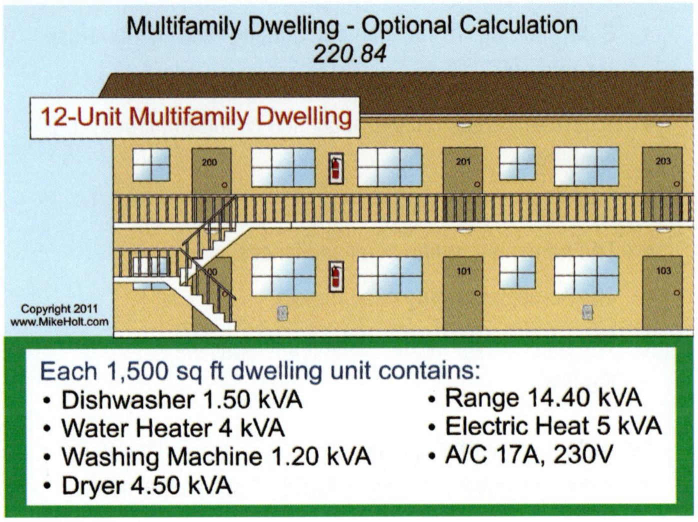

Figure 10–13

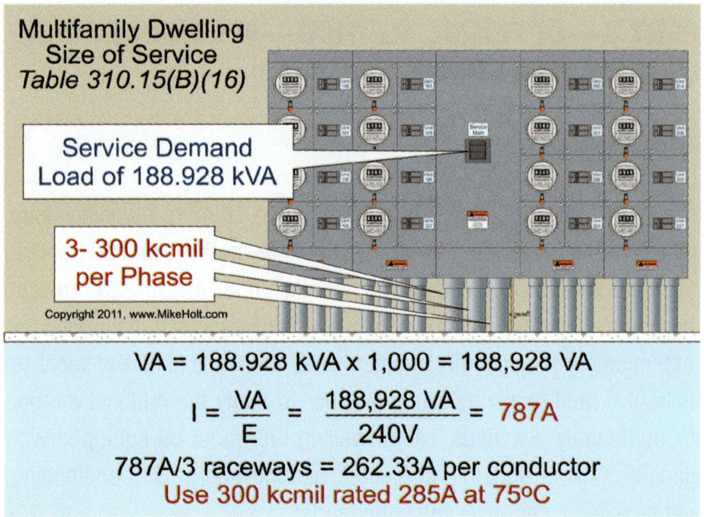

Figure 10–14

► Parallel Service Conductor Sizing Example 1

Question: *What size conductor is required if the service is rated 120/240V, single-phase and the conductors are installed in parallel in three separate raceways?*

(a) 300 kcmil (b) 400 kcmil (c) 500 kcmil (d) 600 kcmil

Answer: *(a) 300 kcmil*

Step 1: Total Connected Load

Step a: Determine the General Lighting Load:

General Lighting (1,500 sq ft x 3 VA)	*4,500 VA*		
Small-Appliance Circuits (2 circuits x 1,500 VA)	*3,000 VA*		
Laundry Circuit	*+ 1,500 VA*		
	9,000 VA	*x 12 units =*	*108,000 VA*

Step b: Determine the Appliance Calculated Load:

Dishwasher	*1,500 VA*		
Water Heater	*4,000 VA*		
Dryer (nameplate)	*4,500 VA*		
Range (nameplate)	*+ 14,400 VA*		
	24,400 VA	*x 12 units =*	*292,800 VA*

Step c: Compare the Air-Conditioning versus Heat Load:

Heat	*5,000 VA*	*x 12 units =*	*60,000 VA*

Air-conditioning VA = 240V x 17A, 4,080 VA

Use the heat for this calculation, it Is larger than the a/c [220.60]

Step 2: Total Connected Loads

General Lighting, Receptacles	*108,000 VA*
Appliances Connected Load	*292,800 VA*
Heat	*+ 60,000 VA*
Total Connected Load	*460,800 VA*

Total Calculated Load = Total Connected Load x Demand Factor [Table 220.84]

Total Calculated Load = 460,800 VA x 0.41 [Table 220.84]

Total Calculated Load = 188,928 VA

Step 3: Service Conductor Size **Figure 10–14**

I = VA/E

I = 188,928 VA/240V

I = 787A

Conductor size if paralleled in three raceways [240.4(B)]:

787A/3 raceways = 262.33A per conductor

Feeder/Service Conductors: Parallel 300 kcmil rated 285A at 75°C [Table 310.15(B)(16)].

► Grounding Electrode Conductor Sizing Example 1

Question: *What size grounding electrode conductor is required if the service ungrounded conductors are 300 kcmil with three conductors in parallel in three separate raceways?*

(a) 4 AWG (b) 2/0 AWG (c) 3/0 AWG (d) 4/0 AWG

Answer: *(b) 2/0 AWG*

300 kcmil x 3 = 900 kcmil equivalent area of the ungrounded conductors [Table 250.66, Note 1]

900 kcmil for ungrounded conductors requires a grounding electrode conductor of 2/0 AWG [Table 250.66]

► Grounding Electrode Conductor Sizing Example 2

Question: *What size grounding electrode conductor is required if the service ungrounded conductors are 600 kcmil with two conductors in parallel in two separate raceways?*

(a) 4 AWG (b) 1 AWG (c) 3/0 AWG (d) 4/0 AWG

Answer: *(c) 3/0 AWG*

600 kcmil x 2 = 1,200 kcmil equivalent area of the ungrounded conductors [Table 250.66, Note 1].

Over 1,100 kcmil for ungrounded conductors requires a grounding electrode conductor of 3/0 AWG [Table 250.66].

► Parallel Service Conductor Sizing Example 2

Question: *What size conductor is required if the service with a calculated load of 787A is rated 120/240V, single-phase and the conductors are installed in parallel in three separate raceways?*

(a) 300 kcmil (b) 400 kcmil (c) 500 kcmil (d) 600 kcmil

Answer: *(a) 300 kcmil*

787A/2 raceways = 393.30A

600 kcmil copper is rated 420A at 75°C [Table 310.15(B)(16)], so two 600 kcmil conductors can be paralleled for this service.

► Parallel Service Conductor Sizing Example 3

Question: *What size conductor is required if the service with a calculated load of 787A is rated 120/240V, single-phase and the conductors are installed in parallel in four separate raceways?*

(a) 1/0 AWG (b) 3/0 AWG (c) 500 kcmil (d) 600 kcmil

Answer: *(b) 3/0 AWG*

787A/4 raceways = 196.75A

3/0 AWG copper is rated 200A at 75°C [Table 310.15(B)(16)], so four 3/0 AWG conductors can be paralleled for this service.

► Grounding Electrode Conductor Sizing Example 3

Question: *What size grounding electrode conductor is required if the service ungrounded conductors are 3/0 AWG with four conductors in parallel in four separate raceways?*

(a) 4 AWG (b) 2/0 AWG (c) 3/0 AWG (d) 4/0 AWG

Answer: *(b) 2/0 AWG*

3/0 AWG has an area of 167,800 cmil [Chapter 9, Table 8].

167,800 cmil x 4 = 671,000 cmil equivalent area of the ungrounded conductors [Table 250.66, Note 1].

671,000 cmil for ungrounded conductors requires a grounding electrode conductor of 2/0 AWG [Table 250.66].

Author's Comment: When installing feeders, an equipment grounding conductor is required in every raceway. Section 250.118 lists allowable equipment grounding conductors. To size this conductor using a wire-type equipment grounding conductor, go to Table 250.122 and select the equipment grounding conductor based on the overcurrent device protecting the conductors in the raceway [250.122(F)]. For instance, the equipment grounding conductor in each raceway of an 800A feeder which is paralleled using two 600 kcmil conductors per phase, will require a 1/0 AWG equipment grounding conductor in each raceway.

10.6 Multifamily—Optional Method Example 2 [220.84]

A 120/240V, single-phase system supplies a 20-unit multifamily building. Each 1,500 sq ft unit contains:

Dishwasher	1.50 kVA
Water Heater	4 kVA
Washing Machine	1.20 kVA
Dryer	4.50 kVA
Range	14.40 kVA
Air-Conditioning (230V)	17A
Electric Space Heating	5 kVA

► Multifamily- Optional Method Example

Question: *Using the optional method of calculation, what size conductor is required if the service is rated 120/240V, single-phase and the conductors are installed in parallel in four separate raceways?*

(a) 350 kcmil (b) 400 kcmil (c) 500 kcmil (d) 600 kcmil

Answer: *(d) 600 kcmil*

Step 1: Total Connected Load

Step a: Determine the General Lighting Load:

General Lighting (1,500 sq ft x 3 VA)	*4,500 VA*
Small-Appliance Circuits (1,500 VA each x 2)	*3,000 VA*
Laundry Circuit	*+ 1,500 VA*
Connected Load per Unit	*9,000 VA*

Total Connected Load = Load per Unit x Number of Units
Total Connected Load = 9,000 VA x 20 units
Total Connected Load = 180,000 VA

Step b: Determine the Appliance Calculated Load:

Dishwasher	*1,500 VA*
Water Heater	*4,000 VA*
Dryer (nameplate)	*4,500 VA*
Range (nameplate)	*+ 14,400 VA*
	24,400 VA

Total Appliance Connected Load = Load Per Unit x Number of Units
Total Appliance Connected Load = 24,400 VA x 20 units
Total Appliance Connected Load = 488,000 VA

Step c: Compare the Air-Conditioning versus Heat Load:
Heat Load = VA x Number of Units
Heat = 5,000 VA x 20 Units
Heat = 100,000 VA

Air-conditioning VA = 240V x 17A
Air-conditioning VA Load = 4,080
Use the larger of heat or air-conditioning [220.60]

Step 2: Total Connected Loads

General Lighting, Receptacle	*180,000 VA*
Appliances Connected Load	*488,000 VA*
Heat	*+100,000 VA*
Total Connected Load	*768,000 VA*

Total Calculated Load = Total Connected Load x Demand Factor [Table 220.84]
Total Calculated Load = 768,000 VA x 0.38 [Table 220.84]
Total Calculated Load = 291,840 VA

Step 3: Service Conductor Size
I = VA/E
I = 291,840 VA/240V
I = 1,216A
Note: The calculated load is above 1,200A, so a 1,600A service size is required, which is the next standard size [240.6(A)]. For conductors sized above 800A, we are not allowed to round up to the next size overcurrent device [240.4(C)] so the conductors must have an ampacity of at least 1,600A.
1,600A/4 = 400A minimum conductor ampacity if paralleled in four raceways.
Feeder/Service Conductors: Parallel 600 kcmil each for four parallel conductors, rated 420A in the 75°C Column of Table 310.15(B)(16).

When do you use the standard method versus the optional method? For the purpose of exam preparation, always use the standard load calculation unless the question specifies the optional method. In the field, you'll probably want to use the optional method because it's faster and easier to calculate. Be sure to read 220.84(A) carefully to be certain that your installation qualifies for the optional method. In order to use the optional method for multifamily dwellings, each dwelling must be equipped with electric cooking equipment and either electric space heating or air-conditoning, or both [220.84(A)(2) and (3)].

10.7 Two-Family Dwelling Units [220.85]

220.85 Two Dwelling Units. Where two dwelling units are supplied by a single feeder and the calculated load using the standard calculation method under Part III of Article 220 exceeds that for three identical units calculated under the optional method of Section 220.84, the lesser of the two loads is permitted to be used. **Figure 10–15**

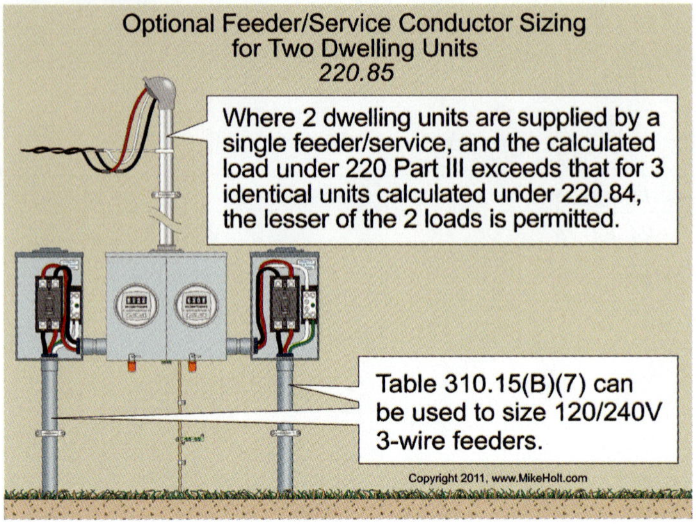

Figure 10–15

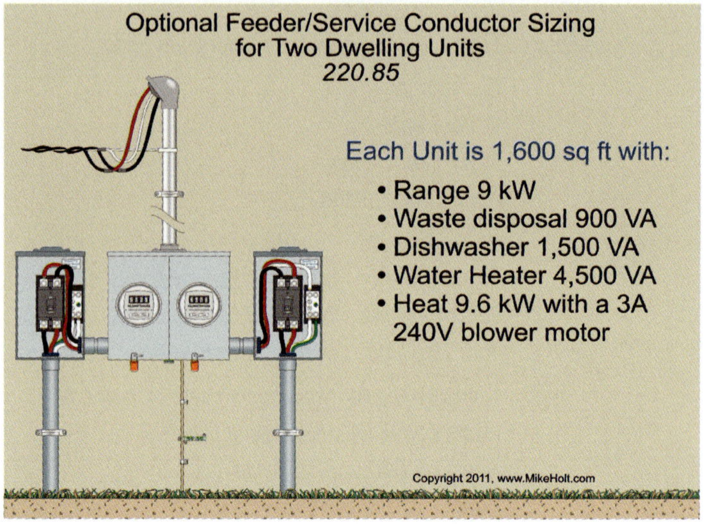

Figure 10–16

▶ Standard Calculation for a Two-Family Dwelling, Calculated under Part III of Article 220

Calculate the service size for a two-family dwelling, where each unit is 1,600 sq ft and contains the following loads: **Figure 10–16**

Range 9 kW
Waste disposal 900 VA
Dishwasher 1,500 VA
Water heater 4,500 VA
Central electric heat, 9.6 kW with 3A, 240V blower motor

Step 1: General lighting, small appliance, laundry loads:

General lighting load [220.12]: 1,600 x 3 VA =	*4,800 VA*		
2 small appliance circuits [220.52(A)]: 1,500 VA x 2 =	*3,000 VA*		
1 laundry circuit [220.52(B)]: 1,500 VA x 1 =	*+1,500 VA*		
	9,300 VA		
Total of general lighting, small appliance and laundry:			
9,300 x 2 dwellings =	*18,600 VA*		
Apply the demand factors of Table 220.42 to:	*18,600 VA*		
First 3,000 VA at 100% =	*-3,000 VA*	*x 1.00 =*	*3,000 VA*
Remainder at 35% =	*15,600 VA*	*x 0.35 =*	*+5,460 VA*
			8,460 VA

Step 2: Air-Conditioning versus Heat [220.51]

Electric heat at 100% [220.51] =

9,600 VA + (3A x 240V) =10,320 VA x 2 = *20,640 VA*

Step 3: Appliance Calculated Load [220.53]

2 disposals at 900VA =	*1,800 VA*		
2 dishwashers at 1,500 VA =	*3,000 VA*		
2 - 4,500 VA water heaters =	*9,000 VA*		
Demand factor [220.53]	*13,800 VA*	*x 0.75 =*	*10,350 VA*

Step 4: Dryer Calculated Load [220.54]: no dryer

Step 5: Cooking Equipment Calculated Load [220.55]

2 - 9 kW Ranges

Step a: Column C demand load for 2 ranges = 11,000 VA [Table 220.55] = *11,000 VA*

Step 6: Service Conductor Size:

Step a: Total general lighting, small appliance, and laundry calculated load	*8,460 VA*
Step b: Total heat calculated load:	*20,640 VA*
Step c: Total appliance calculated load:	*10,350 VA*
Step d: Total dryer calculated load:	*0 VA*
Step e: Range Calculated load:	*+11,000 VA*
Total calculated load	*50,450 VA*

► Optional Method, Assume Three Identical Units Calculated Under 220.84 [220.85]:

Calculate the service size for a two-family dwelling (use 3 units for this method), where each unit is 1,600 sq ft and contains the following loads:

Range 9 kW
Waste disposal 900 VA
Dishwasher 1,500 VA
Water heater 4,500 VA
Central electric heat, 9.6 kW with 3A, 240V blower motor

Step 1: Total Connected Loads, per 220.84(C):

Step a: Determine the General Lighting Load:

General lighting load [220.84(C)(1)]: 1,600 sq ft x 3 VA =	*4,800 VA*
2 small appliance circuits [220.84(C)(2)]: 1,500 VA x 2 =	*3,000 VA*
1 laundry circuit [220.84(C)(2)]: 1,500 VA x 1 =	*+1,500 VA*
	9,300 VA

Step b: Determine the Appliance Connected Load:

Nameplate rating of all appliances [220.84(C)(3)]:

Waste disposal 900 VA =	*900 VA*
Dishwasher 1,500 VA =	*1,500 VA*
Water heater 4,500 VA =	*4,500 VA*
Range 9 kW =	*+ 9,000 VA*
	15,900 VA

Step c: Compare the Air-Conditioning versus Heat Load:

9.60 kW central electric heat [220.84(C)(5)]

9,600 VA + (3A x 240V) = 10,320 VA *10,320 VA*

Step 2: Total Connected Loads

General Lighting, Receptacle	*9,300 VA*
Appliances Connected Load	*15,900 VA*
Heat	*+ 10,320 VA*
Total Connected Load	*35,520 VA*

Total Connected Load = Load per Unit x Number of Units

Total Connected Load = 35,520 VA x 3 Units

Total Connected Load = 106,560 VA

Total Calculated Load = Total Connected Load x Demand Factor [Table 220.84]

Total Calculated Load = 106,560 VA x 0.45 [Table 220.84]

Total Calculated Load = 47,952 VA

In this case, the smaller of the two methods of calculation was the optional method at 47,952 VA

Step 3: Service Conductor Size

I = VA/E

I = 47,952 VA/240V

I = 199.80A

A 200A service will meet the Code minimum.

Conductors for anything more than a single dwelling are sized using Table 310.15(B)(16)

3/0 AWG conductors are rated 200A in the 75 degree column of Table 310.15(B)(16)

CONCLUSION TO UNIT 10—MULTIFAMILY DWELLING CALCULATIONS

As you saw in Unit 10, the sizing of branch circuits, feeders, and service conductors for multifamily dwellings is similar to the process for single-family dwellings. The feeders to individual dwelling units are sized in the same manner whether that dwelling unit is a single-family dwelling or an individual unit of an apartment building. The *Code* allows the use of Table 310.15(B)(7) for sizing the feeders or service conductors to an individual dwelling unit; however, the conductors that feed the service to a multifamily dwelling must be sized using Table 310.15(B)(16).

Some additional demand factors for multifamily dwellings are allowed on the presumption that there will be diversity of usage between the various units. Dryers are allowed the demand factors of Table 220.54, which don't provide less than 100 percent demand until there are five units or more. Perhaps one of the most confusing single tables in the *NEC* is Table 220.55 for household ranges. This table is confusing because the first two columns are percentage multipliers, while the third column is a final kVA value. The notes to this table further complicate matters. Be sure you've studied this part of Unit 10 well and are able to complete the calculations using the range table as well as sizing the service for a multifamily dwelling unit.

UNIT 10

Practice Questions

PRACTICE QUESTIONS FOR UNIT 10—MULTIFAMILY DWELLING CALCULATIONS

PART A—STANDARD METHOD—FEEDER/SERVICE LOAD CALCULATIONS

10.2 Multifamily Dwelling Unit Calculation Examples—Standard Method

1. Each unit of a 20-unit apartment building is 840 sq ft. What's the general lighting and general-use receptacle and small appliance circuits feeder/service calculated load for the building?

   Note: Laundry facilities are provided on the premises for all tenants.

   (a) 5,200 VA
   (b) 40,590 VA
   (c) 60,250 VA
   (d) 160,500 VA

2. Each unit of a 20-unit apartment building is 990 sq ft. What's the general lighting and general-use receptacle and small appliance and laundry circuits feeder/service calculated load for the building?

   (a) 51,300 VA
   (b) 74,700 VA
   (c) 105,600 VA
   (d) 149,400 VA

3. A 40-unit multifamily building has an air conditioner (17A, 230V) and two 3 kW baseboard heaters in each unit. What's the feeder/service calculated load for the air-conditioning and heat?

   (a) 50 kVA
   (b) 60 kVA
   (c) 160 kVA
   (d) 240 kVA

4. Each unit of a 25-unit multifamily building has air-conditioning (17A, 230V) and electric heat (5 kW). What's the air-conditioning and heat feeder/service calculated load?

   (a) 5 kVA
   (b) 6 kVA
   (c) 125 kVA
   (d) 160 kVA

5. In a 16-unit multifamily building, each unit contains a waste disposal (940 VA), a dishwasher (1,250 VA), and a water heater (4,500 VA). What's the feeder/service calculated load for these appliances when sizing the service for the multifamily building?

   (a) 5 kVA
   (b) 80 kVA
   (c) 100 kVA
   (d) 134 kVA

6. Each unit in a 28-unit apartment building contains a waste disposal (900 VA), a dishwasher (1,200 VA), and a water heater (5,000 VA). What's the feeder/service calculated load for the appliances when sizing the service for the multifamily building?

   (a) 107 kVA
   (b) 142 kVA
   (c) 149 kVA
   (d) 186 kVA

7. A multifamily dwelling (40 units) contains a 4.50 kW electric clothes dryer in each unit. What's the feeder/service calculated load for all of the dryers?

   (a) 27 kW
   (b) 53 kW
   (c) 60 kW
   (d) 150 kW

8. What's the feeder/service calculated load for ten 5.25 kW dryers installed in dwelling units of a multifamily building?

(a) 27 kW
(b) 37 kW
(c) 40 kW
(d) 60 kW

9. What's the feeder/service calculated load for twelve 3.25 kW ovens?

(a) 10 kW
(b) 15 kW
(c) 18 kW
(d) 20 kW

10. What's the feeder/service calculated load for eight 7 kW counter-mounted cooktops?

(a) 14.70 kW
(b) 17 kW
(c) 20 kW
(d) 48 kW

11. What's the feeder/service calculated load for five 12.40 kW ranges?

(a) 9 kW
(b) 20 kW
(c) 45 kW
(d) 60 kW

12. What's the feeder/service calculated load for three ranges rated 15.50 kW each?

(a) 14 kW
(b) 15 kW
(c) 17 kW
(d) 21 kW

13. What's the feeder/service calculated load for three ranges rated 11 kW and three ranges rated 14 kW?

(a) 23 kW
(b) 36 kW
(c) 42 kW
(d) 78 kW

14. What size aluminum service conductors are required for a 120/240V, single-phase multifamily building that has a total calculated load of 90 kW?

(a) 500 kcmil AL
(b) 600 kcmil AL
(c) 700 kcmil AL
(d) 800 kcmil AL

15. What size copper service conductors are required for a 120/240V, single-phase multifamily building that has a total calculated load of 90 kW?

(a) 500 kcmil
(b) 600 kcmil
(c) 700 kcmil
(d) 800 kcmil

16. What size copper service conductors are required for a multifamily building that has a total calculated load of 260 kW for a 120/208V wye, three-phase system? The conductors are paralleled in two raceways.

(a) Two–300 kcmil
(b) Two–350 kcmil
(c) Two–500 kcmil
(d) Two–700 kcmil

17. What size aluminum service conductors are required for a multifamily building that has a total calculated load of 260 kW for a 120/208V wye, three-phase system? The conductors are paralleled in two raceways.

(a) Two–300 kcmil AL
(b) Two–350 kcmil AL
(c) Two–500 kcmil AL
(d) Two–700 kcmil AL

The following information applies to the next five questions. A multifamily building has 12 units. The system voltage is 120/240V, single-phase. Each 1,500 sq ft unit contains the following:

Dishwasher	1.50 kVA
Water Heater	4 kW
Dryer	4.50 kW
Washing Machine	1.20 kVA
Range	14.45 kW
Air-Conditioning (230V)	3 hp
Air-Conditioning Fan Motor rated 1A at 230V	
Heat	5 kW

18. What's the building's feeder/service calculated load for the general lighting and general-use receptacles, and the small-appliance and laundry circuits in kVA?

(a) 40 kVA
(b) 90 kVA
(c) 105 kVA
(d) 108 kVA

19. What's the building's feeder/service calculated load for the air conditioner (18A, 230V) versus electric heat (5 kW)?

(a) 30 kVA
(b) 52 kVA
(c) 60 kVA
(d) 105 kVA

20. What's the building's feeder/service calculated load for the appliances in kVA?

(a) 40 kVA
(b) 43 kVA
(c) 50 kVA
(d) 55 kVA

21. What's the building's feeder/service calculated load for the 4.50 kW dryers?

(a) 27.60 kW
(b) 45.70 kW
(c) 55.30 kW
(d) 60.40 kW

22. What's the building's feeder/service calculated load for the 12 14.45 kW ranges?

(a) 27 kW
(b) 30 kW
(c) 35 kW
(d) 168 kW

23. If the total calculated load of a multifamily dwelling unit is 206 kVA, what's the minimum feeder/service conductor ampacity? The system voltage is 120/240, single-phase.

(a) 600A
(b) 800A
(c) 1,000A
(d) 1,200A

24. If a service consists of three sets of parallel 400 kcmil conductors routed in three separate raceways, what size equipment bonding jumper is required for each service raceway?

(a) 1 AWG
(b) 1/0 AWG
(c) 2/0 AWG
(d) 3/0 AWG

25. If three sets of 400 kcmil copper service conductors are paralleled in three raceways, what's the minimum size grounding electrode conductor required?

(a) 1/0 AWG
(b) 2/0 AWG
(c) 3/0 AWG
(d) 4/0 AWG

PART B—OPTIONAL METHOD—FEEDER/ SERVICE LOAD CALCULATIONS

10.4 Multifamily Dwelling Unit Calculations [220.84]—Optional Method

26. When determining the service (using the optional calculation method) for a multifamily dwelling, the total connected load must have the demand factors of Table 220.84 applied. When determining the total connected load, ______ must be used.

    (a) 125 percent of the air-conditioning load plus 100 percent of the space-heating load
    (b) the larger of the air-conditioning load or the space-heating load
    (c) the sum of the air-conditioning load and the space-heating load
    (d) 125 percent of the sum of the air-conditioning load and the space-heating load

27. A multifamily building has 60 units. Each unit is 1,500 sq ft. Using the optional dwelling unit calculations, what's the calculated load for the building's general lighting and general-use receptacles, and small-appliance and laundry circuits?

    (a) 108 kVA
    (b) 130 kVA
    (c) 145 kVA
    (d) 190 kVA

28. A 60-unit multifamily dwelling has an air conditioner (3 hp with 1⁄8 hp blower) and electric heat (5 kW) in each unit. Using the optional calculation method, what's the air-conditioning versus heat calculated load?

    (a) 30 kVA
    (b) 50 kVA
    (c) 61 kVA
    (d) 72 kVA

29. Using the optional method for dwelling unit calculations, what's the fixed appliance portion of the 60-unit multifamily building's calculated load if each unit has a water heater (4 kW) and a dishwasher (1.50 kW)?

    (a) 30 kVA
    (b) 50 kVA
    (c) 60 kVA
    (d) 80 kVA

30. Each unit of a 60-unit apartment building has a 4 kW dryer. Using the optional calculation method, the calculated load added to the service for the dryers is ______.

    (a) 58 kW
    (b) 72 kW
    (c) 75 kW
    (d) 240 kW

31. Using the optional method for dwelling unit calculations, what's the dryer portion of a 60-unit multifamily building's calculated load if there's a 4.50 kW dryer in each unit?

    (a) 25 kW
    (b) 55 kW
    (c) 65 kW
    (d) 75 kW

32. Using the optional method for dwelling unit calculations, what's the electric range portion of a 60-unit multifamily building's calculated load if each apartment has a 14 kW range?

    (a) 50 kW
    (b) 100 kW
    (c) 150 kW
    (d) 200 kW

33. If the total calculated load for a multifamily dwelling is 270 kVA, what's the minimum feeder/service conductor ampacity? The service is 120/208V, three-phase.

    (a) 600A
    (b) 800A
    (c) 1,000A
    (d) 1,200A

34. Each unit of a 20-unit multifamily dwelling has 900 sq ft of living space and contains one of each of the following: water heater (5 kW), range (13 kW), air-conditioning (5 hp, 230V), and heat (5 kW), The calculated load for sizing the single phase 120V/240V service for this apartment building is approximately ______ if the optional method of calculation is used.

(a) 200 kVA
(b) 250 kVA
(c) 280 kVA
(d) 320 kVA

35. If two parallel service conductors per phase are installed in two raceways (500 kcmil in each raceway), what size equipment bonding jumper is required for each service raceway?

(a) 2 AWG
(b) 1 AWG
(c) 1/0 AWG
(d) 2/0 AWG

36. If two parallel service conductors per phase are installed in two raceways (500 kcmil in each raceway), what's the minimum size copper grounding electrode conductor required?

(a) 1/0 AWG
(b) 2/0 AWG
(c) 3/0 AWG
(d) 4/0 AWG

UNIT

10

Challenge Questions

CHALLENGE QUESTIONS FOR UNIT 10—MULTIFAMILY DWELLING CALCULATIONS

PART A—STANDARD METHOD—FEEDER/SERVICE LOAD CALCULATIONS

10.2 Multifamily Dwelling Unit Calculation Examples—Standard Method

General Lighting, Small Appliance, and Laundry Demand [Table 220.42]

1. Each dwelling unit of a 20-unit multifamily building has 900 sq ft of living space. What's the general lighting and general-use receptacle load, before demand factors are applied, for the multifamily apartment building?

   (a) 37 kVA
   (b) 45 kVA
   (c) 54 kVA
   (d) 60 kVA

2. A multifamily apartment building contains 20 units and each unit has 840 sq ft of living space. What's the general lighting, general receptacle, and small appliance circuits portion of the service calculated load for the multifamily building if laundry facilities are provided on the premises for all tenants and no laundry circuit is installed in each unit?

   (a) 35 kVA
   (b) 41 kVA
   (c) 45 kVA
   (d) 63 kVA

Appliance Calculated Load [220.53]

3. A multifamily apartment building contains 20 units. Each unit contains a waste disposal (900 VA), a dishwasher (1,200 VA), and a water heater (5,000 VA). What's the feeder calculated load for the appliances in this building?

   (a) 60,000 VA
   (b) 106,500 VA
   (c) 117,100 VA
   (d) 137,000 VA

Household Dryer Calculated Load [220.54]

4. The nameplate rating for each household dryer in a 10-unit apartment building is 4 kW. This will add ______ to the service size.

   (a) 20 kW
   (b) 25 kW
   (c) 40 kW
   (d) 50 kW

Ranges [Table 220.55, Note 1]

5. The calculated load for thirty 15.80 kW household ranges is ______.

   (a) 31 kW
   (b) 33 kW
   (c) 47 kW
   (d) 54 kW

Ranges [Table 220.55, Note 2]

6. What's the feeder calculated load for five 10 kW, five 14 kW, and five 16 kW household ranges?

   (a) 14 kW
   (b) 30 kW
   (c) 33 kW
   (d) 210 kW

7. What kW needs to be added to service loads for ten 12 kW, eight 14 kW, and two 9 kW household ranges?

(a) 29.35 kW
(b) 33 kW
(c) 35 kW
(d) 36.75 kW

Ranges [Table 220.55, Note 3]

8. What's the minimum service calculated load for five 5 kW cooktops, two 4 kW ovens, and four 7 kW ranges?

(a) 8.80 kW
(b) 15.50 kW
(c) 18.20 kW
(d) 19.60 kW

9. What's the maximum dwelling unit feeder/service calculated load for fifteen 8 kW cooking units?

(a) 30 kW
(b) 38.40 kW
(c) 60 kW
(d) 120 kW

Neutral Calculation [220.61]

10. The service neutral load for household electric clothes dryers must be calculated at ______ percent of the load as determined by 220.54.

(a) 50
(b) 60
(c) 70
(d) 80

11. The feeder neutral demand for fifteen 9 kW cooking units is ______.

(a) 21 kW
(b) 30 kW
(c) 38.40 kW
(d) 120 kW

12. What's the feeder neutral load for ten 5 kW household dryers?

(a) 17.50 kW
(b) 21.50 kW
(c) 27.50 kW
(d) 32.50 kW

13. An 11-unit multifamily dwelling contains a 4 kW electric clothes dryer in each unit. What's the feeder/service neutral calculated load?

(a) 18.10 kW
(b) 22.30 kW
(c) 29.30 kW
(d) 32.90 kW

14. What's the dwelling unit service neutral load for ten 9 kW ranges?

(a) 12.40 kW
(b) 13.50 kW
(c) 15.50 kW
(d) 17.50 kW

15. The optional method of calculation for the feeder/service size of a multifamily dwelling can't be used if there is no electric range present, unless the use of a(n) ______ range in the calculation using the optional method results in a smaller result than the standard calculation of the same building.

(a) 8 kW
(b) 10 kW
(c) 12 kW
(d) 14 kW

16. Each unit of a 20-unit multifamily dwelling has 900 sq ft of living space and contains one of each of the following: water heater (5 kW), air-conditioning (5 hp, 230V), and heat (5 kW), The calculated load for sizing the single phase 120V/240V service for this apartment building is approximately ______ if the optional method of calculation is used. (Carefully read 220.84(A)(2) Ex)

(a) 200 kVA
(b) 205 kVA
(c) 280 kVA
(d) 320 kVA

Notes

UNIT 11 Commercial Calculations

INTRODUCTION TO UNIT 11—COMMERCIAL CALCULATIONS

Commercial buildings have different use patterns than homes or multifamily dwellings. In a commercial building, certain loads (such as store lighting) are used for extended periods of time. Homes have a diversity of usage as discussed in Units 9 and 10, which allow us to apply demand factors to many of the loads used in dwelling units. There are some demand factors for commercial buildings, but they're different from those used in dwelling calculations. It's important to study this unit carefully so you understand the proper application of demand factors in commercial calculations.

Be careful when applying demand factors to commercial installations. For example, the demand factors for dryers in Table 220.54 are for dwelling units only and can't be used for laundromats or similar locations. The range table of 220.55 is allowed only for dwelling unit use and can't be applied to commercial kitchens. There are different rules, and in some cases different demand factors for commercial occupancies.

Commercial occupancies include many different types of businesses and uses. Some of the occupancies that are covered in this unit include banks, stores, restaurants, and office buildings. Some other locations with their own special requirements, such as marinas and mobile home parks, are also discussed.

Unit 11 includes some specific requirements for restaurant equipment, show-window lighting, sign lighting, multioutlet assemblies, and electric welders. As you study this unit, pay careful attention to when demand factors can be applied, and also to when a load must be considered a "continuous duty load" for proper conductor sizing.

PART A—GENERAL

Introduction

The *NEC* contains detailed requirements for calculating service and feeder loads in many types of occupancies (buildings). Although most of these requirements are located in Article 220, other rules effecting service and feeder loads are scattered throughout the *Code*. Units 9 and 10 covered the *NEC* rules for calculating loads in residential buildings. This unit covers commercial occupancies. It's an important and challenging subject, because there are many different types of commercial buildings and installations, and some have unique rules for calculating service and feeder loads.

11.1 General Requirements

Article 220 provides the requirements for branch circuits, feeders, and services. In addition to this article, other articles are applicable such as Branch Circuits—210, Feeders—215, Services—230, Overcurrent Protection—240, Wiring Methods—300, Conductors—310, Appliances—422, Electric Space-Heating Equipment—424, Motors—430, and Air-Conditioning Equipment—440 [220.3].

11.2 Conductor Ampacity [Article 100]

The ampacity of a conductor is the rating, in amperes, that a conductor can carry continuously without exceeding its insulation temperature rating [Article 100]. Figure 11–1

The allowable ampacities listed in Table 310.15(B)(16) are affected by conductor insulation, ambient temperature, and conductor bundling [310.15(B)]. Figure 11–2

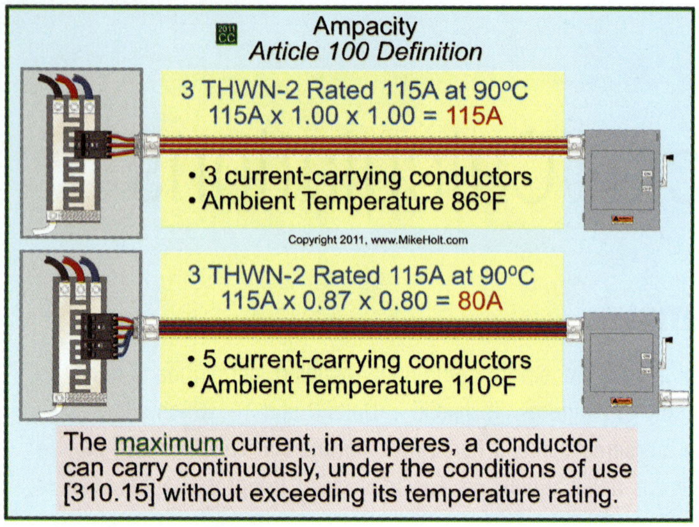

Figure 11–1

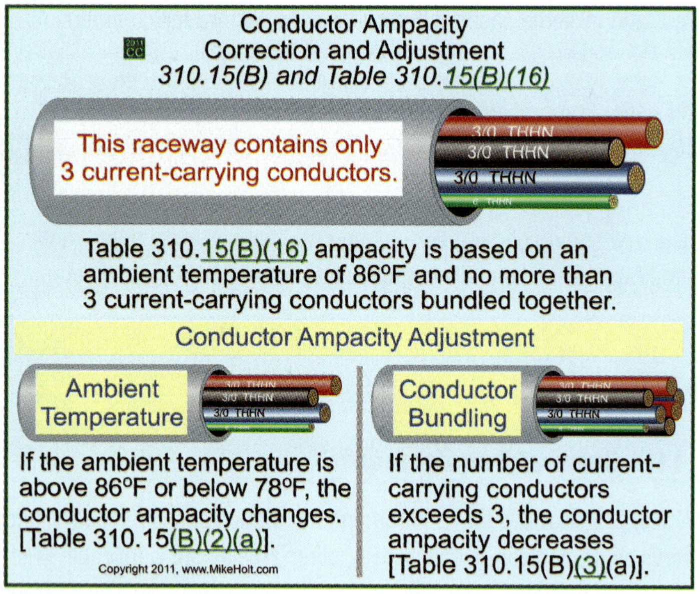

Figure 11–2

Author's Comment: Section 110.14(C)(1)(a) states that terminals are rated 60°C for equipment rated 100A or less unless marked 75°C. In real life, most terminals are now rated 75°C, so in this unit, we'll assume all terminals are rated 75°C unless specified 60°C. For exam purposes, and when answering questions at the end of this unit, read the problem carefully to be certain you know what terminal rating the question specifies. If unspecified, use the rules of 110.14(C).

Continuous Loads

Ungrounded conductors are sized at 125 percent of the continuous load before any adjustment factor and the overcurrent devices are also sized at 125 percent of the continuous load [210.19(A), 215.2(A)(1), and 230.42]. Feeder neutral conductors that aren't connected to an overcurrent device are permitted to be sized at 100 percent of the continuous and noncontinuous load [215.2(A)(1) Ex 2]. **Figure 11–3**

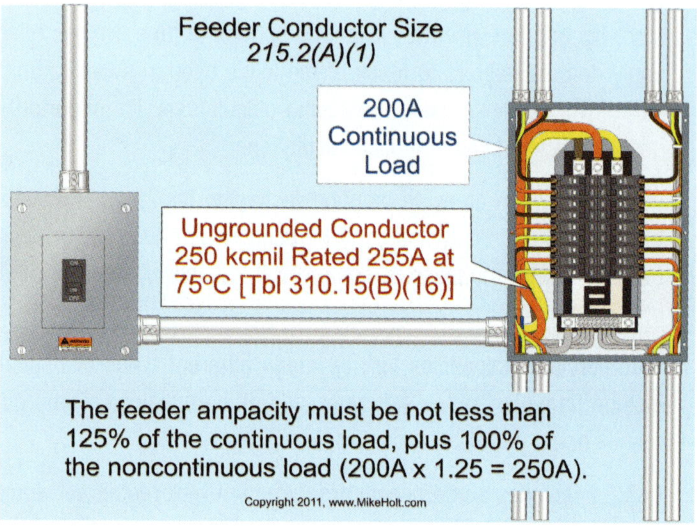

Figure 11–3

Author's Comment: Article 100 defines a continuous load as a load where the maximum current is expected to continue for 3 hours or more. Some *NEC* sections tell you when certain loads are continuous, such as 422.13 for some types of water heaters, or 424.3(B) for fixed electric space-heating equipment. Most commercial lighting and electric signs are considered continuous loads.

Example: *If a 60A continuous load with 75°C rated terminals is supplied by a feeder with four current-carrying conductors, it's necessary to adjust the conductor ampacity for four current-carrying conductors.*

Step 1: Take the continuous load times 125 percent when sizing conductors and overcurrent protection.

60A x 1.25 = 75A

Step 2: Select the conductors using the column of Table 310.15(B)(16) that corresponds with the temperature rating of the terminals [110.14(C)(1)].

4 AWG is rated 85A at 75°C [Table 310.15(B)(16)].

Step 3: Verify that the conductor is large enough for any necessary deratings, using the column that corresponds to the conductor's temperature rating. If you're using THHN conductors, use the 90°C column of Table 310.15(B)(16) [110.14(C)].

Adjust the ampacity by 80 percent for four current-carrying conductors [Table 310.15(B)(3)(a)].

95A x 0.80 = 76A

This verifies that a 4 THHN conductor is large enough. It can be used on an 80A breaker because 240.4(B) allows rounding up to the next standard size listed in 240.6(A).

11.3 Conductor Overcurrent Protection [240.4]

The purpose of an overcurrent device is to protect conductors and equipment against excessive or dangerous temperatures [240.1 FPN]. There are many different rules for protecting conductors and equipment. It isn't simply 12 AWG wire and a 20A breaker. The general rule is that conductors must be protected at the point where they receive their supply in accordance with their ampacities, as listed in Table 310.15(B)(16). **Figure 11–4** Other methods of protection are permitted or required as listed in 240.4, such as:

(B) Overcurrent Devices Rated 800A or Less. The next higher standard rating of overcurrent device (above the ampacity of the ungrounded conductors being protected) is permitted, provided all of the following conditions are met:

(1) The conductors don't supply multioutlet receptacle branch circuits.

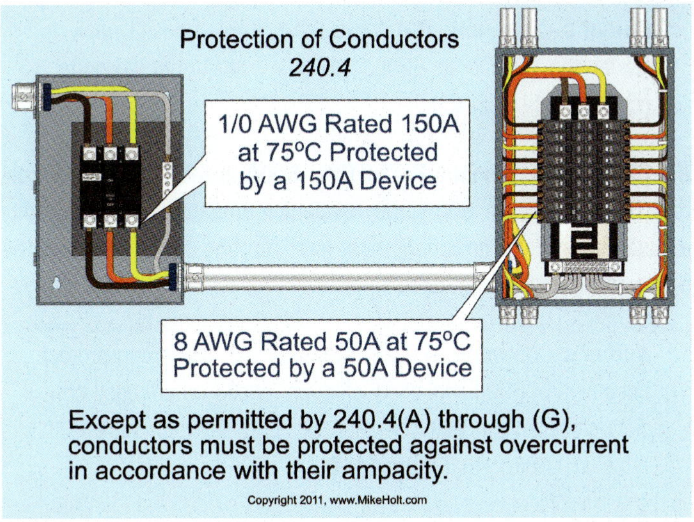

Figure 11–4

(2) The ampacity of a conductor, after ampacity adjustment and/or correction, doesn't correspond with the standard rating of a fuse or circuit breaker in 240.6(A).

(3) The overcurrent device rating doesn't exceed 800A.

Author's Comment: A 400A overcurrent device can protect 500 kcmil conductors, where each conductor has an ampacity of 380A at 75°C, in accordance with Table 310.15(B)(16). **Figure 11–5**

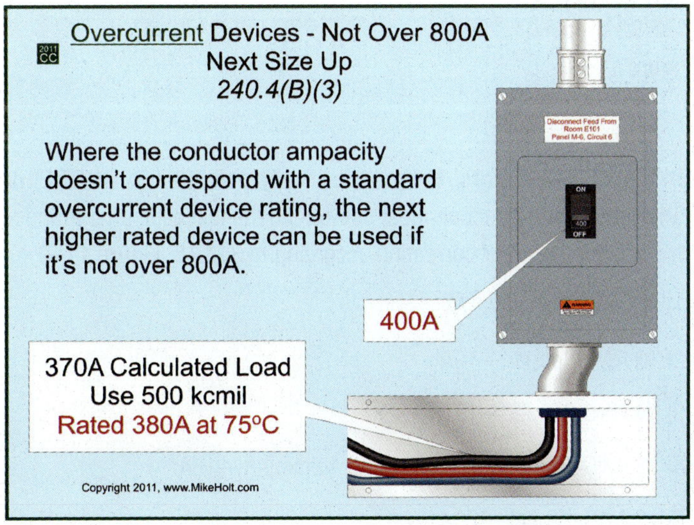

Figure 11–5

Author's Comment: This "next size up" rule doesn't apply to feeder tap conductors [240.21(B)], or transformer secondary conductors [240.21(C)].

(C) Overcurrent Devices Rated Over 800A. If the circuit's overcurrent device exceeds 800A, the conductor ampacity, after ampacity adjustment and/or correction, must have a rating of not less than the rating of the overcurrent device.

Author's Comment: A 1,200A overcurrent device can protect three sets of 600 kcmil conductors per phase, where each conductor has an ampacity of 420A at 75°C, in accordance with Table 310.15(B)(16). **Figure 11–6**

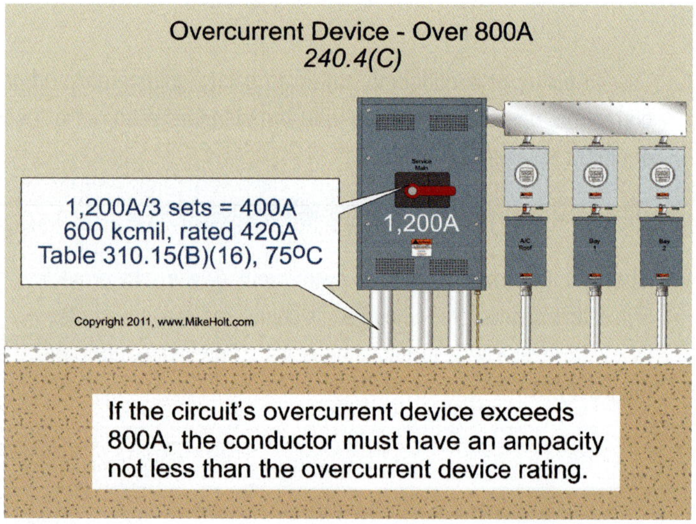

Figure 11–6

(D) Small Conductors. Unless specifically permitted in 240.4(E) or (G), overcurrent protection must not exceed the following after ampacity adjustment and/or correction according to 310.15: **Figure 11–7**

(1) 18 AWG Copper—7A

(2) 16 AWG Copper—10A

(3) 14 AWG Copper—15A

(4) 12 AWG Aluminum/Copper-Clad Aluminum—15A

(5) 12 AWG Copper—20A

(6) 10 AWG Aluminum/Copper-Clad Aluminum—25A

(7) 10 AWG Copper—30A

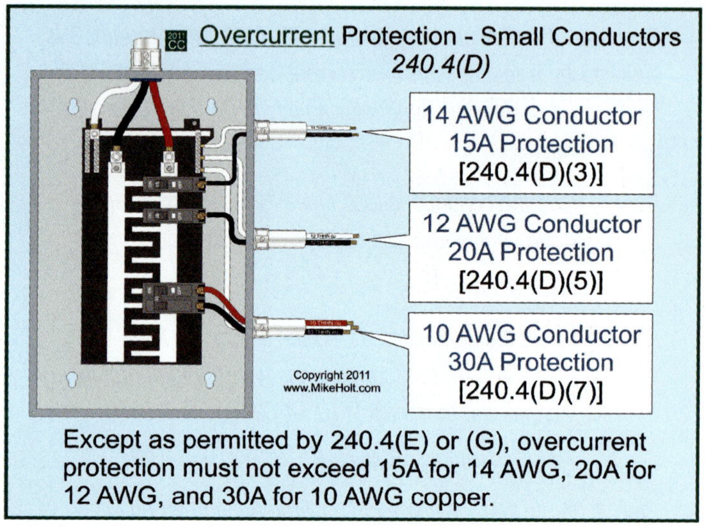

Figure 11–7

Standard Size Overcurrent Devices [240.6(A)]. The following is a list of some of the standard ampere ratings for fuses and inverse time circuit breakers: 15, 20, 25, 30, 35, 40, 45, 50, 60, 70, 80, 90, 100, 110, 125, 150, 175, 200, 225, 250, 300, 350, 400, 500, 600, 800, 1,000, 1,200, and 1,600A. **Figure 11–8**

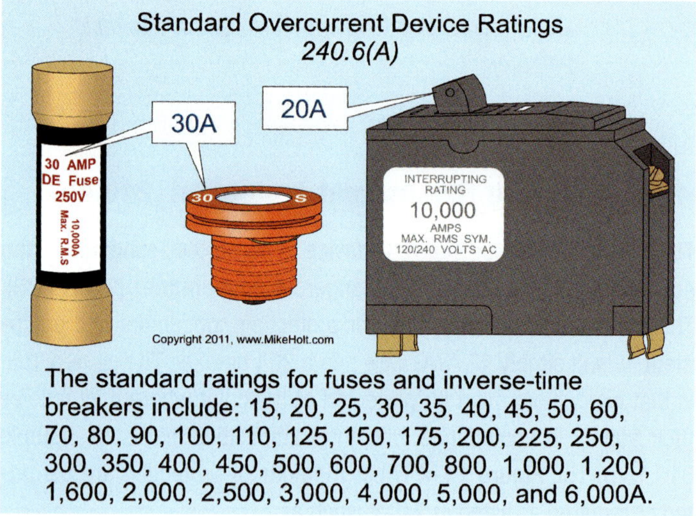

Figure 11–8

11.4 Voltages [220.5(A)]

Unless other voltages are specified, branch-circuit, feeder, and service loads must be computed at a nominal system voltage of 120V, 120/240V, 120/208V, 240V, 277/480V, or 480V. **Figure 11–9**

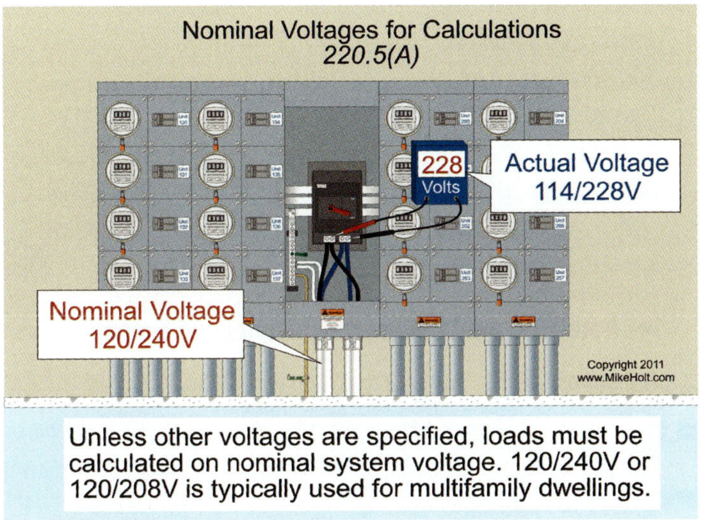

Figure 11–9

11.5 Fractions of an Ampere [220.5(B)]

Calculations are permitted to be rounded to the nearest whole ampere, with decimal fractions smaller than 0.50 dropped [220.5(B)].

Author's Comment: When do you round—after each calculation, or at the final calculation? The *NEC* isn't specific on this issue, so I guess it all depends on the answer you want to see!

► **Rounding Example**

Question: *According to 424.3(B), the branch-circuit conductors and overcurrent device for electric space-heating equipment must be sized no less than 125 percent of the total load. What size conductor is required to supply a 9.60 kVA, 240V, single-phase fixed space heater with a 3A blower motor if the equipment terminals are rated 75°C?* **Figure 11–10**

(a) 10 AWG *(b) 8 AWG* *(c) 6 AWG* *(d) 4 AWG*

Answer: *(c) 6 AWG*

Step 1: Determine the total load

I = VA/E

I = 9,600 VA/240V

I = 40A

Step 2: Conductor sized at 125 percent of the load.

Conductor Size = (40A + 3A) x 1.25

Conductor Size = 53.75A, round up to 54A

If we could round down, then 8 AWG rated 50A at 75°C can be used, but since we have to round up, 6 AWG rated 65A at 75°C is required.

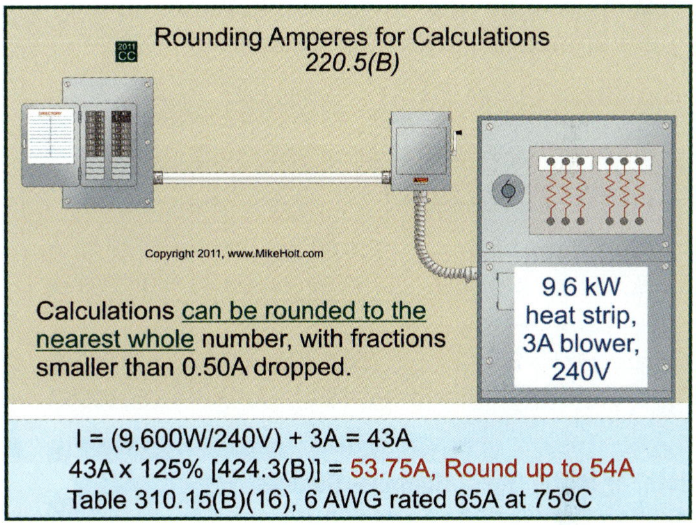

Figure 11–10

11.6 Lighting—Demand Factors [Tables 220.12 and 220.42]

The *NEC* Table 220.12 requires a minimum load per square foot for general lighting depending on the type of occupancy. For the guest rooms of hotels and motels, hospitals, and storage warehouses, the demand factors of Table 220.42 can be applied to the general lighting load. There is usually a diversity of usage in the occupancies that receive demand factors from Table 220.42, meaning that not all of the lighting is in use continuously, so the diversity of usage is reflected in sizing of the electrical service.

Hospital—General Lighting [Tables 220.12 and 220.42]

The general lighting unit load of 2 VA per sq ft [Table 220.12] for hospitals is permitted to be reduced according to the demand factors listed in Table 220.42.

General Lighting Demand Factors

- First 50,000 VA at 40 percent demand factor
- Remainder VA at 20 percent demand factor

► Hospital General Lighting Calculated Load Example

Question: *What's the general lighting calculated load for a hospital which contains a total of 100,000 sq ft?*

(a) 20 kVA (b) 30 kVA (c) 50 kVA (d) 75 kVA

Answer: *(c) 50 kVA*

[Tables 220.12 and 220.42]

100,000 sq ft x 2 VA	200,000 VA		
First 50,000 VA at 40%	– 50,000 VA	x 0.40	20,000 VA
Remainder over 50,000 VA at 20%	150,000 VA	x 0.20	+30,000 VA
			50,000 VA

Hotel or Motel Guest Rooms—General Lighting [Tables 220.12 and 220.42]

The general lighting unit load of 2 VA per sq ft [Table 220.12] for the guest rooms of hotels and motels is permitted to be reduced according to the demand factors listed in Table 220.42. These are units without provisions for cooking. Units that have permanent cooking provisions may be considered multifamily dwellings rather than hotels.

General Lighting Demand Factors

- First 20,000 VA at 50 percent demand factor
- Next 80,000 VA at 40 percent demand factor
- Remainder VA at 30 percent demand factor

► Hotel General Lighting Calculated Load Example 1

Question: *What's the general lighting calculated load for a hotel which contains a total of 100,000 sq ft of living area?*

(a) 20 kVA (b) 21 kVA (c) 24 kVA (d) 72 kVA

Answer: *(d) 72 kVA*

[Tables 220.12 and 220.42]

100,000 sq ft x 2 VA	200,000 VA		
First 20,000 VA at 50%	– 20,000 VA	x 0.50	10,000 VA
Next 80,000 VA at 40%	80,000 VA	x 0.40	32,000 VA
Remainder at 30%	100,000 VA	x 0.30	+30,000 VA
			72,000 VA

► Hotel General Lighting Calculated Load Example 2

Question: *What's the general lighting calculated load for a 40-room hotel? Each unit contains 600 sq ft of living area.* **Figure 11–11**

(a) 20 kVA (b) 21 kVA (c) 24 kVA (d) 48 kVA

Answer: *(b) 21 kVA*

[Tables 220.12 and 220.42]

40 units x 600 sq ft x 2 VA	48,000 VA		
First 20,000 VA at 50%	– 20,000 VA	x 0.50	10,000 VA
Next 80,000 VA at 40%	28,000 VA	x 0.40	+11,200 VA
			21,200 VA

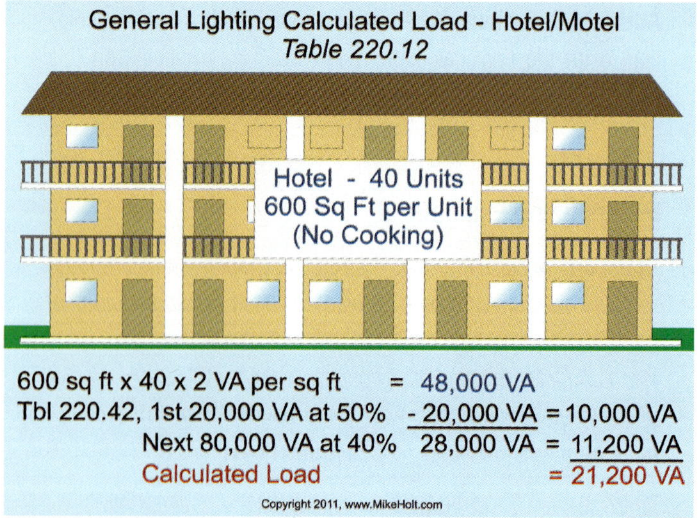

Figure 11–11

Warehouses—General Lighting [Tables 220.12 and 220.42]

The general lighting unit load of ¼ VA per sq ft [Table 220.12] for warehouses is permitted to be reduced according to the demand factors listed in Table 220.42.

General Lighting Demand Factors

- First 12,500 VA at 100 percent demand factor
- Remainder VA at 50 percent demand factor

▶ Warehouse General Lighting Calculated Load Example

Question: *What's the general lighting calculated load for a warehouse which contains a total of 100,000 sq ft of area?*

(a) 19 kVA (b) 25 kVA (c) 55 kVA (d) 75 kVA

Answer: *(a) 19 kVA*

[Tables 220.12 and 220.42]

100,000 sq ft x 0.25 VA	25,000 VA		
First 12,500 VA at 100%	– 12,500 VA	x 1.00	12,500 VA
Remainder over 100,000 VA at 50%	12,500 VA	x 0.50	+6,250 VA
			18,750 VA

11.7 Lighting Without Demand Factors [215.2(A) (1), 230.42(A)(1), and Table 220.12]

The feeder/service general lighting load for commercial occupancies other than guest rooms of motels and hotels, hospitals, and storage warehouses is calculated with a 100 percent demand factor. Additionally, this is assumed to be a continuous load and when sizing the feeder/service conductors for continuous loads, that portion of the load must be calculated at 125 percent of the general lighting load as listed in Table 220.12.

> **Author's Comment:** The lighting loads listed in Table 220.12 are minimum requirements. If the actual lighting load is known and it's larger than the Table 220.12 value, then the actual load must be used.

▶ Office Lighting Example

Question: *What's the general lighting feeder/service calculated load for a 100,000 sq ft office building?*

(a) 240 kVA (b) 250 kVA (c) 375 kVA (d) 438 kVA

Answer: *(d) 438 kVA*

Offices are 3 1/2 VA per sq ft [Table 220.12]

General Lighting Load = 100,000 sq ft x 3.50 VA
General Lighting Load = 350,000 VA
For sizing the feeder/service conductors, this is a continuous load and would be included at 125%

General Lighting Feeder/Service Calculated Load = 350,000 VA x 1.25
General Lighting Feeder/Service Calculated Load = 437,500 VA (437.50 kVA)

▶ Restaurant Lighting Example

Question: *What's the general lighting feeder/service calculated load for a 100,000 sq ft restaurant?*

(a) 240 kVA (b) 250 kVA (c) 375 kVA (d) 438 kVA

Answer: *(b) 250 kVA*

Restaurants are 2 VA per sq ft [Table 220.12]

General Lighting Load = 100,000 sq ft x 2 VA
General Lighting Load = 200,000 VA
For sizing the feeder/service conductors, this is a continuous load and would be included at 125%

General Lighting Feeder/Service Calculated Load = 200,000 VA x 1.25
General Lighting Feeder/Service Calculated Load = 250,000 VA (250 kVA)

▶ School Lighting Example

Question: *What's the general lighting feeder/service calculated load for a 100,000 sq ft school?*

(a) 240 kVA (b) 250 kVA (c) 375 kVA (d) 438 kVA

Answer: *(c) 375 kVA*

Schools are 3 VA per sq ft [Table 220.12]

General Lighting Load = 100,000 sq ft x 3 VA
General Lighting Load = 300,000 VA
For sizing the feeder/service conductors, this is a continuous load and would be included at 125%

General Lighting Feeder/Service Calculated Load = 300,000 VA x 1.25
General Lighting Feeder/Service Calculated Load = 375,000 VA (375 kVA)

▶ Store Lighting Example

Question: *What's the general lighting feeder/service calculated load for a 21,000 sq ft store?* **Figure 11–12**

(a) 40 kVA (b) 63 kVA (c) 79 kVA (d) 81 kVA

Answer: *(c) 79 kVA*

Store is 3 VA per sq ft [Table 220.12]

General Lighting Load = 21,000 sq ft x 3 VA
General Lighting Load = 63,000 VA
For sizing the feeder/service conductors, this is a continuous load and would be included at 125%

General Lighting Feeder/Service Calculated Load = 63,000 VA x 1.25
General Lighting Feeder/Service Calculated Load = 78,750 VA

11.8 Sign Circuit [220.14(F) and 600.5]

The *NEC* requires each commercial occupancy accessible to pedestrians to have at least one 20A branch circuit for a sign [600.5(A)]. The load for the required exterior sign or outline lighting must be a minimum of 1,200 VA [220.14(F)]. A sign outlet is considered to be a continuous load and the feeder/service conductor must be sized at 125 percent of the continuous load [215.2(A)(1) and 230.42].

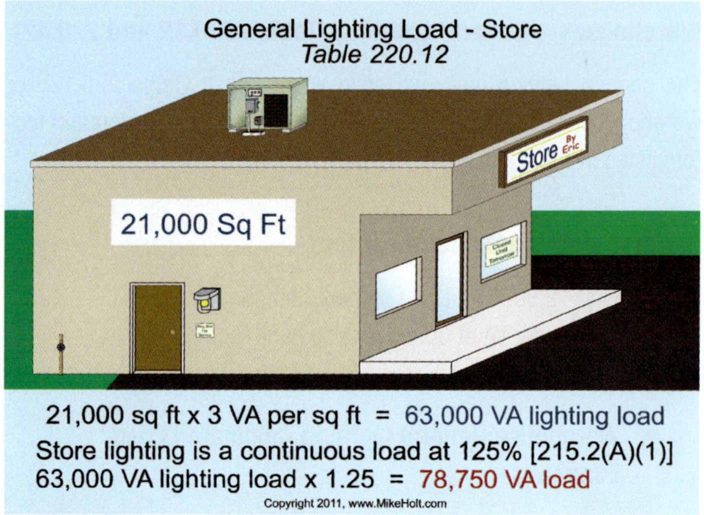

Figure 11–12

▶ Sign Calculated Load Example

Question: *What's the feeder/service conductor calculated load for one electric sign?* **Figure 11–13**

(a) 1,200 VA (b) 1,500 VA (c) 1,920 VA (d) 2,400 VA

Answer: *(b) 1,500 VA*

Feeder/Service Calculated Load = 1,200 VA x 1.25
Feeder/Service Calculated Load = 1,500 VA

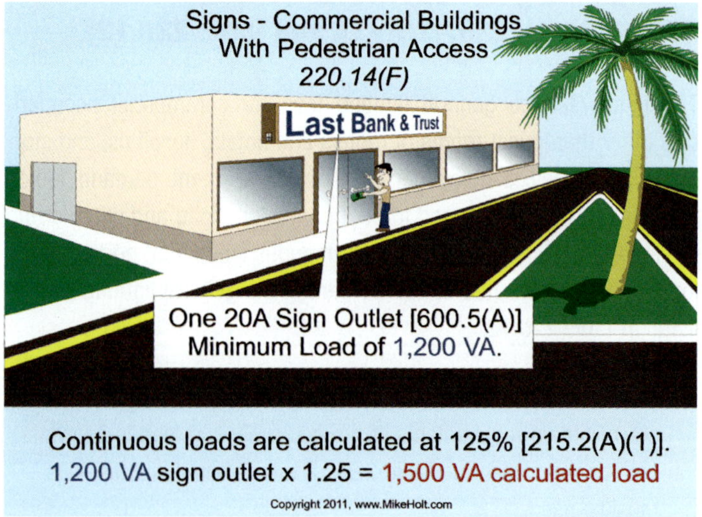

Figure 11–13

11.9 Lighting—Miscellaneous

The feeder/service calculated load for each linear foot of show-window lighting must be calculated at 200 VA per ft. Show-window lighting is assumed to be a continuous load. See Example D3 in Annex D of the *NEC* for an example calculation including show-window branch circuits.

► Show-Window Load Example1

Question: *What's the feeder/service calculated load in kVA for 50 ft of show-window lighting?* **Figure 11–14**

(a) 6 kVA (b) 7.50 kVA (c) 9 kVA (d) 12.50 kVA

Answer: *(d) 12.50 kVA*

Lighting Load = 50 ft x 200 VA per ft
Lighting Load = 10,000 VA

Lighting Feeder/Service Calculated Load = 10,000 VA x 1.25
Lighting Feeder/Service Calculated Load = 12,500 VA

Lighting Feeder/ServiceCalculated Load in kVA = 12,500 VA/1,000
Lighting Feeder/Service Calculated Load in kVA = 12.50 kVA

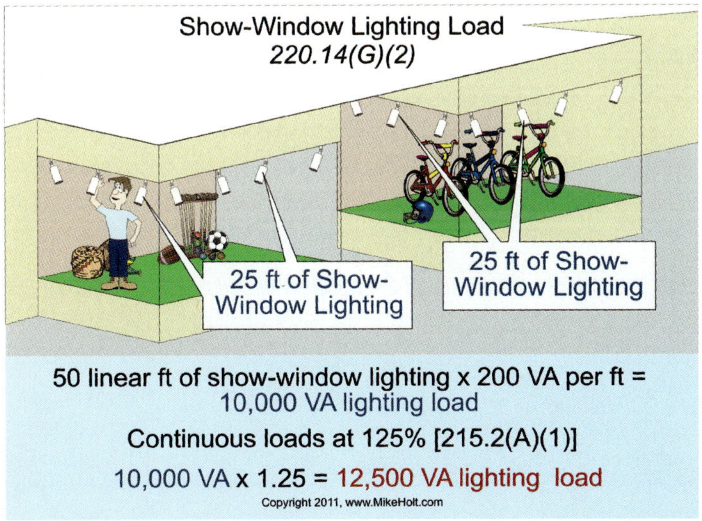

Figure 11–14

► Show-Window Load Example 2

Example: *A 3,000 sq ft store has 30 ft of show window. The service is 120/240V, single-phase. The actual connected lighting load is 8,500 VA [Annex D, Example D3].*

General Lighting = 3,000 sq ft at 3 VA per sq ft*
General Lighting = 9,000 VA*

Window Lighting Load [220.14(G)] = 30 ft at 200 VA per ft
Window Lighting Load = 6,000 VA

Outside Sign Circuit [220.14(F)] = 1,200 VA

Lighting Total = 9,000 VA + 6,000 VA + 1,200 VA

Lighting Total =16,200 VA

**In the example, 125% of the actual connected lighting load (8,500 VA x 1.25 = 10,650 VA) is less than 125% of the load from Table 220.12, so the minimum lighting load from Table 220.12 is used in the calculations. Had the actual lighting load been greater than the value calculated from Table 220.12, 125% of the actual connected lighting load would have been used. See the NEC Annex D, Example D3 for the full calculation on a store building.*

11.10 Multioutlet Receptacle Assembly [220.14(H)]

Each 5 ft or fraction thereof of a multioutlet receptacle assembly must be considered to be 180 VA for feeder/service calculations where it's unlikely that appliances will be used simultaneously. **Figure 11–15**

When a multioutlet receptacle assembly is expected to have a number of appliances used simultaneously, each foot or fraction of a foot must be considered as 180 VA for feeder/service calculations. **Figure 11–16** A multioutlet receptacle assembly isn't generally considered to be a continuous load.

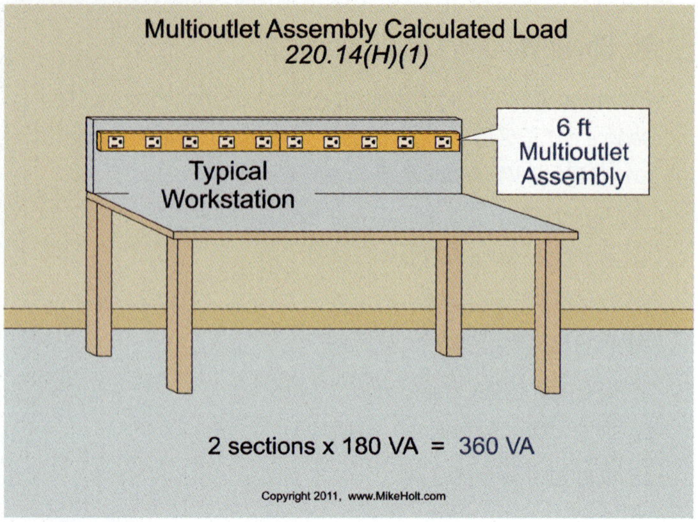

Figure 11–15

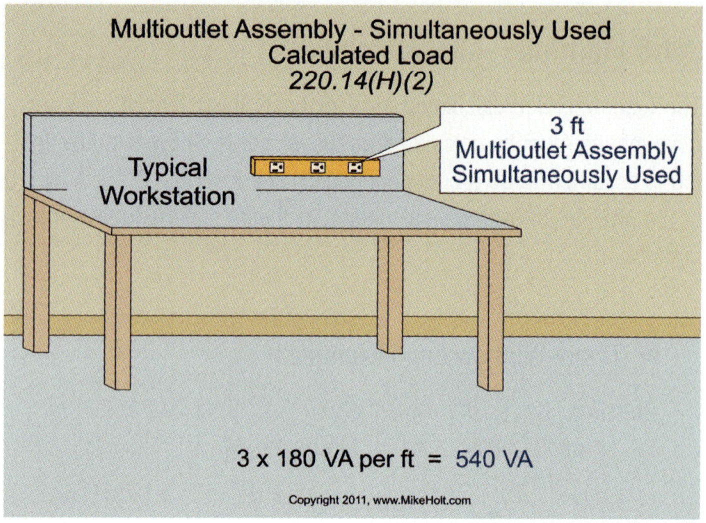

Figure 11–16

▶ Multioutlet Receptacle Assembly Example

Question: *What's the calculated load for 10 work stations, each of which has 6 ft of multioutlet receptacle assembly not used simultaneously and 3 ft of multioutlet receptacle assembly simultaneously used?* **Figure 11–17**

(a) 5 kVA *(b) 6 kVA* *(c) 7 kVA* *(d) 9 kVA*

Answer: *(d) 9 kVA*

10 stations with 6 ft per station = one 5 ft length plus a fraction of multioutlet assembly not simultaneously used per station count as two 180VA sections

10 stations with 3 ft per station = each foot of multioutlet assembly simultaneously used per station counts as one 180 VA section

Non-simultaneous sections:	*2 sections x 180 VA x 10 stations =*	*3,600 VA*
Simultaneous used sections:	*3 sections x 180 VA x 10 stations =*	*+ 5,400 VA*
Calculated Load		*9,000 VA*

This example shows how to size the feeder to accommodate this load. To size the branch circuits using 20A branch circuits, first find the VA allowed per circuit:

- 120V x 20A = 2,400 VA for noncontinuous loads
- Then divide by 180 VA to find how many 180 VA sections can be served by a 20A circuit
- 2,400 VA/180 VA = 13 so a 20A branch circuit can serve two tables.

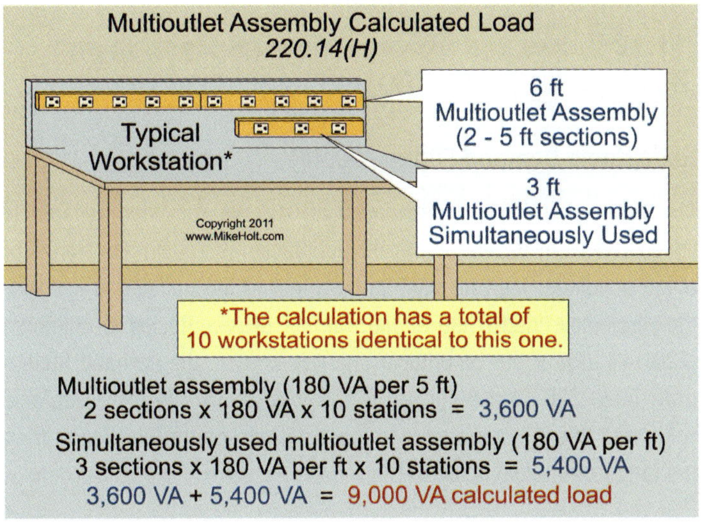

Figure 11–17

11.11 Receptacle VA Load

The load for a general-use receptacle outlet in a nondwelling occupancy is 180 VA per yoke [220.14(I)]. Receptacles aren't considered to be a continuous load. **Figure 11–18**

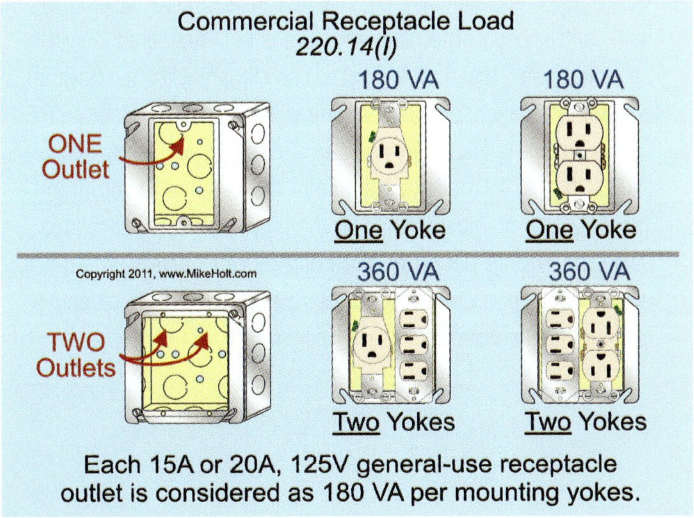

Figure 11–18

Number of Receptacles Permitted on a Circuit

The maximum number of receptacle outlets permitted on a commercial or industrial circuit depends on the circuit rating. The number of receptacles per circuit is calculated by dividing the VA rating of the circuit by 180 VA for each receptacle yoke (also called a "strap"). Based on the Article 100 definition, a duplex receptacle is two receptacles on the same yoke. For the purposes of this calculation, a single receptacle or a duplex receptacle each count as 180 VA.

▶ Receptacles per 20A Circuit [220.14(I)] Example

Question: *How many 15A and 20A, 125V duplex receptacles are permitted on a 20A, 120V circuit in a nondwelling occupancy?* **Figure 11–19**

(a) 10 *(b) 13* *(c) 15* *(d) 20*

Answer: *(b) 13*

Total circuit VA load for a 20A circuit = 120V x 20A
Total circuit VA load for a 20A circuit = 2,400 VA

Number of receptacle outlet yokes per circuit =
2,400 VA/180 VA

Number of receptacle outlet yokes per circuit =
13 receptacles

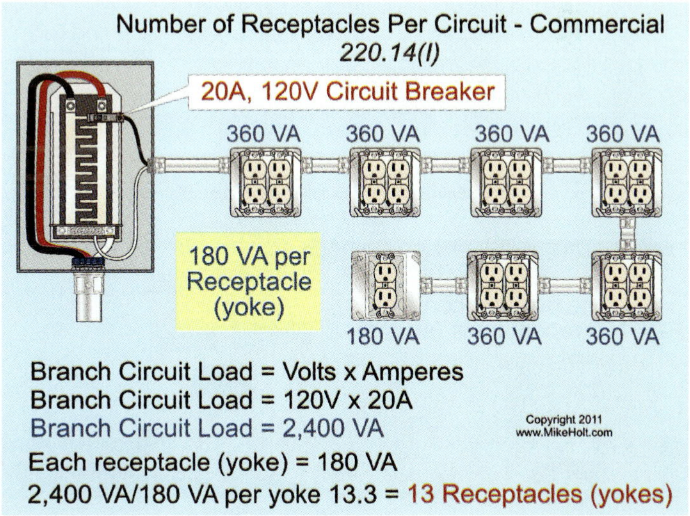

Figure 11–19

Receptacle Feeder/Service Calculated Load [220.44]

In other than dwelling units, receptacle loads computed at not less than 180 VA per outlet yoke in accordance with 220.14(I), and fixed multioutlet assemblies computed in accordance with 220.14(H), can be added to the lighting loads and made subject to the demand factors given in Table 220.42 for those occupancies that are included in Table 220.42. Or they're permitted to be made subject to the demand factors given in Table 220.44. Receptacles are generally not considered to be continuous loads.

Table 220.44 Receptacle Demand Factors

- First 10 kVA at 100 percent demand factor
- Remainder kVA at 50 percent demand factor

► Receptacle Feeder/Service Calculated Load Using Table 220.44 Example

Question: *What's the feeder/service calculated load for one hundred and fifty 15A and 20A, 125V duplex receptacles in a nondwelling occupancy?* **Figure 11–20**

(a) 4 kVA (b) 14 kVA (c) 19 kVA (d) 27 kVA

Answer: *(c) 19 kVA*

Total Receptacle Load

(150 receptacles x 180 VA)	*27,000 VA*		
First 10 kVA at 100%	*– 10,000 VA*	*x 1.00*	*10,000 VA*
Remainder at 50%	*17,000 VA*	*x 0.50*	*+ 8,500 VA*
Total Receptacle Calculated Load			*18,500 VA*

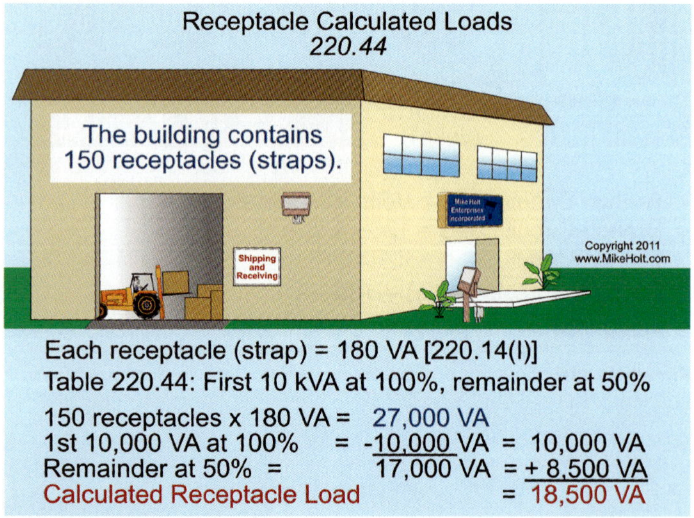

Figure 11–20

11.12 Banks and Offices—General Lighting and Receptacles [220.14(K)]

Receptacle Demand [Table 220.44]

The receptacle load is calculated at 180 VA for each receptacle yoke [220.14(I)] if the number of receptacles is known. For banks or office buildings, 1 VA for each square foot of the building is used for the receptacle load if the actual number of receptacles is unknown [220.14(K)(2)]. If the receptacle count is known, the demand factors from Table 220.44 are applied to the total of 180 VA per receptacle yoke, and this is compared it to the 1 VA per square foot figure, then the larger of the two is used.

Office Buildings and Banks. The receptacle calculated load for office buildings and banks is the larger calculation of (1) or (2).

(1) Determine the receptacle calculated load at 180 VA per receptacle yoke [220.14(I)], then apply the demand factor from Table 220.44. [220.44]

(2) Determine the receptacle calculated load at 1 VA per sq ft.

Author's Comment: Not knowing the exact number of receptacles that will eventually be installed in an office building or bank isn't unusual. The main structure is built first, then individual office space that's rented out to each tenant will often have a custom installation, or a new tenant will remodel. 1 VA per sq ft allows a generic feeder/service demand for general receptacles. Notice that 220.44 allows the use of the demand factors from Table 220.42 or Table 220.44 to the receptacle load calculated using the 180 VA per sq ft figure of 220.14(H) and (I). There is no allowance given to use these demand tables for the receptacle load that is based on the 1 VA per sq ft.

► Bank/Office Building Receptacle Load Example 1

Question: *What's the receptacle calculated load for an 18,000 sq ft bank/office building containing one hundred and sixty 15A and 20A, 125V receptacle yokes?* **Figure 11–21**

(a) 15,400 VA (b) 19,400 VA (c) 28,800 VA (d) 142 kVA

Answer: *(b) 19,400 VA*

[220.14(K)(1)]

160 receptacle yokes x 180 VA [220.14(I)] = 28,800 VA

Total Receptacle Load =	*28,800 VA*		
First 10,000 at 100%	*– 10,000 VA*	*x 1.00*	*10,000 VA*
Remainder at 50%	*18,800 VA*	*x 0.50*	*+ 9,400 VA*
[Table 220.44]			
Receptacle Calculated Load			*19,400 VA*

Compare this to the 1 VA method [220.14(K)(2)] and use only the larger of the two.

18,000 x 1 VA per sq ft = 18,000 VA

Use 19,400 VA, the larger of the two.

► Bank/Office Building Receptacle Load Example 2

Question: *What's the receptacle calculated load for an 18,000 sq ft bank/office building containing one hundred and forty 15A and 20A, 125V duplex receptacles?* **Figure 11–22**

(a) 15,000 VA (b) 18,000 VA (c) 23,000 VA (d) 31,000 VA

Answer: *(b) 18,000 VA*

[220.14(K)(1)]

140 receptacles (straps) x 180 VA = 25,200 VA [220.14(I)]

Total Receptacle Load	*25,200 VA*		
First 10,000 VA at 100%	*– 10,000 VA*	*x 1.00*	*10,000 VA*
Remainder at 50%	*5,200 VA*	*x 0.50*	*+ 7,600 VA*
[Table 220.44]			
Receptacle Calculated Load			*17,600 VA*

Compare this to the 1 VA method [220.14(K)(2)] and use the larger of the two.

18,000 sq ft x 1 VA per sq ft = 18,000 VA

Use 18,000 VA, the larger of the two.

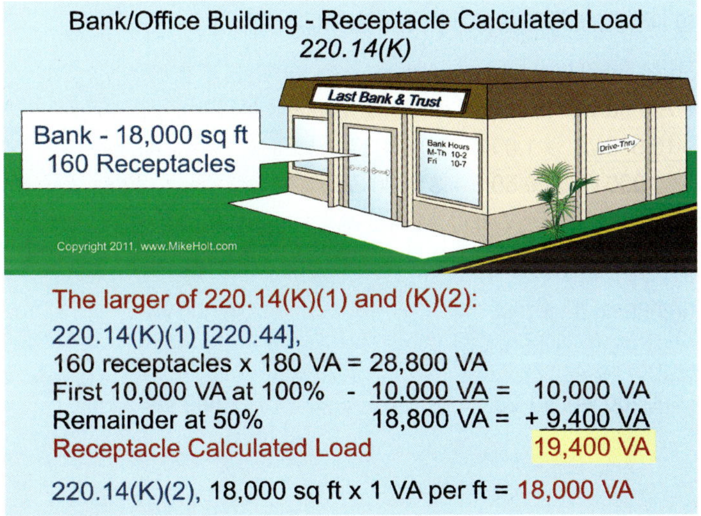

Figure 11–21

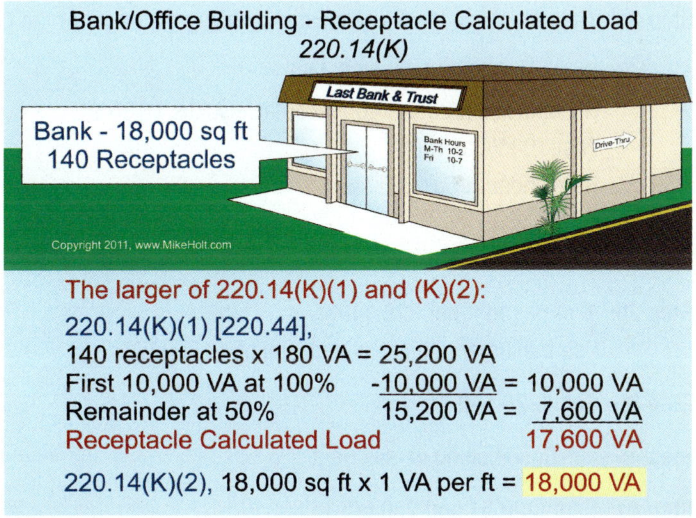

Figure 11–22

PART B—EXAMPLES

11.13 Bank/Office Building Example

Determine the feeder/service calculated load for an office building/bank with a single phase 120/240V service. The building has the loads listed in Figure 11–23

Determine the feeder/service calculated load:

Bold indicates neutral load. [215.2(A)(1) Ex 2].

Step 1a:	Lighting [Table 220.12]				
	Use the larger of the actual lighting load listed or the VA per sq ft from Table 220.12				
	General Lighting = 30,000 sq ft x 3.50 VA				
	General Lighting = 105,000 VA				
	General Lighting Calculated Load = 105,000 VA x 1.25				**131,250 VA**
Step 1b:	Actual Lighting				
	Actual Lighting Connected Load = 200 units x 120V x 1.65A				
	Actual Lighting Connected Load = 39,600 VA				
	Actual Lighting Calculated Load = 39,600 VA x 1.25				49,500 VA (omit)
	Use the larger: the calculated load of 131,250 VA				
Step 2a:	The receptacle load is calculated by using the larger of the computed load from 220.44 or 1 VA per sq ft [220.14(K)].				
	Computed Load from 220.44				
	Receptacles [220.44] 400 receptacle yokes x 180 VA	72,000 VA			
	First 10 kVA at 100%	–10,000 VA	x 1.00	10,000 VA	
	Remainder at 50%	62,000 VA	x 0.50	+ 31,000 VA	
				41,000 VA	
	Receptacle Calculated Load				41,000 VA
Step 2b:	1 VA per sq ft per 220.14(K)	30,000 sq ft	x 1 VA		30,000 VA
	Use the larger: the calculated load of 41,000 VA				
Step 3:	Sign [220.14(F)]	1,200 VA	x 1.25		**1,500 VA**
Step 4:	Air-Conditioning versus Heat				
Step 4a:	Heat [220.51 and 220.60] 15,000 VA				15,000 VA
Step 4b:	Air-Conditioning 10 hp, single phase, 230V, FLC = 50A [Table 430.248]				
	VA = (240V x 50A)				
	VA = 12,000VA				
	Air-Conditioning Calculated Load				12,000 VA
	Use the electric heat, the larger at 15,000 VA				
Step 5:	Lawn Sprinkler Pump Motor 5 hp, single-phase, 230V FLC = 28A [Table 430.248]				
	VA = V x A				
	VA = 240V x 28A	6,720 VA	x 1.25		8,400 VA

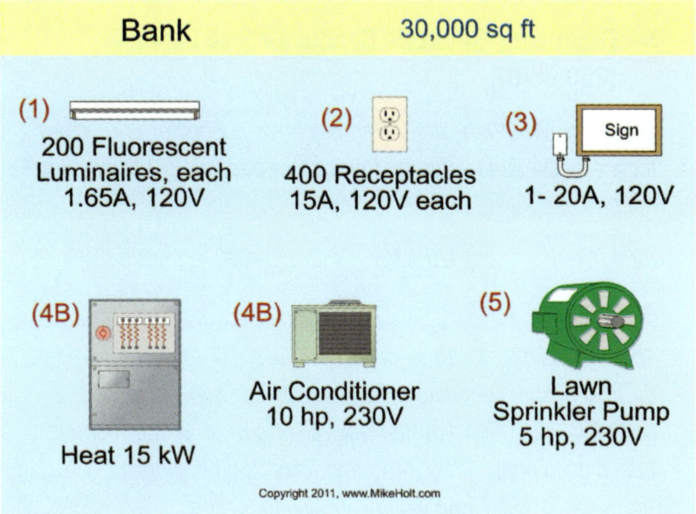

Figure 11–23

Summary

The following list includes:

- A Total Load column which is the total load calculated following Article 220 requirements
- A Conductor Sizing column which includes continuous loads at 125% and noncontinuous loads at 100%.
- A Neutral column which provides the neutral loading for sizing the neutral conductor.

		Total Load	Conductor Sizing	Neutral
Step 1:	Lighting	105,000 VA	131,250 VA	105,000 VA
Step 2:	Receptacles	41,000 VA	41,000 VA	41,000 VA
Step 3:	Sign	1,200 VA	1,500 VA	1,200 VA
Step 4:	Heat	15,000 VA	15,000 VA	0 VA
Step 5:	Sprinkler Pump	6,720 VA	8,400 VA	0 VA
		168,920 VA	197,150 VA	147,200 VA*

*The neutral conductor is sized at 100 percent of the continuous load [215.2(A)(1) Ex 2].

Feeder/Service Calculated Load:

I = VA/E
I = 197,150 VA/240V
I = 821.45A

Neutral Amperes: The neutral conductor is permitted to be reduced according to the requirements of 220.61(B)(2) for that portion of the unbalanced load that exceeds 200A. Since this system is a 120/240V, single-phase system, we're permitted to reduce the neutral by multiplying the portion that exceeds 200A by 70 percent.

Neutral Conductor:

I = VA/E
I = 147,200 VA/240V
I = 613A

220.61(B)(2) allows reduction of the neutral load over 200A to 70%

First 200A at 100%	200A	x 1.00	200A
Remainder at 70%	413A	x 0.70	+ 289A
			489A

The service conductors and overcurrent device must be sized no less than 821A, and the neutral conductor must be sized to carry not less than 489A.

Summary Questions

► Overcurrent Protection Example

Question: *What size service overcurrent device is required to supply an 821A calculated load?*

(a) 800A *(b) 1,000A* *(c) 1,200A* *(d) 1,600A*

Answer: *(b) 1,000A [240.6(A)]*

► Service Ungrounded Conductor Size Example

Question: *What size service conductors are required in each raceway if the conductors are paralleled in four raceways to supply an 821A calculated load? Use 75°C rated conductors.*

(a) 250 kcmil *(b) 300 kcmil* *(c) 350 kcmil* *(d) 400 kcmil*

Answer: *(a) 250 kcmil*

When the overcurrent device is over 800A, the ampacity of the conductors must be equal to, or greater than, the rating of the overcurrent device. In this example, the overcurrent device is 1,000A, so the ampacity of the conductors must be 1,000A or more [240.4(C)].

1,000A/4 raceways = 250A per raceway, sized based on the 75°C terminal rating [110.14(C)(1)(b)]

250 kcmil has an ampacity of 255A x 4 = 1,020A [Table 310.15(B)(16)]

► Service Neutral Conductor Size Example

Question: *What size neutral service conductor is required in each of the four raceways to supply a 489A calculated neutral load if using four conductors in parallel per phase?*

(a) 1/0 AWG (b) 2/0 AWG (c) 3/0 AWG (d) 4/0 AWG

Answer: *(a) 1/0 AWG*

The neutral service conductor must have the capacity to carry 489A and be sized no smaller than 1/0 AWG to meet the paralleling requirements of 310.10(H). [220.61(B)(2)].

489A/4 raceways = 123A; 1 AWG has an ampacity of 130A at 75°C [110.14(C)(1)(b) and Table 310.15(B)(16)], but the smallest size conductor permitted for paralleling is 1/0 AWG. The neutral must also be not smaller than called for by Table 250.66, based on the ungrounded conductors in the same raceway [250.24(C)(2)].

The neutral service conductor must have an ampacity of not less than 489A and it must not be smaller than 1/0 for paralleling [310.10(H)], and meet the requirements of 250.24(C)(1).

If using three neutral conductors in parallel per phase:

- 489A/3 raceways = 163A
- 2/0AWG has an ampacity of 175A at 75°C [Table 310.15(B)(16)]

► Parallel Service Conductors Sizing Example

Question: *What size service conductors are required in each raceway if the conductors are paralleled in three raceways to supply an 821A calculated load?*

(a) 250 kcmil (b) 300 kcmil (c) 350 kcmil (d) 400 kcmil

Answer: *(d) 400 kcmil*

1,000A/3 raceways = 333A for each conductor, if fed by 3 parallel conductors

400 kcmil has an ampacity of 335A at 75°C [Table 310.15(B)(16)].

► Grounding Electrode Conductor Size Example [250.66(B)]

Question: *What size grounding electrode conductor is required for a 1,000A service fed by four sets of parallel 250 kcmil conductors per phase?*

(a) 4 AWG (b) 1/0 AWG (c) 2/0 AWG (d) 3/0 AWG

Answer: *(c) 2/0 AWG*

The grounding electrode conductor is sized to the four sets of 250 kcmil conductors in accordance with Table 250.66 [250.24(C)(2)]. First find the equivalent size of all four conductors in each phase [250.24(C) and Table 250.66, Note 1]:

250 kcmil x 4 = 1,000 kcmil equivalent size

1,000 kcmil will require a 2/0 grounding electrode conductor [Table 250.66].

► Feeder Equipment Grounding Conductor Example

Question: *If a 1,000A feeder is installed using four sets of parallel 250 kcmil conductors per phase in four raceways, what size equipment grounding conductor will be required in each raceway?*

(a) 4 AWG (b) 1/0 AWG (c) 2/0 AWG (d) 3/0 AWG

Answer: *(c) 2/0 AWG*

The equipment grounding conductor for a feeder is based on the size of the overcurrent device protecting the feeder [250.122(F)].

For a feeder with 1,000A overcurrent protection, a 2/0 equipment grounding conductor is required [Table 250.122].

11.14 Mobile/Manufactured Home Park [550.31]

The service calculated load for a mobile/manufactured home park is sized according to the demand factors of Table 550.31 to the larger of 16,000 VA for each mobile/manufactured home lot, or the calculated load for each mobile/manufactured home site according to 550.18. It's also permitted to size service and feeder conductors to an individual mobile home in accordance with 310.15(B)(7).

▶ Mobile/Manufactured Home Park Example

Question: *What's the feeder/service calculated load for a mobile/manufactured home park that has facilities for 35 sites? The system is 120/240V, single-phase.* **Figure 11–24**

(a) 400A (b) 560A (c) 800A (d) 1,000A

Answer: *(b) 560A*

A mobile home park's electrical wiring system must be calculated at 120/240V based on the larger of the following [550.31]:

(1) 16,000 VA for each mobile home lot.

(2) The load calculated in accordance with 550.18 for the largest typical mobile home that each lot will accept.

The feeder or service load can be calculated in accordance with the demand factor percentages in Table 550.31

Since no calculated load in accordance with 550.18 is given, just use 16,000 VA per site [550.31(1)].

Calculated Load = VA x Sites x Demand Factor
Table 550.31, 35 sites = 0.24 demand factor.
Calculated Load = 16,000 VA x 35 sites x 0.24
Calculated Load = 134,400VA

I = VA/E
I = 134,000 VA/240V
I = 560A

Paralleling two conductors per phase: 560A/2 raceways = 280A

300 kcmil has an ampacity of 285A at 75°C [Table 310.15(B)(16)]: 285A x 2 = 570A
This is large enough for the calculated load, 600A overcurrent protection can be used according to 240.4(B), which allows us to round up to the next standard size overcurrent protection not exceeding 800A.

The neutral must be large enough to serve the neutral load [220.61] but the minimum neutral size when paralleling conductors is 1/0 AWG [250.24(C)(2) and 310.10(H)].

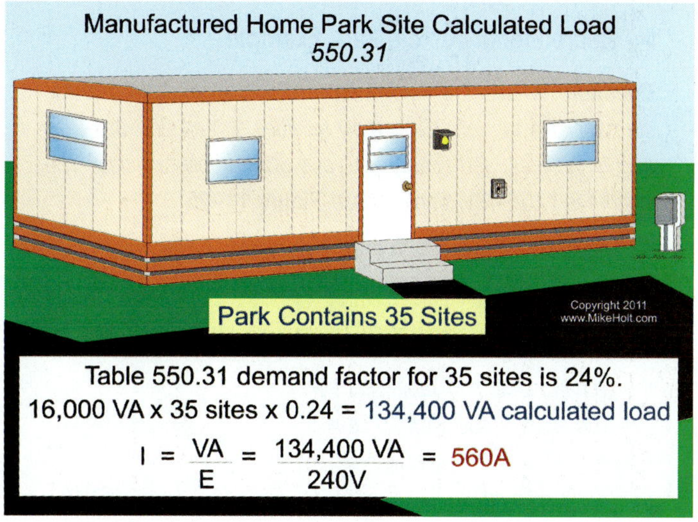

Figure 11–24

11.15 Recreational Vehicle Park [551.73]

Recreational vehicle parks are typically equipped with several different sizes of receptacles. Each size of receptacle must be present based on a minimum percentage requirement provided In 551.71. Dedicated tent sites can be excluded when calculating these percentages.

Recreational vehicle parks are calculated according to the demand factors of Table 551.73. The total calculated load is based on the VA per site values listed in 551.73(A):

- 2,400 VA for each site with 20A, 120V supply facilities,
- 3,600 VA for each site with 20A and 30A, 120V supply facilities, and
- 9,600 VA for each site with 50A, 120/240V supply facilities.

► Recreational Vehicle Park Example

Question: *What's the calculated load for a recreational vehicle park that has ten 20A supply facilities, fifteen 20A and 30A supply facilities, and twenty 30A and 50A supply facilities? The system is 120/240V, single-phase.* **Figure 11–25**

(a) 420A (b) 461A (c) 520A (d) 600A

Answer: *(b) 461A*

The service for the recreational vehicle park is sized according to the demand factors of Table 551.73

Ten 20A sites (2,400 VA x 10 sites)	*24,000 VA*
Fifteen 20A and 30A sites (3,600 VA x 15 sites)	*54,000 VA*
Twenty 50A sites (9,600 VA x 20 sites)	*+ 192,000 VA*
Connected Load	*270,000 VA*

Calculated Load = 270,000 VA x 0.41 [Table 551.73]
Calculated Load = 110,700 VA

I = VA/E
I = 110,700 VA/240V
I = 461A

Paralleling two conductors per phase: 461A/2 raceways = 230.50A

250 kcmil has an ampacity of 255A at 75°C [Table 310.15(B)(16)]: 255A x 2 = 510A

The neutral must be large enough to serve the neutral load [220.61] but the minimum neutral size when paralleling conductors is 1/0 AWG [250.24(C)(2) and 310.10(H)].

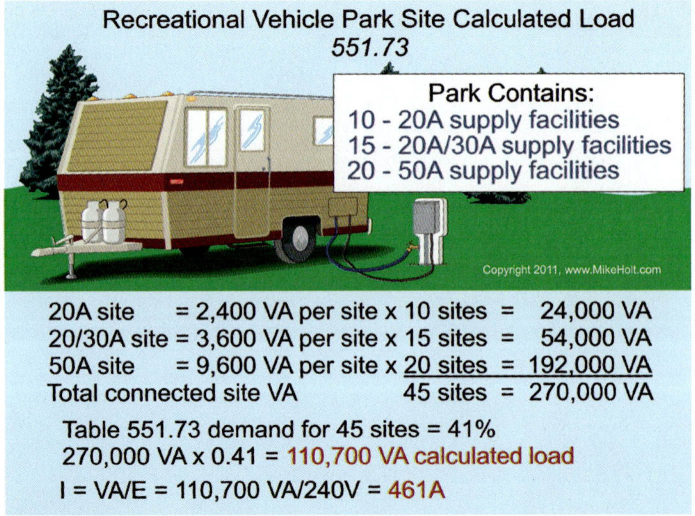

Figure 11–25

11.16 Marina [555.12]

The *NEC* permits a demand factor to apply to the receptacle outlets for boat slips at a marina. The demand factors of Table 555.12 are based on the number of receptacles on the feeder. The receptacles must also be balanced between the phases to determine the number of receptacles on any given line.

► Marina Receptacle Outlet Demand Example [555.12]

Question: *What is the calculated load for a 120/240V, single-phase service is required for a marina that has twenty 30A, 250V receptacles and twenty 20A, 125V receptacles?* **Figure 11–26**

(a) 200A (b) 420A (c) 560A (d) 720A

Answer: *(c) 560A*

The calculated load is based on the number of receptacles. Try to divide the receptacles equally on each line in order to determine the connected load per line.

	Line 1	**Line 2**
Twenty 30A, 250V	*20 x 30A*	*20 x 30A*
Ten 20A, 125V	*+ 10 x 20A*	*+ 10 x 20A*
Thirty receptacles	*30—800A*	*30—800A*

Table 555.12, 30 receptacles = 0.70 demand factor

Calculated Load Per Line =
Connected Load Per Line x Demand Factor

Calculated Load per Line = 800A x 0.70
Calculated Load per Line = 560A per line

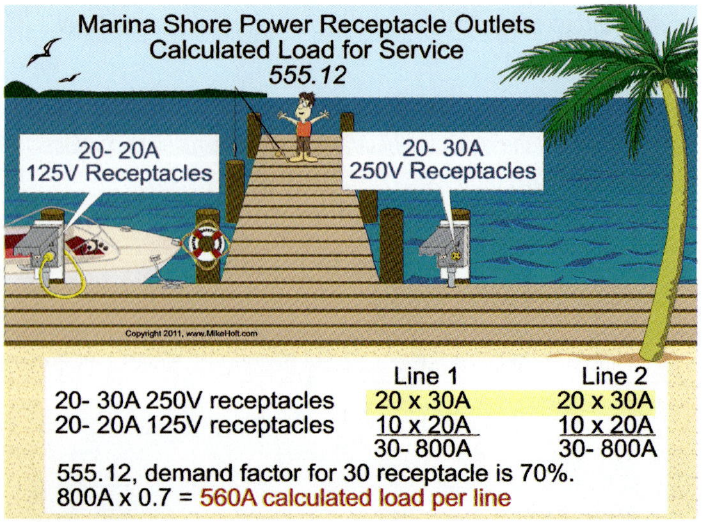

Figure 11–26

▶ Overcurrent Device Sizing Example

Question: *What size overcurrent device will be required for this service?*

(a) 200A (b) 400A (c) 600A (d) 800A

Answer: *(c) 600A*

For overcurrent protection, use a 600A overcurrent device [240.6(A)]

Paralleling two conductors per phase: 560A/2 raceways = 280A

300 kcmil has an ampacity of 285A at 75°C [Table 310.15(B)(16)]: 285A x 2 = 570A

The minimum neutral size when paralleling conductors is 1/0 AWG [250.24(C)(2) and 310.10(H)].

▶ Grounding Electrode Conductor Sizing Example

Question: *What size grounding electrode conductor will be required for this service, using two sets of 300 kcmil conductors in parallel?*

(a) 4 AWG (b) 1/0 AWG (c) 2/0 AWG (d) 3/0 AWG

Answer: *(b) 1/0 AWG*

300 kcmil x 2 = 600 kcmil [Table 250.66, Note 1]

600 kcmil requires a 1/0 grounding electrode conductor [250.66].

Author's Comment: The largest size grounding electrode conductor required to a ground rod is 6 AWG and to a concrete encased electrode (uffer) is 4 AWG [250.66(A) and 250.66(B)].

PART C—OPTIONAL METHOD—FEEDER/SERVICE LOAD CALCULATIONS

Introduction

An optional method of calculating the service load is permitted for a new restaurant that has electric space heating or electric air-conditioning, or both.

11.17 New Restaurant—Optional Method [220.88]

The following steps can be used to determine the service size for a new restaurant using the optional method described in the *NEC* 220.88:

Step 1: Determine the total connected load. Add the nameplate rating of all loads at 100 percent and include both the air-conditioning and heat load [Table 220.88 Note].

Step 2: Apply the demand factors from Table 220.88 to the total connected load calculated in Step 1.

▶ All-Electric Restaurant Example

Question: *What's the calculated load for an all-electric restaurant (120/208V, three-phase) that has a total connected load of 300 kVA?*

(a) 420A (b) 472A (c) 520A (d) 600A

Answer: *(b) 472A*

Total Connected Load	*300 kVA*	
First 200 kVA at 80%	*– 200 kVA x 0.80*	*160 kVA*
Next 201-325 kVA at 10%	*100 kVAx 0.10*	*+ 10 kVA*
Total Calculated Load		*170 kVA*

I = VA/(E x 1.732)

I = 170,000 VA/(208V x 1.732)

I = 170,000 VA/360V

I = 472A

Paralleling two conductors per phase: 472A/2 raceways = 236A

250 kcmil has an ampacity of 255A at 75°C [Table 310.15(B)(16)]: 255A x 2 = 510A

The neutral must be large enough to serve the neutral load [220.61] but the minimum neutral size when paralleling conductors is 1/0 AWG [250.24(C)(2) and 310.10(H)].

▶ Grounding Electrode Conductor Sizing Example

Question: *What size grounding electrode conductor will be required for this service, using two sets of 250 kcmil conductors in parallel?*

(a) 4 AWG (b) 1/0 AWG (c) 2/0 AWG (d) 3/0 AWG

Answer: *(b) 1/0 AWG*

250 kcmil x 2 = 500 kcmil [Table 250.66, Note 1]

500 kcmil requires a 1/0 AWG grounding electrode conductor [250.66].

Author's Comment: The largest size grounding electrode conductor required as a sole connection to a ground rod is 6 AWG and as a sole connection to a concrete encased electrode (uffer) is 4 AWG [250.66(A) and 250.66(B)].

▶ Not All-Electric Restaurant Example

Question: *What's the calculated load for a not all-electric restaurant (120/208V, three-phase) that has a total connected load of 300 kVA?*

(a) 420A (b) 460A (c) 520A (d) 695A

Answer: *(d) 695A*

Total Connected Load	*300 kVA*		
First 200 kVA at 100%	*– 200 kVA*	*x 1.00*	*200 kVA*
201-325 kVA at 50%	*100 kVA*	*x 0.50*	*+ 50 kVA*
Total Calculated Load			*250 kVA*

I = VA/(E x 1.732)

I = 250,000 VA/(208V x 1.732)

I = 250,000 VA/360V

I = 694A

This will require a minimum of a 700A overcurrent device [240.6(A)], standard service size from most power suppliers is 800A.

Paralleling two conductors per phase: 694A/2 raceways = 347A

500 kcmil has an ampacity of 380A at 75°C [Table 310.15(B)(16)]: 380A x 2 = 760A

The neutral must be large enough to serve the neutral load [220.61] but the minimum neutral size when paralleling conductors is 1/0 AWG [250.24(C)(2) and 310.10(H)]

Or-

Paralleling three conductors per phase: 694A/3 raceways = 231A

250 kcmil has an ampacity of 255A at 75°C [Table 310.15(B)(16)]: 255A x 3 = 765A

The neutral must be large enough to serve the neutral load [220.61] but the minimum neutral size when paralleling conductors is 1/0 AWG [250.24(C)(2) and 310.10(H)]

▶ Grounding Electrode Conductor Sizing Example

Question: *What size grounding electrode conductor will be required for this service, using two sets of 500 kcmil conductors in parallel?*

(a) 4 AWG (b) 1/0 AWG (c) 2/0 AWG (d) 3/0 AWG

Answer: *(c) 2/0 AWG*

500 kcmil x 2 = 1,000 kcmil [Table 250.66, Note 1]

1,000 kcmil requires a 2/0 AWG grounding electrode conductor [Table 250.66].

Author's Comment: The largest size grounding electrode conductor required as a sole connection to a ground rod is 6 AWG and as a sole connection to a concrete encased electrode (uffer) is 4 AWG [250.66(A) and 250.66(B)].

PART D—WELDERS

Introduction

Electric welding equipment is a very specialized load, compared to occupancies such as schools, banks, stores, and dwellings. Electric welders operate by either creating an electric arc between two surfaces, or by heating a metal rod until it melts. Both techniques result in high momentary current draws. Article 630 of the *NEC* requires that information about current rating and duty cycle be marked on the nameplate of the equipment.

11.18 Arc Welders

Ampacity of Supply Conductors—Individual Welders

The supply conductors for arc welders must have an ampacity not less than the welder nameplate rating. If the nameplate rating isn't available, the supply conductors must have an ampacity not less than the rated primary current as adjusted by the multiplier in Table 630.11(A), based on the duty cycle of the welder.

Table 630.11(A) Duty Cycle Multiplication Factors for Arc Welders		
Duty Cycle	Nonmotor Generator	Motor Generator
100	1.00	1.00
90	0.95	0.96
80	0.89	0.91
70	0.84	0.86
60	0.78	0.81
50	0.71	0.75
40	0.63	0.69
30	0.55	0.62
20 or less	0.45	0.55

► Individual Welder Example

Question: *A nonmotor-generator arc welder has a primary current rating of 40A with a duty cycle of 50 percent. The branch-circuit conductor for the welder must not be sized less than:* **Figure 11–27**

(a) 15A (b) 20A (c) 25A (d) 30A

Answer: *(d) 30A*

Calculated Load = Primary Rating x Multiplier [Table 630.11(A)]

Calculated Load = 40A x 0.71

Calculated Load = 28.40A

Conductor: 10 AWG has an ampacity of 35A at 75°C [110.14(C) and Table 310.15(B)(16)].

Ampacity of Supply Conductors—Group of Welders

Feeder conductors that supply a group of welders must have a minimum ampacity not less than the sum of the currents as determined in 630.11(A), based on 100 percent of the two largest welders, 85 percent for the third largest welder, 70 percent for the fourth largest welder, and 60 percent for all remaining welders [630.11(B)].

Author's Comment: This calculation method provides an ample margin of safety under high-production conditions.

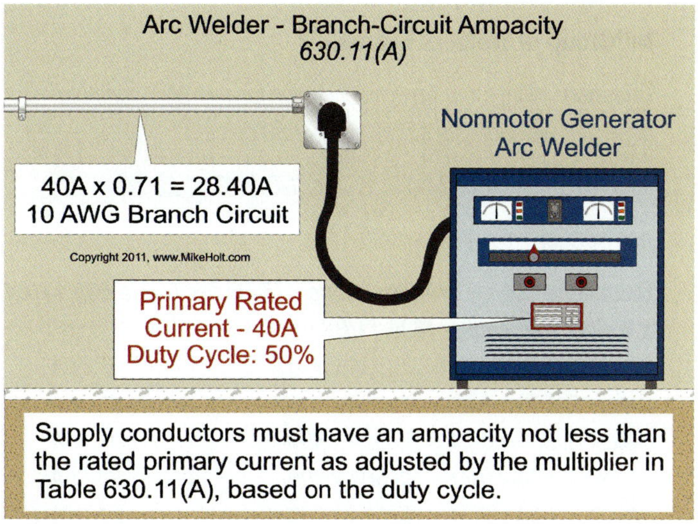

Figure 11–27

► Group of Welders Example 1

Question: *What's the feeder conductor for five 40A nonmotor-generator welders with a duty cycle of 50 percent?*

(a) 4 AWG (b) 1 AWG (c) 1/0 AWG (d) 2/0 AWG

Answer: *(b) 1 AWG*

Calculated Load = Primary Rating x Multiplier [Table 630.11(A)] x Welder Percentage [630.11(B)]

Welder 1: 40A x 0.71 = 28.40A x 100%	*28.40A*
Welder 2: 40A x 0.71 = 28.40A x 100%	*28.40A*
Welder 3: 40A x 0.71 = 28.40A x 85%	*24.14A*
Welder 4: 40A x 0.71 = 28.40A x 70%	*19.88A*
Welder 5: 40A x 0.71 = 28.40A x 60%	*17.04A*
Total Calculated Load	*117.86A*

Conductor size: 1 AWG has an ampacity of 130A at 75°C [110.14(C) and Table 310.15(B)(16)]

► Group of Welders Example 2

Question: *What's the feeder conductor for five 50A nonmotor-generator welders with a duty cycle of 50 percent?*

(a) 4 AWG (b) 3 AWG (c) 1/0 AWG (d) 2/0 AWG

Answer: *(c) 1/0 AWG*

Calculated Load = Primary Rating x Multiplier [Table 630.11(A)] x Welder Percentage [630.11(B)]

Welder 1: 50A x 0.71 = 35.50A x 100%	*35.50A*
Welder 2: 50A x 0.71 = 35.50A x 100%	*35.50A*
Welder 3: 50A x 0.71 = 35.50A x 85%	*30.18A*
Welder 4: 50A x 0.71 = 35.50A x 70%	*24.85A*
Welder 5: 50A x 0.71 = 35.50A x 60%	*21.30A*
Total Calculated Load	*147.33A*

Conductor size: 1/0 AWG has an ampacity of 150A at 75°C [110.14(C) and Table 310.15(B)(16)]

Overcurrent Protection

Where the calculated overcurrent protection value doesn't correspond to the standard overcurrent device ratings in 240.6(A), the next higher standard rating is permitted.

Welders. Each welder must have an overcurrent device rated at not more than 200 percent of the maximum rated supply current at the maximum rated output nameplate, or not more than 200 percent of the rated primary current of the welder [630.12(A)].

Conductors. The conductors must be protected by an overcurrent device rated at not more than 200 percent of the conductor rating [630.12(B)].

► Overcurrent Protection Example

Question: *What's the maximum overcurrent protection device rating for 10 THHN used for an arc welder branch circuit?*

(a) 30A (b) 40A (c) 50A (d) 70A

Answer: *(d) 70A*

10 AWG has an ampacity of 35A at 75°C [110.14(C) and Table 310.15(B)(16)]

35A x 2 = 70A maximum overcurrent protection device size

Disconnecting Means

A disconnecting means is required for each arc welder that isn't equipped with an integral disconnect [630.13].

11.19 Resistance Welders

Ampacity of Supply Conductors—Individual Welders

The ampacity of the supply conductors for varied duty-cycle welders must not be less than 70 percent of the rated primary current for seam and automatically fed welders, and 50 percent of the rated primary current for manually operated welders [630.31(A)(1)].

The ampacity of the supply conductors for welders with a specific duty cycle and nonvarying current levels must have an ampacity not less than the rated primary current as adjusted by the multipliers in Table 630.31(A)(2), based on the duty cycle of the welder.

Table 630.31(A)(2) Duty Cycle Multiplication Factors for Resistance Welders

Duty Cycle	Multiplier
50	0.71
40	0.63
30	0.55
25	0.50
20	0.45
15	0.39
10	0.32
7.50	0.27
5 or less	0.22

▶ Individual Welders Example

Question: *What size branch-circuit conductors are required for a 50A resistance welder having a duty cycle of 50 percent?*

(a) 8 AWG *(b) 6 AWG* *(c) 4 AWG* *(d) 2 AWG*

Answer: *(a) 8 AWG*

Calculated Load = Primary Rating x Multiplier [Table 630.31(A)(2)]
Calculated Load = 50A x 0.71
Calculated Load = 35.50A

8 AWG has an ampacity of 50A at 75°C [110.14(C) and Table 310.15(B)(16)]

Ampacity of Supply Conductors—Group of Welders

Feeder conductors that supply a group of resistance welders must have an ampacity not less than the sum of the value determined using 630.31(A)(2) for the largest welder in the group, plus 60 percent of the values determined for all remaining welders [630.31(B)].

▶ Group of Welders Example

Question: *What's the minimum size feeder conductor for five 50A resistance welders with a duty cycle of 50 percent?*

(a) 4 AWG *(b) 3 AWG* *(c) 2 AWG* *(d) 1 AWG*

Answer: *(d) 1 AWG*

Conductor size: 1 AWG, has an ampacity of 130A at 75°C [110.14(C) and Table 310.15(B)(16)].

Calculated Load = Primary Rating x Multiplier [Table 630.31(A)(2)] x Welder Percentage [630.31(B)]

Welder 1: 50A x 0.71 = 35.50A x 100%	*35.50A*
Welder 2: 50A x 0.71 = 35.50A x 60%	*21.30A*
Welder 3: 50A x 0.71 = 35.50A x 60%	*21.30A*
Welder 4: 50A x 0.71 = 35.50A x 60%	*21.30A*
Welder 5: 50A x 0.71 = 35.50A x 60%	*21.30A*
Total Calculated Load	*120.70A*

1 AWG has an ampacity of 130A at 75°C [110.14(C) and Table 310.15(B)(16)]

Overcurrent Protection

Where the calculated overcurrent protection value doesn't correspond with the standard overcurrent device ratings in 240.6(A), the next higher standard rating is permitted.

Welders. Each welder must have an overcurrent device set at not more than 300 percent of the rated primary current [630.32(A)].

Conductors. Branch-circuit conductors must be protected by an overcurrent device rated at not more than 300 percent of the conductor rating [630.32(B)].

Disconnecting Means

A switch or circuit breaker is required to disconnect each resistance welder and its control equipment from the supply circuit [630.33].

11.20 Light Industrial Calculation

Calculate the service size for a light industrial manufacturing building with the following loads:

- Lighting, 11,600 VA, comprised of electric-discharge luminaries operating at 277V
- Twenty-two 20A, 125V receptacle outlets on general-purpose branch circuits, supplied by a separately derived system
- Air compressor, 460V, three-phase, 7½ hp
- Grinder, 460V, three-phase, 1½ hp
- Five 50A nonmotor-generator arc welders with a duty cycle of 50 percent (nameplate: 50A, 480V)
- Three industrial process dryers, 480V, three-phase, 15 kVA each (assume continuous duty during shifts)

Step 1: Determine the noncontinuous loads and motor loads. The noncontinuous and motor loads can be combined [430.24].

(1) Noncontinuous Loads

(a) Receptacle Load [220.44] 22 receptacles at 180 VA	3,960 VA	
(b) Welder Load [630.11(A) and Table 630.11(A)]		

A multiplication factor of 0.71 is allowed for 50% duty cycle
Each welder: 480V x 50A x 0.71 = 17,040 VA

Welder demand factors for 5 welders: [630.11(B)]

First welder	100%
Second welder	100%
Third welder	85%
Fourth welder	70%
Fifth welder	60%

17,040 VA x 100%	17,040 VA
17,040 VA x 100%	17,040 VA
17,040 VA x 85%	14,484 VA
17,040 VA x 70%	11,928 VA
17,040 VA x 60%	+ 10,224 VA
	70,716 VA

Welder Total Calculated Load =	+ 70,716 VA	
Total Noncontinuous Loads (receptacles and welders) =	74,676 VA	74,676 VA

(2) Motor Loads [430.24 and Table 430.250]

(a) Air Compressor: 7½ hp FLC = 11A [Table 430.250] 460V x 11A x 1.732	8,764 VA	
(b) Grinder: 1½ hp FLC = 3A [Table 430.250] 3A x 460V x 1.732 =	2,390 VA	
(c) Largest Motor, Additional 25 percent: 8,764 x 25% =	+ 2,191VA	
Total Motor Loads =	13,345 VA	+ 13,345
Total Noncontinuous Loads and the Motor Loads [430.24] =		88,021 VA

Step 2: Determine the continuous loads:

(1) General Lighting	11,600 VA	
(2) Three Industrial Process Dryers 15 kVA each	+45,000 VA	
Total Continuous Loads	56,600 VA	56,600 VA

Step 3: Determine the overcurrent protection [215.3]:

The overcurrent device must be sized at 125 percent of the continuous loads, plus the noncontinuous loads:

(1) Noncontinuous Loads =	88,021 VA
(2) Continuous Loads (56,600 VA x 1.25) =	+ 70,750 VA
Total VA	158,771 VA

Step 4: Convert to amperes to size the overcurrent device:

I = VA/(E x 1.732)

I = 158,771 VA/(480V x 1.732)

I = 158,771 VA/831V

I = 191A

Overcurrent Device = 200A [240.6]

Conductors: 3/0 AWG has an ampacity of 225A at 75°C [110.14(C)(1)(b) and Table 310.15(B)(16)]

CONCLUSION TO UNIT 11—COMMERCIAL CALCULATIONS

This unit showed that the calculations used to size feeders and service conductors for commercial installations don't include the same demand factors allowed for dwelling units. The nature of nondwelling occupancies doesn't create the same kinds of diversity found in homes and apartment buildings. Accordingly, Unit 11 provided a variety of examples to help you learn the *Code* requirements for commercial service sizing.

Article 220 isn't the only *Code* article where service calculation requirements are contained. We referred to Article 550 for mobile home parks, Article 551 for recreational vehicle parks, Article 555 for marinas, Article 630 for electric welders, Article 440 for hermetic air-conditioning equipment, and Article 430 for motors. When performing commercial service calculations, be careful to look at all of the components of the installation to determine if some other *NEC* article includes information pertinent to your installation.

Certain demand factors may be applied to commercial services. When dealing with individual branch circuits and feeders for continuous loads, remember to use a 125 percent multiplier for the ungrounded conductors. This carries over to the continuous duty portions of loads when determining the actual feeder and service conductors for commercial occupancies. The neutral conductor is allowed to be sized at 100 percent of the continuous and noncontinuous load for branch circuits and feeders when it's not connected to an overcurrent device [210.19(A)(1) Ex 2 and 215.2(A)(1) Ex 2]. Optional calculations are allowed for some commercial installations, so be certain to read problems carefully so you'll employ the correct method.

UNIT
11 Practice Questions

PRACTICE QUESTIONS FOR UNIT 11—COMMERCIAL CALCULATIONS

PART A—GENERAL

11.2 Conductor Ampacity [Article 100]

1. The ______ of a conductor is the rating in amperes it can carry continuously without exceeding its insulation temperature rating. The allowable ampacities listed in Table 310.15(B)(16) are affected by ambient temperature, current flow, conductor insulation, and conductor bundling [310.10].

(a) load rating
(b) ampacity
(c) calculated load
(d) continuous factor

11.3 Conductor Overcurrent Protection [240.4]

2. The purpose of ______ is to protect circuit conductors against excessive or dangerous temperatures. If the ampacity of a conductor doesn't correspond with the standard ampere rating of a fuse or circuit breaker, the next size up overcurrent device is permitted. This applies only if the conductors don't supply branch circuits for multiple receptacles and if the next size up overcurrent device doesn't exceed 800A.

(a) short-circuit protection
(b) ground-fault protection
(c) overload protection
(d) overcurrent protection

3. The following is a partial list of standard ampere ratings for overcurrent devices (fuses and inverse time circuit breakers): 15, 25, 35, 45, 80, 90, 110, 175, 250, and 350A.

(a) True
(b) False

11.5 Rounding an Ampere [220.5(B)]

4. Where a calculation results in a fraction of an ampere, the results are permitted to be rounded to the nearest whole ampere, with decimal fractions smaller than ______ dropped.

(a) 0.05
(b) 0.40
(c) 0.50
(d) 0.59

11.6 Lighting—Demand Factors [Tables 220.12 and 220.42]

5. What's the general lighting and general-use receptacle feeder/service calculated load for a 24-room motel, where each unit is 685 sq ft?

(a) 10 kVA
(b) 16 kVA
(c) 20 kVA
(d) 25 kVA

6. What's the general lighting and general-use receptacle feeder/service calculated load for a 250,000 sq ft storage warehouse that has 200 receptacles? (Note: the receptacle load can be calculated using Table 220.44 or combining with the lighting load and using Table 220.42 (see 220.44). For this problem, use Table 220.44 for the receptacle load.)

(a) 25 kVA
(b) 61 kVA
(c) 95 kVA
(d) 105 kVA

11.7 Lighting Without Demand Factors [215.2(A)(1), 230.42(A)(1), and Table 220.12]

7. What's the feeder/service general lighting calculated load for a 3,200 sq ft dance club?

   (a) 3,200 VA
   (b) 5,400 VA
   (c) 8,000 VA
   (d) 12,000 VA

8. What's the feeder/service general lighting load for a 90,000 sq ft school?

   (a) 90 kVA
   (b) 120 kVA
   (c) 230 kVA
   (d) 338 kVA

11.8 Lighting—Miscellaneous

9. When calculating the load for the feeder/service conductor load, how much is included for 130 ft of show-window lighting?

   (a) 29 kVA
   (b) 33 kVA
   (c) 35 kVA
   (d) 38 kVA

11.9 Multioutlet Receptacle Assembly [220.14(H)]

10. What's the feeder/service conductor calculated load for ten 5 ft sections of multioutlet assembly not used simultaneously and five 2 ft sections of multioutlet assembly simultaneously used?

    (a) 3,600 VA
    (b) 5,500 VA
    (c) 7,200 VA
    (d) 12,000 VA

11.10 Receptacle VA Load

11. How many receptacle outlet yokes are permitted on a 20A, 120V circuit in a commercial occupancy?

    (a) 10
    (b) 13
    (c) 15
    (d) 20

12. What's the service calculated load for 110 receptacle yokes (15A or 20A, 125V) in a commercial building?

    (a) 5 kVA
    (b) 10 kVA
    (c) 15 kVA
    (d) 20 kVA

11.11 Banks and Offices—General Lighting and Receptacles [220.14(K)]

13. What's the service calculated load for the general lighting and receptacles for a 30,000 sq ft bank?

    (a) 111 kVA
    (b) 123 kVA
    (c) 162 kVA
    (d) 175 kVA

14. What's the general lighting and receptacle calculated load for a 10,000 sq ft office building with 75 receptacles?

    (a) 25 kVA
    (b) 35 kVA
    (c) 45 kVA
    (d) 56 kVA

11.12 Sign Circuit [220.14(F) and 600.5]

15. What's the feeder calculated load contribution from one electric sign circuit?

    (a) 1,400 VA
    (b) 1,500 VA
    (c) 1,920 VA
    (d) 2,400 VA

PART B—EXAMPLES

11.14 Mobile/Manufactured Home Park [550.31]

16. What's the feeder and service calculated load for a mobile home park that has the facilities for 42 sites? The system is 120/240V, single-phase.

(a) 452A
(b) 512A
(c) 644A
(d) 732A

11.15 Recreational Vehicle Park [551.73]

17. A recreational vehicle park has 17 dedicated tent sites with only 20A, 125V receptacles; 35 sites with 20A and 30A, 125V receptacles; and 10 sites with 50A, 125/250V receptacles. The feeder/service calculated load is approximately _____.

(a) 355A
(b) 400A
(c) 789A
(d) 1,114A

11.16 Marina [555.12]

18. A marina has 24 slips with 20A, 250V receptacles, and 30 slips with 30A, 250V receptacles. What size service is required for the marina?

(a) 400A
(b) 600A
(c) 900A
(d) 1,000A

19. What size conductor is required for a marina service if the total calculated load for each phase is 570A and the service is paralleled in two raceways?

(a) 4/0 AWG
(b) 250 kcmil
(c) 300 kcmil
(d) 350 kcmil

PART C—OPTIONAL METHOD—FEEDER/ SERVICE LOAD CALCULATIONS

11.17 New Restaurant—Optional Method [220.88]

20. A new restaurant has a total connected load of 400 kVA and is all electric. What's the calculated load for the service?

(a) 210 kVA
(b) 275 kVA
(c) 300 kVA
(d) 325 kVA

21. A new restaurant has a total connected load of 400 kVA and isn't all electric. What's the calculated load for the service?

(a) 275 kVA
(b) 297 kVA
(c) 300 kVA
(d) 325 kVA

UNIT 11 Challenge Questions

CHALLENGE QUESTIONS FOR UNIT 11—COMMERCIAL CALCULATIONS

PART A—GENERAL

11.6 Lighting—Demand Factors [Tables 220.12 and 220.42]

1. Each unit of a 100-unit hotel is 12 x 15 ft. In addition, there's a 60 x 20 ft office and there are hallways with a total of 120 sq ft. What's the calculated load for general lighting and receptacles?

   (a) 23 kVA
   (b) 25 kVA
   (c) 29 kVA
   (d) 37 kVA

11.10 Receptacle VA Load

2. If in the hall and other areas of a motel there are 100 receptacle outlets (not in the motel rooms), the calculated load added to the service for these receptacles is ______.

   (a) 0 VA
   (b) 10,000 VA
   (c) 14,000 VA
   (d) 20,000 VA

3. What's the receptacle calculated load for a 20,000 sq ft office building?

   (a) 10,000 VA
   (b) 20,000 VA
   (c) 30,000 VA
   (d) 40,000 VA

PART B—EXAMPLES

11.13 Bank/Office Building Example

4. What's the general lighting and general-use receptacle load for a 30,000 sq ft bank?

   (a) 123 kVA
   (b) 136 kVA
   (c) 162 kVA
   (d) 173 kVA

11.14 Mobile/Manufactured Home Park [550.31]

5. A 75-site mobile home park is designed for mobile homes that have a 14,000 VA load per site. The service calculated load for the park is ______.

   (a) 201 kVA
   (b) 222 kVA
   (c) 264 kVA
   (d) 1,200 kVA

11.15 Recreational Vehicle Park [551.73]

6. A recreational vehicle park has 42 sites: nine sites are equipped with 50A, 120/240V supply facilities; 30 sites are equipped with 20A and 30A, 120V supply facilities; and three sites are equipped with 20A, 120V supply facilities. The minimum feeder calculated load for these sites is ______.

   (a) 83 kVA
   (b) 101 kVA
   (c) 139 kVA
   (d) 158 kVA

11.16 Marina [555.12]

7. A marina shore power facility has twenty 20A, 240V receptacles; seventeen 30A, 240V receptacles; and seven 50A, 240V receptacles. After applying demand factors, the service calculated load for the shore power boxes is _____.

   (a) 625A
   (b) 630A
   (c) 1,160A
   (d) 1,260A

PART C—OPTIONAL METHOD—FEEDER/ SERVICE LOAD CALCULATIONS

11.17 New Restaurant—Optional Method [220.88]

8. A new restaurant has a total connected lighting load of 30 kVA. The kitchen equipment includes two gas stoves, one gas grill, three gas ovens, one 75-gallon gas water heater, one 5 kW dishwasher, two 2 kW coffee makers, five 2 kW kitchen appliances on their own circuit, and ten 1.50 kVA small-appliance circuits. Using the optional method, the service calculated load is closest to _____.

   (a) 38 kVA
   (b) 45 kVA
   (c) 50 kVA
   (d) 64 kVA

UNIT

12 Transformer Calculations

INTRODUCTION TO UNIT 12—TRANSFORMER CALCULATIONS

Transformers are essential to electric power distribution. For this reason, you must understand several important concepts about transformers to be successful when doing electrical work.

If you remove the cover of a transformer and look inside, you'll see two sets of windings. And you'll immediately understand why they're called that–the manufacturer literally winds wire into a coil. Now, think back to the basic transformer concepts introduced in Unit 4.

The ratio of the number of turns in the primary side (supply side) to the number on the secondary side (load side) is what determines how the unit *transforms* the power supplied to it. This is a key concept in transformer theory and application.

Typically, the transformation is that of raising or lowering the voltage. Using a transformer, we can step down the 480V facility distribution voltage to the 120V needed at the wall receptacles in the offices or wherever else we want to supply with 120V.

If you look on the nameplate of a typical three-phase wye-connected transformer, you'll see it has a 4:1 ratio and a 120/208V secondary. You get 208V by connecting between two sets of windings (two lines). You get 120V by connecting between one line and the transformer center tap.

Transformers are connected into different configurations. Industrial and commercial applications use the delta-wye configuration extensively, so it's important that you understand delta and wye line currents.

We'll look at such concepts as current flow and power loss, and show you how to size the conductors. We'll conclude by discussing the grounding and bonding of transformers. This is an area where mistakes are common. Those are mistakes that, thanks to what you'll learn here, you won't be making.

PART A–GENERAL

Introduction

A transformer is a stationary device used to raise or lower voltage. It transfers electrical energy (power) from one system to another by induction with no physical connection between the two systems. For this reason, the National Electrical *Code* refers to transformers as "separately derived systems." Figure 12–1

Some transformers, called "isolation transformers," don't raise or lower the voltage. They're simply for the purpose of decoupling the primary from the secondary.

> **Author's Comment:** This unit is based on the use of solidly grounded ac systems, 600V or less, using 90°C insulated copper conductors sized to 75°C terminals unless otherwise specified.

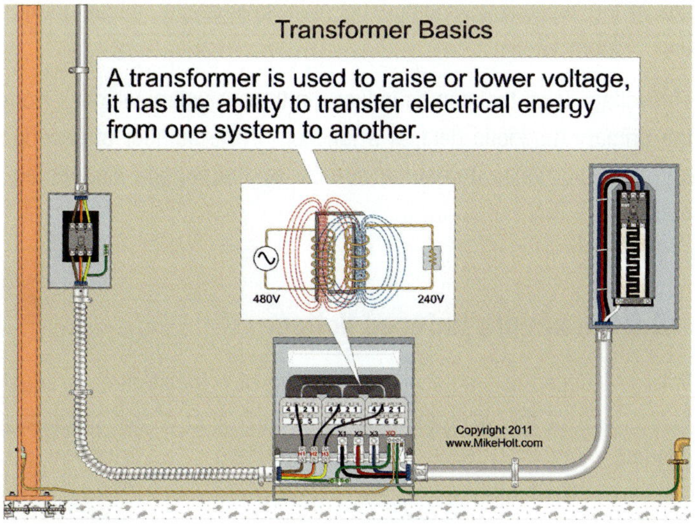

Figure 12–1

12.1 Transformer Basics

Primary versus Secondary

The transformer winding connected to the voltage source is called the "primary." The transformer winding connected to the load is called the "secondary." Transformers can be used to either raise or lower voltage. **Figure 12–2**

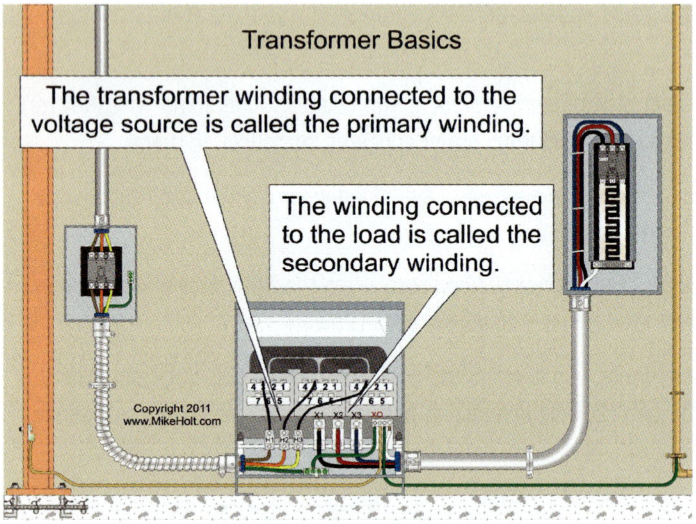

Figure 12–2

Mutual Induction

The energy transfer of a transformer is accomplished because the electromagnetic lines of force from the primary winding induce a voltage in the secondary winding. This process is called "mutual induction." **Figure 12–3**

The voltage level that can be induced in the secondary winding, from the primary magnetic field, is a function of the number of secondary conductor loops (turns) that are cut by the primary electromagnetic field.

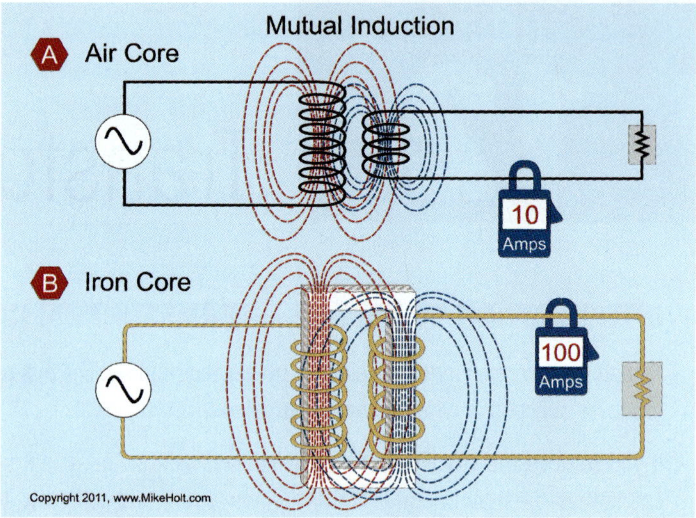

Figure 12–3

For example, if a transformer has three windings on the secondary and each secondary winding has 80V induced, the secondary voltage is 240V. **Figure 12–4**

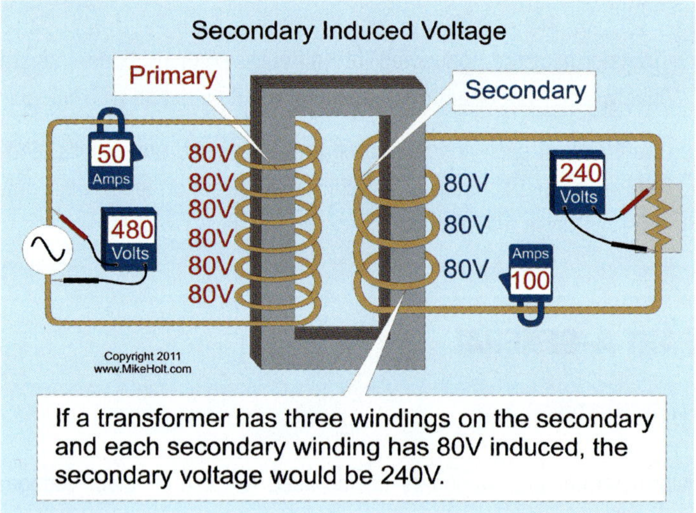

Figure 12–4

12.2 Secondary Induced Voltage

Voltage induced in the secondary winding of a transformer is equal to the sum of the voltages induced in each loop of the secondary winding.

The induced voltage in each loop of the secondary winding depends on the number of secondary conductor loops (turns), as compared to the number of primary turns. If both windings have the same number of turns, and if all of the magnetism set up by the primary passes through the secondary, the secondary will deliver the same voltage and power as the primary. This is how an isolation transformer works. **Figure 12–5**

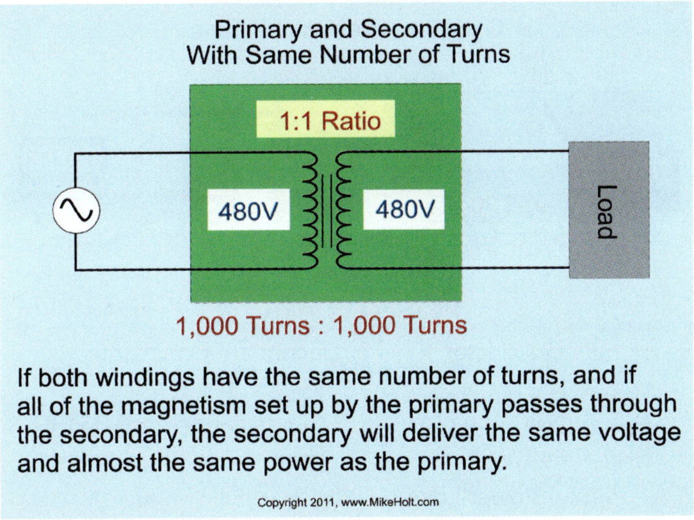

Figure 12–5

12.3 Autotransformers

Autotransformers use a single winding for both the primary and secondary.

Autotransformers are often used to increase or decrease the voltage by a small amount, such as to step the voltage up from 208V to 240V, or down from 240V to 208V. **Figure 12–6 and 12–7**

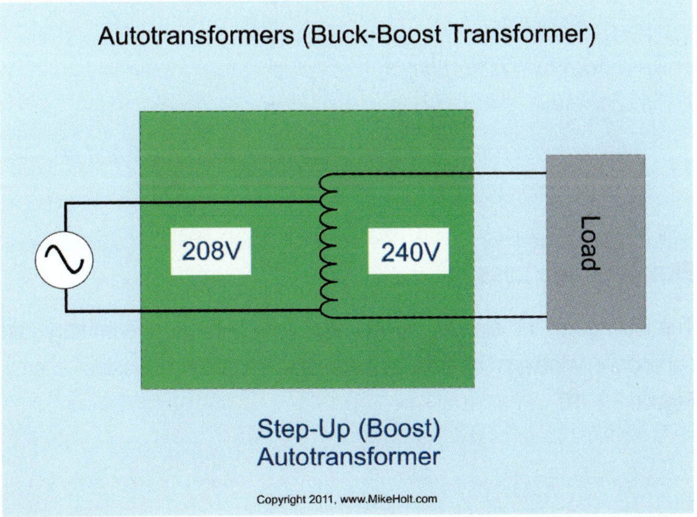

Figure 12–6

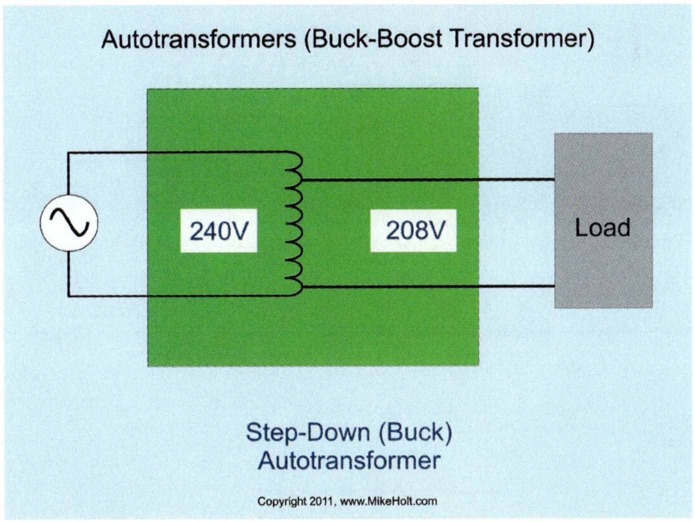

Figure 12–7

Step-Down Transformer

The secondary winding of a step-down transformer has fewer turns than the primary winding, resulting in a lower secondary voltage as compared to the primary.

Step-Up Transformer

The secondary winding of a step-up transformer has more turns than the primary winding, resulting in a higher secondary voltage as compared to the primary.

> **Author's Comment:** "Buck-Boost" transformers used to make small increases or decreases in voltage are sometimes autotransformers and are available with multiple voltage taps to meet the needs of various situations.

Autotransformers are not the only type of buck-boost transformers, however. A transformer can have separate primary and secondary windings connected together in configurations to provide small amounts of increase or decrease in the voltage level, and these are also called buck-boost transformers . **Figure 12–8**

Lack of Isolation

The disadvantage of an autotransformer is the lack of electrical isolation between the primary and secondary conductors. But they're often used because they're inexpensive.

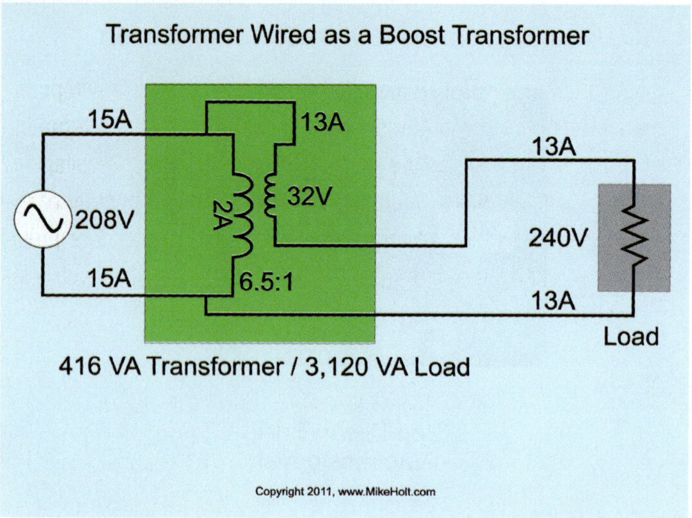

Figure 12–8

Figure 12–9

12.4 Power Losses

In an ideal transformer, all the primary power is transferred from the primary winding to the secondary winding. But real-world transformers have power losses because of conductor resistance, flux leakage, eddy currents, and hysteresis losses.

Conductor Resistance Loss

Transformer primary and secondary windings are generally made of many turns of copper. Conductor resistance is directly proportional to the length of a conductor and inversely proportional to the cross-sectional area of a conductor.

► Primary Power Loss Example

Question: *What's the primary conductor power loss of a 75 kVA transformer if the primary current rating is 90A and the winding has a resistance of 0.08 ohms?* **Figure 12–9**

(a) 400W (b) 648W (c) 1,150W (d) 1,300W

Answer: *(b) 648W*

Power = I^2 x R

$I = 90A$

$R = 0.08$ ohms

$P = 90A^2 \times 0.08$ ohms

$P = 648W$

► Secondary Power Loss Example

Question: *What's the secondary conductor power loss of a 75 kVA transformer if the secondary current rating is 208A and the winding has a resistance of 0.0313 ohms? See* **Figure 12–9**

(a) 1,354W (b) 1,800W (c) 2,100W (d) 2,700W

Answer: *(a) 1,354W*

Power = I^2 x R

$I = 208A$

$R = 0.0313$ ohms

$P = 208A^2 \times 0.0313$ ohms

$P = 1{,}354W$

The total power loss of the transformer is the primary and secondary losses combined: 648W + 1,354W = 2,002W

Flux Leakage Loss

The leakage of the electromagnetic flux lines between the primary and secondary windings of transformers also represents wasted energy. **Figure 12–10**

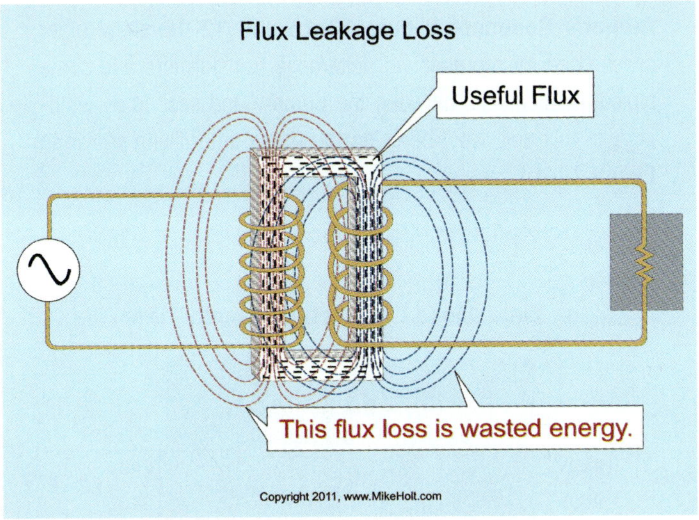

Figure 12–10

Eddy Currents

Iron is the only metal used for transformer cores because it's easy to magnetize. However, the expanding and collapsing electromagnetic field from alternating current induces a voltage in the iron core. These circulating eddy currents cause the core to heat up without any useful purpose. To reduce losses because of eddy currents, long laminated iron cores, separated by insulation (usually lacquer), are used. Figure 12–11

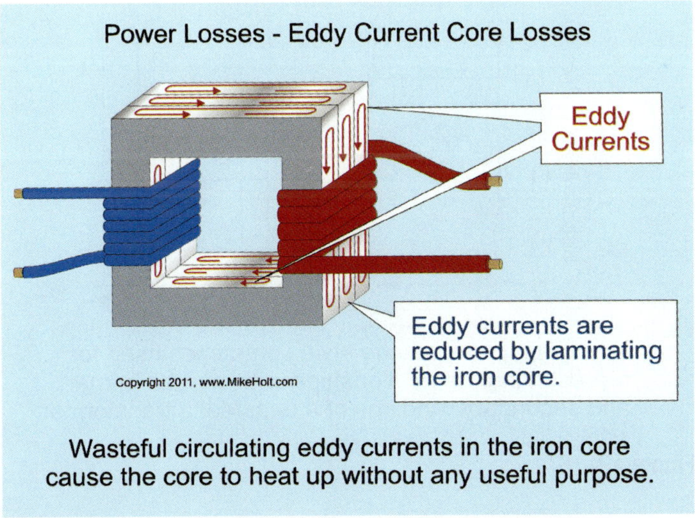

Figure 12–11

Hysteresis Losses

As current flows through a transformer, the iron core is temporarily magnetized by the electromagnetic field created by the alternating current. Each time the primary magnetic field expands and collapses, the core molecules realign themselves to the changing polarity of the electromagnetic field. The energy required to realign the core molecules to the changing electromagnetic field is called the hysteresis loss of the core. Figure 12–12

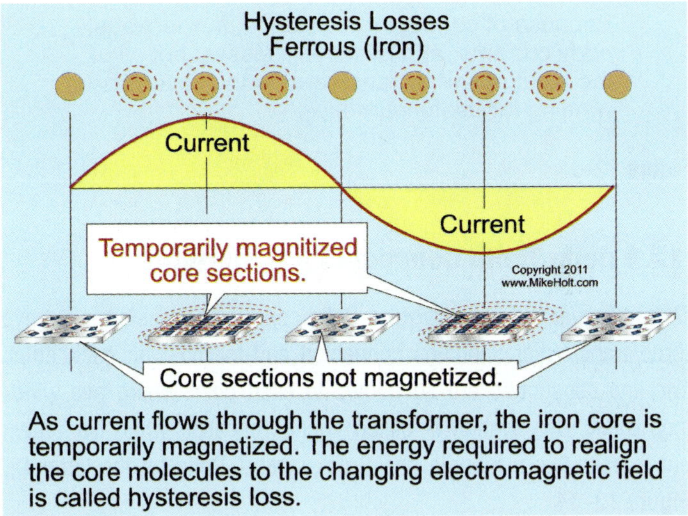

Figure 12–12

Hysteresis losses are directly proportional to the alternating-current frequency. The higher the frequency, the more times per second the molecules must realign. Hysteresis loss is one of the main reasons why iron-core transformers aren't used in applications involving high frequencies and nonlinear loads.

12.5 Efficiency

Because of conductor resistance, flux leakage, eddy currents, and hysteresis losses, not all of the input power is transferred to the secondary winding of a transformer for useful purposes. Transformer losses are typically quite small with efficiency approaching 95 to 97 percent. Thus, for most practical purposes, transformer efficiency can be ignored. Figure 12–13

The ratio between the output power and the input power is described as efficiency, and is found with the formula:

Efficiency = Output Power/Input Power

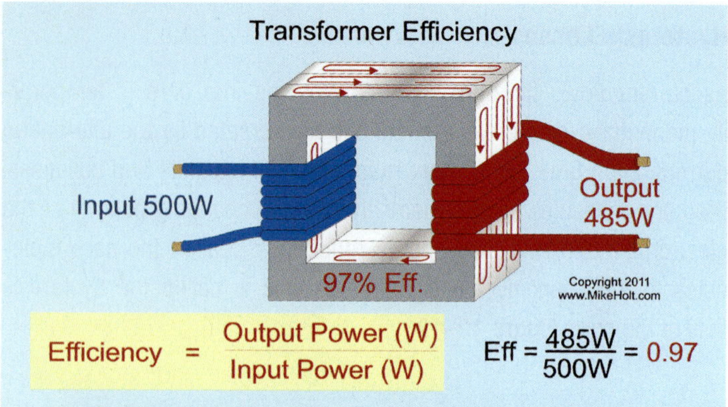

Because of conductor resistance, flux leakage, eddy currents, and hysteresis losses, not all of the input power is transferred to the secondary winding for useful purposes.

Figure 12–13

12.6 Delta/Delta Connected Transformers

Delta-Connected Transformer. Delta-connected transformers have three transformer windings connected end-to-end with each other. The line conductors are connected to each point where two windings meet. This system is called "Delta" because when it's drawn out it looks like a triangle (the Greek symbol Delta for the letter D). **Figure 12–14**

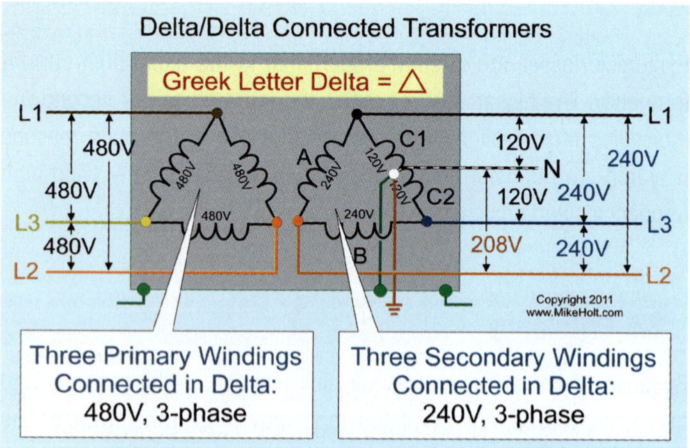

Delta-connected transformers have three windings connected end-to-end with each other.

Figure 12–14

Author's Comment: Figure 12–15 and 12–16 show other styles used for representing delta/delta transformers and some typical relationships between the primary and secondary windings. In this unit, we'll be using the Greek letter Delta shown in **Figure 12–14**

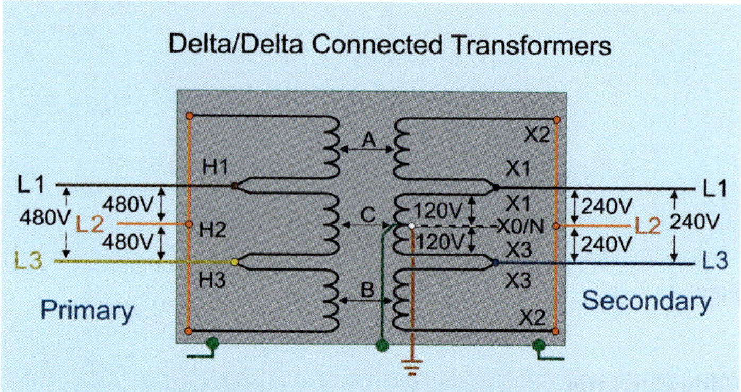

This graphic shows one style sometimes used for representing the relationships between the primary and secondary windings of a delta/delta transformer.

Copyright 2011, www.MikeHolt.com

Figure 12–15

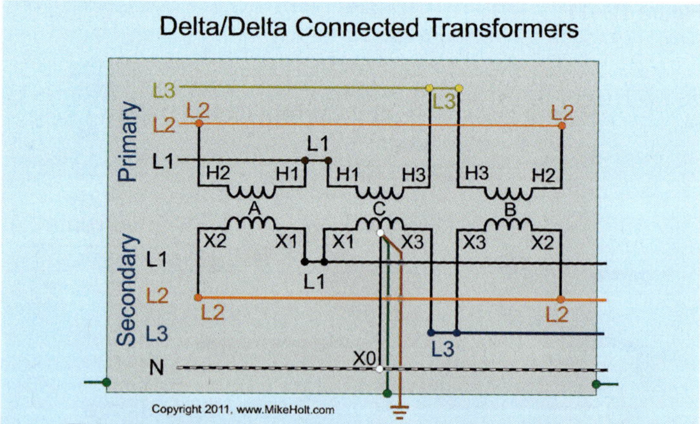

This graphic shows one style sometimes used for representing the relationships between the primary and secondary windings of a delta/delta transformer.

Figure 12–16

The transformer winding connected to the voltage source is called the "primary." The transformer winding connected to the load is called the "secondary." Transformers can be used to either raise or lower voltage. **Figure 12–17**

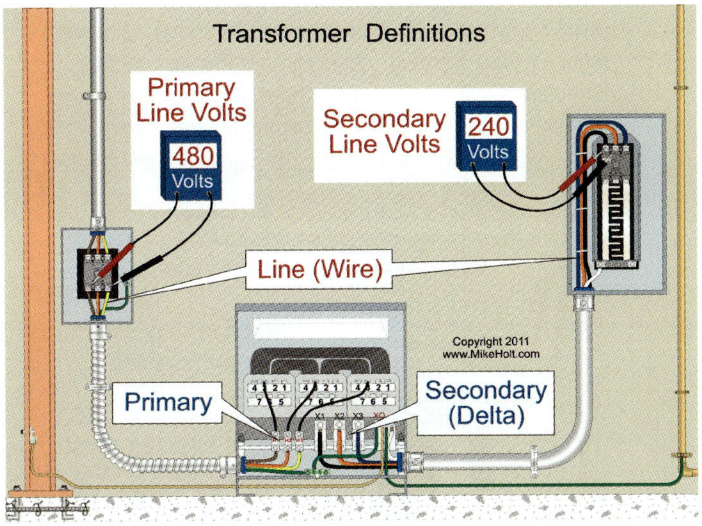

Figure 12–17

The voltage measured on the primary side is the primary line voltage while the voltage measured on the secondary side is referred to as the secondary line voltage. Figure 12–18

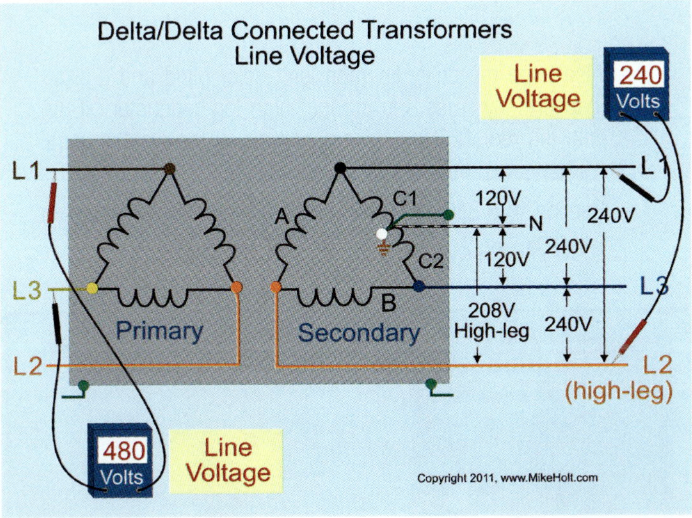

Figure 12–18

The terms "high-leg," "wild-leg," "stinger-leg" or "bastard-leg" are used to identify the conductor of a delta-connected system that has a voltage rating of 208V to ground. The high-leg voltage is the vector sum of the voltage of transformers A and C1, or transformers B and C2, which equal 120V x 1.732 = 208V for a 120/240V secondary. Figure 12–19

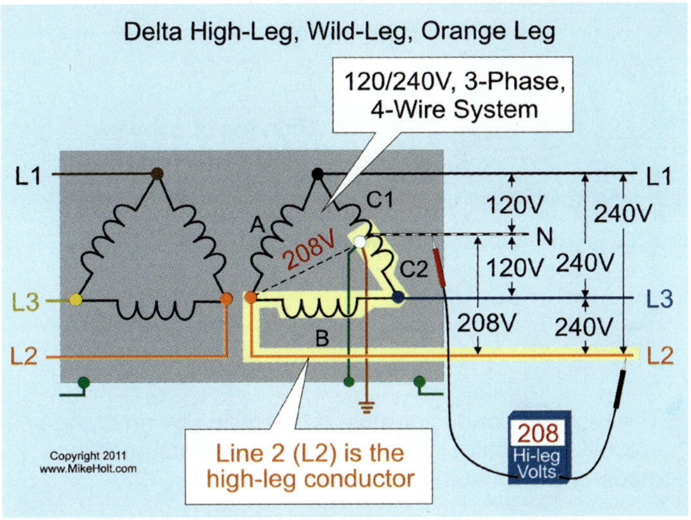

Figure 12–19

Author's Comment: The actual voltage of the high-leg is often less than the nominal system voltage because of voltage drop and transformer loading.

► High-Leg Voltage Example

Question: *What's the actual voltage of the high-leg if the delta-configured secondary is 115/230V, three-phase?*

(a) 115V *(b) 199V* *(c) 230V* *(d) 240V*

Answer: *(b) 199V*

High-Leg Voltage = (Line Voltage/2) x 1.732

High-Leg Voltage = 115V x 1.732

High-Leg Voltage = 199.18V

High-Leg Conductor Identification [110.15]

On a 4-wire, delta-connected, three-phase system, where the midpoint of one phase winding is grounded (high-leg system), the conductor with 208V to ground must be durably and permanently marked by an outer finish orange in color, or other effective means. Such identification must be placed at each point on the system where a connection is made if the neutral conductor is present [110.15, and 230.56]. Figure 12–20

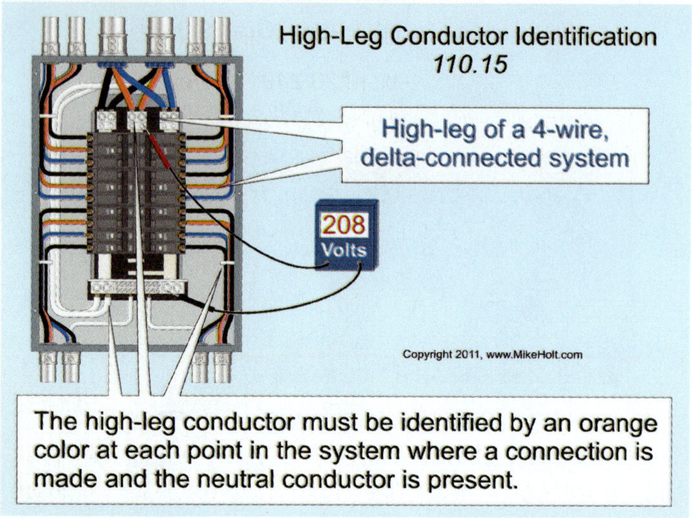

Figure 12–20

Author's Comments:

- The high-leg conductor is also called the "wild-leg," "stinger-leg," or "bastard-leg."
- Other important *NEC* rules relating to the high-leg are as follows:
  - Panelboards. Since 1975, panelboards supplied by a 4-wire, delta-connected, three-phase system must have the high-leg conductor terminate to the "B" phase of a panelboard [408.3(E)]. **Figure 12–21**

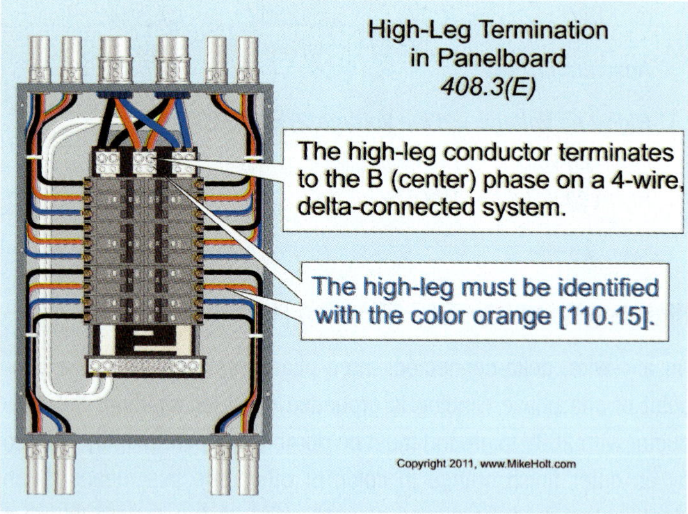

Figure 12–21

  - Disconnects. The *NEC* doesn't specify the termination location for the high-leg conductor in switch equipment (Switches Article 404), but the generally accepted practice is to terminate this conductor to the "B" phase.
  - Utility Equipment. The ANSI standard for meter equipment requires the high-leg conductor (208V to neutral) to terminate on the "C" (right) phase of the meter socket enclosure. This is because the demand meter needs 120V, and it gets that voltage from the "B" phase. **Figure 12–22**

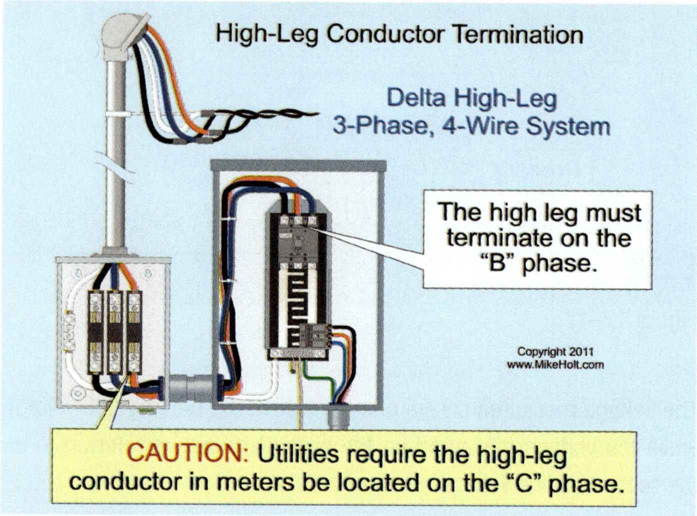

Figure 12–22

  - Also hope the utility lineman isn't color blind and doesn't inadvertently cross the "orange" high-leg conductor (208V) with the red (120V) service conductor at the weatherhead. It's happened before!
  - Section 408.3(F) requires panelboards to be field-marked with "Caution 208V to ground." **Figure 12–23**

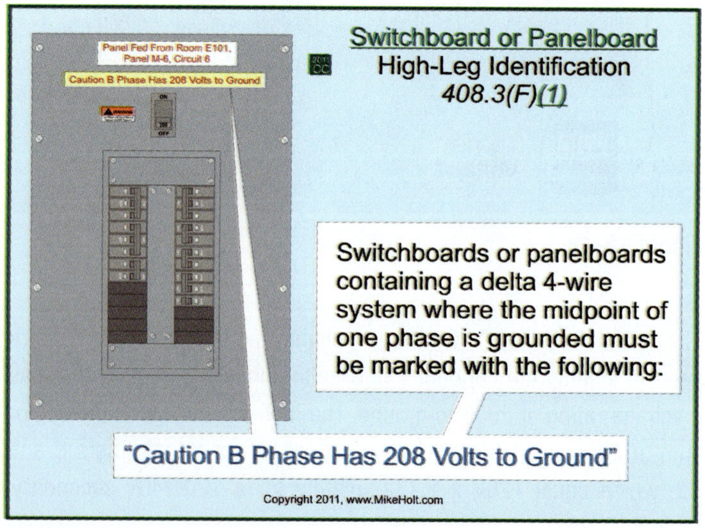

Figure 12–23

WARNING: *When replacing equipment in existing facilities that contain a high-leg conductor, care must be taken to ensure the high-leg conductor is replaced in the original location. Prior to 1975, the high-leg conductor was required to terminate on the "C" phase of panelboards and switchboards. Failure to re-terminate the high-leg in accordance with the existing installation can result in 120V circuits inadvertently connected to the 208V high-leg, with disastrous results.*

Ungrounded Conductors [215.12(C)]

Where the premises wiring system contains feeders supplied from more than one voltage system, each ungrounded conductor, at all termination, connection, and splice points, must be identified by phase or line and system. Identification can be by color coding, marking tape, tagging, or other means approved by the authority having jurisdiction. Such identification must be documented in a manner that's readily available, or it must be permanently posted at each panelboard. **Figure 12–24**

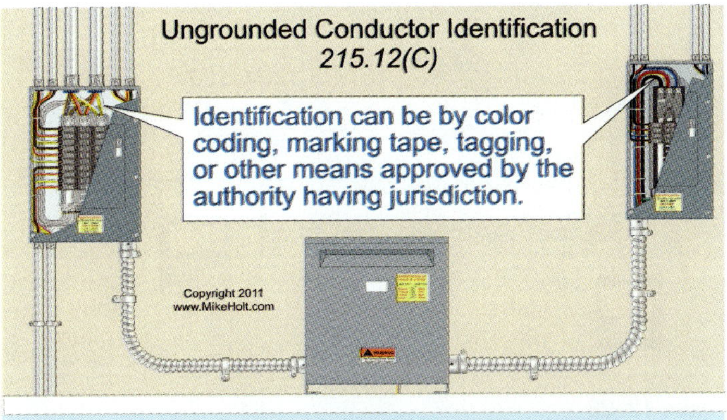

Where the premises wiring system contains feeders supplied from more than one voltage system, each ungrounded conductor must be identified by phase or line and system at termination, connection, and splice points.

Figure 12–24

Author's Comment: Although the *NEC* doesn't require a specific color code for ungrounded conductors, electricians often use the following color system for power and lighting conductor identification:

- 120/240V, single-phase–black, red, and white
- 120/208V, three-phase–black, red, blue, and white
- 120/240V, three-phase–black, orange, blue, and white
- 277/480V, three-phase–brown, orange, yellow, and gray; or, brown, purple, yellow, and gray
- Conductors with insulation that's green or green with one or more yellow stripes can't be used for an ungrounded or neutral conductor [250.119].

12.7 Delta/Wye Connected Transformers

Wye-Connected Transformers. Wye-configured transformers have one lead from each of three windings connected to a common point. The other leads from each of the windings are connected to the line conductors. A wye-configured secondary is often represented with a Y-shaped arrangement of the windings. **Figure 12–25**

Author's Comment: Figure 12–26 and 12–27 show other styles used for representing delta/wye transformers and some typical relationships between the primary and secondary windings.

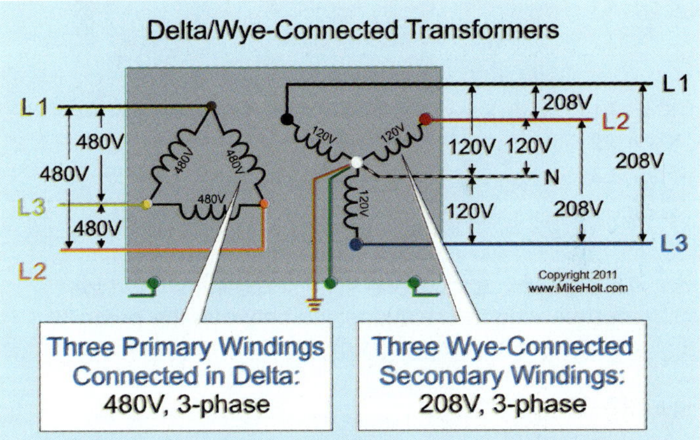

Wye-connected transformers have one lead from each of three windings connected to a common point.

Figure 12–25

The transformer winding connected to the voltage source is called the "primary." The transformer winding connected to the load is called the "secondary." Transformers can be used to either raise or lower voltage. **Figure 12–28**

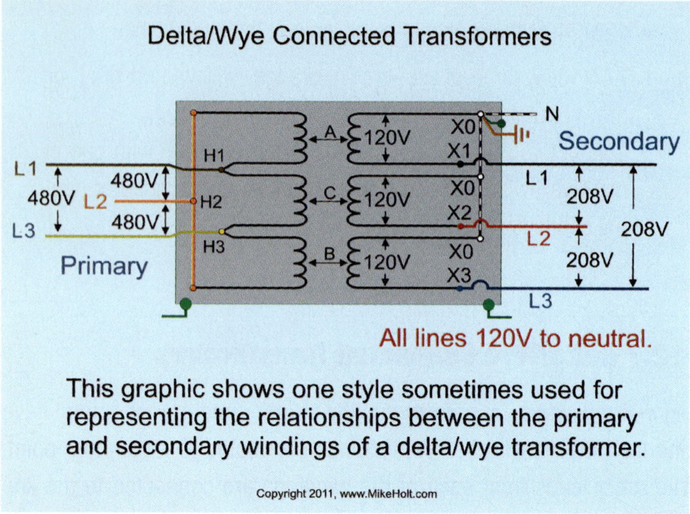

Figure 12–26

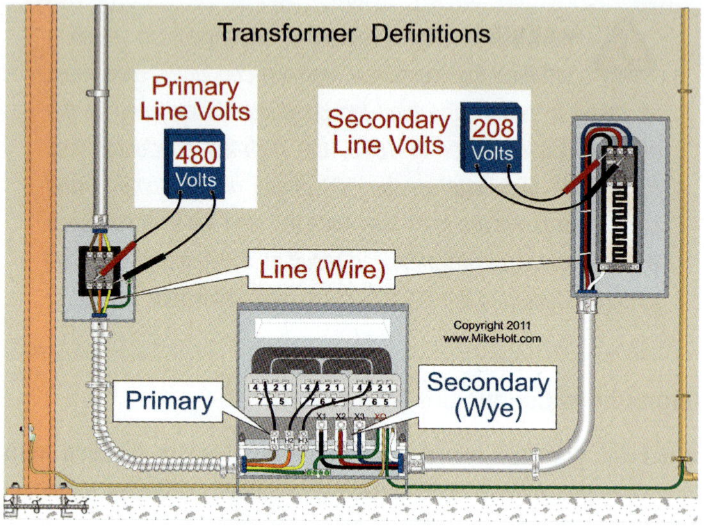

Figure 12–28

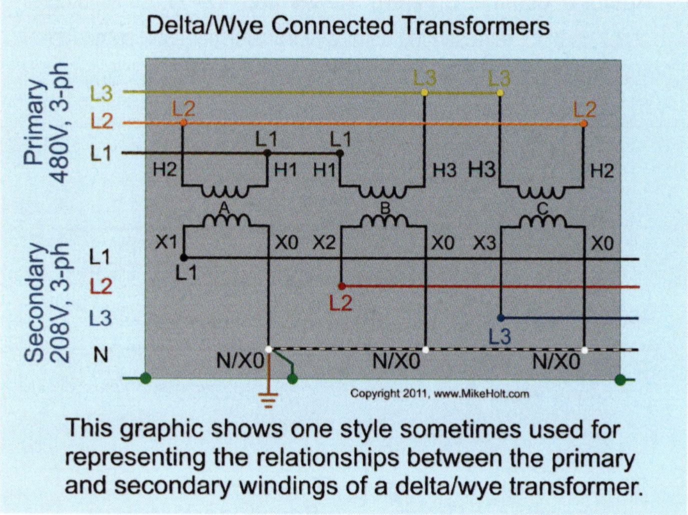

Figure 12–27

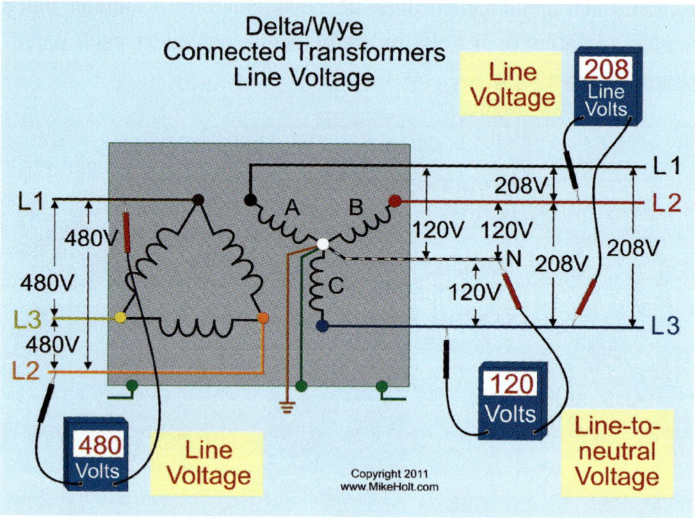

Figure 12–29

The voltage measured on the circuit conductors that supply the primary side is the primary line voltage while the voltage measured on the secondary side circuit conductors that feed the load is referred to as the secondary line voltage. **Figure 12–29**

12.8 Transformer Turns Ratio

The relationship of the primary winding voltage to the secondary winding voltage is the same as the relationship between the number of turns of wire on the primary and the number of turns on the secondary. This relationship is called the "turns ratio." **Figure 12–30**

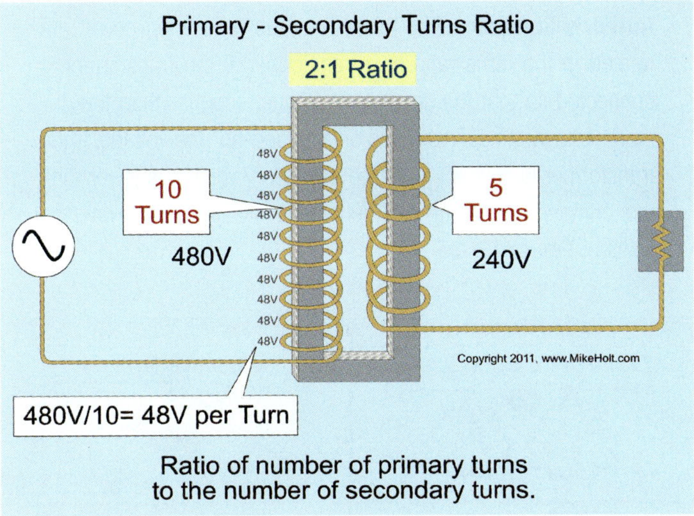

Figure 12–30

► Primary Voltage Example

Question: *What's the primary voltage of the transformer shown in* **Figure 12–31** *if the turns ratio is 10:1 and the secondary voltage is 12V?*

(a) 6V *(b) 24V* *(c) 48V* *(d) 120V*

Answer: *(d) 120V*

The turns ratio is 10:1. This means the voltage ratio is also 10:1. Since the secondary voltage is 12V, the primary voltage is 10 times larger, 12V x 10 Turns= 120V.

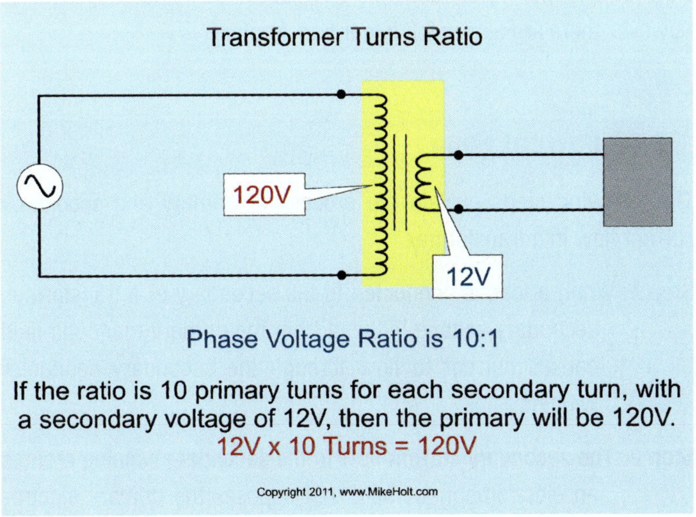

Figure 12–31

► Secondary Voltage Example

Question: *What's the secondary voltage of the transformer shown in* **Figure 12–32** *if the turns ratio is 5:1 and the primary voltage is 120V?*

(a) 6V *(b) 24V* *(c) 48V* *(d) 120V*

Answer: *(b) 24V*

Since the primary voltage is 120V, the secondary voltage is five times smaller, 120V/5 Turns = 24V.

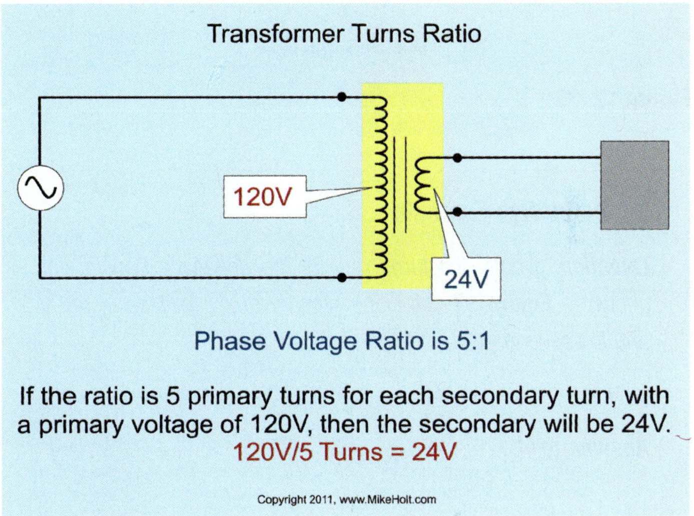

Figure 12–32

► Delta/Delta Example

Question: *What's the turns ratio of the delta/delta transformer shown in* **Figure 12–33** *if the primary phase voltage is 480V and the secondary is 240V?*

(a) 4:1 *(b) 1:4* *(c) 2:1* *(d) 1:2*

Answer: *(c) 2:1*

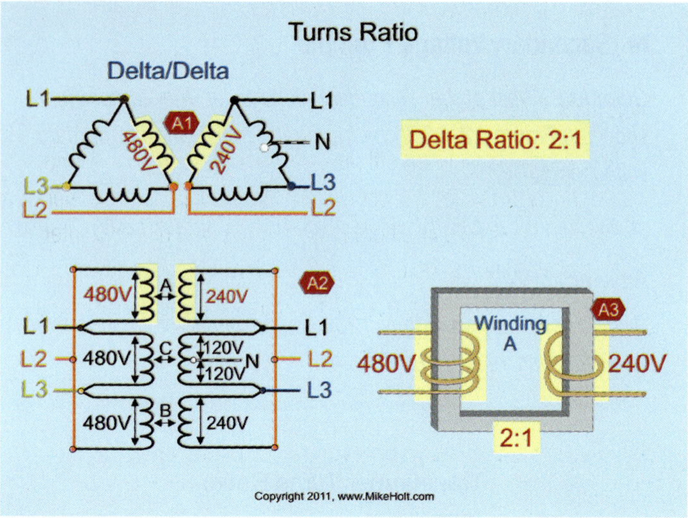

Figure 12–33

Author's Comment: The terms "step-up" and "step-down" are related to the turns ratio of a transformer. If the transformer is connected so that the secondary voltage is higher than the primary voltage, it has increased or "stepped-up" the voltage. If the transformer is connected so the secondary voltage is lower than the primary voltage, it has decreased or "stepped-down" the voltage. **Figure 12–35**

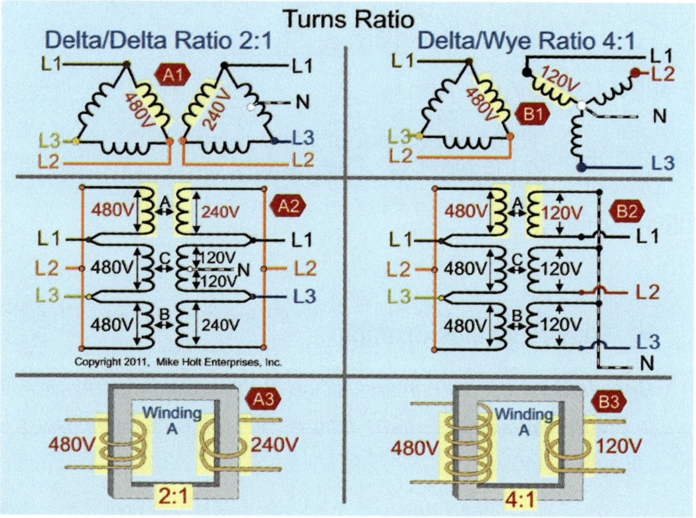

Figure 12–35

▶ Delta/Wye Example

Question: *What's the turns ratio of the delta/wye transformer shown in* **Figure 12–34** *if the primary phase voltage is 480V and the secondary is 120V?*

(a) 4:1 *(b) 1:4* *(c) 2:1* *(d) 1:2*

Answer: *(a) 4:1*

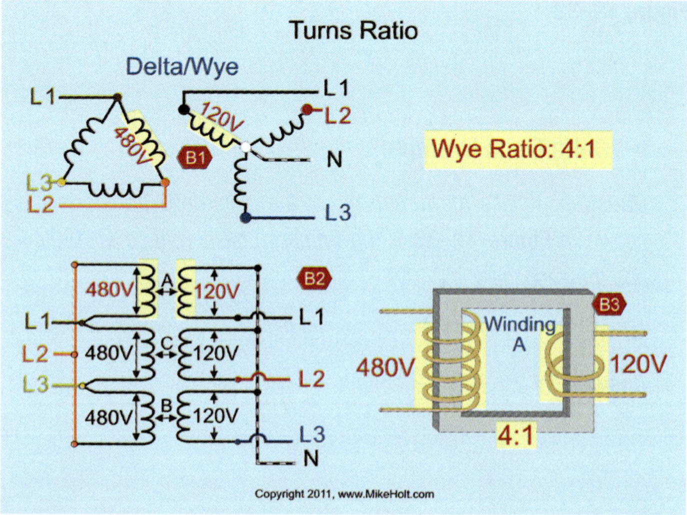

Figure 12–34

12.9 Transformer kVA Rating

Transformers are rated in kilovolt-amperes (kVA), where 1 kilovolt-ampere = 1,000 volt-amperes (VA). **Figure 12–36** lists common standard transformer sizes used in commercial-industrial applications. However, there are also much larger transformers.

12.10 Current Flow

The following steps explain the process of primary and secondary current flow in a transformer.

Step 1: When a load is connected to the secondary of a transformer, secondary voltage induced from the primary magnetic field causes current to flow through the secondary conductor winding.

Step 2: The secondary current flow in the secondary winding creates an electromagnetic field that opposes the primary electromagnetic field.

Standard Transformer Ratings - In kVA	
Single-Phase	Three-Phase
3	15
5	30
10	45
15	75
25	112.5
37.5	150
50	225
75	300
100	500
167	750
250	1,000
333	1,500
500	2,000
833	2,500

Figure 12–36

Step 3: The flux lines from the secondary magnetic field effectively reduce the strength of the primary flux lines, and as a result, less CEMF is generated in the primary winding conductors. With less CEMF to oppose the primary applied voltage, the primary current increases in direct proportion to the secondary current. **Figure 12–37**

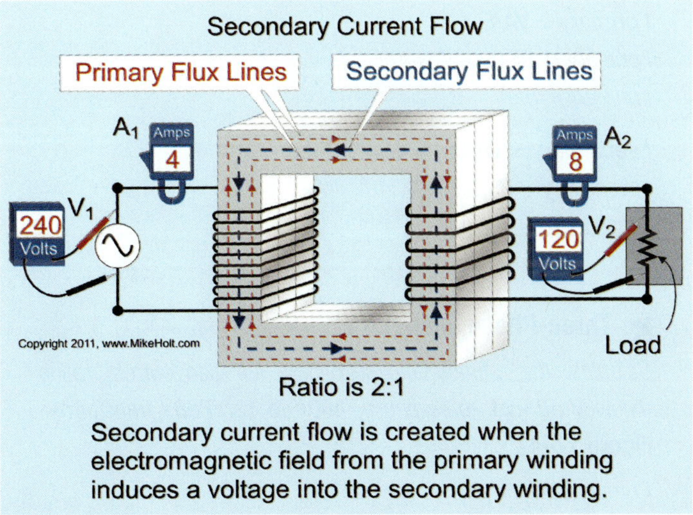

Figure 12–37

12.11 Line Currents

The line current of a transformer can be calculated using the appropriate formula below for single-phase or three-phase:

Single-phase: I = VA/E
Three-phase: I = VA/(E x 1.732)

Author's Comments:

- Delta/Delta connected three-phase transformers (**Figure 12–38**) and Delta/Wye connected three-phase transformers (**Figure 12–39**) have different turns ratios and different internal voltage and current relationships, but the line current can be calculated in each type of transformer using the formula above.

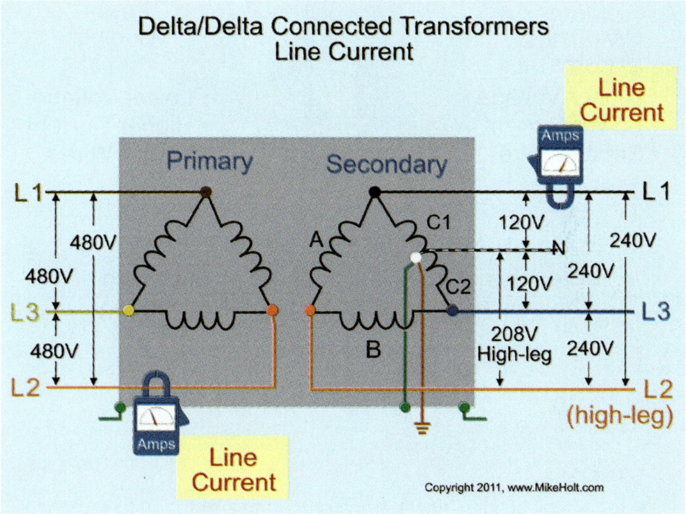

Figure 12–38

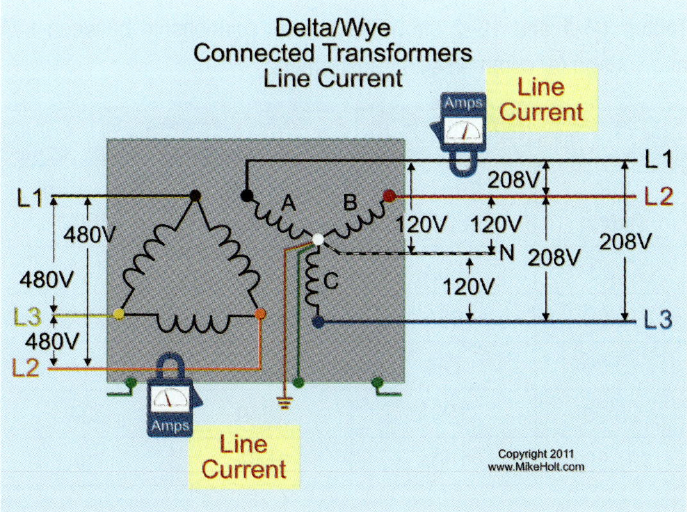

Figure 12–39

- The primary and secondary line currents are inversely proportional to the voltage ratio of the transformer. This means that the winding with the greatest number of turns has a higher voltage and lower current than the winding with the least number of turns, which has a lower voltage and higher current. **Figure 12–40**

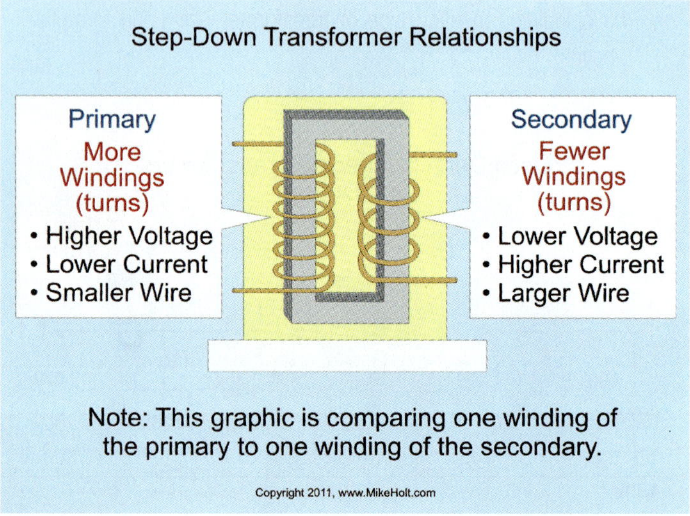

Figure 12–40

- In a typical step-down transformer, the primary has more windings, higher voltage, lower current, and smaller wire. The secondary has fewer windings, lower voltage, higher current, and larger wire. See **Figure 12–40**

Tables 12–1 and 12–2 show the current relationship between kVA and voltage for common size transformers:

Table 12–1. Single-Phase Transformers I = VA/E

kVA Rating	Current at 208V	Current at 240V	Current at 480V
7.50	36A	31A	16A
10.00	48A	42A	21A
15.00	72A	63A	31A
25.00	120A	104A	52A
37.50	180A	156A	78A

Table 12–2. Three-Phase Transformers I = VA/(E x √3)

kVA Rating	Current at 208V	Current at 240V	Current at 480V
15.00	42A	36A	18A
22.50	63A	54A	27A
30.00	83A	72A	36A
37.50	104A	90A	45A
45.00	125A	108A	54A
50.00	139A	120A	60A
75.00	208A	180A	90A
112.50	313A	271A	135A

► Single-Phase Example

Question: *What's the maximum primary and secondary full load line current for a 480V to 240V, 25 kVA single-phase transformer?* **Figure 12–41**

(a) 52/104A (b) 104/52A (c) 104/208A (d) 208/104A

Answer: *(a) 52/104A*

I primary = VA/E
I primary = 25,000 VA/480V
I primary = 52A

I secondary = VA/E
I secondary = 25,000 VA/240V
I secondary = 104A

► Three-Phase Example 1

Calculate the primary and secondary full load current rating for a 37.50 kVA, three-phase, 480V to 120/208V transformer. **Figure 12–42**

Primary Current
I = VA/(E x 1.732)
I = 37,500 VA/(480V x 1.732)
I = 45A

Secondary Current
I = VA/(E x 1.732)
I = 37,500 VA/(208V x 1.732)
I = 104A

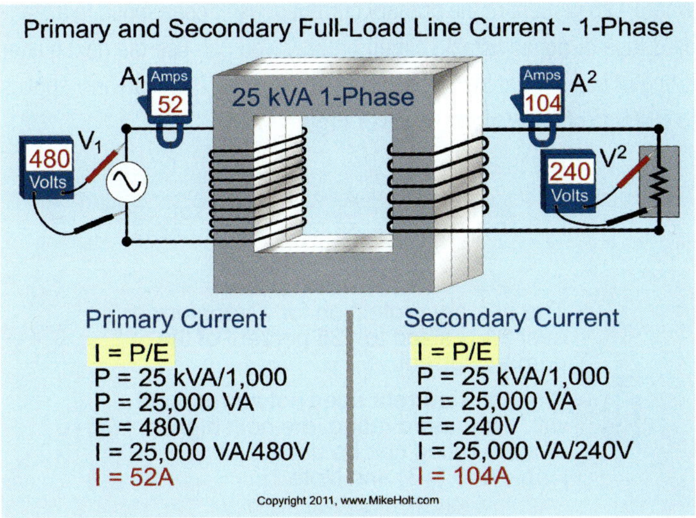

Figure 12–41

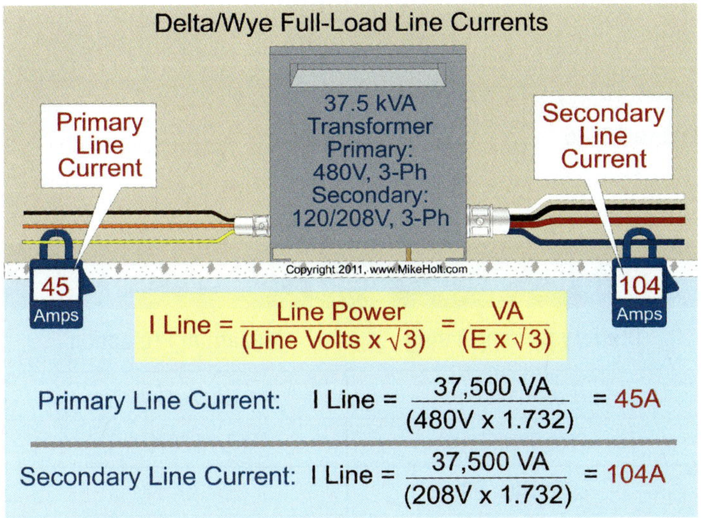

Figure 12–42

▶ Three-Phase Example 2

Calculate the primary and secondary full load current rating for a 45 kVA, three-phase, 480V to 120/208V transformer. **Figure 12–43**

Primary Current

I = VA/(E x 1.732)

I = 45,000 VA/(480V x 1.732)

I = 54A

Secondary Current

I = VA/(E x 1.732)

I = 45,000 VA/(208V x 1.732)

I = 125A

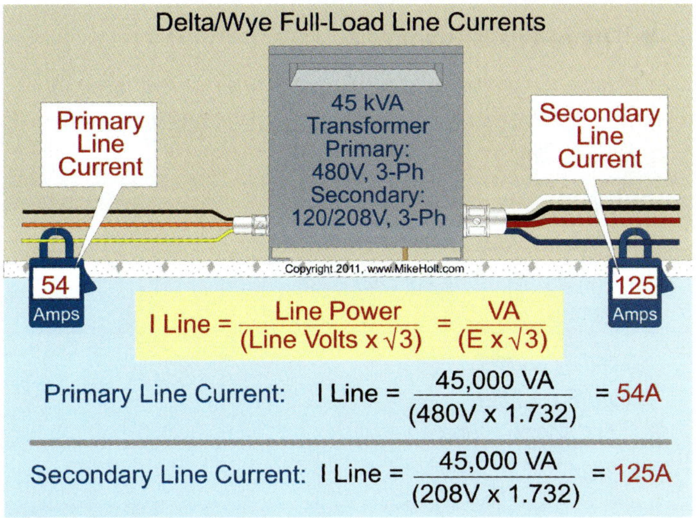

Figure 12–43

▶ Three-Phase Example 3

Calculate the primary and secondary full load current rating for a 75 kVA, three-phase, 480V to 120/208V transformer. **Figure 12–44**

Primary Current

I = VA/(E x 1.732)

I = 75,000 VA/(480V x 1.732)

I = 90A

Secondary Current

I = VA/(E x 1.732)

I = 75,000 VA/(208V x 1.732)

I = 208A

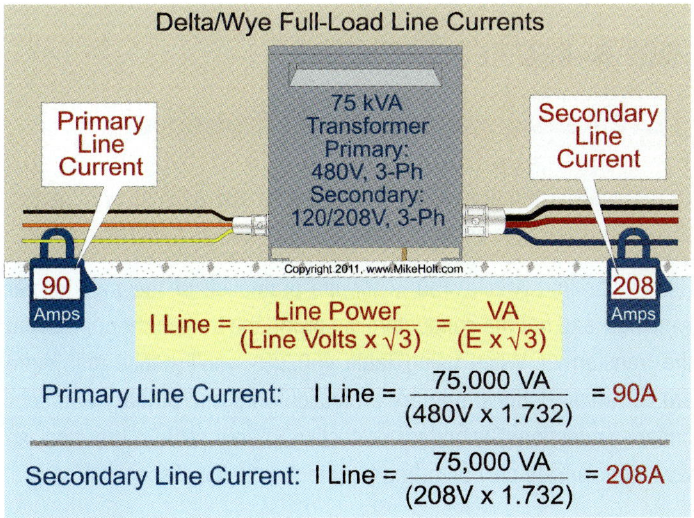

Figure 12–44

▶ Three-Phase Example 4

Calculate the primary and secondary full load current rating for a 112.50 kVA, three-phase, 480V to 120/208V transformer. **Figure 12–45**

Primary Current

I = VA/(E x 1.732)

I = 112,500 VA/(480V x 1.732)

I = 135A

Secondary Current

I = VA/(E x 1.732)

I = 112,500 VA/(208V x 1.732)

I = 313A

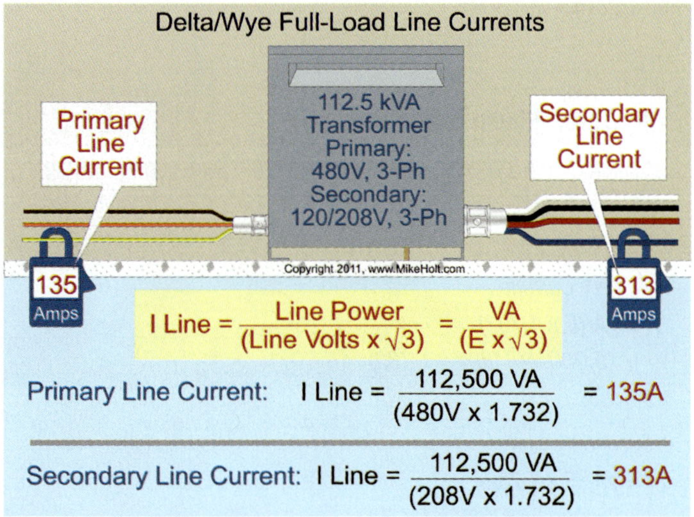

Figure 12–445

PART B—*NEC* REQUIREMENTS

12.12 Transformer Overcurrent Protection

To protect the primary winding of a transformer against overcurrent, use the percentages listed in Table 450.3(B) and its applicable notes.

Remember that Article 450 is for the protection of the transformer windings, and not the conductors supplying the transformer or leaving the transformer. When using Table 450.3(B), you'll notice that there are two main options: primary protection only, and primary *and* secondary protection. Secondary protection is very seldom required, so we'll concentrate only on primary protection in this discussion.

Where 125 percent of the primary current doesn't correspond to a standard fuse or nonadjustable circuit breaker, you can use the next higher rating of overcurrent device, as listed in 240.6(A). This note only applies to currents of 9A or more, however. **Figure 12–46**

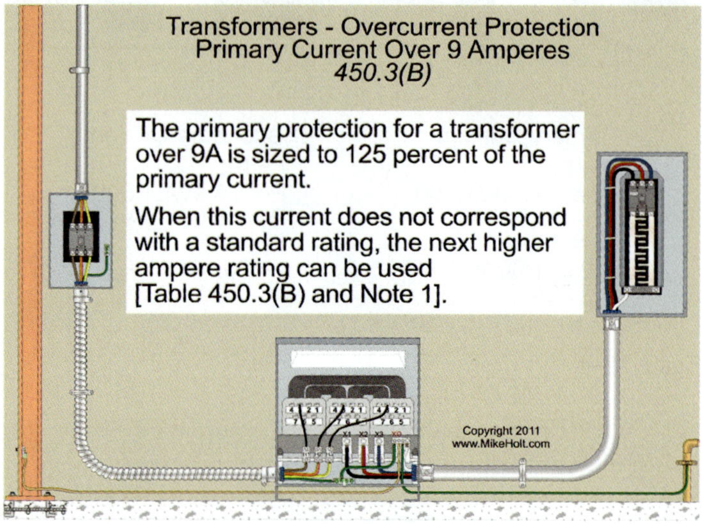

Figure 12–46

Table 450.3(B) Primary Protection Only

Primary Current Rating	Maximum Protection
9A or More	125%, Note 1
Less Than 9A	167%
Less Than 2A	300%

Note 1. Where 125 percent of the primary current doesn't correspond to a standard rating of a fuse or nonadjustable circuit breaker, the next higher rating is permitted [240.6(A)].

▶ Primary Overcurrent Protection Example 1

Question: *What's the maximum primary overcurrent device rating for a 750 VA, single-phase, 480V transformer?*

(a) 2A (b) 4A (c) 6A (d) 10A

Answer: *(b) 4A*

I Line = 750 VA/480V = 1.56A

1.56A x 3.00 = 4.68A, use 4A, [240.6(A) and Table 450.3(B)]

(The Note 1 provision for rounding only applies for primary currents over 9A)

► Primary Overcurrent Protection Example 2

Question: *What's the maximum primary overcurrent device rating for a 2 kVA, single-phase, 240V transformer?*

(a) 4A (b) 5A (c) 13A (d) 17A

Answer: *(c) 13A*

I Line = 2,000 VA/240V = 8.33A

8.33 x 1.67 = 13.92A, use 13A, [240.6(A) and Table 450.3(B)]

(The Note 1 provision for rounding only applies for primary currents over 9A)

► Primary Overcurrent Protection Example 3

Question: *What's the maximum primary overcurrent device rating for a 45 kVA, three-phase, 480V transformer?* **Figure 12–47**

(a) 40A (b) 50A (c) 60A (d) 70A

Answer: *(d) 70A*

I Line = 45,000 VA/(480V x 1.732) = 54A

54A x 1.25 = 68A, next size up 70A, [240.6(A) and Table 450.3(B), Note 1]

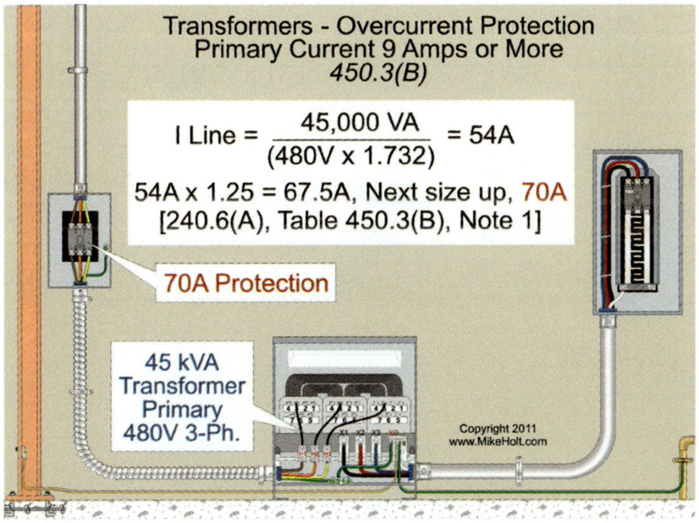

Figure 12–47

► Primary Overcurrent Protection Example 4

Question: *What's the maximum primary overcurrent device rating for a 75 kVA, three-phase, 480V transformer?* **Figure 12–48**

(a) 70A (b) 100A (c) 110A (d) 125A

Answer: *(d) 125A*

I Line =75,000 VA/(480V x 1.732) = 90A

90A x 1.25 = 113A, next size up 125A, [240.6(A) and Table 450.3(B), Note 1]

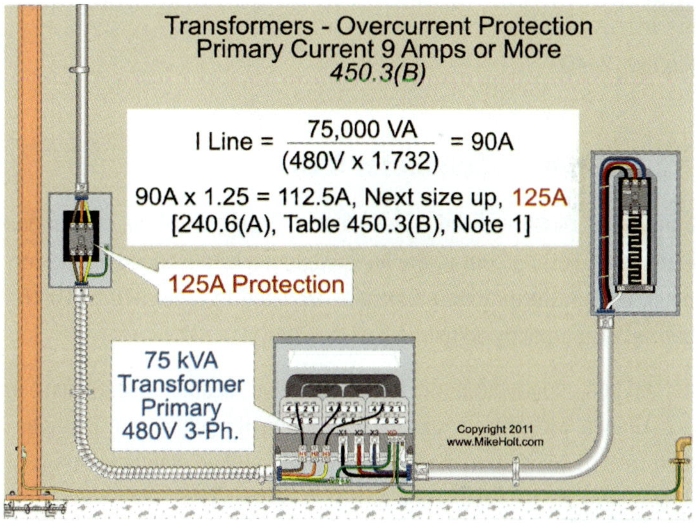

Figure 12–48

► Primary Overcurrent Protection Example 5

Question: *What's the maximum primary overcurrent device rating for a 112.50 kVA, three-phase, 480V transformer?* **Figure 12–49**

(a) 70A (b) 100A (c) 175A (d) 200A

Answer: *(c) 175A*

I Line = 112,500 VA/(480V x 1.732) = 135A

135A x 1.25 = 169A, next size up 175A, [240.6(A) and Table 450.3(B), Note 1]

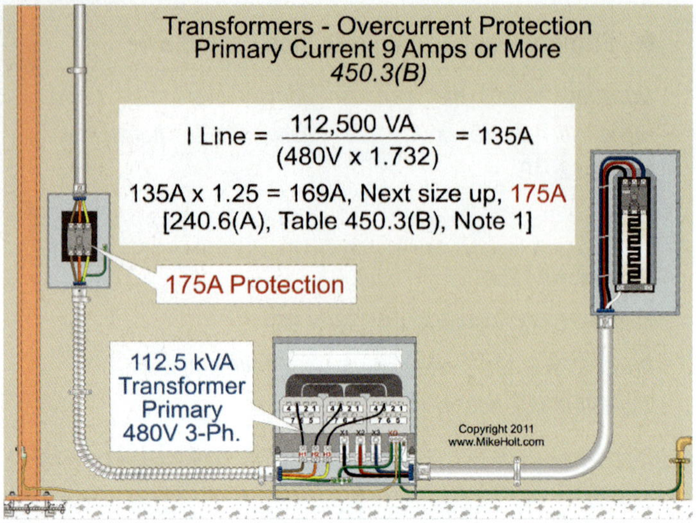

Figure 12–49

12.13 Primary Conductor Sizing

Conductors must be sized no less than 125 percent of the continuous loads, plus 100 percent of the noncontinuous loads, based on the terminal temperature rating ampacities as listed in Table 310.15(B)(16), before any ampacity adjustment [210.19(A)(1)].

In addition, conductors must be protected against overcurrent in accordance with their ampacity after ampacity adjustment, as specified in 310.15 [240.4] However, the next higher standard rating of overcurrent device (above the ampacity of the conductors being protected) is permitted, provided the overcurrent device rating doesn't exceed 800A [240.4(B)].

► Primary Conductor Sizing Example 1

Question: *What size primary conductor could be used for a 45 kVA, three-phase, 480V transformer, where primary overcurrent is sized at 70A?* **Figure 12–50**

(a) 6 AWG *(b) 4 AWG* *(c) 3 AWG* *(d) 2 AWG*

Answer: *(b) 4 AWG*

Step 1: Size the primary conductor at 125% of the primary current rating.

I Line = 45,000 VA/(480V x 1.732) = 54A

54A x 1.25 = 68A, 4 AWG has an ampacity of 85A [110.14(C)(1) and Table 310.15(B)(16)]

Step 2: Verify that the conductors are protected in accordance with their ampacities [240.4].

4 AWG is rated 85A at 75°C, and it's permitted to be protected by the 70A primary overcurrent device.

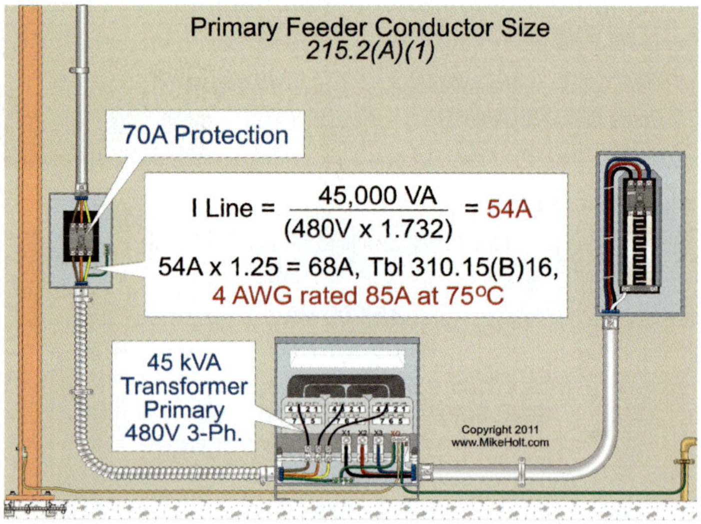

Figure 12–50

► Primary Conductor Sizing Example 2

Question: *What size primary conductor could be used for a 75 kVA, three-phase, 480V transformer, where primary overcurrent is sized at 125A?* **Figure 12–51**

(a) 6 AWG (b) 4 AWG (c) 3 AWG (d) 2 AWG

Answer: *(d) 2 AWG*

Step 1: Size the primary conductor at 125% of the primary current rating.

I Line =75,000 VA/(480V x 1.732) = 90A

90A x 1.25 = 113A, 2 AWG has an ampacity of 115A at 75°C [110.14(C)(1) and Table 310.15(B)(16)]

Step 2: Verify that the conductors are protected in accordance with their ampacities [240.4].

2 AWG has an ampacity of 115A at 75°C, and it's permitted to be protected by the 125A primary overcurrent device [240.4(B)].

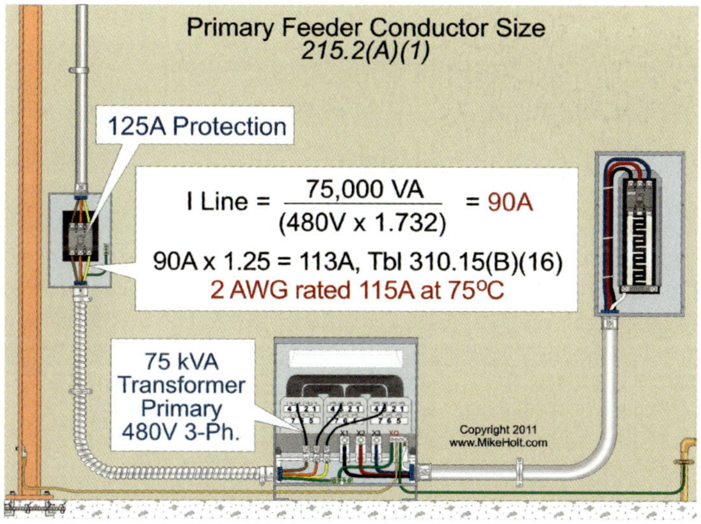

Figure 12–51

► Primary Conductor Sizing Example 3

Question: *What size primary conductor could be used for a 112.50 kVA, three-phase, 480V transformer, where primary overcurrent is sized at 175A?* **Figure 12–52**

(a) 1/0 AWG (b) 2/0 AWG (c) 3/0 AWG (d) 4/0 AWG

Answer: *(b) 2/0 AWG*

Step 1: Size the primary conductor at 125% of the primary current rating.

I Line = 112,500 VA/(480V x 1.732) = 135A

135A x 1.25 = 169A, 2/0 AWG has an ampacity of 175A [110.14(C)(1) and Table 310.15(B)(16)]

Step 2: Verify that the conductors are protected in accordance with their ampacities [240.4].

2/0 AWG is rated 175A at 75°C, and it's permitted to be protected by the 175A primary overcurrent device.

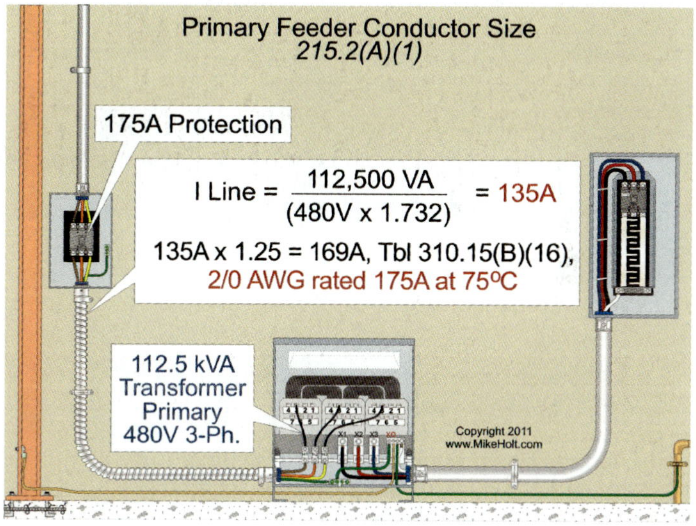

Figure 12–52

12.14 Secondary Conductor Sizing

The ampacity of the secondary conductor must not be less than the rating of the device supplied by the secondary conductors or the overcurrent device at the termination of the secondary conductors [240.21(C)(2)]. Assume the secondary conductors are intended to carry the full capacity of the transformer continuously.

Step 1: Determine the rating of the device supplied by the secondary conductors at 125 percent of the secondary rating.

Step 2: Size the secondary conductors so that they have an ampacity of "not less" than the device rating supplied by the secondary conductors. A panelboard must always have overcurrent protection within the panelboard or at any point on the supply side. **Figure 12–53** When a panelboard is supplied by a transformer, it must have overcurrent protection located on the secondary side of the transformer. **Figure 12–54**

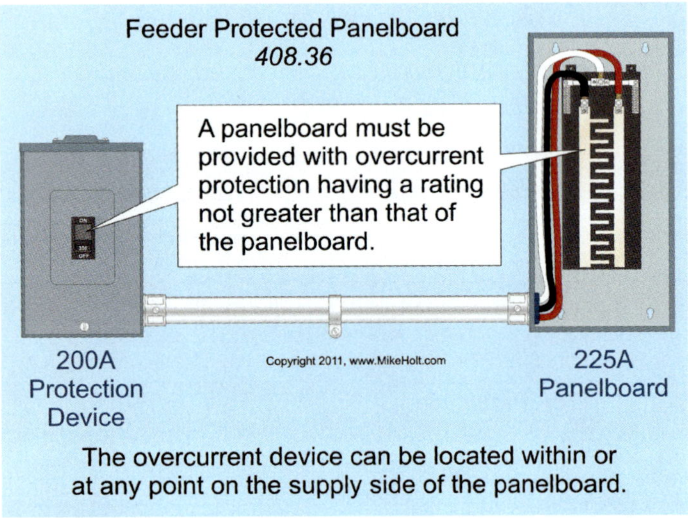

Figure 12–53

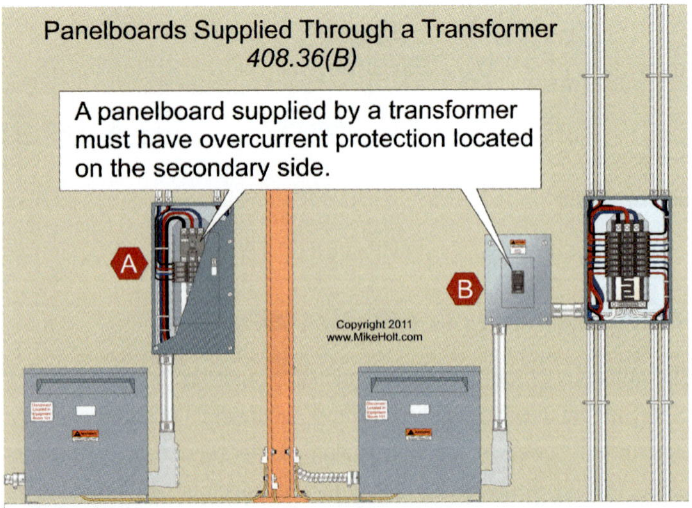

Figure 12–54

► Secondary Conductor Sizing Example 1

Question: *What size secondary conductor could be used for a 45 kVA, three-phase, 480-120/208V transformer?*

(a) 2 AWG *(b) 1 AWG* *(c) 1/0 AWG* *(d) 2/0 AWG*

Answer: *(d) 2/0 AWG*

Step 1: Determine the secondary current rating. **Figure 12–55**

I = VA/(E x 1.732)

I = 45,000 VA/(208V x 1.732)

I = 125A

Step 2: Size the secondary device rating at 125% of the secondary current rating. **Figure 12–56**

125A x 1.25 = 156A, 175A overcurrent device

Step 3: Size the secondary conductor where it has an ampacity of "not less" than the rating of the secondary device [240.21(C)(2)].

2/0 AWG has an ampacity of 175A at 75°C [110.14(C)(1) and Table 310.15(B)(16)].

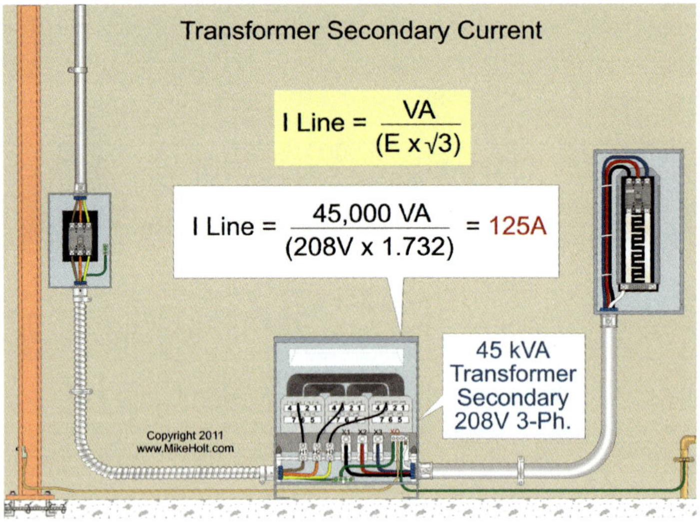

Figure 12–55

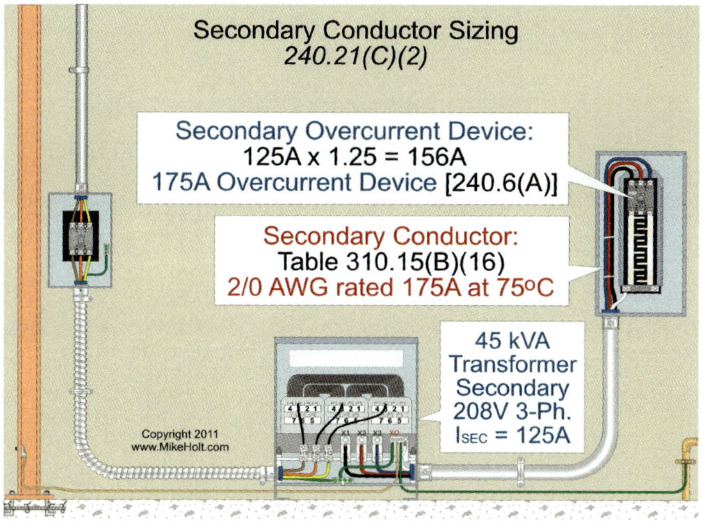

Figure 12–56

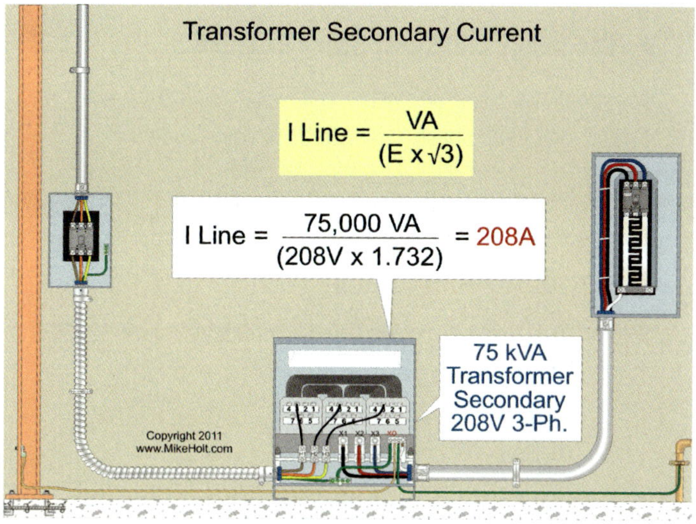

Figure 12–57

▶ Secondary Conductor Sizing Example 2

Question: *What size secondary conductor could be used for a 75 kVA, three-phase, 480-120/208V transformer?*

(a) 3/0 AWG (b) 4/0 AWG (c) 350 kcmil (d) 500 kcmil

Answer: *(c) 350 kcmil*

Step 1: Determine the secondary current rating. **Figure 12–57**

I = VA/(E x 1.732)

I = 75,000 VA/(208V x 1.732)

I = 208A

Step 2: Size the secondary device rating at 125% of the secondary current rating. **Figure 12–58**

208A x 1.25 = 260A, round up to a 300A overcurrent device

Step 3: Size the secondary conductor where it has an ampacity of "not less" than the rating of the secondary device [240.21(C)(2)].

350 kcmil has an ampacity of 310A at 75°C [110.14(C)(1) and Table 310.15(B)(16)].

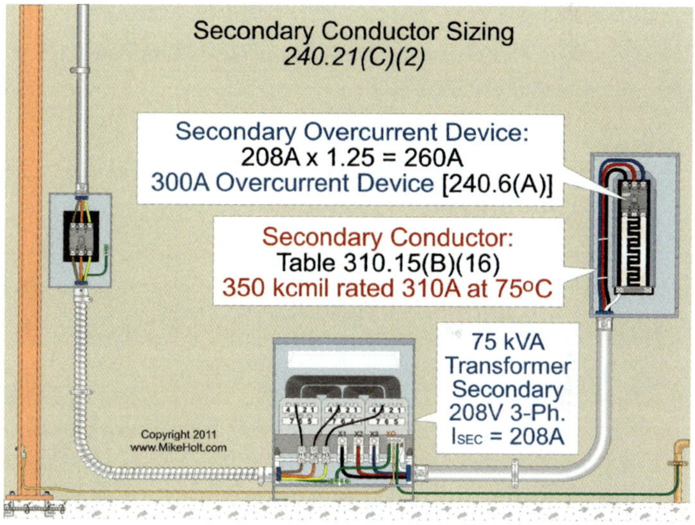

Figure 12–58

▶ Secondary Conductor Sizing Example 3

Question: *What size secondary conductor could be usedfor a 112.50 kVA, three-phase, 480-120/208V transformer?*

(a) Two parallel 1/0 AWG *(b) Two parallel 2/0 AWG*
(c) Two parallel 3/0 AWG *(d) Two parallel 4/0 AWG*

Answer: *(c) Two parallel 3/0 AWG*

Step 1: Determine the secondary current rating. **Figure 12–59**

I = VA/(E x 1.732)

I = 112,500 VA/(208V x 1.732)

I = 313A

Step 2: Size the secondary device rating at 125% of the secondary current rating. **Figure 12–60**

313A x 1.25 = 391A, 400A overcurrent device

Step 3: Size the secondary conductors where they have an ampacity of "not less" than the rating of the secondary device [240.21(C)(2)].

Two sets of parallel 3/0 AWG conductors, each with and ampacity of 200A at 75°C [110.14(C)(1) and Table 310.15(B)(16)]

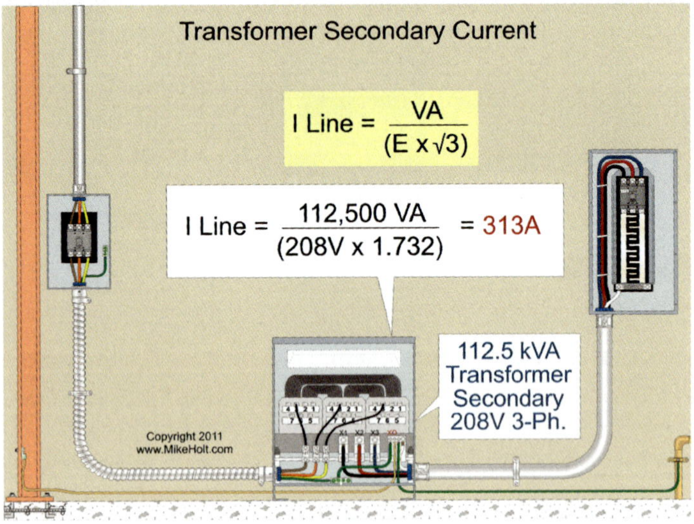

Figure 12–59

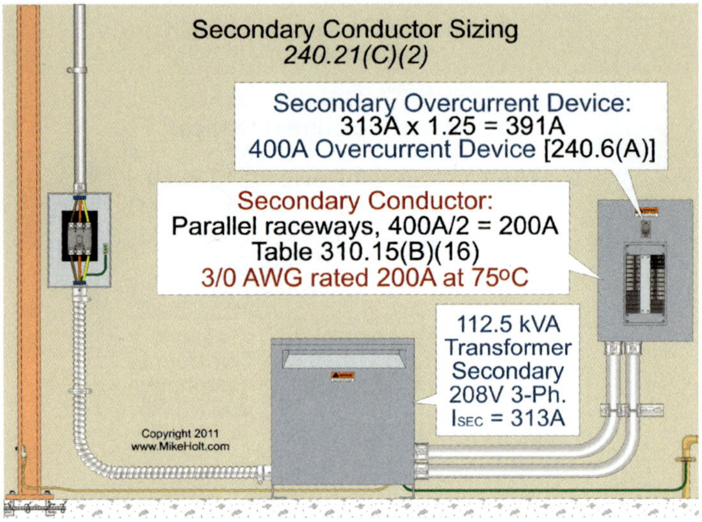

Figure 12–60

12.15 Grounding and Bonding

System Bonding Jumper

A system bonding jumper, sized in accordance with Table 250.66 based on the area of the secondary conductors [250.28(D)], must be installed at the same location where the grounding electrode conductor terminates to the neutral terminal of the separately derived system; either at the separately derived system or the system disconnecting means, but not at both locations [250.30(A)(1) and (A)(3)].

▶ System Bonding Jumper Example 1

Question: *What size system bonding jumper is required for a 45 kVA, three-phase, 480-120/208V transformer, when the secondary conductors are 2/0 AWG?* **Figure 12–61**

(a) 6 AWG *(b) 4 AWG* *(c) 3 AWG* *(d) 2 AWG*

Answer: *(b) 4 AWG [Table 250.66]*

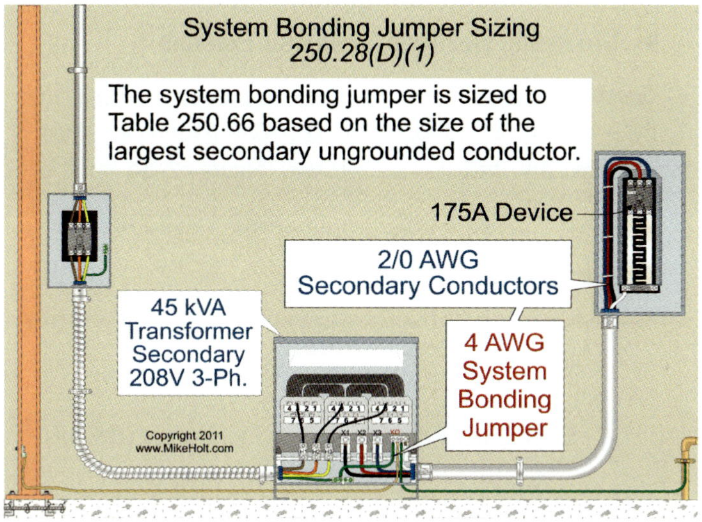

Figure 12–61

► System Bonding Jumper Example 2

Question: *What size system bonding jumper is required for a 75 kVA, three-phase, 480-120/208V transformer, when the secondary conductors are 350 kcmil?* **Figure 12–62**

(a) 6 AWG *(b) 4 AWG* *(c) 3 AWG* *(d) 2 AWG*

Answer: *(d) 2 AWG [Table 250.66]*

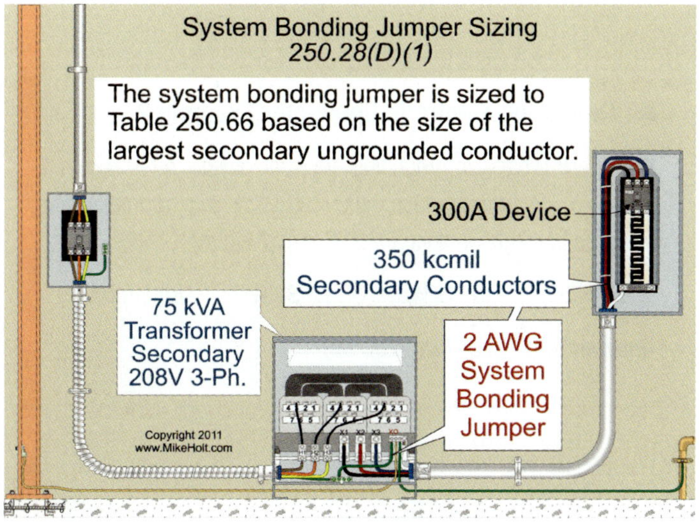

Figure 12–62

► System Bonding Jumper Example 3

Question: *What size system bonding jumper is required for a 112.50 kVA, three-phase, 480-120/208V transformer, when the secondary conductors are two parallel 3/0 AWG conductors?* **Figure 12–63**

(a) 6 AWG *(b) 4 AWG* *(c) 3 AWG* *(d) 2 AWG*

Answer: *(d) 2 AWG*

Cmil area of 3/0 AWG = 167,800 cmil [Chapter 9, Table 8]

167,000 cmil x 2 = 335,600 cmil

Table 250.66 based on 335,600 cmil = 2 AWG

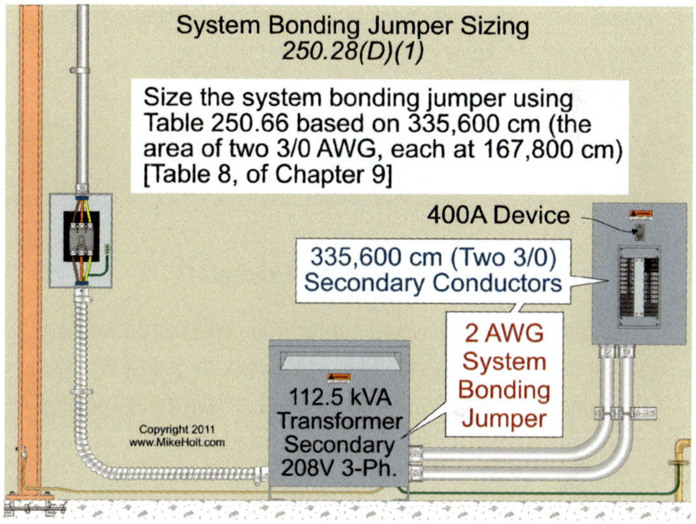

Figure 12–63

Equipment Bonding Jumper

An equipment bonding jumper must be run to the secondary system disconnecting means. Where the secondary equipment grounding conductor is of the wire type, it must be sized in accordance with Table 250.66, based on the area of the largest ungrounded secondary conductor in the raceway or cable [250.30(A)(2)].

► Equipment Bonding Jumper Example 1

Question: *What size equipment grounding conductor of the wire type is required to the secondary disconnect for a 45 kVA, three-phase, 480-120/208V transformer, when the secondary conductors are 2/0 AWG?*

(a) 6 AWG (b) 4 AWG (c) 3 AWG (d) 2 AWG

Answer: *(b) 4 AWG [Table 250.66]*

► Equipment Bonding Jumper Example 2

Question: *What size equipment grounding conductor of the wire type is required to the secondary disconnect for a 75 kVA, three-phase, 480-120/208V transformer, when the secondary conductors are 350 kcmil?*

(a) 6 AWG (b) 4 AWG (c) 3 AWG (d) 2 AWG

Answer: *(d) 2 AWG [Table 250.66]*

► Equipment Bonding Jumper Example 3

Question: *What size equipment grounding conductor of the wire type is required to the secondary disconnect for a 112.50 kVA, three-phase, 480-120/208V transformer, when the secondary conductors are two parallel 3/0 AWG conductors?*

(a) 6 AWG (b) 4 AWG (c) 3 AWG (d) 2 AWG

Answer: *(d) 2 AWG*

Cmil area of 3/0 = 167,800 cmil [Chapter 9, Table 8]

167,000 cmil x 2 = 335,600 cmil

Table 250.66 based on 335,600 cmil = 2 AWG

Grounding Electrode Conductor

A grounding electrode conductor must connect the neutral terminal of a separately derived system to a grounding electrode of a type identified in 250.30(A)(4). The grounding electrode conductor must be sized in accordance with 250.66, based on the area of the ungrounded secondary conductor [250.30(A)(5)].

► Grounding Electrode Conductor Example 1

Question: *What size grounding electrode conductor is required for a 45 kVA, three-phase, 480-120/208V transformer, when the secondary conductors are 2/0 AWG?* **Figure 12–64**

(a) 6 AWG (b) 4 AWG (c) 3 AWG (d) 2 AWG

Answer: *(b) 4 AWG [Table 250.66]*

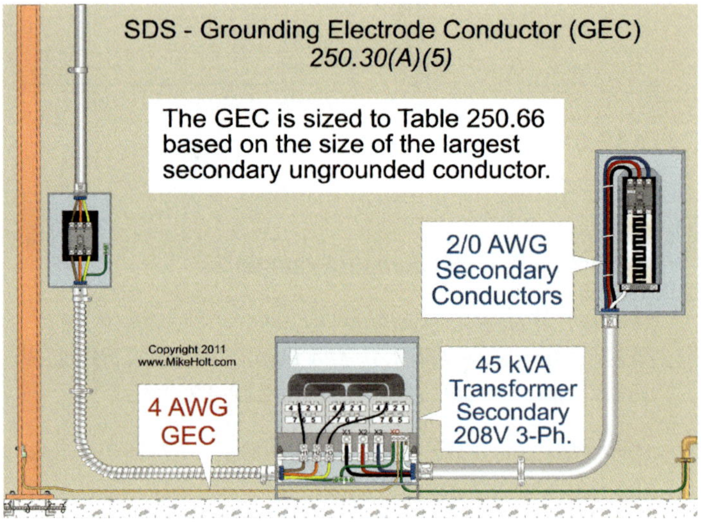

Figure 12–64

► Grounding Electrode Conductor Example 2

Question: *What size grounding electrode conductor is required for a 75 kVA, three-phase, 480-120/208V transformer, when the secondary conductors are 350 kcmil?* **Figure 12–65**

(a) 6 AWG (b) 4 AWG (c) 3 AWG (d) 2 AWG

Answer: *(d) 2 AWG [Table 250.66]*

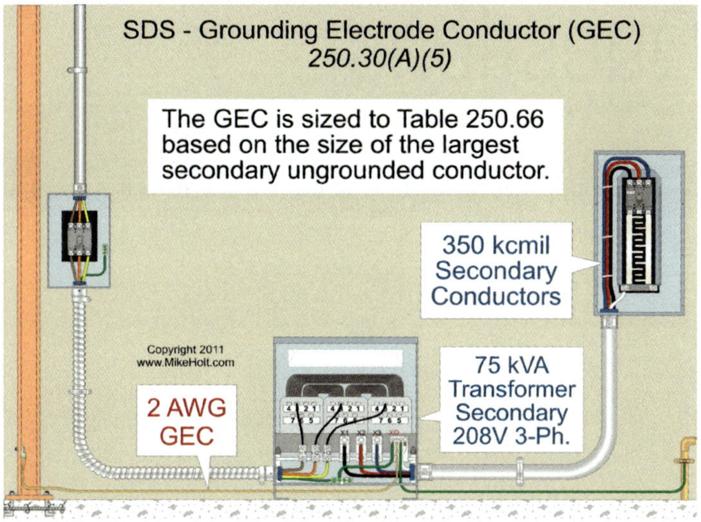

Figure 12–65

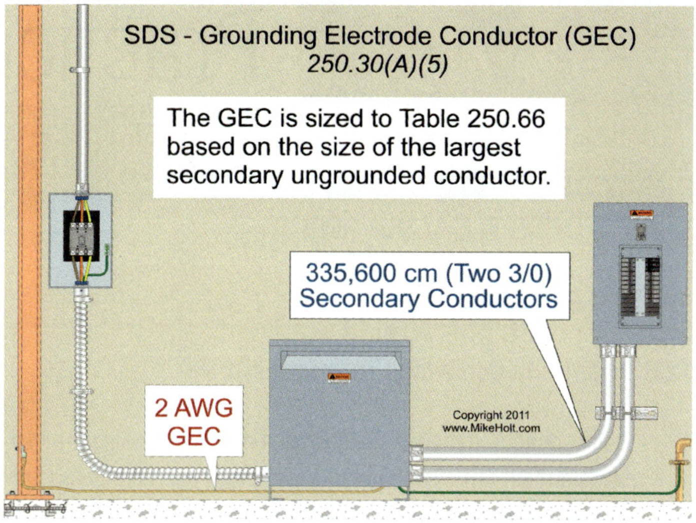

Figure 12–66

► Grounding Electrode Conductor Example 3

Question: *What size grounding electrode conductor is required for a 112.50 kVA, three-phase, 480-120/208V transformer, when the secondary conductors are two parallel 3/0 AWG conductors?* **Figure 12–66**

(a) 6 AWG *(b) 4 AWG* *(c) 3 AWG* *(d) 2 AWG*

Answer: *(d) 2 AWG*

Cmil area of 3/0 AWG = 167,800 cmil [Chapter 9, Table 8]

167,000 cmil x 2 = 335,600 cmil

Table 250.66 based on 335,600 cmil = 2 AWG

CONCLUSION TO UNIT 12—TRANSFORMER CALCULATIONS

If you can remember that transformers really are *transforming* the electricity that goes through them, you'll find it easier to apply transformer theory. Except for autotransformers, all transformers consist of two sets of interacting coils. The turn's ratio of the primary set to the secondary set determines the degree to which the voltage is transformed–that is, raised or lowered.

To keep from making grounding and bonding errors, remember that there's a difference between grounding and bonding. Grounding is the connection to the earth which is accomplished by means of the grounding electrode and the grounding electrode conductor. The connection to earth won't provide an effective ground fault return path. That's the role of proper bonding. With transformers, a vital link in that path is the system bonding jumper that must be installed on the secondary of the transformer, either in the transformer or in the panel. The system bonding jumper completes the bonding path back to the source (the transformer secondary), to provide an effective fault current path.

UNIT 12

Practice Questions

PRACTICE QUESTIONS FOR UNIT 12—TRANSFORMER CALCULATIONS

PART A–GENERAL

12.6 Delta/Delta Connected Transformers

1. Delta configured means that the windings of three single-phase transformers are connected in ______ with each other. A delta-connected transformer is represented by the Greek letter delta.

   (a) series
   (b) parallel
   (c) series-parallel
   (d) a and b

2. What 4-wire system is called the high-leg system because the voltage from one conductor to ground is between 190 volts and 208 volts-to-ground?

   (a) Delta
   (b) Wye

3. The term "______" is used to identify the ungrounded (hot) conductors in an electrical system.

   (a) load
   (b) line
   (c) system
   (d) grounded

4. ______ voltage is the voltage measured between any two ungrounded (hot) conductors.

   (a) Load
   (b) Line
   (c) Grounded
   (d) any of these

5. In a delta-configured transformer, the line voltage is equal to the phase voltage.

   (a) True
   (b) False

6. If the secondary voltage of a delta/delta transformer is 120/240V, the high-leg voltage-to-ground (or neutral) is approximately ______.

   (a) 191V
   (b) 196V
   (c) 202V
   (d) 208V

7. On a 4-wire, delta-connected system where the midpoint of one phase winding is grounded, the conductor having the higher phase voltage-to-ground must be durably and permanently marked by an outer finish that's ______ in color.

   (a) black
   (b) red
   (c) blue
   (d) orange

12.7 Delta/Wye Connected Transformers

8. "______-connected" means a connection of three single-phase transformer windings to a common point (neutral), with the other end of each winding connected to the line conductors.

   (a) Delta
   (b) Wye
   (c) a or b
   (d) none of these

9. In a wye-configured transformer, the line voltage is the same as the phase (winding) voltage.

   (a) True
   (b) False

12.8 Transformer Turns Ratio

10. The turns ratio is the relationship between the number of primary windings compared to the number of secondary windings. This is the same as the turns ratio between the primary phase voltage and the secondary phase voltage. For under 600V, a typical delta/delta system phase voltage ratio is ____ and a typical delta/wye system phase voltage ratio is _____.

    (a) 1:2, 1:4
    (b) 2:1, 4:1
    (c) 4:1, 2:1
    (d) 10:1, 20:1

11. What's the turns ratio for a 480V to 120/208V, three-phase, delta/wye-configured transformer?

    (a) 4:1
    (b) 1:4
    (c) 1:2
    (d) 2:1

12. What's the voltage ratio of a single-phase 480V to 240V transformer?

    (a) 4:1
    (b) 1:4
    (c) 1:2
    (d) 2:1

12.10 Current Flow

13. When a load is connected to the secondary winding of a transformer, current flows through the secondary winding. The current flowing in the secondary creates an electromagnetic field that opposes the primary electromagnetic field.

    (a) True
    (b) False

12.11 Line Currents

14. In a delta-configured transformer, the ratio of the primary-to-secondary line current is directly proportional (the same ratio) to the voltage turns ratio.

    (a) True
    (b) False

15. What's the primary line current for a fully loaded 45 kVA, 480V to 120/240V, three-phase transformer?

    (a) 43A
    (b) 54A
    (c) 108A
    (d) 124A

16. What's the secondary line current for a fully loaded 45 kVA, 480V to 240V, three-phase transformer?

    (a) 43A
    (b) 54A
    (c) 108A
    (d) 124A

17. The line current for both delta- and wye-configured three-phase transformers can be calculated by the formula:

    ILine = VALine/(ELine x 1.732)

    (a) True
    (b) False

18. What's the primary line current for a fully loaded 22 kVA, 480V to 120/208V, three-phase transformer?

    (a) 22A
    (b) 26A
    (c) 54A
    (d) 61A

19. What's the secondary line current for a fully loaded 22 kVA, 480V to 120/208V, three-phase transformer?

(a) 22A
(b) 27A
(c) 54A
(d) 61A

PART B—*NEC* REQUIREMENTS

12.12 Transformer Overcurrent Protection

20. The primary overcurrent protection for a transformer rated 600V, nominal, or less, having a primary current rating of over 9A or more must be set at not more than ______ percent of the primary current when using primary only protection.

(a) 125
(b) 167
(c) 200
(d) 300

21. Overcurrent protection for the secondary of a transformer rated 600V or less having a secondary current rating of 9A or more must be set at not more than ______ percent of the secondary current rating.

(a) 100
(b) 125
(c) 150
(d) 170

12.13 Primary Conductor Sizing

22. A 45 kVA, 480V primary to 120/208V secondary, three-phase transformer with a 70A primary overcurrent device will require at least ______ primary conductors.

(a) 6 AWG
(b) 4 AWG
(c) 2 AWG
(d) 1 AWG

23. A 75 kVA, 480V primary to 120/208V secondary, three-phase transformer with a 125A primary overcurrent device will require at least ______ primary conductors.

(a) 6 AWG
(b) 4 AWG
(c) 2 AWG
(d) 1 AWG

12.14 Secondary Conductor Sizing

24. A 45 kVA, 480V primary to 120/208V secondary, three-phase transformer with a 175A secondary overcurrent device will require at least ______ secondary conductors (secondary conductors are 10 ft).

(a) 2/0 AWG
(b) 4/0 AWG
(c) 350 kcmil
(d) 400 kcmil

25. A 75 kVA, 480V primary to 120/208V secondary, three-phase transformer with a 300A secondary overcurrent device will require at least ______ secondary conductors (secondary conductors are 10 ft).

(a) 2/0 AWG
(b) 4/0 AWG
(c) 350 kcmil
(d) 400 kcmil

12.15 Grounding and Bonding

26. The connection of the system bonding jumper for a separately derived system must be made ______ on the separately derived system from the source to the first system disconnecting means or overcurrent device.

(a) in at least two locations
(b) in every location that the grounded conductor is present
(c) at any single point
(d) none of these

27. The grounding electrode conductor for a single separately derived system is used to connect the grounded conductor of the derived system to the supply-side bonding jumper.

    (a) True
    (b) False

28. In an area served by a separately derived system, the grounding electrode must be as near as practicable and must be the nearest ______ .

    (a) structural metal grounding electrode
    (b) metal water pipe electrode
    (c) metal building skin
    (d) a or b

29. The size of the grounding electrode conductor for a single separetely derived system must not be smaller than that identified in ______, based on the area of the largest derived ungrounded supply conductor.

    (a) 250.66
    (b) 250.122
    (c) Table 310.15(B)(16)
    (d) none of these

30. In an ac system, the size of the grounding electrode conductor to a concrete-encased electrode isn't required to be larger than a(n) ______ copper conductor.

    (a) 10 AWG
    (b) 8 AWG
    (c) 6 AWG
    (d) 4 AWG

UNIT 12

Challenge Questions

CHALLENGE QUESTIONS FOR UNIT 12—TRANSFORMER CALCULATIONS

PART A–GENERAL

12.11 Line Currents

1. The primary line current of a three-phase, 37.50 kVA, delta/delta transformer with a 480V primary and a 120/240V secondary is closest to ______.

    (a) 45A
    (b) 50A
    (c) 65A
    (d) 90A

2. What's the secondary line current for a 45 kVA delta/delta transformer that has a line voltage turns ratio of 2:1, if the primary operates at 480V?

    (a) 36A
    (b) 55A
    (c) 108A
    (d) 240A

3. A 4,160V to 240V, three-phase transformer is connected delta/delta. The secondary phase current is 300A and the secondary line voltage is 240V. How much current will be flowing in the primary conductors supplying the transformer (line current)?

    (a) 17A
    (b) 20A
    (c) 30A
    (d) 50A

4. What's the primary line current for a delta/wye 480V to 120/208V, three-phase transformer that has a secondary line current of 200A?

    (a) 31A
    (b) 53A
    (c) 72A
    (d) 87A

5. The secondary line current for a wye-connected transformer is approximately ______ if the secondary phase voltage is 277V and the load is 10 kVA, three-phase.

    (a) 7A
    (b) 10A
    (c) 12A
    (d) 32A

PART B–*NEC REQUIREMENTS*

12.12 Transformer Overcurrent Protection

6. The maximum size overcurrent device for primary only protection of a three-phase, 37.50 kVA, delta/delta transformer with a 480V primary and a 120/240V secondary is ______.

    (a) 40A
    (b) 45A
    (c) 50A
    (d) 60A

7. The maximum size overcurrent device for primary only protection of a three-phase 45 kVA transformer with a 480V primary and a 120/208V secondary is ______.

    (a) 50A
    (b) 60A
    (c) 70A
    (d) 90A

8. The maximum size overcurrent device for primary only protection of a three-phase 75 kVA transformer with a 480V primary and a 120/208V secondary is ______.

   (a) 90A
   (b) 100A
   (c) 125A
   (d) 150A

9. The maximum size overcurrent device for primary only protection of a three-phase 112.50 kVA transformer with a 480V primary and a 120/208V secondary is ______.

   (a) 100A
   (b) 125A
   (c) 150A
   (d) 175A

Notes

CHAPTER

4

MOTOR CONTROL BASICS

Journeyman and Master's Exams in Some States

Notes

UNIT
13
Motor Control Basics

INTRODUCTION TO UNIT 13—MOTOR CONTROL BASICS

The purpose of this unit is to introduce the basics of motor controls. When beginning this study of basic motor controls, remember that motor controls are basically different kinds of switches that turn things on and off, both manually and automatically. This may help you keep things in perspective.

The basis for most control wiring is either a 2-wire control circuit or a 3-wire control circuit. As controls become more complicated, there may be several 2-wire or several 3-wire control circuits involved. There may even be a combination of both types. The circuitry from a magnetic starter using a 3-wire control circuit to the field pilot devices may also require more than three conductors to meet all circuiting needs. Reversing motor control circuits include forward and reverse contactors, interlocks that prevent those contactors from being energized at the same time (which will cause a phase-to-phase short), and control devices including reversing pushbutton stations and selector switches.

This unit will help you prepare for the type of motor control topics that may be included in a licensing exam. There are many good books available for more advanced studies about this subject. Also check with the manufacturers of motor control equipment for educational material and standard motor control circuits.

PART A BASIC MOTOR CONTROL CONCEPTS

Introduction

Motor control circuits are an effective way to reduce cost by using smaller wire and reduced-amperage devices to control a motor. Imagine trying to wire a pushbutton station for a 100A motor using 3 AWG conductors. Many smaller motors use the same size conductors for both control and power circuits, but as the horsepower increases it becomes impractical to do so, **Figure 13–1**. Motor control circuits are often connected to lower voltages than the motor they control to make it safer for operators and maintenance personnel. A motor control circuit, for the most part, is simply a switch (or group of switches) and a motor. If you keep the word "switch" in mind, it helps keep the intimidating subject of "motor control" in its proper context. For example, the following can be considered motor controls:

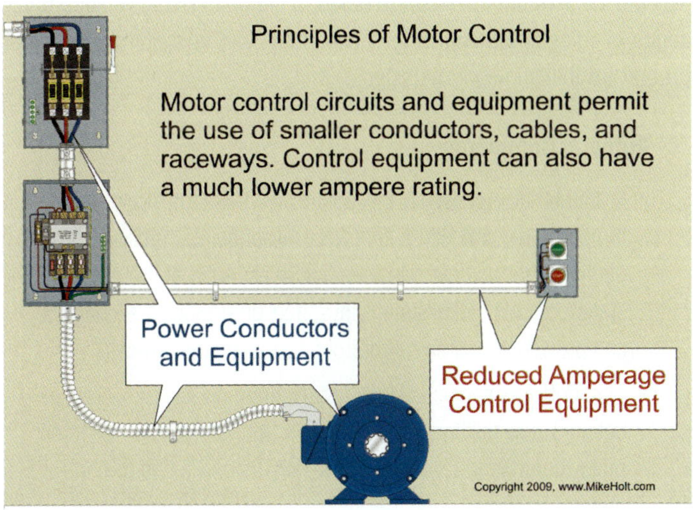

Figure 13–1

A time clock that operates a pool or sprinkler pump is nothing more than an automatic switch. At a preset time, a set of contacts open or close (turn off or on). **Figure 13–2**

An automatic garage door opener uses a radio signal to operate a switch that activates a garage door in much the same manner as a typical "up-down" pushbutton station.

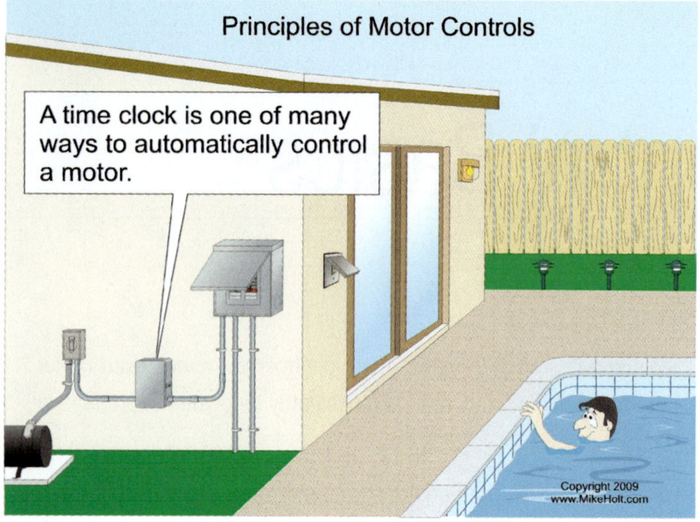

Figure 13–2

Many motors are controlled by computerized control systems, solid-state logic controls, or programmable logic controllers (PLCs). The fundamentals of control systems still apply. The PLC controls an external output based on the logic of a control program, and that output controls the motor or groups of motors by using a magnetic starter, and in some cases additional relays. PLCs and other solid-state control devices were originally invented to provide less expensive replacements for older automated systems that used large numbers of relays and mechanical timers. In some cases, a single PLC can replace thousands of relays resulting in less expensive wiring systems that offer greater flexibility in control designs.

Author's Comments:

- In industrial processes, the control of pressure, flow, speed, temperature, and other items are essential for efficient productivity and safety. Devices such as solid-state sensors, static controls, solid-state relays, and programmable controls can provide very precise control for an industrial process.
- Although the subject of solid-state controls isn't covered in detail in this textbook, the concepts are very similar to other motor controls in that they essentially use switches to control motors.
- Many experts agree that the best way to learn about motor controls is to start with the standard control methods covered in this textbook. This statement also applies when electronic controls are the subject being studied.

Many control circuits include motor overload protection devices. Traditional overload (OL) protectors operate on the relationship between heat and current. As current increases, heat increases. If an overload device is rated 10A, and the current exceeds that rating, the OL device will operate to open the circuit because of the increased heat caused by the current running through it. A magnetic starter or other motor controllers may include overload devices, or they may be an integral part of the motor, particularly with small motors.

Author's Comment: Short circuits and ground faults aren't considered overloads.

There are two basic designs of motor control equipment, NEMA and IEC.

NEMA (National Electrical Manufacturers Association). NEMA is a trade association for manufacturers of electrical equipment and supplies. NEMA standards specify motor horsepower (hp) ratings, speeds, motor frame sizes and dimensions, motor torques, motor starter size ratings, and enclosure specifications.

NEMA-rated products are typically heavy duty, can be used in a broad range of applications, and some starters can be maintained and repaired. For these reasons, they're often more expensive than IEC motor starters. NEMA-rated motors and motor controllers are the type most commonly used in North America.

IEC (International Electrotechnical Commission). IEC is an international standards organization. IEC motor starters are often less expensive, smaller in size, are tailored for specific motor performance requirements, and the selection of the right starter for each application is very important. IEC-rated motor controllers are widely used in Europe and Asia.

13.1 Motor Control Language

Electrical symbols, words, and line diagrams provide the information necessary to understand the operation of motor control circuits. Used together, they create a type of motor control "language" that's used to transfer information and ideas quickly and efficiently.

The symbols in motor control schematics represent devices, power conductors, control conductors, conductor connections and terminals, and sometimes the motor itself.

The words, phrases, and abbreviations in a schematic are generally accepted terms that represent functions, describe actions, and list sequences of operation.

In many cases, the symbols and words have a similarity to the items they represent. The basic types of schematics are shown in **Figure 13–3**. Parts A, B, and C of that figure illustrate three different methods of representing the same control circuit.

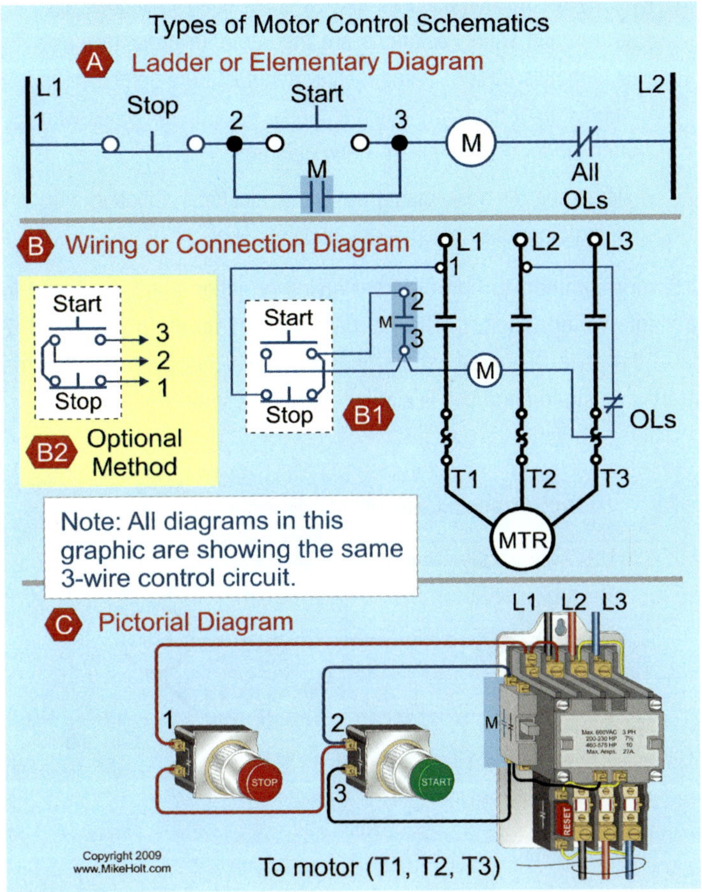

Figure 13–3

(1) Ladder Diagrams (Figure 13–4)

Ladder diagrams are also called "line diagrams" or "elementary diagrams." They're used to represent the function of the control circuit and the associated devices, but don't show the components of the control circuit in their actual positions. As control circuits become more complex, a ladder diagram can be less complicated to read than a wiring or connection diagram. For example, in **Figure 13–4**, notice the set of contacts marked M under the start pushbutton. The M contacts marked 2 and 3 are actually located in the motor starter fairly close to the coil, as shown in **Figure 13–3**, and the normal physical appearance of these contacts often look as shown in **Figure 13–3**. (Notice that all three examples of the M contacts are shown with a blue background in **Figure 13–3**.)

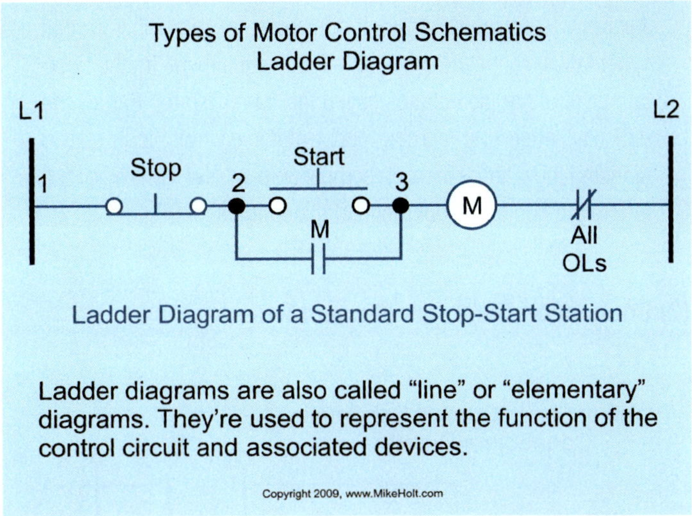

Figure 13–4

The ladder diagrams in **Figures 13–4 and 13–5** illustrates electrical function, showing the M contacts in parallel with the start pushbutton to form what's called a "holding circuit." The physical location of the M contacts isn't shown in the ladder diagram.

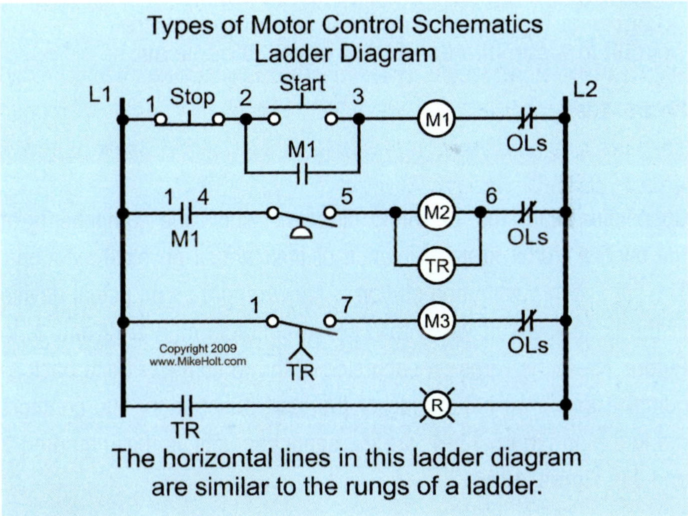

Figure 13–5

Figure 13–5 shows a more complicated version of a ladder diagram. Notice that the horizontal lines in this control circuit are similar to the rungs of a ladder.

Author's Comment: An important point to remember is that schematics show motors and control equipment in the resting, or off state (sometimes called the "shelf" state). Part of the difficulty, when first learning about motor controls, is in understanding how the different components of the control circuit interrelate during the operation of the controls.

(2) Connection Diagrams (Figure 13–6)

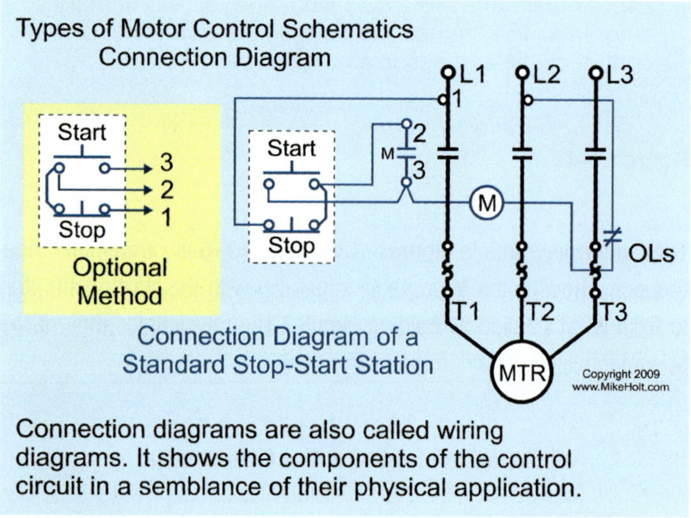

Figure 13–6

Connection diagrams, or wiring diagrams, show the components of the control circuit in a semblance of their actual physical locations. The start-stop pushbutton station is shown more as an actual device in the control circuit wired to a set of contacts marked 2 and 3. In Figure 13–4, the wires on each side of the M contacts trace back to points 2 and 3 on either side of the start pushbutton. The contacts marked M in Figure 13–4 are the same contacts as those marked 2 and 3 in Figure 13–6.

Different manufacturers of control devices, as well as books about motor controls, use different methods of showing the control circuit wiring. For example, in Figure 13–3B1, the control wiring from the start-stop pushbutton station runs to the actual connection points 1, 2, and 3. As the wiring diagrams become more complicated, the optional method shown in Figure 13–3B2 is frequently used to show the connection points for the start-stop pushbutton station. Here, in Figure 13–6, instead of running the control wires to the actual connection point, arrowed lines represent connections to be made by the installer.

Author's Comments:

- Many times you see plain lines (no arrows) with numbers to indicate connections to be made by the installer. We use both methods in this textbook.
- Many of the components and symbols used in ladder diagrams and wiring diagrams are the same. In order to make schematics easier to read, some manufacturers combine the two types of diagrams together. Some equipment comes with both ladder diagrams and wiring diagrams.
- Remember, ladder diagrams show electrical function and wiring diagrams show the actual components.

It's very common to find different styles of schematics combined in a single wiring diagram. The top part of the diagram in Figure 13–7 is in the style of a connection diagram, while the style showing the start-stop station and coil is similar to a ladder diagram.

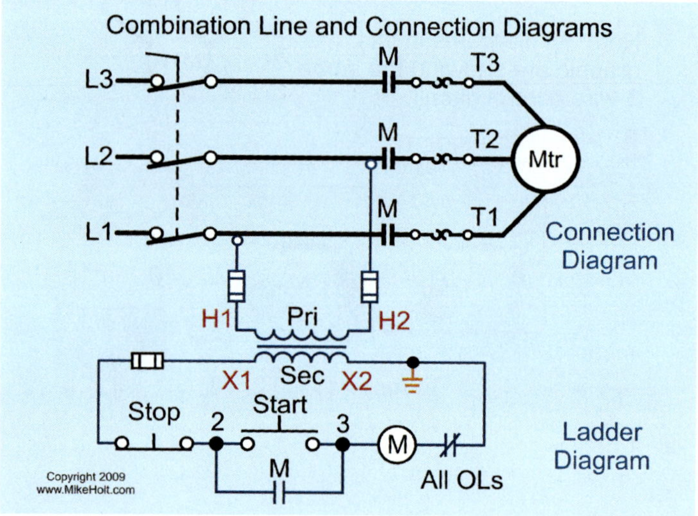

Figure 13–7

(3) Pictorial Diagrams (Figure 13–8)

Pictorial diagrams are often used in educational material and as exploded views or cut-away views in installation and maintenance literature. Pictorial diagrams help students see actual devices and components used in motor control circuits and how they relate to the symbols used in ladder diagrams and wiring diagrams. For example, the start pushbutton we mentioned earlier has wires run to the device that contains the set of contacts M in Figure 13–4, and to contact points 2 and 3 in Figure 13–6.

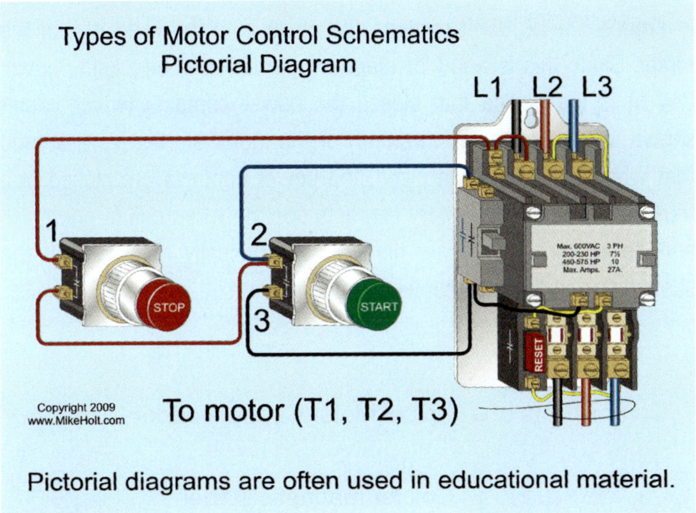

Figure 13–8

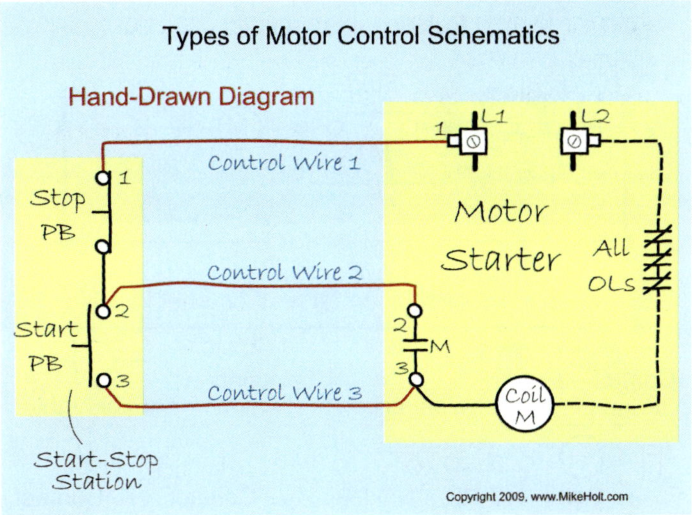

Figure 13–9

Author's Comments:

- Often a hand-drawn diagram of a control circuit constructed in the field helps in understanding how a circuit functions and how to make the necessary connections, especially during the learning process. **Figure 13–9** shows the hand-drawn version of the 3-wire start-stop control circuit shown in **Figure 13–3**. Notice that the stop pushbutton is in series with coil M, and that the start pushbutton is in parallel with M contacts 2–3. The entire control circuit in this example is in parallel between line 1 and line 2. These basic relationships can be found in many control circuits.
- The numbers in this diagram are simply for the aid of the reader and it don't imply that terminal 1 on one device should always be connected to terminal 1 on another device.

Once you understand the terminology and symbols involved in motor control circuit wiring, understanding how it works becomes easier and less intimidating.

13.2 Motor Control Basics

The purpose of this textbook is to introduce the basics of motor controls. Many of the control circuits that are covered are standard control circuits used in many different applications. Each circuit can have several variations and optional devices in addition to those included in the schematics. This textbook won't teach you all of these control circuit variations, but will give you a basic understanding of motor controls, and how to read wiring diagrams and understand the sequences of operation.

When beginning this study of basic motor controls, remember that motor controls are basically different kinds of switches that turn things on and off, both manually and automatically. This may help you keep things in perspective.

There are many good books available for more advanced studies about this subject. Also check with the manufacturers of motor control equipment for educational material and standard motor control circuits.

13.3 Reading a Motor Control Schematic

Figure 13–10 contains some of the devices and associated symbols covered in this unit used in a ladder diagram of a control circuit. Use the symbols legend in the bottom part of this figure to see how symbols are combined to create a schematic. To read schematics, it's important to remember that diagrams are shown in the "at rest" or "shelf" position.

Figure 13–11 shows some of the components related to power and control conductors and terminals. The numbers 1, 2, 3, and 4 are showing points where conductors will need to be terminated. Remember that these terminal numbers aren't found on the devices you'll be connecting in the field. They're just used on schematics as reference points.

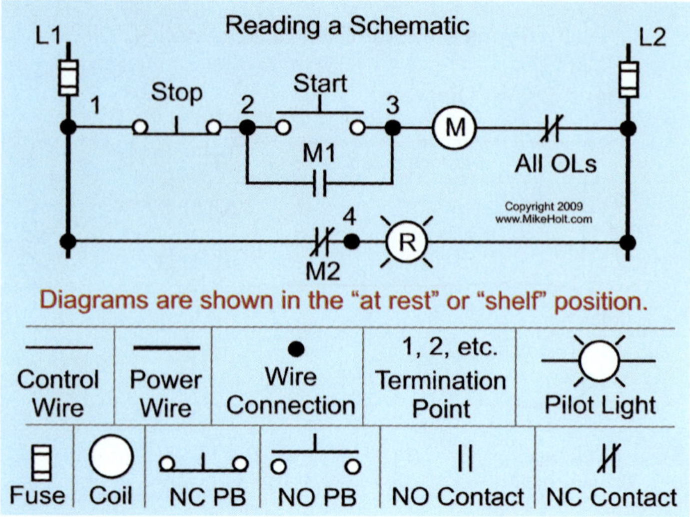

Figure 13–10

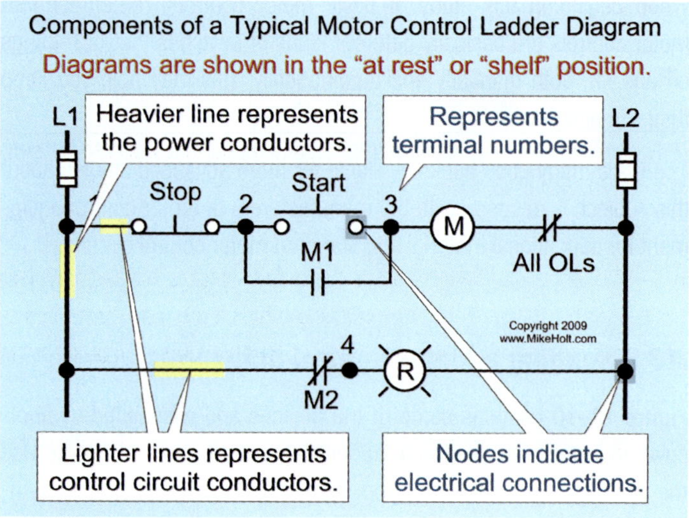

Figure 13–11

CAUTION: *The terminal numbers found on a schematic rarely match the terminal numbers found on some wiring devices. Different manufacturers will use different numbering systems. Wiring must always be based on function, not on terminal numbers. We're matching many terminal numbers in this textbook only for the purpose of making it easier for students to learn.*

In **Figure 13–12**, don't confuse the circle with the M in it with the motor. Since this is a ladder diagram, the actual motor isn't shown. Coil M is the device that closes the power contacts (which aren't shown in a ladder diagram either) of the motor starter. It's assumed that when the coil is energized, the power contacts are closed. You must know that the auxiliary contacts operate when coil M energizes and de-energizes. Auxiliary contacts are typically marked with the same letter as the coil with which they operate.

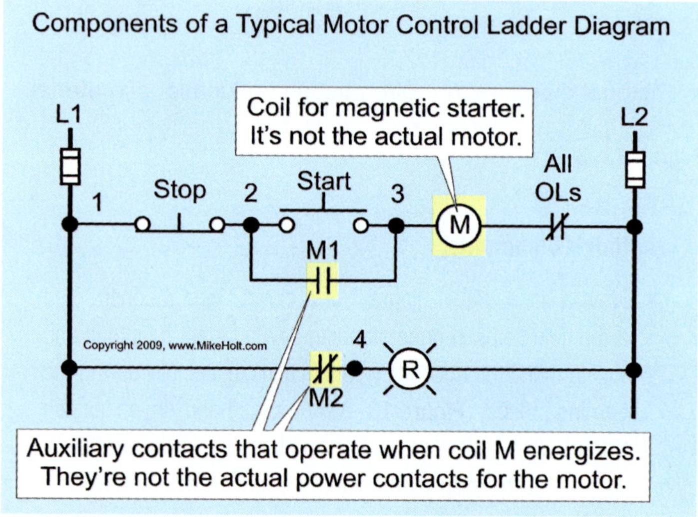

Figure 13–12

Author's Comment: Parent, Child, and Sibling. Many motor control functions are accomplished with sets of contacts that are activated by a coil, such as those found in magnetic motor starters or relays. These devices can have several sets of contacts operated from a single coil. The term "Parent Coil" refers to the coil that operates the group of contacts. The sets of contacts that are activated by the parent coil are sometimes called the "Child" or "Sibling" contacts.

Sometimes the contacts that operate from the parent coil are numbered, such as contacts M1 and M2 that operate with coil M. It's common to have just the letter designator without numbers in the diagram. In that case, the contacts are sometimes referred to with their connection points. For example, contacts M1 in **Figure 13–12** can also be called "M contacts 2-3" because these contacts connect to points 2 and 3 in the control circuit. Contacts M2 can also be called "M contacts 1-4" because these contacts connect to points 1 and 4 in the control circuit. Both methods of identifying contacts will be used in this textbook.

Figure 13–13 points out several symbols representing some the components of a motor control schematic. Schematics frequently use short labels to help identify the function of a device in a control circuit. For example, the word "Stop" is used to indicate what the normally closed pushbutton switch is being used for. The phrase "All OLs" is used to indicate that the normally closed contacts symbol represents the overload protection associated with this control circuit. The letter "R" is used with the pilot light to indicate that a red lamp or lens is required.

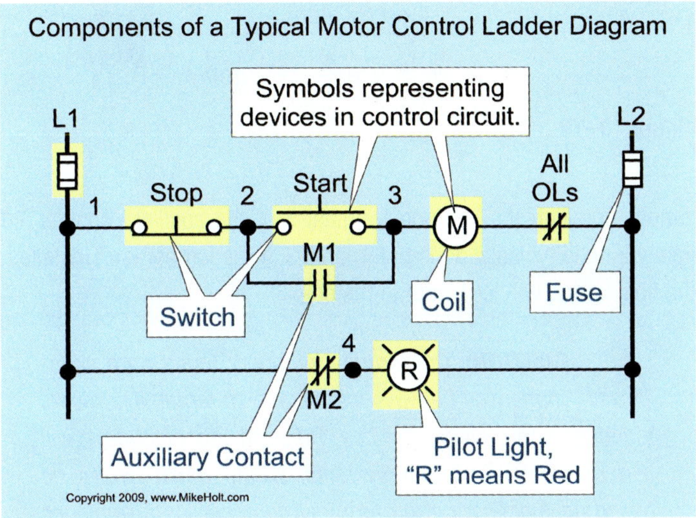

Figure 13–13

Figure 13–14 illustrates one of the learning tools we use in this textbook. The yellow and blue shading aren't found on any control circuits you'll work on in the field. We use this shading to indicate voltage paths to different parts of the control circuit. For example, the yellow shading shows the voltage path between where the control circuit connects to L1 on one side of the start PB, and one side of auxiliary contacts M1 through the stop PB. The blue shading shows the voltage path between where the control circuit connects to L2 on one side of coil M and one side of the pilot light.

Author's Comment: This shading isn't showing the actual voltage through the control circuit. It's just showing the paths required to energize the individual components.

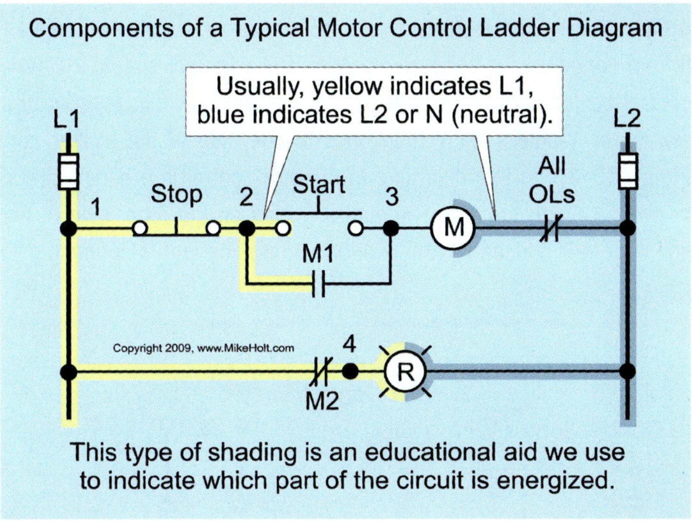

Figure 13–14

PART B MOTOR CONTROL CIRCUITS

13.4 2-Wire Control Circuits

2-wire control circuits are used for applications that need to be self-starting. These include applications such as pumping stations, air-conditioning (HVAC) equipment and fans, and refrigeration equipment.

A 2-wire control circuit doesn't have low-voltage protection. This means that if the equipment is running when there's a power loss or brownout (voltage reduction), the equipment will automatically restart when the power is restored.

CAUTION: *2-wire control circuits shouldn't be used where automatic restart after a power loss will create a safety hazard for personnel working around the restarting equipment. A power loss can be caused by a utility outage, or the equipment disconnect being turned off and back on. In locations where there are a large number of motors, automatic restart can cause an undesirable power surge when power is restored.*

A basic 2-wire control circuit goes from a power supply, which is L1 if from the contactor (for a common control-wiring circuit) to a 2-wire control device such as a float switch, pressure switch, temperature switch, or 1-pole switch, then goes to one side of the starter coil, **Figure 13–15**. In this example, the 2-wire control is a series circuit between L1 and the coil. The control wiring on the other side of the coil is generally used for the overload protection and is connected to L2.

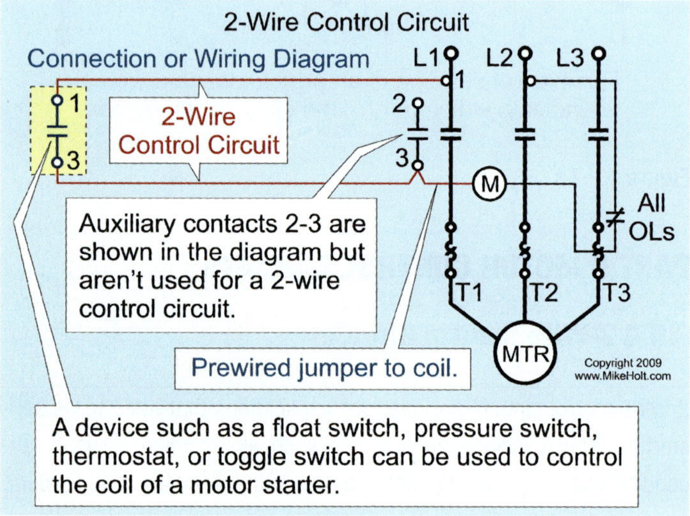

Figure 13–15

Author's Comment: The term "low-voltage release" is used with 2-wire circuits that have a maintained-contact pilot device(s) in series with the coil. See **Figure 13–15**. This type of control is used when the starter must function automatically without a human operator. Don't confuse this phrase with "low-voltage protection" which applies to 3-wire circuits and manual restart after a power failure. This concept is explained more fully later in this unit.

Notice the numbers 1 and 3 at the terminals of the 2-wire control device, **Figure 13–16** The same numbers can be found on the motor starter schematic. These numbers are used to indicate where the control circuit conductors are terminated. The conductor (control wire 1) that terminates to terminal 1 of the control device connects to terminal 1 in the motor starter (next to L1). The conductor (control wire 2) from terminal 3 of the control device connects to terminal 3 of the auxiliary contacts in the motor starter. This is essentially the same as connecting it to the coil because the auxiliary contacts aren't being utilized in this control circuit. There's usually a factory-installed jumper between the coil and terminal 3 of the auxiliary contact, so field wiring is typically done to terminal 3. If the jumper isn't installed, the field wiring will terminate to the coil.

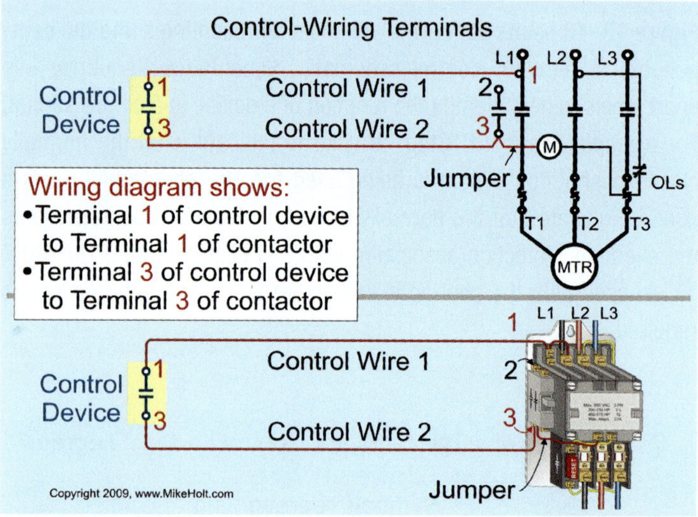

Figure 13–16

CAUTION: *The terminal numbers found on a schematic won't always match up with terminal numbers found on some wiring devices. Different manufacturers will use different numbering systems. Wiring must always be based on function, not on terminal numbers. As a reminder, we're matching many terminal numbers in this textbook only for the purpose of making it easier for students to learn.*

Optional Wiring

Some pilot devices have more than one set of contacts. This allows a single device to be more versatile and used for more applications. A schematic often indicates optional wiring by using dashed lines with instructions. In **Figure 13–17**, a float switch has two different sets of contacts. It's up to the installer or designer of the control circuit to determine how these will be wired. In this example, one end of wire A (solid line) is connecting the NC contacts of the float switch. The optional wiring is the dashed line from the NO contacts. The instructions under the wiring diagram state that wire A must be removed and connected as shown by the dashed line for a sump-pump application.

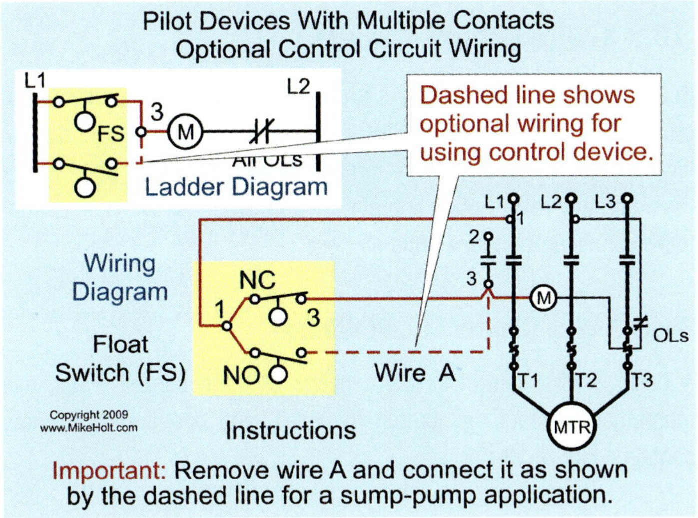

Figure 13–17

Application 1—Tank Filling Application

NC Contacts (Solid Line A). This application leaves wire A on the NC contact as shown in the diagram, Figure 13–18. Since the NC contacts are open when the tank is full, they'll close when the liquid level drops. This function can be used for something like automatically filling a watering tank for livestock.

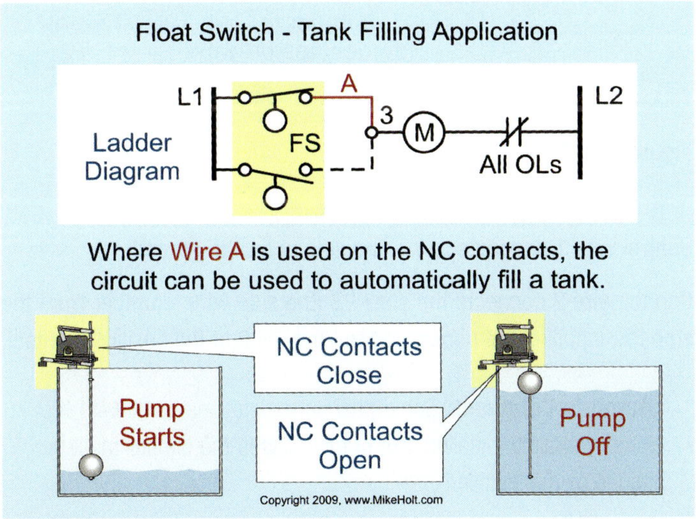

Figure 13–18

Operation Sequence for Automatic Filling. If the tank is full, the NC contacts are open and the motor is off, Figure 13–19. When the liquid level drops to a certain point, the NC contacts close, the M coil energizes, the main power contacts close, and the pump runs, Figure 13–19. As the liquid level rises to a certain point, the NC contacts open, the M coil de-energizes, the main power contacts open, and the pump stops. Figure 13–19

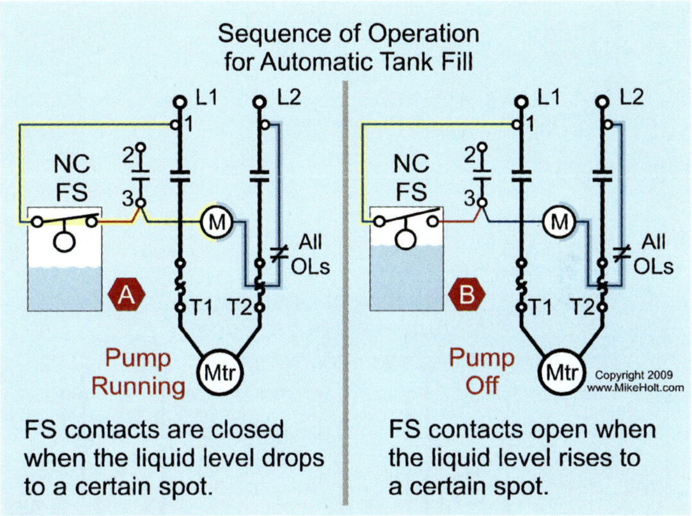

Figure 13–19

Application 2—Sump-Pump Application

NO Contacts (Dashed Line). Since the NO contacts are closed when the tank is full, they'll open when the liquid level drops. If you want to use the NO contacts of the float switch, wire A must be removed from the NC contacts and placed on the NO contacts, Figure 13–20. This function can be used for something like an automatic sump pump.

Operation Sequence for a Sump Pump. If the tank is full, the NO contacts are closed so as soon as power is supplied to the circuit, the NO contacts energize the M coil, the main power contacts close, and the pump runs, Figure 13–21B. When the liquid level drops to a certain point, the NO contacts open, the M coil de-energizes, the main power contacts open, and the pump stops. Figure 13–21A

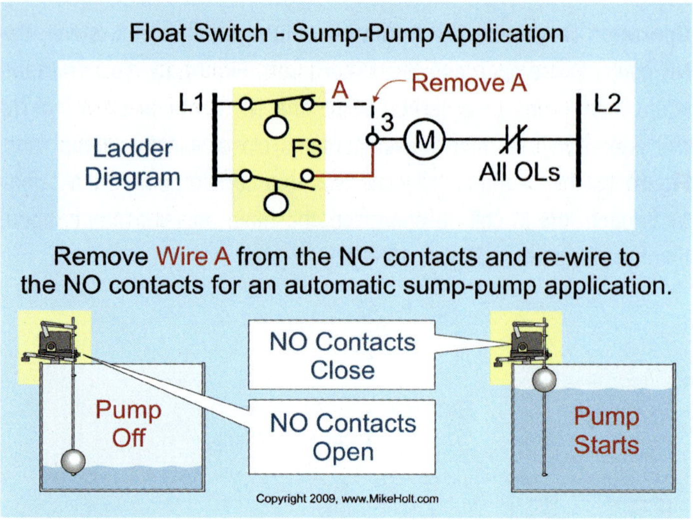

Figure 13–20

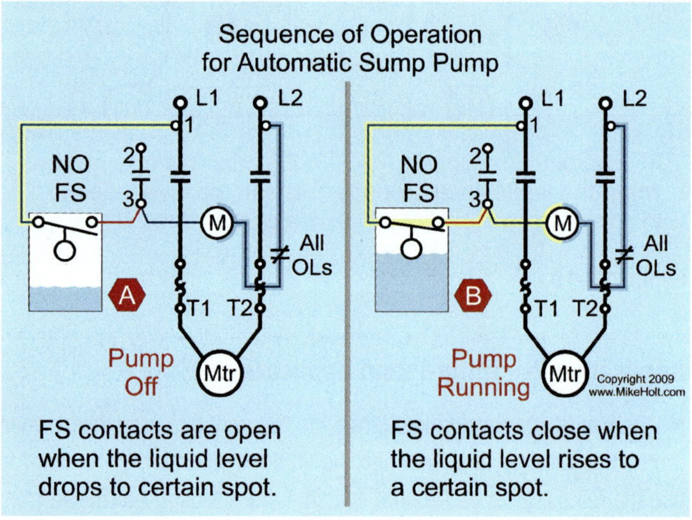

Figure 13–21

If Application 2 is used for a sump pump, it won't be a tank-type container. Sump pumps are often located in or near a small pit in the lowest part of a floor. As liquid seeps into the pit, the float will rise and at a certain point, the contacts will close, energize the coil, and start the pump. When the water is pumped out, the float lowers, the NO contacts open, de-energize the coil, and the pump stops. This automatically keeps the pump from running after the liquid is gone. This same principle is also used for sewage lift pumps.

13.5 3-Wire Control Circuits

Because 3-wire control circuits are more flexible, they're used more often than 2-wire control circuits. A 3-wire control circuit has built-in low-voltage protection. 3-wire circuits should always be used where the automatic restart of equipment after a power loss will be a danger to personnel or to the machine process.

Basic 3-Wire Control Circuit Wiring

A basic 3-wire control circuit consists of three control wires, two momentary-contact pushbutton switches, and one set of auxiliary contacts. Figure 13–22

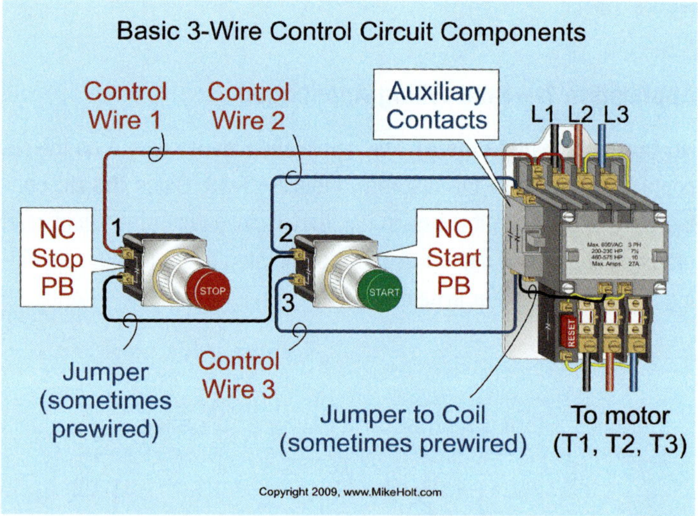

Figure 13–22

Control wire 1 connects to the line side of the NC stop PB.

Control wire 2 connects the start PB (the side with a jumper from the stop PB; install one if necessary) to terminal 2 of the auxiliary contact.

Author's Comment: Some pushbutton stations come with the jumper already installed, but in most cases the jumper must be added by the installer.

Control wire 3 connects the other side of the start PB (the side without a jumper) to terminal 3 of the auxiliary contact.

A NC stop PB is wired in series with the coil of the contactor and a NO start PB is wired in series with the coil, but also connected in parallel with the auxiliary contact. Figure 13–23

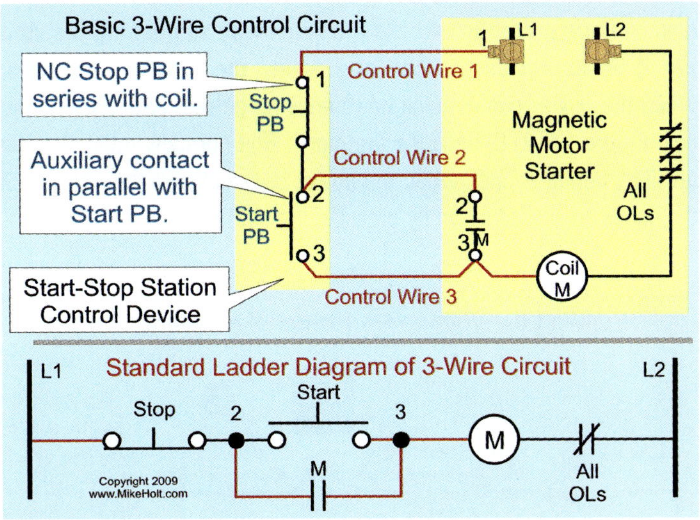

Figure 13–23

Author's Comments:

- Remember, the letter M in the circle symbol in **Figure 13–23** is the coil, not the motor. The contacts marked M are the auxiliary contacts, not the motor branch-circuit power contacts.
- Notice that the start PB, stop PB, coil, and overloads are all in series with each other and this entire circuit is in parallel with the power source (motor starter L1 and L2 in this case). The entire 3-wire circuit is connected between one side of the coil and one line of the power source (L1 in this case), while the overloads are connected between the other side of the coil and the other line of the power source (L2 in this case). These points will be more important later when the 3-wire control circuit(s) become more complicated. When learning about motor controls, it's important to keep things in perspective by remembering the basics.

Sequence of Operation

A sequence of operation is a detailed list of the steps it takes to perform a task. Each action of the sequence is based directly on a previous event. For example, you're sitting in a chair and you want the light over your head turned on. To describe this process, you can simply say, "I get up and turn on the light." But if you describe it as a sequence of operation, it will be something like, "I stand up, take one step with my left leg, take one step with my right leg, raise my right arm, use my right index finger to move the switch handle to the On position, and the light comes on."

To apply this concept to the basic 3-wire control circuit, start with whatever action you're trying to accomplish. The goal is to energize and de-energize the coil. The coil must have power to operate. The overload side of the coil is already taken care of in the example with L2 through the overload relay contacts, so that one side of the coil is hot all the time, **Figure 13–24A1**. The OL contacts aren't opened or closed by the coil.

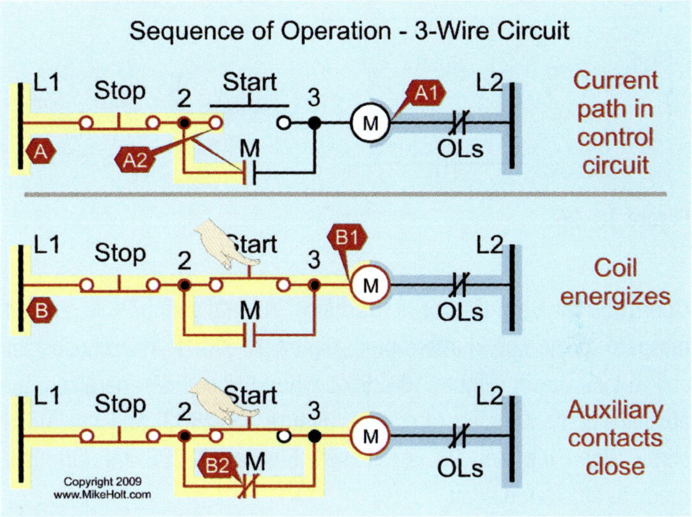

Figure 13–24

Operation from Rest (Motor not Running). In this example, there's a continuous current path from L1 of the power source, through the NC stop PB to the line side of the NO start PB, and to terminal 2 of the auxiliary contact, **Figure 13–24A2** . When the start PB is pushed, a current path is provided through the start PB to the coil, **Figure 13–24B1**, which starts the motor (the power contacts aren't shown).

The coil closes the auxiliary contacts, **Figure 13–24B2**. This closed set of contacts is the "holding circuit" or "sealing circuit." When the start PB is released as shown in **Figure 13–25**, the auxiliary contacts stay closed and maintain a continuous current path to the coil, even though there's no longer a path through the start PB. This held-closed set of auxiliary contacts is electrically holding (or connecting) the circuit to the coil.

Author's Comment: Remember that auxiliary contacts 2-3 are physically closed by the coil when it's energized. These contacts will remain closed as long as power is maintained to the coil.

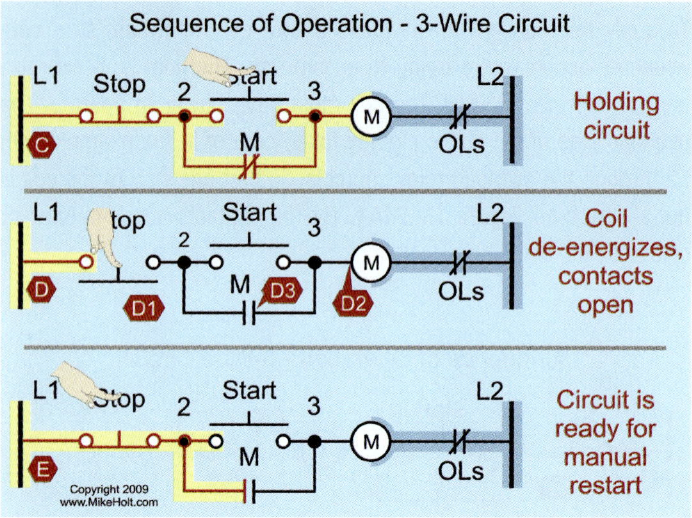

Figure 13–25

Operation for Stop (Motor is Running). When the stop PB is pushed, the path to the coil is interrupted, Figure 13–25D1. This causes the coil to lose power, Figure 13–25D2. When the coil de-energizes, the auxiliary contacts open (drop out), Figure 13–25D3, and the motor stops. When the stop PB is released, Figure 13–25E, the circuit is ready to be started again.

Low-Voltage Protection. This means that if power goes off to the control circuit, the equipment won't automatically restart when power is restored, Figure 13–26B. Someone must manually restart the equipment instead.

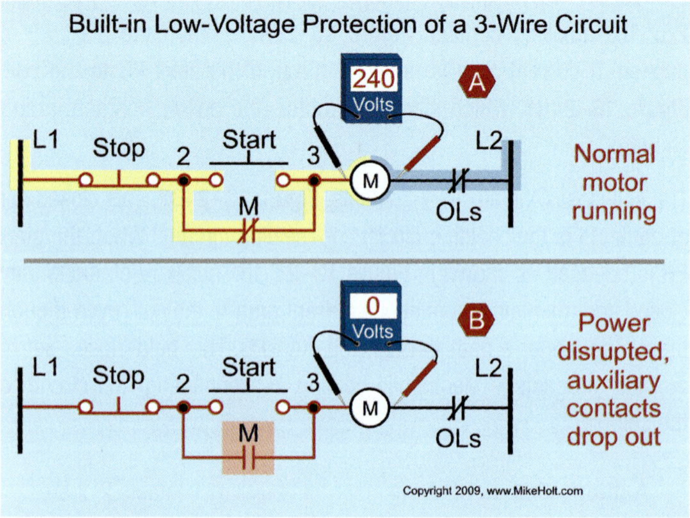

Figure 13–26

Low-voltage protection works the same way as pushing the stop PB; it de-energizes the coil and opens the auxiliary contacts. When the power comes back on, there's no current path back to the coil, Figure 13–27C, because the start PB is normally open and the auxiliary contacts open when the power goes out and stay open until the coil is energized again by pressing the start PB. Figure 13–27D

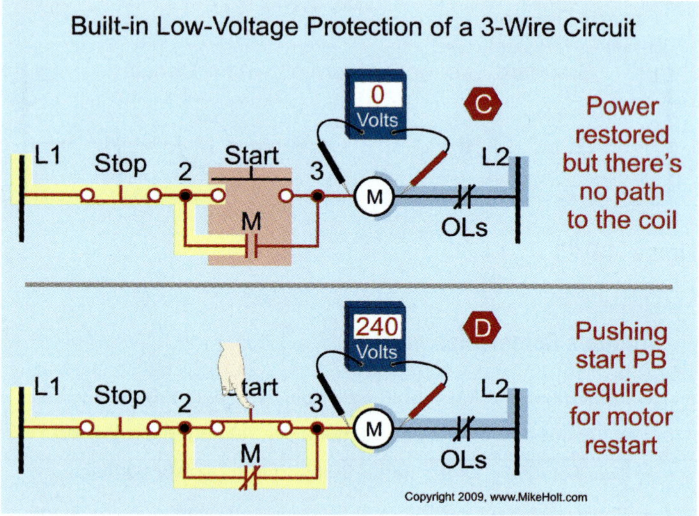

Figure 13–27

Low-voltage protection only applies to magnetic controls. It's an inherent function of 3-wire control circuits because of the use of auxiliary contacts, which are used as holding contacts (also called "sealing contacts," an "electric holding circuit," "memory contacts," or a "maintaining circuit"). This set of holding contacts is electrically held, which means they can only be closed when there's power producing the electromagnetic field which holds them closed.

Safety Function. This is what makes 3-wire control circuits safer than 2-wire control circuits. They work the same way as if a circuit breaker is turned off or tripped, or a disconnect opens. Someone operating or doing maintenance on the equipment won't be caught by surprise when the circuit breaker is reset or the equipment disconnect closes. For example, if a person is working on a lathe controlled by this type of 3-wire circuit, when the power goes out, the lathe stops. The lathe won't automatically restart when the power is restored and the worker won't be injured. The PB must be manually pushed again in order for the motor to restart.

13.6 3-Wire Circuit in a Wiring (Connection) Diagram

It's very common to find the same standard 3-wire control circuit that we just covered in **Figure 13–26** in wiring (connection) diagrams, like the one shown in **Figure 13–28**. The wiring diagram provides more of an actual picture of the components and the physical relationship between those components than do ladder diagrams, which provide more functional-type information.

One of the main differences between wiring diagrams and ladder diagrams is that a wiring diagram shows the branch-circuit contacts and equipment (including the motor) as well as the control circuit contacts and equipment. It's also very common to see both ladder and connection diagrams on the same schematic, **Figure 13–29.** In this figure, the 3-wire circuit is called a "common control circuit" because its power is being taken directly from L1 and L2 of the motor-starter contactor. This is also called a "tapped motor-control circuit."

A common wiring diagram for connecting a start-stop pushbutton station to a motor starter combines a ladder diagram and a start-stop pushbutton station labeled with numbers to show where the control

Wiring (Connection) Diagram of a 3-Wire Control Circuit

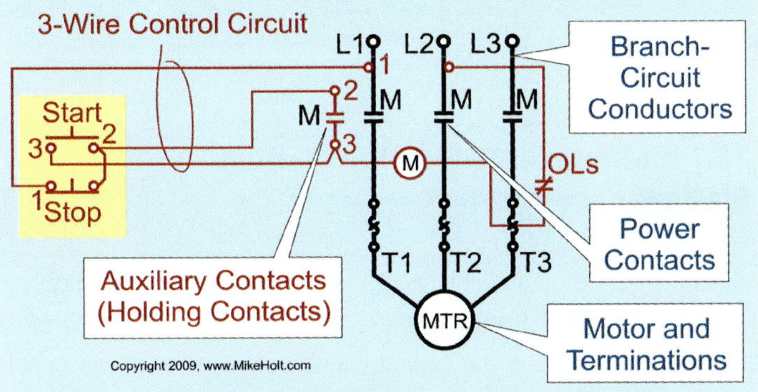

A connection diagram shows the branch-circuit wiring and utilization equipment (including the motor) as well as the control wiring and equipment.

Figure 13–28

Combination Ladder and Connection Diagram

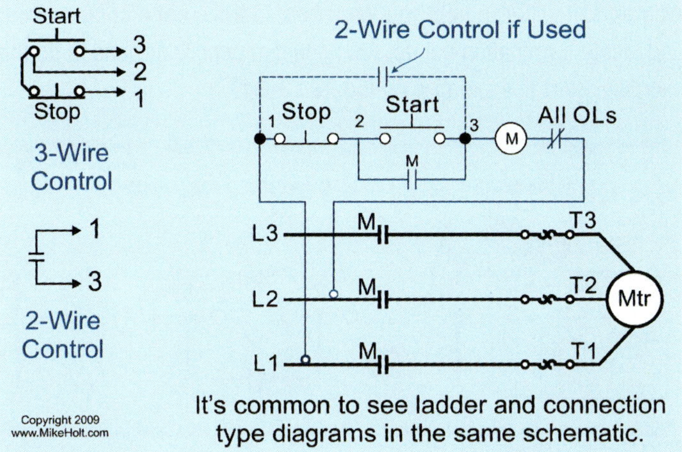

It's common to see ladder and connection type diagrams in the same schematic.

Figure 13–29

conductors are connected in the motor-starter enclosure or control wire cabinet. The arrowed lines indicate connections made by the installer. **Figure 13–30**

Wiring Diagram for Start-Stop Station

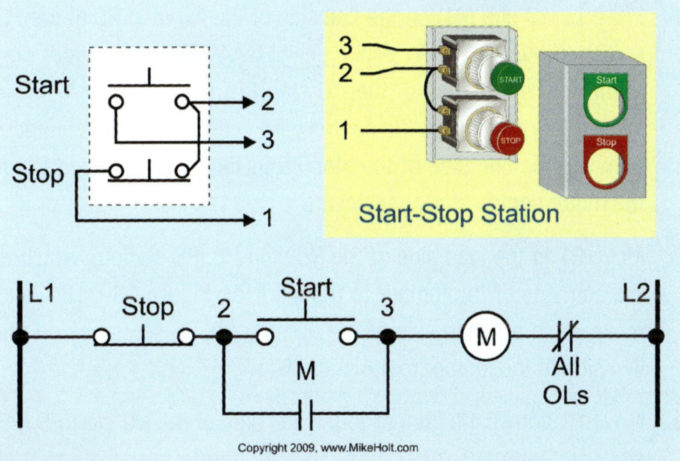

Figure 13–30

Author's Comment: The arrowed lines with terminal numbers in **Figure 13–30** aren't always shown with arrows. Plain lines with terminal numbers are also used.

Exercise. This exercise is designed to teach you how to read wiring diagrams. It will also help you learn how to trace out a control circuit and locate termination points. You need two pencils or pens to do this exercise. Start this exercise on **Figure 13–31**.

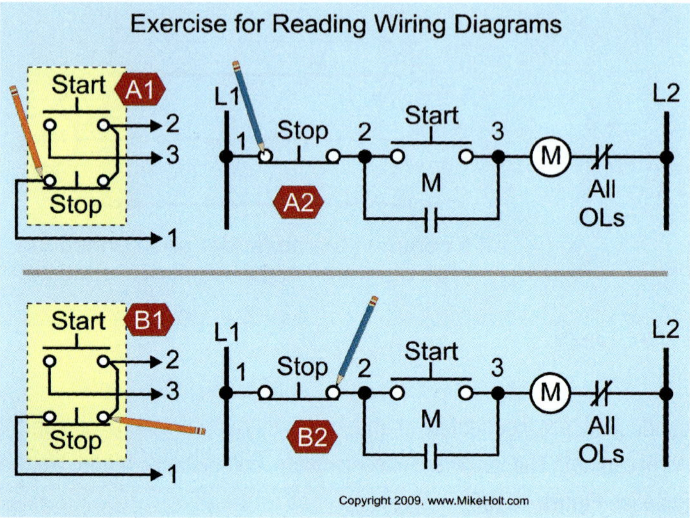

Figure 13–31

1. Place pencil one (P1) on the line side of the NC stop PB of the PB station, **Figure 13–31A1**. Place pencil two (P2) on the ladder diagram on the line side of the NC stop PB, **Figure 13–31A2**. This shows the point where the control wire with a number 1 connects between the line side of the stop PB in the PB station and L1 at the motor control starter enclosure.

2. Move P1 to the load side of the NC stop PB (PB station), which is the line side of the jumper to the start PB, **Figure 13–31B1**, and move P2 to the load side of the NC stop PB. P2 should be on the line side of the jumper to the start PB.

3. Move P1 across the jumper to the line side of the NO start PB (PB station), **Figure 13–32C1**, and move P2 across to the line side of the NO start PB, **Figure 13–32C2**. This shows that control wire 2 in the PB station connects to terminal 2 of the ladder diagram. Note that terminal 2 in the ladder diagram is connected to the auxiliary contact symbol M.

4. Move P1 across to the load side of the NO start PB, **Figure 13–32D1**, and move P2 across to the load side of the NO start PB, **Figure 13–32D2**. This has a control wire labeled with a number 3. It shows that the load side of the NO start PB is connected somewhere between terminal 3 of the auxiliary contacts and the L1 side of the coil.

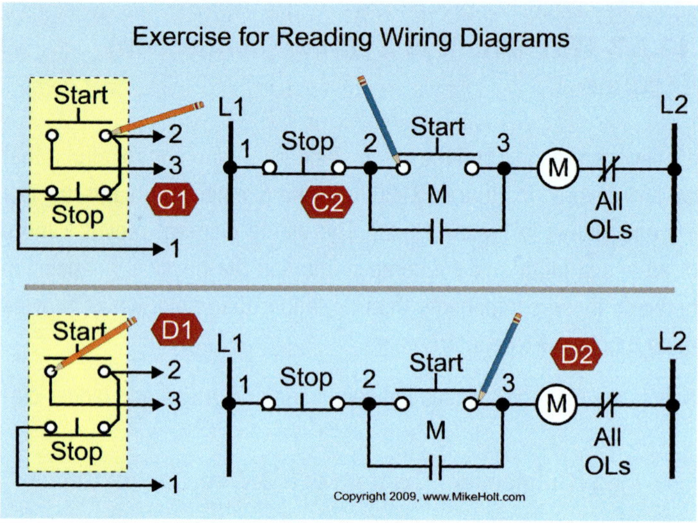

Figure 13–32

13.7 Multiple Start-Stop Pushbutton Stations

Additional start-stop stations can be added to a 3-wire control circuit. The additional stop pushbuttons are wired in series with each other and must be placed in the control circuit between the power supply (such as L1) and the line side of the start pushbutton(s) (the terminal 2 side of the auxiliary contact).

Any number of stations can be added, and pushing any one of the stop pushbuttons will de-energize the coil, **Figure 13–33A**. The additional start pushbuttons are wired in parallel with the other start pushbuttons. **Figure 13–33B**

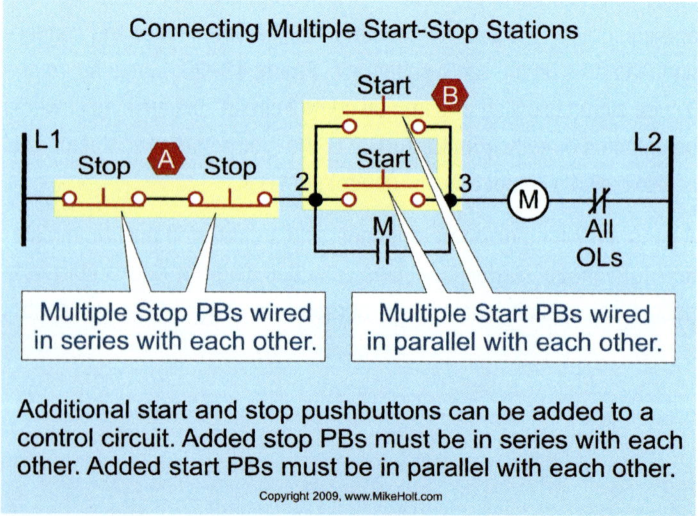

Figure 13–33

Any number of stop stations can be used in a control circuit, as long as they are all wired in series. Any number of start stations can be wired in parallel and paralleled with the holding contacts. A wiring diagram of the same control circuit is shown in **Figure 13–34**

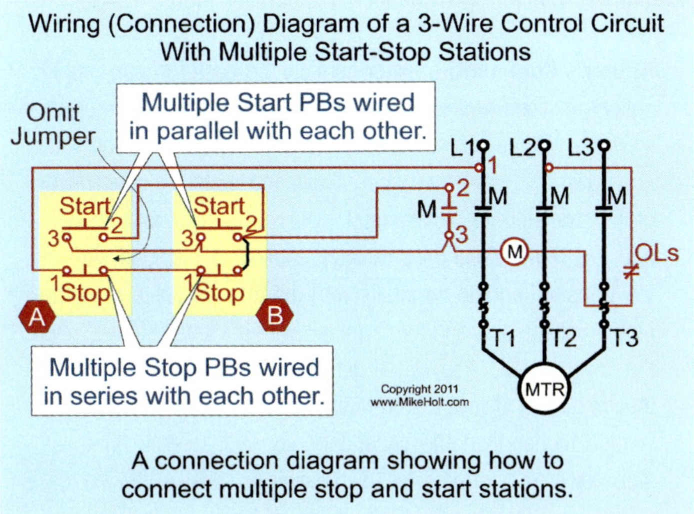

Figure 13–34

To get a better idea of how multiple start-stop stations might be laid out on a job, use a riser-type diagram, **Figure 13–35.** You won't normally find a riser diagram with the control equipment, but they're sometimes found on job blueprints. The lines between boxes represent the raceway and the slashes on that line represent the number of conductors. This type of riser diagram often has raceway and conductor sizes noted on it.

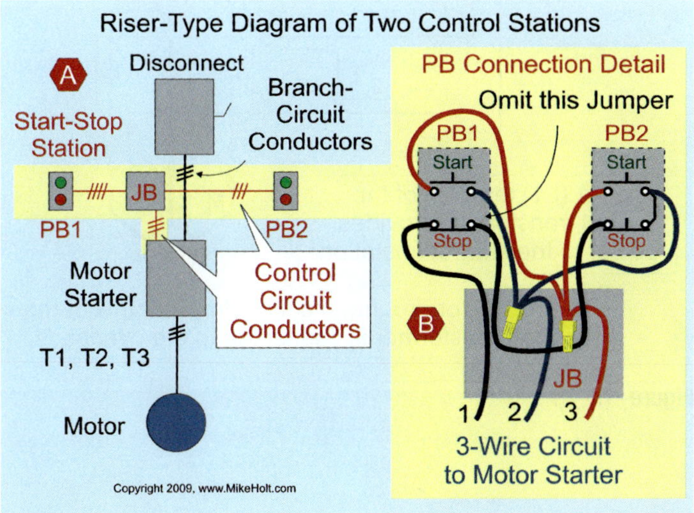

Figure 13–35

Figure 13–35B shows the control wire terminations and splices needed to wire this control circuit. When wiring multiple start-stop PB stations, the jumper between the load side of the stop PB and terminal 2 of the start PB must be removed from all added PB stations except the last one in the circuit.

CAUTION: *Careful consideration should be given to multiple start-stop stations for a motor or equipment. Additional safety features may need to be added to the control circuit to reduce or avoid hazardous starting of equipment. For example, when setting up or doing maintenance on a machine, it can be hazardous to a person whose hand is in the machine if someone else pushes a start button at a different location. To avoid this hazard, the control circuit can be wired to lock out all of the multiple start-stop stations except the one directly at the machine being set up or serviced.*

3-Wire Control Circuit Supplied by a Control Transformer

Control transformers are frequently used in motor controls. They reduce the supply voltage (usually 480V) to control circuit voltage (usually 120V), which provides greater safety to personnel, **Figure 13–36**. Some control transformers have built-in fuseholders on the primary and/or secondary side of the transformer.

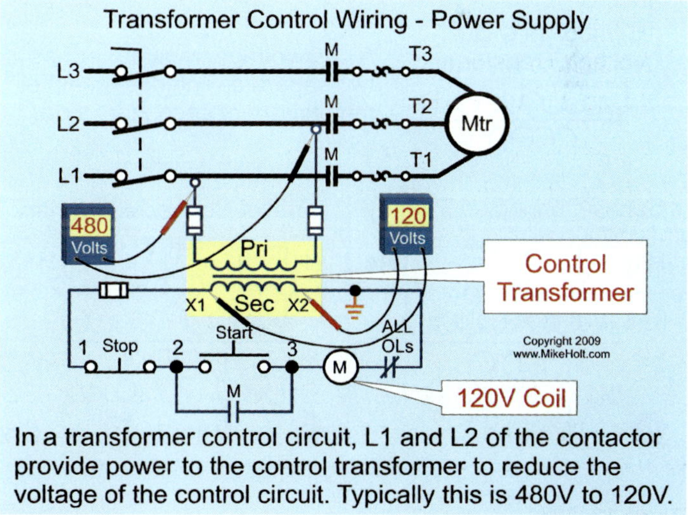

Figure 13–36

When wiring a step-down transformer, the higher voltage terminals have a letter "H" with the terminal numbers. The lower voltage terminals have the letter "X" with the terminal numbers. **Figure 13–37**

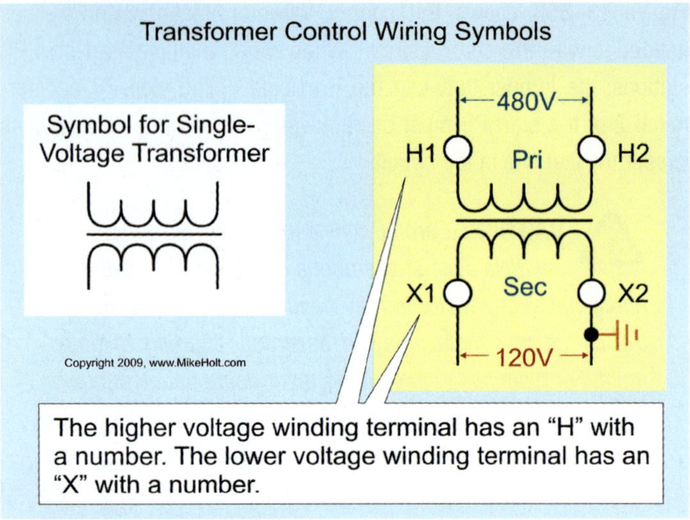

Figure 13–37

Many control transformers have several different connection configurations that allow them to be connected to a variety of primary voltages. Control transformers with a multiple voltage configuration are called "multi-tap transformers," and a transformer with two voltages is commonly called a "dual-voltage transformer." Figure 13–38

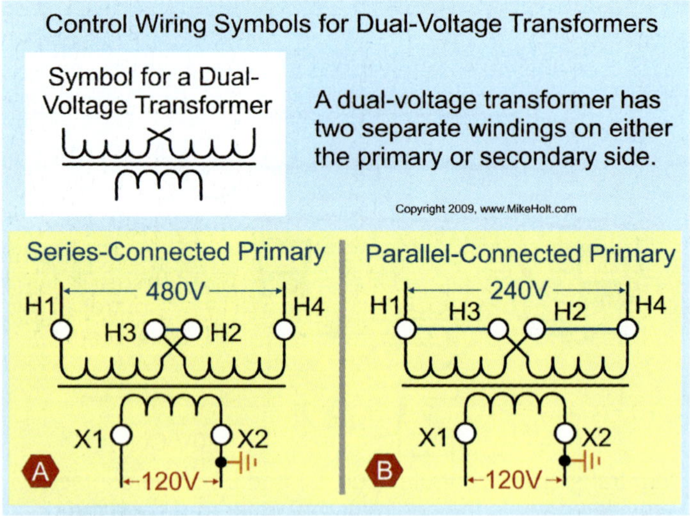

Figure 13–38

A dual-voltage transformer has two separate windings on either the primary or secondary. For example, a control transformer has a primary rated for either 480V or 240V with the secondary being 120V. If the supply conductors are 480V, the two primary windings are connected in series, Figure 13–38. If the supply conductors are 240V, the two primary windings are connected in parallel. Figure 13–38

> **Author's Comment:** Transformers can be used for many applications besides motor control, and sometimes it's desirable to step the voltage up, sometimes it's desirable to step the voltage down. The term "primary" always applies to the supply side of the transformer, which isn't always the high-voltage side, and the term "secondary" always applies to the load side of the transformer. The terminals with the letter H are always the higher-voltage side and the terminals with the letter X are always the lower voltage side. When dealing with control transformers, they're almost always a step-down transformer with the primary voltage higher than the secondary, so we'll refer to them as step-down transformers for this discussion. Just be aware that in a step-up transformer, the primary will be the X terminals and the secondary the H terminals.

Figure 13–39 shows an example of how a 480V motor starter with a 480/120V control transformer is connected to the 120V control circuit. A stop-start PB station is wired on the L1 (X1) side and the OLs are wired on the L2 (X2) side.

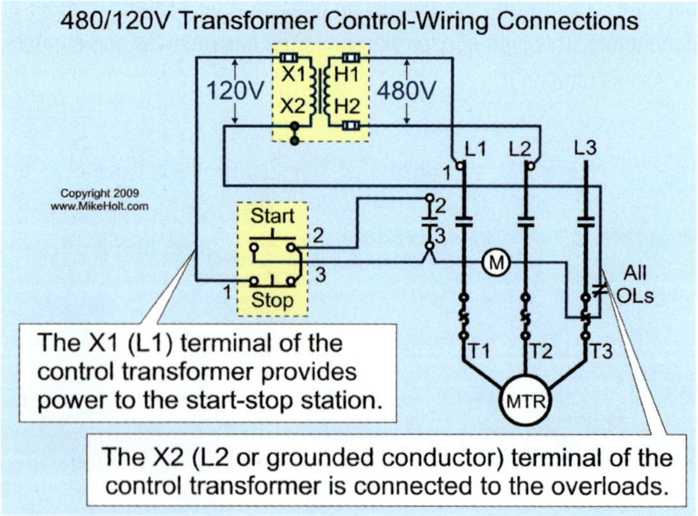

Figure 13–39

Arrangement of a 3-Wire Control Circuit with a Neutral Conductor

Where one side of the motor control circuit is grounded, the circuit and its components must be arranged so that an accidental ground fault in the control circuit remote from the motor controller won't start the motor, or bypass manually operated shutdown devices or automatic safety shutdown devices [430.74].

CAUTION: *Wiring a start-stop station in the neutral conductor can cause accidental starting of the motor if a ground fault occurs on the load side of a start PB wired in the neutral conductor.* **Figure 13–40**

The ground fault, shown in **Figure 13–40**, makes a connection between the neutral conductor and the metal enclosure or metal raceway (equipment grounding conductor). The metal path provided by the metal enclosure or raceway becomes a "parallel conductor" from the power source and provides a bypass around the start PB.

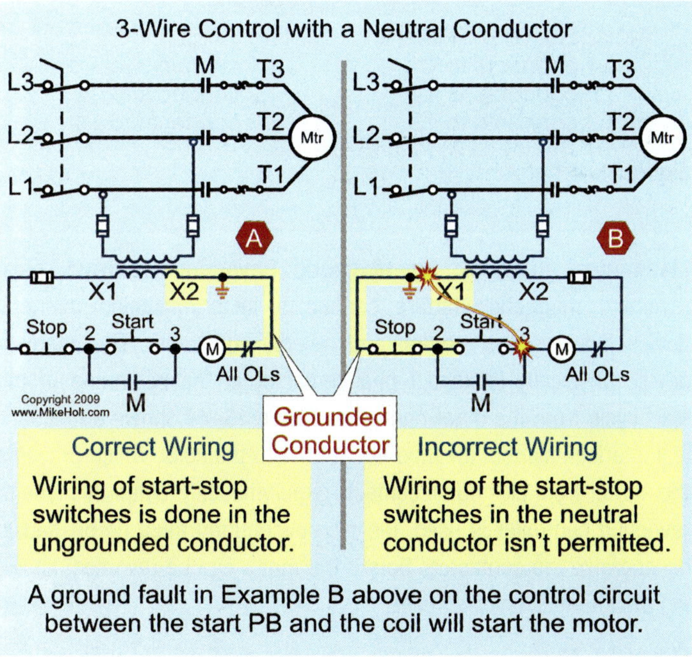

Figure 13–40

Author's Comments:

- The grounding symbol used on the neutral conductor in the schematics represents a connection between the secondary terminal X2 and the case of the transformer, or the case of the equipment in which the transformer is installed. It's not an actual grounding electrode installed at the transformer [250.20(B)]. Remember that metal equipment enclosures, metal raceways, and other noncurrent-carrying metal parts are usually connected to the equipment grounding conductor, which is connected to the earth at the electrical service or separately derived system. Similarly, a separate 120V control circuit (Class 1 circuit) has a neutral conductor and is represented by the same grounding symbol on the schematics, but there isn't a neutral conductor connection to the metal equipment enclosure. The actual grounding electrode connection to the earth is made at the electrical service or separately derived system.
- Neutral-to-ground connections aren't permitted on the load side of the service equipment except under specific conditions [250.142(B)].

13.8 Reversing Three-Phase Motors

Reversing any two lines (power-supply conductors) to a three-phase motor causes the motor to run in the other direction. It's standard industry practice to interchange L1 and L3, **Figure 13–41**

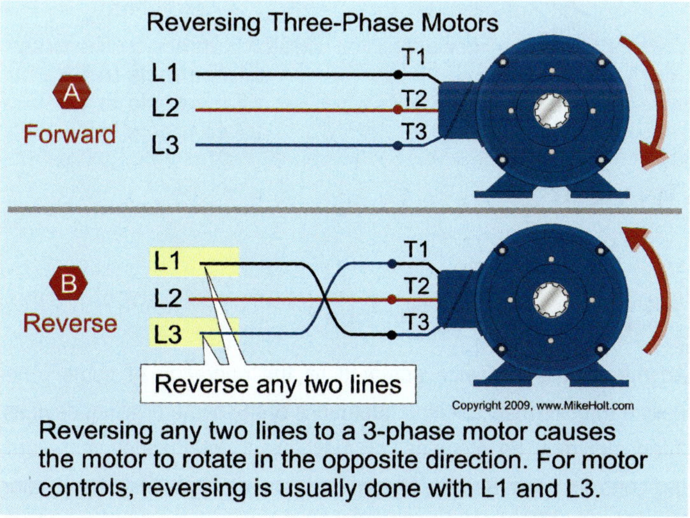

Figure 13–41

A reversing motor starter can be used to interchange L1 and L3. The basic reversing starter has two contactors (one forward and one reverse), and an interlocking arrangement to prevent energizing the forward and reverse contactors at the same time.

Author's Comment: When starting a three-phase motor for the first time, it should be uncoupled from the load and then jogged or bumped to ensure proper rotation.

13.9 Forward and Reverse Contactors

Figure 13–42 shows just the forward and reversing contacts of a reversing starter (the coils and interlock aren't shown). When the forward contacts close, Figure 13–42A, L1 is connected to T1, L2 is connected to T2, and L3 is connected to T3. When the reverse contacts close, Figure 13–42B, L1 connects to T3, L2 connects to T2, and L3 connects to T1. The motor runs in the opposite direction.

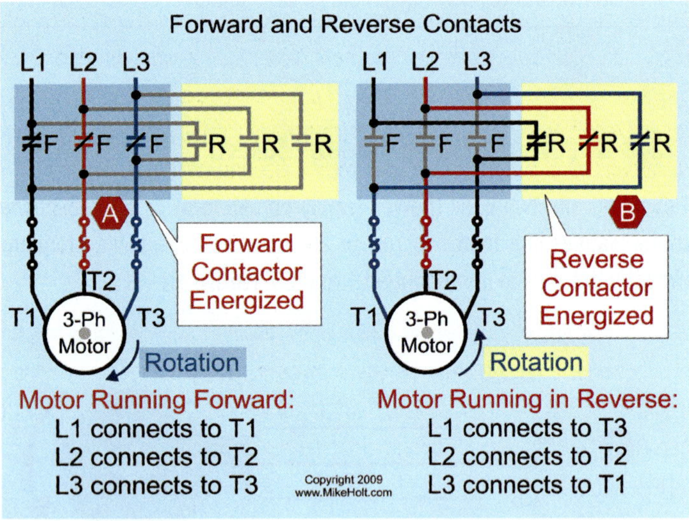

Figure 13–42

13.10 Interlocking Devices

An interlock is a device actuated by the operation of some other device to govern succeeding operations of the same or allied devices. Interlocks may be electrical or mechanical. Interlocking in reversing controls prevents the forward and reverse contactors from being energized at the same time, which will cause a phase-to-phase short.

Mechanical Interlock for a Manual Reversing Starter. A manual reversing starter is two individual 3-pole manual starters connected together. This type of reversing starter is often used for low-horsepower motors without automatic control. In some cases, the installer adds the manual interlock device between the start-stop pushbuttons of each starter, Figure 13–43. It may also be up to the installer to properly mark the starter enclosure "Forward" and "Reverse" because individual manual starter pushbuttons read start and stop.

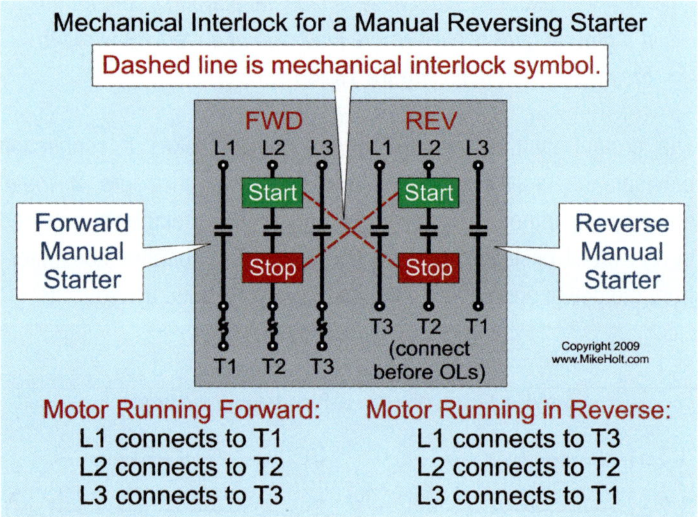

Figure 13–43

Mechanical Interlock for Magnetic Reversing Controls. Most reversing magnetic starters contain a factory-installed interlock device between the forward and reverse contactors. The interlock device physically locks out one contactor at the beginning of the start cycle from the other contactor. Figure 13–44 shows a mechanical interlock symbol (dashed line) between the coils, which prevents the starter from closing all contacts simultaneously. When this type of reversing controller is used, the stop pushbutton must be pushed to de-energize the contactors before the motor can be reversed, allowing the interlock lever to reset.

Figure 13–45 shows the voltage path when the F coil is energized. Coil R is blocked out by the interlock lever. When the motor is running in reverse, coil F is blocked out by the interlock lever. Figure 13–45

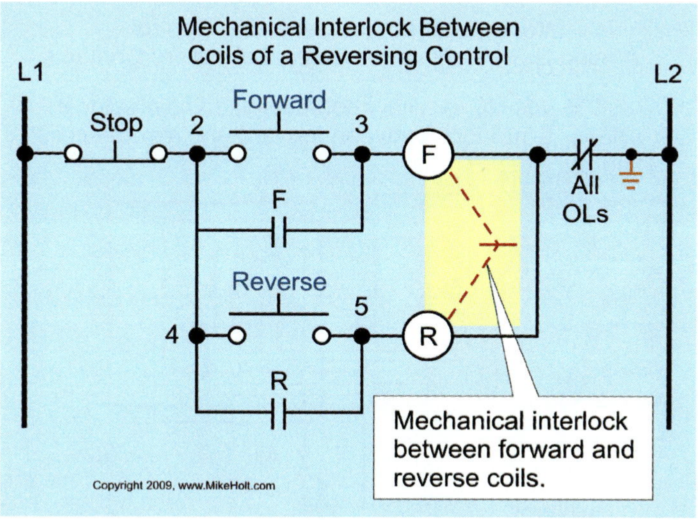

Figure 13–44

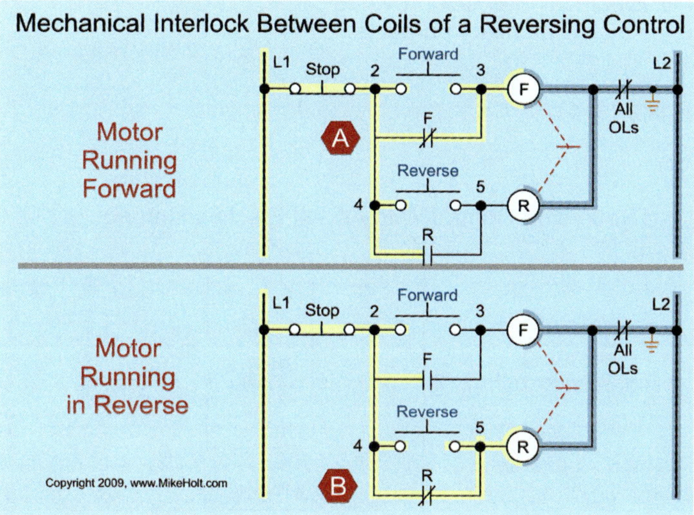

Figure 13–45

Figure 13–46 is the wiring diagram for the same control circuit as the one shown in Figures 13–44 and 13–45. Notice that each contactor has its own set of NO auxiliary contacts that serve as the holding circuit for each coil.

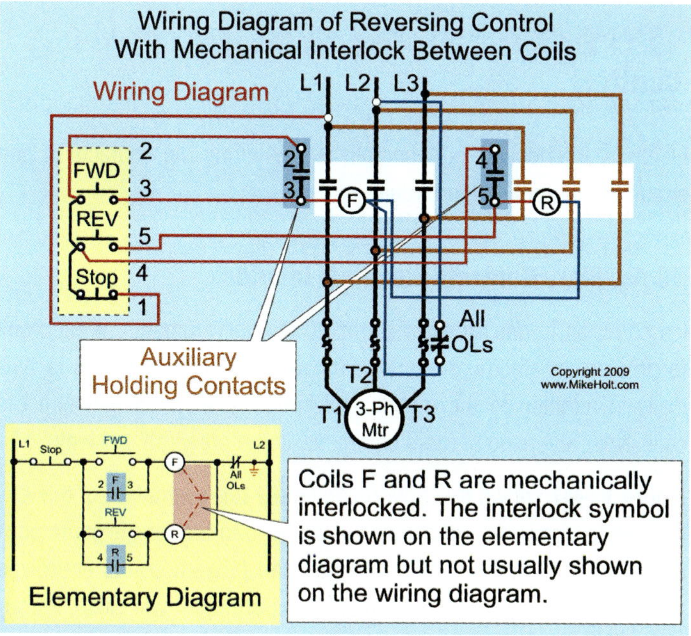

Figure 13–46

This is still an application of a basic 3-wire control circuit, even though there are five wires running to the pushbutton control station. Two 3-wire control circuits (with one shared conductor) are being used, one for each coil. Remember that a 3-wire control circuit has one wire from terminal 1 (L1 or other power source), a second wire that runs to one side of an auxiliary contact, and a third wire that runs to the other side of the auxiliary contact that connects to one side of the coil. The 3-wire circuit to the forward coil consists of control wires 1, 2, and 3.

The 3-wire circuit to the reverse coil consists of control wires 1, 4, and 5. Whenever a control circuit makes use of holding contacts that drop out on power loss, it's called a "3-wire circuit" regardless of the actual number of conductors necessary to provide for all circuit options.

13.11 Electrical Interlock for Magnetic Reversing Controls

Electrical interlocking is accomplished by wiring the contacts of one circuit to control another circuit.

NC Auxiliary Contacts Electrical Interlock

It's common to use an extra set of NC auxiliary contacts at each coil to provide an electrical interlock for reversing controls. This is typically in addition to the mechanical interlock provided between the coils. New reversing starters commonly come prewired this way.

Figure 13–47 shows the ladder/elementary representation of this circuit, while **Figure 13–48** shows the wiring diagram for the same controls. When the forward PB is pushed, the forward coil is energized and all F contacts switch (F contacts that are open will close, F contacts that are closed will open).

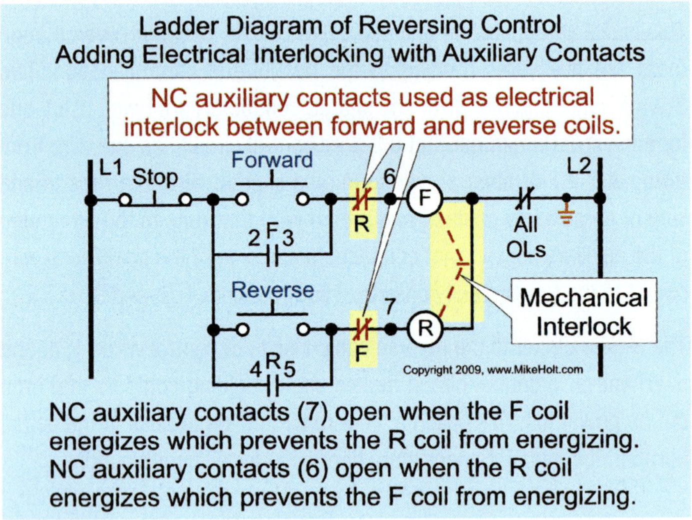

Figure 13–47

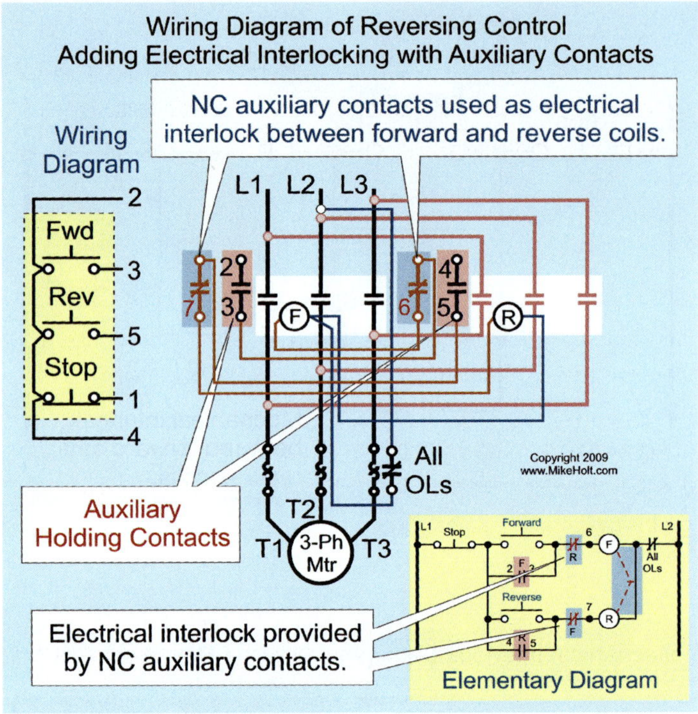

Figure 13–48

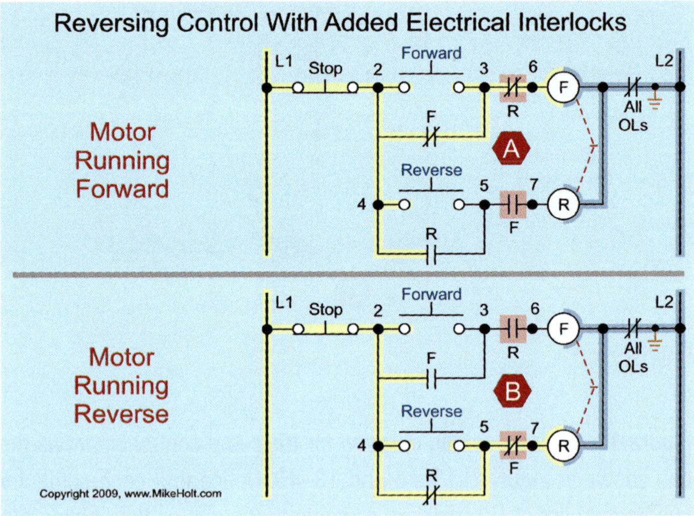

Figure 13–49

The forward NC auxiliary contact interlock (with terminal 7) opens and interrupts the current path to the reverse coil, **Figure 13–49A**. If the reverse PB is pushed, nothing happens. The stop PB must be pushed to de-energize the forward coil and the motor stops. Now if the reverse PB is pushed, the reverse coil is energized and all R contacts switch (R contacts that are open will close, R contacts that are closed will open).

The reverse NC auxiliary contact interlock (with terminal 6) will then open and interrupt the current path to the forward coil, **Figure 13–49B**. If the forward PB is pushed, nothing will happen.The stop PB must be pushed to de-energize the reverse coil and stop the motor before the forward PB will work.

Author's Comment: Auxiliary contacts often come as two sets of contacts in a single device. This device can be two sets of NO contacts, two sets of NC contacts, or one set of NO contacts and one set of NC contacts.

Pushbutton Electrical Interlock

In Figure 13–50, notice that both the forward and reverse pushbuttons have the mechanical interlock symbol. This gives the appearance that there are four individual pushbuttons for the forward and reverse controls (not counting the stop PB). But these are actually just two double-circuit momentary-contact pushbuttons, and the way these two pushbuttons are wired provides the electrical interlock method in this control circuit.

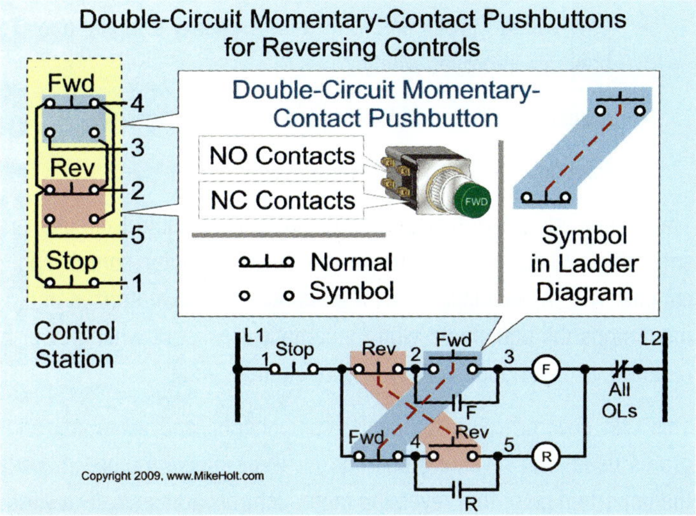

Figure 13–50

Remember that ladder/elementary diagrams show electrical functions and terminations rather than the physical location of devices. Each pushbutton has one set of NO contacts and one set of NC contacts, and when the button is pushed, both sets of contacts operate simultaneously.

The interlock symbol between the double-circuit pushbutton contacts represents the mechanical construction of the pushbuttons, but doesn't represent the electrical interlocking feature that the wiring of these double-circuit pushbuttons adds to the control circuit. Each of these pushbuttons contains two sets of contacts that operate when the pushbutton is pressed.

While each pushbutton controls the circuit it's connected to, it also operates a set of contacts that control another circuit, Figure 13–51. For example, the forward PB is part of the 3-wire circuit that controls the F coil. The NC contacts of the forward PB are the interlocking contacts of the reversing circuit and this set of NC contacts has a major role in controlling the 3-wire circuit for the R coil. The same features in the NC contacts of the reverse PB act exactly the same way on the 3-wire circuit for the F coil.

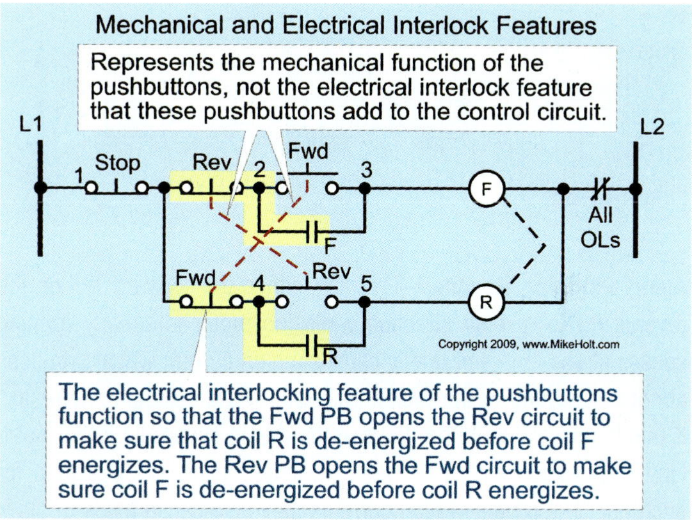

Figure 13–51

Figure 13–52A shows the standard method for using double-circuit pushbuttons as an electrical interlock in reversing controls. Figure 13–52B shows the same circuit configuration without using the dashed lines for the interlock symbol. Although this ladder diagram is seldom used, it shows the double-circuit pushbuttons and electrical interlocking features more clearly. When the forward PB is pressed, the NO forward PB contact is momentarily closed, which energizes the F coil through the NC reverse PB. The NO F holding contacts close, which allows the motor to continue to run forward after the forward PB has been released. When the reverse PB is pressed, the NC reverse PB contacts open and de-energize the F coil. The NO reverse PB contact is then closed, energizing the R coil, which closes the NO R seal-in contacts, allowing the motor to run in reverse after the reverse PB has been released. Pushbuttons used for this type of application are constructed with a "break-before-make" feature, which allows one set of contacts to open before the other set of contacts close.

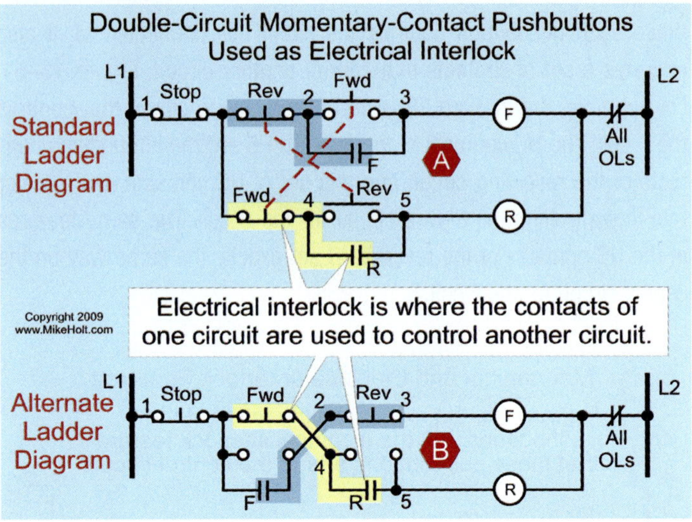

Figure 13–52

Avoid Plugging Reversal. Pressing either the forward PB or the reverse PB to reverse direction while the motor is already running causes stress in it, and briefly causes a high current which produces abnormal heating in the motor. This is called a "plugging reversal." If this is done often it can damage the motor, especially if the motor isn't allowed to cool off between reversals, unless it's designed for such use. The repeated high currents may also cause fuses to blow, the circuit breaker to trip, or the overload relay to trip. It's preferable to push the stop PB and let the motor coast to a stop before reversing it. In some cases, it may be desirable to add a time-delay relay to the reversing process to allow the motor to come to a complete stop before allowing it to start in the opposite direction.

CONCLUSION TO UNIT 13—MOTOR CONTROL BASICS

This unit explained the basic concepts of motor controls, concentrating on how specialized electrical symbols, words, and line diagrams are used to convey information about motor control circuits. It provided an introduction to the following types of diagrams:

- Ladder diagrams (these are also called "line diagrams" or "elementary diagrams").
- Connection diagrams (also called "wiring diagrams").
- Pictorial diagrams.

This unit explained basic control circuits, particularly the differences between 2-wire and 3-wire control schemes. It also covered related subjects such as:

- Holding circuits (also called "sealing circuits").
- Low-voltage protection with 3-wire control circuits, and how this improves safety.
- Reading motor control wiring (connection) diagrams.
- Pilot devices such as start-stop pushbuttons.

This unit made the important point that 3-wire control circuits are safer than 2-wire control circuits for magnetic motor control applications. This is because, if power goes out and the motorized equipment stops the equipment won't automatically restart when power is restored, as can happen with a 2-wire control circuit.

This unit covered basic concepts, components, and schematic diagrams used with reversing controls for three-phase motors. It made the important point that reversing motor controls are basically a variation of 3-wire control circuits, even though they may have four or five conductors.

Another important point made was that combining mechanical interlocking with electrical interlocking incorporates a greater degree of safety by reducing the possibility of phase-to-phase shorts.

UNIT 13 Practice Questions

PRACTICE QUESTIONS FOR UNIT 13—MOTOR CONTROL BASICS

Introduction

1. A motor control circuit, for the most part, is simply a ______ and a motor.

   (a) motor
   (b) switch
   (c) feeder
   (d) magnet

2. Many types of overload protectors operate on the relationship between ______.

   (a) heat and current
   (b) the neutral conductor and the earth
   (c) branch circuits and feeders
   (d) voltage and wattage

13.1 Motor Control Language

3. Schematics show motors and control equipment in their "resting" or "shelf" state.

   (a) True
   (b) False

4. Ladder diagrams are also known as ______.

   (a) line diagrams
   (b) elementary diagrams
   (c) pictorial diagrams
   (d) a or b

5. ______ are used to represent the function of the control circuit and the associated devices, but don't show the components of the control circuit in their actual positions.

   (a) Ladder diagrams
   (b) Connection diagrams
   (c) Wiring diagrams
   (d) Pictorial diagrams

6. Connection diagrams are also called wiring diagrams.

   (a) True
   (b) False

7. ______ are used mostly in educational material and as exploded views or cut-away views in installation and maintenance literature.

   (a) Ladder diagrams
   (b) Connection diagrams
   (c) Wiring diagrams
   (d) Pictorial diagrams

8. The motor control circuit shown in **Figure 13–53** is a ______.

   (a) ladder diagram
   (b) connection diagram
   (c) wiring diagram
   (d) pictorial diagram

9. The motor control circuit shown in **Figure 13–54** is a ______.

   (a) ladder diagram
   (b) connection diagram
   (c) wiring diagram
   (d) pictorial diagram

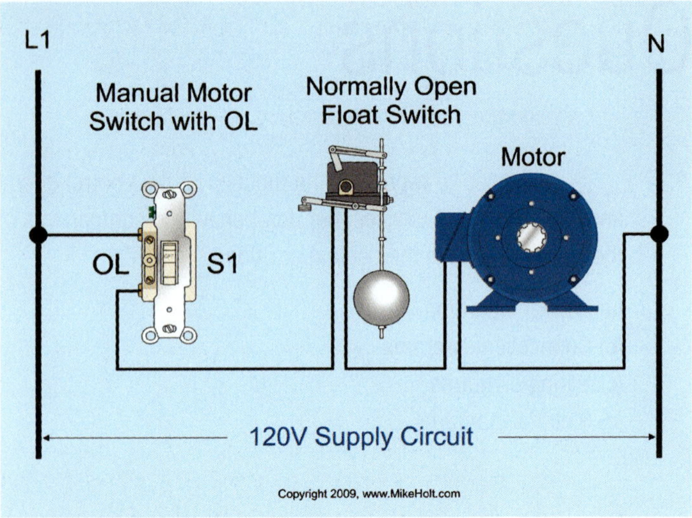

Figure 13–53

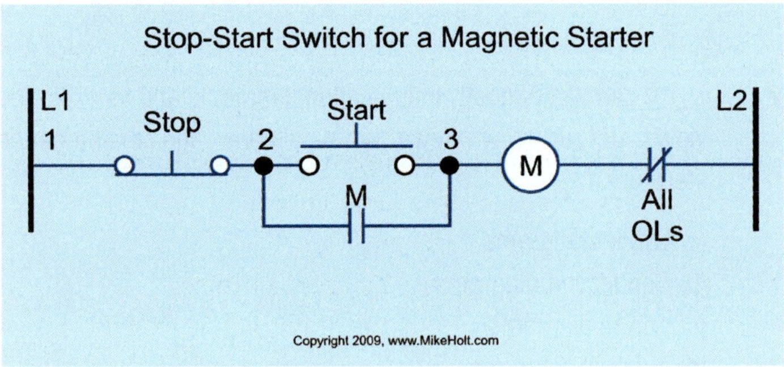

Figure 13–54

13.4 2-Wire Control Circuits

10. A 2-wire control circuit doesn't have low-voltage protection.

(a) True
(b) False

11. A basic 2-wire control circuit goes from a power supply, which is L1 if from the contactor (common control wiring), to a 2-wire control device such as a ______.

(a) float switch
(b) pressure switch
(c) temperature switch
(d) any of these

13.5 3-Wire Control Circuits

12. A 3-wire control circuit has built-in low-voltage protection.

(a) True
(b) False

13. In a basic 3-wire control circuit, the stop PB is in series with the coil, and the start PB is in parallel with the NO auxiliary contacts.

(a) True
(b) False

14. ______ means that if power goes off to the control circuit, the equipment won't automatically restart when power is restored.

(a) Sequence of operation
(b) Low-voltage protection
(c) Operation from rest
(d) Operation from stop

13.11 Electrical Interlock for Magnetic Reversing Controls

15. Pressing either the forward PB or the reverse PB to reverse direction while the motor is already running causes stress in the motor, and briefly causes a high current which produces abnormal heating in the motor. This is called a(n) ______.

(a) plugging reversal
(b) electrical interlock
(c) mechanical interlock
(d) reversing control

16. In the field, most ladder and wiring diagrams don't use numbers such as F1, F2, R1, or R3 for the auxiliary contacts.

(a) True
(b) False

Practice Questions—General

Note: The following questions are based on any part of this unit

17. In **Figure 13–55**, in the 3-wire control circuit, the ______.

(a) stop PB is in series with the M coil
(b) start PB is in series with the M coil
(c) start PB is in parallel with the auxiliary contacts 2-3
(d) all of these

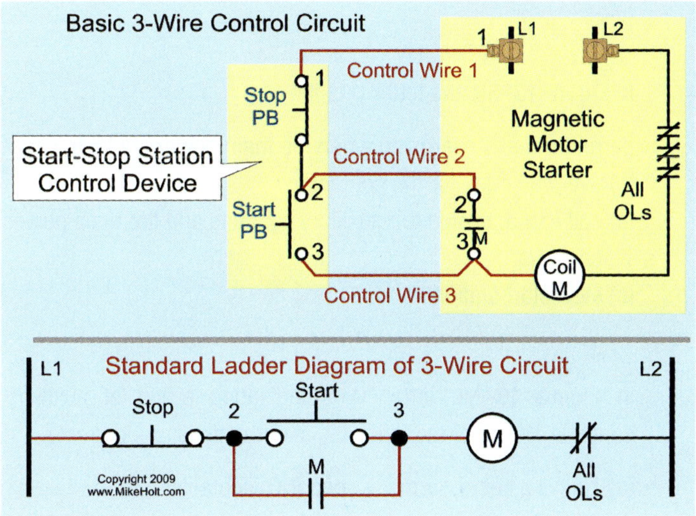

Figure 13–55

18. Based on **Figure 13–55**, which of the following statements is(are) true?

(a) The power from L2 runs through the OLs to get to the M coil.
(b) The power from L1 connects to this control circuit at the stop PB.
(c) The entire 3-wire control circuit (including the coil and OLs) is connected between L1 and L2.
(d) all of these

19. In **Figure 13–55**, the conductor supplying power to the M coil through the OLs is part of the overall control circuit, but it's not part of the 3-wire control circuit.

(a) True
(b) False

20. In **Figure 13–55**, if the motor isn't running, which of the following statements is true?

(a) Pressing the start NO PB de-energizes the M coil.
(b) After the coil energizes, the NO auxiliary contacts open.
(c) After the coil energizes, the NO auxiliary contacts will stay closed after the start PB is released.
(d) Pressing the stop PB energizes the M coil.

21. In **Figure 13–55**, if the motor is running, which of the following statements is true?

(a) Pressing the NO start PB will start the motor.
(b) The NO auxiliary contacts are closed providing a holding circuit to keep the motor running after the start PB is released.
(c) The motor will continue running if the NC stop PB is pressed.
(d) The motor will only run if the NO start PB is held closed.

22. In **Figure 13–55**, if the motor is running, and the power to the magnetic motor starter is interrupted, the ______.

(a) motor will automatically restart when power is restored
(b) NO auxiliary contacts will remain closed
(c) motor won't restart automatically
(d) stop PB must be pressed to restart the motor

23. Reversing any two lines (power-supply conductors) to a three-phase motor causes the motor to run in the other direction.

(a) True
(b) False

24. Whenever a control circuit makes use of holding contacts that drop out on power loss, it's called a "______" circuit regardless of the actual number of conductors necessary to provide for all circuit options.

(a) 1-wire
(b) 2-wire
(c) 3-wire
(d) 4-wire

UNIT 13

Challenge Questions

CHALLENGE QUESTIONS FOR UNIT 13—MOTOR CONTROL BASICS

1. The circuit of a control apparatus or system that carries the electric signals directing the performance of the controller but doesn't carry the main power current is called a ______.

(a) control circuit
(b) service
(c) feeder
(d) branch circuit

2. In **Figure 13–56**, the auxiliary contacts are indicated by the letter ______.

(a) A
(b) B
(c) D
(d) M

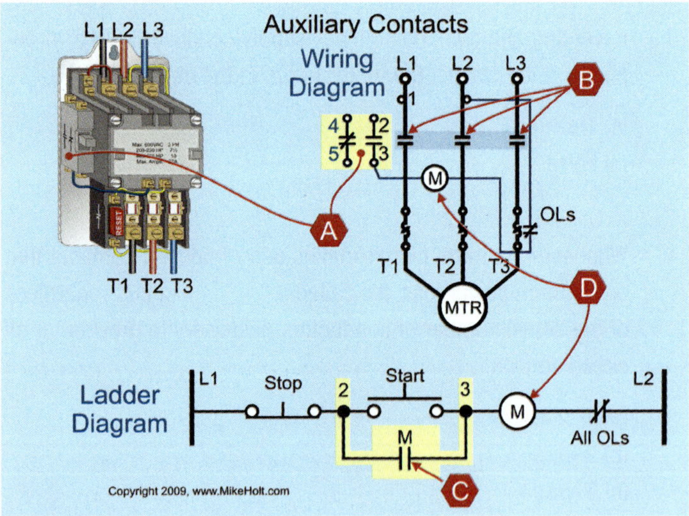

Figure 13–56

3. In **Figure 13–56**, the power contacts in the magnetic starter are indicated by the letter ______.

(a) A
(b) B
(c) C
(d) D

4. In **Figure 13–56**, the letter D is the______.

(a) motor that's energized when the main power contacts close
(b) overload relay for the contactor
(c) coil that activates the auxiliary contacts and the main power contacts
(d) stop-start station

5. In **Figure 13–56**, letter C is indicating a set of auxiliary contacts. Which of the following statements is(are) correct?

(a) This is a set of normally open (NO) contacts.
(b) The M over the auxiliary contacts indicates that coil M activates the contacts.
(c) The NO auxiliary contacts have terminal numbers 2 and 3.
(d) all of these

6. In **Figure 13–57** there is(are) ______ momentary-contact pushbutton(s).

(a) 1
(b) 2
(c) 3
(d) 4

7. In **Figure 13–57**, when the start pushbutton is pressed, the ______.

(a) M coil energizes
(b) NO M1 contacts close
(c) NC M2 contacts open
(d) all of these

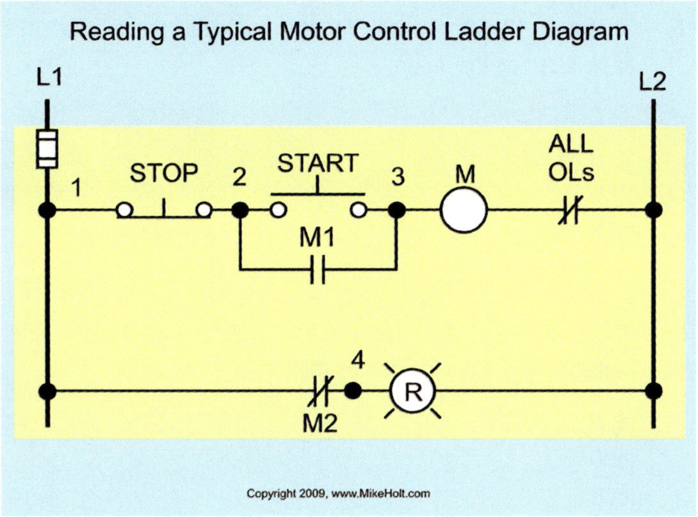

Figure 13–57

8. In **Figure 13–57**, the letter in the middle of the pilot light symbol represents ______.

(a) the direction the motor turns
(b) the color of the pilot light
(c) which coil activates the pilot light
(d) the terminal number to which the pilot light is connected

9. In **Figure 13–57**, the normally closed auxiliary contacts M2 are connected to points ______.

(a) 1-2
(b) 1-3
(c) 1-4
(d) 3-4

10. In **Figure 13–57**, the normally open auxiliary contacts M1 are connected to points ______.

(a) 1-2
(b) 1-3
(c) 1-4
(d) 2-3

11. ______ are devices using coils that can be used to facilitate remote-control functions.

(a) Contactors
(b) Magnetic starters
(c) Solenoids
(d) all of these

12. In **Figure 13–58**, the main power contacts are _____.

(a) not shown in the ladder diagram A
(b) shown in the wiring (connection) diagram B
(c) not shown in either diagram
(d) a and b

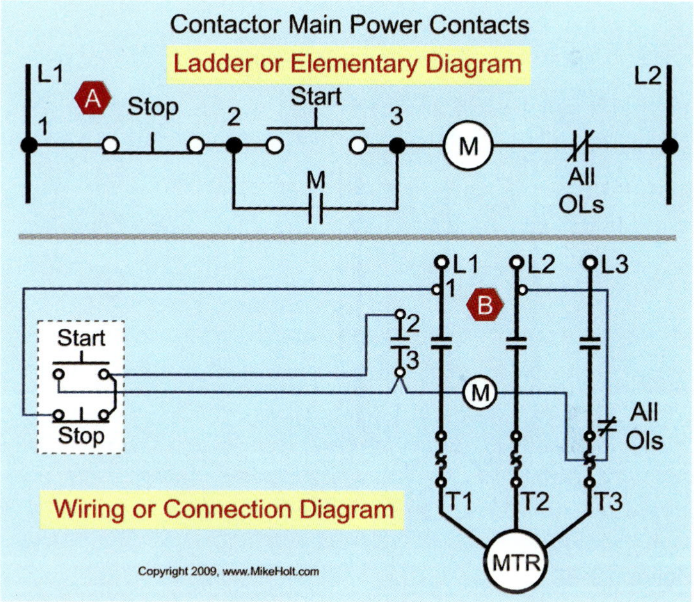

Figure 13–58

13. In **Figure 13–58**, the power for the control circuit is taken from ______.

(a) L1 and L2 for both the ladder and wiring diagrams
(b) L1 and L2 for the ladder diagram and from L1 and L3 for the wiring diagram
(c) L1 and L3 for both diagrams
(d) L2 and L3 for both diagrams

14. In **Figure 13–58**, when the start PB is pushed, the M coil ______.

(a) closes the power contacts
(b) closes the auxiliary contacts 2-3
(c) energizes
(d) all of these

15. In **Figure 13–59**, the magnetic motor starter is designated by the letter ______.

(a) A
(b) B
(c) C
(d) D

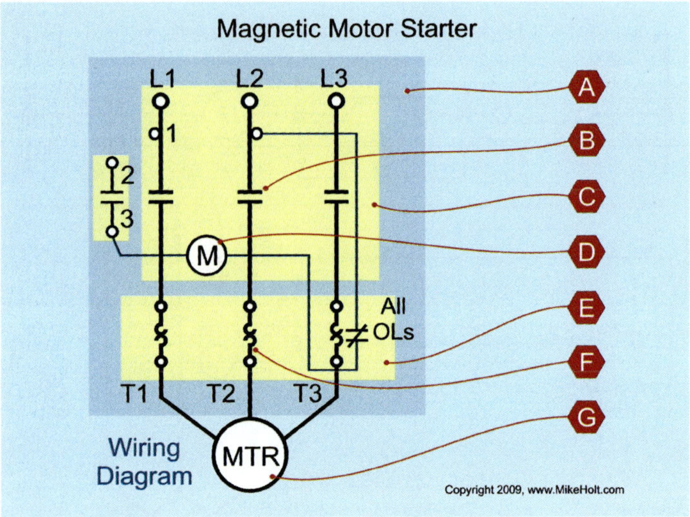

Figure 13–59

16. In **Figure 13–59**, the power contacts for the magnetic motor starter are designated by the letter ______.

(a) A
(b) B
(c) C
(d) D

17. In **Figure 13–59**, the coil for the magnetic motor starter is designated by the letter ______.

(a) C
(b) D
(c) E
(d) F

18. In **Figure 13–59**, the overload relay assembly for the magnetic motor starter is designated by the letter ______.

(a) C
(b) D
(c) E
(d) F

19. In **Figure 13–59**, the motor that's supplied by the magnetic motor starter is designated by the letter ______.

(a) D
(b) E
(c) F
(d) G

20. In **Figure 13–59**, the thermal overload (heater) is designated by the letter ______.

(a) C
(b) D
(c) E
(d) F

CHAPTER

5 *NEC* PRACTICE QUESTIONS

Essential for all Journeyman and Master's Exams

- ***NEC* Practice Quizzes**
- ***NEC* Challenge Quizzes**
- **Final *NEC* Exams**

The first three chapters of this book focused on the theory and calculation topics necessary to pass an exam. This chapter provides a review of *Code* requirements. There are ten sets of Practice Quizzes in Straight Order and 10 sets of Practice Quizzes in Random Order that you should complete to begin with. If you are short on time before your exam, complete all of the straight order questions first, then return to the random order questions. After you have done the practice quizzes to provide a good *Code* review, you should next complete the seven Challenge Quizzes to hone your skills in finding *Code* requirements. To complete your review, there are two 100 question Final Exams that will help you evaluate your exam taking skills.

Answer these questions from the 2011 *NEC* book. Practice using your *Code* book for the straight-order questions, and then as you progress, you may want to see how many of the questions you can answer from memory. Most licensing exams are open book, but check with your testing authority in your region.

Mike Holt's Understanding the National Electrical Code Volume 1 and *Mike Holt's Understanding the National Electrical Code Volume 2* will help if you feel you need more *Code* review.

Notes

Practice Quiz 1

Straight Order [90 through 210.8]

Unit 1 Practice Quiz—Straight Order [90 through 210.8]

Please use the 2011 *Code* book to answer the following questions, which are based on the 2011 *NEC*.

1. The *NEC* is ______.

   (a) intended to be a design manual
   (b) meant to be used as an instruction guide for untrained persons
   (c) for the practical safeguarding of persons and property
   (d) published by the Bureau of Standards

2. The *Code* contains provisions considered necessary for safety, which will not necessarily result in ______.

   (a) efficient use
   (b) convenience
   (c) good service or future expansion of electrical use
   (d) all of these

3. The *Code* isn't a design specification standard or instruction manual for the untrained and unqualified.

   (a) True
   (b) False

4. The *NEC* applies to the installation of ______.

   (a) electrical conductors and equipment within or on public and private buildings
   (b) outside conductors and equipment on the premises
   (c) optical fiber cables
   (d) all of these

5. Installations of communications equipment that are under the exclusive control of communications utilities, and located outdoors or in building spaces used exclusively for such installations ______ covered by the *NEC*.

   (a) are
   (b) are sometimes
   (c) are not
   (d) may be

6. Utilities may be subject to compliance with codes and standards covering their regulated activities as adopted under governmental law or regulation.

   (a) True
   (b) False

7. The *NEC* does not apply to electric utility-owned wiring and equipment ______.

   (a) installed by an electrical contractor
   (b) installed on public property
   (c) consisting of service drops or service laterals
   (d) in a utility office building

8. Communications wiring such as telephone, antenna, and CATV wiring within a building shall not be required to comply with the installation requirements of Chapters 1 through 7, except where specifically referenced in Chapter 8.

   (a) True
   (b) False

9. By special permission, the authority having jurisdiction may waive specific requirements in this *Code* where it is assured that equivalent objectives can be achieved by establishing and maintaining effective safety.

   (a) True
   (b) False

10. If the *NEC* requires new products that are not yet available at the time a new edition is adopted, the ______ may permit the use of the products that comply with the previous edition of the *Code* adopted by that jurisdiction.

    (a) electrical engineer
    (b) master electrician
    (c) authority having jurisdiction
    (d) permit holder

11. When the *Code* uses "_____," it means the identified actions are allowed but not required, and they may be options or alternative methods.
(a) shall
(b) shall not
(c) shall be permitted
(d) a or b

12. Nonmandatory Informative Annexes contained in the back of the *Code* book _____.
(a) are for information only
(b) aren't enforceable as a requirement of the *Code*
(c) are enforceable as a requirement of the *Code*
(d) a and b

13. Capable of being removed or exposed without damaging the building structure or finish, or not permanently closed in by the structure or finish of the building is known as _____.
(a) accessible (as applied to equipment)
(b) accessible (as applied to wiring methods)
(c) accessible, readily
(d) all of these

14. The maximum current in amperes a conductor can carry continuously, where the temperature will not be raised in excess of the conductor's insulation temperature rating is called its "_____."
(a) short-circuit rating
(b) ground-fault rating
(c) ampacity
(d) all of these

15. An arc-fault circuit interrupter is a device intended to de-energize the circuit when it recognizes characteristics unique to _____.
(a) overcurrent
(b) arcing
(c) ground fault
(d) harmonic fundamental

16. Where no statutory requirement exists, the authority having jurisdiction can be a property owner or his/her agent, such as an architect or engineer.
(a) True
(b) False

17. A reliable conductor that ensures electrical conductivity between metal parts of the electrical installation that are required to be electrically connected is called a "_____."
(a) grounding electrode
(b) auxiliary ground
(c) bonding conductor or jumper
(d) tap conductor

18. The connection between the grounded conductor and the supply-side bonding jumper or equipment grounding conductor, or both, at a _____ is called a "system bonding jumper."
(a) service disconnect
(b) separately derived system
(c) motor control center
(d) separate building or structure disconnect

19. A(n) _____ branch circuit supplies energy to one or more outlets to which appliances are to be connected.
(a) general purpose
(b) multiwire
(c) individual
(d) appliance

20. For a circuit to be considered a multiwire branch circuit, it shall have _____.
(a) two or more ungrounded conductors with a voltage potential between them
(b) a grounded conductor having equal voltage potential between it and each ungrounded conductor of the circuit
(c) a grounded conductor connected to the neutral or grounded terminal of the system
(d) all of these

21. _____ is a term indicating that there is an intentional delay in the tripping action of the circuit breaker, which decreases as the magnitude of the current increases.
(a) Adverse time
(b) Inverse time
(c) Time delay
(d) Timed unit

22. Communications equipment includes equipment used for the transmission of ______.

(a) audio
(b) video
(c) data
(d) any of these

23. A conductor encased within material of composition or thickness that is not recognized by the *NEC* as electrical insulation is considered ______.

(a) noninsulating
(b) bare
(c) covered
(d) protected

24. A solderless pressure connector is a device that ______ between conductors or between conductors and a terminal by means of mechanical pressure.

(a) provides access
(b) protects the wiring
(c) is never needed
(d) establishes a connection

25. ______ are designed for surface mounting with a swinging door.

(a) Outlet boxes
(b) Cabinets
(c) Cutout boxes
(d) none of these

26. A unit of an electrical system that carries or controls electric energy as its principal function is a(n) "______."

(a) raceway
(b) fitting
(c) device
(d) enclosure

27. An enclosure or piece of equipment constructed so that dust will not enter the enclosure under specified test conditions is known as "______."

(a) dusttight
(b) dustproof
(c) dust rated
(d) all of these

28. "Varying duty" is defined as ______.

(a) intermittent operation in which the load conditions are regularly recurrent
(b) operation at a substantially constant load for an indefinite length of time
(c) operation for alternate intervals of load and rest, or load, no load, and rest
(d) operation at loads, and for intervals of time, both of which may be subject to wide variations

29. Surrounded by a case, housing, fence, or wall(s) that prevents persons from accidentally contacting energized parts is called "______."

(a) guarded
(b) covered
(c) protection
(d) enclosed

30. Equipment enclosed in a case that is capable of withstanding an explosion of a specified gas or vapor that may occur within it, and of preventing the ignition of a specified gas or vapor surrounding the enclosure by sparks, flashes, or explosion of the gas or vapor within, and that operates at such an external temperature that a surrounding flammable atmosphere will not be ignited thereby defines the phrase "______."

(a) overcurrent device
(b) thermal apparatus
(c) explosionproof equipment
(d) bomb casing

31. For wiring methods, "on or attached to the surface, or behind access panels designed to allow access" is known as ______.

(a) open
(b) uncovered
(c) exposed
(d) bare

32. An accessory, such as a locknut, intended to perform a mechanical function best describes ______.

(a) a part
(b) equipment
(c) a device
(d) a fitting

33. Connected to ground or to a conductive body that extends the ground connection is called "______."

(a) equipment grounding
(b) bonded
(c) grounded
(d) all of these

34. Connected to ground without the insertion of any resistor or impedance device is referred to as "______."

(a) grounded
(b) solidly grounded
(c) effectively grounded
(d) grounding conductor

35. A Class A GFCI protection device is designed to trip when the ground-fault current to ground is ______ or higher.

(a) 4 mA
(b) 5 mA
(c) 6 mA
(d) none of these

36. The installed conductive path(s) that connects normally noncurrent-carrying metal parts of equipment together and to the system grounded conductor or to the grounding electrode conductor, or both, is known as a(n) ______.

(a) grounding electrode conductor
(b) grounding conductor
(c) equipment grounding conductor
(d) none of these

37. A "______" is an accommodation with two or more contiguous rooms comprising a compartment that provides living, sleeping, sanitary, and storage facilities.

(a) guest room
(b) guest suite
(c) dwelling unit
(d) single-family dwelling

38. A hoistway is any ______ in which an elevator or dumbwaiter is designed to operate.

(a) hatchway or well hole
(b) vertical opening or space
(c) shaftway
(d) all of these

39. Within sight means visible and not more than ______ ft distant from the equipment.

(a) 10
(b) 20
(c) 25
(d) 50

40. A device that provides a means to connect bonding conductors for ______ systems to the building grounding electrode system is an intersystem bonding termination.

(a) limited energy
(b) low-voltage
(c) communications
(d) power and lighting

41. An outlet intended for the direct connection of a lampholder or a luminaire is a(n) "______."

(a) outlet
(b) receptacle outlet
(c) lighting outlet
(d) general-purpose outlet

42. A ______ location will be protected from weather and not subject to saturation with water or other liquids; such locations include partially protected locations under canopies, marquees, and roofed open porches.

(a) dry
(b) damp
(c) wet
(d) moist

43. Conduit installed underground or encased in concrete slabs that are in direct contact with the earth is considered a ______ location.

(a) dry
(b) damp
(c) wet
(d) moist

44. A neutral conductor is the conductor connected to the ______ of a system, which is intended to carry neutral current under normal conditions.

(a) grounding electrode
(b) neutral point
(c) intersystem bonding termination
(d) none of these

45. Outline lighting may include an arrangement of ______ to outline or call attention to the shape of a building.

(a) incandescent lamps
(b) electric-discharge lighting
(c) electrically powered light sources
(d) any of these

46. A branch-circuit overcurrent device is capable of providing protection for ______.

(a) service conductors
(b) feeders
(c) branch circuits
(d) all of these

47. An overload is the same as a short circuit or ground fault.

(a) True
(b) False

48. A ______ is a chamber to which one or more ducts are connected and form part of the air distribution system.

(a) riser
(b) plenum
(c) a or b
(d) none of these

49. A raceway is an enclosure designed for the installation of wires, cables, or busbars.

(a) True
(b) False

50. A raintight enclosure is constructed or protected so that exposure to a beating rain will not result in the entrance of water under specified test conditions.

(a) True
(b) False

51. A single receptacle is a single contact device with no other contact device on the same ______.

(a) circuit
(b) yoke
(c) run
(d) equipment

52. When one electrical circuit controls another circuit through a relay, the first circuit is called a "______."

(a) primary circuit
(b) remote-control circuit
(c) signal circuit
(d) controller

53. Service conductors originate at the service point and terminate at the service disconnecting means.

(a) True
(b) False

54. Underground service conductors are the underground conductors between the service point and the first point of connection to the service-entrance conductors in a terminal box, meter, or other enclosure, ______ the building wall.

(a) inside
(b) outside
(c) above
(d) a or b

55. The overhead system service-entrance conductors are the service conductors between the terminals of ______ and a point where they are joined by a tap or splice to the service drop or overhead service conductors.

(a) service equipment
(b) service point
(c) grounding electrode
(d) equipment grounding conductor

56. The ______ is the necessary equipment, usually consisting of a circuit breaker(s) or switch(es) and fuse(s) and their accessories, connected to the load end of service conductors, and intended to constitute the main control and cutoff of the supply.

(a) service equipment
(b) service
(c) service disconnect
(d) service overcurrent device

57. A signaling circuit is any electrical circuit that energizes signaling equipment.

(a) True
(b) False

58. Special permission is the written consent from the ______.

(a) testing laboratory
(b) manufacturer
(c) owner
(d) authority having jurisdiction

59. A surge protective device (SPD) intended for installation on the load side of the service disconnect overcurrent device, including SPDs located at the branch panel, is a ______ SPD.

(a) Type 1
(b) Type 2
(c) Type 3
(d) Type 4

60. An isolating switch is one that is ______.

(a) not readily accessible to persons unless special means for access are used
(b) capable of interrupting the maximum operating overload current of a motor
(c) intended for use in general distribution and branch circuits
(d) intended for isolating an electrical circuit from the source of power

61. A power supply used to provide alternating-current power to a load for some period of time in the event of a power failure is known as a(n) "______."

(a) uninterruptible power supply
(b) power management system
(c) surge protective device
(d) arc fault interrupter

62. The voltage of a circuit is defined by the *Code* as the ______ root-mean-square (effective) difference of potential between any two conductors of the circuit concerned.

(a) lowest
(b) greatest
(c) average
(d) nominal

63. An enclosure constructed so that moisture will not enter the enclosure under specific test conditions is called "______."

(a) watertight
(b) moistureproof
(c) waterproof
(d) rainproof

64. In judging equipment for approval, considerations such as the following shall be evaluated:

(a) mechanical strength
(b) wire-bending space
(c) arcing effects
(d) all of these

65. Wiring shall be installed so that the completed system will be free from ______, other than as required or permitted elsewhere in the *Code*.

(a) short circuits
(b) ground faults
(c) connections to the earth
(d) all of these

66. Equipment intended to interrupt current at fault levels shall have an interrupting rating not less than the nominal circuit voltage and the current that is available at the line terminals of the equipment.

(a) True
(b) False

67. Unless identified for use in the operating environment, no conductors or equipment shall be ______ having a deteriorating effect on the conductors or equipment.

(a) located in damp or wet locations
(b) exposed to fumes, vapors, liquids or gases
(c) exposed to excessive temperatures
(d) all of these

68. The *NEC* requires that electrical work be ______.

(a) installed in a neat and workmanlike manner
(b) installed under the supervision of a licensed person
(c) completed before being inspected
(d) all of these

69. Wooden plugs driven into holes in ______ or similar materials shall not be used for securing electrical equipment.

(a) masonry
(b) concrete
(c) plaster
(d) all of these

70. Conductor terminal and splicing devices must be ______ for the conductor material and they must be properly installed and used.
(a) listed
(b) approved
(c) identified
(d) all of these

71. Many terminations and equipment are marked with ______.
(a) an etching tool
(b) a removable label
(c) a tightening torque
(d) the manufacturer's initials

72. Connection by means of wire-binding screws, studs, or nuts having upturned lugs or the equivalent shall be permitted for ______ or smaller conductors.
(a) 12 AWG
(b) 10 AWG
(c) 8 AWG
(d) 6 AWG

73. For circuits rated 100A or less, when the equipment terminals are listed for use with 75°C conductors, the ______ column of Table 310.15(B)(16) shall be used to determine the ampacity of THHN conductors.
(a) 30°C
(b) 60°C
(c) 75°C
(d) 90°C

74. Separately installed pressure connectors shall be used with conductors at the ______ not exceeding the ampacity at the listed and identified temperature rating of the connector.
(a) voltages
(b) temperatures
(c) listings
(d) ampacities

75. Electrical equipment such as switchboards, panelboards, industrial control panels, meter socket enclosures, and motor control centers that are in other than dwelling units, and are likely to require ______ while energized shall be field-marked to warn qualified persons of potential electric arc flash hazards.
(a) examination
(b) adjustment
(c) servicing or maintenance
(d) any of these

76. Each disconnecting means shall be legibly marked to indicate its purpose unless located and arranged so ______.
(a) that it can be locked out and tagged
(b) it is not readily accessible
(c) the purpose is evident
(d) that it operates at less than 300 volts-to-ground

77. Field markings of maximum available fault current at a service are not required for industrial installations where conditions of maintenance and supervision ensure that only qualified persons service the equipment.
(a) True
(b) False

78. A minimum working space depth of ______ to live parts operating at 277 volts-to-ground is required where there are exposed live parts on one side and no live or grounded parts on the other side.
(a) 2 ft
(b) 3 ft
(c) 4 ft
(d) 6 ft

79. Concrete, brick, or tile walls are considered ______, as applied to working space requirements.
(a) inconsequential
(b) in the way
(c) grounded
(d) none of these

80. The required working space for access to live parts operating at 300 volts-to-ground, where there are exposed live parts on both sides of the workspace is _____.

(a) 3 ft
(b) 3½ ft
(c) 4 ft
(d) 4½ ft

81. The minimum height of working spaces about electrical equipment, switchboards, panelboards, or motor control centers operating at 600V, nominal, or less and likely to require examination, adjustment, servicing, or maintenance while energized shall be 6½ ft or the height of the equipment, whichever is greater, except for service equipment or panelboards in existing dwelling units that do not exceed 200A.

(a) True
(b) False

82. When normally enclosed live parts are exposed for inspection or servicing, the working space, if in a passageway or general open space, shall be suitably _____.

(a) accessible
(b) guarded
(c) open
(d) enclosed

83. For equipment rated 1,200A or more that contains overcurrent devices, switching devices, or control devices; and where the entrance to the working space has a personnel door less than 25 ft from the working space, the door shall _____.

(a) open either in or out with simple pressure and shall not have any lock
(b) open in the direction of egress and be equipped with panic hardware or other devices so the door can open under simple pressure
(c) be equipped with a locking means
(d) be equipped with an electronic opener

84. All switchboards, panelboards, and motor control centers shall be _____.

(a) located in dedicated spaces
(b) protected from damage
(c) in weatherproof enclosures
(d) a and b

85. The dedicated space above a panelboard extends to a dropped or suspended ceiling, which is considered a structural ceiling.

(a) True
(b) False

86. To guard live parts over 50V but less than 600V, equipment is permitted to be _____.

(a) located in a room accessible only to qualified persons
(b) located on a balcony accessible only to qualified persons
(c) elevated 8 ft or more above the floor or other working surface
(d) any of these

87. In locations where electrical equipment is likely to be exposed to _____, enclosures or guards shall be so arranged and of such strength as to prevent such damage.

(a) corrosion
(b) physical damage
(c) magnetic fields
(d) weather

88. The term "rainproof" is typically used in conjunction with Enclosure-Type Number _____.

(a) 3
(b) 3R
(c) 3RX
(d) b and c

89. Grounded conductors _____ and larger can be identified by distinctive white or gray markings at their terminations.

(a) 10 AWG
(b) 8 AWG
(c) 6 AWG
(d) 4 AWG

90. If neutral conductors of different voltage systems are installed in the same raceway, cable, or enclosure, the means of identification of the different neutrals shall be documented in a manner that's _____ or be permanently posted where the conductors of different systems originate.

(a) available to the AHJ
(b) available through the engineer
(c) readily available
(d) included in the as-built drawings

91. If used for single-pole, 3-way or 4-way switch loops, the reidentified conductor with white or gray insulation or three continuous white stripes can be used for the supply to the switch, but not as a return conductor from the switch to the outlet.

(a) True
(b) False

92. Receptacles shall have the terminal intended for connection to the grounded conductor identified by a metal or metal coating that is substantially ______ in color.

(a) green
(b) white
(c) gray
(d) b or c

93. A three-phase, 4-wire, ______ power system used to supply power to nonlinear loads may necessitate that the power system design allow for the possibility of high harmonic current on the neutral conductor.

(a) wye-connected
(b) delta-connected
(c) wye/delta-connected
(d) none of these

94. Multiwire branch circuits shall ______.

(a) supply only line-to-neutral loads
(b) not be permitted in dwelling units
(c) have their conductors originate from different panelboards
(d) none of these

95. Where more than one nominal voltage system supplies branch circuits in a building, each ______ conductor of a branch circuit shall be identified by phase and system at all termination, connection, and splice points.

(a) grounded
(b) ungrounded
(c) grounding
(d) all of these

96. Where two or more branch circuits supply devices or equipment on the same yoke, a means to disconnect simultaneously all ungrounded conductors that supply those devices or equipment shall be provided ______.

(a) at the point where the branch circuit originates
(b) at the location of the device or equipment
(c) at the point where the feeder originates
(d) none of these

97. GFCI protection shall be provided for all 15A and 20A, 125V receptacles in dwelling unit accessory buildings that have a floor located at or below grade level not intended as ______ and limited to storage areas, work areas, or similar use.

(a) habitable rooms
(b) finished space
(c) a or b
(d) none of these

98. All 15A and 20A, 125V receptacles installed in crawl spaces at or below grade level of dwelling units shall have GFCI protection.

(a) True
(b) False

99. In industrial laboratories, 15A and 20A, 125V receptacles used to supply equipment where removal of power would introduce a greater hazard aren't required to be GFCI protected.

(a) True
(b) False

100. All 15A and 20A, 125V receptacles installed in garages, service bays, and similar areas where ______ are to be used must be GFCI protected.

(a) electrical diagnostic equipment
(b) electrical hand tools
(c) portable lighting equipment
(d) all of these

Practice Quiz
1

Random Order [90 through 210.8]

Unit 1 Practice Quiz— Random Order [90 through 210.8]

Please use the 2011 *Code* book to answer the following questions, which are based on the 2011 *NEC.*

1. The dedicated equipment space for electrical equipment that is required for panelboards installed indoors is measured from the floor to a height of _____ above the equipment, or to the structural ceiling, whichever is lower.

   (a) 3 ft
   (b) 6 ft
   (c) 12 ft
   (d) 30 ft

2. Equipment associated with the electrical installation can be located above or below other electrical equipment within their working space when the associated equipment does not extend more than _____ from the front of the electrical equipment.

   (a) 3 in.
   (b) 6 in.
   (c) 12 in.
   (d) 30 in.

3. A load is considered to be continuous if the maximum current is expected to continue for _____ or more.

   (a) one-half hour
   (b) 1 hour
   (c) 2 hours
   (d) 3 hours

4. An insulated grounded conductor of _____ or smaller shall be identified by a continuous white or gray outer finish, or by three continuous white stripes on other than green insulation along its entire length.

   (a) 8 AWG
   (b) 6 AWG
   (c) 4 AWG
   (d) 3 AWG

5. The required working space for access to live parts operating at 300 volts-to-ground, where there are exposed live parts on one side and grounded parts on the other side, is _____.

   (a) 3 ft
   (b) 3½ ft
   (c) 4 ft
   (d) 4½ ft

6. The minimum height of dedicated equipment space for motor control centers installed indoors is _____above the enclosure, or to the structural ceiling, whichever is lower.

   (a) 3 ft
   (b) 5 ft
   (c) 6 ft
   (d) 6½ ft

7. Conductor ampacity shall be determined using the _____ column of Table 310.15(B)(16) for circuits rated 100A or less or marked for 14 AWG through 1 AWG conductors, unless the equipment terminals are listed for use with conductors that have higher temperature ratings.

   (a) 30°C
   (b) 60°C
   (c) 75°C
   (d) 90°C

8. Conductors shall have their ampacity determined using the _____ column of Table 310.15(B)(16) for circuits rated over 100A, or marked for conductors larger than 1 AWG, unless the equipment terminals are listed for use with higher temperature-rated conductors.

   (a) 30°C
   (b) 60°C
   (c) 75°C
   (d) 90°C

9. Entrances to rooms and other guarded locations containing exposed live parts shall be marked with conspicuous ______ forbidding unqualified persons to enter.

(a) warning signs
(b) alarms
(c) a and b
(d) neither a nor b

10. Working space distances for enclosed live parts shall be measured from the ______ of equipment or apparatus, if the live parts are enclosed.

(a) enclosure
(b) opening
(c) a or b
(d) none of these

11. An opening in an outlet box where one or more receptacles have been installed is called "______."

(a) a device
(b) equipment
(c) a receptacle
(d) a receptacle outlet

12. Admitting close approach, not guarded by locked doors, elevation, or other effective means, is referred to as ______.

(a) accessible (as applied to equipment)
(b) accessible (as applied to wiring methods)
(c) accessible, readily
(d) all of these

13. Capable of being reached quickly for operation, renewal, or inspections without resorting to portable ladders and such is known as ______.

(a) accessible (as applied to equipment)
(b) accessible (as applied to wiring methods)
(c) accessible, readily
(d) all of these

14. Compliance with the provisions of the *NEC* will result in ______.

(a) good electrical service
(b) an efficient electrical system
(c) an electrical system essentially free from hazard
(d) all of these

15. A fixed, stationary, or portable self-contained, electrically illuminated equipment with words or symbols designed to convey information or attract attention describes ______.

(a) an electric sign
(b) equipment
(c) appliances
(d) none of these

16. Equipment or materials to which a symbol or other identifying mark of a product evaluation organization that is acceptable to the authority having jurisdiction has been attached is known as "______."

(a) listed
(b) labeled
(c) approved
(d) identified

17. Electrical equipment that depends on ______ for cooling of exposed surfaces shall be installed so that airflow over such surfaces is not prevented by walls or by adjacent installed equipment.

(a) outdoor air
(b) natural circulation of air and convection principles
(c) artificial cooling and circulation
(d) magnetic induction

18. Electrical equipment rooms or enclosures housing electrical apparatus that are controlled by a lock(s) shall be considered ______ to qualified persons.

(a) readily accessible
(b) accessible
(c) available
(d) none of these

19. The *NEC* defines a "______" as all circuit conductors between the service equipment, the source of a separately derived system, or other power-supply source and the final branch-circuit overcurrent device.

(a) service
(b) feeder
(c) branch circuit
(d) all of these

20. The rating of a branch circuit shall be determined by the rating of the ______.

(a) ampacity of the largest device connected to the circuit
(b) average of the ampacity of all devices
(c) branch-circuit overcurrent device
(d) ampacity of the branch-circuit conductors according to Table 310.15(B)(16)

21. The *NEC* defines a(n) "______" as a permanent structure having a roof and walls that stands alone or that is cut off from adjoining structures by fire walls or fire barriers, with all openings therein protected by approved fire doors and used to enclose an occupancy.

(a) unit
(b) apartment
(c) building
(d) utility

22. The continuity of a grounded conductor shall not depend on a connection to a ______.

(a) metallic enclosure
(b) raceway
(c) cable armor
(d) all of these

23. Access and ______ shall be provided and maintained about all electrical equipment to permit ready and safe operation and maintenance of such equipment.

(a) ventilation
(b) cleanliness
(c) circulation
(d) working space

24. A clothes closet is defined as a ______ room or space intended primarily for storage of garments and apparel.

(a) habitable
(b) non-habitable
(c) conditioned
(d) finished

25. A separate portion of a raceway system that provides access through a removable cover to the interior of the system, defines the term ______.

(a) junction box
(b) accessible raceway
(c) conduit body
(d) cutout box

26. A circuit breaker is a device designed to ______ the circuit automatically on a predetermined overcurrent without damage to itself when properly applied within its rating.

(a) energize
(b) reset
(c) connect
(d) open

27. "Bonded" can be described as ______ to establish electrical continuity and conductivity.

(a) isolated
(b) guarded
(c) connected
(d) separated

28. In dwelling units, the voltage between conductors that supply the terminals of ______ shall not exceed 120V, nominal.

(a) luminaires
(b) cord-and-plug-connected loads of 1,440 VA or less
(c) cord-and-plug-connected loads of more than ¼ hp
(d) a and b

29. When modifications to the electrical installation affect the maximum available fault current at the service, the maximum available fault current shall be verified or ______ to ensure the service equipment ratings are sufficient for the maximum available fault current at the line terminals of the equipment.

(a) recalculated
(b) increased
(c) decreased
(d) adjusted

30. A ______ is a single unit that provides independent living facilities for persons, including permanent provisions for living, sleeping, cooking, and sanitation.

(a) one-family dwelling
(b) two-family dwelling
(c) dwelling unit
(d) multifamily dwelling

31. A "______" is an accommodation that combines living, sleeping, sanitary, and storage facilities within a compartment.

(a) guest room
(b) guest suite
(c) dwelling unit
(d) single-family dwelling

32. The following systems shall be installed in accordance with the *NEC* requirements:

(a) signaling
(b) communications
(c) electrical conductors, equipment, and raceways
(d) all of these

33. The connection between the grounded conductor and the equipment grounding conductor at the service is accomplished by installing a(n) ______ bonding jumper.

(a) main
(b) system
(c) equipment
(d) circuit

34. A(n) ______ is an unintentional, electrically conducting connection between an ungrounded conductor of an electrical circuit, and the normally noncurrent-carrying conductors, metallic enclosures, metallic raceways, metallic equipment, or earth.

(a) grounded conductor
(b) ground fault
(c) equipment ground
(d) bonding jumper

35. The screw shell of a luminaire or lampholder shall be connected to the ______.

(a) grounded conductor
(b) ungrounded conductor
(c) equipment grounding conductor
(d) forming shell terminal

36. In other than dwelling locations, GFCI protection is required in ______.

(a) indoor wet locations
(b) locker rooms adjacent to showering facilities
(c) garages, service bays, and similar areas
(d) all of these

37. A switch constructed so that it can be installed in device boxes or on box covers, or otherwise used in conjunction with wiring systems recognized by the *NEC* is called a "______ switch."

(a) transfer
(b) motor-circuit
(c) general-use snap
(d) bypass isolation

38. A circuit conductor that is intentionally grounded is called a(n) "______."

(a) grounding conductor
(b) unidentified conductor
(c) grounded conductor
(d) grounding electrode conductor

39. Each multiwire branch circuit shall be provided with a means that will simultaneously disconnect all ______ conductors at the point where the branch circuit originates.

(a) circuit
(b) grounded
(c) grounding
(d) ungrounded

40. A conducting object through which a direct connection to earth is established is a "______."

(a) bonding conductor
(b) grounding conductor
(c) grounding electrode
(d) grounded conductor

41. Overhead service conductors are the conductors between the ______ and the first point of connection to the service-entrance conductors at the building or other structure.

(a) service disconnect
(b) service point
(c) grounding electrode
(d) equipment grounding conductor

42. The underground system service-entrance conductors are the service conductors between the terminals of _____ and the point of connection to the service lateral or underground service conductors.

(a) service equipment
(b) service point
(c) grounding electrode
(d) equipment grounding conductor

43. A handhole enclosure is an enclosure for use in underground systems, provided with an open or closed bottom, and sized to allow personnel to _____.

(a) enter and exit freely
(b) reach into but not enter
(c) have full working space
(d) examine it visually

44. All 15A and 20A, 125V receptacles located outdoors of dwelling units, including receptacles installed under the eaves of roofs, must be GFCI protected except for a receptacle that's supplied by a branch circuit dedicated to _____ if the receptacle isn't readily accessible and the equipment or receptacle has ground-fault protection of equipment (GFPE) [426.28 or 427.22].

(a) fixed electric snow-melting or deicing equipment
(b) pipeline and vessel heating equipment
(c) holiday decorative lighting
(d) a or b

45. Internal parts of electrical equipment, including _____, shall not be damaged or contaminated by foreign materials such as paint, plaster, cleaners, abrasives, or corrosive residues.

(a) busbars
(b) wiring terminals
(c) insulators
(d) all of these

46. Factory-installed _____ wiring of listed equipment need not be inspected at the time of installation of the equipment, except to detect alterations or damage.

(a) external
(b) associated
(c) internal
(d) all of these

47. The highest current at rated voltage that a device is identified to interrupt under standard test conditions is the _____.

(a) interrupting rating
(b) manufacturer's rating
(c) interrupting capacity
(d) withstand rating

48. A branch circuit that supplies only one utilization equipment is a(n) _____ branch circuit.

(a) individual
(b) general-purpose
(c) isolated
(d) special-purpose

49. GFCI protection shall be provided for all 15A and 20A, 125V receptacles installed in a dwelling ____.

(a) attic
(b) garage
(c) laundry room
(d) all of these

50. Utilization equipment is equipment that utilizes electricity for _____ purposes.

(a) electromechanical
(b) heating
(c) lighting
(d) any of these

Practice Quiz
2

Straight Order [210.8 through 240.54]

Unit 2 Practice Quiz—Straight Order [210.8 through 240.54]

Please use the 2011 *Code* book to answer the following questions, which are based on the 2011 *NEC.*

1. All 15A and 20A, 125V receptacles installed in _____ of dwelling units shall have GFCI protection.

(a) unfinished attics
(b) finished attics
(c) unfinished basements and crawl spaces
(d) finished basements

2. GFCI protection shall be provided for all 15A and 20A, 125V receptacles installed within 6 ft of all dwelling unit sinks located in areas other than the _____.

(a) laundry room
(b) bathroom
(c) den
(d) kitchen

3. All 15A and 20A, 125V receptacles _____ of commercial occupancies shall have GFCI protection.

(a) in bathrooms
(b) on rooftops
(c) in kitchens
(d) all of these

4. All 15A and 20A, 125V receptacles located outdoors or on rooftops in locations other than dwelling units must be GFCI protected except for a receptacle that's supplied by a branch circuit dedicated to _____ if the receptacle isn't readily accessible and the equipment or receptacle has ground-fault protection of equipment (GFPE) [426.28 and 427.22].

(a) fixed electric snow-melting or deicing equipment
(b) pipeline and vessel heating equipment
(c) holiday decorative lighting
(d) a or b

5. 15A and 20A, 125V receptacles located in patient bed locations of general care or critical care areas of health care facilities aren't required to be GFCI protected.

(a) True
(b) False

6. All 15A and 20A, 125V receptacles installed in locker rooms with associated showering facilities must be GFCI protected.

(a) True
(b) False

7. Ground-fault circuit-interrupter protection shall be provided for outlets not exceeding 240V that supply boat hoists installed in dwelling unit locations.

(a) True
(b) False

8. Two or more _____ small-appliance branch circuits shall be provided to supply power for receptacle outlets in the dwelling unit kitchen, dining room, breakfast room, pantry, or similar dining areas.

(a) 15A
(b) 20A
(c) 30A
(d) either 20A or 30A

9. There shall be a minimum of one _____ branch circuit for the laundry outlet(s) required by 210.52(F).

(a) 15A
(b) 20A
(c) 30A
(d) b and c

10. An individual 20A branch circuit can supply a single dwelling unit bathroom for receptacle outlet(s) and other equipment within the same bathroom.

(a) True
(b) False

11. An arc-fault circuit interrupter can be located at the first outlet to provide protection for the remaining portion of the branch circuit if _____.
    (a) the arc-fault circuit interrupter is installed within 8 ft of the branch-circuit overcurrent device
    (b) the circuit conductors up to the arc-fault circuit interrupter are in a metal raceway or steel armored Type AC or Type MC cable with metal outlet and junction boxes
    (c) a and b
    (d) the branch circuit serves only lighting loads

12. Where a listed metal or nonmetallic conduit or tubing is encased in not less than _____of concrete for the portion of the branch circuit between the branch-circuit overcurrent device and the first outlet, an outlet branch circuit AFCI at the first outlet is permitted to provide protection for the remaining portion of the branch circuit.
    (a) 2 in.
    (b) 4 in.
    (c) 6 in.
    (d) 8 in.

13. The recommended maximum total voltage drop on branch-circuit conductors is _____ percent.
    (a) 2
    (b) 3
    (c) 4
    (d) 6

14. A single receptacle installed on an individual branch circuit shall have an ampere rating not less than that of the branch circuit.
    (a) True
    (b) False

15. If a 20A branch circuit supplies multiple receptacles, the receptacles shall have an ampere rating of no less than _____.
    (a) 10A
    (b) 15A
    (c) 20A
    (d) 30A

16. _____ in dwelling units shall supply only loads within that dwelling unit or loads associated only with that dwelling unit.
    (a) Service-entrance conductors
    (b) Ground-fault protection
    (c) Branch circuits
    (d) none of these

17. When applying the general provisions for receptacle spacing to the rooms of a dwelling unit which require receptacles in the wall space, no point along the floor line in any wall space of a dwelling unit may be more than _____ from an outlet.
    (a) 6 ft
    (b) 8 ft
    (c) 10 ft
    (d) 12 ft

18. In dwelling units, when determining the spacing of receptacle outlets, _____ on exterior walls shall not be considered wall space.
    (a) fixed panels
    (b) fixed glass
    (c) sliding panels
    (d) all of these

19. Receptacles installed for countertop surfaces as required by 210.52(C) shall not be used to meet the receptacle requirements for wall space as required by 210.52(A).
    (a) True
    (b) False

20. A receptacle connected to one of the dwelling unit small-appliance branch circuits can be used to supply an electric clock.
    (a) True
    (b) False

21. A receptacle outlet shall be installed in dwelling units for every kitchen and dining area countertop space _____, and no point along the wall line shall be more than 2 ft, measured horizontally, from a receptacle outlet in that space.
    (a) wider than 10 in.
    (b) wider than 3 ft
    (c) 18 in. or wider
    (d) 12 in. or wider

22. For the purpose of determining the placement of receptacles in a dwelling unit kitchen, a(n) ______ countertop is measured from the connecting edge.

(a) island
(b) usable
(c) peninsular
(d) cooking

23. Kitchen and dining room countertop receptacle outlets in dwelling units shall be installed above the countertop surface, and not more than ______ above the countertop.

(a) 12 in.
(b) 18 in.
(c) 20 in.
(d) 24 in.

24. In dwelling unit bathrooms, not less than one 15A or 20A, 125V receptacle outlet must be installed within ______ from the outside edge of each bathroom basin.

(a) 20 in.
(b) 3 ft
(c) 4 ft
(d) 6 ft

25. There shall be a minimum of ______ receptacle(s) installed outdoors at a one-family or two-family dwelling unit.

(a) one
(b) two
(c) three
(d) four

26. A laundry receptacle outlet shall not be required in each dwelling unit of a multifamily building, if laundry facilities are provided on the premises for all building occupants.

(a) True
(b) False

27. Where a portion of the dwelling unit basement is finished into one or more habitable rooms, each separate unfinished portion shall have a receptacle outlet installed.

(a) True
(b) False

28. Foyers with an area greater than ______ sq ft must have a receptacle located in each wall space as 3 ft or more in width unbroken by doorways, floor-to-ceiling windows, and similar openings.

(a) 40
(b) 60
(c) 80
(d) 100

29. At least one receptacle outlet shall be installed within 18 in. of the top of a show window for each ______, or major fraction thereof, of show-window area measured horizontally at its maximum width.

(a) 10 ft
(b) 12 ft
(c) 18 ft
(d) 24 ft

30. At least one wall switch-controlled lighting outlet must be installed in every habitable room and bathroom of a dwelling unit.

(a) True
(b) False

31. In dwelling units, lighting outlets can be controlled by occupancy sensors where equipped with a ______ that will allow the sensor to function as a wall switch.

(a) manual override
(b) photo cell
(c) sensor
(d) none of these

32. When locating lighting outlets in dwelling units, a vehicle door in a garage shall be considered an outdoor entrance.

(a) True
(b) False

33. At least one wall switch-controlled lighting outlet shall be installed in every habitable room and bathroom of a guest room or guest suite of hotels, motels, and similar occupancies. A receptacle outlet controlled by a wall switch may be used to meet this requirement in other than ______.

(a) bathrooms
(b) kitchens
(c) sleeping areas
(d) a and b

34. The minimum feeder conductor ampacity, before the application of any adjustment or correction factors, must be no less than the noncontinuous load plus ______ percent of the continuous load.

(a) 80
(b) 100
(c) 125
(d) 150

35. The feeder conductor ampacity shall not be less than that of the service-entrance conductors where the feeder conductors carry the total load supplied by service conductors with an ampacity of ______ or less.

(a) 30A
(b) 55A
(c) 60A
(d) 100A

36. When a feeder supplies ______ in which equipment grounding conductors are required, the feeder shall include or provide an equipment grounding conductor.

(a) an equipment disconnecting means
(b) electrical systems
(c) branch circuits
(d) electric-discharge lighting equipment

37. When calculations in Article 220 result in a fraction of an ampere that is less than ______, such fractions can be dropped.

(a) 0.49
(b) 0.50
(c) 0.51
(d) 0.80

38. Where fixed multioutlet assemblies are used in other than dwelling units or the guest rooms of hotels or motels, each ______ or fraction thereof of each separate and continuous length shall be considered as 180 VA where appliances are unlikely to be used simultaneously.

(a) 5 ft
(b) 5½ ft
(c) 6 ft
(d) 6½ ft

39. A device comprised of ______ or more receptacles shall be calculated at not less than 90 VA per receptacle.

(a) one
(b) two
(c) three
(d) four

40. Branch circuits that supply lighting units that have ballasts, autotransformers, or LED drivers shall have the calculated load based on ______ of the units, not to the total wattage of the lamps.

(a) 50 percent of the rating
(b) 80 percent of the rating
(c) the total ampere rating
(d) 150 percent of the rating

41. A dwelling unit containing three 120V small-appliance branch circuits has a calculated load of ______VA for the small appliance circuits.

(a) 1,500
(b) 3,000
(c) 4,500
(d) 6,000

42. When sizing a feeder for the fixed appliance loads in dwelling units, a demand factor of 75 percent of the total nameplate ratings can be applied if there are ______ or more appliances fastened in place on the same feeder.

(a) two
(b) three
(c) four
(d) five

43. Using the standard load calculation method, the feeder demand factor for five household clothes dryers is ______ percent.

(a) 50
(b) 70
(c) 85
(d) 100

44. The feeder/service calculated load for a multifamily dwelling containing nine 12 kW ranges is ______.

(a) 13,000W
(b) 14,700W
(c) 16,000W
(d) 24,000W

45. Where it is unlikely that two or more noncoincident loads will be in use simultaneously, only the ______ loads used at one time is required to be used in computing the total load to a feeder.

(a) smaller of the
(b) largest of the
(c) difference between the
(d) none of these

46. There shall be no reduction in the size of the neutral or grounded conductor on ______ loads supplied from a 4-wire, wye-connected, three-phase system.

(a) dwelling unit
(b) hospital
(c) nonlinear
(d) motel

47. A demand factor of ______ percent applies to a multifamily dwelling with ten units if the optional calculation method is used.

(a) 43
(b) 50
(c) 60
(d) 75

48. The point of attachment of overhead premises wiring to a building shall in no case be less than ______ above finished grade.

(a) 8 ft
(b) 10 ft
(c) 12 ft
(d) 15 ft

49. The minimum clearance for overhead feeder conductors that pass over track rails of railroads is ______.

(a) 10 ft
(b) 12 ft
(c) 24.50 ft
(d) 30 ft

50. If a set of 120/240V overhead feeder conductors terminates at a through-the-roof raceway or approved support, with less than 6 ft of these conductors passing over the roof overhang, the minimum clearance above the roof for these conductors is ______.

(a) 12 in.
(b) 18 in.
(c) 2 ft
(d) 5 ft

51. Overhead feeder conductors to a building shall have a vertical clearance of final spans above, or within ______ measured horizontally from the platforms, projections, or surfaces from which they might be reached.

(a) 3 ft
(b) 6 ft
(c) 8 ft
(d) 10 ft

52. Raceways on exterior surfaces of buildings or other structures shall be arranged to drain, and be suitable for use in ______ locations.

(a) damp
(b) wet
(c) dry
(d) all of these

53. The disconnecting means for a building supplied by a feeder shall be installed at a(n) ______ location.

(a) accessible
(b) readily accessible
(c) outdoor
(d) indoor

54. There shall be no more than ______ switches or circuit breakers to serve as the disconnecting means for a building supplied by a feeder .

(a) two
(b) four
(c) six
(d) eight

55. In a multiple-occupancy building, each occupant shall have access to his or her own ______.
(a) disconnecting means
(b) building drops
(c) building-entrance assembly
(d) lateral conductors

56. The disconnecting means for a building supplied by a feeder shall plainly indicate whether it is in the ______ position.
(a) open or closed
(b) correct
(c) up or down
(d) none of these

57. Additional services shall be permitted for a single building or other structure sufficiently large to make two or more services necessary if permitted by ______.
(a) the registered design professional
(b) special permission
(c) the engineer of record
(d) master electricians

58. Where a building or structure is supplied by more than one service, a permanent plaque or directory shall be installed at each service disconnect location denoting all other services supplying that building or structure and the area served by each.
(a) True
(b) False

59. Conductors are considered outside a building when they are installed:
(a) Under not less than 2 in. of concrete beneath a building or structure.
(b) Within a building or structure in a raceway encased in not less than a 2 in. thickness of concrete or brick.
(c) Installed in a vault that meets the construction requirements of Article 450.
(d) all of these

60. Conductors other than service conductors shall not be installed in the same ______.
(a) service raceway
(b) service cable
(c) enclosure
(d) a or b

61. Service conductors shall not be installed beneath openings through which materials may be moved and shall not be installed where they will obstruct entrance to these buildings' openings.
(a) True
(b) False

62. Service-drop conductors shall have ______.
(a) sufficient ampacity to carry the load
(b) adequate mechanical strength
(c) a or b
(d) a and b

63. Overhead service conductors installed over roofs shall have a vertical clearance of ______ above the roof surface, unless a lesser distance is permitted by an exception.
(a) 3 ft
(b) 8 ft
(c) 12 ft
(d) 15 ft

64. The requirement to maintain a 3 ft vertical clearance from the edge of a roof does not apply to the final conductor span where the service drop is attached to ______.
(a) a service pole
(b) the side of a building
(c) an antenna
(d) the base of a building

65. Overhead service conductors shall have a horizontal clearance of ______ from a pool.
(a) 8 ft
(b) 10 ft
(c) 12 ft
(d) 14 ft

66. The minimum point of attachment of the service-drop conductors to a building shall not be less than ______ above finished grade.
(a) 8 ft
(b) 10 ft
(c) 12 ft
(d) 15 ft

67. Underground service conductors shall have ______.
(a) adequate mechanical strength
(b) sufficient ampacity for the loads calculated
(c) a and b
(d) none of these

68. Underground service conductors that supply power to limited loads of a single branch circuit shall not be smaller than ______.
(a) 14 AWG copper
(b) 14 AWG aluminum
(c) 12 AWG copper
(d) 12 AWG aluminum

69. A single family dwelling unit and its accessory structure(s) shall be permitted to have one set of service conductors run to each structure from a single service drop, set of overhead service conductors, set of underground service conductors, or service lateral.
(a) True
(b) False

70. One set of service-entrance conductors connected to the supply side of the normal service disconnecting means shall be permitted to supply standby power systems, fire pump equipment, and fire and sprinkler alarms covered by 230.82(5).
(a) True
(b) False

71. Wiring methods permitted for service-entrance conductors include ______.
(a) rigid metal conduit
(b) electrical metallic tubing
(c) PVC conduit
(d) all of these

72. Service-entrance conductors can be spliced or tapped by clamped or bolted connections at any time as long as ______.
(a) the free ends of conductors are covered with an insulation that is equivalent to that of the conductors or with an insulating device identified for the purpose
(b) wire connectors or other splicing means installed on conductors that are buried in the earth are listed for direct burial
(c) no splice is made in a raceway
(d) all of these

73. Service-entrance cables mounted in contact with a building shall be supported at intervals not exceeding ______.
(a) 24 in.
(b) 30 in.
(c) 3 ft
(d) 4 ft

74. Overhead service-entrance cables shall be equipped with a ______.
(a) raceway
(b) service head
(c) cover
(d) all of these

75. Service heads shall be located ______, unless impracticable.
(a) above the point of attachment
(b) below the point of attachment
(c) even with the point of attachment
(d) none of these

76. Service-entrance and overhead service conductors shall be arranged so that ______ will not enter the service raceway or equipment.
(a) dust
(b) vapor
(c) water
(d) none of these

77. Service disconnecting means shall not be installed in bathrooms.
(a) True
(b) False

78. Each service disconnecting means shall be permanently ______ to identify it as a service disconnect.
(a) identified
(b) positioned
(c) marked
(d) none of these

79. There shall be no more than ______ disconnects installed for each service or for each set of service-entrance conductors as permitted in 230.2 and 230.40.

(a) two
(b) four
(c) six
(d) eight

80. The additional service disconnecting means for fire pumps, emergency systems, legally required standby, or optional standby services, shall be installed remote from the one to six service disconnecting means for normal service to minimize the possibility of ______ interruption of supply.

(a) intentional
(b) accidental
(c) simultaneous
(d) prolonged

81. The service disconnecting means shall plainly indicate whether it is in the ______ position.

(a) open or closed
(b) tripped
(c) up or down
(d) correct

82. For installations consisting of not more than two 2-wire branch circuits, the service disconnecting means shall have a rating of not less than ______.

(a) 15A
(b) 20A
(c) 25A
(d) 30A

83. A meter disconnect switch located ahead of service equipment must have a short-circuit current rating equal to or greater than the available short-circuit current and be capable of interrupting the load served.

(a) True
(b) False

84. Each ______ service conductor shall have overload protection.

(a) overhead
(b) underground
(c) ungrounded
(d) none of these

85. The ground-fault protection system for service equipment shall be ______ when first installed on-site.

(a) a Class A device
(b) identified
(c) turned on
(d) performance tested

86. When service equipment has ground-fault protection installed, it may be necessary to review the overall wiring system for proper selective overcurrent protection ______.

(a) rating
(b) coordination
(c) devices
(d) none of these

87. A device that, when interrupting currents in its current-limiting range, reduces the current flowing in the faulted circuit to a magnitude substantially less than that obtainable in the same circuit if the device were replaced with a solid conductor having comparable impedance, is a(n) ______ protective device.

(a) short-circuit
(b) overload
(c) ground-fault
(d) current-limiting

88. The next higher standard rating overcurrent device above the ampacity of the ungrounded conductors being protected shall be permitted to be used, provided all of the following conditions are met:

(a) The conductors are not part of a branch circuit supplying more than one receptacle for cord-and-plug-connected portable loads.
(b) The ampacity of the conductors doesn't correspond with the standard ampere rating of a fuse or circuit breaker.
(c) The next higher standard rating selected doesn't exceed 800A.
(d) all of these

89. Flexible cord used in listed extension cord sets shall be considered protected against overcurrent when used ______.

(a) in indoor installations
(b) in unclassified locations
(c) within the extension cord's listing requirements
(d) within 50 ft of the branch-circuit panelboard

90. The standard ampere ratings for fuses includes ______.

(a) 1A
(b) 6A
(c) 601A
(d) all of these

91. Supplementary overcurrent devices used in luminaires or appliances are not required to be readily accessible.

(a) True
(b) False

92. A(n) ______ shall be considered equivalent to an overcurrent trip unit for the purpose of providing overcurrent protection of conductors.

(a) current transformer
(b) overcurrent relay
(c) a and b
(d) a or b

93. Tap conductors not over 25 ft shall be permitted, providing the ______.

(a) ampacity of the tap conductors is not less than one-third the rating of the overcurrent device protecting the feeder conductors being tapped
(b) tap conductors terminate in a single circuit breaker or set of fuses that limit the load to the ampacity of the tap conductors
(c) tap conductors are suitably protected from physical damage
(d) all of these

94. Outside feeder tap conductors can be of unlimited length without overcurrent protection at the point they receive their supply if:

(a) The tap conductors are suitably protected from physical damage.
(b) The tap conductors terminate at a single circuit breaker or a single set of fuses that limits the load to the ampacity of the conductors.
(c) a and b
(d) none of these

95. Overcurrent devices shall be ______.

(a) accessible (as applied to wiring methods)
(b) accessible (as applied to equipment)
(c) readily accessible
(d) inaccessible to unauthorized personnel

96. Overcurrent devices shall not be located ______.

(a) where exposed to physical damage
(b) near easily ignitible materials, such as in clothes closets
(c) in bathrooms of dwelling units
(d) all of these

97. Handles or levers of circuit breakers, and similar parts that may move suddenly in such a way that persons in the vicinity are likely to be injured by being struck by them, shall be ______.

(a) guarded
(b) isolated
(c) a and b
(d) a or b

98. Plug fuses of the Edison-base type shall have a maximum rating of ______.

(a) 20A
(b) 30A
(c) 40A
(d) 50A

99. Edison-base fuseholders shall be used only if they are made to accept ______ fuses by the use of adapters.

(a) Edison-base
(b) medium-base
(c) heavy-duty base
(d) Type S

100. Type ______ fuse adapters shall be designed so that once inserted in a fuseholder they cannot be removed.

(a) A
(b) E
(c) S
(d) P

Practice Quiz 2

Random Order [90.2 through 240.60]

Unit 2 Practice Quiz— Random Order [90.2 through 240.60]

Please use the 2011 *Code* book to answer the following questions, which are based on the 2011 *NEC*.

1. "______" means that an object is not readily accessible to persons unless special means for access are used.

   (a) Isolated
   (b) Secluded
   (c) Protected
   (d) Locked

2. "Continuous duty" is defined as ______.

   (a) when the load is expected to continue for 5 hours or more
   (b) operation at a substantially constant load for an indefinite long time
   (c) operation at loads and for intervals of time, both of which may be subject to wide variations
   (d) operation at which the load may be subject to maximum current for 6 hours or more

3. "Ungrounded" describes not connected to ground or a conductive body that extends the ground connection.

   (a) True
   (b) False

4. A "______" is a building or portion of a building in which one or more self-propelled vehicles can be kept for use, sale, storage, rental, repair, exhibition, or demonstration purposes.

   (a) garage
   (b) residential garage
   (c) service garage
   (d) commercial garage

5. A 15A or 20A, 125V receptacle outlet shall be located within 25 ft of heating, air-conditioning, and refrigeration equipment for ______ occupancies.

   (a) dwelling
   (b) commercial
   (c) industrial
   (d) all of these

6. A building disconnecting means that supplies only limited loads of a single branch circuit shall have a rating of not less than ______.

   (a) 15A
   (b) 20A
   (c) 25A
   (d) 30A

7. A building or structure shall be supplied by a maximum of ______ feeder(s) or branch circuit(s), unless specifically permitted otherwise.

   (a) one
   (b) two
   (c) three
   (d) four

8. A building or structure shall be supplied by a maximum of ______ service(s), unless specifically permitted otherwise.

   (a) one
   (b) two
   (c) three
   (d) as many as desired

9. A device that establishes a connection between the conductors of the attached flexible cord and the conductors connected to the receptacle is called a(n) "______."

   (a) attachment plug
   (b) plug cap
   (c) plug
   (d) any of these

10. A dwelling unit containing two 120V laundry branch circuits has a calculated load of ______VA for the laundry circuits.

(a) 1,500
(b) 3,000
(c) 4,500
(d) 6,000

11. A large single panel, frame, or assembly of panels on which switches, overcurrent and other protective devices, buses, and instruments are mounted is a "______." They are generally accessible from the rear as well as from the front and are not intended to be installed in cabinets.

(a) switchboard
(b) panel box
(c) switch box
(d) panelboard

12. A panel, including buses and automatic overcurrent devices, designed to be placed in a cabinet or cutout box and accessible only from the front is known as a "______."

(a) switchboard
(b) disconnect
(c) panelboard
(d) switch

13. A receptacle connected to a dwelling unit small-appliance circuit can supply gas-fired ranges, ovens, or counter-mounted cooking units.

(a) True
(b) False

14. A receptacle outlet shall be installed at each dwelling unit kitchen wall countertop space that is 12 in. or wider and receptacle outlets shall be installed so that no point along the wall line is more than ______, measured horizontally from a receptacle outlet in that space.

(a) 10 in.
(b) 12 in.
(c) 16 in.
(d) 24 in.

15. A service disconnecting means shall be installed at a(n) ______ location.

(a) dry
(b) readily accessible
(c) outdoor
(d) indoor

16. A system intended to provide protection of equipment from damaging line-to-ground fault currents by opening all ungrounded conductors of the faulted circuit at current levels less than the supply circuit overcurrent device defines the phrase "______."

(a) ground-fault protection of equipment
(b) guarded
(c) personal protection
(d) automatic protection

17. A(n) ______ enclosure is constructed or protected so that exposure to the weather will not interfere with successful operation.

(a) weatherproof
(b) weathertight
(c) weather-resistant
(d) all weather

18. A(n) ______ is a point on the wiring system at which current is taken to supply utilization equipment.

(a) box
(b) receptacle
(c) outlet
(d) device

19. Accepted industry workmanship practices are described in ANSI/NECA 1-2006, *Standard Practices for Good Workmanship in Electrical Contracting*, and other ANSI-approved installation standards.

(a) True
(b) False

20. According to the *Code*, "automatic" is performing a function without the necessity of ______.

(a) protection from damage
(b) human intervention
(c) mechanical linkage
(d) all of these

21. Additional services shall be permitted for different voltages, frequencies, or phases, or for different uses such as for ______.

(a) gymnasiums
(b) different rate schedules
(c) flea markets
(d) special entertainment events

22. All 15A and 20A, 125V receptacles installed in dwelling unit boathouses shall have GFCI protection.

(a) True
(b) False

23. Any current in excess of the rated current of equipment or the ampacity of a conductor is called "______."

(a) trip current
(b) fault current
(c) overcurrent
(d) a short circuit

24. As used in the *NEC*, equipment includes ______.

(a) fittings
(b) appliances
(c) machinery
(d) all of these

25. At least one receptacle outlet not more than ______ above a balcony, deck or porch shall be installed within the perimeter at each balcony, deck or porch of a dwelling unit.

(a) 3 ft
(b) 6½ ft
(c) 8 ft
(d) 24 in.

26. Chapters 1 through 4 of the *NEC* apply ______.

(a) generally to all electrical installations
(b) only to special occupancies and conditions
(c) only to special equipment and material
(d) all of these

27. Circuit breakers shall ______ all ungrounded conductors of the circuit both manually and automatically unless specifically permitted otherwise.

(a) open
(b) close
(c) isolate
(d) inhibit

28. Conductor sizes are expressed in American Wire Gage (AWG) or ______.

(a) inches
(b) circular mils
(c) square inches
(d) cubic inches

29. Conductors supplied under the tap rules are allowed to supply another conductor using the tap rules.

(a) True
(b) False

30. Connection of conductors to terminal parts shall ensure a thoroughly good connection without damaging the conductors and shall be made by means of ______.

(a) solder lugs
(b) pressure connectors
(c) splices to flexible leads
(d) any of these

31. Constructed, protected, or treated so as to prevent rain from interfering with the successful operation of the apparatus under specified test conditions defines the term "______."

(a) raintight
(b) waterproof
(c) weathertight
(d) rainproof

32. Each service disconnecting means shall be suitable for ______.

(a) hazardous (classified) locations
(b) wet locations
(c) dry locations
(d) the prevailing conditions

33. Electric utilities may include entities that install, operate, and maintain ______.

(a) communications systems (telephone, CATV, Internet, satellite, or data services)
(b) electric supply systems (generation, transmission, or distribution systems)
(c) local area network wiring on the premises
(d) a or b

34. Enclosures for overcurrent devices shall be mounted in a ______ position unless impracticable.

(a) vertical
(b) horizontal
(c) vertical or horizontal
(d) there are no requirements

35. Equipment enclosed with a means of sealing or locking so that live parts cannot be made accessible without opening the enclosure is said to be "______."

(a) guarded
(b) protected
(c) sealable
(d) lockable

36. Equipment or materials included in a list published by a testing laboratory acceptable to the authority having jurisdiction is said to be "______."

(a) book
(b) digest
(c) manifest
(d) listed

37. Explanatory material, such as references to other standards, references to related sections of the *NEC*, or information related to a *Code* rule, are included in the form of Informational Notes.

(a) True
(b) False

38. Feeder and service loads for fixed electric space heating shall be calculated at ______ percent of the total connected load.

(a) 80
(b) 100
(c) 125
(d) 200

39. Feeder neutral conductors shall be permitted to be sized at ______ percent of the continuous and noncontinuous load.

(a) 80
(b) 100
(c) 125
(d) 150

40. Flexible cords approved for and used with a specific listed appliance or luminaire shall be considered to be protected by the branch-circuit overcurrent device when ______.

(a) not more than 6 ft in length
(b) 20 AWG and larger
(c) applied within the listing requirements
(d) 16 AWG and larger

41. For a one-family dwelling, at least one receptacle outlet shall be required in each ______.

(a) basement
(b) attached garage
(c) detached garage or accessory building with electric power
(d) all of these

42. For attics and underfloor spaces in other than dwelling units that contain heating, air-conditioning, and refrigeration equipment requiring servicing, at least one lighting outlet containing a switch or controlled by a wall switch shall be installed ______.

(a) at the equipment requiring servicing
(b) near the equipment requiring servicing
(c) a or b
(d) none of these

43. For installations that supply only limited loads of a single branch circuit, the service disconnecting means shall have a rating not less than ______.

(a) 15A
(b) 20A
(c) 25A
(d) 30A

44. For other than dwelling occupancies, banks, or office buildings, each receptacle outlet shall be calculated at not less than ______ VA.

(a) 90
(b) 180
(c) 270
(d) 360

45. Fuseholders for cartridge fuses shall be so designed that it is difficult to put a fuse of any given class into a fuseholder that is designed for a _____ lower or a _____ higher than that of the class to which the fuse belongs.

(a) voltage, wattage
(b) wattage, voltage
(c) voltage, current
(d) current, voltage

46. Ground-fault protection of equipment shall be provided for solidly grounded wye electrical services of more than 150 volts-to-ground, but not exceeding 600V phase-to-phase for each service disconnecting means rated _____ or more.

(a) 1,000A
(b) 1,500A
(c) 2,000A
(d) 2,500A

47. Ground-fault protection of equipment shall be required for a feeder disconnect if _____.

(a) the disconnect is rated 800A, 208V
(b) the disconnect is rated 800A, 480V
(c) the disconnect is rated 1,000A, 208V
(d) the disconnect is rated 1,000A, 480V

48. Ground-fault protection that functions to open the service disconnect _____ protect(s) from faults on the line side of the protective element.

(a) will
(b) will not
(c) adequately
(d) totally

49. Guest rooms or guest suites provided with permanent provisions for _____ shall have receptacle outlets installed in accordance with all of the applicable requirements for a dwelling unit as specified in 210.52.

(a) whirlpool tubs
(b) bathing
(c) cooking
(d) internet access

50. If grounded conductors of different voltage systems are installed in the same raceway, cable, or enclosure, each neutral conductor must be identified to distinguish the systems by _____.

(a) a continuous white or gray outer finish for one system
(b) a neutral conductor with a different continuous white or gray outer finish or white or gray with a stripe for one system
(c) Other identification allowed by 200.6(A) or (B) that distinguishes each system from other systems.
(d) a, b, or c

Practice Quiz 3

Straight Order [240.60 through 300.8]

Unit 3 Practice Quiz—Straight Order [240.60 through 300.8]

Please use the 2011 *Code* book to answer the following questions, which are based on the 2011 *NEC*.

1. Fuses shall be marked with their ______.
   (a) ampere and voltage rating
   (b) interrupting rating where other than 10,000A
   (c) name or trademark of the manufacturer
   (d) all of these

2. Cartridge fuses and fuseholders shall be classified according to their ______ ranges.
   (a) voltage
   (b) amperage
   (c) a or b
   (d) a and b

3. Circuit breakers shall be capable of being closed and opened by manual operation. Operation by other means, such as electrical or pneumatic, shall be permitted if means for ______ operation are also provided.
   (a) automated
   (b) timed
   (c) manual
   (d) shunt trip

4. A(n) ______ shall be of such design that any alteration of its trip point (calibration) or the time required for its operation requires dismantling of the device or breaking of a seal for other than intended adjustments.
   (a) Type S fuse
   (b) Edison-base fuse
   (c) circuit breaker
   (d) fuseholder

5. Circuit breakers shall be marked with their ampere rating in a manner that is durable and visible after installation. Such marking can be made visible by removal of a ______.
   (a) trim
   (b) cover
   (c) box
   (d) a or b

6. A circuit breaker having an interrupting current rating of other than ______ shall have its interrupting rating marked on the circuit breaker.
   (a) 5,000A
   (b) 10,000A
   (c) 22,000A
   (d) 50,000A

7. Circuit breakers used to switch high-intensity discharge lighting circuits shall be listed and marked as ______.
   (a) SWD
   (b) HID
   (c) a or b
   (d) a and b

8. A circuit breaker with a ______ rating, such as 120/240V or 277/480V can be used on a solidly grounded circuit where the nominal voltage of any conductor to ground does not exceed the lower of the two values, and the nominal voltage between any two conductors does not exceed the higher value.
   (a) straight
   (b) slash
   (c) high
   (d) low

9. A ground-fault current path is an electrically conductive path from the point of a ground fault through normally noncurrent-carrying conductors, equipment, or the earth to the ______.
   (a) ground
   (b) earth
   (c) electrical supply source
   (d) none of these

10. Grounded electrical systems shall be connected to earth in a manner that will ______.
(a) limit voltages due to lightning, line surges, or unintentional contact with higher-voltage lines
(b) stabilize the voltage-to-ground during normal operation
(c) facilitate overcurrent device operation in case of ground faults
(d) a and b

11. For grounded systems, normally noncurrent-carrying conductive materials enclosing electrical conductors or equipment shall be connected to earth so as to limit the voltage-to-ground on these materials.
(a) True
(b) False

12. In grounded systems, normally noncurrent-carrying electrically conductive materials that are likely to become energized shall be ______ in a manner that establishes an effective ground-fault current path.
(a) connected together
(b) connected to the electrical supply source
(c) connected to the closest grounded conductor
(d) a and b

13. For ungrounded systems, noncurrent-carrying conductive materials enclosing electrical conductors or equipment shall be connected to the ______ in a manner that will limit the voltage imposed by lightning or unintentional contact with higher-voltage lines.
(a) ground
(b) earth
(c) electrical supply source
(d) none of these

14. Electrically conductive materials that are likely to ______ in ungrounded systems shall be connected together and to the supply system grounded equipment in a manner that creates a low-impedance path for ground-fault current that is capable of carrying the maximum fault current likely to be imposed on it.
(a) become energized
(b) require service
(c) be removed
(d) be coated with paint or nonconductive materials

15. The grounding of electrical systems, circuit conductors, surge arresters, surge protective devices, and conductive normally noncurrent-carrying metal parts of equipment shall be installed and arranged in a manner that will prevent objectionable current.
(a) True
(b) False

16. Currents that introduce noise or data errors in electronic equipment are considered objectionable currents in the context of 250.6(D) of the NEC.
(a) True
(b) False

17. ______ on equipment to be grounded shall be removed from contact surfaces to ensure good electrical continuity.
(a) Paint
(b) Lacquer
(c) Enamel
(d) any of these

18. Alternating-current systems of 50V to 1,000V that supply premises wiring systems shall be grounded where the system is three-phase, 4-wire, wye connected with the neutral conductor used as a circuit conductor.
(a) True
(b) False

19. ______ alternating-current systems operating at 480V shall have ground detectors installed on the system.
(a) Grounded
(b) Solidly grounded
(c) Effectively grounded
(d) Ungrounded

20. Alternating current systems from 50V to less than 1,000V that are ungrounded systems must be legibly marked "Ungrounded System" at ______ of the system, with sufficient durability to withstand the environment involved.
(a) the source
(b) the first disconnecting means
(c) every junction box
(d) a or b

21. Where an alternating-current system operating at less than 1,000V is grounded at any point, the ______ conductor(s) shall be routed with the ungrounded conductors to each service disconnecting means and shall be connected to each disconnecting means grounded conductor(s) terminal or bus.

(a) ungrounded
(b) grounded
(c) grounding
(d) none of these

22. The grounded conductor brought to service equipment shall be routed with the phase conductors and shall not be smaller than specified in Table ______ when the service-entrance conductors are 1,100 kcmil copper and smaller.

(a) 250.66
(b) 250.122
(c) 310.16
(d) 430.52

23. Where service-entrance phase conductors are installed in parallel in two or more raceways, the size of the grounded conductor in each raceway shall be based on the total circular mil area of the parallel ungrounded service-entrance conductor in the raceway, sized per 250.24(C)(1), but not smaller than ______.

(a) 1/0 AWG
(b) 2/0 AWG
(c) 3/0 AWG
(d) 4/0 AWG

24. A main bonding jumper shall be a ______ or similar suitable conductor.

(a) wire
(b) bus
(c) screw
(d) any of these

25. A grounded conductor shall not be connected to normally noncurrent-carrying metal parts of equipment on the ______ side of the system bonding jumper of a separately derived system except as otherwise permitted in Article 250.

(a) supply
(b) grounded
(c) high-voltage
(d) load

26. The connection of the system bonding jumper for a separately derived system shall be made ______ on the separately derived system from the source to the first system disconnecting means or overcurrent device.

(a) in at least two locations
(b) in every location that the grounded conductor is present
(c) at any single point
(d) none of these

27. The grounding electrode for a separately derived system shall be as near as practicable to, and preferably in the same area as, the grounding electrode conductor connection to the system.

(a) True
(b) False

28. The grounding electrode conductor for a single separately derived system is used to connect the grounded conductor of the derived system to the grounding electrode.

(a) True
(b) False

29. Tap connections to a common grounding electrode conductor for multiple separately derived systems shall be made at an accessible location by ______.

(a) a connector listed as grounding and bonding equipment
(b) listed connections to aluminum or copper busbars
(c) by the exothermic welding process
(d) any of these

30. In an area served by a separately derived system, the ______ shall be connected to the grounded conductor of the separately derived system.

(a) structural steel
(b) metal piping
(c) metal building skin
(d) a and b

31. A grounding electrode at a separate building or structure shall be required where one multiwire branch circuit serves the building or structure.

(a) True
(b) False

32. For a separate building or structure supplied by a feeder or branch circuit, the neutral conductor can serve as the ground-fault return path for the building/structure disconnecting means for existing installations made in compliance with previous editions of the Code as long as the installation continues to meet the condition(s) that ______.

(a) there are no continuous metallic paths between buildings and structures
(b) ground-fault protection of equipment isn't installed on the supply side of the feeder
(c) the neutral conductor is sized no smaller than the larger required by 220.61 or 250.122
(d) all of these

33. The frame of a portable generator shall not be required to be connected to a(n) ______ if the generator only supplies equipment mounted on the generator or cord-and-plug-connected equipment using receptacles mounted on the generator.

(a) grounding electrode
(b) grounded conductor
(c) ungrounded conductor
(d) equipment grounding conductor

34. When a permanently installed generator ______, the requirements of 250.30 apply.

(a) is a separately derived system
(b) is not a separately derived system
(c) supplies only cord and plug connected loads
(d) none of these

35. Concrete-encased electrodes of ______ shall not be required to be part of the grounding electrode system where the steel reinforcing bars or rods aren't accessible for use without disturbing the concrete.

(a) hazardous (classified) locations
(b) health care facilities
(c) existing buildings or structures
(d) agricultural buildings with equipotential planes

36. The metal frame of a building shall be considered a grounding electrode where one of the NEC-prescribed methods for connection of the metal frame to earth has been met:

(a) True
(b) False

37. Where more than one concrete-encased electrode is present at a building or structure, it shall be permitted to connect to only one of them.

(a) True
(b) False

38. Grounding electrodes that are driven rods require a minimum of ______ in contact with the soil.

(a) 6 ft
(b) 8 ft
(c) 10 ft
(d) 12 ft

39. A buried iron or steel plate used as a grounding electrode shall expose not less than ______ of surface area to exterior soil.

(a) 2 sq ft
(b) 4 sq ft
(c) 9 sq ft
(d) 10 sq ft

40. ______ shall not be used as grounding electrodes.

(a) Underground gas piping systems
(b) Aluminum
(c) Metal well casings
(d) a and b

41. Where a metal underground water pipe is used as a grounding electrode, the continuity of the grounding path or the bonding connection to interior piping shall not rely on ______ and similar equipment.

(a) bonding jumpers
(b) water meters or filtering devices
(c) grounding clamps
(d) all of these

42. When a ground ring is used as a grounding electrode, it shall be buried at a depth below the earth's surface of not less than ______.

(a) 18 in.
(b) 24 in.
(c) 30 in.
(d) 8 ft

43. The upper end of a ground rod electrode shall be ______ ground level unless the aboveground end and the grounding electrode conductor attachment are protected against physical damage.

(a) above
(b) flush with
(c) below
(d) b or c

44. Auxiliary grounding electrodes can be connected to the ______.

(a) equipment grounding conductor
(b) grounded conductor
(c) a and b
(d) none of these

45. Grounding electrode conductors shall be made of ______ wire.

(a) solid
(b) stranded
(c) insulated or bare
(d) any of these

46. Bare aluminum or copper-clad aluminum grounding electrode conductors shall not be used where in direct contact with ______ or where subject to corrosive conditions.

(a) masonry or the earth
(b) bare copper conductors
(c) wooden framing members
(d) all of these

47. Grounding electrode conductors smaller than ______ shall be in rigid metal conduit, IMC, PVC conduit, electrical metallic tubing, or cable armor.

(a) 10 AWG
(b) 8 AWG
(c) 6 AWG
(d) 4 AWG

48. Where service equipment consists of more than one enclosure, grounding electrode connections shall be permitted to be ______.

(a) multiple individual grounding electrode conductors
(b) one grounding electrode conductor at a common location
(c) common grounding electrode conductor and taps
(d) any of these

49. The largest size grounding electrode conductor required is ______ copper.

(a) 6 AWG
(b) 1/0 AWG
(c) 3/0 AWG
(d) 250 kcmil

50. In an ac system, the size of the grounding electrode conductor to a concrete-encased electrode shall not be required to be larger than a(n) ______ copper conductor.

(a) 10 AWG
(b) 8 AWG
(c) 6 AWG
(d) 4 AWG

51. An encased or buried connection to a concrete-encased, driven, or buried grounding electrode shall be accessible.

(a) True
(b) False

52. Exothermic or irreversible compression connections, together with the mechanical means used to attach to fireproofed structural metal, shall not be required to be accessible.

(a) True
(b) False

53. Grounding electrode conductors and grounding electrode bonding jumpers are permitted to terminate to the metal frame of a building/structure that's in direct contact with the earth for 10 ft or more [250.52(A)(2)] or connected to ______

(a) a concrete-encased electrode] or ground ring
(b) a ground rod
(c) other approved earth connection
(d) any of these

54. Metal enclosures and raceways containing service conductors shall be connected to the grounded system conductor if the electrical system is grounded.

(a) True
(b) False

55. Short sections of metal enclosures or raceways used to provide support or protection of ______ from physical damage shall not be required to be connected to the equipment grounding conductor.

(a) conduit
(b) feeders under 600V
(c) cable assemblies
(d) none of these

56. The noncurrent-carrying metal parts of service equipment, such as ______, shall be bonded together.

(a) service raceways or service cable armor
(b) service equipment enclosures containing service conductors, including meter fittings, boxes, or the like, interposed in the service raceway or armor
(c) service cable trays
(d) all of these

57. Service metal raceways and metal-clad cables are considered effectively bonded when using threadless couplings and connectors that are ______.

(a) nonmetallic
(b) made up tight
(c) sealed
(d) classified

58. The intersystem bonding termination shall ______.

(a) be accessible for connection and inspection
(b) consist of a set of terminals with the capacity for connection of not less than three intersystem bonding conductors
(c) not interfere with opening the enclosure for a service, building/structure disconnecting means, or metering equipment
(d) all of these

59. At existing buildings or structures, an external accessible means for bonding communications systems together can be by the use of ______.

(a) nonflexible metallic raceway
(b) an exposed grounding electrode conductor
(c) a connection to grounded raceway or equipment approved by the authority having jurisdiction
(d) any of these

60. Where installed to reduce electrical noise for electronic equipment, a metal raceway can terminate to a(n) ______ nonmetallic fitting(s) or spacer on the electronic equipment. The metal raceway shall be supplemented by an internal insulated equipment grounding conductor.

(a) listed
(b) labeled
(c) identified
(d) marked

61. The supply-side bonding jumper on the supply side of services shall be sized according to the ______.

(a) overcurrent device rating
(b) ungrounded supply conductor size
(c) service-drop size
(d) load to be served

62. Where ungrounded supply conductors are paralleled in two or more raceways or cables, the bonding jumper for each raceway or cable shall be based on the size of the ______ in each raceway or cable.

(a) overcurrent protection for conductors
(b) grounded conductors
(c) ungrounded supply conductors
(d) sum of all conductors

63. What is the minimum size copper equipment bonding jumper for a 40A rated circuit?

(a) 14 AWG
(b) 12 AWG
(c) 10 AWG
(d) 8 AWG

64. Metal water piping system(s) shall be bonded to the ______.

(a) grounded conductor at the service
(b) service equipment enclosure
(c) equipment grounding bar or bus at any panelboard within a single occupancy building
(d) a or b

65. Metal gas piping shall be considered bonded by the equipment grounding conductor of the circuit that is likely to energize the piping.

(a) True
(b) False

66. Lightning protection system ground terminals ______ be bonded to the building grounding electrode system.

(a) shall
(b) shall not
(c) shall be permitted to
(d) none of these

67. Electrical equipment permanently mounted on skids, and the skids themselves, shall be connected to the equipment grounding conductor sized as required by ______.

(a) 250.50
(b) 250.66
(c) 250.122
(d) 310.15

68. Listed FMC can be used as the equipment grounding conductor if the length in any ground return path does not exceed 6 ft and the circuit conductors contained in the conduit are protected by overcurrent devices rated at ______ or less.

(a) 15A
(b) 20A
(c) 30A
(d) 60A

69. The armor of Type AC cable containing an aluminum bonding strip is recognized by the NEC as an equipment grounding conductor.

(a) True
(b) False

70. An equipment grounding conductor shall be identified by ______.

(a) a continuous outer finish that is green
(b) being bare
(c) a continuous outer finish that is green with one or more yellow stripes
(d) any of these

71. An equipment grounding conductor is permitted to be used as a grounding electrode conductor.

(a) True
(b) False

72. When ungrounded circuit conductors are increased in size, the equipment grounding conductor must be proportionately increased in size according to the ______ of the ungrounded conductors.

(a) ampacity
(b) circular mil area
(c) diameter
(d) none of these

73. Equipment grounding conductors for feeder taps are not required to be larger than the tap conductors.

(a) True
(b) False

74. The structural metal frame of a building can be used as the required equipment grounding conductor for ac equipment.

(a) True
(b) False

75. A grounded circuit conductor is permitted to ground noncurrent-carrying metal parts of equipment, raceways, and other enclosures on the supply side or within the enclosure of the ac service-disconnecting means.

(a) True
(b) False

76. A(n) ______ shall be used to connect the grounding terminal of a grounding-type receptacle to a grounded box.

(a) equipment bonding jumper
(b) grounded conductor jumper
(c) a or b
(d) a and b

77. The receptacle grounding terminal of an isolated ground receptacle shall be connected to a(n) ______ equipment grounding conductor run with the circuit conductors.

(a) insulated
(b) covered
(c) bare
(d) solid

78. The arrangement of grounding connections shall be such that the disconnection or the removal of a receptacle, luminaire, or other device does not interrupt the grounding continuity.

(a) True
(b) False

79. Transient voltage surge suppressors (TVSSs) are also known as Type 2 and Type 3 surge protective devices (SPDs).

(a) True
(b) False

80. Surge protective devices shall be listed.

(a) True
(b) False

81. A Type 2 surge protective device is permitted to be connected on either the line or load side of the service equipment.

(a) True
(b) False

82. Conductors shall be installed within a raceway, cable, or enclosure.

(a) True
(b) False

83. Conductors of ac and dc circuits, rated 600V or less, shall be permitted to occupy the same _____ provided that all conductors have an insulation rating equal to the maximum voltage applied to any conductor.

(a) enclosure
(b) cable
(c) raceway
(d) all of these

84. Cables laid in wood notches require protection against nails or screws by using a steel plate at least _____ thick, installed before the building finish is applied.

(a) 1/16 in.
(b) 1/8 in.
(c) 1/4 in.
(d) 1/2 in.

85. Wiring methods installed behind panels that allow access shall be _____ according to their applicable articles.

(a) supported
(b) painted
(c) in a metal raceway
(d) all of these

86. A cable, raceway, or box installed under metal-corrugated sheet roof decking shall be supported so the top of the cable, raceway, or box is not less than _____ from the lowest surface of the roof decking to the top of the cable, raceway, or box.

(a) 1/2 in.
(b) 1 in.
(c) 1 1/2 in.
(d) 2 in.

87. When installed under metal-corrugated sheet roof decking, the rules for spacing from roof decking apply equally to rigid metal conduit and intermediate metal conduit.

(a) True
(b) False

88. A listed expansion/deflection fitting or other approved means must be used where a raceway crosses a _____ intended for expansion, contraction or deflection used in buildings, bridges, parking garages, or other structures.

(a) junction box
(b) structural joint
(c) cable tray
(d) unistrut hanger

89. What is the minimum cover requirement for Type UF cable supplying power to a 120V, 15A GFCI-protected circuit outdoors under a driveway of a one-family dwelling?

(a) 6 in.
(b) 12 in.
(c) 16 in.
(d) 24 in.

90. "_____" is defined as the area between the top of direct-burial cable and the top surface of the finished grade.

(a) Notch
(b) Cover
(c) Gap
(d) none of these

91. Type MC Cable listed for ______ is permitted to be installed underground under a building without installation in a raceway.

(a) direct burial
(b) damp and wet locations
(c) rough service
(d) b and c

92. Direct-buried service conductors that are not encased in concrete and that are buried 18 in. or more below grade shall have their location identified by a warning ribbon placed in the trench at least ______ above the underground installation.

(a) 6 in.
(b) 10 in.
(c) 12 in.
(d) 18 in.

93. When installing direct-buried cables, a ______ shall be used at the end of a conduit that terminates underground.

(a) splice kit
(b) terminal fitting
(c) bushing
(d) b or c

94. Each direct-buried single conductor cable must be located ______ in the trench to the other single conductor cables in the same parallel set of conductors, including equipment grounding conductors.

(a) perpendicular
(b) bundled together
(c) in close proximity
(d) spaced apart

95. Cables or raceways installed using directional boring equipment shall be ______ for this purpose.

(a) marked
(b) listed
(c) labeled
(d) approved

96. Where corrosion protection is necessary for ferrous metal equipment and the conduit is threaded in the field, the threads shall be coated with a(n) ______, electrically conductive, corrosion-resistant compound.

(a) marked
(b) listed
(c) labeled
(d) approved

97. Where exposed to sunlight, nonmetallic raceways, cable trays, boxes, cables with a nonmetallic outer jacket, fittings, and support hardware shall be ______.

(a) listed as sunlight resistant
(b) identified as sunlight resistant
(c) a and b
(d) a or b

98. An exposed wiring system for indoor wet locations where walls are frequently washed shall be mounted so that there is at least a ______ between the mounting surface and the electrical equipment.

(a) ¼ in. airspace
(b) separation by insulated bushings
(c) separation by noncombustible tubing
(d) none of these

99. Where portions of a cable raceway or sleeve are subjected to different temperatures and condensation is known to be a problem, the ______ shall be filled with an approved material to prevent the circulation of warm air to a colder section of the raceway or sleeve.

(a) raceway
(b) sleeve
(c) a or b
(d) none of these

100. Raceways or cable trays containing electric conductors shall not contain any pipe or tube for steam, water, air, gas, drainage, or any service other than ______.

(a) as permitted by the authority having jurisdiction
(b) electrical
(c) pneumatic
(d) as designed by the engineer

Practice Quiz 3

Random Order [90.3 through 300.6]

Unit 3 Practice Quiz— Random Order [90.3 through 300.6]

Please use the 2011 *Code* book to answer the following questions, which are based on the 2011 *NEC.*

1. "______" means that an object is not readily accessible to persons unless special means for access are used.

(a) Isolated
(b) Secluded
(c) Protected
(d) Locked

2. "Continuous duty" is defined as ______.

(a) when the load is expected to continue for 5 hours or more
(b) operation at a substantially constant load for an indefinite long time
(c) operation at loads and for intervals of time, both of which may be subject to wide variations
(d) operation at which the load may be subject to maximum current for 6 hours or more

3. "Ungrounded" describes not connected to ground or a conductive body that extends the ground connection.

(a) True
(b) False

4. A "______" is a building or portion of a building in which one or more self-propelled vehicles can be kept for use, sale, storage, rental, repair, exhibition, or demonstration purposes.

(a) garage
(b) residential garage
(c) service garage
(d) commercial garage

5. A 15A or 20A, 125V receptacle outlet shall be located within 25 ft of heating, air-conditioning, and refrigeration equipment for ______ occupancies.

(a) dwelling
(b) commercial
(c) industrial
(d) all of these

6. A bare 4 AWG copper conductor installed horizontally near the bottom or vertically, and within that portion of a concrete foundation or footing that is in direct contact with the earth can be used as a grounding electrode when the conductor is at least ______ in length.

(a) 10 ft
(b) 15 ft
(c) 20 ft
(d) 25 ft

7. A building disconnecting means that supplies only limited loads of a single branch circuit shall have a rating of not less than ______.

(a) 15A
(b) 20A
(c) 25A
(d) 30A

8. A building or structure shall be supplied by a maximum of ______ feeder(s) or branch circuit(s), unless specifically permitted otherwise.

(a) one
(b) two
(c) three
(d) four

9. A building or structure shall be supplied by a maximum of ______ service(s), unless specifically permitted otherwise.

(a) one
(b) two
(c) three
(d) as many as desired

10. A building or structure that is supplied by a feeder shall have the interior metal water piping system bonded with a conductor sized in accordance with ______.

(a) Table 250.66
(b) Table 250.122
(c) Table 310.15(B)(16)
(d) none of these

11. A connection between equipment grounding conductors and a metal box shall be by ______.

(a) a grounding screw used for no other purpose
(b) equipment listed for grounding
(c) a listed grounding device
(d) any of these

12. A device that establishes a connection between the conductors of the attached flexible cord and the conductors connected to the receptacle is called a(n) "______."

(a) attachment plug
(b) plug cap
(c) plug
(d) any of these

13. A dwelling unit containing two 120V laundry branch circuits has a calculated load of ______VA for the laundry circuits.

(a) 1,500
(b) 3,000
(c) 4,500
(d) 6,000

14. A ground ring encircling the building or structure can be used as a grounding electrode when ______.

(a) the ring is in direct contact with the earth
(b) the ring consists of at least 20 ft of bare conductor
(c) the bare copper conductor is not smaller than 2 AWG
(d) all of these

15. A grounding electrode shall be required if a building or structure is supplied by a feeder.

(a) True
(b) False

16. A large single panel, frame, or assembly of panels on which switches, overcurrent and other protective devices, buses, and instruments are mounted is a "______." They are generally accessible from the rear as well as from the front and are not intended to be installed in cabinets.

(a) switchboard
(b) panel box
(c) switch box
(d) panelboard

17. A means external to enclosures for connecting intersystem ______ conductors shall be provided at service equipment or metering equipment enclosure and disconnecting means of buildings or structures supplied by a feeder.

(a) bonding
(b) ungrounded
(c) secondary
(d) a and b

18. A panel, including buses and automatic overcurrent devices, designed to be placed in a cabinet or cutout box and accessible only from the front is known as a "______."

(a) switchboard
(b) disconnect
(c) panelboard
(d) switch

19. A receptacle connected to a dwelling unit small-appliance circuit can supply gas-fired ranges, ovens, or counter-mounted cooking units.

(a) True
(b) False

20. A receptacle outlet shall be installed at each dwelling unit kitchen wall countertop space that is 12 in. or wider and receptacle outlets shall be installed so that no point along the wall line is more than ______, measured horizontally from a receptacle outlet in that space.

(a) 10 in.
(b) 12 in.
(c) 16 in.
(d) 24 in.

21. A service consisting of 12 AWG service-entrance conductors requires a grounding electrode conductor sized no less than ______.

(a) 10 AWG
(b) 8 AWG
(c) 6 AWG
(d) 4 AWG

22. A service disconnecting means shall be installed at a(n) ______ location.

(a) dry
(b) readily accessible
(c) outdoor
(d) indoor

23. A service is supplied by three metal raceways, each containing 600 kcmil ungrounded conductors. Determine the copper supply-side bonding jumper size for each service raceway.

(a) 1/0 AWG
(b) 3/0 AWG
(c) 250 kcmil
(d) 500 kcmil

24. A system intended to provide protection of equipment from damaging line-to-ground fault currents by opening all ungrounded conductors of the faulted circuit at current levels less than the supply-circuit overcurrent device defines the phrase "______."

(a) ground-fault protection of equipment
(b) guarded
(c) personal protection
(d) automatic protection

25. A(n) ______ enclosure is constructed or protected so that exposure to the weather will not interfere with successful operation.

(a) weatherproof
(b) weathertight
(c) weather-resistant
(d) all weather

26. A(n) ______ is a point on the wiring system at which current is taken to supply utilization equipment.

(a) box
(b) receptacle
(c) outlet
(d) device

27. Accepted industry workmanship practices are described in ANSI/NECA 1-2006, *Standard Practices for Good Workmanship in Electrical Contracting*, and other ANSI-approved installation standards.

(a) True
(b) False

28. According to the *Code*, "automatic" is performing a function without the necessity of ______.

(a) protection from damage
(b) human intervention
(c) mechanical linkage
(d) all of these

29. Additional services shall be permitted for different voltages, frequencies, or phases, or for different uses such as for ______.

(a) gymnasiums
(b) different rate schedules
(c) flea markets
(d) special entertainment events

30. All 15A and 20A, 125V receptacles installed in dwelling unit boathouses shall have GFCI protection.

(a) True
(b) False

31. All conductors of a circuit, including the grounded and equipment grounding conductors, shall be contained within the same ______, unless otherwise permitted elsewhere in the Code.

(a) raceway
(b) cable
(c) trench
(d) all of these

32. All conductors of the same circuit shall be ______, unless otherwise specifically permitted in the Code.

(a) in the same raceway or cable
(b) in close proximity in the same trench
(c) the same size
(d) a or b

33. Alternating-current circuits of less than 50V shall be grounded if supplied by a transformer whose supply system exceeds 150 volts-to-ground.

(a) True
(b) False

34. Alternating-current systems of 50V to 1,000V that supply premises wiring systems shall be grounded where supplied by a three-phase, 4-wire, delta-connected system in which the midpoint of one phase winding is used as a circuit conductor.

(a) True
(b) False

35. Aluminum raceways, cable trays, cablebus, auxiliary gutters, cable armor, boxes, cable sheathing, cabinets, elbows, couplings, nipples, fittings, supports, and support hardware ______ shall be provided with supplementary corrosion protection.

(a) embedded or encased in concrete
(b) in direct contact with the earth
(c) likely to become energized
(d) a or b

36. An effective ground-fault current path is an intentionally constructed, permanent, low-impedance path designed and intended to carry fault current from the point of a ground fault on a wiring system to ______.

(a) ground
(b) earth
(c) the electrical supply source
(d) none of these

37. An important consideration for limiting imposed voltage on electrical systems is to remember that bonding and grounding electrode conductors shouldn't be any longer than necessary and unnecessary bends and loops should be avoided.

(a) True
(b) False

38. An unspliced ______ that is sized based on the derived phase conductors shall be used to connect the grounded conductor and the supply-side bonding jumper, or the equipment grounding conductor, or both, at a separately derived system.

(a) system bonding jumper
(b) equipment grounding conductor
(c) grounded conductor
(d) grounding electrode conductor

39. Any current in excess of the rated current of equipment or the ampacity of a conductor is called "______."

(a) trip current
(b) fault current
(c) overcurrent
(d) a short circuit

40. As used in the *NEC*, equipment includes ______.

(a) fittings
(b) appliances
(c) machinery
(d) all of these

41. At least one receptacle outlet not more than ______ above a balcony, deck or porch shall be installed within the perimeter at each balcony, deck or porch of a dwelling unit.

(a) 3 ft
(b) 6½ ft
(c) 8 ft
(d) 24 in.

42. Bonding jumpers for service raceways shall be used around impaired connections such as ______ .

(a) concentric knockouts
(b) eccentric knockouts
(c) reducing washers
(d) any of these

43. Chapters 1 through 4 of the *NEC* apply ______.

(a) generally to all electrical installations
(b) only to special occupancies and conditions
(c) only to special equipment and material
(d) all of these

44. Circuit breakers rated at ______ amperes or less and ______ volts or less shall have the ampere rating molded, stamped, etched, or similarly marked into their handles or escutcheon areas.

(a) 100, 600
(b) 600, 100
(c) 1,000, 6,000
(d) 6,000, 1,000

45. Circuit breakers shall ______ all ungrounded conductors of the circuit both manually and automatically unless specifically permitted otherwise.

(a) open
(b) close
(c) isolate
(d) inhibit

46. Circuit breakers used to switch 120V or 277V fluorescent-lighting circuits shall be listed and marked ______.

(a) UL
(b) SWD or HID
(c) Amps
(d) VA

47. Conductor sizes are expressed in American Wire Gage (AWG) or ______.

(a) inches
(b) circular mils
(c) square inches
(d) cubic inches

48. Conductors supplied under the tap rules are allowed to supply another conductor using the tap rules.

(a) True
(b) False

49. Conductors with the color ______ insulation shall not be used for ungrounded or grounded conductors.

(a) green
(b) green with one or more yellow stripes
(c) a or b
(d) white

50. Conduits or raceways through which moisture may contact live parts shall be ______ at either or both ends.

(a) sealed
(b) plugged
(c) bushed
(d) a or b

Practice Quiz 4

Straight Order [300.9 through 344.10]

Unit 4 Practice Quiz—Straight Order [300.9 through 344.10]

Please use the 2011 *Code* book to answer the following questions, which are based on the 2011 *NEC*.

1. Where raceways are installed in wet locations above grade, the interior of these raceways shall be considered a ______ location.

(a) wet
(b) dry
(c) damp
(d) corrosive

2. Metal raceways, cable armors, and other metal enclosures shall be ______ joined together into a continuous electric conductor so as to provide effective electrical continuity.

(a) electrically
(b) permanently
(c) metallically
(d) none of these

3. Raceways, cable assemblies, boxes, cabinets, and fittings shall be securely fastened in place.

(a) True
(b) False

4. Where independent support wires of a ceiling assembly are used to support raceways, cable assemblies, or boxes above a ceiling, they shall be secured at ______ ends.

(a) one
(b) both
(c) a or b
(d) none of these

5. The independent support wires for supporting electrical wiring methods in a fire-rated ceiling assembly shall be distinguishable from fire-rated suspended-ceiling framing support wires by ______.

(a) color
(b) tagging
(c) other effective means
(d) any of these

6. Electrical wiring within the cavity of a fire-rated floor-ceiling or roof-ceiling assembly shall not be supported by the ceiling assembly or ceiling support wires.

(a) True
(b) False

7. Raceways can be used as a means of support of Class 2 circuit conductors or cables that connect to the same equipment.

(a) True
(b) False

8. Conductors in raceways shall be ______ between outlets, boxes, devices, and so forth.

(a) continuous
(b) installed
(c) copper
(d) in conduit

9. When the opening to an outlet, junction, or switch point is less than 8 in. in any dimension, each conductor shall be long enough to extend at least ______ outside the opening of the enclosure.

(a) 0 in.
(b) 3 in.
(c) 6 in.
(d) 12 in.

10. A box or conduit body shall not be required where cables enter or exit from conduit or tubing that is used to provide cable support or protection against physical damage.

(a) True
(b) False

11. A box or conduit body shall not be required for conductors in handhole enclosures, except where connected to electrical equipment.

(a) True
(b) False

12. Prewired raceway assemblies shall be used only where specifically permitted in the NEC for the applicable wiring method.

(a) True
(b) False

13. Metal raceways shall not be ______ by welding to the raceway.

(a) supported
(b) terminated
(c) connected
(d) all of these

14. Conductors in ferrous metal raceways and enclosures shall be arranged so as to avoid heating the surrounding ferrous metal by alternating-current induction. To accomplish this, the ______ conductor(s) shall be grouped together.

(a) phase
(b) grounded
(c) equipment grounding
(d) all of these

15. Electrical installations in hollow spaces, vertical shafts, and ventilation or air-handling ducts shall be made so that the possible spread of fire or products of combustion is not ______.

(a) substantially increased
(b) allowed
(c) inherent
(d) possible

16. The space above a hung ceiling used for environmental air-handling purposes is an example of ______, and the wiring limitations of ______ apply.

(a) a specifically fabricated duct used for environmental air, 300.22(B)
(b) other space used for environmental air (plenum), 300.22(C)
(c) a supply duct used for environmental air, 300.22(B)
(d) none of these

17. ______ shall be permitted to support the wiring methods and equipment permitted to be used in other spaces used for environmental air (plenum).

(a) Metal cable tray system
(b) Nonmetallic wireways
(c) PVC conduit
(d) Surface nonmetallic raceways

18. Wiring methods and equipment installed behind suspended-ceiling panels shall be arranged and secured to allow access to the electrical equipment.

(a) True
(b) False

19. Insulated conductors used in wet locations shall be ______.

(a) moisture-impervious metal sheathed
(b) MTW, RHW, RHW-2, TW, THW, THW-2, THHW, THWN, THWN-2, XHHW, XHHW-2, ZW
(c) listed for wet locations
(d) any of these

20. Where conductors in parallel are run in separate raceways, the raceways shall have the same electrical characteristics.

(a) True
(b) False

21. The ______ rating of a conductor is the maximum temperature, at any location along its length, which the conductor can withstand over a prolonged period of time without serious degradation.

(a) ambient
(b) temperature
(c) maximum withstand
(d) short-circuit

22. The ampacities listed in the Tables of Article 310.15(B)(6) do not take ______ into consideration.

(a) continuous loads
(b) voltage drop
(c) insulation
(d) wet locations

23. Each current-carrying conductor of a paralleled set of conductors shall be counted as a current-carrying conductor for the purpose of applying the adjustment factors of 310.15(B)(3)(a).

(a) True
(b) False

24. Where conductors or cables are installed in circular conduits exposed to direct sunlight on or above rooftops, the ambient temperature shall be increased by ______ where the conduits are less than ½ in. from the rooftop.

(a) 30°F
(b) 40°F
(c) 50°F
(d) 60°F

25. A ______ conductor that carries only the unbalanced current from other conductors of the same circuit shall not be required to be counted when applying the provisions of 310.15(B)(3)(a).

(a) neutral
(b) ungrounded
(c) grounding
(d) none of these

26. When determining the number of current-carrying conductors, a grounding or bonding conductor shall not be counted when applying the provisions of 310.15(B)(3)(a) ______.

(a) True
(b) False

27. THWN insulated conductors are rated ______.

(a) 75°C
(b) for wet locations
(c) a and b
(d) not enough information

28. Where installed in raceways, conductors ______ AWG and larger shall be stranded.

(a) 10
(b) 8
(c) 6
(d) 4

29. Surface-type cabinets, cutout boxes, and meter socket enclosures in damp or wet locations shall be mounted so there is at least ______ airspace between the enclosure and the wall or supporting surface.

(a) 1/16 in.
(b) ¼ in.
(c) 1¼ in.
(d) 6 in.

30. Where raceways or cables enter above the level of uninsulated live parts of cabinets, cutout boxes, and meter socket enclosures in a wet location, a(n) ______ shall be used.

(a) fitting listed for wet locations
(b) explosionproof seal
(c) fitting listed for damp locations
(d) insulated fitting

31. Noncombustible surfaces that are broken or incomplete shall be repaired so there will be no gaps or open spaces greater than ______ at the edge of a cabinet or cutout box employing a flush-type cover.

(a) 1/32 in.
(b) 1/16 in.
(c) ⅛ in.
(d) ¼ in.

32. Enclosures for switches or overcurrent devices are allowed to have conductors feeding through where the wiring space at any cross section is not filled to more than ______ percent of the cross-sectional area of the space.

(a) 20
(b) 30
(c) 40
(d) 60

33. Nonmetallic boxes can be used with ______.

(a) nonmetallic cables
(b) nonmetallic raceways
(c) flexible cords
(d) all of these

34. Boxes, conduit bodies, and fittings installed in wet locations shall be required to be listed for use in wet locations.

(a) True
(b) False

35. According to the *NEC*, the volume of a 3 x 2 x 2 in. device box is _____

(a) 8 cu in.
(b) 10 cu in.
(c) 12 cu in.
(d) 14 cu in.

36. Where a luminaire stud or hickey is present in the box, a _____ volume allowance in accordance with Table 314.16(B) shall be made for each type of fitting, based on the largest conductor present in the box.

(a) single
(b) double
(c) single allowance for each gang
(d) none of these

37. Each strap containing one or more devices shall count as a _____ volume allowance in accordance with Table 314.16(B), based on the largest conductor connected to a device(s) or equipment supported by the strap.

(a) single
(b) double
(c) triple
(d) none of these

38. Where one or more equipment grounding conductors enter a box, a _____ volume allowance in accordance with Table 314.16(B) shall be made, based on the largest equipment grounding conductor.

(a) single
(b) double
(c) triple
(d) none of these

39. Conduit bodies that are durably and legibly marked by the manufacturer with their volume can contain splices, taps, or devices

(a) True
(b) False

40. In walls or ceilings constructed of wood or other combustible surface material, boxes, plaster rings, extension rings, or listed extenders shall _____.

(a) be flush with the surface
(b) project from the surface
(c) a or b
(d) be set back no more than ¼ in.

41. Surface extensions shall be made by mounting and mechanically securing an extension ring over the box, unless otherwise permitted.

(a) True
(b) False

42. Surface-mounted outlet boxes shall be _____.

(a) rigidly and securely fastened in place
(b) supported by cables that protrude from the box
(c) supported by cable entries from the top and permitted to rest against the supporting surface
(d) none of these

43. A wood brace used for supporting a box for structural mounting shall have a cross-section not less than nominal _____.

(a) 1 in. x 2 in.
(b) 2 in. x 2 in.
(c) 2 in. x 3 in.
(d) 2 in. x 4 in.

44. Two intermediate metal or rigid metal conduits threaded wrenchtight into the enclosure can be used to support an outlet box containing devices or luminaires, if each raceway is supported within _____ of the box.

(a) 12 in.
(b) 18 in.
(c) 24 in.
(d) 36 in.

45. A wall-mounted luminaire weighing not more than _____ can be supported to a device box or plaster ring with no fewer than two No. 6 or larger screws.

(a) 4 lb
(b) 6 lb
(c) 8 lb
(d) 10 lb

46. A luminaire that weighs more than ______ can be supported by an outlet box that is listed and marked for the weight of the luminaire.

(a) 20 lb
(b) 30 lb
(c) 40 lb
(d) 50 lb

47. Listed outlet boxes to support ceiling-suspended fans that weigh more than ______lb shall have the maximum allowable weight marked on the box.

(a) 35 lb
(b) 50 lb
(c) 60 lb
(d) 70 lb

48. Pull boxes or junction boxes with any dimension over ______ shall have all conductors cabled or racked in an approved manner.

(a) 3 ft
(b) 6 ft
(c) 9 ft
(d) 12 ft

49. Power distribution blocks shall be permitted in pull and junction boxes over 100 cubic inches when ______.

(a) they are listed as a power distribution block.
(b) they are installed in a box not smaller than required by the installation instructions of the power distribution block.
(c) the junction box is sized so that the wire-bending space requirements of 312.6 can be met.
(d) all of these

50. Where the junction box contains a power distribution block, and it has conductors that don't terminate on the power distribution block(s), the through conductors must be arranged so the power distribution block terminals are ______ following installation.

(a) unobstructed
(b) above the through conductors
(c) visible
(d) labeled

51. Listed boxes and handhole enclosures designed for underground installation can be directly buried when covered by ______, if their location is effectively identified and accessible.

(a) concrete
(b) gravel
(c) noncohesive granulated soil
(d) b or c

52. Handhole enclosure covers shall have an identifying ______ that prominently identifies the function of the enclosure, such as electric.

(a) mark
(b) logo
(c) a or b
(d) manual

53. Boxes and conduit bodies, covers, extension rings, plaster rings, and the like shall be durably and legibly marked with the manufacturer's name or trademark.

(a) True
(b) False

54. For angle or U-pulls, the distance between the shielded conductor entry (for systems over 600V, nominal) and the opposite wall of the box shall not be less than ______ times the outside diameter of the largest cable or conductor.

(a) 12
(b) 16
(c) 24
(d) 36

55. Type ______ cable is a fabricated assembly of insulated conductors in a flexible interlocked metallic armor.

(a) AC
(b) MC
(c) NM
(d) b and c

56. Type AC cable installed through, or parallel to, framing members shall be protected against physical damage from penetration by screws or nails.

(a) True
(b) False

57. When armored cable is run parallel to the sides of rafters, studs, or floor joists in an accessible attic, the cable shall be protected with running boards.

(a) True
(b) False

58. Type AC cable can be supported and secured by ______.

(a) staples
(b) cable ties
(c) straps
(d) all of these

59. Type AC cable installed horizontally through wooden or metal framing members is considered supported where support doesn't exceed ______.

(a) 2 ft
(b) 3 ft
(c) 4½ ft
(d) 6 ft

60. Type FC cable is an assembly of parallel conductors with an insulating material specifically designed for field installation in surface metal raceways.

(a) True
(b) False

61. Flat cable assemblies shall not be installed ______.

(a) where subject to corrosive vapors unless suitable for the application
(b) in hoistways
(c) in any hazardous (classified) location
(d) all of these

62. Extensions from flat cable assemblies shall be made by approved wiring methods, within the ______, installed at either end of the flat cable assembly runs.

(a) end-caps
(b) junction boxes
(c) surface metal raceway
(d) underfloor metal raceway

63. Flat cable assemblies shall consist of ______ conductors.

(a) two
(b) three
(c) four
(d) any of these

64. Type FCC systems shall be permitted for individual branch circuits.

(a) True
(b) False

65. General-purpose branch circuits wired with flat conductor cable shall not be rated more than ______.

(a) 15A
(b) 20A
(c) 30A
(d) 40A

66. Use of Type FCC systems in damp locations is ______.

(a) not permitted
(b) permitted
(c) permitted provided the system is encased in concrete
(d) permitted by special permission only

67. No more than ______ layers of flat conductor cable can cross at any one point.

(a) one
(b) two
(c) three
(d) four

68. Receptacles, receptacle housings, and self-contained devices used with flat conductor cable systems shall be ______.

(a) rated a minimum of 20A
(b) rated a minimum of 15A
(c) identified for this use
(d) none of these

69. Metal shields for flat conductor cable shall be electrically continuous to the ______.

(a) floor
(b) cable
(c) equipment grounding conductor
(d) none of these

70. Type IGS cable is defined as a factory assembly of one or more conductors, each individually insulated and enclosed in a loose-fit, nonmetallic flexible conduit as an integrated gas spacer cable rated _____ volts.

(a) 0 through 6,000
(b) 600 through 6,000
(c) 0 through 600
(d) 3,000 through 6,000

71. Type _____ is a factory assembly of insulated circuit conductors within an armor of interlocking metal tape, or a smooth or corrugated metallic sheath.

(a) AC
(b) MC
(c) NM
(d) b and c

72. Bends made in interlocked or corrugated sheath Type MC cable shall have a radius of at least _____ times the external diameter of the metallic sheath.

(a) five
(b) seven
(c) 10
(d) 12

73. Type MC cable shall be secured at intervals not exceeding _____.

(a) 3 ft
(b) 4 ft
(c) 6 ft
(d) 8 ft

74. Type MC cable can be unsupported where _____.

(a) fished between concealed access points in finished buildings or structures and support is impracticable
(b) not more than 2 ft in length at terminals where flexibility is necessary
(c) not more than 6 ft from the last point of support within an accessible ceiling for the connection of luminaires or other electrical equipment
(d) a or c

75. The minimum size copper conductor permitted for Type MC cable is _____.

(a) 18 AWG
(b) 16 AWG
(c) 14 AWG
(d) 12 AWG

76. Bends in Type MI cable shall be made so that the cable will not be _____.

(a) damaged
(b) shortened
(c) a and b
(d) none of these

77. The radius of the inner edge of any bend in Type MI cable shall not be less than _____ times the external diameter of the metallic sheath for any cable having a diameter greater than ¾ in., but not more than 1 in.

(a) three
(b) six
(c) eight
(d) 10

78. Where single-conductor Type MI cables are used, all ungrounded conductors and, when used, the _____ conductor, shall be grouped together to minimize induced voltage on the metal sheath.

(a) larger
(b) neutral
(c) grounding
(d) largest

79. Type MI cable conductors shall be made of _____, nickel, or nickel-coated copper with a resistance corresponding to standard AWG and kcmil sizes.

(a) solid copper
(b) solid or stranded copper
(c) stranded copper
(d) solid copper or aluminum

80. Type NM cable shall be _____.

(a) marked
(b) approved
(c) identified
(d) listed

81. Type NM and Type NMC cables shall be permitted in ______.

(a) one- and two-family dwellings and their attached/detached garages or storage buildings
(b) multifamily dwellings permitted to be of Types III, IV, and V construction
(c) other structures permitted to be of Types III, IV, and V construction, except as prohibited in 334.12
(d) any of these

82. Type NM cable shall not be used ______.

(a) in other than dwelling units
(b) in the air void of masonry block not subject to excessive moisture
(c) for exposed work
(d) embedded in poured cement, concrete, or aggregate

83. Type NM cable shall be protected from physical damage by ______.

(a) EMT
(b) Schedule 80 PVC conduit
(c) RMC
(d) any of these

84. Type NM cable can be supported and secured by ______.

(a) staples
(b) cable ties
(c) straps
(d) all of these

85. Flat Type NM cables shall not be stapled on edge.

(a) True
(b) False

86. For Type NM and NMC cable, the conductor ampacity used for ambient temperature correction [310.15(B)(2)(a)], conductor bundling adjustment [310.15(B)(3)(a)], or both, is based on the 90°C conductor insulation rating [310.15(B)(2)], provided the adjusted or corrected ampacity doesn't exceed that for a ______ rated conductor.

(a) 60°C
(b) 75°C
(c) 90°C
(d) 120°C

87. The difference in construction between Type NM cable and Type NMC cable is that Type NMC cable is ______, which Type NM is not.

(a) corrosion resistant
(b) flame-retardant
(c) fungus-resistant
(d) a and c

88. Type ______ cable is an assembly primarily for services.

(a) NM
(b) TC
(c) SE
(d) none of these

89. Type SE cable shall be permitted to be used as ______ in wiring systems where all of the circuit conductors of the cable are of the thermoset or thermoplastic type.

(a) branch circuits
(b) feeders
(c) a or b
(d) neither a or b

90. Type SE cable can be used for interior wiring as long as it complies with the installation requirements of Part II of Article 334, excluding 334.80.

(a) True
(b) False

91. Type USE cable used for service laterals shall be permitted to emerge from the ground if terminated in an enclosure at an outside location and protected in accordance with 300.5(D).

(a) True
(b) False

92. Type UF cable can be used for service conductors.

(a) True
(b) False

93. Type UF cable shall not be used in ______.

(a) motion picture studios
(b) storage battery rooms
(c) hoistways
(d) all of these

94. Type UF cable shall not be used where subject to physical damage.

(a) True
(b) False

95. The maximum size of conductors in Type UF cable shall be ______ AWG.

(a) 14
(b) 10
(c) 1/0
(d) 4/0

96. Where practicable, contact of dissimilar metals shall be avoided in an IMC raceway installation to prevent ______.

(a) corrosion
(b) galvanic action
(c) shorts
(d) none of these

97. When IMC is cut in the field, reaming is required to remove the burrs and rough edges.

(a) True
(b) False

98. Trade size 1 IMC shall be supported at intervals not exceeding ______.

(a) 8 ft
(b) 10 ft
(c) 12 ft
(d) 14 ft

99. Threadless couplings and connectors used on threaded IMC ends shall be listed for the purpose.

(a) True
(b) False

100. Galvanized steel, stainless steel and red brass RMC can be installed in concrete, in direct contact with the earth, or in areas subject to severe corrosive influences when protected by ______ and judged suitable for the condition.

(a) ceramic
(b) corrosion protection
(c) backfill
(d) a natural barrier

Practice Quiz
4

Random Order [90.2 through 342.26]

Unit 4 Practice Quiz— Random Order [90.2 through 342.26]

Please use the 2011 *Code* book to answer the following questions, which are based on the 2011 *NEC.*

1. A bushing shall be permitted in lieu of a box or terminal where the conductors emerge from a raceway and enter or terminate at equipment such as open switchboards, unenclosed control equipment, or similar equipment.

(a) True
(b) False

2. A device or utilization equipment wider than a single 2 in. device box shall have ______ volume allowances provided for each gang required for mounting.

(a) single
(b) double
(c) triple
(d) none of these

3. A run of IMC shall not contain more than the equivalent of ______ quarter bends between pull points such as conduit bodies and boxes.

(a) one
(b) two
(c) three
(d) four

4. A surface extension can be made from the cover of a box where the cover is designed so it is unlikely to fall off or be removed if its securing means becomes loose. The wiring method shall be ______ for a length sufficient to permit removal of the cover and provide access to the box interior, and arranged so that any grounding continuity is independent of the connection between the box and cover.

(a) solid
(b) flexible
(c) rigid
(d) cord

5. A vertical run of 4/0 AWG copper shall be supported at intervals not exceeding ______.

(a) 40 ft
(b) 80 ft
(c) 100 ft
(d) 120 ft

6. Armored cable used to connect recessed luminaires or equipment within an accessible ceiling can be unsecured for lengths up to ______.

(a) 2 ft
(b) 3 ft
(c) 4½ ft
(d) 6 ft

7. Bare Type FCC cable ends shall ______.

(a) be sealed
(b) be insulated
(c) use listed insulating ends
(d) all of these

8. Boxes used at luminaire or lampholder outlets in a ceiling shall be designed so that a luminaire or lampholder can be attached and shall be required to support a luminaire weighing a minimum of ______.

(a) 20 lb
(b) 30 lb
(c) 40 lb
(d) 50 lb

9. Cabinets, cutout boxes, and meter socket enclosures can be used for conductors feeding through, spliced, or tapping off to other enclosures, switches, or overcurrent devices where ______.

(a) the total area of the conductors at any cross section doesn't exceed 40 percent of the cross-sectional area of the space
(b) the total area of conductors, splices, and taps installed at any cross section doesn't exceed 75 percent of the cross-sectional area of that space
(c) a warning label on the enclosure identifies the disconnecting means for feed-through conductors
(d) all of these

10. Cabinets, cutout boxes, and meter socket enclosures installed in wet locations shall be ______.
(a) waterproof
(b) raintight
(c) weatherproof
(d) watertight

11. Cable wiring methods shall not be used as a means of support for ______.
(a) other cables
(b) raceways
(c) nonelectrical equipment
(d) all of these

12. Conductors, splices or terminations in a handhole enclosure shall be listed as ______.
(a) suitable for wet locations
(b) suitable for damp locations
(c) suitable for direct burial in the earth
(d) none of these

13. Connection of conductors to terminal parts shall ensure a thoroughly good connection without damaging the conductors and shall be made by means of ______.
(a) solder lugs
(b) pressure connectors
(c) splices to flexible leads
(d) any of these

14. Constructed, protected, or treated so as to prevent rain from interfering with the successful operation of the apparatus under specified test conditions defines the term "______."
(a) raintight
(b) waterproof
(c) weathertight
(d) rainproof

15. Direct-buried conductors or cables can be spliced or tapped without the use of splice boxes when the splice or tap is made in accordance with 110.14(B).
(a) True
(b) False

16. Direct-buried conductors, cables, or raceways, which are subject to movement by settlement or frost, shall be arranged to prevent damage to the ______ or to equipment connected to the raceways.
(a) siding of the building mounted on
(b) landscaping around the cable or raceway
(c) the enclosed conductors
(d) expansion fitting

17. Each service disconnecting means shall be suitable for ______.
(a) hazardous (classified) locations
(b) wet locations
(c) dry locations
(d) the prevailing conditions

18. Each tap conductor to a common grounding electrode conductor for multiple separately derived systems shall be sized in accordance with ______, based on the derived phase conductors of the separately derived system it serves.
(a) 250.66
(b) 250.118
(c) 250.122
(d) 310.15

19. Each Type FCC transition assembly shall incorporate means for ______.
(a) facilitating the entry of the Type FCC cable into the assembly
(b) connecting the Type FCC cable to the grounded conductors
(c) electrically connecting the assembly to the metal cable shields and equipment grounding conductors
(d) all of these

20. Electric utilities may include entities that install, operate, and maintain ______.
(a) communications systems (telephone, CATV, Internet, satellite, or data services)
(b) electric supply systems (generation, transmission, or distribution systems)
(c) local area network wiring on the premises
(d) a or b

21. Electrical equipment with ______ and having adequate fire-resistant and low-smoke-producing characteristics can be installed within an air-handling space (plenum).

(a) a metal enclosure
(b) a nonmetallic enclosures listed for use within an air-handling (plenum) space
(c) any type of enclosure
(d) a or b

22. Enclosures for overcurrent devices shall be mounted in a ______ position unless impracticable.

(a) vertical
(b) horizontal
(c) vertical or horizontal
(d) there are no requirements

23. Enclosures not over 100 cu in. having threaded entries and not containing a device shall be considered to be adequately supported where ______ or more conduits are threaded wrenchtight into the enclosure and each conduit is secured within 3 ft of the enclosure.

(a) one
(b) two
(c) three
(d) none of these

24. Equipment and devices shall only be permitted within ducts or plenum chambers specifically fabricated to transport environmental air if necessary for their direct action upon, or sensing of, the ______.

(a) contained air
(b) air quality
(c) air temperature
(d) none of these

25. Equipment bonding jumpers on the supply side of the service shall be no smaller than the sizes shown in ______.

(a) Table 250.66
(b) Table 250.122
(c) Table 310.15(B)(16)
(d) Table 310.15(B)(6)

26. Equipment enclosed with a means of sealing or locking so that live parts cannot be made accessible without opening the enclosure is said to be "______."

(a) guarded
(b) protected
(c) sealable
(d) lockable

27. Equipment grounding conductors, grounding electrode conductors, and bonding jumpers shall be connected by ______.

(a) listed pressure connectors
(b) terminal bars
(c) exothermic welding
(d) any of these

28. Equipment or materials included in a list published by a testing laboratory acceptable to the authority having jurisdiction is said to be ______.

(a) a book
(b) a digest
(c) a manifest
(d) listed

29. Examples of ground-fault current paths include any combination of conductive materials including ______.

(a) equipment grounding conductors
(b) metallic raceways
(c) metal water and gas piping
(d) all of these

30. Explanatory material, such as references to other standards, references to related sections of the *NEC*, or information related to a *Code* rule, are included in the form of Informational Notes.

(a) True
(b) False

31. Exposed live parts on the power distribution block are allowed when the junction box cover is removed.

(a) True
(b) False

32. Exposed noncurrent-carrying metal parts of fixed equipment likely to become energized shall be connected to the equipment conductor where located ______.

(a) within 8 ft vertically or 5 ft horizontally of ground or grounded metal objects and subject to contact by persons
(b) in wet or damp locations and not isolated
(c) in electrical contact with metal
(d) any of these

33. Exposed runs of Type AC cable can be installed on the underside of joists where supported at each joist and located so they are not subject to physical damage.

(a) True
(b) False

34. Exposed structural metal interconnected to form a metal building frame that is not intentionally grounded and is likely to become energized, shall be bonded to the ______.

(a) service equipment enclosure or building disconnecting means
(b) grounded conductor at the service
(c) grounding electrode conductor where of sufficient size
(d) any of these

35. Feeder and service loads for fixed electric space heating shall be calculated at ______ percent of the total connected load.

(a) 80
(b) 100
(c) 125
(d) 200

36. Feeder neutral conductors shall be permitted to be sized at ______ percent of the continuous and noncontinuous load.

(a) 80
(b) 100
(c) 125
(d) 150

37. Ferrous metal enclosures for grounding electrode conductors shall be electrically continuous from the point of attachment to cabinets or equipment to the grounding electrode.

(a) True
(b) False

38. Fittings and connectors shall be used only with the specific wiring methods for which they are designed and listed.

(a) True
(b) False

39. Flat cable assemblies can supply tap devices for ______ loads.

(a) lighting
(b) small appliance
(c) small power
(d) all of these

40. Flat cable assemblies shall have conductors of ______ AWG special stranded copper conductors.

(a) 14
(b) 12
(c) 10
(d) all of these

41. Flat cable assemblies shall not be installed outdoors or in wet or damp locations unless ______ for the use.

(a) special permission is granted
(b) approved
(c) identified
(d) none of these

42. Flexible cords approved for and used with a specific listed appliance or luminaire shall be considered to be protected by the branch-circuit overcurrent device when ______.

(a) not more than 6 ft in length
(b) 20 AWG and larger
(c) applied within the listing requirements
(d) 16 AWG and larger

43. Floor-mounted flat conductor cable and fittings shall be covered with carpet squares no larger than ______.

(a) 24 inches square
(b) 30 sq in. area
(c) 36 inches square
(d) 36 sq in. area

44. For a grounded system, an unspliced ______ shall be used to connect the equipment grounding conductor(s) and the service disconnecting means to the grounded conductor of the system within the enclosure for each service disconnect.

(a) grounding electrode
(b) main bonding jumper
(c) busbar
(d) insulated copper conductor

45. For a one-family dwelling, at least one receptacle outlet shall be required in each ______.

(a) basement
(b) attached garage
(c) detached garage or accessory building with electric power
(d) all of these

46. For a separate building or structure supplied by a separately derived system when overcurrent protection is provided where the conductors originate, the supply conductors must contain a(n) ______.

(a) equipment grounding conductor
(b) copper conductors only
(c) GFCI protection for the feeder
(d) all of these

47. For attics and underfloor spaces in other than dwelling units that contain heating, air-conditioning, and refrigeration equipment requiring servicing, at least one lighting outlet containing a switch or controlled by a wall switch shall be installed ______.

(a) at the equipment requiring servicing
(b) near the equipment requiring servicing
(c) a or b
(d) none of these

48. For circuits over 250 volts-to-ground, electrical continuity can be maintained between a box or enclosure where no oversized, concentric or eccentric knockouts are encountered, and a metal conduit by ______.

(a) threadless fittings for cables with metal sheath
(b) double locknuts on threaded conduit (one inside and one outside the box or enclosure)
(c) fittings that have shoulders that seat firmly against the box with a locknut on the inside or listed fittings
(d) all of these

49. For engineered series combination systems where circuit breakers are installed in series downstream of overcurrent devices with a higher AIC rating, the engineer shall ensure that the ______ device remains passive during the interruption period of the fully rated device.

(a) downstream
(b) upstream
(c) dynamic impedance
(d) current limiting

50. For grounded systems, electrical equipment and conductive material likely to become energized, shall be installed in a manner that creates a ______ from any point on the wiring system where a ground fault may occur to the electrical supply source.

(a) circuit facilitating the operation of the overcurrent device
(b) low-impedance path
(c) path capable of safely carrying the ground-fault current likely to be imposed on it
(d) all of these

Practice Quiz **5**

Straight Order [344.10 through 404.9]

Unit 5 Practice Quiz—Straight Order [344.10 through 404.9]

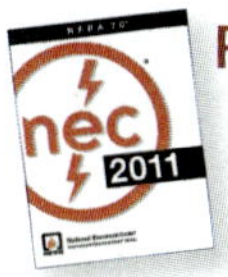

Please use the 2011 *Code* book to answer the following questions, which are based on the 2011 *NEC*.

1. Materials such as straps, bolts, and so forth, associated with the installation of RMC in wet locations shall be ______.

(a) weatherproof
(b) weathertight
(c) corrosion resistant
(d) none of these

2. Aluminum fittings and enclosures can be used with ______ conduit where not subject to severe corrosive influences.

(a) steel rigid metal
(b) aluminum rigid metal
(c) PVC-coated rigid conduit only
(d) a and b

3. A run of RMC shall not contain more than the equivalent of ______ quarter bends between pull points such as conduit bodies and boxes.

(a) one
(b) two
(c) three
(d) four

4. Cut ends of RMC shall be ______ or otherwise finished to remove rough edges.

(a) threaded
(b) reamed
(c) painted
(d) galvanized

5. Horizontal runs of RMC supported by openings through ______ at intervals not exceeding 10 ft and securely fastened within 3 ft of termination points shall be permitted.

(a) walls
(b) trusses
(c) rafters
(d) framing members

6. Threadless couplings and connectors used with RMC in wet locations shall be ______.

(a) listed for wet locations
(b) listed for damp locations
(c) nonabsorbent
(d) weatherproof

7. Running threads shall not be used on RMC for connection at ______.

(a) boxes
(b) cabinets
(c) couplings
(d) meter sockets

8. Each length of RMC shall be clearly and durably identified in every ______.

(a) 3 ft
(b) 5 ft
(c) 10 ft
(d) 20 ft

9. FMC can be installed exposed or concealed where not subject to physical damage.

(a) True
(b) False

10. Bends in FMC ______ between pull points.

(a) shall not be made
(b) need not be limited (in degrees)
(c) shall not exceed 360 degrees
(d) shall not exceed 180 degrees

11. FMC shall be supported and secured ______.

(a) at intervals not exceeding 4½ ft
(b) within 8 in. on each side of a box where fished
(c) where fished
(d) at intervals not exceeding 6 ft

12. Flexible metal conduit shall not be required to be ______ where fished between access points through concealed spaces in finished buildings or structures and supporting is impracticable.

(a) secured
(b) supported
(c) complete
(d) (a) and (b)

13. When FMC is used where flexibility is necessary to minimize the transmission of vibration from equipment or to provide flexibility for equipment that requires movement after installation, ______ shall be installed.

(a) an equipment grounding conductor
(b) an expansion fitting
(c) flexible nonmetallic connectors
(d) none of these

14. The use of LFMC shall be permitted for ______.

(a) direct burial where listed and marked for the purpose
(b) exposed work
(c) concealed work
(d) all of these

15. LFMC shall be supported and secured ______.

(a) at intervals not exceeding 4½ ft
(b) within 8 in. on each side of a box where fished
(c) where fished
(d) at intervals not exceeding 6 ft

16. For liquidtight flexible metal conduit, if flexibility is necessary after installation, unsecured lengths from the last point the raceway is securely fastened must not exceed ______.

(a) 3 ft for trade sizes ½ through 1¼
(b) 4 ft for trade sizes 1½ through 2
(c) 5 ft for trade sizes 2½ and larger
(d) all of these

17. Extreme ______ may cause PVC conduit to become brittle, and therefore more susceptible to damage from physical contact.

(a) sunlight
(b) corrosive conditions
(c) heat
(d) cold

18. PVC conduit can support nonmetallic conduit bodies not larger than the largest entering raceway, but the conduit bodies shall not contain devices, luminaires, or other equipment.

(a) True
(b) False

19. PVC conduit shall not be used ______, unless specifically permitted.

(a) in hazardous (classified) locations
(b) for the support of luminaires or other equipment
(c) where subject to physical damage unless identified for such use
(d) all of these

20. Bends in PVC conduit shall be made only ______.

(a) by hand forming the bend
(b) with bending equipment identified for the purpose
(c) with a truck exhaust pipe
(d) by use of an open flame torch

21. Where PVC conduit enters a box, fitting, or other enclosure, a bushing or adapter shall be provided to protect the conductor from abrasion unless the design of the box, fitting, or enclosure affords equivalent protection.

(a) True
(b) False

22. PVC conduit and fittings for use above ground shall have the following characteristics ______.

(a) flame retardant
(b) resistance to low temperatures and sunlight
(c) resistance to distortion from heat
(d) all of these

23. HDPE shall be permitted ______.
(a) in discrete lengths
(b) in continuous lengths from a reel
(c) in 20 ft lengths
(d) a or b

24. HDPE conduit shall not be subjected to ambient temperatures in excess of ______, unless listed otherwise.
(a) 50°C
(b) 60°C
(c) 75°C
(d) 90°C

25. When HDPE conduit enters a box, fitting, or other enclosure, a(n) ______ shall be provided to protect the conductor from abrasion, unless the box design provides such protection.
(a) bushing
(b) adapter
(c) a or b
(d) reducing bushing

26. HDPE conduit can be joined using ______.
(a) heat fusion
(b) electrofusion
(c) mechanical fittings
(d) any of these

27. HDPE conduit shall be resistant to ______.
(a) moisture
(b) chemical atmospheres
(c) impact and crushing
(d) all of these

28. ______ is a factory assembly of conductors or cables inside a nonmetallic, smooth wall conduit with a circular cross section.
(a) HDPE
(b) ENT
(c) NUCC
(d) RTRC

29. NUCC larger than ______ shall not be used.
(a) trade size 1
(b) trade size 2
(c) trade size 3
(d) trade size 4

30. Bends in NUCC shall ______ between termination points.
(a) not be made
(b) not be limited in degrees
(c) be limited to 360 degrees
(d) be limited to 180 degrees

31. Where NUCC enters a box, fitting, or other enclosure, a bushing or adapter shall be provided to protect the conductor or cable from abrasion unless the design of the box, fitting, or enclosure provides equivalent protection.
(a) True
(b) False

32. RTRC conduit can be described as a rigid nonmetallic conduit of circular cross section, with integral or associated ______ for the installation of electrical conductors and cables.
(a) couplings
(b) connectors
(c) fittings
(d) all of these

33. Bends in LFNC shall ______ between pull points.
(a) not be made
(b) not be limited in degrees
(c) be limited to 360 degrees
(d) be limited to 180 degrees

34. ______ is a listed thin-wall, metallic tubing of circular cross section used for the installation and physical protection of electrical conductors when joined together with listed fittings.
(a) LFNC
(b) EMT
(c) NUCC
(d) RTRC

35. When EMT is installed in wet locations, all supports, bolts, straps, and screws shall be ______.
(a) of corrosion-resistant materials
(b) protected against corrosion
(c) a or b
(d) of nonmetallic materials only

36. EMT shall not be threaded.
(a) True
(b) False

37. ENT is composed of a material resistant to moisture and chemical atmospheres, and is ______.

(a) flexible
(b) flame retardant
(c) fireproof
(d) flammable

38. When a building is supplied with a fire sprinkler system, ENT can be installed above any suspended ceiling.

(a) True
(b) False

39. ENT is not permitted in hazardous (classified) locations, unless permitted in other articles of the Code.

(a) True
(b) False

40. ENT shall not be used where exposed to the direct rays of the sun, unless identified as ______.

(a) high-temperature rated
(b) sunlight resistant
(c) Schedule 80
(d) never can be

41. Bushings or adapters shall be provided at ENT terminations to protect the conductors from abrasion, unless the box, fitting, or enclosure design provides equivalent protection.

(a) True
(b) False

42. The ______ of conductors used in prewired ENT manufactured assemblies shall be identified by means of a printed tag or label attached to each end of the manufactured assembly.

(a) type
(b) size
(c) quantity
(d) all of these

43. Auxiliary gutters shall not be used to extend a distance greater than ______ beyond the equipment that it supplements.

(a) 10 ft
(b) 25 ft
(c) 30 ft
(d) 50 ft

44. The maximum ampere rating of a 4 in. x ½ in. busbar 4 ft long and installed in an auxiliary gutter is ______.

(a) 500A
(b) 650A
(c) 750A
(d) 2,000A

45. Busways shall not be installed ______.

(a) where subject to severe physical damage
(b) outdoors or in wet or damp locations unless identified for such use
(c) in hoistways
(d) all of these

46. Busways shall be securely supported, unless otherwise designed and marked as such, at intervals not to exceed ______.

(a) 3 ft
(b) 5 ft
(c) 8 ft
(d) 10 ft

47. The cablebus assembly is designed to carry ______ current and to withstand the magnetic forces of such current.

(a) service
(b) load
(c) fault
(d) grounded

48. In a cablebus, the size and number of conductors shall be that for which the cablebus is designed, and in no case smaller than ______ AWG.

(a) 1/0
(b) 2/0
(c) 3/0
(d) 4/0

49. Connections from cellular concrete floor raceway headers to cabinets shall be made by means of ______.

(a) listed metal raceways
(b) PVC raceways
(c) listed fittings
(d) a and c

50. In cellular concrete floor raceways, a grounding conductor shall connect the insert receptacles to a ______.

(a) negative ground connection provided in the raceway
(b) negative ground connection provided on the header
(c) positive ground connection provided on the header
(d) grounded terminal located within the insert

51. Except by special permission, no conductor larger than ______ AWG shall be installed in a cellular metal floor raceway.

(a) 1
(b) 1/0
(c) 4/0
(d) no restriction

52. Inserts for cellular metal floor raceways shall be leveled to the floor grade and sealed against the entrance of ______.

(a) concrete
(b) water
(c) moisture
(d) all of these

53. Conductors larger than that for which the wireway is designed can be installed in any wireway.

(a) True
(b) False

54. The ampacity adjustment factors in 310.15(B)(3)(a) shall be applied to a metal wireway only where the number of current-carrying conductors in the wireway exceeds ______.

(a) 30
(b) 40
(c) 50
(d) 60

55. Power distribution blocks installed in metal wireways shall be listed.

(a) True
(b) False

56. ______ is a flame-retardant raceway with hinged or removable covers for housing and protecting electric conductors and cable, and in which conductors are placed after it has been installed as a complete system.

(a) Nonmetallic cable
(b) Nonmetallic raceway
(c) Nonmetallic wireway
(d) none of these

57. Where run horizontally, nonmetallic wireways shall be supported at each end, at intervals not to exceed ______, and at each joint, unless listed for other support intervals.

(a) 3 ft
(b) 6 ft
(c) 8 ft
(d) 10 ft

58. Expansion fittings for nonmetallic wireways shall be provided to compensate for thermal expansion and contraction, where the length change is expected to be ______ or greater in a straight run.

(a) 1⁄16 in.
(b) ¼ in.
(c) ½ in.
(d) 6 in.

59. A multioutlet assembly can be installed in ______.

(a) dry locations
(b) wet locations
(c) a and b
(d) damp locations

60. Metal multioutlet assemblies can pass through a dry partition, provided no receptacle is concealed in the partition and the cover of the exposed portion of the system can be removed.

(a) True
(b) False

61. A strut-type channel raceway is a metallic raceway intended to be mounted to the surface of, or suspended from, a structure with associated accessories for the installation of electrical conductors and cables.

(a) True
(b) False

62. A strut-type channel raceway shall not be installed ______.

(a) in concealed locations
(b) where subject to corrosive influences, if enamel is the only protection from corrosion of ferrous channel raceways and fittings
(c) a or b
(d) none of these

63. A surface mount strut-type channel raceway shall be secured to the mounting surface with retention straps external to the channel at intervals not exceeding ______ and within 3 ft of each outlet box, cabinet, junction box, or other channel raceway termination.

(a) 3 ft
(b) 5 ft
(c) 6 ft
(d) 10 ft

64. Strut-type channel raceway shall be permitted as an equipment grounding conductor in accordance with 250.118(13).

(a) True
(b) False

65. The voltage between conductors in a surface metal raceway shall not exceed ______ unless the metal has a thickness of not less than 0.04 in., nominal.

(a) 150V
(b) 300V
(c) 600V
(d) 1,000V

66. The maximum number of conductors permitted in any surface raceway shall be ______.

(a) no more than 30 percent of the inside diameter
(b) no greater than the number for which it was designed
(c) no more than 75 percent of the cross-sectional area
(d) that which is permitted in Table 312.6(A)

67. Surface metal raceways shall be secured and supported at intervals ______.

(a) in accordance with the manufacturer's installation instructions
(b) appropriate for the building design
(c) not exceeding 4 ft
(d) not exceeding 8 ft

68. Surface metal raceway enclosures providing a transition from other wiring methods shall have a means for connecting a(n) ______.

(a) grounded conductor
(b) ungrounded conductor
(c) equipment grounding conductor
(d) all of these

69. Unbroken lengths of surface nonmetallic raceways can be run through dry ______.

(a) walls
(b) partitions
(c) floors
(d) all of these

70. The maximum number of conductors permitted in any surface nonmetallic raceway shall be ______.

(a) no more than 30 percent of the inside diameter
(b) no greater than the number for which it was designed
(c) no more than 75 percent of the cross-sectional area
(d) that which is permitted in Table 312.6(A)

71. The conductors, including splices and taps, in a nonmetallic surface raceway having a cover capable of being opened in place, shall not fill the raceway to more than ______ percent of its cross-sectional area at that point.

(a) 38
(b) 40
(c) 53
(d) 75

72. Flat-top underfloor raceways over 4 in. but not over 8 in. wide, with a minimum 1 in. spacing between raceways, shall be covered with concrete to a depth of not less than 1 in. Raceways spaced less than 1 in. apart shall be covered with concrete to a depth of ______.

(a) 1 in.
(b) 1½ in.
(c) 2 in.
(d) 4 in.

73. Underfloor raceways shall be laid so that a straight line from the center of one ______ to the center of the next ______ coincides with the centerline of the raceway system.

(a) termination point, termination point
(b) junction box, junction box
(c) receptacle, receptacle
(d) panelboard, panelboard

74. Cable trays can be used as a support system for ______.

(a) service conductors, feeders, and branch circuits
(b) communications circuits
(c) control and signaling circuits
(d) all of these

75. Cable trays and their associated fittings shall be ______ for the intended use.

(a) listed
(b) approved
(c) identified
(d) none of these

76. Cable tray systems shall not be used ______.

(a) in hoistways
(b) where subject to severe physical damage
(c) in hazardous (classified) locations
(d) a or b

77. For raceways terminating at a cable tray, a(n) ______ cable tray clamp or adapter shall be used to securely fasten the raceway to the cable tray system.

(a) listed
(b) approved
(c) identified
(d) none of these

78. Cable trays shall be supported at intervals in accordance with the installation instructions.

(a) True
(b) False

79. Cable ______ made and insulated by approved methods can be located within a cable tray provided they are accessible, and do not project above the side rails where the splices are subject to physical damage.

(a) connections
(b) jumpers
(c) splices
(d) conductors

80. Steel or aluminum cable tray systems shall be permitted to be used as an equipment grounding conductor, provided the cable tray sections and fittings are identified as ______, among other requirements.

(a) an equipment grounding conductor
(b) special
(c) industrial
(d) all of these

81. Where knob-and-tube conductors pass through wood cross members in plastered partitions, conductors shall be protected by noncombustible, nonabsorbent, insulating tubes extending not less than ______ beyond the wood member.

(a) 2 in.
(b) 3 in.
(c) 4 in.
(d) 6 in.

82. Where solid knobs are used for concealed knob and tube wiring, conductors shall be securely tied to them by ______ equivalent to that of the conductor.

(a) tie wires having insulation
(b) conductors having an AWG
(c) nonconductive material
(d) none of these

83. ______ can be installed in messenger-supported wiring.

(a) Multiconductor service-entrance cable
(b) Mineral Insulated (Type MI) cable
(c) Multiconductor underground feeder cable
(d) all of these

84. Open wiring on insulators is a(n) ______ wiring method using cleats, knobs, tubes, and flexible tubing for the protection and support of single insulated conductors run in or on buildings.

(a) temporary
(b) acceptable
(c) enclosed
(d) exposed

85. When nails are used to mount knobs for the support of open wiring on insulators, they shall not be smaller than ______-penny.

(a) six
(b) eight
(c) ten
(d) twelve

86. TPT and TST cords shall be permitted in lengths not exceeding ______ when attached directly to a portable appliance rated 50W or less.

(a) 8 ft
(b) 10 ft
(c) 15 ft
(d) 20 ft

87. Where flexible cords are used in ambient temperatures other than ______ the temperature correction factors from Table 310.15(B)(2)(a) shall be applied to the ampacity from Table 400.5(A)(2).

(a) 30°C
(b) 60°C
(c) 75°C
(d) 90°C

88. Conductors within flexible cords and cables shall not be associated together in such a way that the ______ temperature of the conductors is exceeded.

(a) operating
(b) governing
(c) ambient
(d) limiting

89. Flexible cords and cables shall not be concealed behind building ______, or run through doorways, windows, or similar openings.

(a) structural ceilings
(b) suspended or dropped ceilings
(c) floors or walls
(d) all of these

90. Flexible cords and cables shall be protected by ______ where passing through holes in covers, outlet boxes, or similar enclosures.

(a) bushings
(b) fittings
(c) a or b
(d) none of these

91. One conductor of flexible cords intended to be used as a(n) ______ conductor shall have a continuous marker readily distinguishing it from the other conductors. One means of identification is a braid finished to show a white or gray color on one conductor.

(a) grounded circuit
(b) equipment grounding
(c) ungrounded
(d) all of these

92. The ampacity of 18 TFFN is ______.

(a) 6A
(b) 8A
(c) 10A
(d) 14A

93. Fixture wires shall not be used for branch-circuit wiring, except as permitted in other articles of the Code.

(a) True
(b) False

94. When grouping conductors of switch loops in the same raceway, it is not required to include a grounded conductor in every switch loop.

(a) True
(b) False

95. As a general rule, switches controlling line-to-neutral lighting loads must have a neutral provided at the switch location.
(a) True
(b) False

96. Surface-mounted switches or circuit breakers in a damp or wet location shall be enclosed in a ______ enclosure or cabinet that complies with 312.2.
(a) weatherproof
(b) rainproof
(c) watertight
(d) raintight

97. Switches and circuit breakers used as switches shall be installed so that they may be operated from a readily accessible place.
(a) True
(b) False

98. Snap switches shall not be grouped or ganged in enclosures unless the voltage between adjacent devices does not exceed ______.
(a) 100V
(b) 200V
(c) 300V
(d) 400V

99. Snap switches, including dimmer and similar control switches, shall be connected to an equipment grounding conductor and shall provide a means to connect metal faceplates to the equipment grounding conductor, whether or not a metal faceplate is installed.
(a) True
(b) False

100. A snap switch that does not have means for connection to an equipment grounding conductor shall be permitted for replacement purposes only where the wiring method does not include an equipment grounding conductor and the switch is ______.
(a) provided with a faceplate of nonconducting, noncombustible material with nonmetallic screws
(b) GFCI protected
(c) a or b
(d) none of these

Practice Quiz 5

Random Order [215.10 through 404.8]

Unit 5 Practice Quiz— Random Order [215.10 through 404.8]

Please use the 2011 *Code* book to answer the following questions, which are based on the 2011 *NEC*.

1. _____ connectors shall not be concealed when used in installations of LFMC .
   (a) Straight
   (b) Angle
   (c) Grounding-type
   (d) none of these

2. _____ is a nonmetallic raceway of circular cross section, with couplings, connectors, and fittings for the installation of electrical conductors.
   (a) ENT
   (b) PVC conduit
   (c) LFNMC
   (d) HDPE

3. _____ is a raceway of circular cross section having an outer liquidtight, nonmetallic, sunlight-resistant jacket over an inner flexible metal core.
   (a) FMC
   (b) LFNMC
   (c) LFMC
   (d) none of these

4. A box shall not be required where cables or conductors from cable trays are installed in bushed conduit and tubing used as support or for protection against _____.
   (a) abuse
   (b) unauthorized access
   (c) physical damage
   (d) tampering

5. A cable tray is a unit or assembly of units or sections and associated fittings forming a _____ system used to securely fasten or support cables and raceways.
   (a) structural
   (b) flexible
   (c) movable
   (d) secure

6. A cablebus system shall include approved fittings for dead ends.
   (a) True
   (b) False

7. A multipole, general-use snap switch shall not be fed from more than a single circuit unless it is listed and marked as a 2-circuit or 3-circuit switch, or unless its voltage rating is not less than the nominal _____ voltage of the system supplying the circuits.
   (a) line-to-ground
   (b) line-to-neutral
   (c) line-to-line
   (d) phase-to-phase

8. A strut-type channel raceway can be installed _____.
   (a) where exposed
   (b) as a power pole
   (c) unbroken through walls, partitions, and floors
   (d) all of these

9. An auxiliary gutter is designed to contain _____.
   (a) conductors
   (b) overcurrent devices
   (c) busways
   (d) none of these

10. An exposed wiring support system using a messenger wire to support insulated conductors is known as _____.
   (a) open wiring
   (b) messenger-supported wiring
   (c) field wiring
   (d) none of these

11. Auxiliary gutters shall be constructed and installed so that adequate ______ continuity of the complete system is secured.

(a) mechanical
(b) electrical
(c) a or b
(d) a and b

12. Bends in FMC shall be made so that the conduit is not damaged and the internal diameter of the conduit is ______.

(a) larger than 3/8 in.
(b) not effectively reduced
(c) increased
(d) larger than 1 in.

13. Bends in LFNC shall be made so that the conduit will not be damaged and the internal diameter of the conduit will not be effectively reduced. Bends can be made ______.

(a) manually without auxiliary equipment
(b) with bending equipment identified for the purpose
(c) with any kind of conduit bending tool that will work
(d) by the use of an open flame torch

14. Bends in NUCC can be ______ so that the conduit will not be damaged and the internal diameter of the conduit will not be effectively reduced.

(a) manually made
(b) made only with approved benders
(c) made with RMC bending shoes
(d) made using an open flame torch

15. Bends in PVC conduit shall ______ between pull points.

(a) not be made
(b) not be limited in degrees
(c) be limited to 360 degrees
(d) be limited to 180 degrees

16. Busways can be extended vertically through dry floors if totally enclosed (unventilated) where passing through, and for a minimum distance of ______ above the floor to provide adequate protection from physical damage.

(a) 6 ft
(b) 6½ ft
(c) 8 ft
(d) 10 ft

17. Cablebus is ordinarily assembled at the ______.

(a) point of installation
(b) manufacturer's location
(c) distributor's location
(d) none of these

18. Conductors rated at a temperature ______ than the listed temperature rating of PVC conduit shall not be installed in PVC conduit, unless the conductors are not operated at a temperature above the raceways listed temperature rating of the PVC conduit.

(a) lower
(b) the same as
(c) higher
(d) a or b

19. Conductors smaller than 8 AWG for open wiring on insulators shall be supported within ______ of a tap or splice.

(a) 6 in.
(b) 8 in.
(c) 10 in.
(d) 12 in.

20. Conductors, including splices and taps, shall not fill the nonmetallic wireway to more than ______ percent of its area at that point.

(a) 25
(b) 75
(c) 80
(d) 125

21. Cut ends of FMC shall be trimmed or otherwise finished to remove rough edges, except where fittings ______.

(a) are the crimp-on type
(b) thread into the convolutions
(c) contain insulated throats
(d) are listed for grounding

22. Each run of cable tray shall be ______ before the installation of cables.

(a) tested for 25 ohms resistance
(b) insulated
(c) completed
(d) all of these

23. Each run of nonmetallic extension shall terminate in a fitting that covers the ______.

(a) device
(b) box
(c) end of the extension
(d) end of the assembly

24. EMT couplings and connectors shall be made up ______.

(a) of metal
(b) in accordance with industry standards
(c) tight
(d) none of these

25. EMT, elbows, couplings, and fittings can be installed in concrete, in direct contact with the earth, or in areas subject to severe corrosive influences if ______.

(a) protected by corrosion protection
(b) approved as suitable for the condition
(c) a and b
(d) listed for wet locations

26. ENT and fittings can be______, provided fittings identified for this purpose are used.

(a) encased in poured concrete
(b) embedded in a concrete slab on grade where the tubing is placed on sand or approved screenings
(c) a or b
(d) none of these

27. Fixture wires are used to connect luminaires to the ______ conductors supplying the luminaires.

(a) service
(b) branch-circuit
(c) feeder
(d) none of these

28. Flexible cords and cables can be used for ______.

(a) wiring of luminaires
(b) connection of portable luminaires or appliances
(c) connection of utilization equipment to facilitate frequent interchange
(d) all of these

29. Flexible cords and cables shall be connected to fittings so that tension will not be transmitted to joints or terminal screws by ______.

(a) knotting the cord
(b) winding the cord with tape
(c) fittings designed for the purpose
(d) any of these

30. Flexible cords and cables shall not be used where ______.

(a) run through holes in walls, ceilings, or floors
(b) run through doorways, windows, or similar openings
(c) attached to building surfaces, unless permitted by 368.56(B)
(d) all of these

31. FMC shall not be installed ______.

(a) in wet locations
(b) embedded in poured concrete
(c) where subject to physical damage
(d) all of these

32. For cellular concrete floor raceways, junction boxes shall be ______ the floor grade and sealed against the free entrance of water or concrete.

(a) leveled to
(b) above
(c) below
(d) perpendicular to

33. For flexible metal conduit, if flexibility is necessary after installation, unsecured lengths from the last point the raceway is securely fastened must not exceed ______

(a) 3 ft for trade sizes ½ through 1¼
(b) 4 ft for trade sizes 1½ through 2
(c) 5 ft for trade sizes 2½ and larger
(d) all of these

34. For grounded systems, the earth is considered an effective ground-fault current path.

(a) True
(b) False

35. For installations that supply only limited loads of a single branch circuit, the service disconnecting means shall have a rating not less than ______.

(a) 15A
(b) 20A
(c) 25A
(d) 30A

36. For other than dwelling occupancies, banks, or office buildings, each receptacle outlet shall be calculated at not less than ______ VA.

(a) 90
(b) 180
(c) 270
(d) 360

37. For straight pulls, the length of a pull box shall not be less than ______ times the outside diameter, over the sheath, of the largest shielded or lead-covered conductor or cable entering the box on systems over 600V.

(a) 12
(b) 16
(c) 24
(d) 48

38. For the purposes of determining box fill, each device or utilization equipment in the box which is wider than a single device box counts as two conductors for each ______ required for the mounting.

(a) inch
(b) kilometer
(c) gang
(d) box

39. For ungrounded systems, noncurrent-carrying conductive materials enclosing electrical conductors or equipment, or forming part of such equipment, shall be connected together and to the supply system equipment in a manner that creates a low-impedance path for ground-fault current that is capable of carrying ______.

(a) the maximum branch-circuit current
(b) at least twice the maximum ground-fault current
(c) the maximum fault current likely to be imposed on it
(d) the equivalent to the main service rating

40. Fuseholders for cartridge fuses shall be so designed that it is difficult to put a fuse of any given class into a fuseholder that is designed for a ______ lower or a ______ higher than that of the class to which the fuse belongs.

(a) voltage, wattage
(b) wattage, voltage
(c) voltage, current
(d) current, voltage

41. Galvanized steel, stainless steel, and red brass RMC shall be permitted in or under cinder fill subject to permanent moisture, when protected on all sides by a layer of noncinder concrete not less than ______ thick.

(a) 2 in.
(b) 4 in.
(c) 6 in.
(d) 18 in.

42. Grommets or bushings for the protection of Type NM cable shall be ______ for the purpose.

(a) marked
(b) approved
(c) identified
(d) listed

43. Ground clamps and fittings shall be protected from physical damage by being enclosed in ______ where there may be a possibility of physical damage.

(a) metal
(b) wood
(c) the equivalent of a or b
(d) none of these

44. Ground rod electrodes shall be installed so that at least ______ of the length is in contact with the soil.

(a) 5 ft
(b) 8 ft
(c) one-half
(d) 80 percent

45. Ground-fault protection of equipment shall be provided for solidly grounded wye electrical services of more than 150 volts-to-ground, but not exceeding 600V phase-to-phase for each service disconnecting means rated ______ or more.

(a) 1,000A
(b) 1,500A
(c) 2,000A
(d) 2,500A

46. Ground-fault protection of equipment shall be required for a feeder disconnect if ______.

(a) the disconnect is rated 800A, 208V
(b) the disconnect is rated 800A, 480V
(c) the disconnect is rated 1,000A, 208V
(d) the disconnect is rated 1,000A, 480V

47. Ground-fault protection that functions to open the service disconnect ______ protect(s) from faults on the line side of the protective element.

(a) will
(b) will not
(c) adequately
(d) totally

48. Grounding electrode conductor taps from a separately derived system to a common grounding electrode conductor are permitted when a building or structure has multiple separately derived systems, provided that the taps terminate at the same point as the system bonding jumper.

(a) True
(b) False

49. Grounding electrode conductors ______ and larger that are not subject to physical damage can be run exposed along the surface of the building construction if it is securely fastened to the construction.

(a) 10 AWG
(b) 8 AWG
(c) 6 AWG
(d) 4 AWG

50. Grounding electrodes of the rod type less than ______ in. in diameter shall be listed.

(a) ½ in.
(b) 5/8 in.
(c) ¾ in.
(d) none of these

Practice Quiz **6**

Straight Order [404.9 through 430.87]

Unit 6 Practice Quiz— Straight Order [404.9 through 430.87]

Please use the 2011 *Code* book to answer the following questions, which are based on the 2011 *NEC*.

1. A snap switch with integral nonmetallic enclosure complying with 300.15(E) is required to be connected to an equipment grounding conductor.

   (a) True
   (b) False

2. Snap switches installed in boxes shall have the _____ seated against the finished wall surface.

   (a) extension plaster ears
   (b) body
   (c) toggle
   (d) all of these

3. Metal enclosures for switches or circuit breakers shall be connected to the circuit _____.

   (a) grounded conductor
   (b) grounding conductor
   (c) equipment grounding conductor
   (d) any of these

4. Nonmetallic boxes for switches shall be installed with a wiring method that provides or includes _____.

   (a) a grounded conductor
   (b) an equipment grounding conductor
   (c) an inductive balance
   (d) none of these

5. Alternating-current general-use snap switches are permitted to control _____.

   (a) resistive and inductive loads that do not exceed the ampere and voltage rating of the switch
   (b) tungsten-filament lamp loads that do not exceed the ampere rating of the switch at 120V
   (c) motor loads that do not exceed 80 percent of the ampere and voltage rating of the switch
   (d) all of these

6. Alternating-current or direct-current general-use snap switches may be used for control of inductive loads not exceeding _____ percent of the ampere rating of the switch at the applied voltage.

   (a) 50
   (b) 75
   (c) 90
   (d) 100

7. Switches shall be marked with _____.

   (a) current
   (b) voltage
   (c) maximum horsepower, if horsepower rated
   (d) all of these

8. A child care facility is a building or structure, or portion thereof, used for educational, supervision, or personal care services for more than _____ children seven years in age or less.

   (a) two
   (b) three
   (c) four
   (d) six

9. Receptacles rated _____ or less directly connected to aluminum conductors shall be listed and marked CO/ALR.

   (a) 15A
   (b) 20A
   (c) 25A
   (d) 30A

10. Isolated ground receptacles installed in nonmetallic boxes shall be covered with a nonmetallic faceplate, unless the box contains a feature or accessory that permits the effective grounding of the faceplate.

(a) True
(b) False

11. When replacing receptacles in locations that would require GFCI protection under the current NEC, _____ receptacles shall be installed.

(a) dedicated
(b) isolated ground
(c) GFCI-protected
(d) grounding

12. Listed tamper-resistant receptacles shall be provided where replacements are made at receptacle outlets that are required to be tamper resistant elsewhere in this Code.

(a) True
(b) False

13. Receptacles mounted in boxes set back of the wall surface shall be installed so that the mounting _____ of the receptacle is held rigidly at the surface.

(a) screws or nails
(b) yoke or strap
(c) faceplate
(d) none of these

14. Receptacles mounted to and supported by a cover shall be secured by more than one screw unless listed and identified for securing by a single screw.

(a) True
(b) False

15. Attachment plugs and cord connectors shall be listed and marked with the _____.

(a) manufacturer's name or identification
(b) voltage rating
(c) amperage rating
(d) all of these

16. An outdoor receptacle in a location protected from the weather, or in another damp location, shall be installed in an enclosure that is weatherproof when the receptacle is _____.

(a) covered
(b) enclosed
(c) protected
(d) none of these

17. A receptacle is considered to be in a location protected from the weather when located under roofed open porches, canopies, marquees, and the like, where it will not be subjected to _____.

(a) spray from a hose
(b) a direct lightning hit
(c) beating rain or water runoff
(d) falling or wind-blown debris

18. _____, 125V and 250V receptacles installed in a wet location shall have an enclosure that is weatherproof whether or not the attachment plug cap is inserted.

(a) 15A
(b) 20A
(c) a and b
(d) none of these

19. A 30A, 208V receptacle installed in a wet location, where the product intended to be plugged into it is not attended while in use, shall have an enclosure that is weatherproof with the attachment plug cap inserted or removed.

(a) True
(b) False

20. A receptacle installed in an outlet box flush-mounted in a finished surface in a damp or wet location shall be made weatherproof by means of a weatherproof faceplate assembly that provides a _____ connection between the plate and the finished surface.

(a) sealed
(b) weathertight
(c) sealed and protected
(d) watertight

21. In dwelling units, all nonlocking type 125V, 15A and 20A receptacles installed ______ shall be listed as tamper resistant.

(a) in bedrooms
(b) outdoors, at grade level
(c) above countertops
(d) in all areas except as covered by exceptions

22. Nonlocking type 15A and 20A, 125V receptacles in a dwelling unit shall be listed as tamper resistant except nongrounding receptacles used for replacements for existing nongrounding receptacles as permitted in 406.4(D)(2)(a).

(a) True
(b) False

23. Barriers shall be placed in all service switchboards such that no uninsulated, ungrounded service ______ or service terminal is exposed to inadvertent contact by persons or maintenance equipment while servicing load terminations.

(a) busbar
(b) conductors
(c) cables
(d) none of these

24. In switchboards and panelboards, load terminals for field wiring shall be so located that it is not necessary to reach across or beyond a(n) ______ ungrounded line bus in order to make connections.

(a) insulated
(b) uninsulated
(c) grounded
(d) high impedance

25. A switchboard or panelboard containing a 4-wire, ______ system where the midpoint of one phase winding is grounded, shall be legibly and permanently field-marked to caution that one phase has a higher voltage-to-ground.

(a) wye-connected
(b) delta-connected
(c) solidly grounded
(d) ungrounded

26. Circuit directories can include labels that depend on transient conditions of occupancy.

(a) True
(b) False

27. Conduits and raceways, including end fittings, shall not rise more than ______ above the bottom of a switchboard enclosure.

(a) 3 in.
(b) 4 in.
(c) 5 in.
(d) 6 in.

28. Switchboards shall be placed so as to reduce to a minimum the probability of communicating ______ to adjacent combustible materials.

(a) sparks
(b) backfed
(c) fire
(d) all of these

29. Insulated conductors used within a switchboard shall be ______.

(a) listed
(b) flame-retardant
(c) rated for the highest voltage it may contact
(d) all of these

30. A panelboard shall be protected by an overcurrent device within the panelboard, or at any point on the ______ side of the panelboard.

(a) load
(b) supply
(c) a or b
(d) none of these

31. Each ______ conductor shall terminate within the panelboard at an individual terminal that is not used for another conductor.

(a) grounded
(b) ungrounded
(c) grounding
(d) all of these

32. A panelboard shall be provided with physical means to prevent the installation of more ______ devices than that number for which the panelboard was designed, rated, and listed.

(a) overcurrent
(b) equipment
(c) circuit breaker
(d) all of these

33. Lighting track is a manufactured assembly and its length may not be altered by the addition or subtraction of sections of track.

(a) True
(b) False

34. Cleat-type lampholders located at least _____ above the floor can have exposed terminals.

(a) 3 ft
(b) 6 ft
(c) 8 ft
(d) 10 ft

35. Luminaires located within the actual outside dimension of a bathtub and shower shall be marked for damp locations, or marked for wet locations where they are _____.

(a) below 7 ft in height
(b) below 6 ft 7 in. in height
(c) subject to shower spray
(d) not GFCI protected

36. Lampholders installed over highly combustible material shall be of the _____ type.

(a) industrial
(b) switched
(c) unswitched
(d) residential

37. The following types of luminaires can be installed in a clothes closet:

(a) A surface or recessed incandescent luminaire with completely enclosed light source.
(b) A surface or recessed fluorescent luminaire.
(c) A surface-mounted or recessed LED luminaire with a completely enclosed light source.
(d) all of these

38. Surface-mounted fluorescent luminaires in clothes closets shall be permitted on the wall above the door, or on the ceiling, provided there is a minimum clearance of _____ between the luminaire and the nearest point of a storage space.

(a) 3 in.
(b) 6 in.
(c) 9 in.
(d) 12 in.

39. Surface-mounted fluorescent or LED luminaires are permitted within the closet storage space if identified for this use.

(a) True
(b) False

40. Electric-discharge and LED luminaires supported independently of the outlet box shall be connected to the branch circuit through _____.

(a) raceways
(b) Type MC, AC, MI, or NM cable
(c) flexible cords
(d) any of these

41. The maximum weight of a luminaire permitted to be supported by the screw shell of a lampholder is _____.

(a) 2 lb
(b) 3 lb
(c) 4 lb
(d) 6 lb

42. Poles over 20 ft in height above grade, without a hinged base, that support luminaires shall _____.

(a) have an accessible handhole (sized 2 in. x 4 in.) with a cover suitable for use in wet locations.
(b) have an equipment grounding terminal that is accessible from the handhole.
(c) a and b
(d) none of these

43. Outdoor luminaires and associated equipment can be supported by trees.

(a) True
(b) False

44. Luminaires must be connected to an equipment grounding conductor of a type recognized in 250.118. If of the wire type, the circuit equipment grounding conductor must be sized in accordance with _____.

(a) Table 250.66
(b) Table 250.122
(c) Table 310.16
(d) a and c

45. Replacement luminaires can be installed in an outlet box that doesn't contain an equipment grounding conductor if an equipment grounding conductor is added from the luminaire and is connected to ______.

(a) the grounding electrode system or grounding electrode conductor
(b) the panelboard equipment grounding terminal
(c) the service neutral conductor within the service equipment enclosure
(d) any of these

46. Luminaires shall be wired so that the ______ of each lampholder is connected to the same luminaire or circuit conductor or terminal.

(a) stem
(b) arm
(c) supplemental protection
(d) screw shell

47. No ______ splices or taps shall be made within or on a luminaire.

(a) unapproved
(b) untested
(c) uninspected
(d) unnecessary

48. Luminaires that require adjustment or aiming after installation can be cord-connected without an attachment plug, provided the exposed cord is of the hard-usage type and is not longer than that required for maximum adjustment.

(a) True
(b) False

49. Luminaires can be used as a raceway for circuit conductors only when listed and marked for use as a raceway.

(a) True
(b) False

50. Luminaires designed for end-to-end assembly, or luminaires connected together by ______, can contain a 2-wire branch circuit, or one multiwire branch circuit, supplying the connected luminaires. One additional 2-wire branch circuit supplying one or more of the connected luminaires is permitted.

(a) rigid metal conduit
(b) recognized wiring methods
(c) flexible wiring methods
(d) EMT

51. Lampholders of the screw-shell type shall be installed for use as lampholders only.

(a) True
(b) False

52. Lampholders installed in damp locations shall be listed for use in ______ locations.

(a) damp
(b) wet
(c) dry
(d) a or b

53. Luminaires installed in ______ shall comply with 410.115 through 410.122.

(a) recessed cavities in walls or ceilings
(b) suspended ceilings
(c) Class I classified locations
(d) a and b

54. Recessed incandescent luminaires shall have ______ protection and shall be identified as thermally protected.

(a) physical
(b) corrosion
(c) thermal
(d) all of these

55. The minimum distance that an outlet box containing tap supply conductors is permitted to be placed from a recessed luminaire is ______.

(a) 1 ft
(b) 2 ft
(c) 3 ft
(d) 4 ft

56. Ballasts for fluorescent lighting installed indoors shall have ______ protection.

(a) AFCI
(b) supplementary
(c) integral thermal
(d) none of these

57. In indoor locations other than dwellings and associated accessory buildings, fluorescent luminaires that utilize double-ended lamps and contain ballast(s) and can be serviced in place shall have a disconnecting means either internal or external to each luminaire.

(a) True
(b) False

58. In indoor locations other than dwellings and associated accessory structures, fluorescent luminaires that utilize double-ended lamps (typical fluorescent lamps) and contain ballasts that can be serviced in place must have a disconnecting means except for ______.

(a) emergency illumination required in 700.16.
(b) cord-and-plug-connected luminaires with accessible plugs and receptacles
(c) industrial establishments with restricted public access and written procedures and conditions of maintenance and supervision
(d) all of these

59. Surface-mounted luminaires with a ballast shall have a minimum clearance of ______ from combustible low-density cellulose fiberboard, unless the luminaire is marked for surface mounting on combustible low-density cellulose fiberboard.

(a) ½ in.
(b) 1 in.
(c) 1½ in.
(d) 2 in.

60. Lighting track fittings can be equipped with general-purpose receptacles.

(a) True
(b) False

61. A 120V section of lighting track that is continuously loaded shall not exceed 12 ft in length, in accordance with 220.43(B).

(a) True
(b) False

62. Lighting track shall not be installed less than ______ above the finished floor except where protected from physical damage or where the track operates at less than 30V rms, open-circuit voltage.

(a) 4 ft
(b) 5 ft
(c) 5½ ft
(d) 6 ft

63. Decorative lighting and similar accessories used for holiday lighting and similar purposes shall be ______.

(a) marked
(b) listed
(c) arc fault protected
(d) GFCI protected

64. Lighting systems operating at 30V or less shall be listed or assembled with listed components.

(a) True
(b) False

65. Lighting systems operating at 30V or less shall not be installed within ______ of pools, spas, fountains, or similar locations.

(a) 5 ft
(b) 6 ft
(c) 10 ft
(d) 20 ft

66. A vending machine is defined as any self-service device that dispenses products or merchandise without the necessity of replenishing the device between each vending operation and designed to require insertion of a ______.

(a) coin or paper currency
(b) token or card
(c) key or payment by other means
(d) all of these

67. Infrared lamps for commercial and industrial heating appliances shall have overcurrent protection not exceeding ______.

(a) 30A
(b) 40A
(c) 50A
(d) 60A

68. If a branch circuit supplies a single nonmotor-operated appliance, the rating of overcurrent protection shall not exceed ______ percent of the appliance rated current if the overcurrent protection rating is not marked and the appliance is rated over 13.30A.

(a) 100
(b) 125
(c) 150
(d) 160

69. A fixed storage-type water heater having a capacity of _____ gallons or less shall be considered a continuous load for the purposes of sizing branch circuits.

(a) 60
(b) 75
(c) 90
(d) 120

70. The length of the cord for a dishwasher or trash compactor shall not be longer than _____, measured from the rear of the appliance.

(a) 2 ft
(b) 4 ft
(c) 6 ft
(d) 8 ft

71. For motor-operated appliances rated over _____, a switch or circuit breaker located within sight from the motor operated appliance can serve as the appliance disconnect.

(a) ⅛ hp
(b) ¼ hp
(c) 15A
(d) b and c

72. For cord-and-plug-connected appliances, _____ plug and receptacle is permitted to serve as the disconnecting means.

(a) a labeled
(b) an accessible
(c) a metal enclosed
(d) none of these

73. Appliances that have a unit switch with a marked_____ position that disconnects all the ungrounded conductors can serve as the appliance disconnecting means.

(a) on
(b) off
(c) on/off
(d) all of these

74. Electric drinking fountains shall be _____ protected.

(a) GFCI
(b) AFCI
(c) a or b
(d) none of these

75. Fixed electric space-heating equipment requiring supply conductors with insulation rated over _____ shall be clearly and permanently marked.

(a) 60°C
(b) 75°C
(c) 90°C
(d) all of these

76. Means shall be provided to simultaneously disconnect the _____ of all fixed electric space-heating equipment from all ungrounded conductors.

(a) heater
(b) motor controller(s)
(c) supplementary overcurrent device(s)
(d) all of these

77. Electric space-heating equipment employing resistance-type heating elements rated more than _____ shall have the heating elements subdivided.

(a) 24A
(b) 36A
(c) 48A
(d) 60A

78. Electric space-heating cables shall be furnished complete with factory-assembled nonheating leads at least _____ in length.

(a) 6 in.
(b) 18 in.
(c) 3 ft
(d) 7 ft

79. Electric space-heating cables shall not be installed over cabinets whose clearance from the ceiling is less than the minimum _____ dimension of the cabinet to the nearest cabinet edge that is open to the room or area.

(a) horizontal
(b) vertical
(c) overall
(d) depth

80. Ground-fault circuit-interrupter protection shall be provided for cables installed in electrically heated floors of _____.

(a) bathrooms
(b) hydromassage bathtub locations
(c) kitchens
(d) all of these

81. When installing duct heaters, sufficient clearance shall be maintained to permit replacement and adjustment of controls and heating elements.

(a) True
(b) False

82. Examples of snow-melting resistance heaters include ______.

(a) tubular heaters and strip heaters
(b) heating panels
(c) heating cables or heating tape
(d) all of these

83. Fixed outdoor deicing and snow-melting equipment shall be provided with a means for simultaneous disconnection from all ______ conductors.

(a) grounded
(b) grounding
(c) ungrounded
(d) all of these

84. Fixed electric heating equipment for pipelines and vessels shall be considered a(n) ______ load.

(a) noncontinuous
(b) insignificant
(c) continuous
(d) proprietary

85. Ground-fault protection of equipment shall be provided for electric heat tracing and heating panels installed on pipelines or vessels except in certain industrial installations where there is alarm indication of ground faults.

(a) True
(b) False

86. For general motor applications, the motor branch-circuit short-circuit and ground-fault protection device shall be sized based on the ______ values.

(a) motor nameplate
(b) NEMA standard
(c) NEC Table
(d) Factory Mutual

87. Torque requirements for motor control circuit device terminals shall be a minimum of ______ lb-in. (unless otherwise identified) for screw-type pressure terminals used for 14 AWG and smaller copper conductors.

(a) 7
(b) 9
(c) 10
(d) 15

88. A motor terminal housing enclosing rigidly mounted motor terminals shall have a minimum of ______ between line terminals for a 230V motor.

(a) ¼ in.
(b) ⅜ in.
(c) ½ in.
(d) ⅝ in.

89. Open motors having commutates or collector rings shall be located or protected so that sparks cannot reach adjacent combustible material. This shall not prohibit the installation of these motors ______.

(a) on wooden floors
(b) over combustible fiber
(c) under combustible material
(d) none of these

90. Branch-circuit conductors supplying a single continuous-duty motor shall have an ampacity not less than ______ rating.

(a) 125 percent of the motor's nameplate current
(b) 125 percent of the motor's full-load current as determined by 430.6(A)(1)
(c) 125 percent of the motor's full locked-rotor
(d) 80 percent of the motor's full-load current

91. A separate overload device used to protect continuous-duty motors rated more than 1 hp shall be selected to trip at no more than ______ percent of the motor nameplate full-load current rating if marked with a service factor of 1.15 or greater.

(a) 110
(b) 115
(c) 120
(d) 125

92. Motor overload protection shall not be shunted or cut out during the starting period if the motor is ______.

(a) not automatically started
(b) automatically started
(c) manually started
(d) none of these

93. Overload relays and other devices for motor overload protection that are not capable of ______ shall be protected by fuses, circuit breakers, or motor short-circuit protector.

(a) opening short circuits
(b) clearing overloads
(c) opening ground faults
(d) a or c

94. If a(n) ______ shutdown is necessary to reduce hazards to persons, the overload sensing devices can be connected to a supervised alarm instead of causing immediate interruption of the motor circuit.

(a) emergency
(b) normal
(c) orderly
(d) none of these

95. A motor can be provided with combined overcurrent protection using a single protective device to provide branch-circuit ______ where the rating of the device provides the overload protection specified in 430.32.

(a) short-circuit protection
(b) ground-fault protection
(c) motor overload protection
(d) all of these

96. Overcurrent protection for motor control circuits shall not exceed ______ percent if the conductor is based on Table 310.15(B)(17) and does not extend beyond the motor control equipment enclosure.

(a) 100
(b) 150
(c) 300
(d) 400

97. Motor control circuit transformers, with a primary current rating of less than 2A, can have the primary protection device set at no more than ______ percent of the rated primary current rating.

(a) 150
(b) 200
(c) 400
(d) 500

98. If the motor control circuit transformer is located in the controller enclosure, the transformer shall be connected to the ______ side of the control circuit disconnecting means.

(a) line
(b) load
(c) adjacent
(d) none of these

99. For stationary motors of 2 hp or less and 300V or less on ac circuits, the controller can be an ac-rated only general-use snap switch where the motor full-load current rating is not more than ______ percent of the rating of the switch.

(a) 50
(b) 60
(c) 70
(d) 80

100. Each motor shall be provided with an individual controller.

(a) True
(b) False

Practice Quiz 6

Random Order [210.21 through 430.81]

Unit 6 Practice Quiz—Random Order [210.21 through 430.81]

Please use the 2011 *Code* book to answer the following questions, which are based on the 2011 *NEC*.

1. The combined area of all conductors installed at any point of an underfloor raceway shall not exceed _____ percent of the internal cross-sectional area.

(a) 0
(b) 40
(c) 60
(d) 75

2. The branch-circuit protective device can serve as the controller for a stationary motor rated at _____ or less that is normally left running and cannot be damaged by overload or failure to start.

(a) ⅛ hp
(b) ¼ hp
(c) ⅜ hp
(d) ½ hp

3. A recessed luminaire not identified for contact with insulation shall have all recessed parts spaced not less than _____ from combustible materials, except for points of support.

(a) ¼ in.
(b) ½ in.
(c) 1¼ in.
(d) 6 in.

4. The radius of the inner edge of any bend in Type MI cable shall not be less than five times the external diameter of the metallic sheath for cable not more than _____ in external diameter.

(a) ½ in.
(b) ⅝ in.
(c) ¾ in.
(d) 1½ in.

5. Thermal insulation shall not be installed above or within _____ of the recessed luminaries' enclosure, wiring compartment, ballast, transformer, LED driver, or power supply unless it is a Type IC luminaire.

(a) ½ in.
(b) 3 in.
(c) 6 in.
(d) 12 in.

6. HDPE conduit shall be permitted only in trade sizes _____.

(a) ¾ to 4
(b) ½ to 6
(c) 1 to 5
(d) 1 to 3

7. What size copper grounding electrode conductor is required for a service that has three sets of 600 kcmil copper conductors per phase?

(a) 1 AWG
(b) 1/0 AWG
(c) 2/0 AWG
(d) 3/0 AWG

8. Branch-circuit conductors within _____ of a ballast shall have an insulation temperature rating not lower than 90°C (194°F).

(a) 1 in.
(b) 3 in.
(c) 6 in.
(d) 8 in.

9. The load for electric clothes dryers in a dwelling unit shall be _____ watts or the nameplate rating, whichever is larger, per dryer.

(a) 1,500
(b) 4,500
(c) 5,000
(d) 8,000

10. Noncombustible surfaces that are broken or incomplete around boxes employing a flush-type cover or faceplate shall be repaired so there will be no gaps or open spaces larger than _____ at the edge of the box.

(a) 1/16 in.
(b) 1/8 in.
(c) 1/4 in.
(d) 1/2 in.

11. Where nails or screws are likely to penetrate nonmetallic-sheathed cable or ENT installed through metal framing members, a steel sleeve, steel plate, or steel clip not less than _____ in thickness shall be used to protect the cable or tubing.

(a) 1/16 in.
(b) 1/8 in.
(c) 1/2 in.
(d) 3/4 in.

12. In noncombustible walls or ceilings, the front edge of a box, plaster ring, extension ring, or listed extender employing a flush-type cover, shall be set back not more than _____ from the finished surface.

(a) 1/8 in.
(b) 1/4 in.
(c) 3/8 in.
(d) 1/2 in.

13. In general, the minimum size conductor permitted for use in parallel installations is _____ AWG.

(a) 10
(b) 4
(c) 1
(d) 1/0

14. The minimum clearance for overhead feeder conductors not exceeding 600V that pass over commercial areas subject to truck traffic is _____.

(a) 10 ft
(b) 12 ft
(c) 15 ft
(d) 18 ft

15. The minimum clearance for overhead service conductors not exceeding 600V that pass over commercial areas subject to truck traffic is _____.

(a) 10 ft
(b) 12 ft
(c) 15 ft
(d) 18 ft

16. Motor control circuit conductors that extend beyond the motor control equipment enclosure shall have short-circuit and ground-fault protection sized not greater than _____ percent of value specified in Table 310.15(B)(16) for 60°C conductors.

(a) 100
(b) 150
(c) 300
(d) 400

17. Ungrounded service-entrance conductors shall be sized not less than _____ percent of the continuous load, plus 100 percent of the noncontinuous load.

(a) 100
(b) 115
(c) 125
(d) 150

18. When an overload device sized in accordance with 430.32(A)(1) and (B)(1) is not sufficient to start the motor, higher size sensing elements shall be permitted if the trip current does not exceed _____ percent of the motor nameplate full-load current rating, when the motor is marked with a service factor of 1.12.

(a) 100
(b) 110
(c) 120
(d) 130

19. Receptacles and cord connectors shall be rated not less than _____ at 125V, or at 250V, and shall be of a type not suitable for use as lampholders.

(a) 10A
(b) 15A
(c) 20A
(d) 30A

20. Pilot lights, instruments, potential transformers, current transformers, and other switchboard devices with potential coils shall be supplied by a circuit that is protected by overcurrent devices rated ______.

(a) 10A or less
(b) 15A or less
(c) 15A or more
(d) 20A or less

21. External surfaces of pipeline and vessel heating equipment that operate at temperatures exceeding ______shall be physically guarded, isolated, or thermally insulated to protect against contact by personnel in the area.

(a) 110°F
(b) 120°F
(c) 130°F
(d) 140°F

22. For switchboards that are not totally enclosed, a space of ______ or more shall be provided between the top of the switchboard and any combustible ceiling.

(a) 12 in.
(b) 18 in.
(c) 2 ft
(d) 3 ft

23. In dwelling units, the required bathroom receptacle outlet can be installed on the side or face of the basin cabinet if no lower than ______ below the countertop.

(a) 12 in.
(b) 18 in.
(c) 24 in.
(d) 36 in.

24. In dwelling units, at least one receptacle outlet shall be installed at each peninsular countertop having a long dimension of ______ in. or greater, and a short dimension of ______ in. or greater.

(a) 12, 24
(b) 24, 12
(c) 24, 48
(d) 48, 24

25. Electric-discharge luminaires having an open-circuit voltage exceeding ______ shall not be installed in or on dwelling occupancies.

(a) 120V
(b) 250V
(c) 600V
(d) 1,000V

26. On electric space-heating cables, blue leads indicate a cable rated for use on a nominal circuit voltage of ______.

(a) 120V
(b) 208V
(c) 240V
(d) 277V

27. The maximum rating or setting of an inverse time breaker used as the motor branch-circuit short-circuit and ground-fault protective device for a single-phase motor is ______ percent of the full-load current given in Table 430.248.

(a) 125
(b) 175
(c) 250
(d) 300

28. When connected to a branch circuit supplying two or more 15A receptacles, each receptacle shall not supply a total cord-and-plug-connected load in excess of ______.

(a) 12A
(b) 16A
(c) 20A
(d) 24A

29. The minimum size conductor permitted for branch circuits under 600V is ______ AWG.

(a) 14
(b) 12
(c) 10
(d) 8

30. The maximum length of a feeder tap conductor in a high-bay manufacturing building over 35 ft high shall be ______.

(a) 15 ft
(b) 20 ft
(c) 50 ft
(d) 100 ft

31. The maximum voltage permitted between ungrounded conductors of flat conductor cable systems is ______.

(a) 150V
(b) 250V
(c) 300V
(d) 600V

32. A lighting system covered by Article 411 shall have a power supply rated not more than ______ and not more than 30V.

(a) 15A
(b) 20A
(c) 25A
(d) 30A

33. If a branch circuit supplies a single nonmotor-operated appliance, the rating of overcurrent protection shall not exceed ______ if the overcurrent protection rating is not marked and the appliance is rated 13.30A or less.

(a) 15A
(b) 20A
(c) 25A
(d) 30A

34. The minimum feeder load for show-window lighting is ______ per-linear-foot.

(a) 180 VA
(b) 200 VA
(c) 300 VA
(d) 400 VA

35. In a dwelling unit, each wall space ______ or wider requires a receptacle.

(a) 2 ft
(b) 3 ft
(c) 4 ft
(d) 5 ft

36. Lighting track shall have two supports for a single section of ______ or shorter in length and each individual section of not more than 4 ft attached to it shall have one additional support, unless the track is identified for supports at greater intervals.

(a) 2 ft
(b) 4 ft
(c) 6 ft
(d) 8 ft

37. Lighting track shall not be installed within the zone measured 3 ft horizontally and ______ vertically from the top of the bathtub rim or shower stall threshold.

(a) 2 ft
(b) 3 ft
(c) 4 ft
(d) 8 ft

38. Open wiring on insulators within ______ from the floor shall be considered exposed to physical damage.

(a) 2 ft
(b) 4 ft
(c) 7 ft
(d) 8 ft

39. Where communications cables and electric service drop conductors are supported by the same pole, communications cables must have a minimum separation of ______ at any point in the span, including the point of attachment to the building.

(a) 2 in.
(b) 6 in.
(c) 12 in.
(d) 24 in.

40. Supports for concealed knob-and-tube wiring shall be installed within ______ in. of each side of each tap or splice and at intervals not exceeding ______ ft.

(a) 2, 3½
(b) 3, 2½
(c) 4, 6½
(d) 6, 4½

41. The sum of the cross-sectional areas of all contained conductors at any cross section of a nonmetallic wireway shall not exceed ______.

(a) 20 percent
(b) 30 percent
(c) 40 percent
(d) 50 percent

42. For permanently connected appliances rated over ______ the branch-circuit circuit breaker can serve as the disconnecting means where the circuit breaker is within sight from the appliance, or is capable of being locked in the open position with a permanently installed locking provision that remains in place with or without the lock installed.

(a) 200 VA
(b) 300 VA
(c) 400 VA
(d) 500 VA

43. The smallest size fixture wire permitted by the NEC is ______ AWG.

(a) 22
(b) 20
(c) 18
(d) 16

44. Underground service conductors shall be protected from damage in accordance with ______ including minimum cover requirements.

(a) 240.6(A)
(b) 300.5
(c) 310.15(B)(16)
(d) 430.52

45. In industrial establishments where conditions of maintenance and supervision ensure that only qualified persons service the installation, flexible cords and cables can be installed in aboveground raceways that are no longer than ______, to protect the flexible cord or cable from physical damage.

(a) 25 ft
(b) 50 ft
(c) 100 ft
(d) no limit

46. Duct heater controller equipment shall have a disconnecting means installed within ______ the controller except as allowed by 424.19(A).

(a) 25 ft of
(b) sight from
(c) the side of
(d) none of these

47. The size of the grounding electrode conductor for a building or structure supplied by a feeder shall not be smaller than that identified in ______, based on the largest ungrounded supply conductor.

(a) 250.66
(b) 250.122
(c) Table 310.15(B)(16)
(d) none of these

48. Nonmetallic cables can enter the top of surface-mounted cabinets, cutout boxes, and meter socket enclosures through nonflexible raceways not less than 18 in. or more than ______ ft in length if all of the required conditions are met.

(a) 3
(b) 10
(c) 25
(d) 100

49. Overhead feeder conductors installed over roofs shall have a vertical clearance of ______ above the roof surface, unless permitted by an exception.

(a) 3 ft
(b) 8 ft
(c) 12 ft
(d) 15 ft

50. Overhead service conductors to a building shall maintain a vertical clearance of final spans above, or within, ______ measured horizontally from the platforms, projections, or surfaces from which they might be reached.

(a) 3 ft
(b) 6 ft
(c) 8 ft
(d) 10 ft

Practice Quiz 7

Straight Order [430.103 through 514.11]

Unit 7 Practice Quiz— Straight Order [430.103 through 514.11]

Please use the 2011 *Code* book to answer the following questions, which are based on the 2011 *NEC*.

1. The disconnecting means for the controller and motor shall open all ungrounded supply conductors.

   (a) True
   (b) False

2. The motor disconnecting means for a motor shall ______ whether it is in the open (off) or closed (on) position.

   (a) plainly indicate
   (b) provide current
   (c) be in the upper position
   (d) none of these

3. A motor disconnecting means can be a ______.

   (a) listed molded case circuit breaker
   (b) listed motor-circuit switch rated in horsepower
   (c) listed molded case switch
   (d) any of these

4. The disconnecting means for a motor controller shall be designed so that it does not ______ automatically.

   (a) open
   (b) close
   (c) restart
   (d) shut down

5. Where more than one motor disconnecting means is provided in the same motor branch circuit, at least one of the disconnecting means shall be readily accessible.

   (a) True
   (b) False

6. If a motor disconnecting means is a motor-circuit switch, it shall be rated in ______.

   (a) horsepower
   (b) watts
   (c) amperes
   (d) locked-rotor current

7. A horsepower-rated ______ having a horsepower rating not less than the motor rating shall be permitted to serve as the disconnecting means.

   (a) attachment plug and receptacle
   (b) flanged surface inlet and cord connector
   (c) automatic controller
   (d) a or b

8. An oil switch can be used as both the motor controller and disconnecting means on a circuit whose rating ______ or 100A.

   (a) does not exceed 240V
   (b) does not exceed 300V
   (c) does not exceed 600V
   (d) exceeds 600V

9. The ______ current for a hermetic refrigerant motor-compressor is the current resulting when the motor-compressor is operated at the rated load, rated voltage, and rated frequency of the equipment it serves.

   (a) full-load
   (b) nameplate rating
   (c) selection
   (d) rated-load

10. Equipment such as ______ shall be considered appliances, and the provisions of Article 422 apply in addition to Article 440.

   (a) room air conditioners
   (b) household refrigerators and freezers
   (c) drinking water coolers and beverage dispensers
   (d) all of these

11. An attachment plug and receptacle can serve as the disconnecting means for cord-connected ______.
    (a) room air conditioners
    (b) household refrigerators and freezers
    (c) drinking water coolers and beverage dispensers
    (d) all of these

12. Short-circuit and ground-fault protection for an individual air-conditioner motor-compressor shall not exceed ______ percent of the motor-compressor rated-load current or branch-circuit protection current, whichever is greater.
    (a) 80
    (b) 125
    (c) 175
    (d) 250

13. Conductors supplying more than one air-conditioner motor-compressor shall have an ampacity not less than the sum of the rated load or branch-circuit current ratings, whichever is larger, of all the air-conditioner motor-compressors plus the full-load currents of any other motors, plus ______ percent of the highest motor or motor-compressor rating in the group.
    (a) 25
    (b) 50
    (c) 80
    (d) 100

14. The rating of the attachment plug and receptacle shall not exceed ______ at 250V for a cord-and-plug-connected air-conditioner motor-compressor.
    (a) 15A
    (b) 20A
    (c) 30A
    (d) 40A

15. An attachment plug and receptacle can serve as the disconnecting means for a single-phase room air conditioner rated 250 volts or less if ______.
    (a) the manual controls on the room air conditioner are readily accessible and located within 1.80 meter (6 ft) of the floor
    (b) an approved manually operable disconnecting means is installed in a readily accessible location within sight from the room air conditioner
    (c) a or b
    (d) a and b

16. The ampacity of ungrounded conductors from the generator terminals to the first distribution device containing overcurrent protection shall not be less than ______ percent of the nameplate rating of the generator.
    (a) 75
    (b) 115
    (c) 125
    (d) 140

17. Generators must have a disconnecting means that is lockable in the open position, except where ______.
    (a) the driving means for the generator can be readily shut down
    (b) the generator isn't arranged to operate in parallel with another generator or other source of voltage
    (c) a and b
    (d) a or b

18. A secondary tie of a transformer is a circuit operating at ______, nominal, or less, between phases that connects two power sources or power-supply points.
    (a) 600V
    (b) 1,000V
    (c) 12,000V
    (d) 35,000V

19. Transformers and transformer vaults shall be readily accessible to qualified personnel for inspection and maintenance, except ______.
    (a) dry-type transformers 600V or less, located in the open on walls, columns, or structures
    (b) dry-type transformers rated not more than 50 kVA/ 600V installed in hollow spaces of buildings not permanently closed in by structure
    (c) a or b
    (d) none of these

20. Indoor transformers rated over 35,000V, and insulated with nonflammable dielectric fluid identified as nonflammable, shall be installed in a vault furnished with a ______.
    (a) liquid confinement area
    (b) pressure-relief vent
    (c) means for absorbing or venting any gases generated by arcing
    (d) all of these

21. The walls and roofs of transformer vaults shall be constructed of materials that have adequate structural strength for the conditions with a minimum fire-resistance rating of _____ hours.

(a) 2
(b) 3
(c) 4
(d) 6

22. Personnel doors for transformer vaults shall _____ and be equipped with panic bars, pressure plates, or other devices that are normally latched but open under simple pressure.

(a) be clearly identified
(b) swing out
(c) a and b
(d) a or b

23. Transformer vaults containing more than _____ total kVA transformer capacity shall be provided with a drain or other means that will carry off any accumulation of oil or water in the vault, unless impracticable.

(a) 100
(b) 150
(c) 200
(d) 250

24. Capacitors containing more than _____ of flammable liquid shall be enclosed in vaults or outdoor fenced enclosures.

(a) 3 gallons
(b) 5 gallons
(c) 10 gallons
(d) 11 gallons

25. The residual voltage of a capacitor, rated not over 600V, shall be reduced to 50V or less within _____ after the capacitor is disconnected from the source of supply.

(a) 15 seconds
(b) 45 seconds
(c) 1 minute
(d) 2 minutes

26. An overcurrent device shall be provided in each ungrounded conductor for each capacitor bank. The rating or setting of the overcurrent device shall be _____.

(a) as low as practicable
(b) not to exceed 20A
(c) not to exceed 40A
(d) not to exceed 100A

27. A disconnecting means shall be provided in each ungrounded conductor for each capacitor bank, and shall _____.

(a) open all ungrounded conductors simultaneously
(b) be permitted to disconnect the capacitor from the line as a regular operating procedure
(c) be rated no less than 135 percent of the rated current of the capacitor
(d) all of these

28. For installations of resistors and reactors, a thermal barrier shall be required if the space between them and any combustible material is less than _____

(a) 2 in.
(b) 3 in.
(c) 6 in.
(d) 12 in.

29. The provisions of Article _____ apply to stationary storage battery installations.

(a) 450
(b) 460
(c) 470
(d) 480

30. Nominal battery voltage, as it relates to storage batteries, is defined as the voltage of a battery based on the _____ of cells in the battery.

(a) number
(b) type
(c) a and b
(d) a or b

31. Wiring and equipment supplied from storage batteries must be in accordance with Chapters 1 through 4 of the NEC unless otherwise permitted by 480.4.

(a) True
(b) False

32. Racks (rigid frames designed to support battery cells or trays) must be made of one of the following:

(a) Metal, treated to be resistant to deteriorating action by the electrolyte and provided with nonconducting or continuous insulating material members directly supporting the cells
(b) Fiberglass
(c) Other suitable nonconductive materials
(d) any of these

33. The required working space requirements of 110.26 are measured from the edge of the battery ______.

(a) terminals
(b) enclosure
(c) rack
(d) any of these

34. Combustible dust is defined as a finely divided solid material that's 420 microns or smaller in diameter and ______ when dispersed and ignited in air.

(a) presents a fire hazard
(b) presents an explosion hazard
(c) can't be extinguished
(d) a or b

35. ______ enclosures are constructed so that dust will not enter under specific test conditions.

(a) Dust-ignitionproof
(b) Dusttight
(c) a or b
(d) a and

36. Hazardous (classified) locations shall be classified depending on the properties of the ______ that may be present, and the likelihood that a flammable or combustible concentration or quantity is present.

(a) flammable liquid produced vapors
(b) flammable gases
(c) combustible dusts
(d) all of these

37. Class I, Division 1 locations are those in which ignitible concentrations of ______ can exist under normal operating conditions.

(a) combustible dust
(b) easily ignitible fibers or flyings
(c) flammable gases or flammable liquid produced vapors
(d) pyrotechnics

38. Class II locations are those that are hazardous because of the presence of ______.

(a) combustible dust
(b) easily ignitible fibers/flyings
(c) flammable gases or vapors
(d) flammable liquids or gases

39. Class III locations are those that are hazardous because of the presence of ______.

(a) combustible dust
(b) easily ignitible fibers or materials producing combustible flyings
(c) flammable gases or vapors
(d) flammable liquids or gases

40. Equipment in an area containing ignitible concentrations of acetylene under normal operating conditions shall be classified as a Class I, Group A location.

(a) True
(b) False

41. An atmosphere classified as hazardous Group E contains combustible metal dusts.

(a) True
(b) False

42. An atmosphere classified as hazardous Group G contains combustible dusts such as flour, grain, wood, plastic, and chemicals.

(a) True
(b) False

43. Suitability of identified equipment for use in a hazardous (classified) location shall be determined by:

(a) Equipment listing or labeling.
(b) Evidence of equipment evaluation from a qualified testing laboratory or inspection agency concerned with product evaluation.
(c) Evidence acceptable to the authority having jurisdiction, such as a manufacturer's self-evaluation or an owner's engineering judgment.
(d) any of these

44. Threaded conduits or fittings installed in hazardous (classified) locations shall be made wrenchtight to ______.

(a) prevent sparking when a fault current flows
(b) ensure the explosionproof integrity of the conduit system
(c) a and b
(d) none of these

45. Equipment used in hazardous (classified) locations with metric threaded entries shall be installed using ______ .

(a) NPT threaded fittings
(b) listed conduit fittings
(c) listed cable fittings
(d) b or c

46. Where optical fiber cable is capable of carrying current (composite optical fiber cable), the optical fiber cable must be installed in accordance with Articles 500, 501, 502, or 503.

(a) True
(b) False

47. MI cable terminated with fittings listed for the location is allowed in Class I, Division 1 locations.

(a) True
(b) False

48. Wiring methods permitted in Class I, Division 1 locations are permitted in Class I, Division 2 locations.

(a) True
(b) False

49. ______ are among the wiring methods permitted within a Class I, Division 2 location.

(a) Enclosed gasketed busways and enclosed gasketed wireways
(b) PLTC and Type PLTC-ER cable and ITC and ITC-ER cable terminated with listed fittings
(c) Types MC, MV, or TC cables including installation in cable tray systems and terminated with listed fittings
(d) all of these

50. In a Class I, Division 2 location, if flexibility is necessary, ______ are some of the wiring methods that are permitted.

(a) listed flexible metal fittings
(b) flexible metal conduit, liquidtight flexible metal conduit and liquidtight nonmetallic conduit, all with listed fittings
(c) flexible cords listed for extra-hard usage, containing an equipment grounding conductor, and terminated with listed fittings
(d) all of these

51. In a Class I, Division 2 location, switches and circuit breakers shall be installed in explosionproof enclosures meeting the requirements for Class I, Division 1 locations.

(a) True
(b) False

52. Where the Class I, Division 1 location boundary is below grade, a sealing fitting shall be installed ______, and there must not be any unions, couplings, boxes, or fittings between the sealing fitting and the grade, other than listed explosionproof reducers.

(a) after the conduit emerges from grade
(b) before the conduit emerges from grade
(c) within 10 ft of where the conduit emerges from grade
(d) none of these

53. A sealing fitting shall not be required if a conduit passes completely through a Class I, Division 2 location if the termination points of the unbroken conduit are in unclassified locations and it has no fittings less than ______ beyond each boundary of the hazardous (classified) location.

(a) 6 in.
(b) 12 in.
(c) 18 in.
(d) 24 in.

54. The minimum thickness of sealing compound in Class I shall not be less than the trade size of the conduit or sealing fitting and, in no case, less than ______

(a) ⅛ in.
(b) ¼ in.
(c) ⅜ in.
(d) ⅝ in.

55. When installing shield cables and twisted-pair cables in conduit in a Class I, Division 1 hazardous (classified) location, the removal of shielding material or the separation of the twisted pairs isn't required within the conduit seal fitting.

(a) True
(b) False

56. In Class I, Division 1 locations, a multiwire branch circuit can't be used unless the disconnect device(s) open all ungrounded conductors simultaneously.

(a) True
(b) False

57. Transformers and capacitors installed in Class I, Division 1 locations that do not contain flammable liquids shall not be required to be installed in vaults if they are identified for Class I locations.

(a) True
(b) False

58. Meters, instruments and relays installed in Class I, Division 2 locations can have switches, circuit breakers, and make-and-break contacts installed in general-purpose enclosures if current-interrupting contacts are ______.

(a) immersed in oil
(b) enclosed within a hermetically sealed chamber
(c) a or b
(d) a and b

59. In Class I, Division 2 locations, fused or unfused disconnect and isolating switches for transformers or capacitor banks that are not intended to interrupt current in normal performance can be installed in general-purpose enclosures.

(a) True
(b) False

60. Totally enclosed motors shall have a device to de-energize the motor or provide an alarm if there is an increase in temperature of the motor beyond designed limits when operating in Class I, Division 1 locations.

(a) True
(b) False

61. Luminaires installed in Class I, Division 1 locations shall be protected from physical damage by a suitable ______.

(a) warning label
(b) pendant
(c) guard or by location
(d) all of these

62. Boxes and fittings used to support luminaires in Class I, Division 1 locations shall be identified for Class I locations.

(a) True
(b) False

63. Portable lighting equipment must be ______ for use in a Class I, Division 2 location, unless the luminaire is mounted on movable stands and connected by a flexible cord.

(a) identified
(b) approved
(c) marked
(d) listed

64. In Division 1 or Division 2 locations where the boxes, fittings, or enclosures are required to be explosionproof, if a flexible cord is used it must terminate with a cord connector or attachment plug listed for the location, or a cord connector or attachment plug with a seal that is listed for the location. In Division 2 locations where explosionproof equipment is not required, the cord can terminate ______.

(a) with a listed cord connector
(b) with a listed attachment plug
(c) in a splice of any manner
(d) a or b

65. In Class I locations, receptacles and attachment plugs shall be of the type providing for ______ a flexible cord and shall be identified for the location.

(a) sealing compound around
(b) quick connection to
(c) connection to the equipment grounding conductor of
(d) none of these

66. Raceways permitted as a wiring method in Class II, Division 1 locations include ______.

(a) threaded RMC and steel IMC
(b) PVC conduit
(c) electrical metallic tubing
(d) any of these

67. Where flexibility is required, the following wiring methods are permitted in a Class II, Division 1 location ______.
(a) dusttight flexible connectors
(b) liquidtight flexible metal conduit with listed fittings
(c) flexible cords listed for extra-hard usage with listed dusttight fittings
(d) any of these

68. In Class II locations, dust must be prevented from entering the required dust-ignitionproof enclosure from a raceway by one of the following methods: ______.
(a) a permanent effective seal
(b) a horizontal raceway not less than 10 ft long
(c) a vertical raceway that extends downward for not less than 5 ft
(d) any of these

69. In Class II locations, a permitted method of bonding is the use of bonding jumpers with proper fittings.
(a) True
(b) False

70. In Class II, Division 1 locations, multiwire branch circuits are not permitted unless a disconnect opens all of the ungrounded circuit conductors simultaneously.
(a) True
(b) False

71. In Class II, Division 2 locations, enclosures for fuses, switches, circuit breakers, and motor controllers, including pushbuttons, relays, and similar devices shall be ______.
(a) dusttight or identified for the location
(b) raintight
(c) rated as Class I, Division 1 explosionproof
(d) general duty

72. Luminaires installed in Class II, Division 1 locations shall be identified for the location and shall be clearly marked to indicate the ______.
(a) maximum wattage of lamps for which designed
(b) minimum conductor size
(c) maximum overcurrent protection permitted
(d) all of these

73. Pendant luminaires installed in Class II, Division 1 locations shall be suspended by threaded conduit stems, by chains with approved fittings, or by other approved means. Stems shall be provided with ______ or other effective means to prevent loosening.
(a) set-screws
(b) welded joints
(c) expansion joints
(d) explosionproof flex

74. Luminaires installed in Class II, Division 2 locations shall be protected from physical damage by a suitable ______.
(a) warning label
(b) pendant
(c) guard or by location
(d) all of these

75. Flexible cords used in Class II, Division 1 or 2 locations ______.
(a) shall be listed for hard usage
(b) shall be listed for extra-hard usage
(c) shall not be permitted
(d) none of these

76. Boxes and fittings shall be ______ where installed in a Class III location.
(a) explosionproof
(b) dust-ignitionproof
(c) dusttight
(d) weatherproof

77. Where LFMC is used in a Class III location as permitted in 503.10, it shall ______.
(a) not be unsupported
(b) not exceed 6 ft in length
(c) include an equipment bonding jumper of the wire type
(d) be listed for use in a Class I hazardous (classified) location

78. In Class III locations, ______ used as or in conjunction with control equipment for motors, generators, and appliances shall be provided with dusttight enclosures complying with the temperature limitations in 503.5.
(a) transformers
(b) impedance coils
(c) resistors
(d) all of these

79. Luminaires for fixed lighting in Class III shall have enclosures for lamps and lampholders that are designed to prevent the escape of ______.

(a) sparks
(b) burning material
(c) hot metal
(d) all of these

80. In Class III locations, flexible cords shall ______.

(a) be listed as extra-hard usage
(b) contain an equipment grounding conductor
(c) terminate with a listed dusttight cord connector
(d) all of these

81. The power supply to contact conductors of a crane in Class III locations shall be ______.

(a) electrically isolated from all other systems
(b) equipped with an acceptable ground detector
(c) have an alarm in the case of a ground fault
(d) all of these

82. An intrinsically safe circuit is a circuit in which any spark or thermal effect is incapable of causing ignition of a mixture of flammable or combustible material in air under ______.

(a) water
(b) prescribed test conditions
(c) supervision
(d) duress

83. Intrinsically safe and associated apparatus are permitted to be installed in ______.

(a) any hazardous (classified) location for which they have been identified
(b) Class I locations
(c) Class II locations
(d) Class III locations

84. Intrinsically safe apparatus, metal enclosures, and metal raceways shall be connected to the equipment grounding conductor.

(a) True
(b) False

85. Intrinsically safe conduit or cable runs that leave a Class I or II location shall be sealed. The seal shall be ______.

(a) explosionproof or flameproof
(b) flameproof
(c) a and b
(d) none of these

86. Conduits, cable trays, and other wiring methods used for intrinsically safe systems shall be identified by permanently affixed labels with the wording "Intrinsic Safety Wiring." The labels shall be visible after installation and the spacing between labels shall not exceed ______ ft.

(a) 3
(b) 10
(c) 25
(d) 50

87. Multiwire branch circuits shall be permitted in a Class I, Zone 1 location if all ungrounded conductors of the circuit are opened simultaneously.

(a) True
(b) False

88. Parking garages used for parking or storage can be considered as an unclassified location.

(a) True
(b) False

89. In major repair garages where lighter-than-air gaseous fueled vehicles, such as vehicles fueled by natural gas or hydrogen, are repaired or stored, the area within ______ in. of the ceiling is classified as Class I, Division 2.

(a) 6
(b) 12
(c) 18
(d) 24

90. Any pit for which ventilation is not provided below a minor repair garage floor level of a lubrication or service room is considered to be a Class I, ______ location up to the floor level.

(a) Division 1
(b) Division 2
(c) a or b
(d) a and b

91. Portable lighting equipment used in commercial garages shall be identified for ______ locations, unless the lamp and its cord are supported or arranged in such a manner that they cannot be used in the locations classified in 511.3.

(a) hard usage
(b) Class I, Division 2
(c) Class I, Division 1
(d) general duty

92. A permanently mounted luminaire in a commercial garage, located over lanes on which vehicles are commonly driven, shall be located not less than ______ above floor level.

(a) 10 ft
(b) 12 ft
(c) 14 ft
(d) 16 ft

93. In commercial garages, GFCI protection shall be provided on all 15A and 20A, 125V receptacles installed where ______ is(are) to be used.

(a) electrical diagnostic equipment
(b) electrical hand tools
(c) portable lighting equipment
(d) any of these

94. The entire area of an aircraft hangar, including any adjacent and communicating areas not suitably cut off from the hangar, shall be classified as a Class I, Division 2 or Zone 2 location up to a level of ______ above the floor.

(a) 6 in.
(b) 12 in.
(c) 18 in.
(d) 24 in.

95. Stockrooms and similar areas adjacent to classified locations of aircraft hangars, but effectively isolated and adequately ventilated, shall be designated as ______ locations.

(a) Class I, Division 2
(b) Class II, Division 1
(c) Class II, Division 2
(d) unclassified

96. In aircraft hangars, equipment less than ______ above wings and engine enclosures of aircraft and may produce arcs, sparks, or particles of hot metal shall be of the totally enclosed type or constructed so as to prevent the escape of sparks or hot metal particles.

(a) 2 ft
(b) 3 ft
(c) 10 ft
(d) 20 ft

97. All 15A and 20A, 125V receptacles installed in aircraft hangars in areas where ______ is(are) used shall have GFCI protection.

(a) electrical diagnostic equipment
(b) electrical hand tools
(c) portable lighting equipment
(d) any of these

98. Underground wiring to motor fuel dispensers shall be installed in ______.

(a) threaded rigid metal conduit
(b) threaded steel IMC
(c) PVC conduit when buried under not less than 2 ft of cover
(d) any of these

99. Each circuit leading to or through motor fuel dispensing equipment shall be provided with a clearly identified and readily accessible switch or other approved means located remote from the dispensing device to disconnect all conductors of the circuit including the grounded conductor.

(a) True
(b) False

100. The emergency controls for unattended self-service stations shall be located not less than ______ or more than ______ from motor fuel dispensers.

(a) 10 ft, 25 ft
(b) 20 ft, 50 ft
(c) 20 ft, 100 ft
(d) 50 ft, 100 ft

Practice Quiz 7

Random Order [100 through 514.11]

Unit 7 Practice Quiz—Random Order [100 through 514.11]

Please use the 2011 *Code* book to answer the following questions, which are based on the 2011 *NEC*.

1. Resistors and reactors rated over 600V shall be isolated by ______ to protect personnel from accidental contact with energized parts.

   (a) an enclosure
   (b) elevation
   (c) a or b
   (d) a and b

2. Where equipment grounding is required for an installation of HDPE, a separate equipment grounding conductor shall be ______.

   (a) an insulated copper conductor
   (b) installed within the conduit
   (c) a stranded bare copper conductor
   (d) a solid bare copper conductor

3. Receptacle yokes designed and ______ as self-grounding can establish the grounding circuit between the device yoke and a grounded outlet box.

   (a) approved
   (b) advertised
   (c) listed
   (d) installed

4. Where Type NM cable passes through factory or field openings in metal members, it shall be protected by ______ bushings or ______ grommets that cover metal edges.

   (a) approved
   (b) identified
   (c) listed
   (d) none of these

5. Splices and taps shall not be located within luminaire ______.

   (a) arms or stems
   (b) bases or screw shells
   (c) a and b
   (d) a or b

6. The rules of ______ shall apply to air-conditioning and refrigerating equipment that does not incorporate a hermetic refrigerant motor-compressor.

   (a) Article 422
   (b) Article 424
   (c) Article 430
   (d) all of these

7. In Class II, Division 1 locations, receptacles and attachment plugs shall be identified ______.

   (a) as explosionproof
   (b) for Class II locations
   (c) with laminated tags
   (d) for general duty

8. Where the supply conductors are larger than 1,100 kcmil copper or 1,750 kcmil aluminum, the main bonding jumper shall have an area that is ______ the area of the largest phase conductor when of the same material.

   (a) at least equal to
   (b) at least 50 percent of
   (c) not less than 12½ percent of
   (d) not more than 12½ percent of

9. Service raceways threaded into metal service equipment such as bosses (hubs) are considered to be effectively ______ to the service metal enclosure.

   (a) attached
   (b) bonded
   (c) grounded
   (d) none of these

10. Each circuit leading to or through motor fuel dispensing equipment, including all associated power, communication, data, video circuits, and equipment for remote pumping systems, shall be provided with a switch or other approved means to disconnect _____ from the source of supply all conductors of the circuit, including the grounded conductor, if any.

(a) automatically
(b) simultaneously
(c) manually
(d) individually

11. The standard length of RMC shall _____.

(a) be 10 ft
(b) include a coupling on each length
(c) be threaded on each end
(d) all of these

12. Openings around electrical penetrations into or through fire-resistant-rated walls, partitions, floors, or ceilings shall _____ to maintain the fire-resistance rating.

(a) be documented
(b) not be permitted
(c) be firestopped using approved methods
(d) be enlarged

13. Service conductors supplying a building or other structure shall not _____ of another building or other structure.

(a) be installed on the exterior walls
(b) pass through the interior
(c) a and b
(d) none of these

14. Flexible cords in Class I hazardous (classified) locations must _____.

(a) be listed as extra-hard usage
(b) contain an equipment grounding conductor
(c) be supported by clamps or other suitable means to avoid tension on the terminals
(d) all of these

15. The intersystem bonding termination shall _____.

(a) be securely mounted and electrically connected to service equipment, the meter enclosure, or exposed nonflexible metallic service raceway, or be mounted at one of these enclosures and be connected to the enclosure or grounding electrode conductor with a minimum 6 AWG copper conductor
(b) be securely mounted to the building/structure disconnecting means, or be mounted at the disconnecting means and be connected to the metallic enclosure or grounding electrode conductor with a minimum 6 AWG copper conductor
(c) have terminals that are listed as grounding and bonding equipment
(d) all of these

16. Pipeline resistance heating elements include heating _____.

(a) blankets
(b) tape
(c) cables
(d) all of these

17. Raceways and cables installed into the _____ of open-bottom equipment shall not be required to be mechanically secured to the equipment.

(a) bottom
(b) sides
(c) top
(d) any of these

18. The conductors and equipment from the electric utility that deliver electric energy to the wiring system of the premises is called a "_____."

(a) branch circuit
(b) feeder
(c) service
(d) none of these

19. A _____ rated in amperes shall be permitted as a controller for all motors.

(a) branch-circuit inverse time circuit breaker
(b) molded case switch
(c) a and b
(d) none of these

20. Nonmetallic surface extensions shall be permitted in ______ when occupied for residential or office purposes.

(a) buildings not over three stories high
(b) buildings over four stories high
(c) all buildings
(d) none of these

21. IMC must be secured ______.

(a) by fastening within 3 ft of each outlet box, junction box, device box, cabinet, conduit body, or other conduit termination
(b) within 5 ft of a box or termination fitting when structural members don't permit the raceway to be secured within 3 ft of the termination
(c) except when the IMC is within 3 ft of the service head for an above-the-roof termination of a mast
(d) a, b, or c

22. Resistance heating elements of embedded deicing and snow-melting ______ shall not be installed where they bridge expansion joints unless provision is made for expansion and contraction.

(a) cables
(b) units
(c) panels
(d) all of these

23. Switches or circuit breakers shall not disconnect the grounded conductor of a circuit unless the switch or circuit breaker ______.

(a) can be opened and closed by hand levers only
(b) simultaneously disconnects all conductors of the circuit
(c) opens the grounded conductor before it disconnects the ungrounded conductors
(d) none of these

24. In multi-occupancy buildings, branch circuits for ______ shall not be supplied from equipment that supplies an individual dwelling unit or tenant space.

(a) central alarm
(b) parking lot lighting
(c) common area purposes
(d) all of these

25. The number of conductors permitted in ENT shall not exceed the percentage fill specified in ______.

(a) Chapter 9, Table 1
(b) Table 250.66
(c) Table 310.15(B)(16)
(d) 240.6

26. In Class III locations, switches, circuit breakers, motor controllers, and fuses, including pushbuttons, relays, and similar devices, shall be provided with ______.

(a) Class I enclosures
(b) general duty enclosures
(c) dusttight enclosures
(d) seals at each enclosure

27. Where flammable liquids having a flash point below 100°F (such as gasoline, or gaseous fuels such as natural gas or hydrogen) will not be transferred in a minor repair garage, such location is considered to be a(n) ______ location, provided the entire floor area has mechanical ventilation providing a minimum of four air changes per hour or one cubic foot per minute of exchanged air for each square foot of floor area.

(a) Class I, Division 1
(b) Class I, Division 2
(c) Class II, Division 1
(d) unclassified

28. Any pit or depression below the level of an aircraft hangar floor shall be classified as a ______ location that extends up to said floor level.

(a) Class I, Division 1
(b) Class I, Division 2
(c) Class II, Division 1
(d) Class III

29. Wiring in or under the aircraft hangar floor shall comply with the requirements for ______ locations.

(a) Class I, Division 1
(b) Class I, Division 2
(c) a or b
(d) none of these

30. In Class I, Division 1 locations, control transformers, impedance coils, and resistors, along with any switching mechanism associated with them, shall be provided with enclosures identified for ______.

(a) Class I, Division 1 locations
(b) control transformer duty
(c) general duty
(d) NEMA 3R

31. In Class II, Division 1 locations, control transformers, solenoids, impedance coils and resistors, and any overcurrent devices or switching mechanisms associated with them, shall have enclosures identified for ______.

(a) Class I, Division 1 locations
(b) control transformer duty
(c) general duty
(d) Class II locations

32. Areas designated as hazardous (classified) shall be properly ______ and shall be available to those authorized to design, install, inspect, maintain, or operate electrical equipment at these locations.

(a) cleaned
(b) documented
(c) maintained
(d) all of these

33. Where a premises wiring system contains feeders supplied from more than one nominal voltage system, each ungrounded conductor of a feeder shall be identified by phase and system by ______, or other approved means.

(a) color coding
(b) marking tape
(c) tagging
(d) any of these

34. When a single equipment grounding conductor is used for multiple circuits in the same raceway, cable or cable tray, the single equipment grounding conductor shall be sized according to ______.

(a) combined rating of all the overcurrent devices
(b) largest overcurrent device of the multiple circuits
(c) combined rating of all the loads
(d) any of these

35. Table 220.56 may be applied to determine the load for thermostatically controlled or intermittently used ______ and other kitchen equipment in a commercial kitchen.

(a) commercial electric cooking equipment
(b) dishwasher booster heaters
(c) water heaters
(d) all of these

36. Unbroken lengths of electric nonmetallic tubing shall not be required to be secured where fished between access points for ______ work in finished buildings or structures and supporting is impractical.

(a) concealed
(b) exposed
(c) hazardous
(d) completed

37. Exposed metal conductive parts of luminaires shall be ______.

(a) connected to an equipment grounding conductor
(b) painted
(c) removed
(d) a and b

38. A hermetic motor-compressor controller shall have a ______ current rating not less than the respective nameplate rating(s) on the compressor.

(a) continuous-duty full-load
(b) locked-rotor
(c) a or b
(d) a and b

39. A ______ shall be located in sight from the motor location and the driven machinery location.

(a) controller
(b) protection device
(c) disconnecting means
(d) all of these

40. Provisions shall be made for sufficient diffusion and ventilation of the gases from a storage battery to prevent the accumulation of a(n) ______ mixture.

(a) corrosive
(b) explosive
(c) toxic
(d) all of these

41. In completed installations, each outlet box shall have a ______.

(a) cover
(b) faceplate
(c) canopy
(d) any of these

42. Type NM cable protected from physical damage by a raceway shall not be required to be ______ within the raceway.

(a) covered
(b) insulated
(c) secured
(d) unspliced

43. Letters used to designate the number of conductors within a cable are ______.

(a) D–Two insulated conductors laid parallel
(b) M–Two or more insulated conductors twisted spirally
(c) T–Two or more insulated conductors twisted in parallel
(d) a and b

44. Lampholders installed in wet locations shall be listed for use in ______ locations.

(a) damp
(b) wet
(c) dry
(d) any of these

45. General-use ______ switches shall be used only to control permanently installed incandescent luminaires unless listed for control of other loads.

(a) dimmer
(b) fan speed control
(c) timer
(d) all of these

46. LFNC shall be permitted for ______.

(a) direct burial where listed and marked for the purpose
(b) exposed work
(c) outdoors where listed and marked for this purpose
(d) all of these

47. Where practicable, rod, pipe, and plate electrodes shall be installed ______.

(a) directly below the electrical meter
(b) on the north side of the building
(c) below permanent moisture level
(d) all of these

48. For transformers, other than Class 2 and Class 3, a means is required to disconnect all transformer ungrounded primary conductors. The disconnecting means must be located within sight of the transformer unless the ______.

(a) disconnect location is field-marked on the transformer
(b) disconnect is lockable
(c) disconnect is nonfusible
(d) a and b

49. When an outlet is ______ from a cellular concrete floor raceway, the sections of circuit conductors supplying the outlet shall be removed from the raceway.

(a) discontinued
(b) abandoned
(c) removed
(d) any of these

50. In major repair garages where ventilation is not provided in accordance with 511.3(C)(3)(a), any pit or depression below floor level shall be a Class I, ______ location that extends up to the floor level.

(a) Division 1
(b) Division 2
(c) a or b
(d) a and b

Practice Quiz 8

Straight Order [514.13 through 647.4]

Unit 8 Practice Quiz— Straight Order [514.13 through 647.4]

Please use the 2011 *Code* book to answer the following questions, which are based on the 2011 *NEC*.

1. Each motor fuel dispensing device shall be provided with a means to remove all external voltage sources, including power, communication, data, video circuits, and feedback, during periods of maintenance and service of the fuel dispensing equipment.

   (a) True
   (b) False

2. The requirements of Article 517 apply to buildings or portions of buildings in which medical, _____, or surgical care are provided.

   (a) psychiatric
   (b) nursing
   (c) obstetrical
   (d) any of these

3. A limited care facility is an area used on a(n) _____ basis for the housing of four or more persons who are incapable of self-preservation because of age, physical limitation due to accident or illness, or mental limitations, mental illness, or chemical dependency.

   (a) occasional
   (b) 10-hour or less per day
   (c) 24-hour
   (d) temporary

4. In motor fuel dispensing facilities, all metal raceways, the metal armor or metallic sheath on cables, and all noncurrent-carrying metal parts of fixed and portable electrical equipment _____ shall be grounded and bonded.

   (a) operating at under 600V
   (b) regardless of voltage
   (c) over 300V
   (d) under 50V

5. Locations where flammable paints are dried, with the ventilating equipment interlocked with the electrical equipment, may be designated _____ locations by the authority having jurisdiction.

   (a) Class I, Division 2
   (b) unclassified
   (c) Class II, Division 2
   (d) Class II, Division 1

6. A nursing home is an area used for the housing and nursing care, on a 24-hour basis, of _____ or more persons who, because of mental or physical incapacity, might be unable to provide for their own needs and safety without the assistance of another person.

   (a) two
   (b) three
   (c) four
   (d) five

7. The patient care area is any portion of a health care facility where patients are intended to be _____.

   (a) examined
   (b) treated
   (c) registered
   (d) a or b

8. Wiring methods used in health care locations must comply with the *NEC* Chapter 1 through 4 provisions, except as modified by Article 517.

   (a) True
   (b) False

9. In patient care areas, the grounding terminals of all receptacles, metal boxes and enclosures containing receptacles, and all noncurrent-carrying conductive surfaces of fixed electric equipment _____ shall be connected to an insulated copper equipment grounding conductor.

   (a) operating at over 100V
   (b) likely to become energized
   (c) subject to personal contact
   (d) all of these

10. Each general care area patient bed location shall be provided with a minimum of ______ receptacle(s), which can be single, duplex, or a combination.

(a) one
(b) two
(c) three
(d) four

11. In critical care areas of health care facilities, each patient bed location shall be provided with a minimum of ______ receptacles.

(a) two
(b) four
(c) six
(d) eight

12. Which of the following shall not be connected to the life safety branch in a hospital?

(a) exit signs
(b) elevators
(c) general illumination
(d) communications systems

13. Receptacles or their cover plates, supplied from the emergency electrical system in nursing homes shall have a distinctive color or marking so as to be readily identifiable.

(a) True
(b) False

14. In patient care areas, secondary circuits of transformer-powered communications or signaling systems shall not be required to be enclosed in raceways unless required by Chapters 7 or 8.

(a) True
(b) False

15. Examples of assembly occupancies include ______.

(a) restaurants
(b) conference rooms
(c) pool rooms
(d) all of these

16. Where GFCI protection is supplied by plug-and-cord-connection to the branch circuit or to the feeder for temporary wiring such as exhibition halls in assembly occupancies, the GFCI-protection device ______, whether assembled in the field or at the factory.

(a) shall be listed as portable ground-fault circuit-interrupter protection
(b) provide a level of protection equivalent to a portable ground-fault circuit interrupter
(c) must provide the same level of protection as ground-fault protection for equipment
(d) a or b

17. In assembly occupancies of fire-rated construction, nonmetallic raceways encased in not less than ______ of concrete shall be permitted.

(a) 1 in.
(b) 2 in.
(c) 3 in.
(d) 4 in.

18. Theater fixed stage switchboards that are not completely enclosed, dead-front and dead-rear or recessed into a wall, shall be provided with a metal hood extending the full length of the board to protect all equipment on the board from falling objects.

(a) True
(b) False

19. The pilot light provided within a portable stage switchboard enclosure shall have overcurrent protection rated or set at not more than ______.

(a) 10A
(b) 15A
(c) 20A
(d) 30A

20. Lights and receptacles installed in theater dressing rooms adjacent to the mirrors and above the dressing table counter, shall be controlled by wall switches in the dressing rooms.

(a) True
(b) False

21. The individual responsible for starting, stopping, and controlling an amusement ride or supervising a concession is known as the ______.

(a) operator
(b) director
(c) manager
(d) facilitator

22. Electrical service equipment at carnivals and circuses shall not be accessible to unqualified persons, unless ______.

(a) lockable
(b) readily accessible
(c) accessible
(d) none of these

23. Where multiple services or separately derived systems supply portable structures of carnival, circuses, or fairs, all structures separated by less than ______ shall be bonded together at the portable structures.

(a) 6 ft
(b) 8 ft
(c) 10 ft
(d) 12 ft

24. Cord connectors for carnivals, circuses, and fairs can be laid on the ground when the connectors are ______ for a wet location.

(a) listed
(b) labeled
(c) approved
(d) identified

25. Each portable structure at a carnival, circus, or fair shall be provided with a means to disconnect from all ungrounded conductors within sight of and within ______ of the operator's station.

(a) 3 ft
(b) 6 ft
(c) 8 ft
(d) 10 ft

26. For carnivals and fairs, receptacles of the locking type not accessible from grade level that facilitate quick disconnecting and reconnecting of electrical equipment shall not be required to be provided with GFCI protection.

(a) True
(b) False

27. The ______ of the circuit supplying metal parts of portable structures at a carnival, circuit or fair can serve as the required bonding means.

(a) grounded conductor
(b) equipment grounding conductor
(c) grounding electrode conductor
(d) ungrounded conductor

28. The continuity of the grounding conductor system used to reduce electrical shock hazards at carnivals, fairs, and similar locations shall be verified each time that portable electrical equipment is connected.

(a) True
(b) False

29. A professional motion picture projector is one that uses ______ film and has on each edge 212 perforations per meter, or a type using carbon arc, xenon, or other light source equipment that develops hazardous gases, dust, or radiation.

(a) 35 mm
(b) 70 mm
(c) 105 mm
(d) a or b

30. Plans, specifications, and other building details for construction of manufactured buildings are included in the ______ details.

(a) manufactured building
(b) building component
(c) building structure
(d) building system

31. Agricultural buildings where excessive dust and dust with water may accumulate, including all areas of ______ confinement systems where litter dust or feed dust may accumulate shall comply with Article 547.

(a) poultry
(b) livestock
(c) fish
(d) all of these

32. An equipotential plane is an area where wire mesh or other conductive elements are embedded in or placed under concrete bonded to ______.

(a) all metal structures
(b) fixed nonelectrical equipment that may become energized
(c) the electrical grounding system
(d) all of these

33. The distribution point is an electrical supply point from which ______ to agricultural buildings or structures under single management are supplied.

(a) service drops or service conductors
(b) feeders or branch circuits
(c) a or b
(d) none of these

34. Enclosures and fittings installed in areas of agricultural buildings where excessive dust may be present shall be designed to minimize the entrance of dust and shall have no openings through which dust can enter the enclosure.

(a) True
(b) False

35. In agricultural building locations where surfaces are periodically washed or sprayed with water, boxes, conduit bodies, and fittings shall be listed for use in wet locations.

(a) True
(b) False

36. An equipment grounding conductor installed within an agricultural building shall be a(n) ______ conductor.

(a) aluminum
(b) copper
(c) copper-clad
(d) any of these

37. Where livestock is housed, any portion of a direct-buried equipment grounding conductor run to the building or structure shall be insulated or covered ______.

(a) aluminum
(b) copper
(c) copper-clad aluminum
(d) none of these

38. The equipotential plane in an agricultural building shall be connected to the electrical grounding system with a solid copper, insulated, covered, or bare conductor and not smaller than ______.

(a) 10 AWG
(b) 8 AWG
(c) 6 AWG
(d) 4 AWG

39. A ______ is a structure transportable in one or more sections that is built on a permanent chassis and designed to be used as a dwelling, with or without a permanent foundation.

(a) manufactured home
(b) mobile home
(c) dwelling unit
(d) all of these

40. A mobile home that is factory-equipped with gas or oil-fired central heating equipment and cooking appliances can be provided with a listed mobile home power-supply cord rated ______.

(a) 30A
(b) 35A
(c) 40A
(d) 50A

41. Receptacle outlets over countertops in the kitchen in a mobile home shall ______.

(a) be no more than 2 ft apart
(b) be no more that 4 ft apart
(c) be no more than 6 ft apart
(d) include at least one receptacle outlet on each side of the sink

42. AFCI protection is required for branch circuits of mobile homes and manufactured homes in all the same locations as required for dwelling units by 220.12.

(a) True
(b) False

43. What is the park electrical wiring system load, after applying the demand factors, for a mobile home park having six mobile homes?

(a) 4,640 VA
(b) 27,840 VA
(c) 96,000 VA
(d) 144,000 VA

44. Mobile home service equipment shall be rated not less than ______ at 120/240V.

(a) 50A
(b) 60A
(c) 100A
(d) 200A

45. Feeder conductors to a mobile home shall consist of ______.

(a) a listed cord
(b) a permanently installed feeder consisting of four color-coded, insulated conductors
(c) a or b
(d) none of these

46. A minimum of 20 percent of all recreational vehicle sites with electrical supply shall be equipped with a ______,125/250V receptacle.

(a) 15A
(b) 20A
(c) 30A
(d) 50A

47. Electrical service and feeder loads for a recreational vehicle park shall be calculated at a minimum of ______ per site equipped with only 20A supply facilities (not including tent sites).

(a) 1,200 VA
(b) 2,400 VA
(c) 3,500 VA
(d) 9,600 VA

48. Private, noncommercial docking facilities constructed or occupied for the use of the owner or residents of the associated ______ are not covered by Article 555.

(a) single-family dwelling
(b) multifamily dwelling
(c) a or b
(d) none of these

49. At marinas and boatyards, the electrical datum plane, in land areas subject to tidal fluctuation, is a horizontal plane ______ above the highest high tide under normal circumstances.

(a) 1 ft
(b) 2 ft
(c) 3 ft
(d) 4 ft

50. Electrical connections in marinas and boatyards shall be located ______ unless the conductor splices are contained within sealed wire connector systems listed and identified for submersion.

(a) at least 12 in. above the deck of a floating pier
(b) at least 12 in. above the deck of a fixed pier
(c) not below the electrical datum plane of a fixed pier
(d) all of these

51. Equipment enclosures on piers must be located so as not to interfere with mooring lines.

(a) True
(b) False

52. Where shore power accommodations provide two receptacles specifically for an individual boat slip, and these receptacles have different voltages, only the receptacle with the ______ shall be required to be calculated.

(a) smaller kW demand
(b) larger kW demand
(c) higher voltage
(d) none of these

53. Disconnecting means shall be provided to ______ each boat from its supply connection(s). The disconnecting means shall consist of a circuit breaker, switch, or both, and shall identify which receptacle it controls.

(a) isolate
(b) separate
(c) guard
(d) control

54. Supplying 120/240V 3-wire shore power receptacles from a 120/208V 3-wire supply may cause overheating or malfunctioning of connected equipment.

(a) True
(b) False

55. Fifteen and 20A, single-phase, 125V receptacles used for other than shore power in marinas but not installed in marine power outlets shall be provided with ______.

(a) lockouts
(b) GFCI protection
(c) warning labels
(d) all of these

56. Except as specifically modified by Article 590, all other Code requirements for permanent wiring apply to temporary wiring installations.

(a) True
(b) False

57. Temporary electrical power and lighting installations shall be permitted for a period not to exceed 90 days for ______ decorative lighting and similar purposes.

(a) Christmas
(b) New Year's
(c) July 4th
(d) holiday

58. Type NM cables can be used for feeder temporary installations without height limitation and without concealment.

(a) True
(b) False

59. Receptacles on construction sites shall not be installed on the ______ as temporary lighting.

(a) same branch circuit
(b) the same feeders
(c) a or b
(d) none of these

60. For temporary installations, lamps shall be protected from accidental contact by a suitable ______ or by the use of a lampholder with a guard.

(a) globe
(b) luminaire
(c) fitting
(d) porcelain fitting

61. Flexible cords and flexible cables used for temporary wiring shall ______.

(a) be protected from accidental damage
(b) be protected where passing through doorways
(c) avoid sharp corners and projections
(d) all of these

62. GFCI protection is required for 15A, 20A, and 30A, 125V receptacle outlets that are installed or existing as part of the permanent wiring of the building/structure when used during construction or remodeling. Listed cord sets or adapters that incorporate listed GFCI protection can be used to meet this requirement.

(a) True
(b) False

63. For temporary power outlets existing or installed as permanent wiring, GFCI protection can be incorporated into a ______.

(a) circuit breaker
(b) receptacle
(c) cord set
(d) any of these

64. Listed cord sets or adapters that incorporate listed GFCI protection can be used to meet the GFCI requirement with portable generators manufactured prior to ______.

(a) January 1, 2005
(b) January 1, 2011
(c) January 1, 2014
(d) January 1, 2015

65. A section sign is a sign or ______ , shipped as subassemblies that require field-installed wiring between the subassemblies to complete the overall sign.

(a) outline lighting system
(b) skeleton tubing system
(c) neon system
(d) sign body

66. The markings required on signs and outline lighting systems in 600.4(A) and listing labels are required to be visible after installation, as well as during servicing.

(a) True
(b) False

67. Section signs shall be marked to indicate that field-wiring and ______ are required.

(a) listing
(b) labeling
(c) inspection
(d) installation instructions

68. Branch circuits that supply signs ______.

(a) are to be considered a continuous load for the purposes of calculations
(b) must be rated 30A or less for neon tubing installations
(c) must be rated not more than 20A for signs and outline lighting systems other than neon
(d) all of these

69. Each sign and outline lighting system shall be controlled by an externally operable switch or circuit breaker that opens all ______ conductors.

(a) ungrounded
(b) grounded
(c) equipment grounding
(d) all of these

70. Metal parts of signs and outline lighting systems must be bonded to the transformer or power-supply equipment grounding conductor of the branch circuit or feeder supplying the sign or outline lighting system, with the exception that remote metal parts of a section sign or outline lighting system only supplied by a remote Class 2 power supply are not required to be connected to an equipment grounding conductor.

(a) True
(b) False

71. The bottom of sign and outline lighting system equipment shall be at least ______ above areas accessible to vehicles unless protected from physical damage.

(a) 12 ft
(b) 14 ft
(c) 16 ft
(d) 18 ft

72. Signs and outline lighting systems shall be installed so that adjacent combustible materials are not subjected to temperatures in excess of ______.

(a) 60°C
(b) 75°C
(c) 90°C
(d) 105°C

73. A working space not less than 3 ft high by 3 ft wide by ______ deep is required for each ballast, transformer, and electronic power supply where not installed in a sign.

(a) 2 ft
(b) 3 ft
(c) 4 ft
(d) 6 ft

74. Manufactured wiring systems shall be permitted in ______ locations.

(a) accessible
(b) dry
(c) wet
(d) a and b

75. Manufactured wiring systems constructed with Type MC cable shall be supported and secured at intervals not exceeding ______.

(a) 3 ft
(b) 4 ft
(c) 6 ft
(d) 8 ft

76. Wired partitions for office furnishings that are secured to building surfaces shall be connected to the building electrical system by a Chapter 3 wiring method.

(a) True
(b) False

77. The minimum size conductor for operating control and signaling circuits in an elevator shall be ______.

(a) 20 AWG
(b) 16 AWG
(c) 14 AWG
(d) 12 AWG

78. At least ______ 125V, single-phase, 15A or 20A, duplex receptacle(s) shall be provided in each elevator machine room and elevator machinery space.

(a) one
(b) two
(c) three
(d) four

79. The lighting switch for hoistway pits shall be readily accessible from the ______.

(a) pit access door
(b) elevator car
(c) floor of the pit
(d) machinery room

80. Only wiring, raceways, and cables used directly in connection with an elevator shall be permitted inside the hoistway and the machine room.

(a) True
(b) False

81. The disconnecting means for an elevator or escalator shall be an enclosed externally operable circuit breaker or fused motor-circuit switch capable of ______.

(a) interrupting six times the locked-rotor current
(b) being locked in the open position
(c) including overload protection
(d) serving as a transfer switch

82. All 15A and 20A, 125V receptacles installed in machine rooms and machinery spaces for elevators, escalators, moving walks, and lifts shall have GFCI protection by a ______.

(a) GFCI receptacle
(b) GFCI-circuit breaker
(c) a or b
(d) none of these

83. Each elevator shall have a means for disconnecting all ungrounded main power-supply conductors for each ____.

(a) excluding the emergency power system
(b) including the emergency or standby power system
(c) excluding the emergency power system if it is automatic
(d) and the power supply may not be an emergency power system

84. According to Article 625, automotive-type vehicles for on-road use include ______.

(a) passenger automobiles
(b) trucks
(c) neighborhood electric vehicles
(d) all of these

85. For cord-and-plug-connected electric vehicle supply equipment, the listed system of personnel protection can be______.

(a) an integral part of the attachment plug
(b) in the power-supply cable not more than 12 in. from the attachment plug
(c) a or b
(d) none of these

86. A disconnecting means that is identified shall be provided in the supply circuit for each arc welder not equipped with ______.

(a) a governor
(b) a shunt-trip device
(c) an integral disconnect
(d) GFCI protection

87. Each resistance welder shall have an overcurrent device rated or set at not more than ______ percent of the rated primary current of the welder.

(a) 80
(b) 100
(c) 125
(d) 300

88. A ______ shall be provided to disconnect each resistance welder and its control equipment from the supply circuit.

(a) switch
(b) circuit breaker
(c) magnetic starter
(d) a or b

89. Audio distribution cable not terminated at equipment and not identified for future use with a tag is considered abandoned.

(a) True
(b) False

90. The accessible portion of abandoned audio distribution cables shall be removed.

(a) True
(b) False

91. Audio system equipment supplied by branch-circuit power shall not be located within _____ of the inside wall of a pool, spa, hot tub, fountain, or tidal high-water mark.

(a) 18 in.
(b) 2 ft
(c) 5 ft
(d) 10 ft

92. Metal equipment racks and enclosures for permanent audio system installations shall be grounded.

(a) True
(b) False

93. Loudspeakers of permanent audio systems which are installed in fire-resistance-rated partitions, walls, or ceilings shall be listed for the purpose or installed in an enclosure or recess that _____.

(a) maintains the fire-resistance rating
(b) is no more than 4 in. deep
(c) is no more than 6 ft 6 in. high
(d) all of these

94. Branch-circuit conductors for data processing equipment in information technology equipment rooms shall have an ampacity not less than _____ of the total connected load.

(a) 80 percent
(b) 100 percent
(c) 125 percent
(d) the sum

95. Nonmetallic raceways can be installed within the raised floor area of an information technology equipment room.

(a) True
(b) False

96. Ventilation in the underfloor area of an information equipment room shall be used in that room only, unless provided with fire/smoke dampers at the point of penetration of the room boundary.

(a) True
(b) False

97. _____ conductor cables 4 AWG and marked for use in cable trays shall be permitted for equipment grounding within a raised floor of an information technology equipment room.

(a) Green
(b) Insulated
(c) Single
(d) all of these

98. The remote disconnect controls for the control of electronic equipment power and HVAC systems shall be grouped and identified. A single means to control both shall be permitted.

(a) True
(b) False

99. According to the NEC, sensitive electronic equipment is a separately derived system that operates at _____ volts-to-ground and _____ volts line-to-line.

(a) 30, 60
(b) 60, 120
(c) 120, 120
(d) 120, 240

100. Junction boxes used in sensitive electronic equipment systems shall be clearly marked to indicate _____.

(a) the system frequency
(b) the system voltage
(c) the distribution panel
(d) b and c

Practice Quiz 8

Random Order [200.6 through 640.4]

Unit 8 Practice Quiz— Random Order [200.6 through 640.4]

Please use the 2011 *Code* book to answer the following questions, which are based on the 2011 *NEC*.

1. The demand factor for marina load calculations of 45 shore power receptacles is ______ percent.

   (a) 40
   (b) 50
   (c) 60
   (d) 70

2. Electrical equipment used in hazardous (classified) locations that is designed for use in the ambient temperature range between ______ requires no ambient temperature marking. For equipment rated for a temperature range other than ______, the marking must specify the range of ambient temperatures in degrees Celsius.

   (a) -40°C and +40°C
   (b) –25°C and +40°C
   (c) -10°C and +20°C
   (d) -10°C and +30°C

3. Handhole enclosure covers shall require the use of tools to open, or they shall weigh over ______.

   (a) 45 lb
   (b) 70 lb
   (c) 100 lb
   (d) 200 lb

4. Which of the following is not standard size fuses or inverse time circuit breakers?

   (a) 45A
   (b) 70A
   (c) 75A
   (d) 80A

5. A sealing fitting shall be installed within ______ of either side of the boundary where a conduit leaves a Class I, Division 1 location.

   (a) 5 ft
   (b) 6 ft
   (c) 8 ft
   (d) 10 ft

6. GFCI protection is required for 15A, 20A, and 30A, 125V and 125V/250V receptacles that are part of a portable generator rated not greater than ______.

   (a) 5 kW
   (b) 7.50 kW
   (c) 10 kW
   (d) 15 kW

7. The required ampacity for the supply conductors for a resistance welder with a duty cycle of 15 percent and a primary current of 21A is ______.

   (a) 5.67A
   (b) 6.72A
   (c) 8.19A
   (d) 9.45A

8. If a protective device rating is marked on an appliance, the branch-circuit overcurrent device rating shall not exceed ______ percent of the protective device rating marked on the appliance.

   (a) 50
   (b) 80
   (c) 100
   (d) 115

9. The maximum unbalanced feeder load for household electric ranges, wall-mounted ovens, and counter-mounted cooking units shall be considered as ______ percent of the load on the ungrounded conductors.

   (a) 50
   (b) 70
   (c) 85
   (d) 115

10. The sum of the cross-sectional areas of all contained conductors at any cross-section of a metal wireway shall not exceed ______.

(a) 50 percent
(b) 20 percent
(c) 25 percent
(d) 80 percent

11. Article ______ contains the wiring requirements for service and repair operations in connection with self-propelled vehicles in which volatile flammable liquids or flammable gases are used for fuel or power.

(a) 500
(b) 501
(c) 511
(d) 514

12. What is the minimum size copper supply-side bonding jumper for a service raceway containing 4/0 THHN aluminum conductors?

(a) 6 AWG aluminum
(b) 4 AWG aluminum
(c) 4 AWG copper
(d) 3 AWG copper

13. Closet storage space is defined as a volume bounded by the sides and back closet walls extending from the closet floor vertically to a height of ______ or the highest clothes-hanging rod at a horizontal distance of 2 ft from the sides and back of the closet walls.

(a) 6 ft
(b) 7 ft
(c) 8 ft
(d) 9 ft

14. Liquidtight flexible metal conduit must be securely fastened by a means approved by the authority having jurisdiction within ______ of termination.

(a) 6 in.
(b) 10 in.
(c) 1 ft
(d) 10 ft

15. Noninsulated busbars shall have a minimum space of ______ between the bottom of a switchboard enclosure and busbars or other obstructions.

(a) 6 in.
(b) 8 in.
(c) 10 in.
(d) 12 in.

16. PVC conduit shall be securely fastened within ______ of each box.

(a) 6 in.
(b) 12 in.
(c) 24 in.
(d) 36 in.

17. Receptacle outlets in floors shall not be counted as part of the required number of receptacle outlets for dwelling unit wall spaces, unless they are located within ______ of the wall.

(a) 6 in.
(b) 12 in.
(c) 18 in.
(d) 24 in.

18. The conductors used to connect the surge protective device to ground shall not be any longer than ______ and shall avoid unnecessary bends

(a) 6 in.
(b) 12 in.
(c) 18 in.
(d) necessary

19. The minimum clearance between an electric space-heating cable and an outlet box used for surface luminaires shall not be less than ______.

(a) 6 in.
(b) 8 in.
(c) 14 in.
(d) 18 in.

20. The raceway or cable for tap conductors to recessed luminaires shall have a minimum length of ______

(a) 6 in.
(b) 12 in.
(c) 18 in.
(d) 24 in.

21. Type UF cable used with a 24V landscape lighting system can have a minimum cover of ______.

(a) 6 in.
(b) 12 in.
(c) 18 in.
(d) 24 in.

22. What is the minimum cover requirement for direct burial Type UF cable installed outdoors that supplies a 120V, 30A circuit?

(a) 6 in.
(b) 12 in.
(c) 18 in.
(d) 24 in.

23. When installing PVC conduit underground without concrete cover, there shall be a minimum of ______ of cover.

(a) 6 in.
(b) 12 in.
(c) 18 in.
(d) 22 in.

24. Where used outside, aluminum or copper-clad aluminum grounding electrode conductors shall not be terminated within ______ of the earth.

(a) 6 in.
(b) 12 in.
(c) 15 in.
(d) 18 in.

25. For each floor area inside a major repair garage where ventilation is not provided and flammable liquids having a flash point below 100°F are transferred, the entire area up to a level of ______ above the floor is considered to be a Class I, Division 2 location.

(a) 6 in.
(b) 12 in.
(c) 18 in.
(d) 24 in.

26. The overcurrent device for the main marina feeder conductors must have ground-fault protection not exceeding ______. If ground-fault protection is provided for each individual marina branch or feeder circuit, ground-fault protection is not required for the main marina feeder conductors.

(a) 6 mA
(b) 20 mA
(c) 30 mA
(d) 100 mA

27. THW insulation has a ______ rating when installed within electric-discharge lighting equipment, such as through fluorescent luminaires.

(a) 60°C
(b) 75°C
(c) 90°C
(d) 105°C

28. When bare conductors are installed with insulated conductors, their ampacities shall be limited to ______.

(a) 60°C
(b) 75°C
(c) 90°C
(d) the lowest temperature rating for any of the insulated conductors

29. Handhole enclosures shall be designed and installed to withstand ______.

(a) 600 lb
(b) 3,000 lb
(c) 6,000 lb
(d) all loads likely to be imposed

30. For phase converters serving variable loads, the ampacity of the single-phase supply conductors shall not be less than ______ percent of the single-phase input full-load amperes listed on the phase converter nameplate.

(a) 75
(b) 100
(c) 125
(d) 150

31. On fixed stage equipment, portable strip lights and connector strips shall be wired with conductors having insulation rated suitable for the temperature but not less than ______.

(a) 75°C
(b) 90°C
(c) 125°C
(d) 200°C

32. Where the supplemental electrode is a rod, that portion of the bonding jumper that is the sole connection to the supplemental grounding electrode shall not be required to be larger than ______ AWG copper.

(a) 8
(b) 6
(c) 4
(d) 1

33. Individual open conductors and cables, other than service-entrance cables, shall not be installed within ______ of grade level or where exposed to physical damage.

(a) 8 ft
(b) 10 ft
(c) 12 ft
(d) 15 ft

34. Type MC cable containing four or fewer conductors, sized no larger than 10 AWG, shall be secured within ______ of every box, cabinet, fitting, or other cable termination.

(a) 8 in.
(b) 12 in.
(c) 18 in.
(d) 24 in.

35. Cables installed in agricultural buildings shall be secured within ______ of each cabinet, box, or fitting.

(a) 8 in.
(b) 12 in.
(c) 18 in.
(d) 24 in.

36. The minimum size service-drop conductor permitted is ______ AWG copper or ______ AWG aluminum or copper-clad aluminum.

(a) 8, 8
(b) 8, 6
(c) 6, 8
(d) 6, 6

37. Conductors supplying several motors shall not be sized smaller than ______ percent of the full-load current rating of the highest rated motor, plus the sum of the full-load current ratings of all other motors in the group, plus the ampacity or other loads.

(a) 80
(b) 100
(c) 125
(d) 150

38. The disconnecting means for motor circuits rated 600 volts, nominal, or less shall have an ampere rating not less than ______ percent of the full-load current rating of the motor.

(a) 80
(b) 100
(c) 115
(d) 125

39. Conductors that supply one or more resistance welders shall be protected by an overcurrent device rated or set at not more than ______ percent of the conductor rating.

(a) 80
(b) 100
(c) 125
(d) 300

40. If the circuit's overcurrent device exceeds ______, the conductor ampacity must have a rating not less than the rating of the overcurrent device.

(a) 800A
(b) 1,000A
(c) 1,200A
(d) 2,000A

41. The maximum setting for ground-fault protection in a service disconnecting means is ______.

(a) 800A
(b) 1,000A
(c) 1,200A
(d) 2,000A

42. When service-entrance conductors exceed 1,100 kcmil for copper, the required grounded conductor for the service shall be sized not less than ______ percent of the circular mil area of the largest set of ungrounded service-entrance conductor(s).

(a) 9
(b) 11
(c) 12½
(d) 15

43. Panelboards supplied by a three-phase, 4-wire, delta-connected system shall have the phase with higher voltage-to-ground (high-leg) connected to the ______ phase.

(a) A
(b) B
(c) C
(d) any of these

44. The requirement for maintaining a 3 ft vertical clearance from the edge of the roof shall not apply to the final feeder conductor span where the conductors are attached to ______.

(a) a building pole
(b) the side of a building
(c) an antenna
(d) the base of a building

45. Where IMC enters a box, fitting, or other enclosure, ______ shall be provided to protect the wire from abrasion, unless the design of the box, fitting, or enclosure affords equivalent protection.

(a) a bushing
(b) duct seal
(c) electrical tape
(d) seal fittings

46. If grounded conductors of different voltage systems are installed in the same raceway, cable, or enclosure, each neutral conductor must be identified to distinguish the systems by ______.

(a) a continuous white or gray outer finish for one system
(b) a neutral conductor with a different continuous white or gray outer finish or white or gray with a stripe for one system
(c) other identification allowed by 200.6(a) or (B) that distinguishes each system from other systems.
(d) a, b, or c

47. Amplifiers, loudspeakers, and other equipment shall be located or protected so as to guard against environmental exposure or physical damage that might cause ______.

(a) a fire
(b) shock
(c) personal hazard
(d) all of these

48. Effective January 1, 2014, where a receptacle outlet is supplied by a branch circuit that requires arc-fault circuit-interrupter protection [210.12(A)], a replacement receptacle at this outlet shall be ______.

(a) a listed (receptacle) outlet branch circuit type arc-fault circuit-interrupter receptacle
(b) a receptacle protected by a listed (receptacle) outlet branch circuit type arc-fault circuit-interrupter type receptacle
(c) a receptacle protected by a listed combination type arc-fault circuit-interrupter type circuit breaker
(d) all of these

49. Where branch-circuit wiring in a dwelling unit is modified, replaced or extended in any of the areas specified in 210.12(A), the branch circuit must be protected by ______.

(a) a listed combination AFCI located at the origin of the branch circuit
(b) a listed outlet branch-circuit AFCI located at the first receptacle outlet of the existing branch circuit
(c) a GFCI circuit breaker or receptacle
(d) a or b

50. A manufactured wiring system is a system assembled by a manufacturer, which cannot be inspected at the building site without ______.

(a) a permit
(b) a manufacturer's representative present
(c) damage or destruction to the assembly
(d) an engineer's supervision

Practice Quiz

9

Straight Order [647.4 through 700.12]

Unit 9 Practice Quiz— Straight Order [647.4 through 700.12]

Please use the 2011 *Code* book to answer the following questions, which are based on the 2011 *NEC.*

1. The voltage drop on technical power systems for sensitive electronic equipment shall not exceed ______ percent for feeder and branch-circuit conductors combined.

   (a) 1.50
   (b) 2
   (c) 2.50
   (d) 3

2. Electric pipe organ circuits shall be arranged so that 26 AWG and 28 AWG conductors are protected from overcurrent by an overcurrent device rated not more than ______.

   (a) 2A
   (b) 4A
   (c) 6A
   (d) 8A

3. X-ray equipment mounted on a permanent base equipped with wheels for moving while completely assembled describes ______.

   (a) portable
   (b) mobile
   (c) movable
   (d) room

4. A disconnecting means for X-ray equipment shall have adequate capacity for at least ______ percent of the input required for the momentary rating of the equipment or ______ percent of the input required for the long-time rating of the equipment, whichever is greater.

   (a) 50, 100
   (b) 50, 125
   (c) 100, 100
   (d) 125, 125

5. The ampacity of supply branch-circuit conductors and the rating of the circuit overcurrent devices for X-ray equipment shall not be less than ______.

   (a) 50 percent of the momentary rating
   (b) 100 percent of the long-time rating
   (c) the larger of a or b
   (d) the smaller of a or b

6. Where overcurrent protection is provided as part of an industrial machine, the machine shall be marked ______.

   (a) Overcurrent Protection Provided At Machine Supply Terminals
   (b) This Unit Contains Overcurrent Protection
   (c) Fuses Or Circuit Breaker Enclosed
   (d) Overcurrent Protected

7. Permanently installed swimming pools include those constructed in the ground or partially in the ground, and all others capable of holding water in a depth greater than ______ in.

   (a) 36
   (b) 42
   (c) 48
   (d) 54

8. A wet-niche luminaire is intended to be installed in a ______.

   (a) transformer
   (b) forming shell
   (c) hydromassage bathtub
   (d) all of these

9. Insulated overhead utility service conductors that are cabled together with a bare messenger and operate at not over 750 volts-to-ground shall maintain a ______ clearance in any direction to the water level.

   (a) 14 ft
   (b) 16 ft
   (c) 20 ft
   (d) 22½ ft

10. Overhead network-powered broadband communications systems conductors shall be located no less than ______ from the water's edge of swimming and wading pools, or the base of diving structures.

(a) 10 ft
(b) 12 ft
(c) 18 ft
(d) none of these

11. Complete raceway systems of underground PVC can be located less than 5 ft from the inside wall of a pool when space limitations are encountered and shall be buried not less than ______ with at least 4 in. of concrete cover.

(a) 6 in.
(b) 10 in.
(c) 12 in.
(d) 18 in.

12. The maintenance disconnecting means required for swimming pool equipment shall be ______ and at least 5 ft from the water's edge, unless separated by a permanently installed barrier.

(a) readily accessible
(b) within sight of its equipment
(c) capable of being locked in the open position
(d) a and b

13. Outlets supplying pool pump motors connected to single-phase 120 volt through 240 volt branch circuits rated 15 or 20 amperes, whether by receptacle or by direct connection, shall be provided with ______ protection for personnel.

(a) AFCI
(b) GFCI
(c) a or b
(d) a and b

14. Grounding-type GFCI-protected receptacles of the single and locking type for motors related to the circulation and sanitation system of a pool can be located not less than ______ from the inside walls of the pool.

(a) 3 ft
(b) 6 ft
(c) 8 ft
(d) 12 ft

15. Switching devices shall be at least ______ ft horizontally from the inside walls of a pool unless the switch is listed as being acceptable for use within 5 ft.

(a) 3 ft
(b) 5 ft
(c) 10 ft
(d) 12 ft

16. A GFCI shall be installed in the branch circuit supplying luminaires operating at more than the low-voltage contact limit so there is no shock hazard during ______.

(a) construction
(b) pool pump motor maintenance
(c) relamping
(d) overload conditions

17. When PVC conduit extends from the pool light forming shell to a pool junction box, an 8 AWG ______ conductor shall be installed in the raceway.

(a) solid bare
(b) solid insulated
(c) stranded insulated
(d) b or c

18. Branch-circuit wiring on the supply side of enclosures and junction boxes for underwater luminaires shall be installed in ______.

(a) RMC or IMC
(b) LFNC and PVC conduit
(c) any wiring method
(d) a or b

19. The junction box connected to a conduit that extends to the forming shell of the luminaire that operates at over 15V shall be located not less than ______ above the ground level or pool deck.

(a) 4 in.
(b) 6 in.
(c) 8 in.
(d) 12 in.

20. Junction boxes for pool lighting shall be located not less than_____ from the inside wall of a pool unless separated by a fence or wall.

(a) 3 ft
(b) 4 ft
(c) 6 ft
(d) 8 ft

21. Junction boxes connected to conduits that extend directly to forming shells of swimming pool no-niche luminaires shall be provided with a number of grounding terminals that is at least _____ the number of conduit entries.

(a) one more than
(b) two more than
(c) the same as
(d) none of these

22. The feeder to a swimming pool panelboard at a separate building or structure can be supplied with any Chapter 3 wiring method provided the feeder has a separate insulated copper equipment grounding conductor.

(a) True
(b) False

23. The swimming pool structure, including the structural reinforcing steel of the pool shell and deck, except reinforcing steel encapsulated with a nonconductive compound shall be bonded.

(a) True
(b) False

24. Metal conduit and metal piping within _____ horizontally of the inside walls of the pool shall be bonded unless separated by a permanent barrier.

(a) 4 ft
(b) 5 ft
(c) 8 ft
(d) 10 ft

25. The electric motor and controller for an electrically operated pool cover shall be _____.

(a) GFCI protected
(b) AFCI protected
(c) a and b
(d) a or b

26. All 15A and 20A, 125V receptacles located within _____ of the inside walls of a storable pool shall be GFCI protected.

(a) 8 ft
(b) 10 ft
(c) 15 ft
(d) 20 ft

27. Listed packaged spa or hot tub equipment assemblies, or self-contained spas or hot tubs installed outdoors, are permitted to have flexible connections using _____.

(a) LFMC or LFNC in lengths of not more than 6 ft
(b) cords not longer than 15 ft, where GFCI protected
(c) a or b
(d) none of these

28. The equipotential bonding requirements for perimeter surfaces contained in 680.26(B)(2) don't apply to a listed self-contained spa or hot tub installed above a finished floor.

(a) True
(b) False

29. Receptacles rated 30A or less, 125V located within 10 ft of the inside walls of an indoor spa or hot tub, shall be _____.

(a) GFCI protected
(b) AFCI protected
(c) a or b
(d) none of these

30. Luminaires and ceiling fans located over or within 5 ft, measured horizontally, from the inside walls of an indoor spa or hot tub shall have a mounting height of not less than _____ above the maximum water level when GFCI protected.

(a) 4.70 ft
(b) 5 ft
(c) 7 ft 6 in.
(d) 12 ft

31. Metal raceways and metal piping within _____ of the inside walls of an indoor spa or hot tub, and not separated from the indoor spa or hot tub by a permanent barrier, shall be bonded.

(a) 4 ft
(b) 5 ft
(c) 7 ft
(d) 12 ft

32. The outlet(s) that supplies a ______ shall be GFCI protected except as otherwise provided in 680.44.
(a) self-contained spa or hot tub
(b) packaged spa or hot tub equipment assembly
(c) field-assembled spa or hot tub with a heater load of 50A or less
(d) all of these

33. Luminaires installed in fountains shall be ______.
(a) installed with the top of the luminaire lens below the normal water level
(b) listed for above-water use
(c) have the lens guarded or be listed for use without a guard
(d) any of these

34. Metal piping systems associated with a fountain shall be bonded to the equipment grounding conductor of the ______.
(a) branch circuit supplying the fountain
(b) bonding grid
(c) equipotential plane
(d) grounding electrode system

35. Each circuit supplying a sign within or adjacent to a fountain shall ______.
(a) have GFCI protection
(b) be capable of being locked in the open position
(c) operate at less than 15V
(d) be an intrinsically safe circuit

36. All 15A and 20A, single-phase, 125V through 250V receptacles located within ______ of a fountain edge shall have GFCI protection.
(a) 8 ft
(b) 10 ft
(c) 15 ft
(d) 20 ft

37. Hydromassage bathtubs and their associated electrical components shall be on an individual branch circuit and protected by a(n) ______ GFCI.
(a) exposed
(b) accessible
(c) readily accessible
(d) concealed

38. Metal piping systems and all grounded metal parts in contact with the circulating water of a hydromassage bathtub shall be bonded together using a(n) ______ solid copper bonding jumper not smaller than 8 AWG.
(a) insulated
(b) covered
(c) bare
(d) any of these

39. An alternating-current photovoltaic module is designed to generate ac power when exposed to______.
(a) electromagnetic induction
(b) heat
(c) sunlight
(d) hysteresis

40. A photovoltaic array that has two outputs, each having opposite polarity to a common reference point is known as ______.
(a) bipolar photovoltaic array
(b) polar photovoltaic array
(c) a or b
(d) neither a or b

41. ______ include photovoltaic cells, devices, modules, or modular materials that are integrated into the outer surface or structure of a building and serve as the outer protective surface of that building.
(a) Protective photovoltaics
(b) Building integrated photovoltaics
(c) Bipolar photovoltaic arrays
(d) Bipolar photoconductive arrays

42. For PV systems, a piece of equipment that regulates the charging process of a battery by diverting power from energy storage to direct-current or alternating-current loads or to an interconnected utility service is known as a(n) ______.
(a) alternating charge controller
(b) diversion charge controller
(c) direct charge controller
(d) alternating charge regulator

43. The conductors between the inverter and the battery in a stand-alone system or the conductors between the inverter and the photovoltaic output circuits for electrical production and distribution network are part of the ______.

(a) branch circuit
(b) feeder
(c) inverter input circuit
(d) inverter output circuit

44. A(n) ______ is a complete, environmentally protected unit consisting of solar cells, and other components, exclusive of tracker, designed to generate direct-current power when exposed to sunlight.

(a) interface
(b) battery
(c) module
(d) cell bank

45. For PV systems, a field-installable unit including a collection of modules mechanically fastened together and wired, is called a(n) ______.

(a) panel
(b) array
(c) bank
(d) gang

46. A single array or aggregate of arrays that generates direct-current power at system voltage and current is the photovoltaic ______.

(a) output source
(b) source circuit
(c) power source
(d) array source

47. For PV systems, the ______ is the total components and subsystems that, in combination, convert solar energy into electric energy suitable for connection to a utilization load.

(a) solar photovoltaic system
(b) solar array
(c) a and b
(d) neither a or b

48. A ______ is an electrical subset of a photovoltaic array.

(a) panel
(b) module
(c) circuit
(d) subarray

49. Photovoltaic systems are permitted to supply any building or other structure in addition to any other ______.

(a) electricity supply system
(b) telephone supply system
(c) plumbing supply system
(d) none of the above

50. PV system conductors shall be identified by separate color coding, marking tape, tagging, or other approved means.

(a) True
(b) False

51. The requirement for grouping PV source and output circuit is not required if the circuit enters from a cable or raceway unique to the circuit that makes the grouping obvious.

(a) True
(b) False

52. The connection to a ______ shall be arranged so that removal of either from a photovoltaic source circuit does not interrupt a grounded conductor to other PV source circuits.

(a) panelboard or switchboard
(b) bus or lug
(c) module or panel
(d) array or subarray

53. The location of PV source and output conductors imbedded in built-up, laminate, or membrane roofing materials in areas not covered by PV modules and associated equipment must be clearly marked.

(a) True
(b) False

54. Monopole subarrays in a bipolar photovoltaic system shall be physically _____ where the sum of the photovoltaic system voltages, without consideration of polarity of the two monopole subarrays, exceeds the rating of the conductors and connected equipment.

(a) separated
(b) connected
(c) joined
(d) together

55. Faulted circuits required to have ground-fault protection in a photovoltaic system shall be isolated by automatically disconnecting the _____, or, the inverter charge controller fed by the faulted circuits shall automatically stop supplying power to output circuits.

(a) ungrounded conductors
(b) grounded conductors
(c) equipment grounding conductors
(d) all of the above

56. The PV output circuit conductor of an ac module, which has a built-in dc to ac inverter, is considered an _____ output circuit as defined in 690.2.

(a) inverter
(b) module
(c) PV
(d) subarray

57. The _____ of a dc photovoltaic source circuit or output circuit, must be calculated as the sum of the rated open-circuit voltage of the series-connected photovoltaic modules multiplied by the correction factor provided in Table 690.7.

(a) minimum allowable ampacity of conductors
(b) maximum allowable ampacity of conductors
(c) minimum photovoltaic system voltage
(d) maximum photovoltaic system voltage

58. For one- and two-family dwellings, the maximum PV system voltage is _____V.

(a) 240
(b) 208
(c) 480
(d) 600

59. The maximum PV inverter output circuit current is equal to the _____ output current rating.

(a) average
(b) peak
(c) continuous
(d) intermittent

60. Overcurrent devices for PV systems shall be rated to carry not less than _____ percent of the maximum currents calculated in 690.8(A).

(a) 80
(b) 100
(c) 125
(d) 250

61. Overcurrent devices for PV source circuits must be readily accessible.

(a) True
(b) False

62. In photovoltaic source circuits, one overcurrent device is not permitted to protect the photovoltaic modules and the interconnecting conductors.

(a) True
(b) False

63. For stand-alone PV systems, circuit breakers that are marked line and load can be backfed.

(a) True
(b) False

64. A switch, circuit breaker, or other device is permitted to open the grounded dc conductor of PV circuit conductors.

(a) True
(b) False

65. A PV source circuit isolating switch is permitted on the PV side of the PV disconnecting means, but it's not required.

(a) True
(b) False

66. The PV system disconnecting means must be ______ to identify it as a photovoltaic system disconnect.

    (a) listed
    (b) approved
    (c) permanently marked
    (d) temporarily marked

67. Disconnecting means must be installed for PV output circuits where fuses that must be serviced can't be isolated from energized circuits. The disconnect must be within sight and accessible to the fuse or integral with the fuse holder, be externally operable without exposing the operator to contact with live parts, and plainly indicating whether in the open or closed position [690.17]. Where the disconnecting means is located more than ______ from the fuse, a directory showing the location of the fuse disconnect must be installed at the fuse location.

    (a) 3 ft
    (b) 6 ft
    (c) 10 ft
    (d) 12 ft

68. Disconnects used for PV systems (dc and ac) must be a manually operable switch or circuit breaker ______.

    (a) located where readily accessible
    (b) externally operable without exposing the operator to contact with live parts
    (c) plainly indicating whether in the open or closed position
    (d) all of these

69. ______ must be used to disable an array or sections of an PV array for installation and service.

    (a) Open circuiting
    (b) Short circuiting
    (c) Opaque covering
    (d) any of the above

70. Exposed PV source and output circuits operating at greater than ______ must be installed in a Chapter 3 wiring method anytime the conductors are installed in a(n) ______ location.

    (a) 30V, accessible
    (b) 30V, readily accessible
    (c) 60V, accessible
    (d) 60V, readily accessible

71. Wiring methods for PV systems conductors are not permitted within ______ of the roof decking or sheathing except where located directly below the roof surface that is covered by PV modules and associated equipment.

    (a) 6 in.
    (b) 10 in.
    (c) 12 in.
    (d) none of these

72. Which of the following that contain photovoltaic power source conductors must be marked with the wording "Photovoltaic Power Source" by means of permanently affixed labels or other approved permanent marking?

    (a) Exposed raceways, cable trays, and other wiring methods
    (b) The covers or enclosures of pull boxes and junction boxes
    (c) Conduit bodies in which any of the available conduit openings are unused
    (d) all of the above

73. Photovoltaic wiring methods containing ______ must be terminated only with terminals, lugs, devices, or connectors that are identified and listed for such use.

    (a) flexible, fine-stranded cables
    (b) solid conductors
    (c) flexible raceways
    (d) all of the above

74. The connectors permitted by Article 690 shall ______.

    (a) be polarized
    (b) guard against inadvertent contact with live parts by persons
    (c) require a tool for opening if the circuit operates at over 30V, nominal, maximum dc or 30V ac
    (d) all of these

75. A(n) ______ must be installed between a photovoltaic array and other equipment .

    (a) grounded conductor
    (b) main bonding jumper
    (c) equipment grounding conductor
    (d) system bonding jumper

76. For PV systems, metallic mounting structures used for grounding purposes must be ______ as equipment grounding conductors or have ______ bonding jumpers or devices connected between the separate metallic sections and be bonded to the grounding system.

(a) listed
(b) labeled
(c) identified
(d) a and b

77. Devices ______ for bonding the metallic frames of PV modules shall be permitted to bond the metallic frames of PV modules to the metallic frames of adjacent PV modules.

(a) listed
(b) labeled
(c) identified
(d) a and c

78. Equipment grounding conductors for PV circuits having overcurrent protection must be sized to the rating of the PV circuit overcurrent device in accordance with ______.

(a) 250.122
(b) 250.66
(c) Table 250.122
(d) Table 250.66

79. PV systems having no direct connection between the dc grounded conductor and ac grounded conductor shall have a(n) ______ which shall be bonded to the ac grounding system.

(a) ac grounding system
(b) dc grounding system
(c) separately derived grounding system
(d) none of the above

80. Where the removal of equipment opens the bonding connection between the ______ and exposed conducting surfaces in the PV source or output circuit equipment, a bonding jumper shall be installed while the equipment is removed.

(a) equipment grounding conductor
(b) grounded conductor
(c) grounding electrode conductor
(d) ungrounded conductor

81. A permanent label must be applied by the installer at the PV dc power source disconnect indicating the following:

(a) the rated maximum power-point current and voltage
(b) the maximum system voltage and short-circuit current
(c) the maximum rated output current of the charge controller (if installed)
(d) all of the above

82. Any building or structure with a stand-alone PV system not connected to a utility service source must have a permanent ______ installed on the exterior of the building or structure at a readily visible location acceptable to the authority having jurisdiction. The ______ must indicate the location of the stand-alone PV system disconnecting means and that the structure contains a stand-alone electrical power system.

(a) plaque
(b) directory
(c) a and b
(d) a or b

83. In dwellings, battery cells for PV systems must be series connected so as to operate at less than ______, nominal.

(a) 20V
(b) 30V
(c) 40V
(d) 50V

84. For PV systems, a listed current-limiting overcurrent device must be installed where the available short-circuit current from the battery bank exceeds the interrupting or ______ ratings of equipment it supplies.

(a) short-circuit
(b) withstand
(c) ground-fault current
(d) none of these

85. For PV systems, where flexible cables are installed, they are only permitted between the battery terminals to a nearby junction box where they must connect to an approved wiring method, or between batteries and cells within the battery enclosure.

(a) True
(b) False

86. A fuel cell is an electrochemical system that consumes _____ to produce an electric current.

(a) power
(b) water
(c) heat
(d) fuel

87. Phase converters shall be permitted to be used for fire pump service.

(a) True
(b) False

88. When a fire pump is supplied by an individual source, the _____ shall be selected to carry indefinitely the sum of the locked-rotor current of the fire pump motor(s), pressure maintenance pump motor(s), and full-load current of associated fire pump accessory equipment.

(a) overcurrent device(s)
(b) pump motor conductors
(c) a and b
(d) none of these

89. The primary overcurrent device for a transformer supplying a fire pump shall carry the sum of the locked-rotor current of the fire pump motor(s), pressure maintenance pump motor(s), and the full-load current of associated fire pump accessory equipment _____.

(a) for 15 minutes
(b) for 45 minutes
(c) for 3 hours
(d) indefinitely

90. Feeder conductors supplying fire pump motors and accessory equipment shall be sized no less than _____ percent of the sum of the motor full-load currents, plus 100 percent of the ampere rating of the fire pump accessory equipment.

(a) 100
(b) 125
(c) 250
(d) 600

91. Emergency systems are generally installed where artificial illumination is required for safe exiting and for panic control in buildings occupied by large numbers of persons, such as _____ and similar institutions.

(a) hotels
(b) theaters and sports arenas
(c) health care facilities
(d) all of these

92. Emergency power systems are those systems legally required and classed as emergency by a governmental agency having jurisdiction. These systems are intended to automatically supply illumination and/or power essential for _____.

(a) community activity
(b) safety to human life
(c) public recreation
(d) police and emergency services exclusively

93. Where batteries are used for _____ in auxiliary engines of emergency systems, the authority having jurisdiction shall require periodic maintenance.

(a) starting
(b) control or ignition
(c) a and b
(d) none of these

94. Means for testing all emergency lighting and power systems during maximum anticipated load conditions shall be provided.

(a) True
(b) False

95. Automatic transfer switches shall be _____.

(a) electrically operated
(b) mechanically held
(c) listed for emergency system use if rated 600V ac and below
(d) all of these

96. When practicable, audible and visual signal devices for an emergency system shall be provided to indicate _____.

(a) that the battery is carrying load
(b) derangement of the emergency source
(c) that the battery charger is not functioning
(d) all of these

97. Wiring from an emergency source or emergency source distribution overcurrent protection to emergency loads shall be kept independent of all other wiring and equipment except in ______.

(a) transfer equipment enclosures
(b) exit or emergency luminaires supplied from two sources
(c) load control relay supplying emergency or exit luminaires or a common junction box attached to exit or emergency luminaires supplied from two sources
(d) all of these

98. Emergency circuit wiring shall be designed and located to minimize the hazards that might cause failure because of ______.

(a) flooding
(b) fire
(c) icing
(d) all of these

99. Where an internal-combustion engine is used as the prime mover for an emergency system, an on-site fuel supply shall be provided for not less than ______ hours of full-demand operation of the system.

(a) 2
(b) 3
(c) 4
(d) 5

100. For an emergency system power generator installed outdoors, where conditions of maintenance and supervision ensure that only qualified persons will monitor and service the installation and where documented safe switching procedures are established and maintained for disconnection, the generator disconnecting means is not required to be located within sight of the building or structure served.

(a) True
(b) False

Practice Quiz 9

Random Order [100 through 690.49]

Unit 9 Practice Quiz— Random Order [100 though 690.49]

Please use the 2011 *Code* book to answer the following questions, which are based on the 2011 *NEC.*

1. Flexible cords immersed in or exposed to water in a fountain shall be ______.

(a) extra-hard usage type
(b) listed with a W suffix
(c) encased in not less than 2 in. of concrete
(d) a and b

2. In order to ______ NUCC, the conduit shall be trimmed away from the conductors or cables using an approved method that will not damage the conductor or cable insulation or jacket.

(a) facilitate installing
(b) enhance the appearance of the installation of
(c) terminate
(d) provide safety to the persons installing

3. A separate ______ shall supply the elevator hoistway pit lighting and receptacle(s). The required lighting shall not be connected to the load side of a ground-fault circuit interrupter.

(a) feeder
(b) subpanel
(c) emergency system
(d) branch circuit

4. Lampholders shall be constructed, installed, or equipped with shades or guards so that ______ isn't subjected to temperatures in excess of 90°C (194°F).

(a) ferrous material
(b) the shade or guard
(c) combustible material
(d) a or b

5. Which of the following metal parts shall be protected from corrosion?

(a) Ferrous metal raceways
(b) Ferrous metal elbows
(c) Ferrous boxes
(d) all of these

6. The cut ends of HDPE conduit shall be ______ to avoid rough edges.

(a) filed on the inside
(b) trimmed inside and outside
(c) cut only with a hacksaw
(d) all of these

7. Nonmetallic cable trays shall be made of ______ material.

(a) fire-resistant
(b) waterproof
(c) corrosive
(d) flame-retardant

8. Smooth-sheath Type MC cable with an external diameter not greater than ¾ in. shall have a bending radius not more than ______ times the cable external diameter.

(a) five
(b) 10
(c) 12
(d) 13

9. The radius of the curve of the inner edge of any bend, during or after installation, shall not be less than ______ times the diameter of Type USE or SE cable.

(a) five
(b) seven
(c) 10
(d) 12

10. The radius of the curve of the inner edge of any bend shall not be less than ______ for Type AC cable.

(a) five times the largest conductor within the cable
(b) three times the diameter of the cable
(c) five times the diameter of the cable
(d) six times the outside diameter of the conductors

11. The overall covering of Type UF cable is ______.

(a) flame retardant
(b) moisture, fungus, and corrosion resistant
(c) suitable for direct burial in the earth
(d) all of these

12. The metallic sheath of metal-clad cable shall be continuous and ______.

(a) flame-retardant
(b) weatherproof
(c) close fitting
(d) all of these

13. Portable luminaires shall be wired with ______ recognized by 400.4, and have an attachment plug of the polarized or grounding type.

(a) flexible cable
(b) flexible cord
(c) nonmetallic flexible cable
(d) nonmetallic flexible cord

14. There are four principal determinants of conductor operating temperature, one of which is ______ generated internally in the conductor as the result of load current flow, including fundamental and harmonic currents.

(a) friction
(b) magnetism
(c) heat
(d) none of these

15. Duty on escalator and moving walk driving machine motors shall be rated as ______.

(a) full time
(b) continuous
(c) various
(d) long term

16. Equipment shall be identified not only for the class of hazardous (classified) location, but also for the explosive, combustible, or ignitible properties of the specific ______ present.

(a) gas or vapor
(b) dust
(c) fibers/flyings
(d) all of these

17. In Class III locations, receptacles and attachment plugs shall be of the grounding type, shall be designed so as to minimize the accumulation or the entry of ______, and shall prevent the escape of sparks or molten particles.

(a) gases or vapors
(b) particles of combustion
(c) fibers/flyings
(d) none of these

18. Which of the following switches must indicate whether they are in the open (off) or closed (on) position?

(a) General-use switches
(b) Motor-circuit switches
(c) Circuit breakers
(d) all of these

19. Temporary wiring in exhibition halls for display booths in assembly occupancies is permitted to be in accordance with Article 590, except ______.

(a) GFCI-protection requirements of Article 590 are not required
(b) flexible cords and cables listed for hard or extra-hard usage cords can be laid on floors where protected from contact with the general public
(c) GFCI protection must be provided where required by the *NEC* except for the Article 590 requirements
(d) all of these

20. When the service disconnecting means is a power-operated switch or circuit breaker, it shall be able to be opened by hand in the event of a ______.

(a) ground fault
(b) short circuit
(c) power surge
(d) power supply failure

21. A switching device with a marked OFF position shall completely disconnect all ______ conductors of the load it controls.

(a) grounded
(b) ungrounded
(c) grounding
(d) all of these

22. Metal boxes shall be ______ in accordance with Article 250.

(a) grounded
(b) bonded
(c) a and b
(d) none of these

23. Receptacles and cord connectors having equipment grounding conductor contacts shall have those contacts connected to a(n) ______ conductor.

(a) grounded
(b) ungrounded
(c) equipment grounding
(d) neutral

24. When equipment grounding conductors are installed in panelboards, a ______ shall be secured inside the cabinet.

(a) grounded conductor
(b) terminal lug
(c) terminal bar
(d) none of these

25. Type SE cables shall be permitted to be used for branch circuits or feeders where the insulated conductors are used for circuit wiring and the uninsulated conductor is used only for ______ purposes.

(a) grounded connection
(b) equipment grounding
(c) remote control and signaling
(d) none of these

26. Metal raceways shall be bonded to the metal pole with a(n) ______.

(a) grounding electrode
(b) grounded conductor
(c) equipment grounding conductor
(d) any of these

27. The frame of a vehicle-mounted generator shall not be required to be connected to a(n) ______ if the generator only supplies equipment mounted on the vehicle or cord-and-plug connected equipment, using receptacles mounted on the vehicle.

(a) grounding electrode
(b) grounded conductor
(c) ungrounded conductor
(d) equipment grounding conductor

28. Where the removal of the utility-interactive inverter or other equipment disconnects the bonding connection between the grounding electrode conductor and the photovoltaic source and/or photovoltaic output circuit grounded conductor, a ______ shall be installed to maintain the system grounding while the inverter or other equipment is removed.

(a) grounding electrode conductor
(b) fuse
(c) bonding jumper
(d) overcurrent device

29. For pendants in an aircraft hangar, not installed in Class I locations, flexible cords suitable for the type of service and identified for ______ shall be used.

(a) hard usage
(b) extra-hard usage
(c) general duty
(d) a or b

30. The PV system disconnecting means shall be suitable for ______.

(a) heat
(b) cold
(c) rain
(d) the prevailing conditions

31. A warning label applied by the ______ must be on the PV utility-interactive inverter stating the following: WARNING ELECTRIC SHOCK HAZARD–IF A GROUND FAULT IS INDICATED, NORMALLY GROUNDED CONDUCTORS MAY BE UNGROUNDED AND ENERGIZED

(a) homeowner
(b) inspector
(c) installer
(d) power company

32. An atmosphere containing ignitible concentrations of ______ is classified as a Group C hazardous (classified) location.

(a) hydrogen
(b) ethylene
(c) gasoline
(d) all of these

33. In Class ______ locations for Groups A, B, C, and D, the classification involves determinations of maximum explosion pressure and maximum safe clearance between parts of a clamped joint in an enclosure.

(a) I
(b) II
(c) III
(d) all of these

34. Where raceway-type service masts are used, all raceway fittings shall be ______ for use with service masts.

(a) identified
(b) approved
(c) of a heavy-duty type
(d) listed

35. In Class I, Division 1 locations, all utilization equipment must be ______ for use in a Class I, Division 1 location.

(a) identified
(b) approved
(c) marked
(c) listed

36. All equipment intended for use in photovoltaic power systems shall be ______ for the application.

(a) identified
(b) listed
(c) approved
(d) a and b

37. Devices ______ for grounding the metallic frames of PV modules and other equipment can be used to bond the exposed metal surfaces of the modules and equipment to the mounting structures.

(a) identified
(b) approved
(c) listed
(d) a and c

38. Attachment plugs and receptacles in Class I locations of aircraft hangars shall be ______.

(a) identified for use in Class I locations
(b) designed so that they cannot be energized while the connections are being made or broken
(c) a or b
(d) none of these

39. Wireways can pass transversely through a wall ______.

(a) if the length passing through the wall is unbroken
(b) if the wall is of fire-rated construction
(c) in hazardous (classified) locations
(d) if the wall is not of fire-rated construction

40. The header on a cellular concrete floor raceway shall be installed ______ to the cells.

(a) in a straight line
(b) at right angles
(c) a and b
(d) none of these

41. Type UF cable shall not be used ______.

(a) in any hazardous (classified) location except as otherwise permitted in this Code
(b) embedded in poured cement, concrete, or aggregate
(c) where exposed to direct rays of the sun, unless identified as sunlight resistant
(d) all of these

42. Surface nonmetallic raceways shall be permitted ______.

(a) in dry locations
(b) where concealed
(c) in hoistways
(d) all of these

43. NUCC shall not be used ______.

(a) in exposed locations
(b) inside buildings
(c) in hazardous (classified) locations
(d) all of these

44. Where single conductor cables comprising each phase, neutral, or grounded conductor of a circuit are connected in parallel in a cable tray, the conductors shall be installed ______, to prevent current unbalance in the paralleled conductors due to inductive reactance.

(a) in groups consisting of not more than three conductors per phase or neutral
(b) in groups consisting of not more than one conductor per phase or neutral
(c) as individual conductors securely bound to the cable tray
(d) in separate groups

45. Receptacles in countertops and similar work surfaces in dwelling units shall not be installed ______.

(a) in the sides of cabinets
(b) in a face-up position
(c) on GFCI circuits
(d) on the kitchen small-appliance circuit

46. Constant-voltage generators, except ac generator exciters, shall be protected from overcurrent by ______ or other acceptable overcurrent protective means suitable for the conditions of use.

(a) inherent design
(b) circuit breakers
(c) fuses
(d) any of these

47. Type S fuses, fuseholders, and adapters shall be designed so that ______ would be difficult.

(a) installation
(b) tampering
(c) shunting
(d) b or c

48. Raceways shall be ______ between outlet, junction, or splicing points prior to the installation of conductors.

(a) installed complete
(b) tested for ground faults
(c) a minimum of 80 percent complete
(d) none of these

49. Type NM cable on a wall of an unfinished basement installed in a listed raceway shall have a(n) ______ installed at the point where the cable enters the raceway.

(a) insulating bushing or adapter
(b) sealing fitting
(c) bonding bushing
(d) junction box

50. Premises wiring includes ______ wiring from the service point or power source to the outlets.

(a) interior
(b) exterior
(c) underground
(d) all of these

Practice Quiz 10

Straight Order [700.15 through Chapter 9]

Unit 10 Practice Quiz— Straight Order [700.15 through Chapter 9]

Please use the 2011 *Code* book to answer the following questions, which are based on the 2011 *NEC.*

1. In emergency systems, only appliances and lamps required for emergency use, shall be supplied by ______.

   (a) emergency circuits
   (b) multiwire branch circuits
   (c) HID-rated circuit breakers
   (d) a and b

2. Emergency lighting systems shall be designed and installed so that the failure of any individual lighting element, such as the burning out of a lamp, will not leave in total darkness any space that requires emergency illumination.

   (a) True
   (b) False

3. Branch-circuit overcurrent devices in emergency circuits shall be accessible to ______ only.

   (a) the authority having jurisdiction
   (b) authorized persons
   (c) the general public
   (d) qualified persons

4. The alternate source for emergency systems shall have ground-fault protection of equipment.

   (a) True
   (b) False

5. Overcurrent devices for emergency power systems ______ all supply-side overcurrent devices.

   (a) shall be selectively coordinated with
   (b) can be selectively coordinated with
   (c) shall be the same amperage as
   (d) shall be a higher amperage than

6. A legally required standby system is intended to automatically supply power to ______ in the event of failure of the normal source.

   (a) those systems classed as emergency systems
   (b) selected loads
   (c) a and b
   (d) none of these

7. Legally required standby systems that are tested upon installation and found to be acceptable to the authority having jurisdiction shall not be required to undergo any future tests unless the equipment is modified.

   (a) True
   (b) False

8. A written record shall be kept of required tests and maintenance on legally required standby systems.

   (a) True
   (b) False

9. Transfer equipment for legally required systems, including automatic transfer switches, shall be ______.

   (a) automatic
   (b) identified for standby use
   (c) approved by the authority having jurisdiction
   (d) all of these

10. Automatic transfer switches on legally required standby systems shall be electrically operated and ______ held.

    (a) electrically
    (b) mechanically
    (c) gravity
    (d) any of these

11. A sign shall be placed at the service equipment indicating the ______ of on-site legally required standby power sources.

    (a) type
    (b) location
    (c) manufacturer
    (d) a and b

12. A generator set for a legally required standby system shall ______.
    (a) have means for automatically starting the prime mover
    (b) have 2 hours of fuel supply for full demand operation available on-site if the prime mover is an internal combustion engine
    (c) not be solely dependent on a public utility gas system unless acceptable to the AHJ
    (d) all of these

13. The alternate source for legally required standby systems shall not be required to have ground-fault protection of equipment.
    (a) True
    (b) False

14. Optional standby systems are typically installed to provide an alternate source of power for ______.
    (a) data processing and communication systems
    (b) emergency systems for health care facilities
    (c) emergency systems for hospitals
    (d) none of these

15. A transfer switch shall be required for all fixed or portable optional standby power systems for buildings or structures at which an electric utility is either the normal or standby source, unless permitted by an exception.
    (a) True
    (b) False

16. Audible and visual signal devices shall be provided on optional standby systems to indicate ______, where practicable.
    (a) derangement of the optional standby source
    (b) that the optional standby source is carrying load
    (c) that the battery charger is not functioning
    (d) a and b

17. Where a generator for an optional standby system is installed outdoors and equipped with a readily accessible disconnecting means located ______, an additional disconnecting means is not required where ungrounded conductors serve or pass through the building or structure.
    (a) inside the building or structure
    (b) within sight of the building or structure
    (c) inside the generator enclosure
    (d) a or c

18. For interconnected electric power production sources, a hybrid system is comprised of multiple power sources, such as ______, but not the utility power system.
    (a) photovoltaic
    (b) wind
    (c) micro-hydro generators
    (d) all of these

19. For interconnected electric power production sources, a hybrid system includes ______.
    (a) storage batteries
    (b) flywheel storage equipment
    (c) superconducting magnetic storage equipment
    (d) none of these

20. For interconnected electric power production sources, the circuit conductors from the inverter output terminals that supplies ac power to the utility powered electric system is known as the utility-interactive inverter output circuit.
    (a) True
    (b) False

21. For interconnected electric power production sources, a permanent ______, denoting all electric power sources on or in the premises, must be installed at a service equipment location and all interconnected electric power production sources.
    (a) label
    (b) plaque
    (c) directory
    (d) b or c

22. For interconnected electric power production sources, the sum of the ratings of all overcurrent devices connected to power production sources is permitted to exceed the rating of the service.
    (a) True
    (b) False

23. For interconnected electric power production sources, each utility-interactive inverter connection must terminate to a dedicated circuit breaker or fusible disconnect.
    (a) True
    (b) False

24. For interconnected electric power production sources, conductors from the ac inverter can backfeed dedicated circuit breakers that are not marked ______.

(a) line
(b) load
(c) a or b
(d) a and b

25. For interconnected electric power production sources, upon loss of utility source power, an electric power production source must be manually disconnected from all ungrounded conductors of the utility source and not reconnected until the utility source has been restored.

(a) True
(b) False

26. For circuits and equipment operating at less than 50V, conductors are not permitted to be smaller than ______ AWG copper.

(a) 18
(b) 16
(c) 14
(d) 12

27. Circuits and equipment operating at less than 50V shall have receptacles that are rated at not less than ______.

(a) 10A
(b) 15A
(c) 20A
(d) 30A

28. For circuits and equipment operating at less than 50V, cables shall be supported by the building structure in such a manner that the cable will not be damaged by normal building use.

(a) True
(b) False

29. Class 1, 2, and 3 circuits installed through fire-resistant-rated walls, partitions, floors, or ceilings must be firestopped to limit the possible spread of fire or products of combustion.

(a) True
(b) False

30. When a raceway is used for the support or protection of cables for remote-control, signaling, and power-limited circuits, a bushing to reduce the potential for abrasion must be placed at the location the cables enter the raceway.

(a) True
(b) False

31. Class 2 and Class 3 circuits installed ______ on the surface of ceilings and walls shall be supported by the building structure in such a manner that the cable will not be damaged by normal building use.

(a) exposed
(b) concealed
(c) hidden
(d) a and b

32. Accessible portions of abandoned Class 2 and Class 3 cables shall be removed.

(a) True
(b) False

33. Power-supply conductors and Class 1 circuit conductors can occupy the same cable, enclosure, or raceway ______.

(a) where both are functionally associated with the equipment powered
(b) where the circuits involved are not a mixture of ac and dc
(c) under no circumstances
(d) none of these

34. Equipment supplying Class 2 or Class 3 circuits shall be durably marked where plainly visible to indicate ______.

(a) each circuit that is a Class 2 or Class 3 circuit
(b) the circuit VA rating
(c) the size of conductors serving each circuit
(d) all of these

35. Conductors of Class 2 and Class 3 circuits shall not be placed in any enclosure, raceway, cable, or similar fittings with conductors of Class 1 or electric light or power conductors, unless ______.

(a) insulated for the maximum voltage present
(b) totally comprised of aluminum conductors
(c) separated by a barrier
(d) all of these

36. Raceways shall not be used as a means of support for Class 2 or Class 3 cables.

(a) True
(b) False

37. Class 2 and Class 3 riser cables listed as suitable for use in a vertical run in a shaft, or from floor to floor shall be Type(s) ______.

(a) CL2P and CL3P
(b) CL2R and CL3R
(c) CL2 and CL3
(d) PLTC

38. Type ITC cable is used for instrumentation and control circuits operating at ______.

(a) 150V or less and 5A or less
(b) 300V or less and 0.50A or less
(c) 480V or less and 10A or less
(d) over 600V

39. The conductors contained within Type ITC cable shall be rated 300V, and not smaller than ______ AWG nor larger than ______ AWG.

(a) 22, 12
(b) 18, 10
(c) 16, 8
(d) 14, 1/0

40. Bends in Type ITC cable shall be made ______.

(a) so as not to exceed 45 degrees
(b) so as not to damage the cable
(c) not less than five times the diameter of the cable
(d) using listed bending tools

41. Sprinkler piping shall be permitted to share a cable tray with fire alarm conductors, provided the conductors are supplied by a power limited source.

(a) True
(b) False

42. When a raceway is used for the support or protection of cables for fire alarm circuits, a bushing to reduce the potential for abrasion must be placed at the location the cables enter the raceway.

(a) True
(b) False

43. Accessible portions of abandoned fire alarm cable shall be removed.

(a) True
(b) False

44. Fire alarm circuits shall be identified at all terminal and junction locations in a manner that helps prevent unintentional signals on fire alarm system circuits during ______.

(a) installation
(b) testing and servicing
(c) renovations
(d) all of these

45. Overcurrent devices for nonpower-limited fire alarm circuits shall be located at the point where the conductor to be protected ______.

(a) terminates at the load
(b) is spliced to any other conductor
(c) receives its supply
(d) none of these

46. Conductors for nonpower-limited fire alarm circuits shall be ______.

(a) solid copper
(b) stranded copper
(c) copper or aluminum
(d) a or b

47. The power source for a power-limited fire alarm circuit can be supplied through a ground-fault circuit interrupter or an arc-fault circuit interrupter.

(a) True
(b) False

48. Fire alarm equipment supplying power-limited fire alarm circuits shall be durably marked where plainly visible to indicate each circuit that is ______.

(a) supplied by a nonpower-limited fire alarm circuit
(b) a power-limited fire alarm circuit
(c) a fire alarm circuit
(d) none of these

49. Audio system circuits using Class 2 or Class 3 wiring methods shall not be installed in the same cable or raceway with ______.

(a) other audio system circuits
(b) power-limited fire alarm conductors or cables
(c) a or b
(d) none of these

50. Power-limited fire alarm cable used in a ______ location shall be listed for use in ______ locations or have a moisture-impervious metal sheath.

(a) dry
(b) damp
(c) wet
(d) hazardous

51. Cables used in power-limited fire alarm systems shall have an insulation rating of not less than ______.

(a) 100V
(b) 300V
(c) 600V
(d) 1,000V

52. Nonconductive optical fiber cable is a factory assembly of one or more optical fibers with an overall covering and containing no electrically conductive materials.

(a) True
(b) False

53. Composite optical fiber cables contain optical fibers and ______.

(a) strength members
(b) vapor barriers
(c) current-carrying electrical conductors
(d) none of these

54. Nonconductive optical fiber cable contains no metallic members and no other ______ materials.

(a) electrically conductive
(b) inductive
(c) synthetic
(d) insulating

55. Access to electrical equipment shall not be denied by an accumulation of optical fiber cables that ______ removal of panels, including suspended-ceiling panels.

(a) prevents
(b) hinders
(c) blocks
(d) require

56. Exposed optical fiber cables shall be supported by the building structure using hardware including straps, staples, cable ties, hangers, or similar fittings designed and installed so as not to damage the cable.

(a) True
(b) False

57. Optical fiber cables are not required to be listed and marked where the length of the cable within the building, measured from its point of entrance, does not exceed ______ and the cable enters the building from the outside and is terminated in an enclosure.

(a) 25 ft
(b) 30 ft
(c) 50 ft
(d) 100 ft

58. Where exposed to contact with electric light or power conductors, the noncurrent-carrying metallic members of optical fiber cables entering buildings shall be ______.

(a) grounded as specified in 770.100 as close to the point of entrance as practicable
(b) interrupted as close to the point of entrance as practicable by an insulating joint or equivalent device
(c) a or b
(d) a and b

59. When optical fiber cable is installed in a Chapter 3 raceway, the raceway shall be installed in accordance with Chapter 3 requirements.

(a) True
(b) False

60. Conductive optical fiber cables can occupy the same cable tray or raceway with conductors for electric light, power, and Class 1 circuits.

(a) True
(b) False

61. Types ______ nonconductive and conductive general-purpose optical fiber cables shall be listed as being suitable for general-purpose use, with the exception of risers and plenums, and shall also be listed as being resistant to the spread of fire.

(a) OFNP and OFCP
(b) OFNR and OFCR
(c) OFNG and OFCG
(d) OFN and OFC

62. Communications circuits are circuits that extend ______ and outside wiring for fire alarms and burglar alarms from the communications utility to the customer's communications equipment up to and including equipment such as a telephone, fax machine, or answering machine.

(a) voice
(b) audio and video
(c) interactive services
(d) all of these

63. The circuit that extends voice, audio, video, interactive services, telegraph (except radio), and outside wiring for fire alarm and burglar alarm from the communications utility to the customer's communications equipment up to and including equipment such as a telephone, fax machine or answering machine defines ______.

(a) limited-energy circuit
(b) remote-signaling circuit
(c) power-limited circuit
(d) communications circuit

64. A communications circuit that is in such a position that, in case of failure of supports or ______, contact with another circuit may result, and is considered to be exposed to accidental contact.

(a) insulation
(b) shield
(c) fittings
(d) grounding conductor

65. Equipment intended to be permanently electrically connected to a communications network shall be listed.

(a) True
(b) False

66. Communications cables installed ______ on the surface of ceilings and walls shall be supported by the building structure in such a manner that the cable will not be damaged by normal building use.

(a) exposed
(b) concealed
(c) hidden
(d) a and b

67. Accessible portions of abandoned communications cable shall be removed.

(a) True
(b) False

68. Where overhead communications cables enter buildings, they shall ______.

(a) be located below the electric light or power conductors, where practicable
(b) not be attached to a cross-arm that carries electric light or power conductors
(c) have a vertical clearance of not less than 8 ft from all points of roofs above which they pass
(d) all of these

69. In one- and two-family dwellings, the primary protector bonding conductor or grounding electrode conductor for communications systems shall be as short as practicable, not to exceed ______ in length.

(a) 5 ft
(b) 8 ft
(c) 10 ft
(d) 20 ft

70. Limiting the length of the primary protector grounding conductors for communications circuits helps to reduce voltage between the building's ______ and communications systems during lightning events.

(a) power
(b) fire alarm
(c) lighting
(d) lightning protection

71. Communications grounding electrodes must be bonded to the power grounding electrode system at the building or structure served using a minimum ______ copper bonding jumper.

(a) 10 AWG
(b) 8 AWG
(c) 6 AWG
(d) 4 AWG

72. Communications cables installed in buildings shall be listed except for up to 50 ft past the point of entry as allowed by 800.48.

(a) True
(b) False

73. Communications ______ cables shall be listed as being suitable for use in a vertical run in a shaft, or from floor to floor, and shall also be listed as having fire-resistant characteristics capable of preventing the carrying of fire from floor to floor.

(a) plenum
(b) riser
(c) general-purpose
(d) none of these

74. Soft-drawn or medium-drawn copper lead-in conductors for receiving antenna systems shall be permitted where the maximum span between points of support is less than ______.

(a) 10 ft
(b) 20 ft
(c) 30 ft
(d) 35 ft

75. A receiving station outdoor wire-strung antenna conductor with a span of 75 ft shall be at least ______ if a copper-clad steel conductor is used.

(a) 17 AWG
(b) 14 AWG
(c) 12 AWG
(d) 10 AWG

76. Underground antenna conductors for radio and television receiving equipment shall be separated at least ______ from any light, power, or Class 1 circuit conductors.

(a) 12 in.
(b) 18 in.
(c) 5 ft
(d) 6 ft

77. Antenna discharge units shall be located outside the building only.

(a) True
(b) False

78. Radio and television receiving antenna systems must have bonding or grounding electrode conductors that ______.

(a) are copper or other corrosion-resistant conductive material
(b) are insulated, covered, or bare
(c) are securely fastened in place and mechanically protected where subject to physical damage
(d) all of these

79. The bonding conductor or grounding electrode conductor for an antenna mast or antenna discharge unit shall be run to the grounding electrode in as straight a line as practicable.

(a) True
(b) False

80. The grounding conductor for an antenna mast or antenna discharge unit, if copper, shall not be smaller than 10 AWG.

(a) True
(b) False

81. Article _____ covers the installation of coaxial cables for distributing radio frequency signals typically employed in community antenna television (CATV) systems.

(a) 300
(b) 430
(c) 800
(d) 820

82. Coaxial cable is a cylindrical assembly composed of a conductor centered inside a metallic tube or shield, separated by _____ material and usually covered by an insulating jacket.

(a) insulating
(b) conductive
(c) isolating
(d) dielectric

83. CATV coaxial cable can deliver power to equipment that is directly associated with the radio frequency distribution system if voltage is not over _____ volts and if the current supply is from a transformer or other power-limiting device.

(a) 60
(b) 120
(c) 180
(d) 270

84. CATV coaxial cables installed _____ on the surface of ceilings and walls shall be supported by the building structure in such a manner that the cables will not be damaged by normal building use.

(a) exposed
(b) concealed
(c) hidden
(d) a and b

85. Overhead coaxial cables for a CATV system shall be separated by at least _____ from lightning conductors, where practicable.

(a) 3 in.
(b) 6 in.
(c) 2 ft
(d) 6 ft

86. The outer conductive shield of a CATV coaxial cable entering a building shall be grounded as close to the point of entrance as practicable.

(a) True
(b) False

87. In one- and two-family dwellings, the grounding conductor for CATV shall be as short as practicable, not to exceed _____ in length.

(a) 5 ft
(b) 8 ft
(c) 10 ft
(d) 20 ft

88. Limiting the length of the primary protector grounding conductors for community antenna television and radio systems reduces voltages that may develop between the building's _____ and communications systems during lightning events.

(a) power
(b) fire alarm
(c) lighting
(d) lightning protection

89. Coaxial cables can be installed in listed communications raceways. If coaxial cables are installed in a listed communications nonmetallic raceway, the raceway must be installed in accordance with 362.24 through 362.56 where the requirements applicable to ENT apply.

(a) True
(b) False

90. Coaxial cables installed in buildings for CATV shall be listed except for the first 50 ft that enters a building in compliance with 820.48.

(a) True
(b) False

91. Coaxial cables used for CATV systems shall not be strapped, taped, or attached by any means to the exterior of any _____ as a means of support.

(a) conduit
(b) raceway
(c) raceway-type mast intended for overhead spans of such cables
(d) a or b

92. Type _____ coaxial cables for community antenna television systems shall be listed as suitable of being installed in vertical runs in a shaft, with fire-resistant characteristics capable of preventing the carrying of fire from floor to floor.

(a) CATV
(b) CATVX
(c) CATVR
(d) any of these

93. Network-powered broadband communications cables installed _____ on the surface of ceilings and walls shall be supported by the structural components of the building in such a manner that the network-powered broadband communications cables will not be damaged by normal building use.

(a) exposed
(b) concealed
(c) hidden
(d) a and b

94. Where network-powered broadband communications system aerial cables are installed outside and entering buildings, they shall _____.

(a) be located below the electric light or power conductors, where practicable
(b) not be attached to a cross-arm that carries electric light or power conductors
(c) have a vertical clearance of not less than 8 ft from all points of roofs above which they pass
(d) all of these

95. In one- and two-family and multifamily dwellings, the bonding conductor and grounding electrode conductor for network-powered broadband communications systems shall be as short as practicable, not to exceed _____ in length.

(a) 5 ft
(b) 6 ft
(c) 10 ft
(d) 20 ft

96. In network-powered broadband communications systems, all separate electrodes shall be bonded together using a minimum _____ copper bonding jumper.

(a) 10 AWG
(b) 8 AWG
(c) 6 AWG
(d) 4 AWG

97. When calculating raceway conductor fill, equipment grounding conductors shall _____.

(a) not be required to be counted
(b) have the actual dimensions used
(c) not be counted if in a nipple
(d) not be counted if for a wye three-phase balanced load

98. When the calculated number of conductors, all of the same size, installed in a conduit or in tubing includes a decimal, the next higher whole number shall be used when this decimal is _____ or larger.

(a) 0.40
(b) 0.60
(c) 0.70
(d) 0.80

99. The inside diameter of trade size 1 IMC is _____.

(a) 0.314 in.
(b) 0.826 in.
(c) 1.000 in.
(d) 1.105 in.

100. A trade size 1½ RMC nipple containing three conductors can be filled to an area of _____.

(a) 0.882 sq in.
(b) 1.072 sq in.
(c) 1.243 sq in.
(d) 1.343 sq in.

Practice Quiz 10

Random Order [220.82 through Chapter 9]

Unit 10 Practice Quiz—Random Order [220.82 through Chapter 9]

Please use the 2011 *Code* book to answer the following questions, which are based on the 2011 *NEC.*

1. Unlisted conductive and nonconductive outside plant optical fiber cables shall be permitted to be installed in locations other than risers, ducts used for environmental air, plenums used for environmental air, and other spaces used for environmental air , where the length of the cable within the building, measured from its point of entrance, does not exceed _____ ft and the cable enters the building from the outside and is terminated in an enclosure.

   (a) 25
   (b) 50
   (c) 75
   (d) 100

2. Outside plant communications cables shall not be required to be listed where the length of the cable within the building, measured from its point of entrance, does not exceed_____ and the cable enters the building from the outside and is terminated in an enclosure or on a listed primary protector.

   (a) 25 ft
   (b) 30 ft
   (c) 50 ft
   (d) 100 ft

3. Community antenna television and radio system coaxial cables shall not be required to be listed and marked where the length of the cable within the building, measured from its point of entrance, does not exceed _____, the cable enters the building from the outside and the cable is terminated at a grounding block.

   (a) 25 ft
   (b) 30 ft
   (c) 50 ft
   (d) 100 ft

4. Where no overcurrent protection is provided for the PV dc circuit, an assumed overcurrent device rated at the PV circuit short-circuit current is used to size the equipment grounding conductor in accordance with _____.

   (a) 250.122
   (b) 250.66
   (c) Table 250.122
   (d) Table 250.66

5. For an outline lighting system, the equipment grounding conductor size shall be in accordance with _____, based on the rating of the overcurrent device protecting the conductors supplying the sign.

   (a) 250.66
   (b) 250.122
   (c) 310.13
   (d) 310.16

6. Type MC cable installed horizontally through wooden or metal framing members are considered secured and supported where such support doesn't exceed _____ intervals.

   (a) 3 ft
   (b) 4 ft
   (c) 6 ft
   (d) 8 ft

7. Type MI cable shall be supported and secured at intervals not exceeding _____.

   (a) 3 ft
   (b) 3½ ft
   (c) 5 ft
   (d) 6 ft

8. Unless an individual switch is provided for each luminaire located over combustible material, lampholders shall be located at least _____ above the floor, or shall be located or guarded so that the lamps cannot be readily removed or damaged.

   (a) 3 ft
   (b) 6 ft
   (c) 8 ft
   (d) 10 ft

9. When Type AC cable is run across the top of a floor joist in an attic without permanent ladders or stairs, substantial guard strips within _____ of the scuttle hole, or attic entrance, shall protect the cable.

(a) 3 ft
(b) 4 ft
(c) 5 ft
(d) 6 ft

10. Overhead wiring outside of tents and concession areas of carnivals and circuses which are accessible to pedestrians shall maintain a vertical clearance of _____ above finished grade, sidewalks, or from platforms, projections, or surfaces from which the wiring might be reached.

(a) 3 ft
(b) 6 ft
(c) 8 ft
(d) 10 ft

11. Listed flexible metal conduit or listed liquidtight flexible metal conduit for secondary circuit conductors for neon tubing can be used as a bonding means if the total accumulative length of the conduit does not exceed _____.

(a) 3 ft
(b) 10 ft
(c) 50 ft
(d) 100 ft

12. Luminaires installed above the pool or the area extending _____ horizontally from the inside walls of the pool shall be installed at a height not less than 12 ft above the maximum water level of the pool.

(a) 3 ft
(b) 5 ft
(c) 10 ft
(d) 12 ft

13. In clothes closets, recessed incandescent or LED luminaires with a completely enclosed light source can be installed in the wall or the ceiling, provided there is a minimum clearance of _____ between the luminaire and the nearest point of a storage space.

(a) 3 in.
(b) 6 in.
(c) 9 in.
(d) 12 in.

14. Type FCC cable consists of _____ copper conductors placed edge-to-edge, separated and enclosed within an insulating assembly.

(a) three or more square
(b) two or more round
(c) three or more flat
(d) two or more flat

15. The maximum trade size FMT is _____.

(a) ⅜
(b) ½
(c) ¾
(d) 1

16. The permitted raceway fill for two conductors is _____ percent.

(a) 30
(b) 31
(c) 40
(d) 53

17. Panelboards equipped with snap switches rated at 30A or less shall have overcurrent protection not exceeding _____.

(a) 30A
(b) 50A
(c) 100A
(d) 200A

18. The overcurrent device ratings in photovoltaic systems operated at temperatures greater than _____, shall comply with the manufacturer's temperature correction factors.

(a) 32 degrees C
(b) 40 degrees C
(c) 32 degrees F
(d) 40 degrees F

19. For listed explosionproof equipment, factory threaded entries shall be made up with at least _____ threads fully engaged.

(a) 4
(b) 4½
(c) 5
(d) 6

20. No parts of cord-connected luminaires, chain-, cable-, or cord-suspended luminaires, lighting track, pendants, or paddle fans shall be located within a zone measured 3 ft horizontally and ______ vertically from the top of the bathtub rim or shower stall threshold.

(a) 4 ft
(b) 6 ft
(c) 8 ft
(d) 10 ft

21. Where run vertically, nonmetallic wireways shall be securely supported at intervals not exceeding ______, unless listed otherwise, with no more than one joint between supports.

(a) 4 ft
(b) 6 ft
(c) 8 ft
(d) 10 ft

22. When supplying a room air conditioner rated 120V, the length of a flexible supply cord shall not exceed ______.

(a) 4 ft
(b) 6 ft
(c) 8 ft
(d) 10 ft

23. Under the optional method for calculating a single-family dwelling service, general loads beyond the initial 10 kVA are assessed at a ______ percent demand factor.

(a) 40
(b) 50
(c) 60
(d) 75

24. Where six current-carrying conductors are run in the same conduit or cable, the ampacity of each conductor shall be adjusted by a factor of ______ percent.

(a) 40
(b) 60
(c) 80
(d) 90

25. When a fire pump motor operates at 115 percent of its full-load current rating, the supply voltage at the motor terminals shall not drop more than ______ percent below the voltage rating of the motor.

(a) 5
(b) 10
(c) 15
(d) any of these

26. In the event of failure of the normal supply to the building/structure, emergency power shall be available within ______ seconds.

(a) 5
(b) 10
(c) 30
(d) 60

27. A portable electric sign shall not be placed in or within ______ from the inside walls of a fountain.

(a) 5 ft
(b) 10 ft
(c) 15 ft
(d) 20 ft

28. Markings of PV system raceways and enclosures must be suitable for the environment and be placed with a maximum of ______ of spacing.

(a) 5 ft
(b) 10 ft
(c) 20 ft
(d) none of these

29. In one- and two-family dwellings where it is not practicable to achieve an overall maximum primary protector grounding conductor length of 20 ft, a separate ground rod not less than ______ shall be driven and it shall be connected to the power grounding electrode system with a 6 AWG conductor.

(a) 5 ft
(b) 8 ft
(c) 10 ft
(d) 20 ft

30. A separation of at least ______ shall be maintained between communications wires and cables on buildings and lightning conductors, where practicable.

(a) 6 ft
(b) 8 ft
(c) 10 ft
(d) 12 ft

31. Complete raceway systems of underground PVC can be located less than 5 ft from the inside wall of a pool when space limitations are encountered and shall be buried not less than ______ if not covered with concrete.

(a) 6 in.
(b) 10 in.
(c) 12 in.
(d) 18 in.

32. Wet-niche luminaires shall be installed with the top of the luminaire lens not less than ______ below the normal water level of the pool.

(a) 6 in.
(b) 12 in.
(c) 18 in.
(d) 24 in.

33. Where the conductors of more than one PV system occupy the same junction box or raceway with removable cover(s), the ac and dc conductors of each system shall be grouped separately by wire ties or similar means at least once, and then shall be grouped at intervals not to exceed ______.

(a) 6 in.
(b) 12 in.
(c) 36 in.
(d) 6 ft

34. The circular mil area of a 12 AWG conductor is ______.

(a) 6,100
(b) 6,530
(c) 10,380
(d) 26,240

35. Article ______ contains the installation requirements for the wiring of television and radio receiving equipment, such as digital satellite receiving equipment for television signals and amateur/citizen band radio equipment antennas.

(a) 680
(b) 700
(c) 810
(d) 840

36. The PV output circuit current is equal to the sum of parallel PV source circuit maximum currents as calculated in ______.

(a) 690.8(A)(1)
(b) 690.8(A)(2)
(c) 690.8(A)(3)
(d) none of the above

37. Article ______ covers the installation of electric power production sources operating in parallel with a primary source(s) of electricity.

(a) 700
(b) 701
(c) 702
(d) 705

38. For nonpower-limited fire alarm circuits, an 18 AWG conductor shall be considered protected if the overcurrent device protecting the circuit is not over ______.

(a) 7A
(b) 10A
(c) 15A
(d) 20A

39. The ______ pool bonding conductor shall be connected to the equipotential bonding grid either by exothermic welding or by pressure connectors in accordance with 250.8.

(a) 8 AWG
(b) insulated or bare
(c) copper
(d) all of these

40. An emergency system shall have adequate capacity and rating for ______ to be operated simultaneously.

(a) 80% of the loads
(b) all loads
(c) 125% of the load
(d) none of these

41. The power source for a Class 2 circuit shall be _____.
(a) a listed Class 2 transformer
(b) a listed Class 2 power supply
(c) other listed equipment marked to identify the Class 2 power source
(d) any of these

42. Joints between lengths of ENT, couplings, fittings, and boxes shall be made by _____.
(a) a qualified person
(b) set screw fittings
(c) an approved method
(d) exothermic welding

43. PV systems with dc modules having no direct connection between the dc grounded conductor and ac grounded conductor must be bonded to the ac grounding system by _____.
(a) a separate dc grounding electrode bonded to the ac grounding electrode system with a bonding jumper
(b) a dc grounding electrode conductor sized to 250.166 run from the marked dc grounding electrode connection point to the ac grounding electrode
(c) an unspliced, or irreversibly spliced, combined grounding conductor run from the marked dc grounding electrode connection point along with the ac circuit conductors to the grounding busbar in the associated ac equipment_
(d) a, b, or c

44. Reliable sources of power for a fire pump are considered to include _____.
(a) a separate service or a connection located ahead of but not within the service disconnecting means
(b) an on-site power supply, such as a generator, located and protected to minimize damage by fire
(c) a dedicated feeder derived from a service connection
(d) all of these

45. For information technology equipment, supply circuits and interconnecting cables not terminated to equipment and not identified for future use with a tag are considered to be _____
(a) abandoned
(b) unused
(c) future use
(d) none of these

46. Locations where flammable liquids having a flash point _____, such as gasoline, will not be handled and can be unclassified.
(a) above 100°F
(b) below 100°F
(c) 100°F
(d) none of these

47. In Class I, Division 1 locations, all apparatus and equipment of signaling, alarm, remote-control, and communications systems _____ shall be identified for Class I, Division 1 locations.
(a) above 50V
(b) above 100 volts-to-ground
(c) regardless of voltage
(d) except under 24V

48. Totally enclosed motors shall have no external surface with an operating temperature that exceeds _____ when operating in Class I, Division 1 locations.
(a) absolute zero
(b) 80 percent of ignition temperature of the gas or liquid involved
(c) 100°C
(d) 40°C

49. Type _____ cable is a wiring method that encloses two or more insulated conductors within a nonmetallic jacket.
(a) AC
(b) MC
(c) NM
(d) b and c

50. The location of the disconnecting means for an elevator shall be _____ to qualified persons.
(a) accessible
(b) readily accessible
(c) disclosed only
(d) accessible only with a key

Notes

CHALLENGE QUIZ 1

Article 90 through Chapter 9

Challenge Quiz 1— Article 90 through Chapter 9

Please use the 2011 *Code* book to answer the following questions, which are based on the 2011 *NEC*.

1. ______ can be used to fasten boxes to structural members of a building using brackets on the outside of the enclosure.

   (a) Nails
   (b) Screws
   (c) Bolts
   (d) a and b

2. ______ clips identified for use with the type of ceiling-framing member(s) and luminaires shall be permitted to be used to secure luminaires to the ceiling-framing members.

   (a) Marked
   (b) Labeled
   (c) Identified
   (d) listed

3. ______ equipment excludes dust and doesn't permit arcs, sparks, or heat inside the enclosure to ignite accumulations or atmospheric suspensions of a specified dust on or in the vicinity outside of the enclosure.

   (a) Dust-ignitionproof
   (b) Dusttight
   (c) a or b
   (d) a and

4. ______ identified for use on lighting track shall be designed specifically for the track on which they are to be installed.

   (a) Fittings
   (b) Receptacles
   (c) Devices
   (d) all of these

5. ______ in other than dwelling units must be legibly field-marked with the maximum available fault current, including the date the fault current calculation was performed and be of sufficient durability to withstand the environment involved.

   (a) Service equipment
   (b) Subpanels
   (c) Motor control centers
   (d) all of these

6. ______ is a nonferrous, nonmagnetic metal that has no heating due to hysteresis heating.

   (a) Steel
   (b) Iron
   (c) Aluminum
   (d) all of these

7. ______ is a raceway of circular cross section made of a helically wound, formed, interlocked metal strip.

   (a) Type MC cable
   (b) Type AC Cable
   (c) LFMC
   (d) FMC

8. ______ shall be installed so that the wiring contained can be rendered accessible without removing any part of the building or, in underground circuits, without excavating sidewalks, paving, or earth.

   (a) Boxes
   (b) Conduit bodies
   (c) Handhole enclosures
   (d) all of these

9. ______ shall not be located over the steps of a stairway.

   (a) Disconnect switches
   (b) Overcurrent devices
   (c) Knife switches
   (d) Transformers

10. "______" means acceptable to the authority having jurisdiction.

(a) Identified
(b) Listed
(c) Approved
(d) Labeled

11. "Nonautomatic" is defined as requiring ______ to perform a function.

(a) protection from damage
(b) human intervention
(c) mechanical linkage
(d) all of these

12. 20A, 125V receptacles subject to ______ can have an enclosure that is weatherproof when the attachment plug is removed.

(a) shower spray
(b) beating rain
(c) corrosive conditions
(d) routine high-pressure spray

13. A ______ is a device, or group of devices that governs, in some predetermined manner, the electric power delivered to the apparatus to which it is connected.

(a) relay
(b) breaker
(c) transformer
(d) controller

14. A ______ is an area that includes a basin with a toilet, urinal, tub, shower, bidet, or similar plumbing fixtures.

(a) bath area
(b) bathroom
(c) rest area
(d) none of these

15. A ______ is an enclosed assembly that can include receptacles, circuit breakers, fused switches, fuses, watt-hour meter(s), distribution panelboards and monitoring means approved for marine use.

(a) marine power receptacle
(b) marine outlet
(c) marine power outlet
(d) any of these

16. A ______ is the location of an inpatient sleeping bed; or the bed or procedure table used in a critical care area.

(a) patient bed location
(b) patient care area
(c) a or b
(d) none of these

17. A ______ location may be temporarily subject to dampness and wetness.

(a) dry
(b) damp
(c) moist
(d) wet

18. A ______ must be used to serve as the required shore power receptacle disconnecting means and it must be identified as to which receptacle it controls.

(a) circuit breaker
(b) switch
(c) a and b
(d) a or b

19. A ______ subarray has two conductors in the output circuit, one positive (+) and one negative (-). Two of these subarrays are used to form a bipolar photovoltaic array.

(a) bipolar
(b) monopole
(c) double-pole
(d) module

20. A 10 AWG single strand (solid) copper conductor has a cross-sectional area of ______.

(a) 0.008 sq in.
(b) 0.012 sq in.
(c) 0.101 sq in.
(d) 0.106 sq in.

21. A 10 AWG stranded copper conductor has a cross-sectional area of ______.

(a) 0.007 sq in.
(b) 0.011 sq in.
(c) 0.012 sq in.
(d) 0.106 sq in.

22. A 250 kcmil bare conductor has a diameter of ______.
(a) 0.557 in.
(b) 0.575 in.
(c) 0.690 in.
(d) 0.755 in.

23. A 3-conductor SJE cable (one conductor is used for grounding) has a maximum ampacity of ______ for each 16 AWG conductor.
(a) 9A
(b) 11A
(c) 13A
(d) 15A

24. A battery system includes storage batteries, battery chargers, and can include inverters, converters, and associated electrical equipment.
(a) True
(b) False

25. A blocking ______ is used to block reverse current flow into a PV source circuit.
(a) resistor
(b) potentiometer
(c) diode
(d) all of the above

26. A bonding jumper not smaller than ______ copper or equivalent shall be connected between the CATV system's grounding electrode and the power grounding electrode system at the building or structure served where separate electrodes are used.
(a) 12 AWG
(b) 8 AWG
(c) 6 AWG
(d) 4 AWG

27. A box or conduit body shall not be required for splices and taps in direct-buried conductors and cables as long as the splice is made with a splicing device that is identified for the purpose.
(a) True
(b) False

28. A branch-circuit overcurrent device can serve as the disconnecting means for a stationary motor of 1/8 hp or less.
(a) True
(b) False

29. A building or portions of a building where engine overhauls, painting, body and fender work, and repairs that require ______ of the motor vehicle fuel tank are performed defines the term major repair garage.
(a) removal
(b) replacement
(c) filling
(d) draining

30. A building that contains three or more dwelling units is called a "______."
(a) one-family dwelling
(b) two-family dwelling
(c) dwelling unit
(d) multifamily dwelling

31. A capacitor operating at over 600V shall be provided with means to reduce the residual voltage to 50V or less within ______ after it is disconnected from the source of supply.
(a) 1 minute
(b) 3 minutes
(c) 5 minutes
(d) 7 minutes

32. A circuit breaker with a ______ voltage rating, such as 240V or 480V, can be used where the nominal voltage between any two conductors does not exceed the circuit breaker's voltage rating.
(a) straight
(b) slash
(c) high
(d) low

33. A Class III, Division______ location is where easily ignitible fibers/flyings are stored or handled but not manufactured.
(a) 1
(b) 2
(c) 3
(d) all of these

34. A common dc grounding electrode conductor of a PV system is permitted to serve multiple inverters with the size of the common grounding electrode and the tap conductors in accordance with 250.166. The tap conductors must be connected to the common grounding electrode conductor in such a manner that the common grounding electrode conductor remains ______.

(a) without a splice or joint
(b) inside inverter enclosures
(c) inside a raceway
(d) supported on insulators

35. A communications raceway is an enclosed channel of nonmetallic materials designed for holding communications wires and cables in ______ .

(a) plenum
(b) riser
(c) general-purpose applications
(d) all of these

36. A conductor on the supply side of a service or within a service equipment enclosure or separately derived system to ensure the electrical conductivity between metal parts required to be electrically connected is known as the ______.

(a)supply-side bonding jumper
(b) ungrounded conductor
(c) the electrical supply source
(d) grounding electrode conductor

37. A conductor used for open wiring on insulators that penetrates a wall, floor, or other framing member shall be carried through a ______.

(a) separate sleeve or tube
(b) weatherproof tube
(c) tube of absorbent material
(d) grounded metallic tube

38. A conductor used to connect the system grounded conductor or the equipment to a grounding electrode or to a point on the grounding electrode system is called the "______ conductor."

(a) main grounding
(b) common main
(c) equipment grounding
(d) grounding electrode

39. A conduit seal fitting shall be installed in each conduit that passes from a Class I, Division 2 location into an unclassified location and it is not required to be ______.

(a) listed
(b) installed
(c) explosionproof
(d) accessible

40. A contact device installed at an outlet for the connection of an attachment plug is known as a(n) "______."

(a) attachment point
(b) tap
(c) receptacle
(d) wall plug

41. A device intended for the protection of personnel that functions to de-energize a circuit or portion thereof within an established period of time when the current to ground exceeds the values established for a Class A device, is a(n) "______."

(a) dual-element fuse
(b) inverse time breaker
(c) ground-fault circuit interrupter
(d) safety switch

42. A disconnecting means is required to open ungrounded dc circuit conductors of the PV system.

(a) True
(b) False

43. A disconnecting means is required within sight of the storage battery for all ungrounded battery system conductors operating at over ______ nominal.

(a) 20V
(b) 30V
(c) 40V
(d) 50V

44. A disconnecting means that serves a hermetic refrigerant motor-compressor shall have an ampere rating of at least ______ percent of the nameplate rated-load current or branch-circuit selection current, whichever is greater.

(a) 80
(b) 100
(c) 115
(d) 125

45. A disconnecting switch is permitted to open the grounded dc conductor of a PV system when ______.

(a) the switch is used only for PV array maintenance
(b) the switch is accessible only by qualified persons
(c) the switch is rated for the maximum dc voltage and current, including ground-fault conditions
(d) all of these

46. A feeder supplying fixed motor load(s) shall have a protective device with a rating or setting ______ branch-circuit short-circuit and ground-fault protective device for any motor in the group, plus the sum of the full-load currents of the other motors of the group.

(a) not greater than the largest rating or setting of the
(b) 125 percent of the largest rating of any
(c) equal to the largest rating of any
(d) none of these

47. A field-installed wiring system for branch circuits designed for installation under carpet squares is referred to as ______.

(a) underfloor wiring
(b) undercarpet wiring
(c) flat conductor cable
(d) underfloor conductor cable

48. A flexible cord conductor intended to be used as a(n) ______ conductor shall have a continuous identifying marker readily distinguishing it from the other conductor or conductors. One means of identification is a braid finished to show a continuous green color or a green color with one or more yellow stripes on one conductor.

(a) ungrounded
(b) equipment grounding
(c) service
(d) high-leg

49. A ground-fault protection device or system required for photovoltaic systems shall be capable of ______.

(a) interrupting the flow of fault current
(b) detecting a ground-fault current
(c) provide an indication of the fault
(d) all of the above

50. A grounding electrode conductor shall be permitted to be run to any convenient grounding electrode available in the grounding electrode system where the other electrodes, if any, are connected by bonding jumpers per 250.53(C).

(a) True
(b) False

51. A grounding electrode conductor, sized in accordance with 250.66, shall be used to connect the equipment grounding conductors, the service-equipment enclosures, and, where the system is grounded, the grounded service conductor to the grounding electrode(s).

(a) True
(b) False

52. A heating panel is a complete assembly provided with a junction box or length of flexible conduit for connection to a(n) ______.

(a) wiring system
(b) service
(c) branch circuit
(d) approved conductor

53. A hospital is a building or portion thereof used for the medical, psychiatric, obstetrical, or surgical care, on a 24-hour basis, of ______ or more inpatients.

(a) two
(b) three
(c) four
(d) five

54. A kitchen is defined as an area with a sink and ______ provisions for food preparation and cooking.

(a) listed
(b) labeled
(c) temporary
(d) permanent

55. A legally required standby system shall have adequate capacity and rating for ______ that are expected to operate simultaneously on the standby system.

(a) all of the loads
(b) 80% of the loads
(c) 125% of the loads
(d) none of these

56. A listed exposed work cover can be the grounding and bonding means when the device is attached to the cover with at least ______ permanent fastener(s) and the cover mounting holes are located on a non-raised portion of the cover.

(a) one
(b) two
(c) three
(d) none of these

57. A listed seal for motor fuel dispensers shall be ______.

(a) provided in each conduit run entering a dispenser
(b) provided in each conduit run leaving a dispenser
(c) the first fitting after the conduit emerges from the earth or concrete at a dispenser
(d) all of these

58. A luminaire intended for installation in the floor or wall of a pool, spa, or fountain in a niche that's sealed against the entry of water is called a ______.

(a) wet-niche luminaire
(b) dry-niche luminaire
(c) submersible luminaire
(d) none of these

59. A luminaire marked "Suitable for Wet Locations" ______ be permitted to be used in a damp location.

(a) shall
(b) shall not
(c) a or b
(d) none of these

60. A mechanically integrated assembly of PV modules or panels with a support structure and foundation, tracker, and other components as required to form a dc power-producing unit, is known as a(n) ______.

(a) pulse width modulator
(b) array
(c) capacitive supply bank
(d) alternating-current photovoltaic module

61. A minimum of 70 percent of all recreational vehicle sites with electrical supply shall be equipped with a ______,125V receptacle.

(a) 15A
(b) 20A
(c) 30A
(d) 50A

62. A motor ______ device that can restart a motor automatically after overload tripping shall not be installed if automatic restarting of the motor can result in injury to persons.

(a) short-circuit
(b) ground-fault
(c) overcurrent
(d) overload

63. A motor controller shall open all conductors to the motor where not used as a disconnecting means.

(a) True
(b) False

64. A motor for general use shall be marked with a time rating of ______.

(a) continuous
(b) 5 or 15 minutes
(c) 30 or 60 minutes
(d) any of these

65. A multioutlet assembly shall not be installed ______.

(a) in hoistways
(b) where subject to severe physical damage
(c) where subject to corrosive vapors
(d) all of these

66. A pool light junction box connected to a conduit that extends directly to a forming shell shall be ______ for this use.

(a) listed
(b) identified
(c) marked
(d) a and b

67. A pool transformer used for the supply of underwater luminaires, together with the transformer enclosure, shall be listed for swimming pool and spa use and ______ between the primary and secondary windings

(a) be of the isolated-winding type with an ungrounded secondary and a grounded metal barrier
(b) incorporate an approved system of double insulation
(c) a or b
(d) none of these

68. A portable or mobile electric sign in a wet or damp location shall have GFCI ______.

(a) located on the sign
(b) located in the power-supply cord within 12 in. of the attachment plug
(c) as an integral part of the attachment plug of the supply cord
(d) b or c

69. A portable or temporary alternate source ______ whenever the emergency generator is out of service for major maintenance or repair.

(a) shall not be required
(b) is recommended
(c) shall be available
(d) shall be avoided

70. A receptacle outlet for mobile and manufactured home heat tape that is used to protect cold water inlet piping shall be ______ protected and it shall be connected to an interior branch circuit other than a small-appliance branch circuit where all of the outlets of the circuit are on the load side of the GFCI.

(a) AFCI
(b) GFCI
(c) a or b
(d) none of these

71. A receptacle shall not be installed within, or directly over, a bathtub or shower space.

(a) True
(b) False

72. A recessed luminaire shall be installed so that adjacent combustible material will not be subjected to temperatures in excess of ______°C.

(a) 75
(b) 90
(c) 125
(d) 150

73. A separate ______ shall be provided for the elevator car lights, receptacle(s), auxiliary lighting power source, and ventilation on each elevator car.

(a) branch circuit
(b) disconnecting means
(c) connection
(d) none of these

74. A separate branch circuit shall supply elevator machine room/machinery space lighting and receptacle(s). The required lighting shall not be connected to the load side of ______.

(a) a local subpanel
(b) an SWD-type circuit breaker
(c) an HID-type circuit breaker
(d) a GFCI

75. A separate disconnecting means shall be installed where a capacitor is connected on the load side of a motor controller.

(a) True
(b) False

76. A separate overcurrent device shall not be required for a capacitor connected on the load side of a motor overload protective device.

(a) True
(b) False

77. A sign shall be placed at the service-entrance equipment indicating the ______ of on-site optional standby power sources.

(a) type
(b) location
(c) manufacturer
(d) a and b

78. A sign shall be placed at the service-entrance equipment indicating the type and location of on-site emergency power sources.

(a) True
(b) False

79. A single _____ shall not be used for more than one branch circuit, one multiwire branch circuit, or one set of feeder conductors except as allowed elsewhere in the Code.

(a) equipment grounding conductor
(b) neutral conductor
(c) grounding electrode conductor
(d) bonding conductor

80. A spa or hot tub is a hydromassage pool or tub and is not designed to have the contents drained or discharged after each use.

(a) True
(b) False

81. A stand-alone PV system supplies power in conjunction with and to supplement an electrical production and distribution network.

(a) True
(b) False

82. A storage battery supplying emergency lighting and power shall maintain not less than 87½ percent of normal voltage at total load for a period of at least _____ hour(s).

(a) 1
(b) 1½
(c) 2
(d) 2½

83. A structure is that which is built or constructed.

(a) True
(b) False

84. A switch or circuit breaker can be used as both the controller and disconnecting means if it _____.

(a) opens all ungrounded conductors
(b) is protected by an overcurrent device in each ungrounded conductor
(c) is manually operable, or both power and manually operable
(d) all of these

85. A switchboard or panelboard containing an ungrounded electrical system is required to be legibly and permanently field-marked to caution that the system is ungrounded and include the _____.

(a) contact information for the power supplier
(b) contact information for emergency services
(c) operating voltage between conductors
(d) transformer impedance rating

86. A thermal protector may consist of one or more sensing elements integral with the motor or motor-compressor and an external control device.

(a) True
(b) False

87. A unit switch with a marked _____ position that is part of a fixed space heater, and disconnects all ungrounded conductors, shall be permitted to serve as the required disconnecting means.

(a) on
(b) closed
(c) off
(d) none of these

88. A value assigned to a circuit or system for the purpose of conveniently designating its voltage class, such as 120/240V, is called "_____ voltage."

(a) root-mean-square
(b) circuit
(c) nominal
(d) source

89. A vented alkaline-type battery, as it relates to storage batteries, operating at less than 250V shall be installed with not more than _____ cells in the series circuit of any one tray.

(a) 10
(b) 12
(c) 18
(d) 20

90. A waste disposal can be cord-and-plug-connected, but the cord shall not be less than 18 in. or more than _____ in length.

(a) 30 in.
(b) 36 in.
(c) 42 in.
(d) 48 in.

91. A written record shall be kept of required tests and maintenance on emergency systems.

(a) True
(b) False

92. A(n) _____ disconnecting means is required within sight of the storage battery for all ungrounded battery system conductors operating at over 50V nominal.

(a) accessible
(b) readily accessible
(c) safety
(d) all of these

93. A(n) _____ is a device, or group of devices, by which the conductors of a circuit can be disconnected from their source of supply.

(a) feeder
(b) enclosure
(c) disconnecting means
(d) conductor interrupter

94. A(n) _____ is intended to provide limited overcurrent protection for specific applications and utilization equipment, such as luminaires and appliances. This limited protection is in addition to the protection provided by the required branch-circuit overcurrent protective device.

(a) supplementary overcurrent device
(b) surge protection device
(c) arc-fault circuit interrupter
(d) Class A GFCI

95. A(n) _____ shall be located at the point of entry to an elevator machine room.

(a) directory
(b) lighting switch
(c) control circuit disconnecting means
(d) emergency exit map

96. A(n) _____ system is a premises wiring system whose power is derived from a source of electric energy other than a service and has no direct electrical connection to supply conductors originating in another system other than through the earth, metallic enclosures and raceways, or equipment grounding conductors.

(a) separately derived
(b) classified
(c) direct
(d) emergency

97. Acceptable protection techniques for electrical and electronic equipment in hazardous (classified) locations includes:

(a) Explosionproof Equipment
(b) Dust Ignitionproof
(c) Dusttight
(d) all of these

98. Accepted industry practices for optical fiber installations are described in _____.

(a) ANSI/NECA/BICSI 568, *Standard for Installing Commercial Building Telecommunications Cabling*
(b) ANSI/NECA/FOA 301, *Standard for Installing and Testing Fiber Optic Cables*
(c) other ANSI-approved installation standards
(d) any of these

99. Access to electrical equipment shall not be denied by an accumulation of CATV coaxial cables that _____ removal of suspended-ceiling panels.

(a) prevents
(b) hinders
(c) blocks
(d) require

100. Access to electrical equipment shall not be denied by an accumulation of remote-control, signaling, or power-limited cables that prevent removal of panels, including suspended-ceiling panels.

(a) True
(b) False

CHALLENGE QUIZ 2

Article 90 through Chapter 9

Challenge Quiz 2— Article 90 through Chapter 9

Please use the 2011 *Code* book to answer the following questions, which are based on the 2011 *NEC*.

1. Access to equipment shall not be denied by an accumulation of communications ______ that prevents the removal of suspended-ceiling panels.

   (a) wires
   (b) cables
   (c) ductwork
   (d) a and b

2. Accessible portions of abandoned CATV cable shall be removed unless tagged for future use.

   (a) True
   (b) False

3. Accessible portions of abandoned network-powered broadband cable shall be removed.

   (a) True
   (b) False

4. Accessible portions of abandoned optical fiber cable shall be removed.

   (a) True
   (b) False

5. AFCI protection can be omitted for an individual branch circuit to a ______ in accordance with 760.41(B) and 760.121(B), if the circuit conductors are installed in RMC, IMC, EMT, or steel sheath Type AC or MC cable that qualifies as an equipment grounding conductor in accordance with 250.118, with metal outlet and junction boxes.

   (a) smoke alarm
   (b) communication system
   (c) fire alarm system
   (d) sump pump

6. Agricultural buildings where corrosive atmospheres exist include areas where the following exist:

   (a) poultry and animal excrement
   (b) corrosive particles which may combine with water
   (c) area of periodic washing with water and cleansing agents
   (d) all of these

7. All ______, 125V receptacle outlets that are not part of the permanent wiring of the building or structure and are used by personnel for temporary power shall be GFCI protected.

   (a) 15A
   (b) 20A
   (c) 30A
   (d) all of these

8. All 15A and 20A, 125V receptacles installed in bathrooms of ______ shall have ground-fault circuit-interrupter (GFCI) protection for personnel.

   (a) guest rooms in hotels/motels
   (b) dwelling units
   (c) office buildings
   (d) all of these

9. All 15A and 20A, 125V receptacles installed indoors in wet locations must be GFCI protected.

   (a) True
   (b) False

10. All 15A and 20A, 125V receptacles installed within 6 ft of the outside edge of a sink in locations other than dwelling units must be ______ .

   (a) AFCI protected
   (b) GFCI protected
   (c) tamperproof
   (d) a and b

11. All 15A and 20A, 125V receptacles located within ______ of the inside walls of a pool shall be GFCI protected.
(a) 8 ft
(b) 10 ft
(c) 15 ft
(d) 20 ft

12. All 15A and 20A, 125V, single-phase general-purpose receptacles installed ______ of agricultural buildings shall be GFCI protected.
(a) in areas having an equipotential plane
(b) outdoors
(c) in dirt confinement areas for livestock
(d) any of these

13. All 15A or 20A, 120V branch circuits that supply outlets in dwelling unit family rooms, dining rooms, living rooms, parlors, libraries, dens, bedrooms, sunrooms, recreation rooms, closets, hallways, or similar rooms or areas shall be AFCI protected by a listed arc-fault circuit interrupter of the combination type.
(a) True
(b) False

14. All branch circuits serving patient care areas shall be provided with an effective ground-fault current path by installation in a metal raceway system, or a cable having a metallic armor or sheath assembly. The metal raceway system, or metallic cable armor, or sheath assembly shall itself qualify as an equipment grounding conductor in accordance with 250.118.
(a) True
(b) False

15. All conductors of a circuit, including the equipment grounding conductor, must be installed in the same raceway or cable, or otherwise run with the PV array circuit conductors when they leave the vicinity of the PV array.
(a) True
(b) False

16. All electric pool water heaters shall have the heating elements not exceed ______ amperes.
(a) 20A
(b) 35A
(c) 48A
(d) 60A

17. All raceway and cable wiring methods included in this Code and other wiring systems and fittings specifically intended and identified for use on photovoltaic arrays shall be permitted.
(a) True
(b) False

18. All switchboards and panelboards supplied by a feeder in ______ shall be marked as to the device or equipment where the power supply originates.
(a) other than one- or two-family dwellings
(b) all dwelling units
(c) all nondwelling units
(d) b and c

19. All unused openings in equipment for hazardous (classified) locations must be closed with listed ______ close-up plugs.
(a) nonmetallic
(b) metal
(c) composition
(d) a or b

20. Alternating-current systems from 50V to less than 1,000V that aren't required to be grounded as per 250.20(B) must have ______.
(a) ground detectors installed
(b) the ground detection sensing equipment connected as close as practicable to where the system receives its supply
(c) a and b
(d) ground-fault protection for equipment

21. Aluminum conductors and copper-clad aluminum conductors shall be permitted for branch-circuit wiring in mobile homes.
(a) True
(b) False

22. An 8 AWG or larger solid copper equipotential bonding conductor shall be extended to service equipment to eliminate voltage gradients in the pool area.
(a) True
(b) False

23. An 800A fuse rated at 600V ______ on a 250V system.

(a) shall not be used
(b) shall be used
(c) can be used
(d) none of these

24. An arc welder shall have overcurrent protection rated or set at not more than ______ percent of the rated primary current of the welder.

(a) 100
(b) 125
(c) 150
(d) 200

25. An assembly of interconnected intrinsically safe apparatus, associated apparatus, and interconnecting cables designed so that they are intrinsically safe circuits is a(n) ______.

(a) intrinsically safe system
(b) safe location
(c) reclassified location
(d) associated system

26. An atmosphere containing carbon black, charcoal, coal, or coke dusts that have been sensitized by other materials so they present an explosion hazard is classified as Group F.

(a) True
(b) False

27. An electric vehicle connector is a device that, by insertion into an electric vehicle inlet, establishes an electrical connection to the electric vehicle for the purpose of power transfer and information exchange.

(a) True
(b) False

28. An electrical production and distribution network, such as a utility and connected load is internal to and controlled by a photovoltaic power system.

(a) True
(b) False

29. An electrically driven or controlled machine with one or more motors which is used primarily to transport and distribute water for agricultural purposes, and is not hand portable is called a(n) ______.

(a) irrigation machine
(b) electric water distribution system
(c) center pivot irrigation machine
(d) automatic water distribution system

30. An electric-discharge or LED luminaire or listed assembly can be cord connected if located ______ the outlet, the cord is visible for its entire length outside the luminaire, and the cord is not subject to strain or physical damage.

(a) within
(b) directly below
(c) directly above
(d) adjacent to

31. An electrode encased by at least 2 in. of concrete, located horizontally near the bottom or vertically and within that portion of a concrete foundation or footing that is in direct contact with the earth, shall be permitted as a grounding electrode when it consists of ______.

(a) at least 20 ft of ½ in. or larger steel reinforcing bars or rods
(b) at least 20 ft of bare copper conductor of 4 AWG or larger
(c) a or b
(d) none of these

32. An emergency transfer switch shall supply ______.

(a) emergency loads
(b) computer equipment
(c) UPS equipment
(d) all of these

33. An enclosure for either surface mounting or flush mounting provided with a frame in which a door can be hung is called a(n) "______."

(a) enclosure
(b) outlet box
(c) cutout box
(d) cabinet

34. An equipment bonding jumper can be installed on the outside of a raceway, providing the length of the equipment bonding jumper is not more than ______ and the equipment bonding jumper is routed with the raceway.

(a) 12 in.
(b) 24 in.
(c) 36 in.
(d) 72 in.

35. An equipotential plane shall be installed in all concrete floor confinement areas of livestock buildings, and all outdoor confinement areas with a concrete slab that contains metallic equipment accessible to livestock and that may become energized.

(a) True
(b) False

36. An impedance heating system that is operating at a(n) ______ greater than 30, but not more than 80, shall be grounded at a designated point(s).

(a) voltage
(b) amperage
(c) wattage
(d) temperature

37. An inverter or an ac module in an interactive PV system must automatically de-energize its output to the connected electrical distribution system upon ______ of voltage and remain de-energized until the electrical distribution system voltage has been restored.

(a) surge
(b) spike
(c) loss
(d) unbalance

38. An open span length of 200 ft for antenna conductors of hard-drawn copper located at an amateur transmitting and receiving station requires a minimum conductor size of ______.

(a) 14 AWG
(b) 12 AWG
(c) 10 AWG
(d) 8 AWG

39. An optical fiber cable is a factory assembly of one or more optical fibers having a(n) ______covering that transmits light for control, signaling, and communications.

(a) conductive
(b) nonconductive
(c) overall
(d) metallic

40. An optical fiber raceway is a raceway for optical fiber cables.

(a) True
(b) False

41. An outdoor disconnecting means for a mobile home shall be installed so the bottom of the enclosure is not less than ______ above the finished grade or working platform.

(a) 1 ft
(b) 2 ft
(c) 3 ft
(d) 6 ft

42. An outdoor wire-strung antenna conductor of a receiving station with a 75 ft span using a hard-drawn copper conductor shall not be less than ______.

(a) 17 AWG
(b) 14 AWG
(c) 12 AWG
(d) 10 AWG

43. Annex C contains tables that list the number of conductors or fixture wires permitted in a raceway when the conductors are all of the same size and type.

(a) True
(b) False

44. Antenna conductors for amateur transmitting stations attached to buildings shall be firmly mounted at least ______ clear of the surface of the building on nonabsorbent insulating supports.

(a) 1 in.
(b) 2 in.
(c) 3 in.
(d) 4 in.

45. Any of the following wiring methods can be installed in a cable tray:

(a) metal raceways
(b) nonmetallic raceways
(c) cables
(d) all of these

46. Armored cable shall not be installed ______.

(a) in damp or wet locations
(b) where subject to physical damage
(c) where exposed to corrosive conditions
(d) all of these

47. Article ______ covers the installation of portable wiring and equipment for carnivals, circuses, exhibitions, fairs, traveling attractions, and similar functions.

(a) 518
(b) 525
(c) 590
(d) all of these

48. As defined by 230.95, the rating of the service disconnect shall be considered to be the rating of the largest ______ that can be installed or the highest continuous current trip setting for which the actual overcurrent device installed in a circuit breaker is rated or can be adjusted.

(a) fuse
(b) circuit
(c) conductor
(d) all of these

49. At circuses and carnivals, all equipment to be grounded shall be connected to a(n) ______ conductor of a type recognized by 250.118.

(a) equipment grounding
(b) grounded
(c) grounding electrode
(d) ungrounded

50. At construction sites, boxes are not required for temporary wiring splices of ______.

(a) multiconductor cords
(b) multiconductor cables
(c) a or b
(d) none of these

51. At least ______ 125V, single-phase, 15A or 20A, duplex receptacle(s) shall be provided in the elevator hoistway pit.

(a) one
(b) two
(c) three
(d) four

52. At least one 15A or 20A, 125V receptacle on a general-purpose branch circuit shall be located a minimum of ______ and a maximum of 10 ft from the inside wall of a spa or hot tub installed indoors.

(a) 18 in.
(b) 2 ft
(c) 6 ft
(d) no minimum

53. At least one lighting outlet containing a switch or controlled by a wall switch shall be installed in attic spaces containing ballasts for electric signs. At least one ______ shall be at the usual point of entry to these spaces. The lighting outlet shall be provided at or near the equipment requiring servicing.

(a) receptacle
(b) switch
(c) point of control
(d) luminaire

54. At Type AC cable terminations, a(n) ______ shall be provided.

(a) fitting (or box design) that protects the conductors from abrasion
(b) insulating bushing between the conductors and the cable armor
(c) a and b
(d) none of these

55. Audible and visual signal devices shall be provided on legally required standby systems, where practicable, to indicate ______.

(a) derangement of the standby source
(b) that the standby source is carrying load
(c) that the battery charger is not functioning
(d) all of these

56. Audio cables identified for future use shall be marked with a tag of sufficient durability to withstand _____.

(a) moisture
(b) humidity
(c) the environment involved
(d) none of these

57. Audio system circuits using Class 2 or Class 3 wiring methods, are not permitted in the same cable or raceway with _____.

(a) other audio system circuits
(b) Class 2 conductors or cables
(c) Class 3 conductors or cables
(d) b or c

58. Backfill used for underground wiring shall not _____.

(a) damage the wiring method
(b) prevent compaction of the fill
(c) contribute to the corrosion of the raceway
(d) all of these

59. Ballasts, transformers, and electronic power supplies can be above a suspended ceiling, provided the enclosures are _____.

(a) securely fastened in place
(b) don't use the suspended-ceiling grid for support.
(c) a or b
(d) a and b

60. Bare conductors in auxiliary gutters shall be securely and rigidly supported so that the minimum clearance between bare current-carrying metal parts of different potential mounted on the same surface will not be less than 2 in., nor less than _____ for parts in free air.

(a) ¼ in.
(b) ½ in.
(c) 1 in.
(d) 2 in.

61. Battery chargers and the batteries being charged can be located in any area of a commercial garage.

(a) True
(b) False

62. Bends shall be made in HDPE conduit _____

(a) in a manner that will not damage the raceway
(b) so as not to significantly reduce the internal diameter of the raceway
(c) with mechanical bending tools
(d) a and b

63. Bonding shall be provided where necessary to ensure _____ and the capacity to conduct safely any fault current likely to be imposed.

(a) electrical continuity
(b) fiduciary responsibility
(c) listing requirements
(d) electrical demand

64. Boxes and fittings used for taps, joints, or terminal connections shall be _____ where installed in Class II, Division 1 locations.

(a) explosionproof
(b) identified for Class II locations
(c) dusttight
(d) weatherproof

65. Branch-circuit conductors supplying a single air-conditioner motor-compressor shall have an ampacity not less than _____ percent of either the motor-compressor rated-load current or the branch-circuit selection current, whichever is greater.

(a) 100
(b) 125
(c) 150
(d) 200

66. Branch-circuit conductors to individual appliances shall not be sized _____ than required by the appliance markings.

(a) larger
(b) smaller

67. Buildings or structures containing both utility service and a PV system must have a permanent _____ identifying the location of the service disconnecting means and PV system ac disconnecting means if they are not located at the same location.

(a) plaque
(b) directory
(c) a and b
(d) a or b

68. Buildings or structures supplied by multiple services or feeders must use the same _____ to ground enclosures and equipment in or on that building.

(a) service
(b) disconnect
(c) grounding electrode system
(d) any of these

69. Cable splices or terminations in power-limited fire alarm systems shall be made in listed _____ or utilization equipment.

(a) fittings
(b) boxes or enclosures
(c) fire alarm devices
(d) all of these

70. Cable trays shall _____.

(a) include fittings or other suitable means for changes in direction and elevation
(b) have side rails or equivalent structural members
(c) be made of corrosion-resistant material or protected from corrosion as required by 300.6
(d) all of these

71. Cable trays shall be _____ except as permitted by 392.10(D).

(a) exposed
(b) accessible
(c) concealed
(d) a and b

72. Cable trays used to support service-entrance conductors shall contain only service-entrance conductors _____.

(a) unless a solid fixed barrier separates the service-entrance conductors from other conductors
(b) under 300V
(c) in industrial locations
(d) over 600V

73. Cablebus framework that is _____ shall be permitted as the equipment grounding conductor for branch circuits and feeders.

(a) bonded
(b) welded
(c) protected
(d) galvanized

74. Cables and conductors of Class 2 and Class 3 circuits _____ be placed with conductors of electric light, power, Class 1, nonpower-limited fire alarm circuits, and medium power network-powered broadband communications circuits.

(a) shall be permitted to
(b) shall not
(c) shall
(d) none of these

75. Cables and conductors of two or more power-limited fire alarm circuits can be installed in the same cable, enclosure, cable tray or raceway.

(a) True
(b) False

76. Cables are considered _____ if rendered inaccessible by the structure or finish of the building.

(a) inaccessible
(b) concealed
(c) hidden
(d) enclosed

77. Cables for communications systems such as _____ shall be located no less than 10 ft above swimming and wading pools, diving structures, observation stands, towers, or platforms.

(a) communications
(b) radio
(c) television coaxial cable
(d) all of these

78. Cables installed exposed on the surface of ceilings and sidewalls shall be supported in such a manner that they will not be damaged by normal building use. Cables shall be secured by _____ designed and installed so as not to damage the cable.

(a) straps
(b) staples
(c) cable ties
(d) any of these

79. Capacitors shall be _____ so that persons cannot come into accidental contact or bring conducting materials into accidental contact with exposed energized parts, terminals, or buses associated with them.

(a) enclosed
(b) located
(c) guarded
(d) any of these

80. CATV cable not terminated at equipment other than a coaxial cable connector and not identified for future use with a tag is considered abandoned.

(a) True
(b) False

81. CATV coaxial cable can be placed in a raceway, compartment, outlet box, or junction box with the conductors of light or power circuits, or Class 1 circuits when _____.

(a) installed in rigid metal conduit
(b) separated by a permanent barrier
(c) insulated
(d) none of these

82. CATVP cables are community antenna television coaxial cables that must be listed for installation in ducts, plenums and other spaces used for environmental air and shall also be listed as having adequate fire-resistant and low smoke-producing characteristics.

(a) True
(b) False

83. Ceiling-support wires used for the support of electrical raceways and cables within nonfire-rated assemblies shall be distinguishable from the suspended-ceiling framing support wires.

(a) True
(b) False

84. Central heating equipment, other than fixed electric space-heating equipment, shall be supplied by a(n) _____ branch circuit.

(a) multiwire
(b) individual
(c) multipurpose
(d) small-appliance

85. Circuit breakers in Class I, Division 2 locations that are not hermetically sealed or oil-immersed shall be installed in a Class I, Division 1 enclosure.

(a) True
(b) False

86. Class 2 and Class 3 cable not terminated at equipment and not identified for future use with a tag is considered abandoned.

(a) True
(b) False

87. Class 2 and Class 3 cables listed as suitable for general-purpose use with the exception of risers, ducts, plenums, and other spaces used for environmental air, shall be Type(s) _____.

(a) CL2P and CL3P
(b) CL2R and CL3R
(c) CL2 and CL3
(d) PLTC

88. Class 2 and Class 3 plenum cables listed as suitable for use in ducts, plenums, and other spaces used for environmental air shall be Type _____.

(a) CL2P and CL3P
(b) CL2R and CL3R
(c) CL2 and CL3
(d) PLTC

89. Class 2 cables identified for future use shall be marked with a tag of sufficient durability to withstand _____.

(a) moisture
(b) humidity
(c) the environment involved
(d) none of these

90. Class 2 or Class 3 cables, installed in vertical runs penetrating more than one floor or installed in a shaft without being installed in a raceway, shall be Type _____.

(a) CL2R
(b) CL3R
(c) CL2P
(d) a or b

91. Class III, Division _____ locations include areas where easily ignitible fibers/flyings are handled, manufactured, or used.

(a) 1
(b) 2
(c) 3
(d) all of these

92. Coaxial cables can be installed in any Chapter 3 raceway in accordance with the requirements of Chapter 3.

(a) True
(b) False

93. Color coding shall be permitted to identify intrinsically safe conductors where they are colored light _____ and where no other conductors colored light _____ are used.

(a) red
(b) blue
(c) yellow
(d) any of these

94. Communications cables and raceways identified as suitable for plenum use can be installed above a suspended ceiling or below a raised floor used for environmental air.

(a) True
(b) False

95. Communications cables not terminated at both ends with a connector or other equipment and not identified for future use with a tag are considered abandoned.

(a) True
(b) False

96. Communications circuits and equipment installed in a location that is _____ in accordance with 500.5 shall comply with the applicable requirements of Chapter 5.

(a) designed
(b) classified
(c) located
(d) approved

97. Communications plenum cable shall be _____ as being suitable for use in other spaces used for environmental air.

(a) marked
(b) identified
(c) approved
(d) listed

98. Communications wires and cables shall be separated by at least 2 in. from conductors of _____ circuits, unless permitted otherwise.

(a) power
(b) lighting
(c) Class 1
(d) any of these

99. Compliance with either the metric or the inch-pound unit of measurement system shall be permitted.

(a) True
(b) False

100. Conductive optical fiber cables contain noncurrent-carrying conductive members such as metallic _____.

(a) strength members
(b) vapor barriers
(c) armor or sheath
(d) any of these

CHALLENGE QUIZ

3

Article 90 through Chapter 9

Challenge Quiz 3— Article 90 through Chapter 9

Please use the 2011 *Code* book to answer the following questions, which are based on the 2011 *NEC*.

1. Conductor adjustment factors shall not apply to conductors in raceways having a length not exceeding _____

   (a) 12 in.
   (b) 24 in.
   (c) 36 in.
   (d) 48 in.

2. Conductor overload protection shall not be required where the interruption of the _____ would create a hazard, such as in a material-handling magnet circuit or fire pump circuit. However, short-circuit protection is required.

   (a) circuit
   (b) line
   (c) phase
   (d) system

3. Conductors and busbars on a switchboard or panelboard shall be located so as to be free from _____ and shall be held firmly in place.

   (a) obstructions
   (b) physical damage
   (c) a and b
   (d) none of these

4. Conductors and cables of intrinsically safe circuits run in other than raceway or cable tray systems shall be separated by at least _____ and secured from conductors and cables of any nonintrinsically safe circuits.

   (a) 2 in.
   (b) 6 in.
   (c) 12 in.
   (d) 18 in.

5. Conductors for an appliance circuit supplying more than one appliance or appliance receptacle in an installation operating at less than 50V shall not be smaller than _____ AWG copper or equivalent.

   (a) 18
   (b) 14
   (c) 12
   (d) 10

6. Conductors installed in overhead service masts on the outside surface of the building traveling through the eave of that building are considered to be outside of the building.

   (a) True
   (b) False

7. Conductors located above an electric space-heated ceiling are considered to be operating in an ambient temperature of _____.

   (a) 20°C
   (b) 30°C
   (c) 50°C
   (d) 86°C

8. Conductors of intrinsically safe circuits shall be separated at least _____ from conductors of any nonintrinsically safe circuits within the same enclosures.

   (a) 2 in.
   (b) 6 in.
   (c) 12 in.
   (d) 18 in.

9. Conductors of intrinsically safe circuits shall not be placed in any _____ with conductors of any nonintrinsically safe system.

   (a) raceway
   (b) cable tray
   (c) cable
   (d) any of these

10. Conductors shall be ______ unless otherwise provided.
(a) bare
(b) stranded
(c) of copper
(d) of aluminum

11. Conductors shall be permitted for use in any of the wiring methods recognized in Chapter 3 and as permitted in the NEC.
(a) True
(b) False

12. Conductors smaller than 1/0 AWG can be connected in parallel to supply control power, provided ______.
(a) they are all contained within the same raceway or cable
(b) each parallel conductor has an ampacity sufficient to carry the entire load
(c) the circuit overcurrent device rating does not exceed the ampacity of any individual parallel conductor
(d) all of these

13. Conductors supplying outlets for arc and xenon projectors of the professional type shall not be smaller than ______ and shall have an ampacity not less than the projector rating.
(a) 12 AWG
(b) 10 AWG
(c) 8 AWG
(d) 6 AWG

14. Conductors, including splices and taps, shall not fill a strut-type channel raceway to more than ______ percent of its area at that point.
(a) 25
(b) 75
(c) 80
(d) 125

15. Conduit bodies containing conductors larger than 6 AWG shall have a cross-sectional area at least twice that of the largest conduit to which they can be attached.
(a) True
(b) False

16. Connectors and terminals for conductors more finely stranded than Class B and Class C, as shown in Table 10 of Chapter 9, must be ______ for the specific conductor class or classes.
(a) listed
(b) approved
(c) identified
(d) all of these

17. Cord-and-plug-connected equipment in fountains ______ shall have GFCI protection.
(a) except pumps
(b) including power-supply cords
(c) less than 6 ft high
(d) except power-supply cords

18. Cord-and-plug-connected vending machines manufactured or remanufactured on or after January 1, 2005 shall include a ground-fault circuit interrupter as an integral part of the attachment plug or in the power-supply cord within 12 in. of the attachment plug. Older vending machines not incorporating integral GFCI protection shall ______.
(a) be remanufactured
(b) be disabled
(c) be connected to a GFCI-protected outlet
(d) be connected to an AFCI-protected circuit

19. Coves for luminaires shall be located so that the lamps and equipment can be properly installed and ______.
(a) maintained
(b) protected from physical damage
(c) tested
(d) inspected

20. Critical operations power systems are those systems so classed by municipal, state, federal, or other codes, by any governmental agency having jurisdiction or by facility engineering documentation establishing the necessity for such a system.
(a) True
(b) False

21. Currents of photovoltaic systems are to be considered ______.
(a) safe
(b) continuous
(c) noncontinuous
(d) inverted

22. Cut ends of ENT shall be trimmed inside and ______ to remove rough edges.
 (a) outside
 (b) tapered
 (c) filed
 (d) beveled

23. Devices and systems used for securing PV modules that also provide grounding of the module frames must be ______ for the purpose of grounding PV modules.
 (a) listed
 (b) labeled
 (c) identified
 (d) a and b

24. Dimensions of Type S fuses, fuseholders, and adapters shall be standardized to permit interchangeability regardless of the ______.
 (a) model
 (b) manufacturer
 (c) amperage
 (d) voltage

25. Disconnecting means for air-conditioning or refrigerating equipment can be installed ______ the air-conditioning or refrigerating equipment, but not on panels that are designed to allow access to the equipment, and not over the equipment nameplate.
 (a) on
 (b) within
 (c) a or b
 (d) none of these

26. Disconnecting means must be provided to disconnect a fuse from all sources of supply if energized from both directions and shall be capable of being disconnected independently of fuses in other photovoltaic source circuits.
 (a) True
 (b) False

27. Dry-type transformers installed indoors rated over ______ shall be installed in a vault.
 (a) 1,000V
 (b) 20,000V
 (c) 35,000V
 (d) 50,000V

28. Due to its power limitations, a Class 2 circuit is considered safe from a fire initiation standpoint and provides acceptable protection from electric shock.
 (a) True
 (b) False

29. Duplex receptacles that provide power for pump motors related to the circulation and sanitation system of pools shall be located at least ______ from the inside walls of the pool.
 (a) 3 ft
 (b) 5 ft
 (c) 10 ft
 (d) 12 ft

30. Dwelling unit or mobile home feeder conductors need not be larger than the service conductors and can be sized according to 310.15(B)(7).
 (a) True
 (b) False

31. Each 15A and 20A, 125V receptacle installed in pits, in hoistways, on elevator car tops, and in escalator and moving walk wellways shall be ______.
 (a) on a GFCI-protected circuit
 (b) of the GFCI type
 (c) a or b
 (d) none of these

32. Each appliance shall have a means that ______ disconnects all ungrounded circuit conductors.
 (a) sequentially
 (b) automatically
 (c) simultaneously
 (d) all of these

33. Each cable entering a cutout box ______.
 (a) shall be secured to the cutout box
 (b) can be sleeved through a chase
 (c) shall have a maximum of two cables per connector
 (d) all of these

34. Each commercial occupancy accessible to pedestrians shall have at least one outside sign outlet in an accessible location at each entrance supplied by a branch circuit rated at least _____.

(a) 15A
(b) 20A
(c) 30A
(d) 40A

35. Each doorway leading into a transformer vault from the building interior shall be provided with a tight-fitting door having a minimum fire rating of _____ hours.

(a) 2
(b) 3
(c) 4
(d) 6

36. Each electric appliance shall be provided with a(n) _____ giving the identifying name and the rating in volts and amperes, or in volts and watts.

(a) pamphlet
(b) nameplate
(c) auxiliary statement
(d) owner's manual

37. Each generator shall be provided with a _____ listing the manufacturer's name, the rated frequency, power factor, number of phases (if of alternating current), and its rating in kilowatts or kilovolt-amperes.

(a) list
(b) faceplate
(c) nameplate
(d) sticker

38. Each lead-in conductor from an outdoor antenna shall be provided with a listed antenna discharge unit, unless enclosed in a continuous metallic shield that is either grounded or protected by an antenna discharge unit.

(a) True
(b) False

39. Each length of HDPE conduit shall be clearly and durably marked not less than every _____ ft.

(a) 3
(b) 5
(c) 10
(d) 20

40. Each sign and outline lighting system shall be controlled by an externally operable switch or circuit breaker that opens all ungrounded conductors simultaneously on _____ branch circuits.

(a) 15A
(b) 20A
(c) multiwire
(d) outdoor

41. Each switchboard or panelboard used as service equipment shall be provided with a main bonding jumper within the panelboard, or within one of the sections of the switchboard, for connecting the grounded service-entrance conductor on its _____ side to the switchboard or panelboard frame.

(a) load
(b) supply
(c) phase
(d) high-leg

42. Each vented cell of a battery, as it relates to storage batteries, shall be equipped with _____ that is(are) designed to prevent destruction of the cell due to ignition of gases within the cell by an external spark or flame under normal operating conditions.

(a) pressure relief
(b) a flame arrester
(c) fluid level indicators
(d) none of these

43. Electric equipment, including power-supply cords, used with storable pools shall be _____.

(a) AFCI protected
(b) GFCI protected
(c) a or b
(d) none of these

44. Electric signs and outline lighting shall be ______.
(a) approved by special permission
(b) listed
(c) identified for the location
(d) a or b

45. Electric space-heating cables shall not extend beyond the room or area in which they ______.
(a) provide heat
(b) originate
(c) terminate
(d) are connected

46. Electric swimming pool equipment can be installed in pits where drainage adequately prevents water accumulation during abnormal operation.
(a) True
(b) False

47. Electric vehicle supply equipment identified for and intended to be interconnected to a vehicle, and also serve ______, shall be listed as suitable for that purpose.
(a) as an optional standby system
(b) as an electric power production source
(c) to provide bidirectional power feed
(d) all of these

48. Electric vehicle supply equipment shall have a listed system of protection against electric shock of personnel.
(a) True
(b) False

49. Electrical circuits and equipment must be installed in such a way that the spread of fire or products of combustion won't be substantially increased. Openings into or through fire-rated walls, floors, and ceilings for electrical equipment must be firestopped using methods approved by the authority having jurisdiction to maintain the fire-resistance rating of the fire-rated assembly. This rule is in Section 300.21, but it also applies to information technology equipment rooms.
(a) True
(b) False

50. Electrical continuity at service equipment, service raceways, and service conductor enclosures shall be ensured by ______.
(a) bonding equipment to the grounded service conductor
(b) connections utilizing threaded couplings on enclosures, if made up wrenchtight
(c) by listed bonding devices, such as bonding-type locknuts, bushings, or bushings with bonding jumpers
(d) any of these

51. Electrical equipment and wiring methods in or on portable structures for carnival or circuses shall have mechanical protection where subject to ______.
(a) public access
(b) physical damage
(c) exposure to the weather
(d) operator access

52. Electrical equipment enclosures at marinas must be securely and substantially supported by structural members, independent of any raceway connected to them.
(a) True
(b) False

53. Electrical equipment shall not be connected to the supply side of the service disconnecting means, except for a few specific exceptions such as ______.
(a) Type 1 surge protective devices
(b) taps used to supply legally required optional standby power systems, fire pump equipment, fire and sprinkler alarms, and load (energy) management devices
(c) solar photovoltaic systems
(d) all of these

54. Electrical wiring for______ shall be installed on the side of the wharf, pier, or dock opposite from the liquid fuel piping system.
(a) power
(b) lighting
(c) fuel dispensing equipment
(d) all of these

55. Electronic organs or other electronic musical instruments are included in the scope of Article 640.
(a) True
(b) False

56. Emergency equipment must be designed and located so as to minimize the hazards that might cause complete failure due to ______.

(a) flooding
(b) fires
(c) icing, and vandalism
(d) all of these

57. Emergency systems may provide power for ventilation where essential to maintain life, fire detection and alarm systems, elevators, fire pumps, public safety communications systems, industrial processes where current interruption would produce serious ______.

(a) production slowdowns
(b) life safety or health hazards
(c) a and b
(d) a or b

58. Emergency transfer equipment, including transfer switches, shall be ______.

(a) automatic
(b) identified for emergency use
(c) approved by the authority having jurisdiction
(d) all of these

59. EMT is permitted to contain branch-circuit wiring for underwater pool luminaires where the EMT is installed on or within a building.

(a) True
(b) False

60. EMT shall not be used where ______.

(a) subject to severe physical damage
(b) protected from corrosion only by enamel
(c) used for the support of luminaires
(d) any of these

61. ENT shall be permitted for direct earth burial when used with fittings listed for this purpose.

(a) True
(b) False

62. Equipment bonding jumpers shall be of copper or other corrosion-resistant material.

(a) True
(b) False

63. Equipment grounding conductor(s), and not more than ______ fixture wire(s) smaller than 14 AWG can be omitted from the calculations where they enter the box from a domed luminaire or similar canopy and terminate within that box.

(a) one
(b) two
(c) three
(d) four

64. Equipment grounding conductors for motor branch circuits shall be sized in accordance with Table 250.122, based on the rating of the ______ device.

(a) motor overload
(b) motor over-temperature
(c) branch circuit short-circuit and ground-fault protective
(d) feeder overcurrent protection

65. Equipment installed in hazardous (classified) locations shall be marked to show the ______.

(a) class
(b) group
(c) temperature class (T Code) or operating temperature at a 40°C ambient temperature
(d) all of these

66. Equipotential planes shall be installed in outdoor concrete slabs where metallic equipment is located that may be energized and is accessible to livestock, other than poultry.

(a) True
(b) False

67. Explosionproof equipment is enclosed in a case capable of withstanding a(n) ______ of a specified gas or vapor and of preventing the ignition of a specified gas or vapor surrounding the enclosure. It operates so that the external temperature won't ignite the surrounding flammable atmosphere.

(a) internal explosion
(b) external explosion
(c) pressure imbalance
(d) temperature fluctuation

68. Exposed audio cables shall be secured by ______ or similar fittings designed and installed so as not to damage the cable.
(a) straps
(b) staples
(c) hangers
(d) any of these

69. Exposed CATV cables shall be secured by hardware such as straps, staples, cable ties, hangers, or similar fittings designed and installed so as not to damage the cables.
(a) True
(b) False

70. Exposed Class 2 and Class 3 cables shall be supported by straps, staples, hangers, or similar fittings designed and installed so as not to damage the cable.
(a) True
(b) False

71. Exposed communications cables shall be secured by hardware including straps, staples, cable ties, hangers, or similar fittings designed and installed so as not to damage the cable.
(a) True
(b) False

72. Exposed elements of impedance heating systems shall be physically guarded, isolated, or thermally insulated with a ______ jacket to protect against contact by personnel in the area.
(a) corrosion-resistant
(b) waterproof
(c) weatherproof
(d) flame-retardant

73. Exposed fire alarm circuit cables shall be supported by the building structure using straps, staples, hangers, cable ties or similar fittings designed and installed so as not to damage the cable.
(a) True
(b) False

74. Exposed live parts of motors and controllers operating at ______ or more between terminals shall be guarded against accidental contact by enclosure or by location.
(a) 24V
(b) 50V
(c) 60V
(d) 150V

75. Exposed network-powered broadband communications cables shall be secured to structural components by hardware including straps, staples, cable ties, hangers, or similar fittings designed and installed so as not to damage the cable.
(a) True
(b) False

76. Exposed noncurrent-carrying metal parts of an information technology system shall be ______.
(a) bonded to an equipment grounding conductor
(b) double-insulated
(c) GFCI protected
(d) a or b

77. Exposed secondary circuits of lighting systems operating at 30V or less shall be ______.
(a) installed in a Chapter 3 wiring method
(b) supplied by a Class 2 power source and shall use Class 2 cable in accordance with Article 725
(c) at least 7 ft above the finished floor unless listed for a lower installation height
(d) any of these

78. Feeder tap conductors supplying motor circuits, with an ampacity at least one-third that of the feeder, shall not exceed ______ in length.
(a) 10 ft
(b) 15 ft
(c) 20 ft
(d) 25 ft

79. Feeders for temporary installations can be cable assemblies or multiconductor cords or cables identified for hard usage or extra-hard usage.
(a) True
(b) False

80. Feeders to floating buildings can be installed with ______ where flexibility is required.

(a) extra-hard usage portable power cable listed for both wet locations and sunlight resistance
(b) LFMC with approved fittings
(c) LFNC with approved fittings
(d) all of these

81. Ferrous metal raceways, boxes, fittings, supports, and support hardware can be installed in concrete or in direct contact with the earth or other areas subject to severe corrosive influences, where ______ approved for the conditions.

(a) the soil is
(b) made of material
(c) the qualified installer is
(d) none of these

82. Field-installed skeleton tubing lighting is not required to be ______ where installed in conformance with the Code.

(a) listed
(b) identified for the purpose
(c) marked
(d) none of these

83. Fire alarm cables identified for future use shall be marked with a tag of sufficient durability to withstand ______.

(a) moisture
(b) humidity
(c) the environment involved
(d) none of these

84. Fire alarm cables that are not terminated at equipment and not identified for future use with a tag are considered abandoned.

(a) True
(b) False

85. Fire alarm systems include ______.

(a) fire detection and alarm notification
(b) guard's tour
(c) sprinkler waterflow
(d) all of these

86. Fire pump supply conductors on the load side of the final disconnecting means and overcurrent device(s) can be routed through a building(s) using ______.

(a) 2 in. of concrete encasement
(b) a listed 2-hour fire-rated assembly dedicated to the fire pump circuit
(c) a listed electrical circuit protective system with a minimum 2-hour fire rating
(d) any of these

87. Fittings used for connecting Type MC cable to boxes, cabinets, or other equipment shall ______.

(a) be nonmetallic only
(b) be listed and identified for such use
(c) be listed and identified as weatherproof
(d) include anti-shorting bushings

88. Fixed electric space-heating equipment and motors shall be considered a ______ load for branch circuit sizing.

(a) noncontinuous
(b) intermittent
(c) continuous
(d) none of these

89. Fixed electric space-heating equipment shall be installed to provide the ______ spacing between the equipment and adjacent combustible material, unless it is listed for direct contact with combustible material.

(a) required
(b) minimum
(c) maximum
(d) safest

90. Fixed electrical equipment installed in spaces above a Class I location in a commercial garage shall be ______.

(a) well ventilated
(b) located above the level of any defined Class I location
(c) identified for the location
(d) b or c

91. Fixed wiring in an aircraft hangar not in a Class I location shall be ______.

(a) metal raceways
(b) Type MI, TC, or MC cable
(c) nonmetallic raceways
(d) a or b

92. Fixture wires of 18 AWG or 16 AWG, shall be permitted for the control and operating circuits of X-ray equipment when protected by an overcurrent device not larger than ______.

(a) 15A
(b) 20A
(c) 25A
(d) 30A

93. Fixture wires used as pendant conductors for incandescent luminaires with intermediate or candelabra-base lampholders shall not be smaller than ______ AWG.

(a) 22
(b) 18
(c) 16
(d) 14

94. Flat conductor cable shall not be installed in ______.

(a) residential buildings
(b) schools
(c) hospitals
(d) any of these

95. Flexible conductors used to supply portable stage equipment shall be ______ cords or cables.

(a) listed
(b) extra-hard usage
(c) hard-usage
(d) a and b

96. Flexible cords and flexible cables are permitted for the electrical connection of permanently installed equipment racks of audio systems to facilitate access to equipment.

(a) True
(b) False

97. Flexible cords are not permitted in Class I locations.

(a) True
(b) False

98. Flexible cords for fixed or stationary pool equipment shall ______.

(a) not exceed 3 ft
(b) have a copper equipment grounding conductor not smaller than 12 AWG
(c) terminate in a grounding-type attachment plug
(d) all of these

99. Flexible cords for pendants installed above Class I locations in a commercial garage shall be ______.

(a) suitable for the type of service
(b) listed for hard usage
(c) a and b
(d) shall not be used

100. Flexible cords shall not be used as a substitute for ______ wiring.

(a) temporary
(b) fixed
(c) overhead
(d) none of these

CHALLENGE QUIZ

4

Article 90 through Chapter 9

Challenge Quiz 4—Article 90 through Chapter 9

Please use the 2011 *Code* book to answer the following questions, which are based on the 2011 *NEC.*

1. Flexible metal conduit must be securely fastened by a means approved by the authority having jurisdiction within ______ of termination.

   (a) 6 in.
   (b) 10 in.
   (c) 1 ft
   (d) 10 ft

2. Floor boxes ______ specifically for the application shall be used for receptacles located in the floor.

   (a) identified
   (b) listed
   (c) approved
   (d) none of these

3. FMC to a luminaire or electrical equipment within an accessible ceiling is permitted to be unsupported for not more than 6 ft from the last point where the raceway is securely fastened.

   (a) True
   (b) False

4. FMT can be used ______.

   (a) in dry and damp locations
   (b) for direct burial
   (c) in lengths over 6 ft
   (d) for a maximum of 1,000V

5. For a separate building or structure supplied by a separately derived system when overcurrent protection isn't provided for the supply conductors to the building/structure as permitted by 240.21(C)(4), the installation must be ______ in accordance with 250.30(A).

   (a) AFCI protected
   (b) grounded and bonded
   (c) isolated
   (d) all of these

6. For a single separately derived system, the grounding electrode conductor connects the grounded conductor of the derived system to the grounding electrode at the same point on the separately derived system where the ______ is connected.

   (a) metering equipment
   (b) transfer switch
   (c) system bonding jumper
   (d) largest circuit breaker

7. For a skin-effect heating installation complying with Article 427, the provisions of 300.20 shall apply to the installation of a single conductor in a ferromagnetic envelope (metal enclosure).

   (a) True
   (b) False

8. For buildings with grounding means but without an intersystem bonding termination, the grounding conductor for communications circuits shall terminate to the nearest ______.

   (a) building or structure grounding electrode system
   (b) interior metal water piping system, within 5 ft from its point of entrance
   (c) service equipment enclosure
   (d) any of these

9. For circuits and equipment operating at less than 50V, electrical equipment must be installed in a neat and workmanlike manner.

   (a) True
   (b) False

10. For Class I locations where 501.140(A)(5) is applied, flexible cords shall be ______ from the power source to the temporary portable assembly and from the temporary portable assembly to the utilization equipment.

(a) permitted to be spliced
(b) of continuous length
(c) installed in a metal raceway
(d) spliced only using listed splicing kits

11. For cord-and-plug-connected household electric ranges, an attachment plug and receptacle connection at the rear base of the range can serve as the disconnecting means, if it is ______.

(a) less than 40A
(b) a flush-mounted receptacle
(c) GFCI protected
(d) accessible by the removal of a drawer

12. For equipment rated 1,200A or more and over 6 ft wide that contains overcurrent devices, switching devices, or control devices, there shall be one entrance to and egress from the required working space not less than 24 in. wide and ______ high at each end of the working space.

(a) 5½ ft
(b) 6 ft
(c) 6½ ft
(d) any of these

13. For equipotential bonding of pool and spa equipment, a solid 8 AWG copper conductor shall be run back to the service equipment. This conductor shall be unbroken.

(a) True
(b) False

14. For existing installed luminaires in indoor locations, other than dwellings and associated accessory structures, a disconnecting means ______ in fluorescent luminaires that utilize double-ended lamps (typical fluorescent lamps) at the time a ballast is replaced.

(a) shall be installed
(b) is not required to be added
(c) shall not be installed
(d) can be a screw terminal

15. For grounded systems, electrical equipment and electrically conductive material likely to become energized, shall be installed in a manner that creates a low-impedance circuit capable of safely carrying the maximum ground-fault current likely to be imposed on it from where a ground fault may occur to the ______.

(a) ground
(b) earth
(c) electrical supply source
(d) none of these

16. For grounded systems, noncurrent-carrying conductive materials enclosing electrical conductors or equipment, or forming part of such equipment, shall be connected together and to the ______ to establish an effective ground-fault current path.

(a) ground
(b) earth
(c) electrical supply source
(d) none of these

17. For individual dwelling units of ______ dwellings, Table 310.15(B)(7) can be used to size 3-wire, single-phase, 120/240V service or feeder conductors that serve as the main power feeder.

(a) one-family
(b) two-family
(c) multifamily
(d) any of these

18. For indoor installations, heating, cooling, or ventilating equipment shall not be installed in the dedicated space above a panelboard or switchboard.

(a) True
(b) False

19. For installations consisting of not more than two 2-wire branch circuits, the building disconnecting means shall have a rating of not less than ______.

(a) 15A
(b) 20A
(c) 25A
(d) 30A

20. For interconnected electric power production sources, a hybrid system includes the utility power system.

(a) True
(b) False

21. For interconnected electric power production sources, a permanent warning label must be applied to the panelboard to warn others that the inverter output connection circuit breaker must not be relocated.

(a) True
(b) False

22. For interconnected electric power production sources, an electric power production source is permitted to be connected to the supply side of the service disconnecting means.

(a) True
(b) False

23. For interconnected electric power production sources, dedicated ac inverter circuit breakers that are backfed must be secured in place by an additional fastener as required by 408.36(D).

(a) True
(b) False

24. For interconnected electric power production sources, installation of one or more electrical power production sources operating in parallel with a primary source(s) of electricity must be installed only by ______.

(a) qualified persons
(b) utility company
(c) the authority having jurisdiction
(d) b or c

25. For interconnected electric power production sources, panelboards containing ac inverter circuit breakers must be field-marked to indicate the presence of multiple ac power sources.

(a) True
(b) False

26. For interconnected electric power production sources, the generating source and all distribution equipment associated with it that generates electricity from a source other than a utility supplied service is called a ______.

(a) service drop
(b) power production equipment
(c) service point
(d) utilization equipment

27. For interconnected electric power production sources, the output of a utility-interactive inverter can be connected to the load side of the service disconnecting means at any distribution equipment on the premises.

(a) True
(b) False

28. For interconnected electric power production sources, the point of common coupling is the point where electric power production systems interface.

(a) True
(b) False

29. For interconnected electric power production sources, utility-interactive inverters must be ______ for interconnection service.

(a) listed
(b) labeled
(c) identified
(d) a and c

30. For interconnected electric power production sources, dedicated ac inverter circuit breakers must be located at the opposite end from the input feeder supply conductors.

(a) True
(b) False

31. For optional standby systems, the temporary connection of a portable generator without transfer equipment shall be permitted where conditions of maintenance and supervision ensure that only qualified persons will service the installation, and where the normal supply is physically isolated by ______.

(a) a lockable disconnecting means
(b) the disconnection of the normal supply conductors
(c) an extended power outage
(d) a or b

32. For other than dwelling units or guest rooms of hotels or motels, the feeder and service calculation for track lighting shall be calculated at 150 VA for every _____ of lighting track or fraction thereof unless the track is supplied through a device that limits the current to the track.

(a) 1 ft
(b) 2 ft
(c) 3 ft
(d) 4 ft

33. For other than dwelling units, the branch circuits for pool-associated motors shall be installed in wiring methods including _____. Any wiring method employed shall include an insulated copper equipment grounding conductor sized in accordance with 250.122, but not smaller than 12 AWG.

(a) PVC conduit
(b) electrical metallic tubing where installed on or within buildings
(c) flexible metal conduit
(d) a or b

34. For other than one- or two-family dwellings, when 15A and 20A receptacles are installed in a wet location, the outlet box _____ must be listed for extra-duty use.

(a) sleeve
(b) hood
(c) threaded entry
(d) mounting

35. For PV systems, a _____ controller controls dc voltage, dc current, or both, and is used to charge a battery.

(a) charge
(b) power
(c) photovoltaic
(d) b and c

36. For PV systems, a(n) _____ is a device that changes direct-current input to an alternating-current output.

(a) diode
(b) rectifier
(c) transistor
(d) inverter

37. For PV systems, in one- and two-family dwellings, live parts over 150V to ground must not be _____ while energized.

(a) accessible to an inspector
(b) accessible to an electrician
(c) accessible to an unqualified person
(d) all of the above

38. For PV systems, means must be provided to disconnect equipment, such as batteries, inverters, charge controllers, and the like, from all ungrounded conductors of all sources.

(a) True
(b) False

39. For PV systems, one source for lowest-expected ambient temperature is the "Extreme Annual Mean Minimum Design Dry Bulb Temperature" found in the ASHRAE Handbook — Fundamentals.

(a) True
(b) False

40. For PV systems, the circuit(s) between modules and from modules to the common connection point(s), of the direct-current system is known as the _____.

(a) photovoltaic source circuit
(b) photovoltaic array circuit
(c) photovoltaic input circuit
(d) photovoltaic output circuit

41. For PV systems, the conductors between the inverter and an alternating-current panelboard for stand-alone systems, or the conductors between the inverter and the service equipment or another electric power production source, such as a utility, for an electrical production and distribution network, are part of the _____.

(a) bipolar photovoltaic array
(b) monopole subarray
(c) emergency standby power
(d) inverter output circuit

42. For PV systems, where all terminals of a disconnecting means may be energized when the switch is in the open position, a warning sign must be placed on or adjacent to the disconnecting means. The sign shall be similar to: WARNING ELECTRIC SHOCK HAZARD. DO NOT TOUCH TERMINALS. TERMINALS ON BOTH THE LINE AND LOAD SIDES MAY BE ENERGIZED IN THE OPEN POSITION.

(a) True
(b) False

43. For PV systems, where used for battery interconnections, flexible cables identified as hard-service use and moisture resistant in Article 400, must be a minimum size of ______ AWG.

(a) 1/0
(b) 2/0
(c) 3/0
(d) 4/0

44. For PV systems, where used for battery interconnections, flexible, fine-stranded cables must terminate in terminals, lugs, devices, or connectors that are identified and listed for fine-stranded conductors.

(a) identified
(b) listed
(c) a or b
(d) a and b

45. For stand-alone PV systems, energy storage or backup power supplies are required.

(a) True
(b) False

46. For stand-alone PV systems, the ac current output from a stand-alone inverter(s) can be ______ than the calculated load connected to the disconnect, but not less than the largest single utilization equipment connected to the system.

(a) less
(b) more
(c) greater
(d) any of these

47. For temporary installations, cable assemblies, flexible cords, and flexible cables shall be supported by ______ or similar fittings so as not to damage the wiring.

(a) staples
(b) cable ties
(c) straps
(d) any of these

48. For the purposes of conduit fill, a multiconductor cable or flexible cord of two or more conductors is considered ______ conductor(s).

(a) one
(b) two
(c) three
(d) four

49. Fountain equipment supplied by a flexible cord shall have all exposed noncurrent-carrying metal parts grounded by an insulated copper equipment grounding conductor that is an integral part of the cord.

(a) True
(b) False

50. Fuses or circuit breakers for PV dc circuits must be ______ for use in dc circuits and shall have the appropriate voltage, current, and interrupt ratings.

(a) identified
(b) approved
(c) recognized
(d) listed

51. General purpose Type CL2, CM, or CATV cables are permitted within the raised floor area of an information technology equipment room.

(a) True
(b) False

52. Generally speaking, conductors for lighting or power may occupy the same enclosure or raceway with conductors of power-limited fire alarm circuits.

(a) True
(b) False

53. General-purpose enclosures and fittings are permitted in Class I, Division 2 locations unless the enclosure contains make-and-break contacts for ______ as required by 501.105(B)(1), 501.115(B)(1), 501.150(B)(1).
(a) meters, instruments, and relays
(b) circuit breakers, or motor controllers
(c) signaling, alarm, remote-control, and communications systems
(d) all of these

54. GFCI protection in a mobile home shall be provided for ______.
(a) receptacle outlets installed outdoors and in compartments accessible from outside
(b) receptacles within 6 ft of a wet bar sink
(c) all receptacles in bathrooms including receptacles in luminaires
(d) all of these

55. GFCI protection is not permitted at carnivals, circuses, and fairs for ______.
(a) portable structures
(b) egress lighting
(c) a and b
(d) none of these

56. GFCI protection shall be provided at carnivals, circuses, and fairs for all 15A and 20A, 125V nonlocking-type receptacles that are readily accessible to the general public.
(a) True
(b) False

57. GFCI protection shall be provided for all 15A and 20A, 125V receptacles ______ in dwelling unit kitchens.
(a) installed to serve the countertop surfaces
(b) within 6 ft of the sink
(c) for all receptacles
(d) that are readily accessible

58. GFCI protection shall be required for all 125V receptacles not exceeding 30A and located within 6 ft measured ______ from the inside walls of a hydromassage bathtub.
(a) vertically
(b) horizontally
(c) across
(d) none of these

59. Grounded dc photovoltaic arrays must be provided with direct-current ______ meeting the requirements of 690.5(A) through (C) to reduce fire hazards.
(a) arc-fault protection
(b) rectifier protection
(c) ground-fault monitors
(d) ground-fault protection

60. Ground-fault protection for personnel is required for all temporary wiring used for construction, remodeling, maintenance, repair, or demolition of buildings, structures, or equipment, from power derived from an ______.
(a) electric utility company
(b) on-site generated power source
(c) a or b
(d) none of these

61. Ground-fault protection of equipment ______ for fire pumps.
(a) shall not be permitted
(b) shall be provided
(c) shall be permitted
(d) shall be listed

62. Ground-fault protection of equipment shall be provided for solidly grounded wye electrical systems of more than 150 volts-to-ground, but not exceeding 600V phase-to-phase for each individual device used as a building or structure main disconnecting means rated ______ or more, unless specifically exempted.
(a) 1,000A
(b) 1,500A
(c) 2,000A
(d) 2,500A

63. Ground-fault protection of equipment shall not be required at a feeder disconnect if ground-fault protection of equipment is provided on the ______ side of the feeder and on the load side of any transformer supplying the feeder.
(a) load
(b) supply
(c) service
(d) none of these

64. Grounding and bonding connection devices shall not depend solely on ______.

(a) pressure connections
(b) solder
(c) lugs
(d) approved clamps

65. Grounding electrode conductors shall be installed in one continuous length without a splice or joint, unless spliced ______.

(a) by connecting together sections of a busbar
(b) by irreversible compression-type connectors listed as grounding and bonding equipment
(c) by the exothermic welding process
(d) any of these

66. Grounding-type attachment plugs shall be used only with a cord having a(n) ______ conductor.

(a) equipment grounding
(b) isolated
(c) computer circuit
(d) insulated

67. Guest rooms or guest suites provided with permanent provisions for ______ shall have receptacle outlets installed in accordance with all of the applicable requirements for a dwelling unit as specified in 210.52.

(a) whirlpool tubs
(b) bathing
(c) cooking
(d) Internet access

68. Hallways in dwelling units that are ______ long or longer require a receptacle outlet.

(a) 6 ft
(b) 8 ft
(c) 10 ft
(d) 12 ft

69. Handholds in poles supporting luminaires shall not be required for poles ______ or less in height above finished grade, if the pole is provided with a hinged base.

(a) 5 ft
(b) 10 ft
(c) 15 ft
(d) 20 ft

70. Hazards often occur because of ______.

(a) overloading of wiring systems by methods or usage not in conformity with the *NEC*
(b) initial wiring not providing for increases in the use of electricity
(c) a and b
(d) none of these

71. HDPE conduit can be installed ______.

(a) where subject to chemicals for which the conduit is listed
(b) in direct burial installations in earth or concrete
(c) for conductors operating at a temperature above the rating of the raceway
(d) a and b

72. High-impedance grounded neutral systems shall be permitted for three-phase ac systems of 480 volts to 1,000 volts where ______.

(a) the conditions of maintenance ensure that only qualified persons service the installation
(b) ground detectors are installed on the system
(c) line-to-neutral loads are not served
(d) all of these

73. Horizontal runs of IMC supported by openings through framing members at intervals not exceeding 10 ft and securely fastened within 3 ft of terminations shall be permitted.

(a) True
(b) False

74. HPD cord shall be permitted for ______.

(a) not hard usage
(b) hard usage
(c) extra-hard usage
(d) all of these

75. Hydromassage bathtub electrical equipment shall be ______ without damaging the building structure or building finish.

(a) readily accessible
(b) accessible
(c) within sight
(d) none of these

76. If a generator for emergency system power located outdoors is equipped with a readily accessible disconnecting means located within sight (within 50 ft) of the building/structure, an additional disconnecting means isn't required on or at the building/structure for the generator feeder conductors that serve or pass through the building/structure.

(a) True
(b) False

77. If a permanently installed electric baseboard heater has factory-installed receptacle outlets, the receptacle is permitted to be connected to the heater circuits.

(a) True
(b) False

78. If a separate grounding electrode is installed for the radio and television equipment, it shall be bonded to the building's electrical power grounding electrode system with a bonding jumper not smaller than ______ AWG.

(a) 10
(b) 8
(c) 6
(d) 1/0

79. If a set of 120/240V overhead service conductors terminate at a through-the-roof raceway or approved support, with less than 6 ft of these conductors passing over the roof overhang, the minimum clearance above the roof for these service conductors shall be ______.

(a) 12 in.
(b) 18 in.
(c) 2 ft
(d) 5 ft

80. If an appliance of more than ⅛ hp is provided with a unit switch that complies with 422.34(A), (B), (C), or (D), the switch or circuit breaker serving as the other disconnecting means shall be permitted to be out of sight from the appliance.

(a) True
(b) False

81. If fire alarm conductors are installed in a raceway that is subjected to different temperatures, and where condensation is known to be a problem, the raceway must be filled with a material approved by the authority having jurisdiction that will prevent the circulation of warm air to a colder section of the raceway. An explosionproof seal ______ .

(a) is required for this purpose
(b) has been proven effective for this purpose
(c) isn't required for this purpose
(d) is the only method of doing this

82. If more than one luminaire is installed on a branch circuit that isn't of the multiwire type, a disconnecting means isn't required for every luminaire when the light switch for the space ensures that some of the luminaires in the space will still provide illumination.

(a) True
(b) False

83. If remote-control, signaling, and power-limited circuits are installed in a raceway that is subjected to different temperatures, and where condensation is known to be a problem, the raceway must be filled with a material approved by the authority having jurisdiction that will prevent the circulation of warm air to a colder section of the raceway. An explosionproof seal ______ .

(a) is required for this purpose
(b) has been proven effective for this purpose
(c) isn't required for this purpose
(d) is the only method of doing this

84. If the building or structure served has an intersystem bonding termination, the bonding conductor for an antenna mast shall be connected to the intersystem bonding termination.

(a) True
(b) False

85. If the transfer switch for a portable generator switches the ______ conductor, then it is being used as a separately derived system and the portable generator shall be grounded in accordance with 250.30.

(a) phase
(b) equipment grounding
(c) grounded
(d) all of these

86. If the voltage between overhead service conductors does not exceed 300V and the roof area is guarded or isolated, a reduction in clearance to 3 ft is permitted.

(a) True
(b) False

87. Illumination shall be provided for all working spaces about service equipment, switchboards, panelboards, and motor control centers _____.

(a) over 600V
(b) located indoors
(c) rated 1,200A or more
(d) using automatic means of control

88. IMC can be installed in or under cinder fill subject to permanent moisture _____.

(a) where the conduit is not less than 18 in. under the fill
(b) when protected on all sides by 2 in. of noncinder concrete
(c) where protected by corrosion protection judged suitable for the condition
(d) any of these

89. In a Class III location, pendant luminaires suspended by stems longer than _____ ft shall be provided with a fitting or flexible connector identified for the location, or it shall be provided with effective bracing.

(a) 1
(b) 2
(c) 3
(d) 4

90. In a dwelling unit, at least one lighting outlet _____ shall be located at the point of entry to the attic, underfloor space, utility room, or basement where these spaces are used for storage or contain equipment requiring servicing.

(a) that is unswitched
(b) containing a switch
(c) controlled by a wall switch
(d) b or c

91. In a dwelling unit, illumination for outdoor entrances that have grade-level access can be controlled by _____.

(a) remote
(b) central
(c) automatic control
(d) any of these

92. In a dwelling unit, illumination from a lighting outlet shall be provided at the exterior side of each outdoor entrance or exit that has grade-level access.

(a) True
(b) False

93. In a health care facility, receptacles and attachment plugs in a hazardous (classified) location within an anesthetizing area shall be listed for use in Class I, Group _____ locations.

(a) A
(b) B
(c) C
(d) D

94. In a hospital where flammable anesthetics are employed, the entire area that extends _____ shall be classified as a Class I, Division 1 location.

(a) upward to the structural ceiling
(b) upward to a level 8 ft above the floor
(c) upward to a level 5 ft above the floor
(d) 10 ft in all directions

95. In a multiple-occupancy building where electric service and electrical maintenance are provided by the building management under continuous building management supervision, the service disconnecting means can be accessible to authorized _____ only.

(a) inspectors
(b) tenants
(c) management personnel
(d) qualified persons

96. In a multiple-occupancy building, each occupant shall have access to the occupant's _____.

(a) service disconnecting means
(b) service drops
(c) distribution transformer
(d) lateral conductors

97. In an FMC installation, _____ connectors shall not be concealed.

(a) straight
(b) angle
(c) grounding-type
(d) none of these

98. In anesthetizing locations of health care facilities, low-voltage equipment in frequent contact with persons shall ______.

(a) operate on an electrical potential of 10V or less
(b) be moisture resistant
(c) be intrinsically safe or double-insulated
(d) any of these

99. In assembly occupancies, Type NM cable, AC cable, ENT, and PVC conduit can be installed in those portions of the building not required to be of ______ construction by the applicable building code.

(a) Class I, Division 1
(b) fire-rated
(c) occupancy-rated
(d) aboveground

100. In cellular concrete floor raceways, a cell is defined as a single, enclosed ______ space in a floor made of precast cellular concrete slabs, the direction of the cell being parallel to the direction of the floor member.

(a) circular
(b) oval
(c) tubular
(d) hexagonal

CHALLENGE QUIZ

5

Article 90 through Chapter 9

Challenge Quiz 5—Article 90 through Chapter 9

Please use the 2011 *Code* book to answer the following questions, which are based on the 2011 *NEC.*

1. In Class 1, Division 2 locations, Schedule 80 PVC conduit or reinforced thermosetting resin conduit (RTRC) shall be permitted where ______.

   (a) metal conduit does not provide sufficient corrosion resistance
   (b) only qualified persons service the installation
   (c) installed in industrial locations
   (d) all of these

2. In Class I locations, the locknut-bushing and double-locknut types of contacts shall not be depended on for bonding purposes.

   (a) True
   (b) False

3. In Class I, Division 2 locations, where metallic conduit doesn't provide sufficient corrosion resistance, reinforced thermosetting resin conduit and Schedule 80 PVC conduit can be used, but only in industrial establishments where maintenance and supervision ensure that only qualified persons service the installation.

   (a) True
   (b) False

4. In Class II, Division 1 locations, motors, generators, or other rotating electric machinery shall be ______.

   (a) identified for the location
   (b) totally enclosed pipe-ventilated, and meet the temperature limitations of 502.5
   (c) general duty
   (d) a or b

5. In Class II, Division 1 locations, switches, circuit breakers, motor controllers, and fuses, including pushbuttons, relays, and similar devices shall be provided with enclosures that are ______ .

   (a) explosionproof
   (b) identified for the location
   (c) dusttight
   (d) weatherproof

6. In Class II, Division 2 locations, flexible cord can serve as the supporting means for a pendant luminaire.

   (a) True
   (b) False

7. In Class II, Division 2 locations, motors, generators, or other rotating electrical equipment shall be ______.

   (a) totally enclosed nonventilated or pipe-ventilated
   (b) totally enclosed water-air-cooled or fan-cooled
   (c) dust-ignitionproof
   (d) any of these

8. In Class III locations, locknut-bushing and double-locknut types of fittings may be depended on for bonding purposes.

   (a) True
   (b) False

9. In Class III locations, motors, generators, and other rotating machinery shall be ______.

   (a) totally enclosed nonventilated
   (b) totally enclosed pipe-ventilated
   (c) totally enclosed fan-cooled
   (d) any of these

10. In Class III locations, portable lighting equipment shall be equipped with handles and protected with substantial guards. Lampholders shall be of the unswitched type with no provisions for ______.

    (a) receiving attachment plugs
    (b) grounding connections
    (c) lamp installation
    (d) hooks or hangers

11. In damp or wet locations of agricultural buildings, equipment enclosures and fittings shall be located or equipped to prevent moisture from ______ within the enclosure, box, conduit body, or fitting.

(a) entering
(b) accumulating
(c) a or b
(d) none of these

12. In determining the highest rated motor for purposes of 430.24, the highest rated motor shall be based on the rated full-load current as selected ______.

(a) from the motor nameplate
(b) from Tables 430.247, 430.248, 430.249, and 430.250
(c) from taking the horsepower times 746 watts
(d) using the largest horsepower motor

13. In dwelling units, a 125V receptacle shall be installed a minimum of 6 ft and a maximum of 20 ft from the inside wall of a pool.

(a) True
(b) False

14. In dwelling units, outdoor receptacles can be connected to one of the 20A small-appliance branch circuits.

(a) True
(b) False

15. In general, areas where acids and alkali chemicals are handled and stored may present corrosive conditions, particularly when wet or damp.

(a) True
(b) False

16. In hazardous (classified) locations, intrinsically safe apparatus shall be ______ in accordance with 250.100.

(a) secured
(b) bonded
(c) painted
(d) not be used

17. In health care facilities, installations of communications and signaling systems in other-than-patient-care areas must be in accordance with Chapter 7 and Chapter 8 as applicable.

(a) True
(b) False

18. In health care facilities, receptacles with insulated grounding terminals, as described in 250.146(D) shall be permitted in patient care areas.

(a) True
(b) False

19. In industrial establishments with restricted public access where only qualified persons will service the installation, MC-HL cable is allowed to be used in a Class I, Division 1 location if it is ______, and terminated with fittings listed for the application. Such cable must comply with Part II of Article 330.

(a) listed for use in Class I, Zone 1, or Division 1 locations
(b) has a gas/vaportight continuous corrugated metallic sheath, an overall jacket of suitable polymeric material
(c) has a separate equipment grounding conductor(s) in accordance with 250.122
(d) all of these

20. In industrial establishments with restricted public access, where the conditions of maintenance and supervision ensure that only qualified persons service the installation, Type ITC-HL cable is allowed to be used in a Class I, Division 1 location if it is ______ and installed in accordance with the provisions of Article 727.

(a) listed for use in Class I, Zone 1, or Division 1 locations
(b) has a gas/vaportight continuous corrugated metallic sheath, an overall jacket of suitable polymeric material
(c) is terminated with fittings listed for the application,
(d) all of these

21. In industrial facilities where conditions of maintenance and supervision ensure that only qualified persons will service the installation, cable tray systems can be used to support ______.

(a) raceways
(b) cables
(c) boxes and conduit bodies
(d) all of these

22. In installations where optical fiber cable is terminated on the outside of the building and is exposed to contact with electrical conductors, the metallic sheath members of the cable shall be ______ in accordance with 770.100, or interrupted by an insulating joint or equivalent device.

(a) bonded
(b) connected
(c) grounded
(d) isolated

23. In installations where the communications cable enters a building, the metallic sheath members of the cable shall be ______ as close as practicable to the point of entrance.

(a) grounded as specified in 800.100
(b) interrupted by an insulating joint or equivalent device
(c) a or b
(d) a and b

24. In marinas and boatyards, the bottom of enclosures for transformers shall not be located below ______.

(a) 2 ft above the dock
(b) 18 in. above the electrical datum plane
(c) the electrical datum plane
(d) a dock

25. In marinas or boatyards, the NEC requires a(n) ______ disconnecting means, which allows individual boats to be isolated from their supply connection.

(a) accessible
(b) readily accessible
(c) remote
(d) any of these

26. In mobile/manufactured homes, portable appliances could be ______, if these appliances can be moved from one place to another in normal use.

(a) refrigerators
(b) range equipment
(c) clothes washers
(d) all of these

27. In multiwire branch circuits, the continuity of the ______ conductor shall not be dependent upon the device connections.

(a) ungrounded
(b) grounded
(c) grounding electrode
(d) a and b

28. In one- and two-family dwellings where it is not practicable to achieve an overall maximum bonding conductor or equipment grounding conductor length of ______ for CATV, a separate grounding electrode as specified in 250.52(A)(5), (A)(6), or (A)(7) shall be used.

(a) 5 ft
(b) 8 ft
(c) 10 ft
(d) 20 ft

29. In one- and two-family dwellings where it is not practicable to achieve an overall maximum primary protector grounding conductor length of 20 ft or less for network-powered broadband communications systems, and a grounding means is not present, a separate ______ communications ground rod shall be driven and be bonded to the power grounding electrode system with a 6 AWG conductor.

(a) 5 ft
(b) 8 ft
(c) 10 ft
(d) 20 ft

30. In order for a metal underground water pipe to be used as a grounding electrode, it shall be in direct contact with the earth for ______ .

(a) 5 ft
(b) 10 ft or more
(c) less than 10 ft
(d) 20 ft or more

31. In other than dwelling units, GFCI protection shall be provided for all outdoor 15A and 20A, 125V receptacles.

(a) True
(b) False

32. In rooms other than kitchens and bathrooms of dwelling units, one or more receptacles controlled by a wall switch shall be permitted in lieu of _____.

(a) lighting outlets
(b) luminaires
(c) the receptacles required by 210.52(b) and (D)
(d) all of these

33. In spas or hot tubs, a clearly labeled emergency shutoff or control switch shall be _____, not less than 5 ft away, and within sight of the spa or hot tub.

(a) accessible
(b) readily accessible
(c) available
(d) none of these

34. In straight pulls, the length of the box or conduit body shall not be less than _____ times the trade size of the largest raceway.

(a) six
(b) eight
(c) 12
(d) none of these

35. In terms of Article 770, a cable routing assembly is composed of single or connected multiple channels as well as associated fittings, forming a structural system to _____ high densities of wires and cables, typically communications wires and cables, optical fiber and data (Class 2 and Class 3) cables.

(a) support
(b) route
(c) protect
(d) a, b, and c

36. In the *NEC*, the words "_____" indicate a mandatory requirement.

(a) shall
(b) shall not
(c) shall be permitted
(d) a or b

37. In ungrounded systems, electrical equipment, wiring, and other electrically conductive material likely to become energized shall be installed in a manner that creates a low-impedance circuit from any point on the wiring system to the electrical supply source to facilitate the operation of overcurrent devices should a(n) _____ fault from a different phase occur on the wiring system.

(a) isolated ground
(b) second ground
(c) arc
(d) high-impedance

38. In walls constructed of wood or other _____ material, electrical cabinets shall be flush with the finished surface or project there from.

(a) nonconductive
(b) porous
(c) fibrous
(d) combustible

39. Incandescent luminaires that have open lamps, and pendant-type luminaires, shall be permitted in clothes closets where proper clearance is maintained from combustible products.

(a) True
(b) False

40. Individual circuits for nonmotor-operated appliances that are continuously loaded shall have the branch-circuit rating sized not less than _____ percent of the appliance marked ampere rating, unless otherwise listed.

(a) 80
(b) 100
(c) 125
(d) 150

41. Individual unit equipment for legally required standby illumination shall be permanently fixed in place. Flexible cord-and-plug connection shall be permitted, provided the cord does not exceed _____ in length.

(a) 12 in.
(b) 18 in.
(c) 3 ft
(d) 6 ft

42. Indoor antenna and lead-in conductors for radio and television receiving equipment shall be separated by at least ______ from conductors of any electric light, power, or Class 1 circuit conductors, unless otherwise permitted.

(a) 2 in.
(b) 12 in.
(c) 18 in.
(d) 6 ft

43. Indoor antenna lead-in conductors for radio and television receiving equipment can be in the same enclosure with conductors of other wiring systems where separated by an effective, permanently installed barrier.

(a) True
(b) False

44. Indoor transformers of greater than ______ rating shall be installed in a transformer room of fire-resistant construction.

(a) 75 kVA
(b) 87½ kVA
(c) 112½ kVA
(d) 35,000 kVA

45. Installed supply circuits and interconnecting cables identified for future use in information technology equipment rooms must be marked with a tag of sufficient durability to withstand the environment involved which must include ______.

(a) date cable was identified for future use
(b) date of expected use
(c) intended future use of the cable
(d) all of these

46. Interconnecting cables under raised floors that support information technology equipment shall be Type ______.

(a) RF
(b) Type UF
(c) LS
(d) DP

47. Interior metal water piping located not more than ______ from the point of entrance to the building shall be permitted to be used as a conductor to interconnect electrodes that are part of the grounding electrode system.

(a) 2 ft
(b) 4 ft
(c) 5 ft
(d) 6 ft

48. Intrinsically safe apparatus, associated apparatus, and other equipment must be installed in accordance with the ______ drawing(s).

(a) approved
(b) control
(c) identified
(d) any of these

49. Intrinsically safe circuits must be identified at ______ locations to prevent unintentional interference during testing and servicing.

(a) terminal
(b) junction
(c) a or b
(d) a and b

50. It is frequently possible to locate much of the equipment in less hazardous or unclassified locations and thus reduce the amount of special equipment required.

(a) True
(b) False

51. It shall be permissible to ground meter enclosures located near the service disconnecting means to the ______ circuit conductor on the load side of the service disconnect, if service ground-fault protection is not provided.

(a) grounding
(b) bonding
(c) grounded
(d) phase

52. Joints between HDPE conduit shall be made using ______.

(a) expansion fittings
(b) an approved method
(c) a listed method
(d) none of these

53. Joints between NUCC, fittings, and boxes shall be made by ______.
(a) a qualified person
(b) set screw fittings
(c) an approved method
(d) exothermic welding

54. Joints between PVC conduit, couplings, fittings, and boxes shall be made by ______.
(a) the authority having jurisdiction
(b) set screw fittings
(c) an approved method
(d) expansion fittings

55. Junction, pull, and outlet boxes can be located behind PV modules that are secured by removable fasteners.
(a) True
(b) False

56. Knife switches rated for more than 1,200A at 250V or less ______.
(a) can be used only as isolating switches
(b) shall not be opened under load
(c) shall be placed so that gravity tends to close them
(d) a and b

57. Legally required standby system equipment shall be suitable for ______ at its terminals.
(a) the maximum available fault current
(b) the maximum overload current only
(c) the minimum fault current
(d) a 1-hour rating

58. Legally required standby system wiring can occupy the same raceways, cables, boxes, and cabinets with other general-purpose wiring.
(a) True
(b) False

59. LFMC shall not be required to be secured or supported where fished between access points through ______ spaces in finished buildings or structures and supporting is impractical.
(a) concealed
(b) exposed
(c) hazardous
(d) completed

60. Lighting systems operating at 30V or less can be concealed or extended through a building wall, floor or ceiling without regard to the wiring method used.
(a) True
(b) False

61. Lighting track is a manufactured assembly designed to support and ______ luminaires that are capable of being readily repositioned on the track.
(a) connect
(b) protect
(c) energize
(d) all of these

62. Listed fittings and connectors that are intended to be concealed at the time of on-site assembly are permitted for on-site interconnection of PV modules or other array components.
(a) True
(b) False

63. Listed FMC and LFMC shall contain an equipment grounding conductor if the raceway is installed for the reason of ______.
(a) physical protection
(b) flexibility after installation
(c) minimizing transmission of vibration from equipment
(d) b or c

64. Listed liquidtight flexible metal conduit (LFMC) is acceptable as an equipment grounding conductor when it terminates in listed fittings and is protected by an overcurrent device rated 60A or less for sizes ⊠ in. through ½ in.
(a) True
(b) False

65. Listed or labeled equipment shall be installed and used in accordance with any instructions included in the listing or labeling.

(a) True
(b) False

66. Listed plenum signaling raceways enclosing ______ cable can be installed in other spaces used for environmental air.

(a) Type CL2P
(b) Type CL3P
(c) a or b
(d) none of these

67. Listed spa and hot tub packaged units installed indoors, rated 20A or less, can be cord-and-plug-connected.

(a) True
(b) False

68. Live parts of electrical equipment operating at ______ or more shall be guarded against accidental contact by approved enclosures or by suitable permanent, substantial partitions, or screens arranged so that only qualified persons have access to the space within reach of the live parts.

(a) 20V
(b) 30V
(c) 50V
(d) 100V

69. Live parts of PV storage battery systems for dwellings shall be ______ to prevent accidental contact by persons or objects regardless of voltage.

(a) isolated
(b) grounded
(c) insulated
(d) guarded

70. Local metal underground systems or structures such as ______ are permitted to serve as grounding electrodes.

(a) piping systems
(b) underground tanks
(c) underground metal well casings
(d) all of these

71. Locations in which combustible dust is in the air under normal operating conditions in quantities sufficient to produce explosive or ignitible mixtures are classified as ______.

(a) Class I, Division 2
(b) Class II, Division 1
(c) Class II, Division 2
(d) Class III, Division 1

72. Loop wiring ______ in a cellular metal raceway.

(a) shall not be permitted
(b) shall not be considered a splice or tap
(c) shall be considered a splice or tap when used
(d) none of these

73. Loop wiring in an underfloor raceway ______ to be a splice or tap.

(a) shall be considered
(b) shall not be considered
(c) shall not be permitted
(d) none of these

74. Low-voltage contact limit is a voltage not exceeding ______.

(a) 15 volts (RMS) for sinusoidal ac or 21.20 volts peak for nonsinusoidal ac
(b) 30 volts for continuous dc
(c) 12.40 volts peak for dc that is interrupted at a rate of 10 to 200 Hz
(d) all of these

75. Luminaires and ceiling fans located over or within 5 ft, measured horizontally, from the inside walls of an indoor spa or hot tub shall have a mounting height of not less than ______ above the maximum water level when not GFCI protected.

(a) 4.70 ft
(b) 5 ft
(c) 7 ft 6 in.
(d) 12 ft

76. Luminaires attached to the framing of a suspended ceiling shall be secured to the framing member(s) by mechanical means such as ______.

(a) bolts
(b) screws
(c) rivets
(d) any of these

77. Luminaires can be installed in a commercial cooking hood if the luminaire is identified for use within a ______ cooking hood.

(a) nonresidential
(b) commercial
(c) multifamily
(d) all of these

78. Luminaires containing a metal halide lamp (other than a thick glass PAR lamp) shall be provided with a containment barrier that encloses the lamp, or shall be provided with a physical means that only allows the use of a(n) ______.

(a) Type O lamp
(b) Type CB lamp
(c) a or b
(d) inert gas

79. Luminaires for fixed lighting in Class II, Division 2 locations shall be equipped with enclosures that are ______ or otherwise identified for the location.

(a) dust-ignitionproof
(b) dusttight
(c) dustproof
(d) explosionproof

80. Luminaires identified for ______, with an integral outlet box per 410.21 shall be permitted to be used as a conductor raceway.

(a) through-wiring
(b) wet locations
(c) Class 1, Division 1 locations
(d) b and c

81. Luminaires in Class III locations exposed to physical damage shall be protected by a(n) ______ guard.

(a) plastic
(b) metal
(c) suitable
(d) explosionproof

82. Luminaires installed in a fountain shall ______.

(a) be capable of being removed from the water for relamping or normal maintenance
(b) not be permanently embedded into the fountain structure
(c) a and b
(d) a or b

83. Luminaires installed in Class I, Division 1 locations shall be identified as a complete assembly for the Class I, Division 1 location and shall be clearly marked to indicate the ______.

(a) maximum wattage of lamps
(b) minimum conductor size
(c) maximum overcurrent protection permitted
(d) all of these

84. Luminaires installed in Class I, Division 2 locations shall be protected from physical damage by a suitable ______.

(a) warning label
(b) pendant
(c) guard or by location
(d) all of these

85. Luminaires installed in Class II, Division 1 locations shall be protected from physical damage by a suitable ______.

(a) warning label
(b) pendant
(c) guard or by location
(d) all of these

86. Luminaires located more than 7½ ft above the floor can be connected to the equipment grounding return path complying with 517.13(A), without being connected to an insulated equipment grounding conductor.

(a) True
(b) False

87. Luminaires made of insulating material that are directly wired or attached to outlets supplied by a wiring method that does not provide a ready means for grounding attachment to an equipment grounding conductor shall be made of insulating material and shall have no exposed conductive parts.

(a) True
(b) False

88. Luminaires must maintain a minimum clearance from the closet storage space of ______.

(a) 12 in. for surface-mounted incandescent or LED luminaires with a completely enclosed light source
(b) 6 in. for surface-mounted fluorescent luminaires
(c) 6 in. for recessed fluorescent luminaires or recessed incandescent or LED luminaires with a completely enclosed light source
(d) all of these

89. Luminaires shall be marked with the maximum lamp wattage, manufacturer's _____, trademark, or other suitable means of identification.

(a) address
(b) name
(c) phone number
(d) none of these

90. Luminaires shall be wired with conductors having insulation suitable for the environmental conditions and _____ to which the conductors will be subjected.

(a) temperature
(b) voltage
(c) current
(d) all of these

91. Luminaires used in agricultural buildings shall _____.

(a) minimize the entrance of dust, foreign matter, moisture, and corrosive material
(b) be protected by a suitable guard if exposed to physical damage
(c) be listed for use in wet locations when exposed to water
(d) all of the above

92. Luminaires using a _____ lamp, that is subject to physical damage and installed in playing and spectator seating areas of indoor sports, mixed-use, or all-purpose facilities, shall be of the type that protects the lamp with a glass or plastic lens.

(a) mercury vapor
(b) metal halide
(c) fluorescent
(d) a or b

93. Main bonding jumpers and system bonding jumpers shall not be smaller than the sizes shown in _____.

(a) Table 250.66
(b) Table 250.122
(c) Table 310.15(B)(16)
(d) Chapter 9, Table 8

94. Manual switches controlling emergency circuits shall be convenient to authorized persons responsible for their _____.

(a) maintenance
(b) actuation
(c) inspection
(d) evaluation

95. Manufactured wiring systems shall be constructed with _____.

(a) Type AC cable
(b) Type MC cable
(c) a or b
(d) none of these

96. Materials such as straps, bolts, screws, and so forth, which are associated with the installation of IMC in wet locations shall be _____.

(a) weatherproof
(b) weathertight
(c) corrosion resistant
(d) none of these

97. Means shall be provided to simultaneously disconnect all _____ supply conductors to a phase converter.

(a) ungrounded
(b) grounded
(c) grounding
(d) all of these

98. Means to bypass and isolate transfer switch equipment shall not be permitted on legally required standby systems.

(a) True
(b) False

99. Mechanical elements used to terminate a grounding electrode conductor to a grounding electrode shall be accessible.

(a) True
(b) False

100. Metal cable trays containing only nonpower conductors such as communication, data, signal, conductors and cables must be electrically continuous, through listed connections or the use of an insulated stranded bonding jumper not smaller than _____.

(a) 12 AWG
(b) 10 AWG
(c) 6 AWG
(d) 4 AWG

CHALLENGE QUIZ

6

Article 90 through Chapter 9

Challenge Quiz 6—Article 90 through Chapter 9

Please use the 2011 *Code* book to answer the following questions, which are based on the 2011 *NEC.*

1. Metal enclosures and raceways for other than service conductors shall be connected to the neutral conductor.

(a) True
(b) False

2. Metal faceplates for receptacles shall be grounded.

(a) True
(b) False

3. Metal faceplates for switches and receptacles can be connected to the equipment grounding conductor by means of a metal mounting screw(s) securing the faceplate to a grounded outlet box or grounded wiring device in patient care areas.

(a) True
(b) False

4. Metal or nonmetallic poles used to support signs can contain the sign circuit conductors, provided the installation complies with 410.30(B).

(a) True
(b) False

5. Metal or nonmetallic raceways, cable armors, and cable sheaths _____ between cabinets, boxes, fittings or other enclosures or outlets.

(a) can be attached with electrical tape
(b) are allowed gaps for expansion
(c) shall be continuous
(d) none of these

6. Metal parts associated with an indoor spa or hot tub shall be bonded by _____.

(a) the interconnection of threaded metal piping and fittings
(b) metal-to-metal mounting on a common frame or base
(c) a solid copper bonding jumper not smaller than 8 AWG solid
(d) any of these

7. Metal parts of cord-and-plug-connected equipment shall be connected to an equipment grounding conductor that terminates to a grounding-type attachment plug.

(a) True
(b) False

8. Metal parts of electric equipment associated with an indoor spa or hot tub water circulating system shall be bonded together unless they are a part of a listed self-contained spa or hot tub.

(a) True
(b) False

9. Metal piping systems and metal parts in contact with the circulating water must be bonded together and to the circulating pump motor with an 8 AWG bare solid copper conductor if it's not double-insulated. The solid 8 AWG copper conductor isn't required to be bonded to any remote panelboard, service equipment, or electrode. The solid 8 AWG copper conductor used for bonding hydromassage bathtubs must have sufficient length to terminate on a _____, and must terminate to the equipment grounding conductor of the motor circuit when a double-insulated circulating pump motor is used.

(a) replacement non-double-insulated pump motor
(b) replacement double-insulated pump motor
(c) grounding electrode
(d) b or c

10. Metal wireways are sheet metal troughs with _____ for housing and protecting electric conductors and cable.

(a) removable covers
(b) hinged covers
(c) a or b
(d) none of these

11. Meters, instruments, instrument transformers, resistors, rectifiers, and thermionic tubes in Class I, Division 1 locations shall be installed in enclosures identified for use in Class I, Division 1 locations.

(a) True
(b) False

12. Mobile home and manufactured home feeder-circuit conductors shall have a capacity not less than ______.

(a) 50A
(b) 60A
(c) 100A
(d) 200A

13. Mobile home service equipment shall be located adjacent to the mobile home, located in sight from but not more than ______ from the exterior wall of the mobile home it serves.

(a) 15 ft
(b) 20 ft
(c) 30 ft
(d) 40 ft

14. Motor control circuits shall be arranged so they will be disconnected from all sources of supply when the disconnecting means is in the open position.

(a) True
(b) False

15. Motor controllers and terminals of control circuit devices shall be connected with copper conductors unless identified for use with a different conductor.

(a) True
(b) False

16. Motors shall be located so that adequate ______ is provided and so that maintenance, such as lubrication of bearings and replacing of brushes, can be readily accomplished.

(a) space
(b) ventilation
(c) protection
(d) all of these

17. Motors, generators, or other rotating electric machinery identified for Class I, Division 2 locations can be used in Class I, Division 1 locations.

(a) True
(b) False

18. Multiwire branch circuits for temporary wiring shall be provided with a means to disconnect simultaneously all ______ conductors where the branch circuit originates.

(a) underground
(b) overhead
(c) ungrounded
(d) grounded

19. Neon tubing which is readily accessible to pedestrians shall be protected from physical damage, other than ______.

(a) Class I, Division 1 locations
(b) dry-location portable signs
(c) fixed equipment
(d) wet-location portable signs

20. Network-powered broadband cable not terminated at equipment other than a connector, and not identified for future use with a tag, is considered abandoned.

(a) True
(b) False

21. Network-powered broadband communications system cables shall be separated at least 2 in. from conductors of ______ circuits.

(a) power
(b) electric light
(c) Class 1
(d) any of these

22. NFPA 70E—*Standard for Electrical Safety in the Workplace*, provides information to help determine the electrical safety training requirements expected of a qualified person.

(a) True
(b) False

23. No ______ shall be attached to any terminal or lead so as to reverse designated polarity.

(a) grounded conductor
(b) grounding conductor
(c) ungrounded conductor
(d) grounding connector

24. No conductor shall be used where its operating temperature exceeds that designated for the type of insulated conductor involved.

(a) True
(b) False

25. No wiring of any type shall be installed in ducts used to transport ______.

(a) dust
(b) flammable vapors
(c) loose stock
(d) all of these

26. Nominal battery voltage is typically ______.

(a) 2V per cell for lead-acid systems
(b) 1.20V for per cell for alkali systems
(c) 4V per cell for lithium-ion systems
(d) all of these

27. Non-load-break rated disconnecting means for PV output circuits must be marked "Do not open under load."

(a) True
(b) False

28. Nonlocking 15A and 20A, 125V and 250V receptacles installed in damp locations shall be listed as ______.

(a) raintight
(b) watertight
(c) weatherproof
(d) weather resistant

29. Nonlocking type 15A and 20A, 125V receptacles in ______ must be listed as tamper resistant.

(a) theatres
(b) arcades
(c) child care facilities
(d) major repair garages

30. Nonlocking type 15A and 20A, 125V receptacles in ______ must be listed as tamper resistant.

(a) restaurants
(b) guest rooms and guest suites
(c) office buildings
(d) b and c

31. Nonlocking type 15A and 20A, 125V receptacles in a dwelling unit shall be listed as tamper resistant except ______.

(a) receptacles located more than 5½ ft above the floor.
(b) receptacles that are part of a luminaire or appliance.
(c) a receptacle located within dedicated space for an appliance that in normal use is not easily moved from one place to another
(d) all of these

32. Nonmetallic surface extensions shall be secured in place by approved means at intervals not exceeding ______.

(a) 6 in.
(b) 8 in.
(c) 10 in.
(d) 16 in.

33. A nonmetallic surface metal raceway is a nonmetallic raceway that is intended to be mounted to the surface of a structure, with associated couplings, connectors, boxes, and fittings for the installation of electrical conductors.

(a) True
(b) False

34. Nonmetallic wireways can pass transversely through a wall ______.

(a) if the length through the wall is unbroken
(b) if the wall is not of fire-rated construction
(c) in hazardous (classified) locations
(d) if the wall is of fire-rated construction

35. Nonmetallic wireways shall be permitted for ______.

(a) exposed work
(b) concealed work
(c) wet locations if listed for the purpose
(d) a and c

36. Nonpower-limited fire alarm circuit conductors are permitted to be in the same cable, enclosure, or raceway with power-supply circuits where connected to the same equipment.

(a) True
(b) False

37. NUCC and its associated fittings shall be _____.

(a) listed
(b) metallic
(c) identified
(d) none of these

38. On a 4-wire, delta-connected system where the midpoint of one phase winding is grounded, the conductor having the higher phase voltage-to-ground shall be durably and permanently marked by an outer finish that is _____ in color.

(a) black
(b) red
(c) blue
(d) orange

39. On a three-phase, 4-wire, delta-connected service where the midpoint of one phase winding is grounded, the service conductor having the higher phase voltage-to-ground shall be durably and permanently marked by an outer finish that is _____ in color, or by other effective means, at each termination or junction point.

(a) orange
(b) red
(c) blue
(d) any of these

40. On a three-phase, 4-wire, wye circuit, where the major portion of the load consists of nonlinear loads, the neutral conductor shall be counted when applying 310.15(B)(3)(a) adjustment factors.

(a) True
(b) False

41. Only electrical equipment and wiring associated with the operation of the information technology room is allowed to be installed in the room. This does include HVAC systems, communications systems, telephone, fire alarm systems, security systems, water detection systems, and other related protective equipment.

(a) True
(b) False

42. Only inverters and ac PV modules listed as interactive can be used with interactive systems.

(a) True
(b) False

43. Only wiring methods recognized as _____ are included in this *Code*.

(a) expensive
(b) efficient
(c) suitable
(d) cost-effective

44. Open individual conductors shall not be smaller than _____ AWG copper for spans up to 50 ft in length and _____ AWG copper for a longer span, unless supported by a messenger wire.

(a) 10, 8
(b) 8, 8
(c) 6, 8
(d) 6, 6

45. Openings around penetrations of CATV coaxial cables and raceways through fire-resistant–rated walls, partitions, floors, or ceilings shall be _____ using approved methods to maintain the fire-resistance rating.

(a) closed
(b) opened
(c) draft stopped
(d) firestopped

46. Openings around penetrations of communications cables and raceways through fire-resistant–rated walls, partitions, floors, or ceilings shall be ______ using approved methods to maintain the fire-resistance rating.

(a) closed
(b) opened
(c) draft stopped
(d) firestopped

47. Openings around penetrations of optical fiber cables and raceways through fire-resistant–rated walls, partitions, floors, or ceilings shall be ______ using approved methods to maintain the fire-resistance rating.

(a) closed
(b) opened
(c) draft stopped
(d) firestopped

48. Openings in cabinets, cutout boxes, and meter socket enclosures through which conductors enter shall be ______.

(a) adequately closed
(b) made using concentric knockouts only
(c) centered in the cabinet wall
(d) identified

49. Optical fiber cables installed ______ on the surface of ceilings and walls shall be supported by the building structure in such a manner that the cable will not be damaged by normal building use.

(a) exposed
(b) concealed
(c) hidden
(d) a and b

50. Optical fiber cables not terminated at equipment, and not identified for future use with a tag are considered abandoned.

(a) True
(b) False

51. Optical fiber cables shall not be ______ to the exterior of any raceway as a means of support.

(a) strapped
(b) taped
(c) attached
(d) all of these

52. Optical fiber riser cables listed as suitable for use in a vertical run in a shaft or from floor to floor includes Types ______.

(a) OFNP and OFCP
(b) OFNR and OFCR
(c) OFNG and OFCG
(d) OFN and OFC

53. Optical fibers shall be permitted within the same composite cable as electric light, power, and Class 1 circuits operating at 600V or less, where the functions of the optical fibers and the electrical conductors are associated.

(a) True
(b) False

54. Optional standby system wiring is permitted to occupy the same raceways, cables, boxes, and cabinets with other general wiring.

(a) True
(b) False

55. Optional standby systems utilizing automatic transfer equipment shall have adequate capacity and rating for the supply of ______.

(a) all emergency lighting and power loads
(b) the load, as calculated in Article 220
(c) 100 percent of the appliance loads and 50 percent of the lighting loads
(d) 100 percent of the lighting loads and 75 percent of the appliance loads

56. Other than an energy storage subsystem of a photovoltaic system, such as a battery, a(n) ______ system operates in parallel with and may deliver power to an electrical production and distribution network.

(a) hybrid
(b) inverted
(c) interactive
(d) internal

57. Outdoor antennas and lead-in conductors shall be securely supported and the lead-in conductors shall be securely attached to the antenna, but they shall not be attached to the electric service mast.

(a) True
(b) False

58. Outlet boxes can be secured to suspended-ceiling framing members by mechanical means such as ______, or by other means identified for the suspended-ceiling framing member(s).

(a) bolts
(b) screws
(c) rivets
(d) all of these

59. Outside secondary conductors can be of unlimited length without overcurrent protection at the point they receive their supply if:

(a) The conductors are suitably protected from physical damage.
(b) The conductors terminate at a single circuit breaker or a single set of fuses that limits the load to the ampacity of the conductors.
(c) a and b
(d) none of these

60. Outside wiring shall not be installed beneath openings through which materials may be moved, and shall not be installed where they will obstruct entrance to these buildings' openings.

(a) True
(b) False

61. Overcurrent devices aren't permitted to be located in the bathrooms of ______

(a) dwelling units
(b) dormitories
(c) guest rooms or guest suites of hotels or motels
(d) all of these

62. Overcurrent devices for Class 1 circuits shall be located at the point where the conductor to be protected ______.

(a) terminates to the load
(b) is spliced to any other conductor
(c) receives its supply
(d) none of these

63. Overcurrent devices for legally required power systems shall be ______ with all supply-side overcurrent devices.

(a) series rated
(b) selectively coordinated
(c) installed in parallel
(d) any of these

64. Overcurrent devices shall be readily accessible and installed so the center of the grip of the operating handle of the switch or circuit breaker, when in its highest position, is not more than ______ above the floor or working platform.

(a) 2 ft
(b) 4 ft 6 in.
(c) 5 ft
(d) 6 ft 7 in.

65. Overcurrent protection for conductors and equipment is designed to ______ the circuit if the current reaches a value that will cause an excessive or dangerous temperature in conductors or conductor insulation.

(a) open
(b) close
(c) monitor
(d) record

66. Overcurrent protection for Type ITC cable shall not exceed ______ for 20 AWG and larger conductors.

(a) 3A
(b) 5A
(c) 10A
(d) 15A

67. Overcurrent protection shall not exceed ______.

(a) 15A for 14 AWG copper
(b) 20A for 12 AWG copper
(c) 30A for 10 AWG copper
(d) all of these

68. Overhead feeder conductors shall have a minimum ______ vertical clearance over residential property and driveways, as well as those commercial areas not subject to truck traffic, where the voltage is limited to 300 volts-to-ground.

(a) 10 ft
(b) 12 ft
(c) 15 ft
(d) 18 ft

69. Overhead service conductors can be supported to hardwood trees.

(a) True
(b) False

70. Overhead service conductors shall have a minimum of ______ vertical clearance from final grade over residential property and driveways, as well as over commercial areas not subject to truck traffic where the voltage is limited to 300 volts-to-ground.

(a) 10 ft
(b) 12 ft
(c) 15 ft
(d) 18 ft

71. Overhead service-entrance conductors of Type SE cable can be formed in a ______ and taped with self-sealing weather-resistant thermoplastic.

(a) loop
(b) circle
(c) gooseneck
(d) none of these

72. Overload devices are intended to protect motors, motor control apparatus, and motor branch-circuit conductors against ______.

(a) excessive heating due to motor overloads
(b) excessive heating due to failure to start
(c) short circuits and ground faults
(d) a and b

73. Parallel conductors shall have the same ______.

(a) length
(b) material
(c) size in circular mil area
(d) all of these

74. Pendant luminaires in a Class I, Division 1 location shall be suspended by and supplied through threaded rigid metal conduit stems or threaded steel intermediate conduit stems, and threaded joints shall be provided with ______ or other effective means to prevent loosening.

(a) set screws
(b) welded joints
(c) expansion joints
(d) explosionproof flex

75. Performance area includes the stage and audience seating area associated with a ______ stage structure, whether indoors or outdoors.

(a) temporary
(b) permanent
(c) a or b
(d) a and b

76. Photovoltaic alternating-current module systems are permitted to use one device to detect only ______ ground faults and to disable the array by removing ac power to the ac module(s).

(a) line-to-line
(b) direct-current
(c) line-to-neutral
(d) alternating-current

77. Photovoltaic source circuits and photovoltaic output circuits are not permitted to be contained in the same raceway, cable tray, cable, outlet box, junction box, or similar fitting, with non-photovoltaic systems unless the two systems are separated by a partition.

(a) True
(b) False

78. Photovoltaic source circuits shall be identified at all points of termination, connection, and splices.

(a) True
(b) False

79. Plug fuses of 15A or less shall be identified by a(n) ______ configuration of the window, cap, or other prominent part to distinguish them from fuses of higher ampere ratings.

(a) octagonal
(b) rectangular
(c) hexagonal
(d) triangular

80. Plug fuses of the Edison-base type shall be used ______.

(a) where overfusing is necessary
(b) as a replacement in existing installations
(c) as a replacement for Type S fuses
(d) 50A and above

81. Plug-in type backfed circuit breakers connected to a stand-alone PV system are not required to be secured in place by an additional fastener that requires other than a pull to release the breaker from the panelboard.

(a) True
(b) False

82. Plug-in-type circuit breakers that are backfed shall be ______ by an additional fastener that requires more than a pull to release.

(a) grounded
(b) secured in place
(c) shunt tripped
(d) none of these

83. Portable carnival or circus structures shall be maintained not less than ______ in any direction from overhead conductors operating at 600V or less.

(a) 7½ ft
(b) 10 ft
(c) 12½ ft
(d) 15 ft

84. Portable distribution and termination boxes installed outdoors at carnivals, circuses, or fairs shall be weatherproof and mounted so the bottom of the enclosure is not less than ______ above the ground.

(a) 6 in.
(b) 8 in.
(c) 10 in.
(d) 12 in.

85. Portable or transportable equipment with a self-contained power supply, such as battery-operated equipment, could potentially become an ignition source in hazardous (classified) locations.

(a) True
(b) False

86. Power distribution blocks installed in metal wireways shall ______.

(a) allow for sufficient wire-bending space at terminals
(b) not have uninsulated exposed live parts
(c) a or b
(d) a and b

87. Power distribution blocks shall be permitted in pull and junction boxes over 100 cubic inches when they comply with the provisions of 314.28(E).

(a) True
(b) False

88. Power to fire pump motors must be supplied by a reliable source of power that has the capacity to carry the ______.

(a) locked-rotor current of the fire pump motor(s)
(b) locked-rotor current of the pressure maintenance pump motors
(c) full-load current of any associated fire pump equipment
(d) all of these

89. Power-limited fire alarm cables can be supported by strapping, taping, or attaching to the exterior of a conduit or raceway.

(a) True
(b) False

90. Power-limited fire alarm cables installed within buildings shall be ______ as being resistant to the spread of fire.

(a) marked FR
(b) listed
(c) identified
(d) color-coded

91. PV source and output conductors must be routed along building structural members ______ where the location of those structural members can be determined by observation.

(a) beams and rafters
(b) trusses and columns
(c) windows and doors
(d) a and b

92. PVC conduit shall be permitted for exposed work where subject to physical damage if identified for such use.

(a) True
(b) False

93. Raceway fill limitations of 300.17 apply to coaxial cables installed in a raceway.

(a) True
(b) False

94. Raceways enclosing cables and conductors for fire alarm systems must be large enough to permit the ______ of conductors without damaging conductor insulation as limited by 300.17.

(a) installation
(b) removal
(c) splicing
(d) a and b

95. Raceways permitted as a wiring method in Class II, Division 2 locations include ______.

(a) RMC and IMC
(b) EMT
(c)ENT
(d) a or b

96. Raceways permitted in a Class III location include ______.

(a) RMC and IMC
(b) Type MC cable with listed termination fittings
(c) electrical metallic tubing
(d) any of these

97. Raceways shall be provided with expansion fittings where necessary to compensate for thermal expansion and contraction.

(a) True
(b) False

98. Raceways, cable trays, cablebus, auxiliary gutters, cable armor, boxes, cable sheathing, cabinets, elbows, couplings, fittings, supports, and support hardware shall be of materials suitable for ______.

(a) corrosive locations
(b) wet locations
(c) the environment in which they are to be installed
(d) none of these

99. Radiant heating cables embedded in or below a pool deck ______.

(a) shall not be installed within 5 ft horizontally from the inside walls of the pool
(b) shall be mounted at least 12 ft vertically above the pool deck
(c) shall not be permitted
(d) none of these

100. Receptacle outlet assemblies listed for the application can be installed in countertops of dwelling unit bathrooms.

(a) True
(b) False

CHALLENGE QUIZ 7

Article 90 through Chapter 9

Challenge Quiz 7—
Article 90 through Chapter 9

Please use the 2011 *Code* book to answer the following questions, which are based on the 2011 *NEC*.

1. Receptacle outlets can be installed below the countertop surface in dwelling units when necessary for the physically impaired, or if there is no means available to mount a receptacle above an island or peninsular countertop.

   (a) True
   (b) False

2. Receptacle outlets for mobile and manufactured homes are not allowed to be installed ______.

   (a) within or directly over a bathtub or shower space
   (b) in a face-up position in any countertop
   (c) underneath the skirting of the home
   (d) a or b

3. Receptacle outlets installed for a specific appliance in a dwelling unit, such as laundry equipment, shall be located within ______ of the intended location of the appliance.

   (a) sight
   (b) 3 ft
   (c) 6 ft
   (d) none of these

4. Receptacles incorporating an isolated grounding conductor connection intended for the reduction of electrical noise shall be identified by ______ on the face of the receptacle.

   (a) an orange triangle
   (b) a green triangle
   (c) the color orange
   (d) the engraved word ISOLATED

5. Receptacles installed behind a bed in the guest rooms in hotels and motels shall be located to prevent the bed from contacting an attachment plug, or the receptacle shall be provided with a suitable guard.

   (a) True
   (b) False

6. Receptacles installed in a dwelling unit kitchen to serve countertop surfaces shall be supplied by not fewer than ______ small-appliance branch circuits.

   (a) one
   (b) two
   (c) three
   (d) four

7. Receptacles installed outdoors, in a location protected from the weather or other damp locations, shall be in an enclosure that is ______ when the receptacle is covered.

   (a) raintight
   (b) weatherproof
   (c) rainproof
   (d) weathertight

8. Receptacles located within the rooms, bathrooms, playrooms, activity rooms, and patient care areas of designated pediatric locations shall be listed as ______, or shall employ a listed ______ cover.

   (a) tamper resistant
   (b) isolated
   (c) GFCI-protected
   (d) specification grade

9. Receptacles mounted in boxes flush with the finished surface or projecting beyond it shall be installed so that the mounting yoke or strap of the receptacle is ______.

   (a) held rigidly against the box or box cover
   (b) mounted behind the wall surface
   (c) held rigidly at the finished surface
   (d) none of these

10. Receptacles of dc plugging boxes shall be rated at not ______ when used on a stage or set of a motion picture studio.

(a) more than 30A
(b) less than 20A
(c) less than 30A
(d) more than 20A

11. Receptacles or their cover plates, supplied from the emergency electrical system in hospitals shall have a distinctive color or marking so as to be readily identifiable.

(a) True
(b) False

12. Receptacles rated other than 125V, single-phase, 15, 20, and 30A for temporary installations shall be protected by a ______.

(a) GFCI device
(b) written assured equipment grounding conductor program
(c) AFCI device
(d) a or b

13. Receptacles shall be located not less than ______ from the inside walls of a storable pool.

(a) 5 ft
(b) 6 ft
(c) 15 ft
(d) 20 ft

14. Receptacles shall not be grouped or ganged in enclosures unless the voltage between adjacent devices does not exceed ______.

(a) 100V
(b) 200V
(c) 300V
(d) 400V

15. Receptacles that provide shore power for boats shall be rated not less than ______.

(a) 15A
(b) 20A
(c) 30A
(d) 60A

16. Receptacles, cord connectors, and attachment plugs shall be constructed so that the receptacles or cord connectors do not accept an attachment plug with a different ______ or current rating than that for which the device is intended.

(a) voltage rating
(b) ampere interrupting capacity (AIC)
(c) temperature rating
(d) all of these

17. Recognized as suitable for the specific purpose, function, use, environment, and application is the definition of "______."

(a) labeled
(b) identified (as applied to equipment)
(c) listed
(d) approved

18. Reinforcing bars for use as a concrete-encased electrode can be bonded together by the usual steel tie wires or other effective means.

(a) True
(b) False

19. Remote-control circuits to safety-control equipment shall be classified as ______ if the failure of the equipment to operate introduces a direct fire or life hazard.

(a) Class 1
(b) Class 2
(c) Class 3
(d) Class I, Division 1

20. Replacement luminaires aren't required to be connected to an equipment grounding conductor if no equipment grounding conductor exists at the outlet box and the luminaire is ______.

(a) more than 20 years old
(b) mounted to the box using nonmetallic fittings and screws
(c) mounted more than 6 ft above the floor
(d) GFCI protected

21. Resistance-type heating elements in electric space-heating equipment shall be protected at not more than ______.

(a) 24A
(b) 36A
(c) 48A
(d) 60A

22. Rigid metal conduit and IMC shall not be required to be threaded when used in Class II, Division 2 locations.

(a) True
(b) False

23. Rigid metal conduit that is directly buried outdoors shall have at least ______ of cover.

(a) 6 in.
(b) 12 in.
(c) 18 in.
(d) 24 in.

24. Running threads shall not be used on IMC for connection at couplings.

(a) True
(b) False

25. Sealing compound shall be used in Type MI cable termination fittings to ______

(a) prevent the passage of gas or vapor
(b) exclude moisture and other fluids from the cable insulation
(c) limit a possible explosion
(d) prevent the escape of powder

26. Seals in Class II hazardous (classified) locations shall be explosionproof.

(a) True
(b) False

27. Separate data processing units can be interconnected by means of listed cables and cable assemblies. Where exposed to physical damage, the installation shall be protected.

(a) True
(b) False

28. Separately derived system generators must have the ______ conductor sized not smaller than required to carry the maximum unbalanced current as determined by 220.61.

(a) neutral
(b) grounding
(c) a and b
(d) none of these

29. Service conductors can supply ______ service disconnecting means as permitted in 230.71(A).

(a) only one
(b) only two
(c) up to six
(d) an unlimited number of

30. Service conductors installed as unjacketed multiconductor cable shall have a minimum clearance of ______ from windows that are designed to be opened, doors, porches, stairs, fire escapes, or similar locations.

(a) 3 ft
(b) 4 ft
(c) 6 ft
(d) 10 ft

31. Service equipment for floating docks or marinas shall be located ______ the floating structure.

(a) adjacent to
(b) on
(c) in
(d) any of these

32. Service equipment shall be securely fastened to a solid backing and be installed so as to be protected from the weather, unless of weatherproof construction.

(a) True
(b) False

33. Service raceways for overhead service drops or overhead service conductors shall have a weatherhead listed for ______.

(a) wet locations
(b) damp locations
(c) Class 2 locations
(d) NEMA 3R

34. Service-entrance cables which are not installed underground, where subject to physical damage, shall be protected by ______.

(a) rigid metal conduit
(b) IMC
(c) Schedule 80 PVC conduit
(d) any of these

35. Short sections of raceways used for ______ shall not be required to be installed complete between outlet, junction, or splicing points.
(a) meter to service enclosure connection
(b) protection of cables from physical damage
(c) nipples
(d) separately derived systems

36. Short-radius conduit bodies such as capped elbows, and service-entrance elbows that enclose conductors 6 AWG and smaller shall not contain ______.
(a) splices
(b) taps
(c) devices
(d) any of these

37. Signaling, alarm, remote-control and communications system circuits containing contacts installed in Class II, Division 2 locations shall be in enclosures that are ______ or otherwise identified for the location.
(a) dust-ignitionproof
(b) dusttight
(c) dustproof
(d) explosionproof

38. Signs and outline lighting systems shall be marked with ______.
(a) the manufacturer's name, trademark, or other means of identification
(b) input voltage
(c) current rating
(d) all of these

39. Since Class 3 control circuits permit higher allowable levels of voltage and current than Class 2 control circuits, additional ______ are specified to provide protection against the electric shock hazard.
(a) circuits
(b) safeguards
(c) conditions
(d) requirements

40. Single-conductor Type USE-2 and single conductor cable ______ as PV wire can be run exposed at outdoor locations for PV source circuits for PV module interconnections within the PV array.
(a) approved
(b) listed or labeled
(c) listed and labeled
(d) none of the above

41. Single-pole breakers utilizing identified handle ties are not permitted to be used for the required disconnecting means for motor fuel dispensing equipment.
(a) True
(b) False

42. Single-pole breakers with identified handle ties can be used to protect each ungrounded conductor for line-to-line connected loads.
(a) True
(b) False

43. Single-throw knife switches shall be installed so that gravity will tend to close the switch.
(a) True
(b) False

44. Snap switches are considered to be part of the effective ground-fault current path when ______.
(a) the switch is connected to the intersystem bonding termination
(b) the switch is mounted with metal screws to a metal box or a metal cover that's connected to an equipment grounding conductor of a type recognized in 250.118
(c) an equipment grounding conductor or equipment bonding jumper is connected to the grounding terminal of the metal mounting yoke.
(d) b or c

45. Snap switches in listed assemblies aren't required to be connected to an equipment grounding conductor if ______.

(a) the device is provided with a nonmetallic faceplate that cannot be installed on any other type of device and the device does not have mounting means to accept other configurations of faceplates
(b) the device is equipped with a nonmetallic yoke
(c) all parts of the device that are accessible after installation of the faceplate are manufactured of nonmetallic material
(d) all of these

46. Snap switches rated ______ or less directly connected to aluminum conductors shall be listed and marked CO/ALR.

(a) 15A
(b) 20A
(c) 25A
(d) 30A

47. Soldered splices shall first be spliced or joined so as to be mechanically and electrically secure without solder and then be soldered.

(a) True
(b) False

48. Some cleaning and lubricating compounds can cause severe deterioration of many plastic materials used for insulating and structural applications in equipment.

(a) True
(b) False

49. Supplementary overcurrent protection ______.

(a) shall not be used in luminaires
(b) may be used as a substitute for a branch-circuit overcurrent device
(c) may be used to protect internal circuits of equipment
(d) shall be readily accessible

50. A surface metal raceway is a metallic raceway that is intended to be mounted to the surface of a structure, with associated couplings, connectors, boxes, and fittings for the installation of electrical conductors.

(a) True
(b) False

51. Surface metal raceways shall not be used ______.

(a) where subject to severe physical damage
(b) where subject to corrosive vapors
(c) in hoistways
(d) all of these

52. Surface nonmetallic raceways shall be supported in accordance with the ______ installation instructions.

(a) vendor's
(b) supplier's
(c) manufacturer's
(d) engineer's

53. Surface-mounted luminaires ______ located over or within 5 ft, measured horizontally, from the inside walls of an indoor spa or hot tub can be installed at less than 7 ft 6 in. above the maximum water level when GFCI protected.

(a) with a glass or plastic globe
(b) with a nonmetallic body or a metallic body isolated from contact
(c) suitable for use in a damp location
(d) all of these

54. Surge protective devices shall be marked with a short-circuit current rating and shall not be installed where the available fault current is in excess of that rating.

(a) True
(b) False

55. Surge protective devices shall only be located outdoors.

(a) True
(b) False

56. Switchboards that have any exposed live parts shall be installed in permanently ______ locations, and then only where under competent supervision and accessible only to qualified persons.

(a) dry
(b) mounted
(c) supported
(d) all of these

57. Switches and circuit breakers used as switches can be mounted ______ if they are installed adjacent to motors, appliances, or other equipment that they supply and are accessible by portable means.
(a) not higher than 6 ft 7 in.
(b) higher than 6 ft 7 in.
(c) in the mechanical equipment room
(d) up to 8 ft high

58. Switches controlling line-to-neutral lighting loads must have a neutral provided at the switch location unless ______.
(a) the conductors for switches enter the device box through a raceway that has sufficient cross-sectional area to accommodate a neutral conductor
(b) cable assemblies for switches enter the box through a framing cavity that's open at the top or bottom on the same floor level, or through a wall, floor, or ceiling that's unfinished on one side
(c) the lighting consists of all fluorescent fixtures with integral disconnects for the ballasts
(d) a or b

59. Switches not required for projectors, flood or other special effect lamps shall not be installed in projection rooms.
(a) True
(b) False

60. Switches shall be located at least ______, measured horizontally, from the inside walls of an indoor spa or hot tub.
(a) 4 ft
(b) 5 ft
(c) 7 ft 6 in.
(d) 12 ft

61. Switches shall not be installed within wet locations in tub or shower spaces unless installed as part of a listed tub or shower assembly.
(a) True
(b) False

62. Tap connections to a common grounding electrode conductor for multiple separately derived systems may be made to a copper or aluminum busbar that is ______.
(a) not over ½ in. x 4 in.
(b) not over ¼ in. x 2 in.
(c) at least ¼ in. x 2 in.
(d) a and c

63. Tap devices used in Type FC assemblies shall be rated not less than ______ or more than 300 volts-to-ground.
(a) 15A
(b) 20A
(c) 30A
(d) 40A

64. Temporary currents resulting from abnormal conditions, such as ground faults, are not considered to be objectionable currents.
(a) True
(b) False

65. Temporary electrical power and lighting shall be permitted during emergencies and for ______.
(a) tests
(b) experiments
(c) developmental work
(d) all of these

66. Temporary wiring methods shall be acceptable only if ______, based on the conditions of use and any special requirements of the temporary installation.
(a) listed
(b) identified
(c) approved
(d) any of these

67. Temporary wiring shall be ______ immediately upon the completion of construction or purpose for which the wiring was installed.
(a) disconnected
(b) removed
(c) de-energized
(d) any of these

68. Testing legally required standby system lighting and power systems during maximum anticipated load conditions shall be avoided so as not to tax the standby system unnecessarily.

(a) True
(b) False

69. The _____ conductor terminals of a junction box (pool deck box), transformer enclosure, or other enclosure in the supply circuit to a wet-niche luminaire shall be connected to the equipment grounding terminal of the panelboard.

(a) equipment grounding
(b) grounded
(c) grounding electrode
(d) ungrounded

70. The _____ has the responsibility for deciding on the approval of equipment and materials.

(a) manufacturer
(b) authority having jurisdiction
(c) testing agency
(d) none of these

71. The _____ is the basic photovoltaic device that generates electricity when exposed to light.

(a) solar battery
(b) solar cell
(c) solar atom
(d) solar ray

72. The _____ is the point of connection between the facilities of the serving utility and the premises wiring.

(a) service entrance
(b) service point
(c) overcurrent protection
(d) beginning of the wiring system

73. The _____ of a circuit shall be selected and coordinated to permit the circuit protective devices to clear a fault without extensive damage to the electrical equipment of the circuit.

(a) overcurrent devices
(b) total circuit impedance
(c) equipment short-circuit current ratings
(d) all of these

74. The _____ of any system is the ratio of the maximum demand of a system, or part of a system, to the total connected load of a system.

(a) load
(b) demand factor
(c) minimum load
(d) calculated factor

75. The _____ shall conduct or witness a test of the complete legally required standby system upon installation.

(a) electrical engineer
(b) authority having jurisdiction
(c) qualified person
(d) manufacturer's representative

76. The _____ shall conduct or witness an acceptance test of the complete emergency system upon installation and periodically afterward.

(a) electrical engineer
(b) authority having jurisdiction
(c) qualified person
(d) manufacturer's representative

77. The 3 VA per-square-foot general lighting load for dwelling units does not include _____.

(a) open porches
(b) garages
(c) unused or unfinished spaces not adaptable for future use
(d) all of these

78. The 3 VA per-square-foot general lighting load for dwelling units includes general-use receptacles and lighting outlets.

(a) True
(b) False

79. The 8 AWG solid bonding jumper required for hydromassage bathtubs shall not be required to be extended to any _____.

(a) remote panelboard
(b) service equipment
(c) electrode
(d) all of these

80. The ac ohms-to-neutral impedance per 1,000 ft of 2/0 AWG copper conductor in a steel raceway is ______.

(a) 0.06 ohms
(b) 0.10 ohms
(c) 0.11 ohms
(d) 0.22 ohms

81. The ac ohms-to-neutral impedance per 1,000 ft of 4/0 AWG aluminum conductor in a steel raceway is ______.

(a) 0.06 ohms
(b) 0.10 ohms
(c) 0.11 ohms
(d) 0.22 ohms

82. The ac ohms-to-neutral impedance per 1,000 ft of 4/0 AWG aluminum in a steel raceway is the same as the ohms-to-neutral impedance of 1,000 ft of ______ copper installed in a steel raceway.

(a) 1 AWG
(b) 1/0 AWG
(c) 2/0 AWG
(d) 250 kcmil

83. The accessible portion of abandoned interconnecting cables under an information technology room raised floor shall be removed, unless the cables are contained within a ______.

(a) raceway
(b) panelboard
(c) a and b
(d) none of these

84. The allowable ampacity of flexible cords and cables is found in ______.

(a) Table 310.15(B)(16)
(b) Tables 400.5(A)(1) and (2)
(c) Chapter 9, Table 1
(d) Table 430.52

85. The ampacity adjustment factors of 310.15(B)(3)(a) shall not apply to conductors installed in strut-type channel raceways where ______.

(a) the cross-sectional area of the raceway is at least 4 sq in.
(b) the number of current-carrying conductors does not exceed 30
(c) the sum of the cross-sectional areas of all contained conductors does not exceed 20 percent of the interior cross-sectional area of the strut-type channel raceway
(d) all of these

86. The ampacity adjustment factors of 310.15(B)(3)(a) shall not apply to conductors installed in surface metal raceways where ______.

(a) the cross-sectional area exceeds 4 sq in.
(b) the current-carrying conductors do not exceed 30 in number
(c) the total cross-sectional area of all conductors does not exceed 20 percent of the interior cross-sectional area of the raceway
(d) all of these

87. The ampacity adjustment factors of Table 310.15(B)(3)(a) does not apply to Type AC or Type MC cable without an overall outer jacket, if which of the following conditions are met?

(a) Each cable has not more than three current-carrying conductors.
(b) The conductors are 12 AWG copper.
(c) No more than 20 current-carrying conductors are installed without maintaining spacing.
(d) all of these

88. The ampacity of a conductor can be different along the length of the conductor. The higher ampacity can be used beyond the point of transition for a distance of no more than ______ ft, or no more than ______ percent of the circuit length figured at the higher ampacity, whichever is less.

(a) 10, 10
(b) 10, 20
(c) 15, 15
(d) 20, 10

89. The ampacity of capacitor circuit conductors shall not be less than ______ percent of the rated current of the capacitor.
(a) 100
(b) 115
(c) 125
(d) 135

90. The ampacity of the supply conductors to an individual electric arc welder shall not be less than the effective current value on the rating plate.
(a) True
(b) False

91. The ampacity of Type UF cable shall be that of ______ in accordance with 310.15.
(a) 60°C conductors
(b) 75°C conductors
(c) 90°C conductors
(d) 105°C

92. The area in sq in. for a 1/0 AWG bare aluminum conductor is ______.
(a) 0.087 sq in.
(b) 0.109 sq in.
(c) 0.137 sq in.
(d) 0.173 sq in.

93. The area used for ______ of alcohol-based windshield washer fluid into motor vehicles in repair garages shall be unclassified.
(a) storage
(b) handling
(c) dispensing into motor vehicles
(d) any of these

94. The authority having jurisdiction has the responsibility for ______.
(a) making interpretations of rules
(b) deciding upon the approval of equipment and materials
(c) waiving specific requirements in the *Code* and permitting alternate methods and material if safety is maintained
(d) all of these

95. The authority having jurisdiction shall not be allowed to enforce any requirements of Chapter 7 (Special Conditions) or Chapter 8 (Communications Systems).
(a) True
(b) False

96. The bonding conductor or grounding electrode conductor for a radio/television antenna system must be mechanically protected where subject to physical damage, and where installed in a metal raceway both ends of the raceway must be bonded to the ______ conductor.
(a) contained
(b) grounded
(c) ungrounded
(d) b or c

97. The bonding jumper used to bond the metal water piping system shall be sized in accordance with ______.
(a) Table 250.66
(b) Table 250.122
(c) Table 310.15(B)(16)
(d) Table 310.15(B)(6)

98. The branch circuit supplying submersible fountain equipment shall be ______, unless the equipment is listed for operation at not more than 15V.
(a) 240V
(b) GFCI protected
(c) a and b
(d) none of these

99. The branch-circuit overcurrent devices for legally required standby systems shall be accessible only to ______.
(a) the authority having jurisdiction
(b) authorized persons
(c) the general public
(d) qualified persons

100. The choice of overcurrent devices so that an overcurrent condition will be localized and restrict outages to the circuit or equipment affected, is called "______."
(a) overcurrent protection
(b) interrupting capacity
(c) selective coordination
(d) overload protection

FINAL EXAM
1

Questions in Random Order for Article 90 through Annex C

Final Exam 1—Questions in Random Order for Article 90 through Annex C

Please use the 2011 *Code* book to answer the following questions, which are based on the 2011 *NEC*.

1. The circuit conductors between the inverter or direct-current utilization equipment and the photovoltaic source circuit(s) is part of the ______.

   (a) photovoltaic output circuit
   (b) photovoltaic input circuit
   (c) inverter input circuit
   (d) inverter output circuit

2. The *Code* covers underground mine installations and self-propelled mobile surface mining machinery and its attendant electrical trailing cable.

   (a) True
   (b) False

3. The Code provides rules for the minimum number of receptacle outlets required in a dwelling unit. The minimum required receptacle outlets shall be in addition to receptacle outlets that are ______.

   (a) part of a luminaire or appliance
   (b) controlled by a wall switch for use as required illumination
   (c) located more than 5½ ft above the floor
   (d) all of these

4. The Code requires the installation of an equipment grounding conductor of the wire type in ______.

   (a) Rigid metal conduit (RMC).
   (b) Intermediate metal conduit (IMC).
   (c) Electrical metallic tubing (EMT).
   (d) Listed flexible metal conduit over 6 ft in length

5. The combination of all components and subsystems that convert solar energy into electrical energy is called a "______ system."

   (a) solar
   (b) solar voltaic
   (c) separately derived source
   (d) solar photovoltaic

6. The common grounding electrode conductor installed for multiple separately derived systems shall not be smaller than ______ copper when using a wire-type conductor.

   (a) 1/0 AWG
   (b) 2/0 AWG
   (c) 3/0 AWG
   (d) 4/0 AWG

7. The common point on a wye-connection in a polyphase system describes a neutral point.

   (a) True
   (b) False

8. The conductor ampacity adjustment factors only apply to the number of current-carrying conductors in the cable and not to the number of conductors in the cable tray.

   (a) True
   (b) False

9. The conductor insulation of Type MI cable shall be a highly compressed refractory mineral that provides proper ______ for all conductors.

   (a) covering
   (b) spacing
   (c) resistance
   (d) none of these

10. The conductor used to ground the outer cover of a CATV coaxial cable shall be permitted to be ______.

    (a) insulated
    (b) 14 AWG minimum
    (c) bare
    (d) all of the above

11. The conductors between the final overcurrent device protecting the circuit and the outlet(s) are known as "_____ conductors."
(a) feeder
(b) branch-circuit
(c) home run
(d) none of these

12. The conductors of PV output circuits and inverter input and output circuits shall be identified at all points of termination, connection, and splices.
(a) True
(b) False

13. The conductors, including splices and taps, in a metal surface raceway having a removable cover shall not fill the raceway to more than _____ percent of its cross-sectional area at that point.
(a) 38
(b) 40
(c) 53
(d) 75

14. The connected load on lighting track is permitted to exceed the rating of the track under some conditions.
(a) True
(b) False

15. The connection of the grounding electrode conductor to a buried grounding electrode (driven ground rod) shall be made with a listed terminal device that is accessible.
(a) True
(b) False

16. The continuous current-carrying capacity of 1½ sq in. copper busbar mounted in an unventilated sheet metal auxiliary gutter is _____.
(a) 500A
(b) 650A
(c) 750A
(d) 1,500A

17. The cross-sectional area (sq in.) of a single 12 THHN conductor is _____.
(a) 0.0133
(b) 0.0147
(c) 0.0233
(d) 0.0321

18. The cross-sectional area of the conductors permitted in a sealing fitting shall not exceed _____ percent of the cross-sectional area of RMC of the same trade size.
(a) 25
(b) 50
(c) 100
(d) 125

19. The cross-sectional area of trade size 1 IMC is approximately _____.
(a) 0.62 sq in.
(b) 0.96 sq in.
(c) 1.22 sq in.
(d) 2.13 sq in.

20. The cut ends of PVC conduit must be trimmed to remove the burrs and rough edges.
(a) True
(b) False

21. The demand factors of Table 220.56 apply to space heating, ventilating, or air-conditioning equipment.
(a) True
(b) False

22. The direct-current system grounding connection must be made at any _____ point(s) on the photovoltaic output circuit.
(a) single
(b) two
(c) three
(d) four

23. The disconnecting means for a shore power connection shall be not more than _____ from the receptacle it controls.
(a) 12 in.
(b) 24 in.
(c) 30 in.
(d) 36 in.

24. The disconnecting means for a torque motor shall have an ampere rating of at least ______ percent of the motor nameplate current.
(a) 100
(b) 115
(c) 125
(d) 175

25. The disconnecting means for air-conditioning and refrigerating equipment shall be ______ from the air-conditioning or refrigerating equipment.
(a) readily accessible
(b) within sight
(c) a or b
(d) a and b

26. The distance between a shielded cable or conductor entry and its exit from the box shall not be less than ______ times the outside diameter of that cable or conductor on a system of over 600V.
(a) 12
(b) 16
(c) 24
(d) 36

27. The distribution point is also known as the ______.
(a) center yard pole
(b) meter pole
(c) common distribution point
(d) all of these

28. The electric motors, controllers, and wiring for an electrically operated pool cover shall be ______.
(a) located at least 5 ft from the inside wall of the pool
(b) separated from the pool by a permanent barrier
(c) a and b
(d) a or b

29. The emergency controls for attended self-service stations shall be located no more than ______ from motor fuel dispensers.
(a) 20 ft
(b) 50 ft
(c) 75 ft
(d) 100 ft

30. The enclosure for a transformer or ground-fault circuit interrupter connected to a conduit that extends directly to a pool light forming shell shall be ______ for this purpose.
(a) labeled
(b) listed
(c) approved
(d) a and b

31. The equipment grounding conductor at a marina is required to be an insulated copper conductor for all circuits.
(a) True
(b) False

32. The equipment grounding conductor shall not be required to be larger than the circuit conductors.
(a) True
(b) False

33. The essential electrical systems in a health care facility shall be supplied from ______.
(a) a normal source generally supplying the entire electrical system
(b) one or more alternate sources for use when the normal source is interrupted
(c) a or b
(d) a and b

34. The fire alarm circuit disconnecting means for a power-limited fire alarm system must ______.
(a) have red identification
(b) be accessible only to qualified personnel
(c) be identified as FIRE ALARM CIRCUIT
(d) all of the above

35. The fuel cell system shall be evaluated and ______ for its intended application.
(a) approved
(b) identified
(c) listed
(d) marked

36. The general requirement for each service drop, set of overhead service conductors, set of underground service conductors, or service lateral is that it shall supply ______ set(s) of service-entrance conductors.

(a) only one
(b) only two
(c) up to six
(d) an unlimited number of

37. The GFCI protection required by 210.8(A) and (B) must be ______.

(a) the circuit breaker type only
(b) accessible
(c) readily accessible
(d) concealed

38. The grounded conductor of an alternating-current system operating at less than 1,000V shall be routed with the ungrounded conductors and connected to each disconnecting means grounded conductor terminal or bus, which is then connected to the service disconnecting means enclosure via a(n) ______ that's installed between the service neutral conductor and the service disconnecting means enclosure.

(a) equipment bonding conductor
(b) main bonding jumper
(c) grounding electrode
(d) intersystem bonding terminal

39. The grounding conductor connection to the grounding electrode shall be made by ______.

(a) listed lugs
(b) exothermic welding
(c) listed pressure connectors
(d) any of these

40. The grounding conductor for an antenna mast shall be ______ protected where subject to physical damage.

(a) electrically
(b) mechanically
(c) arc-fault
(d) none of these

41. The grounding conductor for CATV coaxial cable shall be ______ protected where subject to physical damage.

(a) electrically
(b) arc-fault
(c) physically
(d) none of these

42. The grounding electrode conductor shall be connected to the grounded service conductor at the ______.

(a) load end of the service drop
(b) load end of the service lateral
(c) service disconnecting means
(d) any of these

43. The grounding electrode used for grounding strike termination devices of a lightning protection system can be used as a grounding electrode system for the buildings or structures.

(a) True
(b) False

44. The identification of ______ to which a grounded conductor is to be connected shall be substantially white in color.

(a) wire connectors
(b) circuit breakers
(c) terminals
(d) ground rods

45. The insulation temperature rating of conductors in Type NM cable shall be ______.

(a) 60°C
(b) 75°C
(c) 90°C
(d) 105°C

46. The interior of underground raceways shall be considered a ______ location.

(a) wet
(b) dry
(c) damp
(d) corrosive

47. The markings required on signs and outline lighting systems in 600.4(A) must be permanent, durable, and ______ when in wet locations.

(a) weatherproof
(b) laminated
(c) rainproof
(d) indelible

48. The material located in the *NEC* Annexes are part of the requirements of the *Code* and shall be complied with.

(a) True
(b) False

49. The maximum size conductors permitted in a metal surface raceway shall not be larger than that for which the wireway is designed.

(a) True
(b) False

50. The maximum size conductors permitted in a nonmetallic surface raceway shall not be larger than that for which the wireway is designed.

(a) True
(b) False

51. The messenger of messenger-supported wiring shall be supported at dead ends and at intermediate locations so as to eliminate ______ on the circuit conductors.

(a) static
(b) magnetism
(c) tension
(d) induction

52. The metal mounting yoke of a replacement switch isn't required to be connected to an equipment grounding conductor if the wiring at the existing switch doesn't contain an equipment grounding conductor, and ______

(a) the switch faceplate is nonmetallic with nonmetallic screws
(b) the replacement switch is GFCI protected.
(c) a or b
(d) the circuit is AFCI protected

53. The minimum radius of a field bend on trade size 1¼ RMC is ______.

(a) 7 in.
(b) 8 in.
(c) 10 in.
(d) 14 in.

54. The minimum size parallel conductors permitted for elevator lighting shall be ______, provided the combined ampacity is equivalent to at least that of a 14 AWG conductor.

(a) 20 AWG
(b) 16 AWG
(c) 14 AWG
(d) 1/0 AWG

55. The minimum working space on a circuit that is 120 volts-to-ground, with exposed live parts on one side and no live or grounded parts on the other side of the working space, is ______.

(a) 1 ft
(b) 3 ft
(c) 4 ft
(d) 6 ft

56. The mobile home park secondary electrical distribution system to mobile home lots shall be ______.

(a) 120/208V, single-phase
(b) 120/240V single-phase
(c) a or b
(d) none of these

57. The motor ______ currents listed in Tables 430.247 through 430.250 shall be used to determine the ampacity of motor circuit conductors and short-circuit and ground-fault protection devices.

(a) nameplate
(b) full-load
(c) power factor
(d) service factor

58. The motor branch-circuit short-circuit and ground-fault protective device shall be capable of carrying the ______ current of the motor.

(a) varying
(b) starting
(c) running
(d) continuous

59. The motor controller shall have horsepower ratings at the application voltage not ______ the horsepower rating of the motor.

(a) lower than
(b) higher than
(c) equal to
(d) none of these

60. The motor disconnecting means shall not be required to be in sight from the motor and the driven machinery location, provided ______.

(a) the controller disconnecting means is capable of being individually locked in the open position
(b) the provisions for locking are permanently installed on, or at, the switch or circuit breaker used as the controller disconnecting means
(c) locating the motor disconnecting means within sight of the motor is impractical or introduces additional or increased hazards to people or property
(d) all of these

61. The NEC allows a lighting outlet on the wall in a clothes closet when it is at least 6 in. away from storage space.

(a) True
(b) False

62. The *NEC* defines a(n) "______" as one who has skills and knowledge related to the construction and operation of the electrical equipment and installations and has received safety training to recognize and avoid the hazards involved.

(a) inspector
(b) master electrician
(c) journeyman electrician
(d) qualified person

63. The *NEC* does not cover electrical installations in ships, watercraft, railway rolling stock, aircraft, or automotive vehicles.

(a) True
(b) False

64. The *NEC* requires tested series-rated installations of circuit breakers or fuses to be legibly marked in the field to indicate the equipment has been applied with a series combination rating.

(a) True
(b) False

65. The NEC specifies wiring methods for manufactured buildings.

(a) True
(b) False

66. The number and size of conductors permitted in a raceway is limited to ______.

(a) permit heat to dissipate
(b) prevent damage to insulation during installation
(c) prevent damage to insulation during removal of conductors
(d) all of these

67. The number of conductors in a raceway for permanent audio system installations shall not be limited by the percentage fill specified in Chapter 9, Table 1.

(a) True
(b) False

68. The number of conductors permitted in LFNC shall not exceed the percentage fill specified in ______.

(a) Chapter 9, Table 1
(b) Table 250.66
(c) Table 310.15(B)(16)
(d) 240.6

69. The number of conductors permitted in PVC conduit shall not exceed the percentage fill specified in ______.

(a) Chapter 9, Table 1
(b) Table 250.66
(c) Table 310.15(B)(16)
(d) 240.6

70. The number of fixture wires in a single conduit or tubing shall not exceed the percentage fill specified in ______.

(a) Chapter 9, Table 1
(b) Table 250.66
(c) Table 310.15(B)(16)
(d) 240.6

71. The number of nonpower-limited fire alarm conductors in a raceway shall not be required to comply with the fill requirements contained in 300.17.

(a) True
(b) False

72. The number of receptacle outlets for guest rooms in hotels and motels shall not be less than that required for a dwelling unit. These receptacles can be located to be convenient for permanent furniture layout, but at least ______ receptacle outlets shall be readily accessible.

(a) one
(b) two
(c) three
(d) four

73. The outer sheath of Type MI cable is made of ______.

(a) aluminum
(b) steel alloy
(c) copper
(d) b or c

74. The patient care area of a health care facility does not include business offices, corridors, lounges, day rooms, dining rooms, or similar areas.

(a) True
(b) False

75. The permitted conduit fill for five conductors is ______ percent.

(a) 35
(b) 40
(c) 55
(d) 60

76. The phase converter disconnecting means shall be ______ and located in sight from the phase converter.

(a) protected from physical damage
(b) readily accessible
(c) easily visible
(d) clearly identified

77. The photovoltaic system voltage is the direct-current voltage of any photovoltaic source or photovoltaic output circuit.

(a) True
(b) False

78. The point of entrance ______ of a network-powered broadband cable is the point at which the cable emerges from an external wall, from a concrete floor slab, or from a rigid metal conduit (Type RMC) or an intermediate metal conduit (Type IMC) connected by a bonding conductor or grounding electrode conductor to an electrode in accordance with 830.100(B).

(a) outside a building
(b) within a building
(c) on the building
(d) none of these

79. The point of entrance of a CATV coaxial cable is the point ______ at which the coaxial cable emerges from an external wall, from a concrete floor slab, or from a rigid metal conduit (Type RMC) or an intermediate metal conduit (Type IMC) connected by a grounding conductor to an electrode in accordance with 820.100(B).

(a) outside a building
(b) within a building
(c) on the building
(d) none of these

80. The point of entrance of a communications circuit is the point ______ at which the communications cable emerges from an external wall, from a concrete floor slab, or from a RMC or an IMC connected by a grounding conductor to an electrode.

(a) outside a building
(b) within a building
(c) on the building
(d) none of these

81. The point of entrance of an optical fiber installation is the point ______ at which the optical fiber cable emerges from an external wall, from a concrete floor slab, or from a rigid metal conduit or an intermediate metal conduit connected by a grounding conductor to an electrode in accordance with 770.100(B).

(a) outside a building
(b) within a building
(c) on the building
(d) none of these

82. The point of interconnection of the PV system power source to other sources must be marked at an accessible location at the ______ as a power source and with the rated ac output current and nominal operating ac voltage.

(a) disconnecting means
(b) array
(c) inverter
(d) none of the above

83. The power source for a nonpower-limited fire alarm circuit shall not be supplied through a(n) ______.

(a) ground-fault circuit interrupter
(b) arc-fault circuit interrupter
(c) inverse time circuit breaker
(d) a or b

84. The power source for a nonpower-limited fire alarm circuit shall not operate at more than ______.

(a) 120V
(b) 300V
(c) 600V
(d) 20A

85. The primary overcurrent protection for a transformer rated 600V, nominal, or less, with no secondary protection and having a primary current rating of over 9A must be set at not more than ______ percent.

(a) 125
(b) 167
(c) 200
(d) 300

86. The prospective symmetrical fault current at a nominal voltage to which an apparatus or system is able to be connected without sustaining damage exceeding defined acceptance criteria is known as the "______."

(a) short-circuit current rating
(b) arc flash rating
(c) overcurrent rating
(d) available fault current

87. The provisions of Article 690 apply to ______ systems, including inverter(s), array circuit(s), and controller(s) for such systems.

(a) solar photoconductive
(b) solar photovoltaic
(c) solar photogenic
(d) solar photosynthesis

88. The purpose of sensitive electronic equipment is to reduce objectionable noise in sensitive electronic equipment in ______ locations.

(a) commercial
(b) industrial
(c) a and b
(d) institutional

89. The purpose of the equipotential plane is to prevent a difference in voltage from developing within the plane area.

(a) True
(b) False

90. The purpose or use of panelboard circuits and circuit ______, including spare positions, shall be legibly identified on a circuit directory located on the face or inside of the door of a panelboard, and at each switch or circuit breaker on a switchboard.

(a) manufacturers
(b) conductors
(c) feeders
(d) modifications

91. The PV source circuit current is calculated by multiplying the sum of the parallel module nameplate short-circuit current ratings (Isc) by 125 percent.

(a) True
(b) False

92. The PV system dc disconnect must be placed at a readily accessible location ______ of a building or structure to disconnect the ungrounded PV system dc circuit conductors.

(a) outside
(b) inside, nearest the point of entrance
(c) anywhere inside
(d) a or b

93. The receptacle outlet for a dwelling unit bathroom must be located on a ______ adjacent to the basin counter surface, or on the side or face of the basin cabinet not more than 12 in. below the countertop.

(a) wall
(b) partition
(c) light fixture
(d) a or b

94. The removal of shielding material or the separation of the twisted pairs isn't required within the conduit seal fitting in a Class I, Division 2 hazardous (classified) location provided the termination is by an approved means to minimize the entrance of gases or vapors and prevent flame propagation.

(a) True
(b) False

95. The service conductors shall be connected to the service disconnecting means by ______ or other approved means.

(a) pressure connectors
(b) clamps
(c) solder
(d) a or b

96. The service disconnecting means shall be marked as suitable for use as service equipment and shall be ______.

(a) weatherproof
(b) listed
(c) approved
(d) acceptable

97. The service drop is defined as the overhead conductors between the utility electric supply system and the ______.

(a) service equipment
(b) service point
(c) grounding electrode
(d) equipment grounding conductor

98. The space between 5 ft and 10 ft from the open end of a vent, extending in all directions, shall be classified as ______in a bulk storage plant.

(a) Class I, Division 1
(b) Class I, Division 2
(c) Class II, Division 1
(d) Class II, Division 2

99. The supply conductors shall directly connect the power source to either a listed fire pump controller or listed combination fire pump controller and power transfer switch.

(a) True
(b) False

100. The temperature rating associated with the ampacity of a ______ shall be so selected and coordinated so as not to exceed the lowest temperature rating of any connected termination, conductor, or device.

(a) terminal
(b) conductor
(c) device
(d) all of these

FINAL EXAM

2

Questions in Random Order for Article 90 through Annex C

Final Exam 2—Questions in Random Order for Article 90 through Annex C

Please use the 2011 *Code* book to answer the following questions, which are based on the 2011 *NEC.*

1. The term "luminaire" includes an individual lampholder.

   (a) True
   (b) False

2. The term "mobile home" includes manufactured homes, unless otherwise indicated.

   (a) True
   (b) False

3. The terminal of a wiring device for the connection of the equipment grounding conductor shall be identified by a green-colored, _____.

   (a) not readily removable terminal screw with a hexagonal head
   (b) hexagonal, not readily removable terminal nut
   (c) pressure wire connector
   (d) any of these

4. The top shield installed over all floor-mounted Type FCC cable shall completely _____ all cable runs, corners, connectors, and ends.

   (a) cover
   (b) encase
   (c) protect
   (d) none of these

5. The total rating of a cord-and-plug-connected room air conditioner, connected to the same branch circuit which supplies lighting units, other appliances, or general-use receptacles, shall not exceed _____ percent of the branch-circuit rating.

   (a) 40
   (b) 50
   (c) 70
   (d) 80

6. The total rating of utilization equipment fastened in place, shall not exceed _____ percent of the branch-circuit ampere rating where lighting units and cord-and-plug-connected utilization equipment are supplied.

   (a) 50
   (b) 75
   (c) 100
   (d) 125

7. The total volume occupied by two internal cable clamps, six 12 AWG conductors, and a single-pole switch is _____.

   (a) 2.00 cu in.
   (b) 4.50 cu in.
   (c) 14.50 cu in.
   (d) 20.25 cu in.

8. The two to six disconnects for a disconnecting means for a building supplied by a feeder shall be _____.

   (a) the same size
   (b) grouped
   (c) in the same enclosure
   (d) none of these

9. The underground conductors between the utility electric supply system and the service point are known as the "_____."

   (a) utility service
   (b) service lateral
   (c) service drop
   (d) main service conductors

10. The ungrounded and grounded conductors of each _____ shall be grouped by wire ties or similar means at the panelboard or other point of origination.

    (a) branch circuit
    (b) multiwire branch circuit
    (c) feeder circuit
    (d) service-entrance conductor

11. The use of NUCC shall be permitted ______.

(a) for direct burial underground installations
(b) to be encased or embedded in concrete
(c) in cinder fill
(d) all of these

12. The voltage at the line terminals of a fire pump motor controller shall not drop more than ______ percent below the controller's normal rated voltage under motor-starting conditions.

(a) 5
(b) 10
(c) 15
(d) any of these

13. The voltage drop on technical power systems for sensitive electronic equipment shall not exceed ______ percent for branch circuits.

(a) 1.50
(b) 2
(c) 2.50
(d) 2.80

14. The white conductor within a cable can be used for a(n) ______ conductor where permanently reidentified to indicate its use as an ungrounded conductor at each location where the conductor is visible and accessible.

(a) grounded
(b) ungrounded
(c) a and b
(d) none of these

15. The wiring methods permitted in theaters, audience areas of motion picture and television studios, performance areas, and similar locations are ______.

(a) any metal raceway
(b) nonmetallic raceways encased in 2 in. of concrete
(c) Type MC or AC cable with an insulated equipment grounding conductor
(d) any of these

16. The word "Earth" best describes what *NEC* term?

(a) Bonded
(b) Ground
(c) Effective ground-fault current path
(d) Guarded

17. The working clearance for a distribution panelboard in a recreational vehicle shall be not less than ______.

(a) 24 in. wide
(b) 30 in. deep
(c) 30 in. wide
(d) a and b

18. The working space in front of the electric equipment shall not be less than ______ wide, or the width of the equipment, whichever is greater.

(a) 15 in.
(b) 30 in.
(c) 40 in.
(d) 60 in.

19. This *Code* covers the installation of ______ for public and private premises, including buildings, structures, mobile homes, recreational vehicles, and floating buildings.

(a) optical fiber cables
(b) electrical equipment
(c) raceways
(d) all of these

20. Threadless couplings and connectors used with RMC buried in masonry or concrete shall be the ______ type.

(a) raintight
(b) wet and damp location
(c) nonabsorbent
(d) concrete-tight

21. Threadless couplings approved for use with IMC in wet locations shall be ______.

(a) rainproof
(b) listed for wet locations
(c) moistureproof
(d) concrete-tight

22. Three-way and four-way switches shall be wired so that all switching is done only in the ______ circuit conductor.

(a) ungrounded
(b) grounded
(c) equipment ground
(d) neutral

23. To determine the feeder calculated load for ten 3 kW household cooking appliances, use _____ of Table 220.55.

(a) Column A
(b) Column B
(c) Column C
(d) none of these

24. To limit the voltage induced by lightning, one conductor of a 2-wire PV system operating at over _____ must be solidly grounded (connected to the earth) in accordance with 250.4(A)(1).

(a) 15V
(b) 30V
(c) 50V
(d) none of these

25. To prevent moisture from entering service equipment, service-entrance conductors shall _____.

(a) be connected to service-drop conductors below the level of the service head
(b) have drip loops formed on the individual service-entrance conductors
(c) a or b
(d) a and b

26. Track lighting shall not be installed _____.

(a) where likely to be subjected to physical damage
(b) in wet or damp locations
(c) a and b
(d) none of these

27. Transformer vaults shall be located where they can be ventilated to the outside air without using flues or ducts, where _____.

(a) permitted
(b) practicable
(c) required
(d) all of these

28. Transformers and capacitors installed in Class I, Division 1 locations containing a liquid that will burn shall be installed in vaults.

(a) True
(b) False

29. Transformers that supply a fire pump motor shall be sized no less than _____ percent of the sum of the fire pump motor(s) and pressure maintenance pump motors, and 100 percent of associated fire pump accessory equipment.

(a) 100
(b) 125
(c) 250
(d) 300

30. Transformers with ventilating openings shall be installed so that the ventilating openings _____.

(a) are a minimum 18 in. above the floor
(b) are not blocked by walls or obstructions
(c) are aesthetically located
(d) are vented to the exterior of the building

31. Two or more grounding electrodes bonded together are considered a single grounding electrode system.

(a) True
(b) False

32. Two-family dwellings, multifamily dwellings, and multiple occupancy buildings shall be permitted to have one set of service entrance conductors to supply branch circuits for public or common areas.

(a) True
(b) False

33. Type _____ cable is a factory assembly of conductors with an overall covering of nonmetallic material suitable for direct burial in the earth.

(a) NM
(b) UF
(c) SE
(d) TC

34. Type _____ cable is a factory assembly of insulated conductors under a nonmetallic sheath for installation in cable trays or raceways.

(a) NM
(b) TC
(c) SE
(d) UF

35. Type ______ is a multiconductor cable identified for use as underground service-entrance cable.
    (a) SE
    (b) NM
    (c) UF
    (d) USE

36. Type 3 surge protective devices can be installed on the load side of a branch-circuit overcurrent device up to the equipment served. If ______, the Type 3 SPD connection must be a minimum 30 ft of conductor distance from the service or separately derived system disconnect.
    (a) voltage drop is excessive
    (b) installed in a metal raceway or cable
    (c) included in the manufacturer's instructions
    (d) b and c

37. Type AC cable installed in thermal insulation shall have conductors that are rated at 90°C. The ampacity of the cable in this application shall be based on ______.
    (a) that of 60°C conductors
    (b) that of 75°C conductors
    (c) that of 90°C conductors
    (d) none of these

38. Type AC cable is permitted in ______ installations.
    (a) wet
    (b) cable tray
    (c) exposed
    (d) b and c

39. Type AC cable shall be secured at intervals not exceeding 4½ ft and within ______ of every outlet box, cabinet, conduit body, or fitting.
    (a) 6 in.
    (b) 8 in.
    (c) 10 in.
    (d) 12 in.

40. Type CMX communications cables can be installed in ______.
    (a) one- or two-family dwellings
    (b) multifamily dwellings in nonconcealed spaces
    (c) a or b
    (d) none of these

41. Type FCC cable shall be clearly and durably marked ______.
    (a) on the top side at intervals not exceeding 30 in.
    (b) on both sides at intervals not exceeding 24 in.
    (c) with conductor material, maximum temperature, and ampacity
    (d) b and c

42. Type FCC cable systems are permitted on wall surfaces in ______.
    (a) surface metal raceways
    (b) cable trays
    (c) busways
    (d) any of these

43. Type IC recessed luminaires are permitted to make contact with combustible material at ______.
    (a) recessed parts
    (b) points of support
    (c) portions passing through or finishing off the opening in the building structure
    (d) all of these

44. Type ITC cable shall be installed in industrial establishments where the conditions of maintenance and supervision ensure that only ______ will service the installation.
    (a) the authority having jurisdiction
    (b) authorized persons
    (c) the general public
    (d) qualified persons

45. Type MC cable installed through, or parallel to, framing members shall be protected against physical damage from penetration by screws or nails by 1¼ in. separation or protected by a suitable metal plate.
    (a) True
    (b) False

46. Type MC cable provides an effective ground-fault current path and is recognized by the NEC as an equipment grounding conductor when ______.

(a) it contains an insulated or uninsulated equipment grounding conductor in compliance with 250.118(1)
(b) the combined metallic sheath and uninsulated equipment grounding/bonding conductor of interlocked metal tape–type MC cable is listed and identified as an equipment grounding conductor
(c) a or b
(d) only when it is hospital grade Type MC cable

47. Type MC cable shall not be ______ unless the metallic sheath or armor is resistant to the conditions, or is protected by material resistant to the conditions.

(a) used for direct burial in the earth
(b) embedded in concrete
(c) exposed to cinder fill
(d) all of these

48. Type MV cable is defined as a single or multiconductor solid dielectric insulated cable rated ______ volts or higher.

(a) 601
(b) 1,001
(c) 2,001
(d) 6,001

49. Type NM cable can be installed above a Class I location in a commercial garage.

(a) True
(b) False

50. Type NM cable can be installed as open runs in dropped or suspended ceilings in other than one- and two-family and multifamily dwellings.

(a) True
(b) False

51. Type NM cable shall be permitted in agricultural buildings.

(a) True
(b) False

52. Type NM cable shall closely follow the surface of the building finish or running boards when run exposed.

(a) True
(b) False

53. Type NM cables can be used for branch-circuit temporary installations without height limitation and without concealment.

(a) True
(b) False

54. Type NM cables shall not be used in one- and two-family dwellings exceeding three floors above grade.

(a) True
(b) False

55. Type OFNG, OFN, OFCG, and OFC optical fiber cables can be installed in vertical riser runs when ______.

(a) encased in a metal raceway
(b) having firestops at each floor
(c) a or b
(d) none of these

56. Type TC cable can be used ______.

(a) for power and lighting circuits
(b) in cable trays
(c) in Class 1 control circuits
(d) all of these

57. Type TC cable shall not be installed ______.

(a) where it will be exposed to physical damage
(b) outside of a raceway or cable tray system, unless permitted in 336.10(7)
(c) direct buried unless identified for such use
(d) all of these

58. Type UF cable can be used in commercial garages.

(a) True
(b) False

59. Type UF cable is permitted to be used for inside wiring.

(a) True
(b) False

60. Type USE cable is not permitted for ______ wiring.

(a) underground
(b) interior
(c) a or b
(d) a and b

61. Types ______ nonconductive and conductive optical fiber cables shall be listed as being suitable for general-purpose use, with the exception of risers, plenums, and other spaces used for environmental air, and shall also be listed as being resistant to the spread of fire.

(a) OFNP and OFCP
(b) OFNR and OFCR
(c) OFNG and OFCG
(d) OFN and OFC

62. Unbroken lengths of surface metal raceways can be run through dry ______.

(a) walls
(b) partitions
(c) floors
(d) all of these

63. Underground copper service conductors supplying more than a single branch circuit shall not be smaller than ______ AWG copper.

(a) 3
(b) 4
(c) 6
(d) 8

64. Underground PVC conduit shall be not less than ______ from the inside wall of the pool, unless space limitations prevent otherwise.

(a) 5 ft
(b) 8 ft
(c) 10 ft
(d) 25 ft

65. Underground raceways and cable assemblies entering a handhole enclosure shall extend into the enclosure, but they are not required to be ______.

(a) bonded
(b) insulated
(c) mechanically connected to the handhole enclosure
(d) below minimum cover requirements after leaving the handhole

66. Underground raceways entering a ______ from an underground distribution system shall be sealed or plugged at either or both ends to prevent moisture from contacting energized live parts.

(a) building
(b) structure
(c) highway right-of-way
(d) a or b

67. Underground service-entrance conductors shall be protected against physical damage.

(a) True
(b) False

68. Unit equipment for emergency systems shall be on the same branch circuit that serves the normal lighting in the area and connected ______ any local switches.

(a) with
(b) ahead of
(c) after
(d) downstream of

69. Unless overload protection is provided by other approved means, the minimum number of overload units required for a three-phase ac motor is ______.

(a) one
(b) two
(c) three
(d) any of these

70. Unless supplemented or modified by Article 690, Chapters 1, 2, 3, and 4 in the NEC shall apply. However, if any provisions of Article 690 differ with other articles of the Code, Article 690 requirements apply within the scope of Article 690 installations.

(a) True
(b) False

71. Unused openings for circuit breakers and switches in switchboards and panelboards shall be closed using ______ or other approved means that provide protection substantially equivalent to the wall of the enclosure.
(a) duct seal and tape
(b) identified closures
(c) exothermic welding
(d) sheet metal

72. Unused openings other than those intended for the operation of equipment, intended for mounting purposes, or permitted as part of the design for listed equipment shall be ______.
(a) filled with cable clamps or connectors only
(b) taped over with electrical tape
(c) repaired only by welding or brazing in a metal slug
(d) effectively closed to afford protection substantially equivalent to the wall of the equipment

73. Utilities may include entities that are designated or recognized by governmental law or regulation by public service/utility commissions.
(a) True
(b) False

74. Utilization equipment weighing less than 6 lb can be supported to any box or plaster ring secured to a box, provided the equipment is secured with at least two ______ or larger screws.
(a) No. 6
(b) No. 8
(c) No. 10
(d) self tapping

75. Vegetation shall not be used to support overhead conductor spans of ______for temporary installations.
(a) branch circuits
(b) feeders
(c) a or b
(d) none of these

76. Vegetation such as trees shall not be used for support of ______.
(a) overhead conductor spans
(b) surface wiring methods
(c) luminaires
(d) electric equipment

77. Ventilation openings for transformer vaults must be as far as possible from ______.
(a) doors
(b) windows
(c) combustible material
(d) any of these

78. Wall-mounted ovens and counter-mounted cooking units shall be permitted to be ______.
(a) permanently connected
(b) cord-and-plug-connected
(c) a or b
(d) none of these

79. Weather-resistant receptacles ______ where replacements are made at receptacle outlets that are required to be so protected elsewhere in the Code.
(a) shall be provided
(b) are not required
(c) are optional
(d) are not allowed

80. Wet-niche luminaires installed in swimming pools shall be removable from the water for inspection, relamping or other maintenance. The luminaire maintenance location shall be accessible ______.
(a) while the pool is drained
(b) without entering the pool water
(c) during construction
(d) all of these

81. Wet-niche luminaires shall be connected to an equipment grounding conductor not smaller than ______ AWG.
(a) 12
(b) 10
(c) 8
(d) 6

82. When a building is supplied with a(n) ______ fire sprinkler system, ENT shall be permitted to be used within walls, floors, and ceilings, exposed or concealed, in buildings exceeding three floors above grade.
(a) listed
(b) identified
(c) NFPA 13-2010
(d) none of these

83. When an outlet from an underfloor raceway is discontinued, the circuit conductors supplying the outlet ______.

(a) may be spliced
(b) may be reinsulated
(c) may be cut and capped off
(d) shall be removed from the raceway

84. When an underground metal water piping system is used as a grounding electrode, bonding shall be provided around insulated joints and around any equipment that is likely to be disconnected for repairs or replacement.

(a) True
(b) False

85. When applying the demand factors of Table 220.56, the feeder or service demand load shall not be less than the sum of ______.

(a) the total number of receptacles at 180 VA per receptacle outlet
(b) the VA rating of all of the small-appliance branch circuits combined
(c) the largest two kitchen equipment loads
(d) the kitchen heating and air-conditioning loads

86. When bonding enclosures, metal raceways, frames, and fittings, any nonconductive paint, enamel, or similar coating shall be removed at ______.

(a) contact surfaces
(b) threads
(c) contact points
(d) all of these

87. When breaks occur in dwelling unit kitchen countertop spaces for rangetops, refrigerators or sinks, each countertop surface shall be considered a separate counter space for determining receptacle placement.

(a) True
(b) False

88. When conduit nipples having a maximum length not exceeding 24 in. are installed between boxes, the nipple can be filled to 60 percent.

(a) True
(b) False

89. When connected to multiwire branch circuits, the fluorescent luminaire disconnect must simultaneously break all circuit conductors of the ballast, including the neutral conductor.

(a) True
(b) False

90. When counting the number of conductors in a box, a conductor running through the box with an unbroken loop or coil not less than twice the minimum length required for free conductors shall be counted as ______ conductor(s).

(a) one
(b) two
(c) three
(d) four

91. When determining a Class I, Division 2 location, ______ is a factor that should be considered in determining the classification and extent of the location.

(a) the quantity of flammable material that might escape in case of an accident
(b) the adequacy of ventilating equipment
(c) the record of the industry or business with respect to explosions or fires
(d) all of these

92. When devices or plug-in connections for tapping off feeders or branch circuits from the busway include an externally operable fusible switch that is out of reach, ______ shall be provided for operation of the disconnecting means from the floor.

(a) ropes
(b) chains
(c) hook sticks
(d) any of these

93. When electric-discharge and LED luminaires that are designed not to be supported solely by the outlet box are surface mounted over a concealed outlet box, the luminaire shall provide access to the wiring within the outlet box by means of suitable openings in the back of the luminaire.

(a) True
(b) False

94. When FMC or LFMC is used as permitted in Class I, Division 2 locations, it shall include an equipment bonding jumper of the wire type in compliance with 250.102.

(a) True
(b) False

95. When installed indoors for carnivals, circuses, and fairs, flexible cords and flexible cables shall be listed for wet locations and shall be sunlight resistant.

(a) True
(b) False

96. When installed under metal-corrugated sheet roof decking, cables, raceways, and enclosures are permitted in concealed locations of metal-corrugated sheet-decking type roofing if they are at least 2 in. away from a structural support member.

(a) True
(b) False

97. When installing auxiliary electrodes, the earth shall not be used as an effective ground-fault current path.

(a) True
(b) False

98. When LFMC is used to connect equipment where flexibility is necessary to minimize the transmission of vibration from equipment of for equipment requiring movement after installation, a(n) ______ conductor shall be installed.

(a) main bonding
(b) grounded
(c) equipment grounding
(d) none of these

99. When LFNC is used to connect equipment requiring flexibility after installation, a separate ______ shall be installed.

(a) equipment grounding conductor
(b) expansion fitting
(c) flexible nonmetallic connector
(d) none of these

100. When mounting an enclosure in a finished surface, the enclosure shall be ______ secured to the surface by clamps, anchors, or fittings identified for the application.

(a) temporarily
(b) partially
(c) never
(d) rigidly

Save 25% On These Great Libraries

when you use discount code 11EXB25

2011 Master/Journeyman Comprehensiv Exam Preparation **Library**

Want to pass your Journeyman or Master Exam the first time? Then order one of Mi Holt's Comprehensive Exam prep libraries. Mike's dynamic teaching style and detail graphics easily explain the most difficult subjects. Each of these libraries inclu Theory, Code and Calculations – teaching you everything you need from the ground u

This package includes:

Electrical Exam Preparation Textbook
Electrical Theory Textbook
Understanding the National Electrical Code Volumes 1 and 2 Textbooks
Simulated Exam
Code Review [10 DVDs]
Theory Review [3 DVDs]
Calculations Review [Masters 8 DVDs; Journeyman 5DVDs]

Master Library List Price: ~~$1025.00~~ $768.75
Journeyman Library List price: ~~$925.00~~ $693.75

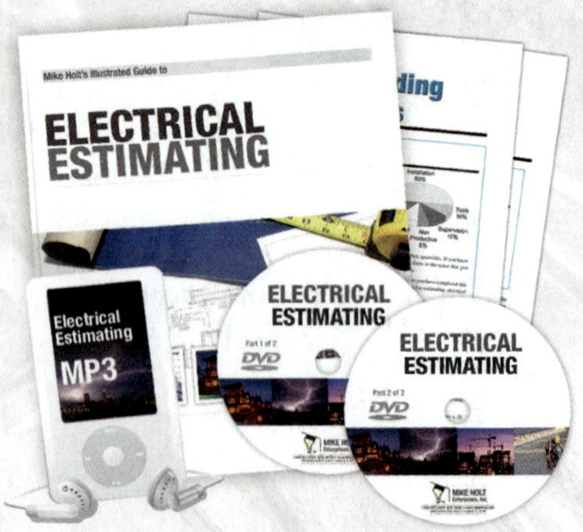

Supreme Estimating **Library**

Running a business requires an understanding of how to estimate a job. T program will show you how to take-off a job, how to determine material cost a how to accurately estimate the labor cost. You'll learn the importance of knowi how to determine your overhead, profit and break-even point, and much mo

This package includes:

Electrical Estimating textbook/workbook and Instructor's guide
Estimating Part 1 DVD
Estimating Part 2 DVD
MP3 audio

List Price: ~~$345.00~~ $258.75

2011 Detailed Code **Library**

The Detailed Code Library includes three textbooks and 10 DVDs:
Understanding the NEC Volume 1
Understanding the NEC Volume 2
Practice Questions Book
General Requirements DVDs [Part 1 and Part 2]
Grounding vs. Bonding DVD
Wiring Methods DVDs [Part 1 and Part 2]
Equipment for General Use DVD
Special Occupancies DVD
Special Equipment DVD
Limited Energy and Communication Systems DVD
List Price- ~~$569.00~~ $426.75

r Now - Call 888.NEC.CODE (632.2633